The Treasury of Knowledge

Book Six, Parts One and Two:

Indo-Tibetan Classical Learning and Buddhist Phenomenology

The translation and publication of this work have been made possible through the generous support of the Tsadra Foundation.

The Treasury of Knowledge

Book Six, Parts One and Two

Indo-Tibetan Classical Learning and Buddhist Phenomenology

Jamgön Kongtrul Lodrö Tayé

KALU RINPOCHÉ TRANSLATION GROUP
under the direction of Khenpo Lodrö Dönyö Rinpoché

This volume translated, introduced,
and annotated by Gyurme Dorje

SNOW LION
BOSTON & LONDON
2012

Snow Lion
An imprint of Shambhala Publications, Inc.
Horticultural Hall
300 Massachusetts Avenue
Boston, Massachusetts 02115
www.shambhala.com

9 8 7 6 5 4 3 2 1

First Edition
Printed in the United States of America

♾ This edition is printed on acid-free paper that meets the American National Standards Institute z39.48 Standard.
♻ Shambhala makes every attempt to print on recycled paper. For more information please visit www.shambhala.com.

Distributed in the United States by Random House, Inc., and in Canada by Random House of Canada Ltd

Designed and typeset by Gopa & Ted2, Inc.

Library of Congress Cataloging-in-Publication Data

Koṅ-sprul Blo-gros-mtha'-yas, 1813–1899.
[Śes bya mtha' yas pa'i rgya mtsho. English. Selections]
The treasury of knowledge. Book six, parts one and two, Indo-Tibetan classical learning and Buddhist phenomenology / Jamgön Kongtrul Lodrö Tayé; Kalu Rinpoché Translation Group under the direction of Khenpo Lodrö Dönyö Rinpoché; this volume translated, introduced, and annotated by Gyurme Dorje.
p. cm.
Includes bibliographical references and index.
ISBN 978-1-55939-389-8 (alk. paper)
1. Buddhism—Study and teaching. 2. Buddhist philosophy. 3. Koṅ-sprul Blo-gros-mtha'-yas, 1813–1899. Śes bya kun khyab. I. Gyurme Dorje. II. Kalu Rinpoché Translation Group. III. Title. IV. Title: Indo-Tibetan classical learning and Buddhist phenomenology.
BQ158.K6613 2012
294.3'42042—dc23
2011042842

Contents

Illustrations and Credits

All drawings are by Chris Banigan except where otherwise noted.

Foreword
by Zenkar Rinpoche, Thubten Nyima

The text contained in this volume, to which these comments refer, corresponds to Book Six of *The Treasury of Knowledge*, composed by Jamgon Kongtrul Rinpoche, Yonten Gyatso, entitled a Graduated Exposition of the Fields of Classical Learning, and more specifically, to Part One of Book Six, which offers a systematic presentation of the ordinary classical sciences and mundane spiritual paths, and Part Two, which offers a systematic presentation of phenomenological structures common to both the Greater Vehicle and the Lesser Vehicle. The original sources respectively comprise 150 pages (pp. 204–356) and 83 pages (pp. 359–442) of Volume Two of the *Shes bya kun khyab mdzod* (Beijing Nationalities Publishing House, 1982)—totalling 343 pages altogether. At the outset I wish to express my immense gratitude, out of affection, respect, and joy, that this book, excellently translated into English by the *lotsāwa chen mo* Gyurme Dorje, whose other translations include *An Encyclopaedic Tibetan-English Dictionary*, has been successfully published.

Although there are all sorts of subjects actually included within the fields of the ordinary classical sciences, and it would take many years to master even a fraction of any one of these disciplines, let alone comprehend them in their totality, even so, all the innermost essentials of these diverse subjects were condensed and refined by Jamgon Kongtrul Rinpoche. I consider that the composition of synopses of this nature—terse and meaningful, succinct and precise—is within the perceptual range of omniscient beings alone, and otherwise inconceivable.

The task of understanding all the points expressed in this scripture, which integrates the many different classical sciences, and then rendering it in English, is one of great difficulty, and there are without doubt many complexities. However, Gyurme Dorje (PhD London University) is a learned, intelligent, courageous, painstaking, capable, and diligent scholar. On the basis of such excellent talents, this unsurpassed achievement has been realized. So, when

Gyurme Dorje, my old colleague from the years when we were translating and editing the *Encyclopaedic Tibetan-English Dictionary*, requested me to write a foreword, not to disappoint, I offered this bouquet of eulogy as a foreword.

Thubten Nyima
21 September, 2011

དབྱིན་བསྒྱུར་ཤེས་བྱ་ཀུན་ཁྱབ་ཀྱི་མགོ་བརྗོད།

དེ་ལ་འདིར་སྐབས་ཀྱི་གླེང་བར་བྱ་བ་ནི། འཇམ་མགོན་ཀོང་སྤྲུལ་རིན་པོ་ཆེ་ཡོན་ཏན་རྒྱ་མཚོ་མཆོག་གིས་ལྷུགས་རྩོམ་གནང་བའི་ཤེས་བྱ་ཀུན་ཁྱབ་ཀྱི་གནས་དྲུག་པ་ཐོས་པའི་རིམ་པར་ཕྱེ་བ་ལས། སྐབས་དང་པོ་ཐུན་མོང་རིག་པའི་གནས་དང་འཇིག་རྟེན་པའི་ལམ་རྣམ་པར་གཞག་པ་པེ་ཅིན་མི་རིགས་དཔེ་སྐྲུན་ཁང་གིས1982ལོར་དཔེ་སྐྲུན་བྱས་པའི་དེབ་གཉིས་པའི་ལྡེབ་ངོས204པ་ནས356བར་ཤོག་ངོས་ཆིག་བརྒྱ་ལྔ་བཅུ་དང་། སྐབས་གཉིས་པ་ཐེག་པ་ཆེ་ཆུང་སྤྱིའི་གནས་རྣམ་པར་གཞག་པ་ལྡེབ་ངོས359པ་ནས442པའི་བར་ཤོག་ངོས་ཆིག་བརྒྱ་གོ་གསུམ་བཅས་ངོས་བསྡོམ343ཡོད་པ་རྣམས་བོད་དབྱིན་ལོ་ཙཱ་བ་ཆེན་མོ། བོད་དབྱིན་ཚིག་མཛོད་ཆེན་མོའི་ཡིག་བསྒྱུར་ཆེན་མོ། འགྱུར་མེད་རྡོ་རྗེ་ལགས་ཀྱིས་དབྱིན་ཡིག་ཐོག་ལེགས་བསྒྱུར་གནང་གྲུབ་པའི་དཔེ་ཆ་དེ་ཉིད་དཔེ་སྐྲུན་བྱེད་ཐུབ་པ་ལ་དགའ་ཀུས་སྤྲོ་གསུམ་འཕེལ་བཞིན་པའི་ངང་ནས་ཐུགས་རྗེ་ཚད་མེད་ཆེ་ཞེས་ཐོག་མར་ཞུ་བ་ཡིན།

ཡར་ཐུན་མོང་གི་རིག་གནས་གང་དང་གང་ཡིན་ཀྱང་། ཕྱོགས་མཐའ་དག་ནས་ཤེས་ཐུབ་པ་ལྟ་ཅི། དེ་དག་རེ་རེའི་ཆ་ཤས་ཙམ་ཞིག་སྦྱང་རྒྱུ་ལའང་ལོ་མང་པོ་འགོར་ནའང་། འཇམ་མགོན་ཀོང་སྤྲུལ་རིན་པོ་ཆེ་ནས་དེ་དག་གི་སྙིང་བཅུད་ཐམས་ཅད་གནད་ནས་གནད་དུ་བསྡུས་ཏེ། ཚིག་ཉུང་ལ་དོན་འདུས་པ། ཞལ་གསལ་ལ་གནད་ཐེགས་པ་འདི་འདྲ་བ་ཞིག་ནི་ཐམས་ཅད་མཁྱེན་པ་ཁོ་ནའི་སྤྱོད་ཡུལ་ལས་གཞན་གྱི་བསམ་ཡུལ་འདས་པ་ཞིག་ཡིན་པར་སེམས།

དེ་ལྟ་བུའི་རིག་གཞུང་སྣ་མང་གཅིག་ཏུ་འདྲིལ་བའི་གསུང་རབ་འདི་ཉིད་ཀྱི་བརྗོད་བྱ་ཐམས་ཅད་ལ་གོ་བ་ལོན་ནས་རྗོད་བྱེད་དབྱིན་ཡིག་གི་ཐོག་ཕབ་བསྒྱུར་གནང་བ་དེ་ནི་དཀའ་ཚེགས་ཆེ་ལ་རྙོག་འཛིང་མང་བ་ཡོད་པ་གོར་མ་ཆག འོན་ཀྱང་ལྷུན་ཏུན་སློབ་གྲྭ་ཆེན་མོའི་འབུམ་རམས་པ་འགྱུར་མེད་རྡོ་རྗེ་ལགས་ནི་ཤེས་རྒྱ་ཆེ་ཞིང་བློ་གྲོས་རྣོ་བ། སྙིང་སྟོབས་ཆེ་ཞིང་དཀའ་ཚེགས་བཟོད་པ། འཛོན་ཐང་ཆེ་ལ་བརྩོན་འགྲུས་ལྡན་པ་སོགས་ཀྱི་ཁྱད་འཕགས་ཀྱི་ཡོན་ཏན་ལྡན་པ་ལ་བརྟེན་ནས་གྲུབ་འབྲས་བླ་ན་མེད་པ་ཐོབ་པ་འདི་ལ་བོད་དབྱིན་ཚིག་མཛོད་བསྒྱུར་སྒྲིག་སྐབས་ཀྱི་ལས་གྲོགས་རྒན་པ་སྐུ་ཞབས་འགྱུར་མེད་རྡོ་རྗེ་ལགས་ཀྱིས་མགོ་བརྗོད་ཅིག་བྲི་རོགས་གྱིས་ཞེས་བསྐུལ་མ་གནང་བར་ངོ་མ་ལྡོག་ཙམ་དུ་བསྔགས་བརྗོད་མེ་ཏོག་གི་ཆུན་པོ་མགོ་བརྗོད་ཀྱི་ཚུལ་དུ་ཕུལ་བ་ལགས།

ཕྲན་ཐུབ་བསྟན་ཉི་མས་ཕུལ།

2011/9/21

Introduction

The life of Jamgon Kongtrul (1813–1899), author and compiler of the *Treasury of Knowledge*, is well known from various sources. In Tibetan, there are two extant autobiographical accounts, not to mention the writings of his student Karma Tashi Chopel and the later abridged biographies contained in the Buddhist histories of Zhechen Gyaltsab (1910) and Dudjom Rinpoche (1964). Gene Smith was the first Western scholar to appraise the life and works of Kongtrul in his ground-breaking introduction to the Indian edition of the *Treasury of Knowledge*, published in 1970. The longest account in English is Richard Barron's translation, entitled *The Autobiography of Jamgon Kongtrul* (2003); while short hagiographies are also be found in the English translation of Dudjom Rinpoche's *The Nyingma School of Tibetan Buddhism: Its Fundamentals and History* (1991) and in Ringu Tulku's *The Ri-me Philosophy of Jamgon Kongtrul the Great* (2006).

Revered as a spiritual emanation of the great eighth-century translator Vairocana, Jamgon Kongtrul was born into a Bon family at Rongyab Pema Lhatse in Drida Zelmogang, within the principality of Derge. After familiarizing himself with the teachings and iconography of the Bon tradition in childhood, and mastering the local pharmacopeia, he was introduced to the formal study and practice of Buddhism from his eighteenth year onwards—initially at Zhechen under the tutelage of Gyurme Tutob Namgyal (b. 1787) and subsequently at Palpung, which had been founded by Situ Chokyi Jungne (1700–1774). In these institutions he twice received the vows of monastic ordination, according to the lower and upper Vinaya lineages respectively. During these formative years, Kongtrul accepted Situ Pema Nyinje (1774–1853) as his main teacher, receiving the Kagyu and Jonangpa transmissions from him and some sixty other teachers in all. His exhaustive studies are fully documented in the record of his received teachings (*gsan yig*), which was devotedly compiled by Karma Tashi Chopel.

In 1842, Situ Pema Nyinje granted Kongtrul permission to leave the monastery and enter into a three-year solitary retreat at Tsadra Rinchen Drak, revered as one of the twenty-five foremost power-places in Kham, specifically associated with the "mind aspect of Padmasambhava's enlightened attributes" (*yon tan gyi thugs*). At Tsadra, on a concealed ridge, high above Palpung Monastery, Kongtrul founded the hermitage of Kunzang Dechen Oseling. It was here that he completed his prodigious writings, passed long periods in isolated meditation, and first liaised with his closest associates—Jamyang Khyentse Wangpo of Dzongsar (1820–1892), Chogyur Dechen Lingpa of Nangchen (1829–1870), and others—to establish the dynamic and all-embracing non-sectarian (*ris med*) tradition of eastern Tibet. Together, they sought to preserve and integrate the diverse lineages of Tibetan Buddhism, large and small, without fear of persecution, in an age of increasing strife. Receptive to Padmasambhava's spiritual revelations, they also mapped out the twenty-five ancient sacred sites of eastern Tibet which had been imbued with his blessings.

While Kongtrul uniquely juxtaposed the realizations of Tibet's diverse spiritual traditions, Buddhist and Bon, he had a special affinity with the Jonangpa and Shangpa Kagyu teachings maintained in the lineage of Tāranātha (1575–1634). His writings display a particular penchant for the views and expositions of this multi-talented renaissance figure and later scholars who empathized with his approach—Nyingma masters such as Rigdzin Tsewang Norbu (1698–1755) and Gyurme Tsewang Chokdrub (1761–1829) of Katok, and Sarma masters including the aforementioned Situ Chokyi Jungne of Palpung.

After dedicating a lifetime to the preservation of Tibet's spiritual traditions in their entirety, Kongtrul passed away at Tsadra in his eighty-seventh year. By that time he had ensured the successful transmission of his diverse teachings to the foremost lineage-holders of a younger generation, who resolved to continue this legacy of eclecticism into the twentieth century.

Derge

It is true that the success of Jamgon Kongtrul's all-embracing non-sectarian approach can be measured in terms of his outstanding attributes and talents alone, yet his activities were undeniably facilitated by the political climate in which he lived and worked. The principality of Derge, where Jamgon Kongtrul was born, is characterized by fast-flowing rivers that, in summertime, carry fertile red silt downstream through alpine woodlands and small farming villages, discharging into the turbid Yangtze Gorge. The villages, which exude an air of quiet prosperity—their houses constructed distinctively of red-painted horizontal timbers, with surrounding barley fields—were renowned for their craftsmen and artisans, working in metal and wood-carving.

The rulers of Derge, who had been granted hegemony in Kham by Chogyal Phakpa and assumed outright power from the mid-fourteenth century onwards, claimed their descent from Lonpo Gar—an illustrious seventh-century emissary of the Tibetan emperor Songtsen Gampo. Under their authority, the Bon, Nyingma, and Sakya traditions all flourished in Derge—their best known sites being at Dzong-nying, Katok, and Dzongsar, respectively. In the early fifteenth century, Lodro Tobden relocated his capital and palace to a sheltered ravine abutting the Zi-chu River, where, in 1448, Tangtong Gyalpo consecrated the site for the building of Gonchen Monastery.

Later, in the eighteenth century, Tenpa Tsering (1678–1738) brought Derge to the zenith of its power by conquering the outlying northern grasslands of Dzachuka and the Jomda region to the west of the Yangtze. Under his auspices, two imposing, free-standing buildings were constructed in a strikingly similar architectural style, both of them destined to become vital centers of learning and repositories of Tibetan culture. One was Palpung Monastery, founded in 1717 above the village of Rashenda in the Pa-chu Valley, which the king bequeathed to Situ Chokyi Jungne, the eighth incumbent of the Tai Situpa lineage of the Kagyu school. The other was the Derge Parkhang, founded between 1729 and 1750 within the Gonchen monastic complex of the Sakya-Ngor tradition. This treasure-store of Tibet's great literary endeavors still houses the largest and most eclectic collection of xylographs and printed texts on the plateau. It was here that Situ Chokyi Jungne, Zhuchen Tsultrim Rinchen, and Gyurme Tsewang Chokdrub respectively edited newly commissioned xylographic editions of the Kangyur, Tengyur, and Nyingma Gyudbum, the woodblocks of which are still used for printing at the present day.

This remarkably tolerant and culturally stimulating environment provided the setting for Jamgon Kongtrul's refreshing non-sectarian approach. The eclectic patronage of the Derge rulers during the seventeenth to mid-nineteenth centuries stood in marked contrast to the fortress-like mentality of the neighboring lands of Eastern Tibet—Jyekundo, Sershul, and Beri, where a Bon chieftain had been deposed and his lands occupied by Gushi Qan in the 1640s. In those regions, large Gelukpa monasteries had been established by Mongol force of arms, often uprooting or supplanting the earlier traditions.

Yet, even Derge could not remain aloof from the turbulence of the age. In 1863, the principality succumbed to Gonpo Namgyal, the chieftain of Nyarong, around the time when Jamgon Kongtrul was composing his supremely eclectic treatise, *The Treasury of Knowledge*. Then, shortly after this work was completed, in 1865, the forces of Nyarong were defeated by an expeditionary force from Lhasa. During this period, Jamgon Kongtrul is said to have personally averted a forced conversion of Kagyu monasteries, including Palpung, to the Gelukpa school by successfully offering medical treatment to Dongkam Tulku of Drayab. Although the principality relinquished its independence in 1909, one short decade after Kongtrul's passing, when the Chinese warlord Zhao Erfeng incorporated it within his new but short-lived Xikang Province, Derge even now retains its prestige as the cultural center of Kham.

Doxographical Traditions

Just as Western literature can be said to have, in the words of the encyclopedist Robert Hutchins, maintained a "great conversation," handing down and reworking ideas, insights, and methodologies in successive literary contexts since the time of Homer, the world of Indo-Tibetan Buddhism has continued its own parallel great conversation, one that can be traced back to the canonical works of the Buddha, the classical Indian commentaries, and Tibet's indigenous commentarial literature. While this conversation has continued unabated into the modern era, in the writings of Dudjom Jigdral Yeshe Dorje, Dungkar Lobzang Trinle, Tseten Zhabdrung, and so forth, many historians share the view that Jamgon Kongtrul's writings and those of his contemporaries, notably Jamyang Khyentse Wangpo and Mipham Namgyal Gyatso, represent the culmination of the trend towards syncretism in those works of Tibetan literature that focus on the theoretical understandings and practical application of the Buddhist teachings.

There are some early canonical sūtras that might be considered doxographical in content, such as the *Net of Brahmā* (*Brahmajālasūtra*), which identifies sixty-two distinct inauthentic views with regard to the limits of past and future time. However, the Indian master Bhāvaviveka (ca. 500–570) is reckoned to have been the first exponent of classical Mahāyāna Buddhism to construct a formal, hierarchical doxography of all the Indian philosophical systems (*siddhānta, grub mtha'*). In his *Flame of Dialectics* (*Tarkajvālā*), he in fact differentiates one hundred and ten primary and three hundred and sixty-three derivative philosophical views. The trend which he set in motion continues in the elaborate commentarial writings of subsequent scholars, including Kamalaśīla (740–795), Vitapāda (fl. late ninth century), Avalokitavrata, and Bodhibhadra (fl. 1000). Later texts generally focus on the four commonly accepted philosophical systems of Indian Buddhism—Vaibhāṣika, Sautrāntika, Cittamātra, and Madhyamaka—preceded by a Buddhist analysis of the non-Buddhist systems of ancient India, including materialism, Jainism, and various strands of Brāhmaṇism.

From the eighth century onwards, the Indian Buddhist doxographical tradition began to take root in Tibet, initially in the writings of Kawa Peltsek and Zhang Yeshede, and later during the new wave of translations that flourished in Tibet from the eleventh century onwards. Each of the main Tibetan schools gradually evolved its distinctive standpoints with regard to the four main Indian Buddhist philosophical systems. Among the Nyingmapa, this trend is exemplified by the writings of Rongzom Chokyi Zangpo (fl. eleventh century) and Longchen Rabjampa (1308–1363); among the Sakyapa, by the works of Sakya Paṇchen Kunga Gyaltsen (1182–1251) and Zilungpa Shākya Chokden (1428–1507); in the Kadampa school, by the systematic presentations of Chomden Rigpei Raldri (1227–1305) and his student Upa Losal (fl. thirteenth century); in the Kagyu school, by the likes of Karmapa Rangjung Dorje (1284–1339) and Drukchen Pema Karpo (1527–1592); in the Jonangpa school, by Dolpopa Sherab Gyaltsen (1292–1361) and Tāranātha (1575–1634); and among the Gelukpa, by Tsongkhapa (1357–1419), Khedrub Gelek Pelzangpo (1385–1438), and the incumbents of Labrang and Gonlung monasteries in Amdo, notably Jamyang Zhepa II Konchok Jigme Wangpo (1728–1791), Jangkya Rolpei Dorje (1717–1786), and Tuken Lobzang Chokyi Nyima (1732–1802).

While many of these great masters naturally tended to focus on the perspectives of their own traditions and often highlighted their differences rather than their common ground, Tibet's greatest literati of the eighteenth century made concerted efforts, in the wake of the civil war and persecutions of the seventeenth century, towards a more ecumenical approach, giving more emphasis to the commonality of the various traditions rather than the nuances that divided them. This eclectic approach found its inspiration in the long career of Tangtong Gyalpo (1361–1485), and was presaged during the eighteenth century by the non-partisan activities of Rigdzin Tsewang Norbu of Katok (1698–1755) and Situ Chokyi Jungne of Palpung (1700–1774).

There were, in addition to those exponents of the Buddhist systems of philosophy, others who adopted an encyclopedic perspective, striving in their works to encompass the full range of secular and spiritual knowledge that had been handed down and preserved within the Indo-Tibetan classical tradition. Such works include the *Elucidation of Knowledge* (*Shes bya rab gsal*) by Chogyal Phakpa Lodro Gyaltsen (1235–1280), the *Compendium of Facts*

(*De nyid 'dus pa*) by Bodong Paṇchen (1376–1451), and the *Exegetical Treasury: A Wish-fulfilling Gem* (*bShad mdzod yid bzhin nor bu*), attributed to Dondam Mawei Senge (fl. fifteenth century), which syncretizes ideas derived from Buddhism, Bon, and the mundane sciences—astrology, medicine, linguistics, and rhetoric. Later, during the early life of Jamgon Kongtrul, another important encyclopedia entitled *Treasury of Sūtras and Tantras* (*mDo rgyud mdzod*) was compiled at Keude Monastery in Repkong by Tobden Choying Dorje (1785–1848). In five recently republished volumes, this work covers the full range of the classical sciences, sūtras, and tantras, principally from a Nyingma perspective, and it may be considered an Amdowa precursor to Jamgon Kongtrul's encyclopedia.

Jamgon Kongtrul's Writings

The collected writings of Jamgon Kongtrul are known as the "five great treasuries" (*mdzod chen lnga*), a title prophetically bestowed upon them by Kongtrul's closest associate, Jamyang Khyentse Wangpo, in 1864 when only the first of the five had been composed. As Dudjom Rinpoche writes, "When the vase of Jamgon Kongtrul's mind had been filled with the textual exegeses and oral explanations of the transmitted precepts, treatises, tantras, transmissions and esoteric instructions, along with their rituals, practical techniques, and fine points, he too composed treatises. These form the wonderful legacy of his studies, reflections and meditations."[1]

Among these works, the earliest was *The Treasury Encompassing All Knowledge* (*Shes bya kun khyab mdzod*) in three volumes—ten books (*gnas bcu*) and forty parts (*skabs bzhi bcu*)—covering the entire corpus of the sūtra and mantra traditions, from the common sciences of Indo-Tibetan classical learning, all the way up to the uncommon teachings of Atiyoga, which is the culmination of the nine vehicles of Buddhist practice. (2) *The Treasury of Precious Instructions* (*gDams ngag rin po che'i mdzod*), in twelve volumes and nine books, collates the empowerment rites and oral instructions pertaining to the eight instructional lineages that are extant in Tibet—those of the Nyingma, Kadam, Sakya, Marpa Kagyu, Shangpa Kagyu, Kālacakra, Pacification, and Oḍḍiyāna tradition of ritual service and attainment. (3) *The Treasury of Kagyu Mantra* (*bKa' brgyud sngags kyi mdzod*), in six volumes, contains descriptions of thirteen principal maṇḍalas along with guidance on the perfection stage of meditation and integrated empowerment rites according to tantras of both the ancient and new transmissions, with an emphasis on the cycles of Marpa and Ngok. (4) *The Treasury of Precious Spiritual Revelations* (*Rin chen gter mdzod*), now expanded in 72 and 111 volumes, anthologizes the revealed teachings disclosed over the centuries by Tibet's greatest treasure-finders, structured according to the hierarchy of Atiyoga, Anuyoga, and Mahāyoga. (5) *The Treasury of Uncommon Teachings* (*Thun mong ma yin pa'i mdzod*), in seven volumes, contains the actual spiritual revelations of Jamgon Kongtrul, headed by the *Gathering of the Three Roots' Enlightened Intention* (*rTsa gsum dgongs 'dus*), while Kongtrul's miscellaneous textual commentaries are contained in the supplementary *Treasury of Extensive Transmitted Teachings* (*rGya chen bka' mdzod*).

The Encompassment of All Knowledge

The first of these five treasuries, from which the present work derives, comprises the terse root verses entitled the *Encompassment of All Knowledge* (*Shes bya kun khyab*) and an interlinear commentary (*tshig 'grel*), written largely in prose, entitled the *Infinite Ocean of Knowledge* (*Shes bya mtha' yas pa'i rgya mtsho*), which includes copious citations from authoritative Indian and Tibetan sources. The former was composed at the Tsadra Hermitage in 1862, at the behest of Dabzang Ngedon Tenpa Rabgye, who had requested Kongtrul to write more narrowly, on the integration of monastic, bodhisattva, and mantra vows. Kongtrul purposefully widened the scope of his treatise, following in the tradition of the earlier encyclopedists, and successfully integrated the full range of traditional Buddhist studies and practice in his work. It is said that the commentary was compiled and written at the behest of Jamyang Khyentse Wangpo in only four months, during the year 1863, and revised in its final form the following year, with the assistance of Tashi Ozer of Palpung.

This work, as mentioned above, contains ten books, the first four of which are historically oriented, focussing respectively on cosmology, the Buddha, his teachings, and their propagation in ancient India and Tibet. The fifth book concerns the integration of monastic, bodhisattva, and mantra vows, while the next three concern the cultivation of discriminative awareness, which is to be achieved respectively by study, reflection, and meditation. The last two books offer Kongtrul's syncretic analysis of the spiritual paths and goals attained through the causal and fruitional vehicles of Buddhist practice.

Each of the ten books is also divided into four parts, through which the author moves gradually from general or foundational levels of exegesis towards more specialized and advanced themes, objectively explaining the distinctions between different theories and practices, without adopting a partisan stance.

Book Six: The Cultivation of Discriminative Awareness through Study

Among the ten books, the sixth specifically concerns the range of traditional studies through which discriminative awareness may be cultivated. The first part focuses on the so-called common fields of knowledge (*sādhāraṇavidyā*) and the meditative techniques of calm abiding (*śamatha*) and higher insight (*vipaśyana*) through which spiritual progress can be achieved, with or without successfully terminating the cycle of rebirth. The second part highlights the distinctions between non-Buddhist and Buddhist philosophical systems and goes on to present three nuanced perspectives of Buddhist phenomenology (*abhidharma*), based on the commentarial traditions associated with the three successive promulgations of the sūtras. Part three outlines the philosophical systems of the so-called causal vehicles—those of the pious attendants, hermit buddhas, and bodhisattvas, culminating in the elaborate presentation of Madhyamaka philosophy, from the perspectives of intrinsic emptiness, independent reasoning, consequential reasoning, extrinsic emptiness, and its integration with the view of the tantras. Part four presents the philosophical systems of the resultant or fruitional vehicles—those of Action Tantra, Conduct Tantra, Yoga Tantra, and Unsurpassed Yoga Tantra—emphasizing the distinctive continua of the ground, path, and result, and outlining the scriptures and exegetical techniques favored by exponents of both the new (*gsar ma*) and ancient (*rnying ma*) traditions.

The present work contains an annotated English translation of parts one and two, under the collective title *Indo-Tibetan Classical Learning and Buddhist Phenomenology*. The two subsequent parts of Book Six have already been translated and published—part three by Elizabeth Callahan under the title *Frameworks of Buddhist Philosophy*, and part four by Elio Guarisco and Ingrid McLeod under the title *Systems of Buddhist Tantra*.

Part One: Indo-Tibetan Classical Learning

Early in Book Six, Jamgon Kongtrul remarks that since the enlightened attributes of erudition are limitless, studies should be thoroughly pursued in an impartial manner—as if explaining his own non-sectarian motivation in writing this treatise. He begins by defining the purpose of learning, with the preamble:

> In order that persons who have become well grounded in the higher ethical disciplines that form the basis of all those virtuous teach-

> ings [discussed in Book Five] might understand without error the spiritual paths that lead to freedom [from cyclic existence] and to omniscience [as expounded in Books Seven and Eight], it will be necessary to investigate the discriminative awareness (*prajñā*, *shes rab*) that arises through studying the [various] fields of knowledge, which are as vast as an ocean in their extent.

He then concisely crystallizes the content of Books Five, Six, Seven, and Eight—the core of his treatise—in the following words:

> It is through knowledge of non-Buddhist and Buddhist philosophical and spiritual systems (*siddhānta*, *grub mtha'*) [i.e., Book Six] that one will come to discern those things that should be adopted and those things that should be renounced. Then, after one has studied the training of ethical discipline (*śīlaśikṣā*, *tshul khrims kyi bslab pa*) [i.e., Book Five], negative actions will be reversed. After studying the training of the mind (*cittaśikṣā*, *sems kyi bslab pa*) [through meditation, i.e., Book Seven], pointless desires will be completely abandoned; and after studying the training of discriminative awareness (*prajñāśikṣā*, *shes rab kyi bslab pa*) [i.e., Book Eight], the state of nirvāṇa that is actually free from corruption will be attained.

The range of general subjects that fall within the scope of Indo-Tibetan classical learning traditionally include the "five major sciences" of Sanskrit grammar, logic, fine arts, medicine, and Buddhist philosophy, along with a further group of "five minor sciences"—astrology, poetics, prosody, lexicography or synonymics, and dramaturgy. The latter classification appears to have evolved from the Vedic doxography of the six subsidiary sciences necessary for the comprehension of ritual texts (*ṣadvedāṅga*) in the Brāhmaṇical tradition, namely, ritual sacrifice (*kalpa*), elocution (*śikṣā*), prosody (*chandas*), etymology (*nirukta*), grammar (*vyākaraṇa*), and astronomy/ astrology (*jyotiṣa*). The rationale for including these disparate subjects as an aid to spiritual cultivation is offered in a scriptural passage from the *Sūtra of Great Skillful Means Repaying [the Buddha] with Gratitude* (*Thabs mkhas pa drin lan bsabs pa'i mdo*), which says:

> In this regard, if you ask why bodhisattvas continue to pursue these studies, bodhisattvas continue to investigate thoroughly

> the teachings of the Buddha because they are obliged to master earnestly and authentically all doctrines that are in conformity with the sacred teaching and because they impart those doctrines extensively and authentically to others.
>
> Bodhisattvas continue to investigate the science of logic because they have to thoroughly and qualitatively understand the eloquence and solecism found in the treatises themselves, because they are obliged to refute the critiques of others, because they have to convince those lacking faith in this teaching [of Buddhism], and because they have to reinvigorate those who already have faith.
>
> Bodhisattvas continue to investigate the science of grammar because, while constructing refined Sanskrit syntax with fine words and syllables and an elegant use of etymological definitions, they inspire confidence in those wishing them to speak, and because they have to employ terminology in conformity with diverse etymological nuances, even though their shades of meaning might be identical.
>
> Bodhisattvas continue to investigate the science of medicine because they are obliged to alleviate the various ailments that afflict sentient beings, and because they can benefit the great mass of living creatures.
>
> Bodhisattvas continue to investigate the aspects of knowledge concerning the status of mundane past actions because they acquire resources without difficulty for the sake of sentient beings, and because they are obliged to cherish all sentient beings.

And:

> The five ordinary sciences cultivated by bodhisattvas are also to be investigated because bodhisattvas are obliged to perfect the great provision of pristine cognition (*jñānasambhāra*, *ye shes kyi tshogs*) of unsurpassed and genuinely perfect enlightenment. If they do not study all those subjects, they will not in due course attain the unobscured all-knowing pristine cognition.

Prior to commencing the study of the classical sciences, it will be essential to grasp the intricacies of phonetics and semantics. To this end, Kongtrul starts by emphasizing the importance of articulation, etymology, graphology, phonology, syntax, and morphology in respect of the Sanskrit and Tibetan languages. He also summarizes Che Khyidruk's *Eight Elements of Linguistic Application* (*'Jug pa'i gnas brgyad*), where the semantic concepts of objective referent, sound generation, shared ideation, commonality, and adhesion are introduced.

Armed with these linguistic tools, the neophyte may commence the study of the classical sciences, keeping in mind that in Book Six, Kongtrul discusses the actual content of the various classical sciences rather than their historical transmission and the literary sources, which he has already covered in Book Four. Generally speaking, he notes that:

> Grammar and logic eradicate wrong understandings of word and meaning. Fine arts and medicine bring into the fold students [seeking] both general and particular [skills]. The inner science [of Buddhism] brings about an understanding of all aspects of the path to omniscience. Therefore, the classical sciences may also be grouped in three categories: those that eradicate [wrong understandings], those that bring [seekers] into the fold, and the one through which omniscience is attained.

Sanskrit Grammar

Kongtrul's presentation of Sanskrit grammar (*śabdavidyā, sgra'i rig gnas*) owes much to the writings of Situ Chokyi Jungne of Palpung (1699–1774), who was one of the most influential Tibetan authorities on Sanskrit language and the related *vedāṅga* literature. The ancient *Grammar of Pāṇini* had been translated into Tibetan only during the seventeenth century. Instead, Sanskrit grammatical studies had been traditionally pursued in Tibet through the medium of the three medieval grammars—the *Kalāpasūtra*, the *Candravyākaraṇa*, and the *Sārasvatavyākaraṇa*. Among these, the Shaivite *Kalāpasūtra* (also known as the *Kātantra*) had great popularity in northern India and Nepal from the thirteenth century onwards and was translated by Pang Lodro Tenpa and Buton Rinchendrub during the fourteenth century. The Buddhist *Candravyākaraṇa* is a masterful abridgement of *Pāṇini* composed by Candragomin, one of the great scholars of the Nālanda tradition, which had great prestige in Tibet. The *Sārasvatavyākaraṇa*, revealed in a vision to Anubhūtisvarūpa, was translated from the seventeenth century onwards on three occasions—by Tāranātha, by Darpa Lotsāwa, and by Situ Chokyi Jungne.

The traditional presentation of Sanskrit grammar outlined here is based on the distinctions between primary bases (*prakṛti, rang bzhin*), affixation (*pratyaya*, *rkyen*), and morphological derivation (*vikāra*, *rnam 'gyur*), as presented in the writings of Pang Lodro Tenpa. There are two different sorts of primary base—verbal roots (*dhātu*, *byings*) and nominal stems (*nāman*, *ming*). Affixation is applied to these stems or roots through the agency of verbal or nominal suffixes, which can differentiate tense, mood, voice, number, declension, gender, and case. The processes of morphological derivation are more complex and are traditionally understood through the so-called Pāṇinian technical markers (*anubandha*, *rjes su 'brel ba*), which prescribe certain rules for forming derivatives, as well as through the diverse verbal prepositions, augments, and affixes which can be appended, and the compex rules for elision, vowel strengthening, and euphonic conjunction (*sandhi*, *sbyor ba*). Many examples are offered in the course of this terse summary, which concludes with a short section on the nuances of nominal compounding (*samāsa*, *tshig sdud*), a distinctive feature of Sanskrit syntax, that enables several conjoined word-forms to take a single termination.

Following in the footsteps of Situ Chokyi Jungne, who encouraged the study of Sanskrit grammatical and related literature, Kongtrul concludes this section by stating that "for one who would learn the phonetic articulations of the Sanskrit language, an intelligence that easily understands both word and meaning will arise if one becomes undeluded with regard not only to the words but also to their meaning."

Buddhist Logic

Buddhist logic (*pramāṇavidyā*, *tshad ma'i rig gnas*) is founded on the classical Sanskrit treatises of Dignāga, Dharmakīrti, and their commentators. All the main schools of Tibetan Buddhism also developed distinctive interpretations and points of emphasis. Among them, the earliest Tibetan interpretations include the Kadampa writings of Chapa Chokyi Senge (1109–1169), Chomden Rigpei Raldri (1227–1305), and Bodong Paṇchen (1376–1451). Within the Sakya tradition, the most influential text is the *Tshad ma rigs gter* of Sakya Paṇchen Kunga Gyaltsen (1182–1251) and its commentaries by Gorampa Sonam Senge (1429–1489) and Zilungpa Shākya Chokden (1428–1507). For Kagyupas, the most influential source is the *Rigs pa'i gzhung lugs kyi rgya mtsho* of Karmapa VII Chodrak Gyatso (1454–1506), although Kongtrul also cites the work of Zhamarpa VI Garwang Chokyi Wangchuk (1584–1630).

Noteworthy Nyingma exponents, who by and large have adopted a more utilitarian approach to the study of logic, include Sodokpa Lodro Gyaltsen (b. 1552) and more recently Mipham Namgyal Gyatso (1846–1912). On the other hand, Gelukpa writers have tended to emphasize the study of logic as an elaborate preliminary exercise that hones the mind for spiritual practice. Followers of Tsongkhapa who have exemplified this approach include Khedrubje Gelek Pelzangpo (1385–1438), Paṇchen Sonam Drakpa (1478–1554), and more recently Phurbuchok Tsultrim Jampa Gyatso Pelzangpo (1825–1901). The last mentioned authored the *Magic Key of the Path of Reason: A Presentation of the Collected Topics, Analyzing the Meaning of Valid Cognition* (*Tshad ma'i gzhung don 'byed pa'i bsdus grva rnam gzhag rigs lam 'phrul gyi lde mig*), which has become a bible for structured debate.

Kongtrul begins by reiterating that the purpose of Buddhist logic is to "eradicate wrong understandings, with regard to all objects of knowledge that are not directly evident but held to be indirectly evident to one's own mind." His main exegesis appears to follow the tradition of Phurbuchok, although parallels are found also in Sakya Paṇchen's *Tshad ma rigs gter*. There are three main topics to be analyzed: appraisable objects (*viṣaya, yul*), subjects (*viṣayin, yul can*), and processes of logical understanding.

Appraisable objects are categorized as either substantial (*dngos po*) or insubstantial (*dngos med*) in nature, the former comprising external and internal matter, and the latter cognitive phenomena. Among them, substantial objects have causal efficiency (*kāraṇa, byed pa*), either in terms of direct or indirect causes; they may be compounded or uncompounded (*'dus byas dang 'dus ma byas*); and they may be permanent or impermanent (*rtag pa dang mi rtag pa*). In terms of their process of objectification, objects are also classed as apparent (*snang yul*), apprehended (*grāhyakaviṣaya, bzung yul*), conceived (*adhyavasāyaviṣaya, zhen yul*), or engaged (*'jug yul*). In terms of their understanding, however, they are said to include specifically or generally characterized phenomena, directly or indirectly evident objects of appraisal, and signified phenomena (*vākya, brjod bya*).

Subjects are, by contrast, defined as signifiers (*vācaka, brjod byed*), comprising nouns (*nāman, ming*), syntactically bound phrases (*pada, tshig*), and sentences (*vāk, ngag*). They include words that signify types (*rigs brjod kyi sgra*) or sets (*tshogs brjod kyi sgra*); words signifying predicate expressions (*chos brjod kyi sgra*); and words signifying subject expressions (*chos can brjod pa'i sgra*), or preclusion (*vyavaccheda, rnam gcod*). In terms of their theoretical presentation, subjects are also analyzed as directly or implicitly conceived signifiers (*zhen pa'i brjod byed*) and actual signifiers (*dngos kyi brjod byed*).

Having then defined what is meant by the terms "syllable" (*varṇa, yi ge*) and "individual person" (*gang zag*), Kongtrul shows how valid, reliable cognition (*pramāṇa, tshad ma*) takes place either through direct perception (*mngon *sum tshad ma*) or inference (*rjes dpag tshad ma*)—the former including direct perception of the senses, mental consciousness, intrinsic awareness, and yoga, and the latter including inference through the cogent power of facts, popular acclaim, and conviction. On the other hand, cognition may also be unreliable (*apramāṇa, tshad min*), just as it may be conceptual or non-conceptual, and mistaken or unmistaken. Distinctions are then drawn between intrinsic or reflexive awareness (*svasaṃvedana, rang rig*) and extraneous awareness (*anyasaṃvid, gzhan rig*), and between mind (*citta, sems*) and its diverse mental states (*caitta, sems byung*).

The logical understanding acquired in relation to the aforementioned objects and subjects may result from the presence of contradiction (*virudha, 'gal ba*), relation (*saṃbandha, 'brel ba*), negation (*pratiṣedha, dgag pa*), proof (*vidhi, sgrub pa*), universals (*sāmānya, spyi*), particulars (*viśeṣa, bye brag*), identity and difference (*abhinnabhinna, gcig dang tha dad*), eliminative engagement (*apohapravṛtti, sel 'jug*), affirmative engagement (*vidhipravṛtti, sgrub 'jug*), or extraneous elimination (*anyāpoha, gzhan sel*). Specific expressions are also categorized as exemplars of definition (*lakṣaṇa, mtshan nyid*) or definiendum (*lakṣya, mtshon bya*); and as substance phenomena (*dravyadharma, rdzas chos*) or distinguishing counterpart phenomena (*vyāvṛttidharma, ldog chos*).

When inference is employed for one's own sake (*rang don rjes dpag*), the property of the thesis (*pakṣadharma, phyogs chos*) may be subject to either forward logical entailment (*anvayavyāpti, rjes khyab*) or counter logical entailment (*vyatirekavyāpti, ldog khyab*). Genuine evidence may be obtained in three ways (*gtan tshigs gsum*): through the axiom of the result (*kāryahetu, 'bras bu'i rtags*), the axiom of identity (*svabhāvahetu, rang bzhin gyi rtags*), and the axiom of the absence of the objective referent (*ma dmigs pa'i rtags*). On the other hand, untenable evidence (*khas mi len pa'i rtags*) may be rejected as ostensible, contradictory, uncertain, or unestablished. The examples employed in the construction of logical arguments (*dṛṣṭānta, dpe*) are classified as correct analogous examples, non-analogous examples, or ostensible examples.

When inference is employed for others' sake (*gzhan don rjes dpag*), the argument may take the form of either a correctly formulated statement of proof (*sgrub ngag*) with qualitative similarity or dissimilarity, or an ostensible statement of proof (*sgrub ngag ltar snang*), in which case the evidence (*rtags*) that has been presented may be subject to elimination, refutation, or consequential reasoning. Kongtrul also describes the defining characteristics of an ideal antagonist (*snga rgol*) and an ideal respondent or protagonist (*phyi rgol*) in the context of debate.

The author ends this section by mentioning other important logical traditions that evolved in Tibet prior to Phurbuchok, including that of Sakya Paṇchen's *Treasure of Logical Reasoning* (*Tshad ma rigs gter*), Karmapa Chodrak Gyatso's *Oceanic Textbook of Uncommon Logical Reasoning* (*Thun min rig gzhung rgya mtsho*), and the ancient Kadampa logical traditions.

He then goes on to summarize the techniques employed in debate or dialectics. These include correct and ostensible forms of direct perception and inference, correct and ostensible forms of proof and refutation, and appraisable objects that may be directly evident, indirectly evident, or indirectly evident to an extreme degree. Moreover, according to the particular Kagyu presentation of Zhamarpa Chokyi Wangchuk, five essential modes of logical reasoning are identified.

The practicalities of debate include how to recognize evidence and specific predicates (*rtags gsal gyi ngos 'dzin*), and what are the suitable rejoinders made by respondents to antagonists upon recognizing or accepting a valid cognition, or a non-valid cognition, on the basis of non-establishment of the argument, contradictory reasoning, or unascertained reasoning. The dialectician should know that there are eight possible approaches to logical entailment (*khyab pa sgo brgyad*), namely, forward logical entailment (*anvayavyāpti, rjes khyab*), contrary entailment (*viruddhavyāpti, 'gal khyab*), backward entailment (*heṣṭhavyāpti, thur khyab*), and counter entailment (*vyatirekavyāpti, ldog khyab*), each of which may be positive or negative.

Fine Arts

The indigenous Indian literature concerning the fine and applied arts (*śilpaśāstra, bzo rig*) includes commentaries on specific chapters or elements of the tantras. Among them are the works of Kuladatta, Jaggadarpaṇa, Śākyamitra, and Ātreya. In emphasizing the importance of the arts, Kongtrul remarks that

> All the [material] things that are deemed necessary for the Buddhist teachings and mundane activities cannot be created or achieved without relying on this science [of fine arts].

And:

> Although the [diverse] artistic traditions are infinite, all aspects of knowledge—not only the arts—can be categorized in terms of the "fine arts of the three media" [body, speech, and mind].

In this section, which is the most extensive in Book Six, Part One, Kongtrul considers the physical, vocal, and mental arts in succession. Each of these has supreme and common forms; and in the case of the supreme arts of the body, these comprise

> sculptures, paintings, and sculpted images of the buddhas, which are all representations of buddha body; the literary works of India and Tibet, which are representations of buddha speech; and the stūpas and [various] kinds of symbolic hand-held emblem, which are representations of buddha mind.

The section on the representations of buddha body (*sku rten*) is preceded by a passage discussing the virtues and faults exhibited by artists and patrons of the arts. Sculptures and paintings depicting the icons of sacred Buddhist art are to be drawn in accordance with the prescribed rules of iconometric proportion (*brten pa lha'i cha tshad*). In general, it is said that there are five iconometric scales and six categories of icons, which accords with the distinctions found in the *Tantra of the Wheel of Time* (*Kālacakra Tantra*), the *Tantra of the Emergence of Cakrasaṃvara* (*Saṃvarodaya Tantra*), and the *Tantras of Black and Red Yamāri* (*Kṛṣṇayamāri Tantra/ Raktayamāri Tantrarāja*). More specifically, however, in terms of current practice, there are two main traditions of iconographic measurement extant in Tibet—the Encampment style (*gar bri*) of Eastern Tibet, which bases itself on Buton Rinchendrub's identification of eleven distinct categories of icon, and the Menri (*sman ris*) style, based on Menla Dondrub's system, which recognizes eight distinct categories of icon.

The essential elements of iconographic painting and sculpture that require the undivided attention of the artist include the demeanor (*nyams*), posture (*'dug stangs*), ornaments (*rgyan*), hand emblems (*phyag mtshan*), thrones, and backrests (*khri rgyab*), as well as the application of colors and shading (*tshon mdangs*), stylistic features (*rnam 'gyur*), and the correction of errors in draftsmanship (*skyon sel*). Special procedures and iconometric rules are applied when drawing and painting celestial palaces (*rten gzhal yas khang*) and the elements of the maṇḍalas they contain. Colored sand may be applied to represent the distinct bands of a maṇḍala—its walls, gates, and pedimental arches. Furthermore, the symbols emblematic of the deities may be represented as either two-dimensional painted forms or three-dimensional sculpted forms.

The representations of buddha speech (*gsung rten*) include the ancient Indic scripts, some of which, such as Rañjanā and Vartula, are still well-known in Tibet, and the various categories of Tibetan scripts. Kongtrul, in the latter case, emphasizes the evolution and functions of the headed and headless block-letter forms of Tibetan script (*gzab chen/chung*). He includes pith instructions concerning the eight important strokes in block-letter calligraphy, the ten calligraphic points to be memorized and recited, the twenty-one primary characteristics, the sixteen secondary characteristics, the three general characteristics, and the calligraphic gridlines. The functions and usefulness of other Tibetan scripts are then examined, among them the headless thick-stroked italic script (*'bru chen*), the headless thin-stroked italic script (*'bru chung*), the handwriting scripts (*bshur ma*) and the cursive shorthand scripts (*'khyug yig*). In a long passage of verse, he describes the technicalities of paper-making (*bris gzhi*), the cutting of bamboo pens (*rgya smyug*), and the preparation of vermilion and black ink (*mtshal snag*).

The representations of buddha mind (*thugs rten*) include stūpas, which are essentially of five types: those that are spontaneously present by nature, those that are unsurpassed, those that are consecrated by blessings, those that have arisen from spiritual accomplishments, and those that correspond to the different vehicles. In terms of actual stūpa construction, however, there are different designs to be followed, including the model stūpas prescribed for ordinary persons, pious attendants, hermit buddhas, and buddhas. The last, which are most widely constructed in the Indo-Tibetan tradition, themselves comprise eight distinct types, symbolic of eight distinct deeds in the life of the Buddha, namely, the Stūpa of the Sugatas (*bde gshegs mchod rten*), the Stūpa of Supreme Enlightenment (*byang chub chen po'i mchod rten*), the Stūpa of the Wheel of the Sacred Teachings (*chos 'khor mchod rten*), the Stūpa of Miracles (*cho 'phrul mchod rten*), the Stūpa of the Divine Descent (*lha babs mchod rten*), the Stūpa of Resolving Schism (*dbyen bzlums mchod rten*), the Stūpa of Victory (*rnam rgyal mchod rten*), and the Stūpa of Nirvāṇa (*myang 'das mchod rten*).

Kongtrul then goes on to describe the dimensions and symbolism of the different elements of the stūpa (*mchod rten gyi tshad*), concluding with an account of certain miraculous stūpas which are said not to have been made by human hand, such as the Jñānabimbakāya Stūpa (*ye shes gzugs kyi sku*) of southwest India and the Svayambhū Stūpa (*rang byung mchod rten*) of Nepal, as well as other distinctive models that are mentioned in the Nyingma tradition.

In addition to stūpas, the hand-held emblems of the deities, such as the vajra and bell (*rdo rje dril bu*), are also classed among the supreme representations of buddha mind.

This long section concerning the supreme arts of the body concludes with a discussion on the playing of sacred percussion instruments—various sorts of drums and cymbals (*rnga dang sbub chol*)—and the choreographic movements (*stangs stabs*) of sacred masked dances. Here, Kongtrul summarizes the writings of Lochen Dharmaśrī, describing the preparation of the dance arena, the sacred offering dances, the nine dramatic dance moods, the thirteen procedures in the basic dance of the herukas, and the masked dances of exorcism.

By contrast, the common physical arts (*lus bzo phal pa*) are said to include construction of high-rise buildings, such as royal palaces, sports stadia, meeting halls, and the residences of ordinary people, as well as ocean-faring ships and small ferry boats, the particular styles of clothing and ornaments suitable for men and women, culinary techniques, palanquins, irrigation turbines, and military contraptions—armor, arrows, bows, swords, artillery, stone-catapults, naval cannons, Greek fire, curved knives, wind machines, siege catapults, and war chariots.

The supreme arts of speech (*ngag gi bzo gnas*) are the techniques of debate, teaching, and composition (*rtsod 'chad rtsom gsum*). They also include the expression of the four melodic contours (*nga ro*) of sacred chanting (*gdangs*). Among them:

(1) The sustaining note (*sthāyī, 'dren pa*) may be of five types, because it may be induced by the vowel A, which is level or neutral; E, which is sharp; I, which is flat; O, which is high; or U, which is low.
(2) The descending note (*avarohī, bkug pa*), through its undulations, may last for a single beat or multiple beats.
(3) The changing note (*sañcārī, bsgyur ba*) occurs due to repetition and includes three types—guttural variation, lingual variation, and nasal variation.
(4) The ascending note (*ārohī, ltengs pa*) occurs by raising [the voice an octave], and may be of two sorts—long and short.

Kongtrul remarks that the preliminary training in chanting should emphasize three essentials—courage or brilliance (*spobs pa'i gnad*), tempo (*dus kyi gnad*), and refinement (*sbyangs pa'i gnad*), through which the six defects (*skyon drug*) and their five causes (*rgyu lnga*) also should be abandoned. Then, citing Candraśrī, he adds that sacred chanting should be performed in six great ceremonial contexts: offering rites of attainment (*sgrub mchod*), empowerments (*dbang bskur*), consecrations (*rab gnas*), anniversary offering ceremonies (*dus mchod*), funeral rites (*gshin don*), and elaborate burnt offerings (*sbyin sreg*). In conclusion, he notes that Sakya Paṇchen's *Treatise on Music* (*Rol mo'i bstan bcos*) refers to twelve ancillary modes of chanting, while Candraśrī alludes to twelve modalities of voice pitch.

The common vocal arts (*ngag bzo phal pa*) include the songs performed at secular festivals recounting tales of yaks or wealth and contests of repartee between the sexes, along with the musical accompaniment of flutes, assorted percussion, and string instruments. Rhetoric, comprising informal discursive talks (*'bel gtam*) and formal speeches (*gral 'phros*), is also included here.

The supreme arts of mind (*yid gi bzo gnas mchog tu gyur pa*) include study, reflection, and meditation (*thos bsam sgom gsum*), through which discriminative awareness is cultivated, in accordance with the exposition Kongtrul himself offers in Books Six through Eight of *The Treasury of Knowledge*. By contrast, the common mental arts include the so-called eighteen great topics of knowledge (*rigs gnas chen po bco brgyad*), as well as the scrutiny of land (*sa gzhi brtag pa*), gems and precious metals (*rin po che brtag pa*), trees and elephants (*ljong shing dang glang po che brtag pa*), treasures (*gter brtag pa*), horses (*rta brtag pa*), and men and women (*pho mo brtag pa*).

In addition, there are several treatises on human behavior (*lugs kyi bstan bcos*) preserved in the Tengyur, along with various listings of the sixty-four crafts (*sgyu rtsal drug cu rtsa bzhi*), the thirty designated arts (*bzo la sogs par gtogs pa sum cu*), the eighteen requisites of musical performance (*rol mo'i bye brag bco brgyad*), the seven tones of the musical scale (*glu dbyangs kyi nges pa bdun*), and the nine dramatic moods (*gar gyi cha byad dgu*). According to Śīlapālita, the common mental arts are differentiated on the basis of whether they pertain to wealth or objects, to desire, to religion, or to liberation. More elaborately, Longchen Rabjampa in his *Treasury of Wish-fulfilling Gems* (*Yid bzhin mdzod*) identifies the arts of mind with the full diversity of ordinary human activities, which he summarizes in twenty-two aspects, starting with the characteristics of the six classes of sentient beings.

Medicine

The Indian medical science of Āyurveda straddles the Brāhmaṇical and Buddhist traditions. At its roots are the compilations (*saṃhitā*) of two celebrated physicians of antiquity—Caraka and Suśruta, but specifically within the Buddhist tradition, there are treatises by Candranandana, Nāgārjuna, and Vāgbhaṭa, extant in the Tengyur. Among them, Vāgbhaṭa's *Eight Divisions of Medical Science* (*Aṣṭāṅgahṛdayasaṃhitā*) has been particularly influential. Within the Tibetan medical tradition, however, primacy is given to the *Great Tantra of Secret Instructions on the Eight Branches of the Essence of the Glorious*

Elixir of Immortality (*dPal ldan bdud rtsi snying po yan lag brgyad pa gsang ba man ngag gi rgyud chen po*). This text is said to have been transmitted in Tibet by the great translator Vairocana during the eighth century, based on teachings he received from Candranandana and Padmasambhava in the lifetime of the great physician Yutok Yonten Gonpo the Elder, and to have been concealed as a "treasure-doctrine" (*gter chos*) at Samye, from where it was subsequently revealed by Drapa Ngonshe of Dratang on 19 July 1038. Subsequently the text was redacted and came to be known as the *Four Tantras of Dratang* (*Grva thang rgyud bzhi*). Some contemporary scholars consider the work to have been adapted by Yutok Yonten Gonpo himself from an earlier Bon medical treatise by Chebu Trishe (*dpyad bu khri shes*), entitled *Four Collections of Medical Science* (*gSo rig 'bum bzhi*). Whatever its origin, the *Four Tantras of Dratang* has become the primary sourcebook for the practice of Buddhist medicine in Tibet, surpassing in its importance the aforementioned Sanskrit treatises.

By the fifteenth century, two main schools of interpretation had evolved: the Jangpa school, stemming from Rigdzin Namgyal Trakzangpel and including Namgyal Dorje (fl. sixteenth century); and the Zurkhar lineage, stemming from Wangchuk Drak and including Zurkhar Nyamnyi Dorje (1439–1475). These and other medical lineages were integrated during the seventeenth century by Sangye Gyatso (1653–1705), the author of the authoritative *Blue Beryl* (*Baiḍūrya sngon po*) treatise. Sangye Gyatso additionally composed further texts on medicine—the *Survey of Medicine* (*sMan gyi khog 'bubs*) and his concise appraisal in chapter thirty-four of the *Removal of the Tarnish of Deluded Appearances* (*'Khrul snang gYa' sel*), which is an addendum to the *White Beryl* (*Baiḍūrya dkar po*).

Concerning the *Four Tantras of Dratang*, Kongtrul remarks that the text is "easy to comprehend and well-intentioned. It perfectly reveals the meanings of the eight aspects [of medicine] and is great on account of its extensive benefits for all [sentient beings], regardless of their status."

Each of the *Four Tantras of Dratang* is presented for pedagogic reasons in the form of a graphic arboreal metaphor, comprising roots, stems, branches, leaves, flowers, and fruits. On this analogy, the "root" of physiology and pathology gives rise to eighty-eight "leaves," the "root" of diagnosis to thirty-eight "leaves," and the "root" of the methods of remedial treatment to ninety-six "leaves." The "flowers" symbolize the freedom from disease and longevity acquired by those who have properly understood and implemented medical science, while the "fruits" symbolize the endowments of the sacred teachings, wealth, and well-being.

The promulgation of the *Four Tantras of Dratang* is attributed to the hermit sage Vidyājñāna, appearing in succession as an emanation of Bhaiṣajyaguru's buddha mind, body, attributes, and activities. Among them, the *Root Tantra* (*rTsa ba thugs kyi rgyud*) describes the tree of medicine, which has three roots—those of physiology (*gnas lugs*), diagnosis (*ngos 'dzin rtags*), and methods of treatment (*gso byed thabs*). The second is the *Exegetical Tantra* (*bShad pa sku yi rgyud*), which concerns the four therapeutic principles (*tshul bzhi*) outlined below. The third is the *Instructional Tantra* (*Man ngag yon tan rgyud*), which concerns the treatment of humoral and internal disorders of the body in general, as well as pediatrics, gynecological diseases, demonic possession, traumas, poisoning, elixirs of rejuvenation in the treatment of old age, the restoration of virility, and the treatment of infertility. The fourth is the *Subsequent Tantra* (*Phyi ma phrin las kyi rgyud*), which elaborates on the diseases afflicting the patient (*gso yul gyi nad*), the remedies (*gso byed gnyen po*), and the methods of treatment (*gso ba'i thabs*) from the standpoint of medical practice.

Kongtrul dwells briefly on the themes of the *Subsequent Tantra:* All ailments are generally classified as either imaginary diseases due to demonic possession (*kun brtags gdon*), ostensible diseases that suddenly occur (*ltar snang 'phral*), absolute diseases that harm the life span (*yongs grub tshe*), or dependent diseases due to past actions (*gzhan dbang sngon las kyi nad*). The remedies that may be applied include medications (*sman*), external therapies (*dpyad*), diet (*zas*) and regimen (*spyod lam*). Treatment begins with diagnostics (*brtag thabs*) based on pulse palpation (*reg pa rtsa*) and urinalysis (*mthong ba chu la brtag pa*). Then, keeping in mind nine therapeutic principles (*gso tshul rnam pa dgu*), the following curative methods (*bcos thabs*) may be applied: eight classes of tranquilizing agents (*zhi byed sde tshan brgyad*), seven cathartic procedures (*sbyong byed bdun*), and six techniques of external therapy (*dpyad pa drug*).

At this juncture, Kongtrul returns to the theoretical basis outlined in the second of the *Four Tantras of Dratang*, to introduce the four therapeutic principles (*gso ba'i tshul bzhi rgyas par bshad pa*), namely, the patient to be treated (*gso bya'i yul*), the remedy (*gso byed gnyen po*), the method of treatment (*gso thabs*), and the practicing physician (*gso mkhan*).

Among them, the patient is considered in terms of physiology and pathology. Under physiology, the text elaborates on the themes of human embryology, anatomy, bodily constituents, interconnecting channels, vulnerable points, passageways, and orifices. The defining characteristics of human physiology are the seven bodily constituents; the three impurities; the humors that may be harmful; physical activities, distinctions based on sex, age, and constitution; and the signs of physical decay. Pathology, by contrast, concerns the remote and immediate primary causes of disease as well as the secondary causes of disease, such as the affected sensory activity fields, the covert gathering and overt arising of the three humors, the full manifestation of disease, the inception of disease, its characteristics, and classification according to primary causes, the sex or age of the patient, and the actual humoral disorders that manifest.

The second therapeutic principle concerns the remedy, which may include daily, seasonal, or occasional regimen; dietetics; the prescription of compounded medications, which have their distinctive tastes, potencies, and post-digestive tastes; and the techniques of external therapy, whether mild, rough, or rigorous. This section ends with a listing of the various surgical instruments and their functions.

The third therapeutic principle concerns suitable methods of treatment, including prophylactics (*nad med gnas shing 'tsho ba*) and actual treatment (*na ba gso bar bya'o*). The latter entails effective diagnostics, whether based on genuine understanding, subterfuge, or the so-called four parameters (*spang blang mu bzhi'i brtag pa*), followed by the application of general and specific therapeutic principles as well as anabolic and catabolic methods of treatment.

The fourth therapeutic principle concerns the practicing physician, who should be distinguished by six primary attributes and avoid the twelve defects of inferior doctors.

Minor classical sciences

Among the five minor sciences (*rigs gnas chung ba*), poetics, prosody, lexicography, and dramaturgy are all considered subsidiary to Sanskrit grammar, while astrology is most closely affiliated with medicine in the Tibetan tradition.

Astrology

In India, the non-Buddhist traditions of astrology (*jyotiḥśāstra, skar rtsis*) are exemplified by the works of Varāhamihira, whose *Fivefold Textbook Calculation* (*Pañcasiddhāntikā*) exhibits indigenous and Bactrian Greek influences. Buddhist sources on astrology include canonical works, such as the *Sūtra of the Nucleus of the Sun* (*Sūryagarbhasūtra*), the *Tantra of the Wheel of Time* (*Kālacakra Tantra*), Puṇḍarīka's *Taintless Light* (*Vimalaprabhā*), and

Vasubandhu's *Treasury of Phenomenology* (*Abhidharmakośa*). The extensive Tibetan commentarial literature, upon which different calendrical systems are based, includes the following traditions:

(1) Sakya, exemplified by the works of Chogyal Phakpa Lodro Gyaltsen (1235–1280) and Yungton Dorjepel (1284–1365);
(2) Tsurphu, exemplified by the writings of Karmapa Rangjung Dorje (1284–1339) and Pawo Tsuklak Trengwa (1504–1566);
(3) Go Lotsāwa Zhonupel (1392–1481), who introduced the practical "error correction" system;
(4) the Phugpa system, represented by the writings of Phugpa Lhundrub Gyatso (fl. fifteenth century) and Norzang Gyatso (1423–1513);
(5) the New Phugpa system, represented by Sangye Gyatso (1653–1705) and Lochen Dharmaśrī (1654–1717); and
(6) the Jonang system, represented by the works of Drakpa Pelzang (fl. sixteenth to seventeenth centuries) and Banda Gelek Gyatso (1844–1904).

Kongtrul begins by observing that "Since this science [of astrology] is undeluded with respect to the mathematical calculations and circumstances applicable in the relative world, it should disclose without error [the appropriate courses or actions] that are to be adopted and those that are to be abandoned."

The *Tantra of the Wheel of Time* in particular emphasizes the correlation between the microcosmic precision of the inner world (*nang gi nges pa*) and the precision of the calculations that pertain to the macrocosm—constellations and planets. The former refers to the cycles of exhalation and inhalation of breath through the left and right nostrils of the body respectively, setting in motion the five elements—space, wind, fire, water, and earth—in progressive and retrograde sequences. Here, it is said that the step index of slow (*dal rkang*) and fast planetary motion (*myur rkang*) may be correlated with the calculations applicable to the fire element and the wind element respectively. Each of these minor elemental cycles (*'pho chung*) is equivalent to three hundred and sixty breaths, and when all five elements have been completely set in motion, that is known as a major cycle (*'pho chen*), equivalent to one thousand eight hundred breaths.

Furthermore, it is said that there are six major cycles of breath associated with Aries and the other odd-numbered solar mansions (*mi mnyam pa'i khyim*), correlating with the right-side energy channel, and six major cycles of breath associated with Taurus and the other even-numbered solar mansions (*mnyam pa'i khyim*), correlating with the left-side energy channel. Collectively, the breaths corresponding to the twelve solar mansions number twenty-one thousand six hundred, which is reckoned to be the total number of breaths in a single solar day. In the interval between any two major cycles, the breath is said to re-enter the central energy channel of the subtle body from the left- and right-side channels. This moment correlates with the state of vacuity (*stong par gnas*) that endures when the cycle of cosmological formation and dissolution has ended, or when consciousness enters naturally into a state of natural inner radiance (*rang bzhin 'od gsal*) in the interval between the cycle of birth and death.

In terms of the macrocosm, when the twelve solar mansions (*khyim bcu gnyis*) and the twenty-eight constellations (*rgyu skar nyer brgyad*) become manifest upon the zodiac, they seem to move clockwise, while the Sun and the planetary bodies appear to move anti-clockwise—with the exception of Rāhu, the eclipser, who ostensibly moves clockwise, devouring the Moon and the Sun at regular and predictable lunar and solar eclipses.

There are three distinct ways of calculating the duration of the day, in terms of the zodiacal or sidereal day (*khyim zhag*), the calendar day (*tithi, tshes zhag*), and the solar day (*dina, nyin zhag*). Among them, the zodiacal day is a measure of time equivalent to one thirtieth of a single sign of the zodiac, there being three hundred and sixty of them in a zodiacal year. The calendar or lunar day is dependent on the phases of the moon, thirty of them corresponding in duration to the lunar month. The solar day comprises twelve two-hour periods, commencing from daybreak (*nam langs, pratyūṣa*) at approximately 5AM, and ending with pre-dawn (*tho rangs*) around 3AM. The solar days are therefore of equal length and correspond to the days of the week, from Monday through to Sunday.

Kongtrul then examines conventional divisions of time, contrasting the three different months which may traditionally herald the lunar new year; and he shows how there are different views as to whether the waning or waxing half of the lunar month has precedence.

When practically applied, there are five aspects of astrological calculation (*yan lag lnga/ lnga bsdus*) which are to be determined: the seven alternating days of the week, the twenty-seven constellations that demarcate lunar and solar longitude individually, the twenty-seven combined calculations of solar and lunar longitude (*yoga, sbyor ba*), and the eleven impacts of the lunar month (*karaṇa, byed pa*), four of which are "fixed" and seven "transient." Further calculations then take into account the apparent motion of the five main planetary bodies against the zodiacal band of the constellations, the predictions of solar and lunar eclipses, and the current ascendant conjunction or rising sign (*tatkāla, dus sbyor*).

Outside astrology, subsidiary calculations also have to be made in respect of other systems of divination, especially the Svarodaya system (*dbyangs 'char*), which derives from Jumla in northwest Nepal, and the system of elemental divination (*'byung rtsis*) which derives from China.

Poetics

The Tibetan appreciation of Sanskrit poetics (*kāvya, snyan dngags*) is based almost exclusively on Daṇḍin's *Mirror of Poetics* (*Kāvyādarśa*), in contrast to the works of Bhamāha and Udbhaṭa, which were never translated. Later Tibetan writers also refer to the Sanskrit commentaries on Daṇḍin's work by Ratnaśrī and Vāgindrakīrti. According to the *Mirror of Poetics*, the body of poetry (*śarīra, lus*) comprises metrical compositions (*padya, tshigs bcad*), prose compositions (*gadya, lhug pa*), and compositions of mixed verse and prose (*miśra, spel ma*). The first includes detached verse, clustered verses, intricate verse, compound verse, and cantos. Prose, by contrast, includes both narrative and legend; while the versatile or mixed composition may take the form of courtly drama or Campū-style composition and employ any of the four established literary languages of ancient India—the "refined language of Sanskrit, the common language of Prākrit, the corrupted language of Apabhraṃśa, and the hybrid language of Miśrabhāṣā."

There are various poetic devices or ornaments (*alaṃkāra, rgyan*) that may be employed, including the ten uncommon ornaments of the mellifluous South Indian or Vaidarbha style, and the somewhat harsher and more uneven East Indian or Gauḍa style. Kṣemendra's *Wish-granting Tree: Narrative of the Bodhisattva* (*Bodhisattvāvadānakalpalatā, dPag bsam 'khri shing*) is extolled as an exemplary text according to the tradition of the easterners, and Śūra's *Garland of Birth Stories* (*Jātakamālā*) has a similar status according to the tradition of the southerners.

The common ornaments, of which both styles partake, include the thirty-five recognized ornaments of sense (*arthālaṃkāra, don rgyan*), namely, natural description, simile, metaphor, poetic association, repetition, denial, corroboration, contrast, peculiar causation, concise suggestion, hyperbole, poetic fancy, cause, misrepresentation, subtlety, respective ordering of words and meaning, flattery, sentiment, vigor, indirect speech, coincidence, exaltation, obfuscation, double entendre, expressions of distinction, equal pairing, incongruity, artful praise, damning with faint praise, co-mention, illustrative simile, exchange, benediction, conjunction of poetic figures, and underlying intention.

In addition, there are phonetic ornaments (*śabdālaṃkāra, sgra rgyan*), including repetition; complex ornaments employing acrostic verse and alliteration; as well as sixteen "ornaments of enigmatic innuendo" (*ṣoḍaśaprahelikā, gab tshig bcu drug*), which are employed to incite laughter.

The *Mirror of Poetics* concludes with a summary of the ten potential defects of poetic composition, which, along with vernacular slang, are to be avoided. These include incoherence, incongruity, tautology, ambiguity, syntactical disorder, grammatical error, discordance of metrical pause, prosodic deviation, absence of euphonic conjunction, and non-sequitur with regard to place, time, fine arts, the mundane world, scriptural authority, or logical reasoning.

Prosody

The Tibetan understanding of prosody (*chandas, sdeb sbyor*) derives largely from Ratnākaraśānti's *Precious Source of Prosody* (*Chandoratnākara*) and its auto-commentary. Prosody includes metric rules governing syllabic quantity (*vṛtta*) or moric instants (*jāti*), either of which may be applied in the context of a traditional stanza (*śloka*) comprising four metrical lines of verse.

The former entails the scansion of the syllabic quantity of meters with equal lines (*samāvṛtta, mnyam pa'i vṛttta*), unequal lines (*viṣamavṛtta, mi mnyam pa'i vṛtta*), or semi-equal lines (*ardhavṛtta, phyed mnyam pa'i vṛtta*). Among them, when the lines are of equal length, Ratnākaraśānti holds, in common with earlier traditional Sanskrit sources such as Piṅgala's *Discourse on Prosody* (*Chandaḥsūtra*), that meter classes may begin with verses comprising only a single syllable and range up to verses of twenty-seven syllables or more. Seven of the most commonly employed meter classes are named after the mythic seven horses that pull the chariot of Aditya—the sun—across the heavens in the course of a solar day, viz. Gāyatrī (six syllables), Uṣṇih (seven syllables), Anuṣṭubh (eight syllables), Bṛhatī (nine syllables), Paṅktī (ten syllables), Triṣṭubh (eleven syllables), and Jagatī (twelve syllables).

By contrast, when lines of verse are divided according to the number of moric instants (*jāti*), there are three possible meters—the Āryā, Vaitālya, and Paiṅgala meters—in which the eight kinds of trimeter (*gaṇa, tshogs*) that are well known from classical Greek poetry are scanned:

> [Trimeters] adopting a "heavy" stress in the first, middle, and last syllables
> Are [respectively known as]
> The dactyl (BHA), the amphibrach (DZA), and the anapaest (SA).
> Those adopting a "light" stress [in the first, middle, and last syllables]
> Are [respectively known as]
> The bachius (YA), the cretic (RA), and the antibachius (TA).

While the molossus (MA) and the tribach (NA) respectively
Have [all three syllables] "heavy" and "light."

The final section of the *Precious Source of Prosody* concerns certain astonishing applications (*adbhutaprayoga, ngo mtshar rtogs byed kyi sbyor ba*). These relate to the mathematical field of combinatorics—examining possible combinations or permutations, in response to the basic question posed by Rachel Hall in "The Mathematics of Poetry," namely, how many ways are there to do or make something. In all, there are six astonishing calculations that can be made:

(1) The first is the preparation of a table of metrical variants (*prastāra, 'god tshul*), indicating how the number of possible permutations of heavy and light syllables doubles as the number of syllables in a line of verse increases incrementally by one.
(2) The second facilitates the process of understanding the general calculations applicable to each distinct meter class—as for example in the case of the tabular chart for the ten-syllable meter class, there are 1,024 variant meters, so that the table is nineteen units wide, 2,047 units deep, and comprises 38,893 square units in its extent.
(3) The third is the so-called "reductionist" calculation (*naṣṭa cho ga*) of Piṅgala, which shows how any specific meter in a given class can be spontaneously applied and the cadence of its heavy and light syllables easily understood, without the need for setting out all the tabular variations. This is achieved by dividing the number of the specific meter (e.g., the fourteenth permutation of the six-syllable class) by two, repeatedly until there is no remainder. An even quotient indicates that the first syllable will be "light," and an odd quotient, that it will be "heavy." This calculation ranks as the earliest known description of the binary numeral system.
(4) The fourth, also known as the "grouping of patterns," is used to calculate the specific position of a given meter within its class (*uddiṣṭa*), by placing the sequence of heavy and light syllables sequentially below the incremental tabular numbers (1, 2, 4, 8, 16, 32, 64, etc.). One thus obtains the numbers corresponding to the light syllables in the given meter, ignoring those that correspond to the heavy syllables. The numbers corresponding to the light syllables should then be tallied, and the number one added to the total. The answer indicates that the given meter is *x*th among the possible permutations in its meter class.

(5) The fifth is the formation of a triangular chart of light syllables (*yang ba'i bya ba*), which exactly resembles Pascal's triangle, enabling one to understand, with regard to a specific meter class, how many permutations have all their syllables "heavy" (*lci ba 'ba zhig pa du*), how many have one "light" syllable (*gcig yang ba du*), how many have two "light" syllables (*gnyis yang ba du*), and so on.

(6) The sixth is the *adhva* calculation of the exact point of cadence (*adhva, ji tsam 'gro ba*) in a given meter, formed on the basis of a grid comprising horizontal and vertical units, which shows the variations of heavy and light syllables and the intermediate units that are left blank.

Lastly, there are also three common ways of calculating the number of syllables, the number of moric instants, and the number of heavy and light syllables in a given line of verse.

Synonymics

Synonymics (*abhidāna, mngon brjod*) is a form of lexicography, based on the format of a traditional thesaurus containing lists of homonyms and synonyms appropriate for the composition of Sanskrit poetry (*kāvya, snyan ngag*). Foremost among the texts of this genre is the *Treasury of Amarasiṃha* (*Amarakośa*), also known as the *Treatise on Nouns and Gender* (*Nāmaliṅgānuśāsana*). The author, Amarasiṃha, is revered as one of the "nine gems" (*navaratna*) in the imperial court of Candragupta II (fl. 400 CE), although other sources assign him to the much later period of Vikramāditya (fl. seventh century). The popularity of this thesaurus among exponents of classical Indian poetry is attested by its forty-one Sanskrit commentaries, which are formally listed in Radhakāntadeva's *Śabdakalpadruma* lexicon, and about twenty further commentaries which exist in manuscript form—some in other Indic languages. Amarasiṃha is considered to have been a Buddhist, based on the prominence given in the text to synonyms of the word *buddha*, although others suggest that he may have followed the Jain tradition. Among the commentaries, only one—the *Wish-fulfilling Commentary* (*Amaraṭīkākāmadhenu*), composed by the Buddhist scholar Subhūticandra—was translated into Tibetan.

The *Treasury of Amarasiṃha* contains three chapters (*khāṇḍa*) The first, entitled "Celestial Realms and so forth" (*svargavargādikhāṇḍa*), is divided into ten sections concerning celestial realms, time, abstract terms, speech, sound, dramaturgy, subterranean abodes, serpents, hells, and water. The second chapter, entitled "Terrestrial Realms and so forth" (*bhūmivargādikhāṇḍa*), is divided into ten sections concerning earth, towns, minerals, vegetables, animals, humans, the priestly class, the royal class, the mercantile class, and the laboring class. The third chapter, entitled "General Topics and so forth" (*samānyādikhāṇḍa*), concerns adjectives, compounds, homonyms (*nānārtha-varga*), indeclinables, and gender.

At the outset, Kongtrul defines "names" (*nāman*, *ming*) as signifiers, capable of subsuming multi-syllabic forms as the basis of their designation (*prajñāptivastu*, *gdags gzhi*), and indicating the bare essential nature of a given object that is not syntactically bound. They include primary radical names, derived names, proper names, and imputed names. The application of synonyms and homonyms in poetry and literary composition requires knowledge of the paradigms of Sanskrit roots and the definitions of the terms expressed in both Sanskrit and Tibetan.

Dramaturgy

Although the essential Sanskrit treatise on dramaturgy (*nāṭya*, *zlos gar*), Bharata's *Nāṭyaśāstra*, was not translated into Tibetan, there are a small number of indigenous Tibetan compositions on this subject, which is distinct from the Tibetan operatic tradition. Among the few classical Sanskrit dramas that were translated into Tibetan, Harṣadeva's *Utter Delight of the Nāgas* (*Nāgānandanāmanāṭaka*) is contained within the Tengyur.

Kongtrul summarizes the significance of drama in the following paragraph:

> [Dramatic performances informed by] the science of Indian dramaturgy are endowed with sentiments or moods which give rise to joy in the people who see and hear [them], because the physical and verbal moods [that they evoke] are repeatedly recreated in the context of a play which captivates the minds [of the audience]. Although [this science] is known to be particularly amazing, the relevant [classical Indian] treatises are not extant in [Tibet,] the Land of Snows, and they are not immediately useful for the purpose of attaining liberation [from cyclic existence]. Even so, all the actions of the bodhisattvas, which are reminiscent of such [dramatic sentiments] and bring delight to sentient beings, should be studied.

Dramaturgy is considered by Kongtrul in terms of three topics: the sixty-five aspects of the five sequences of dramatic juncture (*samdhyaṅga*, *mtshams sbyor gyi yan lag*), the sixteen contexts of the four dramatic elements (*vṛty-aṅga, 'jug pa'i yan lag*), and the thirty-six characteristics of stagecraft (*lakṣaṇa, mtshan nyid*).

The five dramatic junctures, each of which has multiple aspects, indicate the different phases of a play or plot. Among them, the first is the dramatic juncture of the introduction (*mukhasaṃdhi, sgo'i mtshams sbyor*), in which an initial proposal (*'dri ba*) is made. The second is the dramatic juncture of the progression (*pratimukhasaṃdhi, lan gyi sgo'i mtshams sbyor*), in which a multitude of causes provoke a dialogue of proposals and rejoinders. The third is the dramatic juncture of the development (*garbhasaṃdhi, snying po'i mtshams sbyor*), in which, following many verbal exchanges exemplified by episodic discussions, the plot is decisively determined. The fourth is the dramatic juncture of the plot-crisis (*vimarśasaṃdhi, mi bzod pa'i mtshams sbyor*), in which words that seek to expose the wrongdoings of another backfire, exposing the speaker's own wrongdoings, which cannot be tolerated. The fifth is the dramatic juncture of the conclusion (*nirvahaṇasaṃdhi, nges pa thob byed kyi mtshams sbyor*), in which, following many statements expressing hesitation, a singular resolution or positive outcome is obtained.

The four dramatic elements are those of dialogue (*bhāratī*), grandeur (*sātvatī*), intimacy (*kauśikī*), and conflict (*ārabhaṭī*), each of which may occur in four distinct dramatic contexts. For example, dialogue may occur in the context of stimulating prologues, preludes, single-act dramas, or farce.

The thirty-six characteristics of stagecraft are enumerated as embellishment, abbreviation, beauty, declarations, reasons, doubts, objectives, attainments, prosperity, evidence, explanations, accomplishments, distinctions, disqualifications, hyperbole, similarity of ideas, versification, observations, suggestion, discrimination, opposition, solecism, conciliation, the bestowal of flower garlands, concord, reproach, presumption, proof, interrogation, mistaken identity, imagination, the use of disparaging metaphor, agitation, the proclamation of talents, understated achievements, and words of endearment.

Plays should also evoke key sentiments (*rasa, nyams*), including the "sentiment of extreme anger, the sentiment of anguish caused by desire, the sentiment of suffering caused by sorrow, the sentiment of astonishment caused by amazement, and other dramatic moods."

Mundane Spiritual Paths

Having examined the major and minor classical sciences, in the final section of Book Six, Part One, Kongtrul considers the advantages and disadvantages of worldly spiritual pursuits. In general, the term "philosophical system" (*siddhānta, grub mtha'*) implies that a specific level of realization may be attained but cannot be transcended. "Although reality (*tattva, de nyid*) is true, the perspectives of it which are known in the world are uncertain in terms of their truthfulness." Some of them, such as the views expressed in the so-called "exalted" vehicle (*abhyudayayāna, mngon mtho'i theg pa*), are deemed to be authentic, while others espousing eternalism (*nityadṛṣṭi, rtag lta*) or nihilism (*ucchedadṛṣṭi, chad lta*) are considered inauthentic. The doxographical penchant of Indian philosophers has already been noted.

Among the exponents of the non-Buddhist traditions of ancient India, who are labeled as "extremists" or "forders" because they cannot transcend the temporary props on which they rely and are therefore incapable of transcending the sufferings of cyclic existence, there are those classed as nominal extremists (*btags pa ba'i mu stegs pa*), emanational extremists (*sprul pa'i mu stegs pa*), and independently minded extremists (*rang rgyud kyi mu stegs pa*). The first are exemplified by virtuous ascetics (*śramaṇa, dge sbyong*) who advocate materialism, and even the Vātsīputrīya Buddhists, who held the psycho-physical aggregates (*skandha, phung po*) to be truly existent. The second include those extremists who have power to emanate in diverse forms on account of their meditative abilities and supernormal cognitive powers. The third include three types of meditator (*dhyāyī, bsam gtan pa*)—lower, middling and superior—who respectively have the ability to recollect thirty, sixty, and ninety aeons of time, as well as the dialecticians (*tārkika, rtog ge pa*) who developed the nihilistic and eternalistic philosophical systems.

Following the presentation of Chomden Rigpei Raldri, Kongtrul then enumerates twelve distinct categories of nihilistic and eternalistic view that are to be refuted and transcended.

1. Mundane Materialism

Firstly, the mundane materialists (*lokāyatika, rgyang 'phen pa*) are regarded as

> the lowest of all those propounding spiritual and philosophical systems; and they are the most severely [deluded] among deluded beings. Let us not even mention [the possibility of them aspiring to] liberation [from cyclic existence]! Since they lack the causal basis for attaining simply a physical body compatible with the exalted realms (*svarga, mtho ris*) [of gods and humans], the result that they accrue is exclusively compatible with the inferior realms (*durgati, ngan 'gro*).

The mundane materialists seek to establish four points: (1) that there is an indiscernible soul or self (*avyaktātma, mi gsal ba'i bdag*) existing when the elements are in their causative or formative state; (2) there is a discernible soul or self (*vyaktātma, gsal ba'i bdag*) existing when the elements are in their resultant or fruitional state; (3) that gods (*deva*), anguished spirits (*preta*), and denizens of the hells (*naraka*) do not exist, whereas animistic spirits do exist, as do people and animals; and (4) that the syllogistic concept of an inanimate object such as a "vase" may also be applicable to sentient beings in whom the physical body and the mind are of a single material substance. At the same time, they reject the existence of non-visible causes, denying the existence of past and future lives as well as the processes of past actions, causes and results, the existence of invisible phenomena, the validity of logical inference, and the revered status of the "three precious jewels" (*triratna, dkon mchog gsum*).

2. Sāṃkhya

The Sāṃkhya (*grangs can pa*) hold that all appraisable objects of knowledge may be considered in terms of the "twenty-five categories of reality" (*pañcaviṃśatitattva, de nyid nyer lnga*): primal matter (*pradhāna, gtso bo*); great intelligence (*mahat/ buddhi, chen po/ blo*); the threefold ego-principle (*ahaṃkāra, nga rgyal gsum*); the five quidities of subtle matter (*pañcatanmātra, de tsam lnga*), identified with the potentialities of sound, touch, color, taste, and smell; the five elements (*pañcabhūta, 'byung po lnga*); the five inner sense organs (*pañcantarendriya, nang blo'i dbang po lnga*); the five motor organs (*pañcabāhyendriya, phyi las kyi dbang po lnga*), namely, speech, handling, walking, excretion, and reproduction; the mind or mental faculty (*manas, yid*); and the "soul" (*ātma, bdag*) or "intelligent self" (*puruṣa, shes rig gi skyes bu*). These twenty-five categories may also be reduced to primal matter and "intelligent self," the former comprising nature (*prakṛti, rang bzhin*) and the latter the absence of nature (*aprakṛti, rang bzhin min pa*).

The "self" is essentially conceived as permanent—an actor or creator (*byed pa po*) and a consumer (*za ba po*), devoid of lightness (*sattva, snying stobs*), motility (*rajas, rdul*), and dullness (*tamas, mun pa*), but intelligent with regard to the nature of primary matter. Primal matter, in which all the other twenty-four categories are subsumed, is identified with nature (*prakṛti, rang bzhin*) at the causal level. It is the circumstance in which motility, dullness, and lightness are present in a state of perfect equilibrium. The "soul," or "cognizant self," being ignorant of the impurity of "nature" which gives rise to the aforementioned modifications, then becomes attached through a series of events, and as long as it enjoys or partakes of the sense objects, it will remain within the cycle of existence. But when it becomes dissatisfied with such enjoyments of the sense objects, through the supernormal cognitive powers associated with meditative concentration, it will directly behold the impurity of this engagement in "nature," and flee away in shame. Separated from this involvement in "nature," all the modifications produced by "nature" will be reversed in turn, and dissolve into the reality of unmodified nature itself. When the "self" abides in an absolutely radiant state, it is held that it will attain release from the cycle of existence.

In addition to the valid cognition of sense-perception (*pratyakṣapramāṇa*), accepted by mundane materialists, the Sāṃkhya school also upholds the valid cognition of inference for one's own sake (*svārthānumāna*), which entails seven kinds of relation (*saptasaṃbandhana, 'brel ba bdun*), and inference for the sake of others (*parārthānumāna*), which may include syllogisms based or not based on yogic experience.

3. Vaiśeṣika

The Vaiśeṣika (*bye brag pa*) hold that knowable phenomena comprise six categories (*śaṭpadārtha, tshig don drug*): (1) substance (*dravya, rdzas*) including "self," time, relative direction, space, and mind, along with the primary elements; (2) the nine attributes of the "self" (*ātmanavaguṇa, bdag gi yon tan dgu*), such as intellect, happiness, sorrow, effort, merit, demerit, and velocity; (3) actions (*karma, las*); (4) universals (*sāmānya, spyi*); (5) particulars (*viśeṣa, bye brag*); and (6) relational inherence (*samavāya, 'du ba*).

They hold that these six categories may be appraised by means not only of direct perception and the two kinds of inference but also through Vedic testimony (*śabdapramāṇa, sgra byung tshad ma*). As long as the nine attributes are all inherent in the soul, it will remain trapped within the cycle of existence, performing virtuous and non-virtuous actions. However, once the six categories that pertain to the "self" (*puruṣa, skyes bu*) are known, the nine attributes and their roots will be cut off, leaving the self or soul isolated, whereupon it will be released from the cycle of existence.

4. Naiyāyika

The Naiyāyika (*rig pa can pa*) uphold the same categorization of phenomena and modes of valid cognition as do the Vaiśeṣika. In addition, any appraisable object is implicitly classed as partaking of one of twelve possible kinds of entity (*bhāva, dngos po*), namely, self, body, sense organs, sense objects, understanding, mind, sensory engagement, defiled emotion, rebirth, future lives, suffering, and final emancipation.

5. *Aiśvarya*

The Aiśvarya (*dbang phyug pa*) hold that almighty Īśvara, through his eight emanational forms, is endowed with eight distinct supernormal powers: subtlety (*sūkṣmatā, phra ba*), agility (*laghutva, yang ba*), worthiness of offering (*pūjya, mchod par 'os pa*), supremacy (*īśitva, bdag por gyur pa*), dominion (*vaśitva, dbang du gyur pa*), the power to move freely and obtain anything (*prāpti, gar yang phyin pa*), irresistible will-power (*prākāmya, 'dod dgur sgyur ba*), and teleportation (*yatrakāmāvasāyitva, dga' mgur gnas pa*). As such, he is the creator of the inanimate and living world, the sun and moon, the five elements, and sacrificial offering rites. Mundane beings have no control over their own actions, but by making offerings to Īśvara, a non-symbolic knowledge and liberation will be attained.

6. *Vaiṣṇava*

The Vaiṣṇava (*khyab 'jug pa*) revere the ten incarnations of Viṣṇu (*daśāvatāra, 'jug pa bcu*), and claim that Bhagavān Vāsudeva or Kṛṣṇa is the omniscient, all-seeing creator of all living beings, the conferrer of release from the cycle of existence. At the same time, their view may be considered as either eternalist or nihilist, since some of them hold the nature of mind, which they call the "self" (*ātman*) or the sacred Vāsudeva, to be eternal, free from creation and destruction, and to be without duality (*advaita*) in terms of substantial existence and non-existence; while others emphasize the nihilist view, expressed at the time when Viṣṇu was on the verge of being defeated in battle with the antigods. In terms of meditation, they engage in the Vaiṣṇavite yoga of the six branches (*ṣaḍaṅgayoga*).

7. *Brāhmaṇa*

The Brāhmaṇa (*tshangs pa ba*) maintain that the Vedas are eternal and not created because they are the recollections of Brahmā, and as such they represent a valid form of cognition in their own right. They hold that those who die in battle will be reborn in exalted realms, that negative actions can be cancelled out by bathing in sacred rivers such as the Ganges, and that the whole world and its living organisms were created by Brahmā.

8. *Vedāntaupaniṣadika*

The Vedāntaupaniṣadika (*rigs byed kyi mtha' gsang ba pa*) hold that there is a shining immortal person (*amṛtamayapuruṣa, 'chi med bdud rtsi'i skyes bu*) submerged within the sphere of terrestrial darkness (*pṛthivītalatamomaṇḍala*), in which the eternal "self" (*ātman*), "consciousness" (*cit*), and "being" (*sat*, *dam pa*) are all gathered together as a single entity, in the manner of space, and that both the container world and living beings originated through its modifications. When all phenomena are seen to be illusory, at that time, by cultivating the view concerning the creator "self" (*kartṛkapuruṣa, byed pa po'i skyes bu*), they hold that one will awaken from darkness, and, perceiving all things as golden light, one will then be liberated by merging with the immortal person or *brahman* in a single savor.

9. Vaiyākaraṇa

The Grammarians (*vaiyākaraṇa, brda sprod pa*) hold that the valid cognition of direct perception and inference are not definitive. Instead, the foundations of all knowledge are the treatises on Sanskrit grammar, while the Vedas offer genuine valid cognition. All phenomena are embodiments of sound, and the ultimate among all sounds (*sgra don*) is the syllable OṂ, which is the pure source (*brahman, tshangs pa*) of sound, free from creation, destruction, and preservation, and entirely without relative direction. Although this sound is eternal and unchanging, it has become sullied by ignorance and consequently appears as form. But when this apparitional aspect is reversed, the pure source of non-apparitional sound is realized to be immortal.

10. Mīmāṃsaka

The Mīmāṃsaka followers of Jaimini (rGyal dpogs pa) hold that there are twelve defining characteristics that apply to ritual sacrifices: (1) validity or authority of Vedic ritual and tradition; (2) general rules on lack of precedence and improper implementation of rites; (3) particular rules on the context and sense of specific Vedic rites; (4) the impact of general and particular rules on other ritual practices; (5) the relative sequence of the stages of ritual practices and textual passages; (6) the basic obligations and prescriptions regarding officiating priests and ritual materials; (7–8) the general and specific prescriptions concerning the transfer from one rite to another, based respectively on the direct injunctions of the Vedic texts and overt or covert signs; (9) the discussion on the adaptation of Vedic hymns, sāman, and mantra; (10) the debate concerning the preclusion of secondary rites; (11) the continuous performance of several autonomous rites in sequence; and (12) the contiguity between primary and secondary rites.

The Mīmāṃsaka accept six modes of valid cognition: direct perception, inference, scriptural testimony, comparison, presumption, and absence or non-entity. They also propound the ideas that (1) since the self (*ātman*) is the progenitor of the psycho-physical constituents (*skandha, phung po*), permanence is a condition of mankind (*mānava, shed las skyes*); (2) impurity is a condition of the nature of mind; and (3) once it has expired, release from the cycle of existence will occur.

11. Cāraka

The followers of Caraka (Cāraka, Tsa ra ka pa) are largely similar to the Mīmāṃsaka (*dpyod pa ba*), while recognizing that objects may be appraised by means of eight modes of valid cognition, because they differentiate between inferences that refer to the past, present, and future.

12. Jainism

The Nirgrantha Jains (*gcer bu pa*) hold that knowable phenomena comprise nine categories (*navapadārtha, tshig don dgu*): animate substances (*jīva, srog ldan*), inanimate substances (*ajīva, zag pa*), controlled actions (*saṃvara, sdom pa*), rejuvenation (*nirjara, nges par dga'*), bondage (*bandha, 'ching*), deeds (*karma, las*), negative acts (*pāpa, sdig pa*), merits (*puṇya, bsod nams*), and release (*mokṣa, thar pa*). Since animate substances include the elementary life-forms of earth, water, wood, fire, and wind, as well as the four classes of living creatures, namely, animalcules, ants, bees, and human beings, they hold that earth and other elements are living organisms, and that consequently the excavation of land and construction of monastic gardens is a causal basis of negativity.

The path followed by Nirgrantha Jains entails the observance of controlled actions, the vows of ascetic restraint, and the cultivation of knowledge, each of which has five aspects, as well as the thirteen modes of conduct, and various austerities designed to terminate the impact of past actions. They hold that by subjecting the physical body to austerities, the knots that bind the mind are destroyed, and they are known to esteem three hundred and sixty-three modes of ascetic discipline, including the control of the three "staffs" of body, speech, and mind (*tridaṇḍin, dbyu gu gsum pa*) and the "possession of only a tree" (*palāśin, lo ma can*).

The objects that may be appraised by means of the three modes of valid cognition—direct perception, inference, and scriptural authority—include the three times and the six substances (animate things, matter, time, space, merit, and negativity), along with the aforementioned nine categories of phenomena, and the nine kinds of animate substance.

The fruit of the practice of Jainism is that, on bringing an end to the impact of past actions, the animate abode known as the "aggregate of worlds" (*lokasaṃgraha, 'jig rten 'dus pa*) will still remain, present at the summit of the three world-systems, and that even when one has been released from cyclic existence, the release that is attained will still be a positive state of being, "pure and resembling an upturned parasol, fragrantly scented and pleasant, extending to a distance of four million five hundred thousand fathoms."

Barbarous Views

In addition to those nihilistic and eternalistic non-Buddhist systems of Indian philosophy, Kongtrul briefly alludes to the inappropriate practices advocated by so-called barbarians (*mleccha*, *kla klo*), such as the ritual killing of animals in Islam, the amoral acts of killing condoned by the Ājīvaka of ancient India and the unreformed Bon of Tibet, as well as Daoist numerology and Chinese Confucianism.

The Exalted Vehicle

At this juncture, Kongtrul differentiates between two modes of spiritual practice that are advantageous, the vehicle that aspires to the exalted realms (*abhyudaya*) and the level of definitive excellence (*niḥśreyasa*, *nges legs kyi go 'phang*), noting that the former brings "immediate release from the sufferings [of rebirth] in the three inferior realms in which the happiness of gods and humans is accrued by means of a ripening [of virtuous past actions] in conformity with their [appropriate] causes." The latter, by contrast, is the result attained through practice of the Buddhist teachings, bringing "release, passing beyond sorrow and into nirvāṇa, which is a perpetual liberation from the sufferings of all [classes of beings] within cyclic existence."

From the perspective of gradual spiritual development, initially one should become secure in the vehicle of the exalted realms, and then subsequently aim to attain the conclusive path of definitive excellence. However, faith and discriminative awareness are both regarded as common prerequisites for the attainment of these two goals. This is because "in the case of the exalted realms, when one is motivated principally by the faith born of conviction in the results of past actions, among the three kinds of faith, one can effectively adopt virtuous actions and reject negative actions." Also, it is because, "in the case of the attainment of definitive excellence, the roots of cyclic existence are severed by means of discriminative awareness that is non-discursive with respect to the three spheres of subject, object, and their interaction."

Mundane vehicle of gods and humans

The vehicle of the exalted realms itself has two aspects—the mundane vehicle of gods and humans (*devamanuṣyayāna*, *lha mi'i theg pa*) and the more refined vehicle of Brahmā (*brahmāyāna, tshangs pa'i theg pa*). The former is defined by Kongtrul as the means of attaining an exalted physical form through fear of rebirth in the inferior realms (*durgati, ngan song*) and by striving for the result of happiness, which is associated with the higher realms (*svarga, mtho ris*). This is a spiritual path suited for persons of inferior ability, relying on protection from fear and auspicious aspirational prayers. It is the path influenced by the impact of past actions, which conforms to the practice of the ten virtuous actions (*daśakuśala, dge ba bcu*) but which is not yet apprehended by means of meditative concentration (*dhyāna, bsam gtan*).

The correct view maintained by followers of this vehicle is the conviction that there are other worlds, and that past actions do have causes and results. In conduct, ten non-virtuous actions are to be continuously rejected and ten virtuous actions actively pursued. Consequently, those who adopt this course will traverse the various realms of the world-system of desire as far as the Paranirmitavaśavartin realm, experiencing the conclusive happiness of the human beings of the four continents and the six species of Kāma divinities.

Vehicle of Brahmā

The vehicle of Brahmā requires not only ethical observances but the cultivation of the four meditative concentrations associated with the world-system of form (*rūpadhātu, gzugs khams*), and the four meditative absorptions (*samāpatti, snyoms 'jug*) associated with the world-system of formlessness (*ārūpyadhātu, gzugs med khams*).

Calm abiding and higher insight

In preparing for the attainment of the first meditative concentration, the beginner is required to cultivate the experiences of calm abiding (*śamatha, gzhi gnas*) and higher insight (*vipaśyanā, lhag mthong*). In the former case, meditative stability (*samādhi, ting nge 'dzin*) will be secured by means of nine techniques: mental placement, perpetual placement, integrated placement, intensified placement, control, calmness, quiescence, one-pointedness, and meditative equipoise that is effortlessly free from all mental dullness and agitation. Consequently, a state of happiness, characterized by both physical and mental refinement will be experienced.

In higher insight, one cultivates a continual alertness that accords with six modes of attention (*ṣaḍmanaskāra, yid la byed pa drug*), namely, attention that is aware of individual characteristics, attention that arises through resolve, attention that arises through isolation, attention imbued with encompassing joy, attention imbued with scrutiny, and attention imbued with perfected application. Consequently, even the subtlest and most minute dissonant mental states associated with the world system of desire will be overcome. For this reason, these modes of higher insight are equivalent to the spiritual realizations attained by pious attendants, hermit buddhas, and mundane gods and humans.

Attainments of the four meditative concentrations

Following these preparations, the actual attainment (*maula, dngos gzhi*) of the four successive meditative concentrations will ensue. Among them, the first meditative concentration is endowed with ideation, scrutiny, joy, bliss, and one-pointed mind. The second meditative concentration is endowed with intense inner clarity, joy, and bliss arising from meditative stability, and continuous meditative stability (*samādhisthāṅga, ting nge 'dzin gnas kyi yan lag*). The third meditative concentration is endowed with recollection, alertness, equanimity, bliss in which joy has been renounced, and continuous meditative stability. Finally, the fourth meditative concentration is endowed with purity of recollection, purity of equanimity, equanimity of feelings, and continuous meditative stability.

The result attained by those who have mastered the four meditative concentrations is rebirth in the twelve successive realms of the world-system of form, three of which are each attained through the lesser, mediocre, and greater realizations of the four successive meditative concentrations.

Attainments of the four meditative absorptions

Having traversed the world-system of form, the practitioner may then focus on the four successive meditative absorptions associated with the world system of formlessness, namely, the meditative absorption of the sensory activity field of infinite space (*ākāśānantyāyatana, nam mkha' mtha' yas skye mched kyi snyoms 'jug*), the meditative absorption of the sensory activity field of infinite consciousness (*vijñānāntyāyatana, rnam shes mtha' yas skye mched kyi snyoms 'jug*), the meditative absorption of the sensory activity field of nothing-at-all (*akiṃcanyāyatana, ci yang med pa'i skye mched kyi snyoms 'jug*), and the meditative absorption of neither perception nor non-perception (*naivasaṃjñānāsaṃjñāyatana, 'du shes med min gyi snyoms 'jug*). This is the conclusive perfection of the path that leads to the summit of mundane cyclic existence (*bhavāgra, srid pa'i rtse*).

Kongtrul adds that the rebirth in the four levels of the world-system of formlessness is distinguished on the basis of their superior and inferior degrees of meditative absorption, the duration of the life span enjoyed by their inhabitants, and other hierarchical aspects.

Conclusion

The distinctive attributes acquired by those who have successively attained the world-systems of form and formlessness include the four immeasurable aspirations (*caturaprameya, tshad med bzhi*)—loving-kindness, compassion, empathetic joy and equanimity—along with five supernormal cognitive powers (*pañcābhijñā, mngon shes lnga*)—clairvoyance, clairaudience, knowledge of the minds of others, recollection of past lives, and knowledge of death and rebirth.

All those who would enter upon the Buddhist vehicles are initially required to cultivate these meditative stabilities and attributes, familiarizing themselves with the distinctive features of the higher realms. In particular, the conclusive meditative absorption of cessation (*nirodhasamāpatti, 'gog pa'i snyoms 'jug*) is obtained dependent on the mind that has successfully reached the summit of existence (*bhavāgra, srid pa'i rtse*) by cultivating the fourth meditative concentration and the meditative absorption of neither perception nor non-perception. It is for this reason that the higher realms are objectives of the pious attendants and hermit buddhas, who follow the Lesser Vehicle of Buddhism, as well as of non-Buddhist sages and philosophical extremists.

Part Two: Buddhist Phenomenology

In the second part of Book Six, Kongtrul examines the various traditions of phenomenology, corresponding to the three promulgations of the Buddhist teachings. As a preamble to the main discussion, he begins by differentiating Buddhist and non-Buddhist philosophical systems according to their view, meditation, conduct, and result:

> The "view" (*lta ba*) on the basis of which one embarks upon any philosophical and spiritual system is differentiated according to whether it accepts or does not accept the four hallmarks [of impermanence, suffering, selflessness, and quiescent nirvāṇa], which are indicative of the Buddhist transmitted teachings.
>
> The "meditation" (*sgom pa*) is differentiated on the basis of whether it acts or does not act as an antidote for [attachment to] the summit of existence.
>
> "Conduct" (*spyod pa*) is differentiated on the basis of whether it renounces or does not renounce the two extremes of self-mortification and over-indulgence.

> Release [from cyclic existence], which is the "result," is differentiated on the basis of whether it upholds or does not uphold the extraordinary truth of the cessation [of suffering], which is [completely] free from the corruption [of past actions] that are to be renounced.

Then, with regard to the actual Buddhist teachings, although many diverse classifications have been attempted, the hierarchy of the four spiritual and philosophical systems (*grub mtha' bzhi*) is the one that gained greatest currency in the Indo-Tibetan tradition. These comprise the Vaibhāṣika (*bye brag smra ba*), the Sautrāntika (*mdo sde pa*), the Yogacārin (*rnal 'byor spyod pa*) and the Mādhyamika (*dbu ma pa*) systems—the first two being maintained by followers of the Lesser Vehicle (*hīnayānin, theg dman pa*), and the last two by followers of the Greater Vehicle (*mahāyānin, theg chen pa*).

Phenomenological structures

Once the causal basis of cyclic existence has been abandoned, in order that release from cyclic existence might be attained, it will be essential to establish the defining characteristics of all objects of knowledge by means of discriminative awareness (*prajñā, shes rab*), which thoroughly discerns all phenomena. This is effected by structuring all phenomena in terms of the five psycho-physical aggregates (*pañcaskandha, phung po lnga*), the eighteen sensory bases (*aṣṭadaśadhātu, khams bco brgyad*), the twelve sensory activity fields (*dvādaśāyatana, skye mched bcu gnyis*), and the processes of dependent origination (*pratītyasamutpāda, rten cing 'brel bar 'byung ba*), which collectively function as an antidote for the deluded apprehension of wholeness.

These structures of Buddhist phenomenology—the psycho-physical aggregates, sensory bases, and sensory activity fields—may be differently understood in the context of the three promulgations of the Buddhist teachings, exemplified in the "Higher Abhidharma" tradition (*mngon pa gong ma'i lugs*) of Asaṅga, the "Lower Abhidharma" tradition (*mngon pa 'og ma*) of Vasubandhu, and the "third turning" expositions of Maitreya, Tāranātha and so forth.

Phenomenological structures according to the tradition of Higher Abhidharma

According to the system of Higher Abhidharma, the psycho-physical continuum that constitutes an individual person or living being comprises five aggregates (*skandha, phung po*), which are so called because they "function heaps of multiple phenomena, partaking of a common class, or because they bundle together all the distinctive attributes of their respective classes." They are the aggregate of physical forms (*rūpaskandha, gzugs kyi phung po*), the aggregate of feelings (*vedanāskandha, tshor ba'i phung po*), the aggregate of perceptions (*saṃjñāskandha, 'du shes kyi phung po*), the aggregate of formative predispositions (*saṃskāraskandha, 'du byed kyi phung po*), and the aggregate of consciousness (*vijñānaskandha, rnam par shes pa'i phung po*).

Aggregate of physical forms

The aggregate of physical forms includes primary matter (*heturūpa, rgyu'i gzugs*), derivative matter (*phalarūpa, 'bras bu'i gzugs*), and forms associated with the sensory activity field of phenomena (*dharmāyatanarūpa, chos kyi skye mched pa'i gzugs*). Primary matter refers to the four elements—earth, water, fire, and wind—which are known through their respective properties—solidity, cohesion, warmth, and motion. Derivative matter includes the five sense organs—eyes, ears, nose, tongue, and body—in their subtle or sensitive and gross material aspects, as well as the corresponding five sense objects—visible forms, sounds, odors, tastes, and tangibles.

There are intricate sub-classifications. For example, in the case of visible forms (*rūpa, gzugs*), twenty-five aspects have been enumerated individually: blueness, yellowness, redness, whiteness, longness, shortness, squareness, roundness, subtle particles, coarse particles, evenness, unevenness, highness, lowness, shadow, sun, light, darkness, cloud, smoke, dust, mist, atmospheric forms, apperceived but intangible forms, and monochrome sky. These can then be reduced to four categories: visual forms differentiated on the basis of color, shape, appearance, and circumstances.

There are eleven recognized categories of sound (*śabda, sgra*), comprising pleasant, unpleasant, and neutral sounds, as well as sounds produced by the primary elements, which may either be organic, such as human sounds; inorganic, such as rustling trees; or both, such as the sound of a musical instrument. Then there are sounds that are known in the world, demonstrated by accomplished spiritual masters, or imagined; and those that are designated as originating from sublime beings (*ārya, 'phags pa*) and from those who are not sublime. These eleven categories may then be reduced to three: sounds differentiated on the basis of the feelings they evoke, i.e., pleasant, unpleasant, and neutral sounds; sounds differentiated on the basis of whether they are produced organically or inorganically; and sounds differentiated on the basis of imputed symbols and conventional terms.

There are six recognized categories of odor (*gandha, dri*): fragrant, strong, and neutral odors that are differentiated on the basis of the feelings they evoke, along with natural, compounded and developmental odors that are differentiated on the basis of circumstances. In the case of taste (*rasa, ro*), there are twelve types: sweet, astringent, bitter, sour, spicy, salty, pleasant, unpleasant, neutral, natural, compounded, and modified. Then, there are twenty-two types of tangible sensation (*spraṣṭavya, reg bya*): softness, roughness, lightness, heaviness, suppleness or flexibility, languidness, tension, warmth, coldness, hunger, thirst, satisfaction, strength, weakness, faintness, itchiness, putrefaction, sickness, aging, death, fatigue, rest, and energy. The latter may be reduced to three categories: tangible sensations differentiated on the basis of mutual contact or interaction, tangible sensations differentiated on the basis of whether the outer and inner elements are balanced or imbalanced, and tangible sensations differentiated on the basis of circumstances.

As for forms associated with the sensory activity field of phenomena, the "sensory activity field of phenomena" (*dharmāyatana, chos kyi skye mched*) refers to the appearances of physical form that are exclusively within the range of the sense faculty of the mind (*mana indriya, yid kyi dbang po*), and are therefore neither revealed to visual consciousness nor obstructed by tangible objects. There are recognized to be five types of form within this range:

(1) forms that are extremely small and concentrated, such as indivisible atomic particles, which appear as the objects of mental consciousness;
(2) forms that are widespread and spacious, including atmospheric phenomena which appear to mental consciousness but not to visual consciousness;
(3) forms that derive from genuine meditative commitment, including uninterrupted forms indicative of spiritual progress. These are also called "non-apperceived forms" (*avijñaptirūpa, rnam par rig byed ma yin pa'i gzugs*) because they are imperceptible to those with different motivations.
(4) forms that are imagined, including the skeleton that is visualized while practicing the meditative stability on impure phenomena; and
(5) forms that derive from supernormal powers, including the form of the earth element that derives from the meditative stability of the all-consuming earth element (*zad par sa'i ting nge 'dzin*). The latter are also called "images that appear within the perceptual range of meditative stability" (*ting nge 'dzin gyi spyod yul gzugs brnyan*).

In addition, physical forms may be classified as revealed and obstructed (*sanidarśanasapratigha, bstan yod thogs bcas*), unrevealed and obstructed (*anidarśanasapratigha, bstan med thogs bcas*), or unrevealed and unobstructed (*anidarśanāpratigha, bstan med thogs med*), and so forth.

Aggregate of feelings

The aggregate of feelings, when considered according to its essential nature, is sixfold, comprising feelings that are conditioned by sensory contact that is visually, audibly, nasally, lingually, tangibly, or mentally compounded. In addition, there are also six kinds of feelings that are differentiated according to their affinity (*sabhāga, mtshungs ldan*):

(1) physical feelings or sensations originating in affinity with the five types of sensory consciousness;
(2) mental feelings originating in affinity with mental consciousness;
(3) disturbed feelings originating in affinity with attachment to self;
(4) undisturbed feelings acting as an actual antidote for the aforementioned attachment;
(5) feelings associated with greed, originating in affinity with attachment to the objects of the five senses; and
(6) feelings dependent on renunciation which function as an actual antidote for the aforementioned greed.

There is also a further fivefold classification, comprising feelings of sensual happiness, which has affinity with the five types of sensory consciousness; mental happiness, which has affinity with mental consciousness; physical pain, which has affinity with the five types of sensory consciousness; mental unhappiness, which has affinity with mental consciousness; and equanimity, which is free from both happiness and sorrow.

Aggregate of perceptions

The aggregate of perceptions, when considered according to its essential nature, is also sixfold, including perceptions conditioned by sensory contact that is either visually, audibly, nasally, lingually, tangibly, or mentally compounded. There are also six categories of perception that are differentiated according to their circumstances or objects of reference:

(1) non-symbolic perceptions (*animittasaṃjñā, mtshan ma med pa'i 'du shes*), coincidental with meditative equipoise in reality, and those compounded by the levels of meditative equipoise at the summit of existence within the formless realms;
(2) symbolic perceptions (*sanimittasaṃjñā, mtshan ma dang bcas pa'i 'du

shes), comprising all perceptions compounded by the three world systems, excluding those [belonging to the following categories];

(3) limited perceptions (*parīttasaṃjñā, chung ngu'i 'du shes*), compounded by the world system of desire;

(4) extensive perceptions (*mahadgatasaṃjñā, chen po'i 'du shes*), compounded by the word-system of form;

(5) infinite perceptions (*aprameyasaṃjñā, tshad med pa'i 'du shes*), compounded by the sensory activity fields of infinite space and infinite consciousness;

(6) the perception of nothing-at-all (*akiṃcanyasaṃjñā, ci yang med pa'i 'du shes*), compounded by the level of nothing-at-all.

Aggregate of formative predispositions

The aggregate of formative predispositions refers to the mental processes whereby the mind, through an accumulation or combination of various conditions, directly interacts with its objects or points of reference and is driven or motivated towards diverse objects. In terms of their essential nature, these include formative predispositions originating from sensory contact that is visually, audibly, nasally, lingually, tangibly, or mentally compounded. Then, when differentiated according to their circumstances, they include formative predispositions which are either associated with the mind (*cittaprayuktasaṃskāra, sems dang mtshungs ldan gyi 'du byed*) or disassociated with the mind (*cittaviprayuktasaṃskāra, mtshungs par ldan pa ma yin pa'i 'du byed*).

Formative predispositions associated with the mind

Since this class of formative predispositions is identified with the various mental states, Kongtrul begins this long section by examining the defining characteristics of mind (*citta, sems*) and its mental states (*caitasika, sems byung*). Here, mind comprises either eight or six modes of consciousness (*vijñānakāya, rnam par shes pa'i tshogs*), and it objectively refers to the essential nature of its corresponding sense-data—visual form, sound, and so forth. Mental states, on the other hand, objectively refer to the distinguishing characteristics of a given sense datum, such as states of happiness and suffering, or moods that are pleasant and unpleasant. In all, the concomitance of mental states with mind is fivefold (*pañcasamprayuktaka, mtshungs ldan rnam pa lnga*), in that they are said to share a concomitance of location or support (*gnas sam rten*), of objective referent (*dmigs pa*), of sensum (*rnam pa*), of time (*dus*), and of substance (*rdzas*). However, as Kongtrul observes, there is no unanimity of opinion as to whether mind and its mental states are of a single substance or different. Śāntarakṣita and Dharmakīrti appear to hold the former view, and Candrakīrti the latter. Asaṅga suggests that there would be six defects if mind and mental states were identical in substance, while ambiguously stating that this difference is ascertained with respect to material rather than immaterial phenomena.

In addition, mental states may be classified in term of whether they are substantial existents (*dravyataḥ, rdzas yod*) or imputed existents (*prajñaptitaḥ, btags yod*). According to Asaṅga's interpretation, only autonomy (*svatantra, rang rkya thub pa*) can determine whether things are substantially existent—an autonomous object being something that arises as an intrinsic object-universal (*svārthasāmānya, kho'i don spyi*), without dependence on the arising of an extraneous object-universal (*anyārthasāmānya, gzhan gyi don spyi*). Similarly, in his view, only imputation on the basis of its parts can determine whether an object is an imputed existent; that is to say, existents may be acceptably imputed through their partial or incomplete presence because they are the fragments of whole phenomena which are the basis of their designation. In accordance with these criteria, twenty-two of the following fifty-one mental states are classed as substantial existents and the remaining twenty-nine as imputed existents.

Classification of mental states

Kongtrul points out that although various other classifications are found, the prevailing view of Asaṅga is that the mental states are fifty-one in number and divided into the following six categories:

(1) The five ever-present mental states (*sarvatraga, kun 'gro*) comprise feeling (*vedanā, tshor ba*), perception (*saṃjñā, 'du shes*), volition (*cetanā, sems pa*), contact (*sparśa, reg pa*), and attention (*manaskāra, yid byed*). They are designated as "ever-present" because they shadow all aspects of consciousness assumed by the central mind.

(2) The five object-determining mental states (*viṣayaniyata, yul nges*) comprise will (*chanda, 'dun pa*), resolve (*adhimokṣa, mos pa*), mindfulness (*smṛti, dran pa*), meditative stability (*samādhi, ting nge 'dzin*), and discriminative awareness (*prajñā, shes rab*). These are all designated as "object-determining mental states" because they determine their objects, which are respectively conceived, ascertained, experienced, and investigated, without the mind grasping anything apart from these objects.

(3) The eleven wholesome mental states (*kuśalacaitasika, dge ba'i sems byung*) comprise faith (*śraddhā, dad pa*), conscience (*hrī, ngo tsha shes pa*), shame (*apatrāpya, khrel yod*), non-attachment (*alobha, ma chags pa*), non-hatred (*adveṣa, zhe sdang med pa*), non-delusion (*amoha, gti mug med pa*), perseverance (*vīrya, brtson 'grus*), refinement (*praśrabdhi, shin sbyangs*), vigilance (*apramāda, bag yod*), equanimity (*upekṣā, btang snyoms*), and non-violence (*ahiṃsa, mi 'tshe ba*).

(4) The six primary dissonant mental states (*mūlakleśa, rtsa nyon*) comprise desire (*rāga, 'dod chags*), hostility (*pratigha, khong khro*), pride (*māna, nga rgyal*), ignorance (*avidyā, ma rig pa*), doubt (*vicikitsā, the tshom*) ,and wrong view (*mithyādṛṣṭi, lta ba*).

(5) The twenty subsidiary dissonant mental states (*upakleśa, nye bar nyon mongs*) comprise anger (*krodha, khro ba*), enmity (*upanāha, 'khon 'dzin*), hypocrisy (*mrakṣa, 'chab pa*), annoyance (*pradāśa, 'tshig pa*), jealousy (*īrṣyā, phrag dog*), miserliness (*mātsarya, ser sna*), deceit (*māyā, sgyu*), pretentiousness (*śāṭhya, gYo*), self-satisfaction (*mada, rgyags pa*), violence (*vihiṃsa, rnam par 'tshe ba*), lack of conscience (*āhrikya, ngo tsha med pa*), shamelessness (*anapatrāpya, khrel med pa*), dullness (*styāna, rmugs pa*), mental agitation (*auddhatya, rgod pa*), faithlessness (*aśraddhya, ma dad pa*), indolence (*kausīdya, le lo*), carelessness (*pramāda, bag med*), forgetfulness (*muṣitasmṛtitā, brjed ngas pa*), distraction (*vikṣepa, gYeng ba*), and inattentiveness (*asaṃprajanya, shes bzhin ma yin pa*).

(6) The four variable mental states (*anyathika, gzhan 'gyur*) comprise regret (*kaukṛtya, 'gyod pa*), drowsiness (*niddha, gnyid pa*), ideation (*vitarka, rtog pa*), and scrutiny (*vicāra, dpyod pa*), which are all designated as "variable" because their application may change according to circumstances and they are unspecified in terms of wholesome and unwholesome phenomena.

Relation between mental states and modes of consciousness

The diverse mental states relate to the eight modes of consciousness, as follows: The so-called "five ever-present mental states" arise within the periphery of the substratum consciousness (*ālayavijñāna, kun gzhi'i rnam par shes pa*). They also, in conjunction with four of the six primary dissonant mental states (desire, pride, ignorance, and wrong views) and six of the twenty subsidiary dissonant mental states (distraction, carelessness, mental agitation, faithlessness, indolence, and dullness), arise within the periphery of the dissonant mental consciousness (*kliṣṭamanovijñāna, nyon yid kyi rnam par shes pa*).

In the case of the six modes of engaged consciousness (*pravṛttivijñāna, 'jug pa'i rnam shes*), there are two distinct mental processes entailing either involuntary or voluntary perception. Only the five ever-present mental states arise within the periphery of an involuntary or passive consciousness; but, in the case of voluntary perception, when the consciousnesses of the five senses (*pañcadvāravijñāna, sgo lnga rnam shes*) willingly engage in virtuous actions, there are twenty-three mental states which may arise, and another twenty-five when they are engaged in defiled actions, or twelve when they are engaged in ethically unspecified or indeterminate actions. In addition, twenty-five of these mental states may arise within the periphery of mental consciousness (*manovijñāna*) when it is engaged in virtuous actions, forty when it is engaged in defiled actions, but only fourteen when it is engaged in ethically unspecified or indeterminate actions.

Formative predispositions disassociated with the mind

The formative predispositions that are disassociated with the mind are so called because they do not share the five concomitant characteristics when the mind engages with its object of reference. Even so, they are designated as "formative predispositions" (*saṃskāra, 'du byed*) because they partake of their distinctive predisposed circumstances. In the view of Asaṅga, they number twenty-three: acquisition (*prāpti, thob pa*), meditative absorption devoid of perception (*asaṃjñisamāpatti, 'du shes med pa'i snyoms 'jug*), meditative absorption of cessation (*nirodhasamāpatti, 'gog pa'i snyoms 'jug*), the state of non-perception (*āsaṃjñika, 'du shes med pa*), the faculty of the life-force (*jīvitendriya, srog gi dbang po*), homogeneity of sensory experience (*nikāyasabhāga, rigs mthun pa*), birth (*jāti, skye ba*), aging (*jarā, rga ba*), duration (*sthiti, gnas*), impermanence (*anityatā, mi rtag pa*), nominal clusters (*nāmakāya, ming gi tshogs*), phrasal clusters (*padakāya, tshig gi tshogs*), syllabic clusters (*vyañjanakāya, yi ge'i tshogs*), the status of an ordinary individual (*pṛthagjanatva, so so'i skye bo*), engagement (*pravṛtti, 'jug pa*), distinctive regularity (*pratiniyama, so sor nges pa*), connection (*yoga, 'byor 'brel ba*), rapidity (*java, mgyogs pa*), sequence (*anukrama, go rim*), time (*kāla, dus*), location (*deśa, yul*), number (*saṃkhyā, grangs*), and grouping (*sāmagrī, tshogs pa*).

Aggregate of consciousness

The aggregate of consciousness includes "mind" (*citta, sems*), "mentation" (*manas, yid*), and "consciousness" (*vijñāna, rnam par shes pa*), which correlate with either the "six modes" of consciousness or the "eight modes" of consciousness. In the latter case, these three terms correspond respectively to the substratum consciousness, the dissonant mental consciousness, and the six modes of engaged consciousness.

Substratum consciousness

The substratum consciousness is the unobscured and unspecified consciousness, functioning as the ground from which propensities are distributed, cognizing the essential nature of its objects dependent on both maturational (*vipākabhāga, rnam smin gyi cha*) and seminal aspects (*bījabhāga, sa bon gyi cha*). The former are the causal conditions giving rise to distinct fruitional phenomena, while the latter are the latent propensities atemporally present within the substratum.

The workings of the substratum consciousness are demonstrated in those sense data which, with reference to the psycho-physical aggregates and the external physical world, are invisible and fractional, and, therefore, barely capable of appearing objectively. Such sensa are associated with the five ever-present mental states and particularly with equanimity (*upekṣā, btang snyoms*), and they are essentially unobscured by dissonant mental states, ethically indeterminate, and uninterrupted for the duration of cyclic existence. In addition, the seminal aspect of the substratum consciousness is demonstrable in propensities which are capable of regenerating the content of the substratum itself, while the maturational aspect is demonstrable in maturational phenomena that have already been ripened or projected by means of corrupt past actions.

The sense data associated with the substratum consciousness include the aggregates of feelings, perceptions, formative predispositions, and consciousness, which are subtle, invisible to engaged sensory consciousness, and imprecisely ascertained. The substratum's process of engagement occurs continuously through a succession of lives, expiring at the moment of death and reviving through the propensities of past actions at the moment of rebirth. Although this process takes place exclusively in association with the five ever-present mental states, it is concurrent with the dissonant mental consciousness, the mental consciousness, or all the other seven modes of consciousness. By contrast, the reversal of the substratum consciousness occurs when the status of either an arhat or non-residual nirvāṇa has been attained and the adamantine meditative stability (*vajropamasamādhi, rdo rje lta bu'i ting nge 'dzin*) has arisen, transforming consciousness into the mirror-like pristine cognition (*ādarśajñāna, me long lta bu'i ye shes*).

Kongtrul at this point elaborates on the distribution of propensities (*vāsanā, bag chags*) within the substratum consciousness, pointing out that this occurs because the substratum has a stable continuum, is ethically unspecified, and lacks the well-defined clarity of the six modes of engaged consciousness, or the clarity and limitations of the dissonant mental consciousness. This distribution of propensities occurs on the level of an individual's mental continuum, where the substratum is concurrent with the other seven modes of consciousness that act as distributors, and it cannot occur when these are apart because they and their associated mental states have the function of localizing the propensities. Following this act of distribution, the production and cessation of propensities continues so that even if the mental phenomena that originally distributed them cease to exist, the stream of propensities will still continue to adhere to the substratum. So it is that the causal propensities (*niṣyandavāsanā, rgyu mthun gyi bag chags*) have an extraordinary capacity to homogeneously regenerate their own locus, which is the substratum itself; whereas the maturational propensities (*vipākavāsanā, rnam par smin pa'i bag chags*) are new imprints, generating distinctly different phenomena or newly acquired propensities.

The term *seed* (*bīja, sa bon*), which is used synonymously with "propensity," may convey six distinct shades of meaning: external seeds such as those of the sal tree; internal seeds present in the substratum; the two kinds of invisible and unspecified seeds; the relative seeds comprising objects of external, conventional appearance; and the absolute seed, which is the support for all the seeds that can be detected internally. In addition, these seeds display five natural properties (*prakṛti, rang bzhin*):

(1) They originate co-emergently, intending to produce their appropriate results in an immediate manner, uninterrupted by the instant when they perish, which immediately follows their production, or by any other intervening instant of time.
(2) They originate continuously, until their continuum is destroyed by an appropriate antidote.
(3) They originate exclusively with distinctive regularity.
(4) They originate through proximate conditions.
(5) They originate indirectly from beginningless seeds.

It is for these reasons that an intrinsic result may be established as being present in its seed, or a result may be established on the basis of its seed.

According to Asaṅga, Asvabhāva, and others, such seeds or propensities are neither identical nor different in substance to the unspecified substratum consciousness. While they are merely propensities they do not appear diversified, but when their appropriate ripening occurs, they themselves are transformed into the diversity of phenomena. In the Greater Vehicle, this process is called the "profound and subtle dependent origination" (*zab cing phra ba'i rten 'brel*). Indeed, Dharmapāla observes that "if one could think of all the classes of the propensities one would be well acquainted with beginningless cyclic existence!"

Dissonant mental consciousness

The dissonant mental consciousness cognizes the bare objects of the substratum and has the capacity to initiate extremely agitated mental activity. As long as the sublime path of the buddhas has not been attained, it refers objectively to the substratum consciousness, obscured by the dissonant mental states of perpetual egotism, and it is ethically unspecified. Its associated mental states include egotistical delusion, view, attachment, and pride, along with the aforementioned five "ever-present" mental states.

The dissonant mental consciousness initiates the processes of mental consciousness (*manovijñāna, yid shes*) and functions as the locus that binds the six modes of engaged consciousness to substantialist views and corrupt states, ensuring that seeds are implanted in the substratum. In ordinary mundane circumstances, it refers objectively to the substratum consciousness and engages routinely with the six modes of engaged consciousness. It still persists while a bodhisattva or pious attendant is traversing the four paths of learning (*śaikṣamārga*) and undertaking post-meditative activities, even though subject to reversal during this process, but it finally ceases to exist during the meditative equipoise of sublime arhats and the meditative absorption of cessation, when its most subtle latent tendencies are reversed, in tandem with the reversal of the substratum consciousness itself. On the buddha level, it is then transformed into the conclusive pristine cognition of sameness (*samatājñāna, myam nyid kyi ye shes*).

Six modes of engaged consciousness

The six modes of engaged consciousness are the processes through which consciousness becomes localized on account of its ability to cognize dissimilar sense objects. There are six aspects: visual consciousness (*cakṣurvijñāna, mig gi rnam par shes pa*), auditory consciousness (*śrotravijñāna, rna'i rnam par shes pa*), olfactory consciousness (*ghrāṇavijñāna, sna'i rnam par shes pa*), gustatory consciousness (*jihvāvijñāna, lce'i rnam par shes pa*), tactile consciousness (*kāyavijñāna, lus kyi rnam par shes pa*), and mental consciousness (*manovijñāna, yid kyi rnam par shes pa*).

Each of these six modes of engaged consciousness arises dependent on four conditions. For example, in the case of visual consciousness, the referential condition (*ālambanapratyaya, dmigs pa'i rkyen*) comprises the visual forms that appear as if they were external to itself. The predominant condition (*adhipatipratyaya, bdag rkyen*) comprises the sense organs of the eyes. The immediate condition (*samanantarapratyaya, de ma thag rkyen*) comprises an uninterrupted preceding moment of mental attention. The causal condition (*hetupratyaya, rgyu'i rkyen*) comprises the visual consciousness that arises, dependent on the propensities of the substratum, endowed with the characteristic of apperceiving individual visual forms.

In the case of mental consciousness, the referential condition comprises the knowable phenomena which appear as if they were different to itself; the predominant condition comprises, with one special exception, the dissonant mental consciousness; the immediate condition is the mental activity preceding it; and the causal condition is the mental consciousness that arises, dependent on the propensities of the substratum, endowed with the characteristic of apperceiving individual mental phenomena.

The "special exception" (*dmigs gsal*) is that the predominant condition of the uncorrupted pristine cognition of sublime minds is its necessity to continue functioning by means of mentation immediately after the six modes of engaged consciousness have been reversed.

The functions (*kāritrakarma, byed las*) of these six modes of engaged consciousness are to facilitate the apprehension of their respective sense objects. Among them, the five modes of sensory consciousness (*sgo lnga*) engage in virtuous and non-virtuous actions, pursuing positive and negative motivations, and they consequently engage with the corresponding results which are imbued with suffering or the absence of suffering. On the other hand, mental consciousness only has the functions of engaging with virtuous or non-virtuous phenomena, and otherwise does not in itself engage with those consequential results. Mental consciousness originates without interruption in all circumstances, except the following five which are characterized by an absence of mind: rebirth as a deity devoid of perception in the world-system of formlessness, the two kinds of meditative absorption, sleep, and unconsciousness.

Conclusion

Summarizing the foregoing presentation of the five psycho-physical aggregates, Kongtrul emphasizes that sentient beings inhabiting the world-system of desire (*kāmadhātu, 'dod khams*) are endowed with all five of them, but these are progressively diminished in higher realms of experience, such as the world-system of form (*rūpadhātu, gzugs khams*), the world-system of formlessness (*ārūpyadhātu, gzugs med khams*), and the exalted states attained through the sublime path of the Lesser Vehicle.

Eighteen sensory bases

The diversity of physical and mental phenomena encompassed in the five psycho-physical aggregates may also be restructured, repackaged, and presented for the sake of those of varying intellectual abilities in terms of the eighteen sensory bases (*aṣṭadaśadhātu, khams bco brgyad*). These comprise the six internal sensory bases (*nang gi khams drug*), exemplified by the eyes; the six external sensory bases (*phyi'i khams drug*), exemplified by visual form; and the six cognizant sensory bases (*rnam par shes pa'i khams drug*), exemplified by visual consciousness. They in turn may be reduced to the following three categories: sensory bases that are subsumed in the psycho-physical aggregates (*phung pos bsdus pa'i khams*); those that are not subsumed in the psycho-physical aggregates (*des ma bsdus pa'i khams*); and the sensory base of mental phenomena (*dharmadhātu, chos kyi khams*).

Sensory bases subsumed in the aggregates

Here, the single aggregate of physical forms is restructured as the "ten physical sensory bases" (*daśarūpakadhātu, gzugs can gyi khams bcu*), comprising the sensory bases of the five physical sense organs (*dbang po gzugs can lnga'i khams*) and the sensory bases of the five physical sense objects (*yul gzugs can lnga'i khams*). Classed alongside these is the "material portion of the sensory activity field of phenomena" (*dharmāyatanarūpa, chos kyi skye mched kyi gzugs*), which may be exemplified by intangible atomic forms that are extremely small and concentrated. Then, the three aggregates of feelings, perceptions, and formative predispositions are restructured as the "mental portion of the sensory activity field of phenomena" (*dharmāyatandhātu, chos kyi skye mched kyi khams*), forming a separate sensory base because they are exclusively objects of the mental faculty. Lastly, the single aggregate of consciousness is restructured as the "seven sensory bases of consciousness" (*saptavijñānadhātu, rnam par shes pa'i khams bdun*), comprising the six modes of engaged consciousness, extending from visual consciousness as far as mental consciousness, along with the sensory base of the dissonant mental consciousness.

Sensory bases not subsumed in the aggregates

The sensory bases which are not subsumed in the five psycho-physical aggregates include one portion of the sensory base of phenomena (*dharmadhātu, chos kyi khams*), comprising unconditioned phenomena such as the three aspects of reality, space, cessation obtained through non-analytical or analytical means, the immovable state, and the cessation of perception and feeling.

Sensory base of phenomena

The sensory base of phenomena (*dharmadhātu, chos kyi khams*) includes objects that are exclusively within the range of mental consciousness, such as the aforementioned five subtle aspects of form; the three aggregates of feelings, perceptions, and formative predispositions; and the eight unconditioned states.

Twelve sensory activity fields

In a further refinement, all physical and mental phenomena may then be restructured in terms of the twelve sensory activity fields. Here, they comprise the six inner sensory activity fields (*nang gi skye mched drug*), such as the eye (*cakṣurāyatana, mig gi skye mched*), and six outer sensory activity fields (*phyi'i skye mched drug*), such as visible form (*rūpāyatana, gzugs kyi skye mched*). Ten of these subjectively or objectively activate the five sensory gates where the five modes of sensory consciousness arise. The eleventh is the sensory activity field of the mental faculty (*mana āyatana, yid kyi skye mched*), which activates the sensory gate where mental consciousness arises on the basis of its immediate condition, and the twelfth is the sensory activity field of phenomena (*dharmāyatana, chos kyi skye mched*), which activates the sensory gate where mental consciousness arises on the basis of its referential or objective condition.

Sensory bases subsumed in the sensory activity fields

In this context, the ten physical sensory bases, comprising the five sense organs and the five sense objects, are re-designated as the "ten physical sensory activity fields." The seven sensory bases of consciousness are restructured as the single "sensory activity field of the mental faculty"; while the sensory base of phenomena is re-designated as the "sensory activity field of phenomena."

Phenomenological structures according to the tradition of Lower Abhidharma

Another presentational method, generally associated with the Lower Abhidharma tradition of Vasubandhu but also found in Asaṅga's writings, structures all physical and mental phenomena in terms of five basic categories (*pañcajñeya, shes bya thams cad gzhi lnga*): apparent forms (*snang ba gzugs kyi gzhi*), the central mind (*gtso bo sems kyi gzhi*), the peripheral mental states (*'khor sems byung gi gzhi*), the circumstantial formative predispositions disassociated with mind and mental states (*gnas skabs ldan pa ma yin pa'i 'du byed kyi gzhi*), and the unconditioned states (*'gag pa 'dus ma byas kyi gzhi*).

Among them, apparent forms comprise eleven substances—the five sense organs, their corresponding five sense objects, and imperceptible form (*avijñaptirūpa, rnam par rig byed ma yin pa'i gzugs*), which includes those forms belonging to the sensory activity field of phenomena that arise during distracted periods of apperception (*rnam par rig byed*) and during any meditative stability, providing continuity of experience, and which have the characteristics of imperceptible universals (*avijñaptisāmānya, rig min spyi'i mtshan nyid*).

The central mind, in this context, refers only to the six modes of engaged consciousness, excluding the substratum and the dissonant mental consciousness. Also, the peripheral mental states are forty-six in number (rather than fifty-one), and they are divided into the following six groups:

(1) the ten mental states found in all minds (*daśacittamahābhūmika, sems kyi sa mang po bcu*);
(2) the ten mental states found in all virtuous minds (*daśakuśalamahābhūmika, dge ba'i sa mang bcu*);
(3) the six mental states found in all afflicted minds (*ṣaṭkleśamahābhūmika, nyon mongs can gyi sa mang drug*);
(4) the two mental states found in all non-virtuous minds (*dvyayākuśalamahābhūmika, mi dge ba'i sa pa chen po gnyis*);
(5) the ten mental states found in all slightly afflicted minds (*parīttakleśabhūmika, nyon mongs chung ngu'i sa pa bcu*);
(6) the eight indeterminate mental states (*aṣṭāniyatabhūmika, ma nges pa'i sa pa brgyad*).

In addition, there are eight or fourteen formative predispositions disassociated with mind (*cittaviprayuktacaitasika, ldan min 'du byed kyi gzhi*), and three kinds of unconditioned phenomena (*asaṃskṛta, 'dus ma byas kyi gzhi*): space, cessation obtained through analytical means, and cessation obtained through non-analytical means.

Phenomenology of the definitive promulgation

In a further refinement of the phenomenological presentations of the Higher and Lower Abhidharma, Kongtrul now reaches the culmination of Book Six, Part Two, where physical and mental phenomena are restructured in accordance with the interpretations of Maitreya and Tāranātha, who elaborated on the definitive sūtras of the Buddha's third promulgation. The analysis here comprises the "twenty-one phenomenological categories of the ground" (*gzhi'i chos nyer gcig*); the "spiritual path and goal" (*lam dang 'bras bu*); the "five foundational factors" of epistemology (*pañcadharma, chos lnga*); the "three natures" (*trilakṣaṇa, mtshan nyid gsum*); and the "twelve links of dependent origination" (*dvādaśāṅgapratītyasamutpāda, rten 'brel gyi yan lag bcu gnyis*).

Twenty-one aspects of the ground

Once all the aforementioned phenomenological structures of the Higher and Lower Abhidharma have been established, it becomes apparent that the eighteen sensory bases derive from the five psycho-physical aggregates, and the twelve sensory activity fields derive from the eighteen sensory bases. All of these phenomena may then be further reconstituted under three simpler headings: the aggregate of physical forms, the sensory base of mental phenomena, and the sensory activity field of the mental faculty. This is the starting point for the phenomenological interpretation of the so-called definitive promulgation.

Tāranātha enumerates the twenty-one phenomenological categories of the ground (*gzhi'i chos nyer gcig*) as follows: (1) the aggregate of physical forms (*gzugs kyi phung po*); (2) the sensory base of mental phenomena (*chos kyi khams*); (3) the sensory activity field of the mental faculty (*yid kyi skye mched*). Each of these also has three further subdivisions. Among them, the aggregate of physical forms comprises (4) the sensory base of the elements (*'byung ba'i khams*), (5) the containing physical world (*snod kyi 'jig rten*), and (6) its sentient inhabitants (*bcud kyi sems can*). The sensory activity field of the mental faculty comprises (7) mind (*sems*), (8) mentation (*yid*), and (9) consciousness (*rnam par shes pa*). The sensory base of mental phenomena comprises (10) mental phenomena denoting demonstrations (*mtshan gzhi'i chos*), (11) mental phenomena denoting defining characteristics (*mtshan nyid kyi chos*), and (12) non-substantial mental phenomena (*dngos med kyi chos*). Then, among the last three, demonstrations comprise the aggregates of (13) feelings, (14) perceptions, and (15) formative predispositions. Defining characteristics comprise those that are imputed (16) with regard to space (*yul la btags pa*), (17) with regard to time (*dus la btags pa*), and (18) with regard to substance (*dngos la btags pa*). Finally, non-substantial mental phenomena may also be subdivided into (19) those that arise through the transformation of substance (*dngos po gzhan 'gyur gyi dngos med*), (20) those that are dependent on substance (*dngos po la brten pa'i dngos med*), and (21) those that do not exist (*mi srid pa'i dngos med*).

Spiritual path and goal

On this phenomenological basis, three approaches of the spiritual path are then charted. These comprise (1) the common path pursued in the vehicles of the gods and of Brahmā (*lha dang tshangs pa'i theg pa*), (2) the uncommon path followed in the vehicles of pious attendants and hermit buddhas (*nyan rang gi theg pa*), and (3) the extraordinary path of the Greater Vehicle (*theg pa chen po*) through which the abiding nature or level of the Buddha might be reached. This conclusive goal, identified with the expanse of reality (*dharmadhātu, chos kyi dbyings*), or ultimate truth (*paramārthasatya, don dam pa'i bden pa*), is uniquely considered to be uncompounded, whereas all the unconditioned phenomena posited by pious attendants are merely classed as "symbolic or imputed unconditioned phenomena" (*rnam grangs sam btags pa'i 'dus ma byas*).

Five factors

Following Tāranātha, Kongtrul now proceeds to analyze mundane and supramundane phenomena in terms of the five epistemic factors (*pañcadharma, chos lnga*). Here, the term "factor" (*chos*) suggests a foundation facilitating the understanding of phenomena. Elsewhere, the five factors are also known as the "five entities" (*pañcavastu, dngos po lnga*), indicating that they have the causal efficacy of substantial entities, or that they form the "ground that subsumes all phenomenological structures" (*shes bya bsdu ba'i gzhi*). Together, they comprise appearances (*nimitta, rgyu mtshan*), names (*nāma, ming*), false imaginations (*vikalpa, rnam par rtog pa*), absolute reality (*tathatā, de bzhin nyid*), and genuine non-conceptual knowledge (*nirvikalpajñāna, yang dag pa'i ye shes*).

1. Appearances

Appearances are defined as "universal images of states or objects, which may be signified verbally or conceptually." They include (1) natural appearances (*svabhāvanimitta, rang bzhin gyi rgyu mtshan*)—the signs of diversely appearing propensities that manifest to the innate mind in cyclic existence; (2) projected appearances (*bimbanimitta, gzugs brnyen gyi rgyu mtshan*), such as the apprehension of a self, which is imputed by erroneous philosophical systems; and (3) polarizing appearances (*dvandvanimitta, rgyu mtshan gnyis gnyis*), such as the dichotomies of the realized and unrealized, clear and unclear, or symbolic and non-symbolic.

2. Names

Names are defined as verbally designated universals which, on being imputed with respect to a given appearance, will be perceived and labeled, as in the example of the name "vase," which is perceived as the term-universal (*sgra spyi*) corresponding to its given object, even without it being audibly sensed. Here, there is a sixfold classification comprising (1) substantive names (*dngos po'i ming*), (2) relational names (*'brel ba'i ming*), (3) integrating names (*'dus pa'i ming*), (4) diversifying names (*tha dad pa'i ming*), (5) known names (*grags pa'i ming*), and (6) unknown names (*ma grags pa'i ming*).

3. False imaginations

False imaginations denote the mind and its mental states. There are both symbolic and non-symbolic aspects (*nimittavikalpa cānimittavikalpa*, *mtshan bcas dang mtshan ma med pa'i rnam rtog*). The former refers principally to imaginations associated with the mind and mental states prevalent in the world-system of desire, as well as those prevalent as far as the first meditative concentration. The latter refers to imaginations that are prevalent from that first meditative concentration as far as the summit of existence (*bhavāgra*, *srid rtse*), as well as the temporary mind and mental states associated with unconsciousness and sleep.

Other classifications are also found. For example, imaginations may include those associated with dissonant mental states (*kliṣṭavikalpa*, *nyon mongs can gyi rnam rtog*) and those associated with non-dissonant mental states (*akliṣṭavikalpa*, *nyon mongs can ma yin pa'i rnam rtog*). The former are the non-virtuous notions prevalent in the world system of desire, while the latter are the imaginations compounded by uncorrupted states.

4. Absolute reality

The actual reality that transcends objects of verbal expression and mental conception is also known as "suchness" or "absolute reality," which is within the perceptual range of the non-conceptual pristine cognition (*rnam par mi rtog pa'i ye shes*) alone, experienced during the meditative equipoise of sublime beings.

5. Genuine non-conceptual knowledge

The genuine non-conceptual knowledge is that of the authentic spiritual paths, which characteristically intermingle supramundane meditative equipoise (*samāhita, mnyam gzhag*) with supramundane post-meditative experience (*pṛṣṭhalabdha, rjes thob*).

Three natures

The five factors are then analyzed in terms of the three natures of which they partake. Accordingly, postulated concepts which are not apprehended on the basis of appearances are assigned, along with names, to the imaginary nature (*parikalpita, kun brtags*). Conceptual thoughts and genuine knowledge are assigned to the dependent nature (*paratantra, gzhan dbang*); while the absolute reality is assigned to the unchanging consummate nature (*pariniṣpanna, yongs grub*).

1. Imaginary nature

When the imaginary nature is classified, it comprises

(1) the imaginary nature of delimited characteristics (*paricchedaparikalpita, mtshan nyid yongs su chad pa'i kun btags*), exemplified by objects apprehended through the deluded apprehension of individual selfhood;
(2) the nominal imaginary (*paryāyaparikalpita, rnam grangs pa'i kun btags*), which is exemplified by the dualistic appearances of the subject-object dichotomy; and
(3) the referentially imputed imaginary (*ltos nas btags pa*), which may be exemplified by imputed dichotomies such as "large" and "small," "west" and "east," or "basis of designation" (*gdags gzhi*) and "designator" (*gdags byed*).

Other enumerations are also found, such as the twelve aspects of false imagination that are listed in the *Sūtra of the Descent to Laṅkā*, and the ten aspects of distracting imagination.

2. Dependent nature

The dependent nature which entails "apperception alone," or "ideation alone" (*vijñaptimātra, rnam par rig pa tsam*), arising through its own intrinsic causes and conditions, has two aspects: the dependent nature comprising the seeds of all dissonant mental states, and the dependent nature in which neither deluded nor purified mental states inherently exist because conscious awareness is pure and unmodified by propensities.

Alternatively, the dependent nature may be classified according to the impure mundane dependent nature (*ma dag 'jig rten pa'i gzhan dbang*), in which the mind and mental states of the three world systems manifest as real existents through the power of propensities, and the pure mundane dependent nature (*dag pa 'jig rten pa'i gzhan dbang*), in which appearances devoid of substantial existence manifest in an illusory manner during the post-meditative experiences of sublime beings.

Further enumerations are also found, such as the six aspects of the dependent nature that are listed in the *Sūtra of the Descent to Laṅkā* and the eleven aspects of apperception (*rnam rig bcu gcig*) mentioned by Tāranātha.

3. Consummate nature

The consummate nature is the actual reality of all phenomena, the original ultimate truth, which is known under diverse epithets such as the "reality of physical form" (*rūpatathatā, gzugs kyi de bzhin nyid*) and the "reality of feeling" (*vedanātathatā, tshor ba'i de bzhin nyid*). Asaṅga identifies four aspects, for the consummate nature is natural, immaculate, dynamic in terms of its spiritual path, and fruitional in terms of its objectives. Maitreya, in the *Analysis of the Middle and Extremes* (*Madhyāntavibhāga*), differentiates the unchanging consummate nature and the incontrovertible consummate nature.

Other enumerations are also found, such as the nine aspects of the consummate nature identified in the *Extensive Mother* (*Yum rgyas pa*), which have been interpreted by Vasubandhu; the sixteen aspects of emptiness (*ṣoḍdaśaśūnyatā, stong nyid bcu drug*); and so forth.

Integration of the three natures

From a reductionist perspective, the three natures can in turn be reconstituted as two: the imaginary nature that relates to phenomena (*chos kun brtags kyi mtshan nyid*) and the consummate nature that relates to actual reality (*chos nyid yongs su grub pa'i mtshan nyid*). Elsewhere it is said that they are all "inexpressible apart from the absolute reality"; for the imaginary is the aspect which imputes reification or exaggeration, the dependent is the object of this reification or exaggeration, and the consummate is the actual reality of those other two aspects. For example, "Whether there are appearances that arise before visual consciousness or appearances that arise before mental consciousness, at the time when [this visual or mental object] appears, e.g., as a 'vase,' the aspect which apprehends the vase is the imaginary nature. The bare consciousness, radiant and aware, which distinguishes it, is the dependent nature, and the pristine cognition that remains when the imaginary and dependent natures have ceased to exist is held to be the consummate nature."

Alternatively, "it can certainly be asserted that all phenomena are mind, that the nature of this mind—described by many synonyms, including inner radiance (*prabhāsvara*), emptiness (*śūnyatā*), ultimate reality (*paramārtha*), buddha nature (*dhātu*), the nucleus of those gone to bliss (*sugatagarbha*), and so forth—is the consummate nature, that the relative appearances of this mind as mere illusory apperception are the dependent nature, and that the aspect imputed as the dualistic phenomena of the subject-object dichotomy and so forth, even while apperception is non-existent, is the imaginary nature."

In terms of the three corresponding aspects of emptiness (*stong pa nyid gsum*), the imaginary nature is designated as the "emptiness of non-existence" (*med pa'i stong pa nyid*) and is entirely devoid of inherent existence. The dependent nature is designated as the "emptiness of existence" (*yod pa'i stong pa nyid*) and is non-existent from the standpoint of ultimate truth (*paramārthasatya, don dam bden pa*) but does exist in terms of the relative truth (*saṃvṛtisatya, kun rdzob bden pa*). The consummate nature is designated as the "emptiness of inherent existence" (*rang bzhin stong pa nyid*) and abides as the actual reality of all things.

Conclusion

Kongtrul ends this discussion by emphasizing that three natures are established, not only in the sūtras of the final promulgation but also in the commentarial writings of Maitreya, in Nāgārjuna's *Commentary on the Śālistambhaka Sūtra* (*Śālistambhakasūtraṭīkā*), and in Vasubandhu's *Dissertation on the Thirty Verses* (*Triṃśikāprakaraṇa*). He rejects the view that three natures are known only to the Cittamātrins and not to the Mādhyamika, citing various other sources such as Candrakīrti's *Auto-commentary on the Introduction to Madhyamaka* (*Madhyamakāvatārabhāṣya*), Śāntarakṣita's *Auto-commentary on the Ornament of Madhyamaka* (*Madhyamakālaṃkāravṛtti*), Kamalaśīla's *Lamp of Madhyamaka* (*Madhyamakāloka*), and Nāgārjuna's *Commentary on Enlightened Mind* (*Bodhicittavivaraṇa*).

Twelve links of dependent origination

In the final section of Book Six, Part Two, Kongtrul offers an extensive exegesis of dependent origination (*pratītyasamutpāda, rten 'brel*) according to the common inclusive standpoint of both the Greater and Lesser Vehicles, because, as he states, "In whatever ways the first two of the three natures—the imaginary and the dependent—arise, it is the case that they do so through the power of dependent origination. The consummate nature may also be explained in terms of dependent origination with an intention directed towards the ultimate aspect of dependent origination, even though it is not actually subject to relative dependent origination."

Generally speaking, dependent origination is "endowed with generated and generative aspects" (*utpādyotpādakapratītyasamutpāda, bskyed bya skyed byed kyi rten 'brel*), which are respectively the fruitional and causal processes associated with the arising of the physical environment and its sentient inhabitants, along with the internal modes of consciousness. These processes principally fall within the scope of the dependent nature, as does the "genuine dependent origination" (*samyakpratītyasamutpāda, yang dag pa'i rten 'brel*), which determines the composition of the substratum consciousness and its propensities. However, the term may also refer to the relativistic "dependent origination endowed with determined and determinative aspects" (*sthāpanīyasthāpakapratītyasamutpāda, gzhag bya 'jog byed kyi rten 'brel*), which principally falls within the scope of the imaginary nature.

When all phenomena are investigated, although they ultimately abide as emptiness, without inherent existence in any respect, the essential nature of dependent origination is that this is an empirical process that occurs only with regard to their appearances. Although there are many distinct shades of meaning, generally this term refers to the interconnecting causal nexus through which birth and rebirth within the cycle of existence are perpetuated. As such, this causal nexus comprises the twelve successive links of dependent origination (*dvādaśāṅgapratītyasamutpāda, rten 'brel gyi yan lag bcu gnyis*): fundamental ignorance (*avidyā, ma rig pa*), formative predispositions (*saṃskāra, 'du byed*), substratum consciousness (*ālayavijñāna, kun gzhi'i rnam shes*), name and form (*nāmarūpa, ming gzugs*), the six sensory activity fields (*ṣaḍāyatana, skye mched drug*), sensory contact (*sparśa, reg pa*), sensation (*vedanā, tshor ba*), craving (*tṛṣṇā, sred pa*), grasping (*upādāna, len pa*), rebirth process (*bhava, srid pa*), actual birth (*jāti, skye ba*), and aging and death (*jarāmaraṇa, rga shi'i yan lag*). The individual functions of the twelve links are also analyzed by Kongtrul.

Processes and scopes of dependent origination

There are two processes through which these twelve links unfold: a static process whereby they manifest the propensities imposed on the substratum, and a dynamic process whereby they are manifested through the maturation of the seeds of past actions.

Furthermore, there are several scopes of dependent origination that have been differentiated. For example:

(1) The dependent origination that distinguishes the essential nature (*svabhāvavibhāgapratītyasamutpāda, ngo bo nyid rnam par 'byed pa'i rten*

'brel) refers to the emanation of all outer and inner phenomena from the substratum consciousness, and to the appearances that manifest through its power as being deposited upon it. This realization accords only with the scope of the Greater Vehicle.

(2) The dependent origination that distinguishes attractive and unattractive goals (*priyāpriyavibhāgapratītyasamutpāda, sdug pa dang mi sdug pa rnam par 'byed pa'i rten 'brel*) accords with the views of pious attendants and hermit buddhas, among whom the latter extensively understand both the "arising process" (*anuloma, lugs 'byung*) of dependent origination and its "reversal process" (*pratiloma, lugs ldog*), whereas the pious attendants' understanding is less complete.

(3) The dependent origination associated with sensory engagement (*aupabhogikapratītyasamutpāda, nyer spyod can gyi rten 'brel*) is the process through which the six modes of engaged consciousness generate dissonant mental states of attachment, aversion, and delusion, dependent on sensory contact, respectively with agreeable, disagreeable, and indifferent sensations. To counter this, the pious attendants seek to control the dependent dissonant mental states.

Serial, instantaneous, and interconnected dependent origination

It is said that the twelve links of dependent origination unfold in three different ways: serially, instantaneously, or interconnectedly.

Among them, serial or circumstantial dependent origination (*prākarṣikapratītyasamutpāda, rgyun chags pa'am gnas skabs pa'i rten 'brel*) includes the process whereby one cycle of the twelve links is completed over two lifetimes within the world system of desire, the process through which one cycle is completed over three lifetimes, and the process through which one cycle is completed within a single lifetime. On the other hand, instantaneous dependent origination (*kṣaṇikapratītyasamutpāda, skad cig ma'i rten 'brel*) refers to the completion of all twelve links of dependent origination in a single instant, as may occur when the act of murder is willfully committed.

Eight aspects and two interpretations of interconnected dependent origination

The "interconnected dependent origination" (*sāṃbandhikapratītyasamutpāda, 'brel ba can gyi rten 'brel*) that relates to the causal nexus has eight aspects:

(1) the dependent origination through which consciousness arises;
(2) the dependent origination through which birth and death arise;

(3) the uninterrupted dependent origination of the external world;
(4) the dependent origination which is an extensive analysis of the physical environment
(5) the dependent origination distinguished by the nourishing sustenance of the sensory bases, sensory contact, volition, and consciousness;
(6) the dependent origination that distinguishes living beings according to desirable and undesirable realms of rebirth on the basis of virtuous and non-virtuous past actions;
(7) the dependent origination that is well distinguished by means of purity acquired by cultivating the three higher trainings and the five spiritual paths;
(8) the dependent origination that is well distinguished by means of the six supernormal cognitive powers.

The first six of these fall within the range of dissonant mental states, and the last two are associated with purified states.

There are also two distinct interpretations of interconnected dependent origination, based on the textual commentaries of Maitreya (*rje btsun byams pa'i gzhung don*) and Vasubandhu (*slob dpon dbyig gnyen gyi gzhung don*).

Interpretation of Maitreya

Maitreya explains that three links—fundamental ignorance, craving, and grasping—are classed as dissonant mental states arising from other dissonant mental states (*kleśasaṃkleśa, nyon mongs pa'i kun nas nyon mongs pa*); whereas two links—formative predispositions and rebirth process—are classed as dissonant mental states arising from past actions (*karmasaṃkleśa, las kyi kun nas nyon mongs pa*); and the remaining seven are classed as dissonant mental states arising from the birth of sufferings (*janmasaṃkleśa, sdug bsngal rnams skye ba'i kun nas nyon mongs pa*). Alternatively, five links—fundamental ignorance, formative predispositions, craving, grasping, and the rebirth process—may be designated as causal dissonant mental states (*hetusaṃkleśa*), and the remainder as fruitional dissonant mental states (*phalasaṃkleśa*).

Interpretation of Vasubandhu

Vasubandhu explains that when the cycle of the twelve links of dependent origination is completed over two lifetimes, it comprises "seven projective and formative aspects" (*'phen grub rgyu bdun*). Moreover, there are differences in the distribution of the twelve links of dependent origination. All of them are fully present in the world-system of desire, whereas in the two higher world-systems they are only partly present, because the link of aging exists therein in the manner of formative predispositions that are old and putrid, while in the world-system of formlessness specifically, the physical aspects of dependent origination are absent.

Conclusion

Asaṅga notes, in conclusion, that the processes of dependent origination have five inherent contradictions, for which reason their reality is only fully understood by buddhas. These are summarized as follows:

(1) Although dependent origination is momentary, it is also observed to have duration.
(2) Although dependent origination arises from unmoving conditions, it is also observed that its potencies are idiosyncratic.
(3) Although dependent origination occurs without reference to sentient beings, it is also observed in respect of sentient beings.
(4) Although dependent origination has no creator, it is also observed that past actions are not fruitless.
(5) Although dependent origination does not arise from the four extremes, it does not arise with reference to any other agency.

Furthermore, all phenomena, just as they appear, are established as the relative dependent origination, whereas their actual reality is merely designated as the dependent origination of emptiness, the ultimate truth. This crucial point is "extremely profound and subtle, for which reasons it is an object known by the Buddha alone."

The real nature of dependent origination is to be understood in terms of the four hallmarks of the Buddha's teachings: impermanence, suffering, emptiness, and selflessness. Briefly stated, phenomena are uncreated by the dynamics of conceptual thought present in the mind of a creator divinity, and they are impermanent because that which is permanent and steadfast would not be subject to the arising and cessation of causes and conditions. Since phenomena have a nature that partakes of arising and cessation, and substantial things are seeds endowed with potency, they are produced by causes capable of generating their respective results. Without knowing the processes of arising and cessation in respect of substantial things in accordance with the three natures of which they partake, non-Buddhist philosophers propound their diverse perspectives of eternalism and nihilism. However, when the meaning of dependent origination is properly understood, "the reality will be known, and by also comprehending the three natures, one will obtain certainty with regard to dependent origination."

From the ultimate perspective, although emptiness is identified with dependent origination, the pristine cognition of natural inner radiance (*rang bzhin 'od gsal ba'i ye shes*), which is the ultimate truth, actually transcends dependent origination because it is beyond all objects of verbal expression and mental conception, being liberated from the dichotomies between generative causes and generated results, or determined and determinative aspects. This natural inner radiance has not been generated by any cause whatsoever because it does not produce an extraneous result, nor is it a causal action of extraneous production. On the other hand, it is not contradictory to say that although the ultimate truth is not dependent origination, it can be realized by meditating on dependent origination.

The Translation

The root verses of Jamgon Kongtrul's *Encompassment of All Knowledge* (*Shes bya kun khyab*) are terse and pithy, designed as a mnemonic aid for erudite exponents of the various Tibetan traditions, and they are virtually unintelligible without reference to his auto-commentary, the *Infinite Ocean of Knowledge* (*Shes bya mtha' yas pa'i rgya mtsho*), which was written in prose, in an encyclopedic style. The latter is replete with quotations from classical Indian sources and the Tibetan commentarial tradition, in keeping with the "great conversation" of the ongoing Indo-Tibetan philosophical tradition. Among Tibetan sources, specific mention should be made of Tāranātha, an inspirational writer for Jamgon Kongtrul, whose ghostly presence at times seems to permeate the *Treasury of Knowledge*. In general, Kongtrul takes great care to cite his sources, but references to Tāranātha and his disciple Khewang Yeshe Gyatso are not always acknowledged, possibly for diplomatic reasons, as his new treatise was to gain great currency throughout Tibet—even in the central regions where the works of Tāranātha had been proscribed during the seventeenth century.

There are several challenges to be faced in translating this complex text into readable English. Despite its encyclopedic vastness, the *Treasury of Knowledge* is remarkably terse and concise in style. It contains many passages and observations requiring further elucidation or annotation, even for the educated Tibetan reader. Since accuracy has to be the benchmark, often at the expense of elegance, words have sometimes been added in brackets to assist the reader's understanding. More frequently, endnotes have been added to explain obscure points or to refer the reader to more detailed works in Tibetan, Sanskrit, or Western languages for further reading. Wherever possible, I have also sought to cross-reference Jamgon Kongtrul's observations to other volumes in this series.

In preparing this translation, the range of the English terminology for technical language has had to match the wide diversity of the book's subject-matter, covering the disparate fields of linguistics, logic, fine art, medicine, astrology, poetics, metrics, lexicography, dramaturgy, and Buddhist phenomenology. The full range of terminology employed can be ascertained from the trilingual thematic concordance of technical terms, at the end of the book. In addition, I have frequently opted to retain Tibetan and Sanskrit technical terms in parenthesis, in the body of the text, as an aid for the educated reader, even at the risk of diminishing fluency.

In view of the technical nature of the subject matter, the intricacies of Sanskrit grammar which are explained in the text and so forth, I have deliberately followed the standard academic system of romanization for Sanskrit. In transcribing Tibetan technical terms, I have utilized the standard modifications of extended Wylie for romanized Tibetan, except in the case of personal names or place-names, where a more simplified phonetic system has been employed.

In addition to Kongtrul's root verses and prose commentary, this volume also contains an outline (*sa bcad*) of the headings used by Jamgon Kongtrul in his treatise, following the traditional convoluted style which academic Tibetan treatises employ for pedagogic and mnemonic purposes. This outline has its basis in the *Outline of the Encompassment of All Knowledge* (*Shes bya kun khyab kyi sa bcad*), which was written and published in Tibetan by Professor Thubten Nyima (Zenkar Rinpoche) in 1990.

The bibliography at the end of the book is in two sections. The first contains references to Indic and Tibetan works cited by the author, and the second includes other works—in Sanskrit, Tibetan and other languages—which have been recommended for further reading in the introduction and endnotes.

Acknowledgments

This project—the English translation of the entire *Treasury of Knowledge*—was initiated by the previous Kalu Rinpoche during the winters of 1988 and 1989 and subsequently maintained by his lineage-holder, Bokar Rinpoche. The first volume in the series, *Myriad Worlds*, was published in 1995. When Lama Drupgyu (Anthony Chapman) of the Tsadra Foundation approached me in early 2007 and asked if I would like to undertake the translations contained in this present volume, I was delighted to contribute and thereby establish a connection with the great teacher who had inspired the project from its inception.

In my younger years, from 1968 onwards, I had had the good fortune to meet some of the greatest Nyingma teachers of the previous generation—the lords of refuge Kangyur Rinpoche, Dudjom Rinpoche, and Dilgo Khyentse Rinpoche—and have been translating and familiarizing myself with the sacred texts of this tradition for over forty years. While undertaking this present translation, I also felt a sense of joy in re-establishing a Kagyu connection that I had had when, as an undergraduate, I first met the previous Trungpa Rinpoche at Samye Ling in Scotland. I would like to thank Eric Colombel of the Tsadra Foundation for providing this opportunity, and for all the support he has generously given over the last three years—dedicated, as he is, to fulfilling this long-term vision of Kalu Rinpoche.

The disparate themes and the wide ranging technical terminology found in *Indo-Tibetan Classical Learning and Buddhist Phenomenology* are complex and challenging, even for a jack-of-all-trades. Translation is inevitably a solitary and painstaking pursuit, and I have been able to draw upon my background knowledge in Nyingma and general Buddhist studies, however flawed, acquired under the guidance of the aforementioned peerless teachers, alongside Tulku Pema Wangyal and Zenkar Rinpoche. It also helped immensely to have studied the subjects contained in this volume with authoritative teachers, east and west.

My introduction to Sanskrit grammar, poetics, prosody, and Indian philosophy owes much to the instruction of Dr. Michael Coulson and Dr. John Brockington at the University of Edinburgh during the 1960s. Subsequently, I studied Tibetan grammar under the venerable Lobsang Jamspal at Sanskrit University in Varanasi in 1968–69. During the 1970s I worked briefly with Terry Clifford on the translations from the *Four Medical Tantras of Dratang* contained in her *Tibetan Buddhist Medicine and Psychiatry*, and in the early 1990s I translated numerous passages from Desi Sangye Gyatso's *Blue Beryl* treatise on Tibetan medicine, in connection with my work with Fernand Meyer on *Tibetan Medical Paintings*.

During the 1990s, I also had the good fortune to work at close quarters for four years with Professor Thubten Nyima (Zenkar Rinpoche) at London University, on the translation of the *Greater Tibetan-Chinese Dictionary* (*Bod rgya tshig mdzod chen mo*), which is replete with technical terms drawn from all the subjects contained in this volume, including logic, fine art, astrology, dramaturgy, phenomenology, and others already mentioned. Towards the end of that same decade, I studied astrology and especially elemental divination in some depth, with the late Khenpo Tsultrim Gyaltsen at the Lhasa Mentsikhang, working on an illuminated manuscript, in conjunction with the commentaries of Sangye Gyatso's *White Beryl* treatise and the writings of Lochen Dharmaśrī. The fruits of this research were subsequently published in *Tibetan Elemental Divination Paintings*.

At various times I had also acquired a limited knowledge of sources relevant for the study of Tibetan art, working on specific texts with Philip Denwood at SOAS, with the art historian Jane Casey, and in discussions with Robert Beer, as well as through my fieldwork in researching the successive editions of Footprint *Tibet* and *Jokhang: Tibet's Most Sacred Buddhist Temple*.

While translating and researching this present volume between 2007 and 2010, source materials were generously provided by Gene Smith and his colleagues at the Tibetan Buddhist Resource Center in New York, as well as by Burkhard Quessel of the British Library, Robert Chilton of the Asian Classics Input Project, and Yangchen Lhamo of the Sichuan Nationalities Publishing House in Chengdu. I also made good use of my own private library in Crieff, and the Indological collection at the library of the University of Edinburgh. I am grateful to all those who kindly helped bring this project to fruition.

Teachers, colleagues, and friends in various parts of the world have also contributed by helping to resolve obscurities and difficulties in the text. Professor Thubten Nyima worked intensively and carefully through my list of unresolved issues in London, in October 2009, over a number of days. Specific points were also resolved in discussion with Peter Verhagen (on Sanskrit grammar); Thupten Jinpa Langri, Dzongsar Khyentse Rinpoche, and Georges Dreyfus (on logic); David Jackson, Robert Beer, and Khenpo Kalsang Gyaltsen (on fine art); Gene Smith and Paldor (on various subjects); Ricardo Canzio (on Tibetan music and chanting); Edward Henning (on astrology and art); Christopher Fynn (on calligraphy); and Karl Brunnhölzl, Michael Sheehy, and Bhikkhu Bodhi (on phenomenology). I would like to express my gratitude to them; and, last but not least, to my friend and colleague Martin Boord, who carefully proofread the text and its Sanskrit terminology over several months. The inevitable faults that will be found in this work are entirely mine.

In the course of translating this volume, I soon realized that there are some sections that would uniquely benefit from the inclusion of graphics or illustrations—particularly the chapters on fine art and medicine. In all, fifty-two illustrations have been added; thirty-seven of these have been finely redrawn by Chris Banigan.

Over these recent years, I have enjoyed establishing or re-establishing connections with respected colleagues who worked on the other volumes in the series, among them Ingrid McLeod, Elio Guarisco, Elizabeth Callahan, Richard Barron, Drupgyu Anthony Chapman, Ngawang Zangpo, Sarah Harding, and Dechen Yeshe Wangmo.

In conclusion, I would like to thank Sidney Piburn, one of the cofounders of Snow Lion Publications, and Susan Kyser, who worked carefully through my manuscript prior to publication. May the good work of all those committed to the endeavors of the Tsadra Foundation continue to flourish!

Gyurme Dorje
Crieff
November, 2010

The Treasury of Knowledge

Book Six

A Graduated Exposition of Classical Studies

PART ONE

Indo-Tibetan Classical Learning:
A Systematic Presentation of the Ordinary Classical Sciences and Mundane Spiritual Paths

The Root Verses

[Chapter 1: The Purpose and Scope of Learning]

At the outset, studies should be pursued impartially
Because they are the basis of all erudition and enlightened attributes.
Whatever one investigates—scriptural compilations, treatises, or fine arts—
One should be aided by humility and perseverance.
Why so? In order to accumulate genuine [analytic] knowledge and so forth!

[Chapter 2: Articulation and Semantics]

Articulation of syllables is the basis of all knowledge.
Although the number of languages and scripts may be limitless,
Their [common] foundation comprises the vowels and consonants.
Actual sounds are held to be not fruitional [in nature],
But they are either produced in conformity with their causes, or cumulatively.

The essential nature of syllabic articulation is vocal pulsation,
Which may be short, long, or diphthong in its duration,
Enduring [respectively] for one, two, or three blinks of an eye.
Each fraction [of a vocal pulsation] lasts but a single instant,
And, along with others, forms a continuum.
[Syllables] are categorized in the *Treasury* [*of Phenomenology*]
Among the disassociated [formative predispositions].
The etymological definitions [of "syllable"] include "unchanging nature,"
"Elucidator of nouns and words," and "signifier of meanings."
The syllabic scripts include Rañjanā, and so forth.

As for the analysis that is commonly made,
In Sanskrit, the foremost of the four classical languages of India,
The vowels include simple vowels and diphthongs,
And the consonants include basic phonetic sets, semi-vowels, and spirants.
The vowels [according to the *Grammar of Candragomin*]
Number one hundred and thirty-two,
And the basic consonants thirty-seven, which, when multiplied
by the vowels,
Become four thousand three hundred and fifty-six.
These all arise dependent on eight places of articulation,
Their articulators, and the modes of inner and outer articulation.

The Tibetan language has four represented vowels, I and so forth,
And thirty consonants, analyzed as prefixes, suffixes, and radicals.
These may occur as isolates, or [in conjunction with] prefixes, superscripts,
Stacks, subscripts, and suffixes.

Meaning is disclosed by adding inflections, particles, and so forth;
And [action] is conveyed by verbal agentives and objectives, and the
three tenses.

At first [Tibetan] phonics should be practiced,
And this should be followed by the spelling aloud of constructed syllables.
These [syllables] are produced and expressed in conformity with
Their distinct places of articulation, articulators, and modes of articulation.
Having mastered [spelling], the technique of affixation—
The process determining which [affixes] are attached to which [radicals]—
As well as the need for [affixation]
Should all be studied with reference to the excellent texts of Tonmi,
The oldest of [all the Tibetan treatises on] language,
Which were [composed] through the enlightened activity of the buddhas.

All [constructions depend on] the following eight elements of linguistic
application:
Apprehended sounds and languages,
Names and attributes,
Communicative symbols and conventional terms,
And words and meanings.
Through the convergence of sounds and meanings,

An apprehending intelligence arises
In association with five successive factors:
Objective reference, sound generation, shared ideation,
Commonality, and adhesion.

[Chapter 3: Sanskrit Grammar]

There exist no branches of knowledge
That should remain unstudied by the sons of the Conquerors.
Therefore the classical sciences should be studied
Because they eradicate [wrong understanding],
Bring [seekers] into the fold,
And achieve the all-knowing [path of omniscience].

Grammar—[the science] that eliminates wrong understandings with
regard to words—
Comprises three aspects: primary bases, affixation, and derivation.

Among primary bases, the verbal roots can be subsumed in six categories:
Those that have been listed or formally conjugated,
Those that have not been listed or formally conjugated,
And those that have both been and not been formally conjugated;
As well as denominative verbal roots, affixed verbal roots,
And those that are both denominative and affixed.
When subsumed, they comprise active and reflexive verbs.

Nominal stems are of six types:
Those of exclusive gender, those of mixed gender,
And those of obscure, congruent, universally applicable, and
indeterminate [gender].

Affixation includes desiderative suffixes,
Enabling verbal roots to be formed as [other] verbal roots,
Verbally conjugated suffixes, enabling verbal roots to be formed as phrases,
Primary nominal suffixes associated with verbal action,
Enabling verbal roots to be formed as nouns,
Denominative suffixes, enabling nouns to be formed as verbal roots,
Feminine-forming suffixes, enabling gender to be formed as
[another] gender,

Secondary nominal suffixes, enabling nouns to be formed as [other] nouns,
And nominal case suffixes, enabling nouns to be formed as phrases.

Nouns, adjectives, verbs, and pronouns—
These are the four [categories of words].
Alternatively, [words] can be classified as agents, verbal actions, and objects.

Derivation comprises both actual [derivation] and nominal compounding.
The essential elements of derivation concern the substitution [of retroflex syllables for dentals],
And the classification of technical markers attached to verbal roots, affixes,
Gender terminations, augments, indeclinable and [permitted final] words.
Elision should be carried out in respect of [final vowels] that facilitate pronunciation
And [final letters] denoting peculiarities [of inflection],
As well as those that are [merely] technical markers.[2]

The verbal prepositions that modify meaning and form, and the augments
Constitute the ancillary aspects of derivation.
As for [derivations due to] affixation,
All three elements—syllables, affixes, and inflections—
Undergo infinite transformations,
Including those due to euphonic conjunction.

There are six kinds of nominal compound:
Descriptive, pre-numerical, uncountable,
Initially dependent, exocentric, and coordinative.

The essence [of grammar] is subsumed in nouns, words, and derivations.
To learn the language, one should be undeluded with respect to meaning.

[Chapter 4: Logic]

Valid cognition, which eradicates wrong understanding with respect to meaning,
Refers to the object, subject, and processes of [logical] understanding.

The object is the knowable or appraisable which is to be understood.
Objects may be substantial or insubstantial,

Compounded or uncompounded, permanent or impermanent.
Substantial [objects] include material and cognitive phenomena,
Causes and results, along with their subdivisions.

In terms of their functionality [objects] fall into three categories,
Namely, apparent, conceived, and applied objects.
In terms of the processes of understanding objects that are to be appraised:
[Objects] include specifically and generally characterized phenomena,
Or else they are established as directly evident, indirectly evident,
And indirectly evident to an extreme degree,
Or else [they comprise] signified [phenomena] and their supplementary [definitions].

The subject is both the signifier, which engenders comprehension, and the cognizer.
Signifiers essentially include nouns, phrases, and speech.
In terms of the signified they include type signifiers,
Set signifiers, and modes of signification,
As well as the predicate, the subject, and preclusion without or with [predicate].
Theoretically, [signifiers] may be conceived or directly evident.
[Also incidentally defined here] are the term "syllable" and the term "individual person."

Consciousness or awareness [has ten aspects]:
Valid and non-valid cognition,
Conceptual and non-conceptual cognition,
Mistaken and unmistaken cognition,
Intrinsic and extraneous awareness,
Mind and mental states.

With regard to direct perception,
There are four modes of direct perception:
Sense organs, mind, intrinsic awareness, and yoga.
Inference is made through the power of facts,
Popular acclaim, and conviction.
There are many such categories and approaches,
And the conclusions of valid cognition
Should also be incidentally understood.

With regard to [the logical processes of genuine] understanding,
There are contradictions [that may be determined],
Along with relations, negations, proofs, universals and particulars,
Identity and difference, eliminative and affirmative engagement,
As well as extraneous [elimination], definition, definiendum,
Substance and counterpart [phenomena], and the two modes
of inference.

[The first of these] is inference for one's own sake—
This requires genuine evidence endowed with the three criteria.
One should reject ostensible and contradictory evidence
In which [these criteria] are incomplete.
The [given] examples should also be determined accordingly.
[The second of these] is inference for the sake of others—
This requires a statement of proof endowed with the three criteria,
Acceptable to both the antagonist and the respondent,
And endowed with the two aspects.
In the case of evidence, elimination, refutation,
Consequential reasoning, and so forth,
The ostensible [types] should be rejected,
And the correct [types] should be established.
While these [processes of logical understanding] are prestigious
in modern circles,
There are also different [logical presentations],
Exemplified by the *Treasure of Logical Reasoning*,
The *Oceanic Textbook of Uncommon Logical Reasoning*,
And the traditions of the ancient [Kadampas].

All points signified in the texts on valid cognition may be personally
understood
Through direct perception, inference, and their ostensible forms,
Whereas proof, refutation, and their ostensible forms engender
understanding in others:
These are the eight aspects of dialectics.

In brief, there are three kinds of objects to be appraised:
The directly evident, the indirectly evident,
And the indirectly evident to an extreme degree.
As for their means of appraisal, they comprise [respectively]

Direct perception, logical inference, and scriptural authority,
Of which the purity is established by the three types of scrutiny.
There are four kinds of direct perception,
Three logical axioms of inference,
And various technical terms that derive from these.

The analytical basis or topics [for discussion],
The analysis of phenomena,
The systematic framework to be determined,
Consequential reasoning which is the process of determination, and [correct] view—
These are the five modalities offering an introduction to the Middle Way,
Subsumed in [the teachings] of the mighty lords of knowledge.
Through conventional terms, ultimate objects of appraisal
Are established as valid cognition.

[Chapter 5: Fine Arts]

Although the arts that can be earnestly pursued are limitless,
All knowledge may in fact be subsumed within the fine arts of the three media.
The supreme arts of the body are the representations
Of buddha body, speech, and mind.
Artists are skilled and maintain the one-day observances (*upavāsa*).
They have received empowerments and maintain the commitments
Associated with the inner [classes of] the way of secret mantra,
And they are endowed with blessings, as are their materials and tools.

Painted icons representing [visualized deities] of meditative commitment
That accord with the texts are the best.
With regard to iconometric proportion, the number of relative finger-widths
Allocated [for buddha images] is one hundred and twenty-five
According to the *Tantra of the Wheel of Time*,
While, according to the *Tantra of the Emergence of Cakrasaṃvara*,
It should be one hundred and twenty.
The [*Tantra of the*] *Four* [*Indestructible*] *Seats* is similar [to the latter],
While the [*Tantras of*] *Red* and *Black* [*Yamāri*] calculate eight face-length measures.

The *Sūtra* [*Requested by Śāriputra*] and [other ancient] Indic texts
Are [generally] in conformity with those [works],
And there are [contemporary] traditions that follow them as well.

Among the five anthropometric scales applied in certain circumstances,
[Including the scale of] twelve and a half finger-widths,
[The scale of] twelve finger-widths, and the palm-length measures,
The first and second accord with the *Wheel of Time*
And the *Emergence of Cakrasaṃvara*,
While the third and fourth comprise the nine and eight palm-length measures.
These all correspond to the actual teachings of the sūtras and tantras,
And painstaking efforts should be made [in applying them].
The [first three of these anthropometric scales] are applied, as appropriate,
To the [drawing of] tathāgatas, bodhisattvas,
Wrathful deities, and icons without consort.
The fourth is applied to the most wrathful deities [alone].
The [fifth] is the Tibetan tradition of six mid-finger span measures which emerged later.

As for the typology of the deities, they may be classified as follows:
[Icons depicting] renunciant forms without a consort, universal monarchs,
Peaceful icons without ornaments [including] hermit sages and beings of inferior class,
[Wrathful] buddhas, emanational wrathful forms, and kings among wrathful deities,
Supreme and common bodhisattvas, servants, and intermediaries.

However, among well-known contemporary [traditions],
[Including] those that identify eleven distinct iconometric scales,
All of them concur that the axial lines of Brahmā are drawn first.
Then, [as for the elevenfold classification,] this comprises
[Renunciant buddhas] without a consort,
And the buddha body of perfect resource,
Which are scaled at one hundred and twenty-five finger-widths;
Bodhisattvas scaled at one hundred and twenty finger-widths;
Wrathful hermit sages scaled at twelve palm-lengths;
Female consorts scaled at nine palm-lengths;

Acolytes of Yama and yakṣas scaled at eight [palm-lengths];
Ogre-like wrathful deities scaled at six, five, or three [palm-lengths];
Pious attendants and hermit buddhas who are similar in scale to
human figures;
[Mundane protectors] such as Brahmā, scaled at nine large units;
And human beings of the four continents,
Scaled at seven mid-finger spans in length, and eight in width.
All such measurements are said to depend
On the degree to which the vital energy of past actions is impeded.

[Icons should be depicted] with the major and minor marks,
Or they should be peaceful, amorous, wrathful, graceful,
Or expressive of the dramatic airs.
[Icons may also be adorned with] religious robes,
The eight ornaments made of precious gems,
And two kinds of silken clothes,
With [hand] gestures and
The eight or ten categories of glorious charnel ground accoutrements,
As well as the vajra, *khaṭvāṅga*, and so forth,
Which are foremost among the symbolic hand-held emblems.

There are seven aspects to the construction of a throne or palanquin,
[Which symbolize respectively the seven] categories of the branches of
enlightenment,
While the six ornaments of the backrest symbolize
The six transcendental perfections, and so forth.

[Draftsmanship] should be without defects
In respect of long, short, thick, thin, and curving [lines], and so forth.
The basic and secondary color pigments and their shadings should then
be applied
And the stylistic features should correspond to the traditions maintained
in different lands.

The three-dimensional and two-dimensional celestial palaces,
The abodes in which [these icons] reside,
Are widely [constructed] in accordance with the *Indestructible Garland.*
But there are also other symbolic conventions and meanings,
Including [those represented by] the tradition of the *Magical Net.*

As for the representations of buddha speech, according to the sūtras
There are sixty-four types of [ancient] script,
But Rañjanā, Vartula, and so forth are supreme
Among all the writing systems of different lands.
[In Rañjanā] it is approximately the case
That there are two calligraphic grid squares
For the head stroke and neck stroke [of each letter],
And three for the body strokes [of each letter].
Among these, the head stroke is [drawn] last.

In Tibetan calligraphy, all [writing systems] can be subsumed
Within the following six scripts:
The headed block-letter script, the headless [block-letter] script,
The headless thick and thin italic scripts,
The formal handwriting script, and the cursive shorthand script.
The block-letter scripts [evolved through] nine successive
  [modifications],
Including the "ancient and new styles."
Thereafter, among the followers of Yutri, two traditions arose—
The "frog" tradition and the "popular" tradition.

There are eight [strokes] to which one should pay attention,
Ten [points of calligraphy] to be accentuated,
Twenty-one primary characteristics, sixteen secondary characteristics,
And three general characteristics that should all be applied.

As for the headless thick-stroked italic script,
There were two [original] traditions—those of Li and Den—
From which many [others] gradually evolved.

One should proficiently study the calligraphic proportions,
Writing surfaces, ink and pens;
One should cherish all major and minor [characteristics of composition],
Maintaining neatness, elegance, and accuracy.
One should write, without contravening the hierarchy [of the various
  scripts],
Whereby the sacred scriptures [of the Buddhas]
Are copied in the block-letter script, and so forth.

I cannot digress [to consider here] other kinds of calligraphy because they are limitless.

As for the representations of buddha mind,
There are explained to be five particular types [of stūpa]:
Those that are spontaneously present by nature, those that are unsurpassed,
Those that are consecrated by blessings,
Those that arise through spiritual accomplishments,
And those that correspond to the different vehicles.
The practical techniques [of stūpa construction] that are applicable
Include those suitable for ordinary persons, pious attendants,
Hermit buddhas, and conquerors,
As described in the transmissions [of monastic discipline].

With regard to the eight stūpas of the conquerors,
Although their measurements are indefinite,
The scholars of Tibet generally attest to [the method outlined in]
The [*Commentary*] *on the Taintless* [*Crown Protuberance*].
Accordingly, they refer to the height [of a stūpa]
As sixteen large units, and the width as slightly more than half of that.

As far as the uncommon stūpa of pristine cognition
Mentioned in the [*Tantra of*] *the Wheel of Time* is concerned,
When the Buddha is seated in a cross legged-posture,
The area from his navel downwards corresponds to the terraces [of the stūpa];
The abdomen, to the dome plinth;
The [chest] from there as far as the shoulders, to the bulging dome;
The throat, to the high pavilion; [the face] as far as the hair ringlet,
To the face [painted] on the high pavilion;
And the [hair knot] from there upwards, to the [stacked] wheels
Of the sacred teachings and the crest [of the stūpa].
These collectively and accurately correlate [in their proportions]
To the external [world], the inner [subtle body], and even to other [divine forms].

In particular, there were many [stūpas of extraordinary] measurement and shape
Which existed from antiquity and are unheard of by arrogant scholars,

Such as the Stūpa of Intangible Glory,
And the Naturally Arisen [Svayambhū] Stūpa of Nepal.

The Nyingma tradition also speaks of the stūpas of the eight
virtuous abodes,
Of the dimensions and designs [of the stūpas]
Corresponding to the nine sequences of the vehicle, and so forth.

The proportions and systematic presentation
Of the vajra, bell, ritual spike, tantric staff, and so forth
Are clearly set forth in the *Collection of Rites*, and so forth.
[The playing of] drums and cymbals, sacred masked dances, and so forth
Are all ritual activities associated with the body.

The ordinary [physical arts] comprise [the making of] residences,
Ships, clothing, ornaments, food,
Armaments—both aggressive and defensive—weapons, and so forth.

The supreme arts of speech are debate, explanation, and composition.
Innate musical sound comprises [four melodic contours]:
The sustaining note, the descending note,
The changing note, and the ascending note,
Which [are exemplified] respectively by [four metaphors]:
A wish-granting tree, a creeping flower plant,
The [changing reflections of the] moon [in water],
And the [traverse of a slow] river.[3]
By undertaking preliminaries that focus on three essentials,
The six defects and five causes should be abandoned.
[Chanting] should then be undertaken in a timely manner, in six great
[ceremonial contexts].
In congregations twelve distinctive [ancillary modes of chanting]
Including the lion's roar should also be employed, as appropriate.
The common [vocal arts] include songs, flutes, and formal speeches.

The supreme arts of mind are those of study, reflection, and meditation
With regard to the eloquently expressed [teachings of the Buddha].
The common [mental arts] comprise the eighteen topics of knowledge,
As well as Sanskrit grammar, logic, and so forth.
There are also eight subjects of scrutiny

Comprising land, gems, trees, chariots, horses, elephants, treasures,
And men and women; and commonly too
There are the treatises on [human] conduct, and the sixty-four crafts,
Along with all sorts of [other] enumerations, including the four categories.

[Chapter 6: Medicine]

Among all the works of medical science
Which concern the physical body and its vitality,
The structure of the *Glorious Great Tantra*
Entitled "Essence of Nectar" is of crucial importance.

The roots [of medical science, as expounded in the *Root Tantra*],
Namely, physiology, diagnosis, and treatment,
Are explained in terms of the patient, the remedy,
The application of the remedy, and the practicing physician.

There are eight branches in the *Instructional Tantra*:
[Treatment of] the physical body [in general], pediatrics, gynecological diseases,
Demonic possession, wounds and injuries, poisoning,
Old age, and the restoration of virility and fertility.

Diseases and remedial techniques are integrated in the *Subsequent* [*Tantra*].

The patient includes [the topics of] physiology for which [treatment is prescribed]
And the diseases which are treated.
The remedy includes [the topics of] regimen, diet, medication, and external therapy.
The method of treatment includes [the topics of] the prevention of disease,
And the treatment of pathological transformations,
While the practitioner of medical science [includes the physician].
[Medical science] is subsumed in these primary and ancillary [topics].

Within physiology [the following] are determined:
The understanding of human embryology,
Based on primary and secondary causes,
And the indications [of parturition],

As well as the understanding [of human anatomy] in metaphorical terms,
And the natural condition of the bodily constituents,
The channels, the vulnerable points,
And the passageways and orifices,
Along with the defining characteristics [of the elements]
Which may be subject to harm,
And [the humors] which may be harmful,
As well as the physical activities, distinctions,
And signs of physical decay.

With regard to diseases, the remote and immediate primary causes
Are [respectively] the three poisons and the three humors.
While the secondary causes that aggravate [the basis of disease]
Include the activity fields of the senses
As well as their gathering, arising, and [fully manifest] arising.
The characteristics [of humoral imbalance],
Which has its inception in the six pathways,
Are excess, deficiency, and [mutual] aggravation.
[Diseases] are then classified on the basis of their primary causes,
The [sex or age of] the patient, and their [four] aspects.

Regimen comprises continuous [daily] regimen, seasonal regimen, and occasional regimen.
Dietetics includes [knowledge of] the [diverse] types [of food and beverages],
As well as dietary restrictions and moderation in the quantity of food.
Medication includes taste, potency, post-digestive taste, and compounding methods.
External therapy includes [the application of] mild, rough, and rigorous [treatments],
Along with the [appropriate] surgical instruments.
[Prophylactics] maintain [the body] in good health, free from disease,
And prolong [the life] of the aged, free from disease.

[Understanding] the primary causes and characteristic [symptoms] of disease,
And relying on [familiarity with] the advantages and disadvantage [of certain remedies],
[The physician] should [also] undertake diagnosis through subterfuge

And through the four alternative parameters,
On the basis of which [treatment] is to be abandoned or prescribed.
Treatment should then be administered
According to general, specific, and special [therapeutic] principles.
Both the common and special methods of treatment should be mastered.

Physicians should be endowed with the six primary attributes.
They should be supreme [in all their other qualities],
And masters of [medical and spiritual] practices.
[Thus,] they themselves and others will enjoy
The results of immediate happiness and long-term well-being.

[Chapter 7: Astrology and Divination]

Among the [subjects] known as the five minor sciences,
Astrology discloses things to be adopted or rejected
From the perspective of relative appearances.
The gross apparitional forms of reality or emptiness
Underlie the astrological calculations to be made,
While the techniques of astrological calculation
Are mathematical computations of interdependence or correlation.
The stepping of the planets derives from the breath within the central channel,
But at the end of the four ages, they will enter a state of vacuity.
The precision of time arises through repeated scrutiny.
The inner [world] qualitatively manifested as the [phenomena of] the external world,
Among which the solar mansions and constellations
Which [the planets] traverse took form;
And the planetary bodies that traverse them [also] arose.
The Sun marks out its [anti-clockwise] longitude through the solar mansions,
While the four [terrestrial] seasons rotate in a clockwise manner.
The solar mansions of the constellations and the zodiac,
Dependent on the motion of the wind element,
Also rotate clockwise in the course of each solar day,
While the planets demarcate celestial [longitude], through their respective motions.

Rāhu encounters the Sun and the Moon
In the interval which follows the passing of three "seasons."

The zodiacal, calendar, and solar days then emerged,
Dependent on the epicycles of the Sun, Moon, and the wind element.
[The Sun and the planets in a single solar day] rotate along the zodiac,
[Divided] according to three "periods" of time, four "junctures,"
Eight "watches," twelve "[ascendant] conjunctions,"
Thirty "hours," twenty-one thousand six hundred "breaths,"
Three thousand six hundred "intervals" of time,
Or sixty "clepsydra measures" of time.

Through the five aspects [of astrological calculation]—
Weekdays, lunar days, constellations, combined calculations, and impacts—
The longitude of the five planets and of Rāhu
As well as the conjunctions and [other] aspects should be examined.
Elective prediction and other minor calculations should also be studied.

[Chapter 8: Poetics]

The body [of composition] that conveys the desired meaning of poetry
Includes verse, prose, or mixed verse and prose.
Verses may be detached, clustered, intricate, or compounded,
And they may [also] be divided into cantos.
But they [invariably] consist of four metrical lines.
Prose may comprise narrative and legend,
While mixed verse and prose refers to the main style of [courtly] drama
And the ordinary style of Campū.

Embellishments include the ten uncommon sentiments of composition
As well as the common ornaments of sense, sound, and enigmatic innuendo.
Abandoning defects, one's composition should adorn the world.

[Chapter 9: Prosody]

The prosody of verse should observe the metric rules governing syllabic quantity,
Which may be calculated commencing from the six-syllable meter [class],

As far as the [twenty-seven syllable] Saṃtāna meter [class].
The syllabic quantity [of a given stanza] is demarcated
[By four metrical lines] which may be of equal, unequal, or semi-equal length.

The metric rules governing the scansion of moric instants concern
The Āryā meter, the Vaitālya meter, and the Paiṅgala meter,
But there are also other explanations.

One should then examine the arrangement [of metrical variations] in tabular form,
The general calculation [of the permutations in each meter class],
The reductionist calculation which differentiates [the cadence of each specific meter],
The calculation of the specific position [of a given meter within its meter class],
The [triangular] chart of the light syllables,
And the calculation of the point of cadence that has been reached [in the table].

[Chapter 10: Synonymics]

There are primary names and derivative names which have meaning,
Proper names and, similarly, imputed names.
The latter include names based on similarity and causal relationship,
And the contrariety of these,
While [those based on causal relationships] include
Names that impute the result from its cause
And names that impute the cause from its result,
As well as collective names applicable to individuals,
And the contrariety of these.
Through homonyms and synonyms
[The science of] synonymics should be comprehended,
Along with the tables [of verbal roots] and definitions.

[Chapter 11: Dramaturgy]

One should study all acts that bring delight to sentient beings,
Evoking dramatic performances endowed with the sentiment of joy,

Including the aspects of the five dramatic junctures
And the aspects of the [four] dramatic elements,
As well as the thirty-six characteristics [of stagecraft],
And the [trappings of] graceful [song and dance],
[The wearing of] garlands, and so forth.

[Chapter 12: Mundane Spiritual Paths]

There are common understandings concerning merely the happiness of this life
And there are philosophically inclined persons, endowed with a spiritual path.
There are many views, authentic and inauthentic.
For every hundred lower [views] there is but a single higher view,
But when they are [all] subsumed, they comprise
The outer [non-Buddhist] and inner [Buddhist perspectives].

The non-Buddhists are designated as "extremists."
[Extremists] are of three sorts:
Nominal, emanational, and independently established.
The last of these include meditators
Who possess the fivefold supernormal cognitive powers.

The basic [divisions] of the dialecticians
Are the eternalist and nihilist schools.
Among them, [the latter] are the materialists
Who hold that life forms are of three types—
Discernable, indiscernible, and animistic.
They espouse nihilism, denying the existence of unseen causes,
And they refute the existence of past and future lives,
Along with [the impact of] past actions, and so forth,
For which reasons they cannot attain even the higher realms [of gods and humans].

The oldest of all the eternalist schools is the Sāṃkhya,
Who through three modes of valid cognition
Appraise the twenty-five aspects of reality.
In particular, they hold that the "self,"

Endowed with five [characteristics],
Relates to the fundamental state of "nature,"
[Identified with] primal matter in which the three attributes
Are in a state of equilibrium,
And from which evolves the "[great] intelligence."
From that in turn the ego principle evolves,
Along with the five aspects of subtle matter,
The motor organs, the sense organs, and the mind.
As they unfold in series, they give rise to cyclic existence,
But if these modifications are reversed,
The "self" will attain release.

The Vaiśeṣika are followers of Īśvara
Who hold that within substance and its attributes
All subtypes are subsumed,
And they propound the six categories [of reality]
While being similar to the Naiyāyika
In maintaining four kinds of valid cognition,
Eight aspects of radiant form, and so forth.
There are also the Vaiṣṇava, originating from the ten incarnations [of Viṣṇu],
The Brāhmaṇa, who uphold valid cognition that accords with the Vedas,
The Aupaniṣadika, who [regard] the underworld and "soul" in a single savor,
And the Vaiyākaraṇa, who [regard] all things as embodiments of sound.
There are the followers of Jaiminī,
Who maintain twelve defining characteristics and so forth,
The followers of Caraka, who maintain there are eight kinds of valid cognition,
And the Nirgrantha Jains, who propound the ten objects of knowledge and so forth.

All of these are merely on the path to the exalted realms,
But they are to be rejected
Because [the attainment of] release [from the cycle of existence]
Is obscured by their views of the "self."

There are also barbarians,
Who claim harmful or violent acts as their sacred teaching,
Including those in Tibet and China,
Who are beyond the pale in terms of the [Buddhist] scriptures.
All of them should be rejected and given a wide berth.

[Chapter 13: The Exalted Vehicle]

The god [realms] and the [worlds of] Brahmā
Are within [reach of] the exalted vehicle.
Among the three kinds of faith,
Which are the prerequisites[4] of all [spiritual paths],
It is through the conviction that [the impact of] past actions
Is of primary importance, and so forth,
And through the four correct ways of progressing [on the path],
That the ten non-virtuous actions are abandoned,
While the ten virtuous actions and their peripheral acts are adopted.
In this way, laws are maintained concerning [conduct] to be rejected and accepted,
While confused [virtuous and non-virtuous actions]
And disharmonious [goals] are abandoned.
Those who perfect the path of [virtuous] actions
And are disciplined [in respect of their vows]
Will, in the higher reams, attain excellent results,
Mastering the ripening fruits that conform to their causes.

The vehicle of Brahmā is that which traverses the higher world systems.
The four meditative concentrations associated with the world-system of form
Have both causal and fruitional phases.

In the causal phase [of the first meditative concentration],
Preparation entails the meditative stability of calm abiding,
In which physical and mental refinement occurs,
By means of the nine techniques [for settling the mind],
Namely, placement, perpetual placement, integrated placement, intensified placement,
Control, calmness, quiescence, one-pointedness, and meditative equipoise.
Having accomplished [calm abiding],

Then, through the six kinds of attention—
Namely, defining characteristics, resolve, isolation,
Encompassing joy, scrutiny, and perfected application,
One will accomplish the higher insight,
Of attention to the fruit of perfected application.
These coarse and quiescent aspects [of higher insight] constitute the
    common mundane path.
The actual foundation of the first meditative concentration has five aspects:
Ideation, scrutiny, joy, bliss, and one-pointed mind.

Those for whom the first [meditative concentration]
Is defective and the second without defect
Then [focus on the causal phase of the second meditative concentration].
Here, the extraordinary preparation entails [cultivation of]
The attention that is aware of individual characteristics [and so forth].
The actual foundation [of this second meditative concentration]
Has four aspects, starting with intense inner clarity.

Similarly, the third [meditative concentration] will ensue
When preparation entails progressive scrutiny,
By means of the higher insight endowed with attention.
[Its actual foundation] has five aspects, starting with recollection.
Then, [the actual foundation of] the fourth [meditative concentration]
Has four aspects, purified of the eight defects.

In this way, the results will be greater, mediocre, or lesser,
Corresponding to the actual foundation of each [meditative
    concentration].
The ripening fruit appropriate for each of these states and so forth will
    be experienced.

The four meditative absorptions
Associated with the world-system of formlessness
Also have both causal and fruitional phases.
One whose mind has obtained the fourth meditative concentration
And has not relapsed
After inhibiting [the world system of] form,
And its [interactions] of contact, vision, and perception,
Should conclusively perfect the summit of existence

Through the meditative absorptions
Which experience infinite space and consciousness,
Where there is nothing-at-all to be grasped,
And where there is neither perception, coarse or subtle,
Nor is there non-perception.
The results are particularly sublime,
On account of their meditative stability, life span, and so forth.

This basis of enlightened attributes,
Including the [four] immeasurable aspirations,
The [five] supernormal cognitive powers, and so forth
Is the supreme objective to be striven after by both non-Buddhists
And [by followers of] the Lesser Vehicle.
This is a prerequisite for those who would progressively embark
Upon the vehicle of the Conquerors.

The Auto-commentary

Introduction

In order that persons who have become well grounded in the higher ethical disciplines that form the basis of all those virtuous teachings [discussed in Book Five] might understand without error the spiritual paths that lead to freedom [from cyclic existence] and to omniscience (*sarvajñatā, thams cad mkhyen pa*), it will be necessary to investigate the discriminative awareness that arises through studying the [various] fields of knowledge, which are as vast as an ocean in their extent. Therefore, this sixth book [of *The Treasury of Knowledge*], which is a graduated exposition of the [fields of classical learning], is divided into the following four parts:

(1) a systematic presentation of the ordinary classical sciences and mundane spiritual paths;
(2) a systematic presentation of phenomenological structures common to both the Greater Vehicle and the Lesser Vehicle;
(3) a systematic presentation of the vehicles that emphasize causal characteristics;
(4) a systematic presentation of the vehicles that emphasize the [fruitional] indestructible reality according to the way of secret mantra.[5]

1. The Purpose and Scope of Learning

I. The Purpose of Learning [I]
II. Three General Areas of Study—Scriptures, Treatises, and Fine Arts
III. Introduction to the Actual Texts of Classical Learning

The first part [of Book Six] has three topics: (1) a preamble that relates to the purpose [of learning], (2) an exegesis of the three ways in which studies can be pursued, and (3) an introduction to the actual content [of classical learning].

The Purpose of Learning [I]

As to the first [it is said in the root verses]:

> **At the outset, studies should be pursued impartially**
> **Because they are the basis of all erudition and enlightened attributes.**

In addition to maintaining a foundation in pure ethical discipline,[6] the study of all the fields of knowledge in general, and particularly of the multiple approaches of the sūtras and the way of [secret] mantra, which expound the sacred teachings [of Buddhism], is the basis of all enlightened attributes.[7] It is said in the *Scriptural Compilation of the Bodhisattvas*:

> Through study, all things are known.
> Through study, negative actions are reversed.

> Through study, pointless pursuits are abandoned.
> Through study, nirvāṇa is attained.

These four steps are explained sequentially in the *Rational System of Exposition*. That is to say, it is through knowledge of non-Buddhist and Buddhist philosophical and spiritual systems that one will come to discern those things that should be adopted and those things that should be renounced. Then, after one has studied the training of ethical discipline, negative actions will be reversed. After studying the training of the mind [through meditation], pointless desires will be completely abandoned; and after studying the training of discriminative awareness, the state of nirvāṇa that is actually free from corruption will be attained.[8]

In the transmission [entitled] *Analysis* [*of Monastic Discipline*], it is said that an erudite person has five advantages;[9] and elsewhere, it is said in various sūtras and treatises that the enlightened attributes of erudition are limitless.[10] It is for this reason that, at the outset, studies should be thoroughly pursued in an impartial manner.

Three General Areas of Study—Scriptures, Treatises, and Fine Arts [II]

Secondly, the three ways in which studies can be pursued are explained in accordance with the *Level of the Bodhisattvas*:[11]

> **Whatever one investigates—scriptural compilations, treatises,**
> **or fine arts—**
> **One should be aided by humility and perseverance.**
> **Why so? In order to accumulate genuine [analytic] knowledge**
> **and so forth!**

Whenever bodhisattvas who are in pursuit of the sacred teachings engage in any investigation, it is actually the knowledge of the scriptural compilations (*piṭaka*, *sde snod*), the treatises (*śāstra*, *bstan bcos*), the mundane fine arts (*śilpa*, *bzo*), and the status of past actions (*karma*, *las*) that they are investigating.

The "scriptural compilation" [of the Buddhist canon] includes the scriptures of the bodhisattvas and the scriptures of the pious attendants.[12] Among the so-called twelve branches of the scriptures, the category of extensive teachings (*mahāvaipulya*) is said to comprise the former, while the remaining eleven branches comprise the scriptures of the pious attendants.[13] Together, these form the [canonical] subject matter of the Buddhist treatises or Buddhist studies.

"Treatises," when abbreviated in this context, comprise three categories, namely, commentaries on logic, grammar, and medicine;[14] but these may also be designated as non-Buddhist on account of their allegiance to two [or more] teachers [and not only Śākyamuni].[15]

Third, as for the "arts," the commentaries on the thirty designated arts (*bzor btags pa sum cu*)[16] and so forth are established as fields of mundane science, and for this reason are not [formally] categorized as treatises.

When [bodhisattvas] investigate [the sciences] accordingly, those who know that seeds are conducive to their [appropriate] fruits should conduct their research, aided by humility that never slackens and perseverance that is never interrupted, until the objective of their studies is conclusively comprehended. If you ask why they should conduct their investigations in this way, it says in the *Sūtra of the Ascertainment of the Characteristics of Phenomena*:[17]

> Mañjuśrī! One who knows the essence and defining characteristics of all teachings attains genuine analytic knowledge of their meaning. One who knows their various distinctions and their systematic presentations attains the genuine analytic knowledge of intellectual brilliance. One who knows the range of various synonyms attains the genuine analytic knowledge of the teaching. One who knows etymological definitions attains the genuine analytic knowledge of etymological definition.[18] Therefore, Mañjuśrī, if one strives after omniscience, one should initially cultivate the discriminative awareness that arises from study and reflection.[19] This is because she is the mother of all the buddhas!

Also it is said in the *Discourse on Designations*:[20]

> The genuine analytic knowledge of the teaching will be attained through scholarship with regard to names, [syntactically bound] phrases, and syllables. The genuine analytic knowledge of meaning will be attained through scholarship with regard to their meaning. The genuine analytic knowledge of etymological definition will be attained through scholarship with regard to words and designations. The genuine analytic knowledge of intellectual brilliance will be attained through unimpeded mastery of all these topics, and so forth.

The explanation given in the *Commentary on the Treasury of Phenomenology* is in conformity with these citations.[21]

The *Sutra of [Great] Skillful Means Repaying [the Buddha] with Gratitude*, in particular, refers extensively to the necessity of learning the five classical sciences. The following summary, derived from that work, is relevant in the context of bodhisattvas who investigate the empirical teachings:[22]

> In this regard, if you ask why bodhisattvas continue to pursue these studies, bodhisattvas continue to investigate thoroughly the teachings of the Buddha because they are obliged to master earnestly and authentically all doctrines that are in conformity with the sacred teaching and because they impart those doctrines extensively and authentically to others.
>
> Bodhisattvas continue to investigate the science of logic because they have to thoroughly and qualitatively understand the eloquence and solecism found in the treatises themselves, because they are obliged to refute the critiques of others, because they have to convince those lacking faith in this teaching [of Buddhism], and because they have to reinvigorate those who already have faith.
>
> Bodhisattvas continue to investigate the science of grammar because, while constructing refined Sanskrit syntax with fine words or syllables and an elegant use of etymological definitions, they inspire confidence in those wishing them to speak, and because they have to employ terminology in conformity with diverse etymological nuances, even though their meaning may be identical.
>
> Bodhisattvas continue to investigate the science of medicine because they are obliged to alleviate the various ailments that afflict sentient beings, and because they can benefit the great mass of living creatures.
>
> Bodhisattvas continue to investigate the aspects of knowledge concerning the status of mundane past actions because they acquire resources without difficulty for the sake of sentient beings, and because they are obliged to cherish all sentient beings.

The same text concludes that:[23]

> The five ordinary sciences cultivated by bodhisattvas are also to be investigated because bodhisattvas are obliged to perfect the great provision of pristine cognition (*jñānasambhāra, ye shes kyi tshogs*)

> of unsurpassed and genuinely perfect enlightenment.[24] If they do not study all those subjects, they will not in due course attain the unobscured all-knowing pristine cognition.

When these extensive comments are abbreviated, [bodhisattvas] are obliged to persevere for the sake of their objective—the causal basis of the provisions through which the all-knowing pristine cognition is attained.

Introduction to the Actual Texts of Classical Learning [III]

Thirdly, the exegesis of the actual content [of classical learning] has three parts: the articulation of syllables which is the basis of all knowledge, the ordinary sciences and their branches, and the mundane spiritual paths that focus on this life.

2. Articulation and Semantics

A. Linguistic Theory and Articulation of Syllables [III.A]
- 1. Essential Nature of Articulation
- 2. Etymology
- 3. Graphology
- 4. Phonological Analysis of Sanskrit and Tibetan
- 5. Morphology
- 6. Pronunciation
- 7. Eight Elements of Linguistic Application
  - a. Sounds
  - b. Languages
  - c. Names
  - d. Attributes
  - e. Communicative Symbols
  - f. Conventional Terms
  - g. Words
  - h. Meanings

Linguistic Theory and Articulation of Syllables [A]

The first of these topics comprises both an introduction to the nature [of articulation] and a detailed exegesis of its defining characteristics.

Regarding the former [it is said in the root verses]:

> **Articulation of syllables is the basis of all knowledge.**
> **Although the number of languages and scripts may be limitless,**

Their [common] foundation comprises the vowels and consonants.
Actual sounds are held to be not fruitional [in nature],
But they are either produced in conformity with their causes, or cumulatively.

Articulation of syllables (*yi ge'i sbyor ba*) is the basis of all knowledge because the techniques of training enunciated by the Buddha are maintained with reference to it, because it is also the causal basis of [those teachings that] propound the *Four Vedas* of the non-Buddhists,[25] and because all linguistic expressions throughout the world commonly depend on [articulated] syllables. Therefore, at the outset, it is important that the articulation of syllables should be studied and skillfully comprehended. As Tonmi Sambhoṭa himself has said [in his *Thirty Verses*]:[26]

It should be explained that articulation of syllables
Is the basis of all [higher] spiritual trainings,[27]
As well as being a causal basis for exponents of the Vedas;
And it is the foundation of all forms of linguistic expression.

Although the number of different languages in the world and the scripts that have been intellectually devised to represent them may be limitless and indefinable, the [common] foundation of all languages and scripts comprises vowels and consonants, including both phonemes and their character representations.

Among these, it is said that the basic element of sound—the phoneme (*śabdadhātu, sgra'i khams*)—is not produced from a ripening cause (*vipākahetu, rnam smin gyi rgyu*), because it arises whenever its articulation is desired and does not arise when this condition is absent. By contrast, [results] produced from a ripening [cause] may not arise voluntarily but do arise involuntarily. For this reason sound is held by the Vaibhāṣikas to be produced either [as a result] in conformity with its own cause (*niṣyandaphala, rgyu mthun*), or from a causal basis of homogeneity (*sabhāgahetu, skal mnyam*), or else through the four cumulative experiences (*caturaupacāyika, rgyas byung bzhi*). The four cumulative experiences are enumerated as eating, sleeping, good conduct, and meditative stability.[28]

Secondly, the detailed exegesis of the defining characteristics of syllabic articulation is presented through the following seven topics: essential nature, etymology, graphology, phonological analysis, morphology, pronunciation, and the eight elements of linguistic application (*'jug pa'i gnas brgyad*).

Essential Nature of Articulation [1]

Concerning the essential nature of the syllables (*yi ge'i ngo bo*) [it is said in the root verses]:

> **The essential nature of syllabic articulation is vocal pulsation,**
> **Which may be short, long, or diphthong in its duration,**
> **Enduring [respectively] for one, two, or three blinks of an eye.**
> **Each fraction [of a vocal pulsation] lasts but a single instant,**
> **And, along with others, forms a continuum.**
> **[Syllables] are categorized in the *Treasury [of Phenomenology]***
> **Among the disassociated [formative predispositions].**

The essential nature of the syllables is simply vocal pulsation (*skad kyi gdangs*). It is said in the *Exposition of Valid Cognition*:[29]

> Having understood the motility of articulation,
> Sound is produced by one who knows how to produce it.

The air-stream of vital energy (*vāyu, rlung*) is activated voluntarily, and the pulsation of the syllables arises from that. Depending on whether a pulsation endures for one, two, or three blinks of the eye, it is conventionally termed short, long, or diphthong in its duration. As the previous source also states:[30]

> The full extent of a syllable
> May be measured in the blinking of an eye.

Now, each fraction of a syllable is equivalent to an instant or indivisible time moment (*kṣana, skad cig*), and a series or continuum is formed when the other [fractions] are gathered along with it. The *Treasury of Phenomenology* explains that among the [identifiable] phenomenological categories, [syllables] are held by both the Vaibhāṣikas and Sautrāntikas to belong to the category of formative predispositions that are disassociated from mind (*cittaviprayuktasaṃskāra*).[31]

Etymology [2]

Concerning the etymological definition [of the term "syllable" (*yi ge'i nges tshig*), it is said in the root verses]:

The etymological definitions [of "syllable"] include "unchanging nature,"
"Elucidator of nouns and words," and "signifier of meanings."

The etymological definitions (*nirukta, nges tshig*) of the term *yi ge* ("syllable") include the following: In Sanskrit, the tri-syllabic *a-kṣa-ra* [which is rendered in English as "syllable"] means "unchanging." Even when translated into different languages, the nature of the vowels and consonants is unchanging—for example, a single character, such as [the vowel] A or [the consonant] KA, does not transform into a syllable with another phonetic value.

The Sanskrit term *vyañjana* ("consonant") means "elucidator" in the sense that the consonants elucidate or specify all nouns and words. The Sanskrit term *varṇa* ("letter" or "syllable") means "signifier" in the sense that [the syllables] signify all meanings.

Graphology [3]

Concerning the graphology or character representation of syllables (*yi ge'i rnam pa*) [it is said in the root verses]:

The syllabic scripts include Rañjanā, and so forth.

There exist an almost limitless number of syllabic scripts (*yig gzugs*), the foremost of which are the sixty-four [traditional Indic scripts], including Brāhmī (*tshangs pa'i yi ge*) and Rañjanā (*lānydza*).[32]

Phonological Analysis of Sanskrit and Tibetan [4]

The phonological analysis of the syllables (*yi ge'i dbye ba*), [in this context] includes the Sanskrit tradition and the Tibetan tradition.

[Sanskrit Phonology]

With regard to the former [it says in the root verses]:

As for the analysis that is commonly made,
In Sanskrit, the foremost of the four classical languages of India,
The vowels include simple vowels and diphthongs,
And the consonants include basic phonetic sets, semi-vowels, and spirants.

The vowels [according to the *Grammar of Candragomin*]
Number one hundred and thirty-two,
And the basic consonants thirty-seven, which, when multiplied by the vowels,
Become four thousand three hundred and fifty-six.
These all arise dependent on eight places of articulation,
Their articulators, and the modes of inner and outer articulation.

While there are many systematic presentations of phonological analysis found in the traditions derived from each of the [eight renowned] grammatical treatises[33] and also in the uncommon tantra texts, the one that is commonly made refers to the four major classical languages of India,[34] of which the foremost is known as Sanskrit.

The Sanskrit language includes both vowels and consonants. The vowels comprise the ten simple vowels (*samānākṣara, mtshungs pa'i yi ge*), from A and Ā to Ḷ, and Ḹ, as well as the four diphthongs (*saṃdhyakṣara, mtshams sbyor gyi yi ge*), E, AI, O, and AU—sixteen altogether.[35] The consonants comprise five phonetic sets (*pañcavarga, sde pa lnga*) [of stops/ *sparśa*], including the [velar/ *kaṇṭha*] set beginning with KA, as well as the four semi-vowels (*antaḥsthā, mthar gnas*), YA, RA, LA and VA, and the four spirants (*ūṣmān, dro ba'i yi ge*), ŚA and so forth. Thus there are said to be thirty-three consonants. These are the basic syllables.[36]

Places of articulation	Unvoiced non-aspirate surds	Unvoiced aspirate surds	Voiced non-aspirate sonants	Voiced aspirate sonants	Nasals	Aspirate H and semi-vowels	True spirants	Short vowels	Long vowels	Diphthongs
Velar	KA	KHA	GA	GHA	ṄA	HA	ḤKA	A	Ā	
Palatal	CA	CHA	JA	JHA	ÑA	YA	ŚA	I	Ī	E AI
Retro-flex	ṬA	ṬHA	ḌA	ḌHA	ṆA	RA	ṢA	Ṛ	Ṝ	
Dental	TA	THA	DA	DHA	NA	LA	SA	Ḷ	Ḹ	
Labial	PA	PHA	BA	BHA	MA	VA	ḤPA	U	Ū	O AU

Fig. 1. Phonetic tabulation of the Sanskrit consonants and vowels

Derived from this analysis, the *Grammar of Candragomin* classifies each of the four vowels A, I, U and Ṛ as threefold—short (*hrasva*), long (*dīrgha*), and extra long (*pluta*), each of which has three distinct accents or tones—acute or high (*udātta*), grave or low (*anudātta*), and circumflex or middle (*svarita*), making thirty-six variations.[37] These, in turn, are subdivided into two further categories, depending on whether they accept nasalization (*anunāsika, rjes su sna ldan can*) or not, making seventy-two.[38]

Each of the four diphthongs is subdivided into long and extra-long forms, there being no short forms, while Ḷ has no long form and is subdivided into short and extra-long forms. Each of these five also may have the three tones, high, low, or middle, making thirty, and these are doubled to sixty when a distinction is made between those that accept nasalization and those that do not. Added to the aforementioned category, the vowels now number one hundred and thirty-two.[39]

The consonants, meanwhile, include the basic thirty-three, along with Ḥ (*visarga, rnam gcad*), AṂ (*anusvāra, nga ro*), ḤKA (*jihvāmūlīya, lce rtsa can*), and ḤPA (*upadhmānīya, mchu can*), making thirty-seven.[40] Then, each of the basic thirty-three consonants, including KA, may take each of the hundred and thirty-two vowels, making a total of four thousand three hundred and fifty-six combinations.[41]

All these consonants arise dependent on their appropriate places of articulation, articulators, and processes of articulation. Among them, concerning the places of articulation (*vacanāvasthā, rtsol ba'i gnas*), it is said:[42]

> The chest, the throat, the head,
> And similarly the tip of the tongue, the teeth,
> The nose, the lips, and the palate
> Comprise the eight places of syllabic [articulation].

The syllable A, the stops of the velar phonetic set (*kaṇṭhavarga*) beginning with KA,[43] and the spirant syllable HA all have their place of articulation in the velum or the throat.[44] The vowels I, E, and AI are produced by contact with the throat and the palate; and the vowels U, O, and AU by contact between the throat and the lips.[45]

The vowel Ṛ, the stops of the retroflex phonetic set (*mūrdhanyavarga*) beginning with ṬA,[46] the semi-vowel RA,[47] and the spirant syllable ṢA have their place of articulation in the head.[48] The *jihvāmūlīya* has its place of articulation at the root of the palate.

The vowel Ḷ, the stops of the dental phonetic set (*dantyavarga*) beginning with TA,[49] the semi-vowel LA, and the spirant syllable SA all have their place of articulation in the teeth.[50]

The *anusvāra* (AṂ) has its place of articulation in the nose. The nasal syllables ṄA, ÑA, ṆA, NA, and MA all have their place of articulation in the nose, consequent on their respective contact with the velum, and so forth.[51]

The vowel I, along with the stops of the palatal phonetic set (*tālavyavarga*) beginning with CA,[52] the semi-vowel YA, and the spirant syllable ŚA all have their place of articulation in the palate.[53]

The vowel U, the stops of the labial phonetic set (*oṣṭhyavarga*) beginning with PA,[54] and the *upadhmānīya* (ḤPA) have their place of articulation in the lips. The semi-vowel VA is formed by contact with the teeth and the lips.[55]

[Incidentally], the chest or trunk is said to be included here [among the places of articulation] because the velar or guttural syllables are produced with reference to it [as chest pulses], and the other syllables also inevitably have some association with the throat and thereby with the chest.

With regard to the articulators [of the syllables] (*karaṇa*, *byed pa*], the articulator of the *jihvāmūlīya* (ḤKA) is the root of the tongue. The articulator of the palatal syllables is the blade of the tongue. The articulator of the retroflex or cacuminal syllables is the tip of the tongue in proximity [with the upper incisors]. The articulator of the dental syllables is the tip of the tongue. The remaining syllables all have articulators corresponding to their places of articulation.[56]

The actual process of articulation (*rtsol ba*) includes both inner and outer aspects.[57] There are four inner modes of articulation: closure or occlusion of the vocal tract (*saṃvāra*, *btsums pa*), opening of the vocal tract (*vivāra*, *phye ba*), contact or plosion (*spṛṣṭa*, *phrad pa*), and partial contact (*īṣatspṛṣṭa*, *cung zad phrad pa*).[58] Among these, the syllable A is articulated in coincidence with occlusion, while the other vowels and the spirants are articulated in coincidence with the opening of the vocal tract. In this context, the spirants (*ūṣmān*, *dro ba'i yi ge*) accord with the explanation that is given below [in the next paragraph]. Contact characterizes the inner articulation of the [stop consonants, i.e., the syllables of the various] phonetic sets, which are emitted energetically and loudly expressed. Partial contact characterizes the inner articulation of the semi-vowels.

There are five modes of outer articulation: unvoiced surds (*aghoṣa*, *sgra med*), non-aspirates (*alpapāṇa*, *srog chung*), aspirates (*mahāpāṇa*, *srog chen*), voiced sonants (*ghoṣavant*, *sgra ldan*), and spirants (*ūṣmān*, *dro ba*).[59] Among them, the unvoiced surds comprise the first and second syllables of each phonetic set, along with spirants ŚA, ṢA, SA, the *jihvāmūlīya* (ḤKA), and the *upadhmānīya* (ḤPA). The non-aspirates comprise the first, third, and fifth syllables of each phonetic set, along with the semi-vowels. The aspirates comprise the second and fourth syllables of each phonetic set, along with the spirants ŚA, ṢA, SA, and HA. The voiced sonants comprise the third, fourth, and fifth syllables of each phonetic set, along with the *anusvāra*, the semi-vowels, and the syllable HA. The spirants comprise the second and fourth syllables of each set, along with the [true] spirant syllables ŚA, ṢA, SA, and HA.[60] However, we should note that in other [grammatical] texts, only the syllables ŚA, ṢA, SA, and HA are included among the spirants.[61]

At this juncture it would be useful to include [an explanation of] the methods of reciting [Sanskrit syllables] according to the way of [secret] mantra (*sngags kyi bklag thabs*), but owing to my inability to present these points succinctly, in few words, this is a subject that should be solely understood from the compositions of the authentic [teachers] of the past.[62]

[Tibetan Phonology]

With regard to the latter, the phonological analysis of the syllables according to the Tibetan tradition, [it is said in the root verses]:

> **The Tibetan language has four represented vowels, I and so forth,**
> **And thirty consonants, analyzed as prefixes, suffixes, and radicals.**
> **These may occur as isolates, or [in conjunction with] prefixes, superscripts,**
> **Stacks, subscripts, and suffixes.**

The syllables of which the Tibetan language is composed include the basic vowels and consonants, known as the garland of vowels (*a phreng*) and the garland of consonants (*ka phreng*).[63]

The vowels that are clearly represented [in Tibetan] are four in number: I (*gi gu*), U (*zhabs kyu*), E (*'dreng bu*) and O (*nga ro*). These are combined with the syllable A because they cannot be expressed in isolation. The thirty basic consonants, commencing with KA and ending with A, are analyzed as follows. There are five—GA, DA, BA, MA and 'A—which may also occur as prefixes (*sngon 'jug lnga*); and ten—GA, NGA, DA, NA, BA, MA, 'A, RA, LA, and SA—which may also occur as suffixes (*rjes 'jug bcu*); the remaining twenty consonants can only occur as radicals (*ming gzhi*). The prefixes precede the radical, while the suffixes follow the radical. The radicals themselves are the basis of affixation and cannot, as such, be attached to any prefix or suffix.[64]

When these syllables are formed into words, they may occur as isolates (*rkyang pa*), as in the example *ka ba* (meaning "pillar"); in conjunction with

ཀ་	KA	ཁ་	KHA	ག་	GA	ང་	NGA
ཅ་	CA	ཆ་	CHA	ཇ་	JA	ཉ་	NYA
ཏ་	TA	ཐ་	THA	ད་	DA	ན་	NA
པ་	PA	ཕ་	PHA	བ་	BA	མ་	MA
ཙ་	TSA	ཚ་	TSHA	ཛ་	DZA	ཝ་	VA
ཞ་	ZHA	ཟ་	ZA	འ་	‘A	ཡ་	YA
ར་	RA	ལ་	LA	ཤ་	SHA	ས་	SA
ཧ་	HA	ཨ་	A				
ཨི་	I	ཨུ་	U	ཨེ་	E	ཨོ་	O

Fig. 2. Consonants and vowels of the Tibetan language

prefixes (*sngon 'jug gis 'phul ba*), as exemplified by *mgo bo* ("head"); with subscripts (*'dogs 'phul*), as in the example *dbye ba* ("analysis"); or in stacks (*brtsegs 'phul*), as in the example *bsgrub bya* ("probandum"). There are three syllables that can appear in superscript form (*mgo can*)—RA, LA, and SA—as in the example *sgra* ("sound"), and four that can appear in subscript form (*'dogs bzhi*)—YA, RA, LA, and VA.[65]

The ten suffixes are employed in simple suffixation (*rkyang 'jug*), as exemplified by *rtag* ("always"), but [DA and SA] may also be employed in post-suffixation (*yang 'jug*), as exemplified by *rtags* ("sign").

MORPHOLOGY [5]

Concerning the morphology of syllables (*yi ge sbyor tshul*) [it is said in the root verses]:

> **Meaning is disclosed by adding inflections, particles, and so forth;**
> **And [action] is conveyed by verbal agentives and objectives, and the three tenses.**

ར་མགོ་བཅུ་གཉིས་ནི།

The twelve letters with superscribed RA:

རྐ་	རྒ་	རྔ་	རྗ་	རྙ་	རྟ་	རྡ་	རྣ་	རྦ་	རྨ་	རྩ་	རྫ་
RKA	RGA	RNGA	RJA	RNYA	RTA	RDA	RNA	RBA	RMA	RTSA	RDZA

ལ་མགོ་བཅུ་ནི།

The ten letters with superscribed LA:

ལྐ་	ལྒ་	ལྔ་	ལྕ་	ལྗ་	ལྟ་	ལྡ་	ལྤ་	ལྦ་	ལྷ་
LKA	LGA	LNGA	LCA	LJA	LTA	LDA	LPA	LBA	LHA

ས་མགོ་བཅུ་གཅིག་ནི།

The eleven letters with superscribed SA:

སྐ་	སྒ་	སྔ་	སྙ་	སྟ་	སྡ་	སྣ་	སྤ་	སྦ་	སྨ་	སྩ་
SKA	SGA	SNGA	SNYA	STA	SDA	SNA	SPA	SBA	SMA	STSA

ཡ་བཏགས་བརྒྱད་ནི།

The eight letters with subscribed YA:

ཀྱ་	ཁྱ་	གྱ་	པྱ་	ཕྱ་	བྱ་	མྱ་	ཧྱ་
KYA	KHYA	GYA	PYA	PHYA	BYA	MYA	HYA

ར་བཏགས་བཅུ་བཞི་ནི།

The fourteen letters with subscribed RA:

ཀྲ་	ཁྲ་	གྲ་	ཏྲ་	ཐྲ་	དྲ་	ནྲ་	པྲ་	ཕྲ་	བྲ་	མྲ་	ཤྲ་	སྲ་	ཧྲ་
KRA	KHRA	GRA	TRA	THRA	DRA	NRA	PRA	PHRA	BRA	MRA	SHRA	SRA	HRA

ལ་བཏགས་དྲུག་ནི།

The six letters with subscribed LA:

ཀླ་	གླ་	བླ་	རླ་	སླ་	ཟླ་
KLA	GLA	BLA	RLA	SLA	ZLA

ཝ་ཟུར་བཏགས་པ་བཅུ་གསུམ་ནི།

The thirteen letters with subscribed VA (WA-ZUR):

ཀྭ་	ཁྭ་	གྭ་	ཉྭ་	དྭ་	ཙྭ་	ཚྭ་	ཞྭ་	ཟྭ་	རྭ་	ལྭ་	ཤྭ་	ཧྭ་
KVA	KHVA	GVA	NYVA	DVA	TSVA	TSHVA	ZHVA	ZVA	RVA	LVA	SHVA	HVA

Fig. 3. Superscript and subscript letters of the Tibetan language

When nouns (*nāman, ming*) are formed into [syntactically bound] phrases (*pada, tshig*), phrases that disclose meaning and nuances of meaning may be formed by the addition of [variable] particles and case endings that will change contingent on the preceding suffix. [In Tibetan,] the latter include the reduplicated particles [that mark the end of a sentence; *slar bsdu*], the oblique case particles (*la don*), and the genitive and instrumental case particles (*i ldan*);[66] as well as the six non-variable particles (*phrad gzhan dbang can*), including the thematic particle *ni* that demarcates or emphasizes a subject.[67]

The various combinations of prefixes and suffixes are then applied, distinguishing agentives and objectives (*bdag gzhan*), the three tenses (*dus gsum*), and verbal categories (*bya byed*).[68]

Nouns are formed from multiple combinations of syllables, and [syntactically bound] phrases are formed from multiple combinations of nouns. Concerning the functionality [of nouns, phrases, and syllables], the master [Pang] Lodro Tenpa [1276–1342] has said [in his *Clarification of the Three Clusters*],[69]

> Nouns signify the essential nature of their meaning.
> [Syntactically bound] phrases convey their particular nuances;
> And syllables convey nothing at all.

Take, for example, the nouns "vase" (*bum pa*) and "ox" (*ba lang*). These do convey the essential nature of their meanings, whereas [the relevant syntactically bound] phrases convey particular nuances—[a vase being] "something compounded and impermanent" (*'dus byas mi rtag*), and [an ox] "something endowed with corrupt [psycho-physical aggregates] and subject to suffering" (*zag bcas sdug bsngal*). On the other hand, [a string of] syllables, such as A, Ā, KA, KHA, GA, GHA, and ṄA will convey nothing at all.

[Case Inflections]

The particular nuances of meaning cannot be fully conveyed unless the appropriate inflections and particles are attached to the stems of [the relevant] words and phrases. Among these, inflections (*vibhakti, rnam dbye*; lit. "differentiators") are so called because they differentiate cases—accusative, instrumental, and so forth—and number—singular, dual, and plural. With regard to the relationship between inflections and nominal stems, in Sanskrit the words *buddha, dharma* ("teaching"), *deva* ("deity"), and *ātman* ("self") are not differentiated in themselves, apart from conveying the bare essential nature of their [respective] meanings, but they become differentiated when their appropriate first case [nominative or substantive, *prathamā*] inflections are affixed.[70] In Tibetan, on the other hand, no such distinction is made between the first case inflection (*rnam dbye dang po*) and the noun isolate (*ming rkyang*).

With regard to [the distinctions of number], let us take for example, the noun "buddha" (*sangs rgyas*). One may say "one buddha" (*buddhaḥ, sangs rgyas*) in the singular, "two buddhas" (*buddhau, sangs rgyas dag*) in the dual, and "buddhas" (*buddhāḥ, sangs rgyas rnams*) in the plural. Such [inflections] can be applied to the other examples listed here, in turn.[71]

The second or accusative case (*dvitīyā, las su bya ba*) may be illustrated by the expressions "homage to the buddha" (*sangs rgyas la phyag 'tshal lo*), or "going to India" (*rgya gar du 'gro*), where the object is identified by the particles *la* and *du*.

The third or instrumental case (*tṛtīyā, byed sgra*) may be illustrated by the expressions "the teachings spoken by the buddha" (*sangs rgyas kyis chos gsungs*) and "the actions I have to do" (*bdag gis las bya*), where the agent or instrument is identified respectively by the particles *kyis* and *gis*.

The fourth or dative case (*caturthā, dgos ched du bya ba*) may be illustrated by the expressions "offering food to a beggar" (*slong mo la zas sbyin*) and "irrigating the fields" (*zhing la chu 'dren*), where the indirect object of benefit is identified by the particle *la*.

The fifth or ablative case (*pañcamā, 'byung khungs*) may be illustrated by the expressions "teachings derived from the buddha" (*sangs rgyas las chos*) and "gemstones from the ocean" (*rgya mtsho nas rin po che*), where the source is identified respectively by the particles *las* and *nas*.

The sixth or genitive case (*ṣaṣṭhī, 'brel sgra*) may be illustrated by the expressions "body of the buddha" (*sangs rgyas kyi sku*) and "realm of sentient beings" (*sems can gyi khams*), where the possessive relationship is identified respectively by the particles *kyi* and *gyi*.

The seventh or locative case (*saptamā, gnas gzhi*) may be illustrated by the expressions "he remained seated in steadfastness" (*brtan par bzhugs*) and "man in the house" (*khyim du mi*), where the spatio-temporal location or locus is identified respectively by the [terminal] *-r* and the particle *du*.[72]

Among these cases, the second (accusative), the fourth (dative) and the seventh (locative) all employ the six variants of the oblique particle *la* (*la don gyi sgra drug*) as their case indicator. These are *la, na, tu, du, su,* and *ru*. The [third or] instrumental case employs the five variant forms *kyis, gyis, gis, yis,* and *-'i*. The [fifth or] ablative case employs the particles *las* and *nas*, while the [sixth or] genitive case employs the variant forms *kyi, gyi, gi, yi* and *-'i*.[73]

[Variable Particles That Cannot Stand Alone]

Apart from these, there are some particles which may stand alone, without functioning as inflections, and others [which cannot meaningfully stand alone]. The latter include the particles of reduplication (*slar bsdu*), *go*, *ngo*, and so forth [which demarcate the end of a sentence] and assume [variable forms] depending on the final letters to which they are attached.[74]

The [mnemonic] verses cited in the following paragraph [and translated in the endnotes] illustrate [those variable particles that cannot meaningfully stand alone. They include (1) the oblique particle *la*; (2) the locative particle *na*; (3–6) the genitive particles *kyi*, *gyi*, *gi*, and *yi*; (7–17) the final particles of reduplication *go*, *ngo*, *do*, *no*, *bo*, *mo*, *-'o*, *ro*, *lo*, *so*, and *to*; (18–20) the possessive particles (*bdag sgra*) *pa*, *po*, and *bo*; (21–22) the negative particles (*dgag sgra*) *ma* and *mi*; (23) the possessive particle *can*; (24) the emphatic or thematic particle *ni*; (25) the causal particle *phyir*; (26–27) the vocative particles (*'bod pa'i sgra*) *kye* and *kva*; (28–30) the conjunctive particles *cing*, *zhing*, and *shing*; (31–33) the indirect speech particles *ces*, *zhes*, and *shes*; (34–36) the indefinite or imperative particles *cig*, *zhig*, and *shig*; (37–39) the final speech particles *ce'o*, *zhe'o*, and *she'o*; (40–42) the conditional particles *ce na*, *zhe na*, and *she na*; (43) the optative particle *gu*; (43–45) the conjunctive modifying particles (*rgyan sdud kyi sgra*) *kyang*, *-'ang*, and *yang*; (46–55) the disjunctive-adjunctive connecting particles (*'byed sdud kyi sgra*) *gam*, *ngam*, *dam*, *nam*, *bam*, *mam*, *-'am*, *ram*, *lam*, and *sam*; (56–57) the dual and plural particles *dag* and *rnams*; (58–60) the connecting particles (*lhag bcas*) *te*, *ste*, and *de*; (61) the quantitative pronoun (*spyi sgra*) *snyed*; (62) the conjunctive particle (*dang sgra*) *dang*; and (63) the auxiliary particle *lo*]:[75]

dag **la** gsal **na** legs mod **kyi**/
bstan **gyi** 'jug **gi** 'chad bya **yi**/
mkhas par byas **nas** tshul brtag **go**/
bya ba bzang **po** legs bkod **do**/
'byon **no** grub **bo** don bsam **mo**/
bya'**o** phyar **ro** lha rgyal **lo**/
bltas **so** bstan **to** lha chos **pa**/
sgrub po dga' **bo** gsar ma **pa**/
ma rnyog **mi** lhung dge ba **can**/
da **ni** ci **phyir kye kye** bu/
kva ye grogs dag bgrod **cing** mchis/
bde **zhing** dgyes **shing** yod **ces** thos/

gsal **zhes** mdzes **shes** zhad **cig** gda'/
nam **zhig** gros **shig** gdab **ce'o**/
su yod **ce na** gang **zhe na**/
ma byas **she na** byos shig **gu**/[76]

'khod **kyang** 'gro ba'**ang** dran na **yang**/
rgyug **gam** 'dong **ngam** sdod **dam** ci/
mdun **nam** rgyab **bam** legs bsam **mam**/
bya'**am** 'char **ram** cang thal **lam**/
rgyas **sam** de **dag** dpal 'byor **rnams**/
mkhas **te** 'chad **de** kun chub **ste**/
ji **snyed** bde **dang** ldan **no lo**//[77]

[Nonvariable Particles That Can Stand Alone]

On the other hand, the particles which do convey meaning when they stand alone, and have no variable forms due to affixation, include single-syllable particles (*phrad rkyang pa*) such as (1) *gang* ("what"), (2) *ci* ("what"), (3) *de* ("that"), (4) *'di* ("this"), (5) *su* ("who"), (6) *yang* ("again"), (7) *nam* ("ever"), (8) *slar* ("again"), (9) *'o na* ("but"), (10) *la la* ("some"), and (11) *ji* ("how"); as well as the many disyllabic or trisyllabic particles and so forth, such as (12) *gang dag* ("which two"), (13) *de dag* ("those two"), (14) *gang rnams* ("which"), (15) *de rnams* ("those"), (16) *ji snyed* ("however many"), (17) *de snyed* ("so many"), and (18) *ci nas kyang* ("by all means").[78]

[The Agentive-Objective Distinction and the Three Tenses]

When verbal action is analyzed, with regard to those [transitive] verbs which establish a subject-object relationship (*byed po gzhan dang dngos su 'brel ba*), [the following semantic distinction is made]: the instrument by which the subject effects an action upon the object (*byed pa po'i dngos po*) and the verbal action occurring in the present tense (*byed pa*) are collectively known as the agentive (*bdag*), while the object of the action that is to be achieved (*bsgrub bya'i yul gyi dngos po*) and the action occurring in the future tense (*bya ba*) are collectively known as the objective (*gzhan*).[79]

Whether verbs establish or do not establish a subject-object relationship, the completed action occurs in the past tense (*dus 'das pa*), the action that is yet to be completed occurs in the future tense (*dus ma 'ongs pa*), and the action that is presently being completed occurs in the present tense (*dus da lta ba*).

Although verbs are classified elsewhere according to the action of the subject (*byed pa'i las*) and the action of the object (*bya ba'i las*), these distinctions are subsumed, from the standpoint of the three tenses, by assigning the action of the subject to the present tense and the action of the object to the future tense; or from the standpoint of the agentive-objective distinction, a present action that establishes a [transitive] subject-object relationship is classed as agentive and a future action that does so is classed as objective, as has just been explained. Therefore, the distinction between the three tenses is found universally in sentence construction pertaining to the action of the subject, and the distinction between agentive and objective, though not quite as all-embracing, is made alongside [the distinction of tense] because sentences include constructions expressive of both the subject and the object.[80]

Examples of constructions expressing the agentive or subject include [nominal forms such as] *sgrub pa po* ("achiever"), *ston pa po* ("teacher"), *sgrub byed* ("means of achievement," "practice"), and *ston byed* ("means of teaching," "instruction"); and verbal forms such as *gsal bar byed pa* ("is clarifying"), *sgrub par byed pa* ("is achieving"), *ston par byed pa* ("is teaching"), *sgrub bo* ("is achieving"), and *ston to* ("is teaching").

Examples of constructions expressing the objective include [nominal forms such as] *sgrub par bya ba* ("object to be achieved," "goal"), *bstan par bya ba* ("object to be taught," "student"), *bsgrub bya* ("goal"), and *bstan bya* ("teaching"), as well as their verbal forms—*sgrub par bya* ("is to be achieved"), *bstan par bya* ("is to be taught"), *brgrub bo* ("will be achieved"), and *bstan no* ("will be taught").[81]

As for the distinctive forms of the three tenses, which are not subsumed in that [agentive-objective] classification, there are many examples. Those illustrating the past tense include *bsgrubs* ("achieved"), *bstan* ("taught"), and *grub* ("been attained"). Examples of the present tense include *sgrub bzhin pa* ("is achieving"), *ston bzhin pa* ("is teaching"), *'grub par byed* ("is being attained"), and *'chad par byed* ("is being explained"). Examples of the future tense include *'grub par 'gyur* ("will be achieved"), *'chad par 'gyur* ("will be explained"), *'grub bo* ("will be attained"), *'chad do* ("will teach"), *'grub par bya* ("will be attained"), and *'chad par bya* ("will be explained").[82]

An example of a [transitive] construction that establishes a relationship with the subject (*byed pa po dang dngos su 'brel ba*) is *lcags gser du bsgyur* ("he transformed iron into gold"), and an example of a [non-transitive] construction that that does not establish a relationship with the subject is *lcags gser du 'gyur* ("iron turned into gold").[83]

Pronunciation [6]

Concerning the pronunciation of syllables (*yi ge klag thabs*) [it is said in the root verses]:

> **At first [Tibetan] phonics should be practiced,**
> **And this should be followed by the spelling aloud of constructed syllables.**
> **These [syllables] are produced and expressed in conformity with**
> **Their distinct places of articulation, articulators, and modes of articulation.**
> **Having mastered [spelling], the technique of affixation—**
> **The process determining which [affixes] are attached to which [radicals]—**
> **As well as the need for [affixation]**
> **Should all be studied with reference to the excellent texts of Tonmi,**
> **The oldest of [all the Tibetan treatises on] language,**
> **Which were [composed] through the enlightened activity of the buddhas.**

Now, with regard to the sequential steps of training [in pronunciation], at first one should practice [traditional Tibetan] phonics (*nga ro*). Since sound is conveyed by phonemes, one should perfect the pronunciation of each syllable, ensuring that the individual syllables conform to their respective places of articulation, and that even the vowels have their own distinctive modes of phonetic production.

Then, after acquiring experience [in phonetic diction], one should practice spelling aloud, which entails the composition, in a single syllabic stack, of prefixes, suffixes, and radical letters.[84]

As stated above in the section on Sanskrit phonetics, these [syllables] are produced and expressed in conformity with their own distinctive places of articulation, articulators, and inner and outer modes of articulation. For more detail [on the phonetic diction of Tibetan], readers should refer to the writings of the venerable Sonam Tsemo, and others.[85]

Having mastered spelling, one should then study the excellent works of Tonmi Sambhoṭa—the *Thirty Verses* and the *Introduction to Gender*, in which the definitive rules concerning affixation are presented in detail.[86] These determine which [radicals] may take prefixes and suffixes, which prefixes and suffixes may be attached to a given radical, the actual techniques of affixation, and the need for affixation. Tonmi Sambhoṭa's texts, which are the oldest or most fundamental of all the Tibetan treatises on language, were composed through the enlightened activity of the buddhas, and they cannot simply be examined through the intelligence of ordinary persons.[87]

Eight Elements of Linguistic Application [7]

Concerning the eight elements of linguistic application (*'jug pa'i gnas brgyad*), [it is said in the root verses]:

> **All [constructions depend on] the following eight elements of linguistic application:**
> **Apprehended sounds and languages,**
> **Names and attributes,**
> **Communicative symbols and conventional terms,**
> **And words and meanings.**
> **Through the convergence of sounds and meanings,**
> **An apprehending intelligence arises**
> **In association with five successive factors:**
> **Objective reference, sound generation, shared ideation,**
> **Commonality, and adhesion.**

All constructions that convey meaning by employing syllables are dependent on the eight elements of linguistic application (*'jug pa'i gnas brgyad*).[88] These eight are enumerated and grouped as follows: sounds and languages, names and attributes, communicative symbols and conventional terms, and words and meanings.

Sounds and Languages [a, b]

Among them, sounds (*śabda, sgra*) here refers to phonemes originating from organic or animate sources[89] that are conveyed grammatically to sentient beings. Languages (*bhāṣā, skad*) facilitate the comprehension of communicative symbols applicable in different countries, such as India, Tibet, and China, and so forth.

Names and Attributes [c, d]

Names (*nāman, ming*) are the designations (*adhivacana, tshig bla dvags*) of substantives, such as "vase" and "lion," through which the intellect appraises objects. According to the tradition of the Abhidharma, they comprise an "aggregate of syllables" (*yi ge 'dus pa*), whereas according to the grammarians (*brda sprod pa*) they comprise inflected stems (*vibhaktyanta, rnam dbye'i mtha'*).[90] Attributes (*lakṣaṇa, mtshan ma*) [such as color and form] are so termed because they have the capacity to illustrate and manifest a given object.

Communicative Symbols and Conventional Terms [e, f]

Communicative symbols (*saṃketa, brda*) partake of a [shared] moment of comprehension and verbalization that occurs once names have been imputed, in order to associate a given conventional term with a given meaning. Conventional terms (*vyavahāra, tha snyad*) embody semantic usage, which naturally partakes of three [successive] phases: cognition, signification, and semantic application or engagement (*shes brjod 'jug gsum*). Among these, the imputative cognition (*btags pa'i shes pa*) is the consciousness that thinks [for example], "This is a pillar." From this there follows signification—the verbalization of the word "pillar"—and application, which is [the understanding that] since there is a pillar, building work may be undertaken.

Although universals (*spyi*) do not exist in reality, they are superimposed in order that [terms] might be meaningfully applied, just as, for example, a "piece of wood that supports a beam" is imputed to be a "pillar."[91]

Regarding these [semantic distinctions], names have the function of signifying the bare essential nature (*ngo bo tsam*) of a given object. Attributes [of form and color] have the function of illustrating a given object. Communicative symbols are applied because they are held to arise spontaneously and without precedent in order to facilitate [a given] conventional term. Conventional terms are verbalized in order that a given [term] might be meaningfully applied.

Words and Meanings [g, h]

Syntactically bound words or phrases (*pada, tshig*), according to the tradition of Buddhist phenomenology, are composed of names, which then come to signify or denote particular nuances of meaning, as in the expression, "compounded things are impermanent." However, according to the tradition of the grammarians, it is by suffixing the inflections *tiṄ* (indicating verbal desinence) and *sUP* (indicating nominal desinence),[92] as appropriate, that the essential nature of an object and its particular nuances are suitably signified. Meanings (*don*) are inherent, being analogous to the abiding nature of all phenomena (*chos rnams kyi gnas lugs*).

Now, with respect to these eight elements of linguistic application, when syllables are conjoined in an appropriate manner, there is a convergence of sound and meaning; and the usage then takes effect owing to the apprehending intellect.

Furthermore, with regard to the arising of this intelligence, at the moment when communication takes place, the intellect necessarily experiences five [successive] factors that distinguish this [cognition] from other cognitions. These are objective reference (*don la dmigs pa*), sound generation (*sgra la byung ba*), shared ideation (*mthun par snang ba*), universality or commonality (*thun mongs du grags pa*), and adhesion (*mngon par zhen pa*).

These [five factors] have their own distinctive functions: Objective reference generates the functionality of object-universals (*don spyi*). The production of sound generates the representations of sound-universals (*sgra spyi*).[93] Shared ideation and commonality give rise to adhesion and facilitate comprehension in others. Adhesion generates an association between names and denoted meanings (*ming can*). It is therefore by experiencing these sequentially arising factors that [the intelligence of] names and so forth arises. The phase of adhesion itself has four distinct sub-phases.[94]

For details concerning such distinctions, readers should understand [the discussion] contained in the *Root Verses* and *Commentary on the Eight Elements of Linguistic Application*, and so forth.[95]

3. Sanskrit Grammar

B. The Ordinary Classical Sciences and Their Branches [III.B]
- 1. Usefulness of the Classical Sciences
- 2. Actual Exegesis of the Classical Sciences
  - a. Major Classical Sciences
    - i. Sanskrit Grammar
      - aa. Brief Introduction to Sanskrit Grammar
      - bb. Detailed Explanation of Sanskrit Grammar
        - 1' Primary Bases
          - a' Verbal Roots—Six Categories, Two Voices
          - b' Nominal Stems—Six Aspects of Gender
        - 2' Affixation
        - 3' Derivation
          - a' Actual Derivation
          - b' Nominal Compounding
      - cc. Synopsis of Sanskrit Grammar

The Ordinary Classical Sciences and Their Branches [B]

The second topic [of the exegesis of the actual content of classical learning] concerns the ordinary sciences and their branches. This has two aspects: the usefulness [of the classical sciences] and their actual exegesis.

Usefulness of the Classical Sciences [1]

As to the former [it is said in the root verses]:

There exist no branches of knowledge
That should remain unstudied by the sons of the Conquerors.
Therefore the classical sciences should be studied
Because they eradicate [wrong understanding],
Bring [seekers] into the fold,
And achieve the all-knowing [path of omniscience].

When [bodhisattva] sons of the Conqueror, entering the path of the Greater Vehicle, seek the [sacred] teachings, there exist no branches of knowledge at all, including the five classical sciences (*pañcavidyā, rig gnas lnga*), which should remain unstudied. This is because, when the level of omniscience (*sarvajñātā, thams cad mkhyen pa nyid*) is attained, results will emerge that are in conformity with their causes. So it is said in the *Introduction to the Conduct of a Bodhisattva*:[96]

There is nothing at all which is not to be studied
By the sons of the Conqueror.
For one who has such learning,
Nothing at all will be without merit.

Nāgārjuna has also said [in his *Eulogy to the Expanse of Actual Reality*]:

From all such seeds fruits will emerge that resemble their causes.
Which learned one can prove that fruits come into being without
seeds!

The principal that similar classes of results are derived from similar classes of cause is one that conforms to the norms of worldly folk. Therefore it is accepted that [bodhisattvas] should train their minds in all aspects of knowledge. On this point, too, Nāgārjuna says at the outset [in his *Fundamental Stanzas of Madhyamaka*]:[97]

Without relying on conventional terms,
Ultimate reality cannot be demonstrated.
Without realizing the ultimate reality,
Nirvāṇa will not be attained.

So, even to realize the abiding nature of ultimate reality (*don dam pa'i gnas lugs*), it is necessary to rely upon conventional terminology.

When the fields [of knowledge] are subsumed, they can be classified according to the ten classical sciences, but there are actually only five main classical sciences, since the five minor sciences (*rigs gnas chung ba lnga*) are all considered to be branches of Sanskrit grammar [and medicine]. Among the [five major sciences], grammar and logic eradicate wrong understandings of word and meaning. Fine arts and medicine bring into the fold students [seeking] both general and particular [skills]. The inner science [of Buddhism] brings about an understanding of all aspects of the path to omniscience. Therefore, the classical sciences may also be grouped in three categories: those that eradicate [wrong understandings], those that bring [seekers] into the fold, and the one that attains omniscience.[98]

These then are [the fields of knowledge] that are to be studied. It is said in the *Sūtra of* [*Great*] *Skillful Means, Repaying the Buddha with Gratitude*:[99]

> If a bodhisattva does not study the five sciences, he can never obtain all-knowing pristine cognition in the unsurpassed, genuine, and perfect enlightenment. This being the case, in order to obtain unsurpassed enlightenment, the five sciences should be studied.

And the regent Maitreya has said [in the *Ornament of the Sūtras of the Greater Vehicle*]:[100]

> If one does not persevere with regard to the five classical sciences,
> Even a supremely sublime being will not attain omniscience.
> Therefore, one should persevere in these [studies]
> In order to eradicate [wrong understandings], bring [others] into the fold,
> And understand all natures.

Actual Exegesis of the Classical Sciences [2]

As to the latter, the actual exegesis of the classical sciences comprises both the major pathway of science (*rigs lam che ba*) and the minor pathway of science (*rigs lam chung ba*).

Major Classical Sciences [a]

The major pathway includes four subjects: Sanskrit grammar (*śabdavidyā*), logic (*pramāṇavidyā*), fine arts (*śilpavidyā*), and medicine (*cikitsāvidyā*) [which will now be examined in turn].

Sanskrit Grammar [i]

Sanskrit grammar will be considered in terms of a brief introduction, a detailed explanation, and a synopsis.[101]

Brief Introduction to Sanskrit Grammar [aa]

As to the brief introduction to Sanskrit grammar [it is said in the root verses]:

> **Grammar—[the science] that eliminates wrong understandings with regard to words—**
> **Comprises three aspects: primary bases, affixation, and derivation.**

The classical science of Sanskrit grammar that eradicates and eliminates wrong understandings with regard to signifying [words] comprises three [essential] elements: primary bases (*prakṛti, rang bzhin*), affixation (*pratyaya, rkyen*), and derivation (*vikāra, rnam 'gyur*).[102]

Detailed Explanation of Sanskrit Grammar [bb]

The detailed explanation considers these three elements individually: primary bases, affixation, and derivation.

Primary Bases [1']

The first includes both verbal roots (*dhātu, byings*) and nominal stems (*nāman, ming*).

Verbal Roots—Six Categories, Two Voices [a']

As to verbal roots [it is said in the root verses]:

> **Among primary bases, the verbal roots can be subsumed in six categories:**
> **Those that have been listed or formally conjugated,**
> **Those that have not been listed or formally conjugated,**
> **And those that have both been and not been formally conjugated;**
> **As well as denominative verbal roots, affixed verbal roots,**

And those that are both denominative and affixed.
When subsumed, they comprise active and reflexive verbs.

Primary bases are the stems upon which [words] are to be formed by affixation. They comprise both genuine (*dngos*) and imputed or conventional (*btags*) bases, among which the primary element or the verbal root is considered to be the genuine basis of word formation.[103]

When verbal roots are analyzed, they partake of the following six categories:[104]

(1) [primary] verbal roots that have been listed or formally conjugated (*paripāṭhitadhātu, yongs su bklags pa'i byings*) in the nine chapters of the *Paradigms of Verbal Roots*, commencing with [chapter one, which concerns the Class One] verbs *bhū* ("become"), and *cit* ("think of");[105]

(2) verbal roots that have not been listed or formally conjugated (*viparipāṭhitadhātu, yongs su ma bklags pa'i byings*) in any of the *Commentaries on Verbal Roots* (*mDo 'grel*), including [derivative Class Ten] forms such as *adolayati* ("raises up"), which have acquired wide conventional usage;[106]

(3) verbal roots that have both been and not been listed or formally conjugated (*gnyis ldan*), which are mentioned incidentally in the paradigms and Indian commentaries, such as the verbal root of *jū* ("hasten," *dzu mdo'i byings*) and the verbal root of *skambhu* ("impede," *skambhu'i byings*), but have not been formally listed or conjugated in any table of verbal roots (*dhātupaṭha, byings kyi tshogs*);[107]

(4) denominative verbal roots (*nāmadhātu, ming gi byings*), including twenty that are formed from nouns such as *kaṇḍū* ("itching") by affixing *-ya* (*yaK*)[108] from among the desiderative and related suffixes (*saN*) to the nominal stem, thereby making a denominative verbal root [*kaṇḍūyati*];[109]

(5) affixed verbal roots (*pratyayadhātu, rkyen gyi byings*), including those formed by affixing any of the twelve desiderative and related suffixes (*saN la sogs pa*) to a verbal root as appropriate, so that its ending also becomes a derivative verbal root;[110]

(6) verbal roots that can be both denominative and affixed (*gnyis ka*), since their void terminations, formed by a zero suffix *-v* (*KvIP la sogs pa*)[111] may be classed as nouns or affixes, in order that a conjugated verbal root may take the form of a noun, or vice versa, and then be reconstituted as a verbal root, in accordance with the applied rules of verbal morphology (*ākhyāta, kun bshad*).

When these [six categories of verbal roots] are subsumed, they comprise transitive verbs [of the active voice] (*sakarmaka, las bcas*) and intransitive or reflexive verbs [of the middle voice] (*akarmaka, las med*).[112] With regard to the former, it says in Puñjarāja's commentary:[113]

> When one "conceives," "knows," or "sees,"
> "Eats," or "quarrels,"
> "Makes," "sells," "holds," or "steals,"
> "Gives," "offers," "desires," or "touches,"
> "Pays homage," "eulogizes," "likes," or "tolerates,"
> "Nourishes," "considers," or "impedes," and so forth,
> "Speaks" or "kills," and so forth—
> All such verbs are known as transitive.
> This is because they take a direct object.

Thus, any verbal root such as these which takes a direct object (*karman, bya ba'i yul*), including, for example, the verbs to "conceive," to "know," to "see," and to "hear," and those which are [classed as] agentive (*kartṛ, byed pa*) because they are required to attach a second case accusative inflection to the direct object, are considered to be transitive.

With regard to the latter, it says in the *Analysis of the Grammar of Sārasvata*:[114]

> When one is "embarrassed," "sitting," or "keeping watch,"
> "Waxing," "waning," "decaying," "living," or "dying,"
> "Lying down," "playing," or "shining,"
> These categories of verbal roots are explained to be intransitive.

Since verbal roots such as *śīṄ* ("to lie down") accomplish their action of their own accord, without requiring a direct object in the accusative, they are classed as intransitive or reflexive.[115]

To illustrate [the forming of derivatives from verbal roots], here [in Tibet], for the sake of those who have not studied Sanskrit grammar, the verbal root does not in itself signify anything, just like the Tibetan syllable *ka*. However, just as when prefixes and suffixes are added to *ka* making *bka'* ("Buddhist teachings"), so the Sanskrit verbal root *bhū* (to "become," to "be") through moderate vowel strengthening (*guṇa, aC*) may assume the form *bhava* ("existence") and through extreme vowel strengthening (*vṛddhi, GHaÑ*) assumes the form *bhāva* ("object").[116] In ways such as these, verbal roots assume the form of nouns.

On the subject of derivation (*vikāra, rnam 'gyur*), just as in Tibetan the subscript letters *la, ya* and *ra* assume other forms [when subscripted], so in Sanskrit also, the verbal root *bhū* assumes a great number of other character representations, such as *bhava*, through the application of moderate vowel strengthening. In Sanskrit there are two types of inflected endings: verbal suffixes (*tiṄ*, indicating verbal desinence) and nominal suffixes (*sUP*, indicating nominal desinence),[117] whereas in Tibetan there is only one. This distinction has already been mentioned above.[118]

Nominal Stems—Six Aspects of Gender [b']

Secondly, concerning nominal stems [it is said in the root verses]:

> **Nominal stems are of six types:**
> **Those of exclusive gender, those of mixed gender,**
> **And those of obscure, congruent, universally applicable, and indeterminate [gender].**

With regard to nominal stems, which are the imputed stems to which nominal suffixes are added as inflections (indicated by *sUP*), in general such stems will have masculine, feminine or neuter endings, as appropriate. When these are analyzed, they comprise the so-called six stems indicative of gender (*rtags drug*), which are enumerated as follows:[119]

(1) stems of specific gender (*dag pa'i rtags*), including masculine stems as in *vṛkṣaḥ* ("tree"), feminine stems as in *khaṅḍā* ("bed"), and neuter stems as in *kuṇṭaṃ* ("stove"), which are so called because their gender-based terminations cannot be applied to [nouns of] other genders;

(2) stems of mixed gender (*'dres pa'i rtags*), including some nouns indicating male and female, such as *puruṣa* ("man") and *puruṣī* ("woman"), which can be declined as both masculine and feminine, or those such as *ghṛtaḥ* and *ghṛtaṃ* ("butter"), which may be declined as masculine and neuter;

(3) stems of obscure gender (*gtibs pa'i rtags*), including those single nouns which can partake of all three genders, such as *pātraḥ, patrī*, and *patraṃ* ("bowl");

(4) stems of congruent gender (*nye bar sgrub pa'i rtags*), which assume adjectival forms, indicating color, attributes, and so forth, rather than nouns, as in the examples *śuklaḥ, śuklā*, and *śuklaṃ* ("white") or *paṭuḥ, paṭīḥ*, and *paṭu* ("learned");

(5) stems of universally applicable gender (*kun tu 'jug pa'i rtags*), including words such as *prakṛti*, which have multiple homonyms, and on which, according to the *Wish-fulfilling Commentary* (*Amaraṭīkākāmadhenu*), Vyāḍi says:[120]

> *Prakṛtiḥ* can mean "citizen," "minister," and so forth,
> Or "pattern," "nature," and "womb,"
> As well as the natural equilibrium of lightness, motility and dullness.[121]

Other synonyms are also enumerated:[122]

> When meaning "worldly path" or "orifice of sexual delight"
> *Prakṛtiḥ* assumes a feminine form.

These lists [of synonyms] are found in the *Addendum to Part Three* [*of the Amarakośakāmadhenu*] (*sKabs gsum gyi lhag ma*).[123]

Since single words such as *prakṛti*, may partake of many meanings, it is in the context of the versification that the gender applicable to a given word should be determined. Thus, when it assumes the masculine form, *prakṛtiḥ* may mean "nature" or "citizen," "wine seller," "potter," and so forth, and when it assumes the feminine form, *prakṛti* should be understood to mean "womb."

(6) stems of indeterminate gender (*mi gsal ba'i rtags*), including many words that are derived from an indeclinable class (*avyayībhāvavarga*, *mi zad pa'i sde tshan*), such as *ucchi* ("high") which have no variant forms because all their inflections are elided.[124]

These are the six types of nominal stem.

Affixation [2']

With regard to the second part of the detailed explanation [of Sanskrit grammar], on the subject of affixation (*pratyaya*) [it is said in the root verses]:

> **Affixation includes desiderative suffixes,**
> **Enabling verbal roots to be formed as [other] verbal roots,**
> **Verbally conjugated suffixes, enabling verbal roots to be formed as phrases,**
> **Primary nominal suffixes associated with verbal action,**
> **Enabling verbal roots to be formed as nouns,**

Denominative suffixes, enabling nouns to be formed as verbal roots,
Feminine-forming suffixes, enabling gender to be formed as [another] gender,
Secondary nominal suffixes, enabling nouns to be formed as [other] nouns,
And nominal case suffixes, enabling nouns to be formed as phrases.

Although there are a great many types of affixation that enable verbal roots to be formed as [syntactically] denoting words or phrases, when these are subsumed, they are classed according to the following seven types:

(1) desiderative and related suffixes (*saN la sogs pa*),[125] which are attached externally to the termination of the verbal root, enabling verbal roots to be reformed as [other] verbal roots;

(2) the eighteen suffixes of verbal conjugation (*tiṄ'i rnam dbye bco brgyad*),[126] which alter tense and mood (*l-akāra*)[127] without the need for an intervening vowel, enabling verbal roots to be formed as phrases.[128] These [syntactically] denote the agent (*karaṇa*), the verbal action (*bhāva*) and the direct object (*karman*), and in [Sarvadhara's] verbal morphology section (*akhyāta*) of the *Kalāpa Grammar*, they are known as the hundred and eighty personal verb inflections (*tyādi*, *ti la sogs pa'i rnam dbye brgya dang brgyad cu*).[129]

(3) primary nominal suffixes (*kṛṭ*), enabling verbal roots to be formed as substantives. As described in the first half of the third *pāda* of the first chapter of the *Grammar of Candragomin*[130] and extensively explained in the fifth chapter of the *Kalāpa Grammar*,[131] these are attached exclusively to verbal roots.[132]

(4) the denominative suffix *-ya* (*KyaC*), along with *-kāmya* (*kāmyaT*), among its subsidiary forms, and causative-forming suffixes such as *-i* (*ṆiC la sogs pa*) that are attached to nominal stems, enabling nouns themselves to be formed as denominative verbs;[133]

(5) feminine-forming suffixes (*strīliṅgapratyaya*, *bud med rkyen sbyar*), such as *ī*-stems (*DīŚ*), and *ā*-stems (*TāP* and *CāP*),[134] that are added to nominal stems, enabling [nouns of one] gender to be formed as [nouns of another] gender;

(6) secondary nominal suffixes (*taddhita*, *de la phan pa*) which are attached principally to nominal stems and in some cases to phrases, enabling nouns to be formed as [other] nouns, and in some cases to

resemble phrases, even though they do not actually include inflections that would enable phrases to be formed. These are elucidated at great length through some nine *pādas* (*rkang pa dgu tsam gyis*) in the *Grammar of Candragomin*.[135]

(7) the twenty-one nominal case suffixes (*sUB-vibhakti, sUP'i rnam dbye nyer gcig*), divided into three groups of seven, denoting the genitive (*ṣaṣṭhīvibhakti*) and the other [six] cases, [in singular, dual, and plural forms], which may be attached to the three gender terminations, enabling nouns to be formed as phrases.[136]

Nouns, adjectives, verbs and pronouns—
These are the four [categories of words].
Alternatively, [words] can be classified as agents, verbal actions, and objects.

Although there are many exegeses concerning the formation of words from verbal roots by means of affixation, when these are subsumed, the exegesis expounded by master Vararuci who was of the *miśra* caste,[137] categorizes words as belonging to one of four types: nouns, such as *puruṣaḥ* ("man"), *gauḥ* ("ox"), and *aśvaḥ* ("horse"); adjectives, such as *nīlaḥ* ("blue") and *śuklaḥ* ("white"); verbs, such as *pacati* ("is cooking") and *paṭhati* ("is reading"); and pronouns (*yuṣmad, ji lta bur'i sgra*), which pertain to substantives alone and do not convey any particular action. Alternatively, all words can be considered in terms of the [threefold] classification, denoting agents (*karaṇa, byed pa*), verbal actions (*bhāva, dngos po*), and objects (*karman, las*).[138]

Derivation [3']

With regard to the third part of the detailed explanation [of Sanskrit grammar], on the subject of derivation [it is said in the root verses]:

Derivation comprises both actual [derivation] and nominal compounding.
The essential elements of derivation concern the substitution [of retroflex syllables for dentals],
And the classification of technical markers attached to verbal roots, affixes,
Gender terminations, augments, indeclinable and [permitted final] words.

Elision should be carried out in respect of [final vowels] that facilitate pronunciation
And [final letters] denoting peculiarities [of inflection],
As well as those that are [merely] technical markers.[139]

Derivation refers to the morphological transformations that the verbal roots undergo through contact with affixes and so forth. This includes actual derivation and the nominal compounds that are considered as a subcategory.

Actual Derivation [a']

Concerning the former, the substitution of initial [retroflex] *ṣ* of a verbal root for dental *s* (*ṣatva*), the substitution of initial [retroflex] *ṇ* [of a verbal root] for *n* (*ṇatva*),[140] and the various classifications of the technical markers (*anubandha, rjes su 'brel ba*) are the essential elements of derivation.

Concerning the classifications [of the technical markers]:[141]

(1) Technical markers may be attached directly to verbal roots (*dhātvanubandha, byings kyi rjes su 'brel ba*), in which case they may take the form of [following] vowels, such as *-A*, [preceding] consonants such as [the nominal derivation markers] *Ṭu-* and *Ḍu-*, or combined [vowels and consonants] such as [the following] *-IR*.[142]

(2) Technical markers may be attached to affixes (*pratyayānubandha, rkyen gyi rjes su 'brel ba*), in which case they may take the form of consonants such as the *-N* in *saN* and the *-Ñ* in *GHaÑ*,[143] or of vowels and consonants combined, such as the *–AṬ* in *lAṬ*, or the *Ṅ* and *I* in *ṄasI*.[144]

(3) Technical markers may be attached to long or short gender terminations (*dīrghahrasvaliṅgānubandha, ring thung rtags kyi rjes su 'brel ba*), in which case they take the form of a [following] *-T* (*takāra, t-yig*).[145]

(4) Technical markers may be attached to augments (*āgamānubandha, glo bur gyi rkyen gyi rjes su 'brel ba*), in which case they may be exemplified by the *-M* in *nUM*.[146]

(5) Moreover, there are certain technical markers that may be attached to indeclinable words (*avyayībhāvānbandha, mi zad pa'i sde tshan gyi rjes su 'brel ba*), as well as to [permitted] final letters (*padānta, tshig mtha'*).[147] The latter entail elision (*dbyi ba*) which occurs in the following circumstances:

   (a) [Certain final vowels] such as *-A* have the function of facilitating the pronunciation of a given sound that would otherwise lack a vowel and be unpronounceable, even though they can only occur in conjunction with a consonantal syllable, such as *KA*, when denoting the actual object to which a [given] sound refers. These should be elided, for example, when the vowel *A* attached to *K-* comes into contact with other affixes.[148]

(b) Some [final letters] denote peculiarities [of inflection] (*khyad don*), and these should be elided once the [corresponding] peculiarities [of inflection] have been applied.[149]

(c) Some [final letters] are merely technical markers denoting the function of a substantive or primary base, and should be elided once the rules they prescribe have been implemented.[150]

The verbal prepositions that modify meaning and form, and the augments
Constitute the ancillary aspects of derivation.
As for [derivations due to] affixation,
All three aspects—syllables, affixes, and inflections—
Undergo infinite transformations,
Including those due to euphonic conjunction.

There are twenty verbal prepositions (*upasarga*) that can modify both the meaning and the form [of a word].[151] For example, when the verbal preposition *pra-* is placed before the root *nī* (meaning "control"),[152] it forms *pranī* (meaning "lead"); or when the same verbal preposition *pra-* is placed before *māna*, it forms *pramāṇa* (meaning "valid cognition"); whereas when *anu-* is placed before *māna*, it forms the word *anumāna* (meaning "inference"). Similarly, there are a great many such combinations [that can be formed by this and the other verbal prepositions], e.g., *upamā* ("simile"), *pratimā* ("image"), and *abhimā* ("arrogance").

Also there is the class of augments (*āgama'i rkyen*) which are indefinite with regard to their placement, as initial prefixes, medial infixes, or final suffixes, as when the augment *-s* (*saK*)[153] is inserted between *aya-* and *-kāra*, forming the word *ayaskāra* ("iron"). These are classed among the ancillary aspects of derivation.

Then, with regard to derivations that are due to affixation (*nipātavikāra*, *phrad pa'i rnam gyur*), these occur when verbal roots make contact with affixes, so that consequently

(1) the syllables undergo transformation, as when *sthā* becomes *tiṣṭha*, or *pṛśya* becomes *paśya*, and subsidiary [syllabic] transformations occur

through the strengthening gradations of *guṇa* (*yon tan*) and *vṛddhi* (*'phel ba*), and so forth;[154]

(2) the affixes undergo transformation, as when the primary nominal suffix *-yu* is transformed into *-ana*, and *-vu* is transformed into *-aka*,[155] or when the secondary nominal suffix final *-ch* is transformed into *-īya*;[156] and

(3) the inflections undergo transformation, as when the eighteen verbal inflections (*tiṄ sogs*) derived from the paradigms of verbal morphology or conjugation, modify mood and tense (*l*) without the need for an intervening vowel,[157] or when the nominal inflections (*su sogs*) undergo transformation, as when *Ṭā* is transformed into *-ina*,[158] and *Ṅe* is transformed into *-ya*.[159]

In short, all three categories—syllables, affixes, and inflections—can undergo an infinite number of morphological transformations, including the [elaborate] transformations brought about by the euphonic conjunction (*sandhi*) of vowels and consonants.[160] These are exemplified by the formation of long Ā through the combination of A and A, E through the combination of A and I, and O through the combination of A and U.[161]

Nominal Compounding [b']

There are six kinds of nominal compound:
Descriptive, pre-numerical, uncountable,
Initially dependent, exocentric, and coordinative.

The second part of the detailed explanation on derivation concerns the changes that occur in the formation of nominal compounds (*samāsa*, *tshig sdud*). Nominal compounds combine two or multiple nouns, thereby forming a phrase, with a final nominal suffix (*su sogs*) attached, indicating name or gender. There are six [main] types of nominal compound:[162]

(1) descriptive determinative compounds (*karmadhāraya*, *las 'dzin pa*), the function of which is to combine an appositional noun or adjective with its object for descriptive purposes;

(2) dual compounds (*dvigu*, *ba gnyis pa*) in which the [main word of] the compound is preceded by a numeral—"two," for example;

(3) adverbial compounds (*upakumbha*, *nye ba'i bum pa*) which principally form an indeclinable phrase (*avyayībhāva*);

(4) dependent determinative compounds (*tatpuruṣa*, *de'i skyes bu*) in

which the first member of the compound forms one of twenty-one possible oblique relations [i.e., seven cases times three genders] with the main part, exemplified by the term *tatpuruṣa* [lit. "his man"], which entails a genitive relation;

(5) exocentric compounds (*bahuvṛhi, 'bru mang po*) in which the subject with which the compound forms a possessive relation is external to the compound;

(6) coordinative compounds (*dvandva, zlas dbye ba*) in which pairs [of nouns or adjectives] are conjoined.

All these types of compound are capable of subsuming many meanings in a single point, and they may also combine many expressions and multiple case inflections in a single [phrase, with a single inflection]. The purpose of nominal compounding is to facilitate the construction of complicated expressions in few words. In general, they number six types, but in fact there are explained to be twenty-eight subcategories altogether.[163]

Synopsis of Sanskrit Grammar [cc]

As to the synopsis of Sanskrit grammar [it is said in the root verses]:

> **The essence [of grammar] is subsumed in nouns, words, and derivations.**
> **To learn the language, one should be undeluded with respect to meaning.**

When the essence of all these [aspects of Sanskrit grammar] is summarized, they may be subsumed together under the headings of nouns, words, and morphological derivations. For one who would learn the phonetic articulations of the Sanskrit language, an intelligence that easily understands both word and meaning will arise if one becomes undeluded with regard not only to the words but also to their meaning.

4. Logic

ii. Logic [III.B.2.a.ii]
- aa. The Purpose of Logical Reasoning
- bb. The Actual Exegesis of Logical Reasoning
  - 1' Extensive Exegesis of the *Collected Topics*
    - a' Appraisable Objects
      - i' Objects in Terms of Their Essential Nature
      - ii' Objects in Terms of Their Functionality
      - iii' Objects in Terms of Their Understanding
    - b' Signifying Subjects
      - i' Signifiers in Terms of Their Essential Nature
      - ii' Signifiers in Terms of the Signified
      - iii' Signifiers in Terms of the Modes of Signification
      - iv' Signifiers in Terms of Preclusion
      - v' Signifiers in Terms of Their Theoretical Presentation
      - vi' Defining Characteristic of the Term "Syllable"
      - vii' Defining Characteristic of the Term "Individual Person"
      - viii' Valid Cognition
        - aa' The Valid Cognition of Direct Perception
          - 1'' Direct Perception of the Sense Organs
          - 2'' Direct Perception of Mental Consciousness
          - 3'' Direct Perception of Intrinsic Awareness
          - 4'' Direct Perception of Yoga
        - bb' Valid Cognition of Inference
          - 1'' Inference Proceeding from the Cogent Power of Facts
          - 2'' Inference Based on Popular Acclaim
          - 3'' Inference on the Basis of Conviction
        - cc' Internally Ascertained Valid Cognition
        - dd' Externally Ascertained Valid Cognition

c' Processes of Logical Understanding
- i' Contradiction
- ii' Relation
- iii' Negation
- iv' Proof
- v' Universals
- vi' Particulars
- vii' Identity and Difference
- viii' Eliminative Engagement
- ix' Affirmative Engagement
- x' Extraneous Elimination
- xi' Definition
- xii' Definiendum
- xiii' Substance Phenomenon
- xiv' Distinguishing Counterpart Phenomenon
- xv' The Two Modes of Inference
  - aa' Inference for One's Own Sake
    - 1" Property of the Thesis
    - 2" Forward Logical Entailment
    - 3" Counter Logical Entailment
    - 4" Genuine Evidence
    - 5" Ostensible Evidence
    - 6" Examples
      - a" Correct Analogous Examples
      - b" Nonanalogous Examples
      - c" Ostensible Examples
  - bb' Inference for the Sake of Others
    - 1" Correct Statement of Proof
    - 2" Ostensible Statement of Proof
    - 3" Probandum Based on Correct Evidence
    - 4" Elimination
    - 5" Refutation
    - 6" Consequential Reasoning
    - 7" Defining Characteristics of an Antagonist
    - 8" Defining Characteristics of a Respondent/Protagonist

d' Incidental Comments regarding Other Logical Traditions

2' Synopsis of the Eight Aspects and Three Scopes of Dialectics

a' Eight Aspects of Dialectics

i' Correct and Ostensible Forms of Direct Perception and Inference
ii' Correct and Ostensible Forms of Proof and Refutation
b' Three Scopes of Dialectical Application
i' Directly Evident Objects of Appraisal
ii' Indirectly Evident Objects of Appraisal
iii' Objects of Appraisal Indirectly Evident to an Extreme Degree
3' Synopsis of Five Essential Modes of Logical Reasoning
a' Analytical Basis of Knowable Phenomena
b' Actual Analysis of Phenomena
c' Systematic Presentation of Logical Reasoning
d' Consequential Reasoning
e' Genuine Conclusion of Valid Cognition
4' The Implementation of Logical Reasoning
a' Recognizing Evidence and Specific Predicates
b' Rejoinders Made by Respondents to Antagonists
i' Rejoinders Recognizing Valid Cognition
ii' Rejoinders Recognizing Invalid Cognition
aa' Rejoinders Recognizing Unestablished Reasoning
bb' Rejoinders Recognizing Contradictory Reasoning
cc' Rejoinders Recognizing Unascertained Reasoning
c' Summary of the Rejoinders
i' Eight Approaches to Logical Entailment

. . . .

Logic [ii]

The exegesis of valid cognition (*pramāṇa, tshad ma*), or logic (*hetuvidyā, gtan tshigs rigs pa*), the second [subject of the major pathway of science; see above, p. 127] is in two parts—an introduction to the purpose [of logical reasoning] and the actual exegesis of logical reasoning (*rig lam*).[164]

The Purpose of Logical Reasoning [aa]

As to the former [it is said in the root verses]:

> **Valid cognition, which eradicates wrong understanding with respect to meaning...**

[The exercise of] valid or reliable cognition is the science which eradicates wrong understandings with regard to all objects of knowledge that are not directly evident but held to be indirectly evident to one's own mind, and so forth. Here, based on [the commentarial traditions of] the adherents of the two masters of logical reasoning [Dignāga and Dharmakīrti], I will now present, to some extent, the *Collected Topics* on valid cognition that are prestigious in modern circles,[165] while [also] gathering and specifying [points] derived from certain dissimilar traditions that were established in defense of their distinctive logical positions.

The Actual Exegesis of Logical Reasoning [bb]

The latter, the actual exegesis, has three parts: an extensive exegesis of the *Collected Topics*, a synopsis of these in terms of the eight aspects and three scopes of dialectics, and a synopsis of them in terms of the five essential modes [of logical reasoning].

Extensive Exegesis of the *Collected Topics* [1']

The first of these includes both a brief introduction and a detailed exegesis.

[Brief Introduction]

As to the former [it is said in the root verses]:

> **...Refers to the object, subject, and processes of [logical] understanding.**

All aspects of the science of logic (*hetuvidyā*) are established on the basis of three parameters: the object, the subject, and the processes of [logical] understanding.

[Detailed Exegesis]

As to the latter [the detailed exegesis], it has four parts, which are respectively headed (1) the object, (2) the subject, (3) a detailed exegesis of the process of understanding, and (4) incidental comments regarding other [logical] traditions.

Appraisable Objects [a']

Among them, concerning the first [the object, it is said in the root verses]:

> **The object is the knowable or appraisable which is to be understood.**

That which is to be understood through valid cognition is "the knowable." The terms "object" (*viṣaya, yul*), "knowable" (*jñeya, shes bya*), and "appraisable" (*prameya, gzhal bya*) are all essentially equivalent, but it is the defining characteristic of the "object" that it is to be comprehended or known, it is the defining characteristic of the "knowable" that it can be objectified by the intellect, and it is the defining characteristic of the "appraisable" that it is to be understood through valid cognition.[166]

Objects in Terms of Their Essential Nature [i']

> **Objects may be substantial or insubstantial,**
> **Compounded or uncompounded, permanent or impermanent.**

When objects are analyzed in terms of their essential nature, they may be substantial or insubstantial, compounded or uncompounded, and permanent or impermanent. The defining characteristics of these respectively are that "substantial objects" (*vastu, dngos po*) are causally effective (*arthakriyākāraṇa, don byed nus pa*); "insubstantial objects" (*avastu, dngos med*) are not causally effective, like space, for example; "compounded objects" (*saṃskṛta, 'dus byas*) can be produced from their own primary causes and secondary conditions; "uncompounded objects" (*asaṃskṛta, 'dus ma byas*) cannot be produced from their own primary causes and secondary conditions; "permanent objects" (*nitya, rtag pa*) are imperishable phenomena; and "impermanent objects" (*anitya, mi rtag pa*) do not endure from the moment of their formation into a second moment.[167]

> **Substantial [objects] include material and cognitive phenomena,**
> **Causes and results, along with their subdivisions.**

When substantial objects are analyzed in terms of their essential nature, they comprise both material phenomena (*rūpa, bem po*) and cognitive phenomena (*vidyā, rigpa*). The defining characteristic of material phenomena is that they are composed of atomic particles, while the defining characteristic of cognitive phenomena is that the object is cognitive.[168]

Material phenomena, when analyzed, comprise both outer material phenomena and inner material phenomena. Their defining characteristics are respectively that the former are composed of external atomic particles and the latter of internal atomic particles. External matter (*phyi don bem po*), when analyzed, comprises the five objects of visual form, sound, smell, taste, and touch. Their defining characteristics are that external matter comprises the substantial objects of visual, auditory, and olfactory consciousness, and so forth. Internal matter (*nang don bem po*), when analyzed, comprises the five physical sense organs of the eye, ear, nose, tongue, and body—their defining characteristics being that they are capable of functioning as the predominant condition (*adhipatipratyaya, bdag rkyen*) [prerequisite] for visual consciousness and so forth.[169]

When substantial objects are analyzed in terms of their efficiency (*kāraṇa, byed pa*), they include both causes (*hetu, rgyu*) and results (*phala, 'bras bu*). The defining characteristic is whether or not *x*, the given property, assumes a subsequent existence as a distinct object, either through positive logical concomitance (*anvaya, rjes 'gro*) or through negative logical concomitance (*vyatireka, ldog byed*).[170]

When causes are analyzed in terms of their essential nature, there are both direct causes (*sākṣātkāraṇa, dngos rgyu*) and indirect causes (*avedhahetu, brgyud rgyu*). The defining characteristics of these are respectively that in the case of the [direct] cause of a given property *x*, there are no [extraneous factors intervening] between the cause of the property *x* and its result *y*, as in the example of a seed and a shoot; whereas [in the case of an indirect cause], there are [extraneous intervening factors] between the cause of the given property *x* and its result *y*, just as a shoot is sequentially produced from a seed and finally [ripens] as a fruit.[171]

Causes have many subdivisions, when analyzed in terms of primary and ordinary [causes], or when analyzed in terms of their four secondary conditions, and so forth.[172]

Incidentally, with regard to the three tenses and so forth, the defining characteristic of the past is that it has elapsed, the defining characteristic of the future is that it has not yet arrived, [and the defining characteristic of the present is that it is here], just like one edge of the atom that appears before one here and now.[173] The defining characteristic of the continuum of time (*santāna, rgyun*) is something that has many sequential temporal moments (*kṣaṇa*, *skad cig*) which serve to establish its identity, like "year," for example. The defining characteristic of an indivisible time moment (*nivirbhāgakṣaṇika*, *skad cig cha med*) is something that is without a sequential series of time-moments that serve to establish its identity, like, for example, the first of the sixty time-moments that constitute a fraction of a syllable.[174]

Objects in Terms of Their Functionality [ii']

> **In terms of their functionality [objects] fall into three categories,**
> **Namely, apparent, conceived, and applied objects.**

When objects are analyzed in terms of their different functionalities as objects (*yul du byed tshul*), they fall into three distinct categories, namely, apparent (*snang yul*) or apprehended objects (*grāhyakaviṣaya*, *bzung yul*), conceived objects (*adhyavasāyaviṣaya*, *zhen yul*), and applied or engaged objects (*pravṛttiviṣaya*, *'jug yul*). The defining characteristic of apprehended objects is that they appear and are then apperceived, as is, for example, an "object-universal" (*arthasāmānya*, *don spyi*).[175] The defining characteristic of conceived objects is that they are conceived and then apperceived, just as, for example, the [imagined] seated posture of a man dwelling in another house. The defining characteristic of applied objects is that when they are utilized either as objects to be accepted or rejected, they are [consistently] unfailing (*avisaṃvādi*, *mi slu ba*) [in their results], as, for example, when a farmer has a [productive] field that has absorbed seeds, water, fertilizer, heat, and humidity. These three categories also have many subdivisions.[176]

Objects in Terms of Their Understanding [iii']

> **In terms of the processes of understanding objects that are to be appraised:**
> **[Objects] include specifically and generally characterized phenomena,**
> **Or else they are established as directly evident, indirectly evident,**
> **And indirectly evident to an extreme degree,**
> **Or else [they comprise] signified [phenomena] and their supplementary [definitions].**

When objects to be appraised (*prameya*, *gzhal bya*) are analyzed in terms of the processes of understanding, they are said to include both specifically characterized phenomena (*svalakṣaṇa, rang mtshan*) and generally characterized phenomena (*sāmānyalakṣaṇa, spyi mtshan*). Alternatively, they fall into three [categories]—appraisable objects that are directly evident (*abhimukhī, mngon gyur*), those that are indirectly evident (*parokṣa, lkog gyur*), and those that are indirectly evident to an extreme degree (*atyantaparokṣa, shin tu lkog gyur*).[177]

Now, the defining characteristic of specifically characterized phenomena is that ultimately they are causally effective, as, for example, the color blue. The defining characteristic of generally characterized phenomena is that ultimately they are not causally effective, inasmuch as they are objects that appear conceptually but are indeterminate with regard to place and time, just as, for example, the image [of a vase] as something bulbous in the middle and narrow at the base.[178]

The defining characteristic of appraisable objects that are directly evident is that they are to be understood through the valid cognition of direct perception (*pratyakṣapramāṇa, mngon sum tshad ma*), like, for example, the color blue. The defining characteristic of appraisable objects that are indirectly evident is that they are to be understood through the valid cognition of inference (*anumānapramāṇa, rjes dpag tshad ma*), as for example, when the color blue is inferred to be impermanent. Alternatively, the distinguishing characteristics of those two is that [in the valid cognition of direct perception] superimpositions (*adhyāropa, sgro 'dogs*) are to be eliminated through the power of experience (*anubhava, myong stobs*), while [in the valid cognition of inference], superimpositions are to be eliminated through the power of logical evidence (*liṅga, rtags*).[179]

The defining characteristic of appraisable objects that are indirectly evident to an extreme degree is that they are to be understood by reliance on scriptural authority (*āgama, lung*), the purity of which is established by means of the three types of scrutiny (*dpyad pa gsum*),[180] just as, for example, the meaning demonstrated in the following [sacred] verse [from Nāgārjuna's *Precious Garland*] is deemed to be infallible: "resources ensue through generosity, and comfort ensues through ethical discipline."[181]

The defining characteristic of signified [phenomena] (*vācya, brjod bya*) is that they are to be understood through symbols (*saṃketa, brda*). This includes both phenomena that are termed the "conceived signified" (*zhen pa'i brjod bya*) and the "directly evident signified" (*dngos kyi brjod bya*).[182] Alternatively, there is a distinction made between theoretically signified (*'chad dus kyi brjod bya*) and practically signified [phenomena] (*'jug dus kyi brjod bya*).[183] These have all been established as supplementary definitions of the term "object."

Signifying Subjects [b']

As for the second part of the extensive exegesis, concerning the subject [it is said in the root verses]:

> **The subject is both the signifier, which engenders comprehension, and the cognizer.**

The defining characteristic of the subject (*viṣayin, yul can*) by which these [aforementioned] objects are understood is that it effects comprehension and apperception, as exemplified respectively in the terms "signifier" (*vācaka, brjod byed*) and "cognizer" (*jñāna, shes pa*).[184]

The defining characteristic of the signifier is that, through the power of communicative symbols (*saṃketa, brda*), it generates comprehension of the signified.[185] The defining characteristic of the cognizer is that it is radiant and aware—the opposite of material phenomena.[186]

Signifiers in Terms of Their Essential Nature [i']

> **Signifiers essentially include nouns, phrases, and speech.**
> **In terms of the signified they include type signifiers,**
> **Set signifiers, and modes of signification,**
> **As well as the predicate, the subject, and preclusion without or with [predicate].**
> **Theoretically, [signifiers] may be conceived or directly evident.**
> **[Also incidentally defined here] are the term "syllable" and the term "individual person."**

When signifiers (*vācaka, brjod byed*) are analyzed in terms of their essential nature, they include nouns (*nāman, ming*), [syntactically bound] phrases (*pada, tshig*), and statements (*vāk, ngag*).

The defining characteristic of nouns is that they signify or express the bare essential nature of an object (*yul gyi ngo bo tsam*), exemplified, for example, by the term "vase."

The defining characteristic of phrases is that they signify or express the essential nature of an object, conjoined with its attributes as well, exemplified by the expression "small vase."

The defining characteristic of statements is that they signify, in addition to such descriptive attributes, an [illustrative] base upon which meaning may be applied or predicated,[187] as exemplified, for instance, in the sentence, "Pour water from the small vase!"

Signifiers in Terms of the Signified [ii']

When signifiers are analyzed in terms of the signified, they include both words that signify types (*rigs brjod kyi sgra*) and words that signify sets (*tshogs brjod kyi sgra*). The defining characteristic of the former is that words are [designated as] "type-universals" (*jātisāmānya, rigs spyi*) when *x* is the signified concept that they apprehend, as in, for example, the word "form" [which has multiple instances].[188]

The defining characteristic of words that signify sets is that they are [designated as] a "conglomerate of the eight atomic substances" (*aṣṭāṇudravya, rdul rdzas brgyad*)[189] when *x* is the signified concept that they apprehend, as in, for example, the expression, "snow mountain."

Signifiers in Terms of the Modes of Signification [iii']

When signifiers are analyzed in terms of the ways they signify their objects, they include both words that signify predicates, or predicate-oriented expressions (*chos brjod kyi sgra*), and words that signify subjects, or subject-oriented expressions (*chos can brjod pa'i sgra*).

The defining characteristic of the former [a predicate-oriented expression] is that the comprehension of the signified ensues from having eliminated, with regard to its own signifying statement, other [possible] attributes of the signified concept that it apprehends, as exemplified in the statement, "an ox is explicitly the state of not being a horse" (*ba lang rta min pa nyid yin no*).

The defining characteristic of a subject-oriented expression is that the comprehension of the signified ensues from having not eliminated, with regard to its signified concept, other [possible] attributes of the signified concept that it apprehends, as exemplified in the statement, "an ox is implicitly non-horse" (*ba lang rta ma yin pa yin no*).[190]

Signifiers in Terms of Preclusion [iv']

When signifiers are analyzed in terms of preclusion (*vyavaccheda, rnam gcod*), they includes three subcategories: statements expressing preclusion without a predicate (*mi ldan rnam gcod kyi sgra*), statements expressing preclusion with an extraneous [predicate] (*gzhan ldan rnam gcod*), and statements expressing preclusion of the impossible (*mi srid rnam gcod*).

Their defining characteristics are respectively that, [in the case of statements expressing preclusion without a predicate,] the statement is made by appending the enclitic grammatical particle [indicating preclusion] directly after the attribute (*khyad chos*), that [in the case of statements expressing preclusion with an extraneous predicate] the statement is made by appending [the enclitic particle indicating preclusion] directly after the subject of the attribute (*khyad gzhi*), and that [in the case of words expressing preclusion of the impossible] the statement is made by appending [the enclitic particle indicating preclusion] directly to the verb "to be possible." These three categories may be illustrated respectively as follows: The first is exemplified by the statement "Citrā, the skilled archer alone,..." (*nag pa 'phongs skyen pa kho na...*); the second by the statement "Arjuna alone is a skilled archer" (*srid sgrub kho na 'phongs skyen...*); and the third by the statement "a lotus can only be blue" (*mtsho skyes la sngon po srid pa kho na...*).[191]

Signifiers in Terms of Their Theoretical Presentation [v']

When signifiers are analyzed in terms of their theoretical presentation (*'chad dus*), they comprise both the conceived signifier (*zhen pa'i brjod byed*) and the directly evident signifier (*dngos kyi brjod byed*), which is differentiated from the former. The latter is exemplified by the term-universal (*śabdasāmānya, sgra spyi*) "vase."

When the conceived signifier is analyzed, it includes both the directly evident conceived signifier (*dngos kyi zhen pa'i brjod byed*) and the implicitly conceived signifier (*shugs kyi zhen pa'i brjod byed*).[192] These may be exemplified respectively in the context of the following statement: "A vase is permanent insofar as the impermanence of the vase that is directly [conceived] and the impermanence of the vase that is implicitly [conceived] are both implicatively negated."

Defining Characteristic of the Term "Syllable" [vi']

As an addendum [to this discussion on the subject, let us consider], both syllables (*varṇa, yi ge*) and individual persons (*pudgala, gang zag*):

The defining characteristic of syllables is that though individually they are not causally effective, when they form a set comprising anything from one and a half [syllables] upwards, the words that they form are an amalgam of many indivisible time moments and can be causally effective. When analyzed they comprise the vowels, such as Ā (*āli*) and the consonants, beginning with KA and KHA.

Defining Characteristic of the Term "Individual Person" [vii']

The defining characteristic of individual persons is that they are nominally or imputedly existent (*vijñaptisat, btags yod*) as a continuum in which the five or four psycho-physical aggregates (*skandha, phung po*) are gathered together,[193] as [embodied], for example, [in the person known as] Devadatta.

[Ten Further Aspects of Cognizance]

> **Consciousness or awareness [has ten aspects]:**
> **Valid and non-valid cognition,**
> **Conceptual and non-conceptual cognition,**
> **Mistaken and unmistaken cognition,**
> **Intrinsic and extraneous awareness,**
> **Mind and mental states.**

The terms "intellect" (*buddhi, blo*), "awareness" (*vidyā, rig pa*), and "consciousness" (*jñāna, shes pa*) are all coextensive. When analyzed, [this cognizance] comprises ten aspects, namely, valid or reliable forms of cognition (*pramāṇa, tshad ma*), non-valid or unreliable forms of cognition (*apramāṇa, tshad min*), conceptual cognition (*kalpanā, rtog pa*), non-conceptual cognition (*nirvikalpanā, rtog med*), mistaken cognition (*bhrānti, 'khrul pa*), unmistaken cognition (*abhrānti, ma 'khrul*), intrinsic or reflexive awareness (*svasaṃvedana, rang rig*), and extraneous awareness (*anyasaṃvid, gzhan rig*), along with mind (*citta, sems*) and mental states (*caitta, sems byung*).

Among them, the defining characteristic of valid cognition is that the intellect understands its own objects as they newly arise. The defining characteristic of non-valid cognition is that the intellect does not understand its own objects as they newly arise.[194]

The defining characteristic of conceptual cognition is that, if it has its own apparent object, then that must be a generally characterized phenomenon (*sāmānyalakṣaṇa, spyi mtshan*).[195] The defining characteristic of non-conceptual cognition is that if the given consciousness has its own apparent object, then that must be without any specifically characterized phenomenon or any established basis whatsoever.[196]

The defining characteristic of mistaken consciousness is that it apprehends *x* although *x* does not exist, while the defining characteristic of unmistaken consciousness is that it cognizes the real nature of its object.

The defining characteristic of intrinsic or reflexive awareness is that it is the apprehending consciousness (*'dzin pa'i rnam shes*), while the defining characteristic of extraneous awareness is that it is consciousness of the apprehended (*gzung ba'i rnam shes*).[197]

The defining characteristic of mind is that, with regard to the object and the attributes of an object, it cognizes only the object. When analyzed, the mind comprises the six or eight modes of consciousness (*rnam shes tshogs drug gam brgyad*).[198] The defining characteristic of mental states is that they cognize the particular attributes of an object. When analyzed, they comprise the fifty-one mental states (*sems byung lnga bcu rtsa gcig*).[199]

Although these aforementioned [aspects of the cognizing subject] have a great many subcategories, I will not digress further at this point.

Valid Cognition [viii']

With regard to direct perception,
There are four modes of direct perception:
Sense organs, mind, intrinsic awareness, and yoga.
Inference is made through the power of facts,
Popular acclaim, and conviction.
There are many such categories and approaches,
And the conclusions of valid cognition
Should also be incidentally understood.

When valid cognition is quantifiably analyzed, it comprises both the valid cognition of direct perception (*pratyakṣapramāṇa*, *mngon sum tshad ma*) and the valid cognition of inference (*anumānapramāṇa*, *rjes dpag tshad ma*).

The Valid Cognition of Direct Perception [aa']

The defining characteristic of the valid cognition of direct perception is [cognition] which, without conceptuality and without bewilderment, understands its own objects as they newly arise. It comprises the four designated modes of direct perception. The defining characteristic of direct perception is consciousness without conceptuality and without bewilderment.[200]

When analyzed, [direct perception] comprises four modes, namely, direct perception of the sense organs (*indriyapratyakṣa, dbang po'i mngon sum*), direct perception of mental consciousness (*mana pratyakṣa, yid kyi mngon sum*), direct perception of intrinsic or reflexive awareness (*svasaṃvedanapratyakṣa, rang rig gi mngon sum*), and direct perception of yoga (*yogapratyakṣa, rnal 'byor gyi mngon sum*).

Direct Perception of the Sense Organs [1"]

The defining characteristic of the first of these is [bare] consciousness consisting of extraneous awareness, which arises without conceptuality and without bewilderment, directly from the physical sense organs that constitute an individual's own predominant condition. It has five aspects, corresponding to the direct perception of the [five] sense organs [the eye and so forth] which apprehend their respective sense objects.[201]

Direct Perception of Mental Consciousness [2"]

The defining characteristic of the second is [bare] consciousness consisting of extraneous awareness, which arises without conceptuality and without bewilderment, directly from the sense faculty of the mind that constitutes an individual's own predominant condition. It too has five aspects, corresponding to the direct perception of the [five aspects of] mind, which apprehend their respective sense objects.[202]

Direct Perception of Intrinsic Awareness [3"]

The defining characteristic of the third is [bare] consciousness transcending all the other aspects of consciousness, which is exclusively introverted (*kha nang kho nar 'phyogs pa'i shes pa*).[203]

Direct Perception of Yoga [4"]

The defining characteristic of the fourth is the [bare] consciousness of a sublime being (*ārya, 'phags pa*), free from conceptuality and without bewilderment, which derives from the power of genuine meditation (*bhāvanā*, *sgom*). When the last of these is analyzed, there are in fact three modes of the direct perception of yoga, corresponding to [the meditations of] the pious attendants, the hermit buddhas (*pratyekabuddha*, *rang rgyal*), and the [bodhisattva] followers of the Greater Vehicle—these are exemplified respectively by the path of insight (*darśanamārga*, *mthong lam*) attained by the pious attendants, the path of insight attained by the hermit buddhas, [and so forth].[204]

Valid Cognition of Inference [bb']

The defining characteristic of the valid cognition of inference is that the intellect [correctly] understands its own indirectly evident objects as they newly arise, dependent on logical reasoning or evidence (*liṅga*, *rtags*) in which the threefold criteria (*trairūpya*, *tshul gsum*) are fully present.[205]

Inference Proceeding from the Cogent Power of Facts [1"]

It has three subdivisions. Among them, inference proceeding from the cogent power of facts (*vastubalapravṛrttānumāna*, *dngos po stobs zhugs kyi rjes dpag*) is exemplified by the intellect that understands that sound is impermanent, dependent on factual evidence.

Inference Based on Popular Acclaim [2"]

Inference based on popular acclaim (*yaśo 'numāna*, *grags pa'i rjes dpag*) is exemplified by the understanding that the name Śaśin (*ri bong can*) may be given to the moon, based on the evidence of its [widespread] acceptance as a conceptual object.

Inference on the Basis of Conviction [3"]

Inference on the basis of conviction (*āptatānumāna*, *yid ches rjes dpag*) is exemplified by the intellect that understands that the meaning presented in authoritative scriptures, such as the [previously cited] verse, "resources come through generosity...," is infallible, based on scriptural authority of which the purity is established by the three types of scrutiny.[206]

Internally and Externally Ascertained Valid Cognition [cc', dd']

There are many [other] illustrative categories and approaches that issue from this [analysis], such as the distinction between internally ascertained valid cognition (*rang las nges kyi tshad ma*) and externally ascertained valid cognition (*gzhan las nges kyi tshad ma*), which belong here.[207]

[The Conclusions of Valid Cognition]

It is explained that the conclusions of valid cognition (*pramāṇaphala, tshad 'bras*) should also be understood on the basis of the following incidental comments that relate to these [categories of direct perception and inference].

Although there are many systematic presentations [that could be made], briefly stated, the successful conclusion (*grub 'bras*) of a given presentation is achieved with reference to its causal basis. [Therefore, in the case of direct perception,] let us take, for example, the unmistaken apprehension of the color "blue" as an illustration (*mtshan gzhi*). The defining characteristic is that consciousness arises in conformity with its object. The conclusion of the valid cognition is that the term [blue] on the basis of which the material object in question is understood can then be applied.

Similarly, in the case of inference, let us take the statement that "sound is impermanent" as the object of appraisal. An image of sound being impermanent arises from the understanding of the proof that sound is impermanent, in which all the three criteria are fully present. Valid cognition then refers to the consciousness which is infallible with regard to the statement "sound is impermanent" whenever it newly arises. The conclusion of this inference is that sound is directly understood to be impermanent.

Processes of Logical Understanding [c']

As for the third part of the extensive exegesis, concerning [processes of] logical understanding [it is said in the root verses]:

> **With regard to [the logical processes of genuine] understanding,**
> **There are contradictions [that may be determined],**
> **Along with relations, negations, proofs, universals and particulars,**
> **Identity and difference, eliminative and affirmative engagement,**

As well as extraneous [elimination], definition, definiendum,
Substance and counterpart [phenomena], and the two modes of inference.

The processes of understanding objects or knowable [phenomena] are established to include the following determinations: contradiction (*virudha, 'gal ba*), relation (*saṃbandha, 'brel ba*), negation (*pratiṣedha, dgag pa*), proof (*vidhi, sgrub pa*), universals (*sāmānya, spyi*), particulars (*viśeṣa, bye brag*), identity and difference (*abhinnabhinna, gcig dang tha dad*), eliminative engagement (*apohapravṛtti, sel 'jug*), affirmative engagement (*vidhipravṛtti, sgrub 'jug*), extraneous elimination (*anyāpoha, gzhan sel*), definition (*lakṣaṇa, mtshan nyid*), definiendum (*lakṣya, mtshon bya*), substance phenomena (*dravyadharma, rdzas chos*), distinguishing counterpart phenomena (*vyāvṛttidharma, ldog chos*), and the two modes of inference (*anumāna, rjes dpag rnam gnyis*).

Contradiction [i']

Among them, the defining characteristic of contradiction is that it indicates mutually exclusive or disharmonious factors, such as "light and darkness."[208]

Relation [ii']

The defining characteristic of relation is that [the attribute] *y* is different from the given phenomenon *x*, but if it is negated the phenomenon will explicitly be negated as well, as in the example, "golden vase." [209]

Negation [iii']

The defining characteristic of negation is that in the case of a given phenomenon, for every object-universal (*don spyi*) *x* that arises, a corresponding object-universal of its negandum (*dgag bya*) *y* also arises.[210]

Proof [iv']

The defining characteristic of proof is that in the case of a given phenomenon, for every object-universal *x* that arises, a corresponding object-universal of its negandum *y* does not arise, as in the example "vase" [where the negandum is absent].[211]

Universals [v']

The defining characteristic of a universal is that it has a positive concomitance (*anvaya, rjes 'gro*) with a multiplicity [of attributes].[212]

Particulars [vi']

The defining characteristic of a particular is that (1) a particular [attribute] *x* must be phenomenon *y*; (2) *x* and *y* have a relation of essential identity (*tādātmyasambandha, bdag gcig 'brel*); and (3) there are established to be many other instances of *y* which are not *x*.[213]

For example, taking "gold" and "vase" respectively as the particular and the phenomenon, there is a relation of essential identity between "vase" and "gold," but there are also established to be many other particulars, such as "copper vase," "clay vase," and so forth, which are identified with the phenomenon "vase" and are not the [particular] "golden vase."

Identity and Difference [vii']

The defining characteristic of identity is that in the case of a given phenomenon, different conceptual thoughts will not arise with respect to it, as in the case of the "color white." The defining characteristic of difference is that the established basis (*gzhi grub*), phenomenon *x*, is to be comprehended in terms of different explicit names (*dngos ming*), such as "pillar" and "vase" which refer to different substances (*rdzas tha dad*), or [in terms of different predicates] such as "created" and "impermanent" which refer to different distinguishing counterparts (*ldog tha dad*).[214]

Eliminative Engagement [viii']

The defining characteristic of eliminative engagement is that in the case of the given subject of a [conceptual] predicate *x*, even though there are all sorts of phenomena that are coextensive or congruent in their logical entailment (*yin khyab mnyam*) with the given predicate *x*, it does not engage with object *y*. This is exemplified by the certainty that comes from [correctly] understanding that a vase [is not permanent].

Affirmative Engagement [ix']

The defining characteristic of affirmative engagement is that in the case of the given subject of a [perceptual] predicate *x*, even though there are all sorts of phenomena that are coextensive or congruent with the given predicate *x*, it does engage with object *y*. This is exemplified by the focusing on object-universals.[215] Alternatively, the defining characteristic of these two is that [in the case of eliminative engagement,] [the subject] does not engage with its object, having differentiated its parts, and [in the case of affirmative engagement, the subject] does engage with its object, having differentiated its parts.

Extraneous Elimination [x']

The defining characteristic of extraneous elimination is that the predicate is to be understood, once its own [counterpart] that is to be eliminated has been verbally negated, as when the statement "this is a man" eliminates [the counterpart] "this is a woman," or just as the statement "there is no mountain" eliminates [the counterpart] "there is a mountain."[216]

Definition [xi']

The defining characteristic of a definition is that all the three real properties (*don chos gsum*) are fully present, whereas the defining characteristic of the absence of defining characteristics is that the three real properties are not fully present.[217] In this context, the term "three real properties" refers to the three substantially existent properties [of defining characteristics] (*rdzas yod chos gsum*),[218] that is to say, they exist materially (*rdul rdzas su grub pa*), they exist as entities (*dngos por yod pa*), and they are phenomenally existent (*chos su yod*) because the terms "phenomenon" (*chos*) and "knowable object" (*shes bya*) are equivalent.

Definiendum [xii']

The defining characteristic of a defined object or definiendum is that the three properties of conventional terminology (*tha snyad chos gsum*) are fully present, whereas the defining characteristic of the absence of a defined object is that the three properties of conventional terminology are not fully present. The three properties of conventional terminology are cognition, signification, and application or engagement (*shes brjod 'jug gsum*).[219] Incidentally, the defining characteristic of the term "illustration" (*mtshan gzhi*) is that it is the basis upon which a defined object is defined to be in accordance with its defining characteristic.[220]

When the defects of a definition are analyzed, there are said to be three such defects, namely, the defect of a definition that has no logical entailment (*vyāpti, khyab pa*), the defect of a definition that has excessive logical entailment, and the defect of a definition that is not present in its [proposed] illustration. These [defects] are exemplified respectively as follows:

(1) When "stripes, including the hump" are presented as the definition of an ox, the expression "stripes including the hump" has no logical entailment in respect of an ox.
(2) When "cephalic" is presented as the definition of an ox, the expression "cephalic" has excessive logical entailment in respect of an ox.
(3) When "humped and so forth" is presented as the definition of a horse and an ox, the [proposed] illustration "humped and so forth" is not present in respect of the [definiendum] horse.

Alternatively, the term "definition" can be analyzed in terms of the so-called eight ostensible factors (*ltar snang brgyad*).[221]

SUBSTANCE PHENOMENON [xiii']

The defining characteristic of substance (*dravya, rdzas*) is exemplified by physical form, which is the necessary efficient condition of a human being. The defining characteristic of the term "substance-phenomenon" (*dravyadharma, rdzas chos*) is exemplified by an attribute of physical form, such as the impermanence of form, which is the basis underlying the identity of a substance-phenomenon.

DISTINGUISHING COUNTERPART PHENOMENON [xiv']

The defining characteristic of the term "distinguishing counterpart" (*vyāvṛtti, ldog pa*) is a given phenomenon that conceptually appears to be the opposite of [phenomena] of a dissimilar class but is not actually existent, such as the appearance of form in conceptual thought. The defining characteristic of a "counterpart phenomenon" (*ldog chos*) is a given phenomenon which conceptually appears as a substantial attribute but is not actually existent, such as the appearance of form as impermanent in [the mind of] a logician.[222]

The Two Modes of Inference [xv']

Inference for One's Own Sake [aa']

[Concerning the first of the two modes of inference, it is said in the root verses:]

> **[The first of these] is inference for one's own sake—**
> **This requires genuine evidence endowed with the three criteria.**
> **One should reject ostensible and contradictory evidence**
> **In which [these criteria] are incomplete.**
> **The [given] examples should also be determined accordingly.**

When inference (*anumāna, rjes dpag*) which is to be undertaken for one's own sake is analyzed in particular, the defining characteristic of genuine reasoning or genuine evidence is that the three criteria—property of the thesis (*pakṣadharma, phyogs chos*), forward logical entailment (*anvayavyāpti, rjes khyab*), and counter logical entailment (*vyatirekavyāpti, ldog khyab*)—are fully present.[223]

Property of the Thesis [1"]

The defining characteristic of the property of the thesis is that the reason or evidence *x* is ascertained by valid cognition to be in conformity with the statement proposed on the basis of the subject of interest (*shes 'dod can*) that is to be proven.

Forward Logical Entailment [2"]

The defining characteristic of forward logical entailment is that the reason or evidence *x* is ascertained [by valid cognition] to be present exclusively in the analogous term or compatible factor (*sapakṣa, mthun phyogs*), in accordance with the logical proof that is presented.

Counter Logical Entailment [3"]

The defining characteristic of counter logical entailment is that the reason or evidence *x* is ascertained [by valid cognition] to be absent exclusively in the non-analogous term or incompatible factor (*vipakṣa, mi mthun phyogs*), in accordance with the logical proof that is presented.[224]

These three criteria may be exemplified as follows: "When sound is presented or stated to be impermanent, sound, the subject for discussion, is impermanent because it has been created. Just like a vase, for example, so has sound also been created." Here, sound is the subject for discussion, the basis for the debate (*adhikaraṇa, rtsod gzhi*). "Impermanent" is the property of the probandum (*sādhyadharma, bsgrub bya'i chos*). "Sound is impermanent" is the probandum (*sādhya, bsgrub bya*). "Created" is the evidence (*liṅga, rtags*) or reason (*hetu, gtan tshigs*); and "vase" is the analogous example (*sādharmyadṛṣṭānta, mthun dpe*). Now, the criterion of "sound" (*x*), presented [here] as the subject for discussion, the basis for the debate, being "created" (*y*), which is presented as the evidence, requires an acceptance (*mthung snang*) in the mind of both the [antagonist] who presents the statement of proof and [the respondent or protagonist] who is the focus of this presentation. The correct formulation of this [criterion] is the property of the thesis that is to be established through valid cognition. [The second criterion,] forward logical entailment, is represented [in this example] by the words "is created," and [the third criterion,] inverse or negative logical entailment, is represented by the [implied] statement, "permanent things are uncreated."[225]

Genuine Evidence [4"]

When genuine reason or evidence is quantifiably analyzed, there are said to be three kinds of [genuine] evidence, namely, the [genuine] evidence associated with the axiom of the result (*kāryahetu, 'bras bu'i gtan tshigs*), the axiom of identity (*svabhāvahetu, rang bzhin gyi gtan tshigs*), and the axiom of the absence of the objective referent (*anupalabdhihetu, ma dmigs pa'i gtan tshigs*).[226]

When analyzed in terms of its objectives, [genuine reason] may be applied both for one's own sake (*rang don gyi rtags*) and for the sake of others (*gzhan don gyi rtags*). Then, when analyzed in terms of its modes of establishing proof, there are many subcategories, such as the distinction between proof of a meaning (*don sgrub*) and proof of a conventional term (*tha snyad sgrub*).[227]

Ostensible Evidence [5"]

When the three criteria [of genuine evidence] are incomplete, the evidence is said to be ostensible (*ābhāsaliṅga, rtags ltar snang*). There are many types of ostensible evidence that have to be rejected, such as contradictory evidence (*viruddhaliṅga, 'gal ba'i rtags*), unascertained evidence (*anaikāntikaliṅga, ma nges pa'i rtags*) and unestablished evidence (*asiddhaliṅga, ma grub pa'i rtags*).[228]

Examples [6'']

Correct Analogous Examples [a'']

In such contexts, even the examples that are given are to be determined accordingly, as correct or ostensible. The defining characteristic of a correct example is that it is the basis of a definitive logical entailment, preceding a definitive probandum. When analyzed, there are two sorts of [correct example], among which the defining characteristic of the first, correct analogous examples (*sādharmyadṛṣṭānta, mthun dpe yang dag*), is that they are the definitive basis preceding a logical entailment that precedes a definitive probandum, as in the [aforementioned] proposition where the analogous example proving that sound is impermanent is stated to be a vase.

Nonanalogous Examples [b'']

The defining characteristic of correct non-analogous examples (*vaidharmyadṛṣṭānta, mi mthun dpe yang dag*) is that they are the definitive basis of an authentic inverse logical entailment, made in respect of a definitive probandum, as when space is given as a non-analogous example, while proving that sound is impermanent because it is created.[229]

Ostensible Examples [c'']

The defining characteristic of ostensible examples is that they start out as the definitive basis for logical entailment with regard to a definitive probandum, but they are incapable of being definitive. Moreover, although there are many other defective types of evidence and examples, they may be illustrated by the aforementioned.[230] These should all be determined and then rejected.

Inference for the Sake of Others [bb']

> **[The second of these] is inference for the sake of others—**
> **This requires a statement of proof endowed with the three criteria,**
> **Acceptable to both the antagonist and the respondent,**

And endowed with the two aspects.
In the case of evidence, elimination, refutation,
Consequential reasoning, and so forth,
The ostensible [types] should be rejected,
And the correct [types] should be established.
While these [processes of logical understanding] are prestigious in modern circles...

The defining characteristic of inference for the sake of others, or correct statement of proof (*sgrub ngag*), is that the statement of proof should be presented, endowed with the three criteria, without addition or omission, that are definitively acceptable to both the antagonist (*vādin, rgol mkhan*) and the protagonist or respondent (*prativādin, phyir rgol*).[231]

Correct Statement of Proof [1"]

Statements of proof are said to have two aspects: The [first of these] is a statement of proof applying a qualitative similarity (*chos mthun sbyor gyi sgrub ngag*), as in the statement, "That which is created is logically entailed to be impermanent, just, for example, like a vase. Sound too is created." The [second] is a statement of proof applying a qualitative dissimilarity (*chos mi mthun sbyor gyi sgrub ngag*), as in the statement, "That which is permanent is logically entailed to be uncreated, just, for example, like space. Sound by contrast is created."

Ostensible Statement of Proof [2"]

The defining characteristic of an ostensible statement of proof is that, in the case of a given statement of proof, either the cognizing intellect, or the object, or the words [that are employed] are defective and in contradiction of the three criteria of logical reasoning.

Probandum Based on Correct Evidence [3"]

The defining characteristic of a probandum endowed with correct evidence is that it should be comprehended from its inception on the basis of correct evidence, as exemplified in the statement, "Created things, the subject for discussion, are impermanent, like a vase, for example."

For these reasons it is said that both [aspects of inference], for one's own sake and for the sake of others, may be correct or ostensible.[232]

Elimination [4″]

The defining characteristic of elimination (*bsal ba*) is that, in the case of a given ostensible thesis (*pratijñā*, *dam bcas*) *x*, the object of the opposite standpoint (*ldog phyogs*) *y* is established by valid cognition, as in the statement, "It would follow that sound, the subject for discussion, is not an audible object."

Refutation [5″]

The defining characteristic of correct refutation (*duṣaṇa*, *sun 'byin*) is that a statement can be comprehended as defective by expressing or signifying its defect as a defect. The defining characteristic of ostensible [refutation] is the opposite of that.[233]

Consequential Reasoning [6″]

The defining characteristic of a correct consequence (*prasaṅga*, *thal 'gyur*) is that the following or consequential statement (*thal ngag*) cannot be countered by a rejoinder. The defining characteristic of an ostensible consequence is the opposite of that.[234]

Defining Characteristics of an Antagonist [7″]

The defining characteristic of the antagonist who employs such [logical techniques] is an individual person who holds his position in order to sustain the original premise (*phyogs snga ma*).

Defining Characteristics of a Respondent/Protagonist [8″]

The defining characteristic of the respondent or protagonist is an individual person who holds his position in order to refute the original premise.

Also, the defining characteristic of the witness (*dpang po*) [or mediator] is an individual person who holds his position in order to differentiate between which of the two contestants is the victor in the debate and which is the vanquished.

In all such cases, the ostensible and defective [types of argument] should be rejected and, instead, knowable objects should be appraised and standpoints established in accordance with the correct [types of argument].

[Purpose of the *Collected Topics*]

The [reasoning of the] *Collected Topics*, [summarized above,] is valuable because it facilitates the education of newcomers (lit. those of fresh intelligence) with regard to objects of knowledge. By presenting an uncommon subject for discussion, the basis for the debate should be recognized as directly evident. Once this recognition has dawned, the essential points of negation and proof should be applied. These will arise in the mind and it is through them that one's own thesis can be presented. If a respondent engages, one can then ensure that his evidence is not proven, that his argument is without logical entailment, and that he will categorically accept your position three times.[235] Thereby, the intellectual brilliance of the other party will be eclipsed, and the other party will conclusively accept your logical concomitance, entailments, and observations with regard to scriptural authority and logical reasoning.

This merely partial exegesis [of the *Collected Topics*] leaves unchanged the special technical terms that are employed in the tradition of logical reasoning that is prestigious nowadays in modern circles.[236]

The particle *ste* at the end of this verse is a connecting particle (*lhag bcas kyi sgra*).

Incidental Comments regarding Other Logical Traditions [d']

The fourth part of the extensive exegesis comprises incidental comments regarding other [logical] traditions. On this [it is said in the root verses]:

> **. . . There are also different [logical presentations],**
> **Exemplified by the *Treasure of Logical Reasoning*,**
> **The *Oceanic Textbook of Uncommon Logical Reasoning*,**
> **And the traditions of the ancient [Kadampas].**

The *Treasure of Valid Logical Reasoning* (*Tshad ma rigs gter*), along with its *Auto-commentary* (*rang 'grel*), which were composed in eleven chapters by Sakya Paṇchen, is known as the first pathway of the chariot [of logic], in which the combined twofold approach called "knowable objects to be ascertained through universal distinguishing counterparts" (*shes bya spyi ldog nas nges par bya ba*) and "cognitive process establishing the nature of valid cognition" (*shes byed tshad ma'i rang bzhin gtan la dbab pa*) are perfected, along with the processes of logical reasoning [based upon them].[237]

The *Oceanic Textbook of Uncommon Logical Reasoning* composed by the omniscient Gyalwang [Karmapa] VII Chodrak Gyatso, which perfects the enlightened intention of [Dharmakīrti's] *Seven Sections* [*of Valid Cognition*], summarizing and elucidating them through his own ability, without reference to the exegetical traditions of India and Tibet or to the Indian and Tibetan commentaries (*'grel ṭīk*), is known as the second pathway of the chariot [of logic], containing, [as it does], modes of logical reasoning that were not previously existing.[238]

There are also different traditions, including the one known as the ancients' tradition of valid cognition (*tshad ma snga rabs pa'i lugs*), which was widely propagated by [Kadampa masters] such as the great Ngok Lotsāwa and Chapa Choseng, which are similar in their treatment of universal distinguishing counterparts of the signified object (*brjod bya'i spyi ldog*) but slightly dissimilar in their defense of standpoints concerning the signifier (*brjod byed khas len skyong tshul*).[239]

[This last mentioned system] includes, for example, the following summarization [of the terminology of logical reasoning] in eighteen collected topics (*bsdus tshan bco brgyad*):[240]

> O monks of Kyetshal! [The topics] are (1) the colors white and red (*kha dog dkar dmar*); (2) substance phenomena and distinguishing counterpart phenomena (*rdzas chos ldog chos gnyis*); (3) contradictions and non-contradictions (*'gal dang mi 'gal*); (4) universals and particulars (*spyi dang bye brag gnyis*); (5) relation and non-relation (*'brel dang mi 'brel*); (6) difference and non-difference (*tha dad dang tha min gnyis*); (7) positive and negative concomitance (*rjes su 'gro ldog*); (8) cause and result (*rgyu dang 'bras bu gnyis*); (9) cogency of the antagonist, mediator, and respondent (*snga btsan bar btsan phyi btsan*);[241] (10) definition and definiendum (*mtshan mtshon gnyis*); (11) multi-faceted evidence and multi-faceted elimination (*rtags mang bsal mang*); (12) the two procedures for adding negation (*dgag pa 'phar tshul gnyis*); (13) direct contradiction and indirect contradiction (*dngos 'gal brgyud 'gal*); (14) the two aspects of logical congruence (*khyab mnyam rnam pa gnyis*); (15) presence

and absence (*yin gyur min gyur*), and (16) their opposites (*yin log min log gnyis*); (17) understanding of existence and understanding of non-existence (*yod rtogs med rtogs*); and (18) explicit understanding and evidential understanding (*dngos rtogs rtags rtogs gnyis*).

Although there are many such [categorizations of the terminologies of logical reasoning], they can be principally subsumed under these [eighteen topics].[242]

Synopsis of the Eight Aspects and Three Scopes of Dialectics [2']

The second [part of the actual exegesis] is a synopsis [of logical reasoning] in terms of the eight aspects of dialectics and the three scopes [of dialectical application].

Eight Aspects of Dialectics [a']

All points signified in the texts on valid cognition may be personally understood
Through direct perception, inference, and their ostensible forms,
Whereas proof, refutation, and their ostensible forms engender understanding in others:
These are the eight aspects of dialectics.

Correct and Ostensible Forms of Direct Perception and Inference [i']

When all the points that are signified in the textbooks of valid cognition are abbreviated, the four categories of direct perception and inference, comprising their correct and ostensible forms, are the means whereby [the conclusions of logical reasoning] are personally known or comprehended.

Correct and Ostensible Forms of Proof and Refutation [ii']

Similarly, the four categories of proof and refutation, comprising their correct and ostensible forms, cause others to comprehend [the conclusions of logical reasoning]. Altogether, these are known as the eight aspects of dialectics (*tarka*, *rtog ge*). [When condensed] they may be gathered under two headings: [logical reasoning undertaken] for one's own sake and [logical reasoning undertaken] for the sake of others.

Three Scopes of Dialectical Application [b']

[Then, with regard to the three scopes of dialectical application, it is said in the root verses:]

> **In brief, there are three kinds of objects to be appraised:**
> **The directly evident, the indirectly evident,**
> **And the indirectly evident to an extreme degree.**
> **As for their means of appraisal, they comprise [respectively]**
> **Direct perception, logical inference, and scriptural authority,**
> **Of which the purity is established by the three types of scrutiny.**
> **There are four kinds of direct perception,**
> **Three logical axioms of inference,**
> **And various technical terms that derive from these.**

When all the topics of valid cognition are abbreviated, they are gathered under the three headings of appraisable objects (*gzhal bya*) that are directly evident (*abhimukhī*, *mngon gyur*), indirectly evident (*parokṣa*, *lkog gyur*), and indirectly evident to an extreme degree (*atyantaparokṣa*, *shin tu lkog gyur*). As for the means of appraisal (*gzhal byed*), they may all be subsumed under the three [respective] headings of appraisal by direct perception (*pratyakṣa*, *mngon sum*), logical inference (*anumāna*, *rjes dpag*), and scriptural authority (*āgama*, *lung*), of which the purity is established by three kinds of scrutiny (*dpyad gsum*).

Directly Evident Objects of Appraisal [i']

Directly evident objects of appraisal include

(1) the five sensory activity fields (*pañcāyatana*, *skye mched lnga*) comprising visible, audible, olfactory, gustatory, and tangible forms, which can eliminate superimposition through the experiential power of direct perception, an extraneous or non-apperceptive awareness of external objects that refers to the immediately visible [world];[243]

(2) the sensory activity fields of the six modes of consciousness (*ṣadvijñāna*,

rnam shes tshogs drug),[244] which are experienced through the valid cognition of intrinsic or reflexive awareness[245] and only with reference to objects of experience (*myong bya*) based on the consciousness that can eliminate superimpositions through logical reasoning;

(3) the aspects of experiential awareness associated with mental states that relate collectively to the sensory activity field of phenomena (*dharmāyatana, chos kyi skye mched*).[246]

Although there are realists (*dngos por smra ba rnams*) who [additionally] hold that, in the case of a sublime being, the abiding nature of selflessness including the sixteen aspects of the four truths (*ṣodaśākāravisāritacaturārya satya, bden chung bcu drug*), beginning with impermanence (*anitya, mi rtag pa*),[247] and in the case of a buddha, all quantifiable objects of knowledge[248] are directly evident, Dharmakīrti has said that the processes of cognition that a buddha experiences are inconceivable.[249] Therefore, direct perception, as a means of appraising the [range of] objects that are to be appraised, is said to comprise the four following categories: direct perception of the sense organs, direct perception of mental consciousness, direct perception of intrinsic awareness, and direct perception of yoga.

Indirectly Evident Objects of Appraisal [ii']

Indirectly evident objects of appraisal include the physical sense faculties (*dbang po gzugs can*); the sixteen aspects of the four truths, such as impermanence, the suffering of change (*vipariṇāmaduḥkhatā, 'gyur ba'i sdug bsngal*), the emptiness of self (*ātmaśūnyatā, bdag gi bas stong pa*), and selflessness (*anātmaka, bdag med*);[250] the selflessness of the individual person (*pudgalanairātmya, gang zag gi bdag med*), exemplified by these [aspects of the four truths], and the selflessness of phenomena (*dharmanairātmya, chos kyi bdag med*);[251] as well as [the concepts of] identical nature (*ekātman, bdag gcig*) and relation of identical nature (*tadātmyasaḥbandha, de byung gi 'brel ba*),[252] primary causes (*hetu, rgyu*) or potentialities (*śakti, nus pa*), the seeds of dissonant and purified mental states (*sems kyi steng gi kun byang*),[253] the activities associated with renunciation and antidotes (*spang gnyen*),[254] and so forth. These are all indirectly evident—the second category of objects of appraisal—because they have to be established exclusively through logical axioms proceeding from the cogent power of facts (*vastubalapravṛrttahetu, dngos po stobs zhugs kyi gtan tshigs*).

There are also objects of appraisal that cannot be established through the direct perception of an individual person and require reference to pure [authoritative] sources [see below].[255]

There are three kinds of logical axiom dependent on inference, which appraise and establish these [indirectly evident] objects of appraisal through the cogent power of facts. These are termed the axiom of the result, the axiom of identity, and the axiom of the absence of the objective referent.[256]

Objects of Appraisal Indirectly Evident to an Extreme Degree [iii']

Objects that are indirectly evident to an extreme degree include those such as virtuous and non-virtuous actions which cannot be established by either direct perception or the axioms of the cogent power of facts, and therefore have to be understood on the basis of scriptural authority alone. For this reason, scriptures of which the purity is not established by three kinds of scrutiny only obstruct or impede certainty because they demonstrate or represent heretical [views]. On the other hand, [scriptures] of which purity can be established by the three kinds of scrutiny contain words of definitive meaning (*nītārtha, nges don*), without resorting to terms that express a flawed conviction, the need for a [concealed] intention, and so forth.[257]

The diverse technical language employed in logical reasoning exclusively derives from these basic categories.

As far as the three kinds of scrutiny are concerned, [reasoning based on scriptural authority] is not contradicted by direct perception with regard to directly evident objects, nor by inference through the cogent power of facts with regard to indirectly evident objects, nor by contradictions inherent in the sequence of [authoritative] utterances with regard to objects that are indirectly evident to an extreme degree.

Synopsis of Five Essential Modes of Logical Reasoning [3']

The third [part of the actual exegesis] is a synopsis of these [categories of logical reasoning] in terms of their five essential modalities. On this [it says in the root verses]:

> **The analytical basis or topics [for discussion],**
> **The analysis of phenomena,**
> **The systematic framework to be determined,**

Consequential reasoning which is the process of determination, and [correct] view—
These are the five modalities offering an introduction to the Middle Way,
Subsumed in [the teachings] of the mighty lords of knowledge.
Through conventional terms, ultimate objects of appraisal
Are established as valid cognition.

Analytical Basis of Knowable Phenomena [a']

[In Garwang Chokyi Wangchuk's commentary, concerning the first modality, the topics of logical reasoning (*dharmin*, *chos can*),] it is said:[258]

> Objects of knowledge and objects of appraisal have an established basis.
> This means that phenomena, foundational [factors],
> Dependent origination, objective referents, subjects and objects
> Are all [valid] topics for discussion,
> Forming an analytical basis for logical congruence.

Those verses refer to the analytical basis (*dbye gzhi*) of knowable phenomena, which includes such terminology.

Actual Analysis of Phenomena [b']

[Concerning the second modality, the actual analysis of phenomena, the same text] then says:

> When analyzed, [phenomena] may suggest dichotomies
> Between substance and permanence, negation and proof,
> Or defining characteristics, defined objects, and their demonstrations,
> As well as [a plethora of specific dichotomies]
> Such as between the created and uncreated,
> The produced and non-produced,
> The compounded and non-compounded,
> Entity and non-entity, or the perishable and imperishable.

Those verses refer to the analysis of phenomena (*chos kyi dbye ba*), which includes an analysis of universals (*spyi'i dbye ba*) and also an analysis of the extensive particulars derived from that [analysis of universals].

Systematic Presentation of Logical Reasoning [c']

[Concerning the third modality,] the systematic presentation [of logical reasoning] that is to be determined, the text then goes on to say:

> There are thirteen [logical topics to be examined]:
> Substance and counterpart, contradiction and relation,
> Universal and particular, definition and definiendum,
> Cause and result, and understanding of existence and non-existence,
> Along with presence, absence, and their opposites,
> Positive and negative concomitance,
> Assessment of the basis of negation,
> Cogency of the antagonist, cogency of the respondent,[259]
> And iterations [employed in the course of formal debate].[260]

Those [understandings] and their subdivisions form the systematic presentation [of the dialectic] that is to be determined (*nges bya'i rnam gzhag*).

Consequential Reasoning [d']

[Concerning the fourth modality, the consequential reasoning that forms the actual process of determination, the text] says:

> The subject of interest (*shes 'dod chos can*),
> The property of the probandum that is to be apprehended,
> And the three axioms of the cognitive process
> Together form a causal basis for making consequential statements.

Those verses therefore refer to consequential reasoning (*thal 'gyur*), which, along with logical entailment (*khyab*) and rejoinders (*lan*), form the process of determination (*nges byed*).

Genuine Conclusion of Valid Cognition [e']

[Concerning the fifth modality, the correct view, the text] continues:

> Moreover, according to the logical reasoning of the *Collected Topics*,
> Upon scrutiny, neither beginning nor end will be found,
> Nor will there be any abiding in a middle position.
> All standpoints will be destroyed.

When one is without beginning or end,
Without referring to a middle [position],
Without standpoints, and without philosophical systems,
That is the Great Madhyamaka.[261]

Those verses therefore refer to the conclusion of valid cognition, the direct determination that all things are without self (*anātmaka, bdag med*) and free from conceptual elaboration (*niḥprapañca, spros bral*).[262] This is the view that offers an introduction to the Middle Way, as summarized systematically by mighty lords of logical reasoning, great beings endowed with the precious [teachings of] *sādhana* and *tantra* (*sgrub rgyud*), such as [Zhamar VI] Garwang Chokyi Wangchuk.[263]

This text should be examined in detail, though I am unable to summarize it here. In any case, all of these [citations from it] are in conformity with the ultimate reality, appraised through the logical reasoning of conventional terms and reliably established.

The Implementation of Logical Reasoning [4']

Since [at this juncture,] it would be inappropriate not to establish the points of the textual traditions through the scrutiny of logical reasoning, if I may incidentally make some ad-hoc comments concerning preliminary engagement in the logical techniques, according to the *Collected Topics*, this will have two parts: The first concerns the modes of recognizing evidence and specific predicates (*rtags gsal gyi ngos 'dzin*) and the second concerns the rejoinders made by the respondent to the antagonist (*snga rgol la phyi rgol gyis lan brjod tshul*).

Recognizing Evidence and Specific Predicates [a']

The former is exemplified by the statement, "It follows that the vase, the subject for discussion, is impermanent, because it has been created." Here, it should be recognized that "vase" is the given subject for discussion (*chos can*) (*x*) or basis of the debate (*rtsod gzhi*), "impermanent" is the probandum (*bsgrub bya*) or the specific predicate (*gsal ba*), and "created" is the proof (*sādhana, sgrub byed*), evidence (*liṅga, rtags*), or reason (*hetu, gtan tshigs*).

Rejoinders Made by Respondents to Antagonists [b']

Secondly, concerning the rejoinders made by the respondent to the antagonist in the course of debate, I will offer a slightly detailed explanation and a summary. First, [concerning the detailed explanation,] there are both valid and non-valid forms of cognition.

Rejoinders Recognizing Valid Cognition [i']

The former requires a definitive logical axiom, [presented] through valid cognition in which the three criteria are fully present. Let us take, for example, the statement, "It follows that the vase, the subject for discussion, is impermanent, because it has been created." For the antagonist who accepts this statement:

(1) the criterion of the property of the thesis (*phyogs chos kyi tshul*) is certain because the given evidence "created" (*x*) is applicable to the subject of discussion, the "vase";
(2) the criterion of positive concomitance is certain because the given evidence "created" (*x*) is not contradicted by either the property of the probandum or the specific predicate (*gsal*) "impermanent"; and
(3) the criterion of the distinguishing counterpart is certain because, in respect of the given evidence "created" (*x*), there is no absence of certainty with regard to the specific predicate "impermanent."

If a given [proposition] in which these three criteria are fully present is to be determined through valid cognition, the respondent is required to answer.

Rejoinders Recognizing Invalid Cognition [ii']

In the case of the second, [invalid cognition,] there is no such certainty because [the reasoning] is unestablished, contradictory, and [consequently] unascertained.[264]

Rejoinders Recognizing Unestablished Reasoning [aa']

Among these [invalid forms], first, concerning non-establishment with regard to the proof of the thesis, the defining characteristic of the term "unestablished" (*ma grub pa*) is illustrated, for example, by the statement, "It follows that the vase, the subject for discussion, is impermanent, because it has not been created." Here, the given evidence "not been created" (x) does not apply to the subject for discussion, the "vase." Also, in the statement, "It follows that the vase, the subject for discussion, is permanent, because it has not been created," both the evidence and the specific predicate are inapplicable to the subject for discussion, the "vase."

Again, in the statement, "Taking 'in many places over here' as the subject for discussion, it follows that there are peacocks, because the sound of the peacock is heard," in this case, the evidence is not established because there is room for doubt with regard to the subject of the discussion.

Also, in the statement, "Taking 'this ground over there' as the subject for discussion, it follows that there is fire, because there is some kind of smoky vapor," here the evidence is not established because there is room for doubt with regard to the evidence.

Also, in the statement, "Taking the children of a barren woman as the subject for discussion, it follows that they are noble because they are of a good family," in this case the evidence is not established on account of the non-existence of the subject for discussion. In all these cases, the respondent should say, "The evidence is unestablished!"[265]

Rejoinders Recognizing Contradictory Reasoning [bb']

Second, contradictory reasoning (*'gal ba'i gtan tshigs*) is that in which the probandum is established by a contradictory proof. The defining characteristic of contradictory reasoning may be illustrated, for example, by the statement, "It follows that sound, the subject for discussion, is permanent, because it has been created." Here, although the given evidence "created" (x) does apply to the subject for discussion, "sound," even so, because the specific predicate is contradicted by the term "impermanent," the respondent should say, "The logical entailment is contradicted!"[266]

Rejoinders Recognizing Unascertained Reasoning [cc']

Third, concerning unascertained reasoning (*ma nges pa'i gtan tshigs*), the defining characteristic is that there is uncertainty and room for doubt because there are both analogous or compatible factors (*sapakṣa, mthun phyogs*) and non-analogous or incompatible factors (*vipakṣa, mi mthun phyogs*). This may be illustrated, for example, by the statement, "It follows that the color of a ruby, the subject for discussion, is red, because it is a color." Here, the given evidence "color" (*x*) is compatible with the red of ruby, but because it may also be applied to other properties of the thesis, such as a white conch, it is incompatible or contradictory. Therefore, [the respondent should say,] "It is unascertained!"[267]

Summary of the Rejoinders [c']

Second, concerning the summary [of the rejoinders made by the respondent to the antagonist in the course of debate]:

(1) If the evidence *x* does not apply to the subject for discussion, which is the basis of the debate, the evidence is not established.
(2) If the specific predicate of the probandum is contradictory, logical entailment is contradicted.
(3) [Even] though the specific predicate of the probandum is certain, the logical entailment may be unascertained.

If the evidence *x* does not at all apply to the subject under discussion, even though there is some uncertainty with regard to contradiction of the specific predicate, one may respond that the evidence is not established. If none of the three—non-establishment, contradiction, or uncertainty—is present, one should respond by accepting [the proposition].

Eight Approaches to Logical Entailment [i']

Moreover, when the eight approaches to logical entailment (*khyab pa sgo brgyad*) are considered:

(1) [Positive] forward logical entailment (*anvayavyāpti*, *rjes khyab*) takes the form, "If *x* is the evidence, it is logically entailed that the specific predicate is *y*."
(2) [Positive] contrary entailment (*viruddhavyāpti*, *'gal khyab*) takes the form, "If *x* is the evidence,[268] it is logically entailed that the distinctive predicate is not *y*."
(3) [Positive] backward entailment (*heṣṭhavyāpti*, *thur khyab*)[269] takes the form, "If *y* is the specific predicate, it is logically entailed that the evidence is *x*."
(4) [Positive] counter entailment (*vyatirekavyāpti*, *ldog khyab*) takes the form, "If *y* is not the specific predicate, it is logically entailed that the evidence is not *x*."

In brief, one should know also that, in the case of four kinds [of logical entailment]—comprising forward and contrary positive entailment and their negative forms—the specific predicate arises from the evidence, whereas in the case of the other four kinds [of logical entailment]—comprising backward and counter positive entailment and their negative forms—the evidence arises from the specific predicate, and so forth.

[Conclusion]

In general, with regard to the reasons for engaging in debate, innate discriminative awareness will be enhanced, the mind will be trained in Sanskrit grammar and logic, and the mind will be trained in one's own [Buddhist] textual traditions and in those of others.

As for the graceful trappings or finery associated with debate, [debate will engender] a clear complexion; pleasant and gentle speech, refraining from verbal assaults that would humiliate an opponent; clarity and sharpness with regard to scriptural authority and logical reasoning; avoidance of idleness and arrogance; avoidance of deception, attachment, and aversion that forsake the path of logical reasoning; and dedication to the well-being of oneself and others, along with the Buddhist teaching.

With regard to the similes that illustrate the term "debate," "debate" is purposefully said to resemble a wheel that cuts off one's own delusions and those of others, or to resemble a mountain that cannot be shaken by the winds of refutation, or else to resemble a child of Munīndra, undeluded with regard to words and their meanings.

Then, as for the result of engaging in debate, one's own mind will be satisfied by the increasing understanding that is contingent on the reasons for engaging in debate, as well as by its fine trappings, [stimulating] ideas, and excellently constructed syllogisms (*sbyor ba*). [In addition,] good reputation will permeate all directions, and one will become a king of the sacred teachings, intent on protecting the Buddhist teaching. It is for such ends that [debate] should be studied.

5. Fine Arts

iii. The Fine Arts [III.B.2.a.iii]
- aa. Introductory Preamble
- bb. Physical, Vocal, and Mental Arts
  - 1' Physical Arts
    - a' Supreme Arts of the Body
      - i' Brief Presentation
      - ii' Detailed Discussion
        - aa' Representations of Buddha Body
          - 1" Defining Characteristics of an Artist
            - a" Defining Characteristics of a Patron
          - 2" Iconometric Proportions
            - a" Painted Icons Depicting Visualized Deities
            - b" The Actual Exegesis on Iconometry
              - i" General Explanation of Canonical Iconometric Systems
                - aa" According to the *Tantra of the Wheel of Time*
                - bb" According to the *Tantra of the Emergence of Cakrasaṃvara*
                - cc" According to the *Yamāri Tantras*
                - dd" According to the *Sūtra Requested by Śāriputra*
                - ee" Five Anthropometric Scales
                - ff" The Sixfold Typology of Deities
              - ii" Contemporary Iconometric Systems
                - aa" Eleven Iconometric Scales of the Encampment Style
                - bb" Eight Great Iconometric Scales of Menla Dondrub
              - iii" Essential Elements of Iconography

b'' Unsurpassed
c'' Consecrated by Blessings
d'' Arisen from Spiritual Accomplishments
e'' Corresponding to the Different Vehicles
2'' Techniques of Stūpa Construction
a'' The Ordinary Techniques
i'' Stūpas Associated with Ordinary Persons
ii'' Stūpas Associated with Pious Attendants
iii'' Stūpas Associated with Hermit Buddhas
iv'' Eight Stūpas Suitable for Buddhas
aa'' Stūpa of the Sugatas
bb'' Stūpa of Supreme Enlightenment
cc'' Stūpa of the Wheel of the Sacred Teachings
dd'' Stūpa of Miracles
ee'' Stūpa of the Divine Descent
ff'' Stūpa of Resolving Schism
gg'' Stūpa of Victory
hh'' Stūpa of Nirvāṇa
v'' Dimensions of the Stūpa
vi'' Symbolism of the Stūpa
b'' Uncommon Techniques
3'' Stūpas according to Extraordinary Traditions
a'' The Jñānabimbakāya Stūpa
b'' The Svayambhū Stūpa
c'' Stūpas according to the Nyingma Tradition
4'' Hand-held Emblems and the Associated Ritual Arts
a'' Vajra and Bell
b'' Other Hand-held Emblems
c'' The Playing of Drums and Cymbals
d'' Choreography of the Sacred Dances
i'' Choreography in the Nyingma Tradition
aa'' Thirteen Procedures in the Basic Sacred Dance of the Herukas
bb'' Sacred Dances of Exorcism
ii'' Other Traditions of Sacred Dance
b' Common Physical Arts
2' Vocal Arts
a' Supreme Arts of Speech
i' Chanting

aa' Melodic Contour
bb' Three Essentials, Six Defects, and Five Negative Causes
cc' Six Ceremonial Contexts
dd' Twelve Distinctive Modes of Chanting
ii' Defining Characteristics of Voice Pitch
b' Common Vocal Arts
3' Mental Arts
a' Supreme Arts of Mind
b' Common Mental Arts
i' Eighteen Great Topics of Knowledge
ii' Eight Subjects of Scrutiny
aa' Treatises on Human Behavior
bb' Sixty-four Crafts
1" Thirty Designated Arts
2" Eighteen Requisites of Musical Performance
3" Seven Tones of the Musical Scale
4" Nine Dramatic Moods
iii' Śīlapālita's Classification of the Sixty-four Crafts
iv' Longchen Rabjampa's Classification of Knowledge

The Fine Arts [iii]

The exegesis of the fine arts (*śilpavidyā, bzo rig pa*), the third [field of the major pathway of classical science; see above, p. 127], is in two parts—an introductory preamble concerning the purpose [of the arts] and a detailed exegesis of the particular aspects of the fine arts, in terms of the three media [body, speech, and mind].

Introductory Preamble [aa]

As to the former [it is said in the root verses]:

> **Although the arts that can be earnestly pursued are limitless,**
> **All knowledge may in fact be subsumed within the fine arts of the three media.**

With regard to the arts, which may be earnestly pursued for all intents and purposes, it is said in the *Transmissions on Monastic Discipline*:[270]

The [construction of] monastic campuses (*ārāma*),
The [building of] great temples (*vihāra*),
The [making of] mattresses,
The prolonging of life,
The nursing of those who suddenly fall ill,
Acts of charity [undertaken] in places and times of destitution:
These are the so-called "seven merits derived from material things."[271]
Among them, the first, second, and fourth generate pure merit.

It is also said that the building of stūpas containing essential relics in places where they did not previously exist, the construction of monastic campuses endowed with [appropriate] resources, the act of reconciling monastic disputes, and the engagement, during periods [of meditative absorption], in the fourfold meditation of the four immeasurable aspirations (*caturaprameya*)—loving-kindness (*maitrī*), and so forth—which are foremost among the [diverse] modes of spiritual practice,[272] all have the same ripening effect, generating pure merit.

[Furthermore,] all [material] things that are deemed necessary for the Buddhist teachings and mundane activities cannot be created or achieved without relying on this science [of fine arts]; and it has even been suggested that disrespect for the arts is a philosophical tenet associated [not with the Buddhists but] with the Nirgrantha Jains.[273] Therefore, it is most important to understand this subject.

Although the [diverse] artistic traditions are infinite, all aspects of knowledge—not only the arts—can be categorized in terms of the "fine arts of the three media" [body, speech, and mind], for which reason scholars have formulated the systematic presentation, outlined here:

(1) While mental activity precedes all [forms of artistic expression], the arts of the body (*lus bzo*) are so called because they emphasize physicality, motivated by [mind]. They may be exemplified by the first two items in the series "dancing, drawing, and singing."
(2) The arts of speech (*ngag bzo*) are so called because they emphasize verbal and vocal forms of expression, exemplified by the third item in that same series.
(3) The arts of the mind (*yid bzo*) [by contrast] are those that are achieved by means of mental activity [alone], without emphasizing either body or speech, and they may be exemplified by the extraordinary knowledge (*rig shes*) associated with processes of thought.[274]

Physical, Vocal, and Mental Arts [bb]

As to the latter, this comprises the [detailed] exegeses of the physical, vocal, and mental arts.

Physical Arts [1']

The first of them [the physical arts] comprise both supreme and common [forms], among which the former will be briefly presented and then discussed in detail.

Supreme Arts of the Body [a']

Brief Presentation [i']

Concerning the first [the brief presentation of the supreme arts of the body, it says in the root verses]:

> **The supreme arts of the body are the representations**
> **Of buddha body, speech, and mind.**

Among the supreme and common aspects of the arts of the body, it should be known that the foremost or supreme forms respectively comprise sculptures, paintings, and sculpted images of the buddhas, which are all representations of buddha body; the literary works of India and Tibet, which are representations of buddha speech; and the stūpas and [various] kinds of symbolic hand-held emblem, which are representations of buddha mind.

Detailed Discussion [ii']

The second [the detailed discussion of the supreme fine arts of the body] is in three parts, respectively comprising the exegeses of the representations of buddha body (*sku rten*), the representations of buddha speech (*gsung rten*), and the representations of buddha mind (*thugs rten*).

Representations of Buddha Body [aa']

The first of these also has three aspects:

(1) an exegesis of the defining characteristics, blessings, and so forth of an artist (*bzo bo*);
(2) the iconometric proportions of the images contained [within the celestial palace] (*brten pa'i lha'i cha tshad*); and
(3) some further remarks concerning the celestial palace that contains them (*rten gzhal yas khang*).

Defining Characteristics of an Artist [1"]

With regard to the first of these [the exegesis of the defining characteristics, blessings, and so forth of an artist, it says in the root verses]:

> **Artists are skilled and maintain the one-day observances (*upavāsa*).**
> **They have received empowerments and maintain the commitments**
> **Associated with the inner [classes of] the way of secret mantra,**
> **And they are endowed with blessings, as are their materials and tools.**

The artists who create these representations [of buddha body] potentially possess both faults and virtues. Firstly, as to their [possible] faults, the following verses are found in the *Ocean of Wealth*:[275]

> Poorly trained and arrogant,
> Unsociable but desirous of veneration,
> Scornful [of newly offered commissions] in the short term
> But over-interested in the long term,
> Satiated with donations while demanding extravagant fees,
> Unsatisfied even by that and pilfering materials,
> Stopping work for mere trifles,
> Menacing people and seeking [solace] in dark wine,
> They transform virtuous actions into negative acts.

Faults such as these should not be acquired.

[Conversely, the virtues of an artist] are mentioned in the following verses from the *Tantra of Embrace*:[276]

> They should be disciplined, pious, and in the prime of life,
> Endowed with lucid sense-faculties and free from doubt,

Without anger, avoiding secretive behavior and procrastination,
But highly skilled and jovial,
Patient, and compassionate.

And in the *Ocean of Wealth*:[277]

Not over-ambitious but honorable,
They should be skilled, humble, and obedient,
Respectful of the deities, and well-behaved.

When one who is naturally endowed with these defining characteristics of an artist and possessed of skilled attributes begins working, he or she should perform rites of ablution and cleanliness and assume the observances of the one-day vows (*upavāsa*) in the presence of an image [of a deity] that is not in sexual union, and in accordance with the outer [vehicles] of the way of secret mantra.[278] He or she should also have received the empowerments (*abhiṣeka*) of the deities, according to the inner [vehicles] of the way of secret mantra, and while maintaining the [relevant] commitments (*saṃvara*) and deity yoga in an isolated retreat, unseen by ordinary people, should have repeatedly presented offering *tormas* (*mchod gtor*) and sacraments (*dam rdzas*).[279]

It is also said that all artists should generate [the visualization of] themselves as Vairocana or Vighnāntaka, and even visualize their materials and tools as Vairocana.[280] The marking threads and colors should be consecrated or blessed through a rite derived from the [appropriate] maṇḍala ritual (*maṇḍalavidhi*).[281] [Similarly,] scribes or writers (*yig mkhan*) should also generate [the visualization] of themselves as Amitābha, and the method of consecrating their pens and ink is explained to resemble [the consecration of] a rosary and so forth.[282] It is important that these procedures are unequivocally implemented when commencing work for the first time.

Defining Characteristics of a Patron [a"]

Incidentally, the [potential] faults and virtues of the patrons who commission sacred images are also outlined. The former are described as follows in the *Ocean of Wealth*:[283]

Not avoiding negative actions, and poorly motivated,
Neglectful of benefits and lacking conviction,
Ambitious for fame in this life
Whether having or lacking the will to achieve [the task in hand],

Broad-minded in inappropriate circumstances,
Short-tempered, fickle, and intolerant,
Cursing the deities and the artists,
While interrupting [their projects] out of regret.

It is essential that a [patron] should never possess these faults. As for the latter, [their potential virtues,] the same text says:[284]

They should be endowed with insight that discerns advantages,
Endowed with one-pointed concentration,
Endowed with perseverance that is stable and joyful,
Unmoved by hardships, and tolerant,
Slow-tempered, gentle in speech, and ethically disciplined,
Undeceitful and endowed with generosity,
Full of faith and respect for the deities and the artists,
And they should joyfully meditate in an orderly manner.[285]

It also says in the *Tantra of Acala*:

One who commissions an authentic painting
Should offer whatever fee is requested.

And in the *Tantra of Consecration*:

The being of pristine cognition (*jñānasattva*) will not enter
[The image of] a deity fashioned by an artist who is displeased.[286]
At the start of the consecration, the artist should be pleased.

In many sūtras and tantras such as these the commitment of the patron to satisfy the artist is emphasized. Since to criticize the artist is tantamount to criticizing the deity [he has recreated], it is important that faith and respect should be awarded the artist, like that directed towards a deity, or as if attending upon a [revered] spiritual advisor. Nowadays, though representations of buddha body, speech, and mind are bought and sold, the outcome might still be positive when the artists and their patrons bravely assess the value [of their works], determining the price appropriate in [particular] places and times. However, I would incidentally comment that the kind of salesman's talk in which Newars and Tibetans currently indulge is, by contrast, a causal basis giving rise to serious criminality in respect of both parties.[287]

Iconometric Proportions [2"]

With regard to the second topic, the exegesis of the iconometric proportions of the sacred images or deities that are contained [within the celestial palace], there are two aspects: the painted icons depicting [visualized deities of] meditative commitment and the actual exegesis on iconometry.

Painted Icons Depicting Visualized Deities [a"]

With regard to the former [it says in the root verses]:

> **Painted icons representing [visualized deities] of meditative commitment**
> **That accord with the texts are the best.**

Painted icons (*bris sku*) representing [the visualized deities of] meditative commitment (*dam tshig*), which accord with the texts of their respective tantras, are the best of all images. In chapter six of the second part of the *Tantra of Hevajra* this is explained from the standpoint of the unsurpassed [tantras], in the following verses:[288]

> In this [Hevajra tradition], the painter who maintains the commitments,
> And also the practitioner who maintains the commitments,
> Should create this fearsome icon [of Hevajra].
> Unsurpassed paintings should be created
> With the five colors reposing in a human skull,
> And a brush made from the hair of a corpse.
> Those [assistants] who spin the threads and those who weave the canvases
> Should certainly maintain the same commitments![289]
> In this way, a yogin who maintains the commitments
> And has received the [appropriate] blessings
> [Should proceed] to an isolated place
> At midday on the fourteenth day of the waning moon,
> And in a ferocious state of mind,
> Having consumed a little wine,
> He should visualize the body
> Adorned with human bone ornaments (*niraṃśuka*)

And having removed his clothes,
He should consume the sacraments,
However foul and impure they are,
Having placed to the left side his own female medium (*mudrā*),
She who is of fine complexion, compassionate,
Youthful and auspicious,
Adorned with flowers, and loved by the practitioner.

It is also said that paintings should be executed in accordance with the eloquent explanations given in the *Root Tantra of Mañjuśrī* concerning the very extensive ritual procedures that pertain to the size of the canvases and the painting, as well as to their limitless advantages and benefits.[290]

Furthermore, it is said in the *Tantra of the Emergence of Cakrasaṃvara*:

Novice mantrins should fashion images and so forth.
If they make paintings, they will swiftly
Attain extensive spiritual accomplishments!

The Actual Exegesis on Iconometry [b″]

With regard to the latter, the actual exegesis on iconometry has three parts: (1) the general explanation [of canonical iconometric systems]; (2) the particular explanation [of contemporary iconometric systems]; and (3) the essentials [of iconography] derived from these iconometric systems.

General Explanation of Canonical Iconometric Systems [i″]

First [concerning the general explanation of canonical iconometric systems, it says in the root verses]:

With regard to iconometric proportion, the number of relative finger-widths
Allocated [for buddha images] is one hundred and twenty-five
According to the *Tantra of the Wheel of Time*,
While, according to the *Tantra of the Emergence of Cakrasaṃvara*,
It should be one hundred and twenty.
The [*Tantra of the*] *Four* [*Indestructible*] *Seats* is similar [to the latter],

While the [*Tantras of*] *Red* and *Black* [*Yamāri*] calculate eight face-length measures.
The *Sūtra* [*Requested by Śāriputra*] and [other ancient] Indic texts
Are [generally] in conformity with those [works],
And there are [contemporary] traditions that follow them as well.

The iconometric proportions (*cha tshad*) of icons or images are prescribed in the sūtras and tantras.[291]

According to the *Tantra of the Wheel of Time* [aa"]

In this regard, it is said in the *Wheel of Time*, king of tantras:[292]

> As for [the standing image of the Buddha,] lord among conquerors, [the vertical measurement] from the protuberance on the crown of the head (*uṣṇīsa*) to the hair ringlet between the eyebrows (*ūrṇākeśa*) should be twelve and a half relative finger-widths (*sārdhasūrya, phyed dang bcas pa nyi ma'i sor*).[293]
>
> Then, from that point to the lotus of his throat, and similarly from that point to the heart, and from that point to the lotus of his navel and from there to the genitalia, the measurements are each the same [i.e., 12.5 finger-widths].[294]
>
> The soles of the feet are fourteen (*manu*) fingerwidths [in length and four and a half in height],[295] while the calves, the thighs, the hips and also [the knees][296] are respectively twenty-five (*tattva*), twenty-five (*tattva*), four (*veda*), [and four finger-widths].[297]
>
> [As for the horizontal measurements,] each half of the chest is twelve and a half [finger-widths], while the upper arm, the forearm, [the elbow and wrist] and the hand are respectively twenty (*khākṣi*), sixteen (*rāja*), [two] and twelve (*arka*) [finger-widths].[298]
>
> These one hundred and twenty-five [finger-widths][299] correspond to the mundane [physical] dimensions of human beings of diverse times. However, [the vertical measurements of the Buddha's head are distinctive]: From the protuberance on the crown of his head downwards, as far as the the glorious forehead and nose of the lord among conquerors, and from the nose down to the point of the chin and from there to the center of the lotus at the base of the throat, the measurements are respectively four finger-widths [for the protuberance], four and a half [skull to hairline],[300] four

(*jalanidhi*)[301] [hairline to *ūrṇākeśa*], four [*ūrṇākeśa* to the tip of the nose], four and a half [tip of the nose to the point of the chin], and four [point of the chin to the throat].[302]

The iconometric measurements made in respect of [the Buddha], lord of men, from the throat to the heart, navel, and genitalia, in succession, are each twelve and a half finger-widths.

With these words, [the *Tantra of the Wheel of Time*] clearly mentions only the [overall iconometric scale] of one hundred and twenty-five finger-widths, an interpretation which is found extensively also in the outer and inner virtuous practices (*phyi nang gi dge sbyor*) associated with the maṇḍala [rites of the *Wheel of Time*], and so forth.[303]

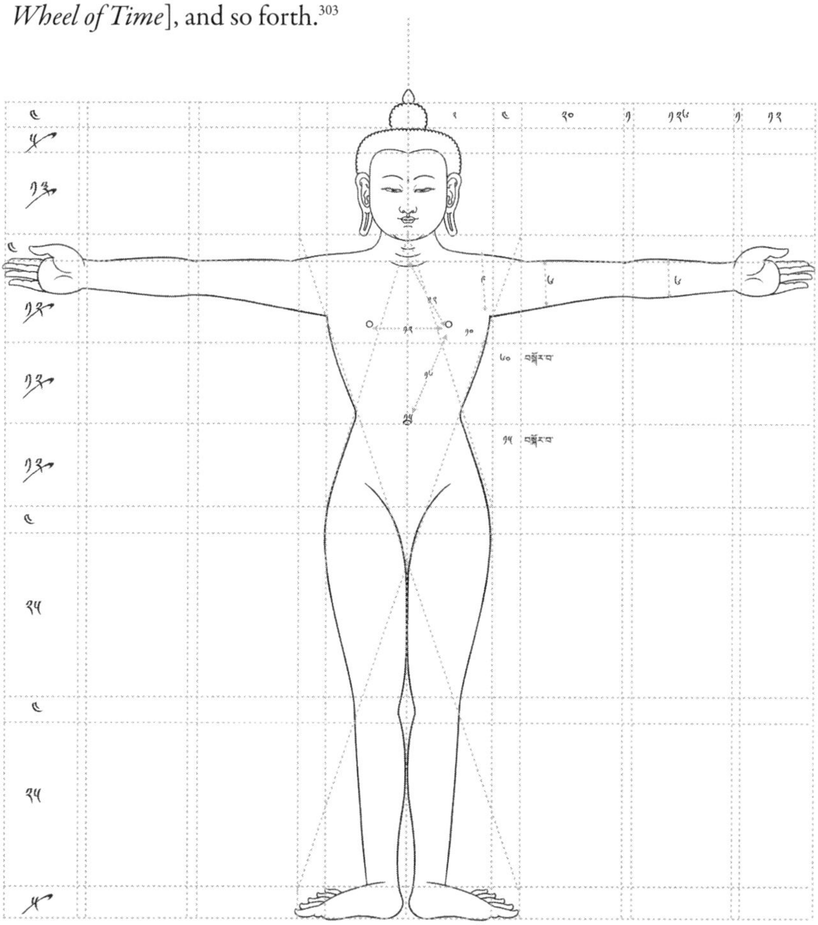

Fig. 4. Iconometry of the buddha body of emanation according to the *Tantra of the Wheel of Time* (scale: 125 *sor*)

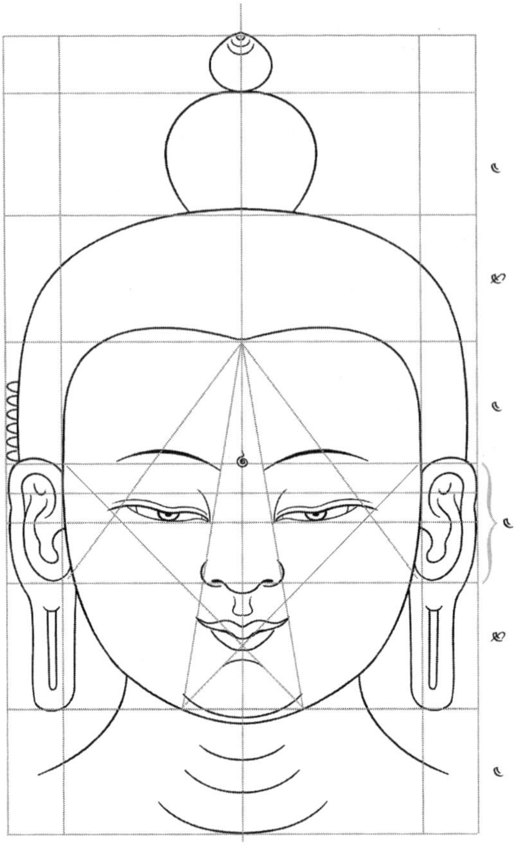

Fig. 5. Iconometry of the head of the buddha body of emanation according to the *Tantra of the Wheel of Time* (scale: 125 *sor*)

According to the *Tantra of the Emergence of Cakrasaṃvara* [bb"]

By contrast, in Chapter Thirty of the [*Tantra of*] *the Emergence of Cakrasaṃvara*, which is an exegetical tantra pertaining to [the cycle of] Cakrasaṃvara, it is said:

> There are measurements and defining characteristics of form [prescribed],
> In respect of the drawn [or painted] images of a deity.[304]
> Before the axial Brahmā lines are formed,[305]
> Five units are [reserved] for the plinth [of the image],
> And the body [of the icon] has three sections...

This passage clearly goes on to mention [the scales] of twelve, ten, and nine relative palm-length measures (*tāla*, *thal mo*) and so forth, which are all based on [an overall iconometric scale comprising] one hundred and twenty finger-widths.[306]

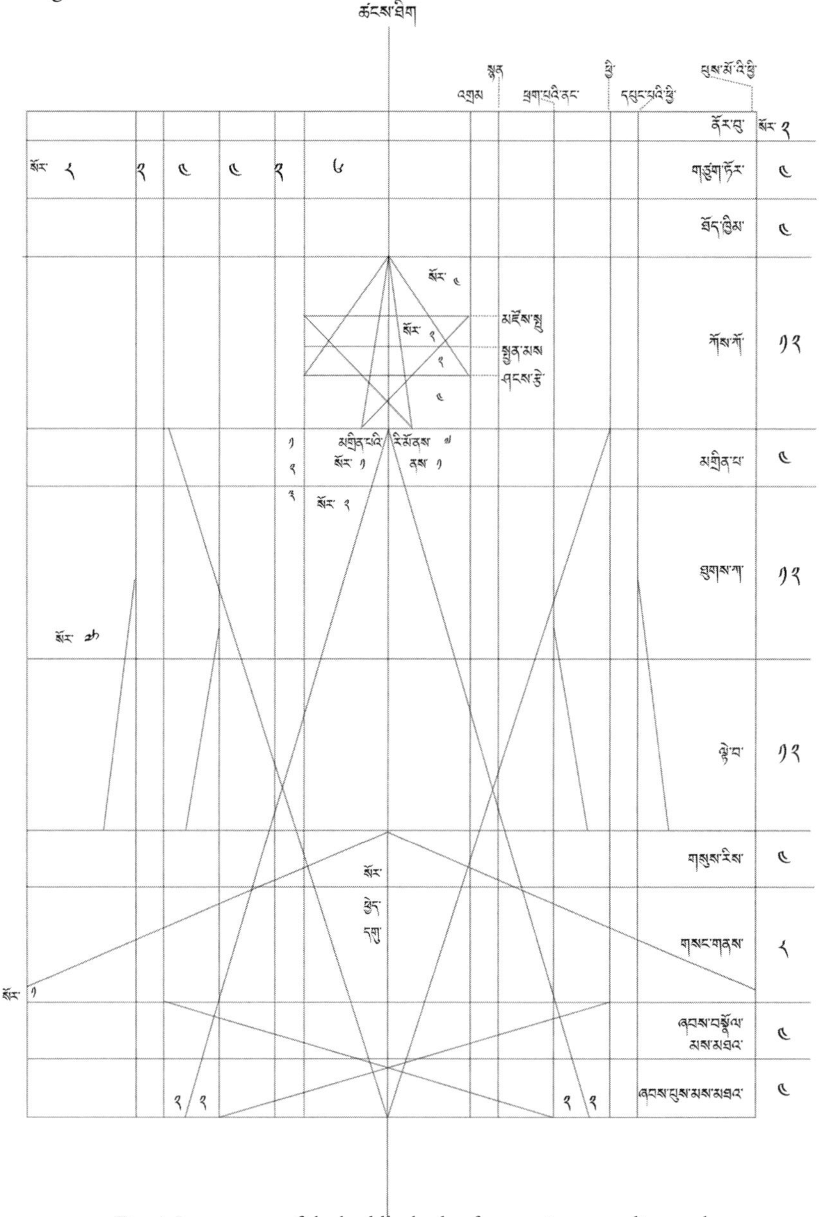

Fig. 6. Iconometry of the buddha body of emanation according to the *Tantra of the Emergence of Cakrasaṃvara* (scale: 120 *sor*)

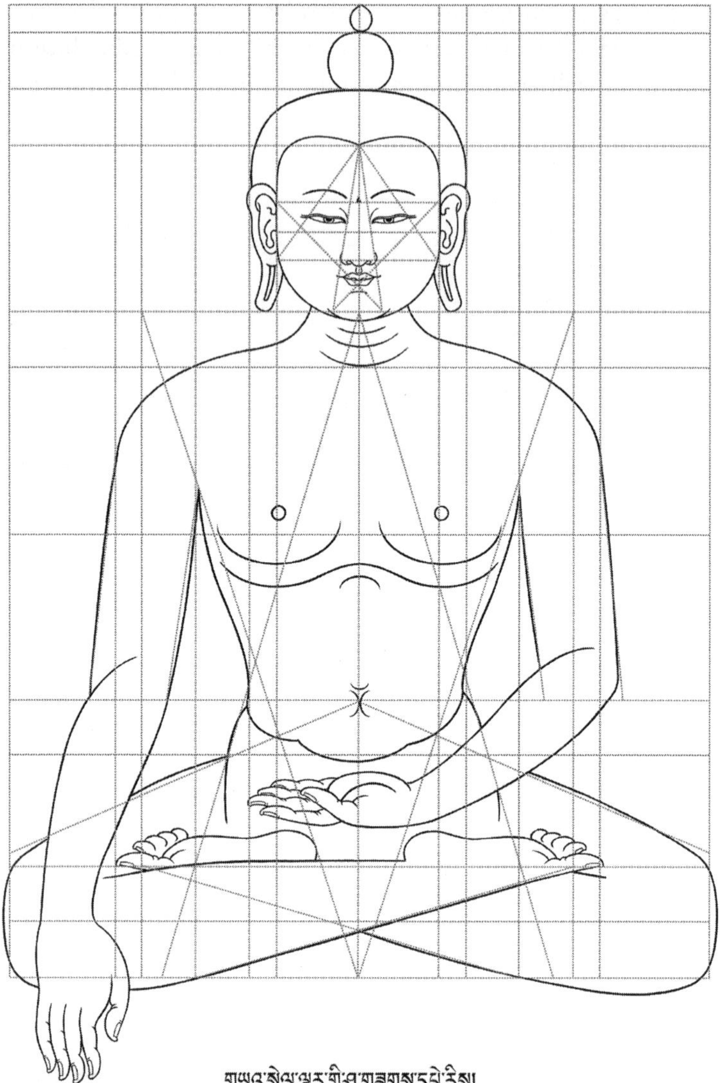

གཡའ་སེལ་ལྷུར་གྱི་ཞ་གཟུགས་དཔེ་རིས།

Fig. 7. The buddha body of emanation according to Desi Sangye Gyatso and the *Tantra of the Emergence of Cakrasaṃvara* (scale: 120 *sor*)

The explanation given in the *Exegetical Tantra of the Four Indestructible Seats: Mantra Section* is mostly similar to this, except for [a few] distinctive variations, and it omits any reference to the scale of nine face-length measures (*zhal tshad*).[307] However, master Ratnarakṣita's "evasive exegesis" (*kyog *bshad*) [on iconometry], contained in his *Lotus Commentary on the Tantra of the Emergence of Cakrasaṃvara*, is incapable of grasping the meaning of that tantra text because his presentation failed to examine [the work of] renowned contemporary Magadhan and Newar artists.[308]

According to the *Yamāri Tantras* [cc"]

A scale of eight face-length measures is mentioned in the *Tantra of Black Yamāri* and in the *Tantra of Red Yamāri*.[309]

According to the *Sūtra Requested by Śāriputra* [dd"]

Moreover, the [iconometric scales] suggested in the *Sūtra Requested by Śāriputra*, certainly in its [earlier] translation based on the Newar manuscript, and also in its later translation, largely conform with those given in the [*Tantra of the*] *Wheel of Time*.[310] The *Compendium of Rituals*[311] also quotes various passages from this same sūtra text.

[It should be pointed out that] there are some citations well known from Indic texts that were prevalent in ancient times, which are in conformity with the aforementioned sources; and where there are slight discrepancies, these are even now discernible in the [contemporary artistic] traditions that follow those [distinctive] tantra texts. It is utterly pointless, therefore, for later scholars [of the present day] to seek to refute any of these [traditions]. For this reason, the venerable Jonang Jetsun Chenpo [Tāranātha] has said:[312]

> The fine arts, the compounding of medicines,
> The rites of the [way of secret] mantra and the profound reality—
> These are not [subjects] to be intellectually scrutinized by sophistry.
> It is right to abandon egotistical assertions and pride.

Five Anthropometric Scales [ee"]

> **Among the five anthropometric scales applied in certain circumstances,**
> **[Including the scale of] twelve and a half finger-widths,**
> **[The scale of] twelve finger-widths, and the palm-length measures,**
> **The first and second accord with the *Wheel of Time***
> **And the *Emergence of Cakrasaṃvara*,**

While the third and fourth comprise the nine and eight palm-length measures.
These all correspond to the actual teachings of the sūtras and tantras,
And painstaking efforts should be made [in applying them].

With regard to the particular terminology of [anthropometric] measurement, twelve and a half or twelve finger-widths (*aṅgulī, rang sor*) are equivalent to one face-length measure (*mukha, zhal tshad*); and [one should know that] the face-length measure itself has five other synonymous terms, including the mid-finger span (*vitasti, mtho*),[313] the palm-length measure (*tāla, thal mo*), the palm or sole measure (*tāla, mthil*), and the large unit (*cha chen*). Different sizes of face-length measure may be applied, according to the circumstances of the two [aforementioned] tantra traditions [those of the *Wheel of Time* and the *Emergence of Cakrasaṃvara*].

A single relative finger-width is also known as a small unit (*plava, cha chung*), one fourth of a [small unit] is known as a quarter (*pada, rkang pa*), and one eighth [of a small unit] is known as a barley grain (*java, nas*).[314]

There are five basic [anthropometric] scales which are to be applied. The first is the measurement [of icons] scaled at one hundred and twenty-five finger-widths and the second is the scale of one hundred and twenty finger-widths, which correspond respectively to the [aforementioned] traditions of the *Wheel of Time* and the *Emergence of Cakrasaṃvara*. The third and fourth are the measurements [of icons] scaled respectively at nine and eight palm-lengths. All these four [anthropometric] scales appropriate for deity icons are actually presented in the sūtras and the tantras; and since these [sources] are uncorrupted with regard to the artistic heritage of the learned, intelligent persons should make painstaking efforts [to master them].[315]

The [first three of these anthropometric scales] are applied, as appropriate,
To the [drawing of] tathāgatas, bodhisattvas,
Wrathful deities, and icons without consort.
The fourth is applied to the most wrathful deities [alone].
The [fifth] is the Tibetan tradition of six mid-finger span measures which emerged later.

The first three of these iconometric scales [respectively comprising 125, 120, and 108 finger-widths] are applied, in the appropriate manner, when drawing male and female tathāgatas, male and female bodhisattvas, and male and female wrathful deities who preside over a maṇḍala, as well as the forms of the supreme buddha body of emanation (*nirmāṇakāya*), which are depicted without consort, and so forth.[316] The fourth category [comprising ninety-six finger-widths] should be applied in respect of extremely wrathful deities, such as Yamāntaka and Vajrapāṇi.[317]

The fifth category represents an [indigenous] tradition associated with the learned and accomplished masters of Tibet that later emerged.[318] It includes the exegetical tradition according to which [protector deities], such as Mahākāla, who assume the forms of intermediaries (*pho nya*) and ogres (*srin po*) are drawn against a scale of [seventy-two relative finger-widths or] six palm-length measures, and another exegetical tradition according to which Mahākāla may also be drawn against a [smaller] scale of three face-length measures.[319] Ratnarakṣita and certain Newar scholars also explain that Gaṇapati and related figures [should be drawn] against a scale of [sixty finger-widths or] five face-length measures.[320]

Since there is no space here to detail the practical application of these [anthropometric scales], those who wish to understand the subject should consult the *Origin of Happiness: A Description of Iconometric Proportions*, which is among the Collected Works of Jetsun [Tāranātha] Rinpoche, and surpasses even ordinary Indic texts.[321] Concerning the application of the [first] four of these scales, this text says:[322]

> There is a similarity between the male and female tathāgatas
> depicted in union,
> And the male and female bodhisattvas depicted in union.
> Since [the latter] are the offspring of the conquerors,
> Born into the buddha family,
> The bodhisattvas and buddhas are similar.
> Therefore, the [first] three iconometric scales
> Are applicable when all the buddhas and bodhisattvas are depicted
> in union.
>
> If one wishes to differentiate between them,
> Since there is a distinction between the slender and stocky
> [physiques],
> Appropriate for the peaceful and wrathful deities respectively,
> The scale of one hundred and twenty-five [finger-widths]
> Applies in the case of peaceful buddhas,

And the scale of one hundred and twenty [finger-widths]
Applies in the case of the [wrathful] herukas,
But there are also certain distinctive features of the glorious bodies of the herukas
That may require them [to be drawn]
Utilizing the scale of eight palm-lengths.[323]

[Female] forms such as Buddhalocanā and Tārā are similar to the peaceful [deities],
While [wrathful female forms such as] Vajravārāhī are similar to the herukas.[324]
Even though these [female forms] lack the crown protuberance (*uṣṇīṣa*),
It is not wrong to include a crown jewel as a substitute.
All female deities should have [the following attributes]
Because they typify the feminine form:
No crown protuberance, but breasts and pudendum,
A slender waist, tapering torso, fullness of the hips and lower body,
Tapering brows, wide sidelong-glancing eyes, and so forth.
The male consorts should be depicted oppositely.

The remainder [of the deities] should be [drawn] along those lines,
And the great bodhisattvas [of the tenth level] are similar,[325]
Whereas the scale of nine mid-finger spans applies to ordinary bodhisattvas,
Mundane peaceful deities such as Śakra,[326]
Emanational wrathful figures [apart from the herukas],
And female deities, conforming to their respective families.[327]
If these [icons] are to be drawn correctly and according to scale,
By following this categorization, the drawing will turn out well.

With regard to the iconometric scale used for depicting human figures which is mentioned in the *Wheel of Time*, although it is applicable for the drawing of pious attendants (*śrāvaka*), it is not included among the categories of iconometric scale appropriate for representing deity [icons].[328] However, since the hermit buddhas (*pratyekabuddha*) are more sublime on account of their [small] crown protuberances, and so forth, they are said to be included among [figures drawn] according to the scale of nine relative palm-lengths.[329]

[The same source] continues:[330]

There are also some individual images which should be depicted
According to their own idiosyncratic forms,
Without the need for conformity in their iconometric proportions.
Iconometric scales are established so as to prevent [the execution of] poor art,
But when works are created by saintly beings
Who have excellently refined their magical skill with respect to the essentials of art,
[The need for such scales] is uncertain.

The Sixfold Typology of Deities [ff"]

As for the typology of the deities, they may be classified as follows:
[Icons depicting] renunciant forms without a consort, universal monarchs,
Peaceful icons without ornaments [including] hermit sages and beings of inferior class,
[Wrathful] buddhas, emanational wrathful forms, and kings among wrathful deities,
Supreme and common bodhisattvas, servants, and intermediaries.

Although the deities that may be analyzed in accordance with these iconometric scales have many aspects, when [the correct] typology is formally applied, they are [generally] classified as follows:

(1) icons depicting renunciant forms, without a consort (*chags bral*);
(2) peaceful and ornate icons depicting universal monarchs (*'khor los sgyur ba*);
(3) peaceful icons without ornaments (*zhi ba rgyan med*), including those depicting hermit sages (*ṛṣi, drang srong*) and those depicting beings of inferior class (*rigs ngan tshul*);
(4) wrathful buddhas or herukas, including Cakrasaṃvara, Hevajra and Kālacakra;[331]
(5) wrathful deities drawn against a scale of nine palm-lengths, including the ordinary emanational wrathful forms (*rol pa'i khro bo*) or the wrathful aspects of bodhisattvas,[332] and the kings among wrathful deities (*khro bo'i rgyal po*), such as Black Yamāri, Red Yamāri, Vajrabhairava, and Hayagrīva;[333]
(6) supreme bodhisattvas, such as the "eight closest sons" (*nye sras brgyad*), including Mañjughoṣa, Avalokiteśvara, and Samantabhadra,[334] along

> with their particular retinues—the peaceful male and female icons that comprise common bodhisattvas (*byang sems phal pa*), servants (*phyag brnyan*), and intermediaries (*pho nya*), including [the protectors of the sacred teachings] Mahākāla and the goddess Rematī.[335]

The term "hermit sage" (*drang srong*) is [in this context] a synonym or epithet of buddha, and therefore denotes a "wrathful buddha." Although Tibetans hold that the other [lesser] wrathful figures, including wrathful *yakṣas* (*gnod sbyin khros pa*), wrathful ogres (*rākṣasa, srin po khros pa*), and wrathful acolytes of Yama (*gshin rje khros pa*),[336] should all have different demeanors according to their respective classifications, it is said that [traditionally] this is not certain.[337]

Contemporary Iconometric Systems [ii"]

Second, concerning the particular explanation [of contemporary iconometric systems, it says in the root verses]:

> **However, among well-known contemporary [traditions],**
> **[Including] those that identify eleven distinct iconometric scales,**
> **All of them concur that the axial lines of Brahmā are drawn first.**
> **Then, [as for the elevenfold classification,] this comprises**
> **[Renunciant buddhas] without a consort,**
> **And the buddha body of perfect resource,**
> **Which are scaled at one hundred and twenty-five finger-widths;**
> **Bodhisattvas scaled at one hundred and twenty [finger-widths];**
> **Wrathful hermit sages scaled at twelve palm-lengths;**
> **Female consorts scaled at nine palm-lengths;**
> **Acolytes of Yama and yakṣas scaled at eight [palm-lengths];**
> **Ogre-like wrathful deities scaled at six, five, or three [palm-lengths];**
> **Pious attendants and hermit buddhas who are similar in scale to human figures;**
> **[Mundane protectors] such as Brahmā, scaled at nine large units;**
> **And human beings of the four continents,**
> **Scaled at seven mid-finger spans in length, and eight in width.**
> **All such measurements are said to depend**
> **On the degree to which the vital energy of past actions is impeded.**

Although there are some standard but obsolete [iconometric] techniques which were once widespread [in Tibet], nowadays all practical styles of painting and sculpture reflect two [surviving contemporary] traditions—the Encampment style (*sgar lugs*) and the Menri style (*sman gyi lugs*).[338]

The former holds, in accordance with the venerable lord of the teachings [Buton] Rinchendrub [1290–1364] and others, that there are eleven categories of iconometric scale (*cha tshad bcu gcig*), while the latter is well known for the classification known as the eight great iconometric scales (*thig chen brgyad*).[339] All sources, however, concur that the vertical and horizontal axial lines of Brahmā (*tshangs thig*) should first be drawn.[340]

Eleven Iconometric Scales of the Encampment Style [aa"]

Then, as for the eleven [iconometric] scales [of the Encampment style]:

(1) The first includes the [renunciant and emanational] forms of the Buddha, depicted without a consort.

(2) The second includes the buddha bodies of perfect resource, comprising the [buddhas of] the five enlightened families. These two classes are drawn against a scale of one hundred and twenty-five finger-widths.[341]

(3) The third category includes peaceful bodhisattvas who are [drawn against a scale] of one hundred and twenty finger-widths.[342]

(4) The fourth includes hermit sages of wrathful demeanor, including Kālacakra, which are [drawn against a scale] of twelve palm-lengths [i.e., 125 finger-widths].[343]

(5) The fifth includes the queens presiding over the maṇḍala, such as the various female consorts [of the five buddhas], as well as female consorts associated with the families [in the four directions of the maṇḍala], exemplified by the deity Tārā, which are all attractively [drawn against a scale] of nine palm-lengths [i.e., 108 finger-widths].[344]

(6) The sixth includes the wrathful acolytes of Yama, headed by Yamāntaka.

(7) The seventh includes the wrathful yakṣas, headed by Vajrapāṇi. These last two classes are both to be drawn against a scale of eight palm-lengths [i.e., 96 finger-widths].[345]

(8) The eighth includes the ogre-like wrathful deities, which have three subdivisions. Among them, [the first] refers to this tradition [of ours] which holds that [the protectors] such as Bhagavān Mahākāla are scaled at six palm-lengths [i.e., 72 finger-widths],[346] as explained in the commentaries on *Black Yamāri*.

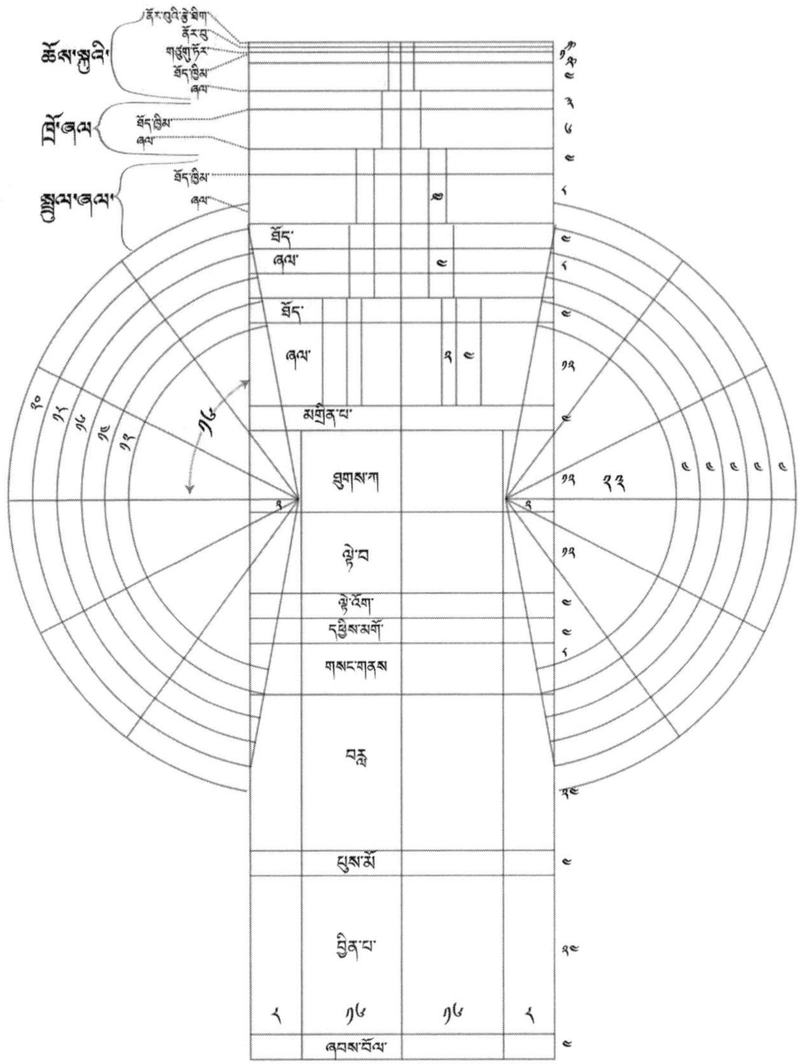

Fig. 8. Iconometry of the standing bodhisattva Mahākāruṇika

Fig. 9. Iconometry of the seated bodhisattva Amitāyus (scale: 120 *sor*)

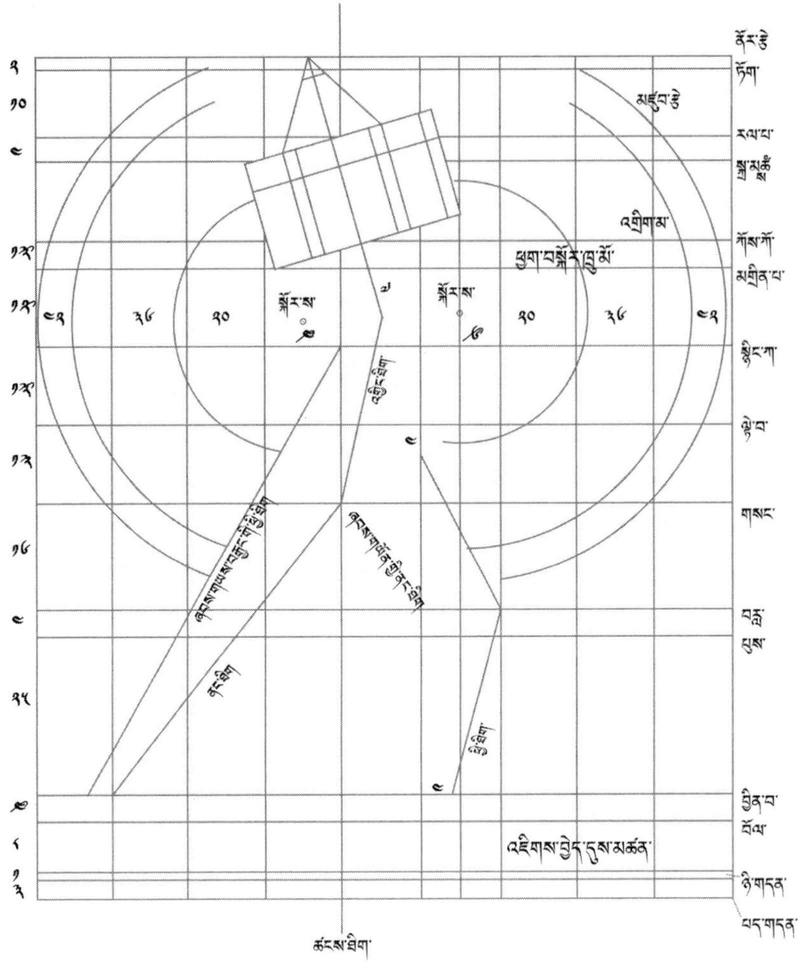

Fig. 10. Iconometry of the wrathful Cakrasaṃvara (scale: 125 *sor*)

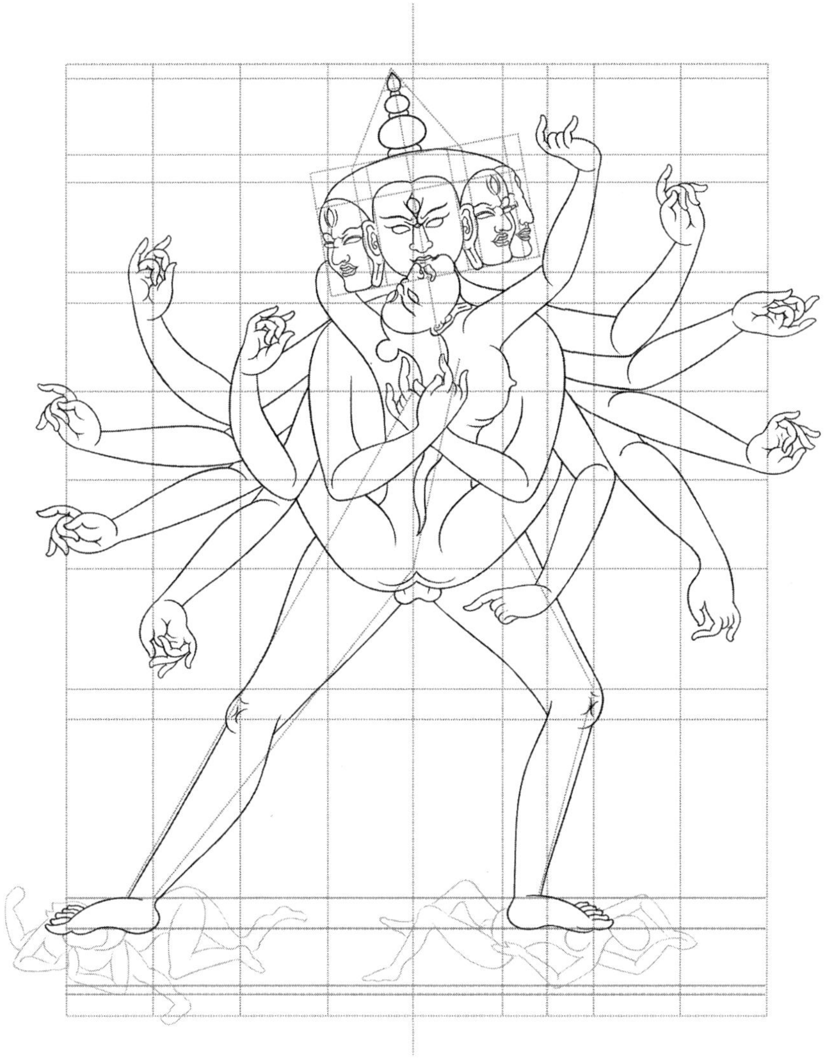

Fig. 11. Cakrasaṃvara (scale: 125 *sor*)

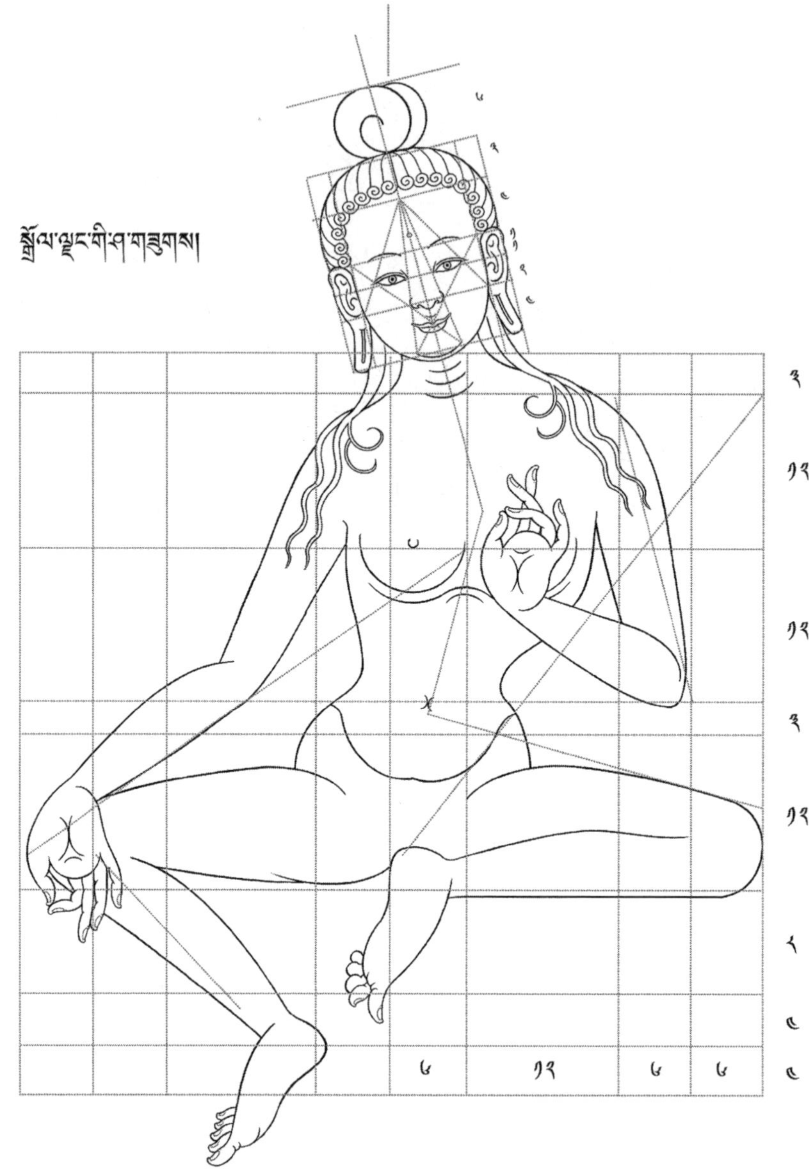

Fig. 12. Iconometry of the female deity Tārā

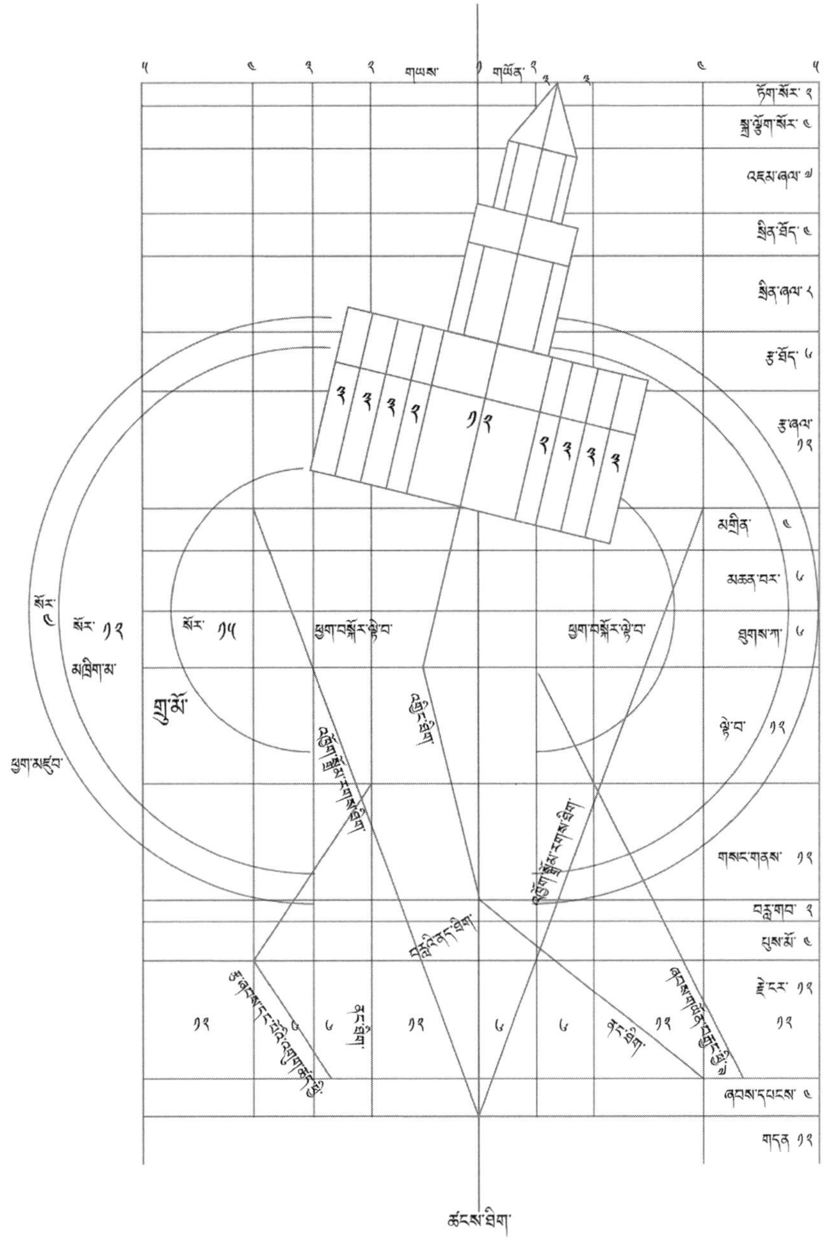

Fig. 13. Iconometry of Vajrabhairava

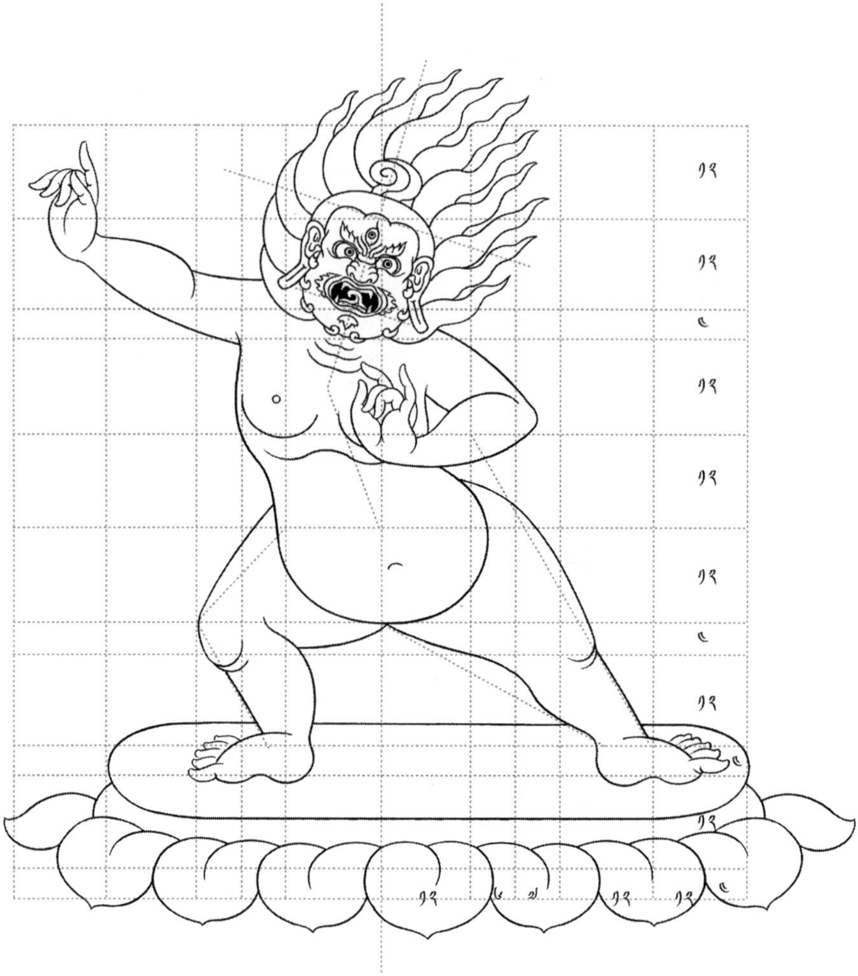

Fig. 14. Iconometry of Vajrapāṇi (scale: 96 *sor*)

[The second] refers to dwarf-like figures such as Gaṇapati, which are [drawn against a scale] of five mid-finger-spans [i.e., 60 finger-widths].[347]

The third refers to the most wrathful of deities, such as those that are based upon the vision of Dorje Berchen, which have a scale of three face-length measures [i.e., 36 finger-widths].[348]

(9) The ninth category includes pious attendants and hermit buddhas, which are [drawn] similar [in scale] to the humans of this continent [i.e., 96 finger-widths].[349]

(10) The tenth includes mundane protectors (*laukikadharmapāla, 'jig rten skyong ba*), such as Brahmā and Śakra, which are [drawn against a scale] of nine large units [i.e., 108 finger-widths].[350]

(11) [Finally], the eleventh category [of iconometric proportion] includes the dimensions of the human figures of the four continents who, according to the *Wheel of Time* and the master Śūra, are said to be drawn on a scale of seven mid-finger spans [i.e., 84 finger-widths] in height and eight mid-finger spans [i.e., 96 finger-widths] in width because their height and width are unequal.[351]

There are some who hold the opposite view, asserting that [human figures] are of equal height and width, and that the spiritual teachers (*guru, bla ma*) who have assumed human form should be depicted as if they were [divine] images, corresponding to their own physiognomy. However, it is certainly ascertained from the indestructible buddha speech of Kyopa Jigten Sumgon [of Drigung] [1143–1217] that the physical form of an authentic root spiritual teacher (*mūlaguru, rtsa ba'i bla ma*) which is introduced to [the practitioner's] own mind as the buddha, should be drawn in accordance with the iconometric proportions of the body of a perfect buddha.[352]

It should be understood in detail from the *Mirror of Great Sunlight* composed by the venerable [Karmapa] VIII[353] and other sources that the iconometric proportions of all sculptures (*'bur sku*) are generally identical to those of painted icons (*bris sku*) but that additional calculations are to be made in respect of the figures forming the retinue, to the front and the rear [of the central statue].[354]

Eight Great Iconometric Scales of Menla Dondrub [bb"]

The second [contemporary] tradition is the systematic presentation subsumed in the eight great iconometric scales, the techniques of which accord

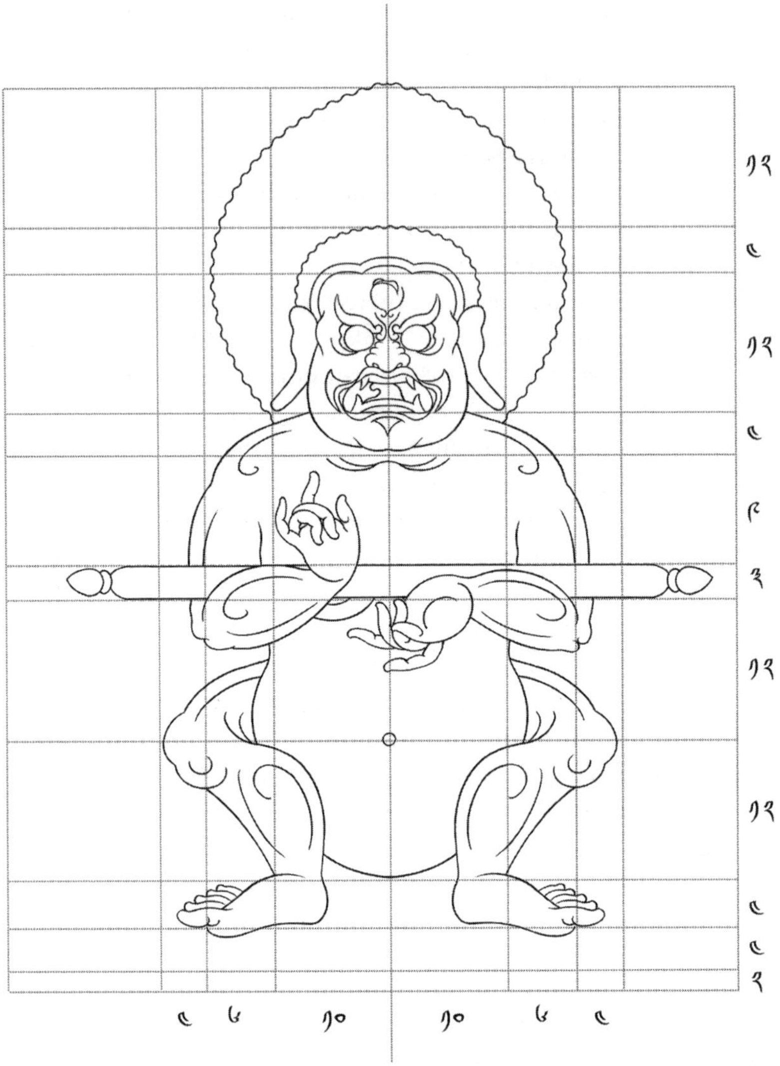

Fig. 15. Iconometry of Pañjaranātha Mahākāla (scale: 72 *sor*)

Fig. 16. Iconometry of Gaṇapati (scale: 60 *sor*)

Above:
Fig. 17. Iconometry of Mahākāla in the form Dorje Berchen (scale: 36 *sor*)

Opposite:
Fig. 18. Iconometry of pious attendants/ hermit buddhas (scale: 96 *sor*) and human beings (imbalanced scale: 84 *sor*)

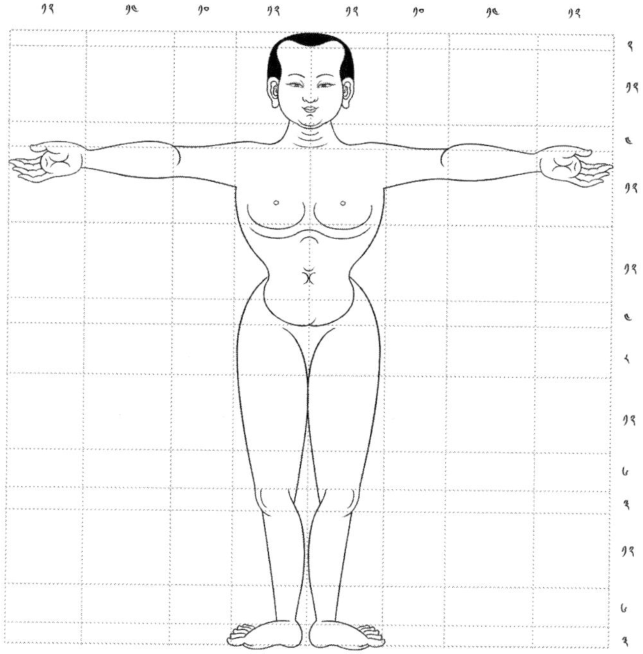

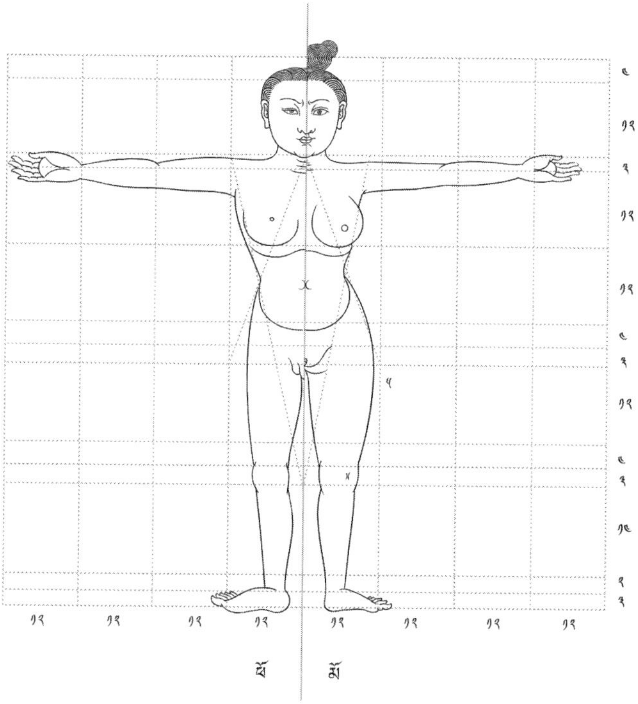

with the *Wish-fulfilling Jewel of Iconometry*, composed by Menla Dondrub [fl. late fifteenth century].[355] Since the *Removal of the Tarnish [of Deluded Appearances]* and the other works which include incidental instructions on many distinctive points derived from that system are detailed and extensive, I will not digress here.[356]

It is also said that the [actual] measurement of the relative palm-length and finger-width can be distinguished by degrees, depending on whether the vital energy of past actions (*karmavāyu, las rlung*) is impeded within the central channel (*avadhūti, dbu ma*) of the subtle body or not.[357]

Essential Elements of Iconography [iii"]

Third, the systematic explanation of the essential elements [of iconography] that evolved on the basis of these [iconometric traditions] consists of the following seven topics: demeanors, ornaments, symbolic hand-held emblems, thrones and backrests, corrections, colors and shadings, and stylistic features.

Demeanors [aa"]

Regarding the first of these [iconic demeanor, *nyams*, it says in the root verses]:

> **[Icons should be depicted with] the major and minor marks,**
> **Or they should be peaceful, amorous, wrathful, graceful,**
> **Or expressive of the dramatic airs.**

Among all these [aforementioned] categories of icon, the aspects of the buddha body of perfect resource and the buddha body of emanation should all be clearly and perfectly drawn, explicitly on the basis of the thirty-two major marks (*dvātriṃśanmahāpuruṣalakṣaṇa, mtshan bzang so gnyis*) and the eighty minor marks (*asītyānuvyañjana, dpe byad brgyad cu*) that characterize them.[358] The tathāgatas and so forth should be peaceful and endowed with a smiling radiance. The female deities should, for the most part, be amorous and youthful. The wrathful deities should be awesome and unpleasant.

[In particular,] the emanational wrathful deities (*rol pa'i khro bo*) and so forth should have a demeanor that is [simultaneously] wrathful, smiling, and graceful. Furthermore, they should also be depicted expressing the nine dramatic airs (*navanāṭyarasa, gar gyi nyams dgu*), that is to say, they should be (1) graceful (*śṛṅgāra, sgeg pa*) on account of their ornaments and radiance; (2) heroic (*vīra, dpa' ba*) on account of their display of dignity; (3) ugly (*bībhatsa, mi sdug pa*) on account of their menacing stares and frowns; (4) jovial (*hāsya, dgod pa*) on account of their smiles and bursts of laughter (*ha ha'i sgra*); (5) fierce (*raudra, drag shul*) on account of their thunderous exclamation of HI HI and HŪṂ PHAṬ; (6) fearsome (*bhayānaka, 'jigs su rung ba*) on account of the gnashing of their teeth, the bowing of their heads, and the brandishing of their weapons; (7) compassionate (*karuṇā, snying rje*) on account of the blinking of their red eyes and their youthfulness; (8) awesome (*adbhūta, rngam pa*) on account of the radiance of their faces and their clicking of the palate; and (9) peaceful (*śānta, zhi ba*) on account of their supple, slender, and gentle eyes that are focused on the tip of the nose.

All the [emanational wrathful deities] should be depicted by the artist on the basis of these nine dramatic airs.[359]

Moreover, it is said:[360]

> There are four sorts of facial physiognomy:
> [The faces] of saintly male figures and female deities
> Respectively have the shape of a hen's egg and a sesame seed.

And:

> As for the [facial] moods or physiognomy of the wrathful deities,
> They are round and square.[361]

The facial physiognomy (*zhal dbyibs*) [of these categories of deities] will differ accordingly.[362]

Then, with regard to the different shapes of their eyes, it is said:[363]

> The eyes of the buddha figure, seated in meditative equipoise,
> Have the shape of a bow, a cowrie shell, or the shape of a lotus petal.
> Like a lily are the eyes of a semi-wrathful deity.
> The eyes of a peaceful female deity resemble a fish's stomach,
> While the eyes of a courtesan resemble a bamboo bow,
> And the eyes of an extremely wrathful deity are round or square.[364]

Then, with regard to the distinctive postures of their legs and so forth, it is said:[365]

> The posture of indestructible reality (*vajraparyaṅka, rdo rje skyil krung*)
> That is universally known
> Requires the left calf to be folded over the right,

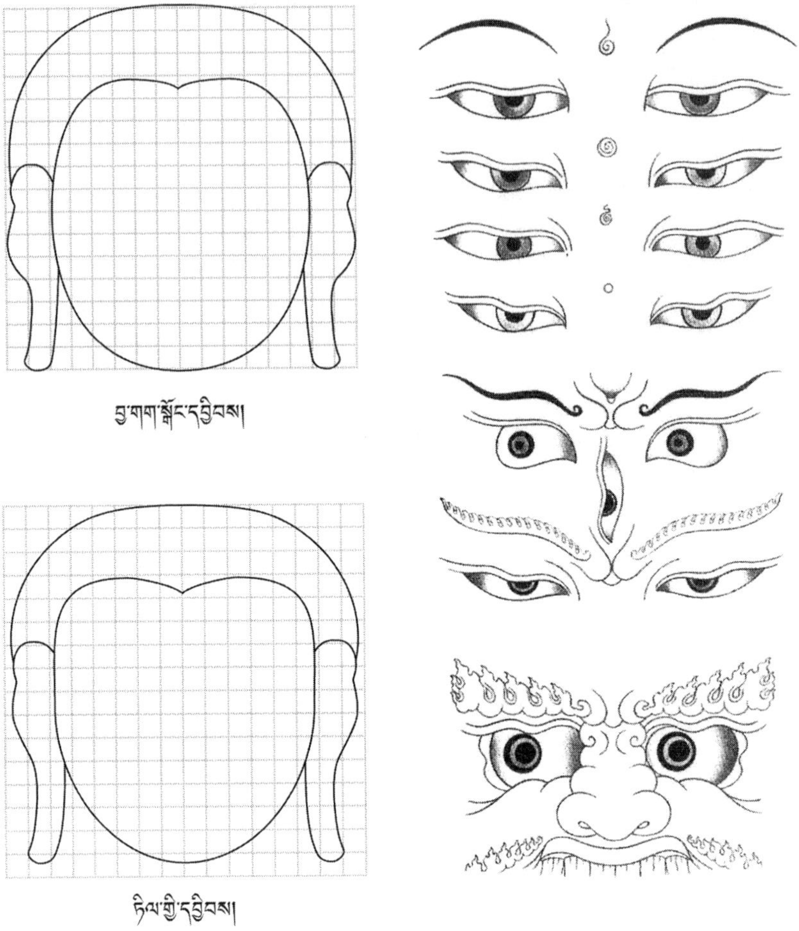

Fig. 19. Male and female facial representations, along with peaceful and wrathful eyes

The legs below the knees then assume the lotus position,
With the ankles crossed,
While it is also said that [in certain instances]
The tips of the big toes may even touch.

When the right leg is in the posture of indestructible reality
And the left leg is folded under the right thigh,
This is called the posture of the bodhisattvas (*sattvaparyaṅka, sems dpa'i skyil krung*).

When the toes of the [contracted] left leg, facing upwards,
Almost but do not quite touch the right thigh,
And the right leg is haughtily extended,
This is called the semi cross-legged posture (*ardhaparyaṅka, skyil krung phyed pa*).

When the left leg is extended,
With the ball of the foot supported on the ground,
And the sole of the right foot positioned at the left thigh,
This is the dancing posture of standing on one leg (*ardhaparyaṅkapratyālīḍha, bzhengs pa'i phyed skyil gar stabs*).

When the calf of the left leg is contracted,
And the right leg assumes an [outstretched] elegant dancing step,
This is the extended right leg posture (*ālīḍha, gYas brkyang*),
And the opposite is the extended left leg posture (*pratyālīḍha, gYon brkyang*).

When the body is standing upright,
With the thighs and calves extending one cubit and two finger-widths,
As far as the heels, with the toes pointing outwards,
This is the [nativity] posture of Vaiśākha (*vaiśākhapada, sa ga'i stabs*).

When, on that basis, the lower limbs of the body [bend] two cubits,
As far as the knees, so as to resemble the wings of a swan,
This is called the squatting posture (*parimaṇḍala, logs su brkyangs pa zlum po*).

When the body is standing upright
With the ten toes aligned together, in front,
This is the posture of balance (*sampada, mnyam pa'i stabs*).

When both legs extend down from the [teaching] throne,
With the toes pointing outwards,
This is the auspicious seated posture [of Maitreya] (*bhadrapada, bzang po'i stabs*).

When the soles of the feet are touching together firmly (*bde legs can*),
And the two legs assume a seated position,
A full palm-width [above the ground],
This is the crouching posture (*tsog bu'i stabs*).

When the toes of the right foot are in the semi cross-legged posture,
And pressing against the ankle of the [extended] left foot,
This is the left-sided [posture] of royal ease (*rājalalita, gYon rol*),
And the right-sided posture of royal ease (*ardhaparyaṅkalalita, gYas rol*) is the opposite.
These [terms] can also be applied when standing upright.

When the left leg is in the semi cross-legged position,
And the extended knee of the right leg almost touches it,
This is called the hero's posture (*vīralīla, dpa' bo'i sdug stangs*).

When the left leg is in the same position,
And the right knee is crossed over it,
So that the thighs of both the left and right legs rest upon the soles,
This is called the heroine's posture (*vīrālīla, dpa' mo'i sdug stangs*).

I shall not digress here, upon other contorted postures,
Such as the [bow-legged] "turtle" posture (*kūrmabandha, rus sbal*)
And the "fly" posture (*bung ba'i stabs*).[366]

One should understand, therefore, that there are exceedingly many [aspects of demeanor], including these postures of the legs [that can be depicted].

Ornaments [bb"]

Regarding the second topic [ornaments (*rgyan*), it says in the root verses]:

> **[Icons may also be adorned with] religious robes,**
> **The eight ornaments made of precious gems,**
> **And two kinds of silken clothes,**
> **With [hand] gestures and**
> **The eight or ten categories of glorious charnel ground accoutrements...**

Icons representing the buddha body of emanation, which is [renunciant and] without a consort, are depicted wearing the three kinds of religious robe (*chos gos gsum*) [i.e., the upper and lower robes and *saṅghāṭī* of a Buddhist monk].

Those representing the buddha body of perfect resource wear the eight ornaments made of precious gemstones (*rin po che'i rgyan brgyad*), namely, the crown (*dbu rgyan*), earrings (*snyan rgyan*), neck-band (*mgul rgyan*), shoulder-straps (*dpung rgyan*), mid-length necklace (*do shal*), long necklace (*se mo do*), bracelets (*gdu bu*), and girdle (*ska rags*) or its tassles (*'og pag*), which are also called the primary ornaments (*rtsa ba'i rgyan*) [of the buddha body of perfect resource]. In addition, there are the lily-shaped earrings (*snyan gong utpala*), anklets (*rkang gdub*), small tinkling bells (*gYer kha*) and so forth, which are known as the subsidiary ornaments (*nye ba'i rgyan*).[367]

[Elsewhere] it has been said:[368]

> With regard to these [ornaments], the scholars of the past hold
> That the earrings, the neck-band, and the bracelets
> Should be of similar weight,
> While the crown, shoulder-straps, anklets, and girdle (*sked*)
> Should also be of a similar [weight].

Concerning the two kinds of silken garment (*dar gos gnyis*), these comprise the upper robe or jacket (*stod gYogs*) and the lower robe or skirt (*smad sham*), whereas in the transmitted oral teachings (*bka' ma*) of the Nyingma school,[369] the enumeration of five silken garments (*dar gyi chas gos lnga*) is well known. These comprise the [patterned] silken scarf (*zi ldir*), the [five-colored] silken crown-pendants (*cod pan*), the long silken dance sleeves (*gar gyi phu rung*), the silken undergarment (*gsang khebs*), and the silken skirt (*tshi gu'i smad dkris*).[370]

Fig. 20. The buddha body of emanation (*nirmāṇakāya*) wearing the three monastic robes

Fig. 21. The buddha body of perfect resource (*saṃbhogakāya*), replete with the eight gemstone ornaments

Fig. 22. Silken garments worn by the buddha body of perfect resource

Then, according to the class of tantra texts that emphasize the [approach of] the Mother Tantras (*ma rgyud*), the male deities are endowed with the so-called six seals (*phyag rgya drug*), namely, a bone wheel (*rus pa'i 'khor lo*) with a half-vajra crest on the crown of their heads, earrings, neck-band, bracelets, girdle, and the thread of Brahmā (*tshangs skud*) or thread of sacrificial investiture (*yajñopavīta, mchod phyir thogs*).[371] Similarly, the female deities should be adorned with five of these seals, excluding the thread of Brahmā.[372]

The dimensions and [prerequisite] purity of these [ornaments] are also mentioned in the *Tantra of the Habitual Practice of the Yoginī* and the [*Tantra of*] *the Indestructible Sky-farers*.

In general the wrathful deities are endowed with the eight accoutrements of the charnel ground (*dur khrod kyi chas brgyad*).[373] These comprise the three garments to be worn (*bgo ba'i gos gsum*), namely, a flayed human hide (*mi lpags kyi gYang gzhi*), the fresh hide of an elephant (*glang chen gyi ko rlon*), and a skirt of tiger skin (*stag lpags kyi sham thabs*),[374] as well as the two ornaments to be affixed (*gdags pa'i rgyan gnyis*), namely, snakes (*sbrul*) and skulls (*thod pa*). Among them, [the snakes] form a white-spotted crown ornament symbolizing the kingly class (*kṣatrīyavarṇa, rgyal rigs*), yellow-spotted earrings symbolizing the mercantile class (*vaiśyavarṇa, rje'u rigs*), a red-spotted neckband symbolizing the priestly class (*brāhmaṇavarṇa, bram ze'i rigs*), and a black-spotted girdle symbolizing the laboring class (*śudravarṇa, dmangs rigs*). They also form green-spotted bracelets and anklets symbolizing the outcastes (*caṇḍāla, gdol rigs*).[375] Crown ornaments are also formed of dry human skulls, side-bands (*se ral kha*) of fresh human skulls, and bandoleers of [human skull] fragments.[376] Lastly, there are the three sacraments to be smeared upon [the body, *byug pa'i rdzas gsum*]: the eyebrows are smeared with pinches of human ashes (*thal chen*), the cheeks are smeared with drops of human blood (*rakta*), and the throat is smeared with markings of human fat (*zhag*).[377]

Fig. 23. Ornaments and garb of the wrathful deities:
the eight accoutrements of the charnel ground

The eight glorious accoutrements (*dpal gyi chas brgyad*), which are known within the Nyingma tradition, are enumerated as follows:[378]

The accoutrement of a glorious sea-monster hide,
Blazing with magnificence;
The accoutrements of sun and moon discs,
Union of skillful means and discriminative awareness;
The accoutrement of the fire of pristine cognition,
Incinerating venomous beings;
The accoutrements of their crescent-shaped fangs,
Eradicating birth and death;
The accoutrements of their indestructible wings,
Pervasive and fulfilling aspirations;
The accoutrement of their indestructible garments,[379]
Perfecting all dominion;
The accoutrement of their rhino-hide armor,
With power to reach the buddha level;
And the accoutrement of their iron discus
Averting harmful and venomous spirits.[380]

This enumeration expands to the ten glorious accoutrements (*dpal gyi chas bcu*) with the addition of two insignia [that are drawn] on the lower robe, namely, the half-vajra crown emblem (*spyi gtsug rdo rje phyed pa*) indicative of the unchanging [reality], and the ritual spike (*phur bu*) that pulverizes venomous spirits. The former [enumeration of eight] is mentioned in the *Tantra of the Flash of the Splendor* [*of Pristine Cognition*] and the latter is emphasized in the *Eight Transmitted Teachings*. Between these [descriptions], therefore, there are some slight discrepancies.

Hand Emblems [cc"]

Regarding the third topic [symbolic hand-held emblems (*cinha, phyag mtshan*), it says in the root verses]:

. . . As well as the vajra, *khaṭvāṅga*, and so forth,
Which are foremost among the symbolic hand-held emblems.

There are many explanations that seek to classify the hand-held emblems associated with the multi-armed central deities, in maṇḍalas such as the [*Tan-*

Fig. 24. Yangdak Heruka, displaying most of the eight glorious accoutrements, according to the Nyingma tradition

tra of the] *Ocean of Sky-farers*, but when these are somewhat abridged, for illustrative purposes, with respect to the vajra (*rdo rje*), the *khaṭvāṅga*, and so forth, which are the primary hand emblems of the central [Heruka], it is said:[381]

As for the vajra which is the foremost of the symbolic hand-held
emblems,
The four side-prongs of the reddish [bronze] vajra,
That is associated with wrathful deities,

Are splayed out in the four directions,
Not quite touching the central [axial prong].[382]

The *khaṭvāṅga* staff has a vajra, [surmounting] three human heads,
[Below which are] a vase, a crossed vajra, and the handle,
Its length equaling that of the body [of the deity];
Silken streamers, a bell, and a hand-drum are suspended from it.[383]

The club (*ga da'i dbyug pa*) and the fox-skin bow (*va gzhu*)
With its far-reaching arrow (*dpag chen mda'*) are similarly [ornate].[384]

The ritual dart (*bhindipāla*) and the sharp-pointed spear (*mdung*)
Have a handle [decorated] with a plume of peacock feathers.[385]

The five-pointed vajra (*rdo rje rtse lnga*) has closed side-prongs,[386]
The *ekasūcikavajra* and the short harpoon (*kaṇaya*) both have single-pointed vajras.[387]

The hand-held skull-drum (*ḍamaru*),
Fashioned of the upper portions of [two human] skulls,
May have or lack hanging valances.[388]

[Other hand-held emblems] include the sword (*ral gri*), the sharp knife (*chu gri*),
The spear-flag (*peṭaka*), the curved knife (*gri gug*),
The battle-axe (*dgra ste*), and the wooden pestle (*gtun shing*),[389]
The long spear, the pike, and the shield[390]—these three,
The copper trumpet (*bho kang*),[391] the kettledrum (*rdza rnga*),
The round drum (*rnga zlum*), the large drum (*rnga chen*),
The *ḍāka* drum, the *paṭaha* drum,[392]
The vajra and bell,[393] and so forth.

Fig. 25. Twenty-two assorted hand-held emblems

Thrones and Backrests [dd"]

Regarding the fourth topic [thrones and backrests (*khri rgyab*), it says in the root verses]:

> **There are seven aspects to the construction of a throne or palanquin,**
> **[Which symbolize respectively the seven] categories of the branches of enlightenment,**
> **While the six ornaments of the backrest symbolize**
> **The six transcendental perfections, and so forth.**

With regard to the teaching-throne (*gdan khri*) and its backrest (*rgyab yol*), as explained in the *Tantra That Completely Apprehends the Attributes of a Spiritual Teacher*, there are seven aspects to the construction of a teaching-throne or palanquin (*khri 'gyogs*), namely, the throne seat (*khri gdan*), the throne front (*khri gdong*), the throne legs (*khri rkang*), the two throne supports (*khri rmang*), the pedestal (*ba gam*), and the railings (*lan kan*).[394]

[More specifically], the supporting [animal figurines]—(1) lion, (2) elephant, (3) peacock, and (4) *cīvaṃcīvaka*—along with the (5) sun, (6) moon, and (7) lotus cushions are imbued respectively with (1) the ten powers (*stobs bcu*), (2) the ten dominions (*dbang bcu*), (3) the [four higher transcendental perfections] from aspiration (*smon lam*) to pristine cognition (*ye shes*), (4) the branches of enlightenment (*byang chub kyi phyogs*), (5) the ultimate reality (*don dam e*), (6) relative appearances (*kun rdzob vaṃ*), and (7) the enlightened attributes that are untainted by the three obscurations (*sgrib gsum gyis ma gos pa'i yon tan*).[395]

The essential nature of the six transcendental perfections (*phyin drug*) is symbolized by the six ornaments of the backrest (*khri rgyab rgyan drug*). These comprise (1) the garuḍa (*mkha' lding*), (2) the sea monsters (*chu srin*), (3) the children (*byis pa*), (4) the elephants (*glang po che*), (5) Śarabha (*bse kha sgo*) [the eight-footed king of deer],[396] and (6) the youthful serpentine water spirits (*klu phrug*), which are imbued respectively with the six transcendental perfections (*pha rol du phyin pa drug*), in reverse order, namely, (1) discriminative awareness (*shes rab*), (2) meditative concentration (*bsam gtan*), (3) perseverance (*brtson 'grus*), (4) patience (*bzod pa*), (5) ethical discipline (*tshul khrims*), and (6) generosity (*sbyin pa*).[397]

The expression "and so forth" (*sogs*) here refers to more elaborate [constructions], including thrones with twenty-one tiers.

Fig. 26. Teaching-throne with seven distinctive features and ornamental backrest

There are also many categories of backrest—elaborate, middling, and simple. These include the elaborate form when the lower part [of the backrest] is woven in an [oval] shield-like design (*phub la zhol btags pa*), the middling form [of backrest] that resembles a lotus petal, and the simplest form which [may have an oblong shape] resembling the best sheet metal (*lcags rtse ma*), or a [semi-circular shape] resembling a hedgehog (*sgang gzugs ma*), and so forth. The middling sort is detailed in Taktsang Lotsāwa's *Ocean of Wealth*.[398]

Although in recent times the throne and its backrest are seldom depicted in either painted icons or sculpture, when they are represented, they are a source of great merit.

Many Tibetan scholars hold that this design of the throne with six [figurines] was [originally] an ornamental feature of the gateway to an [ancient] Indian temple, and that it was erroneously transposed upon the backrest of the deity's [throne], and that this tradition [subsequently] became prevalent only in Tibet but lacks authenticity. They also assert that all the three tantras [translated] by Tsami [Sangye Drakpa], including the [aforementioned] *Tantra That Completely Apprehends the Attributes of a Spiritual Teacher*, are not authentic tantras. However, the omniscient Dharmākara [Situ Chokyi Jungne] has said that we [Kagyupas] should hold these [texts] to be valid, (1) because one can see in certain definitive [sources] that such ornamental features of the throne and its backrest are found within the scope of Indian art, and (2) because [Karmapa III] Rangjung [Dorje] asserted these original tantra texts to be genuine tantras.[399]

CORRECTIONS [ee"]

Regarding the fifth topic [the correction of errors (*skyon sel*), it says in the root verse]:

> **[Draftsmanship] should be without defects**
> **In respect of long, short, thick, thin, and curving [lines], and so forth.**

It says in the *Tantra of the Emergence of Cakrasaṃvara*:

> The three long [lines] that may be flawed
> Are those representing the chin, throat, and calves.
> The three short [lines] that may be defective
> Are those representing the nose, ears, and fingers.

The three thick [lines] that may be defective
Are those representing the calves, feet, and cheeks.
The three thin [lines] that may be defective
Are those representing the jaw, chest, and ribs.
The three curving [lines] that may be defective
Are those representing the breasts, ears, and forehead.
The three thin [lines] that may be defective
Are [also] those representing the thighs, hips, and neck muscles.

Each of these flaws [in draftsmanship] gives rise to its own particular defect or transgression. The same text continues:

In this context, if mistakes are made
With regard to the curves of the eyes and so forth,
Or in respect of the hand gestures and hand-held emblems,
One will be afflicted by sorrow and suffering,
And the icons [one has made] will be characterized as flawed and so forth.
Therefore, defects should be inspected and rectified.
Lesser though still serious defects may also be associated
With [the draftsmanship of] the backrest, the parasol, and the seat.
[If these are poorly executed,] friends will say unpleasant things,
And one's prestige [as an artist] will fade.
These therefore are the major defects
Which skilled [artists] should carefully scrutinize.

For this reason, it is most important that [the work of an artist] should be free from defects.

Furthermore, it is said that the actual being of pristine cognition (*jñānasattva, ye shes sems dpa'*) will not enter into a [visualized or created] deity image that is [iconographically] below standard.[400] In such cases, only negativity will ensue; and even good deeds carried out in a locality where a defective icon has been installed will diminish. Such places are to be abandoned in favor of pure locations.

Colors and Shading [ff"]

Regarding the sixth topic [colors and shadings (*tshon mdangs*), it says in the root verses]:

> **The basic and secondary color pigments and their shadings should then be applied. . . .**

As for the application of color, the five basic colors (*rtsa ba'i tshon*) are white, yellow, red, blue, and green.[401] The intermediate or secondary colors (*yan lag gi tshon*) comprise[402]

> The trio of minium orange (*li khri*), flesh pink (*sha kha*), and dark pink (*na ros*);
> The trio of pale mauve (*mon kha*), smoke grey (*dud kha*), and earthen brown (*sa kha*);[403]
> The trio of brown (*smug po*), bone ivory (*rus kha*), and turquoise blue-green (*gYu kha*).

These all have many subdivisions. Indeed it has also been said:[404]

> The elaborate [index] of the thirty-two secondary [colors] comprises
> White, yellowish white (*dkar ser*), reddish white (*dkar dmar*), and crystal (*chu shel*),
> Yellow, pale yellow (*ser skya*), reddish yellow (*dmar ser*), and minium orange (*li khri*),
> Red, pale red (*dmar skya*), reddish brown (*dmar smug*), and shellac (*rgya skag*),
> Blue, pale blue (*sngo skya*), azure (*mthing nag*), and turquoise (*gYu kha*),
> Green, yellowish green (*ljang ser*), pale green (*ljang skya*), and dark green (*ljang nag*),
> Flesh pink (*sha kha*), tea brown (*ja kha*), pale mauve (*mon kha*), and ash grey (*thal kha*),
> Brown (*smug po*), dark brown (*smug nag*), dark pink (*na ros*), and lung purple (*glo ba kha*),
> Smoke grey (*dud kha*), birch (*re kha*), bone ivory (*rus kha*), and gloomy black (*mun ldog*).

These are the well-known combinations, but the distinctions of color, over and above these, are limitless. It is explained that color combinations are of good quality when they are rich, bright, and lustrous.

With regard to shading (*mdangs*), granular shading (*btsag mdangs*) resembles mustard seeds fading out gradually [across the canvas], fiery shading (*'bar*

Fig. 27. Shading techniques

mdangs) resembles blades of kuśa grass, and lineal shading (*bshal mdangs*) resembles fading bands of rainbow light. Along with outlining (*bcad kyi tshul*), each of these [techniques] should be mastered individually.[405]

Stylistic Features [gg"]

Regarding the seventh topic [stylistic features (*rnam gyur*), it says in the root verses]:

> **. . . And the stylistic features should correspond to the traditions maintained in different lands.**

There are many distinctions of form (*gzugs*) and style (*rnam gyur*) that are dissimilar, exemplified by the eight [distinctive] patterns of basic design (*patra rigs brgyad*)[406] and the three types of flames (*me ris rigs gsum*).[407]

Fig. 28. Motifs of the four elements

In particular, stylistic features should accord with the [artistic] traditions prevalent in different countries—India, China, Tibet, and the like. As has been said:[408]

> Mansions, and so forth, the Tree of Enlightenment,
> Various types of flowers, and offering clouds,
> Auspicious designs, gemstone garlands,
> Individual motifs that are not intermingled—
> These are the distinctive features of Indian art.
>
> Beautiful designs, golden imprints (*mdangs ldan par*),
> Auspicious forms, silken threads,
> Thrones and wondrous details—
> These are the distinctive features of Chinese art.
>
> Aquatic creatures, lakes and pools,
> Fragrant forests, sacraments of the nāgas,
> Medicinal incense, pulsating lines—
> These are the distinctive features of Kashmiri art.
>
> Designs of the four elements, rainbows and clouds,
> Forested glades, gemstones and ornaments with a thread design
> (*snal ris rgyan*),
> Arial creatures, sacraments of the gods—
> These are the distinctive features of Newar art.

Fig. 29. Different types of flames

Cliffs and grassy hills, wild ungulates,
Canopies, bouquets, drapes, and beauteous ornaments,
Diverse images, and snow mountain ranges—
These are the distinctive features of Tibetan art.

The [various] stylistic features, such as those described in this passage should be practically applied.

The Celestial Palace [3"]

Third, [the final topic on the representations of buddha body] comprises certain further remarks concerning the celestial palace that contains [the aforementioned icons]. In this regard, [it says in the root verses]:

The three-dimensional and two-dimensional celestial palaces,
The abodes in which [these icons] reside,
Are widely [constructed] in accordance with the *Indestructible Garland.*

With regard to the celestial palace (*gzhal yas khang*), which is the receptacle of [those] divine icons, the [corresponding Sanskrit] term *vimāna* conveys the sense of "immeasurable" (*gzhal du med pa*). For example, in the [*Tantra of the*] *Ocean of Sky-farers*, the celestial palace is explained to take the form of a lotus flower;[409] while in the *Sūtra of Final Nirvāṇa*, among the sūtras of the Greater Vehicle, the array of the palace is explained to be limitless.

Among the [various descriptions of maṇḍalas] in the tantra texts that are to be applied in practice, there are passages that exclusively describe the palatial mansion (*khang bzang*), which is endowed with four corners, four gates, and arched pediments in order to symbolize that it is imbued with the purity of the thirty-seven aspects of enlightenment (*byang phyogs so bdun*).[410] Such palaces may be either three-dimensional (*blos bslang*) or two-dimensional (*bri cha*) in structure. However, if one wishes to understand [the techniques of] draftsmanship [in relation to the celestial palace] in detail, one should [first] understand the general plan [of the maṇḍala] rather than the particular features of relief and the upright structures that are applicable in three-dimensional [constructions].

Dimensions of the Celestial Palace [a"]

In general, it is said that there are two kinds of maṇḍala—those that have precise measurements (*tshad bcas*) and those that lack precise measurements (*tshad ma nges pa*). As to the former, when precise measurements are laid down on the basis of [the various families of] the deities, it says in the [*Tantra of the Indestructible*] *Tent*:[411]

> The [maṇḍala] of the Vajra [family] should measure three cubits,
> The maṇḍala of the Buddha [family] should measure four cubits,
> The [maṇḍala] of the [Ratna family],
> That of Bhāskara (*snang byed*), should measure five cubits,
> The [maṇḍala] of the [Padma family],
> That of Naṭeśvara, should measure six cubits,
> And the [maṇḍala] of the [Karma family],
> That of the Lord of Horses (Kubera), should measure seven cubits.

This passage indicates that the dimensions of the maṇḍalas of [the five enlightened families]—Akṣobhya, Vairocana, Ratnasambhava, Amitābha, and Amoghasiddhi—respectively range from three to seven cubits.[412]

Then, in chapter four of the *Tantra of the* [*Secret*] *Assembly*, it says that the maṇḍala of buddha mind (*thugs dkyil*) should measure twelve cubits, while in chapter sixteen it adds that the maṇḍala of buddha body (*sku dkyil*) should measure sixteen cubits and the maṇḍala of buddha speech (*gsung dkyil*) twenty cubits. These measurements are all with reference to the four sides of the base line (*rtsa thig*).[413]

When precise measurements are prescribed on the basis of the [different sorts of] patrons [who commission these maṇḍalas], it says in an authoritative passage from a tantra text quoted in the [*Indestructible*] *Garland*:[414]

> A lord of Jambudvīpa, or universal monarch,
> Should draw an external maṇḍala,
> Extending in its dimensions from infinity to one *yojana*.[415]

Elsewhere, Jayasena mentions in [his *Commentary on*] *the Tantra of the Ocean of Sky-farers* that [the size of such maṇḍalas] should be estimated in accordance with the particular wealth of the patron:

> [In this context] it is held that the maṇḍala should measure eight cubits,
> But otherwise, it is said that, in the case of kings,
> It should measure one hundred cubits,
> Half of that in the case of [arhats] in their final birth,[416]
> And, in the case of important persons, half of that again.
> Those commissioned by merchants should measure twelve cubits,
> And those commissioned by practitioners should measure six cubits.

Secondly, with regard to maṇḍalas that have no precise measurement, it says in the *Four Hundred and Fifty Verse* [*Maṇḍala Rite of the Secret Assembly*]:[417]

> Although precise measurements and so forth can be made
> On the basis of the aspirations of sentient beings,
> With regard to the spiritual accomplishments
> Which derive from skillful means and discriminative awareness,
> How can measurements and the like be made precisely!
> Therefore [the maṇḍala] should measure [whatever is appropriate],
> Starting from a single cubit,
> And [possibly] extending as far as one thousand cubits.
> The lines should be marked accordingly in respect of this [maṇḍala] wheel.

The *Indestructible Garland* and other sources also offer similar explanations.

Proportions of the Maṇḍala [b"]

With regard to the contemporary construction techniques employed in respect of those [maṇḍalas] that do have precise measurements, two different traditions are well known, based on the tantras—those of Abhayā[karagupta] and Śraddhākara[varman]—and among them, [the tradition of the former, who authored] the *Indestructible Garland*, has many adherents. Accordingly, it has been said:[418]

> The terms "gate-width" (*sgo tshad*)
> And "large unit" (*cha chen*) are synonymous.
> Each large unit comprises four small units,
> And half of one of these is known as a quarter unit.[419]

The longer [line demarcating the top of the palace wall],
Which is mentioned in the *Indestructible Garland*,
Measures twenty-four large units or ninety-six small units,
Extending from [one end of] the parapet
To [the other end of] the parapet,
And this should be twice the length of the maṇḍala and its
surrounding area.[420]

The shorter [line demarcating the bottom of the palace wall],
Which is mentioned by Śraddhākaravarman,
Measures sixteen large units or sixty-four small units,
Extending from [one end of] the base line
To [the other end of] the base line,
And this should be twice the length of the actual basic maṇḍala.[421]

Since the base line demarcates the actual [basic] maṇḍala,
It is known to be stated in the ordinary tantras
That the gate-width measure should be one eighth of the base line.[422]
However, according to the *Four Indestructible Seats* and the
Emergence of Cakrasaṃvara,
It should be one fifth;
According to the *Victory over the Three Worlds*, it should be one
ninth;
And according to the maṇḍala array [of the *Indestructible Peak*], it
should be one tenth.[423]

The gates are also explained to be of three types—
One in which [the four parts of the gate][424] form two pairs of equal
measure,[425]
One in which [the four parts of the gate] form one pair of equal
measure
And another pair of unequal measure,[426]
And one in which all four [parts] are of equal measure.[427]

As for the tiered pediments [above the gates],[428]
They may be precise or imprecise in their measurement,
Or else they may have a combination [of precise and imprecise
measurements].
Although the size [of the pediments] may be uncertain,

As the second [of these options] suggests,
Even so, painted scrolls [depicting maṇḍalas]
Have all sorts [of measurements inscribed] on their reverse sides.[429]

Ratnākara[śānti] holds, in accordance with the last [of these options],
In his *Illuminator of the World*
That the width [of the pediment] should be three gate-width
measures,
But that its height is imprecise.[430]

Then, according to the first option,
The ancient learned and accomplished masters of India and Tibet
Mostly hold that the [small] pediment with four beams (*snam bu*)
Should be one gate-width in height.[431]

There are also four [different] pediment designs
According to the [*Indestructible*] *Garland*,
And another according to the *Wheel of Time*,
Prescribing eleven beams.[432]

The beams themselves may be arranged in three distinctive ways:
When the pediment is three gate-widths [in height],
It may take the form of two beams of equal width
Combined with nine beams of equal width;
Or else it may take the form of five beams of equal width,
Combined with two sets of three beams of equal width.[433]

In the case of a pediment that is one gate-width in height,
It may resemble the last [design],
Forming three equal beams [and one unequal beam],
But there are [different] extant traditions.[434]

There are also many [tantras prescribing]
Whether the crossed-vajra emblem (*sna tshogs rdo rje*)
[Drawn around the four gateways] should be included or not.[435]

Skilled persons, [after attending to] the six features of the gates,
May thereafter construct the seats [of the deities], with precision.[436]

With regard to four [features]—the roof, its stūpas, battlements,
And tented spire, symbolizing the peak of Rājagṛha[437]—
There are many skillful techniques
Contingent on the longer [parapet] line and shorter [base] line measurements,
And the line measurements [prescribed] in the [various] esoteric instructions.[438]

This will suffice as a brief description of the traditions common to both painted and sculpted maṇḍalas.

Application of Color [c"]

When color pigments (*tshon rtsi*) are applied to maṇḍalas that have been drawn, it is said in the tantras that the best should be prepared from the powders of the most excellent gemstones and precious metals—sapphire, ruby, and so forth. The mediocre [pigments] include dyes made from the powders of various grains, the inferior sort include those prepared from powders derived from flowers or red earth, and the unsurpassed sort, with which [maṇḍalas] are to be painted, are powders derived from the charcoal and bones of a charnel ground, and so forth.

As far as contemporary usage is concerned, there are indeed many artistic techniques for applying colored powders, corresponding to the [distinctions of] place and time, so it will be necessary to follow different technical traditions, without being restricted to one facile approach.[439]

It says in the [*Indestructible*] *Garland*:

Within the circumference [of the maṇḍala],
The lines [of colored sand] should be correctly laid,
Corresponding to the twenty elements that comprise [each of] the gates.[440]
The lines should be even and straight, without break,
And [laid] in the appropriate manner,
With the spaces between them being only the width of a barley grain.
The lower and upper parts [of the maṇḍala] should also be appropriately decorated.
If [the colored lines] are laid too thickly, one will fall ill,
And if they are too thin, wealth will diminish,

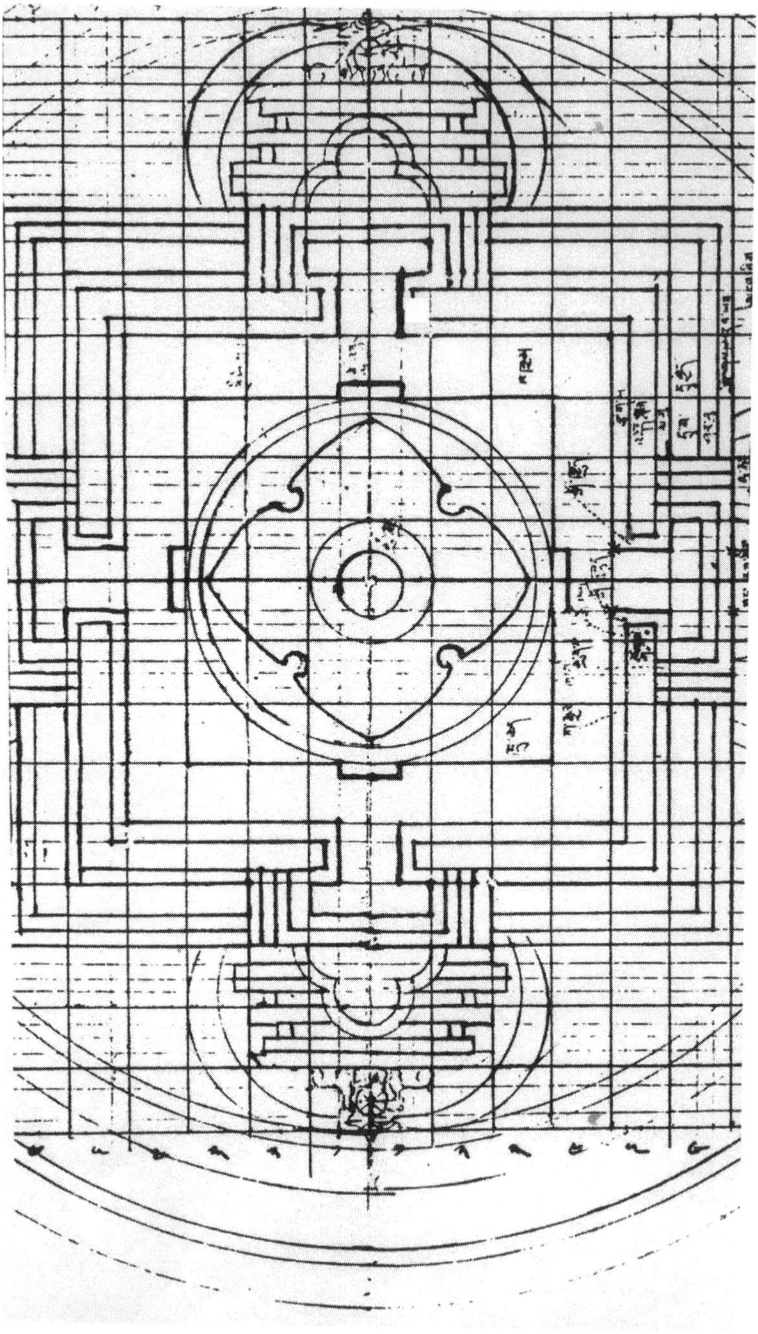

Fig. 30. Maṇḍala of the Guhyagarbha, indicating the parapet and base lines, along with two of the four gates

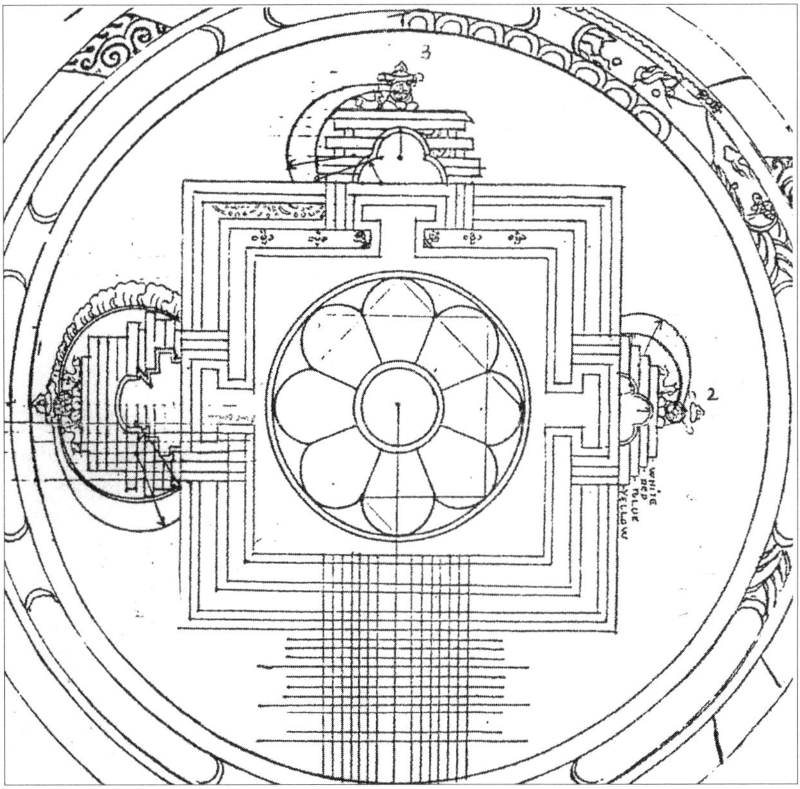

Fig. 31. Composite maṇḍala for didactic purposes, illustrating three different pediment designs

Fig. 32. The Kālacakra sand maṇḍala

If they are crooked, enmity will arise, and
If they are broken, a spiritual teacher or student will die.
If they are not laid out clockwise,
The colors should be pierced with a ritual spike.

Since the disadvantages of defective draftsmanship have been precisely indicated in these verses, one should earnestly concentrate and draw [the lines] with care.

Arraying the Symbols of the Deities [d"]

With regard to the ways in which the symbols representing the deities contained [within the palace] are arrayed, there are some who hold that the body [of the deity] alone should be represented; and, in general, it is held that a pinch or drop of color alone will suffice by way of representation. However, it is said in the *Great* [*Commentary*] *on the Wheel of Time* [entitled *Taintless Light*]:[441]

> In this context, at all times, three aspects should be arrayed upon the sun and moon cushions in the maṇḍala of colored powders because there are gross, subtle, and extraneous categories to be symbolically represented. Among these, the extraneous category (*gzhan gyi dbye ba*) refers to the arrayal of the mantra seed-syllables (*sngags kyi sa bon*). The subtle category (*phra ba'i dbye ba*) refers to the arrayal of the symbolic hand-held emblems such as the vajra which are manifested from the mantra seed-syllables; and the gross category (*rags pa'i dbye ba*) refers to the arrayal of the images or icons of the deities which are manifested from the symbolic [hand-held emblems] such as the vajra.

Nāgabodhi also said [in his *Twenty Rituals of the Maṇḍala of the Secret Assembly*]:[442]

In accordance with one's ability,
The seed syllables should be arrayed within the maṇḍala,
Or else the [corresponding] symbolic [hand-held] emblems,
Or the [actual] deity icons should be arrayed,
Either fashioned of cast metal, or in a composite form.

Similar passages are found in the *Tantra of Embrace* and in the *Cornucopia of Esoteric Instructions*.[443] Also in the [*Secret*] *Tantra of General* [*Rites*], it says:[444]

> An intelligent person, without having [prior] training,
> Should array the [symbolic] emblems.
> Even one who has prior training will have difficulty
> Perfectly representing all the distinct subsidiary [symbols of the maṇḍala],
> But if the subsidiary [emblems] are perfectly fashioned, in detail,
> They should be held in place for the duration of the rite.
> Even if the [corresponding] icons are well sculpted,
> [The maṇḍala] will not hold a great many [of them].
> [In short], it has been well explained that
> There will be no blessings if the subsidiary [emblems] are reduced,
> Nor will spiritual accomplishments be attained.
> So it is that skilled persons should array the deities
> In the form of their [respective] emblems.

[The point here is that] if the forms of the deities are to be drawn perfectly and completely, it will be time-consuming, and the ritual will not be completed [for lack of time]. [Similarly,] if the subsidiary [emblems representing] the deities are reduced, no blessings will accrue. For these reasons, the drawing of the hand-held emblems will be highly esteemed.

With regard to the techniques employed by contemporary skilled [artists] who are of the appropriate standard, it will turn out well and be most satisfactory if the main deity is arrayed as a statue, the retinue in the form of their corresponding symbolic hand-held emblems, and the gatekeepers and other peripheral figures in the form of their corresponding seed-syllables. In this regard, it also says in the [*Indestructible*] *Garland*:

> If the circumstances are inauspicious
> The symbols and the hand-held emblems should be correctly drawn.
> But if the circumstances are not inauspicious,
> The icons of the [various] deities should be drawn,
> And these painted icons should be positioned [in the maṇḍala],
> Or else sculpted images which have been well crafted by an artist
> Should be placed [therein].

In the *Cornucopia of Esoteric Instructions* it is also explained that the icon of a deity in union with a female consort should not be drawn in places where they could be seen by those such as the eternalistic extremists who lack faith [in the Buddhist teachings].[445] Also, according to the *Empowerment of Vajrapāṇi*, a hand-held emblem should be laid out in the place of the central deity, but only drops [of colored powder] should be arrayed in the sectors occupied by the figures forming the retinue.[446]

Furthermore, it says in the *Supreme Tantra of Manifest Expression*:[447]

> Painters should adorn the forms [within the maṇḍala],
> Either with paint, or by using brushes.

Therefore, when seed-syllables and so forth are arrayed within a maṇḍala, they may indeed be painted or drawn with a brush or a pen.

Layout of the Celestial Palace according to the Nyingma Tantras [e″]

> **But there are also other symbolic conventions and meanings,**
> **Including [those represented by] the tradition of the *Magical Net*.**

According to the transmitted teachings (*bka' ma*) and treasures (*gter ma*) of the ancient translation school of secret mantra, such as the [*Tantra of the*] *Magical Net of Vajrasattva*, there are also other distinctions of symbolism and meaning with regard to the layout of the celestial palace which are slightly dissimilar to the prevailing description of the Unsurpassed [Yoga Tantras].[448] These may be exemplified by [the account of the celestial palace in] the [*Tantra of the*] *Secret Nucleus*, which the *Short Commentary* analyzes in terms of the following eleven aspects:

> The celestial palace, its ground, its extent, and its material basis,
> Its shape, projecting bays, and spire,
> Its ornaments, gate passageways, and tiered pediments,
> And the forms assumed by the seats within it,
> Which have their own defining characteristics ...

Among these aspects, it is explained that, below the [vajra] finial (*tog*), the spire (*rtse mo*) [of the celestial palace] is encircled by a round vase-shaped structure—a particular feature of the tradition of the *Magical Net*.[449]

Fig. 33. Three-dimensional celestial palace of the Hundred Peaceful and Wrathful Deities according to *Guhyagarbha*

As for the ornaments (*rgyan*) [of the celestial palace], seven types are enumerated: lower ornaments, side ornaments, upper ornaments, gateway ornaments, external ornaments, ornaments indicative of the essential nature, and ornaments possessed by the lord [of the maṇḍala].

Then, as for the tiered pediments (*rta babs*), the causal pediments (*rgyu'i rta babs*) are known to resemble a rider's dismounting platform and to have eight aspects, since the outer and inner roofs (*sgo phub*) of the gatehouse each have four steps. By contrast, the fruitional pediments (*'bras bu'i rta babs*) are explained to have eight [stacked] beams (*snam bu brgyad*).[450] There are many such classifications.

Representations of Buddha Speech [bb']

The second part of the detailed exegesis, concerning the representations of buddha speech (*gsung rten*), comprises three sections: a general presentation of [Indic and other ancient] scripts (*yig rigs spyir bstan*); a particular analysis of Tibetan scripts (*bod kyi yi ge khyad par du bye ba*); and a presentation of calligraphic technique (*'bri thabs bstan pa*).

General Presentation of Indic and Other Ancient Scripts [1"]

Concerning the first [the general presentation of Indic and other ancient scripts, it says in the root verses]:

> **As for the representations of buddha speech, according to the sūtras**
> **There are sixty-four types of [ancient] script,**
> **But Rañjanā, Vartula, and so forth are supreme**
> **Among all the writing systems of different lands.**
> **[In Rañjanā] it is approximately the case**
> **That there are two calligraphic grid squares**
> **For the head stroke and neck stroke [of each letter],**
> **And three for the body strokes [of each letter].**
> **Among these, the head stroke is [drawn] last.**

The representations of buddha speech (*gsung gi rten*) which are to be created by artists include volumes of written texts [and sacred scriptures]. [Traditionally, it is said that] the following sixty-four scripts (*catuṣṣaṣṭīlipi, yig rigs drug cu rtsa bzhi*), enumerated in the *Sūtra of Extensive Play*, [were known by Prince Siddhārtha]:[451]

[1] Brāhmī (*tshangs pa*);
[2] Kharoṣṭhī;
[3] Puṣkarasārin (*padma'i snying po*);
[4] Aṅga;
[5] Vaṅga;
[6] Magadhā;
[7] Maṅgalya (*bkra shis pa*);
[8] Aṅgulīya (*sor gdub*);
[9] Śakāri;
[10] Svāddhyari;
[11] Brahmavallī (*a hu*);
[12] Pāruṣya (*rtsub mo*);
[13] Drāviḍa (*'gro lding*);
[14] Kirāta (*mon yul*);
[15] Dākṣiṇya (*lho phyogs*);
[16] Ugra (*drag po*);

[17] Saṃkhyā (*grangs*);
[18] Anuloma (*rjes mthun*);
[19] Avamūrdha (*spyi'u tshugs*);
[20] Darada;
[21] Khāṣya;
[22] Chinese/Cīna (*rgya nag*); [Lūna (*lu na'i yi ge*)];
[23] Hūṇa (*hu na*);
[24] Madhyākṣaravistara (*dbus* [*dang rgyas par bri ba'i yi ge*]);
[25] Puṣpa (*rgyal gyi yig*);
[26] Deva (*lha*);
[27] Nāga (*klu*);
[28] Yakṣa (*gnod sbyin*);
[29] Gandharva (*dri za*);
[30] Kinnara (*mi'am ci*);
[31] Mahoraga (*lto 'phye* [*chen po*]);
[32] Asura (*lha min*);
[33] Garuḍa (*mkha' lding*);
[34] Mṛgacakra (*ri dvags 'khor lo*);
[35] Vāyasarūta (*bya rog skad*);
[36] Bhaumadeva (*sa'i lha*);
[37] Antarīkṣadeva (*bar snang lha*);
[38] Aparagoḍānī (*nub*);
[39] Uttarakurūdvīpa (*byang*);
[40] Pūrvavideha (*shar gling*);
[41] Utkṣepa (*'degs*);
[42] Nikṣepa (*bzhag*);
[43] Prakṣepa (*rab tu bzhag*);
[44] Sāgara (*rgya mtsho*);
[45] Vajra (*rdo rje*);
[46] Lekhapratilekha (*'phrin dang rab tu 'phrin*);
[47] Vikṣepa (*rnam gzhag*);
[48] Anudruta (*chung min*);
[49] Śāstravartā (*bstan bcos*);
[50] Gaṇanāvarta (*rtsis*);
[51] Utkṣepāvarta (*'degs skor*); [Nikṣepāvarta (*gzhag pa bskor ba*)];
[52] Pādalikhita (*rkang pas bris*);
[53] Dviruttarapadasaṃdhi (*phyi ma'i tshig gnyis grub*);
[54] Yāvaddaśottarapadasaṃdhi (*phyi ma bcu grub*);
[55] Madhyāhāriṇī (*bar ma sgrub pa*);

[56] Sarvarūtasaṃgrahaṇī (*sgra kun bsdus pa*);
[57] Vidyānulomāvimiśritā (*rigs mthun rnam bsres*);
[58] Ṛṣitapastaptā (*drang srong dka' thub gdungs*);
[59] Rocamānā (*gsal ba*);
[60] Dharaṇīprekṣiṇī (*sa rab lta*);
[61] [Gaganaprekṣiṇī (*nam mkha' blta ba*)];
[62] Sarvauṣadhiniṣyandā (*sman rgyu mthun*);
[63] Saravasārasaṃgrahaṇī (*snying po thams cad kun tu bsdus pa*); and
[64] [Sarvabhūtarūtaprahaṇī (*'byung po thams cad kyi sgra sdud pa*)].[452]

Among these, Rañjanā derives from the Brāhmī script, and it has two forms: the hollow-bodied script (*khog seng*) and the full-bodied script (*sha chen*).[453] There are also, in conformity with that [prototype Guptan script], the five versions of the Dharika script (*dharika'i yig rigs lnga*), as well as six different versions of the Nāgarī script (*na g a ra la rigs mi 'dra ba drug*) in which the heads [of the letters] are [similarly] raised.[454] In addition there is the Vartula script of the nāgas in which the heads [of the letters] are curled downwards.[455]

Furthermore, there are those [scripts employed in more remote lands] at the extremities of the oceans, and those which are not included within the [aforementioned] list of the sixty-four scripts, such as the three different [scripts] of Kashmir,[456] the Gauḍa [script of Bengal/Orissa],[457] the Ghahura script,[458] the Sindhu script,[459] the two kinds of Ghaula script,[460] the Magadhā script,[461] the Kamata script,[462] Puṅkka,[463] the script of Markkola, the script of Tāmaralipti,[464] and the script of the *rākṣasas* (*srin po*),[465] all of which once had stylized calligraphic transmissions, even in Tibet.[466]

Exemplified by these, there is a [seemingly] limitless number of different scripts or writing systems prevalent in each different country, but supreme among them all are the two scripts [known as] Rañjanā and Vartula. For among all these [scripts] if one knows how to write these two, one will have no difficulty with the [contemporary] Nāgarī scripts, and so forth.

[Rañjanā Calligraphy]

Those who have not learned how to apply the calligraphic measurements (*bris thig*) in detail [should know that] the rough guidelines for [Rañjanā] calligraphy are as follows: Longwise, there are [approximately] two grid squares (*kha do*) allocated for the pen strokes representing the head and the neck [of each letter] and three grid squares (*kha gsum*) for those representing the body [of each letter]. Collectively these are known as the "five vertical grid squares for pen strokes" (*dpang smyug khams lnga*).[467]

Then, the letters that lack the long tail [*ring cha*, of the *a shad*] and the extended backhand stroke of the letter *pha* (*pha'i rgyab lag*) [and so forth][468] generally have three horizontal grid squares (*zheng la rang khams gsum*) [allocated for pen strokes].[469] These [strokes] are generally drawn in a downwards movement, starting from the body of the letter, and the head is subsequently drawn.[470]

Fig. 34. Vowels and consonants of the Rañjanā script, showing calligraphic gridlines and Tibetan equivalents

Above:
Fig. 35. Remaining consonants of the Rañjanā script, showing calligraphic gridlines and Tibetan equivalents

Right:
Fig. 36. Examples with (PHA) and without (BA) the extended backstroke in Rañjanā calligraphy

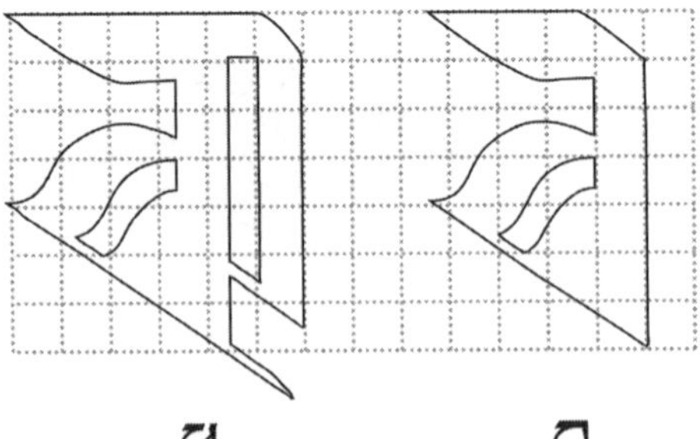

Particular Analysis of Tibetan Scripts [2″]

Secondly, [there is the particular analysis of Tibetan scripts, on which the root verses say]:

> **In Tibetan calligraphy, all [writing systems] can be subsumed**
> **Within the following six scripts:**
> **The headed block-letter script, the headless [block-letter] script,**
> **The headless thick and thin italic scripts,**
> **The formal handwriting script, and the cursive shorthand script.**

Although there are many different categories of Tibetan script that gradually gained currency in recent times, all of them may be subsumed within the following six: the basic headed block-letter script (*gzab chen*) and its headless form (*gzab chung*), the headless thick-stroked italic script (*'bru chen*) and its thin-stroked form (*'bru chung*), the [formal] handwriting script (*bshur ma*), and the cursive shorthand script (*'khyug yig*) [which is a derivative of common writing, *dkyus yig*].[471]

Evolution of the Headed and Headless Block-Letter Scripts [a″]

> **The block-letter scripts [evolved through] nine successive [modifications],**
> **Including the "ancient and new styles."**
> **Thereafter, among the followers of Yutri, two traditions arose—**
> **The "frog" tradition and the "popular" tradition.**

The block-letter script (*gzab ma*), also known as the headed script (*dbu can*), which is [regarded as] the best of the Tibetan fonts, was originally modeled on the calligraphy of Tonmi Sambhoṭa [during the reign of King Songtsen Gampo], and is said to have resembled the "spreading out of black frogs in a swamp" (*sbal nag na la rgyangs pa*).[472] Subsequently, [during the reign of King Mangsong Mangtsen], one Changar[473] Rinchen Bar employed a style of calligraphy that resembled a "shattered brick" (*so phag gshibs pa*). Later still, [during the reign of Dusong Mangpoje], Chabkar Beutse employed a style of calligraphy that resembled a "male finch" (*bya pho 'jol ba*). After that, [during the reign of King Tride Tsukten], Tsang Genyen [Konchok] Wang developed the style that resembled "dark barley grains spread out" (*nas nag bkram pa*).[474]

Subsequently [during the reign of King Trisong Detsen], one Dre-o Trom [engraved the inscription of the Samye obelisk] and thereby developed the style that resembled a "string of pearls" (*mu tig bstar la brgyus pa*).[475] After that [during the reign of King Mune Tsenpo], Tsepong Jangchub developed a style that resembled the "spreading out of dung beetles" (*sbur nag bgrad pa*). Thereafter [during the reign of King Mutik Tsenpo], one Te Yonten developed the style that resembled a "fish brought out of the water" (*nya chu nas phyungs pa*).[476] Subsequently [during the reign of King Relpachen], the two known as Dra and Go developed the style that resembles a "lion leaping through the air" (*seng ge gnam du mthong pa*).[477] All these [methods of writing] are collectively known as the "ancient styles" (*snga ma*).[478]

Later, during the lifetimes of Dro Nyashari and Tongwar Dorje, master and students, at the start of the later dissemination of the [Buddhist] teachings (*phyi dar*), the rectangular style of writing (*grub bzhi*) known as the "new style" (*gsar sleb*) was introduced.[479] [In this way] the evolution of Tibetan writing can be traced through nine successive [generations].[480]

Later still, there was one Khyungpo Yutri Bar who composed a treatise on measurements, bamboo pens, paper-making, calligraphy (*smyu gu shog chag 'bri lugs*), and so forth, modeled on the iconometric measurements of a maṇḍala, which divided [the paper] into grids of large and small units (*cha chen cha chung*), and so forth.[481] He educated an inconceivable number of students, including those who diverged into two streams—some following the so-called "frog tradition" (*sbal lugs*) [of Tonmi Sambhoṭa] and others following the "popular tradition" (*mang lugs*) [of Changar Rinchen Bar], which is reported to have survived down to the present day [i.e., the lifetime of Jamgon Kongtrul], in Phenyul and Ngor.[482]

Eight Important Strokes in Block-Letter Calligraphy [i"]

There are eight [strokes] to which one should pay attention,
Ten [points of calligraphy] to be accentuated,
Twenty-one primary characteristics, sixteen secondary characteristics,
And three general characteristics that should all be applied.

With regard to all these traditions [associated with the writing of the block-letter Tibetan scripts] in general, there are eight [strokes] on which [the scribe's] attention should be focused (*gces brgyad*). As has been said:[483]

When drawing letters [such as CHA] with a curved line (*snag lam zlum*),
One should pay attention to the [convex] "lip" stroke (*gong chags*).[484]
When drawing letters [such as NGA]
Which occupy a single [unit] (*gcig pur skyes*),[485]
One should pay attention to the short "shoulder "stroke (*dpung thung*).[486]
When drawing subjoined letters [such as YA] (*gdags pa can*),
One should pay attention to the corner grid-line (*zur thig*).[487]
When drawing letters [such as NYA] with an upper "shield-like" curve (*stod phub can*), [488]
One should pay attention to the "abdominal" stroke (*sbo*).[489]
When drawing letters [such as TA] with a lower "shield-like" curve (*smad phub can*),[490]
One should pay attention to the delineation of the "body" stroke (*khog 'dren*).[491]
When drawing letters [such as KA] with a "leg" [or tail] line (*rkang pa*),[492]
One should pay attention to delineating the final stroke, as if riding a horse.[493]
When drawing letters [such as PA] with an upright stroke (*yar phul*)
Or [ZA] with a thick-ended (*mthar rgyas*) stroke,[494]
One should pay attention when exerting calligraphic pressure (*sgros gnon*).
When drawing letters [such as NA] with eyes (*mig can dag*),[495]
One should pay attention to the correct drawing of the "neck" stroke (*ske gtsang*).

Ten or Fourteen Accentuated Points of Calligraphy [ii"]

The following is a listing of ten or fourteen points of calligraphy that are to be accentuated (*'don pa bcu'am bcu bzhi*):[496]

A noble "head" stroke (*bzang mgo*) should be accentuated,[497]
A robust "shoulder" stroke (*mkhrangs dpung pa*) should be accentuated,
As should an elegant "abdominal" or "threshold" stroke (*sgros sbo them*),
A graceful "downward" stroke (*bshan mar 'then*),[498]

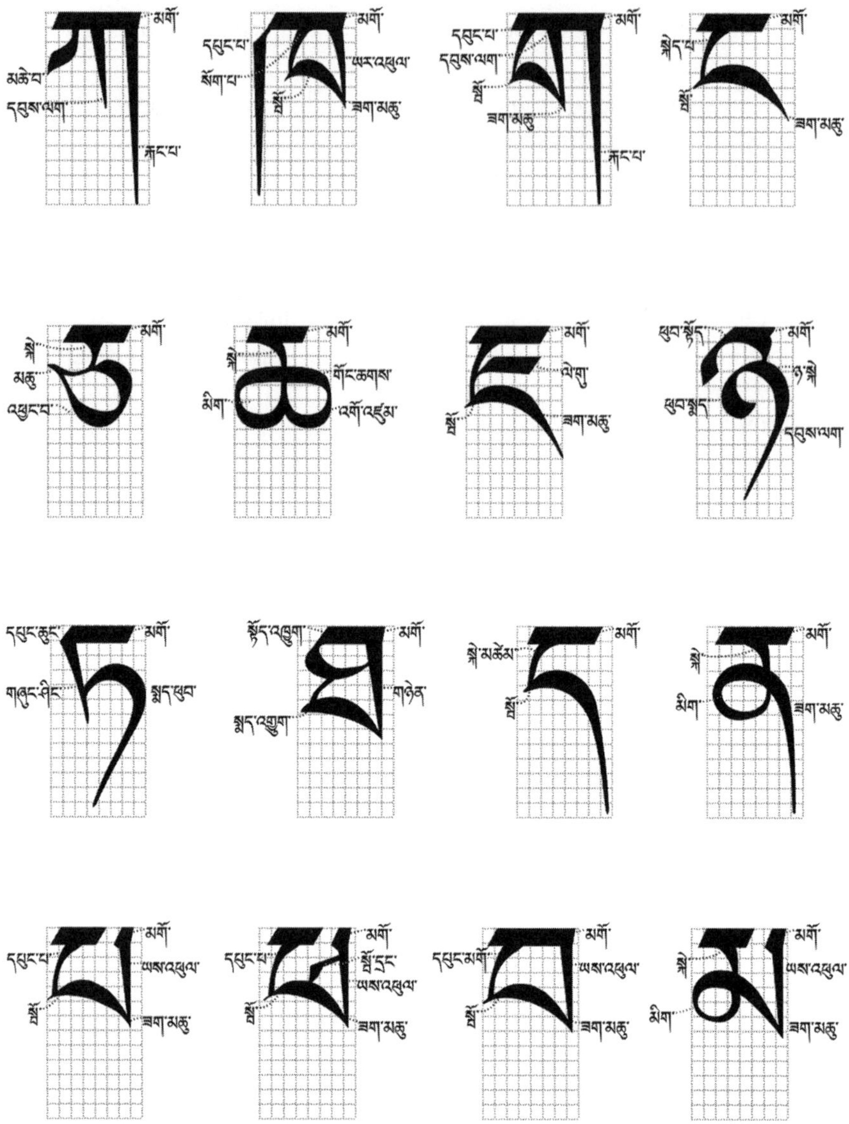

Fig. 37. Tibetan vowels and consonants, showing calligraphic gridlines

A skillful "body" stroke (*sbyang khog pa*),
A precise "ink edge" stroke (*hram snag sna*),
A brightly drawn "eye" stroke (*hur mig 'dril ba*),
A stylish "upright" stroke (*gYer yar 'phul*),
A lightly drawn "subjoined" YA (*yang ya btags*)
And a smartly drawn "tapering lip" stroke (*grung zags mchu*),

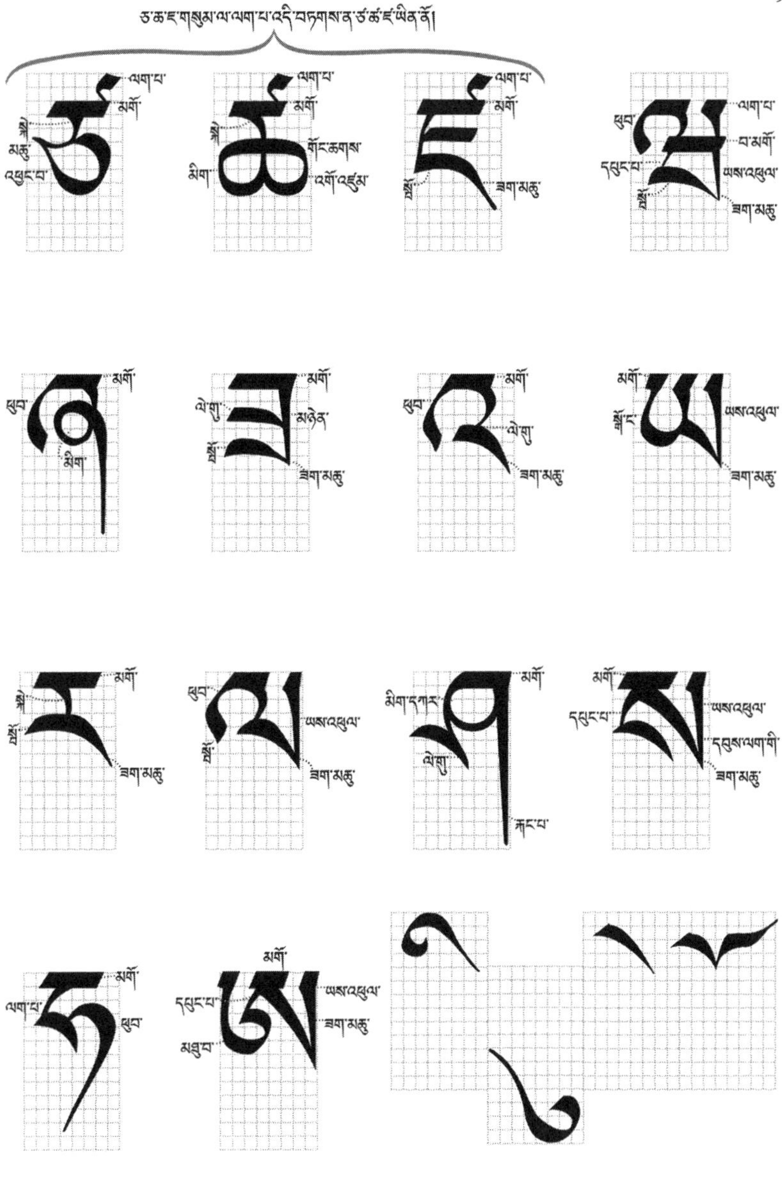

Along with a noble "head" stroke
And a noble "shoulder" stroke (*bzang mgo dpung*),
A closing edge stroke "where the inked and blank grids adjoin"
(*'dzum dkar nag sna*),
A flexible "waist" stroke (*mnyen bsnol mtshams*),
And a curving "extended" stroke (*'khyug yan lag*).

Twenty-one Primary Characteristics [iii"]

There are also twenty-one primary characteristics (*ma chos nyer gcig*),[499] [which are all associated with the radical letters]:

(1–3) Among them, there are three kinds of "head" stroke (*mgo gsum*). The best resembles a round rope that has been cut [diagonally at both ends] by a knife (*thag zlum gris bcad pa*); the average sort resembles the bow-shaped [capital of a pillar, which is cut diagonally at one end]; and the worst resembles the head of a punctuation mark (*tsheg mgo*),[500] [which is slender and pointed at both ends but short and thick in the middle].

(4–6) There are three kinds of "shoulder" stroke (*dpung gsum*). The best resembles a vajra held at the heart (*thugs kar rdo rje 'dzin pa*) [drawn at an angle, curving from left to right, starting thin and increasing in thickness]; the average sort resembles an arrow in flight (*mda' 'phen*) [drawn straight downwards]; and the worst resembles a broken arm, limply lying sideways (*lag chag 'phrod nyal*) [drawn directly from left to right].

(7–9) There are three kinds of "abdominal" stroke (*sbo gsum*). The best resembles the back of a lip-shaped knife (*sgros chags gri ltag*) [or a crescent moon, thick in the middle and thin at both curved ends]; the average sort resembles a taut rope of hair (*spu thag sgrim*); and the worst resembles an ant's waist (*grog sked*) [or a saddle that is thin in the middle and thick at both ends].

(10–12) There are three kinds of "tapering lip" stroke (*zags mchu gsum*). The best takes the form of a short and finely pointed intersection of angled strokes (*gsegs sbyor thung rno*) [where the "abdominal" stroke and the "upright" stroke join together]. The average sort resembles an indented [and thick] pig's snout (*'gye'o phag sna*), and the worst resembles a crooked elephant's trunk (*sgur po glang sna*).

(13–15) There are three kinds of "upright" stroke (*yar 'then/yar 'phul gsum*). The best resembles a raised needle (*rgya khab bslang*) [thick at the top end and becoming gradually thinner]. The average sort resembles [an arm] brandishing a drum or a pole (*rnga dbyug 'phyar*) [which sways crookedly towards the top], and the worst resembles a decapitated arm (*lag mgo bcad*) [where the stroke is drawn straight but without a head].

(16–18) There are three kinds of "downward tail" [or "leg"] stroke (*mar 'then gsum*). The best resembles the stem of a key (*sgo lcags rkang*) [becoming increasingly slender]. The average sort resembles the tail of a puppy (*khyi gu'i mjug*) [which curls slightly at the upper end], and the worst resembles the tail of an insect or the legs of a bee (*'bu mjug sbrang rkang*) [with many crooked lines].

(19–21) Finally, there are three kinds of curving "eye" stroke (*mig gsum*). The best resembles the eye of a fish (*nya mig*) [which is completely round]. The average sort resembles a grain of barley (*nas*) [which is oval shaped], and the worst resembles the triangular-shaped eye of a wrathful deity (*zur gsum khro mig*) [which is almost rounded at the top and thin or flat at the bottom].

Sixteen Secondary Characteristics [iv"]

Then, as for the sixteen secondary characteristics (*bu chos bcu drug*),[501] [which are all associated with superscript and subjoined letters]:

(1–3) The three characteristics of the letter O (*na ro chos gsum*) are that it has two separate parts, it is closed [at the bottom], and it is evenly aligned.

(4–5) The two characteristics of the letter E (*'greng bu'i chos gnyis*) are that it glides down at an angled incline and it is differentiated at the top and bottom.

(6–8) The three characteristics of the letter I (*gi gu'i chos gsum*) are that it is rounded, rolling, and curved.

(9–11) The three characteristics of the letter U (*zhabs kyu'i chos gsum*) are that it is subjoined (*gdags pa can*), extended in the manner of a seat (*gdan thabs brkyang pa*),[502] and endowed with the [sharp] properties of a trident spear.

(12–13) The two characteristics of the subjoined RA (*ra ta'i chos gnyis*) are that it resembles a horse tether and its prominence is restrained.

(14–16) The three characteristics of the subjoined YA (*ya btags kyi chos gsum*) are that it is curved, balanced and rising [at the tail], and light in the middle.

Three General Characteristics [v"]

The following three general characteristics (*spyi chos gsum*) should also be observed:[503] (1) The forms [of the letters] should not be mistaken in length, (2) the length should not deviate from the [permissible] total [dimensions], and (3) the lengths of the forms [of different letters] should be correctly distinguished.

Calligraphic Gridlines [vi"]

For those who wish to know how the square gridlines are formed according to the [traditional] techniques, [once the twelve vertical and eight horizontal gridlines have been drawn, they are divided into upper, middle, and lower sectors]. [In the middle sector, which has six vertical units and is reserved for the main letters,][504] the "shield-like" convex curves (*phub*) and "shoulder" strokes (*dpung*) occupy [only] one unit, the "tapering lip" strokes (*zags mchu*) occupy two units, and the "leg" strokes (*rkang pa*) occupy three units. Therefore, if CA, CHA, RA, and 'A [which have convex curves or shoulder strokes] are too long, they will be defective. If DA, NA, and ZHA [which have tapering strokes] are too long or too short, they will be defective. If KA, GA, and SHA [which have leg strokes] are too short, they will be defective. The subjoined letters [of the lower sector] occupy four units and the superscripts (*steng gi yan lag*) [of the upper sector] occupy two units.

Therefore, [all potential] defects can be avoided when a ruler is used to measure [the middle sector of] six units [in which the main letters are inscribed]. This is but a rough explanation [of how the block-letter script] is to be drawn. One will still have to learn the practical techniques in detail.[505]

Italic Scripts [b"]

> **As for the headless thick-stroked italic script,**
> **There were two [original] traditions—those of Li and Den—**
> **From which many [others] gradually evolved.**

With regard to the headless thick-stroked italic script (*'bru chen*), which is the best of the cursive Tibetan scripts (*bod yig gshar ma*), the letters are drawn against a large grid (*thig tshad che ba*), either in accordance with the Li calligraphic tradition (*li lugs*), which has long been extinct, or the Den calligraphic tradition (*ldan lugs*). The latter is so-called either because it was the tradition of Denma Tsemang, or because it "possesses" (*ldan pa*) an authoritative calligraphic standard.[506]

Then there is the headless thin-stroked italic script (*'bru chung*), in which the letters have a similar form but are drawn against a small grid (*thig tshad chung ba*). These headless italic scripts (*'bru tsha rnams*) which [originally] had only eighteen distinct letters (*yig 'bru*), formed the earliest basic transmission of calligraphy [in Tibet], and it was from them that the "punctuated script" (*tsheg bris*), in which letters forming syllables aligned in squares, separated by punctuation marks, [subsequently] evolved.[507]

Handwriting and Shorthand Scripts [c"]

The "gentle rounded script" (*'jam pa zlum bris*) developed out of the italic scripts, and it had variant forms known as the "tailed script" (*sug po*) and the derivative Baho script (*'ba' ho*), in which elongated tails are accentuated. The latter gave rise to the "short-tailed script" (*sug thung*), and that in turn to the "finely executed style" (*mnyen gra ris*), in which the letters of the "tailed script" were contracted by one-third. That in turn gave rise to the "finely rounded tailed script" (*mnyen pa sug skor*), and that to the [contemporary] "easy and common letter-writing script" (*bde ba phrin yig dkyus ma*). So with regard to these [scripts], there are a great many different practical traditions (*lag rgyun*) in different parts of the country.[508]

Presentation of Calligraphic Technique [3"]

Concerning the third [section on the representations of buddha speech, which is a presentation of calligraphic technique, it says in the root verses]:

> **One should proficiently study the calligraphic proportions,**
> **Writing surfaces, ink, and pens;**
> **One should cherish all major and minor [characteristics of composition],**
> **Maintaining neatness, elegance, and accuracy.**
> **One should write, without contravening the hierarchy [of the various scripts],**
> **Whereby the sacred scriptures [of the Buddhas]**
> **Are copied in the block-letter script, and so forth.**
> **I cannot digress [to consider here] other kinds of calligraphy because they are limitless.**

Before one starts to write, it is important to study the calligraphic proportions (*cha tshad*) and shapes (*dbyibs*) of the letters. In this regard, it is explained that scribes who voluminously copy the sacred scriptures (*gsung rab*) esteem the block-letter script (*dbu can*), as well as the headless italic scripts (*'bru ma*), the "punctuated script" (*tsheg sgrig*), and the "rounded script" (*zlum ris*). Scholar monks (*dge ba'i bshes gnyen*) esteem the "short-tailed script" (*sug thung*) and the finely executed script (*gra ris*). Administrators (*sde dpon*) esteem the "long-tailed" script (*'ba' ho*) and the "finely rounded tailed script" (*sug skor*), while other persons esteem the common letter-writing script (*'phrin yig*). Therefore, individuals should perfect and refine the [scripts] that are particularly useful for their own needs.

After mastering [the appropriate scripts], when one begins to write, one should [initially] study the techniques [for making] paper, the writing surface (*'bri gzhi*), as well as vermilion and black ink (*mtshal snag*), and bamboo pens (*smyu gu*), until one has become proficient in accordance with the ancient treatises and the authentic practical traditions derived from them. Then, by earnest practical application, one should seek to emulate the contributions of past masters.

There are indeed [many] long and short compositions [on these techniques] based on the treatises of past generations, and an infinite number of distinctive practical traditions [of calligraphy], but among them, if I may offer a partial explanation, subsuming and evoking those that are still practiced at the present day:[509]

> [Let us examine] the writing surface (*bris gzhi*),
> As well as the utensils and the substances used for writing.

Paper-Making [a'']

> Writing surfaces may be made from superior, average, and inferior materials.
> The best [writing surface] is paper made from
> *Stellera chamaejasme* with conch-shaped leaves (*shog ldum dung lo ma*),[510]
> Which grows well where the soil is dark, there are juniper trees [nearby],
> And the ground is free from slate and rock.
> The yellow-colored variety that grows in red sandy soil and slate
> Is difficult to prepare and [rather] hard.
> Bark that is thick and harboring insects is inferior.
>
> After collecting [the bark] in the proper way,
> Small particles of earth should be washed away,
> The outer bark should be scraped and rubbed, and the pith extracted.
> Alkaline pebbles (*bya rdo*) are then heated,
> Immersed in ice-cold water, and shaken.
> When the consistency of this solution has become like whey,
> A good test will be if it pricks the tongue, like salt ammoniac (*rgya tshva*).
> Without completing this process, there will be no potency.
> Once the [desired] potency has been reached and impurities removed,
> The stellera [pith] should be cooked in this solution.
> However if it is cooked in an ashy solution, there will be some blemishes.

When [the fibers] have been cooked,
They should be crushed firmly in a stone mortar,
And once the pulp has taken on the consistency of paste,
It should be divided, proportionate to the dimensions
Of the [requisite] sheets [of paper],
And [each batch] should be stirred in a container,
With an equal quantity of water.
This pulpy solution should then be poured into a paper-making tray (*shog bre*),
And it should be left standing in a clear and unsullied film of water,
Without being stirred, [until it dries out].
Due to this [superior] ingredient,
However thick or thin the [desired] paper may be,
The outcome will be successful.

The average sort of [writing surface] is made
From the bark of *Daphne anrantica*.[511]
After peeling off the green shoots,
The inner bark should be cooked for a while,
And the initial liquid then strained off.
The procedures for cooking, grinding,
Sieving, and pouring [the pulpy fibers]
Resemble those already described.
This [ingredient] is particularly well suited for thick paper used in [writing] books.

The worst [writing surfaces] are made
From the roots of common *Stellera chamaejasme*,[512]
Which are to be unearthed.
The inner bark (*bar shun*), the pith clearly visible inside the outer layer,
Should be cooked in an alkaline solution.
[In this regard,] the fibers will become soft, like wool,
When cooked in an ashy solution (*thal khu*).
A dose of myrobalan is then added to draw out the poison.
This ingredient is best when [the plant] is growing in soft and sandy soil,
And in places where soft dark soil predominates.

It produces a hard paper which is good for writing letters
But not very suitable for books.

Since the various qualities of paper
Originating from different countries
Have their [distinctive] materials and manufacturing techniques,
One could digress much [on this subject],
But despite the usefulness [of this approach],
I am bereft [of further knowledge].

Then, [after these preparations, the writing surface] should be rubbed
And polished with a soft, white [pumice] stone
That is used for cutting hairs, and [removing] other residual impurities,
And in this way any holes should be erased.
If the paper is clean, it should be beaten and then rubbed,
So that any traces of earth and stone are removed.
When it retains a whiteness of color,
It is explained to be excellent.

Then, wheat that has not been damaged by frost
Should be washed in water from a hot spring,
Pulverised and stirred in water, until it has the consistency of milk.
Any bubbles that appear should be popped and dissolved.
This size solution should then be filtered for a short while [before use],
But if it is left standing for too long a time,
There is a risk that it will become thin and weak.
If the size has been left standing for more than twenty days
It should be thrown away because it will be old
And its adhesive quality will have diminished.[513]
The pure essence [of the size] should be divided into two parts,
One part should be boiled until it is cooked,
And then it should be mixed with the other part.
Then, in a sunny and humid place where there is no wind,
The paper should be dipped [in the size] and left out to dry.
Alternatively, the size should be mixed in a pan
With one quarter of whey, strained free of butter,
And [the paper] should then be dipped [in this solution] for a while.

If [the solution] is too hot, the paper will be torn,
And if it is too cold, the adhesive quality will be weak
And [the paper surface] will be stained by the size.
Once [the sheets of paper] have definitely dried,
Any [remaining] particles of earth should be removed.

Then, even if it is said that [the paper] is free from green shoots
or sand,
Because there could still be some blemishes,
A wet [sheet of paper] that has been dipped in water
Should be inserted between every sheath of ten dry sheets,
And [the whole bundle] should be compressed.
The sheets should be left like this for one day at the most,
Or, at the very least, for the duration of a tea-break.
However long they are bound together,
The dampness should evenly permeate [the whole sheath].
Then, [the sheath] should be placed upon a smooth liver-shaped
stone,
And it should be beaten and rubbed with a yak horn
That is free from dark stains.
If these utensils are not available, there will be no fault
If [the sheath] is beaten and rubbed using a wooden board and pestle.

It is said that if there is too much size,
The size will smear [the paper surface],
But if there is too little, the glue will adhere to the edges.
If [the sheath] is too dry, it will be somewhat difficult to iron,
But if it is slightly damp, it will be easy [to iron],
And the outcome will be excellent.

The ironing board (*dbur gdan*) should be steady, without wobbling.
If the [ironing stone, *dbur rdo*] is made of conch,
[The paper surface] will turn bluish,
And if it is made of agate,[514]
It will have many lines or marks.
The best [ironing stones] are made of fine gold or banded chalcedony
(*gzi*),
But if these are not available, even the dark and oily horn
Of a wild yak will suffice.[515]

[Once the paper is ready for writing, one should employ]
A measuring ruler (*thig shing*) that is straight and even.
The horizontal calligraphic lines (*byang chub rgyun lam*)
[Should be drawn or plucked]
With a fragrant solution of turmeric and barberry bark,
While the outer and inner margin lines (*phyi nang thig skor*)
Should be drawn or plucked with vermilion.[516]
[These lines] should correspond in their dimensions
To those of the [intended] volume.
Erasures and uneven or crooked [lines] are defects [to be avoided].

Fig. 38. Folio calligraphic and margin lines

BAMBOO PENS [b"]

Then, with regard to the Chinese bamboo pen (*rgya smyug*) used for writing,
Those that are made from tall, thick, and heavy bamboo canes,
Yellow in color, untwisted, and without a [large] hole,
With tips that are soft [and lustrous],

And [a hard exterior] that causes the teeth to slip when biting
down on it[517]
Are praiseworthy for all kinds of writing—in ink, gold,
[and so forth].[518]

The Naxi bamboo pen (*'jang smyug*) which is black in color
And hollow, is well-suited for shorthand letter-writing scripts,[519]
The metal-nib pen (*lcags smyug*) is best
For [copying] large scriptures,
While the "southern" pen (*lho smyug*)
And the "ravine" pen (*rong smyug*) are also acceptable.[520]

[When making a bamboo pen],[521]
The bamboo [stalks] should be secured [and fumigated]
Within a chimney [or a smoky place] for a long time,
And then smeared, at best, with the old marrow of a cow,
Or, if that is not available, with [some other kind of old] marrow.
They should then be inserted within a pile of [freshly] roasted grain,
And gently polished until they become as hard as bone.

Then one should get a knife of a quality suitable for making
[bamboo pens].
Those made of various types of iron are good,
And the metal should be smelted and refined.
The [ideal] knife, combining sharpness, suppleness, and strong
temper,
Should have its point and blade sharpened until they feel cold
[to the touch],[522]
While the back [of the knife] should be straight and [the blade] flat.[523]

The blade should be sharpened on a whetstone (*bdar rdo*)
Of suitable size, flat, and supple:
The outer edge only once and the inner edge six times.[524]
In this way, the sharpness of the blade should be capable of splitting a
hair.
However, if the blade is sharpened too much, it will turn into iron
filings,
So if it is sharpened somewhat less,[525]
The blade will be [suitably] thick and sharp.

The length of a bamboo pen should not exceed one span,
And it should be no shorter than the index finger,
While it should also be of suitable thickness,
And it should be planed down until it comfortably fits
Between the thumb and the fingers.[526]

Then, at a place measured at one and a half relative "finger-widths"
From the tip of the pen ([*smyug*] *rtse*),
[The two tines of the nib-point should be planed down,][527]
Allocating two thirds for the nib (*smyug rdzing*)
And one third for the actual point (*mchu*)
A small cleft (*gas chung*) [should be made in the point]
If one wishes to write the block-letter script (*gzab*),
Or a larger cleft if one wishes to write quickly.
It is said that "[the size of] the vent hole (*smyug yur*)
Should correspond to [the size of] the actual nib."[528]

When looking [at a pen] from the rear,
The left and right [tines of the nib] should be symmetrical,
And the point of the nib (*rdzing mchu*) should not be too flat.
Rather, the surface [of the point] that is cut should be cut at
an angle.[529]

It is said that if one is skilled [in cutting] bamboo nibs
Which are said to be "endowed with the [requisite] three [parts]
And replete with the five [attributes],"[530]
One will become skillful in calligraphy.

With dexterity that [distinguishes] good and bad calligraphy,
Dependent on one's proficiency in [writing] speed,
[One should overcome] hesitation
And master refinement with regard to spelling.
With suitable pressure and balance of the thumb and fingers,
And suitable [attention to] flow and pause,
Understanding verbosity, but endowed with brevity,[531]
The best [calligraphy] is that which combines elegance
With accuracy of spelling and dexterity.[532]

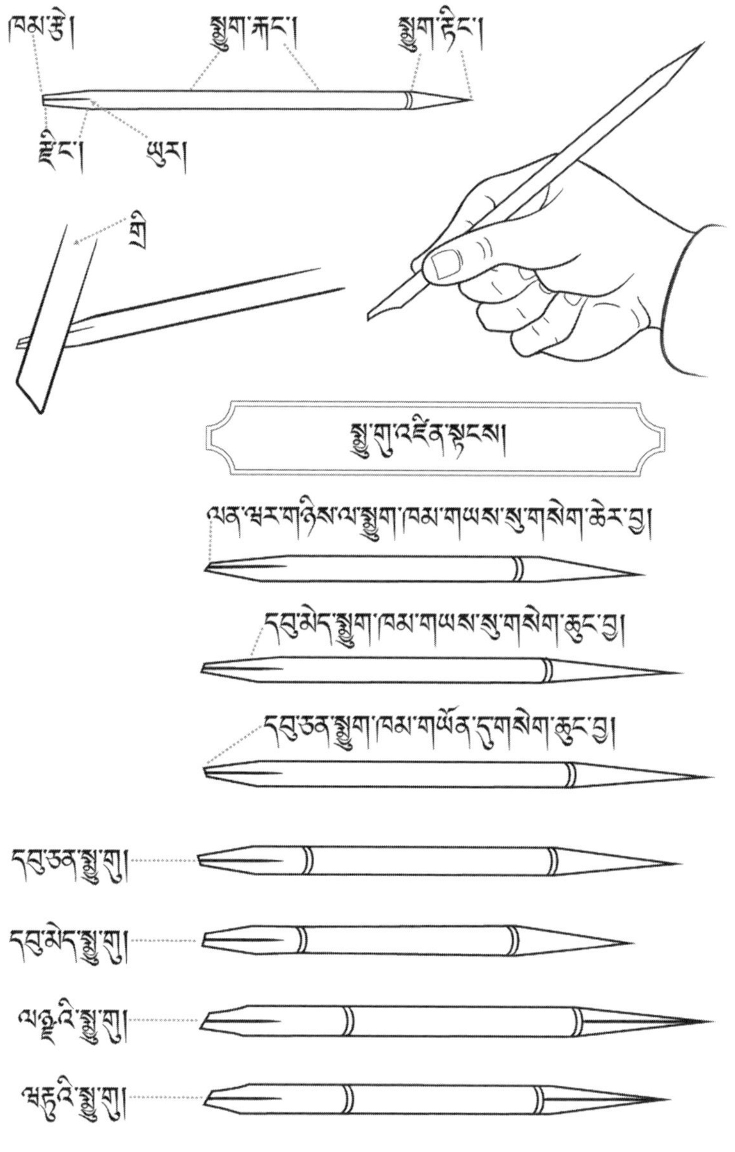

Fig. 39. Bamboo pens: their parts, nib cuts, and hold

Preparing Black Ink [c"]

The substances used for writing comprise both ink-black and vermilion.
First, with regard to the materials used for making [black] ink,
The best are accumulated flakes of lampblack soot or pinewood,
While the average sort includes the bark of the cherry tree—[533]
These last two should be stripped and peeled.
Birch bark (*gro ga*) is also somewhat similar to the latter.
The worst is pine resin (*thang tshil*), which resembles fat—
If it is too old it will resemble [congealed] blood
And if it is too fresh it will not be adhesive.

Having accumulated a large quantity [of these appropriate ingredients],
A clay pot with five to seven holes in its base should be raised
Upon a [specially] constructed circular hearth
Or upon a stove for roasting grain,
And when the wood is burned in the stove,
The soot from within the upper parts of the pot should be gathered—
Grime from the lower parts is inferior and should be thrown away.
In case it should be hard to collect or if it should spill down,
This should be undertaken with care, and in an isolated place.

Then [the soot] should be placed in a metal pot, along with clear glue,[534]
And simmered for a while, under fire.
When the glue has melted,
The solution should be poured [into a bag] and kneaded.
[It is said that] one dry measure per day should be ground,
And that when the grinding emits a crackling sound,
It will reach the required consistency.
However, the grinding should continue until the [desired] potency is obtained,
And the longer it takes, the better the outcome.
Repeated kneading until [the ink] has dried
Is held to be the best technique for making vermilion and [black] ink.[535]

Then, when the [dry ink] is brought to a paste-like consistency,
If it sticks to the hand, its adhesiveness will be weak,
Or if it is hard and solid, these will be the greatest faults.
If it leaves an imprint on the skin but does not stick,
It is held to have suitable adhesiveness.

Moreover, it is mentioned in an ancient treatise that
With [an infusion of] elecampane (*manuratha*, *Inula helenium*),
[The ink] will become soft and freckled.
With an infusion of sandalwood, it will be held by the pen.[536]
Shellac (*rgya skyegs*) will add a reddish lustre,
And with an infusion of musk (*gla rtsi*), the fragrance [of the ink] will linger.
With an infusion of orchid (*dbang lag*) and campion (*sug pa*),[537]
The lustre and richness [of the ink] will be unsurpassed.
With an infusion of saussurea (*spyi bzhur*), [538]
[The ink] will flow well.
With a solution of camphor (*ga bur*), it will not spoil in summer.
With a solution of galangal and long pepper (*Piper longum*),
It will not solidify in winter, and so forth.
Although there are many other techniques for mixing [herbs],
Including solutions of old pine resin (*thang khrag*),
Wheat, barley, parched grain, and the like,
They are mostly defective,
With the exception of some of [the aforementioned] infusions,
Such as campion and saussurea.
Those are not good [techniques] because they entail too much compounding.
It is essential to understand the essential properties
Of the appropriate materials [for mixing with soot].
If one can only make a small amount,
It will be best if the kneading is undertaken [vigorously]
By the hand of a younger person.

Preparing Vermilion Ink [d'']

The best quality of vermilion (*mtshal*) resembles crushed and lustrous crystal,
The average sort has a bright red hue,

And the worst is reddish brown.
It should be ground finely in a smooth, white mortar,
And then a clear solution of myrobalan should be poured in,
Causing the vermilion to sink.
The [yellow] surface water should be drained off, up to three times.
[During the grinding] one should take care to slightly rotate the pestle.[539]
Then, when this refining has gone on for a long time,
One should pour in some binder—
The best is Chinese glue (*rgya spyin*), but if that is not available,
A clear solution of some solid glue will do.
For a quick result, the vermilion powder should be compounded
In the glue solution,
And kneaded slowly, in a container that is without rust,
So that it takes on a strong dark color.
This is an essential technique that will prevent the vermilion from aging.

In whatever ways [the powder] is compounded,
When the time comes to write,
If one wishes to add a decoction
Of "cubeb and long pepper six" (*ka pi drug sbyor*),
In a clean container that is free from rust and stains,
Pour about one third of cubeb and long pepper mixture and glue
Into two thirds of vermilion,
And expose it to the sun for a while.

Or, when adding a decoction of salt ammoniac,
A measure of curd, borax, and
A little sal wood ash (*spos dkar thal, Shorea robusta*)
Should also be included with the salt.
The attributes of these respectively are that
[The first] adds luster, [the second] improves adhesiveness,
And [the third] eliminates traces of moisture.

To enhance the redness [of the vermilion],
It should be [kneaded until] it dries out.

If it flows with difficulty [being too viscous] and is yellowish,
Pour in some clean water.
If it is pale brown in color, add some cubeb and long pepper mixture.

Now, as for the method of compounding cubeb and long pepper,
One should thoroughly clean some campion (*lug sug*)
That has been unearthed in spring or at the end of autumn,
And cook it in a non-metallic container, until it dissolves.
When it has been strained,
Add the aforementioned ingredients to the decoction,
And stir it slowly and gently while it simmers on a fire.
To this triple compounded decoction of vermilion, cubeb, and long pepper,
One should add a little sugar (*rgyal mo ka ra*).
With regard to this technique for enhancing the color quality,
The compound of vermilion and glue is easily made,
But, in any event, one should take care not to burn it in the fire.

Moreover, there are those who would add [other ingredients],
Including a compound of egg albumen and clear serum.
Although these techniques do have short-term positive results,
They will be defective [in the long term],
For which reason they should be rejected.[540]

Conclusion [e"]

The best of ingredients for writing books
Are vermilion and carbon black inks which are bright, shiny, and lustrous.
Even after many years have passed, their color will not fade,
And even though they may get wet, they will not stick or smudge.
If, diverging from this authentic transmission,
A scribe does not care for the ink, paper, and bamboo pen,
Even though he wishes to write carefully, he will make mistakes.

Since this is the case, one should take care of one's [writing] materials and utensils, and greatly cherish all the major and minor characteristics of calligraphy, which are [encapsulated in] the following three defining characteristics: (1) the ink strokes (*snag lam*) should be neat; (2) the body of the letters (*'bru khog*) should be elegant; and (3) the spelling should be accurate, without omissions, additions, or errors.

It is best to follow the ancient tradition of calligraphy in which the hierarchy [of the scripts], based on the greatness [of their content] is not contravened. Thus, the block-letter script (*gzab chen*) and its headless variant (*gzab chung*) should be used for copying the great scriptures [of the buddhas], the large format italic script (*'bru chen*) should be used for copying the textual commentaries of learned Indian masters, and the small format italic script (*'bru chung*) should be used for copying texts of the Tibetan commentarial traditions.

I cannot digress here to consider the other kinds of calligraphy, exemplified by the new scripts (*yig gsar*),[541] the symbolic script [of the ḍākinīs] (*brda' yig*), and the scripts used in transcribing revealed teachings (*gter yig*) because they are limitless in number.[542]

Representations of Buddha Mind [cc']

The third part of the detailed exegesis, concerning the representations of buddha mind (*thugs rten*), comprises four sections: (1) a general presentation of the types of stūpa; (2) a particular exegesis of the practical techniques [for constructing stūpas]; (3) additional remarks on extraordinary traditions [concerning stūpas]; and (4) an explanation of hand-held emblems and certain subsidiary points.

The Types of Stūpa [1"]

Concerning the first [the general presentation of the types of stūpa, it says in the root verses]:

> **As for the representations of buddha mind,**
> **There are explained to be five particular types [of stūpa]:**
> **Those that are spontaneously present by nature, those that are unsurpassed,**
> **Those that are consecrated by blessings,**
> **Those that arise through spiritual accomplishments,**
> **And those that correspond to the different vehicles.**

It is explained that the generic term "stūpa" refers to a "receptacle of the offerings of buddha mind or the buddha body of actual reality" (*thugs sam chos sku'i mchod rten*)[543] and, as such, it may be applicable in five particular contexts.

For, generally speaking, stūpas (*mchod rten*) may comprise structures that are spontaneously present by nature (*rang bzhin lhun gyis 'grub*), those that are unsurpassed (*bla na med*), those that are consecrated by blessings (*byin gyis brlabs pa*), those that arise through spiritual accomplishments (*dngos grub 'byung ba*), and those that correspond to the different vehicles (*theg pa so so*).[544]

Spontaneously Present by Nature [a'']

With regard to [stūpas that are spontaneously present by nature], it is said in the *Tantra of the Indestructible Array*:[545]

> The supreme bone relics [of the buddhas] (*sku gdung chen po*)
> Are always present
> In [the form of] mighty Mount [Sumeru]
> Within the world-system of desire,
> As an exalted tiered throne
> Within the world-system of form,
> And as a dome-shaped receptacle and plinth
> Within the world-system of formlessness.[546]

The *Supreme Transmission of Monastic Discipline* also explains [the distinction between] the aspects of the offering receptacles (*stūpa*) of the outer container world (*phyi snod*) and its inner contents (*nang bcud*); while the *Tantra of the Wheel of Time* clearly explains that the four maṇḍalas (*dkyil 'khor bzhi po*) [of the four elements—earth, water, fire, and wind] are respectively visualized in the forms of (1) the tiers [of the stūpa] (*vedī, bang rim*); (2) the dome [symbolic] of Mount Sumeru (*sumerukumbha, ri rab bum pa*); (3) the section from the high pavilion (*harmikā/ droṇa, 'bre*) downwards, [which symbolizes] the neck and face of Mount Sumeru; and (4) the rain gutter (*varṣasthālī, char khebs*), along with the [stacked] rings of the sacred teachings (*chos 'khor*), above [the high pavilion, which symbolize] the hair [of Mount Sumeru].[547]

Unsurpassed [b'']

With regard to [stūpas that are unsurpassed], it is said:

> As for the fruits that emerge from the immeasurable and
> limitless [abode]:

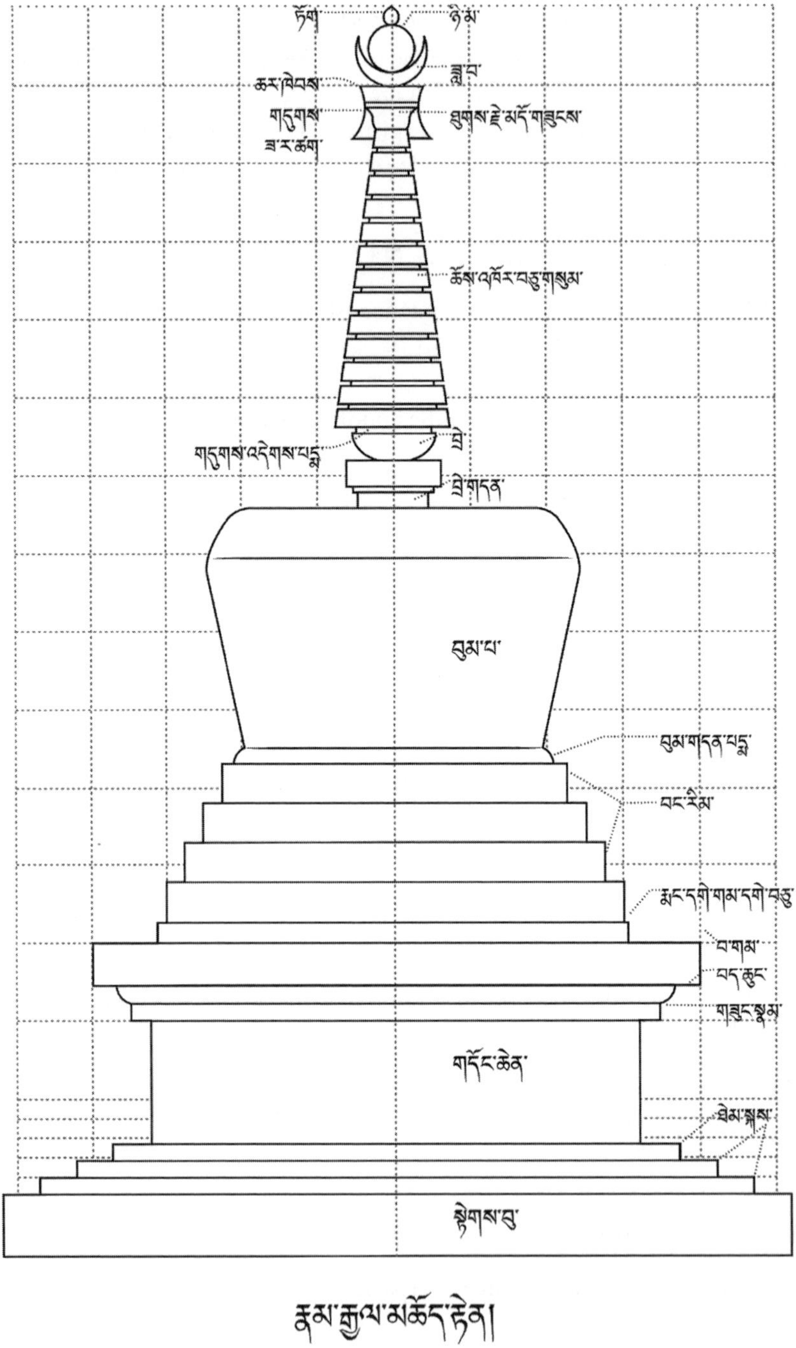

རྣམ་རྒྱལ་མཆོད་རྟེན།

Fig. 40. The distinct elements of a stūpa

In the east there is the [stūpa named]
Vajra Mountain of loving-kindness (*byams pa*),
In the south there is the [stūpa named]
Gemstone Mountain of compassion (*snying rje*),
In the west there is the [stūpa named]
Lotus Mountain of empathetic joy (*dga' ba*),
And in the north, there is the [stūpa named]
Crossed-Vajra Mountain of equanimity (*btang snyoms*).[548]

With these words, the *Tantra of the Empowerment of the Seminal Point*[549] is known to explain that there are four [unsurpassed] aspects, including the limitless Vajra Mountain of immeasurable loving-kindness in the east.

Consecrated by Blessings [c"]

With regard to [stūpas that are consecrated by blessings], in a well-known passage from the *Tantra of the Emergence of Cakrasaṃvara*, it is said:

The bone relics consecrated by blessing
Appeared in eight parts on the four continents.

And in its commentary,[550] the following explanation is given:

> In the eastern continent of Videha, there are two stūpas known as the "treasure of resplendent equanimity" (*byin ldan snyoms gter*) and the "svāstika crest with its well-fashioned arms" (*mthar legs gYung drung tog*). In the southern continent of Jambudvīpa, there are two stūpas known as the "emanation of compassionate spirituality" (*thugs rje sprul pa*) and the "wish-fulfilling spontaneous presence" (*yid bzhin lhun grub*). In the western continent of Aparagodanīya, there are two stūpas known as "the peerless and inconceivable [reality]" (*dpe med bsam 'das*) and the "wondrous and renowned expanse of reality" (*rmad grags chos dbyings*). Then, in the northern continent of Uttarakuru, there are two stūpas known as the "gemstone mountain of enlightened attributes" (*yon tan rin chen brtsegs pa*) and the "lamp of extensive bliss" (*bde rgyas sgron me*).[551]

Arisen from Spiritual Accomplishments [d"]

With regard to [stūpas that arise through spiritual accomplishments], in the *Tantra of Supreme Nectar* it is said:[552]

> The Eight Mātaraḥ are established
> As the great protectresses of corpses,
> While the eight stūpas are also established
> As their great power places.

The [commentary] on this text explains that "In ancient times, when Rudra was disciplined by Heruka, eight stūpas arose through spiritual accomplishment as the receptacles of the eight Mataraḥ in the charnel grounds of eight [distinct] lands.[553] These included the Śaṅkara [Stūpa] in Magadha, the Mount Potala [Stūpa] in Siṅghala, the Bodhnath (*bya khri kha shor*) [Stūpa] in Nepal, the Geudosha[554] [Stūpa] in Siṃhadvīpa, the Gandha [Stūpa] at Gomasa in Khotan (*li yul go ma sa la gan dha*), the Kanaka [Stūpa] in Kashmir, and the Sukhakumāra (*bde skyid gzhon nu*)[555] Stūpa in Sahor.[556]

Corresponding to the Different Vehicles [e"]

With regard to [stūpas corresponding to the different vehicles], there are three sorts: those constructed in accordance with the vehicle of pious attendants (*śrāvakayāna*), the vehicle of hermit buddhas (*pratyekabuddhayāna*) and the greater vehicle (*mahāyāna*).[557] Among them, the first type resembles a monk's staff fixed upon an upturned begging bowl, resting upon a monastic robe folded in four (*chos gos bzhi bltabs*). The second resembles a cube, resting upon a square foundation, surmounted by twelve round tiers and an eight-spoke wheel. The third is said by the master Nāgārjuna to include eight [distinct] stūpa [designs]—one that is round as a *bimpa* berry, resembling an upturned begging bowl; one that is shaped like a small house; one that resembles a victory banner (*dhvaja*); and so forth.[558]

Then, with reference to the different classes of the tantras, the stūpas of the Action and Conduct Tantras are said to have tiers that are internally cut short and externally projecting, or else projecting at the center with the two sides truncated, and surmounted by twelve [stacked] wheels and so forth. [By contrast,] the stūpas of the Yoga Tantras include the aforementioned Vajra Mountain type, while those of the Unsurpassed Yoga Tantras (*Yoganiruttaratantra*) include those described in the *Tantra of the Wheel of Time*, and so forth.[559]

Techniques of Stūpa Construction [2"]

The second section, which is a particular exegesis of the practical techniques [for constructing stūpas] has two parts, the ordinary [techniques] and the uncommon [techniques].

The Ordinary Techniques [a"]

With regard to the former [it says in the root verses]:

> **The practical techniques [of stūpa construction] that are applicable**
> **Include those suitable for ordinary persons, pious attendants,**
> **Hermit buddhas, and conquerors,**
> **As described in the transmissions [of monastic discipline].**

Among all those [types of stūpa] that have just been described, with regard to the actual practical techniques [for the construction of stūpas] that are applicable at the present day, there are [four extant] types of stūpa: those suitable [as reliquaries] for ordinary persons, for pious attendants, for hermit buddhas, and for [the buddhas, or] "conquerors."

Stūpas Associated with Ordinary Persons, Pious Attendants, Hermit Buddhas [i"–iii"]

Now, it is said in the transmissions of monastic discipline (*'dul ba lung*) that, for holding the relics of an ordinary person, [stūpas] should be bare, without an umbrella spire (*catrāvalī*). For pious attendants, they should have umbrella spires, the number [of rings] corresponding to the degree of their fruitional [realization]. For hermit buddhas, stūpas should have an umbrella spire with seven [rings]; and for buddhas they should have an umbrella spire with thirteen [rings].[560] All of them should have a rain gutter (*varṣasthālī*, *char khebs*) and a [gemstone] crest (*ketu*, *tog*).

In this context, the term "umbrella spire" should be recognized as referring to the [stacked] "rings" or "wheels symbolizing the sacred teachings" (*dharmacakra*), while the term "rain gutter" is synonymous here with "umbrella veil" (*gdugs*).

EIGHT STŪPAS SUITABLE FOR BUDDHAS [iv"]

With regard to the eight stūpas of the conquerors,
Although their measurements are indefinite,
The scholars of Tibet generally attest to [the method outlined in]
The [*Commentary*] *on the Taintless* [*Crown Protuberance*].
Accordingly, they refer to the height [of a stūpa]
As sixteen large units, and the width as slightly more than half of that.

It is said in the esoteric instructions of particular lineages that since all stūpas contain within them relics of the sacred teachings, they are all [to be identified as] offering receptacles of the buddha body of reality (*chos sku'i mchod rten*). Therefore, all types of stūpa emblematic of the conquerors (*rgyal ba'i mchod rten*) are conscientiously made at the present day, so that there exist [stūpas of] many different shapes and aspects constructed by living [masters], some of which contain relics of the transcendent lord [Śākyamuni Buddha] and can be classed as offering receptacles for his teeth, hair, nails, small bone relics (*ring bsrel*), and so forth, and others which do not. With regard to the foremost among them all, it is said in the *Sūtra That Expresses the Goals of Activity*:[561]

The bone relics should be placed within eight stūpas,
Which correspond respectively to the deeds of an emanational [buddha],
Once they have been revealed!

Therefore, when the extraordinary [eight] principal deeds of the Teacher [Śākyamuni Buddha] had been fully revealed [in the human world], the people of different lands constructed stūpas [to commemorate these enlightened acts], establishing the traditions of their [respective] festivals. Among them, the [following series of] eight stūpas accords with the systematic presentation found in the glorious master Nāgārjuna's *Euolgy to the Stūpas of the Eight Supreme Sacred Places*, and it is universally esteemed, conforming as it does to the generally accepted norm.[562]

STŪPA OF THE SUGATAS [aa"]

The Stūpa of the Sugatas (*bde gshegs mchod rten*), or Stūpa of Auspicious Origin (*bkra shis 'byung ba'i mchod rten*), which was built [by King Śuddhodhana in the Lumbinī Grove] at Kapilavastu to commemorate the time when our Teacher [Śākyamuni Buddha] was born, is round and adorned with lotus petals, stacked in four or seven lotus tiers.[563]

Stūpa of Supreme Enlightenment [bb"]

The Stūpa of Supreme Enlightenment (*byang chub chen po'i mchod rten*), which [was built by King Bimbisāra] to commemorate the time when the Buddha attained manifest enlightenment (*abhisambodhi*) at Vajrāsana,[564] is square, with four tiers.[565]

Stūpa of the Wheel of the Sacred Teachings [cc"]

The Stūpa of Pristine Cognition (*ye shes kyi mchod rten*), or Stūpa of the Wheel of the Sacred Teachings (*chos 'khor mchod rten*), which [was built by Ājñātakauṇḍinya and his band of monks] to commemorate the time when the Buddha turned the wheel of the sacred teachings at Vārānasī, is square, with four tiers and projecting bays—the best forming one hundred and eight gates, the average sort forming six gates, and the worst sixteen gates.[566]

Stūpa of Miracles [dd"]

The Stūpa Defeating Extremists (*mu stegs pham byed kyi mchod rten*), or Stūpa of Miracles (*cho 'phrul mchod rten*), which [was built by the Licchāvis] to commemorate the time when the Buddha revealed a miraculous display [of emanational forms] at the Jetāvana Grove in Śrāvastī, is square, with four tiers, and a projecting bay (*'bur*) on each of its four sides. Alternatively, it may be round, with four tiers in the form of lotus petals.[567]

Stūpa of the Divine Descent [ee"]

The Stūpa of the Divine Descent (*lha babs mchod rten*), or Stūpa of the Thirty-three Gods (*sum cu rtsa gsum lha'i mchod rten*), which [was built by the inhabitants of Dyutimat] to commemorate the time when the Teacher, sojourning at Dyutimat in Vaiśālī, performed a rain retreat ceremony in the celestial realm (*sum rtsen*) of Tuṣita, but interrupted [the retreat] in the morning to establish his [deceased] mother in the truth, and then descended to [Laṅkā in] Jambūdvīpa in the afternoon, has four or eight tiers with a projecting bay on each side, and a ladder in the center of each projecting bay.[568]

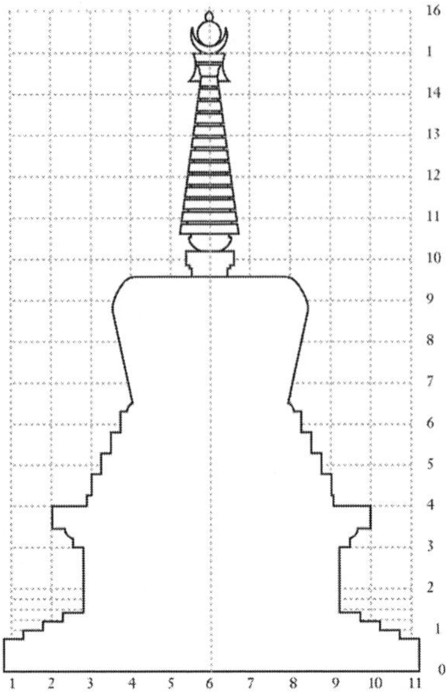

བྱང་ཆུབ་མཆོད་རྟེན།

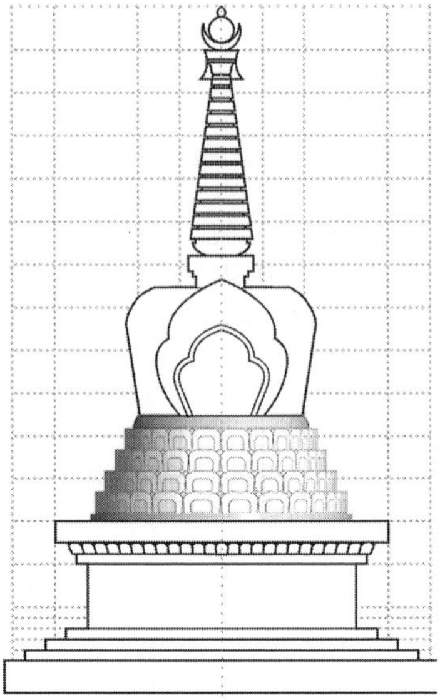

པད་སྤུངས་མཆོད་རྟེན།

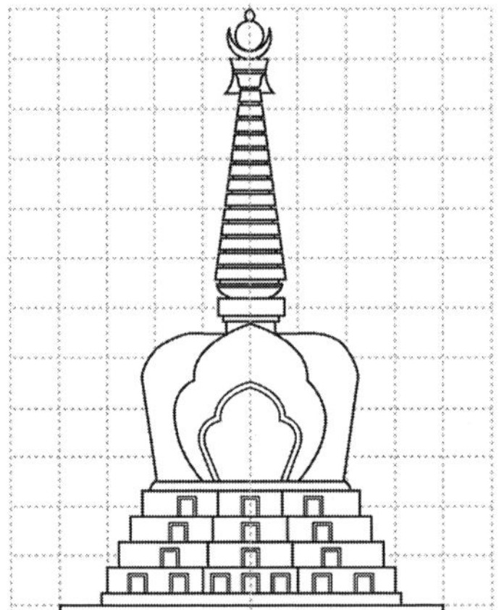

སྒོ་མང་མཆོད་རྟེན།

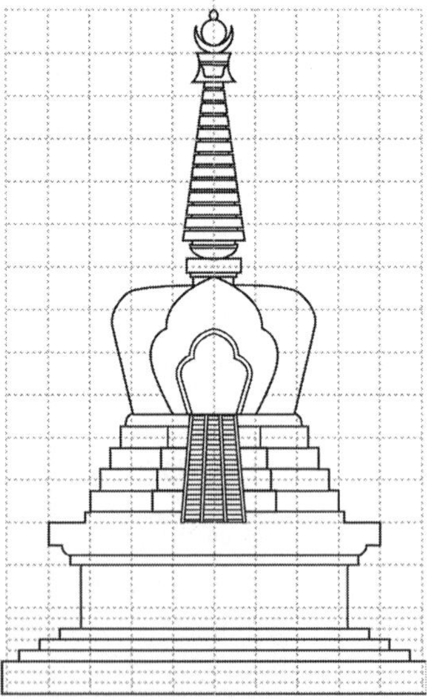

ལྷ་བབས་མཆོད་རྟེན།

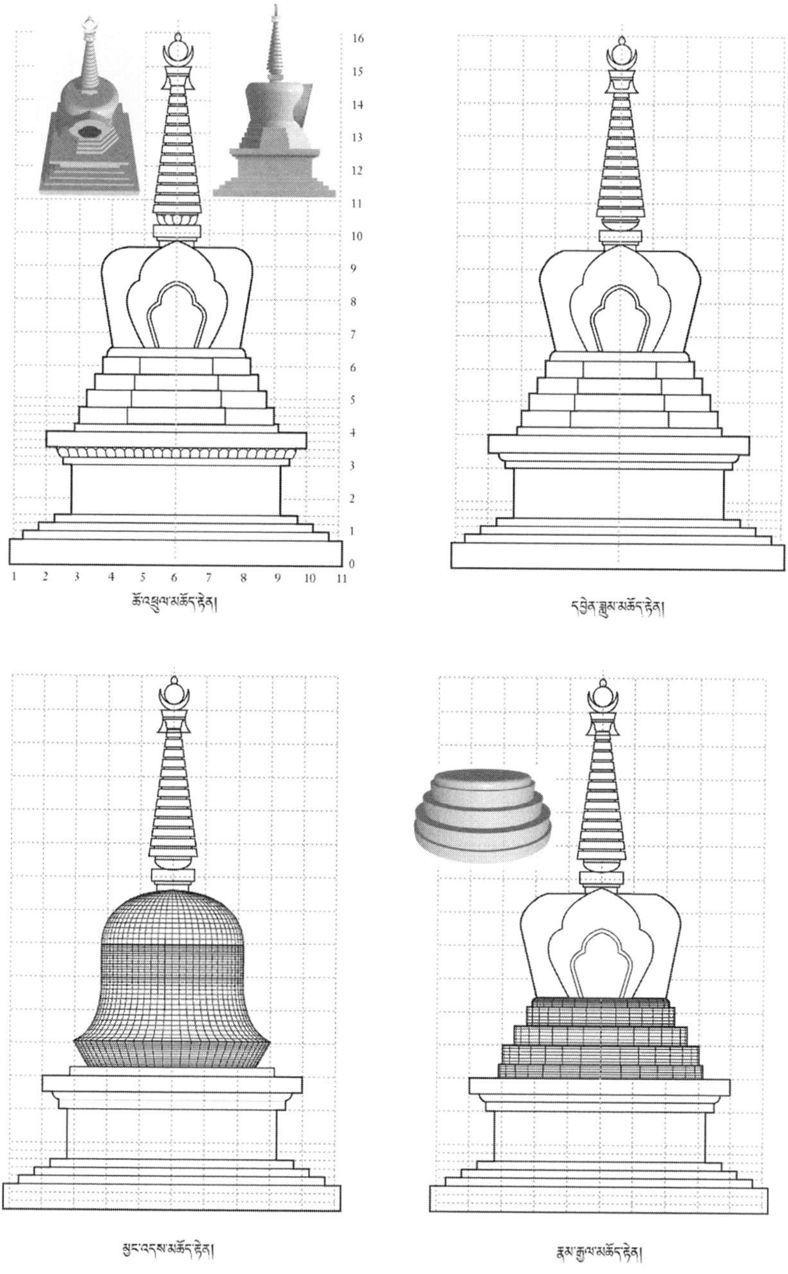

Fig. 41. The eight types of stūpa suitable for Buddhas

Stūpa of Resolving Schism [ff"]

The Stūpa of Resolving Schism (*dbyen bzlums mchod rten*), also known as the Stūpa of Solar Rays (*'od zer can gyi mchod rten*) or the Stūpa of Manifest Loving-kindness (*byams dngos mchod rten*), which [was built by the Magadhans] to commemorate the time when the supreme pair [Śāriputra and Maudgalyāyana] were reconciled after Devadatta had provoked schism within the monastic community, has four tiers and is square, but the four corners are all evenly truncated.[569]

Stūpa of Victory [gg"]

The Stūpa of Blessings (*byin rlabs mchod rten*), or Stūpa of Victory (*rnam rgyal mchod rten*), which [was built by the citizens of Vaiśālī] to commemorate the time when the Buddha [empowered and] consecrated the formative predispositions of his own life span (*sku tshe'i 'du byed*) [so as to prolong his life] for a [further] three months at Vaiśālī, is round, with three tiers.[570]

Stūpa of Nirvāṇa [hh"]

The Stūpa of Nirvāṇa (*myang 'das mchod rten*), which [was built by the local Mallas] to commemorate the time when the Buddha passed into [final] nirvāṇa at Kuśinagara, is tierless, positioned directly above the "dome plinth" (*bum gdan*) slab, which rests upon the podium (*gdan khri*).[571]

Dimensions of the Stūpa [v"]

In general, the measurements and the shapes of stūpas are indefinite. According to the sūtras it is said that the area covered by a stūpa containing relics of the Buddha may be [as large as] one *yojana*.[572] But it is also explained in the *Sūtra of the Stacked Mansion House* that a stūpa could be as small as a grain of emblic myrobalan, the umbrella spire as small as a leaf of Indian juniper, and the life-supporting pole or axis (*yūpa, srog shing*) [within it] as small as a needle.[573] Therefore, [the size of a stūpa] should be measured in accordance with the mental capacity of each individual and their particular degree of wealth. That said, the practical techniques for the proportional measurement [of stūpas] are important, so that constructional defects can be avoided.

Tibetan scholars generally attest to the method of [proportional measurement] that is documented in the *Commentary on the Taintless Crown Protu-*

berance, which was [originally] a renowned Chinese text, while there are also [indigenous] treatises [on this subject] composed by Buton [Rinchendrub], Taktsang Lotsāwa, Tulku Trengkheb Palden Zangpo, and others.[574] The proportional measurements of the regent Sangye Gyatso which combine the best aspects of all these [systems] have great currency throughout [Tibet] at the present day.[575]

According to the tradition of the *Taintless* [*Crown Protuberance*], sixteen large units (*cha chen*) should be measured from the "virtuous foundation" slab (*rmang dge ba*) [of a stūpa] to its crest (*uṣṇīṣa*, *tog*), but according to the other [indigenous Tibetan sources], it is prescribed that the actual [height of the stūpa] should measure twelve large units, from the "small capping" slab (*bad chung*) upwards. Since decorative features are permissible from the "lion throne" podium (*nemī*, *seng khri*) upwards, there appear to be many [different] traditions [of measurement].[576] These measurements all refer to the height [of a stūpa]. The width [of the stūpa] is said to be half the height, or slightly more than half the height.

Symbolism of the Stūpa [vi"]

The venerable Eighth [Karmapa] elucidated the particularly sublime measurement grids (*thig tshad*) appropriate for the eight stūpas, basing his appraisal on the measurements given in the Chapter on Pristine Cognition (*jñānapaṭala*, *ye shes le'u*) from the *Tantra of the Wheel of Time*.[577] These can be examined in his *Mirror of Great Sunlight*.[578]

Therein, with regard to the particular symbolism which it is essential [to know], it is said:[579]

> Upon the podium base (*gdan gyi sa 'dzin*) there are three steps (*them skad gsum*),
> Above which are [successively] the "lion throne" podium,
> And the "small capping" slab, which acts as a base for the gridlines (*thig gdan*).
> Above these [in succession] are the [decorative] frieze of retentive mantra (*gzungs sa*),
> The "large capping" slab (*bad chen*),[580]
> And the "virtuous foundation" slab (*rmang dge ba*).
> Above these in general there are the four tiers (*caturvedī*, *bam rim bzhi*),
> Followed [in succession] by the "dome plinth" (*bum rten*),[581]

The actual dome (*kumbha, bum pa*) and the "high pavilion plinth"
(*'bre gdan*),
And then by the high pavilion (*harmikā, 'bre*),
The [lotus] support of the umbrella spire (*padmamūla, gdugs 'degs*),
And the thirteen [stacked] rings
With their protruding "male" rims and truncated "female" rims,[582]
Forming a garland of lotus light rays.
Above these is [the finial known as]
The "cross-beam containing sūtras and retentive mantra
Of great compassion" (*thugs rje mdo gzungs zhu gya gram*).
This in turn supports the umbrella veil,
Surmounted [in succession] by a rain gutter,
A crescent moon, a solar disc, and a gemstone crest.

Concerning the natural purities that these represent, the meaning is elucidated as follows, based on the *Differentiation of the Parts of a Stūpa*, composed by the master Śāntigarbha:[583]

The "small capping" slab and the "frieze of retentive mantra"
Symbolize the six recollections.
The "large capping" slab and the "tenfold virtuous foundation" slab
Symbolize the [four] immeasurable aspirations.
Alternatively, it is also said that these last two are reversed.
The four tiers respectively symbolize
The [four] foundations of mindfulness, the [four] trainings,
The four supports for miraculous ability, and the five faculties;
While the dome plinth symbolizes the five powers,
And the dome itself symbolizes the [seven] branches of
enlightenment.
The high pavilion symbolizes the [eightfold] sublime path.
All these are the naturally pure causal attributes [of the stūpa].[584]

The life-supporting pole or axis symbolizes
The essential nature of the ten aspects of knowledge,
Namely, [knowledge of the sacred teachings, knowledge of] relative
appearances,
Recollection [of past lives], [knowledge of] other minds,
[Knowledge of] the four truths, [knowledge of] the cessation
[of corruption],

And [knowledge that] it will not be regenerated.[585]
The lotus [support for the rings] symbolizes
Skillful means and discriminative awareness.
The [thirteen] rings symbolize the ten powers,
And the three essential recollections.
The rain gutter symbolizes compassion,
While the crest symbolizes the buddha body of reality.
Those [attributes] are explained to embody the essential nature of the stūpa.[586]

The decorative features [of the stūpa] symbolize enlightened attributes.
Among them, the long stone slab [of the base] symbolizes
Possession of the four fearlessnesses,
The steps [above it] symbolize the four [commitments] that are not to be guarded,
The victory banner symbolizes victory in battle over the four demonic forces,
The flower garlands symbolize the blazing major and minor marks,
The four victory banners symbolize the reality of the four truths,
The bells symbolize the buddha speech that is endowed
With the sixty attributes of the voice of Brahmā,
The sun and moon symbolize the dawning of pristine cognition,
The mirror symbolizes possession of the four facets of pristine cognition,
The crown symbolizes attainment of the kingdom of the sacred teachings,
And the streamers symbolize that the pleasant sound
Of the sacred teachings is pervasive—
Those are the naturally pure fruitional attributes [of the stūpa].[587]

Then, [specifically with regard to
The Stūpa of the Wheel of the Sacred Teachings,]
The multiple gates symbolize the four truths
And the eight approaches to liberation,
As well as [the twelve links of] dependent origination,
And the sixteen types of emptiness.[588]
The projecting bays symbolize that acts of benefit are performed
For the sake of living beings

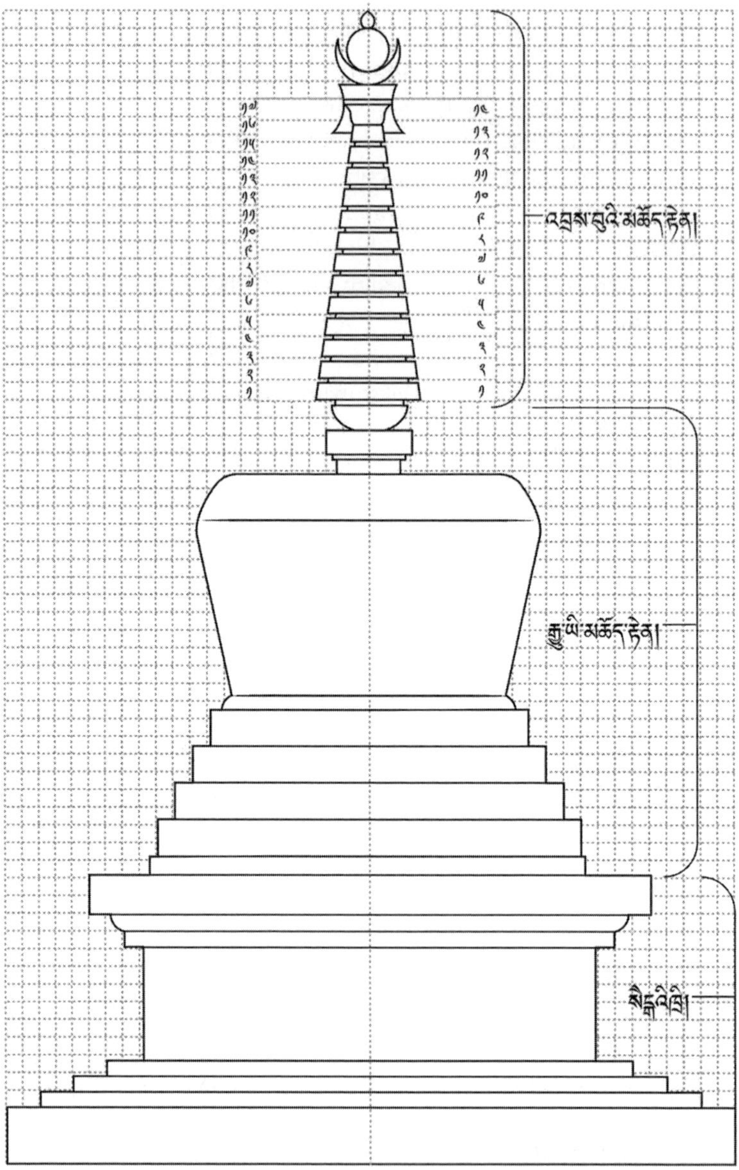

བྱང་ཆུབ་མཆོད་རྟེན།

Fig. 42. Model grid showing the proportions of the Stūpa of Supreme Enlightenment

By means of extraordinary and sublime emanational forms.
The step ladder symbolizes that the Buddha appeared
For the sake of others,
The lotus symbolizes that he is uncovered by the stains of cyclic existence,
While the absence of tiers symbolizes
Freedom from engagement in the rebirth process,
And also freedom from conceptual elaboration.[589]

With regard to the [Stūpa of] Resolving Schism,
The causal attributes symbolize [control of] the three poisons,
And the evenly truncated tiers of the mid-section symbolize
The eight approaches to liberation.[590]

Uncommon Techniques [b″]

Concerning the uncommon [techniques for constructing stūpas, it says in the root verses]:

As far as the uncommon stūpa of pristine cognition
Mentioned in the [*Tantra of*] *the Wheel of Time* is concerned,
When the Buddha is seated in a cross legged-posture,
The area from his navel downwards corresponds to the terraces [of the stūpa];
The abdomen, to the dome plinth;
The [chest] from there as far as the shoulders, to the bulging dome;
The throat, to the high pavilion; [the face] as far as the hair ringlet,
To the face [painted] on the high pavilion;
And the [hair knot] from there upwards, to the [stacked] wheels
Of the sacred teachings and the crest [of the stūpa].
These collectively and accurately correlate [in their proportions]
To the external [world], the inner [subtle body], and even to other [divine forms].

The uncommon stūpas (*thun mong ma yin pa'i mchod rten*) may be [exemplified by] the stūpa of pristine cognition (*ye shes kyi mchod rten*), [which is formed by the indestructible buddha body] and described in the [*Tantra of*] *the Wheel of Time*.[591] In this regard, when the Buddha is seated in a cross-legged posture, the area from his navel downwards corresponds to the tiers [of the podium]; and the swelling of his navel or abdomen, to the dome plinth. Then, [the chest] as far as the shoulders corresponds to the bulging dome; the throat, to the high pavilion; and [the face] from the chin to the tip of the nose and the hair ringlet corresponds to the face [painted] on the high pavilion (*'bre gdong*). From there [upwards], as far as the top-knot, [the crown of the head] corresponds to the [stacked] wheels of the sacred teachings, along with the rain gutter and the crest.[592]

The measurement of the height [of this stūpa] is said by Taktsang Lotsāwa to be 57.5 [lit. five times eleven and a half] finger-widths, and this [measurement], which is generally accepted, accurately correlates to the five energy centers (*'khor lo lnga*) [within the subtle body], extending from the secret center (*gsang gnas*) as far as the crown protuberance.[593]

However, according to Belo Tsewang Kunkhyab, the height should be fifty finger-widths, and the width half of that.[594] The vertical grid is divided into four bands, each measuring twelve and a half finger-widths. This correlates proportionately to four hundred thousand *yojana*—the distance from the circle of wind [below the world] as far as the world-system of formlessness [at the summit of existence],[595] and as such it accurately corresponds to [the extent of] the outer world. It similarly correlates [in proportion] to the inner [or subtle] indestructible body (*rdo rje'i lus*) [of the meditator], extending from the soles of the feet as far as the crown protuberance; and it is also said to incidentally and accurately correlate to the bodies of other deities as well. In short, this measurement correlates collectively and accurately to [the proportions of] the external [world], the inner [human form], and also to other [subtle visualized and divine forms].[596]

Stūpas according to Extraordinary Traditions [3"]

With regard to the third section [of the detailed exegesis concerning the representations of buddha mind], which offers additional remarks on certain extraordinary traditions [concerning stūpas, it says in the root verses]:

> **In particular, there were many [stūpas of extraordinary] measurement and shape**
> **Which existed from antiquity and are unheard of by arrogant scholars,**
> **Such as the Stūpa of Intangible Glory,**
> **And the Naturally Arisen [Svayambhū] Stūpa of Nepal.**

The Jñānabimbakāya Stūpa [a″]

Apart from all those stūpas that are commonly and universally known, there is the particularly sublime Jñānabimbakāya—"the form body of pristine cognition" (*ye shes gzugs kyi sku*), also known as the Stūpa of Intangible Glory (*dpal reg pa med pa'i mchod rten*). This is [said] to be present in the form of rainbow-colored light, in the sky above the so-called "town stūpa" (*mchod rten grong*), in the land of Koṅkana, which hugs the ocean shore in South [West] India.[597] The venerable Sakya Paṇḍita has referred to the whole region that lies beneath this stūpa in the following verse:[598]

> This land, known as Cāritra,
> Is located by the ocean shore, in the south.

With regard to that land known as Cāritra, it is where Vajravārāhī is known to have ritually summoned or brought together all the ale of the three levels of existence (*srid pa gsum*).[599] After she had mixed all the yeast and grain liquor that there was, the quantity increased manifoldly, and when the essence [of that yeast] had been exhausted, she let it set for a while, so that [its potency] was renewed. After this had happened on seven occasions, [subsequently] at auspicious times, the whole region [of Koṅkana] was permeated by the fragrance of the wine.

In that place there was a large reclining stone image of Mañjuśrī, named Jñānakāya, located by the ocean. On auspicious occasions many [extraordinary] phenomena would [naturally] manifest around both [the place and the statue], various sounds of music and fragrances of incense offered by deities would be perceived, along with red fires in the night-time [sky]. These events were witnessed and heard by all. The [aforementioned] stūpa too would at all times be perceived in common by ordinary persons in a form resembling a smoky apparition in the sky, for which reason it became known as the Smoky Stūpa (*du ba can gyi mchod rten*). The awareness-holder Tsewang Norbu established its dimensions, based on the verbal description of Jestun Rinpoche [Tāranātha], and with regard to its symbolic meaning, it has been said:[600]

> There is also another explanation whereby
> The steps symbolize the three levels of going for refuge,
> While the vajra seat (*rdor gdan*), the gold leaf (*gser phye*),
> The lotus (*padma*) and the cornice (*pha gu*)

Symbolize the four philosophical systems.[601]
The three great faces [painted on the high pavilion]—
Upper, middle, and lower—and their peripheral features
Symbolize respectively the maṇḍalas of the buddha mind,
Buddha speech, and buddha body of the Glorious and Supreme
[Kālacakra].[602]
The dome symbolizes the ascendance of the Sugatas,
While the high pavilion and its peripheral features
Symbolize the four delights.[603]
The [stacked] wheels of the sacred teachings
Symbolize the thirteen [buddha] levels (*sa bcu gsum*),
While the crest symbolizes the buddha body of supreme bliss,
And the rain gutter symbolizes the pure deeds of the three
buddha bodies.[604]
The image [within the niche of] the dome (*bum sku*)
Symbolizes the buddha bodies of reality and perfect resource,
While its pediment symbolizes the buddha body of emanation.
The lowest of the great faces symbolizes the slow stepping
Of the glorious constellations,[605]
While the upper two, with the dome and so forth,
Symbolize the maṇḍala of the power of buddha speech,
Which pertains to the expanse of reality.[606]

In this way, the beneficial attributes [of this stūpa] in particular are more sublime than those of the stūpas constructed according to the traditions of the ordinary [causal] vehicles and the traditions of the lower tantras. Furthermore, it is said that in the place where this stūpa is located [i.e., Koṅkana] there is an abundant [harvest of] grain, and it is endowed with an abundance of food and beverages—fruits, molasses, wine, and so forth.

The Svayambhū Stūpa [b″]

On the Lotus Hill (*padmagiri, padma'i ri*) or Ox Horn Hill (*gośṛṇgaparvata, glang ru'i ri*) in Nepal, there is also a self-originated great stūpa that is called venerable and sacred (*rang byung mchod rten chen po rje bo dam pa*). When the guide and king of the sacred teachings [Buddha] Śikhin appeared in the world during the age when living creatures had a life span of seventy-thousand years, the expanse of reality (*dharmadhātu*) naturally arose in a crystalline form from the anthers at the heart of a lotus, fashioned of gemstones. Then, during the age of [the Buddha] Kanakamuni, in order that Dharmaśrīmitra might be accepted into his following, [the bodhisattva] Mañjuśrī emanated the maṇḍala of the power of buddha speech from the expanse of reality into this stūpa, so that the stūpa was named accordingly. [Later] during the age of [the Buddha] Kāśyapa, it was covered with earth and concealed by the accomplished master Śāntaśrī. Subsequently, during the age when our Teacher [Śākyamuni] appeared in the world, it manifested in its [present] form.[607]

As indicated in the new translations of the omniscient Tenpa Nyinje [i.e., Situ Chokyi Jungne], who formerly highlighted these [extraordinary] traditions, there were many [such stūpas] of extraordinary dimensions and shape that existed in the past, which were mostly unheard of by those [later individuals] who arrogantly boasted of their scholarship.

Stūpas according to the Nyingma Tradition [c"]

> **The Nyingma tradition also speaks of the stūpas of the eight virtuous abodes,**
> **Of the dimensions and designs [of the stūpas]**
> **Corresponding to the nine sequences of the vehicle, and so forth.**

In the tantras of the Nyingma tradition of the secret mantra, there are said to be many categories [of extraordinary stūpas] derived from the transmitted teachings (*bka' ma*) and the treasures (*gter ma*), such as the aforementioned "stūpas of the eight virtuous abodes" (*dge gnas brgyad kyi mchod rten*),[608] as well as the exegesis on the dimensions and designs [of the stūpas] corresponding to the nine sequences of the vehicle (*theg rim dgu yi tshad dbyibs*) that derive from the empowerment of the bodhisattva's conduct (*byang chub sems dpa'i spyod dbang*), and so forth.[609] However, these are basically subsumed in the abovementioned description.

The classifications of the types [of stūpa] outlined above can also be found in the authoritative and earliest account, entitled *Source of Enlightened Attributes: The Methods of Constructing the Three Representational Supports*, which was composed by Tsamorong Sonam Ozer, a student of Drogon Chogyal Phakpa. Furthermore, they are also identical in meaning to the [account found in] the *Method of Constructing Stūpas*, derived from the *Eight Transmitted Teachings: Consummation of Secrets* [which was revealed by Guru Chowang]. Takstang Lotsāwa's *Ocean of Wealth* is based upon [these two sources], for which reason his version can be said to represent their common ground.[610]

Hand-held Emblems and the Associated Ritual Arts [4"]

The fourth section of the detailed exegesis on the fine arts of buddha mind is an explanation of hand-held emblems and certain associated [ritual arts, concerning which it says in the root verses]:

> **The proportions and systematic presentation**
> **Of the vajra, bell, ritual spike, tantric staff, and so forth**
> **Are clearly set forth in the *Collection of Rites*, and so forth.**

Vajra and Bell [a"]

Previous generations have established the conventional meanings of the vajra and the bell, which are foremost among the symbolic hand-held emblems included among the representations of buddha mind.[611] Among them, the bell corresponding to the outer [tantras] (*phyi dril*) accords with the defining characteristics presented in the *Tantra of the Indestructible Peak*, which is an exegetical tantra (*bshad rgyud*) of the Yoga Tantras; and the bell corresponding to the inner [tantras] (*nang dril*) accords with the explanations derived from the *Tantra of the Wheel of Time*, the *Tantra of the Emergence of Cakrasaṃvara*, and the *Tantra of Embrace*.[612]

Although systematic presentations have been extensively offered by Gangkar Dorjedenpa and Khedrub Gelek Pel [-zangpo], there is no need to discuss them [here] because their respective traditions are widely known,[613] but with regard to the distinctions between these two [outer and inner approaches], Taktsang Lotsāwa explains:[614]

> Whether vajras have five prongs (*rtse lnga*) or nine prongs (*rtse dgu*), there are some which do not have their prongs emerging from the mouths of [ornamental] sea-monsters but instead rest [directly] on their lotus bases; and there are some which at their [outer] extremities do not have the tips of the [peripheral] prongs actually touching the central prong (*dbus rva*), while the [other] end of the central prong is fixed into [a hub], encircled by symbolic motifs such as the lotus and the [moon] disc. The prongs may be as sharp as the thorns of acacia, and round, and fluted.[615]
>
> As for the bells, some may have an open ring (*bugpa*) in place of the vase [of nectar], which is positioned below the head of Brahmā

> motif [on the handle]. Above the motif known as the "[eight faces of] glory" (*kīrtimukha, grags pa*), on the bulbous body [of the bell], [there is the motif of eight lotus petals]. Bells corresponding to the outer [tantras] have the seed-syllable or symbolic hand emblem of [Buddha]locanā on the eastern petal [of the lotus], while, by contrast, those corresponding to the inner [tantras] have the seed-syllable or symbolic hand emblem of [Samaya]tārā.

According to the tradition of the Yoga [Tantras], the vajras and bells corresponding to the five enlightened families are all differentiated; while according to the Unsurpassed [Tantras], there are two traditions—that of the *Tantra of the Wheel of Time* and that corresponding to the [Unsurpassed] Tantras in general (*rgyud sde spyi 'gro'i lugs*).[616]

Other Hand-held Emblems [b"]

[Similarly,] in the case of the hand-drum (*ḍamaru, cang te'u*), the defining characteristics and craftsmanship techniques of their long-tassled valances (*dra ba can*) and back-to-back skulls (*thod pa ltag sprod*) are [also] distinguished [in the outer and inner tantras].[617]

[The same goes for] all six ornamental [hand emblems] (*rgyan drug*)[618] and the pair of *homa* ladles (*dgang gzar blugs*), as well as the two kinds of hand

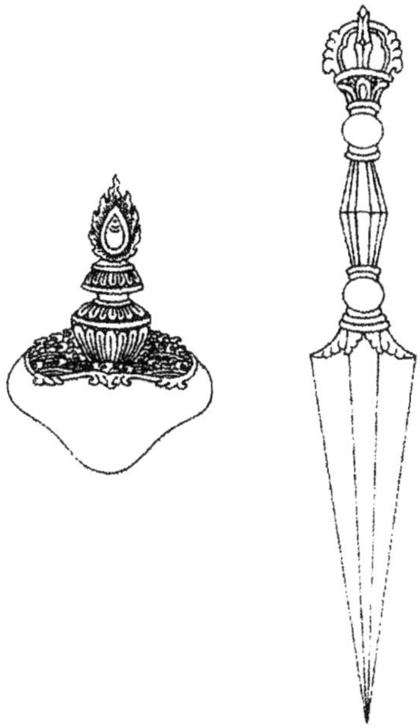

Fig. 43. The skull-cup and ritual spike

emblem that are widely mentioned in the tantra texts of the Nyingma tradition, namely the ritual spike surmounted by the five-pronged vajra (*phur bu rdo rje rtse lnga*) and the tantric staff emblazoned with the motif of the crossed vajra (*sna tshogs rdo rjes mtshan pa'i khaṭvāṅga*), and so forth.[619]

While it is very important to master in detail the proportions and shapes of the [various] hand emblems, exemplified by the sword, axe, and trident, which are [also] included here, I shall not digress at this juncture, fearful of the large number of texts [on this subject]. If one wishes to understand their modes, these can be learned from the clear [explanations] given in the *Collection of Rites* by the master Kuladatta and in the aforementioned Tibetan texts, and so forth.[620]

The Playing of Drums and Cymbals [c"]

> **[The playing of] drums and cymbals, sacred masked dances, and so forth**
> **Are all ritual activities associated with the body.**

In contrast to [mundane music and dance], which cause the mind to wander in all directions due to fleeting attachments and the desire to dress provocatively, the [ritual] playing of large and small drums, as well as big-boss cymbals (*sbub chol*) and small-boss cymbals (*sil snyan*) is integral to the way of [secret] mantra, with the purpose of making offerings to the [three] precious jewels (*dkon mchog*). Along with the choreographic techniques of the sacred masked dances (*gar 'chams stangs stabs*), and so forth, these are all included within the extraordinary aspects of the physical arts.

[At first,] the material of the drum wood, the techniques for attaching the [drum-skin] covers, and the positive and negative qualities of the big-bossed and small-bossed cymbals should be understood, in accordance with the descriptions found in the [relevant] ancient treatises and practical instructions (*dpyad don*).[621]

Then, with regard to the ways of beating the drum, Candraśrī has said [in the *Systematic Presentation of Drums and Cymbals*]:[622]

> Do not stir the middle of the great ocean,
> Do not circumvent Mount Sumeru and the four continents,
> Do not pass the rocky boundary between the mountains and the plains,
> And do not strike the "face of the king of wild beasts."[623]

Also:[624]

There are eight unacceptable drumming styles (*mi bskul ba'i tshul brgyad*),
Including one [that is top-heavy like the crack of] a thunderbolt,
One that is like the [lamentable] beating of the chest,
One that is like the plaintive cry of a beggar,
And one that is like the flapping of a small bird's wings.[625]

One should strike with the drumstick's own weight,
Flexing the finger [joints of the drumming hand slightly],
At an area of the [drum] surface one "knuckle-width" above the lower rim,[626]
And then immediately let [the drumstick] rebound.[627]

When the [mass drummers] are playing, aligned in a row,
They should just keep the beat in turn, one after the other,
And avoid disparities of height and arrangement,
Aligning the drums evenly and elegantly,
Like a threaded string of gemstones.[628]

And:[629]

When one beats the drum during rites of pacification,
The drumming technique should be slow and relaxed.
When one beats the drum during rites of enrichment,
The drumming technique should be clear and resonant.
When one beats the drum during rites of subjugation,
The drumming technique should be pleasant and melodious.
When one beats the drum [imposingly] during rites of wrath,
The drumming technique should be strong and swift.[630]
When beating during the rite of wrath continues without interruption,
It should resemble the fall of a meteor.[631]

There are extensive explanations such as this concerning the different moods to be evoked, and so forth.[632]

Also, with regard to [the playing of] the big-bossed cymbals and the small-bossed cymbals, the same [author] says:[633]

> The low sounds (*pho sgra*) resonate noisily and charismatically,
> The high sounds (*mo sgra*) resonate sweetly and elegantly,
> While the neutral sounds (*phyed ma*) resonate clearly and resoundingly.
> During rites of pacification, [the roll of the cymbals] should resemble light drizzle,
> During rites of enrichment, it should resemble the blustering of wind and rain,
> During rites of pacification, it should resemble torrential rainfall,
> And during the rites of wrath, it should resemble a crescendo of lightning and hail...

There are thus twelve similes (*'dra dpe bcu gnyis*) describing the ways in which [the cymbals] and the drums are played.

It is also said in the *Treatise on Musical Instruments entitled The Single Knowledge that Liberates All*, which was composed by Jamyang Sonam Wangpo:[634]

> In general, whatever type of cymbals (*rol mo*) is being played,
> The advice is that one should not hold them tightly,
> And that the chest and the hands should not come into contact.
> Do not raise [the big-bossed cymbals] up like a club,
> And do not hold [the small-bossed cymbals] straight as a pillar.

And in the words of Candra[śrī]:[635]

> Do not forsake the [necessary] space,
> And do not constrict the [natural] resonance [of the cymbals].
> They should not touch the chest and the knees.

And with regard to the defining characteristics of the [postures] that are to be rejected and adopted, the same text says:[636]

> With the shoulders and the arms relaxed from the wrists,
> Play with a flexing movement of the palm,
> And strike with [the cymbals'] own weight!
> Do not shake [the cymbals] with the tips of the fingers...

And:[637]

> One should refine one's understanding of the different striking techniques:
> Decrescendo (*'jab*), rebounding (*'phar*), loud, soft, harsh,
> Light, heavy, clear, and resonant.[638]

In this way, it is explained that one should master the different striking techniques (*sgra thabs*), which accord with specific rituals.[639]

Choreography of the Sacred Dances [d"]

Choreographic rituals include those for preparing the [dance] arena (*sa bzung ba'i stangs stabs*) and the specific sacred offering dances (*mchod pa'i gar*), which are explained in the *Tantra of the Wheel of Time*, the *Tantra of the Ocean of Sky-farers*, the *Tantra of the Indestructible Tent*, the Yoga Tantra entitled *Indestructible Garland*, and so forth. Also included here are the genre of the basic sacred masked dance of the herukas (*khrag 'thung rtsa 'chams*) and the sacred masked dance of exorcism (*brub 'chams*), which are performed in accordance with the [tantras of] the Nyingma tradition, such as the *Wrathful Deities of the Magical Net*, the *Gathering of the Great Assembly*, the *Eight Transmitted Teachings: Means for Attainment*, and above all the [cycles of] *Vajrakīla*.[640] Moreover, there are also the sacred masked dances of Lord [Mahākāla] (*mgon 'chams*) which are found throughout both the Ancient and New Traditions (*gsar rnying*).[641]

All of these [choreographic rituals] generally employ the nine dramatic demeanors of the dance (*gar gyi nyams dgu*), concerning which the master Candra[śrī], in particular, has said:[642]

> The upper part of one's body should maintain the demeanor of a lion (*seng chags*),
> The waist should maintain a demeanor of elegance (*'khril chags*),
> The wrists and ankles should maintain a demeanor of dexterity (*'phrul chags*),
> The thigh muscles should maintain a relaxed demeanor (*lhod chags*),
> The blood should maintain a fiery red demeanor (*mer chags*),
> The countenance should maintain a handsome demeanor (*'gying chags*),

The movements should maintain a slow demeanor (*dal chags*),
The knees should maintain a supple demeanor (*ldem chags*),
The feet and the head should maintain a demeanor of happiness
(*bde chags*),
And overall [the dancer] should maintain a demeanor
That is both heroic and magnificent (*dpa' zhing brjid chags pa*).

And he also says:

Dances evoking fear and awe are defective if they are too vigorous.
Dances evoking grace and suppleness are defective
If they are too carefree.
Dances evoking speed and ease are defective if they are too hasty.
Dances evoking slowness and relaxation are defective
If they are too indolent.
Dances evoking elegance and attractiveness are defective
If they are too fickle.

With regard to the particulars that should be avoided and evoked [during the performance of a sacred masked dance]: after generally learning the detailed and common instructions, one should study to the point of mastery whatever the unbewildered primary sources of one's own particular tradition happen to be.[643] Above all, it goes without saying that it is essential for the preparatory dances (*sa gar*) and the offering dances (*mchod gar*) to be undertaken in an authentic manner because they are associated with the tantras and the practical traditions of [Ancient] India.

Choreography in the Nyingma Tradition [i'']

At this point, I should refer to those tantra texts from which there derives the "basic sacred masked dance of the herukas" (*khrag 'thung rtsa 'chams*), according to the Nyingma tradition. The following verses are found in the *Tantra of the Flash of the Splendor of Pristine Cognition*:

It is said by the heroes [*vīras*] that,
Once the disposition in which all things are sameness has been
understood,
Everything that stirs or moves becomes the seal [of that reality].
[Therefore], one who maintains these [sacred] dance steps

With meditative stability in his or her own [meditational] deity,
Would terrify even the Buddhas themselves,
Let alone the host of arrogant spirits!

The *Tantra of the Lasso of Skillful Means* also mentions the necessity of these [choreographic] techniques for securing the seals.[644]

The individual practitioner who engages in this practice should maintain the perspective of the indivisible truth, realize the superior great buddha body of reality (*lhag pa'i chos sku chen po*), and, through the appropriate meditative stability, master the indestructible sacred dances (*rdo rje'i zlos gar*), securing all appearances and conduct with the seal of the [meditational] deity.[645]

The ways of achieving this [realization] are the objectives of the teachings derived from the unsurpassed tantras of the Vajra family, including the root and exegetical tantras of the *Magical Net*, and the *Supramundane Sūtra entitled Heruka Galpo*.[646] These teachings descended from King Indrabhūti [in ancient India] through to the [era of the] three wise men (*mkhas pa mi gsum*), in a transmission that included the Tibetan translators Ma [Rinchenchok] and Nyak [Jñānakumāra], the eight "glorious" sons (*dpal gyi bu brgyad*), Nub [chen Sangye Yeshe], the Zur [family], and Dar [charuwa]. Later, the transmission was widely propagated by the brothers from Mindroling [Terdak Lingpa and Lochen Dharmaśrī], who were lords of the most secret teachings.[647] [Among them] Lochen Rinpoche composed and thoroughly established the *Choreographic Treatise of the Sacred Dances entitled The Display of Samantabhadra*. This [text] includes both the basic sacred dance of the Herukas (*khrag 'thung rtsa 'chams*), which is associated with the maṇḍala rituals, and the exorcist dance of the hostile and obstructive spirits (*dgra bgegs brub 'chams*), which is associated with the application of the wrathful rites [of sorcery] (*drag po'i las sbyor*).[648]

Thirteen Procedures in the Basic Sacred Dance of the Herukas [aa"]

The former contains the following thirteen sections (*don tshan bcu gsum*):[649]

(1) In order that their bodies might be unharmed by obstructive spirits, [at the outset, the dancers] don the dance costumes (*chas gos*) and hold the hand emblems that have been consecrated through the pride of the [meditational] deities.[650]

(2) In order that the radiance of the [mundane] gods and ogres might not

infiltrate, [the dancers] dedicate the merit of an oblation (*gser khyems*) [to the protector deities].[651]

(3) In order that the crimes of proclaiming the secret [teachings] might be rejected, [the dancers] visualize the world and its contents as the maṇḍala, so that they come to possess the ten aspects of physical movement that are commonly esteemed, as well as the three masteries of the seals, and the enlightened attributes that conform with the three similes of the bodily ornaments.[652] In this way, they proceed into the maṇḍala arena.

(4) [The dancers] then stand in their respective sectors, corresponding to their [respective] enlightened families.[653]

(5) The master [of the sacred dances] visualizes himself as the lord of the circle, while the others assume the actions of the offspring, so that the maṇḍala [of deities] is completely emanated. The consecratory blessings (*bskur brlab*) should then be directly absorbed [into the dancers], and the [appropriate] offerings made.[654]

(6) The students [positioned] in the [four] directions should then be consecrated, so as to assume the forms of the female consorts of the four enlightened families (*rigs bzhi'i yum*).[655]

(7) After making their preparatory offerings and eulogies, the female consorts of the four directions then pray that the maṇḍala might be explained.[656]

(8) The master [of the sacred dances] arouses the meditative commitments of the conquerors who permeate all space.[657]

(9) Aversion and hatred are exorcised by the sacred dance step of indestructible reality (*rdo rje'i gar*) and the obstructive forces are expelled.[658]

(10) [Following this exorcism,] the [dance] arena is prepared (*sa bzung ba*) through the choreographic movements of the deities of the maṇḍala, which comprise[659]

The three [initial] dance moves,[660]
The [dance movement] creating the *dharmodaya* symbol,[661]
The [dance movement] overpowering [phenomenal existence],[662]
The [dance movement] visualizing the ḍākinīs as heroines,[663]
The [dance movement] drawing in the vitality of [oath-]
breakers,[664]
The [dance movement] summoning the oath-bound
[protectors],[665]
The three [dance movements] consecrating the celestial,

Intermediate, and terrestrial abodes respectively as a wheel,
The eight auspicious symbols, and a lotus,[666]
And the three [dance movements] of the half-vajra, single vajra, and double vajra,
Through which the dance arena is respectively
Staked out, tamed, and consecrated.[667]

In this way the general consecration is carried out by means of these twelve preliminary choreographic movements (*sngon 'gro'i stangs stabs bcu gnyis*).

Then, the seven visualizations of the receptacles that support [this maṇḍala] (*rten bskyed bdun*) are to be made. These comprise[668]

The [protective] circles of space, wind, blood,
Human corpses, skeletons, and fire,
Along with the [actual] celestial palace.

Thereafter, the visualizations of the [deities] supported [by this purified and protected receptacle] are to be undertaken. These comprise the following nine classes [of deities] who perform the graceful dance of the central Mahāśrī [Heruka] (*gtso bo dpal chen po'i 'gying 'chams*):[669]

The central [*heruka*] and those of the four [surrounding] families,
The female consorts of all five enlightened families,
The eight *gaurī*, the eight female [*piśācī*] headed by Siṃhamukhī,
And the four female gatekeepers,
The *īśvarī*, the [lesser] *piśācī*, and their corpse-wielding retainers (*bam len*)
All perform the powerful sacred dance of Mahāśrī [Heruka].[670]

In this way, in the main part [of the sacred dance], the consecrations of the particular [deities] take place through their individual choreographic movements.

(11) The obstructive forces (*vighna*) of the ten directions are transfixed by the ritual spike.[671]

(12) Extreme views of eternalism and nihilism are eliminated.[672]

(13) [Finally], the dedication of merit and aspirational prayers (*bsngo smon*) are undertaken, along with the benedictions (*shis pa brjod pa*), which [altogether] comprise an ornate finale.[673]

By performing [the sacred dances] in this way, based on the movement and actions of the indestructible body (*rdo rje'i lus*), the great waves of the two provisions [of merit and pristine cognition] are increased.[674] This therefore is a marvelous technique for attaining the [four] rites and the [supreme] spiritual accomplishment with ease.[675]

Sacred Dances of Exorcism [bb"]

As for the sacred dances of exorcism (*brub 'chams*), although there are distinctive purposes behind the fearsome choreographic movements that are associated with the application of the wrathful rites [of sorcery] (*drag po'i las*), I will not digress here.[676]

Other Traditions of Sacred Dance [ii"]

[Among other traditions,] the basic sacred dance of Vajrakīla (*phur pa'i rtsa 'chams*) that accords with the tradition of Sakya is integrated (*kha bsgyur ba*) in the context of the ceremony dedicated to their [lineage of] glorious and sacred spiritual teachers (*dpal ldan bla ma dam pa*).[677]

Also, it is claimed that the three hundred and sixty aspects of the dance known as the great masked dance of the assembly of Cakrasaṃvara (*bde mchog tshogs gar chen mo*) which accords with the auspicious [lineage] of Zurmang (*bkra shis zur mang*), was conferred upon Drungpa Ma-se Lodro Rinchen, an emanation of the buddha Tilopā, after he had constructed an actual image of the tathāgata and lord of the [sacred] teachings Cakrasaṃvara.[678] These [sacred dances] offer a great approach to the most exalted blessings that were conferred upon him, favored as he was by the body of pristine cognition (*ye shes kyi sku*) in the buddha-field of the buddha [Tilopā].

Again, in a pure vision, when Guru Chokyi Wangchuk came into the presence of the great master [Padmasambhava] on the Glorious Copper-colored Mountain (*zangs mdog dpal ri*), the vision that was imparted and the content of the advice he received is contained without error in the renowned sacred dances of the tenth day ceremony (*tshes bcu'i gar 'chams*), according to which all sentient beings—even animals—who see [these dances] will become students of the great master [Padmasambhava]. It is said that [Guru Chowang's revelations] have such beneficial attributes.[679]

Therefore, since all [sacred dances], exemplified by these, have their [distinctive] purposes, even the most minute aspects of their respective traditions should be observed without error.

Common Physical Arts [b']

Secondly, concerning the explanation of the common physical arts (*lus bzo phal pa*) [it is said in the root verses]:

> **The ordinary [physical arts] comprise [the making of] residences,**
> **Ships, clothing, ornaments, food,**
> **Armaments—both aggressive and defensive—weapons, and so forth.**

As for the common physical arts, these include the construction of high-rise buildings, such as royal palaces, and buildings with as many as five hundred rooms, as well as the residences of ordinary people. They also include [the construction of] large ships which can traverse the great oceans and small boats which can cross the rivers of India, Nepal, China, and the like. They include the particular styles of clothing and ornaments suitable for men and women, as well as the culinary preparation of food and beverages.[680]

Moreover, the astonishing contraptions that are used for acts of aggression against enemies are mentioned in the *Tantra entitled Summation of the Real.*[681] These include artillery or stone-catapults, which are used to destroy fortresses on the plains; naval cannons, which are used to destroy fortresses at sea or on rivers; catapults of [Greek] fire, which are used to destroy fortresses in the mountains; catapults of curved knives, which are used against a [protective] circle of swords; catapults of wind, which are used to expose the summit [of a fortress]; tented [siege] catapults, which are used to destroy walls; catapults of metal barbs or arrows, which are used for destroying armor; and catapults of swords or lances, which are used to defend one's own position.[682]

Also [included in this category of common physical arts] are the specifications of war chariots for the ruling classes, the specifications of stadia or grand buildings used for holding spectacular events, the specifications for palanquins used at festivals, and turbines that channel water upstream for irrigating gardens.[683]

Moreover, [the common arts] also include the knowledge and technologies pertaining to the making of armor—breastplates, helmets, shields, and the like—as well as arrows, bows, swords, and other types of weaponry.[684]

Vocal Arts [2']

The second part [of the "fine arts of the three media"] concerns [the detailed exegeses of] the vocal arts, which comprise both supreme and common [art forms].

Supreme Arts of Speech [a']

As to the former [it says in the root verses]:

> **The supreme arts of speech are debate, explanation, and composition.**

Supreme among the arts of speech are the following three: the [techniques of] debate (*rtsod pa*) which can destroy the erroneous conceptions of others, the [modes of] teaching (*'chad pa*) which enable one to accept students, and the [modes of] composition (*rtsom pa*) which can elucidate the [Buddhist] teaching. It is essential that these [three techniques] should be devoid of [potential] defects and replete with [genuine] qualities, ensuring that they do not become merely stereotypic.

Chanting [i']

> **Innate musical sound comprises [four melodic contours]:**
> **The sustaining note, the descending note,**
> **The changing note, and the ascending note,**
> **Which [are exemplified] respectively by [four metaphors]:**
> **A wish-granting tree, a creeping flower plant,**
> **The [changing reflections of the] moon [in water],**
> **And the [traverse of a slow] river.**[685]
> **By undertaking preliminaries that focus on three essentials,**
> **The six defects and five causes should be abandoned.**
> **[Chanting] should then be undertaken in a timely manner, in six great [ceremonial contexts].**

The master Candraśrī has explained in his *Treatise on Melody entitled Neck Ornament of Clear Intelligence*:[686]

> Through knowledge of speech, endowed with elegance,
> The causal basis of the two kinds of spiritual accomplishment[687]
> Becomes an offering to sublime beings
> And a boon to sentient beings.

Innate or natural musical sound (*lhan skyes rol mo*), including the particular aspects of melody which have this specific purpose, refers to the offering hymns that are sung to the [three] precious jewels (*triratna*). It says in the [transmissions of] monastic discipline:[688]

> At first the Teacher [Śākyamuni] prohibited actions associated with singing, dancing, instrumental music, and the like, for which reason the liturgical prayers recited as a eulogy to the Buddha and so forth became nonsensical and garbled. Consequently they were ridiculed by extremist [teachers], and householders had no faith [in them]. Therefore, the householder Anāthapiṇḍada made a [specific] entreaty. At that time, the Teacher granted permission for melodic chants to be intoned as an offering to the [three] precious jewels. [The householder] again said that he did not know how to intone melodic chants, whereupon [the Teacher] replied that they should be intoned like the hymns of the Brāhmaṇa Vedas.[689]

More specifically, in the context of the way of [secret] mantra, there is the Chant of Yoga (*yo ga'i gdangs*) which was propagated by Lochen Rinchen Zangpo, as well as the Greater and Lesser Melodic Chants of Lord [Mahākāla] and his sister (*mgon po lcam dral*), while according to the Nyingma tradition of the way of [secret] mantra, there are the [special] intonations of the awareness-holders (*rig 'dzin gyi gsung*).[690] All of these, which have unbroken transmissions, are the oldest [chants in Tibet].

Later, [the melodic chants] familiar to the diverse [Tibetan] schools were formulated in accordance with their respective purposes, but I shall not digress here to generalize on these traditions which should be [carefully] studied, or indeed the masters who taught them, the students who were their recipients, the ways in which they should be imparted, or their [potential] pitfalls and advantages, and so forth.[691]

MELODIC CONTOUR [aa']

The essence of melodic contour (*nga ro*) which is to be studied and refined comprises the four [primary] aspects of melodic contour, along with their twelve subsidiary aspects, and the infinite variety of [melodic] permutations that arise when these notes are intermingled (*spel ma'i sbyor ba*).[692]

Among the four primary aspects of melodic contour[693]

(1) The sustaining note (*sthāyī*, *'dren pa*) may be of five types, because it may be induced by the vowel A, which is level or neutral (*drang po*), E

which is sharp (*bsgreng ba*), I which is flat (*bkug pa*), O which is high (*bstod pa*), or U which is low (*smad pa*).[694]

(2) The descending note (*avarohī, bkug pa*), through its undulation (*khug*), may last for a single beat (*rkyang pa*) or multiple beats (*brtsegs pa*).[695]

(3) The changing note (*sañcārī, bsgyur ba*) occurs due to repetition (*nyis 'gyur*) and includes three types—guttural variation (*mgrin bsgyur*), lingual variation (*lce bsgyur*), and nasal variation (*sna ldan bsgyur*).[696]

(4) The ascending note (*ārohī, ltengs pa*) occurs by raising [the voice an octave] and may be of two sorts—long and short.[697]

Concerning [the functions of these primary aspects of melodic contour], Sakya Paṇchen has said:[698]

> The changing note is most important for offering chants,
> The sustaining note is most important for songs,
> The changing note of short duration is suitable for narratives,[699]
> While short combinations of the changing and sustaining notes
> Are suitable for recapitulations.[700]
> Although in general all [four primary melodic contours]
> May be applicable in all instances,
> The sustaining note is regarded as the most important among them.

In order that these [primary aspects of intonation and chant] might be understood, the following similes are applied: Melodies that emphasize the sustaining note are said to resemble a wish-granting tree; those that emphasize the descending note resemble a creeping flower plant; those that emphasize the ascending note resemble a river that is slowly crossed because the current is weak in mid-stream; and the undulations of the changing note (*'gyur khug*) are explained to resemble the moon [reflected] on [the surface of] an ocean.[701]

THREE ESSENTIALS, SIX DEFECTS, AND FIVE NEGATIVE CAUSES [bb']

In all these [aspects of chant and intonation], the preliminary training that is undertaken should emphasize three essentials—courage or brilliance (*spobs pa'i gnad*), tempo (*dus kyi gnad*), and refinement (*sbyangs pa'i gnad*), through which the six defects (*skyon drug*) and their five causes (*rgyu lnga*) also should be abandoned. The former comprise mental flaws of distraction and the like, verbal flaws of imperfect diction and the like, melodic flaws of excessive or deficient intonation and the like, physical flaws of decrepit posture and the like, the flaw of having unsuitable associates, and the flaw of having an audience that is scornful or prone to ridicule.[702] Moreover, the following five causes which may give rise to negativity should also be abandoned:[703]

> The cause that provokes reproach
> When [chanters] are ignorant of the words,
> The cause that provokes ridicule
> When they do not employ [the correct] melody,
> The cause that provokes sadness when it is untimely,
> The cause that provokes negativity when there is no need to do so,
> And the cause that provokes suffering
> Due to [the chanters'] inadequate training,
> Faint-heartedness, or feeble intelligence,
> Whenever learned persons are present,
> Whenever they are surrounded by a large gathering,
> Or whenever they have evil associates and many enemies.

Six Ceremonial Contexts [cc']

It has also been said [in Candraśrī's *Treatise on Melody entitled Neck Ornament of Clear Intelligence*]:[704]

> The teachings on the melodic chanting of the Yoga [Tantras] will decline
> If chanting is not employed in the six great contexts.

With regard to these six great ceremonial events (*chen po drug*), the master Candraśrī continues:[705]

> Melodic chanting should be undertaken
> Within six great contexts:
> Offering rites of attainment (*sgrub mchod*),
> Empowerments (*dbang bskur*) and consecrations (*rab gnas*),
> Anniversary offering ceremonies (*dus mchod*),
> Funerary rites (*gshin don*), and elaborate burnt offerings (*sbyin sreg rgyas*).

Therefore chanting should be undertaken in a timely manner and in accordance with these [ceremonial] contexts.

Twelve Distinctive Modes of Chanting [dd']

In congregations twelve distinctive [ancillary modes of chanting]
Including the lion's roar should also be employed, as appropriate.

When [chanting] is undertaken at the right time and in the right circumstances, the melodic intonations that are chanted in congregations are designated as the "roar of the lion" (*sengge'i nga ro*) because the voice has to be loud. Altogether, there are twelve distinctive modes of chanting (*len tshul gyi khyad par bcu gnyis*) including [this "lion's roar"], and these should be employed as and when appropriate. Therefore it is explained [in Sakya Paṇchen's *Treatise on Music*]:[706]

Like a lion's roar in congregations,
Like the buzzing of a bee in isolated retreats,
Like the melody of a parrot in the company of the learned,
Like the beauty of the peacock among the ignorant,[707]
Like a leader[708] who inspires confidence in all at times of sadness,
Like the arrow of Kāmadeva, in pursuit of a lover,
Like a virtuous flower among offerings,[709]
Like a saline river, refining negativity,
Like a divine drum when praising one's own side,
Like an overpowering wheel [of sharp weapons]
When subduing the other party,
Like melodies of perfume that waft sweetly in all directions,
And like one with a garland of flowers,
Intermingling [these modes of chanting].
Through [metaphors] such as these,
The distinctions [achieved] by the intermingling[710]
[Of the primary and ancillary melodic contours]
Should be well examined.
There are also other sorts of melodic composition,
Which should also be applied, as and when appropriate.[711]

Defining Characteristics of Voice Pitch [ii']

When the defining characteristics [of voice pitch] applicable in ordinary contexts are abbreviated, it is said:[712]

There are [also] twelve [modalities of voice pitch]—
Rising (*'degs*), pausing (*'jog*), deep (*sbom*), high (*phra*),
Tense (*grim*), relaxed and variable (*lhod du 'gyur*),
Pliant (*ldem*), sweet (*snyan*), covert (*gsang*),
Decisive (*gcod*), and connective (*sbrel*).

On these, Candra[śrī] has said [in his *Treatise on Melody entitled Neck Ornament of Clear Intelligence*]:[713]

Long but balanced, short but perfect,
Majestic but graceful, pleasant but regular,[714]
Firm but yielding, inarticulate but intelligible,
Manifold in voice but in unison,
In unison but enriched with many melodic contours.
In short, [these modalities of voice] should be capable
Of being retained by the simple-minded,
And they should cause the wise to rejoice.
Those [endowed with such voices] are worthy of veneration
By erudite persons, and they are pleasing to all.
They should attract the high-minded and gratify the common man.
They majestically stand out among the crowd,
They captivate the learned and are praised by all.
Separated from enemies and obstacles,
They gather spiritual accomplishments,
And on this basis they will certainly attain the genuine result.

Common Vocal Arts [b']

As to the latter, [the common vocal arts, it says in the root verses]:

The common [vocal arts] include songs, flutes, and formal speeches.

As for the common vocal arts (*ngag bzo phal pa*), there are festivals and public gatherings adorned with singers (*glu len pa*) who desire to sing, their sweet voices expressing the meanings of their respective customs—tales of yaks or wealth (*nor gyi gtam*) and the like. There are also contests of repartee between the sexes (*kha gshags*), and so forth in which [the participants] are unimpeded with regard to noble meanings.[715]

Accompanying musical instruments are also played:[716]

Flutes, lutes, clay drums, gongs (*mkhar lnga*),
Round drums and kettledrums,
Tambours, large-bossed cymbals (*cha lang*), and chimes (*kanaḍi*),
Conches, multi-string lutes, and so forth,
As many [instruments] as are said
To accompany[717] the small-bossed cymbals,
All of them should be mastered.

There are also [different] rhetorical styles [for debate, including informal] discursive talks (*'bel gtam*) and formal speeches (*gral 'phros*), in which [participants] are required to express fine points [in public gatherings], in a loud voice, and with clear diction, using words that are untainted by defects, and so forth.

Mental Arts [3']

The third part is [the detailed exegeses of] the mental arts, which comprise both supreme and common [art forms].

Supreme Arts of Mind [a']

As to the former [it says in the root verses]:

The supreme arts of mind are those of study, reflection, and meditation
With regard to the eloquently expressed [teachings of the Buddha].

Supreme or extraordinary among the arts of mind are the activities pursued in relation to the particularly sublime transmitted teachings [of the Buddha], which are eloquently expressed (*subhāṣitapravacana*), and the treatises (*śāstra*) which comment upon their enlightened intention (*abhisandhi*).[718]

These activities firstly comprise the opening of the eyes by means of study or learning (*śruti, thos pa*) with regard to [virtuous actions] that are to be adopted and [negative actions] that are to be abandoned. Secondly, they comprise the cutting off of indecisive doubts by means of thorough reflection (*cintā, bsam pa*). Lastly, they comprise the establishment of the abiding nature [of reality] (*gnas lugs*) by means of meditation (*bhāvanā, bsgoms pa*) that is undertaken in the correct manner.[719]

Common Mental Arts [b']

As to the latter [it says in the root verses]:

> **The common [mental arts] comprise the eighteen topics of knowledge,**
> **As well as Sanskrit grammar, logic, and so forth.**
> **There are also eight subjects of scrutiny**
> **Comprising land, gems, trees, chariots, horses, elephants, treasures,**
> **And men and women; and commonly too**
> **There are the treatises on [human] conduct, and the sixty-four crafts,**
> **Along with all sorts of [other] enumerations, including the four categories.**

Eighteen Great Topics of Knowledge [i']

Enumerating the common mental arts (*yid bzo phal pa*), it says in the *Auto-commentary on the* [*Great*] *Treasury* [*of Detailed Exposition*]:[720]

> Music (*gandharva, rol mo*), love-making (*vaiśika, 'khrig thabs*),
> Sustenance (*vārtā, 'tsho tshis*), arithmetic (*sāṃkhyā, grangs can*),
> Grammar (*śabda, sgra*), medicine (*cikitsita, gso dpyad*),
> Behavior (*nīti, chos lugs*), fine arts (*śilpa, bzo*), archery (*dhanurveda, 'phongs*),
> Logic (*hetu, gtan tshigs*), yoga (*rnal 'byor*), study (*śruti, thos pa*),
> Recollection (*smṛti, dran pa*), astronomy (*jyotitiṣa, skar ma'i dpyad*),
> Astrology (*gaṇita, rtsis*), optical illusions (*māyā, mig 'phrul 'khor*),
> Antiquity (*purāṇa, sngon gyi rabs*), and history (*itihāsaka, sngon byung ba*):
> These are the eighteen great topics of knowledge.

Also included here are the aforementioned [sciences of] Sanskrit grammar, Buddhist logic, and so forth.[721]

Eight Subjects of Scrutiny [ii']

In addition, there is the category known as the eight subjects of scrutiny (*brtag pa brgyad*). Among them, the scrutiny of land (*sa gzhi brtag pa*) and the scrutiny of water (*chu brtag pa*) are discussed in works such as the master

Dahura [Nagpo]'s *Tantra of the White, Black and Variegated Hundred Thousand Stanzas.*[722]

The *Scrutiny of Gems and Precious Metals* is a treatise composed by the scholar (*paṇḍita*) Mahoṣadhi, and, based upon that, discussions are found in many early and later works composed in Tibet, such as the *White Lotus Bouquet of Investigation.*[723]

As far as "human gems" (*mi'i nor bu*) are concerned, the cranium or skull-cup (*kapāla*), the so-called "inner begging bowl" (*nang gi lhun bzed*), according to the way of secret mantra, is also included in this category. Therefore, [the scrutiny of skulls] is clearly mentioned in works such as the *Great Tantra of the Emergence of Cakrasaṃvara* and discussed in the writings of Tibetan scholars as well as in the esoteric instructions and spiritual revelations based on the *Tantra entitled Mountain of Corpses, Fortress of Skulls*, the *Private Tantra: Black Skull of the Charnel Ground*, the *Citadel of the Wind Goddess*, and similar works.[724]

[Works on] the scrutiny of trees and the scrutiny of elephants (*ljong shing dang glang po brtag pa*) were not translated in Tibet; and the scrutiny of underground treasures (*gter brtag pa*) is only mentioned partially and for illustrative purposes in certain tantra texts, other than which the authentic Indian texts were not translated.

The scrutiny of horses (*rta brtag pa*) is discussed in *Śālihotra's Compendium on the Inspection of the Life Span of Horses*, composed by the hermit sage [Śālihotra], and in the *Mirror Trilogy* translated by Drugu Sengdo Ochen, as well as in the different treatises composed by thirteen royal ministers (*rje blon bcu gsum*), headed by [the Tibetan emperor] Trisong Detsen.[725]

The scrutiny of men and women (*pho mo brtag pa*) is found in the miscellaneous tracts on human nature (*mi dpyad thor bu*) and in the discussions on yoga found in particular tantra texts, as well as in the eightfold scrutiny of women (*bud med brtag pa bcas brgyad*) that is explained in the *Hundred Thousand Scrutinies of the Ḍākinīs* within the Nyingma tradition of the way of secret mantra.[726]

Treatises on Human Behavior [aa']

In [Nāgārjuna's] *Stem of Discriminative Awareness* it is said:

> If the religious traditions of human beings are well investigated,
> The god realms will not be far distant,
> And if the ladder of gods and humans is scaled,
> Liberation will be near.

There are treatises on [human] behavior (*lugs kyi bstan bcos*) which offer an initial introduction to the common foundation or starting point applicable to both aspects of science (*gtsug lag gnyis*) [i.e., verbal expression and meaningful content].[727] Such works include the *Letter to a Friend*, the *Hundred Verses on Discriminative Awareness*, the *Stem of Discriminative Awareness*, the *Point of Human Sustenance*,[728] the *Treasury of the Collection of Topics*, the *Hundred Verses on the Collection of Topics*, the *Answers to the Questions of Vimala[kīrti]*, *Cāṇakya's Treatise on the Behavior of Kings*, [the *Treatise on Human Behavior*] composed by Masurakṣa, and the *Eloquence of Sakya*, which essentializes all of these [aforementioned Indic] works.[729]

Furthermore, it will also be necessary to master related texts, such as the *Garland of the Essential Points of the Religion of the Gods and the Religion of Humans*, which were composed in Tibet by Gyalwa Te-ne and Dromtonpa.[730]

Sixty-four Crafts [bb']

In addition, there is an enumeration of sixty-four crafts (*catuḥṣaṣṭikalā*, *sgyu rtsal drug cu rtsa bzhi*), according to the *Mahāvyutpati*,[731] which include [the thirty designated arts, the eighteen requisites of musical performance, the seven harmonious tones of the musical scale, and the nine dramatic moods].[732]

Thirty Designated Arts [1"]

Among them, the thirty designated arts (*śilpavidyākalā*, *bzo la sogs par gtogs pa sum cu*) comprise (1) writing (*lipi*, *yi ge*); (2) gestures (*mudrā*, *lag rtsis*); (3) arithmetic (*gaṇana*, *grangs*); (4) astrology (*saṃkhya*, *rtsis chen*); (5) hair-binding (*śikhābandha*, *thor tshugs*); (6) deportment (*padabandha*, *gom stabs*); (7) elephant goading (*aṅkuśagraha*, *lcags kyus bsgyur thabs*); (8) swordsmanship (*khaḍgika/ sarau*, *ral gri'i thabs*); (9) lassoing or snaring (*pāśagraha*, *zhags pa gdab pa*); (10) javelin-throwing (*tomaragraha*, *mda' bo che 'phen pa*), (11) advancing (*upayāṇa*, *mdun du bsnur ba*), (12) retreating (*apayāna*, *phyir bsnur ba*); (13) cutting (*chedya*, *bcad pa*); (14) breaking (*bhedya*, *dral ba*); (15) poisoning (*dālana*, *dbug pa*); (16) striking from afar (*dūravedha*, *rgyang nas 'phog pa*); (17) verbal assault (*śabdavedha*, *sgra grags par 'phog pa*); (18) vital assault (*marmavedha*, *gnad du 'phog pa*) or stealthy assault (*avedanīyavedha*, *mi tshor bar 'phog pa*); (19) hard assault (*dṛḍhaprahāritā*, *tshabs che bar 'phog pa*); (20) jumping (*laṅghita*, *mchongs pa*); (21) wrestling (*sālambha*, *gyad kyi 'dzin stangs*); (23) running (*javita*, *bang*); (24) swimming (*plavita*, *rkyal brgal ba*); (25) elephant riding (*hastigrīvā*, *glang po che'i gnyar zhon pa*); (26) horse-riding (*aśvapṛṣṭha*, *rta la zhon pa*); (27) charioteering (*ratha*, *shing rta'i thabs*); (28) archery (*bāṇa, mda'*); (29) bows (*dhanuḥ, gzhu*); and (30) trials of strength (*vikramabala, gyad stobs*).

Eighteen Requisites of Musical Performance [2"]

The eighteen requisites of musical performance (*aṣṭadaśavādyaviśeṣa, rol mo'i bye brag bco brgyad*) comprise (1) the dancer (*nartaka, gar mkhan*); (2) the dance (*nāṭya, bro*); (3) the kettledrum (*bherī, rnga bo che*); (4) clay drum (*mṛdaṅga, rdza rnga*); (5) tambour (*muraja, rnga phran*); 6) large kettledrum (*dundubhi, rnga chen po*); (7) small cymbal (*paṇava, 'khar rnga*); (8) single string lute (*tuṇava, pi vang rgyud gcig pa*); (9) one-sided clay drum (*ekamukha mṛdaṅga, rdza rnga kha gcig pa*); (10) metal bell (*illarī, lcags kyi sil khrol*); (11) bell-metal cymbals (*sampa, mkhar ba'i sil khrol*); (12) three-string lute (*ballarī, pi vang rgyud gsum pa*); (13) mukunda drum (*mukunda, rnga mu kunda*); (14) harmony of percussion and singing (*gītopakṣipyatūrya, sil snyan glu dbyangs dang bstun pa*); (15) musical tempo (*tālāvacara, pheg rdob*); (16) instrumentation (*vādyaśabda, rol mo'i sgra*); (17) lute (*vīṇā, pi vang*); and (18) flute (*veṇu, gling bu*).

Seven Tones of the Musical Scale [3"]

The seven harmonious tones of the musical scale (*saptasvara, glu dbyangs kyi nges pa bdun*) are as follows:[733] (1) the [peacock-like] sixth tone (*ṣaḍja, drug ldan*); (2) the [ox-like] sage tone (*ṛṣabha, drang srong*); (3) the [goat-like] third tone (*gandhāra, sa 'dzin*); (4) the [crane-like] middle tone (*madhyama, bar ma*); (5) the [cuckoo-like] fifth tone (*pañcama, lnga pa*); (6) the [horse-like] clear tone (*dhaivata, blo gsal*); and (7) the [elephant-like] base tone (*niṣāda, 'khor nyan*).

Nine Dramatic Moods [4"]

The nine dramatic moods (*navanāṭyarasa, gar gyi cha byad dgu*) comprise those of (1) grace (*śṛṅgāra, sgeg pa*); (2) heroism (*vīra, dpa' ba*); (3) ugliness (*bībhatsa, mi sdug pa*); (4) ferocity (*raudra, drag shul*); (5) joviality (*hāsya, bzhad gad*); (6) fearsomeness (*bhayānaka, 'jigs rung*); (7) compassion (*karuṇā, snying rje*); (8) awesomeness (*adbhūta, rngam pa*); and (9) peace (*śānta, zhi ba*).[734]

Śīlapālita's Classification of the Sixty-four Crafts [iii']

In the *Extensive* [*Commentary*] *on the Minor Transmissions*, composed by the master Śīlapālita, a quite different classification [of the sixty-four crafts] is presented.[735]

According to such texts, the common arts are mainly to be performed with mind as their precursor, and when all of them are subsumed together, they may be gathered within the following four categories (*sde bzhi*):

(1) The category of wealth or objects (*nor ram don gyi sde*) comprises the things one studies or learns and so forth, as well as the material objects, merchandise, gemstones, precious metals, and other resources that are acquired with effort and their accumulation then guarded.
(2) The category of desire (*'dod pa'i sde*) comprises the desired attributes of the senses experienced by [mundane] gods, humans, and other beings who do not inhabit the inferior realms of existence, which are partaken of as objects [of enjoyment].[736]
(3) The category of religion (*chos kyi sde*) comprises the limitless number of positive teachings which are the causal basis for [rebirth in] the three exalted (*abhyudaya, mngon mtho*) or higher realms of existence (*trisvarga, mtho ris gsum*), and for [the attainment of] definitive excellence (*niḥśreyasa, nges legs*) and the three degrees of enlightenment (*byang chub gsum*).[737]
(4) The category of liberation (*thar pa'i sde*) comprises the enlightenment attained through the three vehicles, which reverse suffering and its causes.[738]

Among all these categories, the first two are with reference to cyclic existence (*saṃsāra, 'khor ba*), since those who strive after objects of desire seek to acquire wealth as their causal basis. The last two are with reference to nirvāṇa, since those who strive after liberation [from cyclic existence] persevere to acquire the sacred teachings, and, if one were to distinguish between them, they correspond to two [distinct] modes [of liberation], causal and fruitional.

Longchen Rabjampa's Classification of Knowledge [iv']

All the many classifications of knowledge, including those just mentioned, may therefore be subsumed within the arts of the mind. This is why, for example, the omniscient Dri-me Ozer [Longchen Rabjampa] has said [in his *Treasury of Wish-fulfilling Gems*]:[739]

> These [arts of mind] are known to include
> The six classes of sentient beings, the four modes of birth,
> The six grounds, the ten measures of time,
> The seventeen material objectives (*dngos po bcu bdun*),
> The fourteen useful devices (*yo byad bcu bzhi*),
> The eight pursuits of daily life (*rjes su spyod pa brgyad*),
> The ten mundane pastimes (*'jig rten spyod bcu*),
> The three kinds of discourse (*gtam rnam pa gsum*),
> The twenty-two kinds of misconduct (*nyes rtsom nyer gnyis*),
> And similarly the sixty-three categories of sentient being (*sems can rigs*),
> The eight phases of the life-cycle (*dus brgyad*),
> The four ways of entering [the womb] (*'jug pa bzhi*),
> The six [acceptable] modes of livelihood (*'tsho ba drug*),
> And the six things to be well guarded (*kun nas bsrung ba drug*),
> The seven kinds of pride (*nga rgyal bdun*),
> And the seven kinds of self-satisfaction (*rgyags pa rnam pa bdun*),
> The four kinds of conventional expression (*tha snyad bzhi*),
> And the manifold bases of conventional expressions (*tha snyad mang po'i gzhi*),
> The six kinds of knowledge (*mkhas pa drug*),
> And the nine themes of [the Buddha's] transmitted teachings (*bka'i dngos po dgu*),
> Along with the eight themes of cyclic existence (*'khor gyi dngos po brgyad*).[740]

6. MEDICINE

aa. Introduction [III.B.2.a.iv.aa]
bb. Exegesis of the Actual Principles of Medicine
  1' Brief Presentation of the *Four Tantras of Dratang*
    a' *Root Tantra*
      i' The Root of Physiology and Pathology
        aa' Physiology
        bb' Pathology
      ii' The Root of Diagnosis
        aa' The Stem of Visual Observation
        bb' The Stem of Pulse Palpation
        cc' The Stem of Inquiry
      iii' The Root of the Methods of Treatment
        aa' The Stem of Diet
        bb' The Stem of Regimen
        cc' The Stem of Medication
        dd' The Stem of External Therapy
    b' *Exegetical Tantra*
    c' *Instructional Tantra*
    d' *Subsequent Tantra*
      i' Classification of Diseases Affecting the Patient
      ii' Classification of Remedies
      iii' Classification of Methods of Treatment
  2' Four Therapeutic Principles
    a' Introductory Preamble
    b' Detailed Explanation of Therapeutic Principles
      i' Patients
        aa' Physiology
        bb' Pathology

ii' Remedies
iii' Methods of Treatment
aa' Prophylactics
bb' Treatment
1" Diagnostics
2" Administering Treatment
a" Therapeutic Principles
b" Methods of Treatment
iv' The Practicing Physician

. . . .

The exegesis of medicine (*cikitsāvidyā, gso ba rig pa*), the fourth [subject of the major pathway of science; see above, p. 127], is in two parts: an introduction identifying the subject matter that is to be explained, along with its purpose, and a detailed exegesis of the actual principles of medicine.

Introduction [aa]

As to the former [it is said in the root verses]:

Among all the works of medical science
Which concern the physical body and its vitality,
The structure of the *Glorious Great Tantra*
***Entitled "Essence of Nectar"* is of crucial importance.**

It should be briefly explained that, although there are limitless textual traditions advocating the maintenance of good health and the treatment of disease in respect of the physical body (*lus*) and the vitality (*srog*) it imbues, among them all the most essential or crucially important is entitled the *Great Tantra of Secret Instructions on the Eight Branches of the Essence of the Glorious Elixir* [*of Immortality*].[741] This [text] is easy to comprehend and well-intentioned. It perfectly reveals the meanings of the eight aspects [of medicine][742] and is great on account of its extensive benefits for all [sentient beings], regardless of their status. Therefore, among all the transmitted teachings and treatises that were translated in Tibet, if one can comprehend even approximately the structure or framework of this amazing and marvelous [text], one will easily discern the objectives of all medical science.

Exegesis of the Actual Principles of Medicine [bb]

The latter, [the detailed exegesis of the actual principles of medicine,] is in two parts—a brief presentation of physiology according to the *Four Tantras of Dratang* and a detailed exegesis of the four therapeutic principles (*gso ba'i tshul bzhi*).

Brief Presentation of the *Four Tantras of Dratang* [1']

First, the brief presentation of physiology accords with the *Root Tantra*, the *Exegetical Tantra*, the *Instructional Tantra*, and the *Subsequent Tantra*.[743]

Root Tantra [a']

With regard to the first of these [it says in the root verses]:

> **The roots [of medical science, as expounded in the *Root Tantra*],**
> **Namely, physiology, diagnosis, and treatment...**

In the *Root Tantra* [expounded by Vidyājñāna, the emanation] of the buddha mind of [Bhaiṣajyaguru],[744] the following three "roots" (*rtsa ba gsum*) are expounded [in the context of an elaborate arboreal metaphor]:[745] (1) physiology (*gnas lugs*) and pathology (*nad gzhi*), (2) diagnosis (*ngos 'dzin rtags*), and (3) methods of treatment (*gso byed thabs*).

Among these, the first ["root"] has two "stems" (*sdong po gnyis*)—unmodified physiology (*rnam par ma gyur pa lus*), which may be exemplified by [naturally occurring] water, and pathological transformation (*rnam par gyur pa nad*) which may be exemplified by ice.[746]

The Root of Physiology and Pathology [i']

Physiology [aa']

The first of these stems has three physiological "branches" (*lus kyi yal ga gsum*), namely, [the humoral basis of] disease (*nad*), the bodily constituents (*lus zungs*), and the three impurities (*dri ma gsum*), which altogether support twenty-five "leaves" (*lo ma*). Among these,

Fig. 44. The first arboreal metaphor: physiology and pathology

(1) The [branch of the humoral basis of] disease comprises the five types of wind (*pañcavāta, rlung lnga*) [leaves 1–5], including life-sustaining breath (*prāṇa, srog 'dzin*); the five types of bile (*pañcapitta, mkhris pa lnga*) [leaves 6–10], including digestive bile (*pācaka, 'ju byed*); and the five types of phlegm (*pañcakapha, bad kan lnga*) [leaves 11–15], including supporting phlegm (*avalambaka, rten byed*).[747]

(2) The branch of the seven [bodily constituents; leaves 16–22] comprises muscle tissue and flesh (*sha*), blood (*khrag*), adipose tissue (*tshil*), bone tissue (*rus*), marrow tissue (*rkang*), reproductive fluids (*khu ba*), and chyle (*dvangs ma*).

(3) The [branch of the] three impurities [leaves 23–25] comprises feces (*bshang*), urine (*gci*), and perspiration (*rngul ba*).

Pathology [bb']

[The second stem, pathological transformation, has nine pathological branches (*nad kyi yal ga dgu*), namely, the primary causes [of disease] (*rgyu*), the secondary causes [of disease] (*rkyen*), the areas of inception [of disease] (*'jug sgo*), the predominant locations of the humors (*rten gnas*), the pathways [affected by pathogenic humors] (*rgyu lam*), the [predominant] rising occasions [of the humors] (*ldang dus*), the results [which bring fatality] (*'bras bu*), the contrary [humoral imbalances] (*ldog rgyu*), and the summary [of diseases] (*mdor dril*). These [branches], in turn, have altogether sixty-three leaves [nos. 26–88]. These are:

(1) The [branch of the] primary causes [of disease] comprises the three poisons (*dug gsum*) [leaves 26–28].[748]

(2) Then, there are four secondary causes [of disease; leaves 29–32]: time (*dus*), demonic possession (*gdon*), diet (*zas*), and regimen (*spyod lam*).

(3) There are six areas of inception [of disease; leaves 33–38], namely, the muscle tissue or flesh (*sha*), the skin (*pags*), the nerves and blood vessels (*rtsa*), the bones (*rus*), the solid viscera (*don*), and the hollow viscera (*snod*).[749]

(4) There are three [predominant] locations of the humors (*rten gsum*) [leaves 39–41], namely, the upper part of the body (*stod*) [where phlegm is predominant], the lower part of the body (*smad*) [where wind is predominant], and the middle part of the body (*bar*) [where bile is predominant].

(5) There are fifteen pathways [affected by pathogenic humors; leaves 42–56], namely, the bodily constituents (*lus zung*), the impurities (*dri ma*), the sense organs (*dbang po*), the solid viscera (*don*), and the hollow viscera (*snod*), each of which has specific associations with pathogenic wind, bile, and phlegm.[750]

(6) There are nine rising occasions [of the three pathogenic humors; leaves 57–65), namely, the three phases of life (*na so gsum*) [old age, adult

maturity, and childhood]; the three kinds of environment (*yul gsum*) [cold, dry, and damp places]; and the three seasons (*dus gsum*) [summer, autumn, and spring].[751]

(7) There are nine results which bring fatality [leaves 66–74], including exhaustion of the three factors that sustain life (*'tsho ba gsum zad pa*) [life span, merit, and past actions].[752]

(8) There are twelve contrary [humoral imbalances; leaves 75–86], comprising the four contrary imbalances of wind, of bile, and of phlegm that may arise when each of the other two humors is tranquilized and when it is not tranquilized.[753]

(9) Then, there are two aspects to the summary [of diseases; leaves 87–88], for all diseases may be subsumed into those that have a hot nature (*tsha ba*) and those that have a cold nature (*grang ba*).

The Root of Diagnosis [ii']

The second [root, diagnosis (*ngos 'dzin rtags*)] has three stems (*sdong po gsum*): visual observation (*lta*), pulse palpation (*reg*), and inquiry (*dri ba*).[754]

The Stem of Visual Observation [aa']

Among them, visual observation has two branches (*lta ba'i yal ga gnyis*), namely, (1) observation of the tongue (*lce*) and (2) [observation of] the urine (*lci*). Each of these "branches" is considered in terms of the three humoral diseases, so that they have altogether six leaves [nos. 89–94].

The Stem of Pulse Palpation [bb']

[The stem of] pulse palpation has three branches (*reg pa'i yal ga gsum*), corresponding to the three humoral diseases, and similarly it has three leaves [nos. 95–97].

The Stem of Inquiry [cc']

[The stem of] inquiry has three branches (*dri ba'i yal ga gsum*), based on the activating or secondary causes (*slong rkyen*) associated with the [three] modes of humoral disease (*na lugs*); and it has altogether twenty-nine leaves [nos. 98–126], which are differentiated when the inquiry focuses on the humoral diseases of wind, bile, and phlegm, complicated by factors of diet and regimen

Fig. 45. The second arboreal metaphor: diagnostics

that are respectively light and harsh [in the case of wind disorders], sharp and hot [in the case of bile disorders], and heavy and oily [in the case of wind disorders], and so forth.[755]

The Root of the Methods of Treatment [iii']

The third [root, the methods of treatment,] has four stems (*sdong po bzhi*): diet (*zas*), regimen (*spyod*), medication (*sman*), and external therapy (*dpyad*).[756]

Fig. 46. The third arboreal metaphor: treatment

THE STEM OF DIET [aa']

Among them, diet has six branches (*zas kyi yal ga drug*), comprising the three types of food (*zas gsum*) and three types of beverage (*skom gsum*) [suitable for imbalances of the three humors]. It has altogether thirty-five leaves [nos. 127–161] since there are fourteen kinds of food [and beverage] suitable for the treatment of wind disorders (*rlung zas bcu bzhi*), twelve for the treatment of bile disorders (*mkhris zas bcu gnyis*), and nine for the treatment of phlegm disorders (*bad kan zas skom dgu*).[757]

The Stem of Regimen [bb']

[The stem of] regimen has three branches (*spyod lam gyi yal ga gsum*), comprising the [modes of conduct] which are the remedies to be applied in [the treatment of] the three respective [imbalances of wind, bile, and phlegm]. Altogether it has six leaves [nos. 162–167] since each [of the three humoral imbalances] is considered in terms of the [recommended] locations (*gnas*) and activities (*spyod lam*) [suitable for recovery].[758]

The Stem of Medication [cc']

[The stem of] medication has fifteen branches (*sman gyi yal ga bcu lnga*), [the first] six of which are differentiated according to the taste (*ro*) and the potency (*nus pa*) of medications suitable for the treatment of the three [humoral disorders], such as the medications for the treatment of wind disorders.[759]

The next six [branches] are differentiated according to the appropriate tranquilizing agents (*zhi byed drug*)—broth (*khu ba*) and medicinal butter (*mar*) for the treatment of wind disorders, decoction (*thang*) and powder (*cur nis*) for the treatment of bile disorders, and pills (*ril bu*) and *tre-sam* powders for the treatment of phlegm disorders.[760]

Then, the last three branches are the cathartic procedures (*sbyong byed gsum*), comprising mild enemata for wind disorders (*rlung 'jam rtsi*), purgatives for bile disorders (*mkhris pa bshal*), and emetics for phlegm disorders (*bad kan skyugs*).[761]

Among them, [the six branches of taste and potency] have eighteen aspects [leaves; nos. 168–185] since the taste [of medications] suitable for wind disorders may be sweet, sour, or salty, and their potency may be oily, heavy or mild, and similar classifications apply to the other two humors as well.[762]

[The six branches of the tranquilizing agents have twenty-three aspects, including] three types of broth (*khu ba gsum*) [leaves 186–188], five types of medicinal butter (*sman mar lnga*) [leaves 189–193], four types of decoction and four types of powder (*thang dang phye ma bzhi bzhi*) [leaves 194–201], two types of pills (*ril bu gnyis*) [leaves 202–203], and five types of *tre-sam* powder (*tre sam lnga*) [leaves 204–208].[763]

[Then the three branches associated with the cathartic procedures] altogether have nine [aspects, including] three types of the first cathartic procedure [i.e., mild enemata] (*sbyong byed snga ma la gsum*) [leaves 209–211]; four types of the second cathartic procedure [i.e., purgatives] (*bar ma la bzhi*) [leaves 212–215]; and two types of the final cathartic procedure [i.e., emetics] (*phyi ma la gnyis*) [leaves 216–217].[764]

In all [the fifteen branches of medication] have fifty leaves [nos. 168–217].

The Stem of External Therapy [dd']

[The stem of] external therapy has three branches (*dpyad kyi yal ga gsum*), comprising the therapeutic techniques suitable for wind, bile, and phlegm disorders. Altogether it has seven leaves [nos. 218–224], including massage (*bsku mnye*) and Mongolian moxibustion (*hor gyi me btsa'*), which are suitable [for treatment of] the first [i.e., wind disorders]; induced perspiration (*rngul dbyung ba*), bloodletting (*gtar ga*), and fomentation (*chu'i 'phrul 'khor*), which are suitable [for the treatment of] the second [i.e., bile disorders]; and compress (*dugs*) and moxibustion (*me btsa'*), which are suitable [for the treatment of] the last [i.e., phlegm disorders].[765]

[The Arboreal Metaphor]

In brief, [the root of] physiology (*gso yul*) and pathology (*nad gzhi*) gives rise to eighty-eight [leaves], [the root of] diagnosis to thirty-eight [leaves], and [the root of] the methods of remedial treatment to ninety-six [leaves]. Since the entire content of medical science is established within [this framework], the [arboreal] metaphor of the Aśoka tree has been justifiably applied.[766] Similarly, the "flowers" (*me tog*) symbolize the freedom from disease and longevity acquired by those who have properly understood and implemented [medical science], as outlined above; while the "fruits" (*'bras bu*) symbolize the endowments of the sacred teachings, wealth, and well-being.

Concerning the application of these appropriate metaphors, the [*Root*] *Tantra* itself says:[767]

> There are nine stems that evolve from the three roots,
> Forty-seven branches that diverge from [these stems],
> Two hundred and twenty-four leaves that flourish,
> And radiant flowers that ripen into the five fruits.
> These are all explained in the paradigms of the *Root Tantra*.

Exegetical Tantra [b']

With regard to the second, [the *Exegetical Tantra*, it says in the root verses]:

> **...Are explained in terms of the patient, the remedy,**
> **The application of the remedy, and the practicing physician.**

All the [theoretical] aspects of medical science which are presented in the *Exegetical Tantra* [expounded by Vidyājñāna, the emanation] of the buddha body of [Bhaiṣajyaguru], are combined within the four [therapeutic] principles (*tshul bzhi*), which will be explained, somewhat, below.[768]

Instructional Tantra [c']

With regard to the third, [the *Instructional Tantra*, it says in the root verses]:

> **There are eight branches in the *Instructional Tantra*:**
> **[Treatment of] the physical body [in general], pediatrics, gynecological diseases,**
> **Demonic possession, wounds and injuries, poisoning,**
> **Old age, and the restoration of virility and fertility.**

The *Instructional Tantra* [expounded by Vidyājñāna, the emanation] of the buddha-attributes of [Bhaiṣajyaguru] has ninety-two chapters.[769] Among them, seventy chapters[770] [chs. 1–70] concern the treatment of [humoral and internal disorders of] the body [in general]; three chapters each are devoted to pediatrics (*byis pa*) [chs. 71–73] and gynecological diseases (*mo nad*) [chs. 74–76]; five chapters each concern demonic possession (*gdon*) [chs. 77–81] and wounds or injuries (*mtshon*) [chs. 82–86]; three concern poisoning (*dug*) [chs. 87–89]; one concerns the elixirs of rejuvenation in the treatment of old age (*rgas pa gso ba'i thabs bcud len*) [ch. 90], and the remaining two concern the restoration of virility (*ro tsa*) [ch. 91] and its ancillary aspect, the treatment of infertility (*bud med btsa' srung gi thabs*) [ch. 92]. Through these [topics], the instructions that concern the remedies or antidotes [for disease] are perfectly presented.[771]

In general, all matters pertaining to [the health of] the physical body and so forth are well known to accord with these [so-called] "eight categories of patients" (*gso yul gyi yan lag brgyad*). All the major and minor therapeutic techniques that exist [are said to] derive exclusively from this [pathological classification].[772]

Subsequent Tantra [d']

With regard to the fourth, [the *Subsequent Tantra*, it says in the root verses]:

> **Diseases and remedial techniques are integrated in the *Subsequent* [*Tantra*].**

The extensive explanations, classified according to the diseases afflicting the patient (*gso yul gyi nad*), the remedies (*gso byed gnyen po*), and the methods of treatment (*gso ba'i thabs*), are presented quintessentially from the standpoint of medical practice in the *Subsequent Tantra* [expounded by Vidyājñāna, the emanation] of the buddha-activities of [Bhaiṣajyaguru].[773]

Classification of Diseases Affecting the Patient [i']

Diseases that afflict patients (*gso yul nad*) are extensively said to number one thousand two hundred, and when these are subsumed, they comprise four [main] types of disease: (1) the imaginary diseases associated with demonic possession (*kun brtags gdon*), (2) the ostensible diseases that suddenly occur (*ltar snang 'phral*), (3) the absolute diseases which harm the life span (*yongs grub tshe*), and (4) the dependent diseases of past actions (*gzhan dbang sngon las kyi nad*).[774]

Each of these [main categories of disease] has one hundred and one subdivisions, making altogether four hundred and four [main diseases]. These include one hundred and one absolute diseases harmful to the life span, which require the application of [all] curative means and are in fact curable.[775]

Classification of Remedies [ii']

Remedies (*gso byed gnyen po*) number one thousand and two, and when these are subsumed, they comprise the four [methods of treatment]: medication, external therapy, diet, and regimen.

Medications (*sman*) include both tranquilizing agents (*zhi byed*) and cathartic procedures (*sbyong byed*). Tranquilizing agents are either cooling or warming (*bsil drod*), and cathartic procedures are either strong or mild (*drag dang 'jam pa*). External therapies (*dpyad*) are either gentle or harsh (*'jam rtsub*). Diets (*zas*) are either beneficial or harmful (*phan gnod*), and regimen (*spyod lam*) is either vigorous or relaxing (*drag dal*).[776] In short, it is said that there are altogether ten types of remedy (*gnyen po bcu*) that can be applied.

Classification of Methods of Treatment [iii']

The methods of treatment (*gso thabs*) that may be implemented number three hundred and sixty, and when these are subsumed, they comprise three aspects: diagnostics (*brtag thabs*), therapeutic principles (*gso tshul*), and curative methods (*bcos thabs*).

The first of these [diagnostics] includes both pulse palpation (*reg pa rtsa*)[777] and urinalysis through visual observation (*mthong ba chu la brtag pa*).[778] The second includes the nine therapeutic principles (*gso tshul rnam pa dgu*).[779] The third [the curative methods] number twenty-three altogether. These include

(1–8) the eight classes of tranquilizing agents (*zhi byed sde tshan brgyad*), namely, decoctions (*thang*), medicinal powders (*phye ma*), pills (*ril bu*), pastes (*lde gu*), medicinal butters (*sman mar*), medicinal ash (*thal sman*), medicinal concentrates (*khaṇḍa*), and medicinal wine (*sman chang*). There are also gemstone and precious metal compounds (*rin po che'i sbyor ba*) which can counter complications and relapses, and herbal compounds (*sngo sbyor*) which are effective against sudden diseases.[780]

(9–15) the seven cathartic procedures (*sbyong byed bdun*): preliminary oil therapy (*sngon 'gro snum 'chos*), the five main cathartics (*sbyong byed dngos gzhi las lnga*): purgatives or laxatives (*bshal*), emetics (*skyugs*), nasal medications or snuff (*sna sman*), mild enema (*'jam rtsi*), and strong enema (*ni ru ha*), and the [supplementary] procedure of channel cleansing (*rtsa sbyong*), which can counter complications and relapses[781]

(16–23) the [six] techniques of external therapy (*dpyad pa*): bloodletting (*gtar ga*), moxibustion (*bsreg pa*), medicinal compresses (*dugs*), fomentation (*lums*), massage with ointment (*byugs pa*), and minor surgery (*thur ma*), which can counter complications and relapses.[782]

These [twenty-three procedures] may also be reduced to eighteen practical methods of treatment (*lag len bco brgyad*) when the last five types [of tranquilizing agent], such as medicinal ash, are subsumed within the five types of primary tranquilizing agent (*zhi byed rtsa ba'i sde tshan lnga*).[783]

Four Therapeutic Principles [2']

Secondly, the detailed exegesis of the four therapeutic principles (*gso ba'i tshul bzhi*) has two parts: an introductory preamble and a detailed explanation.

Introductory Preamble [a']

As to the former [it says in the root verses]:

> **The patient includes [the topics of] physiology for which [treatment is prescribed]**

And the diseases which are treated.
The remedy includes [the topics of] regimen, diet, medication, and external therapy.
The method of treatment includes [the topics of] the prevention of disease,
And the treatment of pathological transformations,
While the practitioner of medical science [includes the physician].
[Medical science] is subsumed in these primary and ancillary [topics].

Since the paradigm of the aforementioned *Exegetical Tantra* contains the principal aphorisms of medical science in general, I will now elucidate this [paradigm] to some extent. The object that is to be treated (*gso bya'i yul*) [i.e., the patient] includes both [the topics of] physiology (*lus*), in respect of which treatment [is prescribed], and the diseases (*nad*) dependent on this [physiology] which are treated. The remedy (*gso byed gnyen po*) includes the four [topics of] regimen (*spyod lam*), diet (*zas*), medication (*sman*), and external therapy (*dpyad*). The therapeutic principles or methods of treatment (*gso ba'i tshul lam thabs*), in accordance with which remedies are applied to diseases, include both [the topics of] the prevention of disease (*nad med ring du gnas pa*) and the treatment of pathological transformations (*rnam gyur gso ba'i thabs*). The practitioner of medical science (*gso byed kyi mkhan po*) includes [the topic of] the physician (*sman pa*). The entire corpus of medical science is completely subsumed in these four primary and eleven ancillary topics.[784]

Detailed Explanation of Therapeutic Principles [b']

As to the latter [the detailed explanation of the therapeutic principles], there are four parts: (1) the patient to be treated (*gso bya*), (2) the remedy (*gso byed*), (3) the method of treatment (*gso thabs*), and (4) the practicing physician (*gso mkhan*).

Patients [i']

The first [of these therapeutic principles], the patient to be treated, comprises [the ancillary topics of] both physiology (*lus*) and disease (*nad*).

PHYSIOLOGY [aa']

Within physiology [the following] are determined:
The understanding of human embryology,
Based on primary and secondary causes,
And the indications [of parturition],
As well as the understanding [of human anatomy] in metaphorical terms,
And the natural condition of the bodily constituents,
The channels, the vulnerable points,
And the passageways and orifices,
Along with the defining characteristics [of the elements]
Which may be subject to harm,
And [the humors] which may be harmful,
As well as the physical activities, distinctions,
And signs of physical decay.

With regard to the physiology of the human body, in respect of which treatment is applied, the following [seven] topics are established:

(1) the understanding of human embryology (*chags pa'i tshul rtogs*). In this regard, the primary cause (*rgyu*) of human conception refers to [the simultaneous conjunction in the womb] of white and red generative fluids [including sperm and ovum] and a consciousness [inclined to rebirth] (*dkar dmar rnam shes gsum*). The secondary cause (*rkyen*) of [embryonic and fetal] development refers to the nutrients that derive from the navel and the umbilical cord. Also included here are the [various] indications associated with parturition.[785]

(2) the understanding of human anatomy (*lus gnas kyi nyams shes*) based on the application of metaphors, whereby the king [symbolizing the heart], the ministers [symbolizing the lungs], the queens [symbolizing the liver and spleen], and the royal subjects [symbolizing the other organs] are supported within a palatial mansion [symbolizing the tissues and limbs].[786]

(3) the understanding of the natural condition of human physiology, which has four parts:

  (a) the natural condition of the bodily constituents (*lus zungs kyi gnas lugs*), i.e., the exact measurements (*ldang tshad*) of the [three] humors, along with chyle (*dvangs*), its residual impurities (*snyigs*), muscle tissue, bone tissue, and so forth [present in a healthy human organism of average build].[787]

(b) the natural condition of the interconnecting channels (*'brel pa rtsa'i gnas lugs*), comprising the channel of embryonic formation (*chags pa'i rtsa*), the channels of existence (*srid pa'i rtsa*), the channels of connection (*'brel pa'i rtsa*), and the course of the life span principle (*tshe gnas pa'i rtsa*).[788]

(c) the natural condition of the vulnerable points (*gnyan pa gnad kyi gnas lugs*), the seven categories of which include [the vulnerable points of] the muscles, the adipose tissue, the bones, the tendons and ligaments (*chu rgyus*), the solid viscera, the hollow viscera, and the channels.[789]

(d) the natural condition of the [inner] passageways and [external] orifices (*bu ga'i gnas lugs*) which are the digestive tracts (*zas kyi rgyu lam*) for chyle and its residual impurities.[790]

(4) the understanding of the defining characteristics of human physiology (*lus kyi mtshan nyid rtogs*), based on the elements that are subject to harm (*gnod bya khams*), i.e., the seven bodily constituents (*lus zungs bdun*) and the three impurities (*dri ma gsum*), and the humors that may be harmful (*gnod byed nyes pa*), which comprise the fifteen types of wind, bile, and phlegm. These are all considered in terms of their formation (*grub tshul*), their nature (*rang bzhin*), their metabolism (*me drod*), their role in the process of digestion (*lto ba*), their locations [within the human organism] (*gnas pa*), their functionality (*byed las*), and their characteristics (*mtshan nyid*).[791]

(5) [the understanding of] physical activities (*lus kyi las*), including general actions associated with body, speech, and mind which are non-specific (*lung ma bstan*) in terms of virtue and non-virtue, and particular actions through which the five sense faculties (*dbang po lnga*) engage with their own particular sense objects.[792]

(6) the understanding of the [further] distinctions (*dbye ba*) between these [physical activities], based on sex—male, female, and hermaphrodite; age—old age, childhood, and adult maturity; and the natural human constitution (*rang bzhin*)—which includes different human characteristics associated with [combinations of] the three humors, as well as the distinctions between non-pathological humors and their pathological transformations.[793]

(7) the determination of the signs of decay (*'jig pa'i ltas*) in respect of the

physical body, based on the [distinctions between] the four categories [of signs]—those that are observed at a distance [from the patient] (*ring ba*), those that are observed at close proximity [to the patient] (*nye ba*), those that are of uncertain outcome (*ma nges pa*), and those that are of certain outcome (*nges pa can*).[794]

The natural condition or physiology of the [human] body which is to be treated [by the physician] should be understood on the basis of these seven topics, each of which has many subdivisions.

Pathology [bb']

With regard to the latter [it says in the root verses]:

> **With regard to diseases, the remote and immediate primary causes**
> **Are [respectively] the three poisons and the three humors.**
> **While the secondary causes that aggravate [the basis of disease]**
> **Include the activity fields of the senses**
> **As well as their gathering, arising, and [fully manifest] arising.**
> **The characteristics [of humoral imbalance],**
> **Which has its inception in the six pathways,**
> **Are excess, deficiency, and [mutual] aggravation.**
> **[Diseases] are then classified on the basis of their primary causes,**
> **The [sex or age of] the patient, and their [four] aspects.**

With regard to the pathological diseases (*nad*) which are to be treated, there are five topics:[795]

(1) Concerning the primary causes of disease, the remote primary causes (*ring rgyu*) are the three poisons (*dug gsum*), which derive from fundamental ignorance (*ma rig pa*),[796] and the immediate primary causes (*nye ba'i rgyu*) are [the imbalances of] the three humors (*nyes pa gsum*) generated by them.

(2) The three secondary causes (*rkyen gsum*) which aggravate diseases comprise

   (a) the sensory activity fields (*skye mched kyi rkyen*) of the seasons, sense organs, and modes of conduct, which may be deficient (*dman*), excessive (*lhag pa*), or abnormally absent (*log pa*);[797]

   (b) the [covert] gathering and [overt] arising (*gsog rkyen*) [of the three humors] which tend to gather, arise, and subside in accordance with their primary causes, natures, and the [different] seasons (*rgyu ngo bo dus gsum*);[798] and

(c) the [fully manifest] arising (*slong rkyen*)[799] [of diseases], which may be defined in the general context [of the three humors] or in terms of their specific [indications].[800]

(3) The inception of disease (*nad 'jug tshul*) is the process through which the three humors enter into their six [respective] pathways (*lam drug*) or areas of inception (*'jug sgo*), targeted by the four secondary conditions (*rkyen bzhi*) [of season, demonic possession, diet, and regimen] which direct [dysfunctions] towards their respective [humoral] locations or targets, so that they become localized.[801]

(4) The characteristics of [the different types of] disease (*nad kyi mtshan nyid*) are based, following this inception, on the three degrees to which the bodily constituents and the three impurities diverge from the standard measurements (*ldang tshad*) [of a healthy human organism]—whether in excess (*'phel*), deficiency (*zad*), or a state of [mutual] aggravation (*'khrugs pa*).[802]

(5) The classifications of [diverse] diseases (*nad kyi dbye ba*) include
   (a) three that are made on the basis of primary causes (*rgyu*), i.e., those that originate from the actions of past [lives], those originating from the humoral [imbalances] of this life, and those originating from a combination of these two.
   (b) five that are made on the basis of [the sex or age of] the patient (*rten*), i.e., [diseases] specific to males, females, children, the elderly, and those that are common to all [types of patient].
   (c) four[803] that are made when the last [mentioned subcategory of common] diseases are [further] enumerated on the basis of their humoral disorders (*nyes pa*), their main features (*gtso bo*), their types (*rigs*), and their locations (*gnas*).

However, there are [also] limitless classifications based on the typology of the twenty-five vulnerable [humoral disorders] (*gnod bya nyi shu rtsa lnga*) and their subdivisions, including [diseases distinguished by] a single isolated humor (*rkyang pa*), and those [distinguished by] a dependent humor in association with others (*ldan 'dres pa*).[804]

The characteristics of the pathological diseases to be treated [by the physician] should be properly understood on the basis of these five topics.

REMEDIES [ii']

As for the exegesis of the second therapeutic principle, the remedy (*gso byed kyi tshul*) [it says in the root verses]:

> **Regimen comprises continuous [daily] regimen, seasonal regimen, and occasional regimen.**
> **Dietetics includes [knowledge of] the [diverse] types [of food and beverages],**
> **As well as dietary restrictions and moderation in the quantity of food.**
> **Medication includes taste, potency, post-digestive taste, and compounding methods.**
> **External therapy includes [the application of] mild, rough, and rigorous [treatments],**
> **Along with the [appropriate] surgical instruments.**

With regard to the remedies which treat diseases (*nad gso byed gnyen po rnams*), there are four topics:[805]

(1) Among them, the first is the important topic of regimen (*spyod lam*), which has three aspects:
   (a) continuous [daily] regimen (*rgyun du spyod pa*) includes activities which prolong the life span, activities associated with worldly pursuits, and those associated with the sacred [teachings] (*dam pa*);[806]
   (b) seasonal regimen (*dus spyod*) includes reliance on the [different] remedies appropriate for the [different conditions] that [covertly] gather and [overtly] arise during the six seasons [of the year];[807]
   (c) occasional regimen (*gnas skabs kyi spyod pa*) [entails the non-suppression of natural functions] in order that [diseases] might not [suddenly] arise and in order that those that have arisen might be alleviated.[808]

(2) Dietetics (*'tsho ba zas*) also has three aspects:
   (a) the [diverse] types (*tshul*) or categories of food and beverages should be understood;[809]
   (b) there should be dietary restrictions practiced (*bsdam par bya ba*) in respect of [food and beverages that are] incompatible with the body;[810]

(c) moderation should be observed with regard to the quantity of food intake (*zas tshod ran par bza'*).[811]

(3) Compounded medications (*sbyor ba'i sman*) have six [different] tastes (*ro drug*) and seventeen [different] attributes (*yon tan bcu bdun*) that arise from their eight [distinct] potencies (*nus pa brgyad*), as well as three kinds of post-digestive taste (*zhu rjes gsum*).[812]

The compounding methods (*sbyor ba'i thabs*) applied in remedies for all kinds of diseases should be mastered. These include sixty-three [types of compound differentiated according to their taste], which are remedies for the [diverse] diseases that arise. For there are fifty-seven compounded tastes (*ro bsdebs sbyor ba lnga bcu rtsa bdun*) and six [basic or] isolated tastes (*rkyang pa drug*) which may be applied as remedies to counter the seventy-four different degrees of [humoral] excess or deficiency.[813]

Then, when [medications] are compounded according to their potency, they include both tranquilizing and cathartic [compounds].[814]

(4) With regard to external therapy (*dpyad pa*) and surgical instruments (*cha byad*), [there are four aspects]:[815]

(a) mild therapy (*'jam pa'i dpyad*) includes compresses (*dugs*), fomentation (*lums*), and massage with ointments (*byugs pa*);[816]

(b) rough therapy (*rtsub pa'i dpyad*) includes bloodletting (*gtar*), moxibustion (*sreg*), and minor surgery (*dbug pa*);[817]

(c) rigorous therapy (*drag po'i dpyad*) is of four types, including incision (*'dral ba*), excision (*gcod pa*), scraping (*'drud pa*), and extraction (*'byin pa*);

(d) the surgical instruments [utilized in these therapeutic applications] include fourteen sorts of probes (*zug rngu brtag pa'i dpyad bcu bzhi*), such as the "needle-headed" probe [for the exploration of cranial fractures] (*khab mdo*); six kinds of forceps (*skam pa rigs drug*), such as the "lion-mouthed" forceps (*seng ge kha*), used for extracting foreign bodies; six kinds of lancet (*gtsag bu'i sde drug*), such as the "lancet shaped like a sparrow's feather" (*bye'u sgro 'dra*), which are used for incisions of the muscle tissue and to cause bleeding; nine kinds of surgical stylets (*thur ma dgu*), such as the "stylet shaped like a reed nib" (*sbubs thur smyu gu*), which are used for making punctures (*btsag dbugs*) and releasing [fluids or] vapors (*dbugs 'dren*); and assorted minor instruments, such as the cannula [for irrigating wounds and applying anal suppositories] (*gce'u*), the cupping horn [for extracting serum] (*rngabs ra*), and the fire-cupping bowl [used to siphon off fluids from surface boils] (*bum pa*).[818]

[The practicing physician] should persevere compassionately with these [remedies] in order to treat the [various] types of pathological disease.

Methods of Treatment [iii']

The third [of the therapeutic principles, the method of treatment (*gso thabs*), has two parts: prophylactics (*nad med gnas shing 'tsho ba*) and treatment (*na ba gso bar bya'o*).

Prophylactics [aa']

As to the former [it says in the root verses]:

> **[Prophylactics] maintain [the body] in good health, free from disease,**
> **And prolong [the life] of the aged, free from disease.**

The supreme method which prolongs life and maintains good health, not in respect of the ordinary body but of the [balance of] non-pathological [humors] free from disease, is the training in abandoning the primary and secondary causes of disease.[819] Then, when the life span is nearly ended due to old age, once the strength of the bodily constituents has been eclipsed by the passing of many years and months, and the physical frame has deteriorated, the life span should be prolonged and vigor enhanced by compounding elixirs of rejuvenation (*bcud len*).[820]

Treatment [bb']

As to the latter [it says in the root verses]:

> **[Understanding] the primary causes and characteristic [symptoms] of disease,**
> **And relying on [familiarity with] the advantages and disadvantage [of certain remedies],**
> **[The physician] should [also] undertake diagnosis through subterfuge**
> **And through the four alternative parameters,**

On the basis of which [treatment] is to be abandoned or prescribed.
Treatment should then be administered
According to general, specific, and special [therapeutic] principles.
Both the common and special methods of treatment should be mastered.

Diagnostics [1″]

Before treating diseases, [the practicing physician] should first master diagnostics (*ngos bzung rtags*). This entails actual or genuine diagnosis (*dngos su brtag*) of humoral disorders on the basis of three principles: [821]

(1) [understanding] the primary [and secondary] causes that arise (*slong byed rgyu*),
(2) [understanding] the characteristic symptoms [of humoral imbalance] (*mtshan nyid rtags*), and
(3) reliance on familiarity with the advantages and disadvantages [of certain remedies] (*phan gnod goms pa bsten pa*).[822]

[Physicians] may also undertake diagnosis by means of subterfuge (*ngan gYo skyon te thabs kyi sgo nas brtag pa*), in order to [inspire confidence in their skills and] avoid acquiring a reputation for ignorance.[823] Then, they should also make their diagnosis on the basis of the four alternative parameters through which [treatment] is to be abandoned or adopted (*spang blang mu bzhi'i brtag pa*), analyzing whether a disease is (1) easily curable (*gso sla ba*), (2) difficult to cure (*gso dka' ba*), (3) only nominally curable (*gso rung ba tsam*), or (4) [incurable and therefore] to be abandoned (*spang bar bya ba*).[824]

Administering Treatment [2″]

Having completed their diagnosis, [physicians should then consider] the ways in which treatment should be administered. This includes both therapeutic principles (*gso tshul*) and the methods of treatment (*gso thabs*).

Therapeutic Principles [a″]

As to the former, there are three [types of recognized therapeutic principle—general, specific, and special:[825]]

(1) The general therapeutic principle is that [imbalances of] the three humors should be cured by tranquilizing agents (*zhi byed*) at the time when they [covertly] gather and by cathartic procedures (*sbyong byed*) at the time when they [overtly] surface, taking precautions not to arouse [other diseases] while they are being tranquilized.[826]

(2) The specific therapeutic principles concern the curing in the appropriate manner of dysfunctions associated with indigestion (*ma zhu ba*), isolated [or independent] humoral diseases (*rkyang pa*), and dependent [or combined humoral diseases] (*gzhan dbang can*).[827]

(3) Then, there are nine special therapeutic principles, through which diseases are to be treated:[828]

  (a) When [the physician] has not yet understood [whether a specific disease is to be classified as one of heat or cold] and is hesitant, the clinical test (*sad mda'*) should be applied [cautiously, like a creeping cat approaching a mouse].

  (b) When [the physician] is certain [as to the nature of the disease], having diagnosed it correctly, medication or external therapy should be actually [and openly] applied, [as if hoisting a silken banner on a mountain top].

  (c) When [the physician has made a correct diagnosis but] the remedy does not immediately take effect, the course of [secondary] ailments has to be stabilized [as if goading an untamed horse along].

  (d) When an ailment has been previously treated [by another doctor and the prescribed medication is diagnosed] to have been deficient, excessive, or counter-indicative, the remedy should be changed [and the mistake swiftly rectified, like a gull catching a fish].

  (e) When treating the most serious diseases, the remedy should be expertly applied [as if meeting a deadly enemy on a narrow path].

  (f) When treating less serious types of disease, the remedy should be applied gradually [as if scaling the rungs of a ladder].

  (g) When, with regard to the three humors, a disease caused by a single isolated [humoral dysfunction] is treated, the remedy should not harm the other [humors, like a hero vanquishing an enemy].

  (h) When combined humoral disorders are treated, the cure should be applied proportionately [like a chieftain resolving a dispute].

  (i) In all cases, the treatment should be commensurate with the disease and unerring [like the balanced loads carried by hybrid cattle and sheep].

Methods of Treatment [b"]

There are two common methods of treatment (*gso thabs gnyis*) which are to be undertaken: anabolic procedures [for increasing weight] (*brta ba*) in the case of [anorexic] patients with a deficiency of the bodily constituents (*zungs zad*), and so forth; and catabolic procedures [for reducing weight] (*nyams dmad pa, smyung ba*) in the case of those suffering from obesity (*tsho che*), and so forth.[829]

Special methods of treatment should also be mastered [and applied] in the case of different disorders of the three humors: cooling [remedies] should be applied in the treatment of fevers [and bile disorders], warming [remedies] in the treatment of colds [and phlegm disorders], oily and warm [remedies] in the treatment of wind disorders, and so forth.[830]

The Practicing Physician [iv']

As to the fourth [of the therapeutic principles, the practicing physician (*gso mkhan*), it says in the root verses]:

> **Physicians should be endowed with the six primary attributes.**
> **They should be supreme [in all their other qualities],**
> **And masters of [medical and spiritual] practices.**
> **[Thus,] they themselves and others will enjoy**
> **The results of immediate happiness and long-term well-being.**

As for the defining characteristics of the practicing physicians (*sman pa*) who undertake the treatment of disease, they should be endowed with six primary attributes (*rgyu drug*):[831]

(1) They should have an analytical intelligence, which is broad-minded, steadfast, and refined.
(2) They should have a virtuous or positive outlook, endowed with loving-kindness and compassion.[832]
(3) They should keep their commitments, including the six [commitments] that establish an attitude [of respect for medical teachers, texts, and colleagues] (*blo zhag drug*), the two [commitments] that are to be retained (*bzung bya gnyis*), and three that bring about understanding (*shes pa gsum*).[833]
(4) They should be skillful [in therapeutic techniques]—dexterous in

hand, pleasant in verbal communication, and brilliant in their knowledge [of diagnosis and treatment].

(5) They should persevere in their own [medical] studies and training, and be without idleness in attending to their patients.

(6) They should be learned in [basic] human values (*mi chos*), maintaining saintly characteristics (*dam pa'i msthan nyid*) and excellence in all ordinary modes of behavior (*kun spyod*).

In addition, they should have rejected the twelve defects of inferior [doctors] (*tha ma'i skyon bcu gnyis*), such as the absence of an authentic lineage, and the lack of observational skills or experience.[834] Instead, they should be endowed with supreme qualities. Mastering the ordinary medical practices pertaining to body, speech, and mind, and in particular the practices of the [Buddhist] view, meditation, and conduct, they should maintain a [high] standard that accords with the aforementioned therapeutic principles. Consequently, both they themselves and others [who encounter them] will enjoy the results of immediate happiness [in this life] and long-term well-being [in future lives].

7. Astrology and Divination

b. The Minor Classical Sciences [III.B.2.b]
  i. General Introduction
  ii. Actual Exegesis
    aa. Astrology
      1' Overview
      2' Precision of the Inner World
        a' Cycles of Breath within the Energy Channels
        b' Correlation of Microcosm and Macrocosm
      3' The Basis of Astrological Calculations in the Macrocosm
        a' The Zodiac
        b' Calculation of Solar and Lunar Eclipses
        c' Calculation of Zodiacal, Calendar, and Solar Days
        d' Calculation of the Cycle of Months
        e' Precedence of the Waxing and Waning Phases of the Moon
      4' The Techniques of Astrological Calculation
        a' The Fivefold Calculation
        b' Subsidiary Calculations concerning Planetary Motion, Eclipses, and So Forth
        c' Prognostications
          i' Prognostications of the *Wheel of Time* and Svarodaya
          ii' Prognostications of Elemental Divination

The Minor Classical Sciences [b]

The second part of the exegesis of the classical sciences concerns the minor or lesser sciences (*rigs gnas chung ba*), which has two parts: a [general] introduction and the actual [exegesis].

General Introduction [i]

As to the former [it says in the root verses]:

> **Among the [subjects] known as the five minor sciences...**

Although there are a few dissimilar opinions as to what subjects actually constitute the enumeration of the "five minor sciences" (*rigs gnas chung ba lnga*),[835] it is said in the *Tantra of Renunciation*:[836]

> A bodhisattva, in order to inspire sentient beings, should study the treatises of poetics for the sake of others, along with the treatises of synonymics which list both homonyms and synonyms; the treatises of prosody which classify metrical verses according to their varying numbers of heavy and light syllables and the degree to which they are interspersed with [passages of prose]; the treatises of dramaturgy which delight audiences through their discourse, humor, and multi-lingual variation; and the treatises of astrology which make astonishing revelations, appraised on the basis of mathematics. This is because that bodhisattva wishes to attain the unsurpassed and completely perfect enlightenment.

In recent times there has been a consensus that the interpretation [of what constitutes the five minor sciences] should accord with this passage. [The postposition] "among" (*las*) completes this introductory line of verse.

Actual Exegesis [ii]

Secondly, [the actual exegesis of the minor classical sciences] comprises five parts: astrology (*jyotiḥśāstra, skar rtsis*), poetics (*kāvya, snyan dngags*), prosody (*chandas, sdeb sbyor*), synonymics (*abhidāna, mngon brjod*), and dramaturgy (*nāṭya, zlos gar*).

Astrology [aa]

The explanation of astrology has four sections: (1) the overview, (2) the precision of the inner [world], (3) the basis of astrological calculations pertaining to the outer [world], and (4) an exegesis of the techniques employed in astrological calculation.

Overview [1']

With regard to the first [the overview, it says in the root verses]:

> **... Astrology discloses things to be adopted or rejected**
> **From the perspective of relative appearances.**
> **The gross apparitional forms of reality or emptiness**
> **Underlie the astrological calculations to be made,**
> **While the techniques of astrological calculation**
> **Are mathematical computations of interdependence or correlation.**

The point [of astrology] is that since this [science] is undeluded with respect to the mathematical calculations and circumstances applicable in the world of relative appearances, it should disclose without error the things [or courses of action] that are to be adopted or rejected. The well-known [systems] of astrology (*skar rtsis*) which maintain this purpose include both outer [non-Buddhist] traditions and inner [Buddhist] traditions,[837] and among them here [in Tibet, the tradition] which adheres to the [astrological system] enunciated in the *King of Tantras* [*The Wheel of Time*] is [considered to be] the most useful or purposeful.

According to this [system of the *Wheel of Time*], it is important, at the outset, to understand the precision of the inner world (*nang gi nges pa*): The abiding nature of reality (*de kho na nyid kyi gnas lugs*), the emptiness that is free from conceptual elaborations (*stong pa spros bral*) owing to the contamination of fundamental ignorance (*ma rig pa*), its mode of bewilderment, has been fabricated or superimposed in a limitless number of gross apparitional forms.[838] These include dichotomies exemplified by object and subject, or the outer and inner [worlds], and trichotomies, exemplified by the energy channels, winds, and generative essences (*rtsa rlung thig le*) [within the subtle body], or [the three energy channels of] the Sun, Moon, and Rāhu.[839]

It is this mere apparitional aspect [of emptiness] that underlies the astrological calculations to be made in respect of ordinary individuals,[840] while the actual techniques or methods of astrological calculation are mathematical computations applied to [ascertain] the interdependence or correlation [of these apparent phenomena].

Precision of the Inner World [2']

Secondly, with regard to the precision of the inner [world, it says in the root verses]:

The stepping of the planets derives from the breath within the central channel,
But at the end of the four ages, they will enter a state of vacuity.
The precision of time arises through repeated scrutiny.

The breath (*śvāsa, dbugs*) that moves within the central energy channel (*avadhūti, dbu ma*) [of the subtle body] is known as the vital energy of pristine cognition (*ye shes kyi rlung*). Just as the left-side and right-side energy channels manifestly arise in dependence on the central energy channel, the vital energy of past actions (*las kyi rlung*), which embodies the five material elements (*'byung ba lnga'i bdag gnyid*), arises or circulates dependent on the vital energy of pristine cognition.[841]

Cycles of Breath within the Energy Channels [a']

Dependent on the left-side energy channel (*lalanā, gYon rkyang ma*) [of the subtle body], [this vital energy] generates the objective aspect [of the subject-object dichotomy] which is nature endowed with "lightness" (*sattvaprakṛti, snying stobs kyi rang bzhin*), setting in motion the five peaceful planets (*zhi gza' lnga*) respectively through the [progressive elemental] sequence—space, wind, fire, water, and earth. Meanwhile, dependent on the right-side energy channel (*rasanā, gYas ro ma*), the same vital energy manifests as nature endowed with "motility" (*rajaḥprakṛti, rdul kyi rang bzhin*), thereby generating the primal self (*pradhāna, gtso bo*), which is the subjective or conceptualizing aspect [of the same dichotomy], and setting in motion the five wrathful planets (*drag gza' lnga*) respectively through the [regressive elemental] sequence—earth, water, fire, wind, and space.[842] For this reason it is said that, in the case of the external world, the stepping of the planets in a slow orbital motion (*dal rkang*) and the stepping of the planets in a fast orbital motion (*myur rkang*) and so forth[843] may be correlated with the calculations applicable to the fire element and the wind element respectively.[844]

The number of the years (*lo grangs*) and so forth after which these planets will enter into a state of vacuity at the end of the four ages [of time][845] may also be correlated with the inner [or subtle, microcosmic] body, as stated above, in which case a mature adult male, free from ill-health, should be taken as the [ideal] exemplar: At first five maṇḍalas are set in motion through the [progressive] sequence of the elements—space, wind, fire, water, and earth—emerging exhaled from the left nostril, dependent on the left-side energy channel [of the subtle body], and each of these maṇḍalas is equivalent to three hundred and sixty [breaths]. Then, five maṇḍalas are set in motion in the reverse order, through the [regressive] sequence of the elements—earth, water, fire, wind, and space—absorbed or inhaled into the right [nostril], dependent on the right-side energy channel [of the subtle body].

Each of these maṇḍalas or minor cycles (*'pho chung*) is equivalent to three hundred and sixty [breaths], and when all five maṇḍalas are completed, that is known as one major cycle (*'pho chen*), which is equivalent to one thousand eight hundred breaths. Once these two processes of the exhalation and inhalation [of breath] have been completed, in the interval between any two major cycles, [the breath] re-enters the central energy channel.

Correlation of Microcosm and Macrocosm [b']

[On this analogy, it is said that] when the processes associated with the formation and dissolution of the world have come to an end, there will endure a state of vacuity (*stong par gnas*); or else when the spheres (*maṇḍala*) of the planets have come to an end, they will enter into [a state of] vacuity.[846] Corporeal beings, after [completing] the cycle of birth and death, similarly enter into the [state of] natural inner radiance (*rang bzhin 'od gsal*).[847] Such are the points [indicated here].

In accordance with this principle of correlation, there are six major cycles [of breath] (*'pho chen*) associated with the odd-numbered solar mansions (*mi mnyam pa'i khyim*), starting with Aries (*meṣa, lug*), which emerge from the right-side energy channel and six major cycles [of breath] associated with the even-numbered solar mansions (*mnyam pa'i khyim*), starting with Taurus (*vṛṣa, glang*), which emerge from the left-side energy channel.[848] Together, these [solar mansions] form the "twelvefold cycle of the ascendant conjunctions" (*dus sbyor gyi 'pho ba bcu gnyis*),[849] which is [precisely] equivalent [in its duration] to twenty-one thousand six hundred breaths—i.e., the total number of breaths (*rang dbugs*) in a single [solar] day.[850]

Therefore, internally, once the elements have completed their course of exhalation and inhalation over two major cycles [of breath], they come to rest in emptiness or vacuity within the central energy channel [of the subtle body]. This is the meaning that accords with the [Buddhist] teachings.

In other contexts, in order to induce eternalistic extremists to enter upon [the Buddhist path], this [process] is [provisionally and artfully] presented as if it were due to a powerful "self" (*puruṣa, gtso bo*), for whom one single breath is equivalent to one thousand and two hundred human years.[851] When two major cycles of his breath have come to an end, it is said that, externally, one Great Age [of time] (*mahāyuga*) will come to an end;[852] and that in the interval between [these] and [the next] of his [major breathing] cycles, [the breath] will enter the central energy channel [of his subtle body], while externally the planets will enter into a state of vacuity.

Concerning the timing of this entry into [the state of] vacuity (*stong 'jug*), the followers of the Tsurphu tradition hold that the actual calculations presented in the *Tantra* [*of the Wheel of Time*] should be taken literally, while the followers of the Phugpa tradition hold that the [actual] calculations were concealed in order that [non-Buddhist] extremists might not understand them, and that therefore [the comments of the *Tantra*] are not to be taken literally. [On this basis] they invented a new and detailed "textbook system of calculation" (*grub mtha'i zhib rtsis*).[853]

Furthermore, just as sentient beings transmigrate and take birth through vital energy, by the power of their all-[embracing] conceptual thoughts, similarly the precision of time may also be observed sequentially in the external [world]. This is why, at the end of the solar mansion Pisces (*nya khyim*), on the thirtieth day of the month of Phālguna (*dbo zla ba*), in the fire tiger year [which is the last year of the Jovian sexagenary cycle], the exact longitude (*longs spyod rnam par dag pa*) of the planets and constellations is conventionally designated as an "entry into vacuity" [i.e., zero degrees]. Then, once again from the first day of the month of Caitra (*nag zla*) in the [fire hare] year of Prabhāva (*rab byung*), [which is the first year of the next sexagenary cycle], the mean longitudinal positions (*rtag pa'i longs spyod*) pertaining to all the years, months, planets, and constellations newly arise.[854]

The Basis of Astrological Calculations in the Macrocosm [3']

Thirdly [with regard to the basis of astrological calculations pertaining to the outer world, it says in the root verses]:

> **The inner [world] qualitatively manifested as the [phenomena of] the external world,**
> **Among which the solar mansions and constellations**
> **Which [the planets] traverse took form;**
> **And the planetary bodies that traverse them [also] arose.**
> **The Sun marks out its [anti-clockwise] longitude through the solar mansions,**
> **While the four [terrestrial] seasons rotate in a clockwise manner.**

The solar mansions of the constellations and the zodiac,
Dependent on the motion of the wind element,
Also rotate clockwise in the course of each solar day,
While the planets demarcate celestial [longitude], through their respective motions.

The inner abiding nature of the [subtle] body of indestructible reality (*rdo rje'i lus*) qualitatively manifested as [the diverse phenomena of] the external world,[855] among which, at the outset, the twelve solar mansions (*khyim bcu gnyis*)[856] and twenty-eight constellations (*rgyu skar nyer brgyad*)[857] took form upon the zodiac (*go la*), the space in which [the planets] make their traverse. Thereupon, the ten planetary bodies (*gza' bcu*)[858] that traverse [the zodiac also] arose.

The Zodiac [a']

In the sky the Sun marks out its celestial longitude, [moving] anti-clockwise through the twelve solar mansions, while on earth the four seasons rotate cyclically through their [corresponding] twelve terrestrial aspects which are indicative of past actions, changing and moving in a clockwise manner.[859] So it is that the solar mansions of the constellations (*skar gyi khyim*) and the zodiac, dependent on the motion of the wind element (*rlung 'gros*), move clockwise [rising in the east and setting in the west] in the course of each solar day. By contrast, the planetary bodies, [moving anti-clockwise] through their respective motions (*rang 'gros*), demarcate their celestial longitude against the constellations and solar mansions.

Calculation of Solar and Lunar Eclipses [b']

Unlike the other planetary bodies which [appear to] move anti-clockwise [from west to east] around Mount Sumeru [i.e., the Earth] because the motions of their epicycles turn eastwards upon the [band of] constellations, the eclipser Rāhu, by contrast, from the perspective of ultimate [truth], [is said to] steal the power of the other planets because it is endowed with merits, orbiting Mount Sumeru in a clockwise manner [from east to west], since it turns westwards, in conformity with the motion of the wind element that propels the solar mansions. For this reason, Rāhu demarcates its longitude in reverse, starting from [the constellation] Pisces (Revatī, Nam gru) and ending with Aries (Aśvinī, Tha skar).

Furthermore, since Rāhu internally is an aspect of the pristine cognition within the central energy channel [of the subtle body], the nature of Rāhu may also be understood through the adamantine meditative stability (*vajropamasamādhi*) which destroys aspects of bewilderment with regard to relative [truth]. In accordance with this perspective, correlated to the external world, while the other planets demarcate their celestial longitude in an anti-clockwise manner, and are weak in power (*stobs dman*), Rāhu takes an opposite course because it is endowed with the higher power of merit.[860]

Rāhu encounters the Sun and the Moon,
In the interval which follows the passing of three "seasons."

Since Rāhu partakes of the nature of emptiness or vacuity within the central energy channel of [the yogin's] own body, and is unobscured and unimpeded in terms of the physical elements, its upper part (*yar sna*) has [the appearance of] a ball of semen (*dpyid kyi gong bu*), formed of the water element, and its lower part (*mar sna*) has [the appearance of] a blazing seed (*thig le*), formed of the fire element. Moreover, since Rāhu is endowed with a single purity in respect of both external and internal aspects, its body is vacuous, unobscured and unimpeded, like the space element, while its head (*vaktra, gdong*) is black, embodying darkness, the nature of the water element, and its tail (*puccha, mjug ma*) is red and fiery, [embodying] the nature of the fire element. These two [nodes—the head and the tail—] are the coarsely [appearing aspects of Rāhu], which have the power to cause [solar and lunar] eclipses.[861]

Internally [within the subtle body], during the last of a series of three "seasons" (*try ṛtu, dus gsum*) [each lasting two months], which are respectively named motility (*rajas*), lightness (*sattva*), and darkness (*tamas*), [Rāhu] steals the power of the right-side channel through the vital energy of great darkness (*mun pa chen po'i rlung*). Similarly, when the [cycle of the] six elements—earth, water, fire, wind, space, and pristine cognition—comes to an end [after six months], it steals the power of the left-side channel.[862]

By analogy, in the outer [world], the eclipser Rāhu (*mun can*) appears to enter [across the path of] the Sun in the interval between the waxing and waning phases of the Moon [i.e., on the thirtieth day of the lunar month], once three "seasons" [i.e., six lunar months] have elapsed, whether this period is calculated on the basis of a single link [of dependent origination] or a single "season" corresponding to two months [of the year].[863] Furthermore, when six months have elapsed [on the fifteenth day of the lunar month], Rāhu appears to enter [across the path of] the Moon.[864]

According to [the system] whereby [the Sun is considered to] rotate sequentially through the twelve links of dependent origination (*dvādaśāṅga-pratītyasamutpāda*, *rten 'brel yan lag bcu gnyis*), solar eclipses (*nyi 'dzin*) inevitably coincide with the last day [of the lunar month], which is identified with the link of dependent origination known as "contact" (*sparśa*, *reg pa'i rten 'brel*). Commencing from the lunar mansion (*khyim zla*) Aries, one link [of dependent origination] is assigned to each of the twelve months, and within each of these links [or months], the first solar day (*nyin zhag*) [in turn] corresponds to [the link of] "fundamental ignorance" (*ma rig pa*), the second to [the link of] "formative predispositions" (*'du byed*), the third to [the link of] "consciousness" (*rnam shes*), the fourth to [the link of] "name and form" (*ming gzugs*), the fifth to [the link of] the "six sensory activity fields" (*skye mched drug*), the sixth to [the link of] "contact" (*reg pa*), the seventh to [the link of] "feeling" (*tshor ba*), the eighth to [the link of] "craving" (*sred pa*), the ninth to [the link of] [the "grasping" (*len pa*), the tenth to [the link of] the "rebirth process" (*srid pa*), the eleventh to [the link of] "birth" (*skye ba*), and the twelfth [to the link of] "aging and death" (*rga shi*).[865]

Thereafter the cycle is repeated, from "fundamental ignorance" to "aging and death," corresponding to the thirteenth to twenty-fourth [solar days], and again from "fundamental ignorance" on the twenty-fifth day through to "aging and death" on the sixth day [of the following month], and from "fundamental ignorance" on the seventh day [of that second month] to "aging and death" on the eighteenth day, and from "fundamental ignorance" on the nineteenth day to "aging and death" on the thirtieth day.

In brief, [over a two-month cycle] it is said that the thirtieth day will coincide either with [the link of] "contact" or with [the link of] "aging and death," and that an eclipse may occur when [the link of] "contact" is present—[a day] that occurs in rotation [every other month]. At the mid-point (*dbus*) of this [day or] link of "contact," the exact Moon (*zla dag*) and the exact Sun (*nyi dag*) may be eclipsed by the motion of Rāhu.[866]

Calculation of Zodiacal, Calendar, and Solar Days [c']

The zodiacal, calendar, and solar days then emerged,
Dependent on the epicycles of the Sun, Moon, and the wind element.
[The Sun and the planets in a single solar day] rotate along the zodiac,

[Divided] according to three "periods" of time, four "junctures,"
Eight "watches," twelve "[ascendant] conjunctions,"
Thirty "hours," twenty-one thousand six hundred "breaths,"
Three thousand six hundred "intervals" of time,
Or sixty "clepsydra measures" of time.

Dependent on three kinds of zodiacal epicycle (*go la'i 'gros gsum*)—those of the Sun, the Moon, and the wind element—there emerged the zodiacal or sidereal day (*khyim zhag*), the calendar day (*tshes zhag*), and the solar day (*nyin zhag*). The first of these is longer [in its duration], the second is shorter, and the last is intermediate between these two [in its duration], as has been explained in detail above.[867]

The principal aspect among the [various] divisions of time, which include years, months, and so forth, is the solar day, which depends on the epicycle of the Sun. In the course of a single solar day [of twenty-four hours], there are twelve "ascendant conjunctions" (*dus sbyor bcu gnyis*) [with the respective solar mansions], every four of which are equivalent to a single [eight-hour] "period" of time (*dus gcig*), so that [in a single solar day] there are three such [eight-hour] "periods" of time.

Corresponding to every three "ascendant conjunctions," there is a single [six-hour] "juncture" (*sandhyā, thun mtshams*), so that [in the course of a whole solar day] there are four such [six-hour] "junctures."[868] Likewise, corresponding to every one and a half "ascendant conjunctions" there is a single [three-hour] "watch" (*prahara, thun tshod*), so that [in the course of a whole solar day] there are eight such [three-hour] "watches."[869]

Corresponding to every five "gnomon" [of time] (*daṇḍa, dbyu gu*), there is a single "ascendant conjunction," so that [in the course of a whole solar day] there are twelve "ascendant conjunctions."[870]

Corresponding to every two ["gnomon" or] "clepsydra measures" (*ghaṭikā, chu tshod*), there is a single [forty-eight minute] "hour" (*mauhūrtika, yud tsam*), so that [in the course of a whole solar day] there are thirty [forty-eight minute] "hours."

There are also twenty-one thousand six hundred [human] "breaths" (*śvāsa, dbugs*) [each of four seconds in duration, in the course of a solar day], and every six [human] "breaths" are equivalent to a single [twenty-four second] "interval" of time (*pāṇīpala, chu srang*), so that [in the course of a whole solar day] there are three thousand six hundred such "intervals."[871]

Sixty [twenty-four second] "intervals" are equivalent to a single [twenty-four minute] "clepsydra measure," and the Sun [appears] to rotate through sixty of these "clepsydra measures" in its journey across the zodiac, in the course of a single solar day.

The other planets also [appear] to follow the course of this [solar day], their motions impacting in the world and eliciting positive and negative results.[872]

Calculation of the Cycle of Months [d']

At this juncture, incidentally, we should consider the starting point of the monthly cycle, in the course of a year. It says in the *Sūtra of the Nucleus of the Sun*:

> I am referring to the constellation Pleiades.
> When the Moon is full [in Pleiades], [the cycle of] months will be complete.
> Thus, I affirm that the "late autumn month" should herald the start of the year.

On this basis, it is said that the year should start with the month of Kārttika (*smin drug*) [or late autumn] because Pleiades (*kṛttikā*, *smin drug*) was the first of the lunar mansions, according to the sequence originally established for the course of a given year.[873] However, as is known in the world, it is the early spring month (*dpyid ra*) [equivalent to Caitra (*nag pa*)], that is generally considered to start the year.[874]

In addition to those two traditions, which [respectively] reflect [the views of] monastic discipline (Vinaya) and phenomenology (Abhidharma), there are also other sources claiming that the month of Āśvina (*tha skar*) should herald the start the year, while according to Chinese astrology (*rgya rtsis*) the start of the year is assigned to the first Mongolian month (*hor zla ba dang po*), which they identify with the [month of] the tiger, or early spring.[875]

The *Tantra of the Wheel of Time* identifies three different starting points for the year: (1) with reference to the formation of the world systems in this [universe], (2) while emphasizing the solar mansions, and (3) when emphasizing utility. As for these,

(1) The *Tantra* states that, starting from the mid-summer month, in the solar mansion of Cancer (*karkaṭa'i khyim*),[876] not long after the formation of the world, when the autumn, spring, Sun, Moon, and so forth were still non-existent, the Sun was born—its birth-sign, in terms of celestial longitude, commencing from the third quadrant of the

constellation Gemini (*punarvasū, nabs so*) or the first [quadrant] of the solar mansion Cancer. For this reason, the first season of the year [is reckoned] to have been summer.[877]

(2) This refers to the time when the Sun enters Aries (*lug khyim*) because the planets, constellations, and seasons all follow [the passage of] the Sun, and the first of its [zodiacal] mansions is Aries.[878]

(3) It is held that the [months of] the year commence from the first calendar day of the waxing fortnight of the month Caitra (*nag zla*) because this is the month [principally] mentioned in the [*Concise*] *Tantra of the Wheel of Time*.[879]

Precedence of the Waxing and Waning Phases of the Moon [e']

According to the [*Concise Tantra of the Wheel of Time*], as well as the [sources of] mundane [astrology] and non-Buddhist [astrologers], the waxing fortnight of the months has precedence, whereas it states in the *Commentary on the Treasury of Phenomenology* that in the case of every month, the waning fortnight comes first.[880] Many texts concur that although [Śākyamuni]'s ascetic endeavors appear to have been arduous at the start [of the waxing fortnight],[881] in the end, his attainment of buddhahood coincided with the [fifteenth day] when [the moon] had already reached its fullest extent, and that therefore the waning fortnight should have precedence.[882] Consequently, in the commentaries on the tantras, the majority also give precedence to the waning fortnight. Yet there are some [other sources] which purposefully state that the waxing fortnight has precedence.[883]

It is also known that in the *Root Tantra* [*of the Wheel of Time*], the waning fortnight has precedence, whereas in the *Concise Tantra* [*of the Wheel of Time*], the waxing fortnight has precedence in order to [artfully] induce [non-Buddhist] extremists to enter [the path of the sacred teachings].[884]

The Techniques of Astrological Calculation [4']

Fourth [with regard to the exegesis of the techniques of astrological calculation, it says in the root verses]:

Through the five aspects [of astrological calculation]—
Weekdays, lunar days, constellations, combined calculations,
and impacts—

The longitude of the five planets and of Rāhu
As well as the conjunctions and [other] aspects should be examined.
Elective prediction and other minor calculations should also be studied.

Having correctly ascertained the basis of the astrological calculations which are to be made and the essential points of the actual application of astrology, the practical techniques of astrological calculation, determined according to each day [of the month] and so forth [will now be summarized].

The Fivefold Calculation [a']

Here, we shall have to examine in detail the way in which the fivefold astrological calculation (*yan lag lnga*) is specifically made.[885] The calculation takes into account the [computational values of] the following five aspects:

(1) the seven alternating weekdays (*saptavāra, res gza' bdun*), starting with Sunday[886]
(2) the [twenty-seven] constellations which demarcate lunar longitude, starting with Beta and Gamma Arietis (Aśvinī, Tha skar), either in respect of the start of the solar [week] day (*res 'grogs zla skar*) or in respect of the exact end of the previous lunar day (*tshes kyi skar ma*).[887]
(3) the [twenty-seven] constellations which demarcate solar longitude (*nyi mas spyod pa'i rgyu skar*) [starting with Beta and Gamma Arietis (Aśvinī, Tha skar)][888]
(4) the twenty-seven combined calculations [of solar and lunar longitude] (*yoga, sbyor ba*), starting with the "eliminator" (*viṣkambha, sel ba*)[889]
(5) the [eleven] impacts [of the lunar month] (*karaṇa, byed pa*), including the seven "transient impacts" (*carakaraṇa, 'pho ba'i byed pa bdun*) [which rotate in series through fifty-six half-lunar days, starting with Vava (*gdab pa*) on the second half of the first lunar day through to Viṣṭi (*viṣṭi*) on the first half of the twenty-ninth lunar day]; and the four "fixed impacts" (*dhruvakaraṇa, rtag pa'i byed pa bzhi*), [which always coincide with specific half-lunar days, starting with Śakhuni (*bkra shis*) on the second half of the twenty-ninth through to Kintughna (*mi sdug pa*) on the first half of the first lunar day].[890]

Subsidiary Calculations concerning Planetary Motion, Eclipses, and So Forth [b']

Next, we shall have to examine the [apparent] motion of the five planetary bodies, including the three wrathful planets (*drag gza' gsum*) and the two peaceful planets (*zhi gza' gnyis*), through the four phases of their motion (*'gros bzhi*), against the [zodiacal] space of the constellations.[891]

Also, [for the prediction of lunar and solar eclipses], one has to examine the longitude of the head and tail of Rāhu (*sgra gcan gdong mjug*),[892] and one has also to examine the rising of the current ascendant conjunction (*tatkāla, dus sbyor*) [among the twelve solar mansions].[893]

Further calculations take into account the aspects of the primary and secondary Svarodaya calculations (*dbyangs 'char*) in respect of the calendar days and the seasons.[894]

Prognostications [c']

Prognostications of the *Wheel of Time* and Svarodaya [i']

Prognostications concerning positive and negative outcomes are mentioned in the *Tantra of the Wheel of Time*, while the covert techniques for abandoning or adopting [certain courses of action] are manifestly presented in the essential charts of the esoteric instructions, which mainly depend on the Svarodaya system, contained in the *Tantra of Martial Conquest*.[895]

Prognostications of Elemental Divination [ii']

Positive and negative prognostications should also be studied according to other minor astrological systems, such as the system known as elemental divination (*'byung rtsis*) or Chinese divination (*nag rtsis*), in which the five elements (*'byung ba lnga*) are the object of the calculation.[896] Here there are two sets of techniques (*gtsug lag gnyis*):

(1) the technique for making the basic natural calculation [of the order of the elements] (*rtsis byed rang bzhin gzhi*)[897]

(2) the techniques for calculating the bewildered misconceptions of fundamental ignorance (*ma rig 'khrul snang*), which are integrated in the

four "hidden points of divination" (*gab rtse bzhi*). These charts distinguish respectively between

(a) the discrete elements [which are determined according to their external, internal, and secret classifications] (*'byung ba rang rgyud*);
(b) the sense objects which convey these elements to the senses (*snang ba yul*);
(c) the intellect which analyzes the mutual relationships between the elements and sense objects (*gcod byed yid*); and
(d) the mind which grasps the negative and positive attributes of such relationships (*'dzin pa sems*).

Together they are known as the four primary "hidden points of divination."[898]

8. Poetics

bb. Poetics [III.B.2.b.ii.bb]
- 1' The Body of Poetic Composition
  - a' Metrical Compositions
  - b' Prose
  - c' Mixed Verse and Prose
- 2' Poetic Ornaments
  - a' Ten Uncommon Ornaments
  - b' Common Ornaments
    - i' Ornaments of Sense
    - ii' Phonetic Ornaments
    - iii' Ornaments of Enigmatic Innuendo
  - c' Ten Defects of Poetic Composition
  - d' Causes of Excellent Poetic Composition
  - e' Exemplars of the Two Styles of Poetic Composition

Poetics [bb]

The second [of the minor classical sciences] is the exegesis on poetics (*kāvya, snyan dngags*), which has two parts: the body [of poetic composition] (*śarīra, lus*) and the [poetic] ornaments (*alaṃkāra, rgyan*).[899]

The Body of Poetic Composition [1']

As to the former, it says [in the root verses]:

> **The body [of composition] that conveys the desired meaning**
> **of poetry**

Includes verse, prose, or mixed verse and prose.
Verses may be detached, clustered, intricate, or compounded,
And they may [also] be divided into cantos.
But they [invariably] consist of four metrical lines.
Prose may comprise narrative and legend,
While mixed verse and prose refers to the main style of [courtly] drama
And the ordinary style of Campū.

It is said in a *sūtra* that[900]

> Poetry should be composed in order to elucidate the sacred teachings. It should eulogize the three precious jewels, through which the unsurpassed enlightenment will be attained.

Supreme among the three activities of the learned[901] is composition (*rtsom pa*), the quality of which may emulate or contradict the recognized norms of poetics. The main subject matter of this [science] comprises both the body [of poetic composition] and the [various categories of the poetic] ornaments.

Concerning the first [of these aspects], it is said:[902]

> The body comprises a string of words (*padāvalī*),
> Determining the intended sense.

And [in the auto-commentary], it is said:[903]

> Accordingly, the intended or conceived meaning that is to be expressed by poets is known as the body of poetic composition. Once this meaning has been ascertained, the [appropriate] words should be eloquently formed and [the lines] determined, in accordance with the intended sense (*iṣṭārtha*).[904]

The body [of poetry] may be expressed in [verses of] seven or nine metrical syllables, and so forth, as well as [passages of] non-metrical prose, and [passages of] mixed verse and prose.

METRICAL COMPOSITIONS [a']

Among these, when metrical compositions (*padya, tshigs bcad*) are classified according to their typology, they are said to be of four categories—detached verses (*muktaka, grol ba*), clustered verses (*kulaka, rigs*), intricate verses (*kośa, mdzod*), and compound verses (*saṃghāta, 'dus pa*). Respectively, these refer to (1) single verses which independently and fully convey a single point; (2) multiple stanzas[905] governed by a single verb which convey a single point; (3) intricate but unconnected verses with diverse breaks and verbs, and an indeterminate number of metrical lines [which convey multiple points];[906] and (4) compound verses which employ multiple metrical lines and verbs to convey a single point.[907]

When verses are divided into many cantos (*sarga*), i.e., chapters, sections, or parts, [the compositional style] is known as "court poetry" (*mahākāvya, snyan dngags chen po*).[908]

Although the *Compendium of Phenomenology* explains that poetry may form stanzas of anything from one to six metrical lines (*pāda*), according to the tradition of [the *Mirror of*] *Poetics* itself, verses exclusively form [stanzas of] four metrical lines.[909]

Prose [b']

Then, with regard to prose (*gadya, lhug pa*), although two distinct terms, narrative (*ākhyāyikā, brjod pa*) and legend (*kathā, gtam*), [are implied], the master Daṇḍin has asserted that these are identical in meaning.[910] According to *paṇḍita* Vidyāsāgara (Rig byed rgya mtsho),[911] the defining characteristic of narrative is that knowledge is expressed in the poetic medium of prose that is not deduced from historical legends (*itihāsakathā, sngon byung gi gtam rgyud*), whereas the defining characteristic of legend is that it is expressed in the poetic medium of prose that largely commences with ancient tales. Indeed in the *Mirror* [*of Poetics*], the following verse is also found:[912]

> [The style of prose] should derive either from historical legends,
> Or from some true facts.

In conformity with this [verse], there are many scholars of the past who have asserted the factual basis [of their own composition].

Mixed Verse and Prose [c']

With regard to mixed verse and prose (*miśra, spel ma*), there are both important and ordinary sorts [of composition].[913] Among them, the former refers to the compositions of [courtly] drama (*nāṭaka, zlos gar*), embodying verse, prose, and mixed verse and prose, in which the four languages (*skad rigs bzhi*) are fully represented. The latter refers to the so-called Campū style [of composition] in which verse and prose alternate or intermingle and which depends on any one [of the four acceptable] languages, as appropriate.

In this regard, when [mixed verse and prose] is classified according to the language that is employed, it is explained that there are four categories: the refined language [of Sanskrit] (*legs sbyar*), the common language [of Prākrit] (*rang bzhin*), the corrupted language [of Apabhraṃśa] (*zur chag*), and the hybrid language [of Miśrabhāṣā] (*'dres ma*).[914]

Poetic Ornaments [2']

Secondly, with regard to poetic ornaments (*alaṃkāra, rgyan*), it says [in the root verses]:

> **Embellishments include the ten uncommon sentiments of composition**
> **As well as the common ornaments of sense, sound, and enigmatic innuendo.**
> **Abandoning defects, one's composition should adorn the world.**

It is said in the *Mirror* [*of Poetics*]:[915]

> Features which embellish [the body of] poetic composition
> Are designated as "ornaments."

Just as the human body may be embellished by necklaces, shoulder bracelets, and so forth, a body of poetic composition may also be embellished by ornaments of sense (*arthālaṃkāra, don rgyan*), such as double entendre (*śliṣṭha, sbyar ba*), and so forth. It is for this reason that such compositional features are known as "poetic ornaments."

Ten Uncommon Ornaments [a']

In the treatise of Daṇḍin, the traditions of the East [Indian Gauḍa] style and the South [Indian Vaidarbha] style are differentiated on the basis of the following ten uncommon attributes (*asādhāraṇadaśaguṇalakṣaṇa, thun mong min pa'i yon tan* [*mtshan nyid*] *bcu*):[916]

(1) double entendre (*śleṣa, sbyar ba*),[917]
(2) clarity (*prasāda, rab dvangs*),[918]
(3) phonetic balance (*samatā, mnyam nyid*),[919]
(4) sweetness (*mādhurya, snyan*),[920]
(5) tenderness (*sukumāratā, shin tu gzhon pa*),[921]
(6) elucidation (*arthavyakti, don gsal*),[922]
(7) nobleness (*udāratva, rgya che*),[923]
(8) vigor (*ojas, brjid*),[924]
(9) beauty (*kānti, mdzes ldan*),[925] and
(10) mental focus (*samādhi, ting nge 'dzin*)[926]—
These ten attributes are explained
To be the vital characteristics of the tradition of Vaidarbha.
The hallmarks of the traditions of Gauḍa
Are largely the opposite of these.[927]

Common Ornaments [b']

Then, with regard to the common tradition which the easterners and southerners uniformly share, there are [well-defined categories of] the ornaments of sense (*arthālaṃkāra, don rgyan*), the phonetic ornaments (*śabdālaṃkāra, sgra rgyan*), and the [ornaments of] enigmatic innuendo (*prahelikā, gab tshig*).

Ornaments of Sense [i']

These include the following thirty-five ornaments of sense, which themselves have many subdivisions:[928]

(1) natural description (*svabhāvokti, rang bzhin brjod*),
(2) simile (*upamā, dpe*),
(3) metaphor (*rūpaka, gzugs can*),
(4) poetic association (*dīpaka, gsal byed*),
(5) repetition (*āvṛtti, bskor ba*),
(6) denial (*ākṣepa, 'gog*),
(7) corroboration (*arthāntaranyāsa, don gzhan bkod pa*),
(8) contrast (*vyatireka, ldog pa can*),
(9) peculiar causation (*vibhāvanā, srid pa can*),
(10) concise suggestion (*samāsokti, bsdus*),
(11) hyperbole (*atiśayokti, phul byung*),
(12) poetic fancy (*utprekṣā, rab btags*),

(13) cause (*hetu, rgyu*),
(14) misrepresentation (*leśa, phra mo*),
(15) subtlety (*sūkṣma, cha*),
(16) respective ordering of words and meaning (*yathāsaṃkhya, rim*),
(17) flattery (*preyas, dga'*),
(18) sentiment (*rasavat, nyams ldan*),
(19) vigor (*ūrjasvi, gzi brjid can*),
(20) periphrastic or indirect speech (*paryāyokta, rnam grangs brjod*),
(21) coincidence (*samāhita, kun tu phan*),
(22) exaltation (*udātta, rgya che*),
(23) obfuscation (*apahnutti, bsnyon dor*),
(24) double entendre (*śliṣṭha, sbyar ba*),
(25) expressions of distinction (*viśeṣokti, khyad par*),
(26) equal pairing (*tulyayogitā, mtshungs par sbyor ba*),
(27) incongruity (*virodha, 'gal*),
(28) artful praise (*vyājastuti, skabs min bstod pa*),
(29) damning with faint praise (*aprastutapraśaṃsā, zol bstod*),
(30) co-mention (*sahokti, lhan cig brjod pa*),
(31) illustrative simile (*nidarśana, nges par bstan pa*),
(32) exchange (*parivṛtti, yongs*),
(33) benediction (*āśis, brjes shis*),
(34) conjunction of poetic figures (*saṃkirṇa, rab spel*), and
(35) underlying intention (*bhāvika, da nas dgongs pa can*)—
These were presented by past masters
As the ornaments of poetic expression.[929]

Phonetic Ornaments [ii']

Phonetic ornaments include both the distinctive forms of repetition (*yāmaka, zung ldan*)[930] and ornaments which are hard to execute (*duṣkaramārga, bya dka'*).[931]

Ornaments of Enigmatic Innuendo [iii']

There are also sixteen ornaments of enigmatic innuendo, which are employed to incite laughter in amusing gatherings and the like.[932]

Briefly stated, all poetic ornaments may be gathered within the categories of [straightforward] natural description and [indirect] poetic allusion (*'khyog brjod*).

Ten Defects of Poetic Composition [c']

While engaged in poetic composition, there are ten [potential] defects (*skyon bcu*) [outlined in the *Mirror of Poetics*] as follows:[933]

(1) incoherence (*apārtha, don nyams pa*),
(2) incongruity (*vyartha, don 'gal*),
(3) tautology (*ekārtha, don gcig pa*),
(4) ambiguity (*sasaṃśaya, the tshom can*),
(5) syntactical disorder (*apakrama, rim pa nyams pa*),
(6) grammatical error (*śabdahīna, sgra nyams*),
(7) discordance of metrical pause (*yatibhraṣṭa, gcod mtshams nyams pa*),
(8) prosodic deviation (*bhinnavṛtta, sdeb sbyor nyams*),
(9) absence of euphonic conjunction (*visaṃdhika, mtshams sbyor bral*), and
(10) non-sequitur with regard to place and time (*deśadeśādivirodhin, yul dus la sogs 'gal ba*),
Or with regard to fine arts, the mundane world,
Scriptural authority, or logical reasoning.
The poet should abandon these ten defects
[While engaging] in poetic composition.

So it is that these defects and also the use of vernacular (*grong tshig*), imperfect similes, and so forth are to be avoided.

Causes of Excellent Poetic Composition [d']

Furthermore, as has been said:[934]

Brilliance that is naturally achieved,
Immaculate learning in many [fields],
And an absence of indolence while engaging [in composition]—
These are the causes of excellence in poetry.

Compositions endowed with this [appropriate] accumulation of causes indeed function as ornaments of the world, as exemplified by the eulogies composed by the master Śūra.[935]

Exemplars of the Two Styles of Poetic Composition [e']

[Kṣemendra's] *Wish-granting Tree: Narrative of the Bodhisattva* is generally regarded as an exemplary text according to the tradition of the easterners, whereas [Śūra's] *Garland of Birth Stories* in thirty-four cantos has a similar status according to the tradition of the southerners.[936]

9. Prosody

cc. Prosody [III.B.2.b.ii.cc]

- 1' Metric Rules Governing Syllabic Quantity
  - a' The Syllabic Quantity of Meters with Equal Lines
  - b' The Syllabic Quantity of Meters with Unequal Lines
  - c' The Syllabic Quantity of Meters with Semi-equal Lines
- 2' Metric Rules Governing Moric Instants
  - a' The Eight Trimeters
- 3' The Astonishing Calculations of Prosody
  - a' Preparation of a Table of Metrical Variants
  - b' General Calculations Applicable to Each Meter Class
  - c' The Reductionist Calculation
  - d' Calculation of the Specific Position of a Given Meter within Its Class
  - e' The Triangular Chart of Light Syllables
  - f' Calculation of an Exact Point of Cadence
- 4' Ordinary Calculations Determining Precise Syllabic Quantity and Moric Instants

Prosody [cc]

The third topic [of the minor classical sciences] is the exegesis on prosody (*chandas, sdeb sbyor*), which has three parts: (1) metric rules governing syllabic quantity (*vṛtta*), (2) metric rules governing moric instants (*jāti*), and (3) an exegesis of the astonishing applications that facilitate the understandings [of prosody] (*adbhutaprayoga, ngo mtshar rtogs byed kyi sbyor ba*).[937]

Metric Rules Governing Syllabic Quantity [1']

Concerning the first of these, it says [in the root verses]:

> **The prosody of verse should observe the metric rules governing syllabic quantity,**
> **Which may be calculated commencing from the six-syllable meter [class],**
> **As far as the [twenty-seven syllable] Saṃtāna meter [class].**
> **The syllabic quantity [of a given stanza] is demarcated**
> **[By four metrical lines] which may be of equal, unequal, or semi-equal length.**

Concerning this science [of metrics], which is extremely important for the versification of poetry, it is said [in the *Mirror of Poetics*]:[938]

> These four metrical lines of verse
> May be classified according to syllabic quantity,
> Or according to moric instants.

And:[939]

> This science is a boat for those wishing to traverse
> The profound ocean of poetics.

The term "prosody" (*sdeb sbyor*), which is equivalent to [the Sanskrit] *chandas*, denotes two aspects: (1) metric rules governing syllabic quantity (*vṛtta*) and (2) metric rules governing moric instants (*jāti*), both of which may be applied with reference to four metrical lines (*pāda*) [comprising a conventional stanza].

The Syllabic Quantity of Meters with Equal Lines [a']

The metric rules governing syllabic quantity concern the scansion of the number of syllables occurring in the four metrical lines [of a stanza] where the syllables [of each line] are [usually] equal in number (*samāvṛtta, mnyam pa'i bri tta*).[940] In this regard, there are meter classes of precise [syllabic quantity], ranging from the six-syllable Gāyatrī class (*dbyangs sgrog*) and the seven-syllable

Uṣṇih class (*rab dga'*) meters to the twenty-six-syllable Utkṛti class (*lhag par byed ldan*) meter.[941] Those ranging from twenty-seven syllables upwards are called Saṃtāna meters and they also have many subdivisions, including [the actual] Saṃtāna meter and the Pracaya (*rab bsags*) meter, each of which has subcategories numbered one to eight.[942]

[The precise meter classes, for which tables are calculated] starting from the six-syllable Gāyatrī class, also have a great many subcategories. For example, in the case of the ten-syllable [Paṅktī (*phreng ldan*)] meter class, the number of permutations may multiply to one thousand and twenty-four, when the [possible] combinations of heavy and light syllables are analyzed.[943]

Some of the subcategories of the meter classes also have definite names, such as the Tanumadhyā meter (*dbus phra*) [which belongs to the six-syllable Gāyatrī meter class],[944] the Kumāralalitā meter (*gzhon nu rol pa*) [which belongs to the seven-syllable Uṣṇih meter class],[945] the Samānikā (*'dra mtshungs*)[946] and the Vidyunmāla (*glog phreng*) meters [which both belong to the eight-syllable Anuṣṭubh meter class],[947] the Śuddhavirāja meter (*dag pa'i snang ba*) [which belongs to the ten-syllable Paṅktī meter class],[948] and so forth. However, there are also a great many which are not precisely named in the [primary] texts [on prosody]. All of them fall within the scope of the rules governing syllabic quantity.

The Syllabic Quantity of Meters with Unequal Lines [b']

While there are some categories of syllabic quantity, such as the [aforementioned] Tanumadhyā meter, in which the four metrical lines [of a stanza] are equal, in the sense that their number of syllables and the cadence of their heavy and light syllables are similar,[949] by contrast there are also four [main] classes in which [the four metrical lines of a stanza] are unequal (*viṣamavṛtta, mi mnyam pa'i bri tta*), namely, the Upaṣṭhitapracupitā or Vaktradvāra (*kha sgo*) meter class,[950] the Padacaturārdhva meter class (*rkang bzhi 'phel*),[951] the Udgatā meter class (*steng 'gro*),[952] and the Mardākrāntā meter class (*dal gyi 'gro ba*).[953]

The Syllabic Quantity of Meters with Semi-equal Lines [c']

There are also categories of syllabic quantity in which the four metrical lines [of a stanza] are semi-equal (*ardhavṛtta, phyed mnyam pa'i bri tta*), i.e., combining [both equal and unequal features], as when, for example, [a stanza] has the characteristics of one pair of unequal metrical lines and the other pair equal. This category is exemplified by the Upacitraka (*nyer bkra*) meter class.[954]

[Stanzas] should be embellished when [their metrical lines] are demarcated according to these [rules governing syllabic quantity].

Metric Rules Governing Moric Instants [2']

The second part concerns the metric rules governing moric instants (*jāti*) [on which it is said in the root verses]:

> **The metric rules governing the scansion of moric instants concern**
> **The Āryā meter, the Vaitālya meter, and the Paiṅgala meter,**
> **But there are also other explanations.**

The prosody based on the scansion of moric instants, rather than the number of syllables, is known as *jāti*. In the case of the aforementioned eight-syllable Anuṣṭubh meter class, for example, in which each line of a stanza has precisely eight syllables, here one disregards the syllabic quantity and instead has to scan eight complete moric instants (*mātrā, phyi mo*).[955]

A short vowel and a single consonant with a following vowel are both scanned as a single moric instant. A long vowel and a double consonant with a following vowel are long, as are the [four] diphthongs (*mtshams sbyor g.yi yi ge*), the aspirated [consonants] (*srog tu zhugs pa*), and so forth.[956] In short, all these "heavy" (*guru, lci ba*) syllables are scanned as two moric instants; while non-aspirated consonants are scanned as a half [moric instant].

On this basis, the *Precious Source [of Prosody]* explains the arrangement of moric instants (*phyi mo 'god tshul*) and the three subcategories of the Āryā,[957] Vaitālya, and Paiṅgala meters, which are differentiated [respectively] in accordance with the distinctions between [stanzas which have] four metrical lines that are unequal, semi-equal, and equal.[958] Although many [other categories of moric based meters] are also explained in other works, such as [Kṛṣṇamiśra's] *Defining Characteristics of Prosody entitled Mastery through Learning*,[959] all of them may be subsumed within these [three] essential meter classes.

The Eight Trimeters [a']

In all of these moric based meters, each group of three syllables forms a distinct trimeter (*gaṇa, tshogs*). Based on the [possible permutations of] "heavy" (*guru, lci ba*) and "light" (*laghu, yang ba*) [quantities], the trimeter may assume [altogether] eight [variant forms] (*aṣṭagaṇa, tshogs brgyad*).[960] [With regard to these eight], it has been said:[961]

> [Trimeters] adopting a "heavy" stress in the first, middle, and last syllables
> Are [respectively known as]
> The dactyl (BHA), the amphibrach (DZA), and the anapaest (SA).
> Those adopting a "light" stress [in the first, middle, and last syllables]
> Are [respectively known as]
> The bachius (YA), the cretic (RA), and the antibachius (TA).
> While the molossus (MA) and the tribach (NA) respectively
> Have [all three syllables] "heavy" and "light."[962]

And:[963]

> Each of these [types of trimeter] is also said to correspond to a specific deity, indicating virtue or non-virtue. (1) The dactyl (BHA) corresponds to Bhūdevalakṣmī [symbolizing the earth element] and suggests enrichment. (2) The amphibrach (DZA) corresponds to Varuṇa [symbolizing the water element] and suggests prosperity. (3) The cretic (RA) corresponds to Agni [symbolizing the fire element] and portends death. (4) The anapaest (SA) corresponds to Vāyu [symbolizing the wind element] and suggests distant travel to other lands. (5) The antibachius (TA) corresponds to Gagana [symbolizing the space element] and suggests an empty or vacuous result. (6) The bachius (YA) corresponds to Sūrya or Udāra [symbolizing the Sun] and suggests that diseases will be contracted. (7) The molossus (MA) corresponds to Candra [symbolizing the moon] and suggests an immaculate reputation. [Finally,] (8) the tribach (NA) corresponds to the devas [in general] and suggests that the boon of happiness will be granted. In this way, learned [masters of prosody] can suggest certain outcomes on the basis of the [various types of] trimeter they employ.

It is explained that this inspection should be undertaken with regard to the first trimeter [of the hemistich] (*dang po'i tshogs*).

Similarly, it is also held that there is a distinct deity corresponding to each of the precise [categories of meter], starting with the six-syllable [Gāyatrī] meter class and extending as far as the [twenty-seven syllable] Saṃtāna and Pracaya meter classes. Specifically, the deity of the Gāyatrī meter class is explained to be Hayagrīva. Although [this deity] does seem to have the form of Hayagrīva, [one should know that] all of these [presiding gods] actually appear to be non-Buddhist deities.[964]

The Astonishing Calculations of Prosody [3']

The third part [concerns the astonishing applications that facilitate the understandings of prosody] (*adbhutaprayoga, ngo mtshar rtogs byed kyi sbyor ba*). In this regard [it is said in the root verses]:

> **One should then examine the arrangement [of metrical variations] in tabular form,**
> **The general calculation [of the permutations in each meter class],**
> **The reductionist calculation which differentiates [the cadence of each specific meter],**
> **The calculation of the specific position [of a given meter within its meter class],**
> **The [triangular] chart of the light syllables,**
> **And the calculation of the point of cadence that has been reached [in the table].**

The calculations that facilitate the understanding [of prosody] through an astonishing intellectual rigor apply exclusively to [the scansion of stanzas] where the syllabic quantity comprises lines of equal length. There are six distinct methods.[965]

Preparation of a Table of Metrical Variants [a']

The first step requires the preparation of a table of metrical variants (*prastāra, 'god tshul*) which shows the incremental increase in the number of [permutations of] heavy and light syllables, starting from the single-syllable [Uktā (*brjod pa*)] meter class and continuing as far as the [twenty-seven syllable] Saṃtāna meter class.[966]

ཡི་གེ་གཅིག་པ	ཡི་གེ་གཉིས་པ		ཡི་གེ་གསུམ་པ			ཡི་གེ་བཞི་པ				
༡	༡	༢	༡	༢	༣	༡	༢	༣	༤	
ʔ	ʔ	ʔ	ʔ	ʔ	ʔ	ʔ	ʔ	ʔ	ʔ	༡
I	I	ʔ	I	ʔ	ʔ	I	ʔ	ʔ	ʔ	༢
	ʔ	I	ʔ	I	ʔ	ʔ	I	ʔ	ʔ	༣
	I	I	I	I	ʔ	I	I	ʔ	ʔ	༤
			ʔ	ʔ	I	ʔ	ʔ	I	ʔ	༥
			I	ʔ	I	I	ʔ	I	ʔ	༦
			ʔ	I	I	ʔ	I	I	ʔ	༧
			I	I	I	I	I	I	ʔ	༨
						ʔ	ʔ	ʔ	I	༩
						I	ʔ	ʔ	I	༡༠
						ʔ	I	ʔ	I	༡༡
						I	I	ʔ	I	༡༢
						ʔ	ʔ	I	I	༡༣
						I	ʔ	I	I	༡༤
						ʔ	I	I	I	༡༥
						I	I	I	I	༡༦

Fig. 47. A model *prastāra* table, showing the calculation for the meter classes one to four

General Calculations Applicable to Each Meter Class [b']

The second step facilitates the understanding of the aforementioned table, indicating how many [meters] are applicable to each class, as for example, in the case of the ten-syllable [Paṅktī] meter class [which has 1,024 variants].[967]

	བརྗོད་པ	ཤིན་ཏུ་བརྗོད་པ	ལྷན་ཅིག་བར་མ	རབ་གནས	ལེགས་པར་རབ་གནས	དབྱངས་སྒྲོགས	རབ་དགའ	རྗེས་བསྟུགས	བྲི་ཧ་ཏི
Meter Class	༡	༢	༣	༤	༥	༦	༧	༨	༩
Possible Number of Permutations	༢	༤	༨	༡༦	༣༢	༦༤	༡༢༨	༢༥༦	༥༡༢
Total Number of Light Syllables	༡	༨	༢༤	༦༤	༡༦༠	༣༨༤	༨༩༦	༢༠༤༨	༡༦༠༨
Total Number of Heavy Syllables	༢	༤	༡༢	༣༢	༨༠	༡༩༢	༤༤༨	༡༠༢༤	༢༣༠༤
Total Number of Moric Instants	༣	༡༢	༣༦	༩༦	༢༤༠	༥༢༦	༡༣༤༤	༣༠༧༢	༦༩༡༢

	ཕྲེང་ལྡན	གསུམ་བསྟུད	སྐྱེ་འགྲོ	ཤིན་ཏུ་སྐྱེ་འགྲོ	ནུས་ལྡན	ཤིན་ཏུ་ནུས་ལྡན	ལེགས་སྦྱོར	ཤིན་ཏུ་ལེགས་སྦྱོར	བརྟན་འཛིན
Meter Class	༡༠	༡༡	༡༢	༡༣	༡༤	༡༥	༡༦	༡༧	༡༨
Possible Number of Permutations	༡༠༢༤	༨༠༤༨	༤༠༩༦	༨༡༩༢	༡༦༣༨༤	༣༢༧༦༨	༦༥༥༣༦	༡༣༡༠༧༢	༢༦༢༡༤༤
Total Number of Light Syllables	༡༠༢༤༠	༢༢༥༨	༤༩༢༥༢	༡༠༦༤༩༦	༢༢༩༣༢༦	༤༩༡༥༢༠	༡༠༤༨༥༢༦	༢༢༢༨༢༢༤	༤༢༡༨༥༩༢
Total Number of Heavy Syllables	༥༡༢༠	༡༡༢༦༦༤	༢༤༥༢༦	༥༣༢༤༨	༡༡༤༦༨༨	༢༤༥༢༦༠	༥༢༤༢༨༨	༡༡༡༤༡༡༢	༢༣༥༩༢༩༦
Total Number of Moric Instants	༡༥༣༦༠	༣༣༢༩༢	༧༣༧༢༨	༡༥༩༢༤༤	༣༤༤༠༦༤	༢༣༧༢༨༠	༡༥༧༢༨༦༤	༣༣༤༣༣༦	༢༠༢༢༨༨༨

	ཤིན་ཏུ་བརྟན་འཛིན	བྱེད་ལྡན	རབ་བྱེད་ལྡན	ཀུན་བྱེད་ལྡན	རྣམ་བྱེད་ལྡན	ལེགས་བྱེད་ལྡན	ཤིན་ཏུ་ལེགས་བྱེད་ལྡན	ལྷག་པར་བྱེད་ལྡན
Meter Class	༡༩	༡༠	༢༡	༢༢	༢༣	༢༤	༢༥	༢༦
Possible Number of Permutations	༥༢༤༢༨༨	༡༠༤༨༤༥༢༦	༢༠༩༧༡༥༢	༤༡༩༤༣༠༤	༨༣༨༨༦༠༨	༡༦༧༧༢༡༦	༣༣༥༥༤༤༣༢	༦༢༡༠༨༨༦༤
Total Number of Light Syllables	༩༩༦༡༤༧༢	༢༠༩༧༡༥༢༠	༤༤༠༤༠༡༢	༩༢༢༧༤༦༨༨	༡༩༢༩༣༢༩༨༤	༤༠༢༦༥༣༡༨༤	༨༣༨༨༦༠༨༠༠	༨༩༤༤༨༣༠༤༦༤
Total Number of Heavy Syllables	༤༩༨༠༧༣༦	༡༠༤༨༥༧༦༠	༢༢༠༢༠༠༩༦	༤༦༡༣༢༣༤༤	༩༦༤༦༨༩༩༢	༢༠༡༣༢༦༥༩༢	༤༡༩༤༣༠༤༠༠	༨༦༢༤༡༥༢༣༢
Total Number of Moric Instants	༡༤༩༤༢༢༠༨	༣༡༤༥༧༢༨༠	༦༦༠༦༢༨༨	༡༣༨༤༡༢༠༣༢	༢༨༩༤༠༦༩༢༦	༦༠༣༩༧༩༧༧༦	༡༢༥༨༢༩༡༢༠༠	༢༦༡༧༢༤༥༦༩༦

Fig. 48. Comprehensive table showing permutations for the main twenty-six meter classes [Uktā to Utkṛti]

The Reductionist Calculation [c']

The third step is the so-called reductionist calculation (*naṣṭa cho ga*), which facilitates the understanding of how any [specific] meter derived from the general table should be arranged for practical purposes, as when, for example, the fourteenth of the sixty-four [possible] metrical permutations of the six-syllable [Gāyatrī] meter is spontaneously arranged, and the cadence of heavy and light syllables is easily understood, without the need for setting out the [full] tabular arrangement [of all the possible] variations.[968]

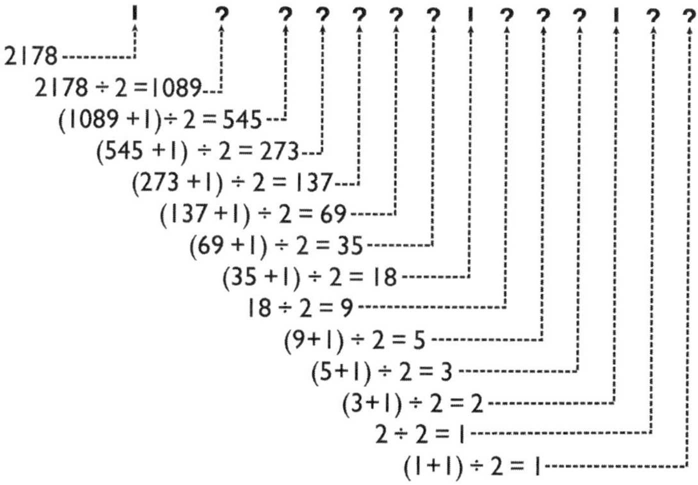

Fig. 49. The reductionist calculation

Calculation of the Specific Position of a Given Meter within Its Class [d']

The fourth step is the calculation of the specific position [of a given meter within its class] (*uddiṣṭa*). Once a lineal table has been arranged in respect of, for example, the meter: molossus (MA) + anapaest (SA) + amphibrach (DZA) + one heavy syllable (GA), from among the [many meters representing] the ten-syllable [Paṅktī] class, one should then implement this calculation, enabling one to easily understand the [exact] position of this meter within the [possible] variations of the ten-syllable meter class.[969]

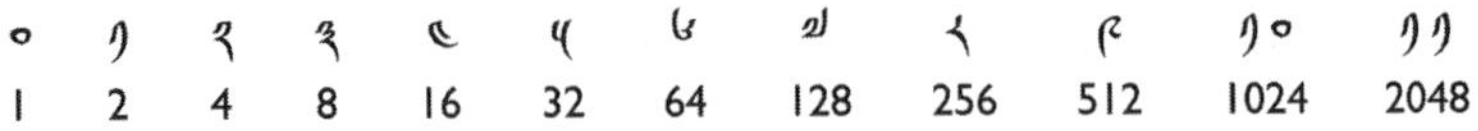
1 2 4 8 16 32 64 128 256 512 1024 2048

Fig. 50. Calculation of the position of a given meter within its meter class

The Triangular Chart of Light Syllables [e']

The [fifth] step is the making of the triangular chart of light syllables (*yang ba'i bya ba*), which facilitates the understanding, with regard to a specific meter class, of how many permutations have all their syllables "heavy" (*lci ba 'ba zhig pa du*), how many have one "light" syllable (*gcig yang ba du*), how many have two "light" syllables (*gnyis yang ba du*), and so forth.[970]

Fig. 51. Triangular chart of light syllables

Calculation of an Exact Point of Cadence [f']

Lastly, one should examine the *adhvā* calculation, which facilitates understanding of the exact point of cadence that has been reached (*adhvā, ji tsam 'gro ba*) [in the *prastāra* table, in the case of a given meter]. To this end, one has to make a grid comprising horizontal and vertical units (*prastara'i phreng steng 'og gi gling*) [indicating the variations of heavy and light syllables] and intermediate units [that are left blank] (*bar gyi sa*).[971]

These are the six procedures through which one may understand specifically the syllabic quantities [of meters forming stanzas with lines] of equal length.

Ordinary Calculations Determining Precise Syllabic Quantity and Moric Instants [4']

There are also three distinct arithmetical calculations that can be made to facilitate the understanding respectively of the number of syllables, [the number of] moric instants, and the [number of] heavy and light syllables [in a given line of verse]. These methods are all [essentially] identical because they are integrated together in the general calculations determining [the rules of precise syllabic quantity and moric instants] (*spyir thun mong rtogs byed*).[972]

These are the points that accord with the text [on prosody] composed by the master Ratnākaraśānti.

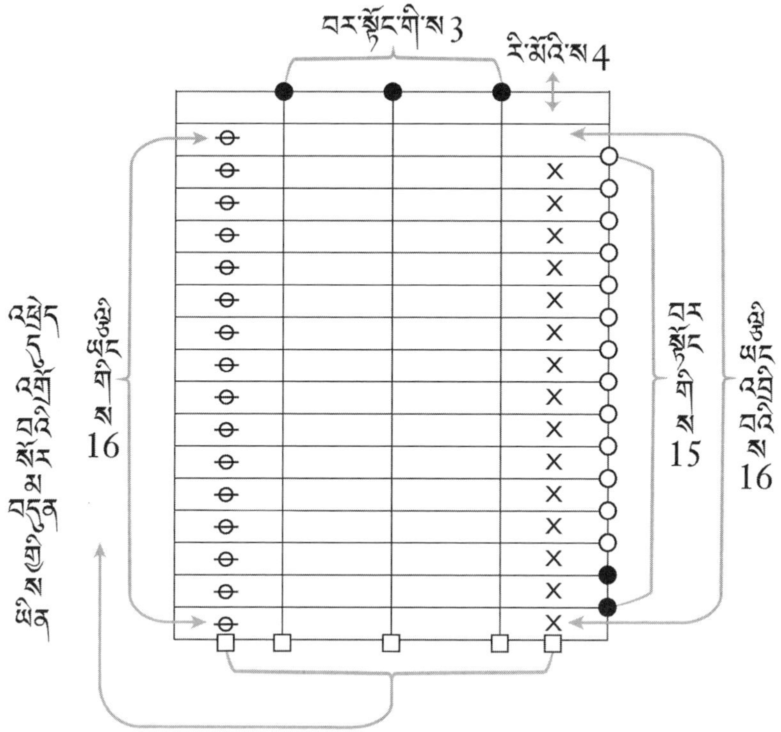

Fig. 52. Calculation of the exact point of cadence in a given meter

[Conclusion]

With regard to that text, it has been said:[973]

> [This text is characterized by]
> Its synopses, its versification, and clarity,[974]
> Its inclusion of illustrative examples based on the sūtras,
> Its exposition in [distinct] steps that are not confused,
> And its [elucidation of] caesurae (*mthar sdod*), trimeters, and their attributes.

Owing to these eight [special] qualities, it is explained to surpass the *Treatise on Prosody by Piṅgala*. The text is also [considered] to be wondrous because its author [Ratnākaraśānti] was particularly sublime.[975]

10. Synonymics

dd. Synonymics [III.B.2.b.ii.dd]
  1' General Exegesis on Names
    a' Primary Radical Names
    b' Derivative Names
    c' Proper Names
    d' Imputed Names
  2' Detailed Exegesis of Synonymics
    a' Homonyms
    b' Synonyms
    c' Derivatives from Sanskrit Roots

Synonymics [dd]

The fourth topic [of the minor classical sciences] is the exegesis on synonymics (*abhidāna*, *mngon brjod*), which has two parts: a general exegesis of the defining characteristics, distinctions, and so forth of names, and a detailed exegesis of the methodology of synonymics.[976]

General Exegesis on Names [1']

With regard to the first [it says in the root verses]:

> **There are primary names and derivative names which have meaning,**
> **Proper names and, similarly, imputed names.**
> **The latter include names based on similarity and causal relationship,**
> **And the contrariety of these,**

While [those based on causal relationships] include
Names that impute the result from its cause
And names that impute the cause from its result,
As well as collective names applicable to individuals,
And the contrariety of these.

The defining characteristic of a name (*nāman, ming*) is that it is a signifier (*vācaka, rjod byed*), [capable of] subsuming multi-syllabic forms as the basis of its designation (*prajñaptivastu, gdags gzhi*), and indicating the bare essential nature of a given object [without syntactically bound stems]. Regarding the necessity for naming substantives [in this way], it is said:

The Sublime One said:
If names are not designated,
The entire world will be deluded.
Therefore, in order to dispel delusion
The Lord designates names.

So it is that the comprehension of conventional terms (*vyavahāra, tha snyad*) and communicative symbols (*saṃketa, brda*) is dependent on names.

Primary Radical Names [a']

Primary names (*yādṛcchikanāman, 'dod rgyal gyi ming*), such as "space," "earth," and "water," convey primary communication, without the need for [establishing] a reason or purpose. [On this basis,] it is explained in the *Sword at the Gateway to Language*:

Any primary name accords with actual reality [or emptiness],
In that it has no basis for etymological definition.

Derivative Names [b']

By contrast, derivative names (*rjes su grub pa'i ming*) designate extraneous objects, having acquired [the status of] conventional terminology. They include primary names that function as derivatives (*rjes grub 'dod rgyal*) which cannot be analyzed in etymological terms, as when a black dog is named Conch, and meaningful derivatives, which can be analyzed in etymological terms, as when a white dog is named Conch.

Proper Names [c']

When names are analyzed further, they comprise both proper names (*mūlanāman, dngos ming*) and imputed names (*prajñaptināman, btags ming*).

[The defining characteristic of] the former is that proper names are either well-known as primary radical names, or else they require the presence of any one of the three appropriate etymological terms for proper [names]. In the latter case, they comprise (1) proper nouns formed from original primary radicals, exemplified by the name "god" (*deva, lha*); (2) proper names formed from primary names functioning as derivatives, which may be exemplified by the expression "drinking at the foot" (*pādapa, rkang 'thung*), which poetically designates a "tree"; and (3) proper nouns unbewildered with regard to their meaning, as when a heroic man is designated "tiger" (*vyāghra, stag*).

Imputed Names [d']

The defining characteristic of imputed names is that any one of three appropriate etymological terms for imputed [names][977] must be present. On analyisis, these comprise (1) imputed names formed on the basis of similarity (*'dra ba rgyu mtshan du byas pa*); (2) imputed names formed on the basis of a causal relationship (*'brel ba rgyu mtshan du byas pa*), or derived therefrom; and (3) imputed names formed on the basis of a causal relationship which is contrary to these two (*de gnyis ka ldog pa rgyu mtshan du byas pa*).

The first category [imputed names based on similarity] is exemplified by the medication *kākapāda* (*bya rog rkang, Delphinium*) [lit. "crow's foot," so called because the plant resembles a crow's foot].

The second category [imputed names based on a causal relationship] includes both names that impute the result from the cause, as when the "disease of indigestion" is termed "indigestion" (*ajīrṇa, ma zhu ba*), and those that impute the cause from the result, as when the names "pine tree" (*devadāru, sgron me'i shing*) or "avaricious" (*īrṣālu, phyug po ser sna can*) are given to an anguished spirit (*preta*).

[In this context], there are instances of collective names (*tshogs pa'i ming*) being applied to an individual, as when certain men are given the name "god," or certain women are given the name "girl"; and by contrast there are instances of individual names (*ya gyal gyi ming*) being applied to a group, as when "gold" and so forth are called "metal."

The third category, imputed names that are based on the contrariety of similarity and causal relationship, includes euphemisms such as "auspicious" (*maṅgala*, *bkra shis*) for [the inauspicious] Tuesday or Mars, and "excellent" (*bhadra*, *bzang po*) for Viṣṭi, which is one of the [negative] impact days of the lunar phases (*karaṇa*, *byed pa*).

Detailed Exegesis of Synonymics [2']

With regard to the second part, concerning the methodology of synonymics, it says in the root verses]:

> **Through homonyms and synonyms**
> **[The science of] synonymics should be comprehended,**
> **Along with the tables [of verbal roots] and definitions.**

Homonyms [a']

With regard to names, [the formation of which] has just been explained, some are characterized as homonyms (*nānārtha*, *don sna tshogs*), and these may be illustrated by the following extracts from the *Treasury of Amarasiṃha*:[978]

> *Kaḥ*, in the masculine, can have [three] meanings:
> "Brahmā" (*tshangs pa*), "wind" (*māruta*, *rlung*), and "sun" (*sūrya*, *nyi*).
> *Kaṃ* can have [two] meanings:
> "Head" (*śiras*, *mgo*) and "water" (*ambu*, *chu*).

And:[979]

> *Kauśikaḥ* can have [four] meanings:
> "Mahendra" (*dbang chen*), "frankincense" (*gu gul*),
> "Owl" (*ūlūka*, *'ug pa*), and "snake-catcher" (*vyālagrāhin*, *sbrul 'dzin*).

And:[980]

> *Artha* can have [five] meanings:
> "Signified object" (*abhidheya*, *brjod bya*), "wealth" (*dhana*, *nor*),
> "Meaning of a word" (*padārtha*, *tshig don*), "purpose" (*prayojana*, *dgos pa*),
> And "prevention" (*nivṛtti*, *ldog pa*).

And:[981]

> *Antaraṃ* can have [thirteen] meanings:
> "Gap" (*avakāśa*, *go skabs*)," "interval" (*avadhi*, *mtshams*),
> "Skirt" (*paridhāna*, *smad gos*), "concealment" (*antardhi*, *sgrib*),

"Difference" (*bheda, dbye*), "for the sake of" (*tādarthya, de'i don*),
"Imperfection" (*chidra, skyon*), "intimate" (*ātmīya, bdag gi ba*),
"Without" (*vinā, bral*),[982] "exterior" (*bahir, phyi rol*),
"Opportunity" (*avasara, skabs*), "between" (*madhye, skabs*),
And "inner soul" (*antarātma, dbus gang gi bdag*).

And:[983]

Svāsti can have [three] meanings:
"Benediction" (*āśī, smon*), "welfare" (*kṣema, bde*),
And "provision of merit" (*puṇyādau, bsod nams tshogs*).

Nāgārjuna has also said:[984]

The learned recognize that the term *go*
Has nine [distinct] meanings, including
"Speech" (*vāg, ngag*), "direction" (*dik, phyogs*), "earth" (*bhūtala, sa*),
"Light ray" (*kiraṇa, 'od zer*), "cattle" (*paśu, phyugs*), "eye" (*netra, mig*),
"Vajra" (*rdo rje*), "higher realms" (*svarga, mtho ris*), and "water" (*lakṣya, chu*).[985]

A [seemingly] limitless number of other [homonyms] are also found in works such as the *Pearl Necklace of Synonymics*[986] and the *Sheaf of Glorious Terms*.[987] Accordingly, Sanskrit has a great many [homonyms].

Also in the Tibetan language, it should be understood that [the use of homonyms] is extensive. For example, the term "twice-born" (*gnyis skyes*; Skt. *dvija*) can mean "moon," "*brāhmaṇa*," "bird," and so forth; while the term "sky-goer" (*mkha' 'gro*, Skt. *ḍākinī*) can mean "accomplished yoginī," a "woman who has been born in a buddha-field such as Oḍḍiyāna," "sun," "bird," and "arrow."[988]

Synonyms [b']

There are also names which are characterized as synonyms. For example, it says in the *Treasury of Amarasiṃha* that the synonyms of *svarga* (*mtho ris*, meaning "higher realms") include[989]

"Absence of endless sorrow" (*nirakṣayaduḥkha, mi zad mi bde med*),
"Paradise" (*susthita, legs gnas*), "third heavenly realm" (*tridiva, sum rtsen*),

"Heavenly abode of the thirty-three gods" (*tridaśālaya, skabs gsum gnas*),
And "the world system of the gods" (*suraloka, lha yi 'jig rten*).

Similarly, the synonyms or epithets of the term "buddha" (*sangs rgyas*) include the following:[990]

"omniscient one" (*sarvajña, kun mkhyen*),
"one gone to bliss" (*sugata, bde gshegs*),
"one who is awakened" (*buddha, sangs rgyas*),
"king of the sacred teachings" (*dharmarāja, chos kyi rgyal po*),
"one who has departed in accord with reality" (*tathāgata, de bzhin gshegs pa*),
"all-positive one" (*samantabhadra, kun tu bzang po*),
"transcendent lord" (*bhagavān, bcom ldan 'das*),
"subduer of malign forces" (*mārajit, bdud 'thul*),
"conqueror" (*jina, rgyal ba*),
"conqueror of the world" (*lokajina, 'jig rten rgyal*),
"one endowed with six supernormal cognitive powers" (*ṣaḍabhijña, mngon shes drug ldan*),
"one endowed with the ten powers" (*daśabalin, stobs bcu pa*),
"one endowed with non-dual speech" (*advayavādin, gnyis med gsung ba*),
"guide" (*vināyaka, rnam par 'dren pa*),
"mighty among sages" (*munīndra, thub dbang*),
"dense with glory" (*śrīghana, dpal stug*), and
"teacher" (*śāstṛ, ston pa*).

As these examples illustrate, there are a great many [classes of] synonyms.

Derivatives from Sanskrit Roots [c']

[The construction of the synonyms and homonyms outlined in] this science of synonymics requires knowledge of the paradigms of Sanskrit roots and the definitions of the terms expressed in both [the Sanskrit and Tibetan] languages. For example, in Sanskrit the term *buddhaḥ* is formed by combining the root *budh*,[991] which means "to realize," with the suffix *–kta*, which indicates a participial substantive (*bhāvārtha, dngos po'i don*). Therefore [the term *buddhaḥ*] is interpreted to mean "one who has awakened," as if free from sleep, or "one who has qualitatively realized all knowable phenomena." In Tibetan the term was rendered by the great translators of the past, relying on its meaning, by the [compound] *sangs rgyas* [lit. "purified and expansive"]. As has been said:[992]

> The buddha is fully purified and expanded like a lotus flower,
> Because he has awakened from the sleep of fundamental ignorance,
> And his mind is extensive with regard to all objects of knowledge.

Since [the construction of synonyms] requires the compounding of such etymologies, illustrative terms [should conform to this standard] and [their meaning] should be inferred accordingly.

11. DRAMATURGY

ee. Dramaturgy [III.B.2.b.ii.ee]
- 1' Aspects of Dramatic Juncture
  - a' Introduction
  - b' Progression
  - c' Development
  - d' Plot Crisis
  - e' Conclusion
- 2' The Contexts of the Four Dramatic Elements
  - a' Dialogue
  - b' Grandeur
  - c' Intimacy
  - d' Conflict
- 3' Thirty-six Characteristics of Stagecraft
- 4' Other Dramatic Sentiments

DRAMATURGY [ee]

The fifth topic [of the minor classical sciences is the exegesis on dramaturgy (*nāṭya, zlos gar*), [on which it is said in the root verses]:

> **One should study all acts that bring delight to sentient beings,**
> **Evoking dramatic performances endowed with the sentiment of joy,**
> **Including the aspects of the five dramatic junctures**
> **And the aspects of the [four] dramatic elements,**
> **As well as the thirty-six[993] characteristics [of stagecraft],**

And the [trappings of] graceful [song and dance],
[The wearing of] garlands, and so forth.

Since the following exegesis on dramaturgy does not for the most part accord with the [normal] exegeses presented by Tibetan writers, utilizing their creative imagination, I will not repeat [their views here]. Rather, I will follow the tradition of the omniscient Tenpei Nyinje, who [personally] inspected the [relevant] Indian manuscripts along with the procedures of [classical Sanskrit] drama and delivered some approximate teachings on the subject.[994]

In general, [the science of] dramaturgy comprises three topics: the aspects of the [five] phases of dramatic juncture (*saṃdhyaṅga, mtshams sbyor gyi yan lag*), the contexts of the [four] dramatic elements (*vṛtyaṅga, 'jug pa'i yan lag*), and the [thirty-six] characteristics [of stagecraft] (*lakṣaṇa, mtshan nyid*).[995]

Aspects of Dramatic Juncture [1']

First, the aspects of dramatic juncture refer to the different sections [of a play], signifying the particular phases of the plot,[996] which require dialogue to be spoken in various languages.[997] These comprise

(1) the dramatic juncture of the introduction or protasis (*mukhasaṃdhi, sgo'i mtshams sbyor*) in which an [initial] proposal (*'dri ba*) is made;
(2) the dramatic juncture of the progression or epitasis (*pratimukhasaṃdhi, lan gyi sgo'i mtshams sbyor*), in which a multitude of causes provoke a dialogue of proposals and rejoinders;
(3) the dramatic juncture of the development or catastasis (*garbhasaṃdhi, snying po'i mtshams sbyor*), in which, following many verbal exchanges, exemplified by episodic discussions (*skabs 'gar gros byed pa*), the deliberations are decisively determined;
(4) the dramatic juncture of the plot crisis or peripeteia (*vimarśasaṃdhi, mi bzod pa'i mtshams sbyor*), in which words that seek to expose the wrongdoings [of another] backfire, exposing the speaker's own wrong-doings, which cannot be tolerated, engendering suffering due to attachment and an unbearable crisis;
(5) the dramatic juncture of the conclusion or catastrophe (*nirvahaṇa-saṃdhi, nges pa thob byed kyi mtshams sbyor*), in which, following many statements expressing hesitation, a singular resolution or [positive] outcome is obtained.

These are known as the five sequences of dramatic juncture.[998]

Also, it is said in an Indian commentary on the *Mirror of Poetics*, which was composed by the master Ratnaśrī:[999]

> The dramatic junctures are explained to number five: the introduction, the progression, the development, the plot crisis, and the conclusion.

Introduction [a']

> Among them the introduction comprises the following [twelve] aspects: (1) suggestive insinuation [alluding to the forthcoming plot] (*upakṣepa, nye bar len pa*); (2) enlargement [indirectly intimating the coming events] (*parikara, nye bar mkho ba*); (3) establishment [of the seed of the plot] (*parinyāsa, yongs su 'jog pa*); (4) allurement [by extolling the qualities of the hero or heroine] (*vilobhana, rnam par sred pa*); (5) resolve [to attain the objective of the plot] (*yukti, rig pa*); (6) accession [to the anticipated joyful conclusion of the plot] (*prāpti, thob pa*); (7) determination of [the purpose or germ of the plot] (*samādhāna, mnyam par 'jog pa*); (8) conflict of [joyful and sorrowful] sentiments (*vidhāna, sgrub pa*); (9) expressions of surprise [giving rise to curiosity] (*paribhāvanā, brnyes pa*); (10) the first disclosure [of the germ of the plot] (*udbheda, dbye ba*); (11) [the initial enactment of the plot (*karaṇa*)];[1000] and (12) [the hatching of a] conspiracy (*bheda, dbye bar byed pa*).

Progression [b']

> The progression comprises the following [thirteen] aspects: (1) longing (*samīhā*) or amorousness (*vilāsa*);[1001] (2) pursuit [of the desired object] (*parisarpa, yongs su 'gro ba*); (3) trembling [due to rejection] (*vidhūta, rnam par 'dar ba*); (4) toleration of anguish [with regard to the desired object] (*tāpana, gdung ba*); (5) amorous playfulness (*narman, rtsed mo*); (6) amusement or deliberate concealment arising from amorous playfulness (*narmadyuti, rtsed mo'i mdangs*); (7) progress [towards the desired objective, achieved through dialogue] (*pragamana, rab tu 'gro ba*); (8) frustration or impediment to the successful progression of the plot (*virodha, 'gal ba*); (9) propitiation or pacification [of an angered person]

(*upāsana, nye bar gnas pa*); (10) sweet words of gallantry (*puṣpa, me tog*);[1002] (11) [an adamant, blunt response made to the face (*vajra, rdo rje*)];[1003] (12) strategic appeasement (*upanyāsa, skye bo 'god par rtsom pa*); and (13) close association, as when characters of different social classes intermingle (*varṇasaṃhāra, yi ge bsdu ba*).[1004]

Development [c']

The development comprises the following [thirteen] aspects:[1005] (1) [deliberate] mis-statement of events that never took place (*abhūtāharaṇa, ma byung ba dper brjod pa*); (2) [clear indication of] the course of action one intends to follow (*mārga, lam gyi rang bzhin*); (3) consequent supposition or hypothesis [expressing doubt] (*vitarka, brtag dpyad*);[1006] (4) employment of [exaggerated] examples or hyperbole (*udāharaṇa, dper brjod*); (5) employment of progressive similes [to obtain knowledge of another person's sentiments] (*krama, rim pa*);[1007] (6) winning over [another person by sweet words and gifts] (*saṅgraha, bsdu ba*); (7) making of an inference or conjecture (*anumāna, rjes su dpag pa*); (8) solicitation (*prārthanā, slong ba*); (9) painful disclosure [of the desired object of the plot] (*ākṣipta, gzer ba*); (10) [quarreling (*toṭaka*)];[1008] (11) outwitting through guile (*adhibala, stobs lhag pa*); (12) distress [caused by separation or exposure to enemies] (*udvega, yid 'byung ba*); and (13) consequent panic or consternation (*vidrava, 'tshab pa*).

Plot Crisis [d']

The plot crisis comprises the following [thirteen] aspects: (1) censure [of another's misdeeds] (*apavāda, rgol ba*); (2) altercation (*saṃpheṭa, 'thor ba*); (3) tumultuous consternation [showing disrespect or insolence] (*adhidrava, 'dzag pa*); (4) powerful placation [of one who is angry] (*śakti, nus pa*); (5) resolute pledge or assertion [with regard to the original objective of the plot] (*vyavasāya, phan tshun du gnas pa*); (6) incidental comments [concerning one's superiors] (*prasaṅga, 'gro ba pa*); (7) disdainful words (*dyuti, gsal ba*); (8) lassitude or depression [arising from over-exertion] (*kheda, 'byed pa*); (9) prohibition or opposition [blocking the desired objective of the plot] (*niṣedha, 'gog pa*); (10) quarrelsome altercation (*virodhana, 'gal ba*); (11) capture [of the germ of the plot within the actions of the plot] (*ādāna, len pa*); (12) words of humiliation (*chādana, 'drid pa*); and (13) words presaging [the denouement] (*prarocanā, rab tu sred pa*).

Conclusion [e']

Lastly, the conclusion comprises the following [fourteen] aspects: (1) [the resurfacing of] the [original] juncture [in which the plot was germinated] (*saṃdhi, mtshams sbyor*); (2) impediment (*virodha, 'gog pa*);[1009] (3) convergence [of the main issues of the plot] (*grathana, spel ba*); (4) settlement [of the plot] (*nirṇaya, gtan la phab pa*); (5) admonition [accepting responsibility for the plot] (*paribhāṣaṇa, smod pa*); (6) confirmation [of the outcome of the plot] (*dyuti, gsal ba*); (7) lucid sense of gratification [following the subsidence of anger] (*prasāda, rab dvangs*); (8) joy [in the attainment of the desired object] (*ānanda, kun dga'*); (9) deliverance [from all misery or misfortune] (*śama, dus*); (10) expressions of wonderment (*upagūhana, nye bas sbed pa*); (11) [conciliatory speech (*bhāṣaṇa*)];[1010] (12) retrospective comments (*pūrvāvākya, bsam pa snga ma 'chad pa*); (13) epilogue (*kāvyāsaṃhāra, snyan ngag bsdu ba*); and (14) formal benediction (*praśasti, rang gis ston pa*).

The Contexts of the Four Dramatic Elements [2']

Second, the aspects of dramatic style are four in number: those of dialogue (*bhāratī*), grandeur (*sātvatī*), intimacy (*kaiśikī*), and conflict (*ārabhaṭī*), each of which also has four contexts.[1011]

Dialogue [a']

Among them, the four contexts for [the element of] "dialogue" are (1) stimulating prologues (*prarocanā, rab tu snang ba*);[1012] (2) preludes (*āmukha, kun tu sgo*); (3) single-act dramas (*vīthī, phreng ba*); and (4) farce (*prahasana, bzo byed*).[1013]

Grandeur [b']

The four contexts for [the element of] "grandeur" are (1) haughty provocations [addressed to an opponent] (*utthāpaka, shin tu 'jog pa*); (2) necessary changes of action [due to exigencies] (*parivartaka, yongs su bsgyur ba*); (3) abusive or intimidating conversations (*saṃlāpa, smra ba dang bcas pa*); and (4) the ending of an alliance [whether by accident or design] (*sāṅghātya, 'phrag tu bzlog pa*).[1014]

Intimacy [c']

The four contexts for [the element of] "intimacy" are (1) amorous play or pleasantries (*narman, rtsed mo*); (2) the partial but lucid manifestation of a recent love [through physical signs and other intimations, combined with fear and other emotions] (*narmasphoṭa, gsal ba*); (3) the covert development of love and affection [by employing disguise and concealment] (*narmagarbha, rtsed mo 'byed pa*); and (4) the ecstatic meeting with a lover or outburst of affection which has troublesome consequences (*narmasphūrja, rtsed mor 'gro ba*).[1015]

Conflict [d']

The four contexts for [the element of] "conflict" are (1) artful devices or adroit moves that compress [or symbolize the plot] (*saṃkṣiptaka, bsdus pa*); (2) commotion [associated with sudden entrances and exits, out of fear or panic] (*avapāta, kun lhung*); (3) elevation of the plot [by intrusion of the supernatural and a plethora of sentiments] (*vastūthāpana, gnas skabs 'jog pa*); and (4) altercations that lead to fighting (*saṃpheṭa, kun tu 'thor ba*).[1016]

Thirty-six Characteristics of Stagecraft [3']

Third, the classification of the characteristics [of stagecraft] is explained in an Indian commentary to include the following thirty-six rhetorical devices or expressions indicating[1017]

> (1) embellishment (*bhūṣana, rgyan*); (2) abbreviation (*akṣarasaṃghātā, yi ge bsdu ba*); (3) beauty (*śobhā, mdzes pa*); (4) declarations (*udāharaṇa, dper brjod*); (5) reasons (*hetu, rgyu yang dag par sbyor ba*); [(6) doubts (*saṃśaya, som nyi/ the tshoms*)];[1018] (7) objectives (*dṛṣṭānta, mthong ba'i mtha'*); (8) attainments (*prāpti, thob pa*); (9) prosperity (*abhyudaya, mngon par mtho ba*); (10) evidence (*nidarśana, nge spar bstan pa*); (11) explanations (*nirukta, nges tshig*); (12) accomplishments (*siddhi, grub pa*); (13) distinctions (*viśeṣana, khyad par byed pa*); (14) disquali-

fications (*guṇātipāta*, *yon tan lhung ba*); (15) hyperbole (*atiśaya*, *phul byung*); (16) similarity of ideas (*tulyatarka*, *rtog ge mtshungs pa*); (17) versification (*padoccaya*, *tshig btus pa*); (18) observations (*diṣṭa*, *bstan pa*); (19) suggestion (*upadiṣṭa*, *nye bar bstan pa*); (20) discrimination (*vicāra*, *rnam par dpyad pa*); (21) opposition (*tadviparyāya*, *go ldog pa*); (22) solecism (*bhraṃśa*, *nyams pa*); (23) conciliation (*anunaya*, *rjes khrid*); (24) [the bestowal of] flower garlands (*mālā*, *phreng ba*); (25) concord (*dākṣiṇya*, *yon sbyin pa*); (26) reproach (*garhaṇa*, *smod pa*); (27) presumption (*arthāpatti*, *don gyi dbang*); (28) proof (*prasiddhi*, *rab tu grub pa*); (29) interrogation (*pṛcchā*, *dri ba*); (30) mistaken identity (*sārūpya*, *'god pa dang bcas pa*); (31) imagination (*manoratha*, *re ba*); (32) the use of disparaging metaphor (*leśa*, *cha shas*); (33) agitation (*saṃkṣobha* or *saṃkṣepa*, *bsdus pa*); (34) the proclamation of talents (*guṇakīrtana*, *yon tan sgrogs pa*); (35) understated achievements (*anuktasiddhi*, *ma brjod pa grub pa*); and (36) words of endearment (*priyavacana*, *dga' ba'i tshig*).

Other Dramatic Sentiments [4']

Moreover, there are also other [essential] elements of drama, including graceful [song and dance] (*lāsya*, *sgeg pa*), [the wearing of] garlands (*phreng ba*), and the aspects of other [additional] dramatic junctures.[1019]

All of these [aspects] are actually experienced, as it were, within the context of [plays enacting] tales and legends of the past and the relevant physical and verbal moods that they evoke, such as the sentiment (*rasa*, *nyams*) of extreme anger, the sentiment of anguish caused by desire, the sentiment of suffering caused by sorrow, the sentiment of astonishment caused by amazement, and other dramatic moods. The extensive characteristics of these [moods and sentiments] should be learned from other [sources] because they are too voluminous for inclusion here.[1020]

[Conclusion]

In brief, the science of Indian dramaturgy is endowed with sentiments or moods which give rise to joy in the people who see and hear [dramatic performances] because the physical and verbal moods [that they evoke] are repeatedly recreated in the context of a play, captivating the minds [of the audience]. Although [this science] is known to be particularly amazing, the relevant [classical Indian] treatises are not extant in [Tibet,] the Land of Snows, and they are not immediately useful for the purpose of attaining liberation [from cyclic existence]. Even so, all the actions of the bodhisattvas, which are reminiscent of such [dramatic sentiments] and bring delight to sentient beings, should be studied. As has been said:[1021]

> There are no methods that please the buddhas
> Apart from those that bring delight to sentient beings.

12. Mundane Spiritual Paths

C. Mundane Spiritual Paths That Focus on This Life [III.C]
- 1. The General Presentation
  - a. Definition of "Spiritual and Philosophical Systems"
  - b. Diverse Enumerations of Philosophical Views
- 2. Particular Classification of the Mundane Spiritual Paths
  - a. Brief Presentation of Non-Buddhist Traditions
    - i. Essential Nature
    - ii. Classification
      - aa. Nominal Extremists
      - bb. Emanational Extremists
      - cc. Independent Non-Buddhist Systems
  - b. Detailed Exegesis of Non-Buddhist Systems
    - i. Meditators
    - ii. Dialecticians
      - aa. Brief Presentation
      - bb. Classificatory Presentation
        - 1' The Nihilist School
        - 2' The Eternalist Schools
          - a' Sāṃkhya
          - b' Vaiśeṣika
          - c' Naiyāyika
          - d' Aiśvarya
          - e' Vaiṣṇava
          - f' Brāhmaṇa
          - g' Vedāntaupaniṣadika
          - h' Vaiyākaraṇa
          - i' Mīmāṃsaka

Mundane Spiritual Paths That Focus on This Life [C]

The third basic topic [of the actual content of classical learning; see above, p. 103] concerns the systematic presentation of the mundane spiritual paths that focus on this life (*tshur mthong 'jig rten pa'i lam*). It has two parts, the general presentation and the particular classifications.

The General Presentation [1]

As to the former [it is said in the root verses]:

> **There are common understandings concerning merely the happiness of this life**
> **And there are philosophically inclined persons, endowed with a spiritual path.**
> **There are many views, authentic and inauthentic.**
> **For every hundred lower [views] there is but a single higher view,**
> **But when they are [all] subsumed, they comprise**
> **The outer [non-Buddhist] and inner [Buddhist perspectives].**

Definition of "Spiritual and Philosophical Systems" [a]

In general, sentient beings designate as "common" those understandings that exclusively concern matters of this life alone—those that are to be adopted in the pursuit of happiness, or abandoned in the avoidance of suffering, without venturing to investigate the [aforementioned] subjects of classical science or the circumstances of the next life and beyond. On the other hand, those who are philosophically inclined and who, to some extent, venture to investigate [the true nature of] phenomena are designated as persons "endowed with a spiritual path." For this reason, they are deemed superior to ordinary worldly folk.

With regard to those in the world who are philosophically inclined, the term "philosophical and spiritual system" (*siddhānta, grub mtha'*) implies that they attain "realization" (*siddhi, grub*) in accordance with their respective classes, but cannot transcend their [particular level of realization]. It has indeed been said that although reality (*tattva, de nyid*) is true, the perspectives of it which are known in the world are uncertain in terms of their truthfulness. In the words of the *Introduction to the Conduct of a Bodhisattva*:[1022]

> When worldly folk perceive phenomena
> They consider them to be real, and not illusory.
> On this point, yogins and worldly folk will enter into debate.

Diverse Enumerations of Philosophical Views [b]

Those who espouse philosophical tenets hold many [diverse] views, some of which, including the [views of the] exalted vehicle (*abhyudayayāna, mngon mtho'i theg pa*), are deemed to be authentic, and others, such as eternalism (*nityadṛṣṭi, rtag lta*) or nihilism (*ucchedadṛṣṭi, chad lta*), are inauthentic.[1023] Among them are the five hundred and seventy [different philosophical] views outlined by the master Vitapāda [in his *Commentary on the Oral Teachings of Mañjuśrī: The Beautiful Flower*],[1024] the hundred and ten primary philosophical views and three hundred and sixty-three derivative views outlined in the *Flame of Dialectics*,[1025] the ninety-six astonishing views outlined in [Bodhibhadra's] *Interlinear Commentary on the Compendium of the Nucleus of Pristine Cognition*,[1026] the sixty-two inauthentic views outlined in the *Sūtra of the Net of Brahmā*,[1027] the twenty-eight inauthentic views outlined in the *Sūtra of the Enhancement of Faith*,[1028] and the twenty-six negative views mentioned in the *Sūtra of the Excellent Meditation on Faith in the Greater Vehicle*.[1029]

Moreover, there are the twenty views concerning mundane aggregates[1030] the sixteen alien interpretations, among the [diverse] analytical views (*vicāradṛṣṭi, rtog dpyod kyi lta ba*),[1031] the fourteen unspecified views,[1032] and the eight, four, or two categories of extremist views (*antagrāhadṛṣṭi, mthar 'dzin gyi lta ba*).[1033]

Since such classifications of inauthentic views have been expounded many times, this [list] is merely illustrative. Among the many hundreds and thousands of ordinary mundane [levels of existence], including those assumed by the denizens of the three inferior realms (*ngan song gsum*)[1034] and most classes of gods and humans, virtually each of them has its own approach to the spiritual and philosophical path. Among them, those who enter [the spiritual path] at the lower end of the scale are greater in number, while those who enter at the higher end are fewer. Accordingly, Jowoje [Atiśa] has said:[1035]

> Nowadays in India, at this time when hundreds are learned in the philosophical systems of the extremists (*tīrthaka*, *mu stegs pa*), for every [hundred of them], there is one who understands the philosophical system of the Vaibhāṣikas, and for every hundred of them there is one Sautrāntika, for every hundred of them there is one Vijñānavādin holding sensa to be veridical (*ākāravādin*, *rnam bden pa*), for every hundred of them there is one Vijñānavādin holding sensa to be false (*nirākāravādin*, *rnam bden pa*), for every hundred of them there is one Mādhyamika upholding independent reasoning (*svātantrikamādhyamika*), and for every hundred of them there is no more than one who understands the tradition of Candrakīrti.

Although there are a great many subdivisions among those espousing spiritual and philosophical systems, when these are subsumed according to their dissimilarity, they comprise (1) the others who are extremists upholding non-Buddhist schools (*gzhan sde phyi rol mu stegs pa*) and (2) the Buddhists of our own tradition. Their [distinctive] positions will now be explained in turn.[1036]

Particular Classification of the Mundane Spiritual Paths [2]

Secondly, the particular classification [of the mundane spiritual paths] has two parts: a brief presentation of the traditions of the non-Buddhist extremists, and an extensive presentation of the exalted vehicle [which may advantageously be pursued by gods and humans].

Brief Presentation of Non-Buddhist Traditions [a]

This comprises three topics: the essential nature, classification, and detailed exegesis [of the non-Buddhist traditions].

Essential Nature [i]

As for the first of these topics [it is said in the root verses]:

> **The non-Buddhists are designated as "extremists."**

Those who maintain standpoints outside [the perspective of] the Buddhist teaching, alien to [the words of] the Teacher [Śākyamuni Buddha], are designated as non-Buddhists or "outsiders" (*phyi rol pa*). This is because, even though they may investigate [the nature of] phenomena through their mundane discriminative awareness, they lack the spiritual path that is in conformity with [the attainment of] nirvāṇa, the abiding nature of reality (*yin lugs*). However, they are also designated as "extremists" or "forders" (*tīrthaka, mu stegs pa*) because, in slightly simulating this attainment, they continue to maintain their extreme [positions] (*mu*) and cling to their [inconclusive] platforms or fords (*stegs*). Therefore, it is said in the *Commentary on the Aspirational Prayer of Good Conduct*,[1037] composed by the great translator Yeshede:

> In the case of the term "extremist" (*mu stegs can*), the word "extreme" (*tīrtha, mu stegs*) designates, for example, a ford (*rab kha*) where a river is easily crossed, or a stepping stone that is reached when negotiating a pool or pond of water. Accordingly, this term comes to refer to the [inconclusive] "fords" (*mu stegs*) encountered while embarking on the lake that leads to [the attainment of] nirvāṇa, and the "fords" encountered on the path of skillful means, whereby the river of cyclic existence (*saṃsāra*) is crossed. Those who maintain and cultivate spiritual paths [fixated on fords and supports] are called "extremists" or "forders" (*tīrthaka*).

Their defining characteristic is that they propound spiritual and philosophical tenets which are contrary to Buddhism in terms of their view, meditation, action, and result.

Classification [ii]

With regard to their classification [it says in the root verses]:

> **[Extremists] are of three sorts:**
> **Nominal, emanational, and independently established.**

In general, philosophical extremists are of three sorts: nominal (*btags pa ba*), emanational (*sprul pa*), and independently established (*rang rgyud pa*).

Nominal Extremists [aa]

Among them, concerning nominal [extremists] it says in the *Sūtra of the Descent to Laṅkā*:[1038]

As long as the mind engages [with sense objects],
So long will there be mundane materialism.

While elsewhere in the sūtras it says, for instance, that those virtuous ascetics (*śramaṇa*, *dge sbyong*) who advocate mundane materialism are corrupt.[1039]

In addition, the Vātsīputrīya and others like them who hold the psycho-physical aggregates (*skandha*, *phung po*) and so forth to be truly existent[1040] may also be nominally designated as extremists, alongside those who are cut off from the seed of buddha nature, maintaining heretical views and imputing disillusionment [with the world] as the bliss of quiescence.[1041]

Emanational Extremists [bb]

With reference to the emanational [sort of extremists], it says in the *Sūtra on Substantialism*:[1042]

When one has encountered a wish-fulfilling gem and quartz,
[The latter] never appears to be genuine.
Similarly, the precious Buddha and the extremist
Never appear in a single field.
Despite that, one should know that this approach of the extremists
Requires mastery of meditative concentration,
Supernormal cognitive powers, and overpowering [means].
Those inclined to engage [in such practices],
Through their discriminative awareness and skilful means,
May display diverse emanational forms.

Many similar passages are found in the sūtras.

Independent Non-Buddhist Systems [cc]

Then, with reference to the independently established [philosophical schools of the non-Buddhists], it says in the *Mother*:

> When a hundred itinerant teachers (*parivrājika*) came, thinking to seek confrontation, I did not discern them to have even a single positive teaching.

And so on.

Detailed Exegesis of Non-Buddhist Systems [b]

Thirdly, the detailed exegesis [of the non-Buddhist systems] presents [the views] of the meditators (*dhyāyī, bsam gtan pa*), the dialecticians (*tārkika, rtog ge pa*), and, incidentally, of the barbarians (*mleccha, kla klo*), which are all to be rejected.

Meditators [i]

Among them, as to the first [it says in the root verses]:

> **The last of these [the independently established extremist schools] include meditators**
> **Who possess the fivefold supernormal cognitive powers.**

With regard to the last of these aforementioned categories, the independently established [extremist schools] (*svātantrikatīrthaka, mu stegs rang rgyud pa*), their spiritual and philosophical systems, which are to be explained here, include both those of the meditators and the dialecticians.

Among them, the former possess the five supernormal cognitive powers (*pañcābhijñā, mngon shes lnga*) associated with formless meditative concentration, as suggested in the [poetic] words of the master Śūra, "The great hermit sage, endowed with five supernormal cognitive powers."[1043]

It is explained in the extensive *Interlinear Commentary on the Compendium of the Nucleus of Pristine Cognition*,[1044] in the *Flame of Dialectics*, and so forth that the extremists include three types of meditator—lower, middling, and superior—who respectively have the ability to recollect thirty, sixty, and ninety aeons of time. Beings such as these hold that cyclic existence is beginningless in its origins, whereas [paradoxically] their spiritual and philosophical systems, which offer an explanation that is generally similar to that of the dialecticians, largely originated during this present aeon of [historical] time.

Dialecticians [ii]

The second has two parts—a brief presentation contextualizing an exegesis of the nihilist school (*ucchedavāda, chad smra*) and a classificatory presentation of the eternalist schools (*nityavāda, rtag smra*).

Brief Presentation [aa]

Concerning the former [it says in the root verses]:

> **The basic [divisions] of the dialecticians**
> **Are the eternalist and nihilist schools.**
> **Among them, [the latter] are the materialists**
> **Who hold that life forms are of three types—**
> **Discernable, indiscernible, and animistic.**
> **They espouse nihilism, denying the existence of unseen causes,**
> **And they refute the existence of past and future lives,**
> **Along with [the impact of] past actions, and so forth,**
> **For which reasons they cannot attain even the higher realms**
> **[of gods and humans].**

The spiritual and philosophical systems espoused by non-Buddhist extremists have many branches. In general, three such subdivisions are identified in the *Compendium of the Nucleus of Pristine Cognition*, comprising the Advocates of the [Three] Attributes (*traiguṇya, yon tan [gsum] can pa*), the Sāṃkhya (*grangs can pa*) and the Brāhmaṇa (*tshangs pa [ba]*). However, according to the *Flame of Dialectics* (*Tarkajvālā*), they fall into four categories, including the Sāṃkhya (*grangs can pa*), the Vaiśeṣika (*bye brag pa*), the Vedāntaupaniṣadika (*rigs byed kyi mtha' gsang ba pa*), and the Mīmāṃsaka (*spyod pa can*).

According to the *Tantra of the Wheel of Time*, there are six categories of extremist, including the Brāhmaṇa, the Aiśvarya (*dbang phyug pa*), the Vaiṣṇava (*khyab 'jug pa*), the Lokāyatika (*['jig rten] rgyang 'phen pa*), the Nirgrantha Jains (*gcer bu pa*), and, in another context, the Sāṃkhya.

Then, according to the eloquent textual tradition of the Sakya school,[1045] there are nine categories, including five eternalist schools—Sāṃkhya, Bārhaspatya (*phur bu pa*), Vaiśeṣika, Naiyāyika (*rig pa can pa*), and the Nirgrantha Jains—along with four nihilist schools, namely, the Cārvāka (*tshu rol mdzes pa*), the Mīmāṃsaka, the Vedāntaupaniṣadika, and those [Advaitavedāntins] who simulate the approach of Madhyamaka (*dbu ma'i tshul du smra ba*).[1046]

Yet again, in the *Ornamental Flower of Philosophical Systems*, composed by Chomden Rigpei Raldri, a twelvefold classification is given, starting with the Lokāyatika, and it is his presentation that I have followed below.[1047]

Exemplified by these [diverse enumerations], many [different] classifications are be found in the [different] textual traditions. However, all these [systems] of the dialecticians may be subsumed within two basic divisions—the eternalist schools and the nihilist schools.

They are all largely similar in their common adherence to Viṣṇu, Īśvara, and Brahmā, in their adherence to the *Four Vedas* as [the revelatory source of] their teachings, in their propounding of the [concepts of] "soul" (*ātmavāda, bdag smras byed pa*) and eternally existing entities (*nityabhava, rtag dngos*), in their inclusion of livelihood or the means of [mundane] sustenance among their tenets, in their polemics directed against the Buddhist tradition, and so forth.

[In short,] all these categories of extremist take refuge in those three [Brāhmaṇical] deities, they uphold [the authority of] the *Four Vedas*, and they propound [the existence of] a "soul" or "self" among the four primary causes (*caturupādāna, nye bar len pa bzhi*) [of involuntary rebirth in the cycle of existence], which [from the Buddhist perspective] is the [misconception] that generally underlies all the other [three] primary causes.[1048] This is because even the mundane materialists uphold [the existence of] a "soul" or "self" comprising the four elements and formed of a single substance.

Classificatory Presentation [bb]

The Nihilist School [1']

Among all these [twelve] schools [identified by Chomden Rigpei Raldri], the Lokāyatika (*rgyang 'phen pa*) are so called because, in holding that past actions (*karma, las*) have no result, they have "deviated far" (*rgyang ring du song ba*) from the genuine view as understood by worldly persons [in general].

In antiquity, during the legendary battles between the gods (*deva*) and the antigods (*asura*), the gods, being of a naturally virtuous disposition, were disinclined to fight and consequently they were nearly defeated in battle. At that time, the hermit sage Bṛhaspati composed and revealed a text on the nihilist view (*chad par lta ba'i gzhung*), in order to induce the gods to fight, with the result that the gods grew confident and emerged victorious in the battle.

Later, hesitating to propagate this negative view in the god realms, Bṛhaspati threw the book into the River Ganges, where it was retrieved by a hermit sage [Vālmīki] and propagated in India. Derived from it, [new treatises] were compiled—the primary text by the hermit sage Lokākṣin ('Jig rten mig) and its commentary by Avatārabalin ('Jug stobs [can]).[1049] Their followers [during the lifetime of Śākyamuni Buddha] were known as the six nihilist teachers who were masters of meditative absorption (*chad smra'i ston pa snyoms 'jug pa drug*), the six who emulated them (*rjes sgrogs pa drug*), and the six dialecticians or teachers (*rtog ge pa'am ston pa drug*).[1050]

Moreover, it is said that the hermit sage Avatārabalin wished to engage in sexual intercourse with his own daughter, and set out to do so. [To vindicate his incestuous intention,] he established four kinds of proof (*sgrub pa bzhi*) and five kinds of refutation (*dgag pa lnga*).[1051] [The four kinds of proof are as follows:]

(1) There is an indiscernible soul or self (*avyaktātma, mi gsal ba'i bdag*) existing when the elements are in their causative or formative state.
(2) There is a discernible soul or self (*vyaktātma, gsal ba'i bdag*) existing when the elements are in their resultant or fruitional state.
(3) There are three classes of sentient beings—the enumeration of six classes being incorrect because the gods (*deva*), anguished spirits (*preta*), and denizens of the hells (*naraka*) do not exist. The three that do exist include human beings and animals which are discernible. They also include animistic spirits of woods, trees, and so forth, composed of the four indiscernible elements, in which the faculty of consciousness has not yet expired.
(4) Although they themselves do not uphold [the deductions of] logical inference (*anumāna, rjes dpag*), they [seek to] establish a reasoned argument which could be communicated to others in logical terms, such as the following [syllogism]: "The [concept] vase, the subject for discussion, may denote sentient beings in whom the physical body and the mind are of a single [material] substance, and it may signify any [actual] vase whatsoever, because it is a material object distinct from the lily [it contains], just as is, for example, a wall [that has a vase upon it].[1052]

As for their five kinds of refutation:

(1) They profess that causes and so forth which are not visible are non-existent because the [diverse] states of sorrow and happiness inherently originate in themselves, just as, for example, a pea is round, a thorn sharp, and so forth. Therefore they deny the existence of past and future lives.
(2) They deny the processes of past actions, causes and results.
(3) They deny the three precious jewels.
(4) They deny that there are invisible phenomena.
(5) They deny the valid cognition of logical inference.

Since these [mundane materialists] hold the basest of all [philosophical] views, they are [regarded as] the lowest of all those propounding spiritual and philosophical systems; and they are the most severely [deluded] among deluded beings. Let us not even mention [the possibility of them aspiring to] liberation [from cyclic existence]! Since they lack the causal basis for attaining simply a physical body compatible with the exalted realms (*svarga, mtho ris*) [of gods and humans], the result that they accrue is exclusively compatible with the inferior realms (*durgati, ngan 'gro*).

The Eternalist Schools [2']

Secondly, there follows the description of the eternalist schools.

Sāṃkhya [a']

The first of the eternalist schools is the Sāṃkhya, [on which it says in the root verses]:

> **The oldest of all the eternalist schools is the Sāṃkhya,**
> **Who through three modes of valid cognition**
> **Appraise the twenty-five aspects of reality.**
> **In particular, they hold that the "self,"**
> **Endowed with five [characteristics],**
> **Relates to the fundamental state of "nature,"**
> **[Identified with] primal matter in which the three attributes**
> **Are in a state of equilibrium,**
> **And from which evolves the "[great] intelligence."**
> **From that in turn the ego principle evolves,**
> **Along with the five aspects of subtle matter,**
> **The motor organs, the sense organs, and the mind.**
> **As they unfold in series, they give rise to cyclic existence,**
> **But if these modifications are reversed,**
> **The "self" will attain release.**

The oldest of all the eternalist schools among the extremist [traditions] is the Sāṃkhya. In antiquity, when the life span was inestimable,[1053] there was a hermit sage named Kapila who boasted of attaining release (*mokṣa, thar pa*) [from rebirth] according to the extremist systems by meditating in his hermitage (*āśramapada, bsti gnas*). In order to reveal to others the reality which he had seen, he composed the *Treatise on the Categories of Reality*.[1054] Later, the hermit sage Patañjali who was a practitioner of yoga, upholding the Shaivite tradition, reworked the *Thirty Chapter and Six Chapter Tantras of Īśvarakṛṣṇa*,[1055] and so forth, for which reason he is held to be their teacher, but, as it is said in the *Introduction to Madhyamaka*:[1056]

> Through minor variations on this theme,
> The extremists form their different traditions.

Accordingly, there were many different traditions that evolved from this [school].

With regard to the tenets of the [Sāṃkhya school],[1057] the valid cognition of direct perception (*pratyakṣapramāṇa*) is held to apply to the sense organs, while inference for one's own sake (*svārthānumāna*) entails seven kinds of relation (*saptasaṃbandhana*), including the relation of implication (*arthāpattisaṃbandhana, nor bdag gi 'brel ba*),[1058] and inference for the sake of others (*parārthānumāna*) may include both [syllogisms in which the inference] is based on yoga and those employing elimination (*bsal ba*). In this way, they hold that through these three modes of valid cognition, appraisable objects will be discerned in terms of the "twenty-five categories of reality" (*pañcaviṃśatitattva, de nyid nyer lnga*).

The twenty-five categories [of reality] are enumerated as follows: (1) primal matter (*pradhāna, gtso bo*); (2) great intelligence (*mahat/ buddhi, chen po/ blo*); (3) the threefold ego-principle (*ahaṃkāra, nga rgyal gsum*); (4–8) the five potentials of subtle matter (*pañcatanmātra, de tsam lnga*), namely, sound-potential, touch-potential, color-potential, taste-potential, and smell-potential; (9–13) the five elements (*pañcabhūta, 'byung po lnga*), including space; (14–18) the five inner sense organs (*pañcantarendriya, nang blo'i dbang po lnga*), namely, ear, skin, eye, tongue, and nose; (19–23) the five motor organs (*pañcabāhyendriya, phyi las kyi dbang po lnga*), namely, speech, handling, walking, excretion, and reproduction; (24) the mind (*manas, yid*), which is a faculty shared by both [categories of sense organs], bringing the number of sense organs up to eleven; and (25) the "soul" (*ātma, bdag*) or "cognizant self" (*puruṣa, shes rig gi skyes bu*).

When these are all subsumed, they may be gathered into two categories, primal matter and cognizant "self," the former comprising nature (*prakṛti, rang bzhin*) and the latter the absence of nature (*aprakṛti, rang bzhin min pa*).

Among them, with regard to the "self," its essential nature is both that of an actor or creator and a consumer. It is said to be a consumer in the sense that it enjoys or partakes of its sense objects. It is [regarded as] permanent because it cannot be destroyed, nor is it created because nothing has produced it. It is devoid of the threefold attributes—lightness (*sattva, snying stobs*), motility (*rajas, rdul*), and dullness (*tamas, mun pa*). It is free from activity because it permeates all space and time. In short, it is endowed with all those five distinctive or defining characteristics. [Therefore] it is known as the [unchanging] soul or self that is cognizant of the nature of primary [matter], subject to various changes.

Then, with regard to the essential nature of primal matter in general, the term "primal matter" (*pradhāna, gtso bo*) is employed as a general term encompassing all twenty-four categories [of reality] distinct from the self. In terms of the dichotomy between sense objects and their subject, it refers to the sense objects, their [three] attributes (*triguṇa, yon tan gsum*), and physical matter. More specifically, primal matter at the causal level (*hetupradhāna, rgyu'i gsto bo*) is identified with nature (*prakṛti, rang bzhin*), the first of the twenty-five categories. It is the circumstance in which the three attributes—motility, dullness, and lightness—are present in a state of equilibrium.

The defining characteristic of these three [attributes] is that [motility] is dynamic and interactive, [dullness] is heavy and obstructive, and [lightness] is light and luminous. This [equilibrium] is said to be an ideal state [of homogeneity] (*prakaraṇa, rab tu byed pa*), because it is [the actual state of] "nature" itself, not subject to modifications or change.

From this primal matter, there [first] originated "intelligence" (*buddhi, blo*), which is designated as "great" (*mahat, chen po*). From that, the threefold ego-principle originated;[1059] and from it there evolved in succession the five quidities or aspects of subtle matter from the modified ego-principle (*vaikārikāhaṃkāra*),[1060] and the five gross elements from those five aspects. Meanwhile, the five motor organs and the five sense organs, along with the single category of the mind (*manas, yid*), which is a faculty shared by both [motor and sense organs], all evolved from the ego-principle imbued with lightness (*sāttvikāhaṃkāra*). As for the ego-principle imbued with dullness (*tāmasikāhaṃkāra*), it interacts with both the other two aspects of the ego-principle.

The [great] intelligence, the ego-principle, and the five aspects of subtle matter all are all modifications when contrasted with the [original and unmodified] nature. On the other hand, from the standpoint of *their* actual modifications, the great intelligence, the ego-principle, and so forth are assigned to the [unmodified] nature, and only the remaining sixteen categories [comprising the five elements, the five sense organs, the five motor organs, and mind] are considered to be [extraneous] modifications.

The "soul" or "cognizant self," being ignorant of the impurity of "nature" which gives rise to [the aforementioned] modifications, then becomes attached through a series of events, and as long as it enjoys or partakes of the sense objects, such as sound, and so forth, it will remain within the cycle of existence. But when it becomes dissatisfied with such enjoyments of the sense objects, through the supernormal cognitive powers associated with meditative concentration (*dhyāna*), it will [directly] behold the impurity of this engagement in "nature" and flee away in shame. Separated from [this involvement], all the modifications produced by nature will be reversed in turn, and dissolve into the reality [of unmodified nature] itself. When the "self" abides in an absolutely radiant state, it is held that it will attain release [from the cycle of existence].

Vaiśeṣika [b']

The Vaiśeṣika are followers of Īśvara
Who hold that within substance and its attributes
All subtypes are subsumed,
And they propound the six categories [of reality]
While being similar to the Naiyāyika
In maintaining four kinds of valid cognition,
Eight aspects of radiant form, and so forth.

Secondly, the Vaiśeṣika (*bye brag pa*) are the followers of the hermit sage Kaṇāda.[1061] They hold that knowable phenomena constitute six categories (*ṣaṭpadārtha, tshig don drug*), namely, (1) substance (*dravya*), which has nine aspects: "self" (*ātma*), time (*kāla*), relative direction (*dik*), space (*ākāśa*), and mind (*manas*), along with the four elements;[1062] (2) "self," which has nine attributes (*ātmanavaguṇa, bdag gi yon tan dgu*), namely, intellect (*buddhi*), happiness (*sukha*), sorrow (*duḥkha*), effort (*yatna*), merit (*dharma*), demerit (*adharma*), velocity (*vega*), [and so forth];[1063] (3) actions (*karma, las*), which are of five sorts: ascending (*'degs*), descending (*'jog*), expanding (*brkyang*), contracting (*bskum*), and moving (*gati*);[1064] (4) universals (*sāmānya, spyi*), which [are characterized as] permeating all particulars;[1065] (5) particulars (*viśeṣa, bye brag*), which differentiate or distinguish object-universals;[1066] and (6) inherence (*samavāya, 'du ba*), which establishes both direct relations and indirect relations between [different] substances.[1067]

The Vaiśeṣika hold that [these phenomenological categories] may be appraised by means of the [aforementioned] three kinds of valid cognition, with the addition of the valid cognition originating from Vedic testimony (*śabdapramāṇa, sgra byung tshad ma*).[1068] They also maintain that as long as the nine attributes are all inherent in the soul, it will remain within the cycle of existence, performing virtuous and non-virtuous actions. However, once the six categories that pertain to the "individual" (*puruṣa, skyes bu*) are known, the nine attributes and their roots will be cut off, leaving the "self" or "soul" alone, whereupon it will be released [from the cycle of existence].

Naiyāyika [c']

Thirdly, the Naiyāyika (*rig pa can pa*) are similar [to the Vaiśeṣika] in holding that there are six phenomenological categories. They also uphold the four kinds of valid cognition, namely, (1) the valid cognition of direct perception, through which objects encountered by the senses are unmistakenly examined; (2–3) the two kinds of inference, which are undertaken for one's own and others' sake; and (4) the valid cognition originating from Vedic testimony, proffering examples which virtually appraise the scriptural testimony [of the Vedas] on the basis of trust.

They hold that if there is an appraisable object, it is implicitly an entity (*bhāva, dngos po*), and they do not accept that it may be a non-entity (*abhāva, dngos med*). In fact, [they enumerate] twelve [different] kinds of entities [or valid objects of knowledge], namely, (1) the "self" (*ātman*); (2) the body; (3) the sense organs; (4) the sense objects; (5) the understanding (*buddhi*); (6) the mind (*manas*); (7) sensory engagement (*pravṛtti, 'jug pa*); (8) defiled emotions (*doṣa, skyon*); (9) rebirth (*bhava, srid pa*); (10) the experience of results in future lives (*aparaphala, phyi ma 'bras bu*); (11) suffering (*duḥkha, sdug bsngal*); and (12) final emancipation (*apavarga, byang grol*).[1069]

Aiśvarya [d']

Fourth, according to the Aiśvarya (*dbang phyug pa*), [almighty] Īśvara is the creator of the world. In order to dispel darkness, [he created] the sun and moon. In order to generate the inanimate world and its living organisms [he created] the five elements; and in order to mature [living beings], [he introduced] sacrificial offerings (*yajña, mchod sbyin*). They also hold that Īśvara emanated in eight distinct forms [Rudra, Bhava, Śarva, Īśāna, Paśupati, Bhīma, Ugra, and Mahādeva],[1070] and that these are endowed respectively with eight [distinct] attributes [or supernormal powers]: (1) subtlety (*sūkṣmatā, phra ba*); (2) agility (*laghutva, yang ba*); (3) worthiness of offering (*pūjya, mchod par 'os pa*); (4) supremacy (*īśitva, bdag por gyur pa*); (5) dominion (*vaśitva, dbang du gyur pa*); (6) the power to move freely and obtain anything (*prāpti, gar yang phyin pa*); (7) irresistible will-power (*prākāmya, 'dod dgur sgyur ba*); and (8) teleportation (*yatrakāmāvasāyitva, dga' mgur gnas pa*).

[By contrast,] they hold that mundane beings have no control over their own actions and so forth, that they should make offerings to Īśvara, and that liberation will be attained, having cultivated a non-symbolic wisdom by relying on sexual union.

The three traditions outlined in this section, starting with the Vaiśeṣika, are all subdivisions, propounding the tenets of the Aiśvarya.

Vaiṣṇava [e']

> **There are also the Vaiṣṇava, originating from the ten incarnations [of Viṣṇu],**
> **The Brāhmaṇa, who uphold valid cognition that accords with the Vedas,**
> **The Aupaniṣadika, who [regard] the underworld and "soul" in a single savor,**
> **And the Vaiyākaraṇa, who [regard] all things as embodiments of sound.**

Fifth, the Vaiṣṇava (*khyab 'jug pa*), according to [authorities] such as [Mahāvīra], teacher of the Nirgrantha Jains, and [the Mīmāṃsaka] Kumārila, claim that the Bhagavān Vāsudeva [i.e., Kṛṣṇa] is the omniscient, all-seeing creator of all living beings, and that he is the conferrer of release [from the cycle of existence]. He himself is also [said to have] exhibited an extraordinary manifest pride, in saying, "I am fire, water, and wind. I am also the [bestower of] food and drink, and the lord of all living creatures. I abide within the physical body of a Brahmin. I am the actor and also the giver!"[1071]

The adherents [of this system] respect the legends composed around the [celebrated] ten incarnations (*daśāvatāra, 'jug pa bcu*) [of Viṣṇu], and they maintain either eternalist or nihilist views.

Now [among the ten incarnations], it is said that (1) Viṣṇu incarnated [first] as Matsya (*nya bo che*), "the great fish," and retrieved the *Four Vedas*, which had sunk into the ocean on account of a primeval [flood]. (2) He then incarnated as Kūrma (*rus sbal*), "the turtle," where he continued to support the world [on his back]. (3) Then, [incarnating] in the form of Varāha (*phag rgod*), "the wild boar," [he assisted by raising] the world realms of Brahmā (*brahmāloka*) [on his tusk] when they had been oppressed [by the demon Hiraṇyakṣa]. (4) Then, having incarnated in the form of Narasiṃha (*mi seng ge'i stod can*), "the man with the torso of a lion," at the time when Asurendra [or Daityendra] had offered sanctuary to living beings, he killed [the demon] Hiraṇyakaśipu with his claws. (5) Then, he incarnated as Vamāna (*mi'i thung*), "the dwarf," and made offerings to the *asura* Bali, whereupon [on being granted a boon] he deceived [the antigod] by taking three strides [to consolidate his celestial, terrestrial, and subterranean dominion] and forced [the demon] underground. (6) Then, he incarnated as the hermit sage Paraśurāma (*dza mā ang'i bu rā ma*), "Rāma with an axe," and [as an act of vengeance] he killed Prince Arjuna among others, and eliminated the princely *kṣatrīya* class. (7) Thereafter, he incarnated as Rāma, son of King Daśaratha, and when his wife Sītā was captured by Daśagrīva, the "ten-headed" [Rāvaṇa, and abducted to Śrī] Laṅkā, charging the [emanational] monkey Hanumant to assist him, he overwhelmed the *rāksaṣa.* (8) Subsequently, he incarnated as Kṛṣṇa (*nag po*) and worked for the benefit of sentient beings during an age of strife.[1072] (9) After incarnating as Buddha Śākyamuni, he offered refuge to all sentient beings, in order to purify his former negative actions [as Paraśurāma] in slaying members of the princely *kṣatrīya* class. (10) In the future, [it is said that] Viṣṇu will also incarnate as Kalkin, the son of a Brahmin of noble family, and after disciplining many sentient beings, he will reverse [the negativity] of that age.[1073]

[The followers of Viṣṇu] also hold that when an aeon [of cyclical time] is destroyed, the hermit sages [who are his devotees] will be preserved within his stomach.

As for the tenets which they espouse, they include eternalism in that [some of them] hold the nature of mind, which they call the "self" (*ātman*) or the sacred Vāsudeva, to be eternal, free from creation and destruction, and to be without duality (*advaita*) in terms of substantial existence and non-existence. Yet they also propound the nihilist view, which may be exemplified by the many verses [in their own scriptures] concerning the view of non-existence, [particularly] at the time when Viṣṇu was [on the verge of] being defeated in battle [with the antigods]; and also by the passages from the *Ornament of the Madhyamaka*, which explain that the view of the Vaiṣṇava is partly in conformity with Madhyamaka.[1074]

In terms of meditation, the Vaiṣṇava engage in the yoga of the six branches (*ṣaḍaṅgayoga*) and so forth.[1075]

Moreover, their subdivisions include the Mīmāṃsaka (*spyod pa po*), the

Vaidika (*rig byed pa*), the Vaiyākaraṇa (*brda sprod pa*), the Cāraka (*tsa ra ka pa*), and the Aupaniṣadika (*gsang ba pa*).[1076]

Brāhmaṇa [f']

Sixth, there are the Brāhmaṇa (*tshangs pa ba*), who maintain that the Vedas are eternal, and not created because they are the recollections of Brahmā, and as such they represent a valid form of cognition [in their own right]. They hold that those who die in battle will be reborn in exalted realms, that negative actions can be cancelled out by bathing in [sacred rivers] such as the Ganges, and that the whole world and its living organisms were created by Brahmā. The hermit sages and the Brahmins are also regarded as the children of Brahmā (*brahmaputra*).[1077]

Vedāntaupaniṣadika [g']

Seventh, there are the Vedāntaupaniṣadika (*rigs byed kyi mtha' gsang ba pa*), who hold that there is a [shining] immortal person (*amṛtamayapuruṣa, 'chi med bdud rtsi'i skyes bu*)[1078] submerged within the maṇḍala of terrestrial darkness (*pṛthivītalatamomaṇḍala*), in which the eternal "self" (*ātman*), "consciousness" (*cit*), and "being" (*sat, dam pa*) are all gathered together as a single entity, in the manner of space, and that both the container world and living beings originated through its modifications.

According to Vedānta, when all phenomena are seen to be illusory, at that time, by cultivating the view concerning the creator "self" (*kartṛkapuruṣa, byed pa po'i skyes bu*), they hold that one will awaken from darkness, and, perceiving [all things] as golden [light], one will then be liberated by merging with [the immortal person or *brahman*] in a single savor, and so forth.

Vaiyākaraṇa [h']

Eighth, there are the Vaiyākaraṇa or grammarians (*brda sprod pa*), such as Bhartṛhari,[1079] who hold that although the valid cognition of direct perception and inference ostensibly exist, they are not definitive, and that the foundations of all knowledge are the treatises on Sanskrit grammar, while the Vedas offer genuine valid cognition. All phenomena are embodiments of sound, and the ultimate among all sounds is the syllable OṂ, which is the pure source (*brahman, tshangs pa*) of sound, free from creation, destruction, and preservation, and entirely without relative direction. Although this [sound] is eternal and unchanging, it has become sullied by ignorance and consequently appears as form. But when this apparitional aspect is reversed, the pure source of non-apparitional sound is realized to be immortal.

Mīmāṃsaka [i']

There are the followers of Jaiminī,
Who maintain twelve defining characteristics and so forth,
The followers of Caraka, who maintain there are eight kinds of valid cognition,
And the Nirgrantha Jains, who propound the ten objects of knowledge and so forth.
All of these are merely on the path to the exalted realms,
But they are to be rejected
Because [the attainment of] release [from the cycle of existence]
Is obscured by their views of the "self."

Ninth, the [Mīmāṃsaka] followers of Jaiminī (rGyal dpogs pa) uphold the following twelve [defining characteristics that apply to ritual sacrifices], namely, (1) the validity or authority [of Vedic ritual and tradition] (*pramāṇa, tshad ma*); (2) the general [rules on lack of precedence and improper implementation of rites] (*sāmānya, spyi*); (3) the particular [rules on the context and sense of specific passages] (*viśeṣa, bye brag*); (4) the impact [of general and particular rules on other ritual practices] (*prayojana, dgos pa*); (5) the relative sequence [of the stages of ritual practices and the passages of their texts] (*anukrama, go rim*); (6) the basic [obligations and prescriptions regarding officiating priests and ritual materials] (*adhikaraṇa, gnas gzhi*); (7) the general prescriptions [concerning the transfer from one rite to another based on the direct injunctions of the Vedic texts] (*sāmānyanirdeśa, spyi nges bstan*); (8) the specific prescriptions [concerning the transfer from one rite to another based on overt or covert signs] (*viśeṣanirdeśa, bye brag nges bstan*); (9) the discussion [on the adaptation of Vedic hymns, *sāman*, and mantra] (*ālāpa, gleng ba*); (10) the debate [concerning the preclusion of secondary rites] (*vivāda, rtsod pa*); (11) the continuous [performance of several autonomous rites in sequence] (*svatantra, rang rgyud*); and (12) the contiguity [between primary and secondary rites] (*prasaṅga, thal 'gyur*).[1080]

As for valid cognition, they accept the following six modes: direct perception, inference, scriptural testimony, comparison (*upamāna, nyer 'jal*), presumption (*arthāpātti, don gyis go ba*), and absence or non-entity (*abhāva, dngos med*).[1081] They also propound [the ideas] that since the "self" (*ātman*) is the progenitor of the psycho-physical constituents, permanence is a condition of mankind (*mānava, shed las skyes*); that impurity is a condition of the nature of mind; and that once it has expired, release [from the cycle of existence] will occur.

Cāraka [j']

Tenth, the Cāraka or followers of Caraka are largely similar to the Mīmāṃsaka. In terms of the aforementioned [six modes of] valid cognition, they maintain that objects may be appraised by means of eight categories [of valid cognition] because they also differentiate between inferences that refer to the past, present, and future.[1082]

Nirgrantha Jains [k']

Eleventh, the Nirgrantha Jains (*gcer bu pa*) hold that knowable phenomena comprise nine categories (*navapadārtha, tshig don dgu*), or ten with the addition of "self" (*ātman*). Included among them are the three modes of valid cognition: direct perception, inference, and scriptural authority.[1083]

They also hold that there are nine types of animate substance (*navajīva, srog ldan dgu*), and that since earth and other [such elements] are living organisms, the construction of monastic gardens (*ārāma, kun dga' ra ba*) and so forth is a causal basis of negativity.

Jains revere the hermit sage Vardhamāna Mahāvīra (rGyal ba dam pa) as a god, and follow the [tradition of] the twenty-five Jain mendicant teachers (*kṣapaṇaka, zad byed pa*),[1084] beginning with Ṛṣabha (Khyu mchog), Ajita (sNod kyi rje) and so forth.

They hold that by subjecting the physical body to austerities (*tapas, dka' thub*), the knots that bind the mind are destroyed, and they are known to possess about three hundred and sixty-three modes of ascetic discipline (*vrata, brtul zhugs*), including the control of the three "staffs" [of body, speech, and mind] (*tridaṇḍin, dbyu gu gsum pa*) and the "possession of only a tree" (*palāśin, lo ma can*).[1085]

The objects that may be appraised by means of the three modes of valid cognition, including the three times, the six substances, the nine categories, and the nine animate substances, are all [considered as] the ground, [when analyzed] in terms of ground, path, and result.

Here, the three times include the past and so forth. The six substances (*ṣaḍ-dravya, rdzas drug*) include animate substances (*jīva, srog ldan*), matter (*pudgala, gang zag*), time (*kāla, dus*), space (*ākāśa, nam mkha'*), merit (*puṇya, bsod nams*), and negativity (*pāpa, sdig pa*).

In particular, as far as the nine categories and nine animate substances are concerned, the hermit sage Jina [Mahāvīra] has explained:[1086]

> Animate substances (*jīva, srog ldan*), inanimate substances (*ajīva, zag pa*),
> And commitments (*saṃvara, sdom pa*),
> Rejuvenation (*nirjara, nges par dga'*), bondage (*bandha, 'ching*),
> And deeds (*karma, las*),
> Negative acts (*pāpa, sdig pa*), merits (*puṇya, bsod nams*),
> And release (*mokṣa, thar pa*)—
> These are held to be the nine categories [of knowable phenomena].
> As for animate substances, they [also] have nine classes:
> [The elementary life-forms of] earth, water, wood, fire, and wind,
> As well as [the four classes of living creatures, namely,]
> Animalcules, ants, bees, and human beings,[1087]
> Which possess anything from one up to five sense faculties.[1088]

The path [followed by the Nirgrantha Jains] entails the observance of controlled actions (*saṃvara*), the minor vows of ascetic restraint (*aṇuvrata*), and the cultivation of knowledge (*jñāna, ye shes*), each of which has five aspects, as well as the thirteen modes of conduct (*pratimā, spyod pa bcu gsum*) and various austerities (*tapas*) designed to terminate [the impact of] past actions (*karma, las*).[1089]

The result or fruit [of the practice] is that, on bringing an end to [the impact of] past actions, the animate abode known as the "aggregate of worlds" (*lokasaṃgraha, 'jig rten 'dus pa*) will still remain, present at the summit of the three world systems (*tridhātu*), and therefore, although one has been released from material forms and cyclic existence, the release [that is attained] will be immaterial but still a positive state of being, pure, and resembling an upturned parasol, fragrantly scented and pleasant, extending to a distance of four million five hundred thousand fathoms (*yojana, dpag tshad*).[1090]

Conclusion [I']

These different traditions have their own scriptures which [seek to] refute [the view and practice of] Buddhism, establishing their respective frameworks for the ground, path, and result, [applying] reason to analyze objects of appraisal, rejecting [the teachings of] the omniscient Buddha, and so forth. Although they have many [different] views and modes of conduct, [they have been summarized as follows] in the *Exposition of Valid Cognition*:[1091]

> Those who propound the Vedas as authoritative,
> Who speak mistakenly [of an eternal "self"],
> Who seek the [sacred] teachings through physical [ablutions],
> Who speak of class [distinctions],[1092]
> And say they have to engage in ascetic mortification
> In order to overcome arrogance and negativity,
> All of them represent the fivefold reasoning of foolish persons,
> Chattering about discriminative awareness!

Among them, there are [spiritual and philosophical systems] that form a view concerning future [lives and] worlds, while engaging in practices that reject negative actions and adopt positive actions, but they are merely focused on the pathway of the exalted realms. Indeed, since these are all similar in maintaining the [mistaken] view of the "self," beginners engaging in Buddhist practice should reject them, giving them a wide berth, so that they might eliminate, in particular, the obscurations covering the path that [actually] leads to release [from cyclic existence].

Barbarous Views [iii]

The third part [of the detailed exegesis of non-Buddhist schools] incidentally concerns other distinctive teachings espoused by barbarians (*mleccha*, *kla klo*) and so forth, which are to be rejected.

> **There are also barbarians,**
> **Who claim harmful or violent acts as their sacred teaching,**
> **Including those in Tibet and China,**
> **Who are beyond the pale in terms of the [Buddhist] scriptures.**
> **All of them should be rejected and given a wide berth.**

Furthermore, there are also extremists and others in conformity with them who are not included within the Brāhmaṇical and Buddhist traditions, who consider the three precious jewels to be heretical, and so forth.[1093] And there are also the most debased of all the extremists who hold harmful or violent acts as their sacred teaching. [For example,] in West India there are the followers of the god Rahman from the country of Mecca (*ma kha*), who are also known as the Mughals or "barbarous Tajiks."[1094] They eat the flesh of cattle, having slit their throats with knives charmed by the spell of Bismillah, and, on account of their own karma, they do not eat the flesh of a creature that has died [naturally].

Then, there are also those who maintain ascetic disciplines [pertaining to diet] such as drinking only the [raw] eggs of a hen—nowadays these traditions are prevalent exclusively in India.

Among those upholding [other] purported philosophical systems that are said to confer liberation from cyclic existence, there are some in the aboriginal borderlands who claim that killing many living creatures is a means of attaining release [from the cycle].

Then, among adherents of the [Ājīvaka] school, the so-called teaching of Maskarī Gośālaputra,[1095] there were also those who held that by piercing ants in a golden bowl with a golden needle they would still be liberated from cyclic existence.[1096] Then again, there are some worldly folk who hold that if one repeats the names of the five Pāṇḍava [brothers], one will obtain great merit.[1097]

In Tibet also, there are the followers of Bon who do not uphold the act of taking refuge in the three precious jewels, and among them, in particular, there are [adherents of] the original Bon (*rgyu'i bon*) widespread in some districts in ancient times and even nowadays [to a limited extent], who adopt harmful or violent acts as their sacred teachings.[1098]

Then, in China, there is the [Daoist] tradition associated with [Princess] Jincheng (Gyim shang), which asserts that the entire world originated from a great golden turtle, and those upholding the views and practices espoused by numerologists (*grangs can pa*) and Confucius (Khong spu tse).[1099] Including them, all those who assert eternalist and nihilist views, and claim harmful or violent acts as their sacred teachings, are beyond the pale in terms of the Buddhist scriptures; all of them should be treated circumspectly, rejected and given a wide berth by those who [genuinely] seek release [from cyclic existence].

In general, with regard to [the distinction between] impure and pure textual traditions, one should know that these are differentiated on the basis of whether or not they emphasize the extraordinary appreciation of great compassion (*mahākaruṇā*) or skillful means (*upāya*), and the abiding nature of reality (*gnas lugs kyi don*), which is discriminative awareness.

13. The Exalted Vehicle

3. Systematic Presentation of the Exalted Vehicle [III.C.3]
  a. Brief Introduction
  b. Detailed Explanation of the Exalted Realms
    i. The Common Preliminaries
    ii. The Vehicle of Gods and Humans
    iii. The Vehicle of Brahmā
      aa. Recognition of This Vehicle
      bb. Exegesis of the Actual Path
        1' The World-Systems of Form and the Four Meditative Concentrations
          a' Brief Introduction
          b' Detailed Explanation
            i' The Causal Phase of Meditative Concentration
              aa' The First Meditative Concentration
                1" Preparation
                  a" Calm Abiding
                  b" Higher Insight
                2" Actual Foundation
              bb' The Second Meditative Concentration
                1" Preparation
                2" Actual Foundation
              cc' The Third Meditative Concentration
                1" Preparation
                2" Actual Foundation
              dd' The Fourth Meditative Concentration
                1" Preparation
                2" Actual Foundation
            ii' The Fruitional Phase

SYSTEMATIC PRESENTATION OF THE EXALTED VEHICLE [3]

The latter [aspect of the classification of mundane spiritual paths; see p. 398] is the extensive exegesis of the exalted vehicle (*abhyudayayāna, mngon mtho'i theg pa*) [which may be advantageously pursued by gods and humans]. This has three parts: a brief presentation, a detailed explanation, and a synopsis.

BRIEF INTRODUCTION [a]

First, concerning the brief presentation [it says in the root verses]:

> **The god [realms] and the [worlds of] Brahmā**
> **Are within [reach of] the exalted vehicle.**

In general, the exalted realms (*abhyudaya, mngon mtho*) and the level of definitive excellence (*niḥśreyasa, nges legs kyi go 'phang*)[1100] are the objectives to be attained by intelligent beings. The defining characteristics of these are, respectively, (1) the immediate release from the sufferings [of rebirth] in the three inferior realms, accruing the happiness of gods and humans through the ripening [of virtuous past actions] in conformity with their [appropriate] causes; and (2) the release passing beyond sorrow and into nirvāṇa, which is a perpetual liberation from the sufferings of all [classes of beings] within cyclic existence.

With regard to these two [goals], initially one has to become secure in the vehicle of the exalted realms, and then subsequently one should attain the conclusive path of definitive excellence. It says in the *Precious Garland*:[1101]

> First there are the teachings of the exalted [vehicle],
> And subsequently the [level of] definitive excellence will emerge.
> For this reason, having attained the exalted [realms],

One should successively [attain] definitive excellence.
We hold that the exalted [realms are states] of happiness,
While definitive excellence is release [from cyclic existence].

Among them, the vehicle of the exalted realms which is first to be attained comprises both the vehicle of gods and humans (*devamanuṣyayāna, lha mi'i theg pa*) and the vehicle of Brahmā (*brahmāyāna, tshangs pa'i theg pa*).

Detailed Explanation of the Exalted Realms [b]

Secondly, the detailed explanation has three parts: (1) an explanation of the common preliminaries, followed by the distinctive explanations of (2) the vehicle of gods, and (3) the vehicle of Brahmā.[1102]

The Common Preliminaries [i]

Concerning the first [it says in the root verses]:

Among the three kinds of faith,
Which are the prerequisites[1103] of all [spiritual paths],
It is through the conviction that [the impact of] past actions
Is of primary importance, and so forth,
And through the four correct ways of progressing [on the path]...

The teaching presented in this section is preliminary, to be actually undertaken before engaging in the vehicle of the exalted realms. Yet, as if to supplement [the main instructions] by way of incidental commentary, it says in the *Precious Garland*:[1104]

When the means of attaining this [path] are abbreviated,
They comprise faith and discriminative awareness.
In order to acquire faith,
One should consult the [sacred] teachings,
And in order to acquire discriminative awareness,
One should [cultivate] genuine awareness.
The most important of these two is discriminative awareness,
But it should be preceded by faith.

Accordingly, the foremost of all the means of attaining both the exalted realms and the definitive excellence are faith and discriminative awareness. This is because [in the case of the exalted realms], when one is motivated principally by the faith born of conviction in the results of past actions, among the three kinds of faith, one can effectively adopt virtuous actions and reject negative actions. Also, it is because [in the case of the attainment of definitive excellence,] the roots of cyclic existence are severed by means of discriminative awareness that is non-discursive with respect to the three spheres [of subject, object, and their interaction].

The defining characteristics of these two [prerequisites] are, respectively, that (1) faith reverses, without any special reason, the four erroneous ways of progressing [on the spiritual path], namely, (a) progressing with attachment to one's own affairs, (b) with aversion for others, (c) with delusion in respect of what should be adopted and rejected, and (d) with fear of officialdom and so forth. Consequently, [with faith,] one will not transgress the things that should be [properly] accepted and rejected by means of the four correct ways of progressing [on the path]. (2) Discriminative awareness engages body, speech, and mind while being non-discursive with respect to the three spheres [of subject, object, and their interaction], whether one possesses or lacks the great compassion that emphasizes the well-being of others.

Accordingly, it says in the same source:[1105]

> A faithful person is one who does not transgress the [sacred]
> teachings
> Through attachment, aversion, fear, and delusion—
> That one is a supremely excellent recipient [of the teachings].
> Discriminative awareness is that which knows
> And always engages in actions of body, speech, and mind,
> Which are beneficial to both self and others,
> Without being discursive with respect to the three spheres.

Therefore, as one should generally know, it is said that if one is not motivated by [genuine] faith, one will not progress [effectively] towards [engagement in] even a modicum of virtuous activity. Equally, if one does not realize selflessness [with respect to individual persons and phenomena] through discriminative awareness that is non-discursive with respect to the three spheres [of subject, object, and their interaction], one will never progress on the path that leads to release [from cyclic existence].

This being the case, the prerequisites of all those who would enter upon the vehicle of [any spiritual] path are the three kinds of faith.[1106] When, among these, one is motivated mainly by the faith born of conviction in the results of past actions, [it is clear that] the attainment of virtuous actions by means of the four correct ways of progressing [on the path] will itself be preliminary to engaging in the vehicle of the exalted realms.

THE VEHICLE OF GODS AND HUMANS [ii]

Concerning the second, [it says in the root verses]:

> **...That the ten non-virtuous actions are abandoned,**
> **While the ten virtuous actions and their peripheral acts are adopted.**
> **In this way, laws are maintained concerning [conduct] to be rejected and accepted,**
> **While confused [virtuous and non-virtuous actions]**
> **And disharmonious [goals] are abandoned.**
> **Those who perfect the path of [virtuous] actions**
> **And are disciplined [in respect of their vows]**
> **Will, in the higher reams, attain excellent results,**
> **Mastering the ripening fruits that conform to their causes.**

The mundane vehicle of gods and humans is the means of attaining an exalted physical form through fear of [rebirth in] the inferior realms (*durgati, ngan song*) and by striving for the result of happiness, which is associated with the higher realms (*svarga, mtho ris*).[1107] This is the [spiritual] path suited for persons of inferior ability, which relies on protection from fear and auspicious aspirational prayers. It is the path influenced by [the impact of] past actions, which is in conformity with [the practice of] the ten virtuous actions (*daśakuśala, dge ba bcu*) but which is not yet apprehended by means of meditative concentration (*dhyāna, bsam gtan*)—the actual attainment of experiential cultivation.

Since there are no [higher] vehicles that do not engage in [the basic virtuous practices associated with] this [vehicle], it is [regarded as] the foundation of all vehicles and precedes them all. As it is said in the *Tantra of Hevajra*:[1108]

> Having commenced from the ten virtues
> His teachings are disclosed.

It is said in the *Sūtra of the Descent to Laṅkā* that this [vehicle] is called the "vehicle of the gods" (*devayāna*) with reference to the foremost [levels of the world system of desire] which are to be traversed [through it], but, in respect of its peripheral [attainments], it also encompasses all the [lower] paths that progress to the happiness [of humans], experienced in the [world system of] desire (*kāma*[*dhātu*]).[1109]

With regard to this [vehicle], the view (*lta ba*) is [deemed to be] correct in its convictions that there are other worlds and that past actions do have causes and results. Conduct (*spyod pa*) requires an uninterrupted familiarity with practices in which the ten non-virtuous actions are renounced and the path of the ten virtuous and peripheral actions is pursued. Thereby, as a result (*'bras bu*), one will traverse [the various realms of the world-system of desire], as far as the Paranirmitavaśavartin realm, experiencing the conclusive happiness of the human beings of the four continents and the six species of Kāma divinities.[1110]

[At the outset] it is important for followers of this [vehicle] to retain the authentic worldly view, which functions as an antidote for the wrong view that past actions have no result, and so forth. For this reason, it says in the *Letter to a Friend*:[1111]

> If one espouses the release associated with the higher realms,
> One should cultivate familiarity with the correct view.
> Even though an individual may have practiced well,
> With a wrong view, all that matures will be unbearable.

Thereafter, it will be important for them to maintain the ethical discipline (*śīla*, *tshul khrims*) which does not confuse the things that are to be rejected and those that are to be accepted. For this reason, it says in the *Four Hundred Verses* (*Catuḥśataka*):[1112]

> Through ethical discipline,
> Progress towards happiness will be attained.

And in the *Introduction* [*to Madhyamaka*]:[1113]

> Apart from ethical discipline,
> There is no other cause of [rebirth in] the exalted realms.

If the ethical discipline associated with this vehicle is analyzed to some extent, it generally requires that, motivated by modesty and decency, one should train oneself in the three modes of conduct (*spyod pa gsum*) that are in conformity with principled physical and verbal behavior. On these, it says in the *Treatise on Behavior entitled Holy Ornament*:[1114]

> To honor well those who are worthy of reverence,
> To be especially benevolent to those who are unprotected,
> And not to forget to repay kindness
> Are [the modes of] conduct of saintly persons.

One should also train oneself, more specifically, in the sixteen [commonly accepted] human laws, which are explained as follows in the *Short Chapter on Discrimination*:[1115]

> One should develop faith in the three precious jewels without sorrow or weariness; search ultimately for the sacred teachings; skillfully study the excellent sciences; and first recollect and then appraise anything that is to be undertaken. One should not hanker after unassigned work; but one should look to a higher level and emulate the ancients and those of superior conduct; repay kindness to one's parents of the past, present, and future; be broad-minded and hospitable in one's dealings with elder and younger siblings and paternal relatives; ensure that the young respect their elders by degrees; show loving-kindness to one's neighbors; arduously assist one's acquaintances who are spiritual advisors (*dge bshes*); perfectly fulfill the needs of those nearby who are connected through the worldly round; help others through one's skill in science and the arts; provide a refuge with kindness to those who depend upon it; resist bad advice and establish advice which will increase the happiness of the country; and, entrusting the goals of one's past actions to the [sacred] teachings, one should bring one's spouse to obtain the ground of enlightenment in future lives.

Therefore, one should train oneself in the pure behavior which accords with these [sixteen] human laws.

In particular, as previously mentioned, one should abandon, both directly and indirectly, the ten kinds of non-virtuous actions, such as killing, and adopt to the best of one's ability the ten virtuous actions, which include saving lives, charity, and so forth.

Among the [various nuances of] this view, meditation, and conduct, the lowest are those who engage in confused [virtuous and non-virtuous] actions, where the parameters [of the actions] that propel [sentient beings into subsequent rebirths] and those that fulfill [the diverse positive and negative experiences of the present lifetime] are in a state of disharmony.[1116] The average or mediocre sort are those who fulfill the path of virtuous actions [in the present lifetime], and the superior sort are those disciplined in the essential nature of the vows that regulate the ten virtuous actions and cyclic existence.

When [such beings] are born in the exalted realms, by mastering the fully ripened effects [of past actions] and effects that conform to their causes, they will consequently obtain excellent results that are respectively inferior, average, and superior.[1117]

The Vehicle of Brahmā [iii]

Concerning the third topic [the vehicle of Brahmā], there are two parts: recognizing [the nature of] this vehicle and an exegesis of its actual path.

Recognition of This Vehicle [aa]

The former [comments on the root verse]:

> **The vehicle of Brahmā is that which traverses the higher world systems.**

If one were to ask why this [vehicle] is called ["the vehicle of Brahmā"], the term "Brahmā" (*tshangs pa*) suggests a state of cleanliness or purity, [free] from the dissonant mental states of desire and attachment, while the term "vehicle" (*yāna, theg pa*) designates the means by which that state is reached. Therefore, with reference to the wide range of the term, as explained by Ārya Vimuktisena, everything subsumed within the levels of the two higher world-systems [of form and formlessness] is designated by the term "Brahmā"; while the path that traverses and reaches that [goal] along with its peripheral [activities] is called the "the vehicle of Brahmā."[1118]

Exegesis of the Actual Path [bb]

The latter has two parts: an exegesis of the four meditative concentrations associated with the world-system of form (*gzugs khams kyi bsam gtan bzhi*), and an exegesis of the four meditative absorptions associated with the world-system of formlessness (*gzugs med khams kyi snyoms 'jug bzhi*).

The World-Systems of Form and the Four Meditative Concentrations [1']

The first of these includes both a brief introduction and a detailed explanation.

Brief Introduction [a']

The brief introduction [comments on the root verse]:

> **The four meditative concentrations associated with the world-system of form**
> **Have both causal and fruitional phases.**

The world-system of form (*rūpadhātu*, *gzugs khams*) comprises [the realms attained through] the first meditative concentration (*prathamadhyāna*, *bsam gtan dang po*), the second meditative concentration (*dvitīyadhyāna*, *bsam gtan gnyis pa*), the third meditative concentration (*tṛtīyadhyāna*, *bsam gtan gsum pa*), and the fourth meditative concentration (*caturthadhyāna*, *bsam gtan bzhi pa*). Each of these has both causal and fruitional aspects.[1119]

Detailed Explanation [b']

The detailed explanation has four parts, corresponding to the meditative concentrations, from the first to the fourth. The causal phase of the practice, comprising meditative concentration on the absorptions (*rgyu snyoms 'jug gi bsam gtan*), will be described first, and this will then be followed by the corresponding fruitional meditative concentrations (*'bras bu skye ba'i bsam gtan*).

The Causal Phase of Meditative Concentration [i']

With regard to the causal phase, the four meditative concentrations will be described in turn.

The First Meditative Concentration [aa']

The first [meditative concentration] entails both preparation (*sāmantaka, nyer bsdogs*) and actual foundation (*maula, dngos gzhi*).

Preparation [1"]

The preparation includes both calm abiding (*śamatha, gzhi gnas*) and higher insight (*vipaśyanā, lhag mthong*).

Calm Abiding [a"]

Concerning [calm abiding, it says in the root verses]:

> **In the causal phase [of the first meditative concentration],**
> **Preparation entails the meditative stability of calm abiding,**
> **In which physical and mental refinement occurs,**
> **By means of the nine techniques [for settling the mind],**
> **Namely, placement, perpetual placement, integrated placement, intensified placement,**
> **Control, calmness, quiescence, one-pointedness, and meditative equipoise.**

As a technique enabling one to engage in meditative absorption during the actual phase [of attainment] through which the fruit of meditative concentration will be obtained, right here and now, it is said that one should first master the causal phase [of this practice]. To that end, the preparation entails the attainment of meditative stability (*samādhi, ting nge 'dzin*) by means of the nine techniques of mental calm abiding (*śamathanavakārayacittasthiti, sems zhi bar gnas pa'i thabs dgu*).[1120]

These [nine techniques] are as follows:

(1) Mental placement (*cittasthāpanā, sems 'jog pa*). This is the placement that focuses the mind on an image or referential object within the scope of meditative stability, such as a [divine] icon with a luster resembling that of gold, without permitting the mind to wander externally.

(2) Perpetual placement (*saṃsthāpana, rgyun 'jog*). Here, the mind is not only focused upon its object, but the placement is continued without interruption for even an instant.

(3) Integrated placement (*avasthāpanā, bslan 'jog*). Here, even when the

mind is distracted elsewhere from its object, it is immediately drawn back and refocused.

(4) Intensified placement (*upasthāpanā, nye bar 'jog pa*). Here, the mind is intensely focused inwardly upon its object, without allowing it to settle [elsewhere], for as long as it is distracted.

(5) Control (*damana, 'dul ba*). This is the process through which the thoroughly disturbed streams of conscious thought caused by dissonant mental states such as greed are properly controlled.

(6) Calmness (*śamana, zhi ba*). Here, the waves of non-discursive mental states are becalmed.

(7) Quiescence (*vyupaśamana, rnam zhi*). Here, even the most subtle conceptual thoughts are again calmed.

(8) One-pointedness (*ekotīkaraṇa, rtse gcig*). Here, the mind focuses one-pointedly and without differentiation upon its object, with minimal effort.

(9) Meditative equipoise (*samasaṃsthāpa, mnyam bzhag*). Here, the mind is equipoised in a state of spontaneous presence, without effort, having dispelled all mental dullness and agitation.[1121]

When meditative stability is attained by means of these nine [techniques], it is implicit that one will be transported to a state of happiness, characterized by both physical and mental refinement (*praśrabdhi, shin tu sbyangs pa*).[1122]

One who develops meditative stability endowed with refinement characteristically focuses on the calm abiding associated with the mundane [realms], but when [one's meditative stability] lacks this refinement, [the aspirational experience] is known as the "level of conduct brought about through resolve in accord with calm abiding" (*śamathānulobhādhimukticaryābhūmi, zhi gnas rjes mthun pa'i mos pas spyod pa'i sa*).[1123]

Higher Insight [b"]

Concerning the second part [of the preparation, the cultivation of higher insight (*vipaśyana, lhag mthong*), it says in the root verses]:

Having accomplished [calm abiding],
Then, through the six kinds of attention—
Namely, defining characteristics, resolve, isolation,
Encompassing joy, scrutiny, and perfected application,
One will accomplish the higher insight,
Of attention to the fruit of perfected application.

These coarse and quiescent aspects [of higher insight] constitute the common mundane path.

Having accomplished the defining characteristics of calm abiding, one should then focus on the six modes of attention (*ṣaḍmanaskāra, yid la byed pa drug*) [associated with higher insight],[1124] which are defined as follows:

(1) The attention that is aware of individual characteristics (*lakṣaṇa-pratisaṃvedanāmanaskāra, mtshan nyid rab tu rig pa yid la byed pa*)[1125] implies that those for whom the [world system of] desire is defective and for whom the first meditative concentration [is appealing because it] is endowed with positive attributes, engage coarsely in ideation and subtly in scrutiny, by means of study and reflection combined.

(2) The attention that arises through resolve (*ādhimokṣikamanaskāra, mos pa las byung ba yid la byed pa*) implies that they generate the [same] essential nature that [also] arises in the course of meditation (*sgom byung gi ngo bor skyes pa*).

(3) The attention that arises through isolation (*prāvivekyamanaskāra, dben pa las skyes pa'i yid la byed pa*) implies that they are isolated from the three great kinds of overt dissonant mental states associated with the world system of desire.[1126]

(4) The attention imbued with encompassing joy (*ratisaṃgrāhakamanaskāra, dga' ba sdud ba yid la byed pa*) implies that they have also renounced the three middling kinds of overt dissonant mental states associated with the world system of desire.

(5) The attention that is imbued with scrutiny (*mīmāṃsāmanaskāra, dpyod pa yid la byed pa*) implies that they continue to engage in ideation and scrutiny whether their minds are covered or uncovered by the three subtle kinds of overt dissonant mental states associated with the world system of desire.

(6) The attention that is imbued with perfected application (*prayoganiṣṭhamanaskāra, sbyor ba'i mtha' yid la byed pa*) implies that they have renounced by means of the [appropriate] antidote even the subtlest and minute traces of overt dissonant mental states associated with the world system of desire, which derive from that [aforementioned] scrutiny.[1127]

Through these six kinds of attention, one will then accomplish the conclusive higher insight attainable by mundane beings, which is called "attention to the fruit of perfected application" (*prayogeṣṭhāphalamanaskāra, sbyor ba'i mtha'i 'bras bu yid la byed pa*).

These forms of [higher insight] have both coarse and quiescent aspects—in that beings of the lower levels whose meditative stability is defective coarsely inspect [their objects], while those of the higher levels who are without such defects inspect [their objects] in a state of quiescence. As such, [these modes of higher insight] are the manifest realizations of the spiritual paths that are commonly pursued in the [diverse] vehicles of pious attendants, hermit buddhas, and mundane [gods and humans] (*laukika, 'jig rten pa*).[1128]

Actual Foundation [2"]

Next, there is the explanation of the actual foundation [of the first meditative concentration] [on which the root verses say]:

> **The actual foundation of the first meditative concentration has five aspects:**
> **Ideation, scrutiny, joy, bliss, and one-pointed mind.**

The actual foundation of meditative concentration will be achieved through those [aforementioned] preparations [of calm abiding and higher insight]. Now, the defining characteristics of the first meditative concentration are that it is endowed with the following five aspects: (1) ideation (*vitarka, rtog pa*), (2) scrutiny (*vicāra, dpyod pa*), (3) joy (*prīti, dga' ba*), (4) bliss (*sukha, bde ba*), and (5) one-pointed mind (*cittaikāgratā, sems rtse gcig pa*).

Among them, when [one's meditative concentration] possesses both ideation and scrutiny, this is [known as] the "ordinary actual foundation" (*dngos gzhi tsam po*), and when it possesses scrutiny but no ideation, this is [known as] the "extraordinary actual foundation" (*dngos gzhi khyad par can*).[1129]

The Second Meditative Concentration [bb']

The second [meditative concentration] also entails both preparation and actual foundation.

Preparation [1"]

Concerning the former [it says in the root verses]:

Those for whom the first [meditative concentration]
Is defective and the second without defect
Then [focus on the causal phase of the second meditative concentration].
Here, the extraordinary preparation entails [cultivation of]
The attention that is aware of individual characteristics [and so forth].

Having established the extraordinary actual foundation of the first meditative concentration as a base, those for whom the first [meditative concentration] is still defective and the second appealing because it is endowed with positive attributes and without defect should meditate by means of the six [aforementioned] kinds of attention, starting with the attention that is aware of individual characteristics, while applying [in particular] the higher insight endowed with scrutiny (*vicāravipaśyanā, dpyod pa'i lhag mthong*).

Consequently, when one has cultivated both calm abiding and higher insight in an integrated manner, the actual attainment of the second meditative concentration may be obtained. This is also [known as] the extraordinary aspect of preparation.

Actual Foundation [2"]

Concerning the latter [the actual foundation, it says in the root verses]:

The actual foundation [of this second meditative concentration]
Has four aspects, starting with intense inner clarity.

The actual foundation of the second [meditative concentration] has four [aspects], starting with intense inner clarity (*adhyātmasamprasāda, rab tu dang ba*). [Altogether,] these comprise (1) the antidotal aspect (*pratipakṣāṅga, gnyen po'i yan lag*), which is intense inner clarity; (2–3) the two beneficial aspects (*anuśaṃsāṅga, phan yon gyi yan lag*) of joy and bliss which arise from meditative stability (*samādhijaprītisukhā, ting nge 'dzin las skyes pa'i dga' bde*); and (4) the aspect of abiding in meditative stability (*samādhisthāṅga, ting nge 'dzin gnas kyi yan lag*).

Among them, intense inner clarity activates three [subsidiary aspects] with regard to the present moment, right here and now, namely, (1) mindfulness or recollection (*smṛti, dran pa*), (2) alertness (*samprajanya, shes bzhin*), and

(3) equanimity (*upekṣā, btang snyoms*). It is called "intense inner clarity" because [in this state] internal ideation (*vitarka, rtog pa*) has been thoroughly abandoned.[1130]

The Third Meditative Concentration [cc']

The third [meditative concentration] similarly entails both preparation and actual foundation.

Preparation [1"]

Concerning the former [it says in the root verses]:

> **Similarly, the third [meditative concentration] will ensue**
> **When preparation entails progressive scrutiny,**
> **By means of the higher insight endowed with attention.**

Similarly, by means of the preparations comprising the mental focus (*cittasthiti*) [of calm abiding] and the higher insight endowed with attention (*manaskāra*) and scrutiny, the mode of scrutiny will become progressively more sublime. In this way, it is said that "the third and fourth meditative concentrations will be achieved." Although, according to the root verses, the third and the fourth [meditative concentrations] may be explained in conjunction, here, to facilitate understanding, they will be described individually.

Those who have achieved the extraordinary calm abiding of the second meditative concentration, and for whom the second meditative concentration is still defective and the third appealing because it is endowed with positive attributes, should meditate by means of the six [aforementioned] kinds of attention, applying [in particular] the higher insight endowed with scrutiny.

Consequently, when both calm abiding and higher insight have been cultivated in an integrated manner, the actual attainment of the third meditative concentration may be obtained.

Actual Foundation [2"]

Concerning the latter [the actual foundation, it says in the root verses]:

> **[Its actual foundation] has five aspects, starting with recollection.**

The actual foundation of the third [meditative concentration] has five aspects, namely, (1–3) the three antidotal aspects comprising recollection, alertness, and equanimity; (4) the beneficial aspect, comprising bliss in which joy has been renounced (*prītiprahāṇasukha, dga' ba spangs pa'i bde ba*); and (5) the aspect of abiding in meditative stability.[1131]

The Fourth Meditative Concentration [dd']

The fourth [meditative concentration] also entails both preparation and actual foundation.

Preparation [1"]

Concerning the former, those who have achieved the extraordinary calm abiding of the third meditative concentration, and for whom the third meditative concentration is still defective and the fourth appealing because it is endowed with positive attributes, should meditate by means of the six [aforementioned] kinds of attention, applying [in particular] the higher insight endowed with scrutiny.

Consequently, when both calm abiding and higher insight have been cultivated in an integrated manner, the actual attainment of the fourth meditative concentration may be obtained.

Actual Foundation [2"]

Concerning the latter [it says in the root verses]:

> **Then, [the actual foundation of] the fourth [meditative concentration]**
> **Has four aspects, purified of the eight defects.**

The actual foundation of the fourth [meditative concentration] has four aspects, namely, (1–2) the two antidotal aspects, comprising purity of recollection (*smṛtipariśuddhi, dran pa yang dag*) and purity of equanimity (*upekṣāpariśuddhi, btang snyoms yang dag*); (3) the beneficial aspect, comprising equanimity of feelings (*vedanopekṣā, tshor ba btang snyoms*); and (4) the aspect of abiding in meditative stability.

In this context, purity of recollection implies complete purity of the eight defects associated with meditative concentration (*dhyānāṣṭadoṣa, bsam gtan gyi skyon brgyad*). These defects comprise (1–2) ideation and scrutiny with respect to the first meditative concentration, which are said to resemble fire; (3–4) feelings of bliss and sorrow with respect to the second meditative concentration, which originate within the range of sensory consciousness; (5–6) [feelings of] mental comfort and discomfort with respect to the third meditative concentration, which originate within the range of mental consciousness; and (7–8) exhalation and inhalation of breath with respect to the fourth meditative concentration.

In this way, [the actual foundation of the fourth meditative concentration] is completely purified of these eight defects.[1132]

THE FRUITIONAL PHASE [ii']

The second part [of the detailed explanation] is an exegesis of the fruitional phase of meditative concentration (*'bras bu skye ba'i bsam gtan*). In this regard, [it says in the root verses]:

> **In this way, the results will be greater, mediocre, or lesser,**
> **Corresponding to the actual foundation of each [meditative concentration].**
> **The ripening fruit appropriate for each of these states and so forth will be experienced.**

As for the results that are attained by means of these meditative absorptions (*snyoms 'jug*), by meditating [successively] on the lesser, mediocre, and greater actual foundations of the first meditative concentration, one will obtain [rebirth] in three other [god] realms, starting with the Stratum of Brahmā (*brahmakāyika, tshangs ris*), and so on, until, by meditating [successively] on the lesser, mediocre, and greater actual attainments of the fourth meditative concentration, one will obtain [rebirth] in three other realms, starting with the Cloudless (*anabhraka, sprin med*). Having conclusively perfected the lesser, mediocre, and greater actual foundations of each [of the four meditative concentrations] in this way, one will experience the ripening fruit and so forth of the realms or states associated with each [in turn].[1133]

Here, the term "ripening result" (*vipākaphala, rnam smin gyi 'bras bu*) includes both the locations, i.e., those [twelve god] realms and the [divine] forms assumed [by the gods] who take birth therein. These attributes [are considered to be] "results in conformity with their causes" (*niṣyandaphala, rgyu mthun 'bras bu*)—in this case the meditative absorptions. The term "predominant result" (*adhipatiphala, bdag po'i 'bras bu*) here refers to the [distinctive] resources that are perceived to be associated with [these distinctive god] realms.

The World-Systems of Formlessness and the Four Formless Absorptions [2']

The exegesis of the four meditative absorptions associated with the world system of formlessness (*gzugs med khams kyi snyoms 'jug bzhi*) includes both a brief introduction and a detailed explanation.

Brief Introduction [a']

The former [comments on the root verses]:

> **The four meditative absorptions**
> **Associated with the world-system of formlessness**
> **Also have both causal and fruitional phases.**

Detailed Explanation [b']

The detailed explanation has two parts: the meditative absorptions of the causal phase and the [corresponding] fruitional phase that will arise.

The Causal Phase [i']

The former [comments on the root verses]:

> **One whose mind has obtained the fourth meditative concentration**
> **And has not relapsed**
> **After inhibiting [the world system of] form,**
> **And its [interactions] of contact, vision, and perception,**
> **Should conclusively perfect the summit of existence**
> **Through the meditative absorptions**
> **Which experience infinite space and consciousness,**
> **Where there is nothing-at-all to be grasped,**
> **And where there is neither perception, coarse or subtle,**
> **Nor is there non-perception.**

The [four meditative absorptions] known to be in association with the four extremes of the formless sensory activity fields (*ārūpyāyatana, gzugs med skye mched*) are enumerated as follows:[1134]

(1) The first is the meditative absorption of the sensory activity field of infinite space (*ākāśānantyāyatana, nam mkha' mtha' yas skye mched kyi snyoms 'jug*), in which the mind, in addition to obtaining the fourth meditative concentration and not relapsing from that state, has inhibited the [world system of] form and its threefold interaction of sensory contact, vision, and perception (*reg mthong snang gsum*), and completely perfected meditation on the thought that all things are infinite like the sky.

(2) The second is the meditative absorption of the sensory activity field of infinite consciousness (*vijñānāntyāyatana, rnam shes mtha' yas skye mched kyi snyoms 'jug*), in which, in addition to that [first meditative absorption], one has completely perfected meditation on the thought that consciousness is infinite, just as space is infinite.

(3) The third is the meditative absorption of the sensory activity field of nothing-at-all (*akiṃcanyāyatana, ci yang med pa'i skye mched kyi snyoms 'jug*), in which, having discerned these two [previous meditative absorptions] to be symbolic, one has completely perfected meditation on the thought that there is nothing at all to be grasped.

(4) The fourth is the meditative absorption of neither perception nor non-perception (*naivasaṃjnāsaṃjnāyatana, 'du shes med min gyi snyoms 'jug*), in which, having discerned these three [previous meditative absorptions] to be symbolic, one has completely perfected meditation on the thought that there is neither perception, coarse or subtle, nor non-perception. This is the conclusive perfection of the path that leads to the summit of [mundane] existence (*bhavāgra, srid pa'i rtse*).[1135]

The Fruitional Phase [ii']

The latter, concerning the corresponding fruitional phases that will arise, [comments on the root verses]:

> **The results are particularly sublime,**
> **On account of their meditative stability, life span, and so forth.**

With regard to the results achieved through these four meditative absorptions, although the world-system of formlessness is not differentiated like the other [aforementioned] locations or [god] realms which may be distinguished on the basis of their coarse material form, there are still differences [therein], based on the superior and inferior [degrees of meditative absorption], the duration of the life span [enjoyed by its denizens], the higher and lower [levels], and so forth.

Among the Mahāsaṅghikas, there are some who explain that [these results] may also be differentiated on the basis of their [distinctive] locations or realms.[1136] However that may be, it is on account of their ever-increasing meditative stability, which becomes more extensive and more steadfast, and on account of the duration of the life span and so forth, that the results of happiness experienced in the exalted realms are particularly sublime.

Synopsis [c]

The third and final part [of the extensive exegesis of the exalted vehicle which may be followed by gods and humans] is the synopsis:

> **This basis of enlightened attributes,**
> **Including the [four] immeasurable aspirations,**
> **The [five] supernormal cognitive powers, and so forth**
> **Is the supreme objective to be striven after by both non-Buddhists**
> **And [by followers of] the Lesser Vehicle.**
> **This is a prerequisite for those who would progressively embark**
> **Upon the vehicle of the Conquerors.**

Dependent on the actual attainments of the four meditative concentrations, the distinctive attributes associated with the two higher world-systems [of form and formlessness] will become familiar. They include the four immeasurable aspirations (*caturaprameya, tshad med bzhi*), starting with loving-kindness (*maitrī, byams pa*),[1137] and the five mundane supernormal cognitive powers (*pañcābhijnā, mngon shes lnga*), namely, clairvoyance (*divyacahkṣurabhijnā, lha'i mig gi mngon shes*), clairaudience (*divyaśrotrābhijnā, lha'i rna ba'i mngon shes*), knowledge of the minds of others (*paracittābhijnā, gzhan sems gyi mngon shes*), recollection of past lives (*pūrvanivāsānusmṛtyabhijñā, sngon gyi gnas rjes su dran pa'i mngon shes*), and knowledge of the nature of passing away and rebirth (*cyutyupapādajñāna, 'chi 'pho dang skye ba shes pa*).[1138]

All who enter upon the [Buddhist] vehicles initially must cultivate those meditative stabilities and their associated attributes, and repeatedly attain the distinctive features of the higher realms. Therefore, [the vehicle of the exalted realms] is the basis of all enlightened attributes that may be cultivated, including the supernormal cognitive powers.

In particular, the meditative absorption of neither perception nor non-perception is obtained dependent on the mind that has attained the actual foundation of the fourth meditative concentration, and the [conclusive] meditative absorption of cessation is obtained dependent on the mind that has attained the actual foundation of the summit of existence, and so forth.[1139] Consequently, this is the supreme objective to be striven after and attained even by the non-Buddhist hermit sages and philosophical extremists, as well as by the pious attendants and hermit buddhas, who follow the Lesser Vehicle of Buddhism.

Since [the vehicles of gods and humans, and the vehicle of Brahmā] are the preliminary or prerequisite teachings practiced by all those who progressively embark on the Buddhist teachings of the Conqueror, one should understand them and master their experiential application.

This completes the auto-commentary on Book Six, Part One: A Systematic Presentation of the Ordinary Classical Sciences and Mundane Spiritual Paths.

Part Two

Buddhist Phenomenology: A Systematic Presentation of Phenomenological Structures Common to Both the Greater Vehicle and the Lesser Vehicle

The Root Verses

[Chapter 1: Non-Buddhist and Buddhist Philosophical Systems]

Endowed with four special seals or hallmarks,
Acting as an antidote for [attachment to] the summit of existence,
Renouncing the two extremes,
And realizing the truth of the cessation [of suffering]—
This is why the teaching of the Conqueror is one of definitive excellence,
Surpassing [the philosophical systems] of non-Buddhists.

[Chapter 2: Doxography of the Buddhist Traditions]

Though there are many classifications,
The generally accepted [view] is that
[The Buddha's teachings] are known
According to the three vehicles and the four philosophical systems,
But all of these, indeed, agree that once the apprehension of self,
Which is the causal basis of cyclic existence, has been abandoned,
Nirvāṇa will then be attained.

[Chapter 3: Phenomenological Structures]

It is discriminative awareness that thoroughly discerns [the nature of] phenomena—
The causal basis of this [cyclic existence].
The psycho-physical aggregates, sensory bases, and sensory activity fields,
Along with dependent origination,
Constitute the [actual phenomenological structures] which are to be established.

Although there are many such classifications
Made in accordance with the Greater and Lesser Vehicles,
These [that are presented here] reflect the tradition in general.
These [constituents of phenomenology] were sequentially presented
As antidotes for the deluded view of self.
As such, they are differentiated in respect of the apprehension of
wholeness,
And the [scope of individual] faculties, and volitions,
Each of which has three aspects.

[Chapter 4: The Tradition of Higher Abhidharma]

[The Five Psycho-Physical Aggregates]

The bundle of the psycho-physical aggregates is fivefold,
Comprising physical forms, feelings, perceptions,
Formative predispositions, and consciousness.

[The Aggregate of Physical Forms]

[The aggregate] capable of assuming physical forms
Includes the four elements of primary matter
Which [respectively] have solidity, fluidity, heat, and motion.
With these [primary elements] acting as the causal basis,
There is also derivative matter, including the five sense organs,
Such as the eye, which supports [visual] consciousness,
And the five types of external object, such as visual form,
Which are to be apprehended.
There are twenty-five aspects of visual form,
Divided into six or four categories.
Sounds are of eleven types,
Comprising four categories,
[The last of which] when classified is fivefold.
Odors are of six types, tastes of twelve types,
And tangibles are of twenty-two types.
The physical forms that constitute the sensory activity field of phenomena,
Being unrevealed and unobstructed,
Are of five types, including [atomic] forms that are extremely concentrated.

[The Aggregate of Feelings]

Mental processes experienced through sensory contact
Are endowed with happiness, sorrow, and neutrality.
There are six types of feeling,
Conditioned by sensory contact that is compounded,
And there are two ways in which [feelings] may be differentiated
According to their affinity.

[The Aggregate of Perceptions]

Compounded perceptions are differentiated according to their essential nature,
And there are also six types of [perception]
Compounded by [different] levels [of experience],
Starting with non-symbolic [perception].

[The Aggregate of Formative Predispositions]

Formative predispositions interact with their points of reference.
According to their essential nature, they are of six types.
According to their circumstances, [formative predispositions]
Comprise those both associated and disassociated with the mind.
The mind perceives the essential nature of a [given] object,
While mental states perceive the distinguishing attributes of a [given] object.

[Mental States Associated with Mind]

[Mental states] adhere to the mind
Through their five concomitant [characteristics],
Such as their [common] location.
Although they have been said to be identical [in substance],
According to this tradition, they are different.
The [five] ever-present [mental] states emerge
[Within the periphery of] the substratum [consciousness].
These [same] five, along with four of the primary dissonant mental states,
And six of the subsidiary dissonant mental states,
Emerge [within the periphery of] the dissonant mental consciousness.

However, all [of the fifty-one mental states] emerge
Within the periphery of the engaged modes of consciousness.
Twenty-two [mental states] are substantial existents
And twenty-nine of them are imputed existents.
Among the four [generally recognized criteria that determine substantial existents],
Here, only autonomous mental states are accepted [as substantial existents],
While partial mental states are accepted [as imputed existents].

The classification [of mental states] comprises
The five ever-present mental states,
The five object-determining mental states,
The eleven wholesome mental states,
And the six primary dissonant mental states.
Among these [six, wrong] view is endowed with afflicted discriminative awareness.
The essential nature [of wrong views] is fivefold,
Including mundane views, extreme views, and so forth.
[These views] have three subcategories and their [respective] subdivisions.
There are also twenty subsidiary dissonant mental states,
And there are the four variable [mental states].

[Mental States Disassociated with Mind]

The formative predispositions disassociated with the mind are twenty-three in number.
They are subsumed in eight categories because they partake of
Increase and decrease, an absence of cognizance,
Abodes, similarity, characteristics, conventional terminology,
And an absence of [spiritual] attainment,
As well as causes and their results.

[The Aggregate of Consciousness]

Mind, mentation, and consciousness
Correlate to the eight modes [of consciousness].

[Substratum Consciousness]

The substratum consciousness, unobscured and unspecified,
Has both seminal and maturational aspects
On the basis of which propensities are [actually] distributed.
It denotes associated [formative predispositions]
Which are invisible and fractional,
But objectively appear.
Compulsively acquiring corrupt [phenomena],
It engages continuously throughout the three world-systems,
But when the adamantine meditative stability arises,
And one becomes an arhat, it will be reversed.

Propensities [are analyzed] according to the ground in which they are distributed,
Their distributors, the distribution process, and their actual content.
The stable continuum [of the substratum], though not clearly [cognized],
Is that in which [propensities] have the capacity to be distributed,
Because it is concurrent with the [other modes of consciousness]
Which are their [actual] distributors.
Seven modes [of consciousness] and their peripheral supports
Are the actual distributors [of these propensities].
Even though [propensities] may have ceased,
They still have the capacity to generate their results.
The distributed [propensities] include those of the causal type,
Which are similar in class [to the original mental phenomena],
And those that are maturational,
And therefore capable of generating other [mental phenomena].

The six kinds of seed comprise those that are external and internal,
[The two] that are invisible, and those that are relative and absolute.
They abide through[1] their [association with] five natural properties.
Though they are localized by whatever localizes them,
They remain unspecified and cannot be described
As identical in substance, or different.
They become localized by regenerating their own habitat,
And by generating [impulses] that did not previously exist.

[Dissonant Mental Consciousness]

Embodying egotism, and unspecified,
Mentation is endowed with associated mental states,
Comprising four of the dissonant mental states.
It has the functions of binding [the modes of engaged consciousness]
To corrupt states, and of implanting seeds.
Referring objectively to the substratum, it engages routinely,
But it is reversed on the sublime [path].

[Six Modes of Engaged Consciousness]

The essential nature of the process of sensory engagement is that
The [modes of] consciousness, referring objectively to their diversely appearing objects,
Arise in conjunction with four conditions.
Their defining characteristic is that, dependent on their predominant condition,
They perceive the sensory activity fields.
Through the locus of the sense organs,
They refer objectively to their sense objects,
And they maintain a concomitance [between mind and mental states].
Their functions include conceptualizing with respect to objects of reference,
Prevarication with respect to objects of reference, and so forth.
They originate in conjunction with conditions, like waves from water.
In particular, mental consciousness is uninterrupted,
Except in the five [special] circumstances, where mind is absent.

[Distribution of the Five Psycho-physical Aggregates]

In the [world-system of] desire, all of the aggregates,
Including the aggregate of physical forms, are possessed,
While in the higher realms, they are progressively reduced.

[The Sensory Bases]

The eighteen sensory bases which support the seeds [of everything]
Or their specifically characterized phenomena

Are divided into [three] groups of six,
Comprising those sensory bases that are internal, external, and cognizant.
There are sensory bases subsumed in the psycho-physical aggregates,
Those that are not subsumed in the psycho-physical aggregates,
And the sensory base of mental phenomena.

The aggregate of physical forms includes the ten physical sensory bases—
Those of the sense organs and sense objects—
Along with one part of the sensory activity field of mental phenomena,
Which are all subsumed within [the category of] form.
Feelings, perceptions, and formative predispositions
Are subsumed within [the category of mental] phenomena,
Because, along with one aspect of the sensory base of mental phenomena,
They are all objects of the mental faculty.
As for the aggregate of consciousness, it is designated as
The "seven sensory bases of consciousness,"
Comprising the six modes [of engaged consciousness]
Along with the dissonant mental [consciousness],
And these are all subsumed within [the category of] mind.

The unconditioned sensory bases
Without causes and conditions, and without agglomeration,
Are included within one part of the sensory base of mental phenomena
That is not subsumed in the psycho-physical aggregates.
These comprise the three aspects of reality, space, the two aspects of cessation,
The immovable state, and the cessation of feeling and perception.
The two sets of eight conditioned and unconditioned things
Together are objects within range exclusively of mental consciousness.
Therefore, these are particularly assigned to the "sensory base of phenomena."

[The Sensory Activity Fields]

There are twelve [sensory activity fields], such as the eye and visual form,
Emerging from the sensory gates
Where the [corresponding modes of] consciousness arise,
Facilitating the extension [of consciousness] to extraneous objects.

Subjective and immediate conditions direct [these modes of consciousness] internally
While objective and referential conditions direct them externally
Toward [their respective] gates that form the sensory activity fields.
[Here,] the ten physical sensory activity fields resemble [their corresponding] sensory bases.
The seven sensory bases of consciousness are [subsumed in]
The sensory activity field of the mental faculty.
The sixteen sensory bases of phenomena are [subsumed in]
The sensory activity field of phenomena.

[Chapter 5: The Tradition of the Lower Abhidharma]

The pious attendants subsume all that is knowable
In these five basic categories:
Apparent forms, the central mind, peripheral mental states,
Formative predispositions disassociated [with mind and mental states],
And unconditioned states.
Form comprises the five sense organs, and their five objects,
Along with imperceptible form.
[Mind comprises] the six modes [of engaged consciousness],
And there are forty-six mental states,
Comprising the group of ten states found in [all] minds,
The group of ten mental states found in [all] virtuous [minds],
The group of six mental states found in dissonant or afflicted [minds],
The group of two mental states found in [all] non-virtuous [minds],
The group of ten mental states found in [all] slightly [afflicted minds],
And the group of eight mental states that are found indeterminately.
There are also fourteen formative predispositions
Disassociated [with mind and mental states], along with their aspects,
And two unconditioned states, comprising cessation and space.

All relative [appearances] are subsumed
In the aggregate of physical forms, the sensory base of mental phenomena,
And the sensory activity field of the mental faculty.
These [appearances] are of three sorts: causally effective phenomena,
Including substantial existents and imputed existents,
And non-causally effective phenomena.

[Chapter 6: Phenomenological Basis according to the Final Promulgation]

When the psycho-physical aggregates, the sensory bases,
And the sensory activity fields are reconstituted,
Each of these [structures] has three further subdivisions:
Respectively, [the aggregate of physical forms] comprises
The sensory bases of the elements, the physical world and its living organisms;
[The sensory base of mental phenomena] comprises
The mind, mentation, and consciousness;
While [the sensory activity field of the mental faculty] comprises
Demonstrations, defining characteristics, and non-substantial mental phenomena.
[Among the latter,] the demonstrations also comprise
Three further aspects—feelings, perceptions, and formative predispositions;
The defining characteristics comprise three further aspects—
Those that are imputed with regard to space, time, and substance;
While the non-substantial mental phenomena comprise
Those arising through the transformation of substance,
Those that are dependent on substance,
And those that do not exist.
These then are the twenty-one aspects associated with the ground.

There are three approaches of the [spiritual] path:
Common, uncommon, and one [extraordinary approach]
Through which the abiding nature of the Conqueror will be reached.
The expanse of reality is the ultimate [truth], unconditioned and unique.
The systematic presentation of the irreversible promulgation
Determines that this object of knowledge
Encompasses all twenty-five realms of phenomenal existence.

[Chapter 7: The Five Foundational Factors]

Moreover, the five foundational factors
Of which [the three] natures partake,
Along with the three natures which partake of them,

And dependent origination and so forth, which derive from them,
Are all subsumed within the Greater Vehicle.

Appearances are universals indicating states or objects,
And they have many variations,
Including those that are natural—
The propensities that manifest to the innate mind—
And those that are projected, such as the imputed self.

Names are verbally designated universals,
Imputed with respect to these [appearances].
They include substantive, relational, integrated,
Diversified, known, and unknown names.

False imagination denotes the mind and its mental states,
Including symbolic and non-symbolic [concepts],
As well as dissonant and non-dissonant mental states.

The absolute reality transcends expression and thought.
Knowledge of the [spiritual] path,
[Intermingling] meditative equipoise and post-meditative experience,
Is the genuine [non-conceptual] knowledge.
The [last two—absolute reality and genuine knowledge—]
Are respectively endowed with objective and subjective characteristics.
All the phenomenological categories associated with the supportive [consciousness]
Are gathered within this [fivefold classification].

[Chapter 8: The Three Natures]

Things imputed by verbal expression and false imagination are imaginary.
These comprise three categories: the imaginary nature of delimited characteristics,
Exemplified by the concept of individual selfhood;
The nominal imaginary,
Exemplified by the dualistic appearances of the subject-object dichotomy;
And the referentially imputed imaginary.
Or, alternatively, there are ten aspects.

The dependent nature is assigned to apperception alone,
Which arises through causes and conditions.
It has two categories: one comprising the seeds of all dissonant mental states
And the other in which neither dissonant nor purified mental states inherently exist.
Or, alternatively, there are six aspects.

The consummate nature is the ultimate actual reality—the absolute reality.
The [consummate] nature has four aspects:
For it is naturally pure, it is free from adventitious stains,
It is the pristine cognition of the spiritual path,
And it is the objective of the scriptures.

In particular, [the three natures] may also be explained
In terms of the ten aspects of distracting false imagination,
The eleven aspects of apperception,
The nine aspects of the consummate nature, and so forth;
But because the apparitional aspect of dependent nature
Partakes of bewildered imagination,
The [three] natures that have been differentiated
May also be subsumed in two.

Respectively, [these three natures are identified] as the emptiness of non-existence,
The emptiness of existence,
And the emptiness of the natural [reality].
When demonstrations [of these three natures] are introduced,
The imaginary is the apparitional aspect,
The dependent is the union of radiance and awareness,
And the consummate is free from conceptual elaboration.

[Chapter 9: Dependent Origination]

The first two [of these three natures] are dependently originated.
[In the case of the dependent nature,]
This [process] is endowed with generative or causal
And generated or fruitional aspects,
And [in the case of the imaginary nature]

It is endowed with interrelated determinative and determined aspects.
However, it is the genuine dependent origination
[That determines] the substratum consciousness.

The essential nature [of dependent origination]
Is that it occurs only with regard to appearances,
And it arises contingent on them.
The etymology implies "origination
Dependent on a complex of causes and conditions."
The literal meanings include "without an agent,"
"Endowed with causal basis," and so forth.

Fundamental ignorance, the opposite of awareness,
Is endowed with three attributes.
Although it has many classifications,
It comprises both [ignorance] endowed with dissonant mental states
And [ignorance] devoid of dissonant mental states.
Fundamental [ignorance] is within the periphery
Of the dissonant mental consciousness,
Deluded with respect to [its imputation of] a self.
Formative predispositions include those associated with meritorious past actions,
Those associated with non-meritorious past actions,
And those associated with past actions that do not transcend [cyclic existence].
The substratum consciousness, along with its propensities,
Includes both causal and fruitional aspects.
[Name and form] comprise the four [aggregates endowed with] names,
Along with physical form in its five stages of embryonic and fetal development;
While the sensory activity fields essentially demarcate the six sense organs.
Sensory contact, which [fully manifests] after birth,
Is an interaction of sense objects, sense organs, and consciousness.
The sensations dependent on that are attachment, aversion, and neutrality.
[Consequently] there is craving desirous [of rebirth]
And craving that grasps after perishable things.
Through grasping after desires, rebirth, erroneous views,
And belief in [an inherently existing] self,

[The rebirth process] is endowed with the potent function
Of implementing reincarnation.
Reaching the moment of conception, birth is obtained,
And commencing from then,
There is a continuous series of indivisible time moments,
Leading to the obstruction of the life essence, aging, and death.

The functions [of the twelve links]
Are respectively to obscure the truth,
To plant seeds, to direct towards [birth],
To offer complete support [to the body],
To perfect it, to delimit [its sense objects],
To partake of [happiness], to acquire [rebirth],
To conjoin [with birth], to propel towards [birth],
[To engender] suffering, and to transform [age].

The detailed analysis [of dependent origination] comprises
A threefold [analysis], an eightfold [analysis],
And a detailed exegesis according to the [twelve] links.
Among the aspects of the threefold analysis,
[The dependent origination] that distinguishes the essential nature
Refers to the emanation of all phenomena from the substratum,
And this is said to be [understood] only by those of highest acumen.
[The dependent origination] that distinguishes attractive and unattractive [goals]
Is said to be [understood] by pious attendants and hermit buddhas.
It has two aspects, referring to dissonant mental states and purification.
[Here] the verb "distinguishes" is understood
To mean "augments" and "magnifies."
[The dependent origination] associated with sensory engagement
Refers to the process that generates and obstructs the six modes [of consciousness],
Which pious attendants then control by means of selflessness.

The eightfold [analysis of dependent origination]
Comprises six aspects that are all within the range of dissonant mental states,
Namely, [the arising of] consciousness;
The arising of birth and death;

The external [dependent origination] of seeds, shoots, stems, and so forth;
The extensive analysis of the physical environment,
Which [appears to undergo] creation, duration and destruction;
Sustenance by means of the four types of nourishment;
And [the distinguishing of] living beings
According to desirable and undesirable [realms of rebirth].
Release [from cyclic existence] contingent on the five [spiritual] paths,
Which is well distinguished by means of purity,
And the attainment of the six supernormal cognitive powers,
Which is well-distinguished by means of [spiritual] power:
These are the [two] aspects within the range of purification.
[All eight aspects] are [established] with reference to
The generated and generative [modes of dependent origination].

As for the detailed [exegesis of] the twelve links,
This includes the circumstantial [dependent origination].
[Accordingly,] when [one cycle] is completed
Over two lifetimes within the world-system of desire,
There are five links that are projected
By means of the two [preceding] projective [links],
And there are three links that are formed
By means of the two formative [links].
A single sequence of the causal and fruitional processes [of dependent origination]
[Is completed] in these four projective and formative phases,
And it is said that these can therefore be known
[To resemble] the planting and nurturing of seeds.

Then, when two links are each associated
With the limits of the [immediately] past and future [lives],
And eight are associated with limits of the [present] intervening [life],
Two causal and fruitional cycles [of dependent origination]
[Are completed] over three lifetimes
Within the [world system] of desire, and so forth.
This is extensively revealed in order to reverse the three aspects of delusion.

There is also [a process whereby] the [cycle of dependent origination]
Will be completed in a single lifetime,

Experiencing [the fruits] of presently perceptible phenomena.
With regard to the instantaneous completion [of the cycle],
Consequent on the completion of a [specific] deed,
As in the case of murder,
This implies a dependent origination of that [instantaneous type].

With regard to the interconnected [dependent origination]
According to the *Analysis of the Middle and Extremes*,
Birth is conjoined with aging and death.
Consequently, there are [only] eleven links.
Then, in terms of the three categories of dissonant mental states,
Fundamental ignorance, craving, and grasping are subsumed
As [dissonant mental states] arising from dissonant mental states;
Formative predispositions and the rebirth process[2] are subsumed
As [dissonant mental states] arising from past actions;
While the remaining [seven] are subsumed
As dissonant mental states arising from the birth of suffering.
These [twelve links] may also be subsumed
Into two categories, in which case
The first five are [designated as]
Causal dissonant mental states arising from past actions,
While the last seven are [designated as] fruitional.

[Dependent origination] may also be presented
According to seven causes of the projective and formative phases,
And these [are said to be] completed over two lifetimes.
Vasubandhupāda has explained,
With reference to the fourfold process of projection and formation,
That this is analyzed according to the following seven aspects:
The projector, the projection process, and the projected,
The former, the formation process, and the formed,
Along with their disadvantages.

The arising and cessation of substantial things
Through uncreated and impermanent seeds
Which are endowed with potency
Accords with the understanding of dependent origination.
Phenomena, just as they appear, are relative.
Their actual reality is merely designated

As the dependent origination of ultimate [truth].
This [point] is extremely subtle.
[Dependent origination] is hard to understand
On account of the profundity of its causal basis,
Defining characteristic, arising, duration, and functioning,
And on account of its five ostensible contradictions.
All phenomena are merely dependently originated and without self.
The real nature of internal [phenomena] is apperception, devoid of self.
Regarding this [mere apperception],
Although it does not primordially exist, it does appear,
Without contradiction,
In the manner of consciousness that is tainted by sleep.
This is the real nature devoid of inherent existence,
The pristine cognition of inner radiance
That transcends the objects of dependent origination,
Because it is liberated from the mutual interdependence
Of determined and determinative aspects.

The Auto-commentary

[Introduction]

The second part [of Book Six, concerning the graduated exposition of knowledge; see p. 97] is a systematic presentation of the phenomenological structures common to both the Greater Vehicle and the Lesser Vehicle. This has three topics: (1) a presentation of the distinctions between the non-Buddhist and Buddhist philosophical systems; (2) a digression concerning the doxography of the Buddhist traditions; and (3) an exegesis of the actual systematic presentation of these phenomenological structures.

1. Non-Buddhist and Buddhist Philosophical Systems

I. Distinctions between the Non-Buddhist and Buddhist Philosophical Systems [I]

Distinctions between the Non-Buddhist and Buddhist Philosophical Systems [1]

Concerning the first [of these topics, it says in the root verses]:

> **Endowed with four special seals or hallmarks,**
> **Acting as an antidote for [attachment to] the summit of existence,**
> **Renouncing the two extremes,**
> **And realizing the truth of the cessation [of suffering]—**
> **This is why the teaching of the Conqueror is one of definitive excellence,**
> **Surpassing [the philosophical systems] of non-Buddhists.**

Concerning the distinctive attributes of the Buddhist and non-Buddhist philosophical systems, which we and others respectively espouse, scholars hold many different opinions, and yet no bias can be distinguished in the [following] qualitative [presentation of] the view, meditation, conduct, and result:

(1) The view (*lta ba*) on the basis of which one embarks upon any philosophical and spiritual system is differentiated according to whether it accepts or does not accept the four hallmarks indicative of [the Buddha's] transmitted teachings.

(2) The meditation (*sgom pa*) is differentiated on the basis of whether it acts or does not act as an antidote for [attachment] to the summit of existence.
(3) Conduct (*spyod pa*) is differentiated on the basis of whether it renounces or does not renounce the two extremes of self-mortification (*ātmaklamathānta, bdag ngal dub kyi mtha'*) and over-indulgence (*kāmasukhallikānta, 'dod pa bsod nyams kyi mtha'*).
(4) Release [from cyclic existence], which is the result (*'bras bu*), is differentiated on the basis of whether it upholds or does not uphold the extraordinary truth of the cessation [of suffering], which is [completely] free from the corruption [of past actions] that are to be abandoned.

Accordingly, it is said in [Śākyaprabha's] *Sun Commentary on Monastic Discipline:*

> The learned realize that the Buddha's speech
> Teaches well the three trainings,
> Is correctly endowed with the four seals,
> And is virtuous in the beginning, middle, and end.[3]

The four seals or hallmarks are [also known as] the four maxims pertaining to the [sacred] teachings [of the Buddha]. As is said in the *Sūtra of Inconceivable Secrets*:[4]

> The Tathāgata has subsumed all the teachings in four aphorisms:
> All that is conditioned is impermanent;
> All that is corrupt is suffering;
> All things are without self;
> And nirvāṇa is peace.

The objection might be raised that this is untenable because the Vatsīputrīyas among the Buddhist schools also uphold [the view] that there is a "self," and they accept that there are compounded [phenomena] which are not perishable, [persisting] through [the series] of indivisible time moments. Even so, there is no defect because they do not hold that there is an object [i.e., a "self"] that is extraneous to the psycho-physical aggregates and permanent, and they do not accept that there are eternal, imperishable, and permanent entities. Therefore, there is a great distinction between them and the [non-Buddhist] extremists.[5]

The "antidote for [attachment to] the summit of existence" (*srid rtse'i gnyen po*) cannot be found in [the philosophical and spiritual traditions of the non-Buddhist] extremists because selflessness (*nairātmya, bdag med*) is diametrically opposed to those [spiritual] paths which maintain [that the "self"] is a truly existent entity, and because above that [summit of existence] there is no other level [of the form or formless realms], and therefore no quiescent or coarse entity existing whatsoever.[6] Therefore, the master Śūra has said:[7]

> The beings who do not side with your teaching
> Have been blinded by delusion.
> Even though they might reach the summit of existence,
> They will achieve a rebirth in which suffering reemerges.
> Those who follow your teaching,
> Even without obtaining the actual realization of meditative
> concentration,
> Will oppose [the cycle of] rebirths,
> As if they were the vision of Māra.

With regard to the defects of conduct [maintained by non-Buddhists], they fall into the two extremes [of self-mortification and over-indulgence]. Through attachment to [material] gain and veneration, such persons are unsatisfied by [resources of] poor quality and scarcity, while indulging in [resources of] excellent quality and abundance. However, when one's own ethical discipline is pure and one realizes through the view of selflessness [the defective nature of] coarse materialism (*dngos 'dzin rags pa*), with a modicum of understanding, at that time one may partake of [one's resources] without hardship, whereupon, if no strong attachment or clinging then arises, even the partaking [of resources] of excellent quality and abundance may be without defect.

Those who do not act accordingly but engage in physical and mental over-indulgence and self-mortification are mainly to be identified, respectively, with the Lokāyatikas and the Nirgrantha Jains.[8] However, the Transcendent Lord [Buddha] emphasized [monastic] discipline with regard to the four [essential] resources—clothing, food, dwelling, and bedding—which does not fall into the two extremes.

Concerning the release [from cyclic existence], which is the result [ensuing from practice of the Buddhist path], it is said in the *Letter to a Friend*:[9]

One should attain [the state] that is free
From earth, water, fire, wind, sun, and moon.

In this context, the Lokāyatikas hold that release [from cyclic existence] and the four elements have a common ground because they define cyclic existence and nirvāṇa respectively as the presence and absence of the four elements, along with the mind. It says in the *Eulogy on Distinctions*:[10]

Parrots are known to say that once the sun has exploded,
There will be release [from cyclic existence].

Passages such as this suggest [the Lokāyatikas] held [the disintegration of] the sun and moon as indicators of release [from cyclic existence]. The Nirgrantha Jains, on the other hand, hold that release occurs in the expanse of celestial space, resembling an upturned parasol.[11] Since beings are deluded with regard to the release that is to be attained according to such [philosophical systems], the corresponding spiritual paths that [are said to] bring about this release are also deluded.

On the other hand, the teaching of the Conqueror [Buddhism] holds that release [from cyclic existence] or nirvāṇa is the truth of the cessation [of suffering, *nirodhasatya*] and it is the source of provisional and conclusive spiritual and temporal well-being, whereby those who achieve it surpass the traditions of the non-Buddhists. For these reasons, the term "definitive excellence" (*niḥśreyasa, nges legs*) applies to the teaching of the Conqueror alone.

2. Doxography of the Buddhist Traditions

II. Digression on Doxographical Analysis and Synthesis within the Buddhist Traditions [II]

Digression on Doxographical Analysis and Synthesis within the Buddhist Traditions [II]

With regard to the second topic [it says in the root verses]:

> **Though there are many classifications,**
> **The generally accepted [view] is that**
> **[The Buddha's teachings] are known**
> **According to the three vehicles and the four philosophical systems,**
> **But all of these, indeed, agree that once the apprehension of self,**
> **Which is the causal basis of cyclic existence, has been abandoned,**
> **Nirvāṇa will then be attained.**

With reference to the [sacred] teachings that comprise the transmissions (*āgamadharma, lung gi chos*) of Buddhism, the distinctions and doxographical classifications made in terms of both the [canonical] transmitted teachings (*vacana, bka'*) [of Buddha word] and the [commentarial] treatises (*śāstra, bstan bcos*) are said to be manifold.[12]

It says in Āryadeva's *Compendium of the Nucleus of Pristine Cognition*:

> The [sacred] teachings of the Buddha
> Are actually discerned by intelligent persons
> To comprise four aspects:

By elucidating the paths of the Vaibhāṣikas and so forth,
The real nature [of the sacred teachings] is attained.

Accordingly, all the sacred Buddhist teachings may be ascertained in terms of the following four spiritual and philosophical systems: the Vaibhāṣika (*bye brag smra ba*), the Sautrāntika (*mdo sde pa*), the Yogacārin (*rnal 'byor spyod pa*) and the Mādhyamika (*dbu ma pa*). These [four systems] may also be subsumed into a threefold classification, comprising the Bāhyārthavādin (*phyi don du smra ba*), the Cittamātrin (*sems tsam pa*), and the Mādhyamika who propound the absence of inherent existence (*niḥsvabhāvikamādhyamika, ngo bo nyid med par smra ba'i dbu ma pa*), because the Vaibhāṣika and the Sautrāntika are both subsumed under the category of those who propound the existence of external objects (*bāhyārthavādin*). Then again, the [four] systems may be further subsumed within the two vehicles because it is certain that the first two are associated with the followers of the Lesser Vehicle (*hīnayānin, theg dman pa*), and the second two with the followers of the Greater Vehicle (*mahāyānin, theg chen pa*).[13]

The *Sūtra of the Descent to Laṅkā* also explains that the entire teaching [of the Buddha] may be subsumed within five vehicles, in the following words:[14]

The vehicle of gods and the vehicle of Brahmā,
And likewise the vehicles of the pious attendants,
Tathāgatas, and hermit buddhas were explained by me.

In this regard, it is said in the *Precious Garland* that, when these [five vehicles] are further subsumed, they may be gathered within two [distinct] vehicles because the first two are associated with the exalted realms and the last three with [the attainment of] definitive excellence.[15]

Similarly, in the context of the pith instructions of the perfection of discriminative awareness (*prajñāpāramitopadeśa, sher phyin gyi man ngag*) [exemplified in the *Ornament of Emergent Realization* and its commentarial literature], these [five vehicles] may also be subsumed according to the [spiritual] paths followed by three types of person (*tripuruṣa, skyes bu gsum*), i.e., the first two [vehicles] correspond to the spiritual path followed by persons of narrow scope (*adhamapuruṣa, skyes bu chung ngu*), the middle two [vehicles] correspond to the spiritual path followed by persons of average scope (*madhyamapuruṣa, skyes bu 'bring pa*), and last [vehicle] corresponds to the spiritual path followed by persons of extensive scope (*mahāpuruṣa, skyes bu chen po*).[16]

On the other hand, if one were to [rigidly] hold that there are [only] five vehicles, it even says in the following verses from [Praśāntamitra's] *Commentary on the Nucleus of Indestructible Reality* that there is no fourth vehicle, nor is there a fifth philosophical system:[17]

> For those who are Buddhists,
> Neither the fourth nor the fifth
> Are the Sage's enlightened intention.

Does this passage not contradict, one might ask, [those references to the five vehicles which have been expressed in texts such as the *Sūtra of the Descent to Laṅkā*]? Indeed, the *Sūtra of the Lotus* also says:[18]

> The teaching of the three vehicles by the Great Sage
> Is the skillful means of the guiding [buddhas].

Although there are passages such as these, stating [the buddha's] enlightened intention to be that the [spiritual] path to liberation has no fourth vehicle, there is not the slightest contradiction because these [different] textual traditions have divergent exegetical bases or starting points.

[While we are on the subject of the threefold doxography,] it is said in the *Lamp Which Subsumes Conduct*:[19]

> With reference to the three kinds of volition possessed by those who require training, conduct comprises the following three categories: for those whose volition is directed towards the low-level [practice] there is the conduct that is free from attachment; for those whose volition is directed towards the extensive [practice], there is the conduct associated with the [bodhisattva] levels and the transcendental perfections; while for those whose volition is directed even higher towards the profound [practice], there is revealed the conduct which engages with desire and attachment.

Also, in the *Lamp of the Three Ways* of the master Tripiṭakamāla, it is said:

> Whatever ways reveal the real nature of the [four] truths,
> Whatever ways are the objective of the [six] transcendental
> perfections,

> Whatever ways are the objectives of the great [vehicle of] secret mantra,
> They are [all] integrated and presented herein.

This latter text therefore seeks to integrate [the teachings] according to their three [established] "ways" (*tshul gsum*): the way of the yogin who pursues the four [sublime] truths, the way of the yogin who follows the [six] transcendental perfections, and the way of the yogin who follows the great [vehicle of] secret mantra. The master Jñānakīrti similarly integrates [the diverse teachings of the Buddha] in his *Abridgement of All Transmitted Teachings Without Exception: A Dissertation on Exegesis.*

Now, it says in the *Ornament of the Sūtras of the Greater Vehicle*:[20]

> The canonical compilations appropriately may number three or two.

According to this [authoritative] text, there are a great many ways in which [the teachings of the Buddha] may be subsumed: integrating them into the two canonical compilations (*piṭaka, sde snod*) or vehicles of the supreme [Mahāyāna] and the lesser [Hīnayāna], or more usually, integrating them into the three vehicles of the pious attendants, hermit buddhas, and bodhisattvas, and so forth.

Even so, the general consensus is that [the teachings of the Buddha] are to be known in terms of either the "three vehicles" or the "four spiritual and philosophical systems.

All of these traditions concur that once the apprehension of the self or egotistical grasping (*ātmagraha, bdag tu 'dzin pa*), which is the causal basis of cyclic existence, has been abandoned, the level of nirvāṇa, which is [a genuine] release [from cyclic existence], will be attained.[21]

Also, with regard to those [diverse vehicles and philosophical systems, one should know that] the more advanced among them will not emerge without relying on those that precede them.[22] This may be exemplified by the following quotation from the *Sūtra of the Ten-Wheeled Kṣitigarbha*:

> Whoever lacks the vehicle of the exalted realms,
> Also lacks the vehicle of the pious attendants.
> Whoever lacks the vehicle of the pious attendants,
> Also lacks the vehicle of the hermit buddhas.
> Whoever lacks the vehicle of the hermit buddhas,
> Also lacks the Greater Vehicle.

3. Phenomenological Structures

III. Systematic Presentation of Phenomenological Structures [III]
- A. The Structures to Be Established and the Means of Establishing Them
- B. Brief Statement on the Essential Purpose Underlying This Structural Analysis
- C. Extensive Exegesis of the Actual Phenomenological Framework
  - 1. A Systematic Presentation of the Psycho-physical Aggregates, Sensory Bases, and Sensory Activity Fields Which the Buddhist Vehicles Commonly Accept

Systematic Presentation of Phenomenological Structures [III]

The third topic is the systematic presentation of phenomenological structures (*jñeya, shes bya),* which has three parts: (1) recognizing the structures to be established and the means of establishing them; (2) a brief statement on the essential purpose underlying this structural analysis; and (3) an extensive exegesis of the actual phenomenological framework.

The Structures to Be Established and the Means of Establishing Them [A]

Concerning the first [it says in the root verses]:

> **It is discriminative awareness that thoroughly discerns [the nature of] phenomena—**
> **The causal basis of this [cyclic existence].**

The psycho-physical aggregates, sensory bases, and sensory activity fields,
Along with dependent origination,
Constitute the [actual phenomenological structures] which are to be established.
Although there are many such classifications
Made in accordance with the Greater and Lesser Vehicles,
These [that are presented here] reflect the tradition in general.

It is said in the *Treasury of Phenomenology*:[23]

> Apart from the thorough discernment of phenomena, there is no means to extinguish the dissonant mental states, and it is by reason of the dissonant mental states that the world roams this ocean of rebirth. Therefore, to enhance this [discernment], the Teacher has taught [phenomenology].

Once the causal basis of cyclic existence has been abandoned, in order that release [from cyclic existence] might be attained, it will be essential to establish the defining characteristics of all objects of knowledge by means of the discriminative awareness (*prajñā, shes rab*) which thoroughly discerns [all] phenomena. Since this is effected by qualitatively establishing the defining characteristics of the five psycho-physical aggregates (*pañcaskandha, phung po lnga*), the eighteen sensory bases (*aṣṭadaśadhātu, khams bco brgyad*), the twelve sensory activity fields (*dvādaśāyatana, skye mched bcu gnyis*), and the processes of dependent origination (*pratītyasamutpāda, rten cing 'brel bar 'byung ba*), it is essential that these [phenomenological constituents] should be understood. Therefore it is said in the sūtras:[24]

> One should understand the psycho-physical aggregates,
> One should understand the sensory bases,
> One should understand the sensory activity fields,
> And one should understand the processes of dependent origination,
> As well as the positive and negative contingencies [of all things].[25]

With regard to these [phenomenological structures], although there are many classifications and presentations of their defining characteristics made in accordance with the Greater Vehicle and the Lesser Vehicle, here I shall briefly discuss the general tradition that is prevalent in all [the Buddhist schools].

Brief Statement on the Essential Purpose Underlying This Structural Analysis [B]

Secondly, concerning the essential purpose that underlies this structural analysis [it says in the root verses]:

> **These [constituents of phenomenology] were sequentially presented**
> **As antidotes for the deluded view of self.**
> **As such, they are differentiated in respect of the apprehension of wholeness,**
> **And the [scope of individual] faculties, and volitions,**
> **Each of which has three aspects.**

The transcendent lord [Buddha] established [all] objects of knowledge by expounding phenomena in terms of the three constituents: psycho-physical aggregates, sensory bases, and sensory activity fields.[26]

With regard to the essential purpose underlying these [phenomenological structures], the Vaibhāṣikas hold that they function as an antidote for the apprehension of wholeness that comes about through three aspects of delusion (*trimoha, rmongs pa gsum*), and they are directed with an intention towards those requiring training, who are endowed with three [distinct] faculties and three [distinct] volitions.[27]

As for these terms, the three aspects of delusion comprise the delusion that comes about through the apprehension of a composite or conglomerate "self" (*piṇḍātmagrāha, ril po'i bdag nyid du 'dzin pa*) with respect to (a) mental states (*caitasika, sems byung*), (b) physical forms (*rūpa, gzugs*), and (c) physical forms and mental states combined (*gzugs sems gnyis ka*).

The three faculties (*dbang po gsum*) [associated with persons of different scopes] are keen faculties, mediocre or average faculties, and dull faculties.

The three volitions [associated with persons of different scopes] include those inclined towards concise explanations (*samāsādhimukti, tshig bsdus pa*), moderate explanations (*madhyamādhimukti, 'bring*), and extensive explanations (*udārādhimukti, rgyas pa 'dod pa*).[28]

As for the teachings of dependent origination, they were expounded in order to dispel delusion with respect to the processes of dependent origination held by some who maintain the view that all things have emerged from an [inherently] existing "self," and by others who maintain the nihilist view that all things have emerged without a causal basis.[29]

In brief, these [constituents of Buddhist phenomenology] were sequentially taught as an antidote for delusion with regard to the abiding nature of [all] objects of knowledge.

Extensive Exegesis of the Actual Phenomenological Framework [C]

Thirdly, [the extensive exegesis of the actual structure of Buddhist phenomenology] has three parts:

(1) a systematic presentation of the psycho-physical aggregates, sensory bases, and sensory activity fields which the [Buddhist] vehicles commonly accept
(2) a systematic presentation of the twenty-five aspects of phenomenal existence and other [related phenomenological] structures, according to the uncommon tradition of the final promulgation[30]
(3) a systematic presentation of the processes of dependent origination, integrating the approaches of both the Greater and Lesser Vehicles

A Systematic Presentation of the Psycho-physical Aggregates, Sensory Bases, and Sensory Activity Fields Which the Buddhist Vehicles Commonly Accept [1]

The first part has two sections: (1) an exegesis emphasizing the distinct phenomenological structures according to the tradition of Higher Abhidharma, and (2) an exegesis summarizing these structures according to Lower Abhidharma.[31]

4. The Tradition of Higher Abhidharma

a. Phenomenological Structures according to Higher Abhidharma [III.C.1.a]

- i. The Five Psycho-physical Aggregates
  - aa. Essential Nature of the Psycho-physical Aggregates
  - bb. Classification of the Psycho-physical Aggregates
    - 1' Brief Presentation
    - 2' Detailed Exegesis
      - a' The Aggregate of Physical Forms
        - i' Essential Nature
        - ii' Classification
          - aa' Primary Matter
          - bb' Derivative Matter
            - 1" Five Sense Organs
            - 2" Five Sense Objects
              - a" Visual Forms
              - b" Sounds
              - c" Odors
              - d" Tastes
              - e" Tangibles
          - cc' Sensory Activity Field of Phenomena
            - 1" Essential Nature
            - 2" Classification
      - b' The Aggregate of Feelings
        - i' Essential Nature
        - ii' Classification
          - aa' Feelings according to Their Essential Nature
          - bb' Feelings according to Their Affinity

c' The Aggregate of Perceptions
- i' Essential Nature
- ii' Classification
  - aa' Perceptions according to Their Essential Nature
  - bb' Perceptions according to Their Circumstances or Referents

d' The Aggregate of Formative Predispositions
- i' Essential Nature
- ii' Classification
  - aa' Formative Predispositions according to Their Essential Nature
  - bb' Formative Predispositions according to Their Circumstances
    - 1" Brief Description
    - 2" Detailed Exegesis
      - a" Formative Predispositions Associated with the Mind
        - i" Standard Account of Mind and Mental States
          - aa" The Essential Nature of Mind and Mental States
          - bb" Are Mind and Mental States Substantially Identical or Different?
          - cc" Relationships between the Central Mind and Peripheral Mental States
        - ii" Particular Explanation of Mental States
          - aa" Distinction between Mental States as Substantial and Imputed Existents
          - bb" Classification of Mental States
            - (1) The Five Ever-Present Mental States
            - (2) The Five Object-Determining Mental States
            - (3) The Eleven Wholesome Mental States
            - (4) Dissonant Mental States
              - (a) The Six Primary Dissonant Mental States
              - (b) Particular Classification of Wrong Views
                - (i) Essential Nature of Wrong Views
                - (ii) Actual Classification of Wrong Views

(aa) Classification That Accords with Their Essential Nature
(bb) Classification That Accords with Their Subcategories
(1') Mundane Views
(2') Extreme Views
(3') Indeterminate or Unspecified Views
(5) Subsidiary Dissonant Mental States
(6) Variable Mental States
b" Formative Predispositions Disassociated with the Mind
i" Essential Nature
ii" Classification
aa" Analysis of Twenty-three Formative Predispositions
bb" Synthesis in Eight Categories
e' The Aggregate of Consciousness
i' Brief Description
ii' Detailed Exegesis
aa' Exegesis of Mind or Substratum Consciousness
1" Defining Characteristics
2" Demonstrations
3" Objective Referents and Sense Data
4" Processes of Sensory Engagement and Reversal
a" Process of Sensory Engagement
b" Process of Reversal
5" Propensities That Issue from the Seminal Aspect of Substratum Consciousness
a" Brief Description
b" Detailed Exegesis
i" The Ground in Which Propensities Are Distributed
ii" The Distributors
iii" The Distribution Process
iv" The Actual Content of the Distributed Propensities
aa" Defining Characteristics
bb" Classification
cc" Natural Properties

dd" Essential Abiding Nature
ee" Localization
bb' Exegesis of Mentation, or Dissonant Mental Consciousness
1" Defining Characteristics
2" Demonstrations
3" Function
4" Processes of Engagement and Reversal
cc' Exegesis of the Six Modes of Engaged Consciousness
1" Essential Nature
2" Defining Characteristics
3" Locus, Sense Objects, and Concomitants
4" Functions and Origins
cc. Combinations of the Five Aggregates
ii. The Eighteen Sensory Bases
aa. Their Essential Nature
bb. Their Subdivisions
1' Brief Description
2' Detailed Exegesis
a' Sensory Bases Subsumed in the Psycho-physical Aggregates
b' Sensory Bases Not Subsumed in the Psycho-physical Aggregates
c' Sensory Base of Mental Phenomena
iii. The Twelve Sensory Activity Fields
aa. Their Essential Nature
bb. Reduction of the Sensory Bases into the Sensory Activity Fields

. . . .

Phenomenological Structures according to Higher Abhidharma [a]

First [in the tradition of Higher Abhidharma], there are three topics, comprising respectively the psycho-physical aggregates, the sensory bases, and the sensory activity fields. Since the *Compendium of Phenomenology*, representing the uncommon phenomenology of the Greater Vehicle, refers to an abundance of phenomenological categories and makes extensive and significant points [with regard to all these three topics], the exegesis that follows accords with that tradition.

The Five Psycho-physical Aggregates [i]

The systematic presentation of the psycho-physical aggregates has three aspects: (1) their essential nature, (2) their classification, and (3) their quantification [within the three world-systems].

Essential Nature of the Psycho-physical Aggregates [aa]

The first comments on the [expression]:

> **The bundle of the psycho-physical aggregates...**

As for the meaning of the term "psycho-physical aggregate," the Tibetan *phung po* corresponds to the Sanskrit *skandha*, a synonym of *rāśi*,[32] conveying the sense of a "collection" (*tshogs pa*) or "heap" (*spungs pa*). The "aggregates" are so called either because they function as heaps of multiple phenomena, partaking of a common class, or because they bundle together all the distinctive attributes of their [respective classes].

Classification of the Psycho-physical Aggregates [bb]

The second includes both a brief presentation and a detailed exegesis.

Brief Presentation [1']

The former [comments on the root verse]:

> **...is fivefold,**
> **Comprising physical forms, feelings, perceptions,**
> **Formative predispositions, and consciousness.**

Detailed Exegesis [2']

The latter has five aspects: (1) the aggregate of physical forms (*rūpaskandha, gzugs kyi phung po*), (2) the aggregate of feelings (*vedanāskandha, tshor ba'i phung po*), (3) the aggregate of perceptions (*saṃjñāskandha, 'du shes kyi phung po*), (4) the aggregate of formative predispositions[33] (*saṃskāraskandha, 'du byed kyi phung po*), and (5) the aggregate of consciousness (*vijñānaskandha, rnam par shes pa'i phung po*).

The Aggregate of Physical Forms [a']

Among them, the aggregate of physical forms is considered in terms of its essential nature and its classification.

Essential Nature [i']

The former comments on the [line]:

> **[The aggregate] capable of assuming physical forms...**

As is said in a sūtra:[34]

> O monks! The compulsively accrued aggregate of physical forms (*rūpopadānaskandha*) is so called because [matter] exists materially (*rūpaṇa*), and [therefore] is capable of assuming [visible] physical forms (*rūpya*).

The *Compendium* [*of Phenomenology*] adds:[35]

> It exists materially through physical contact (*sparśarūpaṇā*), and it exists materially through sensory localization (*viṣayarūpaṇā*).

[The former] refers to unprecedented changes that occur through the contact of physical objects (*rūpin*), as when, for example, a hand touches a flower and the attributes of that [flower] begin to wither. [The latter] refers to the sensa of physical form (*rūpākāra*) arising as mental objects.[36]

Classification [ii']

The latter includes (1) primary matter (*heturūpa, rgyu'i gzugs*), comprising the four gross elements (*'byung ba chen po bzhi*); (2) derivative matter (*phalarūpa, 'bras bu'i gzugs*), comprising the transformations of that primary [matter]; and (3) forms associated with the sensory activity field of phenomena (*chos kyi skye mched pa'i gzugs*).

Primary Matter [aa']

With regard to primary matter comprising the four elements, [it says in the root verses]:

> **. . . Includes the four elements of primary matter,**
> **Which [respectively] have solidity, fluidity, heat, and motion.**

Primary matter comprises the four elements—earth, water, fire, and wind. What, one might ask, are their properties? Although in worldly conventional terms it is [commonly] known that earth has color and form, and so forth, for those who understand the [classical] treatises, with reference to the actual meaning [of the elements], [it is said that] earth enables solidity and hardness to be sustained, water causes moisture and fluidity to cohere, fire causes heat and warmth to ripen, while wind causes lightness and motion to stir.[37]

Derivative Matter [bb']

Derivative matter includes both the five sense organs (*pañcendriya, dbang po lnga*) and their five objects (*pañcārtha, don lnga*).

Five Sense Organs [1"]

The former [comments on the root verses]:

> **With these [primary elements] acting as the causal basis,**
> **There is also derivative matter, including the five sense organs,**
> **Such as the eye, which supports [visual] consciousness...**

Derivative matter refers to that which derives from the four primary elements, acting as the causal basis. Among its particular aspects, there is the clear and sensitive matter (*ādhyātmakarūpa, nang gi gzugs dang ba*) [of the eyes], which is the support or possessive condition of visual consciousness. Similarly, there is the clear and sensitive matter [of the ears, nose, tongue, and body], which are respectively the supports or possessive conditions of auditory consciousness, olfactory consciousness, gustatory consciousness, and tactile consciousness. The five [gross] sense organs, including the eyes, also originate respectively from the corresponding aspects of these seeds, based upon the substratum [consciousness] (*ālaya, kun gzhi*).[38]

The term "clear" (*accha/ svaccha, dang ba*) here refers to the apperception (*pratívid, rnam par rig pa*) that arises when the clear sense organs perceive their [respective] objects on the basis of visual forms, sounds, and so forth, just as reflected images arise on a clear mirror, contingent on the actual forms that it reflects.[39]

Five Sense Objects [2"]

The latter [comments on the root verses]:

> **. . . And the five types of external object, such as visual form,**
> **Which are to be apprehended.**
> **There are twenty-five aspects of visual form,**
> **Divided into six or four categories.**

[As already stated,] derivative matter is that which has emerged from the four primary elements, acting as the causal basis. Its particular aspects include the five external objects (*pañcabāhyārtha, phyi rol gyi don lnga*), such as visual forms, which are to be apprehended respectively by the [five] sense organs, such as the visual forms that are apprehended by the eye.

Visual Forms [a"]

First, with reference to those visual forms which are the sense objects of the eye, the following twenty-five [aspects] have been distinctly enumerated: blueness, yellowness, redness, whiteness, longness, shortness, squareness, roundness, subtle particles, coarse particles, evenness, unevenness, highness, lowness, shadow, sun, light, darkness, cloud, smoke, dust, mist, [atmospheric] forms that are widespread and spacious (*abhiyavakāśikarūpa, mngon par skabs yod kyi gzugs*), apperceived [but intangible] forms (*vijñaptirūpa, rnam par rig byed kyi gzugs*), and monochrome sky (*nam mkha' kha dog gcig pa*).[40]

When these attributes are classified according to their defining characteristics [and so forth], they are explained according to six categories,[41] and when these are further reduced, they comprise the following four categories: (1) visual forms differentiated on the basis of color, including blueness, redness, etc.; (2) visual forms differentiated on the basis of shape, including squareness and roundness, etc.; (3) visual forms differentiated on the basis of appearance, including [atmospheric] forms that are widespread and spacious, exemplified by luminosity in the sky; and (4) visual forms differentiated by circumstances, including apperceived [but intangible] forms, which may be perceived on the basis of other, past impulses (*samutthāna, kun slong*), such as when the body is in motion, bending, rising, or sitting, or when the hands are doing something.

Among them, in this [tradition],[42] [phenomena belonging to] the [last] category, visual forms designated according to circumstances, are considered to be imputed existents (*prajñaptitaḥ, btags yod*), whereas both the pious attendants and the hermit buddhas hold them to be substantial existents (*dravyataḥ, rdzas yod*).[43]

Alternatively, [these twenty-five aspects of visual form] may be subsumed within the following four categories: positive, negative, neutral, and colorful.[44]

> **Sounds are of eleven types,**
> **Comprising four categories,**
> **[The last of which] when classified is fivefold.**
> **Odors are of six types, tastes of twelve types,**
> **And tangibles are of twenty-two types.**

Sounds [b'']

Second, with reference to the classification of sounds (*śabda, sgra*), the following eleven types have been distinctly enumerated: (1–3) pleasant, unpleasant, and neutral [sounds]; (4–6) sounds produced through the cause of the primary elements, which are either organic (*upāttamahābhūtahetukaśabda, zin pa'i 'byung ba las gyur ba'i sgra*) [such as human sounds], or inorganic (*anupāttamahābhūtahetukaśabda, ma zin pa'i 'byung ba las gyur ba'i sgra*) [such as rustling trees], or both [such as the sound of a musical instrument]; (7–9) sounds that are known in the world, or demonstrated by accomplished spiritual masters, or imagined; and (10–11) sounds that are designated as originating from sublime beings (*ārya, 'phags pa*) and from those who are not sublime.

These [eleven] are also explained to be subsumed into four categories, including [sounds] that are differentiated on the basis of their advantages and disadvantages (*phan gnod kyis phye ba*);[45] but when all these are further reduced, they comprise the following [three categories]: (1) the three types of sound differentiated on the basis of the feelings they evoke, namely, pleasant, unpleasant, and neutral sounds; (2) the three types of sound differentiated on the basis of whether they are produced organically or inorganically, such as melodies which are organically produced, the sound of water which is inorganically produced, and the beating of a drum by a human being which is both [organically and inorganically produced]; and (3) the five types of sound differentiated on the basis of imputed symbols and conventions, namely, (i) terms that are imputed or designated by worldly [conventions], such as "vase" and "blanket"; (ii) terms that are expressed by accomplished spiritual masters, such as "emptiness" (*stong pa nyid*) and "selflessness" (*bdag med*); (iii) terms that are imagined by extremists and the like, such as "creator" (*byed po*) and "consumer" (*za bo*); (iv) terms that are designated by sublime beings, such as "purification" (*vyavadāna, rnam byang*); and (v) terms that have been designated by beings who are not sublime, such as the jargon employed by worldly folk.[46]

Odors [c"]

Third, with reference to the classification of odors (*gandha, dri*), the following six types are enumerated: (1–3) the three types of odor differentiated on the basis of the feelings they evoke, namely, those that are fragrant, strong,[47] and neutral; and (4–6) the three types of odor differentiated on the basis of circumstances, namely, those that are natural, compounded, and developmental.[48]

Tastes [d"]

Fourth, with reference to the classification of tastes (*rasa, ro*), the following twelve types are enumerated: (1–6) the six types of taste differentiated on the basis of their essential nature, comprising the three pleasant tastes that are sweet, astringent, and bitter, and the three unpleasant tastes that are sour, spicy, and salty; (7–9) the three types of taste differentiated on the basis of their advantages and disadvantages, namely, those that are pleasant, unpleasant, and neutral; and (10–12) the three types of taste differentiated on the basis of their circumstances, namely, those that are natural, compounded, and modified.[49]

Tangibles [e"]

Fifth, with reference to the classification of tangible objects or sensations (*spraṣṭavya, reg bya*), the following twenty-two types are enumerated: softness, roughness, lightness, heaviness, suppleness or flexibility, languidness, tension, [warmth],[50] coldness, hunger, thirst, satisfaction, strength, weakness, faintness, itchiness, putrefaction, sickness, aging, death, fatigue, rest, and energy.[51]

It is explained that these [twenty-two types of tangible sensation] may also be subsumed within six categories, including tangible sensations that are based on touch (*āmarśanasthita, kun tu brnabs pas bzhag pa*) and so forth.[52] Then, when these are further reduced, they comprise (1) tangible sensations differentiated on the basis of mutual contact or interaction, namely, those of softness, roughness, and so forth; (2) tangible sensations differentiated on the basis of whether the outer and inner elements are balanced or imbalanced, namely, those of warmth, coldness, hunger, thirst, and so forth; and (3) tangible sensations differentiated on the basis of circumstances, namely, those of faintness, itchiness, and so forth.[53]

Sensory Activity Field of Phenomena [cc']

The third [aspect of the aggregate of physical forms] is an exegesis on those physical forms constituting the sensory activity field of phenomena (*dharmāyatana, chos kyi skye mched*). This has two aspects, the essential nature [of the sensory activity field of phenomena] and the classification [of its forms].

Essential Nature [1"]

Concerning the former [it says in the root verses]:

> **The physical forms that constitute the sensory activity field of phenomena,**
> **Being unrevealed and unobstructed...**

The term "sensory activity field of phenomena" refers to the appearances of physical form that are exclusively within the range of the mental faculty (*mana indriya, yid kyi dbang po*) and are [therefore] neither revealed to visual consciousness (*cakṣurvijñāna, mig shes*) nor obstructed by tangible objects.[54]

Classification [2"]

Concerning the latter [it says in the root verses]:

> **. . . Are of five types, including [atomic] forms that are extremely concentrated.**

The classification of those [forms constituting the sensory activity field of phenomena] is fivefold, starting with [atomic] forms that are extremely [small and] concentrated (*ābhisaṃkṣepikarūpa, bsdus pa las gyur pa'i gzugs*). Altogether they are enumerated as follows:

(1) the forms that are extremely [small and] concentrated, such as indivisible atomic particles (*paramāṇu, rdul phra rab*), which appear as the objects of mental consciousness (*manovijñāna, yid shes*)

(2) the forms that are widespread and spacious, such as atmospheric phenomena, which appear to mental consciousness [but not to visual consciousness]

(3) the forms that derive from genuine meditative commitment (*sāmādānikarūpa, yang dag par blangs pa las byung ba*), such as uninterrupted [visualized] forms (*ātyantikarūpa, gtan du ba'i gzugs*) [indicative of spiritual progress], appearing in the mind that has genuinely assumed [monastic or spiritual] vows and achieved renunciation. These are also called "non-apperceived forms" (*avijñaptirūpa, rnam par rig byed ma yin pa'i gzugs*) because they are imperceptible to others with different motivations

(4) the forms that are imagined (*parikalpitarūpa, kun brtags pa'i gzugs*), such as the skeleton that appears [in the mind while practicing] the meditative stability on impure phenomena (*aśucisamādhi, mi gstang ba'i ting nge 'dzin*)[55]

(5) the forms that derive from supernormal powers (*vaibhutvikarūpa, dbang 'byor ba'i gzugs*), such as the form of the earth element that derives from the meditative stability of the all-consuming earth element (*zad par sa'i ting nge 'dzin*). These are also called "images that appear within the perceptual range of meditative stability" (*ting nge 'dzin gyi spyod yul gzugs brnyan*[56]

There are also many other ways in which [forms] may be classified. For example, there is a threefold classification into [forms] that are (1) revealed and obstructed (*sanidarśanasapratigha, bstan yod thogs bcas*); (2) unrevealed and obstructed (*anidarśanasapratigha, bstan med thogs bcas*); and (3) unrevealed and unobstructed (*anidarśanāpratigha, bstan med thogs med*).[57]

And, there is a twofold classification into [forms] that are organically retained (*upāttasaṃkṣipta, zin pas bsdus pa*) and those that are unretained (*anupāttasaṃkṣipta, zin pa ma yin pas bsdus pa*);[58] or into forms with a shared support (*sabhāga, rten mtshungs*) and forms resembling those with a shared support (*tatsabhāga, de'i mtshungs kyi gzugs*).[59]

The Aggregate of Feelings [b']

Secondly, the aggregate of feelings is considered in terms of its essential nature and its classification.

Essential Nature [i']

The former comments on the [verse]:

> **Mental processes experienced through sensory contact**
> **Are endowed with happiness, sorrow, and neutrality.**

The [aggregate of feelings] refers to the mental processes endowed with emotional experiences of happiness, sorrow, or neutrality, ripening through exposure to sensory contact. The term "aggregate," [as before,] denotes a heap of multiple phenomena, partaking of a common class.

Classification [ii']

The latter has two topics: (1) feelings classified according to their essential nature and (2) feelings differentiated according to their affinity.

Feelings according to Their Essential Nature [aa']

As to the first [it says in the root verses]:

> **There are six types of feeling,**
> **Conditioned by sensory contact that is compounded...**

These are the six types [of feelings], beginning with the feelings conditioned by sensory contact that is visually compounded, and ending with the feelings conditioned by sensory contact that is mentally compounded.[60]

Feelings according to Their Affinity [bb']

As to the second [it says in the root verses]:

> **. . . And there are two ways in which [feelings] may be differentiated**
> **According to their affinity.**

There are two ways in which [feelings] may be differentiated according to their affinity (*sabhāga, mtshungs ldan*)—one comprising six categories [of feelings] and the other comprising five categories.

First, the sixfold classification is as follows: (1) physical feelings or sensations originating in affinity with the five types of sensory consciousness, each of which includes feelings of pleasure, pain, and neutrality; (2) mental feelings originating in affinity with mental consciousness; (3) disturbed feelings originating in affinity with attachment to self, which is dependent on the five compulsively acquired psycho-physical aggregates; (4) undisturbed feelings acting as an actual antidote for the [aforementioned attachment]; (5) feelings associated with greed, originating in affinity with attachment to the objects of the five senses; and (6) feelings dependent on renunciation which function as an actual antidote for the [aforementioned greed].[61]

The latter is the fivefold classification, comprising (1) sensual happiness which has affinity with the five types of sensory consciousness; (2) mental happiness which has affinity with mental consciousness; (3) physical pain which has affinity with [the five types of] sensory consciousness; (4) mental unhappiness which has affinity with mental consciousness; and (5) equanimity that is free from both happiness and sorrow.

The Aggregate of Perceptions [c']

Third, the aggregate of perceptions is considered in terms of its essential nature and its classification.

Essential Nature [i']

The former comments on the [expression]:

> **Compounded perceptions...**

The [aggregate of perceptions] refers to the mental processes whereby perceptual activity, compounded of three or four conditions, distinctly apprehends the particular attributes of its object, without confusing a single identifying mark or sign.

Classification [ii']

The latter has two topics: (1) perceptions classified according to their essential nature and (2) perceptions differentiated according to their circumstances or objects of reference.

Perceptions according to Their Essential Nature [aa']

As to the first [it says in the root verses]:

> **... are differentiated according to their essential nature.**

These are the six types [of perception], beginning with perceptions conditioned by sensory contact that is visually compounded, and ending with perceptions conditioned by sensory contact that is mentally[62] compounded.

Perceptions according to Their Circumstances or Referents [bb']

As to the second [it says in the root verses]:

> **And there are also six types of [perception]**
> **Compounded by [different] levels [of experience],**
> **Starting with non-symbolic [perception].**

These six [different types of perception] are enumerated as follows:

(1) perceptions coincidental with meditative equipoise in reality, which are [known as] non-symbolic perceptions (*animittasaṃjñā, mtshan ma med pa'i 'du shes*), unknown in conventional terms; and also perceptions compounded by the levels of meditative equipoise at the summit of existence [within the formless realms]
(2) all perceptions compounded by the levels of the three world systems, excluding the aforementioned, which are classed as symbolic perceptions (*sanimittasaṃjñā, mtshan ma dang bcas pa'i 'du shes*)
(3) perceptions compounded by the levels of the world system of desire, which are [known as] limited perceptions (*parīttasaṃjñā, chung ngu'i 'du shes*)

(4) perceptions compounded by the levels of the world-system of form, which are [known as] extensive perceptions (*mahadgatasaṃjñā, chen po'i 'du shes*)[63]

(5) perceptions compounded by the sensory activity fields of infinite space and infinite consciousness, which are [known as] infinite perceptions (*aprameyasaṃjñā, tshad med pa'i 'du shes*)

(6) perceptions compounded by the level of nothing-at-all, which is [known as] the perception of nothing-at-all (*akiṃcanyasaṃjñā, ci yang med pa'i 'du shes*)[64]

The Aggregate of Formative Predispositions [d']

Fourth, the aggregate of formative predispositions is considered in terms of its essential nature and its classification.

Essential Nature [i']

The former comments on the [line]:

Formative predispositions interact with their points of reference.

The [aggregate of formative predispositions] refers to the mental processes whereby the mind, through an accumulation or combination of [various] conditions, directly interacts with its objects or points of reference, and is driven or motivated towards diverse objects.[65]

Classification [ii']

The latter has two topics: (1) formative predispositions classified according to their essential nature and (2) formative predispositions differentiated according to their circumstances.

Formative Predispositions according to Their Essential Nature [aa']

As to the first [it says in the root verses]:

According to their essential nature, they are of six types.

These are the six types [of formative predispositions], beginning with those through which the mind directly interacts with its point of reference, originating from sensory contact that is visually compounded, and ending with those through which the mind directly interacts with its point of reference, originating from sensory contact that is mentally compounded.

The learned have also designated this [aggregate] by the term "mental processes associated with mental states" (*sems byung sems pa*).

Formative Predispositions according to Their Circumstances [bb']

The second includes both a brief description and a detailed exegesis.

Brief Description [1"]

With regard to the former [it says in the root verses]:

> **According to their circumstances, [formative predispositions]**
> **Comprise those both associated and disassociated with the mind.**

When differentiated according to their circumstances, there are formative predispositions associated with the mind (*cittaprayuktasaṃskāra*, *sems dang mtshungs ldan gyi 'du byed*) and formative predispositions disassociated with the mind (*cittaviprayuktasaṃskāra, mtshungs par ldan pa ma yin pa'i 'du byed*).

Detailed Exegesis [2"]

The latter, the detailed exegesis has two parts, comprising formative predispositions associated with the mind and formative predispositions disassociated with the mind.

Formative Predispositions Associated with the Mind [a"]

The first of these includes both a standard account of mind and mental states, and a particular explanation of mental states.

Standard Account of Mind and Mental States [i"]

The standard account, in turn, has three topics: (1) recognition of the essential nature [of mind and mental states], (2) an investigation into whether [mind and mental states] are [substantially] identical or different, and (3) [the relationships between] the principal [mind] and peripheral [mental states] that are to be ascertained.

The Essential Nature of Mind and Mental States [aa"]

The first of these three topics itself includes (1) the distinctions between the defining characteristics [of mind and its mental states], and (2) a presentation [of mental states] based on their concomitance [with the mind].

With regard to the first [the defining characteristics of mind and its mental states, it says in the root verses]:

> **The mind perceives the essential nature of a [given] object,**
> **While mental states perceive the distinguishing attributes of a [given] object.**

What, in general, you may ask, are the defining characteristics of mind (*citta, sems*) and mental states (*sems byung, caitasika*)? Mind comprises the eight modes of consciousness (*rnam shes tshogs brgyad*), and objectively refers to its given range of objects.[66] As such, its perceptual range is the essential nature of [a given] object, i.e., the supporting substance, exemplified by a visual form or sound. Mental states comprise fifty-one aspects such as feeling (*vedanā, tshor ba*), and objectively refer to their given range of objects.[67] As such, their perceptual range comprises the distinguishing attributes of [a given] object, i.e., the supported qualities, exemplified by states of happiness and suffering, or moods that are pleasant and unpleasant. Therefore, it is said in the *Analysis of the Middle and Extremes* that mind perceives the essential nature of its [given] object and mental states perceive the distinguishing attributes of their [given] object.[68]

With regard to the second [the presentation of mental states based on their concomitance with the mind, it says in the root verses]:

> **[Mental states] adhere to the mind**
> **Through their five concomitant [characteristics],**
> **Such as their [common] location.**

It is explained in [Vasubandhu's *Dissertation on*] *the Five Psycho-physical Aggregates* and in its *Commentary* composed by Sthiramati,[69] that the central mind and its peripheral mental states have a natural concomitance that is acquired through five unrelated factors. That is to say, mental states adhere to mind through their five concomitant characteristics (*pañcasamprayuktaka, mtshungs ldan rnam pa lnga*), starting from their [concomitance of] location or support, and continuing through their [concomitance of] objective referent, their [concomitance of] sensum, their [concomitance of] time, and their [concomitance of] substance.[70]

Among these, first, concomitance of support (*āśrayasamprayukta, rten mtshungs*) means that both the central [mind] and peripheral [mental states] are dependent on a single sense organ. For example, when visual consciousness depends on the sense organ of the eye, its peripheral feelings or sensations also depend on that identical [sense organ].

Second, concomitance of objective referent (*ālambanasamprayukta, dmigs mtshungs*) means that [both the mind and its mental states] refer to an identical object. For example, when visual consciousness refers to a visual form, [the peripheral] feelings or sensations also refer to that [identical object].

Third, concomitance of sensum (*ākārasamprayukta, rnam pa mtshungs*) means that [both the mind and its mental states] share an identical sensum in the course of sensory apprehension. For example, when the sensum of blueness arises in visual consciousness, that [identical sensum] also arises in respect of [the peripheral] feelings or sensations.

Fourth, concomitance of time (*kālasamprayukta, dus mtshungs*) means that [both the mind and its mental states] are active instantaneously. For example, whenever visual consciousness is active, [the peripheral] feelings or sensations are also active [in that same instant].

Fifth, concomitance of substance (*dravyasamprayukta, rdzas mtshungs*) means that [both the mind and its mental states] are of similar class and are identical in number. For example, if visual consciousness refers to a single substance, [the peripheral] feelings or sensations also refer only to a single substance.[71]

The rejection of doubt with regard to [certain apparent] contradictions concerning the concomitance of sensum and time, and so forth, are not discussed here, and these points should therefore be understood from [other] texts.[72]

Are Mind and Mental States Substantially Identical or Different? [bb"]

The second [of these three topics] is an investigation into whether [mind and mental states] are [substantially] identical or different (*gcig dang tha dad brtag pa*) [on which it is said in the root verses]:

> **Although they have been said to be identical [in substance],**
> **According to this tradition, they are different.**

If one were to ask whether mind and mental states are of a single substance or different, [Śāntarakṣita,] who is uniquely called "Bodhisattva" and so forth, along with the glorious Dharmakīrti, hold that both [mind and mental states] are of a single substance, while the master Candrakīrti holds that they are different.[73] Although such [opinions] are found, according to this tradition [of Higher Abhidharma], the sublime Asaṅga suggests that there would be six defects [if mind and mental states were identical in substance]. He disagrees [with this standpoint], stating, for example, that if mind and mental states were not different in substance, the definitive order of the five psycho-physical aggregates would not hold.[74] Therefore, we should follow his position.

[At the same time,] he also states that although they are different, this is with reference to material things. It is hard to investigate this remark in detail because he did not elaborate, and yet one should know that this [distinction between material and immaterial phenomena is understood] dependant on both scriptural authority grounded in conviction and logical reasoning, as when the sense organs focus upon sensitive [inner] forms [which are not objects of external sense perception].[75]

Relationships between the Central Mind and Peripheral Mental States [cc"]

The third [of these three topics] concerns the relationships between the central [mind] and peripheral [mental states] that are to be ascertained. On this [it says in the root verses]:

> **The [five] ever-present [mental] states emerge**
> **[Within the periphery of] the substratum [consciousness].**
> **These [same] five, along with four of the primary dissonant mental states,**

And six of the subsidiary dissonant mental states,
Emerge [within the periphery of] the dissonant mental consciousness.
However, all [of the fifty-one mental states] emerge
Within the periphery of the engaged modes of consciousness.

Here we shall examine how the eight modes of consciousness, subdivided into three groupings, give rise to specific categories among the fifty-one mental states:[76]

[First,] the so-called "five ever-present mental states" (*pañcasarvatraga, kun 'gro lnga*) arise within the periphery of the substratum [consciousness] (*ālayavijñāna, kun gzhi'i rnam par shes pa*).[77]

[Second,] these five, along with four of the six primary dissonant mental states (*sadmūlakleśa, rtsa nyong drug*)—namely, desire or attachment, pride, ignorance, and views concerning mundane aggregates—and six of the [twenty] subsidiary dissonant mental states (*viṃsatyopakleśa, nye nyon nyi shu*)—namely, distraction, carelessness, mental agitation, faithlessness, indolence, and dullness—all arise within the periphery of the dissonant mental consciousness (*kliṣṭamanovijñāna, nyon yid kyi rnam par shes pa*). The other [primary and secondary dissonant mental states] do not arise here because they are essentially dissimilar and lack the [requisite] concomitances of objective referent, sensum, and so forth.[78]

[Third,] in the case of the engaged modes of consciousness *(pravṛttivijñāna, 'jug pa'i rnam shes*), there are two sorts [of mental process]: one in which the conditions are only simulated, as when visual forms are involuntarily perceived, and the other in which the mind has precedence, as when they are voluntarily perceived. In this regard, only the five ever-present mental states arise within the periphery of the former [involuntary or passive consciousness] because if the other [mental] states were to manifest therein, there would be no such thing as blindness, for example.

In the case of the latter [voluntary or active consciousness], there are twenty-three [mental states] which may arise within the periphery of the five sense consciousnesses (*pañcadvāravijñāna, sgo lnga rnam shes*) when they are engaged in virtuous actions, namely, the first twenty-one [of the fifty-one] mental states, along with [the last two], ideation and scrutiny. There are also twenty-five [mental states] which may arise within the periphery of those [five sensory modes of consciousnesses] when they are engaged in defiled actions, namely, the first ten, the "three poisons" among the six primary dissonant mental states, and the last group of ten subsidiary dissonant mental states, along with ideation and scrutiny. In addition, there are twelve [mental states] that may arise within the periphery of [those five modes of sensory consciousness] when they are engaged in unspecified or indeterminate actions, namely, the first ten along with [the last two], ideation and scrutiny.

Furthermore, there are twenty-five [mental states] that may arise within the periphery of mental consciousness (*manovijñāna, yid kyi rnam par shes pa*) when it is engaged in virtuous actions, namely, the first twenty-one and the four variable mental states, which all pertain to the world-system of desire. However, all the mental states, with the exception of the eleven virtuous ones (*dge ba bcu gcig*) may arise within the periphery of that [same mental consciousness] when it is engaged in defiled actions, while [only] the first ten and the last four may arise within its periphery when it is engaged in unspecified or indeterminate actions.

In brief, all [fifty-one] mental states arise according to their respective circumstances. The reasons why they do so can be known through investigation, starting with the defining characteristics of each of them in turn.[79]

Particular Explanation of Mental States [ii"]

The second part [of the account of mental states which are associated with mind] comprises a particular explanation of mental states. It itself has two parts: (1) the distinction between [mental states] that are substantial existents and those that are imputed [existents], and (2) an exegesis differentiating each [of the mental states] individually.

Distinction between Mental States as Substantial and Imputed Existents [aa"]

With regard to the former [it says in the root verses]:

> **Twenty-two [mental states] are substantial existents**
> **And twenty-nine of them are imputed existents.**
> **Among the four [generally recognized criteria that determine substantial existents],**
> **Here, only autonomous mental states are accepted [as substantial existents],**
> **While only partial mental states are accepted [as imputed existents].**

In general, with regard to the determination of things that are substantial existents (*dravyataḥ, rdzas yod*) and those that are imputed existents (*prajñaptitaḥ, btags yod*), the scriptures consider things to be substantially existent when they are causally effective (*arthakriyāsamartha, don byed nus pa*), proven through reason (*rigs pas grub pa*), continuous (*rgyun brtan pa*), and autonomous (*rang rkya thub pa*).

Among these four criteria, here [in this tradition of Higher Abhidharma], only the last [autonomy] can determine whether things are substantially existent. An autonomous object is exemplified by something that arises as an intrinsic object-universal (*svārthasāmānya, kho'i don spyi*) and is not dependent on the arising of an extraneous object-universal (*anyārthasāmānya, gzhan gyi don spyi*).[80]

However, in other [traditions], all [mental states] may be implicitly established as substantial existents on the basis of their causal effectiveness and reasoned proof, while the [mental state known as] "mundane view" or "view of mundane aggregates" (*satkāyadṛṣṭi, 'jig tshogs la lta ba*) may even be implicitly established as a substantial existent on the basis of its enduring continuity.[81]

Similarly, there are also four criteria in respect of imputed existents. Among them, existents imputed on the basis of circumstances are exemplified by [mental states] disassociated with the mind (*cittaviprayuktacaitasika*). Existents imputed through exaggeration, while not actually existing, are exemplified by [the concepts of] "self" and the "horns of a hare." Existents imputed through extraneous [labeling] are exemplified by [the concept of] a "vase." However, existents imputed through their parts are the fragments of the phenomena which are the basis of their designation and these, [being valid,] are not to be rejected.

Accordingly, the master Sthiramati has explained that [a mental state] which has its intrinsic continuity independently established is a substantial existent, while one that does not is an imputed existent.[82]

In this regard, [the mental states that are classed] as substantial existents are twenty-two in number, including the first two groups of five, along with seven [of the eleven] wholesome mental states (*kuśalacaitasika, dge ba'i sems byung*), with the exception of non-delusion, vigilance, equanimity, and non-violence, and five [of the six primary] dissonant mental states, with the exception of [wrong] view. This is because they are autonomous and not dependent on other [object-universals].

[The mental states that are classed] as imputed existents are twenty-nine in number, including the four remaining wholesome mental states, along with [wrong] view [among the six primary dissonant mental states], the twenty subsidiary dissonant mental states, and the four variable mental states (*gzhan 'gyur bzhi*). This is because, in their essential nature, they turn the mind towards its object and are [therefore] dependent on specific phenomena which are the basis of their designation.[83]

In brief, as explained above, these [categories of] substantial and imputed existents are each determined on the basis of four criteria, among which, in this tradition [of Higher Abhidharma], it is maintained that substantial existents are autonomous and imputed existents are partial or incomplete.

The exact number and the sequence [of the mental states] is established on the basis of supposition, and is not precise. Therefore, in the *Minor Transmissions* (*Kṣudrāgama*), the mental states are numbered fifty-seven, while in the texts of the mantra [traditions], other sources give other figures, exemplified by the eighty natural [states of conceptual thought] ([*kun rtog gi*] *rang bzhin brgyad cu*).[84] However, all of them are designated as "mental states" (*caitasika, sems byung*) because they are contingent on the mind and arise from the mind, or because they emerge from the mind and emerge dependent upon the mind, or else because they are modifications of the mind, just as the ripples of a river are modifications of the river. Since they emerge immediately in the manner of the sound of a conch shell and the flames of a fire, there is no need [to state] even that they emerge [in a subsequent moment] respectively from their homogeneous classes (*sajātīya, rigs 'dra las 'byung ba*).[85]

Classification of Mental States [bb"]

The mental states are altogether said to number fifty-one, divided into the following six categories.

The Five Ever-Present Mental States [(1)]

Regarding the first [it says in the root verses]:

> **The classification [of mental states] comprises**
> **The five ever-present mental states...**

It is explained in [Vasubandhu's] *Thirty Verses* that:[86]

> Feeling, perception, volition, contact, and attention
> Are the five ever-present mental states.

Among [the five ever-present mental states (*pañcasarvatraga, kun 'gro lnga*)] (1) feeling (*vedanā, tshor ba*) and (2) perception (*saṃjñā, 'du shes*) are both similar in their essential nature to the corresponding aggregates, apart from [certain] general and particular distinctions. The reason for these two having to be additionally included among the mental states is that they are the roots of disputation, foremost among the causal bases [of the continuity] of cyclic existence—feeling is the basis on which the laity engage in disputations concerning sentiments of happiness and sorrow, while perception is the basis on which renunciant monks engage in disputations concerning different views. (3) Volition (*cetanā, sems pa*) is a modification of the mind, occurring in the circumstances when the mind is propelled towards its object. (4) Contact (*sparśa, reg pa*) is the imposition or confirmation of [certain] modifications of the sense faculties [through the preclusion of others], in conformity with feelings of happiness and sorrow, whenever sense objects, faculties, and consciousness interact. (5) Attention (*manaskāra, yid byed*) is the apprehension of details, through which the mind focuses repeatedly on its object.[87]

If any one of these five [ever-present mental states] is absent, the process through which the mind focuses on its object will be incomplete. They are designated as "ever-present" because they shadow all aspects of consciousness assumed by the central mind, compounded by [all sentient beings within] the three world-systems.[88]

The Five Object-Determining Mental States [(2)]

With regard to the second [category, it says in the root verses]:

> **. . . The five object-determining mental states...**

It is said in the *Thirty Verses*:[89]

> Will, resolve, mindfulness, meditative stability, and discriminative awareness
> Are the five object-determining sensa that arise.

Among [these five object-determining mental states (*pañcaviṣayaniyata, yul nges lnga*)], (6) will (*chanda, 'dun pa*) is the striving towards a conceived objective; (7) resolve (*adhimokṣa, mos pa*) is the focusing exclusively on an ascertained object; (8) mindfulness (*smṛti, dran pa*) is the non-forgetting of an object with which one has experience or familiarity; (9) meditative stability (*samādhi, ting nge 'dzin*) is the one-pointed mental focus on an object to be investigated, such as the coarse and quiescent [objects of higher insight][90] and the four truths;[91] and (10) discriminative awareness (*prajñā, shes rab*) is the analysis of specific and general defining characteristics.[92]

These are all designated as "object-determining mental states" because they determine their objects, which are [respectively] conceived, ascertained, experienced, and investigated, without the mind grasping anything apart from these objects.

The Eleven Wholesome Mental States [(3)]

With regard to the third [category, it says in the root verses]:

> **. . . The eleven wholesome mental states...**

It is said in the *Thirty Verses*:[93]

> Faith, conscience, shame, non-attachment, non-hatred, non-delusion,
> Perseverance, refinement, vigilance, equanimity, and non-violence:
> These eleven are wholesome mental states.

As for [these eleven wholesome mental states (*ekadaśakuśalacaitasika, dge ba'i sems byung bcu gcig*)], (11) faith (*śraddhā, dad pa*) has three qualities—conviction, serenity, and eagerness; (12) conscience (*hrī, ngo tsha shes pa*) is the means of avoiding inadmissible or censurable offences with reference to oneself; (13) shame (*apatrāpya, khrel yod*) is the means of avoiding those [offences] with reference to others; (14) non-attachment (*alobha, ma chags pa*) is the manifest absence of clinging to the five psycho-physical aggregates, which are compulsively acquired, and to mundane resources; (15) non-hatred (*adveṣa, zhe sdang med pa*) is the absence of enmity with regard to inimical objects; (16) non-delusion (*amoha, gti mug med pa*) is the absence of delusion with regard to the practices that are to be adopted and those that are to be rejected; (17) perseverance (*vīrya, brtson 'grus*) is the non-relaxation of enthusiasm for virtuous actions; (18) refinement (*praśrabdhi, shin sbyangs*) is the ability of the mind to engage its object of reference with physical and mental malleability; (19) vigilance (*apramāda, bag yod*) is the means of protecting the mind against things that are corrupt and of meditating on things that are virtuous; (20) equanimity (*upekṣā, btang snyoms*) is the means of abiding effortlessly in sameness when absorbed in meditative equipoise (*samasaṃsthāpa*) without being submerged by mental dullness, agitation, and so forth; (21) non-violence (*ahiṃsa, mi 'tshe ba*) is the means of not harming others owing to the [presence of] the mind's compassionate aspect.[94]

These [eleven] are all designated as "wholesome mental states" and established as virtuous phenomena, ensuring that a pleasant ripening [result] will emerge through the appropriate ethical practices. As such, they are the causal bases [of virtuous conduct], [collectively] named according to their fruitional effect.

Dissonant Mental States [(4)]

The fourth [category of mental states] has two aspects: (1) a general explanation of the six primary dissonant mental states and (2) the particular classifications of [wrong] view.

The Six Primary Dissonant Mental States [(a)]

With regard to the former [it says in the root verses]:

> **. . . And the six primary dissonant mental states.**

[According to the *Thirty Verses*:[95]]

> Desire, anger, pride, ignorance, doubt and [wrong] view
> Are the six primary dissonant mental states.

As for [these six primary dissonant mental states (*sadmūlakleśa, rtsa nyon drug*)] (22) desire (*rāga, 'dod chags*) is attachment to the abodes, physical bodies, and resources associated with the three world-systems; (23) hostility (*pratigha, khong khro*) is a state of total enmity or malevolence, entailing (a) a sentient being intent on inflicting harm, (b) suffering, which is the [actual] harm inflicted, and (c) poisoning, weapons, and so forth, which are the harmful conditions; (24) pride (*māna, nga rgyal*) is an exalted attitude (*cittasyonnatiḥ*) imbued with conceit and dependent on [wrong] views concerning mundane aggregates; (25) ignorance (*avidyā, ma rig pa*) can include both delusion with respect to the nature of reality and delusion with respect to the meaning of the four truths, and in this context it refers to the latter; (26) doubt (*vicikitsā, the tshom*) [can be understood] on many levels, but in this context it refers to hesitation and uncertainty with respect to the [four] truths, as well as to past actions and their results.[96]

Among these, pride also has seven subsidiary aspects (*saptamāna*), namely, (1) conceited pride (*ahaṃkāramāna, khengs pa'i nga rgyal*), thinking of oneself and those of similar talents as peers; (2) exalted pride (*adhimāna, che ba'i nga rgyal*), thinking that one is superior to one's peers; (3) exaggerated pride (*mānātimāna, nga rgyal las kyang nga rgyal*), thinking that one surpasses even the self that exhibits exalted pride; (4) egotistical pride (*asmimāna, nga'o snyam pa'i nga rgyal*), exemplified by holding the view that the psychophysical aggregates are endowed with a "self"; (5) manifest pride (*abhimāna, mngon pa'i nga rgyal*), thinking that one has acquired qualifications that one has not [actually] acquired; (6) perverse pride (*mithyāmāna, 'dzin pa log pa'i nga rgyal*), holding that one is talented when one is actually untalented; and (7) slight pride (*ūnamāna, cung zad snyam pa'i nga rgyal*), thinking that one is [only] slightly lower than extraordinarily sublime beings.[97]

Particular Classification of Wrong Views [(b)]

The latter [the particular classifications of wrong view] includes both the essential nature [of wrong views] and the [actual] classification of [wrong views].

Essential Nature of Wrong Views [(i)]

Regarding the essential nature [of wrong views, it says in the root verses]:

> **Among these [six, wrong] view is endowed with afflicted discriminative awareness.**

Among the [six] primary dissonant mental states, the essential nature of (27) [wrong] view (*mithyādṛṣṭi, log par lta ba*), in particular, is that it is endowed with afflicted discriminative awareness. Dissonant or afflicted states (*kleśa, nyon mongs*) are non-quiescent causal seeds or actions arising within the mind.

Actual Classification of Wrong Views [(ii)]

Secondly, the [actual] classification of [wrong views] includes (1) the classification that accords with their essential nature and (2) the classification that accords with their subdivisions.

Classification That Accords with Their Essential Nature [(aa)]

With regard to the former [it says in the root verses]:

> **The essential nature [of wrong views] is fivefold,**
> **Including mundane views, extreme views, and so forth.**

The essential nature of negative viewpoints or wrong views is fivefold, comprising (1) mundane views (*satkāyadṛṣṭi, 'jig lta*), (2) extreme views (*antadṛṣṭi, mthar lta*), and so forth. The latter additionally include (3) adherence to the supremacy of wrong views (*dṛṣṭiparāmarśa, lta ba mchog 'dzin),* (4) adherence to the supremacy of ethical and ascetic disciplines (*śīlavrataparāmarśa, tshul khrims dang brtul zhugs mchog 'dzin*), and (5) heterodox views (*mithyāyadṛṣṭi, log par lta ba*).[98]

Among these five, concerning the first [mundane views], this comprises the views that regard the five compulsively acquired psycho-physical aggregates, which are composites of many perishable and impermanent [phenomena], as an [imperishable and permanent] "self" and as properties of an [imperishable and permanent] "self." Such viewpoints may be instinctive or imaginary—in the former case they may occur in all sorts of [conventional] circumstances where sentient beings entertain the thought of the first person singular, and in the latter case they refer to the views derived from poor spiritual advisors, such as the foremost of [non-Buddhist] extremists, who maintain that there is a permanent self existing independently of the psycho-physical aggregates.

Concerning the second, extreme views include the views that the self [falsely] apprehended by means of the [aforementioned] mundane view is either eternal or self-annihilating [at death].

As for the third [adherence to the supremacy of wrong view], this is attachment to the notion that mundane view, extreme view, and false view—these three, along with the psycho-physical aggregates, which are their subject-matter—are supreme and genuine.

As for the fourth [adherence to the supremacy of ethical and ascetic discipline], this is the view that poor ethical and ascetic discipline in pursuit of an inferior and poor objective are pure and conducive to liberation [from cyclic existence].

Then, as for the fifth, heterodox views are those which deny causes and results, along with the [four] truths, the [three] precious jewels, and so forth.

[Among these five kinds of view,] the first four are exaggerated viewpoints, while the last is largely one of deprecation.

Classification That Accords with Their Subcategories [(bb)]

With regard to the latter, the classification [of wrong views] that accords with their subdivisions [it says in the root verses]:

> **[These views] have three subcategories and their [respective] subdivisions.**

When [wrong views] are considered in terms of their subcategories, they form three classes, along with their respective subdivisions.

Mundane Views [(1')]

Among them, the subcategory of mundane views (*'jig lta'i char gtogs*) comprises twenty viewpoints concerning mundane aggregates (*viṃśatisatkāyadṛṣṭi, 'jig tshogs la lta ba nyi shu*), namely, the view that physical form is self, the view that physical form is endowed with self, the view that physical form is a possession of the self, and the view that the self abides in physical form; along with four similar viewpoints expressed in respect of each of the other four aggregates—feeling, perception, formative predispositions, and consciousness.[99]

Extreme Views [(2')]

[As for the subcategory of extreme views,] there are sixty-two extreme views [which have been enumerated] (*mthar lta drug cu rtsa gnyis*). Among them there are eighteen extreme views in respect of [speculations about] the limits of past time (*pūrvānta, sngon gyi mtha'*), comprising[100]

> Four views of eternalism, four views of partial eternalism,
> Two views of fortuitous origination, four views of finitude,
> And four views of equivocation regarding finitude.

There are also forty-two extreme views in respect of [speculations about] the limits of future time (*aparānta, phyi mtha'*), comprising[101]

> Sixteen views on percipient [immortality],
> Eight views on non-percipient [immortality],
> Eight views on neither percipient nor non-percipient [immortality],
> Seven views on nihilism,
> And five views on the attainment of liberation in this lifetime.

These are all included within the subcategories of both extreme view and false view. Alternatively, they may all be included among [the subcategory of] mundane view, as is said in the *Verse Summation [of the Transcendental Perfection of Discriminative Awareness]*:[102]

> The view concerning mundane aggregates comprises sixty-two [false] views.

Indeterminate or Unspecified Views [(3')]

There are also fourteen indeterminate or unspecified views (*caturdaśāvyākṛta-vastudṛṣṭi, lung ma bstan gyi lta ba bcu bzhi*). These include the view that the Tathāgata continues to exist after passing into [final] nirvāṇa, which is said to be a deluded view, other than the truth; and similarly the views that he does not continue to exist, that he both continues and does not continue to exist, and that he neither continues nor does not continue to exist. Thus there are four [unspecified] views with reference to [his] attainment of [final] nirvāṇa.

This subcategory also includes four extreme views with reference to future lives, namely, that the self and the world are finite, infinite, both, or neither; as well as four extreme views with reference to past lives, namely, that the self and the world are eternal, not eternal, both eternal and not eternal, and neither eternal nor not eternal. The first position in each of these distinct tetralemmas represents the eternalist view of the Sāṃkhya. The second position in each tetralemma represents the nihilist view of the Lokāyatika. The third position in each tetralemma represents the view of the Nirgrantha Jains that nature (*prakṛti*) is permanent and its actual circumstances impermanent. The fourth position in each of the tetralemmas represents the view of the Vātsīputrīya that nothing at all can be expressed with regard to permanence and impermanence.[103]

In addition, [this subcategory] also includes the view that the vitality or life-force is to be identified with the physical body, and the view that the vitality or life-force and the physical body are independent of one another.

Thus there are [two standpoints] with reference to the physical body and its vitality. The former represents the view of the Naiyāyika and the latter the view of the Sāṃkhya.

These fourteen standpoints are designated as "unspecified or indeterminate views" because when the transcendent lord [Buddha] was asked about them, he said, "Starting from the [concept of] self with regard to individual persons, one may know how to speculate [about these matters] but they cannot be established. Therefore, it is not right to investigate these points particularly, and I will not do so!" For this reason, his enlightened intention was not swayed in that direction, and these [speculations] were deemed to be indeterminate or unspecified.[104]

Subsidiary Dissonant Mental States [(5)]

With regard to the fifth [category of mental states, it says in the root verses]:

> **There are also twenty subsidiary dissonant mental states...**

It is said in the *Thirty Verses*:[105]

> Anger, enmity, hypocrisy, annoyance, jealousy,
> Miserliness, deceit, pretentiousness, self-satisfaction, violence,
> Lack of conscience, shamelessness, dullness, mental agitation,
> faithlessness,
> Indolence, carelessness, forgetfulness, distraction,[106] and
> inattentiveness,
> And similarly regret, drowsiness, ideation, and scrutiny—
> These are the subsidiary dissonant mental states,
> Though the last two pairs may be of two kinds.

The twenty listed here, from inattentiveness backwards, are consistently classed as subsidiary dissonant mental states (*upakleśa, nye bar nyon mongs*), while the [last] four—regret, drowsiness, ideation, and scrutiny—partake of some circumstances when they are dissonant and others when they are not, for which reason, when they do so, they are included alongside the subsidiary dissonant mental states.

Now, with regard to the first of the twenty that are consistently considered to be subsidiary dissonant mental states: (28) Anger (*krodha, khro ba*) is the inability to tolerate harmful [thoughts or deeds]. (29) Enmity (*upanāha, 'khon 'dzin*) deposits harmful [thoughts] in the mind. (30) Hypocrisy (*mrakṣa, 'chab pa*) is the concealment of one's own inadmissible faults. (31) Annoyance (*pradāśa, 'tshig pa*) is the desire to utter harsh words, preceded by anger and enmity. (32) Jealousy (*īrṣyā, phrag dog*) is the inability to tolerate the excellence of another. (33) Miserliness (*mātsarya, ser sna*) is not daring to use one's own resources. (34) Deceit (*māyā, sgyu*) is the physical or verbal fabrication one employs with an intention to deceive others. (35) Pretentiousness (*śāṭhya, gYo*) is the [deliberate] misrepresentation of one's own faults whenever they are seen or heard. (36) Self-satisfaction (*mada, rgyags pa*) is the obsession of those in the prime of life, and so forth, with their own prosperity and prestige. It entails attachment to one's own talents, in contrast to "pride," which entails conceit with regard to the talents of others. (37) Violence (*vihiṃsa, rnam par 'tshe ba*) is the permitting of oneself or others to engage in acts of killing, beating, and so forth. (38) Lack of conscience (*āhrikya, ngo tsha med pa*) is the non-avoidance of wrong-doing with regard to oneself. (39) Shamelessness (*anapatrāpya, khrel med pa*) is the non-avoidance of wrong-doing with regard to others. (40) Dullness (*styāna, rmugs pa*) is the lack of malleability in the mind with regard to its objects or sensa. (41) Mental agitation (*auddhatya, rgod pa*) is the reverting [of the mind] to previously encountered sense objects. (42) Faithlessness (*aśraddhya, ma dad pa*) is an absence of eagerness due to lack of conviction in virtuous teachings or wholesome phenomena. (43) Indolence (*kausīdya, le lo*) is the attachment to inferior activities and the lack of enthusiasm for wholesome phenomena. (44) Carelessness (*pramāda, bag med*) is the means of not protecting the mind [from corruption], permitting it to run carefree. (45) Forgetfulness (*muṣitasmṛtitā, brjed ngas pa*) is the lack of clarity and repeated loss of memory with respect to virtuous objects of reference. (46) Distraction (*vikṣepa, gYeng ba*) is the fascination of the mind for any objects associated with the three poisons. It has six aspects: natural distraction (*svabhāvavikṣepa, ngo bo nyid kyi gYeng ba*), exemplified by the consciousnesses of the five senses; external distraction (*bahirdhāvikṣepa, phyi rol du gYeng ba*), which is consciousness engaging its sense objects; internal distraction (*adhyātmavikṣepa, nang gi gYeng ba*), which occurs in the context of the mental dullness and agitation experienced when one savors meditative stability; the distraction of symbolism (*nimittavikṣepa, mtshan ma'i gYeng ba*), which is the practice of the [sacred] teachings for the sake of the eight [worldly] concerns;[107] distraction due to adverse circumstances (*dauṣṭhulyavikṣepa, gnas ngan len gyi gYeng ba*), which is craving for the happiness associated with physical and mental refinement; and distraction due to mental attention (*manasikāravikṣepa, yid la byed pa'i rnam gYeng*), which

occurs when the mind, without having completed its engagement in one object of reference, engages in another. (47) Inattentiveness (*asaṃprajanya, shes bzhin ma yin pa*) refers to the mental processes of the afflicted discriminative awareness that inappropriately scrutinizes states [of non-virtue] that are to be rejected and those [states of virtue] that are to be adopted.[108]

All of these are established as the [six] primary and [twenty] subsidiary or lesser dissonant mental states.

Variable Mental States [(6)]

With regard to the sixth [category of mental states, it says in the root verses]:

> **. . . And there are the four variable [mental states].**

With regard to these four, which are mentioned at the end of the aforementioned passage quoted from the *Thirty Verses*, (48) regret (*kaukṛtya, 'gyod pa*) refers to the subsequent thought of remorse in respect of an action that one has previously undertaken; (49) drowsiness (*middha, gnyid pa*) occurs when the six modes of the engaged consciousness (*satpravṛttivijñāna, 'jug pa'i sems drug*) are internally absorbed; (50) ideation (*vitarka, rtog pa*) refers to the [process of] coarse [mental] engagement with the phenomena characterized as formative predispositions; and (51) scrutiny (*vicāra, dpyod pa*) refers to the [process of] subtle mental engagement [with regard to the same phenomena].[109]

These four are all designated as "variable mental states" (*gzhan 'gyur bzhi*) because their application varies according to circumstances and they are unspecified in terms of wholesome and unwholesome [phenomena], without being limited to one or the other. They may be exemplified by the negativity that ensues when one regrets virtuous actions, the virtue that ensues when one regrets negative actions, the negativity that ensues when one becomes drowsy while focusing on virtuous actions, and the virtue that ensues when one becomes drowsy while focusing on negative actions.

Formative Predispositions Disassociated with the Mind [b'']

Secondly [see p. 489], the exegesis of formative predispositions disassociated with the mind (*cittaviprayuktasaṃskāra, mtshungs par ldan pa ma yin pa'i 'du byed*) includes (1) [a recognition of] their essential nature and (2) their classification.

Essential Nature [i"]

With regard to the former [it says in the root verses]:

> **The formative predispositions disassociated with the mind...**

This category [of formative predispositions] is designated as "disassociated" (*viprayukta, mi ldan pa*) because they do not, like mental states, partake of [the aforementioned] circumstances where the mind engages with its object of reference through the five concomitant characteristics (*pañcasamprayuktaka, mtshungs ldan rnam pa lnga*).[110] They are nonetheless designated as "formative predispositions" (*saṃskāra, 'du byed*) because they partake of predisposed circumstances.[111]

In this regard, Upa Losal[112] and others have held that these refer to circumstances other than physical form, mind, and mental states. As for [the opinion of] most [masters] of the past, Karma Trinlepa II[113] says that

> There is nothing other than physical form, mind, and mental states, but the designations that are imputed with regard to the circumstantial factors cannot be described as being either the same as or other than physical form, mind, and mental states. That is to say, they are neither established as any distinct substance apart from the triad of physical form and so on, which are the basis of their designation, nor [can they be considered to be] distinguishing counterparts (*vyatireka, ldog pa*) of those three kinds of entity, physical form and the like. They resemble, for example, a fist that cannot be described as identical with or anything other than its fingers.[114]

Classification [ii"]

Secondly, with regard to [the classification of formative predispositions disassociated with the mind], there are two parts: (1) the analysis of twenty-three [formative predispositions] and (2) their synthesis in eight categories.

Analysis of Twenty-three Formative Predispositions [aa"]

With regard to the former [it says in the root verses]:

...are twenty-three [in number].

In this regard, there are various extant enumerations and sequences, such as in the *Sūtra That Reveals the Ten Abodes*, where it is stated that there are seven hundred formative predispositions disassociated [with mind and mental states], and in the [*Dissertation on*] *the Five Psycho-physical Aggregates*, which presents a different account.[115]

However, when these are subsumed principally in accordance with the Higher Abhidharma [of the *Compendium of Phenomenology*, the following twenty-three formative predispositions are enumerated]:[116]

(1) Acquisition (*prāpti, thob pa*) is an imputed existent referring to the [particular or qualitative] circumstances of which all formative predispositions partake, including wholesome and unwholesome phenomena, although the Vaibhāṣika regard it as a substantial existent.[117]

(2) The meditative absorption devoid of perception (*asaṃjñīsamāpatti, 'du shes med pa'i snyoms 'jug*) is characterized as the cessation of the six modes of consciousness, which are non-stable conditions of mind and its mental states, by relying on the state of mind associated with the attainment phase of the fourth meditative concentration.[118]

(3) The meditative absorption of cessation (*nirodhasamāpatti, 'gog pa'i snyoms 'jug*) is characterized as the cessation of the six modes of consciousness, which are non-stable conditions of mind and its mental states, along with the dissonant mental consciousness which is their stable condition. This occurs when a sublime [practitioner] of the Lesser Vehicle, who has mastered calm abiding—his mind reaching the summit of existence—and higher insight, relies on whatever uncorrupted discriminative awareness is present in the mind-stream.[119]

(4) The state of non-perception (*āsaṃjñika, 'du shes med pa*) is characterized as the cessation of directly evident innate feelings and perceptions, deriving from the mind that has attained the fourth meditative concentration. This is a particular [attribute of] Great Fruition (*bṛhatphala, 'bras bu che*), a distinct abode associated with the fourth meditative concentration. This refers to the abode of the so-called "long-living gods" (*dīrghāyuṣadeva, lha tshe ring po*), who lack the leisure [to engage effectively in Buddhist practice] because they maintain a false view that deprecates [the possibility of attaining] release [from cyclic existence] at the time of their death, [knowing that] they would die and transmigrate [away from their exalted state] if perceptions were to arise.[120]

(5) The faculty of the life-force (*jīvitendriya, srog gi dbang po*) is the very substratum of formative predispositions, sustaining living beings for a fixed

period of time, in accordance with their respective classes. As such, it has a time-frame, measured in hundreds or thousands of years, or even lasting as long as an aeon, propelled by the force of the three kinds of deeds, generated in former lives.[121]

(6) Similarity of class or homogeneity (*nikāyasabhāga, rigs mthun pa*) refers to the sentient beings of the three world-systems and the psycho-physical aggregates through which they apprehend their respective objects. In the world-systems of desire and form, [sentient beings] appear to have a continuum comprising five [aggregates], whereas in the world-system of formlessness they have a continuum comprising four [aggregates]. Alternatively, [similarity of class] indicates the interrelationship of bodily parts belonging to sentient beings who may partake of different classes [gods, humans, etc.], assuming different physical appearances, and so forth.[122]

(7) Birth (*jāti, skye ba*) refers to the arising of a [particular] continuum of internal formative predispositions, which precludes [the possibility] of it taking birth in any other form. As such, [this continuum] partakes of a newly emerging [appearance], one that has not previously emerged.[123]

(8) Aging (*jarā, rga ba*) refers to the distinct transformational and sequential circumstances of which this continuum partakes, from the moment of birth through to the moment of death, including childhood, youth, adult maturity, and old age.

(9) Duration (*sthiti, gnas*) refers to the period during which this continuum does not perish, starting from birth and ending with death.

(10) Impermanence (*anityatā, mi rtag pa*) refers to the time of death, when this formerly existing continuum perishes and comes to an end.

(11) Nominal clusters (*nāmakāya, ming gi tshogs*) are the expressive designations which, although the essential nature of the aggregate of knowable phenomena and the like cannot actually be expressed, nonetheless extrapolate the essential nature of [generic] clusters [of phenomena], such as the eye and ears, or individual beings, such as gods and humans. "Names" are so-called because they are the means through which the intellect symbolically appraises conventional circumstances. "Clusters" are so-called because they combine within them many syllables or many similarities pertaining to their own particular classes.[124]

(12)[125] Phrasal clusters (*padakāya, tshig gi tshogs*) express [meaning] by extrapolating particularities, even though the particular attributes of phenomena cannot actually be expressed, as in the sentence, "All formative predispositions are impermanent." "Phrases or words" are so-called because through them particular objects are known. [The designation] "cluster" has already been explained.[126]

(13) Syllabic clusters (*vyañjanakāya, yi ge'i tshogs*) are the basis [of language] in that both nominal [clusters] and phrasal [clusters] emerge from their interrelated combinations. In this case, "cluster" (*tshogs*) means that [the syllables] combine minute phonemes or [syllables] of similar [phonetic] class.[127]

(14) The status of an ordinary individual (*pṛthagjanatva, so so'i skye bo*) refers to birth that is taken among the different distinct classes of living beings under the sway of the individual past actions when one has not obtained the sublime teachings [of Buddhism] that are remote from non-virtuous actions and has not abandoned the seeds of engagement in the three world-systems.[128]

(15) Engagement (*pravṛtti, 'jug pa*) refers to the process of uninterrupted continuity in respect of the [interrelated] circumstances of causes and results, because this [process] cannot cease, even for an instant.

(16) Distinctive regularity (*pratiniyama, so sor nges pa*) refers to the ascertainment made in accordance with actual reality (*dharmatā, chos nyid*) that virtuous and non-virtuous causes are differentiated, and that the results of past actions are also differentiated on the basis of patterns that are wanted and those that are unwanted.

(17) Connection (*yoga, 'byor 'brel ba*) refers to the rightfully obtained conformity of cause and result, exemplified by the resources that derive from generosity and the discriminative awareness that derives from learning.

(18) Rapidity (*java, mgyogs pa*) refers to the swift and fluid [succession of] circumstances on the basis of which particular causal results immediately arise and subside.

(19) Sequence (*anukrama, go rim*) refers to the orderly succession of individual causes and results, from one to the next, which does not emerge spontaneously.

(20) Time (*kāla, dus*) refers to the process whereby causes and results that have originated and then ceased are [designated as] "past," those that have not yet originated are [designated as] "future," and those that have originated but not ceased are [designated as] "present."

(21) Location (*deśa, yul*) refers to the [diverse] presence of causes and results subsumed in corporeal beings in all the ten directions [of space].

(22) Number (*saṃkhyā, grangs*) refers to the separate and distinct enumeration of [all] the formative predispositions, which is made because their differences are incompatible with them numbering only one.

(23) Grouping (*sāmagrī, tshogs pa*) refers to the combination of all interrelated conditions that pertain to [specific] causes and results, as, for example, in the case of the production of sensory consciousness, when sense objects, sense faculties, and mental attention—these three—are all grouped together.

Synthesis in Eight Categories [bb"]

With regard to the latter [it says in the root verses]:

> **They are subsumed in eight categories because they partake of**
> **Increase and decrease, an absence of cognizance,**
> **Abodes, similarity, characteristics, conventional terminology,**
> **And an absence of [spiritual] attainment,**
> **As well as causes and their results.**

Among these twenty-three [formative predispositions that are disassociated with mind and mental states, when they are all grouped together]: (1) the first one [acquisition] partakes of circumstances when it will increase and decrease; (2) the second, third, and fourth all partake of an absence of cognizance; (3) the fifth [the faculty of the life-force] partakes of abodes or realms; (4) the sixth partakes of similarity [of class or species]; (5) the four commencing with the seventh partake of the characteristics [of birth, aging, duration, and impermanence]; (6) the three commencing with the eleventh [i.e., nominal, phrasal, and syllabic clusters] partake of conventional terminology; (7) the fourteenth [the status of an ordinary individual] partakes of an absence of [higher spiritual] attainments; and (8) the nine commencing from the fifteenth partake of the circumstances that pertain to causes and their results.

So it is that all these [formative predispositions disassociated with mind and its mental states] are subsumed into eight categories.[129]

The Aggregate of Consciousness [e']

Fifth, [the explanation of] the aggregate of consciousness has two parts: (1) a brief description and (2) a detailed exegesis.

Brief Description [i']

Concerning the former [it says in the root verses]:

> **Mind, mentation, and consciousness**
> **Correlate to the eight modes [of consciousness].**

It is the case that "mind" (*citta, sems*), "mentation" (*manas, yid*), and "consciousness" (*vijñāna, rnam par shes pa*)—all three—are held by the Vaibhāṣika and Sautrāntika to be "term-universals" (*sāmānyaśabda, spyi sgra*) correlating with the six modes [of consciousness]. By contrast, the Mādhyamika and Cittamātrin apply them as term-universals correlating with the eight modes [of consciousness] (*tshogs brgyad*), whether in the context of the ordinary presentation [of mind] or with reference to the widest sense of these terms.[130]

The defining characteristic which these three terms [commonly] share is that they are all [aspects of] mind, apperceiving the essential nature of objects and differentiating the essential nature of their respective referents by means of cognition.

However, when the [mentalist] teachings are emphasized, or when one refers to these three terms in their narrowest possible sense, "mind," "intellect," and "consciousness" may be separately applied as follows:[131]

(1) The substratum consciousness (*ālayavijñāna, kun gzhi'i rnam par shes pa*) should be exclusively established as "mind" (*citta*) because (a) it accumulates the [latent] propensities or seeds of all the psycho-physical aggregates, sensory bases, and activity fields; (b) it refers objectively to the diversity [of its maturational propensities]; and (c) it cognizes its objects.

(2) The dissonant mental consciousness (*kliṣṭamanovijñāna, nyon yid kyi rnam par shes pa*) should be exclusively established as "mentation" (*manas*) because it is the cognition that at all times is conceited with pride, imposing egotistical thoughts on clear sensory images, for which reason it embodies arrogance and egotism.

(3) The six modes of engaged consciousness (*pravṛttivijñāna, 'jug shes tshogs drug*) should be exclusively established as "consciousness" (*vijñāna*) because they clearly refer to diverse particulars, engaging with their distinctive [sense] objects individually. Therefore, it is said in the [*Sūtra of the*] *Dense Array* (*Ghanavyūhasūtra*):[132]

> Mind pertains to the substratum consciousness,
> Mentation embodies the egotistical mind.
> Consciousness is that which apprehends sense objects.

Detailed Exegesis [ii']

The latter has three parts: (1) [the exegesis of] mind, which is the substratum [consciousness]; (2) [the exegesis of] mentation which is the dissonant mental consciousness; and (3) the exegesis of the six modes of [engaged] consciousness.

Exegesis of Mind or Substratum Consciousness [aa']

The first of these comprises five topics: (1) the defining characteristics [of the substratum consciousness]; (2) its demonstrations; (3) its objective referents and sense data; (4) its processes of engagement and reversal; and (5) an exegesis of the propensities (*vāsanā, bag chags*) that issue from the seminal aspect (*bījabhāga, sa bon gyi cha*) [of the substratum consciousness].

Defining Characteristics [1"]

With regard to the first [it says in the root verses]:

> **The substratum consciousness, unobscured and unspecified,**
> **Has both seminal and maturational aspects**
> **On the basis of which propensities are [actually] distributed.**

The ordinary or general definition of the substratum consciousness is that it is the unobscured and unspecified principal mode of consciousness, functioning as the ground from which propensities are actually distributed, cognizing the essential nature of its objects dependent on both its maturational aspects and its seminal aspects.[133]

Among the nuances implied by the term "aspect" (*cha*) in this context, the definition of the seminal aspect (*bījabhāga, sa bon gyi cha*) [of the substratum consciousness] is that it denotes the [latent] propensities present within the substratum, while the definition of the maturational aspect (*vipākabhāga, rnam smin gyi cha*) is that it is the causal condition giving rise to distinct fruitional phenomena. Therefore, the substratum is designated as "that in which seeds are fully ripened or perfumed, dependent on [latent] propensities that have been atemporally present."[134] In relation to phenomena that will manifest in the future, [the content of the substratum consciousness] is designated as "seminal" or "potential," and in relation to phenomena that have already manifested, it is designated as "maturational."[135]

Since both of [these seminal and maturational aspects] are in association with consciousness when it cognizes the essential nature of its objects, [it is] also [said that] the substratum consciousness in fact has three facets [seminal, maturational, and cognitive], which partake of an identical nature.

Demonstrations [2"]

With regard to the second, the demonstrations [of the substratum consciousness, it says in the root verses]:

> **It denotes associated [formative predispositions]**
> **Which are invisible and fractional,**
> **But objectively appear.**

The demonstrations (*lakṣya, mtshan gzhi*) [of the substratum consciousness] in general may be found in those sense data which, with reference to the internal compulsively acquired [psycho-physical aggregates] and to the external physical world, are invisible and fractional, and, therefore, barely capable of appearing objectively.[136] Such [sensa] are associated with the five ever-present mental states and particularly with equanimity, among the aspects of feeling (*vedanā, tshor ba*), and they are unobscured in their essential nature by dissonant mental states, unspecified in terms of virtuous and non-virtuous actions, and uninterrupted as long as cyclic existence endures.[137]

[More specifically,] the demonstrations of the seminal aspect [of the substratum consciousness] are found in those imprints of it which are endowed with propensities capable of regenerating the content of the substratum itself, while the demonstrations of the maturational aspect [of the substratum] are found in those imprints of it that are endowed with maturational phenomena that have already been ripened or projected by means of corrupt past actions.

Objective Referents and Sense Data [3"]

With regard to the third, the objective referents and sense data (*dmigs rnam*) [associated with the substratum consciousness, it says in the root verses]:

> **Compulsively acquiring corrupt [phenomena]...**

The internal objective referents [of the substratum consciousness] include compulsively acquired corrupt phenomena, such as the [non-material aggregates] "endowed with four names" (*ming bzhi'i phung po*), while the corresponding external [objective referents] comprise the apparent phenomena of the physical world. Even in [the world-system of] formlessness, [the substratum consciousness] refers objectively to its own seeds and to the [non-material aggregates endowed with] four names.

The sense data [associated with the substratum consciousness], though [subtle and] barely capable of appearing objectively, cannot be eliminated by superimposition. Consequently, their corresponding [external] objects are invisible [to consciousness] and imprecisely ascertained, and therefore cannot be delimited.[138]

Processes of Sensory Engagement and Reversal [4″]

Fourth, the processes of engagement and reversal [with respect to the substratum consciousness] are discussed in two parts: (1) the process of sensory engagement (*pravṛtti, 'jug tshul*) and (2) the process of its reversal (*nivṛtti, ldog tshul*).[139]

Process of Sensory Engagement [a″]

With regard to the former [it says in the root verses]:

> **. . . It engages continuously throughout the three world-systems. . .**

The engagement [of the substratum consciousness] occurs in respect of the external and internal objects which form its objective referent, and takes place exclusively in concomitance with the five ever-present mental states (*kun 'gro lnga*), [among] the associated mental states.[140]

This process is characterized as an "engagement based on interacting conditions," in that it depends on the interaction of the substratum consciousness with the engaged consciousness—analogous to the relationship between a structural supporting beam[141] and a building.[142]

Then again, this process may also be [described as] a "concurrent engagement" (*sahabhavapravṛtti, lhan cig 'jug pa*), implying that

(1) with the exception of the meditative equipoise of cessation, in circumstances in which the mind is inactive, [the engagement] will be concurrent with the dissonant mental consciousness;
(2) whereas, in the [world-system of] formlessness, it will be concurrent with both mentation and the mental consciousness; and
(3) in the [world-system] of desire, it will be conditionally concurrent with all the [other] seven modes [of consciousness].

In this way, the process of engagement is considered to be innately concurrent, regardless of whatever world-system the substratum relates to, whatever the class of sentient beings, whatever feelings are present, and whatever unspecified virtuous or non-virtuous mental states happen to arise. It does not function [merely] "in association with" these [respective levels of existence].[143]

Moreover, this engagement [of the substratum consciousness] is one that persists continuously through [a succession of] births. For, when [the substratum consciousness] pertaining to this [present] life expires, it will be revived by the propensities of past actions (*karmavāsanā, las kyi bag chags*) and the propensities of the subject-object dichotomy (*grāhyagrāhakavāsanā, bzung 'dzin gyi bag chags*) and then re-engage as the substratum [consciousness] pertaining to the next life. So, once [this consciousness] has expired, it re-engages with the next life, and so on.[144]

Process of Reversal [b"]

With regard to the latter, the process of reversal [of the substratum consciousness, it says in the root verses]:

> **But when the adamantine meditative stability arises,**
> **And one becomes an arhat, it will be reversed.**

The maturational aspect of [the substratum consciousness] will be reversed, according to the tradition of the followers of the Greater Vehicle, immediately after the adamantine meditative stability (*vajropamasamādhi, rdo rje lta bu'i ting nge 'dzin*) has arisen and [consciousness] is transformed into the mirror-like pristine cognition (*ādarśajñāna, me long lta bu'i ye shes*).[145] According to the tradition of the Lesser Vehicle, this reversal occurs when one has attained [the status of] an arhat and the psycho-physical aggregates have all passed into non-residual nirvāṇa (*niravaśeṣanirvāṇa, lhag ma med par mya ngan las 'das pa*). At that time it is held that the continuity of awareness will also be interrupted.[146]

With regard to the non-virtuous or unwholesome phenomena pertaining to the seminal aspect [of the substratum consciousness], once the antidotes for these unwholesome phenomena have arisen and become steadfast, they [too] will be reversed.

[Synonyms for the Substratum Consciousness]

There are many synonyms for this [substratum consciousness]. In the context of the Greater Vehicle, it is known as the "ground of knowable phenomena" (*jñeyasthiti, shes bya'i gnas*) because it is the locus of the three natures (*trisvabhāva, ngo bo nyid gsum*) into which all knowable phenomena [may be allocated].[147] Also [in the Greater Vehicle], it is known as the "appropriating consciousness" (*ādānavijñāna, len pa'i rnam shes*) because it has the functions of reincarnating (*pratisaṃdhi, nying mtshams sbyor ba*) as well as acquiring and maintaining the psycho-physical aggregates.[148] Elsewhere, it is called the "store-consciousness of all seeds" (*sarvabījakālayavijñāna*) because it has the function of supporting all the seeds. It is known as the "fruitional consciousness" (*vipākavijñāna, rnam smin gyi rnam shes)* because it assuredly ripens and generates past actions and their corrupt deeds; and it is commonly known as the "substratum consciousness" (*ālayavijñāna, kun gzhi'i rnam shes*) because it functions as the ground of all things of cyclic existence and nirvāṇa.[149]

The terms "fundamental consciousness" (*mūlavijñāna, rtsa ba'i rnam shes*), "aggregate that persists for the duration of cyclic existence" (*āsaṃsāraskandha, 'khor ba ji srid pa'i phung po*), "link of the rebirth process" (*bhavāṅga, srid pa'i yan lag*), "maturational consciousness" (*vipākavijñāna, rnam smin gyi rnam shes),* and so forth, which are known in the context of the Lesser Vehicle, are also identical in their meaning.[150]

Although these terms cannot be differentiated in their essential nature, there are indeed many characteristics that differentiate them on the basis of the propensities.

Proofs are also found of [this substratum consciousness] in the *Summation of Ascertainment from the Yogācāra Level*, established by means of scriptural authority and logical reasoning, including the eightfold reasoning [of Asaṅga].[151]

Propensities That Issue from the Seminal Aspect of Substratum Consciousness [5"]

Fifth, the exegesis of the propensities that issue from the seminal aspect [of the substratum consciousness] includes (1) a brief description and (2) a detailed exegesis.

Brief Description [a"]

With regard to the former [it says in the root verses]:

> **Propensities [are analyzed] according to the ground in which they are distributed,**

> **Their distributors, the distribution process, and their actual content.**

Detailed Exegesis [b"]

When the aforementioned description [of the substratum consciousness] as being "endowed with propensities" (*bag chags ldan pa*) is analyzed in greater detail, there are four topics to be considered: (1) the ground in which [propensities] are distributed, (2) the distributors, (3) the [on-going] distribution process, and (4) an exegesis of the actual content of the distributed propensities.

The Ground in Which Propensities Are Distributed [i"]

Concerning the first of these [it says in the root verses]:

> **The stable continuum [of the substratum], though not clearly [cognized],**
> **Is that in which [propensities] have the capacity to be distributed,**
> **Because it is concurrent with the [other modes of consciousness]**
> **Which are their [actual] distributors.**

The distribution of the propensities takes place within the substratum, which has a stable continuum, and not within the six modes [of engaged consciousness] and their external physical forms, which are unstable. That is to say, the distribution of propensities takes place within the substratum, where virtuous and non-virtuous or wholesome and unwholesome [phenomena] are unspecified, and their objective referents, sense data, essential nature, and so forth are not clearly cognized by ordinary persons, pious attendants, hermit buddhas, and the like.[152]

On the other hand, this distribution [of propensities] does not take place within the six modes of engaged consciousness where virtuous and non-virtuous [phenomena] arise, and objective referents and sensa are cognized with great clarity. Nor does it occur within the dissonant mental consciousness because the latter cognizes its objective referents and sense data with great clarity and is delimited, even though [virtuous and non-virtuous phenomena] are unspecified therein.[153]

[Furthermore,] the distribution of propensities takes place within the substratum, which is the apprehending subject, in an impermanent state of flux, because they have the capacity to be distributed [therein]. On the other hand, this distribution does not occur within permanent [phenomena, such as] space, or the cessation obtained through non-analytical means (*apratisaṃkhyānirodha, so sor brtags min gyi 'gog pa*), and the like.[154] Also, the distribution of propensities within the substratum takes place with reference to a single mental continuum, concurrently with [the other seven modes of consciousness] which function as their distributors, and it does not occur when these are in isolation.

The Distributors [ii"]

Concerning the second [the distributors of these propensities, it says in the root verses]:

> **Seven modes [of consciousness] and their peripheral supports**
> **Are the actual distributors [of these propensities].**

The actual distributors [of propensities from within the substratum] are [the other] seven modes [of consciousness] and their associated [or peripheral mental states], which have the capacity to effect this distribution, and are capable of [sensory or mental] engagement. Among them, it is through the virtuous and non-virtuous [phenomena] connected with the corruptible six modes [of engaged consciousness] that propensities of both the maturational and causal types become localized; whereas through the unspecified [phenomena] and the dissonant mental consciousness only the propensities of the causal type become localized, not those of the maturational type.

Furthermore, propensities are not actually distributed by the corporeal actions of body and speech. Rather, it is the mind motivating these [actions] that acts as their distributor, enabling their [ripening] results to emerge.

The Distribution Process [iii"]

Concerning the third, the [ongoing] distribution process [it says in the root verses]:

> **Even though [propensities] may have ceased,**
> **They still have the capacity to generate their results.**

The substratum [consciousness] maintains its association over a long period of time with [the propensities] that give rise to the unspecified virtuous and non-virtuous phenomena of the seven [other] modes [of consciousness]. In fact, the production and cessation [of propensities] is concurrent, so that even though the mental phenomena that act as their distributor may have subsequently ceased [to exist], the stream of propensities still continues to adhere to the substratum, whether they are of the homogeneous [causal] type or the type that has the capacity to generate [specific] results.[155]

The Actual Content of the Distributed Propensities [iv"]

Fourth, [the exegesis of] the actual content of the distributed propensities has five topics: (1) defining characteristics, (2) classification, (3) natural properties, (4) [essential] abiding nature, and (5) localization.

Defining Characteristics [aa"]

Concerning the first [it says in the root verses]:

> **The distributed [propensities] include those of the causal type,**
> **Which are similar in class [to the original mental phenomena],**
> **And those that are maturational,**
> **And therefore capable of generating other [mental phenomena].**

With regard to the defining characteristics of the propensities that are distributed, [the definition of] the causal propensities (*niṣyandavāsanā, rgyu mthun gyi bag chags*) is that, dependent on the concurrent production and cessation of mental phenomena in relation to the substratum, they have an extraordinary capacity to regenerate [as propensities] of the homogeneous type which are similar in class to the [original] phenomena. The definition of the maturational propensities (*vipākavāsanā, rnam par smin pa'i bag chags*) is that they are the causal conditions capable of generating other distinct phenomena and have the capacity to be distributed within the substratum by other phenomena.

Classification [bb"]

Concerning the classification [of propensities, it says in the root verses]:

The six kinds of seed comprise those that are external and internal,
[The two] that are invisible, and those that are relative and absolute.

There are six kinds of seed (*bīja, sa bon rnam pa drug*): (1) external seeds (*phyi'i sa bon*), such as those of the sal tree (*śāli, sā li*); (2i) internal seeds (*nang gi sa bon*), which are present in the substratum;[156] (3–4) two kinds of invisible [seed] (*mi gsal ba gnyis*), which may refer either to virtuous and non-virtuous [mental phenomena] or to the impact of the dissonant mental states on the sense data, which are invisible and unspecified; (5) relative [seeds], comprising objects of external conventional appearance (*phyi tha snyad pa'i yul kun rdzob*); and (6) the absolute [seed], which is the support for all the seeds that can be scrutinized internally (*nang dpyad bzod sa bon thams cad kyi rten don dam*).[157]

Natural Properties [cc"]

Concerning the natural properties [of propensities, it says in the root verses]:

They abide through[158] their [association with] five natural properties.

[Propensities] abide through their association with five natural properties (*rang bzhin lnga*), that is to say:

(1) Seeds or propensities originate co-emergently (*lhan cig 'byung ba*), intending to produce their [appropriate] results in an immediate manner, uninterrupted by the instant when they perish, which immediately follows their production, or by any other intervening instant of time.
(2) They originate continuously (*rgyun chags su 'byung ba*), until [their continuum] is destroyed by [an appropriate] antidote.
(3) Even though many propensities may be spontaneously present, they originate exclusively through the distinctive regular patterning [of their own seeds] (*so sor nges pa kho na las 'byung ba*).
(4) The propensities originate through proximate conditions (*rkyen gang nye ba las 'byung ba*).
(5) They originate indirectly from beginningless seeds (*sa bon thog med nas brgyud de 'byung ba*). Therefore, an intrinsic result may be established as being present in its seed, and a result may be established also on the basis of its seed. These may be exemplified [respectively] by

> the re-emergence of the substratum from the substratum, and by the emergence of a rice shoot from another rice shoot.

These points concerning the seeds and their natural properties have [also] been mentioned by Dignāga.[159]

Essential Abiding Nature [dd"]

Concerning the [essential] abiding nature [of the propensities, it says in the root verses]:

> **Though they are localized by whatever localizes them,**
> **They remain unspecified and cannot be described**
> **As identical in substance, or different.**

If one were to ask what is the essential abiding nature of these propensities, it is that, regardless of the unspecified virtuous or non-virtuous [phenomena] in which they become localized, the propensities themselves remain unspecified. This is because they are identical in substance to the unspecified substratum.

However, you might ask, surely this [process] applies not to the diversity of propensities, but rather to the causes of the diversity of phenomena? [One should know that] while [these propensities] are [merely] propensities they do not appear diversified, but when their [appropriate] results are taking shape, they themselves are transformed into the diversity of phenomena. In the Greater Vehicle, this is also called the "profound and subtle dependent origination" (*zab cing phra ba'i rten 'brel*).[160]

Then, with regard to whether the propensities abide in a manner that is qualitatively identical or different [to the substratum], one might think that if the propensities are identical in substance to the substratum and [consequently] unspecified, there would be a contradiction in them subsequently emerging from it as the manifold diversity of virtuous and non-virtuous [phenomena]; and that if they are different [in substance], the seeds themselves would [have to be identified with] the [diversity of] mind and its mental states, and so it would be implicit that a single individual person could partake of many minds.

The sublime [Asaṅga] has said in this regard that the propensities cannot be described as [phenomena] that are the same or distinct from this [substratum].[161] In the *Combined Commentary* [*on the Summary of the Greater Vehicle*], [Asvabhāva] explains with examples that the Sautrāntika hold the mind which apprehends the sensum of an object and the sensum itself to be neither identical nor different. Accordingly, on that analogy, he states that "the propensities and the substratum cannot be described as counterparts that are identical [in substance], nor can they even be described as different substances."[162]

Localization [ee"]

Concerning the localization [of the propensities, it says in the root verses]:

> **They become localized by regenerating their own habitat,**
> **And by generating [impulses] that did not previously exist.**

In this regard, although there are different explanations which accord with [different] teachers, the master Dharmapāla[163] and others have said that if one could think of [all] the classes of the propensities one would be well acquainted with beginningless cyclic existence! For this reason he identified both of the ways in which [the propensities] become localized: (1) their primary function is to regenerate their own locus or habitat [which is the substratum]; and (2) they also newly generate [imprints] that did not previously exist, as when maturational propensities newly emerge or the propensities associated with what one has heard or studied are newly established.

Exegesis of Mentation, or Dissonant Mental Consciousness [bb']

The second part [of the detailed exegesis of the aggregate of consciousness; see p. 512] is the exegesis of the dissonant mental consciousness (*kliṣṭa-manovijñāna, nyon yid kyi rnam par shes pa*). This has four topics: (1) its defining characteristics, (2) its demonstrations, (3) its function, and (4) its [processes of] engagement and reversal.

Defining Characteristics [1"]

With regard to the first [the defining characteristics of the dissonant mental consciousness, it says in the root verses]:

Embodying egotism, and unspecified...

This is the principal [mode of] consciousness that cognizes the bare objects of the substratum and has the capacity to activate the predominant condition of extremely agitated mental activity. As long as the sublime path [of the buddhas] has not been attained, this [dissonant mental consciousness] refers objectively to the substratum consciousness, obscured by the dissonant mental states of perpetual egotism, and it is unspecified.[164]

Demonstrations [2"]

With regard to the second [the demonstrations of the dissonant mental consciousness, it says in the root verses]:

. . . Mentation is endowed with associated mental states,
Comprising four of the dissonant mental states.

Egotistical mentation (*ngar 'dzin gyi yid*) is endowed with associated [mental states], comprising four of the dissonant mental states, namely, egotistical delusion, egotistical view, egotistical attachment, and egotistical pride, and so forth—the last words implying that it also includes nine altogether: the five ever-present mental states (*kun 'gro lnga*), along with egotistical view, pride, ignorance, and doubt.[165]

Function [3"]

With regard to the third [it says in the root verses]:

It has the functions of binding [the modes of engaged consciousness]
To corrupt states, and of implanting seeds.

[The dissonant mental consciousness] activates the predominant condition of mental consciousness (*manovijñāna, yid shes*) and functions as the locus that binds the six modes [of engaged consciousness] to substantialist [views], after which it binds them to corrupt states, ensuring that seeds are implanted in the substratum.

Processes of Engagement and Reversal [4"]

With regard to the fourth [it says in the root verses]:

> **Referring objectively to the substratum, it engages routinely,**
> **But it is reversed on the sublime [path].**

The directly manifest dissonant mental consciousness, along with its peripheral [mental states], does not emerge during the meditative equipoise of sublime beings, nor while entering the meditative absorption of cessation, nor on the levels associated [with the path] of no-more-learning (*aśaikṣamārga, mi slob pa'i lam*), but it does emerge during the [four paths of] learning (*śaikṣamārga*) and during the post-meditative experiences associated with the meditative absorption of cessation.[166]

Apart from these [special] circumstances, in all [other ordinary] circumstances where it is unspecified in terms of virtuous and non-virtuous [phenomena], the dissonant mental consciousness refers objectively to the substratum [consciousness] and at the same time it engages routinely [with the six modes of engaged consciousness].

Even so, this process may be reversed from the first level of the path of insight (*darśanamārga*), according to the Greater Vehicle; and its [latent] propensities or innate aspects may be reversed through the transformations that occur on the eighth [bodhisattva] level, associated with the path of meditation (*bhāvanāmārga*). Its most subtle latent tendencies (*bag la nyal phra zhing phra ba*) are reversed at the same time when the substratum [consciousness itself is reversed], i.e., at the end of the continuum of the ten [bodhisattva] levels (*daśabhūmi*). On the buddha level, it is then transformed into the conclusive pristine cognition of sameness (*samatājñāna, myam nyid kyi ye shes*).[167]

There are many authoritative passages of the scriptures that establish the proof of this [dissonant mental consciousness].[168] The *Summary of the Greater Vehicle* itself offers six reasons.[169]

Incidentally, if I may digress, there is a passage [in the *Treasury of Phenomenology*] which says:[170]

> Mentation is the [residual] consciousness immediately after
> The sixfold [engaged consciousness] has passed.

In accordance with this passage, Je Rangjungwa has designated the [residual] mentation [that remains] immediately after [any of] the six modes of consciousness have ceased by the term "mentation that is [an aspect of] the sixth [mode of consciousness]" (*drug pa'i yid*).[171] It is [generally] acknowledged that this does not refer to the dissonant mental consciousness, but is, rather, a synonym for mentation (*manas*). However, there are some who also refer to it as the "mentation that serves as a property of the dissonant mental [consciousness]" (*nyon mongs can gyi yid kyi chos can du gyur pa'i yid*).[172]

It is explained that this immediate mentation must also continue to function, after the sixfold [mode of engaged consciousness] has ceased, as the predominant condition of the uncorrupted pristine cognition in the mind of a sublime being.[173]

Also on this point, there are some who employ similar terminology, saying that the principal [aspect of] mind is the substratum, and that mentation has two aspects, comprising absolute mentation (*don dam pa'i yid*) and circumstantial mentation (*gnas skabs pa'i yid*). In this case, the former refers to the dissonant mental [consciousness] and the latter to the [residual] consciousness that remains immediately after the cessation of the six modes of engaged consciousness.[174]

Exegesis of the Six Modes of Engaged Consciousness [cc']

The third part [of the detailed exegesis of the aggregate of consciousness; see p. 512] is the exegesis of the six modes of [engaged] consciousness (*rnam shes tshogs drug*). This has four topics: (1) their essential nature; (2) their defining characteristics; (3) their locus, sense objects, and concomitants; and (4) their functions along with their origins.

Essential Nature [1"]

With regard to the first [the essential nature of engaged consciousness, it says in the root verses]:

> **The essential nature of the process of sensory engagement is that**
> **The [modes of] consciousness, referring objectively to their**
> **diversely appearing objects,**
> **Arise in conjunction with four conditions.**

In general it is the case that consciousness becomes localized on account of its [ability] to cognize dissimilar sense objects. The term "engagement" (*pravṛtti, 'jug pa*) suggests that [consciousness] relates to individual sense objects among those that diversely appear, and consequently a clear sensum repeatedly emerges. The term "consciousness" (*vijñāna, rnam par shes pa*) here suggests that [the subject] refers objectively to the essential nature of its [appropriate] sense object.

This [engaged consciousness] comprises six [modes], extending from visual consciousness (*cakṣurvijñāna, mig gi rnam par shes pa*), as far as mental consciousness (*manovijñāna, yid kyi rnam par shes pa*).

Furthermore, each of these [six modes of engaged consciousness] arises dependent on four conditions. Among them, in the case of visual consciousness, the referential condition (*ālambanapratyaya, dmigs pa'i rkyen*) comprises the visual forms that appear as if they were external to itself. The predominant condition (*adhipatipratyaya, bdag rkyen*) comprises the sense organs of the eyes. The immediate condition (*samanantarapratyaya, de ma thag rkyen*) comprises an uninterrupted preceding moment of mental attention. The causal condition (*hetupratyaya, rgyu'i rkyen*) comprises the [visual] consciousness that arises, dependent on [the propensities of] the substratum, endowed with the characteristic of apperceiving individual visual forms.[175]

These four conditions are similarly applied to each of the [following] four [modes of engaged consciousness], namely, auditory consciousness (*śrotravijñāna, rna'i rnam par shes pa*), olfactory consciousness (*ghrāṇavijñāna, sna'i rnam par shes pa*), gustatory consciousness (*jihvāvijñāna, lce'i rnam par shes pa*), and tactile consciousness (*kāyavijñāna, lus kyi rnam par shes pa*).

As far as mental consciousness is concerned, the referential condition comprises the knowable phenomena which appear as if they were different to itself; the predominant condition comprises, with one special exception, the dissonant mental [consciousness]; the immediate condition is the mental activity preceding it; and the causal condition is the mental consciousness that arises, dependent on [the propensities of] the substratum, endowed with the characteristic of apperceiving individual mental phenomena.

With regard to the [aforementioned] "special exception," the predominant condition of the uncorrupted pristine cognition of sublime minds is its necessity to [continue] functioning by means of mentation immediately after the six [modes of consciousness] have ceased.[176]

Defining Characteristics [2"]

With regard to the second [it says in the root verses]:

Their defining characteristic is that, dependent on their predominant condition,
They perceive the sensory activity fields.

As far as the defining characteristics of these six [modes of engaged consciousness] are concerned, the defining characteristic of visual consciousness is that, dependent on the sense organs of the eyes, which are its predominant condition, sensory consciousness perceives sensa corresponding to the activity field of visual form, and so on [in the case of auditory consciousness, etc.]. The defining characteristic of the sixth, mental consciousness, is that the central consciousness cognizes the activity field of mental phenomena, which is its own object, dependent on the sense faculty of the mind (*mana indriya, yid dbang*), which is its predominant condition, and it is [therefore] different in substance from the [previously mentioned] dissonant mental [consciousness].

Locus, Sense Objects, and Concomitants [3"]

With regard to the third [it says in the root verses]:

Through the locus of the sense organs,
They refer objectively to their sense objects,
And they maintain a concomitance [between mind and mental states].

Regarding the locus [of the six modes of engaged consciousness], (1) in general, the substratum consciousness is the locus for the seeds of all [the six modes of consciousness]. Their former locus—immediately preceding that [subsidence in the substratum]—is the immediate mentation which lingers following their cessation; and their subsequent locus which will re-emerge concurrently with mental consciousness [when they are reactivated] is the dissonant mental consciousness.[177] Thereafter, the peripheral mental states are the locus in which all the six modes [of engaged consciousness] pursue virtuous or non-virtuous actions, and dissonant mental consciousness is the locus in which they pursue corrupt [actions] and are consequently bound to substantialist [views]. (2) In particular, the [distinctive] loci that emerge concurrently with [the consciousnesses of] the five senses comprise the respective sense organs, such as the eye.

It is through these loci that [the six modes of engaged consciousness] refer objectively to their respective six sense objects—visual forms, sounds, odors, tastes, tangibles, and mental phenomena. At the same time, they maintain a concomitance between mind and its mental states, including the five ever-present [mental states].

Functions and Origins [4"]

With regard to the fourth [the functions of the six modes of engaged consciousnesses, along with their origins, it says in the root verses]:

> **Their functions include conceptualizing with respect to objects of reference,**
> **Prevarication with respect to objects of reference, and so forth.**
> **They originate in conjunction with conditions, like waves from water.**
> **In particular, mental consciousness is uninterrupted,**
> **Except in the five [special] circumstances, where mind is absent.**

The functions (*byed las*) of these [six modes of engaged consciousness] are to facilitate the apprehension of their respective sense objects. [Among them,] the five modes of sensory [consciousness] engage in the pursuit of virtuous and dissonant [actions], they engage in the pursuit of the [positive and negative] motivations behind those actions, and they engage in the pursuit of [the corresponding results] which are imbued with suffering or the absence of suffering.[178]

On the other hand, mental consciousness [only] has the functions of engaging in [the pursuit of] virtuous or non-virtuous phenomena and the [associated] actions, whereas the other [five modes of engaged] consciousness also facilitate the complete apprehension of their [respective] results, endowed with suffering or the absence of suffering. The salient point here is that the actions themselves originate, in particular, through mental activity.

In this regard, [the most distinctive activities pursued by the engaged consciousness are outlined in] the following maxim:[179]

> Conceptualizing with respect to objects of reference,
> Prevaricating with respect to objects of reference,
> Being intoxicated, falling sleep, and waking up.
> Fainting and regaining consciousness,
> Engaging in physical and verbal activities,

Experiencing activity devoid of attachment,
Cutting off and connecting with the roots of virtue,
Transmigrating at death and being reborn.

With regard to the origins [of the six modes of engaged consciousness], the Sautrāntika and others hold that there is no multiplicity of immediate conditions and that each [moment of] consciousness arises exclusively due to a single [preceding moment of] consciousness, because an immediate condition comprising a multiplicity [of immediate conditions] would not be causally effective. However, in this [tradition of Higher Abhidharma], it is the referential condition of consciousness that is individually ascertained, and consequently, there is no need to individually ascertain the immediate condition. Indeed, many [moments of] consciousness may originate from a single immediate condition. Therefore, it is explained in the *Thirty Verses* that [the moments of] consciousness that originate may number anything from one to a multiplicity [of moments], according to the conditions that emerge concurrently with the substratum, just as waves emerge from water.[180]

In particular, mental consciousness originates without interruption in all circumstances, except the following five which are characterized by an absence of mind: (1) rebirth as a deity without perception, (2–3) the two kinds of meditative absorption, (4) sleep, and (5) unconsciousness.[181]

Exponents of Buddhist phenomenology explain that in the case of the five modes of sensory consciousness, there are both simulated or proximate conditions, as when visual forms are involuntarily observed, and [instances of] sensory consciousness being preceded by mentation, as when [visual forms] are voluntarily observed.[182]

Combinations of the Five Aggregates [cc]

Third [see p. 477], there is a brief summary concerning the quantification [of the psycho-physical aggregates within the three world-systems]. In this regard [it says in the root verses]:

In the [world-system of] desire, all of the aggregates,
Including the aggregate of physical forms, are possessed,
While in the higher realms, they are progressively reduced.

In the world-system of desire (*kāmadhātu, 'dod khams*), all [the five psycho-physical aggregates] are possessed, starting from the aggregate of physical forms, and continuing with the aggregates of feelings, perceptions, formative predispositions, and consciousness. However, they are progressively diminished in higher and higher realms, such as the world-system of form (*rūpadhātu, gzugs khams*), the world-system of formlessness (*ārūpyadhātu, gzugs med khams*), and the [exalted states] attained through the sublime [path] of the Lesser Vehicle.

Yet that is a gross generalization. At this juncture, the many intricate ways of quantifying [the aggregates] should be studied in the texts of phenomenology. Since these are hard to understand, I fear that my writing [on this subject would be too protracted].[183]

The Eighteen Sensory Bases [ii]

The second topic [of this chapter on Higher Abhidharma; see p. 476] is the systematic presentation of the sensory bases. It has two parts: (1) recognition of their essential nature, and (2) the systematic presentation of their subdivisions.

Their Essential Nature [aa]

With regard to the former [it says in the root verses]:

> **The eighteen sensory bases which support the seeds [of everything]**
> **Or their specifically characterized phenomena**
> **Are divided into [three] groups of six,**
> **Comprising those sensory bases that are internal, external, and cognizant.**

Derived from [the Sanskrit] term *dhātu*, and rendered [in Tibetan] as *khams*, the "sensory bases" are designated as such because they "support the seeds" [of everything] (*sarvadharmabījadhara, sa bon 'dzin pa*) or because they "support their own specifically characterized phenomena" (*rang mtshan 'dzin pa*).[184]

With regard to their essential nature, there are altogether eighteen sensory bases (*aṣṭadaśadhātu, khams bco brgyad*), namely, six internal sensory bases (*nang gi khams drug*), including the eyes; six external sensory bases (*phyi'i khams drug*), including visual form; and six cognizant sensory bases (*rnam par shes pa'i khams drug*), including visual consciousness. It says in the *Commentary on the Treasury [of Phenomenology]*:[185]

The [Sanskrit] term *dhātu* (Tib. *khams*) means "species" or "natural type" (*gotra*). Just as in some parts of the earth, where there are many kinds of [precious metals]—gold, silver, copper, iron, and the like—one speaks of those places and their [various] "constituents" (*dhātu, khams*) or "elements" (*bhūtadhātu, 'byung khams*), in the same way, there are [said to be] eighteen "sensory bases" because a single human body and a single mind with a single continuum of mental states partake of eighteen "natural modes" (*gotra, rigs*) or "constituents" (*dhātu, khams*).

With regard to those [eighteen]:

(1–6) The internal sensory bases, including the eyes, are designated as such because when they engage with their respective sense objects, they do not act [directly] but support specifically characterized phenomena, or else because they support their respective sensory environments (*upacāra, nyer spyod*), or because they support their seeds [of visual consciousness and so forth].

(7–12) The external sensory bases, including visual forms, are designated as such because they support specifically characterized [physical] phenomena.

(13–18) The cognizant sensory bases are designated as such because they support specifically characterized mental phenomena, which apperceive the essential nature of their [respective] sense objects, dependent on their [respective] sense organs.

The defining characteristics of each are extensively explained in [Asaṅga's] *Actual Foundation of the* [*Yogācāra*] *Level*.[186]

Their Subdivisions [bb]

The latter includes both a brief description and a detailed explanation.

Brief Description [1']

With regard to the former [it says in the root verses]:

There are sensory bases subsumed in the psycho-physical aggregates,

Those that are not subsumed in the psycho-physical aggregates,
And the sensory base of mental phenomena.

When all the sensory bases are briefly presented, they comprise three categories: (1) those sensory bases which are subsumed in the psycho-physical aggregates (*phung pos bsdus pa'i khams*); (2) those sensory bases which are not subsumed in the psycho-physical aggregates (*des ma bsdus pa'i khams*); and (3) in particular, the sensory base of mental phenomena (*dharmadhātu, chos kyi khams*).

Detailed Exegesis [2']

[The detailed exegesis presents these three categories in turn.]

Sensory Bases Subsumed in the Psycho-physical Aggregates [a']

With regard to the first [it says in the root verses]:

The aggregate of physical forms includes the ten physical sensory bases—
Those of the sense organs and sense objects—
Along with one part of the sensory activity field of mental phenomena,
Which are all subsumed within [the category of] form.
Feelings, perceptions, and formative predispositions
Are subsumed within [the category of mental] phenomena,
Because, along with one aspect of the sensory base of mental phenomena,
They are all objects of the mental faculty.
As for the aggregate of consciousness, it is designated as
The "seven sensory bases of consciousness,"
Comprising the six modes [of engaged consciousness]
Along with the dissonant mental [consciousness],
And these are all subsumed within [the category of] mind.

The "aggregate of physical forms," which is presented as one [distinct component] in the context of the psycho-physical aggregates, [here,] in the context of the sensory bases, is re-designated as the "ten physical sensory bases" (*daśarūpakadhātu, gzugs can gyi khams bcu*). These ten comprise the sensory bases of the five physical sense organs (*dbang po gzugs can lnga'i khams*), including the eyes, and the sensory bases of the five physical sense objects (*yul gzugs can lnga'i khams*), including visual forms.

Also included here is one part, i.e., half, of the sensory base that derives from the five types of form within the sensory activity field of phenomena (*dharmāyatanapañcarūpa, chos kyi skye mched pa'i gzugs lnga*), including [intangible atomic] forms that are extremely [small and] concentrated (*ābhisaṃkṣepikarūpa, bsdus pa las gyur pa'i gzugs*).[187] Thus there are [altogether] eleven aspects subsumed within [the category of] form.

The "aggregate of feelings," the "aggregate of perceptions," and the "aggregate of formative predispositions," which are presented as three [distinct components] in the context of the psycho-physical aggregates, [here,] in the context of the sensory bases, are [all] localized within one part of the sensory base that derives from the sensory activity field of mental phenomena (*dharmāyatandhātu, chos kyi skye mched pa'i khams*) because they are exclusively objects of the mental faculty. Thus they are [all] subsumed within [the category of mental] phenomena.

The "aggregate of consciousness," which is presented as one [distinct component] in the context of the psycho-physical aggregates, [here,] in the context of the sensory bases, is re-designated as the "seven sensory bases of consciousness" (*rnam par shes pa'i khams bdun*), comprising the six modes of [engaged] consciousness, from visual consciousness as far as mental consciousness, along with the sensory base of the dissonant mental [consciousness].

According to the tradition of the pious attendants (*śrāvaka, nyan thos*), immediately after the six [modes of engaged consciousness] have ceased to function, they still remain localized within the sensory base of the mental faculty (*manodhātu, yid kyi khams*) because this [base] is presented as the locus or habitat of mental consciousness even though there are no [actual circumstances] when it is separated from the six modes.[188] According to the tradition of the Greater Vehicle, on the other hand, the sensory base of the mental faculty is identified with the dissonant mental [consciousness] and also, by implication, with the substratum [consciousness] because it stores the seeds of the [other] seven [modes of consciousness]. Thus, [all these eight modes of consciousness] are subsumed within [the category of] mind.

Sensory Bases Not Subsumed in the Psycho-physical Aggregates [b']

With regard to the second [the sensory bases which are not subsumed in the psycho-physical aggregates, it says in the root verses]:

> **The unconditioned sensory bases**
> **Without causes and conditions, and without agglomeration,**
> **Are included within one part of the sensory base of mental phenomena**
> **That is not subsumed in the psycho-physical aggregates.**
> **These comprise the three aspects of reality, space, the two aspects of cessation,**
> **The immovable state, and the cessation of feeling and perception.**

What, you may ask, are the sensory bases which are not subsumed in the five psycho-physical aggregates? These are designated as the "unconditioned sensory bases" (*asaṃskṛtadhātu, 'dus ma byas kyi khams*), included within one part of the sensory base of phenomena (*dharmadhātu, chos kyi khams*) that is not covered by the five psycho-physical aggregates, because they are not generated by causes and conditions and are not [considered to be] an agglomeration of parts, as is, for example, [the continuum of] past time.

Although there are different exegetical traditions, such as the explanation in the [*Dissertation on the*] *Five Psycho-physical Aggregates* which asserts that there are four unconditioned things (*'dus ma byed bzhi*),[189] according to this tradition [of Higher Abhidharma] there are said to be eight [unconditioned things]. These comprise (1–3) the three aspects of reality, (4) space, (5) cessation obtained through non-analytical means, (6) cessation obtained through analytical means, (7) the immovable state, and (8) the cessation of perception and feeling.[190]

Among them, with regard to the three aspects of reality (*trayatathatā, de bzhin nyid gsum*), although in [actual] reality (*dharmatā, chos nyid*) there are no distinctions, three aspects [of reality] are established on account of their different modes of support (*chos can rten*). Accordingly, they comprise (1) the reality of virtuous phenomena (*kuśaladharmatathatā, chos dge ba rnams kyi de bzhin nyid*), (2) the reality of non-virtuous phenomena (*akuśaladharmatathatā, chos mi dge ba rnams kyi de bzhin nyid*), and (3) the reality of unspecified phenomena (*avyākṛtadharmatathatā, lung ma bstan rnams kyi de bzhin nyid*).[191]

The essential nature of these [three aspects] is the actual reality [or emptiness] present respectively in virtuous, non-virtuous, and unspecified [phenomena]. This is the essential nature that comprises the two aspects of selflessness because it is [characterized by] emptiness in respect of both the self of the individual person (*pudgalātma, gang zag gi bdag*), as when a "self" with permanent, unitary, and independent properties is [mistakenly] apprehended, and the self of phenomena (*dharmātma, chos kyi bdag*), as when phenomena comprising the apprehended [object] and the apprehending [subject] are both [mistakenly] imputed [to have inherent existence].[192]

There are many synonyms of this reality, including emptiness (*śūnyatā, stong pa nyid*), signlessness (*animitta, mtshan nyid med pa*), genuine goal (*bhūtakoṭi, yang dag pa'i mtha'*), ultimate reality (*paramārtha, don dam pa*), and expanse of reality (*dharmadhātu, chos kyi dbyings*).[193]

With regard to the fourth, space (*ākāśa, nam mkha'*), since things become manifest exclusively through physical form, this refers to anything characterized by an absence of material form which is [still] an object of mental consciousness and facilitates or conducts the arising, perishing, and so forth of obstructive matter (*sapratigharūpa, thogs bcas kyi gzugs*). Actually, [space] is not designated as such because it facilitates or conducts [matter] by means of motion but merely because it does not impede the possibility of obstructive matter arising.[194]

With regard to the fifth, cessation obtained through non-analytical means (*apratisaṃkhyānirodha, so sor brtags min gyi 'gog pa*), this refers to the [temporary] cessation [of phenomena] obtained on account of the insufficiency of the causes and conditions [for their arising]. Even so, the seeds or subconscious tendencies of these [phenomena] are, for the while, not destroyed and they are never disconnected because their rejection is not irreversible. This may be exemplified by the non-arising of other modes of consciousness when visual consciousness is distracted by visual forms.[195]

With regard to the sixth, cessation obtained through analytical means (*pratisaṃkhyānirodha, so sor brtags pa'i 'gog pa*), this occurs when the [spiritual] path associated with any uncorrupted antidote is [consciously] cultivated in the mind, and all the corresponding [impurities] that are to be rejected cease, without exception. In this case, the dissonant mental states and their seeds or subconscious tendencies are thoroughly destroyed by means of the antidote in question, and the [impurities] which are to be rejected are perpetually disconnected because their rejection is irreversible.[196]

With regard to the seventh, the immovable state (*āniñjya, mi gYo ba*) is designated as such because when one is free from the desires associated with the third mundane meditative concentration and those below it, and all feelings of happiness and suffering have ceased, one is unmoved by the eight defects [associated with meditative concentration], and, in particular, one is unmoved by transitory happiness and suffering. The eight [defects] comprise ideation and scrutiny, feelings of bliss and sorrow, [feelings of] mental comfort and discomfort, and exhalation and inhalation of breath.[197]

With regard to the eighth, the cessation of perception and feeling (*saṃjñā-vedayitanirodha, 'du shes dang tshor ba 'gog pa*), when one is free from the desires associated with the sensory activity field of nothing-at-all and those below it, and has left behind all sorts of [impurities] that are to be abandoned, passing beyond the very summit of [mundane] existence, the six modes [of engaged consciousness] and the dissonant mental consciousness will cease to function, preceded by the perception that even the perception of moving upwards and the feeling of equanimity will come to rest in a state of quiescence (*śāntavihāra, zhi bar gnas pa*).[198]

Sensory Base of Mental Phenomena [c']

With regard to the third [the sensory base of mental phenomena (*dharmadhātu, chos kyi khams*) in particular, it says in the root verses]:

> **The two sets of eight conditioned and unconditioned things**
> **Together are objects within range exclusively of mental consciousness.**
> **Therefore, these are particularly assigned to the "sensory base of phenomena."**

The aforementioned eight conditioned things comprise the five aspects [of form that constitute the sensory activity field of phenomena], starting with [atomic] forms that are extremely [small and] concentrated (*ābhisaṃkṣepikarūpa, bsdus pa las gyur pa'i gzugs*), along with the three aggregates of feelings, perceptions, and formative predispositions. Together with the eight unconditioned states [described earlier], these two [sets of eight], totaling sixteen, are objects exclusively within the range of mental consciousness. For this reason, they are assigned separately and particularly to the sensory base of phenomena.[199]

The Twelve Sensory Activity Fields [iii]

The third topic [of this chapter on Higher Abhidharma; see p. 476] is the systematic presentation of the sensory activity fields. It has two parts: (1) the recognition of their essential nature, and (2) the reduction [of the sensory bases] into the sensory activity fields.

Their Essential Nature [aa]

With regard to the former [it says in the root verses]:

> **There are twelve [sensory activity fields], such as the eye and visual form,**
> **Emerging from the sensory gates**
> **Where the [corresponding modes of] consciousness arise,**
> **Facilitating the extension [of consciousness] to extraneous objects.**
> **Subjective and immediate conditions direct [these modes of consciousness] internally**
> **While objective and referential conditions direct them externally**
> **Toward [their respective] gates that form the sensory activity fields.**

The "sensory activity fields" (*āyatana, skye mched*) are so designated because their environmental role is to "extend [sense perception] outwards" (*mched pa*) to extraneous objects from the sensory gates (*dvāra, sgo*) where consciousness "arises" (*skye ba*).[200]

There are twelve [sensory activity fields], comprising (1–6) the six inner sensory activity fields (*nang gi skye mched drug*), such as the eye (*cakṣurāyatana, mig gi skye mched*); and (7–12) the six outer sensory activity fields (*phyi'i skye mched drug*), such as visible form (*rūpāyatana, gzugs kyi skye mched*).

It says in the *Commentary on the Treasury* [*of Phenomenology*]:[201]

> The [Sanskrit] term *āyatana* (*skye mched*) [literally meaning "seat" or "abode"][202] is interpreted to mean "sensory gate where [consciousness] arises" (*āyadvā[ra], skye ba'i sgo*).[203] The sensory activity fields are designated as such because they are the portals through which mind and mental states arise and extend or expand outwards, dependent on whichever [internal or external aspect of sense perception is applicable].

When [this definition] is applied in detail to each of [the sensory activity fields] individually, (1) the sensory activity field of the eye (*cakṣurāyatana, mig gi skye mched*) subjectively activates the sensory gate where visual conscious arises, and (2) the sensory activity field of visible form (*rūpāyatana, gzugs kyi skye mched*) objectively activates the sensory gate of visual consciousness. Then, in the same manner, [this dual function] applies to all the remaining [sensory activity fields], since each of them activates the corresponding sensory gate where its respective mode of consciousness [auditory, olfactory, etc.] arises, both subjectively and objectively.

However, as in the case [of the aforementioned sensory bases], one should know in particular that the sensory activity field of the mental faculty (*mano āyatana, yid kyi skye mched*) activates the sensory gate where mental consciousness arises on the basis of its immediate condition (*samanantarapratyaya, de ma thag rkyen*), and the sensory activity field of phenomena (*dharmāyatana, chos kyi skye mched*) activates the sensory gate where mental consciousness arises on the basis of its referential or objective condition (*ālambanapratyaya, dmigs pa'i rkyen*).[204]

In brief, subjective and immediate conditions direct [the modes of] consciousness internally, while referential and objective conditions direct them externally, towards the [respective] gates that form the sensory activity fields.

At this juncture, you may ask why only the sense objects of the eyes are designated as [the sensory activity field of] form (*rūpāyatana, gzugs kyi skye mched*), even though the first ten [of the twelve sensory activity fields] all partake of [the aggregate of] physical forms (*rūpaskandha*), and why only the objects of the mental faculty are designated as [the sensory activity field of] phenomena (*dharmāyatana, chos kyi skye mched*), even though all twelve [of the sensory activity fields] constitute phenomena.

In the former case, the point is that a single item [in a group] is distinguished from the others [in the same group] on account of its distinctive designation [and usage]. Specifically, in this case, only the sense objects of the eyes are designated as [the sensory activity field of] form because they are [held to be] the foremost aspects of form on account of their being both revealed and obstructed (*sanidarsanasapratigha, bstan yod thogs bcas*).

Similarly, [in the latter case,] the point is, just as in the former case, that a single item [in a group] is distinguished from the others [in the same group] owing to its distinctive designation [and usage]. Specifically, only the objects of the mental faculty are designated as [the sensory activity field of] phenomena because they include within them many [diverse mental] phenomena, such as feelings, and they also include nirvāṇa, which is the supreme among all phenomena.[205]

Reduction of the Sensory Bases into the Sensory Activity Fields [bb]

The latter, the reduction [of the sensory bases into the sensory activity fields], has three parts: (1) the reduction that accords with the physical [sensory activity fields], (2) the reduction that accords with the mental [sensory activity fields], and (3) the reduction that accords with [the sensory activity field] of mental phenomena.

With regard to the first [it says in the root verses]:

> **[Here,] the ten physical sensory activity fields resemble [their corresponding] sensory bases.**

The ten physical sensory activity fields (*gzugs can skye mched bcu*) are similar in content to the [corresponding] aforementioned sensory bases, apart from the mere change in their designation. Therefore they are reduced as follows: the physical sensory bases, comprising the five sense organs and the five sense objects, which are presented as ten in number in the context of the sensory bases, [here] in the context of the sensory activity fields are also designated as the "ten physical sensory activity fields."

With regard to the second [it says in the root verses]:

> **The seven sensory bases of consciousness are [subsumed in]**
> **The sensory activity field of the mental faculty.**

The seven sensory bases associated with consciousness (*rnam par shes pa'i khams bdun*), here, in the context of the sensory activity fields, are all reduced within the single "sensory activity field of the mental faculty" (*mano āyatana, yid kyi skye mched*).

Then, with regard to the third [it says in the root verses]:

> **The sixteen sensory bases of phenomena are [subsumed in]**
> **The sensory activity field of phenomena.**

The sixteen sensory bases of phenomena, in the context of the sensory activity fields, are all subsumed in the single "sensory activity field of phenomena."

5. The Tradition of the Lower Abhidharma

b. Summary of Phenomenology according to Lower Abhidharma [III.C.1.b]
  i. Brief Description of Phenomenological Categories
  ii. Detailed Exegesis of This System
    aa. Basic Category of Apparent Forms
    bb. Basic Category of the Central Mind
    cc. Basic Category of Peripheral Mental States
    dd. Basic Category of Formative Predispositions Disassociated with Mind
    ee. Basic Category of Unconditioned Phenomena
  iii. Synopsis of Lower Abhidharma

Summary of Phenomenology according to Lower Abhidharma [b]

The second section [of the systematic presentation of the psycho-physical aggregates, sensory bases, and sensory activity fields which the Buddhist vehicles commonly accept; see p. 472] is the exegesis summarizing these topics from the perspective of Lower Abhidharma. It has three parts: (1) a brief description of [phenomenological] categories, (2) a detailed exegesis of this system [of Lower Abhidharma], and (3) a synopsis of all its points.

Brief Description of Phenomenological Categories [i]

With regard to the first [it says in the root verses]:

The pious attendants subsume all that is knowable
In these five basic categories:
Apparent forms, the central mind, peripheral mental states,
Formative predispositions disassociated [with mind and mental states],
And unconditioned states.

It is said in Buddhist phenomenology that all those phenomena which are differentiated according to the psycho-physical aggregates, sensory bases, and sensory activity fields may also be subsumed in five basic categories (*pañcajñeya, shes bya thams cad kyi gzhi lnga*) with reference to their broad classification.

What, you may ask, are these five? They comprise (1) the basic category of apparent forms (*snang ba gzugs kyi gzhi*), (2) the basic category of the central mind (*gtso bo sems kyi gzhi*), (3) the basic category of peripheral mental states (*'khor sems byung gig zhi*), (4) the basic category of circumstantial formative predispositions disassociated [with mind and mental states] (*gnas skabs ldan pa ma yin pa'i 'du byed kyi gzhi*), and (5) the basic category of unconditioned states [including] cessation (*'gag pa 'dus ma byas kyi gzhi*).[206] The pious attendants hold that all knowable phenomena may be subsumed within these five basic categories, but as Zilung Paṇchen has said, "One cannot agree that the five basic categories are assigned exclusively within the tradition of the Vaibhāṣikas because they are also lucidly explained in the *Compendium of Phenomenology*."[207]

Detailed Exegesis of This System [ii]

With regard to the second [it says in the root verses]:

Form comprises the five sense organs, and their five objects,
Along with imperceptible form.
[Mind comprises] the six modes [of engaged consciousness],
And there are forty-six mental states,
Comprising the group of ten states found in [all] minds,
The group of ten mental states found in [all] virtuous [minds],
The group of six mental states found in dissonant or afflicted [minds],
The group of two mental states found in [all] non-virtuous [minds],

The group of ten mental states found in [all] slightly [afflicted minds],
And the group of eight mental states that are found indeterminately.
There are also fourteen formative predispositions
Disassociated [with mind and mental states], along with their aspects,
And two unconditioned states, comprising cessation and space.

Although the meanings of these [categories] have already been explained in detail, the structures presented according to the [traditions of] Higher and Lower Abhidharma are dissimilar. Since the system of the *Treasury [of Phenomenology]* accords with the tradition of the pious attendants, its principles and theses have been illustrated to some extent [in another section of this book].[208] However, since there is also a need to understand this [text] incidentally, in the present context, I will now briefly discuss it here as well.

Basic Category of Apparent Forms [aa]

Among these [five basic categories], the first is the basic category of apparent forms, which comprises eleven substances—the five sense organs, their [corresponding] five [sense] objects, and imperceptible form. The five sense organs are as [explained] above. Among the five [sense] objects, the sensory activity field of visible forms (*rūpāyatana, gzugs kyi skye mched*), comprising the sense objects of the eye, includes both color and shape:[209]

When these are differentiated there are twenty aspects:
Blueness, yellowness, whiteness, redness,
Light [of the moon and stars], darkness, cloud,
Smoke, dust, mist, sunlight, and shadow,
Along with the long, the short, the square, the round,
The high, the low, the even, and the uneven.
The first twelve of these are [classed as] colors [and shades]—
Four of them are primary colors
And eight are particular or secondary aspects [of shade].
The last eight items [in the list] are [classed as] shapes.[210]

Sounds (*śabda, sgra*) comprise both organically produced sounds [such as human sounds] and inorganically produced sounds [such as rustling trees].

These become four because each [of the two] types includes [sounds] capable of signifying their object and the opposite, and they become eight because each of these [four types] includes sounds that are pleasant and unpleasant.[211]

Odors (*gandha, dri*) include both those that are fragrant and strong, and each of these is differentiated on the basis of whether [it evokes] a neutral [feeling] or one that is not neutral.[212]

Tastes (*rasa, ro*) include the six essential types, namely, those that are sweet, sour, salty, bitter, spicy, and astringent.[213]

Tangibles (*spraṣṭavya, reg bya*) are eleven in number, comprising the four primary elements, which are [classed as] causal tangibles (*rgyu'i reg bya*), and the seven [sensations of] softness, roughness, heaviness, lightness, hunger, thirst, and coldness, which are [classed as] fruitional tangibles (*'bras bu'i reg bya*).[214]

Imperceptible forms (*avijñaptirūpa, rnam min gyi gzugs*) are those forms belonging to the sensory activity field of phenomena, which arise during [distracted periods of] apperception and during any meditative stability, whether virtuous or non-virtuous, [providing continuity of experience,] and which have the characteristics of imperceptible universals. When classified, they comprise both [imperceptible forms] that originate during [distracted] apperception and those that originate during meditative stability. The former includes three types: [distracted apperceptions] that are disciplined, undisciplined, or neutral; while the latter includes two types: [periods of] meditative concentration and [periods of] uncorrupted discipline (*zag med kyi sdom pa*).

Here, "disciplined" (*sdom pa*) implies virtuous [states], "undisciplined" (*sdom min*) implies non-virtuous [states], and "neutral" (*bar ma*) implies any unspecified virtuous or non-virtuous state. The causal bases of these [imperceptible forms] are the four primary elements, as [explained] above.[215]

Basic Category of the Central Mind [bb]

The second is the basic category of the central mind, which refers to the six modes [of engaged consciousness], commencing from visual consciousness and continuing through to mental consciousness.

Basic Category of Peripheral Mental States [cc]

The third is the basic category of peripheral mental states, which partake of the following five classes:

(1) The group of ten mental states that are found in all minds (*daśacitta-mahābhūmika, sems kyi sa mang po bcu*) comprises[216]

Feeling, volition, perception, will, contact, intelligence,
Mindfulness, attention, resolve, and meditative stability.

(2) The group of ten mental states that are found in all virtuous minds (*daśakuśalamahābhūmika, dge ba'i sa mang bcu*) comprises[217]

Faith, vigilance, refinement, equanimity, conscience, shame,
The two roots of virtue, namely, non-attachment and non-hatred,
Along with non-violence and perseverance.

(3) The group of six mental states that are found in all dissonant or afflicted minds (*ṣaṭkleśamahābhūmika, nyon mongs can gyi sa mang drug*) comprises[218]

Delusion, carelessness, indolence,
Faithlessness, dullness, and mental agitation.

(4) The group of two mental states that are found in all non-virtuous minds (*dvayākuśalamahābhūmika, mi dge ba'i sa pa chen po gnyis*) comprises[219]

Lack of conscience and shamelessness.

(5) The group of ten mental states that are found in all slightly dissonant or afflicted minds (*parīttakleśabhūmika, nyon mongs chung ngu'i sa pa bcu*) comprises[220]

Anger, enmity, pretentiousness, jealousy, annoyance,
Hypocrisy, miserliness, deceit, self-satisfaction, and violence.

These thirty-eight [mental states] are actually presented in the *Treasury* [*of Phenomenology*], while the commentaries of Vasubandhu (*bhāṣya*) and Yaśomitra (*ṭīkā*) supplement the list with the addition of the following eight indeterminate mental states (*aṣṭāniyatabhūmika, ma nges pa'i sa pa brgyad*):[221]

Ideation, scrutiny, regret, drowsiness,
Hostility, desire, pride, and doubt.[222]

Basic Category of Formative Predispositions Disassociated with Mind [dd]

The fourth is the basic category of the formative predispositions that are disassociated with mind. When these are all subsumed, there are eight of them, which are enumerated as follows:[223]

> Acquisition (*prāpti, thob pa*), non-acquisition (*aprāpti, ma thob pa*),[224]
> Homogeneity (*sabhāgata, skal mnyam*), [225]
> Non-perception (*āsaṃjñika, 'du shes med pa*),[226]
> Meditative absorptions (*samāpatti, snyoms 'jug*),[227] life-force (*āyus, srog*),[228]
> Characteristics (*lakṣaṇa, mtshan nyid*),[229]
> And nominal clusters (*nāmakāya, ming gi tshogs*), etc.[230]

When these are further differentiated, they number fourteen. For, meditative absorption includes both the meditative absorption devoid of perception and the meditative absorption of cessation. Conditioned characteristics include four aspects: birth, aging, duration [of the life span], and impermanence. Nominal clusters imply three clusters altogether, with the addition of phrasal clusters and syllabic clusters.

Derived from these [fourteen] there are also many further classifications. Thus, it is extensively explained, for example, that acquisition may have three aspects, with the addition of new acquisition (*labdhaprāpti, rnyed thob*) and [uninterrupted] possession (*samanvāgama, ldan thob*). Even "former acquisition" (*pūrvaprāpti, sngar las thob pa*) may include the acquisition of something that had not been acquired (*aprāptiprāpti, ma thob pa las thob pa*), the acquisition of something that had been lost (*vihīnaprāpti, nyams nas thob pa*), and the acquisition of conditioned and unconditioned phenomena (*saṃskṛtāsaṃskṛtaprāpti, 'dus byas dang 'dus ma byas pa'i thob pa*), and so forth.[231]

Basic Category of Unconditioned Phenomena [ee]

The fifth is the basic category of unconditioned phenomena, which are explained to be three in number: space (*ākāśa, nam mkha'*), cessation obtained through analytical means (*pratisaṃkhyānirodha, so sor brtags 'gog*), and cessation obtained through non-analytical means (*apratisaṃkhyānirodha, so sor brtags min gyi 'gog pa*).[232]

Synopsis of Lower Abhidharma [iii]

The third part [of the exegesis according to Lower Abhidharma] is a synopsis of all its points [on which it says in the root verses]:

All relative [appearances] are subsumed
In the aggregate of physical forms, the sensory base of mental phenomena,
And the sensory activity field of the mental faculty.
These [appearances] are of three sorts: causally effective phenomena,
Including substantial existents and imputed existents,
And non-causally effective phenomena.

With regard to all those [phenomenological structures] that have just been explained, the sensory bases are established, having been specially extracted from the psycho-physical aggregates, and the sensory activity fields are [similarly] established, having been specially extracted from the sensory bases. Then, when the psycho-physical aggregates, sensory bases, and sensory activity fields of which this structure is composed are concisely reconstituted, they may all be integrated together under three headings [the aggregate of physical forms, the sensory base of mental phenomena, and the sensory activity field of the mental faculty].

It says in the *Treasury* [*of Phenomenology*]:[233]

Matter comprises the five sense organs,
The five objects, and imperceptible forms.

And:[234]

These sense organs and their objects are exclusively
Held to comprise ten sensory activity fields and ten sensory bases.

So it is that the aggregate of physical forms (*rūpaskandha, gzugs kyi phung po*) [the first of these three headings] subsumes all aspects of form, including the ten physical sensory bases and sensory activity fields, which are mentioned in this passage, along with the physical forms which are the objects of the mental faculty. The sensory base of mental phenomena (*dharmadhātu, chos kyi khams*) [the second of the three headings] subsumes the three aggregates of feelings, perceptions, and formative predispositions, along with one part of form, and the sensory activity field of mental phenomena.[235] The sensory activity field of the mental faculty (*mano āyatana, yid kyi skye mched*) [the third heading] comprises the aggregate of consciousness and the seven sensory bases [associated with consciousness].

Therefore, it says in the *Treasury* [*of Phenomenology*]:[236]

> All [phenomena] may be subsumed in a single aggregate,
> A single sensory base, and a single sensory activity field.

[Reduced in this way,] all relative appearances that are objects of knowledge can be subsumed under these three [headings].

Furthermore, all phenomena may also be classed according to three other modalities, designated respectively as (1) causally effective phenomena which are substantial existents (*dravyataḥ vastu, rdzas yod kyi dngos po*); (2) causally effective phenomena which are imputed existents (*prajñaptitaḥ vastu, btags yod kyi dngos po*); and (3) non-causally effective phenomena (*avastuka, dngos po med pa*).[237]

Among them, the [class of] substantial causally effective phenomena is assigned to inert substances, including atomic particles composed of the primary elements and so forth, and to "conscious substances" (*shes pa'i rdzas*), including the sense data and apperceptions that arise when consciousness relates to its sense objects. The [class of] imputed causally effective phenomena is so designated because, although in general things that are not subject to ideation or scrutiny such as a "vase" are substantially existent, the [concepts of] production and cessation in relation to the vase and so forth are imputed by the intellect. Then, [the class of] non-causally effective phenomena includes [unconditioned phenomena] such as space.

In addition, [phenomena] are also explained to be subsumed within [the categories of] substantial entities (*dravyavastu, rdzas dngos*), imputed entities (*prajñaptivastu, btags dngos*),[238] relative entities (*saṃvṛtivastu, kun rdzob kyi dngos po*), and absolute entities (*paramārthavastu, don dam gyi dngos po*).[239]

6. Phenomenological Basis according to the Final Promulgation

2. Phenomenological Structures according to the Final [Definitive] Promulgation [III.C.2]
   a. Phenomenological Basis Encompassing All Twenty-five Realms of Phenomenal Existence
      i. Ground: The Twenty-one Foundational Categories
      ii. Path: The Three Aspects of the Path
      iii. Result: The Expanse of Reality

Phenomenological Structures according to the Final [Definitive] Promulgation [2]

The second part [of the extensive exegesis on the actual structure of Buddhist phenomenology; see p. 472] is a systematic presentation of phenomenological categories according to the uncommon tradition of the final promulgation.[240] This has three topics: (1) the basis of the phenomenological categories which encompass all twenty-five realms of phenomenal existence (*srid pa nyi shu rtsa lnga*); (2) the five foundational factors (*gzhi chos lnga*) of which the [three] natures partake; and (3) an exegesis of the three natures (*mtshan nyid gsum*) which partake of these [foundational factors].[241]

Phenomenological Basis Encompassing All Twenty-five Realms of Phenomenal Existence [a]

The first of these topics has three aspects: (1) ground (*gzhi*), (2) path (*lam*), and (3) the expanse of reality (*chos kyi dbyings*).

Ground: The Twenty-one Foundational Categories [i]

With regard to the first [it says in the root verses]:

> **When the psycho-physical aggregates, the sensory bases,**
> **And the sensory activity fields are reconstituted,**
> **Each of these [structures] has three further subdivisions:**
> **Respectively, [the aggregate of physical forms] comprises**
> **The sensory bases of the elements, the physical world and its living organisms;**
> **[The sensory base of mental phenomena] comprises**
> **The mind, mentation, and consciousness;**
> **While [the sensory activity field of the mental faculty] comprises**
> **Demonstrations, defining characteristics, and non-substantial mental phenomena.**
> **[Among the latter,] the demonstrations also comprise**
> **Three further aspects—feelings, perceptions, and formative predispositions;**
> **The defining characteristics comprise three further aspects—**
> **Those that are imputed with regard to space, time, and substance;**
> **While the non-substantial mental phenomena comprise**
> **Those arising through the transformation of substance,**
> **Those that are dependent on substance,**
> **And those that do not exist.**
> **These then are the twenty-one aspects associated with the ground.**

As explained above, the five psycho-physical aggregates, the eighteen sensory bases and the twelve sensory activity fields may be reconstituted in the following three aspects: (1) the aggregate of physical forms (*rūpaskandha, gzugs kyi phung po*), (2) the sensory base of mental phenomena (*dharmadhātu, chos kyi khams*), and (3) the sensory activity field of the mental faculty (*mano āyatana, yid kyi skye mched*).[242]

Each of these also has three further subdivisions. Among them, the aggregate of physical forms comprises the following three aspects: (4) the sensory base of the elements (*bhūtadhātu, 'byung ba'i khams*), (5) the containing physical world (*bhājanaloka, snod kyi 'jig rten*), and (6) the sentient beings within it (*sattva, bcud kyi sems can*). The sensory activity field of the mental faculty[243] also comprises the following three aspects: (7) the mind (*citta, sems*), (8) mentation (*manas, yid*), and (9) consciousness (*vijñāna, rnam par shes pa*). The sensory base of mental phenomena similarly has the following three subdivisions: (10) mental phenomena denoting demonstrations (*lakṣyadharma, mtshan gzhi'i chos*), (11) mental phenomena denoting defining characteristics (*lakṣaṇadharma, mtshan nyid kyi chos*), and (12) non-substantial mental phenomena (*abhāvadharma, dngos med kyi chos*).

Among the latter, the demonstrations comprise three further aspects: (13) the aggregates of feelings, (14) perceptions, and (15) formative predispositions. The defining characteristics comprise three further aspects: (16) those that are imputed with regard to space (*dikparikalpita, yul la btags pa*), (17) those that are imputed with regard to time (*kālaparikalpita, dus la btags pa*), and (18) those that are imputed with regard to substance (*bhāvaparikalpita, dngos la btags pa*). Then, the non-substantial mental phenomena may also be subdivided into (19) non-substantial phenomena arising through the transformation of substance (*bhāvanyāthikābhāva, dngos po gzhan 'gyur gyi dngos med*), (20) non-substantial mental phenomena dependent on substance (*bhāvaniśritābhāva, dngos po la brten pa'i dngos med*), and (21) non-substantial mental phenomena which do not exist (*asambhavābhāva, mi srid pa'i dngos med*). These twenty-one are collectively designated as the "aspects associated with the ground" (*gzhi'i chos*).[244]

These largely accord in their meaning with the foregoing [explanations]. However, the "defining characteristics" refer [in this context] to particular aspects of phenomena that are imaginary or imputed (*chos kun tu btags pa*). These include all phenomena that are relatively determined, such as [the dichotomies of] cause and result, greatness and smallness, light and dark, or example and exemplified, which are all said to be imputed with regard to space (*yul la btags pa*). By contrast, those phenomena that are analyzed in terms of past and future are imputed with regard to time (*dus la btags pa*), while those such as "vase" and "pillar" [which may be conceived or imagined] are imputed with regard to substance (*dngos la btags pa*).

Furthermore, non-substantial [phenomena] which were once substantial but subsequently destroyed, such as the cessation [of sensory functions] obtained through analytical means, are [classed as] non-substantial phenomena arising through the transformation [of substance]. Substantial object-universals (*dngos po'i don spyi*), such as the concepts "vase universal" or "pillar universal" (*bum pa dang ka ba'i spyi*), are [classed as] non-substantial [phenomena] dependent on substance. Concepts such as the "horns of a hare" or "non-vase universal" (*bum pa med pa'i spyi)*, are [classed as] non-substantial [phenomena] which do not exist.

Path: The Three Aspects of the Path [ii]

With regard to the second [topic of the phenomenological basis, it says in the root verses]:

> **There are three approaches of the [spiritual] path:**
> **Common, uncommon, and one [extraordinary approach]**
> **Through which the abiding nature of the Conqueror will be reached.**

The three approaches of the [spiritual] path comprise (1) the common path which refers to the vehicles of the gods and of Brahmā,[245] (2) the uncommon path which refers to the vehicles of the pious attendants and hermit buddhas,[246] and (3) the [extraordinary] path of the Greater Vehicle[247] through which the abiding nature or level of the Buddha, our Teacher, the Conqueror, might be reached.[248]

Result: The Expanse of Reality [iii]

With regard to the third [topic of the phenomenological basis, it says in the root verses]:

> **The expanse of reality is the ultimate [truth], unconditioned and unique.**
> **The systematic presentation of the irreversible promulgation**
> **Determines that this object of knowledge**
> **Encompasses all twenty-five realms of phenomenal existence.**

In this context, [unconditioned phenomena,] including the so-called three categories of unconditioned phenomena *('dus ma byas gsum)* posited by pious attendants, are actually [classed as] "symbolic or imputed unconditioned phenomena" (*rnam grangs sam btags pa'i 'dus ma byas*). By contrast, the expanse of reality (*dharmadhātu, chos kyi dbyings*), which is the ultimate truth (*paramārthasatya, don dam pa'i bden pa*), alone is [considered to be] unique and uncompounded.[249]

The systematic presentation of renowned [texts] such as the *Sūtra of Great*

Final Nirvāṇa and the *Sūtra of the Great Drum*, which belong to the irreversible promulgation [of the Buddha's teachings], has determined that all things of phenomenal existence, encompassing all the twenty-five realms (*srid pa'i chos mtha' dag bsdus pa nyi shu rtsa lnga po*) have this field of knowledge, [the actual reality,] as their ground and path.[250]

7. The Five Foundational Factors

b. The Five Foundational Factors of Which the Three Natures Partake [III.C.2.b]
- i. Brief Description
- ii. Detailed Exegesis
  - aa. Five Foundational Factors [of Epistemology]
    - 1' Appearances
    - 2' Names
    - 3' False Imaginations
    - 4' Absolute Reality
    - 5' Genuine Nonconceptual Knowledge
  - bb. Conclusion

The Five Foundational Factors of Which the Three Natures Partake [b]

The second topic [of the systematic presentation of phenomenological categories according to the uncommon tradition of the final promulgation] concerns the five [epistemic] foundational factors of which the three natures partake. This has two parts: (1) a brief description of the five foundational factors, and so forth; and (2) an extensive exegesis.

Brief Description [i]

The former [comments on the root verses]:

> **Moreover, the five foundational factors**
> **Of which [the three] natures partake,**

Along with the three natures which partake of them,
And dependent origination and so forth, which derive from them,
Are all subsumed within the Greater Vehicle.

In the sūtras of the final promulgation, this topic is also known as the "ground that subsumes [all] phenomenological structures" (*shes bya bsdu ba'i gzhi*):[251]

> Here, the five foundational factors (*gzhi chos lnga*) [of epistemology], beginning with appearances, of which the [three] natures partake, along with the three natures (*rang bzhin gsum*) themselves, starting with the imaginary nature (*parikalpita, kun brtags*), which partake of [these foundational factors], and the dependent origination (*pratītyasamutpāda, rten 'brel*) that derives from the first of these [natures], and the two aspects of selflessness (*bdag med gnyis*) and so forth which they also comprise are all subsumed as the phenomenological structures of the Greater Vehicle, and they will be sequentially explained.

Detailed Exegesis [ii]

The latter has two parts, comprising (1) the five foundational factors, and (2) the three natures.

Five Foundational Factors [of Epistemology] [aa]

Firstly, the [five foundational factors of epistemology] comprise (1) perceptual appearances (*nimitta, rgyu mtshan*), (2) names (*nāma, ming*), (3) false imaginations (*vikalpa, rnam par rtog pa*), (4) absolute reality (*tathatā, de bzhin nyid*), and (5) genuine [non-conceptual] knowledge (*nirvikalpajñāna, yang dag pa'i ye shes*).[252]

Appearances [1']

The first [comments on the root verses]:

Appearances are universals indicating states or objects,
And they have many variations,
Including those that are natural—

The propensities that manifest to the innate mind—
And those that are projected, such as the imputed self.

Appearances are universals indicating states or objects which may be signified verbally or through the distracting imagination of the mental faculty. As such, they may be exemplified by the universal image of a given conceived object that arises in the mind due to the apprehending imagination of a "vase."

Among their subdivisions, there are many variations, including (a) natural appearances (*svabhāvanimitta, rang bzhin gyi rgyu mtshan*)—the signs of the diverse imaging or propensities that manifest to the innate mind in cyclic existence; (b) projected appearances (*bimbanimitta, gzugs brnyen gyi rgyu mtshan*), such as the apprehension of a self, which is imputed by erroneous philosophical systems; and (c) dichotomizing or polarizing appearances (*dvandvanimitta, rgyu mtshan gnyis gnyis*), such as [phenomena that are] realized and unrealized, clear and unclear, or symbolic and non-symbolic.[253]

Furthermore, the term "appearance" may also be uniquely applied to each of the five foundational factors, as follows:

(1) The appearance of appearances (*rgyu mtshan gyi rgyu mtshan*) refers to the subjective apprehension of the universal image corresponding to a conceived object, such as a "vase."
(2) The appearance of names (*ming gi rgyu mtshan*) may be exemplified, in this instance, by the universal image of the conceived object [i.e., the "vase"].
(3) The appearance of false imagination (*rnam rtog gi rgyu mtshan*) is exemplified by the workings of the mind and its mental states.
(4) The appearance of absolute reality (*de bzhin nyid kyi rgyu mtshan*) refers to a given object imputed as absolute reality by means of thought processes.
(5) The appearance of genuine [non-conceptual] knowledge (*yang dag pa'i shes pa'i rgyu mtshan*) refers to a given universal image apprehended while one adheres to the [spiritual] path.[254]

Names [2']

The second [comments on the root verses]:

Names are verbally designated universals,
Imputed with respect to these [appearances].

They include substantive, relational, integrated,
Diversified, known, and unknown names.

The essential nature of names is that they are verbally designated universals which, on being imputed with respect to a given appearance, are perceived and then labeled. For example, a "vase" is designated on the basis of a given object apprehended by means of the imagination that conceives a vase; and indeed it is even perceived as the term-universal (*sgra spyi*) corresponding to its given [object], without being audibly sensed.

Although among the subdivisions [of names] almost forty have been enumerated,[255] here they are subsumed in the following six:

(1) Substantive names (*dngos po'i ming*) may be exemplified, in this instance, by the given term-universal (*sgra spyi*) "vase."

(2) Relational names (*'brel ba'i ming*) may be exemplified by the term-universal inherent in the thought, "This vase is large. This vase is small."

(3) Integrating names (*'dus pa'i ming*) are exemplified by term-universals in which multiple aspects are perceived as one, as in the statement, "These golden vases, silver vases, and copper vases are vases."

(4) Diversifying names (*tha dad pa'i ming*) are the opposite of these, exemplified by term-universals in which the details derived from a single descriptive base (*khyad gzhi*) are diversely perceived, as in the statement, "These vases comprise golden, silver, and copper vases."

(5–6) Known names (*grags pa'i ming*) and unknown names (*ma grags pa'i ming*) refer to those that are known and unknown in a given place and time. For example, the Sanskrit term *hasti* (*lag ldan*) is known to mean "elephant," while the same expression (*lag pa dang ldan pa*) is not known to mean "bull."

False Imaginations [3']

The third [comments on the root verses]:

False imagination denotes the mind and its mental states,
Including symbolic and non-symbolic [concepts],
As well as dissonant and non-dissonant mental states.

The essential nature of false imagination is that it denotes the mind and its mental states;[256] while its subdivisions may be either symbolic or non-symbolic (*nimittavikalpa cānimittavikalpa, mtshan bcas dang mtshan ma med pa'i rnam rtog*). The former refers principally to the imaginations associated with the mind and mental states prevalent in the world-system of desire, as well as those prevalent as far as the first meditative concentration. The latter refers to [imaginations that are prevalent] from that [first meditative concentration] as far as the summit of existence, as well as to the temporary mind and mental states associated with unconsciousness and sleep. However, the last mentioned are not designated as "perpetually non-symbolic" (*mtshan ma gtan nas med pa*) but as "inferior states which are subject to cessation."

Alternatively, imaginations may include those associated with dissonant mental states (*kliṣṭavikalpa, nyon mongs can gyi rnam rtog*) and those associated with non-dissonant mental states (*akliṣṭavikalpa, nyon mongs can ma yin pa'i rnam rtog*). Among these, the former are the non-virtuous imaginations prevalent in the world system of desire, while the latter are the imaginations compounded by uncorrupted [states]. Among these, three further types are also distinguished, namely, object-oriented [imaginations] (*ālambanavikalpa, yul la 'jug pa*), investigative [imaginations] (*paryeṣakavikalpa, 'tshol ba po*), and analytical imaginations (*pratyavekṣakavikalpa, so sor rtog pa'i rnam rtog*).[257]

Absolute Reality [4']

The fourth [comments on the root verses]:

> **The absolute reality transcends expression and thought.**

The actual reality that transcends objects of verbal expression and mental conception is [also known as] suchness or absolute reality (*tathatā, de bzhin nyid*), which is within the perceptual range of the non-conceptual pristine cognition (*nirvikalpajñāna, rnam par mi rtog pa'i ye shes*) alone, [experienced during] the meditative equipoise of sublime beings.[258]

Genuine Nonconceptual Knowledge [5']

The fifth [comments on the root verses]:

> **Knowledge of the [spiritual] path,**
> **[Intermingling] meditative equipoise and post-meditative experience,**
> **Is the genuine [non-conceptual] knowledge.**

The [last two—absolute reality and genuine knowledge—]
Are respectively endowed with objective and subjective characteristics.
All the phenomenological categories associated with the supportive [consciousness]
Are gathered within this [fivefold classification].

Knowledge of the [spiritual] path, which characteristically intermingles supramundane meditative equipoise (*samāhita, mnyam gzhag*) with supramundane post-meditative experience (*pṛṣṭhalabdha, rjes thob*) is genuine [non-conceptual] knowledge (*nirvikalpajñāna, yang dag pa'i ye shes*).[259]

The [last] two [foundational factors], absolute reality and the genuine [non-conceptual] knowledge, are endowed with defining characteristics that are respectively objective and subjective.

CONCLUSION [bb]

Elaborating on these [five foundational factors of epistemology], if I might offer some further words of explanation:[260] Since names and appearances are neither identical nor different, they are both [said to be] "inexpressible apart from the absolute reality,"[261] while it is also said of the four other foundational factors in relation to the absolute reality that they too are "inexpressible apart from the absolute reality."

[In terms of their defining characteristics,] appearances are the defining characteristic of the subjective aspect of false imagination. This is because while appearances are the objective aspect of imagination they are also the agent or enactor of a given object of imagination. Names are the defining characteristics of the ground or locus from which conventional expressions originate.

[In term of substantial and imputed existents,] both false imagination that objectifies appearances and genuine knowledge are [classed as] "substantial existents" (*rdzas yod*), while names are [classed as] "imputed existents" (*btags yod*). Those aspects [of imagination] that apprehend [both] names and appearances are [classed as] substantial existents. Absolute reality transcends both substantial and imputed existents.[262]

[In terms of the three natures, those postulated concepts] which are not apprehended on the basis of appearances are assigned, along with names, to the imaginary nature (*parikalpita, kun brtags*). Both false imagination and genuine knowledge are assigned to the dependent nature (*paratantra, gzhan *dbang*). The absolute reality refers to the unchanging consummate nature (*pariniṣpanna, yongs grub*).[263]

With regard to the term "factor" (*chos*) as employed here in the expression "five [foundational] factors" (*chos lnga*), it conveys the sense of a foundation [of epistemology], facilitating the understanding of phenomena. Alternatively, these [five factors] are also known as the "five entities" (*pañcavastu, dngos po lnga*), simply indicating that they have the causal efficacy of substantial entities (*bhāvasadartha, dngos po'i don yod pa*).[264]

The expression "five foundational factors" was mentioned by the Conqueror himself [in the sūtras of the final promulgation],[265] because the factors of demonstration (*lakṣyadharma, mtshan gzhi chos*) among the twofold division of defining characteristics and demonstration, and all phenomenological categories associated with the supportive [consciousness] (*rten gyi shes bya thams cad*) among the twofold division of the supportive [consciousness] and its supported [objects], are subsumed within these five [foundational factors].

8. The Three Natures

bb. The Three Natures [III.C.2.b.ii.bb]
- 1' Imaginary Nature
- 2' Dependent Nature
- 3' Consummate Nature
- 4' Analysis and Synthesis of the Three Natures
  - a' Analysis
  - b' Synthesis
- 5' Three Corresponding Aspects of Emptiness and Their Demonstrations
  - a' Definitive Establishment of the Three Natures as the Three Aspects of Emptiness
  - b' Their Demonstrations
  - c' Indian Commentators on the Three Natures

The Three Natures [bb]

Second, there is the exegesis of the three natures (*trilakṣaṇa, mtshan nyid gsum*), which has five parts: (1) the imaginary nature (*parikalpita, kun brtags*), (2) the dependent nature (*paratantra, gzhan dbang*), (3) the consummate nature (*pariniṣpanna, yongs grub*), (4) their detailed analysis and synthesis (*bye brag gi dbye bsdu*), and (5) an introduction to the three corresponding aspects of emptiness and their demonstrations (*stong nyid gsum dang mtshan gzhir 'jug tshul*).[266]

Imaginary Nature [1']

The first part [concerning the imaginary nature, comments on the root verses]:

Things imputed by verbal expression and false imagination are imaginary.
These comprise three categories: the imaginary nature of delimited characteristics,
Exemplified by the concept of individual selfhood;
The nominal imaginary,
Exemplified by the dualistic appearances of the subject-object dichotomy;
And the referentially imputed imaginary.
Or, alternatively, there are ten aspects.

Designated objects imputed by means of verbal and mental expression and by the false imagination of the mind are assigned to the imaginary nature. In the case of a designated object imputed by the term "vase," for example, the act of designation is carried out by the imaginations of mental consciousness and its peripheral mental states.

When classified, [the imaginary nature] comprises the following three aspects:

(1) the imaginary nature of delimited characteristics (*paricchedaparikalpita, mtshan nyid yongs su chad pa'i kun btags*), exemplified by objects that are apprehended through the [deluded] apprehension of individual selfhood (*pudgalātma, gang zag gi bdag*). In this case even the apprehended object is precluded by nature because despite its apparent image, individual selfhood does not actually exist as a phenomenological category.

(2) the nominal imaginary (*paryāyaparikalpita, rnam grangs pa'i kun btags*), which is exemplified by the dualistic appearances of the subject-object dichotomy

(3) the referentially imputed imaginary (*ltos nas btags pa*), which may be exemplified by [the concept of] "large" imputed in relation to "small," and "west" imputed in relation to "east"[267]

Alternatively, [the imaginary nature] also alludes to the dichotomy between the basis of designation (*gdags gzhi*) and the designator (*gdags byed*), and the dichotomy between the imagining of the essential nature [of an object] and its attributes (*ngo bo nyid dang khyad par gyi kun btags*).[268]

Or else, taking the case of the *Sūtra of the Descent to Laṅkā*, although the verses of the version translated from Sanskrit mention ten aspects (*rnam pa bcu*) [of the imaginary nature, here] in conformity with the version translated from Chinese, where a more detailed explanation is found, referring to twelve [aspects], the text says:[269]

> The imaginary nature has twelve aspects
> And the dependent nature has six aspects.

These [twelve] are said to include false imaginations of verbal expression, false imaginations of absolute reality, false imaginations of defining characteristics, false imaginations of property, false imaginations of nature, false imaginations of causes, false imaginations of philosophical views, false imaginations of reasoning, false imaginations of birth, false imaginations of non-birth, false imaginations of interdependence, and false imaginations of bondage and emancipation.[270]

Dependent Nature [2']

The second part [concerning the dependent nature, comments on the root verses]:

> **The dependent nature is assigned to apperception alone,**
> **Which arises through causes and conditions.**
> **It has two categories: one comprising the seeds of all dissonant mental states**
> **And the other in which neither dissonant nor purified mental states inherently exist.**
> **Or, alternatively, there are six aspects.**

The dependent nature [lit. "that which is subject to extraneous control"] (*paratantra, gzhan dbang*) is assigned to "apperception alone" or "ideation alone" (*vijñaptimātra, rnam par rig pa tsam*), arising through its own intrinsic causes and conditions.

"Intrinsic" implies that the causes and conditions that give rise to this apperceptive consciousness originate from factors that are appropriate or in conformity with it. The term "extraneous" here refers to the diverse propensities which are imprinted upon the substratum, and it is under the "control" of these propensities that the substratum consciousness, congruent with apperception, becomes manifest.

When there is only a radiant and aware consciousness, uncontrolled by propensities, the apperception does not become diversified and abides right where it is, [unmodified,] but otherwise, through its dependence on propensities, the apperception does become diversified.

When classified, [the dependent nature] has two aspects: the dependent nature comprising the seeds of all dissonant mental states (*kun nas nyon mongs pa sa bon gyi gzhan dbang*) and the dependent nature in which neither deluded nor purified mental states inherently exist (*kun byang gi ngo bor ma grub pa'i gzhan dbang*), because conscious awareness is pure and unmodified by propensities.[271]

Alternatively, [the dependent nature] may be classified according to the impure mundane dependent nature (*ma dag 'jig rten pa'i gzhan dbang*), in which the mind and mental states of the three world systems manifest as real existents through the power of propensities, and the pure mundane dependent nature (*dag pa 'jig rten pa'i gzhan dbang*), in which appearances devoid of substantial existence manifest in an illusory manner during the post-meditative experiences of sublime beings.[272]

Or else, it may be classified into six aspects, in accordance with the following sixfold enumeration that is mentioned in the *Sūtra of the Descent to Laṅkā*: (1) visual consciousness and the physical forms that are its object; (2) the mental states that originate within its periphery; (3) the dissonant mental consciousness that closely depends upon these [mental states]; (4) the substratum that is the initial entry-point of diversification; (5) the application of this general process to the other [modes of consciousness]; and (6) the relation of the six modes [of engaged consciousness] to the substratum and the dissonant mental consciousness.[273]

Consummate Nature [3']

The third part [concerning the consummate nature, comments on the root verses]:

> **The consummate nature is the ultimate actual reality—the absolute reality.**
> **The [consummate] nature has four aspects:**
> **For it is naturally pure, it is free from adventitious stains,**
> **It is the pristine cognition of the spiritual path,**
> **And it is the objective of the scriptures.**

The term "consummate nature" (*pariniṣpanna, yongs grub*) refers to the actual reality of all phenomena, the original ultimate [truth]. Although from the perspective of its essential nature, the consummate cannot be differentiated, there are many classifications corresponding to each of its distinct nuances or facets. Therefore, its [synonyms] which have been enumerated [in the sūtras] include the "reality of physical form" (*rūpatathatā, gzugs kyi de bzhin nyid*) and the "reality of feeling" (*vedanātathatā, tshor ba'i de bzhin nyid*).

The sublime Asaṅga, with an enlightened intention directed respectively towards the naturally pure aspect, freedom from adventitious stains, the pristine cognition of the [spiritual] path, and those who have as their objective meditation on the path of the Buddha's scriptures, has said that, without differentiating proper and conventional terms, [the consummate nature] comprises four aspects, namely, (1) the natural consummate nature (*svabhāvapariniṣpanna, rang bzhin yongs grub*), (2) the immaculate consummate nature (*vimalapariniṣpanna, dri med yongs grub*), (3) the consummate nature of the spiritual path (*mārgapariniṣpanna, lam yongs grub*), and (4) the consummate nature of the [scriptural] objectives (*ālambanapariniṣpanna, dmigs pa yongs grub*).[274]

Also, in the *Analysis of the Middle and Extremes*, it is revealed that there are also two aspects: (1) the unchanging consummate nature (*'gyur med yongs grub*) and (2) the incontrovertible consummate nature (*phyin ci ma log pa'i yongs grub*).[275]

Analysis and Synthesis of the Three Natures [4']

The fourth part [concerning the detailed analysis and synthesis of the three natures, comments on the root verses]:

> In particular, [the three natures] may also be explained
> In terms of the ten aspects of distracting false imagination,
> The eleven aspects of apperception,
> The nine aspects of the consummate nature, and so forth;
> But because the apparitional aspect of dependent nature
> Partakes of bewildered imagination,
> The [three] natures that have been differentiated
> May also be subsumed in two.

Analysis [a']

Elaborating on the aspects of the three natures [that have just been summarized], there are also [other] particular analyses that have been mentioned in the *Ornament of the Sūtras of the Greater Vehicle* and in the *Summary of the Greater Vehicle*.

[Analysis of the Imaginary Nature]

Firstly, there are the ten aspects of distracting false imagination (*daśavikṣepavikalpa, rnam gYeng gi rnam rtog bcu*), which are related to the imaginary nature (*parikalpita*). These comprise (1) imaginations of nonexistence (*abhāvavikalpa, med par rtog pa*), (2) imaginations of existence (*bhāvavikalpa, yod par rtog pa*), (3) imaginations of exaggeration or reification (*adhyāropavikalpa, sgro 'dogs par rtog pa*), (4) imaginations of underestimation or repudiation (*apavādavikalpa, skur 'debs kyi rtog pa*), (5) imaginations of singularity (*ekatvavikalpa, gcig tu 'dzin pa'i rtog pa*), (6) imaginations of multiplicity (*nānātvavikalpa, du mar 'dzin pa'i rtog pa*), (7) imaginations of inherent existence (*svabhāvavikalpa, rang gi ngo bo nyid du 'dzin pa'i rtog pa*), (8) imaginations of attribution or qualification (*viśeṣavikalpa, khyad par du rtog pa*), (9) imaginations of meanings that accord with names [i.e., naïve realism] (*yathānāmārthābhiniveśavikalpa, ming la don du rtog pa*), and (10) imaginations of names that accord with meanings [i.e., naïve substantialism] (*yathārthanāmābhiniveśavikalpa, don la ming du rtog pa*).[276] These are enumerated as aspects of false imagination which may be imputed in all sorts of contexts, and it is on this basis that the process of reification actually comes to partake of the imaginary nature.

More generally, it is explained that there are (1) fundamental imaginations—the substratum consciousness (*mūlavikalpa, rtsa ba'i rnam rtog kun gzhi'i rnam shes*), as well as (2) symbolic imaginations that apprehend objects (*nimittavikalpa, yul du 'dzin pa mtshan ma'i rnam rtog*); (3) imaginations that mirror the six modes of [engaged] consciousness (*nimittābhāsavikalpa, rnam shes drug mtshan snang gi rnam rtog*); (4) changeable and symbolic imaginations (*nimittapariṇāmavikalpa, mtshan ma 'gyur ba'i rnam rtog*), which include feelings of happiness, suffering, and so forth; (5) changeable imaginations that mirror the variations of the six modes of [engaged] consciousness (*nimittābhāsapariṇāmavikalpa, rnam shes drug gi 'gyur ba las byung ba mtshan ma snang bar 'gyur ba'i rnam rtog*); (6) imaginations disclosed by other intellectual efforts consequent on having studied Buddhist and non-Buddhist teachings (*parānvayavikalpa, chos dang chos ma yin pa thos pa'i rjes su blo gzhol ba gzhan gyis bstan pa'i rnam rtog*); (7) inappropriate imaginations (*ayoniśovikalpa, tshul bzhin ma yin pa'i rnam rtog*), such as the view that postulates a [permanent] self; (8) appropriate imaginations (*yoniśovikalpa, tshul bzhin gyi rnam rtog*), such as [the view of] impermanence; (9) imaginations that manifestly cling to negative views (*abhiniveśavikalpa, lta ngan la mngon *par zhen pa'i rnam rtog*); and (10) distracting imaginations (*vikṣepavikalpa, rnam par gYeng ba'i rnam rtog*).[277]

Although, on account of the limitless number of imputative imaginations, there are seemingly limitless classifications of the imaginary nature, imputed by them, even so the last-mentioned classifications are explained to be particularly relevant and are listed alongside the objectives of [spiritual] training on the grounds that they are to be rejected by bodhisattvas.[278]

[Analysis of the Dependent Nature]

The eleven aspects of apperception (*rnam rig bcu gcig*), which derive from the dependent nature, comprise[279]

(1) the apperception that the physical manifestations of propensities which are "only consciousness" appear to the sense faculty of the body (*rnam shes tsam bag chags kyi gzugs snang ba lus kyi dbang por snang ba'i rnam rig*)
(2) the apperception that corporeal forms become manifest to the faculty of visual consciousness (*mig shes dbang por snang ba lus can gyi rnam rig*)
(3) the apperception of the consumer mental consciousness (*yid kyi rnam shes za ba po'i rnam rig*)[280]
(4) the apperception of resources that manifest as the six objects [of sensory consciousness] (*yul drug tu snang ba nye bar spyad bya'i rnam rig*)
(5) the apperception of resources associated with visual consciousness and so forth (*mig shes sogs nye bar longs spyod pa'i rnam rig*)
(6) the apperception of temporal divisions that become manifest, such as years and months (*lo dang zla ba sogs dus su snang ba'i rnam rig*)
(7) the apperception of numeric categories that become manifest, such as units, tens, hundreds, and thousands (*gcig bcu brgya stong sogs grangs su snang ba'i rnam rig*)
(8) the apperception of geographical features that become manifest, such as villages, cities, forests, and mountains (*grong dang grong khyer nags tshal dang ri la sogs pa yul gyi snang ba'i rnam rig*)
(9) the apperception [of linguistic concepts] that manifest as conventional terms, phrases, and letters (*tha snyad ming tshig yi ge gsum du snang ba'i rnam rig*)
(10) the apperception of self that becomes manifest with reference to one's

own body, speech, and mind (*rang gi lus ngag yid gsum la dmigs nas bdag tu snang ba'i rnam rig*)

(11) the apperception of others that becomes manifest with reference to the body, speech, and mind of others (*gzhan gyi lus ngag yid gsum la dmigs nas gzhan du snang ba'i rnam rig*)

Among these, with regard to [the first] five, which concern the sense faculties, there is an "apperception only" (*vijñaptimātra, rnam par rig pa tsam*) which manifests as these [faculties]. The middle four originate exclusively through the power of inbuilt propensities (*abhidānavāsanā, mngon brjod kyi bag chags*). The last two originate from the propensities that maintain the [mistaken] view of a [permanent] self.[281]

[Analysis of the Consummate Nature]

The consummate nature also has nine further aspects, as is stated in the *Extensive Mother* (*Yum rgyas pa*), namely, (1) the absolute reality (*tathatā, de bzhin nyid*), (2) the unmistaken absolute reality (*avitathatā, ma nor ba'i de bzhin nyid*), (3) the non-extraneous absolute reality (*ananyatathatā, gzhan ma yin pa'i de bzhin nyid*),(4) the actual reality (*dharmatā, chos nyid*), (5) the expanse of reality (*dharmadhātu, chos kyi dbyings*), (6) the abiding nature of reality (*dharmasthititā, chos gnas pa nyid*), (7) the stainless nature of reality (*dharmanirdoṣatā, chos skyon med pa nyid*), (8) the genuine goal (*bhūtakoṭi, yang dag pa'i mtha'*), and (9) the inconceivable expanse (*acintyadhātu, bsam gyis mi khyab pa'i dbyings*).[282]

These are respectively identified by the master Vasubandhu with (1) the consummate nature devoid of fear (*'jigs pa med pa yongs su grub pa*), (2) the incontrovertible [consummate nature] (*phyin ci ma log pa*), (3) the unchanging [consummate nature] (*'gyur ba med pa*), (4) the [consummate nature] devoid of inherent existence (*ngo bo nyid med pa*), (5) the [consummate nature present] as the seed of all purificatory teachings (*rnam par byang ba'i chos kyi rgyu nyid du*), (6) [the consummate nature] present at all times (*dus thams cad du*), (7) the irreversible [consummate nature] (*phyir mi ldog pa*), (8) the [consummate nature] of the real (*tattva, de kho na nyid*), and (9) [the consummate nature] that transcends the path of sophistry (*rtog ge'i lam las 'das pa*).[283]

The expression "and so forth" (*sogs*) here implies that when the consummate nature is further classified, it may be exemplified by the sixteen aspects of emptiness (*ṣoḍaśaśūnyatā, stong nyid bcu drug*),[284] and that the other two [natures] have also acquired many [additional] aspects.

Synthesis [b']

When these [diverse aspects of the three natures] are all subsumed, the inconceivable appearances which are the bewildering apparitional aspect of the dependent nature, and the substratum consciousness, which is the repository of all seeds and the ground from which that [apparitional aspect] arises, are not extraneous to the imaginary nature. For this reason, the natures that are classified may be reduced to two: (1) the imaginary nature that relates to phenomena (*dharmaparikalpitalakṣaṇa, chos kun brtags kyi mtshan nyid*) and (2) the consummate nature that relates to actual reality (*dharmatāpariniṣpannalakṣaṇa, chos nyid yongs su grub pa'i mtshan nyid*).

More generally, with regard to the relationship between these two natures—one combining the imaginary and the dependent, and the other being the consummate—it is also said that they are [all] "inexpressible apart from the absolute reality."[285] The imaginary is the aspect which imputes reification or exaggeration, and the dependent is the object of this reification or exaggeration. The consummate is the actual reality of those other two aspects. Therefore, when the three natures are analyzed from one perspective they are not identical, but when analyzed from another perspective, they are not different. So it is that they are not established as being identical or different in any respect.[286]

Three Corresponding Aspects of Emptiness and Their Demonstrations [5']

The fifth part [comments on the root verses]:

> **Respectively, [these three natures are identified] as the emptiness of non-existence,**
> **The emptiness of existence,**
> **And the emptiness of the natural [reality].**
> **When demonstrations [of these three natures] are introduced,**
> **The imaginary is the apparitional aspect,**
> **The dependent is the union of radiance and awareness,**
> **And the consummate is free from conceptual elaboration.**

This has two aspects: (1) the definitive establishment of the three natures as the three [corresponding] aspects of emptiness (*stong pa nyid gsum*),[287] and (2) their demonstrations.

Definitive Establishment of the Three Natures as the Three Aspects of Emptiness [a']

It is said in the *Ornament of the Sūtras of the Greater Vehicle* that

(1) The imaginary nature is designated as the "emptiness of non-existence" (*abhāvaśūnyatā, med pa'i stong pa nyid*) and in terms of both the [ultimate and the relative] truths, it is devoid of inherent existence.
(2) The dependent nature is designated as the "emptiness of existence" (*bhāvaśūnyatā, yod pa'i stong pa nyid*) and is non-existent from the standpoint of ultimate [truth] (*paramārthasatya, don dam bden pa*) but does exist in terms of the relative truth (*saṃvṛtisatya, kun rdzob bden pa*).
(3 The consummate nature is designated as the "emptiness of inherent existence" (*svabhāvaśūnyatā, rang bzhin stong pa nyid*) and abides as the actual reality of all things.[288]

This modality is also mentioned in the following passage from the [*Sūtra of the*] *Transcendental Perfection of Discriminative Awareness in Five Hundred Lines*:[289]

> What, you might ask, Subhūti, is the meditative stability of emptiness with regard to physical form? Subhūti, this one-pointed focusing of the mind on physical form, [firstly] with reference to the emptiness of its non-substantiality, and similarly with reference to the emptiness of its substantiality, and [thirdly] with reference to the emptiness of its inherent existence, is known as the meditative stability of emptiness (*śūnyatāsamādhi*). So it is that the bodhisattvas should completely understand meditative stability with regard to physical form.

Their Demonstrations [b']

The second aspect concerns the demonstrations of the three natures, which may be exemplified as follows: Whether there are appearances that arise before visual consciousness or appearances that arise before mental consciousness, at the time when [this visual or mental object] appears [for example] as a "vase," the aspect which apprehends the vase is the imaginary nature. The bare consciousness, radiant and aware, which distinguishes it is the dependent nature, and the pristine cognition that remains when the imaginary and dependent natures have ceased to exist is held to be the consummate nature.

Then, taking as another example a dissonant mental state, such as attachment or hatred: When a strong attachment or hatred arises in the mind, the afflictive apparitional aspect of attachment or hatred is the imaginary nature, the aspect of radiant awareness that cognizes it is the dependent nature, and the pristine cognition, free from conceptual elaboration, that permeates all things in a common savor is the consummate nature.

In this context, the expression "common savor" (*ro mnyam*) may be understood as follows: Although, for example, the radiant and aware aspect of the consciousness of hatred and the radiant and aware aspect of the consciousness of attachment are both very similar, because they relate to different things, they are not mutually inclusive. However, according to the consummate nature of these [apparently dissimilar mental states] they are essentially inseparable, for which reason they are of a common savor in their essential nature.[290]

One should know that this analogy may also be applied to [the apparent dichotomy between all] the phenomenological categories of the path and the result.

Indian Commentators on the Three Natures [c']

The definitive establishment of the three natures is extensively found in the sūtras of the final promulgation, but it can equally be recognized in [the writings of] venerable Maitreya and in Nāgārjuna's *Commentary on the Sūtra of the Shoots of Rice*.[291]

A somewhat different interpretation may be found, however, in Vasubandhu's *Dissertation on the Thirty Verses*, which is well known among the exponents of extraneous emptiness.[292] Accordingly, the mighty lord of awareness [Vasubandhu] has clearly established that[293]

> The objects that are imputed by false imagination
> Are the imaginary nature,
> While the imaginations [themselves] are the dependent [nature],
> And their emptiness is the consummate nature.

I disagree with those who think that the definitive structure of the three essential natures is a tradition that is known only to the Cittamātrins (*sems tsam pa*) and not to the Mādhyamika (*dbu ma pa*).[294] Indeed, it says in the

Chapter Requested by Maitreya from the *Sūtra of the Transcendental Perfection of Discriminative Awareness*:[295]

> Maitreya, the thorough analysis of physical form has three aspects: the thorough analysis of the imaginary nature, the thorough analysis of the imputed nature (*rnam par btags pa'i mtshan nyid*), and the thorough analysis of the nature of actual reality.

The systematic presentation of the three natures of our own tradition is also established in [Candrakīrti's] *Auto-commentary on the Introduction* [*to Madhyamaka*] and in [Śāntarakṣita's] *Auto-commentary on the Ornament of Madhyamaka*.[296] Furthermore, in [Kamalaśīla's] *Lamp of Madhyamaka*, it says:

> It is not the case that the adherents of Madhyamaka do not admit the systematic presentation of the three essential natures. I will reject any contradictory comments, such as those that can be seen in other [writings].

Therefore, the definitive structure of the three essential natures is clearly presented, again and again, in the textual traditions of Madhyamaka.

Furthermore, it says in [Nāgārjuna's] *Commentary on Enlightened Mind*:

> The imaginary, dependent, and consummate natures
> Are all of an identical nature, emptiness,
> But they are imputed within the mind.

On this basis, it can certainly be asserted that all phenomena are mind, that the nature of this mind, described by many synonyms including inner radiance (*prabhāsvara*), emptiness (*śūnyatā*), ultimate reality (*paramārtha*), buddha nature (*dhātu*), the nucleus of those gone to bliss (*sugatagarbha*), and so forth, is the consummate nature, that the relative appearances of this mind as mere illusory apperception are the dependent nature, and that the aspect imputed as the dualistic phenomena of the subject-object dichotomy and so forth, even while apperception is non-existent, is the imaginary nature.

9. Dependent Origination

3. Dependent Origination, Integrating the Approaches of the Greater and Lesser Vehicles [III.C.3]
  a. Brief Introductory Description of Dependent Origination
  b. Extensive Analytical Exegesis of Dependent Origination
    i. Essential Nature [of Dependent Origination]
    ii. Etymology
    iii. Literal Meaning
    iv. The Twelve Individual Links of Dependent Origination
    v. Functions [of the Twelve Links of Dependent Origination]
    vi. Detailed Analysis [of Dependent Origination]
      aa. Brief Introduction
      bb. Extensive Analysis
        1' The Threefold Analysis
          a' Dependent Origination That Distinguishes the Essential Nature
          b' Dependent Origination That Distinguishes Attractive and Unattractive Goals
          c' Dependent Origination Associated with Sensory Engagement
        2' The Eightfold Analysis
          a' The Six Aspects of Dependent Origination Associated with Dissonant Mental States
          b' The Two Aspects of Dependent Origination Associated with Purified Mental States
        3' Detailed Exegesis of the Twelve Links [of Dependent Origination]
          a' Serial or Circumstantial Dependent Origination
            i' Completion of One Cycle in Two Lifetimes

. . .

Dependent Origination, Integrating the Approaches of the Greater and Lesser Vehicles [3]

The third part [of the extensive exegesis of the actual structure of Buddhist phenomenology; see p. 472] is a systematic presentation of the processes of dependent origination, integrating the approaches of both the Greater and Lesser Vehicles.[297]

This has two parts: (1) a brief introductory description, and (2) an extensive analytical exegesis.

Brief Introductory Description of Dependent Origination [a]

The former [comments on the root verses]:

> **The first two [of these three natures] are dependently originated. [In the case of the dependent nature,]**

This [process] is endowed with generative or causal
And generated or fruitional aspects,
And [in the case of the imaginary nature]
It is endowed with interrelated determinative and determined aspects.
However, it is the genuine dependent origination
[That determines] the substratum consciousness.

However the first two of the three natures—the imaginary and the dependent—arise, it is the case that they do so through the power of dependent origination (*pratītyasamutpāda, rten cing 'brel bar 'byung ba*). The consummate nature may also be explained in terms of dependent origination with an intention directed towards the ultimate aspect of dependent origination (*paramārthapratītyasamutpāda*), even though it is not actually subject to relative dependent origination (*samvṛtipratītyasamutpāda*).[298]

In general, [the term] "dependent origination" denotes the dependent origination that is endowed with generated and generative aspects (*utpādyotpādakapratītyasamutpāda, bskyed bya skyed byed kyi rten 'brel*), which are [respectively] the fruitional and causal processes associated with the arising of the physical environment and its sentient inhabitants, along with the inner consciousness. These processes principally fall within the scope of the dependent nature.

The same term may also denote the dependent origination that is endowed with determined and determinative aspects (*sthāpanīyasthāpakapratītyasamutpāda, gzhag bya dang 'jog byed kyi rten 'brel*). Here, the determinative aspects (*'jog byed*) occur with reference to the [just-mentioned] generated and generative [causal nexus] and may be exemplified by the arising of the consciousness in which a shoot appears from the consciousness in which a seed appears. The determined or relational aspects (*gzhag bya*) also occur without reference to this [causal nexus] and may be exemplified by the determination of "small" in relation to "large." In brief, these interrelated aspects [of causality] principally fall within the scope of the imaginary nature.[299]

As far as the genuine dependent origination (*samyakpratītyasamutpāda, yang dag pa'i rten 'brel*) is concerned, it is this that determines [the composition of] the substratum consciousness, along with all its propensities. This is one of the two categories of dependent origination—provisional and genuine—which are identified within the dependent origination of the generative and generated [causal nexus]; and for this reason it is subsumed within the dependent nature.[300]

Extensive Analytical Exegesis of Dependent Origination [b]

The latter, the extensive [analytical] exegesis [of dependent origination], has eight topics: (1) essential nature (*ngo bo*), (2) etymology (*nges tshig*), (3) literal meaning (*sgra don*), (4) recognition of the twelve individual links of dependent origination (*yan lag bcu gnyis so so'i ngos 'dzin*), (5) function (*karmavyavasthāna, byed las*), (6) analysis (*prabheda, rab dbye*), (7) synthesis (*aṅgasamāsa, don bsdu*), and (8) a presentation of the real nature of dependent origination (*rten 'brel gyi de kho na nyid bstan pa*).[301]

Essential Nature [of Dependent Origination] [i]

With regard to the first of these [the essential nature, it says in the root verses]:

> **The essential nature [of dependent origination]**
> **Is that it occurs only with regard to appearances,**
> **And it arises contingent on them.**

When all phenomena are investigated, although they [ultimately] abide as emptiness, without inherent existence in any respect, the characteristic or essential nature of dependent origination is that this is an [empirical process] that occurs only with regard to appearances, and it arises contingent on them. It is said in the *Fundamental Stanzas of Madhyamaka, entitled Discriminative Awareness*:[302]

> Whatever is dependently originated,
> This has been explained as emptiness.
> It is imputed [as existent], dependent on [something else].
> This is indeed the path of Madhyamaka.
> Because there is nothing that is not dependently originated,
> There is nothing that is not empty.

Etymology [ii]

With regard to the second, the etymology [it says in the root verses]:

> **The etymology implies "origination**
> **Dependent on a complex of causes and conditions."**

The Tibetan term *rten 'brel* [translated as "dependent origination"] in the original Sanskrit is rendered as *pratītyasamutpāda*. The prefix *pratītya* [here] conveys the meanings of a "congregation," a "convergence" or an "encounter."[303] *Samutpāda* means "generated" or "originated." The point is that, whatever object one considers, it is impossible for diverse results to arise from a single cause, or for only a single result to arise from diverse causes. Rather, diverse results originate dependent on an encounter or convergence of diverse causes and conditions, or else one might say that [causal] links originate in dependence on previous links.[304]

Literal Meaning [iii]

With regard to the third, the literal meaning [it says in the root verses]:

> **The literal meanings include "without an agent,"**
> **"Endowed with causal basis," and so forth.**

The [Sanskrit] term *pratītyasamutpāda* is generally said to convey eleven literal meanings. As such, it can mean "without an agent" (*niḥkārtṛka, byed pa po med pa*), "endowed with causal basis" (*sahetuka, rgyu dang bcas pa*), "non-sentient" (*niḥsattva, sems can med pa*), "dependent" (*paratantrārtha, gzhan gyi dbang*), "unmoving" (*nirīhaka, gYo ba med pa*),[305] impermanent (*anitya, mi rtag pa*), "momentary" (*kṣaṇika, skad cig pa*), "uninterrupted" (*prabandhānupaccheda, rgyun mi 'chad pa*), "conformity of causes and results" (*anurūpahetuphala, rgyu 'bras mthun pa*), "diversity [of causes and results]" (*vicitrahetuphala, sna tshogs pa*), and a "distinctive regular pattern of causes and results" (*pratiniyatahetuphala, rgyu 'bras so sor nges pa*).[306] For example, it could be understood in the sense, "All phenomena are dependently originated, without an agent," and so forth.

The Twelve Individual Links of Dependent Origination [iv]

[Fundamental Ignorance]

With regard to the fourth, the recognition of the twelve individual links of dependent origination [it says in the root verses]:

> **Fundamental ignorance, the opposite of awareness,**
> **Is endowed with three attributes.**

Although it has many classifications,
It comprises both [ignorance] endowed with dissonant mental states
And [ignorance] devoid of dissonant mental states.
Fundamental [ignorance] is within the periphery
Of the dissonant mental consciousness,
Deluded with respect to [its imputation of] a self.

The essential nature of fundamental ignorance (*avidyā, ma rig pa*), which is the first of the twelve links of dependent origination (*dvādaśāṅgapratītyasamutpāda, rten 'brel gyi yan lag bcu gnyis*), is that it is the opposite or disharmonious counterpoint of awareness (*vidyā, rig pa*) and is endowed with the following three particular attributes: (1) it implies a consciousness that refers objectively to its object; (2) it implies that the sense data of this object are extremely inconspicuous; and (3) it is the gateway through which the mental continuum arises in a non-quiescent dissonant or afflicted state.[307]

Although [fundamental ignorance] has many classifications, it [essentially comprises] both the ignorance endowed with dissonant mental states (*kliṣṭāvidyā, nyon mong pa can gyi ma rig pa*) and the ignorance devoid of dissonant mental states (*akliṣṭāvidyā, nyon mong pa can ma yin pa'i ma rig pa*). The former is the causal basis of cyclic existence, the obscuration comprising dissonant mental states (*kleśāvaraṇa, nyon mong gi sgrib*) that obscures [the attainment of] release [from cyclic existence]. The latter is the obscuration of knowable phenomena (*jñeyāvaraṇa, shes bya'i sgrib*), which obscures [the attainment of] omniscience (*sarvajñā, thams cad mkhyen pa*).

According to this tradition [of Tāranātha], fundamental ignorance (*mūlāvidyā, rtsa ba'i ma rig pa*) actually lies within the periphery of the dissonant mental consciousness and is said to denote "delusion with respect to [the erroneous imputation of] a self."[308]

There are also some who have simplistically stated that, from the perspective of its conspicuousness, [ignorance] is recognized as and identified with the [aforementioned egotistical] views that uphold mundane aggregates (*satkāyadṛṣṭi, 'jig tshogs su lta ba*).[309]

[Formative Predispositions, Consciousness, Name and Form, Sensory Activity Fields]

Formative predispositions include those associated with meritorious past actions,

Those associated with non-meritorious past actions,
And those associated with past actions that do not transcend [cyclic existence].
The substratum consciousness, along with its propensities,
Includes both causal and fruitional aspects.
[Name and form] comprise the four [aggregates endowed with] names,
Along with physical form in its five stages of embryonic and fetal development;
While the sensory activity fields essentially demarcate the six sense organs.

The second link [of dependent origination] comprises formative predispositions (*saṃskāra, 'du byed*) which may be associated with meritorious past actions (*bsod nams kyi las*), non-meritorious past actions (*bsod nams min pa'i las*), or unwavering or non-dynamic past actions (*āniñjyakarma, mi gYo ba'i las*). The first of these are the virtuous past actions pertaining to the world-system of desire; the second are the non-virtuous past actions associated with the world-system of desire; and the third are the past actions, or meditative stabilities, through which the two higher world-systems [of form and formlessness] are attained.[310]

The third link [of dependent origination] is the substratum consciousness (*ālayavijñāna, kun gzhi'i rnam shes*) upon which the propensities of past actions are imposed, for which reason they represent the transformational aspect of this consciousness. It includes both the [substratum] consciousness that is replete with causal imprints and the [substratum] consciousness replete with fruitional imprints.[311]

The fourth link [of dependent origination] comprises name and form (*nāmarūpa, ming gzugs*). Here "name" refers to the four nominal aggregates (*ming bzhi'i phung po*), i.e., the four subsequent aggregates of feelings, and so forth. Although there are reasons for these [feelings, perceptions, formative predispositions, and consciousness] being assigned to the "four nominal aggregates," the aggregate of physical forms should not be understood as being dependent on names because it manifests directly within the perceptual range of the five sensory consciousnesses. By contrast, the four subsequent aggregates, being present in the mental continua of others (*parasāntānika, gzhan gyi rgyud la yod pa*),[312] are understood to be dependent on names.[313]

The link of form comprises the five stages of embryonic and fetal development (*mngal gyi skabs lnga*), known respectively as the clotting of the embryo (*kalala, nur nur po*), the oval formation of the embryo (*arbuda, mer mer po*), the rounded formation or solidification of the embryo (*peśī, gor gor po*), the suspension of the embryo (*ghana, mkhrang 'gyur*), and the limb formation of the fetus (*praśākha, rkang lag rnam par 'gyus pa*).[314]

The fifth link [of dependent origination] comprises the six sensory activity fields (*ṣaḍāyatana, skye mched drug*), the essential nature of which is that they clearly demarcate the six sense organs, consequent on the five stages of embryonic and fetal development.[315]

[Sensory Contact, Sensation, Craving]

Sensory contact, which [fully manifests] after birth,
Is an interaction of sense objects, sense organs, and consciousness.
The sensations dependent on that are attachment, aversion, and neutrality.
[Consequently] there is craving desirous [of rebirth]
And craving that grasps after perishable things.

The sixth link [of dependent origination] is sensory contact (*sparśa, reg pa*). Following birth from the womb, there emerges sensory contact, in which sense objects, sense organs, and consciousness all converge together. However, sensory contact actually refers to a transformation that occurs in consciousness [prior to birth] due to the presence [in the womb] of its sense objects, and consequent on the interaction of consciousness and its sense objects.[316]

The seventh link [of dependent origination] is sensation (*vedanā, tshor ba*). Dependent on that sensory contact, sensations or feelings of happiness, suffering, and neutrality are then experienced. This process may be exemplified as follows: Through the convergence of the sense organ of the eye with its sense objects—comprising pleasant physical forms—and visual consciousness, visual consciousness initially generates sensory contact, which delimits its sense objects. Immediately thereafter, there arises the sensation of happiness, which is experienced through that sensory contact.[317]

Since this analysis of the three types of sensation may be made in relation to all of the six [modes of engaged] sensory consciousness, sensations are collectively designated as the eighteen sensory objects that impact upon the mind (*aṣṭādaśamanopavicāra, yid nye bar rgyu ba bco brgyad*).[318]

The eighth link [of dependent origination] is craving (*tṛṣṇā, sred pa*), which refers to the craving and attachment that occur in relation to the three [just-mentioned] types of sensation—those of happiness, suffering, and neutrality.

Now there are [three aspects of craving] that may arise: the craving that one might not be separated from happiness, the craving that desires separation from suffering, and the craving that desires not to be separated from neutrality.

Alternatively, craving may comprise the craving that desires rebirth (*kāmatṛṣṇā, srid pa la 'dod pa'i sred pa*), the craving associated with the rebirth process (*bhavatṛṣṇā, srid pa'i sred pa*), and the craving associated with decay or perishable phenomena (*vibhavatṛṣṇā, 'jig pa'i sred pa*). The first of these is [the craving] associated with the world-system of desire, the second is [the craving] associated with the two higher world systems, and the third is the craving that grasps after [material] resources.[319]

[Grasping, Rebirth Process, Birth, and Aging and Death]

Through grasping after desires, rebirth, erroneous views,
And belief in [an inherently existing] self,
[The rebirth process] is endowed with the potent function
Of implementing reincarnation.
Reaching the moment of conception, birth is obtained,
And commencing from then,
There is a continuous series of indivisible time moments,
Leading to the obstruction of the life essence, aging, and death.

The ninth link [of dependent origination] is grasping (*upādāna, len pa*), which originates dependent on craving. When, for example, there is craving for and attachment to the sensa of pleasurable objects, such as food, drink, and resources, the desire that these [pleasures] might repeatedly arise, and the potential to engage in diverse activities in pursuit of that goal, are designated as "grasping."

It is said that there are four kinds of grasping (*caturupādāna, nye bar len pa bzhi*), namely, the grasping after desires (*kāmopādāna, 'dod pa'i len pa*), the grasping of rebirth (*bhavopādāna, srid pa'i len pa*),[320] the grasping of [erroneous] views (*dṛṣṭyopādāna, lta ba'i len pa*), and the grasping after belief in an [inherently existing] self (*ātmavādopādāna, bdag tu smra ba'i nye bar len pa*).

Through these [aspects of grasping], the subsequent links [of dependent origination] are formed or fulfilled.[321]

The tenth link [of dependent origination] is the rebirth process (*bhava, srid pa*), which is endowed with the potent function of implementing reincarnation.[322]

The eleventh link [of dependent origination] is actual birth (*jāti, skye ba*). Now, with reference to the [initial] manifestation of the link of birth, this coincides with the moment of conception (*pratisaṃdhi, nying mtshams sbyor ba*), and [from that perspective] everything following the moment of conception [is said to be included within] the twelfth link of aging and death (*jarāmaraṇa, rga shi'i yan lag*).[323]

Having obtained the circumstances of birth, starting with the clotting of the embryo, from then on, there is a continuous series of indivisible time moments, which is [known as] "aging." In this context, [the process of aging] is included within the single link of aging and death. This is said to be the case because if there is no aging, there is also no death.

Therefore, one should know that in respect of all [phenomena] that arise, there are two processes of unfolding (*dvisammukhībhāva, mngon du 'gyur ba gnyis*): one [static process] whereby the twelve links of dependent origination manifest the propensities imposed on the substratum, and one [dynamic process] whereby the twelve links are manifested through the maturation of the seeds [of past actions].[324]

FUNCTIONS [OF THE TWELVE LINKS OF DEPENDENT ORIGINATION] [v]

With regard to the fifth topic [of the extensive exegesis], concerning the functions (*karmavyavasthāna, byed las*) [of dependent origination, it says in the root verses]:

> **The functions [of the twelve links]**
> **Are respectively to obscure the truth,**
> **To plant seeds, to direct towards [birth],**
> **To offer complete support [to the body],**
> **To perfect it, to delimit [its sense objects],**
> **To partake of [happiness], to acquire [rebirth],**
> **To conjoin [with birth], to propel towards [birth],**
> **[To engender] suffering, and to transform [age].**

The individual functions of these [twelve links of dependent origination] are presented in one and a half stanzas from the [*Analysis of the*] *Middle and Extremes*.[325]

[Accordingly, it is said that]

(1) The function of fundamental ignorance is to obscure the vision of the genuine truth, and similarly, through the power of that [fundamental ignorance]:

(2) The function of formative predispositions is to cause the seeds of past actions to be sown in the substratum.

(3) The function of consciousness is to convey [formative predispositions] towards [an appropriate] place of birth, in conformity with those seeds [of past actions].

(4) The function of name and form is to fully embrace a physical body, corresponding to the direction in which [consciousness] has been conveyed.

(5) The function of the six sensory activity fields is to fully perfect a physical body, corresponding to that which is embraced [by name and form].

(6) The function of sensory contact is to integrate the three aspects [of the sense objects, sense organs, and consciousness] through the power of those [sensory activity fields] and to delimit the sense objects.

(7) The function of sensation is to partake of happiness and so forth, corresponding to the [sense objects] that have been delimited [by sensory contact].

(8) The function of craving is to acquire rebirth corresponding to one's past actions, through the power of these [sensations].

(9) The function of grasping is to conjoin the consciousness with birth, corresponding to that craving.

(10) The function of the rebirth process is to manifestly propel a reincarnating [consciousness] towards birth, corresponding to that union [induced by craving].

(11) The function of birth is to engender an aggregate of suffering through the power of that [rebirth process].

(12) The function of aging and death is to transform youth and vitality in accordance with the disadvantages [of birth].

All of these [functions] indeed induce dissonant mental states, conducive [to rebirth] within cyclic existence.

Detailed Analysis [of Dependent Origination] [vi]

The sixth topic, concerning the detailed analysis of dependent origination, includes (1) a brief introduction, and (2) an extensive exegesis.

BRIEF INTRODUCTION [aa]

Concerning the former [it says in the root verses]:

> **The detailed analysis [of dependent origination] comprises**
> **A threefold [analysis], an eightfold [analysis],**
> **And a detailed exegesis according to the [twelve] links.**

Although, in general, the exegeses that offer a detailed analysis of dependent origination have many variations, here I will refer sequentially to the threefold analysis (*gsum du dbye ba*), the eightfold analysis (*brgyad du dbye ba*), and the detailed exegesis of the twelve links (*yan lag bcu gnyis bye brag tub shad pa*).

EXTENSIVE ANALYSIS [bb]

The latter has three parts: (1) the threefold [analysis], (2) the eightfold [analysis], and (3) the detailed [analysis of the twelve links].

THE THREEFOLD ANALYSIS [1']

This also has three topics, namely, (1) the dependent origination that distinguishes the essential nature (*svabhāvavibhāgapratītyasamutpāda, ngo bo nyid rnam par 'byed pa'i rten 'brel*); (2) the dependent origination that distinguishes attractive and unattractive goals (*priyāpriyavibhāgapratītyasamutpāda, sdug pa dang mi sdug pa rnam par 'byed pa'i rten 'brel*); and (3) the dependent origination associated with sensory engagement (*aupabhogikapratītyasamutpāda, nyer spyod can gyi rten 'brel*).[326]

DEPENDENT ORIGINATION THAT DISTINGUISHES THE ESSENTIAL NATURE [a']

Concerning the first of these [it says in the root verses]:

> **Among the aspects of the threefold analysis,**
> **[The dependent origination] that distinguishes the essential nature**
> **Refers to the emanation of all phenomena from the substratum,**
> **And this is said to be [understood] only by those of highest acumen.**

Among the categories of the threefold [analysis], the first is the dependent origination that distinguishes the essential nature. This refers to the emanation of all outer and inner phenomena from the substratum consciousness, and to the appearances that manifest through its power as being deposited upon it. This [realization] was presented as the lot of only bodhisattvas of highest acumen who enter into the Greater Vehicle, but was not disclosed to the other two sorts of spiritual being who follow the way of Buddhism. This means that it is a realization attained uniquely by bodhisattvas or buddhas, whereas the pious attendants and hermit buddhas are not even partly aware of it.[327]

Dependent Origination That Distinguishes Attractive and Unattractive Goals [b']

Concerning the second [it says in the root verses]:

> **[The dependent origination] that distinguishes attractive and unattractive [goals]**
> **Is said to be [understood] by pious attendants and hermit buddhas.**
> **It has two aspects, referring to dissonant mental states and purification.**
> **[Here] the verb "distinguishes" is understood**
> **To mean "augments" and "magnifies."**

Attractive [goals] (*priya, sdug pa*) are pleasant or agreeable, while unattractive [goals] (*apriya, mi sdug pa*) are unpleasant or disagreeable. Distinguishing between these two accords with the twelve links of dependent origination. This [realization] was presented by the transcendent lord [Buddha] to both the pious attendants and the hermit buddhas who follow the way of Buddhism. Although both of these types meditate in accordance with this teaching, the hermit buddhas extensively understand the [two] processes of dependent origination, namely, its "arising process" (*anuloma, lugs 'byung*) and its "reversal process" (*pratiloma, lugs ldog*), whereas the pious attendants do not extensively understand the [processes] of dependent origination through their own comprehension, as do the hermit buddhas.[328]

Now this process [distinguishing attractive and unattractive goals] has two aspects, which refer respectively to dissonant mental states (*saṃkleśa, kun nas nyon mongs pa*) and to purification (*vyavadāna, rnam byang*).[329]

The former, [evolving in association with dissonant mental states,] includes a [positive] process that gives rise to birth within the higher realms (*svarga, mtho ris*) through the power of corrupt virtuous actions that are concomitant with ignorance (*ma rig pa dang mtshungs ldan gyi dge ba zag bcas*) and is designated as the "dependent origination that distinguishes attractive goals" (*sdug pa rnam par 'byed pa'i rten 'brel*). It also includes another [negative] process that gives rise to birth within the three lower realms (*durgati, ngan song*) through the power of non-virtuous actions concomitant with ignorance (*ma rig pa dang mtshungs ldan pa'i las mi dge ba*) and is designated as the "dependent origination that distinguishes unattractive goals" (*mi sdug pa rnam par 'byed pa'i rten 'brel*).

The latter, [evolving in association with purification,] includes one process that gives rise to birth among the six classes of sentient beings through the power of virtuous and negative actions concomitant with ignorance (*ma rig pa dang mtshungs ldan gyi las dge sdig*) and is designated as the "dependent origination that distinguishes unattractive goals" (*mi sdug pa rnam par 'byed pa'i rten 'brel*). It also includes another process that obtains release [from rebirth in cyclic existence] through the power of uncorrupted virtuous actions (*dge ba zag med*) and is therefore designated as the "dependent origination that distinguishes attractive goals" (*sdug pa rnam par 'byed pa'i rten 'brel*).

The verb "distinguishes" (*rnam par 'byed pa*), in this context, means "augments" (*'phel ba*) or "magnifies" (*rgyas pa*). This is because it is by means of all the diverse appearances, including visible forms, sounds, smells, tastes, and tangible phenomena, and all the inauthentic imaginations associated with mind and mental states, that propensities are imposed upon the substratum, causing the substratum itself to be "augmented" or "magnified."

Dependent Origination Associated with Sensory Engagement [c']

Concerning the third [it says in the root verses]:

> **[The dependent origination] associated with sensory engagement**
> **Refers to the process that generates and obstructs the six modes**
> **[of consciousness],**
> **Which pious attendants then control by means of selflessness.**

The dependent origination associated with sensory engagement is the process that causes the six modes of consciousness to arise and cease. In this context, it is said that "sensation" refers to the experiencer or subject of sensory engagement, "sensory contact" to the object of sensory engagement, and the "act of sensory engagement" to the entity where this [interaction] occurs.[330]

For example, [taking] an agreeable visual form as the referential condition (*ālambanapratyaya, dmigs pa'i rkyen*); the sense organ of the eye as the predominant condition (*adhipatipratyaya, bdag po'i rkyen*); visual consciousness as the causal condition (*hetupratyaya, rgyu'i rkyen*), occurring in the first moment [of this perceptual process]; and the mental activity that desires to engage with the object as the immediate condition (*samanantarapratyaya, mtshungs pa de ma thag pa'i rkyen*): through the power of these fully present four conditions, visual consciousness is generated.

The interaction of this visual consciousness with the visual form that is its object is [known as] "sensory contact" (*sparśa, reg pa*). The sensation of happiness experienced through consciousness of that agreeable sensum of the object is [known as] the "gateway that generates attachment" (*'dod chags skye ba'i sgo*), and the [consequent] thought that desires not to be separated from that agreeable mental object is [known as] "volition" (*cetanā, sems pa*). Accordingly, when visual consciousness arises through these four conditions, the mental states that emerge in the periphery of this [visual consciousness]—namely, sensory contact, sensation, and volition—obscure the nature of the central mind and render it impure.

One should know by analogy that when this process depends on a disagreeable sense object, [the unhappy sensation experienced is known as] the "gateway that generates aversion" (*zhe sdang skye ba'i sgo*), and when it depends on a neutral or indifferent sense object, [the neutral sensation experienced is known as] the "gateway that generates delusion" (*gti mug skye ba'i sgo*).

In this way, the six modes of [engaged] consciousness generate the dissonant mental states of attachment, aversion, and delusion, dependent on sense objects that are respectively agreeable, disagreeable, and neutral; and there is an activation of false imagination that ensues. This is why the pious attendants undertake to control the dissonant mental states that arise dependent on those [sensations]. The controls [that they seek to impose] are implemented by means of [their understanding of] impermanence (*anitya, mi rtag pa*), suffering (*duḥkha, sdug bsngal*), emptiness (*śūnyatā, stong pa nyid*), and selflessness (*nairātmya, bdag med*), and above all they exercise control [over dissonant mental states] by meditating on the nature of the selflessness of the individual person (*pudgalanairātmya, gang zag gi bdag med*).[331]

The Eightfold Analysis [2']

The second part [of the extensive exegesis] is the eightfold analysis, which has two topics: (1) the exegesis of the six aspects of dependent origination associated with dissonant mental states (*saṃkleśapratītyasamutpāda, kun nas nyon mongs pa'i rten 'brel*) and (2) the exegesis of the two aspects of dependent origination associated with purified states (*vyavadānapratītyasamutpāda, rnam byang gi rten 'brel*).

The Six Aspects of Dependent Origination Associated with Dissonant Mental States [a']

Concerning the former [it says in the root verses]:

> **The eightfold [analysis of dependent origination]**
> **Comprises six aspects that are all within the range of dissonant mental states,**
> **Namely, [the arising of] consciousness;**
> **The arising of birth and death;**
> **The external [dependent origination] of seeds, shoots, stems, and so forth;**
> **The extensive analysis of the physical environment,**
> **Which [appears to undergo] creation, duration, and destruction;**
> **Sustenance by means of the four types of nourishment;**
> **And [the distinguishing of] living beings**
> **According to desirable and undesirable [realms of rebirth].**

The first topic of the eightfold analysis [of dependent origination] includes the following six aspects, which are [collectively known as] the dependent origination falling within the range of dissonant mental states (*kun nas nyon mongs pa'i phyogs kyi rten 'brel*):[332]

(1) The dependent origination through which consciousness arises (*vijñānotpattipratītyasamutpāda, rnam par shes pa 'byung ba'i rten 'brel*). This is the very same dependent origination associated with sensory engagement which has just been explained [above].

(2) The dependent origination through which birth and death arise (*cyutyupapattipratītyasamutpāda, skye ba dang 'chi 'pho ba 'byung ba'i rten 'brel*). This [process], which is within the range of dissonant mental states, distinguishes between agreeable and disagreeable aspects, starting with the formative predispositions that arise through the condition of fundamental ignorance.

(3) The uninterrupted dependent origination of the external world (*bāhyaśasyotpattipratītyasamutpāda, rgyun mi 'chad pa phyi'i rten 'brel*). This is the process whereby a mass of conditions are present, such as fields, earth, water, and fertilizer, so that shoots then arise from seeds, stems from those [shoots], canes from those [stems] and ears of grain from those [canes], and fruits or harvests from those [ears of grain].

(4) The dependent origination which is an extensive analysis of the physical environment (*saṃvartavivartapratītyasamutpāda, snod kyi rab tu dbye ba'i rten 'brel*).[333] This [is the process] whereby [the physical environment] appears to undergo [successive phases of] creation, duration, and destruction. Also included here are the appearances of the diverse phases of growth and decline, such as [the fluctuations] in the life span which living creatures undergo as well as their positive and negative attributes.

(5) The dependent origination distinguished by means of nourishing sustenance (*āhāropastambhavibhāgapratītyasamutpāda, zas kyi 'tsho bas rnam par dbye ba'i rten 'brel*). This is the process whereby [living beings] are uninterruptedly sustained within the abodes of cyclic existence through the successive and consequential generation of the four kinds of nourishment (*caturāhāra, zas bzhi*), namely, the nourishment of the sensory bases (*kavalikāhāra, kham gyi zas*), the nourishment of sensory contact (*sparśāhāra, reg pa'i zas*), the nourishment of volition (*cetanāhāra, sems pa'i zas),* and the nourishment of consciousness (*vijñānāhāra, rnam par shes pa'i zas).*

(6) The dependent origination that distinguishes living beings according to desirable and undesirable [realms of rebirth] *(iṣṭāniṣṭagativibhāgapratītyasamutpāda, 'dod pa dang mi 'dod par 'gro ba rab tu dbye ba'i rten 'brel*). This is the process whereby living beings abide in the desirable abodes of happy beings through the power of virtuous past actions, and whereby living beings abide in the undesirable abodes of inferior realms of existence through the power of non-virtuous past actions.

Among these [six aspects], the dependent origination of the physical environment and the dependent origination of the external [world] are both contingent on the external container world (*bhājanaloka, snod kyi 'jig rten*), while the other four are all contingent on its sentient inhabitants (*sattvaloka, sems can gyi 'jig rten*).

The Two Aspects of Dependent Origination Associated with Purified Mental States [b']

Concerning the latter [it says in the root verses]:

Release [from cyclic existence] contingent on the five [spiritual] paths,
Which is well-distinguished by means of purity,
And the attainment of the six supernormal cognitive powers,
Which is well-distinguished by means of [spiritual] power:
These are the [two] aspects within the range of purification.
[All eight aspects] are [established] with reference to
The generated and generative [modes of dependent origination].

(7) The [seventh aspect is] the dependent origination that is well-distinguished by means of purity (*viśuddhiprabhedapratītyasamutpāda, rnam par dag pas rab tu dbye ba'i rten 'brel*). This is the process whereby the five spiritual paths (*pañcamārga, lam lnga*) sequentially arise contingent on the three higher trainings (*śikṣātraya, bslab pa gsum*), and [especially] whereby the level of release [from cyclic existence, also known as] the path of no-more-learning (*aśaikṣamārga, mi slob pa'i lam*), is manifested contingent on the four preceding spiritual paths.[334]

(8) The [eighth aspect is] the dependent origination that is well-distinguished by means of [spiritual] power (*prabhāvaprabhedapratītyasamutpāda, mthu stobs kyis rab tu dbye ba'i rten 'brel*). This is the process whereby the six supernormal cognitive powers (*ṣaḍabhijñā, mngon shes drug*) are obtained.[335]

Concerning these six supernormal cognitive powers, it is also said in the *Ornament of the Sūtras of the Greater Vehicle*:[336]

The cognition that becomes manifest
With respect to lives, speech, minds,
[Formerly] generated virtuous and non-virtuous actions,
Abodes, and [ultimate] renunciation,
Is the [spiritual] power of those who have attained a resolve
That is unobstructed[337] throughout space,
In respect of all those distinguished variations.

In this regard:

(1) Knowledge of others' lives is the supernormal cognitive power with respect to their death and subsequent rebirth (*cyutopapādābhijñā, 'chi 'pho dang skye ba mngon par shes pa*).[338]
(2) Knowledge of the speech uttered by those [persons] is the supernormal cognitive power of clairaudience (*divyaśrotrābhijñā, lha'i rna'i mngon par shes pa*).

(3) Knowledge of the minds of those [persons] is the supernormal cognitive power that knows the modalities of [other] minds (*paracittaparyāyābhijñā, sems kyi rnam grangs kyi mngon par shes pa*).
(4) Knowledge of the virtuous and non-virtuous actions which beings have generated in former [lives] is the supernormal cognitive power of past abodes (*pūrvanivāsābhijñā, sngon gyi gnas mngon par shes pa*).
(5) Knowledge of proceeding to the abodes where disciples are situated is the supernormal cognitive power of the domain of miraculous abilities (*ṛddhiviṣayābhijñā, rdzu 'phrul gyi mngon par shes pa*).
(6) Knowledge of the ways in which sentient beings will transcend rebirth [in cyclic existence] is the supernormal cognitive power of the cessation of corruption (*āśravakṣayābhijñā, zag pa zad pa'i mngon par shes pa*).

It is explained that such knowledge in respect of these six objects and their distinguished variations (*rab tu dbye ba dang bcas pa*), manifestly present without obstruction in all world systems, is subsumed in the supernormal cognitive powers of the bodhisattvas.[339]

The six supernormal cognitive powers of sublime bodhisattvas definitively characterize the distinguished variations of [spiritual] power; while the five supernormal cognitive powers acquired by those on the paths of provisions and connection (*tshogs sbyor rnams kyi mngon shes lnga*) are [said to be] in conformity with those same distinguished variations of [spiritual] power.[340] On the other hand, the attainment of [lesser] supernormal cognitive powers, miraculous abilities, and so forth, which is contingent on the mundane non-Buddhist paths, is [said] not to be in conformity with those genuine distinguished variations of [spiritual] power.

These two aspects of dependent origination fall within the range of purification.

In general, all of these eight aspects are collectively designated as the "interconnected dependent origination" (*sāṃbandhikapratītyasamutpāda, 'brel ba can gyi rten 'brel*), i.e., [they are aspects of] dependent origination that relate to generative [causes] and generated [results].[341]

Detailed Exegesis of the Twelve Links [of Dependent Origination] [3']

The third part [of the extensive exegesis] is the detailed exegesis of the twelve links [of dependent origination]. This has three topics: (1) the serial or circumstantial dependent origination (*prākarṣikapratītyasamutpāda, rgyun chags pa'am gnas skabs pa'i rten 'brel*), (2) the instantaneous dependent origination (*kṣaṇikapratītyasamutpāda, skad cig ma'i rten 'brel*), and (3) the interconnected dependent origination (*sāṃbandhikapratītyasamutpāda, 'brel ba can gyi rten 'brel*).[342]

Serial or Circumstantial Dependent Origination [a']

The first of these topics also has three parts: (1) the process through which one cycle of the twelve links is completed over two lifetimes within the world system of desire, (2) the process through which one cycle is completed over three lifetimes, and (3) the process through which one cycle is completed within a single lifetime.

Completion of One Cycle in Two Lifetimes [i']

Concerning the first of these processes [it says in the root verses]:

> **As for the detailed [exegesis of] the twelve links,**
> **This includes the circumstantial [dependent origination].**
> **[Accordingly,] when [one cycle] is completed**
> **Over two lifetimes within the world-system of desire,**
> **There are five links that are projected**
> **By means of the two [preceding] projective [links],**
> **And there are three links that are formed**
> **By means of the two formative [links].**
> **A single sequence of the causal and fruitional processes [of dependent origination]**
> **[Is completed] in these four projective and formative phases,**
> **And it is said that these can therefore be known**
> **[To resemble] the planting and nurturing of seeds.**

Preceded by the [aforementioned] general exegesis of dependent origination, there now follows the detailed exegesis of the actual stages through which the twelve links [of dependent origination] arise. In this regard, the "circumstantial dependent origination" (*gnas skabs kyi rten 'brel*) includes both the process through which [one cycle of the twelve links] is completed over two lifetimes within the world system of desire and the process through which one cycle is completed over three lifetimes, as extensively mentioned in the sūtras delivered by the transcendent lord [Buddha]. At the outset one should understand that these two [dynamics] should not be confused or intermingled, because they have their own distinctive purposes.[343]

Now, with regard to the process through which [one cycle of the twelve links] is completed over two lifetimes, there are two projective links (*ākṣepakāṅga, 'phen byed kyi yan lag gnyis*), namely, fundamental ignorance and formative predispositions; and five projected links (*ākṣiptāṅga, 'phangs pa'i yan lag lnga*), namely, consciousness, name and form, sensory activity fields, sensory contact, and sensation. There are also two formative links (*abhinirvartakāṅga, 'grub pa'i yang lag gnyis*), namely, craving and grasping; and three links that are formed (*abhinirvṛttyaṅga, grub pa'i yan lag gsum*), namely, rebirth process, birth, and aging and death.[344]

A single cycle of the causal and fruitional phases [of dependent origination] is completed through these four processes of projection and formation (*'phen grub kyi tshul bzhi*). It is said that this definitive structure is applicable on the analogy [of farming], since the two links that are projected and formed should be understood to resemble the planting of seeds, and the links that bring about the projection and formation should be known to resemble the nurturing of the seeds.[345]

Completion of One Cycle in Three Lifetimes [ii']

Concerning the second process [it says in the root verses]:

> **Then, when two links are each associated**
> **With the limits of the [immediately] past and future [lives],**
> **And eight are associated with limits of the [present] intervening [life],**
> **Two causal and fruitional cycles [of dependent origination]**
> **[Are completed] over three lifetimes**
> **Within the [world system] of desire, and so forth.**
> **This is extensively revealed in order to reverse the three aspects of delusion.**

[In this context,] two [links], fundamental ignorance and formative predispositions, are associated with the limit of past time (*pūrvānta, sngon gyi mtha'*) [i.e., the immediately previous life]; while another two, birth and aging and death, are associated with the limit of future time (*phyi ma'i mtha'*) [i.e., the immediately following life]; and the eight from consciousness to rebirth process are associated with the limits of the intervening, present [life].

Furthermore, when from the two causal [links] of fundamental ignorance and formative predispositions, the five [fruitional] links from consciousness to sensation arise, this is [regarded as] a single sequence of causal and fruitional phases. Similarly, when from the two causal [links] of craving and grasping, the three fruitional [links] of rebirth process, birth, and aging and death arise, this is also [regarded as] a single sequence of causal and fruitional phases. In this way, two cycles of causal and fruitional phases are completed over three lifetimes within the world system of desire.

This process is extensively revealed by the Buddha in order that sentient beings might reverse the three aspects of delusion, with regard to the limits of the past [life], the future [life], and the present [life].[346]

Completion of One Cycle in a Single Lifetime [iii']

Concerning the third process [it says in the root verses]:

> **There is also [a process whereby] the [cycle of dependent origination]**
> **Will be completed in a single lifetime,**
> **Experiencing [the fruits] of presently perceptible phenomena.**

With reference to the experience of [the fruits of] the presently perceptible phenomena [of this life] (*dṛṣṭadharmavedayitvā, mthong chos myong 'gyur*), [it is said that the cycle of] the twelve links [of dependent origination] may also be completed in a single lifetime.

For example, when sentient beings who have committed an inexpiable crime proceed into the hells, or when, motivated by fundamental ignorance, a man becomes predisposed towards action with a strong thought desirous of being reborn as a woman, through this action, the seeds associated with rebirth in that [corresponding state] are deposited upon consciousness; and then the seeds of [the consequent] links—name and form, the six sensory activity fields, sensory contact, and sensation—are also sequentially deposited [upon that consciousness]. Whenever this occurs, and there is craving desirous of praise on account of that [sensation], as well as grasping that desires praise, motivated by that [craving], and one has consequently disparaged a group of monks, scornfully dismissing them as a group of women, by having committed that action, the previously deposited inclination to take birth as a woman will become extremely powerful, so that the presently perceptible phenomena [of this life] (*mthong ba'i chos*) themselves will assume those characteristics, taking on [the form] of a woman. Being born as such, the link of aging and death inevitably ensues, so that [the cycle of dependent origination] will be completed in a single lifetime.[347]

Instantaneous Dependent Origination [b']

The second topic [in the detailed exegesis of the twelve links of dependent origination] concerns instantaneous dependent origination (*skad cig ma'i rten 'brel*) [on which it is said in the root verses]:

> **With regard to the instantaneous completion [of the cycle],**
> **Consequent on the completion of a [specific] deed,**
> **As in the case of murder,**
> **This implies a dependent origination of that [instantaneous type].**

With regard to the completion of the twelve links [of dependent origination] in a single instant, consequent on the completion of a [specific] deed, this may be exemplified by the act of committing murder, which implies an instantaneous dependent origination.[348]

When, for example, an act of murder is committed, the dissonant mental states present at the time when one kills a sentient being, with thoughts of hatred, motivated by fundamental ignorance, are [considered to be] the link of fundamental ignorance, and the objective of killing is the link of formative predisposition. Consequently, when one's own mind projects negativity, and the propensities to take birth in a [lower realm of existence], such as the hells, contaminate consciousness, this is [considered to be] the link of consciousness. When, at that time, the concerned individual's five psycho-physical aggregates and six sensory activity fields give rise to [further] negativity which contaminates the sensa, these are respectively [considered to be] the links [of name and form and the sensory activity fields]. When, at that time, the sense objects, sense organs, and consciousness all converge and the sense objects are delimited, this is [considered to be] the link of sensory contact. When, on that occasion, he or she experiences the killing of the victim, this is the link of sensation. When, at that time, there is a manifest craving to commit that act of murder, this is the link of craving. When he or she then desires to fulfill that deed through craving, this is the link of grasping. When the propensities for [negative] rebirth in the next life are determined by that [grasping], this is the link of the rebirth process; and when the psycho-physical aggregates determined at that time are actually transformed [into a hellish state of existence], these are [the links of] birth and aging and death.

Interconnected Dependent Origination [c']

The third of these topics, the exegesis concerning interconnected dependent origination (*'brel ba can gyi rten 'brel*), has two parts: (1) the textual interpretation of the venerable Maitreya, and (2) the textual interpretation of the master Vasubandhu.

The Textual Interpretation of Maitreya [i']

The first of these has three topics: (1) analysis, (2) synthesis and (3) the presentation of seven [projective and formative] causes.

[Analysis]

Concerning the first [it is said in the root verses]:

> **With regard to the interconnected [dependent origination]**
> **According to the *Analysis of the Middle and Extremes*,**
> **Birth is conjoined with aging and death.**
> **Consequently, there are [only] eleven links.**

As far as the interconnected dependent origination is concerned, according to the *Analysis of the Middle and Extremes*, [the process of dependent origination] is classified according to [only] eleven links, starting with [the links of] fundamental ignorance and formative predispositions and ending with birth and aging and death, which are all combined together [in a single link].

This integration is made because [the link of] birth is [designated as] the "suffering of the supportive" [physical body] (*ādhāraduḥkha, rten gyi sdug bsngal*), while the diverse manifestations of the aggregate of suffering, including aging, dying, unhappy thoughts, and cries of lamentation, are all [designated as] the "sufferings supported upon it" (*ādheyaduḥkha, de la brten pa'i sdug bsngal*). The structure presented [in this work] holds that a single cycle of these eleven links will be completed over three lifetimes.[349]

[Synthesis]

Concerning the second [it is said in the root verses]:

> **Then, in terms of the three categories of dissonant mental states,**
> **Fundamental ignorance, craving, and grasping are subsumed**

As [dissonant mental states] arising from dissonant mental states;
Formative predispositions and the rebirth process[350] are subsumed
As [dissonant mental states] arising from past actions;
While the remaining [seven] are subsumed
As dissonant mental states arising from the birth of suffering.
These [twelve links] may also be subsumed
Into two categories, in which case
The first five are [designated as]
Causal dissonant mental states arising from past actions,
While the last seven are [designated as] fruitional.

When [these twelve links] are then subsumed together, there are two kinds of synthesis that can be made, one that subsumes them according to the three categories of dissonant mental states and another that subsumes them according to only two categories.[351]

With regard to the former, the lord Nāgārjuna has said [in the *Nucleus of Dependent Origination according to Madhyamaka*]:[352]

The first, eighth, and ninth [links] arise from dissonant mental states,
The second and tenth arise from past actions,
While the remaining seven arise from suffering.

Accordingly, fundamental ignorance, craving, and grasping—these three—are [classed as] dissonant mental states arising from [other] dissonant mental states (*kleśasaṃkleśa, nyon mongs pa'i kun nas nyon mongs pa*); formative predispositions, and rebirth process—these two—are [classed as] dissonant mental states arising from past actions (*karmasaṃkleśa, las kyi kun nas nyon mongs pa*); while the remaining seven are [classed as] dissonant mental states arising from the birth of sufferings (*janmasaṃkleśa, sdug bsngal rnams skye ba'i kun nas nyon mongs pa*).[353]

With regard to these, it is said [by Nāgārjuna, also] in the *Nucleus of Dependent Origination according to Madhyamaka*:

This wheel of the rebirth process,
In which two [links] arise from three [links],
Seven [links] arise from two [links],
And three [links] again arise from seven [links],
Itself revolves repeatedly, in a cyclical manner.

Accordingly, the three categories of dissonant mental states have two functions, among which the basic function is to give rise to the seven [links], and then from these [seven links] the [original] dissonant mental states again arise, so that the process of interaction occurs in a cyclical manner, just as a chicken is produced from an egg and an egg from a chicken.

With regard to the second [kind of synthesis, in two categories], fundamental ignorance, formative predispositions, craving, grasping, and the rebirth process are all subsumed within the dissonant mental states arising from past actions, and are [designated as] the "five causal dissonant mental states" (*hetusaṃkleśa*), while the remainder are [designated as] the "seven fruitional dissonant mental states" (*phala saṃkleśa*).[354]

[Seven Projective and Formative Causes]

Concerning the third [it says in the root verses]:

> **[Dependent origination] may also be presented**
> **According to seven causes of the projective and formative phases,**
> **And these [are said to be] completed over two lifetimes.**

There is also a system according to which [dependent origination] may be presented in terms of the seven projective and formative causes (*'phen grub rgyu bdun*), in which case [the cycle] is completed over two lifetimes:[355]

(1) Fundamental ignorance is the cause [of perversion] (*viparyāsahetu, phyin ci log tu byed pa'i rgyu*) that impedes the vision of the genuine abiding nature of reality (*yang dag pa'i gnas lugs*) and generates an erroneous [perception].

(2) Formative predispositions are the cause [of projection] (*ākṣepahetu, 'debs par byed pa'i rgyu*) that deposits the propensities of past actions upon the substratum consciousness.

(3) Consciousness is the cause [of propulsion] (*upanayanahetu, khrid par byed pa'i rgyu*) that impels [these formative predispositions] towards the birthplace.

(4) Name and form, along with the six sensory activity fields, are the cause [of embrace] (*parigrahahetu, kun tu 'dzin pa'i rgyu*) that sustains all corporeal forms which are compatible in class.[356]

(5) Sensory contact and sensation are the cause [of engagement] (*upabhogahetu, yongs su spyod pa'i rgyu*) that interacts with sense objects.

(6) Craving, grasping, and rebirth process are the cause [of convergence] (*ākarṣaṇahetu, yongs su sdud pa'i rgyu*) that adheres to the next rebirth.
(7) Birth and aging and death are the cause [of distress] (*udvegahetu, skyo ba'i rgyu*) generated by suffering, which [eventually] gives rise to definitive liberation (*niryāṇa/ niḥsaraṇa, nges pas 'byung ba*).

In this way, seven causes are presented, among which fundamental ignorance, formative predispositions and consciousness—these three—are [classed as] the projective links (*ākṣepakāṅga, 'phen byed kyi yan lag*), while name and form, the sensory activity fields, sensory contact, and sensation—these four—are [classed as] the projected links (*ākṣiptāṅga, 'phangs pa'i yan lag*). Together these [links] constitute the "projective dependent origination" (*'phen pa'i rten 'brel*), and they are completed with reference to the previous life. [By contrast,] craving, grasping, rebirth process, birth, and aging and death—these five—are [designated as] the formative links (*abhinirvartakāṅga, grub pa'i yan lag*), and they are completed with reference to the next life.[357]

The Textual Interpretation of Vasubandhu [ii']

With regard to the second part [of the exegesis on the interconnected dependent origination], which accords with the textual interpretation of the master Vasubandhu [it says in the root verses]:

> **Vasubandhupāda has explained,**
> **With reference to the fourfold process of projection and formation,**
> **That this is analyzed according to the following seven aspects:**
> **The projector, the projection process, and the projected,**
> **The former, the formation process, and the formed,**
> **Along with their disadvantages.**

The supreme scholar Vasubandhupāda, in his *Commentary Analyzing the Sūtra of Dependent Origination*, shows that when the structure of the dependent origination that is completed over two lifetimes through the fourfold process of projection and formation (*'phen grub bzhi ldan*) is analyzed according to its subcategories, it comprises seven aspects. [Specifically,] the "projective dependent origination" (*ākṣepapratītyasamutpāda, 'phen pa'i rten 'brel*) is divided into three aspects: the projector (*gang gis 'phen pa*), the projection process (*tshul ji ltar 'phen pa*), and the projected (*gang 'phangs pa*). Then, consequent on this projection, the "formative dependent origination" (*abhinirvartakapratītyasamutpāda, 'grub par byed pa'i rten 'brel*) is also divided into three aspects: the former (*gang gis grub pa*), the formation process (*tshul ji ltar grub pa*), and the formed (*gang 'grub pa*). In addition, the aspect of disadvantage (*ādinava, nyes dmigs*) is also presented.[358]

These seven aspects or points are correlated to the sequence of the twelve links of dependent origination as follows: Among them, "the projector" refers to the two links of fundamental ignorance and the formative predispositions motivated by it. "The projection process" denotes the way in which the seeds of past actions are deposited or projected by the link of formative predispositions upon the single link of consciousness. "The projected" refers to the four [consequent links]—name and form, six sensory activity fields, sensory contact, and sensation—which are projected.

Although the seed of the next rebirth is ripened and fully projected by means of these [just-mentioned] seven links, this same seed merely exists as a potential,[359] and it is uncertain that the [corresponding] rebirth will be swiftly assumed. Therefore, it is the [next four] links of formation (*'grub pa'i yan lag*) that will determine the outcome of the [corresponding] rebirth, in the next life, for example, in a swift and timely manner. In this context, "the former" denotes the two links of craving and grasping through which [the next rebirth] will be formed. "The formation process" denotes the way in which that same seed of the rebirth process, existing in a potential form consequent on the previously projected [links], is actually formed. "The formed" refers to the single link of birth in the next reincarnation.

The seventh aspect, the "disadvantages," correlates with the single link of aging and death.

Alternative Processes of Dependent Origination [iii']

These [processes], for the most part, occur [over sequential lives], just as described in the example [given above]. The alternative [processes], on the other hand, are imprecise because it is possible for many past lives to project a single rebirth, or for a body ripened by certain past actions to endure beyond a hundred aeons, and so forth. Also, as mentioned above, the cycle can be completed within a single lifetime. However, Jetsun Chenpo [Tāranātha] of Jonang has said that those [irregular] modalities that confuse the order [of the links of dependent origination], by appending the three links of craving, grasping, and rebirth process directly to the first three links of the [chain], and so forth, are quite mistaken.[360]

Dependent Origination in the Three World-Systems [iv']

Incidentally, if one were to wonder what sort of dependent origination is applicable in the context of the [three] world systems, and whether these [links] are similar for those abiding on the same level (*sa mtshungs pa*) or not, in the world-system of desire the twelve links [of dependent origination] are fully present, whereas in the two higher world-systems the twelve [links] are partly present because it is explained that [the link of] aging exists therein, in the manner of formative predispositions that are old and putrid. Meanwhile, in the [world system of] formlessness, the physical aspects of dependent origination are absent.

Dependent Origination in respect of the Nine Levels of the Three World-Systems [v']

The nine [experiential] levels that collectively comprise the three world-systems (*khams gsum sa dgu*)[361] may be reduced to the following three circumstances: (1) one's present level (*svabhūmi, rang sa*), (2) the level below it (*adhabhūmi, 'og sa*), and (3) the level above it (*urdhvabhūmi, gong sa*); or alternatively, (1) the level of death (*'chi sa*), (2) the level of birth (*skye sa*), and (3) the level of neither [death nor birth] (*sa gnyis ka ma yin pa*).

In this context, a single link [of dependent origination], with the exception of fundamental ignorance, can only be similar for those who share the level on which they have been born [among these nine levels or three circumstances].

As for fundamental ignorance, when beings are reborn from the world-system of desire back into the [world-system of] desire, this link is similar for all those who continue to abide on this level because it is inherent within the [world system of] desire; but when beings are reborn from their own level among the eight higher levels [of experience, associated with the world-systems of form and formlessness] back into the same [higher] level, [it is said that] there is no fundamental ignorance afflicting those who continue to abide on that same level. This is because the [immediate] past actions that would [ordinarily] project a birth into these [higher levels] are the meditations on quiescent and coarse [appearances] (*zhi rags su sgom pa*), but when one [merely] continues to abide on one's own [previous] level, [the impact of past actions is projected directly, through their own power] and not through the meditations on quiescent and coarse [appearances].[362]

However, when one makes a detailed investigation, there are many particular explanations, which should be understood from the [aforementioned] work of the supreme scholar Vasubandhu, and other texts.[363]

Synthesis [of the Links of Dependent Origination] [vii]

The seventh part [of the extensive exegesis; see p. 578] concerns the synthesis (*aṅgasamāsa, don bsdu*) [of dependent origination]. This has three topics: (1) the understanding of arising and cessation that accords with dependent origination, (2) the synthesis of dependent origination in terms of the two truths, and (3) an explanation of the advantages that accrue when difficult points are incidentally understood in accordance with the five profound contradictions [of dependent origination].

Understanding of Arising and Cessation That Accords with Dependent Origination [aa]

Concerning the first of these topics [it says in the root verses]:

> **The arising and cessation of substantial things**
> **Through uncreated and impermanent seeds**
> **Which are endowed with potency**
> **Accords with the understanding of dependent origination.**

With regard to the arising and cessation of substantial things: Phenomena are uncreated by the dynamics of false imagination present in the mind of a creator, and they are impermanent because anything permanent and steadfast would not be subject to the arising and cessation of causes and conditions. Since phenomena have a nature that partakes of arising and cessation, and substantial things are seeds endowed with potency, they are produced by causes capable of generating their respective results.[364]

Without knowing the processes of arising and cessation in respect of substantial things in accordance with the three natures of which they may partake, non-Buddhists and others propound their diverse [views of] eternalism and nihilism. However, when the meaning of dependent origination is [properly] understood, the reality will be known. By comprehending the three [natures], one will obtain certainty with regard to dependent origination.

Synthesis of Dependent Origination in Terms of the Two Truths [bb]

Concerning the second [it says in the root verses]:

> **Phenomena, just as they appear, are relative.**
> **Their actual reality is merely designated**
> **As the dependent origination of ultimate [truth].**
> **This [point] is extremely subtle.**

All [phenomena], just as they appear, are established in terms of the "relative dependent origination" (*kun rdzob kyi rten 'brel*), whereby emptiness arises as dependent origination. However, their actual reality is the lack of true existence, despite their appearances, and this can merely be designated as the "ultimate dependent origination of emptiness" (*don dam stong pa nyid kyi rten 'brel*). This crucial point is extremely profound and subtle, for which reasons it is an object known by the Buddha alone. Since it is this process of dependent origination that reaches the summit of all the promulgations of buddha speech, it has been extolled as the most genuine of all the [views] that have been propounded.

In this way, the systematic presentation of dependent origination should be known to correspond quantitatively to the essential nature of the two truths.

The Five Profound Contradictions of Dependent Origination [cc]

Concerning the third topic [the advantages that accrue when difficult points are incidentally understood in accordance with the five profound contradictions of dependent origination, it says in the root verses]:

> **[Dependent origination] is hard to understand**
> **On account of the profundity of its causal basis,**
> **Defining characteristic, arising, duration, and functioning,**
> **And on account of its five ostensible contradictions.**

Now, as for the reasons why this [ultimate] reality [of dependent origination] is not understood by others apart from the omniscient Buddha: This [process] is endowed with five [profundities], i.e., it is profound on account of its causal basis (*hetugāmbhīrya, rgyus zab pa*), profound on account of its defining characteristics (*lakṣaṇagāmbhīrya, mtshan nyid kyis zab pa*), profound on account of its arising (*utpattigāmbhīrya, skye bas zab pa*), profound on account of its duration (*sthitigāmbhīrya, gnas pas zab pa*), and profound on account of its functioning (*vṛttigāmbhīrya, 'byung bas zab pa*).[365] And it is endowed with five ostensible contradictions (*ltar snang lnga*), namely,

(1) Although [dependent origination] is momentary, it is also observed to have duration.
(2) Although [dependent origination] arises from unmoving conditions, it is also observed that its potencies are idiosyncratic.
(3) Although [dependent origination] occurs without reference to sentient beings, it is also observed in respect of sentient beings.
(4) Although [dependent origination] has no creator, it is also observed that past actions are not fruitless.
(5) Although [dependent origination] does not arise from the four extremes,[366] it does not arise with reference to any other agency.[367]

One who knows the meaning of this profound dependent origination is endowed with a great sense of purpose because the level of perfect buddhahood will be attained contingent on the pure view that sees emptiness and dependent origination as indivisible. Accordingly, it is said in the *Four Hundred Verses*:

> When dependent origination is perceived,
> Delusion will not arise.
> Therefore, at this juncture,
> And by every possible effort,
> I should explain this point alone.

And in the *Letter to a Friend*:[368]

> This dependent origination is the profound and precious treasure
> Of the compositions of buddha speech of all the conquerors.
> Whosoever genuinely perceives it, discerning this reality,
> Will perceive the tathāgata.

Presentation of the Real Nature of Dependent Origination [viii]

The eighth [and final] part [of the extensive exegesis; see p. 578] presents the real nature of dependent origination. It has three topics: (1) the real nature of selflessness (*bdag med pa'i de kho na nyid*), (2) the real nature of internal [phenomena] (*nang gi de kho na nyid*), and (3) the real nature devoid of inherent existence (*rang bzhin med pa'i de kho na nyid*).

The Real Nature of Selflessness [aa]

Regarding the first of these topics [it says in the root verses]:

> **All phenomena are merely dependently originated and without self.**

Since all relative phenomena, associated with cyclic existence and with the [spiritual] paths and their results, arise from compounded causes and conditions, they are impermanent, they are imbued with suffering, they are empty, and they are without self.[369]

As for these [four hallmarks], with regard to the first, impermanence (*anitya, mi rtag pa*), all substantial things are endowed with a subtle impermanence, whereby they arise and cease instantaneously. This is because although things may not perish immediately after they have arisen, the real nature of things that are arising is that they are also perishing. Since there is not the slightest intervening period of duration [between them], the parameters are the present moment of arising and the present moment of perishing.

With regard to suffering (*duḥkha, sdug bsngal ba*), since things are impermanent, it is established that they are imbued with suffering because they are powerless to endure for more than a mere moment.

With regard to emptiness (*śūnyatā, stong pa nyid*), taking any substantial thing, whether external or internal, into consideration, it is simply the case that from its causes and conditions, which are multifaceted, diverse, and of the nature of impermanence, the results that arise are also diverse and of the nature of impermanence. However, things are also [designated as] empty because they are in all respects devoid of self and devoid of a creator.

With regard to selflessness (*nairātmya, bdag med pa*), these phenomena are not created by any truly existing creator, but they appear merely as the process of dependent origination, which can be analyzed in terms of causes and conditions.

The Real Nature of Internal Phenomena [bb]

Regarding the second topic [it says in the root verses]:

The real nature of internal [phenomena] is apperception, devoid of self.

If one were to wonder whether, although [substantial things] are without self, the processes of dependent origination that apply to internal consciousness and external objects are in reality truly existent, it is the case that *all* dependently originated phenomena are without true or substantial existence in any respect whatsoever, because they are contrived and adventitious.

The [dependent origination] that arises through the power of mere apperception or imagination, focussing on the absence of erroneous bewilderment, is designated as the "real nature of internal phenomena" (*nang gi de kho na nyid*).[370]

The Real Nature Devoid of Inherent Existence [cc]

Regarding the third topic [it says in the root verses]:

Regarding this [mere apperception],
Although it does not primordially exist, it does appear,
Without contradiction,
In the manner of consciousness that is tainted by sleep.
This is the real nature devoid of inherent existence,
The pristine cognition of inner radiance
That transcends the objects of dependent origination,
Because it is liberated from the mutual interdependence
Of determined and determinative aspects.

There is no contradiction [in saying that] although this mere apperception does not truly exist because it has not existed primordially, it is just something that appears. For example, although the appearances that arise diversely in the form of Mount Sumeru, houses, and so forth in the consciousness of the dream state tainted by sleep have never actually existed, there is a dormant consciousness that does exist in that temporary state. In the same way, all the sensa of sense objects and sense data that arise have never truly existed from the beginning, and yet there is a conceptual basis for their arising that is present in this temporary state.[371]

Just as, although the fire that occurs in a dream has never existed from the beginning but it does appear to kindle firewood, this [mere apperception] also transcends all [extremes] of existence and non-existence, eternalism and nihilism. That is to say, since the diverse sensa associated with the dependent origination of causes and conditions do arise as mere appearances, they transcend [the extreme of] non-existence; and since they are without inherent existence, they also transcend [the extreme of] existence.[372]

Similarly, since the appearances associated with the dependent origination of causes and conditions partake of the nature of impermanence, the former [links] ceasing as the subsequent links arise, they also transcend the extreme of permanence; and since the gateways through which these mere appearances arise from their causes and conditions manifest without ceasing, they transcend the extreme of nihilism. This [process] is [designated as] the "real nature devoid of inherent existence" (*rang bzhin med pa'i de kho na nyid*).[373]

For this reason, it is said in the *Compendium* [*of Phenomenology*]:[374]

> It does not arise from itself, or from anything else, nor does it arise from both. It does not arise without a cause. It does not inherently exist in an intrinsic manner, and it does not inherently exist in an extraneous manner. Nor does it inherently exist in a combination of these two.

Although formative predispositions originate through the condition of fundamental ignorance, they do not originate solely from the [concept of] self associated with fundamental ignorance because it is impossible for many [diverse] results to arise from only a single cause. Nor is it the case that they originate from an extraneous substance because they do so with reference to their own cause. Nor indeed do they originate from both [a single intrinsic and an external cause] because [the postulations of] "self" and "other" [as the causes] have been individually refuted. Also, it is not the case that [they can originate] without a cause because one can clearly see that the arising of a result is certainly determined with reference to a cause.[375]

There is an extravagantly proud [view] emphasized by some who have suggested that "this structure of dependent origination associated with Nāgārjuna is the tradition of Madhyamaka, whereas the Cittamātra tradition was expounded by Asaṅga and his brother [Vasubandhu] because they uphold [the concept of] extraneous arising [or production from an external cause]." One can truly understand that this [view] is incorrect on the basis of the foregoing exegesis, which is based on the above citation from the *Compendium of Phenomenology*.[376]

In general, the expression "extraneous arising" (*parata utpāda, gzhan las skye ba*) refers to the appearances that appear to arise extraneously merely within the scope of the relative [truth], and the [corollary] expression "extraneous non-arising" (*gzhan las mi skye*) is refuted because the extraneous arising that truly [or independently] exists is refuted.[377]

Nowadays, those who claim to uphold the content of Nāgārjuna's scriptures unanimously assert the logical congruence that emptiness is dependent origination, and yet it should be understood that the pristine cognition of natural inner radiance (*rang bzhin 'od gsal ba'i ye shes*), which is the ultimate [truth], [actually] transcends dependent origination because it transcends objects of verbal expression and mental conception, and because it is liberated from [the distinctions between] generative causes and generated results, and from the mutual interdependence of determined and determinative aspects (*rnam par gzhag bya 'jog byed kyi ltos bzhag*).[378]

Furthermore, with regard to this natural inner radiance, its essential nature is the original pristine cognition, natural and spontaneously present, which has not been generated by any cause whatsoever. This is because it does not produce an extraneous result, nor is it a causal action of extraneous production. This pristine cognition is not even an object of verbal expression or mental conception. However much one who has never previously seen [Mount] Potala might describe or mentally conceive its defining characteristics, one can never depict it, just as it is. In the same way, too, however much the natural inner radiance can be conceived and determined by means of verbal expressions and mental conceptions, its defining characteristics cannot be qualitatively illustrated by any direct or indirect means.[379]

Since [from the perspective of logical analysis], those [processes] of mutually interdependent origination (*ltos 'jog gi rten 'brel*) are [considered to be] generally characterized phenomena (*sāmānyalakṣaṇa, spyi mtshan*) [which are not causally effective], such processes do not even rank among the properties of [ordinary] material things which are [considered to be] specifically characterized phenomena (*svalakṣaṇa, rang mtshan*) [and therefore causally effective], insofar as they are the directly evident signified objects (*dngos kyi brjod bya*) of verbal signifiers. This being the case, there is no question that natural inner radiance transcends the objective range of dependent origination.[380]

On the other hand, it is not contradictory to say that although the ultimate [truth] is not dependent origination, the ultimate [truth] can be realized by meditating on dependent origination. This is because all phenomena are accepted as dependently originated.[381]

This systematic presentation of dependent origination is expounded as an addendum to the [exegesis of] the three natures, and in order to acquire a more extensive comprehension of it, one should refer to the exegeses that are mainly found in the textual tradition of Asaṅga and his brother [Vasubandhu].

This completes the auto-commentary on Book Six, Part Two: A Systematic Presentation of Phenomenological Structures Common to Both the Greater Vehicle and the Lesser Vehicle.

Appendix: Outline of the Text

This outline derives from the *Shes bya kun khyab kyi sa bcad*, prepared by Zenkar Rinpoche, Thubten Nyima, and published by the Sichuan Nationalities Publishing House in 1990. Entries in italics represent additional levels of nesting which are not found in the chapter or section headings of this book.

[Chapter 4: Logic] 139

ii. Logic [III.B.2.a.ii] 141
aa. The Purpose of Logical Reasoning 141
bb. The Actual Exegesis of Logical Reasoning 142
1' Extensive Exegesis of the *Collected Topics* 142
a' Appraisable Objects 143
i' Objects in Terms of Their Essential Nature 143
ii' Objects in Terms of Their Functionality 145
iii' Objects in Terms of Their Understanding 145
b' Signifying Subjects 147
i' Signifiers in Terms of Their Essential Nature 147
ii' Signifiers in Terms of the Signified 148
iii' Signifiers in Terms of the Modes of Signification 148
iv' Signifiers in Terms of Preclusion 148
v' Signifiers in Terms of Their Theoretical Presentation 149
vi' Defining Characteristic of the Term "Syllable" 149
vii' Defining Characteristic of the Term "Individual Person" 150
viii' Valid Cognition 151
aa' The Valid Cognition of Direct Perception 151
1" Direct Perception of the Sense Organs 152
2" Direct Perception of Mental Consciousness 152
3" Direct Perception of Intrinsic Awareness 152
4" Direct Perception of Yoga 152
bb' Valid Cognition of Inference 153
1" Inference Proceeding from the Cogent Power of Facts 153
2" Inference Based on Popular Acclaim 153
3" Inference on the Basis of Conviction 153
cc' Internally Ascertained Valid Cognition 154
dd' Externally Ascertained Valid Cognition 154
c' Processes of Logical Understanding 154
i' Contradiction 155
ii' Relation 155
iii' Negation 155
iv' Proof 155
v' Universals 156
vi' Particulars 156

[CHAPTER 13: The Exalted Vehicle] 419

PART TWO: BUDDHIST PHENOMENOLOGY: A SYSTEMATIC PRESENTATION OF PHENOMENOLOGICAL STRUCTURES COMMON TO BOTH THE GREATER VEHICLE AND THE LESSER VEHICLE 441

[CHAPTER 1: Non-Buddhist and Buddhist Philosophical Systems] 461

I. Distinctions between the Non-Buddhist and Buddhist Philosophical Systems [I] 461

Thematic Concordance of Terminology

The following tables give precedence to the original Tibetan in the first column, with selected Sanskrit equivalents in the middle column and English translations in the third column.

The Indo-Tibetan Classical Sciences

'jig rten pa'i rig gnas	*laukikavidyā*	mundane science
thun mong gi rig gnas	*sādhāraṇavidyā*	ordinary classical science(s)
rig gnas lnga	*pañcavidyā*	five classical sciences
rigs gnas chung ba	*vedāṅga*	minor/ lesser science(s)
rigs gnas chung ba lnga	*pañcavedāṅga*	five minor sciences

Linguistics and Grammar [Sanskrit and Tibetan]

ka phreng	*kāli*	garland of consonants
kā myaC	*kāmyaC*	denominative suffix *-kāmya*
kun tu 'jug pa'i rtags		stem of universally applicable gender
kun bshad	*ākhyāta*	rules of verbal morphology
kṛṭ	*kṛṭ*	primary nominal suffix
KyaC	*KyaC*	denominative suffix *-ya*
rkan byung gi sde	*tālavyavarga*	palatal phonetic set
rkyang 'jug		simple suffixation
rkyang pa		isolate
rkyen	*pratyaya*	affixation

rkyen gyi rjes su 'brel ba	*pratyayānubandha*	technical marker attached to affixes
rkyen gyi byings	*pratyayadhātu*	affixed verbal root
skad	*bhāṣya*	language
skad kyi gdangs		vocalic pulsation
khyad don		peculiarity [of inflection]
glo bur gyi rkyen gyi rjes su 'brel ba	*āgamānubandha*	technical marker attached to augments
dgag sgra		negative particle
dgos ched du bya ba	*caturthā[vibhakti]*	fourth/ dative case
mgo can		superscript
mgrin byung	*kaṇṭha*	velar
mgrin byung gi sde	*kaṇṭhavarga*	velar phonetic set
rgyan sdud kyi sgra		conjunctive modifying particle
sgra	*śabda*	sound
sgra don	*śabdārtha*	literal meaning
sgra mdo	*śabdasūtra*	grammatical treatise
sgra ldan	*ghoṣavant*	voiced sonant
sgra med	*aghoṣa*	unvoiced surd
sgra la byung ba		sound generation
sgra'i khams	*śabdadhātu*	phoneme/ basic element of sound
sgra'i rigs gnas	*śabdavidyā*	Sanskrit grammar
bsgrub bya'i yul gyi dngos po		agentive of the action to be achieved
GHaÑ	*vṛddhi*	extreme vowel strengthening
nga ro (Skt)	*anusvāra*	anusvāra (AṂ)
nga ro (Tib)		phonics/ phonetic diction
ngag	*vāk*	statement/ speech
nges tshig	*nirukta*	etymology/ etymological definition
ngo bo tsam		bare essential nature [of an uninflected substantive]
dngos [kyi rang bzhin]	*bhāvaprakṛti*	genuine primary base

dngos po	*bhāva*	verbal action
mngon par zhen pa	*abhiniveśa*	adhesion
sngags kyi bklag thabs		method of reciting [Sanskrit syllables] according to the mantras
sngon 'jug		prefix
cung zad phrad pa	*īṣatspṛṣṭa*	partial [phonetic] contact
lce rtsa can	*jihvāmūlīya*	jihvāmūlīya (ḤKA)
mchu can	*upadhmānīya*	upadhmānīya (ḤPA)
mchu byung gi sde	*oṣṭhyavarga*	labial phonetic set
ji lta bu'i sgra	*yuṣmad*	pronoun
'jug ldog byed pa		to apply/ predicate meaningfully
'jug pa'i gnas brgyad		eight elements of linguistic application
rjes 'jug		suffix
rjes su sna ldan	*anunāsika*	nasalization
rjes su 'brel ba	*anubandha*	technical marker
nye ba'i bum pa	*upakumbha*	adverbial compound
nye bar bsgyur ba	*upasarga*	verbal preposition
nye bar sgrub pa'i rtags		stem of congruent gender
gnyis ldan		verbal roots that have and have not been listed/ formally conjugated
ṆiC la sogs pa		causative-forming suffixes such as *–i*
tiṄ (la sogs pa)	*tiṄ/ tyādi*	verbal inflections/ suffixes (numbering eigheen or one hundred and eighty)
gtibs pa'i rtags		stem of obscure gender
btags kyi rang bzhin	*prajñaptiprakṛti*	imputed/ conventional primary base
btags pa'i shes pa		imputative cognition
rtags	*liṅga*	gender
rtags drug		six stems indicative of gender
tha snyad	*vyavahāra*	conventional term

thung ngu['i dbyangs]	*hrasva*	short vowel
thun mongs du grags pa		universality/ commonality
mthar gnas	*antaḥsthā*	semi-vowel
mthun par snang ba		shared ideation
dag pa'i rtags		stem of specific gender
dang sgra		conjunctive particle
dus lta ba	*vartamānā*	present tense
dus 'das pa	*parokṣā*	past tense
dus ma 'ongs pa	*bhaviṣyantī*	future tense
dus gsum	*kālatraya*	three tenses
de la phan pa	*taddhita*	secondary nominal suffix
de'i skyes bu	*tatpuruṣa*	dependent determinative compound
don	*artha*	meaning
don la dmigs pa	*arthālambana*	objective reference
dro ba'i yi ge	*ūṣmān*	spirant
bdag sgra		possessive particle
bdag gzhan		agentive and objective
'dogs 'phul		subscript
'dres pa'i rtags		stem of mixed gender
brda	*saṃketa*	communicative symbol
brda sprod	*vyākaraṇa*	grammar
sde pa lnga	*pañcavarga*	five phonetic sets
nang gi rtsol ba bzhi		four inner modes of articulation
ni sgra		emphatic/ thematic particle
gnas gzhi	*āhāra/ saptamā[vibhakti]*	seventh/ locative case
rnam 'gyur	*vikāra*	derivation
rnam gcad	*visarga*	visarga (Ḥ)
rnam dbye	*vibhakti*	inflection, case-ending
rnam dbye dang po	*prathamā[vibhakti]*	nominative/ substantive/ first case

rnam dbye'i mtha'	*vibhaktyanta*	inflected stem
sna ldan gyi yi ge	*anunāsika*	nasal syllable
spyi	*sāmānya*	universal
spyi sgra		quantitative pronoun
spyi byung gi sde	*mūrdhanyavarga*	retroflex phonetic set
phyi'i rtsol ba lnga		five modes of outer articulation
phye ba	*vivāra*	opening of the glottis/ vocal tract
phrad rkyang pa		single-syllable particle
phrad pa	*spṛṣṭa*	contact/ plosion
phrad pa'i rnam gyur		derivation due to affixation
phrad gzhan dbang can		non-variable particle
ba gnyis pa	*dvigu*	dual compound
bud med rkyen	*strīliṅgapratyaya*	feminine-forming suffix
bya ba		action occurring in the future tense
bya ba'i yul	*karman/ āpya*	direct object
bya ba'i las		action of the object
bya byed		verbal categories [i.e., transitive/ intransitive, or differentiative/ non-differentiative]
byings	*dhātu*	verbal root
byings kyi rjes su 'brel ba	*dhātvanubandha*	technical marker attached directly to verbal roots
byed sgra	*tṛtīyā[vibhakti]*	third/ instrumental case
byed pa	*karaṇa*	articulator (phonetics), agent/ instrument (grammar)
byed pa [po]	*kartṛ*	agentive [verb], subject [of the verb]
byed pa		verbal action occurring in the present tense
byed pa po dang dngos su 'brel ba		[transitive] verb establishing a subject-object relationship
byed pa'i las		action of the subject
dbyi ba	*lopa*	elision

'bod pa'i sgra	*āmantraṇa*	vocative particle
'byung khungs	*pañcamā[vibhakti]/ avadhi*	fifth/ ablative case
'byed sdud kyi sgra		disjunctive-adjunctive connecting particle
'bru mang po	*bahuvṛhi*	exocentric compound
'brel sgra	*ṣaṣṭhī[vibhakti]*	sixth/ genitive case [particle]
mi zad pa'i sde tshan	*avyayībhāvavarga*	indeclinable class of words
mi zad pa'i sde tshan gyi rjes su 'brel ba	*avyayībhāvānubandha*	technical marker attached to the indeclinable class of words
mi gsal ba'i rtags		stem of indeterminate gender
ming	*nāman*	noun, nominal stem, name
ming rkyang		noun isolate
ming gi byings	*nāmadhātu*	denominative verbal root
ming gzhi		radical [letter]
rtsol ba		articulation
rtsol ba'i gnas	*vacanāvasthā*	place of articulation
brtsegs 'phul		stack
tshangs pa'i yi ge	*brāhmīlipi*	Brāhmī script
tshig	*pada*	[syntactically bound] word phrase
tshig mtha'	*padānta*	final letter
tshig sdud	*samāsa*	nominal compound
tshig phreng	*padāvalī*	sentence
tshig bla dvags	*adhivacana*	designation
mtshan ma	*lakṣaṇa*	characteristic
mtshams sbyor	*sandhi*	euphonic conjunction
mtshams sbyor gyi yi ge	*saṃdhyakṣara*	diphthong
mtshungs pa'i yi ge	*samānākṣara*	simple vowel
gzhan		objective
zin pa'i sgra		phoneme originating from sentient sources
zlas dbye ba	*dvandva*	coordinative compound

yang 'jug		post-suffixation
yi ge	*varṇa*	letter/ syllable
yi ge klag thabs		pronunciation of syllables
yi ge 'dus pa		aggregate of syllables
yi ge sbyor tshul		morphology of syllables
yi ge'i rnam pa	*varṇākāra*	graphology/ character representation
yi ge'i dbye ba		phonological analysis of syllables
yig gzugs	*lipi*	writing/ syllabic script
yongs su bklags pa'i byings	*paripāṭhitadhātu*	listed/ formally conjugated verbal roots
yongs su ma bklags pa'i byings	*viparipāṭhitadhātu*	unlisted/ non-formally conjugated verbal roots
rang bzhin	*prakṛti*	primary base [of nouns and verbs]
ring thung rtags kyi rjes su 'brel ba	*dīrghahrasvaliṅgānubandha*	technical marker attached to long or short gender terminations
ring po'i dbyangs	*dīrgha*	long vowel
la don [gyi sgra]		oblique [case] particle
la kāra	*lakāra*	tense and mood
las bcas	*sakarmaka*	transitive verb [of the active voice]
las	*karman*	direct object
las med	*akarmaka*	intransitive/ reflexive verb [of the middle voice]
las 'dzin pa	*karmadhāraya*	descriptive determinative compound
las su bya ba	*dvitīyā[vibhakti]*	second/ accusative case
lānydza	*rañjanālipi*	Rañjanā script
legs sbyar	*saṃskṛta*	Sanskrit
shin tu ring po'i dbyangs	*pluta*	extra long vowel
shes brjod 'jug gsum		cognition, signification and [actual] usage/ application
saN [la sogs pa]	*saNādi*	desiderative and related suffixes
sUP	*sUP*	nominal case suffix

sUB'i rnam dbye nyer gcig	*sUB-vibhakti*	twenty-one nominal case suffixes
so byung gi sde	*dantyavarga*	dental phonetic set
sva ri ta	*svarita*	circumflex/ middle accent
gsal byed	*vyañjana*	consonant
srog chung	*alpaprāṇa*	non-aspirate
srog chen	*mahāprāṇa*	aspirate
slar bsdu		reduplicated particle
lhag bcas		connecting particle
a phreng	*āli*	garland of vowels
aC	*guṇa*	moderate vowel strengthening
a nu data	*anudātta*	grave/ low accent
āgama'i rkyen	*āgama*	augment
i ldan		genitive and instrumental case particle(s)
u data	*udātta*	acute/ high accent

Buddhist Logic

rkyen	*pratyaya*	condition
rkyen bzhi	*caturpratyaya*	four secondary conditions
lkog gyur	*parokṣa*	[appraisable objects that are] indirectly evident
skad cig	*kṣaṇa*	temporal moment
skad cig cha med	*nivirbhāgakṣaṇika*	indivisible time moment
skye mched lnga	*pañcāyatana*	five sensory activity fields
'khrul pa	*bhrānti*	mistaken cognition
khyab mnyam rnam pa gnyis		two aspects of logical congruence
khyab [pa]	*vyāpti*	logical entailment
khyab pa sgo brgyad		eight approaches to logical entailment
gang zag	*pudgala*	individual person
gang zag gi bdag med	*pudgalanairātmya*	selflessness of the individual person
grags pa'i rjes dpag	*yaśo'numāna*	inference based on popular acclaim

grub 'bras	*siddhiphala*	successful conclusion
dgag pa	*pratiṣedha*	negation
dgag pa 'phar tshul gnyis		two procedures for adding negation
dgag bya	*pratiṣedhya*	negandum, antithesis
'gal khyab	*viruddhavyāpti*	contrary entailment
'gal dang mi 'gal	*viruddhāviruddha*	contradiction and non-contradiction
'gal ba	*virodha/ virudha*	contradiction
'gal ba'i gtan tshigs	*viruddhahetu*	contradictory reasoning
'gal ba'i rtags	*viruddhaliṅga*	contradictory evidence
'gyur ba'i sdug bsngal	*vipariṇāmaduḥkhatā*	suffering of change
rgol mkhan	*vādin*	antagonist
rgyu	*hetu*	[primary] cause
rgyu dang 'bras bu gnyis	*hetuphala*	cause and result
rgyun	*santāna*	continuum of time
brgyud 'gal	*avedhaviruddha*	indirect contradiction
brgyud rgyu	*avedhahetu*	indirect cause
sgra spyi	*śabdasāmānya*	term-universal
sgrub ngag	*vidhivākya*	correct statement of proof
sgrub 'jug	*vidhipravṛtti*	affirmative engagement
sgrub pa	*vidhi*	proof
sgrub byed	*sādhana, vidhi*	proof, premise, probens
sgro 'dogs	*adhyāropa*	superimposition, exaggeration
bsgrub bya	*sādhya*	probandum
bsgrub bya'i chos	*sādhyadharma*	property of the probandum
ngag	*vāk*	speech, statement
nges don	*nītārtha*	definitive meaning
dngos kyi brjod bya		directly evident signified [object/ phenomenon]
dngos kyi brjod byed		directly evident signifier
dngos kyi zhen pa'i brjod byed		directly evident conceived signifier
dngos 'gal	*sākṣādviruddha*	direct contradiction
dngos rgyu	*sājñātkāraṇa*	direct cause
dngos rtog	*sākṣādavabodha*	explicit understanding
dngos po	*vastu*	substantial object/ entity
dngos po stobs zhugs kyi rjes dpag	*vastubalapravṛttānumāna*	inference proceeding from the cogent power of facts
dngos po stobs zhugs kyi gtan tshigs	*vastubalapravṛttahetu*	logical axiom proceeding from the cogent power of facts

dngos por smra ba	*vastuvādin*	realist
dngos ming	*mūlanāma*	explicit/ proper name
dngos med	*avastu*	insubstantial object/ non-entity
mngon gyur	*abhimukhī*	directly evident [appraisable object]
mngon sum	*pratyakṣa*	direct perception
mngon sum [gyi] tshad ma	*pratyakṣapramāṇa*	valid cognition of direct perception
snga btsan bar btsan phyi btsan		cogency of the antagonist, mediator, and respondent
gcig dang tha dad	*abhinnabhinna*	identity and difference
chos kyi skye mched	*dharmāyatana*	sensory activity field of phenomena
chos kyi bdag med	*dharmanairātmya*	selflessness of phenomena
chos can	*dharmin*	topic for discussion, subject, theme
chos can brjod pa'i sgra		subject-oriented expression
chos brjod kyi sgra		predicate-oriented expression, specifically predicated expression
chos mthun sbyor gyi sgrub ngag		statement of proof applying qualitative similarity
chos mi mthun sbyor gyi sgrub ngag		statement of proof applying qualitative dissimilarity
'chad dus kyi brjod bya		theoretically signified [phenomenon]
'jug dus kyi brjod bya		practically signified [phenomenon]
'jug ldog gi gzhi		illustrative base demonstrating applied usage
rjes khyab	*anvayavyāpti*	forward logical entailment
rjes 'gro	*anvaya*	positive logical concomitance
rjes dpag	*anumāna*	[logical] inference
rjes dpag tshad ma	*anumānapramāṇa*	valid cognition of inference
rjes su 'gro ldog	*anvayavyatireka*	positive concomitance and its negative counterpart
brjod bya	*vācya*	signified [phenomenon]
brjod bya'i spyi ldog		universal distinguishing counterpart of the signified object
brjod byed	*vācaka*	signifier
brjod byed khas len skyong tshul		defense of standpoints concerning the signifier

brjod tshul		mode of signification
gtan tshigs	*hetu*	axiom, reason
gtan tshigs rigs pa	*hetuvidyā*	logic
btags yod	*vijñaptisat*	nominally/ imputedly existent
rtag pa	*nitya*	permanence, permanent [object]
rtags	*liṅga*	[logical] evidence/ reasoning
rtags rtogs	*liṅgāvabodha*	evidential understanding
rtags ltar snang	*ābhāsaliṅga*	ostensible evidence
rtags mang		multi-faceted evidence
rtags yang dag	*samyagliṅga*	genuine evidence/ reasoning
rtog ge	*tarka*	dialectics
rtog pa	*kalpanā*	conceptual cognition
rtog med	*nirvikalpanā*	non-conceptual/ non-imaginative cognition
ltar snang brgyad	*aṣṭābhāsa*	eight ostensible factors
tha snyad	*vyavahāra*	conventional term
tha snyad sgrub		proof of a conventional term
tha snyad chos gsum		three properties of conventional terminology
tha dad dang tha min	*bhinnābhinna*	difference and non-difference
thal 'gyur	*prasaṅga*	consequential reasoning, [correct] consequence
thal ngag		consequential statement
thur khyab	*heṣṭhavyāpti*	backward [logical] entailment
mthung snang		acceptance
mthun dpe	*sādharmyadṛṣṭānta*	analogous example
mthun dpe yang dag	*samyaksādharmyadṛṣṭānta*	correct analogous example
mthun phyogs	*sapakṣa*	analogous/ compatible factor/ term
de byung gi 'brel ba	*tadātmyasaṃbandha*	relation of identical nature
don sgrub	*arthasiddhi*	proof of a meaning
don gcig	*ekārtha*	coextensive
dam bcas	*pratijñā*	ostensible thesis
don chos gsum		three real properties
don spyi	*arthasāmānya*	object-universal
don byed nus pa	*arthakriyākāraṇa/samartha*	causally effective
don byed mi nus pa	*anarthakriyākāraṇa/samartha*	not causally effective
bdag rkyen	*adhipatipratyaya*	predominant condition

bdag gi bas stong pa	*ātmaśūnyatā*	emptiness of self
bdag gcig	*ekātman*	identical nature
bdag gcig 'brel	*tādātmyasaṃbandha*	relation of essential identity
bden chung bcu drug	*caturāryasatyaṣodaśākāra-visārita*	sixteen aspects of the four truths
bdag med	*nairātmya*	selflessness
bdag med	*anātma[ka]*	selfless
'dus byas	*saṃskṛta*	compounded [object/ phenomenon]
'dus ma byas	*asaṃskṛta*	uncompounded [object/ phenomenon]
rdul rdzas brgyad	*aṣṭāṇudravya*	eight atomic substances
ldog khyab	*vyatirekavyāpti*	counter [logical] entailment
ldog chos	*vyāvṛttidharma*	distinguishing counterpart phenomena
ldog tha dad		different distinguishing counterpart
ldog byed	*vyatireka*	negative logical concomitance
ldog phyogs		opposite standpoint
brda	*saṃketa*	symbol
bsdus tshan bco brgyad		eighteen collected topics
nang don bem po		internal matter
nus pa	*śakti*	potentiality
gnas lugs		abiding/ real nature
rnam gcod	*vyavaccheda*	preclusion
rnam [par] shes [pa]	*vijñāna*	consciousness
rnam shes tshogs brgyad	*aṣṭavijñāna*	eight modes of consciousness
rnam shes tshogs drug	*ṣadvijñāna*	six modes of consciousness
rnal 'byor gyi mngon sum	*yogapratyakṣa*	direct perception of yoga
snang yul		apparent object
dpang po	*sākṣi*	witness
dpyad pa gsum		three types of scrutiny
spang gnyen		renunciation and antidote
spyi	*sāmānya*	universal
spyi mtshan	*sāmānyalakṣaṇa*	generally characterized phenomenon
spros bral	*niḥprapañca*	freedom from conceptual elaboration
phung po	*skandha*	psycho-physical aggregate
phyi don bem po		external matter
phyir rgol	*prativādin*	protagonist/ respondent

phyogs snga ma	*pūrvapakṣa*	original premise
phyogs chos	*pakṣadharma*	property of the thesis
bem po	*rūpa*	material phenomenon
bye brag	*viśeṣa*	particular/ individuation
byed pa	*kāraṇa*	efficiency
blo ['gros]	*buddhi*	intellect
dbang po gzugs can		physical sense faculties
dbang po'i mngon sum	*indriyapratyakṣa*	direct perception of the sense organs
dbang shes	*indriyajñāna*	sensory consciousness
dbu ma'i lam	*madhyamapratipad*	Middle Way
'bras bu	*phala*	conclusion, result
'bras bu'i gtan tshig	*kāryahetu*	axiom of the result
'brel dang mi 'brel		relation and non-relation
'brel ba	*saṃbandha*	relation
sbyor ba	*prayoga*	syllogism
ma 'khrul	*abhrānti*	unmistaken [cognition]
ma grub pa'i gtan tshigs	*asiddhahetu*	unestablished reasoning
ma grub pa'i rtags	*asiddhaliṅga*	unestablished evidence
ma nges pa'i gtan tshigs	*anaikāntikahetu*	unascertained reasoning
ma nges pa'i rtags	*anaikāntikaliṅga*	unascertained evidence
ma dmigs pa'i gtan tshigs	*anupalabdhihetu*	axiom of the absence of the objective referent
ma yin dgag	*paryudāsapratiṣedha*	implicitly affirmative negation
mi rtag pa	*anitya*	impermanence, impermanent [object/ phenomenon]
mi mthun dpe yang dag	*vaidharmyadṛṣṭānta*	correct non-analogous example
mi mthun phyogs	*vipakṣa*	non-analogous/ incompatible factor/ term
mi ldan rnam gcod kyi sgra		statement expressing preclusion without a predicate
mi srid rnam gcod		statement expressing preclusion of the impossible
mi slu ba	*avisaṃvādi*	unfailing
ming	*nāman*	noun, name
med dgag	*prasajyapratiṣedha*	explicit negation
myong stobs	*anubhava*	power of experience
myong bya		object of experience
rtsod gzhi	*adhikaraṇa*	basis for debate
tshad 'bras	*pramāṇaphala*	conclusion of valid/ reliable cognition

tshad ma	*pramāṇa*	valid/ reliable cognition
tshad ma'i rigs gnas	*pramāṇavidyā*	logic
tshad min	*apramāṇa*	non-valid/ unreliable cognition
tshig	*pada*	[syntactically bound] phrase
tshul gsum	*trairūpya*	threefold criteria
tshogs brjod kyi sgra		words signifying sets
mtshan nyid	*lakṣaṇa*	definition, defining characteristic
mtshan gzhi	*lakṣya*	illustration
mtshon bya	*lakṣya*	definiendum, defined/ illustrated object
'dzin pa'i rnam shes		apprehending consciousness
rdzas	*dravya*	substance
rdzas chos	*dravyadharma*	substance phenomenon
rdzas chos ldog chos gnyis		substance phenomena and distinguishing counterpart phenomena
rdzas tha dad	*bhinnadravya*	different substance
rdzas yod chos gsum		three substantially existent properties [of a definition]
zhen pa'i brjod bya		conceived signified [phenomenon]
zhen pa'i brjod byed		conceived signifier
zhen yul	*adhyavasāyaviṣaya*	conceived object
gzhan don gyi rjes dpag	*parārthānumāna*	inference for the sake of others
gzhan ldan rnam gcod	*anyayogavyavaccheda*	statement expressing preclusion with an extraneous [predicate]
gzhan las nges kyi tshad ma		externally ascertained valid cognition
gzhan sel	*anyāpoha*	extraneous elimination
gzhan rig	*anyasaṃvid*	extraneous/ non-apperceptive awareness
gzhal bya	*prameya*	appraisable [object]
gzhal byed		means of appraisal
gzhi grub		established basis
bzung yul	*grāhyakaviṣaya*	apprehended object
yi ge	*varṇa*	syllable
yid kyi mngon sum	*manapratyakṣa*	direct perception of mental consciousness
yid ches rjes dpag	*āptatānumāna*	inference on the basis of conviction

yin khyab mnyam		coextensive, congruent in logical entailment
yin gyur min gyur		presence and absence
yul	*viṣaya*	object
yul can	*viṣayin*	subject
yod rtogs med rtogs		understanding of existence and non-existence
rang don gyi tshad ma	*svārthānumāna*	inference for one's own sake
rang mtshan	*svalakṣaṇa*	specifically characterized phenomenon
rang bzhin gyi gtan tshigs	*svabhāvahetu*	axiom of identity
rang rig	*svasaṃvedana*	intrinsic/ reflexive awareness
rang rig gi mngon sum	*svasaṃvedanapratyakṣa*	direct perception of intrinsic/ reflexive awareness
rang las nges kyi tshad ma		internally ascertained valid cognition
rig pa	*vidyā*	awareness, intelligence, cognitive phenomena
rigs brjod kyi sgra		words signifying types
rigs spyi	*jātisāmānya*	type-universal
lan	*prativacana*	rejoinder
lung	*āgama*	scriptural authority/ testimony
shin tu lkog gyur	*atyantaparokṣa*	indirectly evident to an extreme degree
shugs kyi zhen pa'i brjod byed		implicitly conceived signifier
shes brjod 'jug gsum		cognition, signification and engagement
shes 'dod can		subject of interest
shes pa	*jñāna*	cognition, consciousness
shes bya	*jñeya*	knowable [phenomenon/ object]
sun 'byin	*duṣaṇa*	correct refutation
sems	*citta*	mind
sems byung	*caitta*	mental state
sel 'jug	*apohapravṛtti*	eliminative engagement
gsal ba	*vyakti*	specific predicate
bsal ba	*prativinodha*	elimination
bsal mang		multi-faceted elimination

Fine and Applied Art(s)

1. Iconography: Painting and Sculpture

ka ṇa ya	*kaṇaya*	short harpoon
kun dga' ra ba	*ārāma*	monastic campus
klu	*nāga*	serpentine water spirit
klu phrug	*nāgapota*	youthful serpentine water spirit [motif]
rkang gdub	*nūpura*	anklet [ornament]
rkang pa	*pada*	quarter [measurement]
ska rags	*mekhalā*	girdle [ornament]
sku	*kāya*	buddha body, image, icon
sku rten		representation of buddha body
skyil krung phyed pa	*ardhaparyaṅka*	semi cross-legged posture
skyon sel		correction of errors in draftsmanship
kha ṭvāṅga	*khaṭvāṅga*	khaṭvāṅga staff
khri rkang		throne leg
khri 'gyogs		teaching-throne, palanquin
khri rgyab		throne and back-rest
khri rgyab rgyan drug		six ornaments of the back-rest
khri gdan		throne seat
khri gdong		throne front
khri rmang		throne support
khro bo	*krodha*	wrathful deity
mkha' lding	*garuḍa*	garuḍa
'khor los sgyur ba	*cakravartī*	universal monarch
ga da'i dbyug pa	*gada*	club
gar gyi nyams dgu	*navanāṭyarasa*	nine dramatic airs
gar gyi phu rung		long silken dance sleeve
gri gug	*kartṛkā*	curved knife
glang chen gyi ko rlon	*gajacarma*	fresh hide of an elephant [ornament]
glang po che	*hasti*	elephant [motif]
gling bzhi	*caturdvīpa*	four continents
dgang gzar blugs [gzar]	*pātri/ sruc* and *sruva*	pair of *homa* ladles
dgod pa	*hāsya*	laughter, laughing demeanor
dgra ste	*paraśu*	battleaxe
mgul rgyan	*kaṇṭhābharaṇa*	neck-band [ornament]

rgya bye'u lcags		iron discus
rgyan	*ābharaṇa*	ornament
rgyan drug		six ornamental [hand-emblems]
rgyab yol		back-rest [of a teaching throne]
sgeg pa	*śṛṅgāra*	grace, graceful demeanor
sgang gzugs ma		throne back-rest of semi-circular shape, resembling a hedgehog
sgar lugs		Encampment Style [of painting]
rnga chen	*bherī/ dundubhi*	large drum
rnga zlum		round drum
rngam pa	*adbhūta*	[demeanor of] awe, awesome demeanor
cang te'u	*ḍamaru*	hand-held [skull] drum
cod pan	*mukuṭa*	[five-colored] silken crown-pendant
bcad kyi tshul		outlining
lcags rtse ma		[throne] back-rest resembling sheet metal
cha chung	*plava*	small unit [of measurement]
cha chen		large unit [of measurement]
cha tshad		iconometric proportion
cha tshad bcu gcig		eleven categories of iconometric proportion
chags bral	*virāga*	renunciant icon, without consort
chu gri	*churikā*	sharp knife
chu srin	*makara*	sea monster [motif]
chu srin gyi phags		sea-monster hide, crocodile hide
chos gos gsum	*tricīvara*	three kinds of religious robe
mche ba		indestructible fangs [of wrathful deities]
mchod phyir thogs	*yajñopavīta*	thread of sacrificial investiture
'jig rten skyong ba	*lokapāla*	mundane protector [deity]
'jigs su rung ba	*bhayānaka*	[demeanor of] fearsomeness, fearsome demeanor
nyams	*rasa*	demeanor, sentiment
nyi zla'i chas		accoutrement of sun and moon discs

snyan gong ut pa la	*utpalakarṇika*	lily-shaped earring [ornament]
snyan rgyan	*karṇika*	earring [ornament]
mnyam pa'i stabs	*sampada*	posture of balance
snying rje	*karuṇā*	[demeanor of] compassion, compassionate demeanor
gtun shing	*musala*	wooden pestle
rten 'brel ri mo		auspicious design [motif]
stag lpags kyi sham thabs	*vyāghtacarma*	skirt of tiger skin
stod gYogs	*aṃśuka*	upper robe, jacket
thal chen	*mahābhasma*	human ash [ornament]
thal mo	*tāla*	palm-length measurement
thig chen brgyad		eight major iconometric scales [of the Menri style]
thod pa	*kapāla*	skull
mthil	*tala*	palm-length measurement, sole-length measurement
mtho	*vitasti*	mid-finger span [measurement equal to 12 fingerwidths]
dam tshigs sems dpa'	*samayasattva*	being of commitment [i.e., visualized deity]
ḍā ka	*ḍāka*	ḍāka drum
dur khrod kyi chas brgyad		eight accoutrements of the charnel ground
do shal	*hāra*	mid-length necklace
drag shul	*raudra*	[demeanor of] ferocity, fierce demeanor
drang srong	*ṛṣi*	hermit sage
dril bu	*ghaṇṭā*	bell
gdan khri		teaching-throne
gdu bu	*parihāṭaka*	bracelet
mdangs		shading
mdung	*kunta*	sharp-pointed spear, long spear
mdung thung	*śakti*	short spear, dart
rdo rje	*vajra*	vajra [emblem]
rdo rje skyil krung	*vajraparyaṅka*	posture of indestructible reality
rdo rje glag		indestructible garment, indestructible occiput
rdo rje rtse lnga		five-pointed vajra
rdo rje rtse gcig	*ekapucikavajra*	single-pronged vajra
rdo rje gshogs pa		indestructible wings [of wrathful deities]

nas	*java*	"barley grain" [measurement]
ni raṃ shu	*niraṃśuka*	naked, unclothed [tantric code for human bone ornaments]
gnod sbyin	*yakṣa*	sylvan spirit
rnam gyur	*vikāra*	style, stylistic feature
snal ris rgyan		ornament with a thread design [motif]
sna tshogs rdo rjes mtshan pa'i khaṭvāṅga		tantric staff with crossed vajra motif
pa tra rigs brgyad		eight [distinctive] patterns of basic design
pa ṭa ha	*paṭaha*	paṭaha drum
pad gdab lta bu'i rgyab yol		[throne] back-rest resembling a lotus petal
pe ṭa ka	*peṭaka*	spear-flag
dpa' ba	*vīra*	heroism, heroic demeanor
dpa' bo'i sdug stangs	*vīralīlā*	hero's posture
dpa' mo'i sdug stangs	*vīrālīlā*	heroine's posture
dpal gyi chas brgyad		eight glorious accoutrements
dpung rgyan	*aṅgada*	ornament worn across the shoulders and upper arms
dpe dpyad brgyad cu	*asītyānuvyañjana*	eighty minor marks [of the buddha body]
spyi gtsug rdo rje phyed pa		half-vajra crown crest
sprul sku	*nirmāṇakāya*	buddha body of emanation
phub	*phara*	shield
phub la zhol btags pa		back-rest woven in an [oval] shield-like design
phur bu	*kīla*	ritual spike
phur bu rdo rje rtse lnga		ritual spike surmounted by the five-pronged vajra
pho nya	*dūta*	intermediary, messenger
phyag rgya	*mudrā*	hand gesture, seal
phyag rgya ma	*mudrā*	female spiritual partner/ female medium
phyag brnyan	*parivāra*	servant
phyag mtshan	*hastacihna*	symbolic hand-held emblem
ba gam	*aṭṭāla*	pedestal
bung ba'i stabs		"fly" posture
bhin di pā la	*bhindipāla*	ritual dart
bho kang	*bhokang*	copper trumpet
byis pa	*bāla*	child [motif]

bris sku	*paṭa*	painting, painted icon
dbu rgyan	*mukuṭa/ kiroṭa*	crown [ornament]
'bar mdangs		fiery shading
'bur sku		sculpture, relief
sbrul	*sarpa/ uraga*	snake [ornament]
mi sdug pa	*bibhatsa*	ugliness, ugly demeanor
mi lpags kyi gYang gzhi		flayed human hide
me ris rigs gsum		three types of flames
smad sham	*antaravāsaka*	lower robe/ skirt
sman gyi lugs		Men[ri] Style [of painting]
tsog bu'i stabs	*utkuṭukāsana*	crouching posture
gtsug gtor	*uṣṇīsa*	crown-protuberance
gtsug lag khang	*vihāra*	great temple
btsag mdangs		granular shading
rtsa ba'i tshon		basic color(s) [including the primary colors]
tshangs skud	*brahmāsūtra*	thread of Brahmā
tshangs thig	*brahmāsūtra*	axial line of Brahmā, Brahmā line
tshi gu'i smad dkris		silken skirt [ornament]
tshon mdangs		color and shading
mtshan bzang so gnyis	*dvātriṃśanmahāpuruṣalakṣaṇa*	thirty-two major marks [of the buddha body]
mdzod spu	*ūrṇākeśa*	hair ringlet between the eyebrows
rdza rnga	*mṛdaṅga*	kettledrum
va gzhu		fox-skin bow
zhag	*narataila*	human fat
zhal dbyibs		facial physiognomy
zhal tshad	*mukha*	face-length [measurement]
zhi ba	*śānta*	[demeanor of] peace, peaceful demeanor
zhi ba rgyan med		peaceful iconographic form, without ornaments
bzhengs pa'i phyed skyil gar stabs	*ardhaparyaṅkāpratyālīḍha*	semi-dancing posture
zi ldir		patterned silken scarf [ornament]
gzugs	*rūpa*	form
bzo bo	*śilpin*	artist
bzo [rigs]/ bzo rig pa	*śilpa[vidyā]*	fine [and applied] art

bzang po'i stabs	*bhadrapada*	auspicious seated posture [of Maitreya]
'og pag	*mekhalā*	tassles of a girdle
yan lag gi tshon		intermediate/ secondary color(s)
yab	*pitṛ*	male consort, father
yi dam	*iṣṭadevatā*	meditational deity
yig mkhan		scribe, writer
yum	*matṛ*	female consort, mother
ye shes kyi me		fire of pristine cognition
ye shes sems dpa'	*jñānasattva*	being of pristine cognition [i.e., actual deity]
gYas brkyang	*ālīḍha*	extended right leg posture
gYas rol	*ardhaparyaṅkalalita*	right-sided posture of royal ease
gYon brkyang	*pratyālīḍha*	extended left leg posture
gYon rol	*rājalalita*	left-sided [posture] of royal ease
gYer kha	*kiṅkiṇī*	small tinkling bell
ra kta	*rakta*	[human] blood
rang sor	*aṅgulī*	relative "finger-width" [measurement]
ral gri	*khaḍga*	sword
rigs lnga	*pañcakula*	five enlightened families
rin po che'i rgyan brgyad		eight ornaments made of precious gemstones
rus pa'i 'khor lo	*asthicakra*	bone wheel [ornament]
rus sbal	*kūrmabandha*	"turtle" posture
rol pa'i khro bo	*lalitakrodha*	emanational wrathful deity
lan kan	*vedikā*	[throne] railing, balustrade
lus bzo		physical art(s), art(s) of the body
logs su brkyangs pa zlum po	*parimaṇḍala*	squatting posture
longs [spyod rdzogs pa'i] sku	*saṃbhogakāya*	buddha body of perfect resource
shang shang	*cīvaṃcīvaka*	bird-man [motif]
gshin rje khros pa	*yāmakrodha*	wrathful acolyte of Yama
bshal mdangs		lineal shading
sems dpa'i skyil krung	*sattvaparyaṅka*	relaxed posture of the bodhisattvas
sa ga'i stabs	*vaiśākhapada*	[nativity] posture of Vaiśākha

se mo do	*ardhahāra*	long necklace [ornament]
sor	*aṅgulī*	finger-width measurement
srin po	*rāksaṣa*	ogre
srung ma	*pāla*	protector deity
gsang khebs		silken undergarment
bse kha sgo	*śarabha*	eight-legged deer [motif]
bse khrab		rhino-hide armor [of wrathful deities]
he ru ka	*heruka*	heruka, wrathful male buddha
lha	*deva*	male deity
lha mo	*devī*	female deity
lha bzo	*devakarman*	artist, maker of icons

2. Maṇḍala Construction

ka rgyan	*stambhabhuṣaṇa*	column decoration
ka ba	*stambha*	column, pillar
dkyil 'khor	*maṇḍala*	maṇḍala
sku dkyil	*kāyamaṇḍala*	maṇḍala of buddha body
khang bzang	*prāsāda*	palatial mansion
khru	*śaya/ hasta*	cubit [measurement]
mkhar thab	*kaṃsa*	[rooftop] fortification
glang rgyab mig sum		bow-shaped "ox back" extrados
glo 'bur		projecting bay
rgyan	*bhuṣaṇa*	ornament
rgyal khab ri bo'i gur	*rājagṛhagiripañjara*	tented spire symbolizing Rājagṛha Peak
rgyu'i rta babs	*hetutoraṇa*	causal pediment
sgo	*dvāra*	gate, door, entrance
sgo khang	*niryūha*	gatehouse
sgo rgyan	*dvārabhuṣaṇa*	gateway ornament
sgo drug		six features of the gate
sgo phub		outer and inner ceilings
sgo tshad	*dvāra*	gate-width measure
sngags kyi sa bon	*mantrabīja*	mantra seed-syllable
tog	*ketu*	finial
rta rkang	*aśvapada*	hoofprint design on a supporting pediment beam
rta babs	*toraṇa*	tiered pediment, arched pediment

steng rgyan		upper ornament
thugs dkyil	*cittamaṇḍala*	maṇḍala of buddha mind
them skas	*sopāna*	tiers
thog phub	*channa*	roof
bdag po'i rgyan	*adhipatibhuṣaṇa*	ornament possessed by the lord [of the maṇḍala]
mda' yab	*kramaśīrṣa/ ovidyanakhā*	parapet
rdo rje'i rigs	*vajrakula*	vajra family [of deities]
snam bu	*paṭa*	[pedimental] band, step
sna tshogs rdo rje	*viśvavajra*	crossed-vajra
padma'i rigs	*padmakula*	lotus family [of deities]
dpag tshad	*yojana*	furlong
phyag rgya	*mudrā/ cihna*	symbolic emblem
bri cha		two-dimensional [maṇḍala drawing]
bris thig		outline drawing/ draftsmanship
blos bslang		three-dimensional [maṇḍala palace]
'bras bu'i rta babs	*phalatoraṇa*	fruitional pediment
mun pa	*andhakāra*	dark recess [of the gate]
mun pa pa ti	*munpapati*	bow-shaped keystone
rtsa thig	*mūlasūtra*	base line [of the maṇḍala]
rtse mo	*śikhara*	spire
tshad bcas [kyi dkyil 'khor]		maṇḍala with precise measurement
tshad ma nges pa'i dkyil 'khor		maṇḍala lacking precise measurement
tshon rtsi	*raṅga*	color pigment
gzhal yas khang	*vimāna*	celestial palace
bzhi ba	*caturtha*	quarter unit [measurement]
'og rgyan		lower ornament
rin chen gyi rigs	*ratnakula*	ratna family [of deities]
las kyi rigs	*karmakula*	karma family [of deities]
logs rgyan		side ornament
sangs rgyas kyi rigs	*buddhakula/ tathāgatakula*	buddha family [of deities]
gsung dkyil	*vākmaṇḍala*	maṇḍala of buddha speech

3. Calligraphy and Scripts

klu [yig]	*nāgalipi*	Nāga script
dkyus yig		common writing
bkra shis pa [yig]	*maṅgalyalipi*	Maṅgalya script
rkang pa		leg line, tail line
rkang pas bris [yig]	*pādalikhitalipi*	Pādalikhita script
ske gtsang		"neck" stroke
kha/ khams		[calligraphic] grid square
kha ro ṣṭi [yig]	*kharoṣṭhīlipi*	Kharoṣṭhī script
khog 'dren		"body" stroke
khog seng		hollow-bodied [Rañjanā] script
'khyug yig		cursive shorthand script
mkha' lding [yig]	*garuḍalipi*	Garuḍa script
ga bur	*karpūra*	camphor
gas chung		[nib] cleft
gong chags		[convex] "lip" stroke
gro ga	*bhūrjapatra*	birch bark
grangs [yig]	*saṃkhyālipi*	Saṃkhyā script
grung zags mchu		tapering "lip" stroke
grub bzhi		rectangular style of writing
gla rtsi	*kastūrikā*	musk
'gro lding [yig]	*drāviḍalipi*	Drāviḍa script
rgya skyegs	*alakta*	shellac
rgya nag [yig]	*cīnalipi*	Chinese script
rgya spyin		Chinese glue
rgya smyug		Chinese bamboo pen
rgya tshva		salt ammoniac
rgya mtsho [yig]	*sāgaralipi*	Sāgara script
rgyab lag		extended backhand stroke [in Rañjanā]
rgyal gyi yig	*puṣpalipi*	Puṣpa script
rgyal mo ka ra	*śarkarā*	sugar
sgra kun bsdus pa [yig]	*sarvarūtasaṃgrahaṇīlipi*	Sarvarūtasaṃgrahaṇī script
lcags smyug		metal-nib pen
cha	*kalā*	unit [of measurement]
cha tshad		calligraphic proportion
chung min [yig]	*anudrutalipi*	Anudruta script

'jang smyug		Naxi bamboo pen
'jam pa zlum bris		gentle rounded script
rjes mthun [yig]	*anulomalipi*	Anuloma script
mnyen gra ris		finely executed script
mnyen pa sug skor		finely rounded tailed script
snying po thams cad kun tu bsdus pa [yig]	*saravasārasaṃgrahaṇīlipi*	Saravasārasaṃgrahaṇī script
gter yig	*nidhilipi*	*terma* script [used in transcribing revealed teachings]
lto 'phye chen po [yig]	*mahoragalipi*	Mahoraga script
stod phub can		upper "shield"-like curve
thang khrag/ tshil	*sarala*	pine resin
thal khu		ashy solution
thig tshad		grid
thig shing		measuring ruler
mthar rgyas		thick-ended stroke
dha ri ka'i yig rigs	*dharikalipi*	Dharika script
dha ri ḍa [yig]		Darada script
drag po [yig]	*ugralipi*	Ugra script
drang srong dka' thub gdungs [yig]	*ṛṣitapastaptālipi*	Ṛṣitapastaptā script
dri za [yig]	*gandharvalipi*	Gandharva script
bdar rdo		whetstone
bde ba phrin yig dkyus ma		easy and common letter-writing script
'degs [yig]	*utkṣepalipi*	Utkṣepa script
'degs skor [yig]	*utkṣepāvartalipi*	Utkṣepāvarta script
brda' yig	*ḍākinīlipi*	symbolic script [of the ḍākinīs]
rdo rje [yig]	*vajralipi*	Vajra script
sde dpon		administrator
na ga ra la [yig] rigs	*nāgarīlipi*	Nāgarī script
nam mkha' blta ba [yig]	*gaganaprekṣiṇīlipi*	Gaganaprekṣiṇī script
nub [gling yig]	*aparagoḍānīlipi*	Aparagoḍānī script
gnod sbyin [yig]	*yakṣalipi*	Yakṣa script
rnam gzhag [yig]	*vikṣepalipi*	Vikṣepa script
snag		black ink
snag sna		ink-edge stroke
snag lam		ink stroke
snag lam zlum		curved line

bsnol mtshams		"waist"/ intersecting stroke
padma'i snying po [yig]	*puṣkarasārinlipi*	Puṣkarasārin script
dpung thung		short "shoulder "stroke
spos dkar thal	*śāla*	*Shorea robusta* (sal) ash
spyi bzhur		saussurea
spyi'u tshugs [yig]	*avamūrdhalipi*	Avamūrdha script
phyi nang thig skor		outer and inner margin line(s)
phyi ma bcu grub [yig]	*yāvaddaśottarapadasaṃdhilipi*	Yāvaddaśottarapadasaṃdhi script
phyi ma'i tshig gnyis grub [yig]	*dviruttarapadasaṃdhilipi*	Dviruttarapadasaṃdhi script
'phrin dang rab tu 'phrin [yig]	*lekhapratilekhalipi*	Lekhapratilekha script
'phrin yig		letter-writing script
ba ṅga [yig]	*vaṅgalipi*	Vaṅga script
bar snang lha [yig]	*antarīkṣadevalipi*	Antarīkṣadeva script
bar ma sgrub pa [yig]	*madhyāhāriṇīlipi*	Madhyāhāriṇī script
bar shun		inner bark
bya rdo		alkaline pebble
bya rog skad [yig]	*vāyasarūtalipi*	Vāyasarūta script
byang [gling yig]	*uttarakurūdvīpalipi*	Uttarakurūdvīpa script
byang chub rgyun lam		horizontal calligraphic line
bris thig		calligraphic measurement
bru thabs		stove for roasting grain
dhang lag		orchid
dbu can		headed script, capital letter script
dbur gdan		ironing board [for pressing paper]
dbur rdo		ironing stone [for pressing paper]
dbus dang rgyas par bri ba'i yi ge	*madhyākṣaravistaralipi*	Madhyākṣaravistara script
'ba' ho		Baho script
'byung po thams cad kyi sgra sdud pa [yig]	*sarvabhūtarūtaprahaṇīlipi*	Sarvabhūtarūtaprahaṇī script
'bri thabs		calligraphic technique
'bri gzhi		writing surface
'bru khog		body of a letter
'bru chung		headless thin-stroked italic script
'bru chen		headless thick-stroked italic script

sbo		"abdominal" stroke
ma kko la [yig]	*markkolalipi*	Markkola script
ma ga dhā [yig]	*magadhālipi*	Magadhā script
ma nu ru tha	*manurutha*	*Inula helenium*, elecampane
man ngag	*upadeśa*	[calligraphic] instructions
mar 'then		downward stroke
mar nag		lampblack soot
mig		"eye" stroke
mi'am ci [yig]	*kinnaralipi*	Kinnara script
mon yul [yig]	*kirātalipi*	Kirāta script
smad phub can		lower "shield-like" curve
sman rgyu mthun [yig]	*sarvauṣadhiniṣyandālipi*	Sarvauṣadhiniṣyandā script
smyu gu		bamboo pen
smyug rtse		pen tip
smyug rdzing		nib
smyug yur		[nib] vent hole
rtsis [yig]	*gaṇanāvartalipi*	Gaṇanāvarta script
rtsub mo [yig]	*pāruṣyalipi*	Pāruṣya script
brtsigs thabs 'khor mo		circular hearth
tshangs pa [yig]	*brāhmīlipi*	Brāhmī script
tshva la		borax
tsheg bris		punctuated script
mtshal	*hiṅguli*	vermilion
rdzing mchu		nib-point
va rtu la [yig]	*vartulalipi*	Vartula script
gzhag pa bskor ba [yig]	*nikṣepāvartalipi*	Nikṣepāvarta script
bzhag [yig]	*nikṣepalipi*	Nikṣepa script
zangs gling [yig]	*tāmaraliptilipi*	Tāmaralipti script
zur thig		corner grid-line
gzab chen		headed block-letter script
gzab chung		headless block-letter script
gzab ma		block-letter script
gzi		banded chalcedony
bzang mgo		"head" stroke
yan lag		"extended" stroke
yar phul/ yar 'then		upright stroke
yig gsar		new script(s)
rab tu bzhag [yig]	*prakṣepalipi*	Prakṣepa script

ri dvags 'khor lo [yig]	*mṛgacakralipi*	Mṛgacakra script
rigs mthun rnam bsres [yig]	*vidyānulomāvimiśritālipi*	Vidyānulomāvimiśritā script
ring cha		long tail stroke
rong smyug		"ravine" pen
shar gling [yig]	*pūrvavidehalipi*	Pūrvavideha script
shog ldum dung lo ma		*Stellera chamaejasme* with conch-shaped leaves
shog bre		paper-making tray
bshur ma		[formal] handwriting script
sa rab lta [yig]	*dharaṇīprekṣiṇīlipi*	Dharaṇīprekṣiṇī script
sa'i lha [yig]	*bhaumadevalipi*	Bhaumadeva script
sv ā dhya ni [yig]	*svāddhyarilipi*	Svāddhyari script
si ndhu [yig]	*sindhulipi*	Sindhu script
sug thung		short-tailed script
sug pa/ lug sug		campion
sug po		tailed script
sor gdub [yig]	*aṅgulīyalipi*	Aṅgulīya script
srin po'i yig ge	*rākṣasalipi*	Rākṣasa script
gsal ba [yig]	*rocamānālipi*	Rocamānā script
gsung rten		representation of buddha speech
hu na [yig]	*hūṇalipi*	Hūṇa script
lha [yig]	*devalipi*	Deva script
lha min [yig]	*asuralipi*	Asura script
lho phyogs [yig]	*dākṣiṇyalipi*	Dākṣiṇya script
lho smyug		"southern" pen
a gar u		*Daphne anrantica*
a ṅga [yig]	*aṅgalipi*	Aṅga script
a hu [yig]	*brahmavallīlipi*	Brahmavallī script
a ru ra	*harītakī*	myrobalan

4. Stūpa Construction

bkra shis 'byung ba'i mchod rten		stūpa of auspicious origin
sku gdung chen po	*mahādhātu/ śarīra*	supreme bone relics [of the Buddhas]
'khor lo [bcu gsum]	*trayodaśacakrāvalī*	[thirteen] rings/ wheels [forming the spire]
glo 'bur		projecting bay

dge bcu rmang	*nemīmūla*	"tenfold virtuous foundation" slab
dge gnas brgyad kyi mchod rten		stūpas of the eight virtuous abodes
rgyal mtshan	*dvaja*	victory banner
sgo mang		[stūpa with] multiple gates
cod pan	*mukuṭa*	crown
char khebs	*varṣasthālī*	rain gutter
cho 'phrul mchod rten	*pratihāryastūpa*	stūpa of miracles
chos sku'i mchod rten	*dharmakāyastūpa*	offering receptacle of the buddha body of reality
chos 'khor mchod rten	*dharmacakrastūpa*	stūpa of the wheel of the sacred teachings
chos 'khor	*dharmacakra*	[stacked] rings [of the spire], symbolizing the sacred teachings
mchod rten	*stūpa*	stūpa
nyi ma	*sūrya*	solar disc
tog	*ketu*	[gemstone] crest
thig tshad		measurement grid
thugs rje mdo gzungs zhu gya gram		cross-beam containing sūtras and retentive mantras of great compassion
thugs rten		representation of buddha mind
them skas	*sopāna*	steps/ ladder
gdan khri	*nemī*	podium
gdan gyi sa 'dzin	*nemīmūla*	podium base (see also *dge bcu rmang*)
gdugs	*catrāvalī*	umbrella veil/ parasol
[gdugs] 'degs [padma]	*padmamūla*	[lotus] support of the umbrella spire
bde gshegs mchod rten	*sugatastūpa*	stūpa of the sugatas
rdo ring		long stone slab [of the base]
rdor gdan	*vajrāsana*	vajra seat
nor bu tog	*maṇiketu*	gemstone crest
rnam rgyal mchod rten	*vijayastūpa*	stūpa of victory
pa dma	*padma*	lotus
pha gu		cornice
pho 'khor		ring [of the spire] with projecting "male" rim
ba dan	*patāka*	streamer

bang rim	*vedī*	tier(s) [of the stūpa podium]
bang rim khri 'phang can		exalted tiered throne
bad chung		small capping slab
bad chen/ ba ga	*jagatī*	large capping slab
bad gzungs		frieze of retentive mantras [on the podium]
bum sku		image [within the niche of] the dome
bum rten		see *bum gdan*
bum gdan	*kaṇṭhaka*	dome plinth [slab]
bum ldir		bulging dome
bum pa	*kumbha*	dome
'bur		projecting buttress
'bre	*harmikā/ droṇa*	high pavilion
'bre gdan		high pavilion plinth
byang chub chen po'i mchod rten	*mahābodhistūpa*	stūpa of supreme enlightenment
byams dngos mchod rten		stūpa of manifest loving-kindness
byin rlabs mchod rten	*adhiṣṭhānastūpa*	stūpa of blessings
dbyen bzlums mchod rten	*bhedasaṃvṛtastūpa*	stūpa of resolving schism
mu stegs pham byed kyi mchod rten		stūpa of defeating extremists
mo 'khor		ring [of the spire] with truncated "female" rim
myang 'das mchod rten	*nirvāṇastūpa*	stūpa of nirvāṇa
rmang dge ba	*nemīmūla*	"virtuous foundation" slab
tshangs dbyangs	*brahmaghoṣa*	voice of Brahmā
zla phyed	*ardhacandra*	crescent moon [motif]
gzungs sa		[decorative] frieze of retentive mantras
'od zer can gyi mchod rten		stūpa of solar rays
ye shes kyi mchod rten	*jñānastūpa*	stūpa of pristine cognition
gYung drung tog	*svāstikaketu*	*svāstika* crest
ri rab bum pa	*sumerukumbha*	dome [symbolic] of Mount Sumeru
ring bsrel	*śarīra[dhātu]*	small bone relic
sum cu rtsa gsum lha'i mchod rten	*trayatriṃśastūpa*	stūpa of the thirty-three gods
seng khri	*nemī*	"lion throne" podium
srog shing	*yaṣṭi/ yūpa*	life-supporting pole/ axis

gser phye		gold leaf
lha babs mchod rten	*devāvatārastūpa*	stūpa of the divine descent

5. Sacred Music and Dance

bskur brlab		consecratory blessing
khrag 'thung rtsa 'chams		basic sacred [masked] dance of the herukas
'khril chags		elegant demeanor [of the dance]
gar gyi nyams dgu	*navanāṭyarasa*	nine [dramatic] demeanors of the dance
gar 'chams		sacred masked dance
gar 'chams stangs stabs		choreography of sacred masked dances
dgra bgegs brub 'chams		exorcist dance of the hostile and obstructive spirits
bgegs	*vighna*	obstructive force/ spirit
'gying chags		handsome demeanor [of the dance]
rnga		drum
rnga thabs		drumming technique
rnga gYog		drumstick
sngon 'gro'i stangs stabs bcu gnyis		twelve preliminary choreographic movements
chas gos		[dance] costume
chos dbyings	*dharmodaya*	[dance movement symbolizing] the source of reality
mchod [pa'i] gar		sacred offering dance
'jab		decrescendo [of cymbals]
rten bskyed bdun		seven visualizations of the receptacles [supporting a maṇḍala]
stangs stabs	*pada*	[sacred] dance step
dal chags	*manda*	slow demeanor [of the dance]
drag po'i las sbyor	*raudrakarma*	wrathful rite [of sorcery]
bde chags		happy demeanor [of the dance]
rdo rje'i zlos gar	*vajranāṭya*	indestructible sacred dance
ldem chags		supple demeanor [of the dance]

dpa' zhing brjid chags pa		heroic and magnificent demeanor [of the dance]
pho sgra		low sound [of percussion]
phyag rgya	*mudrā*	seal [of reality]
phyag rgya la mkhas pa gsum		three masteries of the seals
phyag mtshan	*hastacihna*	hand emblem
phyed ma		neutral sound [of percussion]
'phar		rebounding [of cymbals]
'phrul chags		dexterous demeanor [of the dance]
'brub 'chams		sacred [masked] dance of exorcism
sbub chol		big-boss cymbals
mer chags		fiery red demeanor [of the dance]
mo sgra		high sound [of percussion]
gtso bo dpal chen po'i 'gying 'chams		graceful dance of the central Mahāsrī [Heruka]
tshes bcu'i gar 'chams		sacred dance of the tenth-day ceremony
rol mo	*vādya*	cymbals, musical instruments
lus 'gyur thun mong du gces pa'i yan lag bcu		ten commonly esteemed aspects of physical movement
lus rgyan dpe gsum		three similes of bodily ornaments
sa gar		preparatory dance
sa bzung ba'i stangs stabs	*bhūgrahaṇapada*	choreographic rites for preparing the [dance] arena
sil snyan		small-boss cymbals
seng chags		[dancing] demeanor of a lion
gser khyems		oblation [to the protector deities]
lhod chag		relaxed demeanor [of the dance]

6. Physical Applied Arts

rkyal brgal ba	*plavita*	swimming
gar mkhan	*nartaka*	dancer
gur gyi 'phrul 'khor		tented [siege] catapult
gom stabs	*padabandha*	deportment
gyad kyi 'dzin stangs	*sālambha*	wrestling

gyad stobs	*vikramabala*	trial of strength
gri gug gi 'phrul 'khor		catapult of curved knives
gru'i 'phrul 'khor		naval cannon
glang po che'i gnyar zhon pa	*hastigrīvā*	elephant-riding
rgyang nas 'phog pa	*dūravedha*	striking from afar [in combat]
rgyal rigs 'thab pa shing rta		war chariot for the ruling classes
sgyogs		artillery
bcad pa	*chedya*	cutting [in combat]
lcags kyus bsgyur thabs	*aṅkuśagraha*	elephant goading
lcags mda'i 'phrul 'khor		catapult of metal barbs or arrows
mchongs pa	*laṅghita*	jumping
rta la zhon pa	*aśvapṛṣṭha*	horse-riding
thor tshugs	*śikhābandha*	hair-binding
dral ba	*bhedya*	breaking [in combat]
mda'	*bāṇa*	archery
mda' bo che 'phen pa	*tomaragraha*	javelin-throwing
mdun du bsnur ba	*upayāṇa*	advancing [in combat]
rdo'i 'phrul 'khor		stone-catapult
gnad du 'phog pa	*marmavedha*	vital assault [in combat]
phyir bsnur ba	*apayāna*	retreating [in combat]
'phongs	*dhanurveda*	archery
'phrul 'khor	*yantra*	turbine/ machine
bang	*javita/ dhāvana*	running
bro	*nāṭya*	dance
dbug pa	*dālana*	poisoning
mi tshor bar 'hog pa	*avedanīyavedha/ akṣuṇṇavedha*	stealthy assault [in combat]
me'i 'phrul 'khor		catapult of [greek] fire
tshabs che bar 'phog pa	*dṛḍhaprahāritā*	hard assault [in combat]
zhags pa gdab pa	*pāśagraha*	lassoing, snaring
gzhu	*dhanuḥ*	bow
gYos sbyor		cuisine, cooking
ral gri'i thabs	*khaḍgika/ sarau*	swordsmanship
ral gri'i 'phrul 'khor		catapult of swords or lances
lag rtsis	*mudrā*	gesture, divination of gestures
lus kyi bzo phal pa		common physical arts
rlung gi 'phrul 'khor		catapult of wind
shing rta'i thabs	*ratha*	charioteering

7. Vocal and Instrumental Applied Arts

ka na ḍi	*kanaḍi*	chime [percussion]
bkug pa	*avarohī*	descending melodic contour, flat [tone/ note]
rkyang pa		single beat
skyon drug		six defects [in chanting]
kha gshags		repartee between the sexes
khug		undulation
mkhar lnga	*paṇava*	gong
mkhar ba'i sil khrol	*sampa*	bell-metal cymbals
'khar rnga	*paṇava*	small cymbal
'khor nyan	*niṣāda*	[elephant-like] base tone
grim [pa]		tense [vocal pitch]
gling bu	*veṇu*	flute
glu dbyangs kyi nges pa bdun	*saptasvara*	seven harmonious tones of the musical scale
glu len pa		singer
gral 'phros		formal speech
mgrin bsgyur		guttural variation [in tone]
rgyu lnga		five causes [in chanting]
rgyud mangs/ pi vang	*vīṇā*	multi-string lute
sgra grags par 'phog pa	*śabdavedha*	verbal assault [in combat]
bsgyur ba	*sañcārī*	changing melodic contour
bsgreng ba		sharp [tone/ note]
ngag bzo		art(s) of speech
ngag bzo phal pa		common arts of speech
nga ro	*svara*	melodic contour
nga ro rnam pa bzhi		four [primary] aspects of melodic contour
rnga bo che	*bherī*	kettledrum
rnga phran		tambour
rnga chen po	*dundubhi*	large kettledrum
rnga mu kunda	*mukunda*	mukunda drum
rnga zlum	*mṛdaṅga*	round drum
lnga pa	*pañcama*	[cuckoo-like] fifth tone
gcod [pa]		decisive [vocal pitch]
lcags kyi sil khrol	*illarī*	metal bell
lce bsgyur		lingual variation [in tone]

chen po drug		six great [ceremonial] contexts
'chad pa		teaching
'jog [pa]		pausing [vocal pitch]
rjes su brjod pa	*anuvāda/ anubhāṣita*	recapitulation
nyis 'gyur		repetition
snyan [pa]		sweet [vocal pitch]
ltengs pa	*ārohī*	ascending melodic contour
rtogs brjod	*avadāna*	narrative
bstod pa		high [note/ tone]
dung	*śaṅkha*	conch
dus kyi gnad		essential of tempo
drang srong ba	*ṛṣabha*	[ox-like] sage tone
drug ldan	*ṣaḍja*	[peacock-like] sixth tone
'dren pa	*sthāyī*	sustaining melodic contour
drang po		level/ neutral [note/ tone]
gdangs	*ghoṣa*	melodic chant
'degs [pa]		rising [vocal pitch]
ldem [pa]		pliant [vocal pitch]
nor gyi gtam		tales of yaks or wealth
sna ldan bsgyur		nasal variation [in tone]
spobs pa'i gnad		essential of courage/ brilliance
pi vang	*vīṇā*	lute
pi vang rgyud gcig pa	*tuṇava*	single-string lute
pi vang rgyud gsum pa	*ballarī*	three-string lute
pheg rdob	*tālāvacara*	musical tempo
phra [ba]		high [vocal pitch]
bar ma	*madhyama*	[crane-like] middle tone
blo gsal	*dhaivata*	[horse-like] clear tone
'bel gtam		informal discursive talk
sbom [pa]		deep [vocal pitch]
sbyangs pa'i gnad		essential of refinement
sbrel [ba]		connective [vocal pitch]
smad pa		low [note/ tone]
rtsod pa	*vāda/ vigraha*	debate
rtsom pa		composition
brtsegs pa		multiple beats
rdza rnga	*mṛdaṅga*	clay drum

rdza rnga kha gcig pa	*ekamukhamṛdaṅga*	one-sided clay drum
rol mo	*gandharva*	music
rol mo'i sgra	*vādyaśabda*	instrumentation
rol mo'i bye brag bco brgyad	*aṣṭadaśavādyaviśeṣa*	eighteen requisites of musical performance
sa 'dzin	*gandhāra*	[goat-like] third tone
sil snyan glu dbyangs dang bstun pa	*gītopakṣipyatūrya*	harmony of percussion and singing
gsang [ba]		covert [vocal pitch]
lhan skyes rol mo		innate/ natural musical sound
lhod du 'gyur [ba]		relaxed and variable [vocal pitch]

8. Mentally Applied Arts

kun nas bsrung ba drug		six things to be well guarded
bka'i dngos po dgu		nine themes of [the Buddha's] transmitted teachings
skar ma'i dpyad	*jyotiṣa*	astronomy
skye ba rnam bzhi	*catvāro yonayaḥ*	four modes of birth
mkhas pa drug		six kinds of knowledge
'khor gyi dngos po brgyad		eight themes of cyclic existence
'khrig thabs	*vaiśika/ maithuna*	love-making
gar gyi cha byad dgu	*navanāṭyarasa*	nine dramatic demeanors/ moods
grangs	*gaṇana*	arithmetic
grangs can	*sāṃkhyā*	arithmetic
glang po brtag pa		scrutiny of elephants
rgyags pa rnam pa bdun		seven kinds of self-satisfaction
sgeg pa	*śṛṅgāra*	grace
sgyu rtsal drug cu rtsa bzhi	*catuḥṣaṣṭikalā*	sixty-four crafts
sgra	*śabda*	grammar
nga rgyal bdun		seven kinds of pride
dngos po bcu bdun		seventeen material objectives
rngam pa	*adbhūta*	awesomeness
sngon gyi rabs	*purāṇa*	antiquity
sngon byung ba	*itihāsaka*	history
chu brtag pa		scrutiny of water
chos kyi sde		category of religion
chos lugs	*nīti*	behavior

'jig rten spyod bcu		ten mundane pastimes
'jigs rung	*bhayānaka*	fearsomeness
'jug pa bzhi		four ways of entering [the womb]
rjes su spyod pa brgyad		eight pursuits of daily life
ljong shing brtag pa		scrutiny of trees
nyes rtsom nyer gnyis		twenty-two kinds of misconduct
snying rje	*karuṇā*	compassion
gtan tshig	*hetu*	logic
gtam rnam pa gsum		three kinds of discourse
gter brtag pa		scrutiny of underground treasures
rta brtag pa		scrutiny of horses
brtag pa brgyad		eight objects of scrutiny
tha snyad mang po'i gzhi		manifold bases of conventional expressions
tha snyad bzhi		four kinds of conventional expression
thar pa'i sde		category of liberation
thod pa	*kapāla*	cranium, skull, skull-cup
thod pa'i brtag pa		scrutiny of skulls
thos pa	*śruti*	study
dus brgyad		eight phases of the life-cycle
dus bcu		ten measures of time
drag shul	*raudra*	ferocity
dran pa	*smṛti*	recollection
'dod pa'i sde		category of desire
nang gi lhun bzed		inner begging bowl [i.e., the skull]
nor ram don gyi sde		category of wealth or objects
rnal 'byor	*yoga*	union, yoga
dpa' ba	*vīra*	heroism
pho mo brtag pa		scrutiny of men and women
bud med brtag pa bcas brgyad		eightfold scrutiny of women
mi sdug pa	*bibhatsa*	ugliness
mi dpyad thor bu		miscellaneous analyses of human nature
mig 'phrul 'khor	*māyā*	optical illusion
gtsug lag gnyis		two aspects of science [verbal expression and meaningful content]

'tsho tshis	*vārtā*	sustenance
'tsho ba drug		six [acceptable] modes of livelihood
rtsis	*gaṇita*	astrology
rtsis chen	*saṃkhya*	astrology
zhi ba	*śānta*	peace
gzhi drug		six grounds
bzhad gad	*hāsya*	joviality
bzo btags pa sum cu/ bzo la sogs par gtogs pa sum cu	*triṃśatiśilpavidyākalā*	thirty designated arts
yi ge	*lipi*	writing
yid bzo		art(s) of the mind
yid bzo phal pa		common art(s) of mind
yo byad bcu bzhi		fourteen useful devices
rin po che brtag pa	*ratnaparīkṣā*	scrutiny of gems and precious metals
lugs kyi bstan bcos	*nītiśāstra*	treatise on [human] behavior
sa gzhi brtag pa	*bhūmiparīkṣā*	scrutiny of land
sems can rigs		[sixty-three] categories of sentient being

Medicine

kun brtags gdon		imaginary diseases associated with demonic possession
dkar dmar rnam shes gsum		white and red generative fluids, along with consciousness
rkang	*majja*	marrow tissue
rkyang pa		single isolated humor, isolated [or independent] humoral disease
rkyang pa drug		six [basic or] isolated tastes
rkyen	*pratyaya*	secondary cause/ condition [of disease]
rkyen bzhi		four secondary conditions [of disease]
skam pa		forceps
skam pa rigs drug		six kinds of forceps
skom gsum		three types of beverage
skyugs		emetic
skye mched	*āyatana*	sensory activity field(s)

bsku mnye		massage
kha ṇḍa	*khaṇḍa*	medicinal concentrate
khab mdo		"needle-headed" probe [for the exploration of cranial fractures]
khu ba	*śukra*	reproductive fluid, broth
khu ba gsum		three types of broth
khrag	*rakta*	blood
khyad par gyi gso tshul dgu		nine special therapeutic principles
khyab byed	*vyāna*	pervasive wind [associated with metabolism and muscular movement]
mkhris pa	*pitta*	bile, bile disorder
mkhris pa lnga	*pañcapitta*	five types of bile
mkhris pa bshal		purgatives for bile disorders
'khrugs pa		state of [mutual] aggravation
gyen rgyu	*udāna*	ascending wind [associated with the vocal cords]
grang ba		cold, disease with a cold nature
rgas pa gso ba'i thabs bcud len		elixir of rejuvenation in the treatment of old age
rgyu	*hetu*	primary cause [of disease]
rgyu lam		pathway(s) [affected by pathogenic humors]
rgyun du spyod pa		continuous [daily] regimen
sgrub byed	*sādhaka*	energizing bile
ngan gYo skyon te thabs kyi sgo nas brtag pa		diagnosis by means of subterfuge
ngos 'dzin rtags		diagnosis
ngos bzung rtags		diagnostics
dngos su brtag pa		actual/ genuine diagnosis
rngabs ra		cupping horn
rngul ba		perspiration
rngul dbyung ba		induced perspiration
sngo sbyor		herbal compound
sngon gyi las		actions of past [lives]
sngon 'gro snum 'chos		preliminary oil therapy
gci ba	*prasrāva*	urine
gce'u		cannula
gcod pa		excision

bcud len		elixir of rejuvenation
bcos thabs		curative method, therapy
cha byad		surgical instrument
cha byad phran bu		minor [surgical] instrument
chags pa'i rtsa		channel of embryonic formation
chags pa'i tshul rtogs		human embryology
chu rgyu		tendons and ligaments
chu'i 'phrul 'khor		fomentation
'jam pa'i dpyad		mild therapy
'jam rtsi		mild enema
'jig pa'i ltas		sign(s) of decay
'jug sgo		area of inception [of disease]
'ju byed	*pācaka*	digestive bile
nyes pa gsum	*tridoṣa*	three humors
nyams dmad pa		catabolic procedure
gnyan pa gnad kyi gnas lugs		natural condition of the vulnerable points
gnyen po bcu		ten types of remedy
snyigs		residual impurity
tre sam		*tre-sam* powder
tre sam lnga		five types of *tre-sam* powder
gtar [ga]		bloodletting
stod		upper part [of the body]
rten gnas		predominant location [of the humors]
rten byed	*avalambaka*	supporting [phlegm]
lta ba		visual observation [of symptoms]
ltar snang 'phral		ostensible disease(s) that suddenly occur
lte 'khor		navel
lto ba		digestion, abdomen
brta ba		anabolic procedure
brtag thabs		diagnostics
thang		decoction
thang bzhi		four types of decoction
thal sman		medicinal ash
thur ma		surgical stylet, minor surgery
thur ma dgu		nine kinds of surgical stylets

thur sel	*apāna*	descending purgative wind
mthong ba chu la brtag pa		urinalysis through visual observation
mthong byed	*ālocaka*	vision-producing bile
mdog gsal	*bhrājaka*	complexion-clearing bile
mdor dril		summary [of diseases]
dvangs [ma]		chyle
dug		poisoning
dug gsum		three poisons
dugs		[medicinal] compress
dus		time
dus spyod		seasonal regimen
dus gsum		three seasons
don		solid viscera
drag po'i dpyad		rigorous therapy
dri ba		inquiry
dri ma		impurity
gdon		demonic possession
mdangs sgyur	*rañjaka*	color-transforming bile [associated with chyle]
'dral ba		incision
'drud pa		scraping
ldang dus		[predominant] rising occasion [of the humors]
ldang tshad		exact measurement [of the three humors]
ldan 'dres pa		dependent humor in association with others
lde gu		[medicinal] paste
ldog rgyu		contrary [humoral imbalance]
bsdam par bya ba		dietary restriction
gnas skabs kyi spyod pa		occasional regimen
na so gsum		three phases of life
nad		disease
nad 'jug tshul		inception of disease
nad med gnas shing 'tsho ba		prophylactics
nad med ring du gnas pa		prevention of disease
nad gzhi		pathology
nad gso byed gnyen po		remedy
ni ru ha		strong enema

nus pa		potency [of medications]
gnas lugs		physiology
rnam par ma gyur pa lus		unmodified physiology
rnam par gyur pa nad		pathological transformation
rnam gyur gso ba'i thabs		treatment of pathological transformations
sna sman		nasal medication, snuff
snod		hollow viscera
pags		skin
dpyad [pa]		external therapy
spang bar bya ba['i nad]		incurable disease
spyi'i gso tshul		general therapeutic principle
spyod [lam]		regimen, activity, lifestyle
'phel		excess
phye ma		medicinal powder
bad kan	*kapha*	phlegm, phlegm disorder
bad kan skyugs		emetic for phlegm disorders
bad kan lnga	*pañcakapha*	five types of phlegm
bu ga'i gnas lugs		natural condition of the [inner] passageways and [external] orifices
bu snod kyi rtsa		umbilical cord
bud med btsa' srung gi thabs		treatment of infertility
bum pa		fire-cupping bowl
byis pa ['i nad]		pediatrics
byugs pa		massage with ointment
bye brag gi gso tshul		specific therapeutic principle
bye'u sgro 'dra		lancet shaped like a sparrow's feather
dbang po		sense organ(s)
dbug pa		minor surgery
dbugs 'dren		releasing [fluids or] vapors
'byin pa		extraction
'byor byed	*śleṣaka*	adhesive phlegm
'bras bu		result [which bring fatality]
'brel pa rtsa'i gnas lugs		natural condition of the interconnecting channels
'brel pa'i rtsa		channel(s) of connection
sbubs thur smyu gu		stylet shaped like a reed nib
sbyong byed		cathartic procedure

sbyong byed dngos gzhi las lnga		five main cathartics
sbyor ba'i sman		compounded medication
ma zhu ba		indigestion
ma zhur bcas pa		dysfunction associated with indigestion
mar		medicinal butter
mi chos		[basic] human values
me mnyam	*samāna*	fire-accompanying wind [associated with digestion]
me drod		metabolism
me btsa'		moxibustion
mo nad		gynecological disease
mya ngan med pa'i ljon shing	*aśoka*	Aśoka tree, *Jonesia asoka* Roxb.
myag byed	*kledaka*	decomposing phlegm
myong byed	*bodhaka*	gustatory phlegm
dman lhag log pa		deficient, excessive, or counter-indicative
smad		lower part of the body
sman		medication
sman chang		medicinal wine
sman pa	*cikitsaka*	physician
sman mar		medicinal butter
sman mar lnga		five types of medicinal butter
smyung ba		catabolic procedure
tsur nis		powder
gtsag bu		lancet
btsag dbugs		puncture
btsa'		parturition
rtsa		nerve, blood vessel, [energy] channel
rtsa dkar		nerve
rtsa sbyong		channel cleansing
rtsub pa'i dpyad		rough therapy
tsha ba		fever, disease with hot nature
tshe gnas pa'i rtsa		course of the life span principle
tshim byed	*tarpaka*	sensory stimulating phlegm
tshil		adipose tissue, fat
tsho che		obesity
'tsho ba zas		dietetics
'tsho ba gsum zad pa		exhaustion of the three factors that sustain life

mtshon		wound, injury, trauma
zhi byed		tranquilizing agent/ procedure
zhi byed sde tshan brgyad		eight classes of tranquilizing agents
zhu rjes		post-digestive taste
zhu rjes gsum		three kinds of post-digestive taste
gzhan dbang sngon las kyi nad		dependent disease(s) of past actions
gzhan dbang can		dependent [or combined humoral disease]
zad		deficiency
zas		diet
zas kyi rgyu lam		digestive tract
zas tshod ran par bza'		moderation in diet
zas gsum		three types of food
zug rngu brtag pa'i dpyad bcu bzhi		fourteen sorts of probes
zungs zad		under-nourishment, deficiency of the bodily constituents
yul gsum		three kinds of environment
yongs grub tshe		absolute diseases which harm the life span
yon tan bcu bdun		seventeen attributes [of medications]
rang bzhin		natural human constitution
rin po che'i sbyor ba		gemstone and precious metal compound
ril bu		[medicinal] pill(s)
rus		bone, bone tissue
reg pa [rtsa]		pulse palpation
ro		taste [of medications]
ro bsdebs sbyor ba lnga bcu rtsa bdun		fifty-seven compounded tastes
ro tsa		restoration of virility
rlung	*vāta*	wind, wind disorder
rlung lnga	*pañcavāta*	five types of wind
rlung 'jam rtsi		mild enemata for wind disorders
lag len bco brgyad		eighteen practical methods of treatment
lung ma bstan		non-specific [in terms of virtue and non-virtue]

lums		fomentation
lus		physical body
lus gnas kyi nyams shes		human anatomy
lus zungs		bodily constituents
lus zungs kyi gnas lugs		natural condition of the bodily constituents
sha		muscle tissue, flesh
bshang		feces
bshal		purgative, laxative
sad mda'		clinical test
seng ge kha		lion-mouthed forceps
srid pa'i rtsa		channel(s) of existence
sreg [pa]		moxibustion
srog		vitality
srog 'dzin	*prāṇa*	life-sustaining breath
slong rkyen		activating or secondary causes
slong ba		[fully manifest] arising [of diseases]
gso dka' ba		disease difficult to cure
gso mkhan		physician
gso dpyad	*cikitsā*	medicine
gso ba rig pa	*cikitsāvidyā*	medicine
gso [ba'i] thabs		method of treatment
gso ba'i tshul		see *gso tshul*
gso bya'i yul		patient
gso byed [kyi] thabs		method of treatment
gso byed kyi tshul		remedy
gso byed gnyen po		remedy
gso tshul		therapeutic principle
gso yul		physiology
gso yul gyi nad		patient
gso yul gyi yan lag brgyad		eight categories of patients
gso rung ba tsam		nominally curable disease
gso sla ba		easily curable disease
gsog rkyen		[covert] gathering and [overt] arising [of the three humors]
bsam pa dkar ba		virtuous/ positive outlook
bsreg pa		moxibustion
hor gyi me btsa'		Mongolian moxibustion

Astrology and Divination

karkaṭa'i khyim	*karkaṭa*	Cancer, the solar mansion
bkra shis	*śakhuni*	Śakhuni [*karaṇa* of "fixed" impact]
rkang 'dzin		[planetary] step index
skag	*aśleṣā*	Alpha Hydrae [constellation]
skar ma	*tārā*	star
skar gyi khyim	*rāśi*	solar mansion(s) of the constellation(s)
skar rtsis	*jyotiḥśāstra*	astrology
khyim	*rāśi*	solar mansion
khyim bcu gnyis	*dvādaśarāśi*	twelve solar mansions
khyim zhag		zodiacal/ sidereal day
khyim zla		lunar mansion
khrums smad	*uttarabhādrapada*	Gamma Pegasi and Alpha Andromedae [constellation]
khrums stod	*pūrvabhādrapada*	Alpha Pegasi [constellation]
'khyog 'gro	*vakra*	retrograde motion [of the planets]
'khyog 'gros nub		retrograde [planetary] motion in the third/ western quadrant
gab rtse		"hidden point of divination" chart
gab rtse bzhi		four "hidden points of divination"
go la/ khyim 'khor	*rāśicakra*	zodiac
go la'i 'gros gsum		three kinds of zodiacal epicycle
grub mtha'i zhib rtsis		textbook system of calculation
gre	*pūrvaphalguṇī*	Zosma [constellation]
gro zhun	*abhijit*	Vega [constellation]
glang	*vṛṣa*	Taurus [solar mansion]
mgo	*mṛgaśiras*	Lambda Orionis [constellation]
'gros bzhi		four phases of planetary motion
rgya rtsis		Chinese astrology
rgyal	*puṣyā*	Delta Cancri [constellation]
rgyu skar	*nakṣatra*	constellation
sgra gcan gdong mjug		head and tail of Rāhu
lnga bsdus/ yan lag lnga		five aspects [of astrological calculation]

gcod byed yid		intellect that analyses [the relationships of elements and sense objects]
chu stod	*pūrvāṣāḍhā*	Delta Sagittarii [constellation]
chu smad	*uttarāṣāḍhā*	Pelagus [constellation]
chu tshod	*ghaṭikā*	clepsydra [temporal] measure
chu srang	*pāṇīpala*	[twenty-four second] "interval" of time
mchu	*maghā*	Regulus
mjug ma	*puccha*	tail of Rāhu
nya khyim	*mīna*	Pisces solar mansion
nyi ma	*aditya/ sūrya*	Sun, Sunday
nyi mas spyod pa'i rgyu skar		[twenty-seven] constellations demarcating solar longitude
nyi dag		exact Sun [calculation]
nyi 'dzin	*sūryagrahaṇa*	solar eclipse
nyin zhag		solar day
mnyam pa'i khyim		even-numbered solar mansion(s)
snying stobs	*sattva*	lightness
snying stobs kyi rang bzhin	*sattvaprakṛti*	nature endowed with lightness
rtag pa'i byed pa	*dhruvakaraṇa*	"fixed" impact
rtag [pa'i] longs [spyod]		mean celestial longitude
stag zla		tiger month
stong pa	*śūnya*	[state of] vacuity
stong zla tha chung		late autumn month
tha skar	*aśvinī*	Aries [solar mansion], Beta and Gamma Arietis [constellation]
tha skar	*āśvina*	Āśvina [month]
thun mtshams	*sandhyā*	[six-hourly] juncture
thun tshod	*prahara*	[three-hourly] watch
dal ['gros] rkang	*manda*	aphelion, stepping [of the planets] in a slow motion
dal 'gros lho		slow [planetary] motion in the [second or] southern quadrant
dus	*kāla*	time, season
dus gcig		single [eight-hourly] period of time
dus sbyor	*tatkāla/ lagna*	ascendant conjunction, rising sign
dus gsum	*try ṛtu*	three seasons

drag gza' lnga		five wrathful planets
drag gza' gsum		three wrathful planets
gdab pa	*vava*	Vava [*karaṇa* of "transient" impact]
gdong	*vaktra*	head [of Rāhu]
rdul	*rajas*	motility
rdul kyi rang bzhin	*rajaḥprakṛti*	nature endowed with motility
nag [pa]	*citra*	Spica [constellation]
nag pa'i zla	*caitra*	Caitra [month]
nang gi nges pa		precision of the inner [world]
nabs so	*punarvasū*	constellation Gemini/ Pollux [constellation]
nag rtsis		Chinese divination
nam gru	*revatī*	Pisces, Sigma Piscium [constellation]
snang ba yul		sense objects conveying [the elements to the senses]
snar ma	*rohiṇī*	Aldebaran [constellation]
snron	*jyeṣṭhā*	Antares [constellation]
snrubs	*mūlā*	Chaula [constellation]
pa sangs	*śukra*	Venus, Friday
dpyid ra		early spring month
spen pa	*śani/ śanaiścara*	Saturn, Saturday
phur bu	*bṛhaspati*	Jupiter, Thursday
'pho chung		minor cycle [of breaths]
'pho chen		major cycle [of breaths]
'pho ba'i byed pa	*carakaraṇa*	"transient" impact
phyi rol gyi brtsi ba'i gzhi		basis of astrological calculations pertaining to the outer [world]
bi ṣṭi	*viṣṭi*	Viṣṭi [*karaṇa* of "transient" impact]
byi zhin	*śravaṇā*	Altair [constellation]
byed pa [bcu gcig]	[*ekadaśa*] *karaṇa*	[eleven] impacts [of the lunar month]
dbu ma	*avadhūti*	central energy channel [of the subtle body]
dbugs	*śvāsa*	breath, human "breath" [as a unit of time]
dbus		mid-point [of the month]
dbo	*uttaraphalguṇī*	Denebola [constellation]

dbo zla ba	*phālguna*	Phālguna month
dbyangs 'char	*svarodaya*	Svarodaya [divination system]
dbyar 'bring		mid-summer month
dbyu gu	*daṇḍa*	gnomon [device for temporal measurement]
'byung 'gros	*nirgama*	advancing motion [of the planets]
'byung 'gros byang		advancing planetary motion in the [fourth or] northern quadrant
'byung ba	*bhūta*	[material] element
'byung ba lnga	*pañcabhūta*	five [material] elements
'byung ba rang rgyud		discrete elements
'byung rtsis		elemental divination
sbyor ba	*yoga*	combined calculations [of solar and lunar longitude]
mi mnyam pa'i khyim		odd-numbered solar mansion(s)
mi sdug pa	*kintughna*	Kintughna [*karaṇa* of "fixed" impact]
mig dmar	*maṅgala*	Mars, Tuesday
mun can		Rāhu
mun pa	*tamas*	darkness
mun pa chen po'i rlung		vital energy of great darkness
mon gru	*śatabhiṣā*	Lambda Aquarii [constellation]
mon dre	*dhaniṣṭhā*	Beta Delphini [constellation]
me bzhi	*hastā*	Algorab [constellation]
myur ['gros] rkang	*śīghra*	perihelion, stepping [of the planets] in a fast motion
smin drug	*kṛttikā*	Pleiades [constellation]
smin drug [zla ba]	*kārttika*	Kārttika [month]
smyur 'gros shar		perigee, fast [planetary] motion in the [first or] eastern quadrant
gtso bo	*pradhāna*	primal self
rtsa	*nāḍi*	energy channel(s)
rtsi byed		technique/ method of astrological calculation
rtsis byed kyi gnad		essential point of the actual application of astrology
rtsis byed rang bzhin gzhi		basic natural calculation [of the order of the elements]

rtsis bya'i gzhi		basis of the astrological calculations to be made
tshes kyi skar ma		constellation coinciding with the exact end of the previous lunar day
tshes zhag		calendar day
'dzin pa sems		mind that grasps [negative and positive attributes]
zhi gza'	*śubhagraha*	peaceful planet(s)
zla dag		exact Moon [calculation]
zla ba	*soma*	Moon, Monday
zla skar		constellation(s) demarcating lunar longitude
gza'	*graha*	planet
gza' bcu		ten planetary bodies
yud tsam	*muhūrta*	forty-eight minute "hour"
ye shes kyi rlung	*jñānavāyu*	vital energy of pristine cognition
gYas ro ma	*rasanā*	right-side energy channel [of the subtle body]
gYon rkyang ma	*lalanā*	left-side energy channel [of the subtle body]
rang 'gros		individual motion, [planetary] epicycle
rang bzhin 'od gsal		natural inner radiance
rim pa snga rkang		early progressive step [in the planetary step index]
rim pa phyi rkang		later progressive step [in the planetary step index]
rim min snga' rkang		early regressive step [in the planetary step index]
rim min phyi rkang		later regressive step [in the planetary step index]
res 'grogs zla skar		constellation demarcating lunar longitude at the start of the solar day
res gza' bdun	*saptavāra*	seven alternating weekdays
rlung 'gros		motion of the wind element
lag	*ārdrā*	Alpha Orionis [constellation]
las kyi rlung	*karmavāyu*	vital energy of past actions
las kyi sa dum bu bcu gnyis		twelve terrestrial aspects indicative of past actions
lug [khyim]	*meṣa*	Aries [solar mansion]

longs spyod rnam [par] dag [pa]		exact celestial longitude
sa ga	*viśākhā*	Alpha Librae [constellation]
sa ri	*svāti*	Arcturus [constellation]
sel ba	*viṣkambha*	"eliminator" [a combined calculation of solar and lunar longitude]
hor zla ba dang po		first Mongolian month
lha mtshams	*anurādhā*	Delta Scorpii or Iridis [constellation]
lhag pa	*budha*	Mercury, Wednesday

Poetics

kun tu 'khor lo	*sarvotarabhadra*	acrostic verse revolving in all directions
kun tu phan	*samāhita*	coincidence
rkang pa	*pāda*	metrical line
skad rigs bzhi		four languages
skabs min bstod pa	*vyājastuti*	artful praise
skyon bcu	*daśadoṣa*	ten defects [of poetic composition]
bskor ba	*āvṛtti*	repetition
khyad par	*viśeṣokti*	expression of distinction
mkhas pa'i bya ba gsum		three acts of the learned
'khyog brjod	*vakrokti*	poetic allusion
gab tshig	*prahelikā*	enigmatic innuendo
gab tshig bcu drug	*ṣoḍaśaprahelikā*	sixteen ornaments of enigmatic innuendo
grong tshig	*grāmya*	vernacular
grol ba	*muktaka*	detached verse
dga' [ba]	*preyas*	flattery, delightful flattery
'gal [ba]	*virodha*	incongruity
'gog [pa]	*ākṣepa*	denial
rgya che	*udāratva*	nobleness [as an attribute of the Vaidarbha style]
rgya che	*udātta*	exaltation [as an ornament of sense]
rgyan	*alaṃkāra*	poetic ornament
rgyu	*hetu*	cause
sgra rgyan	*śabdālaṃkāra*	phonetic ornament
sgra nyams	*śabdahīna*	grammatical error

nges pa	*niyama*	alliteration
nges par bstan pa	*nidarśana*	illustrative simile
sngon byung gi gtam rgyud	*itihāsakathā*	historical legend
gcod mtshams nyams pa	*yatibhraṣṭa*	discordance of metrical pause
cha	*sūkṣma*	subtlety
brjid	*ojas*	vigor
brjes shis	*āśis*	benediction
brjod pa	*ākhyāyikā*	narrative
nyams ldan	*rasavat*	sentiment
mnyam nyid	*samatā*	phonetic balance
snyan	*mādhurya*	sweetness
snyan dngags	*kāvya*	poetics
snyan dngags chen po	*mahākāvya*	court poetry
bsnyon dor	*apahnutti*	obfuscation
ting nge 'dzin	*samādhi*	mental focus
gtam	*kathā*	legend
thun min yon tan [gyi mtshan nyid] bcu	*asādhāraṇadaśaguṇalakṣaṇa*	ten uncommon attributes
the tshom can	*sasaṃśaya*	ambiguity
da nas dgongs pa can	*bhāvika*	underlying intention
don	*iṣṭārtha*	intended sense
don 'gal	*vyartha*	incongruity
don rgyan	*arthālaṃkāra*	[poetic] ornament(s) of sense
don gcig pa	*ekārtha*	tautology
don nyams pa	*apārtha*	incoherence
don gzhan bkod pa	*arthāntaranyāsa*	corroboration
don gsal	*arthavyakti*	elucidation
'dus pa	*saṃghāta*	compound verse
'dres ma	*miśrabhāṣā*	hybrid language
ldog pa can	*vyatireka*	contrast
sdeb sbyor nyams	*bhinnaavṛtta*	prosodic deviation
bsdus [pa]	*samāsokti*	concise suggestion
rnam grangs brjod	*paryāyokta*	periphrastic/ indirect speech
dpe	*upamā*	simile
spel ma	*miśra*	mixed verse and prose
phul byung	*atiśayokti*	hyperbole
phyed 'khor	*ardhabrahma*	acrostic verse revolving in two directions
phra mo	*leśa*	misrepresentation

bya dka'	*duṣkaramārga*	[ornaments] hard to execute
sbyar ba	*śliṣṭha/ śleṣa*	double entendre
tsa mbu	*campū*	Campū style [of composition]
rtsom pa		composition
tshig gi phreng	*padāvalī*	string of words
tshigs bcad	*padya*	metrical composition
mtshams sbyor bral	*visaṃdhika*	absence of euphonic conjunction
mtshungs par sbyor ba	*tulyayogitā*	equal pairing
mdzes ldan	*kānti*	beauty
mdzod	*kośa*	intricate verse
zung ldan	*yāmaka*	repetition
zur chag	*apabhraṃśa*	Apabhraṃśa [language]
zol bstod	*aprastutapraśaṃsā*	damning with faint praise
zlos gar	*nāṭaka*	courtly drama
gzi brjid can	*ūrjasvi*	vigor
gzugs can	*rūpaka*	metaphor
yul dus la sogs 'gal ba	*deśadeśādivirodhin*	non-sequitur with regard to place and time
yongs [ba]	*parivṛtti*	exchange
rang bzhin	*prākṛta*	Prākrit [language]
rang bzhin brjod [pa]	*svabhāvokti*	[straightforward] natural description
rab btags	*utprekṣā*	poetic fancy
rab dvangs	*prasāda*	clarity
rab spel	*saṃkīrṇa*	conjunction of poetic figures
rigs	*kulaka*	clustered verse
rim [pa]	*yathāsaṃkhya*	respective/ hierarchical ordering of words and meaning
rim pa nyams pa	*apakrama*	syntactical disorder
lus	*śarīra*	body [of poetic composition]
legs sbyar	*saṃskṛta*	Sanskrit [language]
shar [gau ḍa'i] lam srol	*gauḍa*	East [Indian Gauḍa] style
shin tu gzhon pa	*sakumāratā*	tenderness
sa rga	*sarga*	canto
srid pa can	*vibhāvanā*	peculiar causation
gsal byed	*dīpaka*	illuminating poetic association
lhan cig brjod pa	*sahokti*	co-mention
lhug pa	*gadya*	prose
lho [bai darbha'i] lam srol	*vaidarbha*	South [Indian Vaidarbha] style

Prosody

rkang pa	*pāda*	metrical line
rkang bzhi 'phel	*padacaturārdhva*	Padacaturārdhva meter class
skye 'gro	*jagatī*	twelve-syllable meter class
kha sgo	*upaṣṭhitapracupitā/ vaktradvāra*	Upaṣṭhitapracupitā/ Vaktradvāra meter class
glog phreng	*vidyūnmāla*	Vidyūnmāla meter
'god tshul	*prastāra*	table of metrical variants
rgyun chags	*saṃtāna*	twenty-seven syllable meter class
ngo mtshar rtogs byed kyi sbyor ba	*adbhutaprayoga*	astonishing applications that facilitate the understandings [of prosody]
lci ba	*guru*	heavy [syllable]
rjes bsngags	*anuṣṭubh*	eight-syllable meter class
brjod pa	*uktā*	single-syllable meter class
nyer bkra	*upacitraka*	Upacitraka meter class
mnyam pa'i bri ttta	*samāvṛtta*	metrical lines with syllables of equal number
TA		antibachius
steng 'gro	*udgatā*	Udgatā meter class
mthar sdod		caesura
dag pa'i snang ba	*śuddhavirāja*	Śuddhavirāja meter
dang po'i tshogs		first trimeter of a hemistich
dal gyi 'gro ba	*mardākrāntā*	Mardākrāntā meter class
'dra mtshungs	*samānikā*	Samānikā meter
dbyangs sgrog	*gāyatrī*	six-syllable meter class
sdeb sbyor	*chandas*	prosody
NA		tribach
na ṣṭa cho ga	*naṣṭa*	reductionist calculation
prastara'i phreng steng 'og gi gling	*prastāra*	tabular grid with horizontal and vertical units
phyed mnyam pa'i bri tta	*ardhavṛtta*	metrical lines of semi-equal length
phyi mo	*mātrā*	moric/ syllabic instant
phreng ldan	*paṅktī*	ten-syllable meter class
'phags ma	*āryā*	Āryā meter
bri tta	*vṛtta*	metric rules governing syllabic quantity
bri ha tī	*bṛhatī*	nine-syllable meter class

BHA		dactyl
dbus phra	*tanumadhyā*	Tanumadhyā meter
dbyangs sgrog	*gāyatrī*	six-syllable meter class
MA		molossus
mi mnyam pa'i bri tta	*viṣamavṛtta*	metrical lines of unequal length
dmar ser can	*paiṅgala*	Paiṅgala meter
tshogs	*gaṇa*	trimeter
tshogs brgyad	*aṣṭagaṇa*	eight forms of trimeter
tshogs nyid	*gaṇa*	trimeter
DZA		amphibrach
dza ti	*jāti*	metric rules governing morae/ moric instants
gzhon nu rol pa	*kumāralalitā*	Kumāralalitā meter
rab dga'	*uṣṇih*	seven-syllable meter class
YA		bachius
yang ba	*laghu*	light [syllable]
yang ba'i bya ba		triangular chart of light syllables
RA		cretic
rab bsags	*pracaya*	twenty-seven-syllable meter class
ro langs can		Vaitālya meter
SA		anapaest
srog tu zhugs pa		aspirated consonant
gsum bsngags	*triṣṭubh*	eleven-syllable meter class
lhag par byed ldan	*utkṛti*	twenty-six-syllable meter class
adhvā		calculation of a given point of cadence
uddiṣṭa		calculation of the specific position of a given meter within its class

Synonymics and Lexicography

nges tshig	*nirukta*	etymological definition
ngo bo tsam		bare essential nature
dngos kyi sgra bshad gsum po		three appropriate etymological terms for proper [names]
dngos po'i don	*bhāvārtha*	participial substantive
dngos ming	*mūlanāman*	proper name

mngon brjod	*abhidāna*	synonymics, lexicography
rjes su grub pa'i ming		derivative name
rjes grub 'dod rgyal		primary name functioning as a derivative
rjod byed	*vācaka*	signifier
btags ming	*prajñaptināman*	imputed name
tha snyad	*vyavahāra*	conventional term
don gcig la ming mang po dang ldan pa		synonym(s)
gdags	*prajñapti*	designation
gdags gzhi	*prajñaptivastu*	basis of designation
'dod rgyal gyi ming	*yādṛcchikanāman*	primary name
'dra ba rgyu mtshan du byas pa		imputed name formed on the basis of similarity
'brel ba rgyu mtshan du byas pa		imputed name formed on the basis of causal relationship
brda	*saṃketa*	communicative symbol
ming	*nāman*	name
ming gcig kho na don mang po la 'jug pa		homonym(s)

Dramaturgy

kau shi kī	*kauśikī*	intimacy
kun dga'	*ānanda*	joy
kun tu sgo	*āmukha*	prelude
kun tu 'thor ba	*saṃpheṭa*	altercation
kun lhung	*avapāta*	commotion
skad du ma gzhan du bsgyur ba		multi-lingual variation
skabs 'gar gros byed pa		episodic discussion
skye bo 'god par rtsom pa	*upanyāsa*	strategic appeasement
khyad par byed pa	*viśeṣaṇa*	distinction
gar gyi rnam gyur		dramatic mood
go ldog pa	*tadviparyāya*	opposition
grub pa	*siddhi*	accomplishment
dga' ba'i tshig	*priyavacana*	words of endearment
'gal ba	*virodha*	frustration, impediment
'gog pa	*niṣedha*	prohibition/ opposition
'gog pa	*virodha*	impediment
'gal ba	*virodhana*	quarrelsome altercation

'god pa dang bcas pa	*sārūpya*	mistaken identity
'gro ba pa	*prasaṅga*	incidental/ consequential comments
rgol ba	*apavāda*	censure [of another's misdeeds]
rgyan	*bhūṣaṇa*	embellishment
rgyu	*hetu*	reason
sgeg pa	*lāsya*	graceful [song and dance]
sgo['i mtshams sbyor]	*mukha[-saṃdhi]*	introduction, protasis
sgrub pa	*vidhāna*	conflict of sentiments
nges pa thob byed [kyi mtshams sbyor]	*nirvahaṇa[-saṃdhi]*	conclusion, catastrophe
nge spar bstan pa	*nidarśana*	evidence
nges tshig	*nirukta*	explanation
mngon par mtho ba	*abhyudaya*	prosperity
cha shas	*leśa*	use of disparaging metaphor
chags pas gzer ba'i nyams	*śṛṅgārarasa*	sentiment of anguish caused by desire
'jug pa'i yan lag	*vṛtyaṅga*	features/ aspects of the [four] dramatic elements
rjes su dpag pa	*anumāna*	inference, conjecture
nyams pa	*bhraṃśa*	solecism
nye bar mkho ba	*parikara*	enlargement, intimation of forthcoming events
nye bar bstan pa	*upadiṣṭa*	suggestion
nye bar gnas pa	*upāsana*	propitiation, pacification
nye bar len pa	*upakṣepa*	suggestive insinuation
nye bas sbed pa	*upagūhana*	expression of wonderment
mnyam par 'jog pa	*samādhāna*	determination of [the purpose of a plot]
brnyes pa	*paribhāvanā*	expression of surprise
snyan ngag bsdu ba	*kāvyāsaṃhāra*	epilogue
snying po['i mstams sbyor]	*garbha[-saṃdhi]*	development, catastasis
gtan la phab pa	*nirṇaya*	settlement [of the plot]
rtog ge mtshungs pa	*tulyatarka*	similarity of ideas
brtag dpyad	*vitarka*	supposition, hypothesis [expressing doubt]
stobs lhag pa	*adhibala*	outwitting through guile
bstan pa	*diṣṭa*	observation
thob pa	*prāpti*	attainment, accession [to the joyful conclusion of a plot]
mthong ba'i mtha'	*dṛṣṭānta*	objective

'thor ba	*saṃpheṭa*	altercation
dus	*śama*	timely deliverance [from misery/ misfortune]
don gyi dbang	*arthāpatti*	presumption
dri ba	*pṛcchā*	interrogation
gdung ba	*tāpana*	toleration of anguish [with regard to a desired object]
mdo 'dzin pa	*sūtradhāra*	discoursing
'dar ba	*vidhūta*	trembling [due to rejection]
'drid pa	*chādana*	words of humiliation
rdo rje	*vajra*	adamant/ blunt response
bsdu ba	*saṅgraha*	cajolement
bsdus pa	*saṃkṣiptaka*	artful device
bsdus pa	*saṃkṣobha/ saṃkṣepa*	agitation
nus pa	*śakti*	placation
gnas skabs 'jog pa	*vastūthāpana*	supernatural intrusion
rnam par dpyad pa	*vicāra*	discrimination
rnam par sred pa	*vilobhana*	allurement
dper brjod	*udāharaṇa*	declaration, hyperbole
spel ba	*grathana*	convergence [of the main issues of the plot]
phan tshun du gnas pa	*vyavasāya*	resolve, assertion [regarding a plot's objective]
phul byung	*atiśaya*	hyperbole
phreng ba	*vīthī*	single-act drama
phreng ba	*mālā*	[bestowal/ wearing of] flower garlands
'phrag tu bzlog pa	*sāṅghātya*	ending of an alliance [by accident or design]
bhā ra tī	*bhāratī*	dialogue
byed pa	*karaṇa*	initial enactment of a plot
dbye ba	*udbheda*	first disclosure [of the germ of a plot]
dbye bar byed pa	*bheda*	hatching of a conspiracy
'byed pa	*kheda*	lassitude, depression [arising from over-exertion]
ma brjod pa grub pa	*anuktasiddhi*	understated achievement
ma byung ba'i dper brjod pa	*abhūtāharaṇa*	[deliberate] misstatement of events
mi bzod pa['i mtshams sbyor]	*vimarśa[-saṃdhi]*	plot-crisis, peripeteia
me tog	*puṣpa*	sweet/ flowery words of gallantry

mya ngan gyis sdug bsngal	*karuṇārasa*	sentiment of suffering caused by sorrow
smod pa	*garhaṇa/ paribhāṣaṇa*	reproach, admonition
smra ba dang bcas pa	*saṃlāpa*	abusive/ intimidating conversation
rtsed mo	*narman*	amorous playfulness, pleasantry
rtsed mo 'byed pa	*narmagarbha*	covert development of love and affection
rtsed mo'i mdangs	*narmadyuti*	amusement, deliberate concealment
rtsed mor 'gro ba	*narmasphūrja*	ecstatic meeting
tshig btus pa	*padoccaya*	versification
mtshan nyid [so drug]	*lakṣaṇa*	[thirty-six] characteristics [of stagecraft]
mtshams sbyor	*saṃdhi*	dramatic juncture
mtshams sbyor gyi yan lag lnga	*pañcasaṃdhyaṅga*	five sequences/ aspects of dramatic juncture
'tshab pa	*vidrava*	consequent panic, consternation
mdzes pa	*śobhā*	beauty
'dzag pa	*adhidrava*	tumultuous consternation
bzhad gad	*hāsya*	humor
zlos gar	*nātya*	dramaturgy
gzer ba	*ākṣipta*	painful disclosure [of the desired objective of a plot]
bzo byed	*prahasana*	farce
ya mtshan pas ngo mtshar ba'i nyams	*adbhutarasa*	sentiment of astonishment due to amazement
yi ge bsdu ba	*varṇasaṃhāra*	close association, intermingling of social classses
yi ge bsdu ba	*akṣarasaṃghātā*	abbreviation
yon tan sgrogs pa	*guṇakīrtana*	proclamation of talents
yon sbyin pa	*dākṣiṇya*	concord
yongs su 'gro ba	*parisarpa*	pursuit [of a desired object/ goal]
yongs su bsgyur ba	*parivartaka*	necessary change of action [due to exigencies]
yongs su 'jog pa	*parinyāsa*	establishment [of the seed of a plot]
yid 'byung ba	*udvega*	distress [caused by separation/ exposure to enemies]
yon tan lhung ba	*guṇātipāta*	disqualification

rang gis ston pa	*praśasti*	formal benediction
rab tu grub pa	*prasiddhi*	proof
rab tu 'gro ba	*pragamana*	progress [through dialogue]
rab tu snang ba	*prarocanā*	stimulating prologue
rab tu sred pa	*prarocanā*	words presaging [the denouement]
rab dvangs	*prasāda*	lucid sense of gratification
rig pa	*yukti*	resolve [to attain the objective of a plot]
rim pa	*karma*	progressive similes [probing another person's sentiments]
re ba	*manoratha*	imagination
lan gyi sgo['i mtshams sbyor]	*pratimukha[-saṃdhi]*	progression, epitasis
lam gyi rang bzhin	*mārga*	indication of an [intended] course of action
len pa	*ādāna*	capture [of the germ of a plot]
shin tu khros pa'i nyams	*raudrarasa*	sentiment of extreme anger
shin tu 'jog pa	*utthāpaka*	haughty provocation
sā tva tī	*sātvatī*	grandeur
som nyi/ the tshoms	*saṃśaya*	doubt
slong ba	*prārthanā*	solicitation
gsal ba	*dyuti*	disdainful words, confirmation [of the outcome of a plot]
gsal ba	*narmasphoṭa*	partial intimation [of new love]
bsam pa snga ma 'chad pa	*pūrvāvākya*	retrospective comment
ā ra bha ṭī	*ārabhaṭī*	conflict

Non-Buddhist Philosophical Systems

kun dga' ra ba	*ārāma*	(*Jaina*) monastic garden
kun tu rgyu	*parivrājika*	itinerant teacher
kla klo	*mleccha*	barbarian
dka' thub	*tapas*	(*Jaina*) austerity
skyes bu	*puruṣa*	(*Vaiśeṣika*) self
skyon	*doṣa*	(*Naiyāyika*) defiled emotion
brkyang [pa]	*prasāra*	(*Vaiśeṣika*) expanding
bskum [pa]	*kuñcita*	(*Vaiśeṣika*) contracting
khams gsum	*tridhātu*	(*Jaina*) three world systems
khong spu tse		Confucius

khyab 'jug pa	*vaiṣṇava*	(*Vaiṣṇava*) Vaiṣṇava, follower of Viṣṇu
gang zag	*pudgala*	(*Jaina*) matter
gar yang phyin pa	*prāpti*	(*Aiśvarya*) power to move freely and obtain anything
go rim	*anukrama*	(*Mīmāṃsaka*) relative sequence [of rituals]
grangs can pa		(*Chinese*) numerologist
grangs can pa	*sāṃkhya*	(*Sāṃkhya*) Sāṃkhya
grub mtha'	*siddhānta*	philosophical system
gleng ba	*ālāpa*	(*Mīmāṃsaka*) discussion [on Vedic adaptations]
dgag pa lnga		(*Lokāyatika*) five kinds of refutation
dga' mgur gnas pa	*yatrakāmāvasāyitva*	(*Aiśvarya*) teleportation
dge sbyong	*śramaṇa*	virtuous ascetic
dgos pa	*prayojana*	(*Mīmāṃsaka*) impact [of ritual observances]
'gros	*gati*	(*Vaiśeṣika*) movement, motion
rgyang 'phen pa	*lokāyatika*	(*Lokāyatika*) mundane materialist
rgyal dpogs pa	*jaiminī*	(*Mīmāṃsaka*) follower of Jaiminī
rgyal rigs	*kṣatriya*	(*Vaiṣṇava*) ruling/ princely class
rgyu'i bon		original Bon
rgyu'i gsto bo	*hetupradhāna*	(*Sāṃkhya*) primal matter at the causal level
sgra byung tshad ma	*śabdapramāṇa*	(*Vaiśeṣika*) valid cognition originating from Vedic testimony
sgrub pa bzhi		(*Lokāyatika*) four kinds of proof
brgyud 'brel	*anvayasambandha*	(*Vaiśeṣika*) indirect relation
nga rgyal gsum	*ahaṃkāra*	(*Sāṃkhya*) threefold ego-principle
ngan song gsum	*tridurgati*	three inferior realms
nges par dga'	*nirjara*	(*Jaina*) rejuvenation
dngos po	*bhāva*	(*Naiyāyika*) entity
dngos med	*abhāva*	(*Naiyāyika*) non-entity, (*Mīmāṃsaka*) absence
dngos 'brel	*sākṣādsambandhana*	(*Vaiśeṣika*) direct relation

mngon shes lnga	*pañcābhijñā*	five supernormal cognitive powers
mngon sum tshad ma	*pratyakṣapramāṇa*	(*Naiyāyika*) valid cognition of direct perception
gcer bu pa	*nirgrantha[jaina]*	(*Jaina*) naked ascetic, Nirgrantha Jain
chad [par] lta [ba]	*ucchedadṛṣṭi*	(*Lokāyatika*) nihilism, nihilist view
chad [par] smra ba	*uchedavādin*	(*Lokāyatika*) nihilist
chad smra'i ston pa snyoms 'jug pa drug		(*Lokāyatika*) six nihilist teachers who had mastered meditative absorption
chen po/ blo	*mahat/ buddhi*	(*Sāṃkhya*) great intelligence
chos	*dharma*	(*Vaiśeṣika*) merit
chos min	*adharma*	(*Vaiśeṣika*) demerit
mchod par 'os pa	*pūjya*	(*Aiśvarya*) worthiness of offering
mchod sbyin	*yajña*	(*Aiśvarya*) sacrificial offering
'chi med bdud rtsi'i skyes bu	*amṛtamayapuruṣa*	(*Vedānta*) [shining] immortal person
'ching [ba]	*bandha*	(*Jaina*) bondage
rjes sgrogs pa drug		(*Lokāyatika*) six teachers who emulated [the six nihilist teachers]
'jig rten rgyang 'phen pa	*lokāyatika*	(*Lokāyatika*) mundane materialists
'jig rten 'dus pa	*lokasaṃgraha*	(*Jaina*) aggregate of worlds
'jig tshogs la lta ba nyi shu	*viṃśatisatkāyadṛṣṭi*	twenty views concerning mundane aggregates
'jug pa	*pravṛtti*	(*Naiyāyika*) [sensory] engagement
'jug pa	*avatāra*	(*Vaiṣṇava*) incarnation, emanation
'jug pa bcu	*daśāvatāra*	(*Vaiṣṇava*) ten incarnations [of Viṣṇu]
'jog [pa]	*avakṣepaṇa*	(*Vaiśeṣika*) descending
rjes dpag rnam gnyis	*dvayānumāna*	(*Naiyāyika*) two kinds of inference
nye bar len pa bzhi	*caturupādāna*	four primary causes [of involuntary rebirth in cyclic existence]
nyer 'jal	*upamāna*	(*Mīmāṃsaka*) comparison
gnyis ka ma yin pa	*advaita*	(*Vaiṣṇava*) non-dual
snying stobs	*sattva*	(*Sāṃkhya*) lightness

snying stobs nga rgyal	*sāttvikāhaṃkāra*	(*Sāṃkhya*) ego-principle imbued with lightness
btags pa ba['i mu stegs pa]		nominal [extremist]
rtag dngos	*nityabhava*	eternally existing entity
rtag lta	*nityadṛṣṭi*	eternalism
rtag [par] smra [ba]		eternalist
rtog ge	*tarka*	(*Vaiṣṇava*) logic
rtog ge pa	*tārkika*	dialectician
rtog dpyod kyi lta ba	*vicāradṛṣṭi*	analytical view
lta ngan nyi shu rtsa drug		twenty-six negative views
lta ba lnga brgya bdun cu		five hundred and seventy [philosophical] views
lta ba drug cu rtsa gnyis		sixty-two [inauthentic] views
lta ba'i rtsa ba brgya rtsa bcu		hundred and ten primary philosophical views
brtul zhugs	*[aṇu]vrata*	(*Jaina*) ascetic discipline, ascetic restraint
bsti gnas	*āśramapada*	(*Sāṃkhya*) hermitage
thar pa	*mokṣa*	(*Sāṃkhya, Jaina*) release
thal 'gyur	*prasaṅga*	(*Mīmāṃsaka*) contiguity [between primary and secondary rites]
mthar 'dzin gyi lta ba	*antagrāhadṛṣṭi*	extremist view
thar pa gdugs bkan pa lta bu	*īṣaprāgbhāra*	(*Jaina*) release resembling an "upturned parasol"
dam pa	*sat*	(*Vedānta*) being
dam pa ma yin pa'i lta ba nyer brgyad		twenty-eight inauthentic views
de nyid	*tattva*	(*Sāṃkhya*) reality
de nyid nyer lnga	*pañcaviṃśatitattva*	(*Sāṃkhya*) twenty-five categories of reality
de tsam lnga	*pañcatanmātra*	(*Sāṃkhya*) five potentials of subtle matter
de las phye ba['i lta ba] sum brgya drug cu rtsa gsum		three hundred and sixty-three derivative views
dus	*kāla*	(*Vaiśeṣika, Jaina*) time
don gyis go ba	*arthāpatti*	(*Mīmāṃsaka*) presumption
bdag	*ātma*	(*Sāṃkhya, Vaiśeṣika*) soul, self
bdag gi yon tan dgu	*ātmanavaguṇa*	(*Vaiśeṣika*) nine attributes of the "self"
bdag nyid	*ātman*	(*Vaiṣṇava, Mīmāṃsaka, and Vedānta*) "self"

bdag por gyur pa	*īśitva*	(*Aiśvarya*) supremacy
bdag smras byed pa	*ātmavādin*	propounding [the existence] of "soul"
bde ba	*sukha*	(*Vaiśeṣika*) happiness
'du ba	*samavāya*	(*Vaiśeṣika*) inherence
'degs [pa]	*utkṣepa*	(*Vaiśeṣika*) ascending
'dod dgur sgyur ba	*prākāmya*	(*Aiśvarya*) irresistible will-power
rdul	*rajas*	motility
sdig pa	*pāpa*	(*Jaina*) negative act, negativity
sdug bsngal	*duḥkha*	(*Vaiśeṣika, Naiyāyika*) sorrow, suffering
sdom pa	*saṃvara*	(*Jaina*) commitment, controlled action
brda sprod pa	*vaiyākaraṇa*	(*Vaiyākaraṇa*) grammarian
nang blo'i dbang po lnga	*pañcantarendriya*	(*Sāṃkhya*) five inner sense organs
nam mkha'	*ākāśa*	(*Vaiśeṣika, Jaina*) space
nor bdag gi 'brel ba	*arthāpattisaṃbandhana*	(*Sāṃkhya*) relation of implication
gnag lhas bstan pa	*maskarī gośālaputra*	(*Ājīvaka*) Maskarī Gośālaputra
rnam 'gyur nga rgyal	*vaikārikāhaṃkāra*	(*Sāṃkhya*) modified ego-principle
rnam shes	*cit*	(*Vedānta*) consciousness
gnas gzhi	*vāsavastu*	(*Mīmāṃsaka*) basic [ritual obligations]
rnal 'byor ldan pa	*yogayukti*	(*Sāṃkhya*) [inference] based on yoga
dpyod pa ba	*mīmāṃsaka*	(*Mīmāṃsaka*) Mīmāṃsaka
spyi	*sāmānya*	(*Vaiśeṣika*) universal
spyi	*sāmānya*	(*Mīmāṃsaka*) general [rules on ritual observance]
spyi nges bstan	*sāmānyanirdeśa*	(*Mīmāṃsaka*) general prescriptions [on ritual transfer]
spyi don	*sāmānyārtha*	(*Vaiśeṣika*) object-universal
spyod pa can	*mīmāṃsaka*	(*Mīmāṃsaka*) Mīmāṃsaka
spyod pa bcu gsum	*pratimā*	(*Jaina*) thirteen modes of conduct
spyod pa po	*mīmāṃsaka*	(*Mīmāṃsaka*) Mīmāṃsaka
sprul pa['i mu stegs pa]		emanational [extremist]
pha rol smra ba bcu drug	*ṣodaśānuvāda*	sixteen interpretations

phur bu pa	*bārhaspatya*	(*Lokāyatika*) Bārhaspatya, follower of Bṛhaspati
phyi ma 'bras bu	*aparaphala*	(*Naiyāyika*) experience of results in future lives
phyi rol mu stegs pa'i lam srol		tradition(s) of non-Buddhist extremists
phyi rol pa	*bāhya*	non-Buddhist, outsider
phyi las kyi dbang po lnga	*pañcabāhyendriya*	(*Sāṃkhya*) five motor organs
phra ba	*sūkṣmatā*	(*Aiśvarya*) subtlety
phyogs	*dik*	(*Vaiśeṣika*) relative direction
bon		Bon
bon po		Bonpo
bya ba'i shugs	*vega*	(*Vaiśeṣika*) velocity
byang grol	*apavarga*	(*Naiyāyika*) final emancipation
bye brag	*viśeṣa*	(*Vaiśeṣika*) particular
bye brag	*viśeṣa*	(*Mīmāṃsaka*) particular ritual observances
bye brag nges bstan	*viśeṣanirdeśa*	(*Mīmāṃsaka*) specific prescriptions [on ritual transfer]
bye brag pa	*vaiśeṣika*	(*Vaiśeṣika*) Vaiśeṣika
byed pa po	*kartṛ*	(*Sāṃkhya*) actor, creator
byed pa po'i skyes bu	*kartṛkapuruṣa*	(*Vedānta*) creator "self"
blo gros	*buddhi*	(*Vaiśeṣika, Naiyāyika*) intellect, understanding
dbang du gyur pa	*vaśitva*	(*Aiśvarya*) dominion
dbang po	*indriya*	(*Jaina*) sense faculty
dbang phyug pa	*aiśvarya*	(*Aiśvarya*) Aiśvarya, follower of Īśvara
dbyu gu gsum pa	*tridaṇḍin*	(*Jaina*) ascetic possessing three staffs [of body, speech, and mind]
'bad pa	*yatna*	(*Vaiśeṣika*) effort
'byung po lnga	*pañca[mahā]bhūta*	(*Sāṃkhya*) five [gross] elements
'byung ba bzhi	*caturbhūta*	(*Vaiśeṣika*) four elements
'brel ba bdun	*saptasaṃbandhana*	(*Sāṃkhya*) seven kinds of relation
mi gsal ba'i bdag	*avyaktātma*	(*Lokāyatika*) indiscernible soul/ self
mu stegs	*tīrtha*	extreme, ford
mu stegs pa	*tīrthaka*	extremist, forder

mu stegs rang rgyud pa	*svātantrikatīrthaka*	independently established [extremist school]
mun can nga rgyal	*tāmasikāhaṃkāra*	(*Sāṃkhya*) ego-principle imbued with dullness
mun pa	*tamas*	(*Sāṃkhya*) dullness
tsa ra ka pa	*cāraka*	(*Cāraka*) Cāraka, follower of Caraka
gtso bo	*pradhāna*	(*Sāṃkhya*) primal matter
rtsod pa	*vivāda*	(*Mīmāṃsaka*) debate on preclusion of secondary rites
tshangs pa	*brahman*	(*Vaiyākaraṇa*) pure source [of sound]
tshangs pa [ba]	*brāhmaṇa*	(*Brāhmaṇa*) Brāhmaṇa, follower of Brahmā
tshangs pa'i 'jig rten	*brahmaloka*	(*Vaiṣṇava*) world realm(s) of Brahmā
tshangs pa'i bu	*brahmaputra*	(*Brāhmaṇa*) child of Brahmā
tshad ma	*pramāṇa*	(*Mīmāṃsaka*) validity/ authority [of Vedic rites]
tshig don dgu	*navapadārtha*	(*Jaina*) nine categories [of knowable phenomena]
tshig don drug	*ṣaṭpadārtha*	(*Vaiśeṣika*) six categories [of knowable phenomena]
tshur mthong 'jig rten pa'i lam		mundane spiritual path focusing on this life
tshu rol mdzes pa	*cārvāka*	(*Lokāyatika*) Cārvāka, hedonist
rdzas	*dravya*	(*Vaiśeṣika*) substance
rdzas drug	*ṣaḍdravya*	(*Jaina*) six substances
vi shi mallā		Bismillah
zhi ba'i bde ba	*śamasukha*	bliss of quiescence
za ba po	*bhojaka*	(*Sāṃkhya*) consumer
zag pa	*ajīva*	(*Jaina*) inanimate substance
zad byed pa	*kṣapaṇaka*	(*Jaina*) mendicant teacher
bzung ba	*dhāraṇā*	(*Vaiṣṇava*) retention
'og mun pa'i dkyil 'khor	*pṛthivītalatamomaṇḍala*	(*Vedānta*) sphere of terrestrial darkness
ya mtshan gyi lta ba go drug		ninety-six astonishing views
yang ba	*laghutva*	(*Aiśvarya*) agility
yan lag drug gi rnal 'byor	*ṣaḍaṅgayoga*	(*Vaiṣṇava*) yoga of the six branches
yid	*manas*	(*Sāṃkhya, Vaiśeṣika, Naiyāyika*) mind

ye shes	*jñāna*	(*Jaina*) knowledge
yon tan gsum	*triguṇa*	(*Sāṃkhya*) three attributes
yon gtan [gsum] can pa	*[trai]guṇya*	(*Sāṃkhya*) adherent of the [three] attributes
rang rgyud [mu stegs pa]	*svātantrika*	independently established [extremist]
rang rgyud	*svatantra*	(*Mīmāṃsaka*) continuous ritual performance
rang bzhin	*prakṛti*	(*Sāṃkhya*) nature
rang bzhin min pa	*aprakṛti*	(*Sāṃkhya*) absence of nature
rab tu byed pa	*prakaraṇa*	(*Sāṃkhya*) ideal state [of homogeneity]
rig pa can pa	*naiyāyika*	(*Naiyāyika*) Naiyāyika
rigs chad pa'i log rtog can	*kulotsādamithyākalpanā*	cut-off family maintaining heretical views
rigs byed	*veda*	(*Vaidika*) Veda[s]
rigs byed kyi mtha'	*vedānta*	(*Vedānta*) Vedānta
rigs byed kyi mtha' gsang ba pa	*vedāntaupaniṣadika*	(*Vedānta*) follower of the Vedānta Upaniṣadic tradition
rig byed pa	*vaidika*	(*Vaidika*) follower of the Vedas
las	*karma*	(*Vaiśeṣika, Jaina*) action, deed
lung ma bstan gyi lta ba bcu bzhi		fourteen unspecified views
lo ma can	*palāśin*	(*Jaina*) ascetic of no fixed abode (lit. possessing only a tree)
shed las skyes	*mānava*	(*Mīmāṃsaka*) mankind
shes rig gi skyes bu	*puruṣa*	(*Sāṃkhya*) intelligent "self"
sor sdud	*pratyāhāra*	(*Vaiṣṇava*) sense withdrawal, composure
srid pa	*bhava*	(*Naiyāyika*) rebirth
srin po	*rāksaṣa*	(*Vaiṣṇava*) ogre
srin bu	*kṛmi*	(*Jaina*) animalcule
srog ldan	*jīva*	(*Jaina*) animate substance
srog ldan dgu	*navajīva*	(*Jaina*) nine animate substances/ types of living organism
srog 'dzin	*prāṇāyāma*	(*Vaiṣṇava*) breath-control
gsang ba pa	*aupaniṣadika*	(*Aupaniṣadika*) follower of the Upaniṣads
gsal ba'i bdag	*vyaktātma*	(*Lokāyatika*) discernible soul/ self

bsam gtan pa	*dhyāyī*	meditator
bsod nams	*puṇya*	(*Jaina*) merit

Buddhist Phenomenology and General Terms

kun 'gro lnga	*pañcasarvatraga*	five ever-present mental states
kun tu brnabs pas bzhag pa	*āmarśanasthita*	tangible sensation based on irritation
[kun rtog gi] rang bzhin brgyad cu		eighty natural [states of conceptual thought]
kun brtags	*parikalpita*	imaginary [nature]
kun brtags pa'i rnam pa bcu gnyis		twelve aspects of the imaginary [nature]
kun brtags pa'i gzugs	*parikalpitarūpa*	forms that are imagined
kun nas nyon mongs pa	*saṃkleśa*	dissonant mental state
kun nas nyon mongs pa sa bon gyi gzhan dbang		dependent nature comprising the seeds of all dissonant mental states
kun nas nyon mongs pa'i rten 'brel	*saṃkleśapratītyasamutpāda*	dependent origination associated with dissonant mental states
kun nas nyon mongs pa'i phyogs kyi rten 'brel		dependent origination falling within the range of dissonant mental states
kun nas mnar sems pa	*āghāta*	total enmity, malevolence
kun rdzob	*saṃvṛti*	relative appearances
kun rdzob kyi dngos po	*saṃvṛtivastu*	relative entity
kun rdzob kyi rten 'brel	*saṃvṛtipratītyasamutpāda*	relative dependent origination
kun rdzob bden pa	*saṃvṛtisatya*	relative truth
kun rdzob VAṂ	*saṃvṛti* VAṂ	relative appearances, [symbolized by] VAṂ
kun gzhi	*ālaya*	substratum, ground-of-all
kun gzhi'i rnam [par] shes [pa]	*ālayavijñāna*	substratum consciousness
kun gzhi'i rnam smin gyi cha	*ālayavipākabhāga*	maturational aspects of the substratum [consciousness]
kun slong	*samutthana*	past impulse, motivation
dkar po'i chos	*śukladharma*	positive teachings
dkon mchog gsum	*triratna*	three precious jewels
dkyil chog	*maṇḍalavidhi*	maṇḍala ritual
bka'	*vacana*	transmitted [oral] teachings, words of the Buddha
bka' gdams pa		Kadampa

bka' ma		transmitted oral teachings [of the Nyingma school]
bkug pa	*ākarṣaṇa*	convergence
rkang lag rnam par 'gyus pa	*praśākha*	limb formation of the fetus
rkyen gang nye ba las 'byung ba		origin [of seeds] through proximate conditions
skad cig	*kṣaṇa*	instant, indivisible time moment
skad cig pa	*kṣaṇika/ kṣaṇikārtha*	momentary
skad cig ma'i rten 'brel	*kṣaṇikapratītyasamutpāda*	instantaneous dependent origination
skal mnyam	*sabhāgahetu*	[result arising from] a causal basis of homogeneity
sku	*kāya*	buddha body
sku gsum	*trikāya*	three buddha bodies
skur 'debs kyi rtog pa	*apavādavikalpa*	notions of repudiation
skyabs 'gro	*śaraṇagamaṇa*	refuge, seeking refuge
skyur ba	*amla*	sour [taste]
skye mched	*āyatana*	sensory activity field(s)
skye mched bcu gnyis	*dvādaśāyatana*	twelve sensory activity fields
skye mched drug	*ṣaḍāyatana*	six sensory activity fields
skye ba	*jāti*	birth [link of dependent origination]
skye ba rting ma		next life
skye ba dang 'chi 'pho ba 'byung ba'i rten 'brel	*cyutyupapattipratītya-samutpāda*	dependent origination through which birth and death arise
skye bar rnam par rtog pa	*jātivikalpa*	imaginations of birth
skye bas zab pa	*utpattigāmbhīrya*	profundity [of ultimate reality] on account of its arising
skye sa	*janmabhūmi*	level of birth, birthplace
skyes bu chung ngu	*adhamapuruṣa*	person of narrow scope
skyes bu chen po	*mahāpuruṣa*	person of extensive scope
skyes bu 'bring pa	*madhyamapuruṣa*	person of average scope
skyes bu gsum	*tripuruṣa*	three types of person
skyo ba	*udvega*	distress, disillusionment
bska ba	*kaśāya*	astringent [taste]
bskyed bya skyed byed kyi rten 'brel	*utpādyotpādakapratītya-samutpāda*	dependent origination endowed with generated and generative aspects
kha cig rtag smra [bzhi]	*ekasyaśāśvatavāda*	[four] views of partial eternalism
kha na ma tho ba	*avadya*	inadmissible/ censurable offence

kha ba	*tikta*	bitter
kham gyi zas	*kavalikāhāra*	nourishment of the sensory bases
khams	*dhātu*	buddha nature, world-system, sensory base(s)
khams gong ma	*urdhvadhātu*	higher world-systems [of form and formlessness]
khams bco brgyad	*aṣṭadaśadhātu*	eighteen sensory bases
khams gsum	*tridhātu*	three world-systems
khams gsum sa dgu		nine [experiential] levels of the three world-systems
khengs pa'i nga rgyal	*ahaṃkāramāna*	conceited pride
khong khro	*pratigha*	hostility
kho'i don spyi	*svārthasāmānya*	intrinsic object-universal
khyad par du rtog pa	*viśeṣavikalpa*	imaginations of attribution/ qualification
khyad gzhi	*viśeṣya*	descriptive base
khrel med pa	*anapatrāpya*	shamelessness
khrel yod	*apatrāpya*	shame
khro ba	*krodha*	anger
mkhrang 'gyur	*ghana*	suspension of the embryo
'khon 'dzin	*upanāha*	enmity
'khor ba	*saṃsāra*	cyclic existence
'khor ba ji srid pa'i phung po	*āsaṃsāraskandha*	aggregate persisting for the duration of cyclic existence
'khor lo	*cakra*	energy center [within the subtle body]
'khor lo lnga	*pañcacakra*	five energy centers [within the subtle body]
'khor sems byung		peripheral mental states
'khrul pa	*bhrānti*	bewilderment
gang zag	*pudgala*	individual person
gang zag gi bdag	*pudgalātma*	individual selfhood, self of the individual person
gang zag gi bdag med	*pudgalanairātmya*	selflessness of the individual person
go rim	*anukrama*	sequence
gong sa	*urdhvabhūmi*	level above [one's present level]
gor gor po	*peśi*	rounded formation/ solidification of the embryo
grags pa'i ming	*yaśonāma*	known name
grang	*saṃkhyā*	number

grangs su snang ba'i rnam rig		apperception of numeric categories that become manifest
grub mtha'	*siddhānta*	philosophical and spiritual system, tenet
grub mtha' bzhi	*catuḥsiddhānta*	four philosophical systems
grub pa'i yan lag gsum	*abhinirvṛttyaṅga*	three links [of dependent origination] that are formed
gling	*dvīpa*	continent, island
dga' ldan	*tuṣita*	Tuṣita [realm]
dga' ba	*mudita/ prīti/ ānanda*	empathetic joy
dga' ba sdud ba yid la byed pa	*ratisaṃgrāhakamanaskāra*	attention imbued with encompassing joy
dga' ba spangs pa'i bde ba	*prītiprahāṇasukha*	bliss in which joy has been renounced
dga' ba bzhi	*caturānanda*	four delights
dge rgyas	*śubhakṛtsna*	Most Extensive Virtue [realm]
dge chung	*parīttaśubha*	Little Virtue [realm]
dge ba	*kuśala*	virtuous/ wholesome action
dge ba bcu	*daśakuśala*	ten virtuous actions
dge ba zag med	*anāsravakuśala*	uncorrupted virtuous action(s)
dge ba['i sems byung] bcu gcig	*ekadaśakuśalacaitasika*	eleven wholesome/ virtuous mental states
dge ba'i bshes gnyen	*kalyāṇamitra*	spiritual advisor, scholar monk
dge ba'i sa mang bcu	*daśakuśalamahābhūmika*	group of ten mental states found in all virtuous minds
dge ba'i sems byung	*kuśalacaitasika*	wholesome/ virtuous mental state
dgongs pa	*abhisandhi*	enlightened intention
dgra bcom pa	*arhat*	arhat, worthy one, slayer of the foe
mgyogs pa	*java*	rapidity
'gog pa'i snyoms 'jug	*nirodhasamāpatti*	meditative absorption of cessation
'gog pa'i bden pa	*nirodhasatya*	truth of the cessation [of suffering]
'gyur [ba] med [pa'i] yongs [su] grub [pa]	*niṣvikāraparinispanna*	unchanging consummate nature
'gyod pa	*kaukṛtya*	regret
'grub pa'i yan lag	*abhinirvartakāṅga*	formative links [of dependent origination]
'grub par byed pa'i rten 'brel	*abhinirvartakapratītya-samutpāda*	formative dependent origination

'gro ba	*gati*	sentient being, living being
rga ba	*jarā*	aging
rga shi	*jarāmaraṇa*	aging and death [link of dependent origination]
rgod pa	*auddhatya*	mental agitation
rgyags pa	*mada*	self-satisfaction
rgyal chen bzhi	*caturmahārājakāyika*	Caturmahārājakāyika [realm], four guardian kings
rgyal ba	*jina*	Conqueror
rgyal rigs	*kṣatriyavarṇa*	kingly/ princely class
rgyas pa 'dod pa	*udārādhimukti*	extensive explanation
rgyas pa'i las	*vṛṣṭikriyā*	rite of enrichment
rgyas byung bzhi	*caturaupacāyika*	four cumulative experiences
rgyu mthun ['bras bu]	*niṣyanda[phala]*	[result arising] in conformity with its cause
rgyu dang bcas pa	*sahetukārtha*	endowed with causal basis
rgyu 'bras mthun pa	*anurūpahetuphalārtha*	conformity of cause and result
rgyu 'bras so sor nges pa	*pratiniyatahetuphalārtha*	distinctive regular pattern of cause and result
rgyu med [gnyis]	*adhityasamutpannavāda*	[two] views of fortuitous origin
rgyu mtshan	*nimitta*	appearance, indication, perceptual image
rgyu mtshan gyi rgyu mtshan	*nimittanimitta*	appearance of appearances
rgyu mthan gnyis gnyis	*dvandvanimitta*	dichotomizing/ polarizing appearances
rgyud	*tantra*	tantra-text, continuum
rgyud sde 'og ma		lower tantras
rgyun chags pa'am gnas skabs pa'i rten 'brel	*prākarṣikapratītyasamutpāda*	serial/ circumstantial dependent origination
rgyun chags su 'byung ba	*prābandhika*	continuous origin [of seeds]
rgyun 'jog	*saṃsthāpana*	perpetual placement
rgyun mi 'chad pa	*prabandhānupacchedārtha*	uninterrupted
rgyun mi 'chad pa phyi'i rten 'brel	*bāhyaśasyotpattipratītya-samutpāda*	uninterrupted dependent origination of the external world
rgyu'i kun nas nyon mongs	*hetusaṃkleśa*	causal dissonant mental state(s)
rgyu'i rkyen	*hetupratyaya*	causal condition
rgyu'i rnam par rtog pa	*hetuvikalpa*	imagination of causes
rgyu'i gzugs	*heturūpa*	primary matter
rgyu'i reg bya	*hetuspraṣṭavya*	causal tangible [object]

rgyus zab pa	*hetugāmbhīrya*	profundity [of ultimate reality] on account of its causal basis
sgo lnga	*pañcadvāra*	five senses
sgo lnga['i rnam par shes pa]	*pañcadvāra[vijñāna]*	[consciousnesses of] the five senses
sgom [pa]	*bhāvanā*	meditation
sgom lam	*bhāvanāmārga*	path of meditation
sgyu	*māyā*	deceit
sgra	*śabda*	sound
sgra spyi	*śabdasāmānya*	term-universal
sgra mi snyan	*uttarakuru*	Uttarakuru [continent]
sgrib	*āvaraṇa*	obscuration
sgrib gsum gyis ma gos pa'i yon tan		enlightened attributes untainted by the three obscurations
sgrub mchod	*sādhanapūjā*	offering rite of attainment
sgrub pa po	*sādhaka*	practitioner
sgro 'dogs	*adhyāropa*	superimposition, exaggeration, reification
sgro 'dogs par rtog pa	*adhyāropavikalpa*	imaginations of exaggeration/reification
brgyal ba	*mūrcchā*	unconsciousness, fainting
bsgom[s] pa	*bhāvanā*	meditation
nga rgyal	*māna*	pride
nga rgyal bdun	*saptamāna*	seven subsidiary aspects of pride
nga rgyal las kyang nga rgyal	*mānātimāna*	exaggerated pride
nga'i snyams pa'i nga rgyal	*asmimāna*	egotistical pride
ngan 'gro/ song	*durgati*	inferior beings/ realms of existence
ngan song gsum	*tridurgati*	three inferior realms of existence
ngar 'dzin gyi yid	*ahaṃkāramanas*	egotistical mentation
ngar 'dzin pa'i bdag nyid	*ahaṃkārātman*	perpetual egotism
nges pas 'byung ba	*niryāṇa/ niḥsaraṇa*	definitive liberation
nges tshig gi so so yang dag pa rig pa	*niruktapratisaṃvid*	genuine analytic knowledge of etymological definition
nges legs [kyi go 'phang]	*niḥśreyasa*	[level of] definitive excellence
ngo bo	*svabhāva*	essential nature
ngo bo nyid kyi gYeng ba	*svabhāvavikṣepa*	natural distraction
ngo bo nyid med pa'i yongs su grub pa	*niḥsvabhāvikaparinispanna*	consummate nature devoid of inherent existence

ngo bo nyid dang khyad par gyi kun btags		imagining of the essential nature and its attributes
ngo bo nyid med par smra ba'i dbu ma pa	*niḥsvabhāvikamādhyamika*	Mādhyamika propounding absence of inherent existence
ngo bo nyid gsum	*trisvabhāva*	three natures
ngo tsha med pa	*āhrikya*	lack of conscience
ngo tsha shes pa	*hrī*	conscience
dngos grub	*siddhi*	spiritual accomplishment
dngos po	*bhāva/ vastu*	entity, existent, substantial entity/ thing
dngos po lnga	*pañcavastu*	five entities
dngos po med pa	*avastuka*	non-entity, non-causally effective phenomenon
dngos po gzhan 'gyur gyi dngos med	*bhāvanyāthikābhāva*	non-substantial phenomenon arising through the transformation of substance
dngos po la brten pa'i dngos med	*bhāvaniśritābhāva*	non-substantial phenomenon dependent on substance
dngos po'i don spyi	*bhāvārthasāmānya*	substantial object-universal
dngos po'i don yod pa	*bhāvasadartha*	causal efficacy of substantial entities
dngos po'i ming	*bhāvanāman*	substantive name
dngos med kyi chos	*abhāvadharma*	non-substantial [mental] phenomenon
dngos la btags pa'i mtshan nyid	*bhāvaparikalpitalakṣaṇa*	defining characteristics imputed with regard to substance
dngos 'dzin	*bhāvagraha*	materialism
dngos gzhi	*maula*	actual foundation, main practice
mngar ba	*madhura*	sweet
mngal gyi skabs lnga		five stages of embryonic and fetal development
mngon brjod kyi bag chags	*abhidānavāsanā*	inbuilt propensity
mngon mtho	*abhyudaya*	exalted [realm/ vehicle]
mngon mtho'i theg pa	*abhyudayayāna*	exalted vehicle [of gods and humans]
mngon pa gong ma		Higher Abhidharma [of Asaṅga]
mngon pa 'og ma		Lower Abhidharma [of Vasubandhu]
mngon pa'i nga rgyal	*abhimāna*	manifest pride
mngon pa'i chos	*abhidharma*	Buddhist phenomenology, Abhidharma

mngon par skabs yod kyi gzugs	*abhyavakāśikarūpa*	widespread and spacious atmospheric form(s)
mngon par byang chub	*abhisambodhi*	manifest enlightenment
mngon par 'byung ba brten pa'i tshor ba	*naiṣkramyāśritavedanā*	feeling dependent on renunciation
mngon shes	*abhijñā*	supernormal cognitive power
mngon shes lnga	*pañcābhijñā*	five mundane supernormal cognitive powers
mngon shes drug	*ṣaḍabhijñā*	six supernormal cognitive powers
sngags	*mantra*	mantra
snga' bsgyur		Ancient Translation (i.e., Nyingma) School
sngar las thob pa	*pūrvaprāpti*	former acquisition
sngon gyi mtha'	*pūrvānta*	[speculations about the] limits of past time
sngon gyi gnas mngon par shes pa	*pūrvanivāsābhijñā*	supernormal cognitive power of past abodes
sngon gyi gnas rjes su dran pa'i mngon shes	*pūrvanivāsānusmṛtyabhijñā*	supernormal cognitive power of recollecting past lives
bsngo smon	*pariṇāmapraṇidhāna*	dedication of merit and aspirational prayer
ci yang med pa'i skye mched	*akiṃcanyāyatana*	sensory activity field of nothing-at-all
ci yang med pa'i skye mched kyi snyoms 'jug	*akiṃcanyāyatana*	meditative absorption of the sensory activity field of nothing-at-all
ci yang med pa'i 'du shes	*akiṃcanyasaṃjñā*	perception of nothing-at-all
cung zad snyam pa'i nga rgyal	*ūnamāna*	slight pride
gcig tu 'dzin pa'i rtog pa	*ekatvavikalpa*	imaginations of singularity
bcings pa dang ma bcings par rnam par rtog pa	*bandhābandhavikalpa*	imaginations of bondage and emancipation
bcud kyi sems can		sentient inhabitants, living organisms
bcom ldan 'das	*bhagavān*	transcendent lord [Buddha]
lce'i rnam par shes pa	*jihvāvijñāna*	gustatory consciousness
chad lta	*ucchedadṛṣṭi*	nihilistic view
chad lta smra ba	*ucchedavāda*	nihilism
chu	*udaka*	water
chung ngu'i 'du shes	*parīttasaṃjñā*	limited perception
che ba'i nga rgyal	*adhimāna*	exalted pride
chen po'i 'du shes	*mahadgatasaṃjñā*	extensive perception

chos	*dharma*	teaching, doctrine, phenomenon, thing, attribute
chos kun brtags kyi mtshan nyid	*dharmaparikalpitalakṣaṇa*	imaginary nature that relates to phenomena
chos kyi skye mched	*dharmāyatana*	sensory activity field of phenomena
chos kyi skye mched pa'i khams	*dharmāyatanadhātu*	sensory base deriving from the sensory activity field of [mental] phenomena
chos kyi skye mched pa'i gzugs	*dharmāyatanarūpa*	form(s) associated with the sensory activity field of phenomena
chos kyi skye mched pa'i gzugs lnga	*dharmāyatanapañcarūpa*	five types of form associated with the sensory activity field of phenomena
chos kyi khams	*dharmadhātu*	sensory base of [mental] phenomena
chos [kyi] dbyings	*dharmadhātu*	expanse of reality
chos sku	*dharmakāya*	buddha body of reality
chos kyi so so yang dag pa rang rig	*dharmapratisaṃvid*	genuine analytic knowledge of the teaching
chos skyon med pa nyid	*dharmanirdoṣatā*	stainless nature of reality
chos dge ba rnams kyi de bzhin nyid	*kuśaladharmatathatā*	reality of virtuous phenomena
chos lnga	*pañcadharma*	five foundational factors
chos can	*dharmin*	subject, topic, substance, nuance, facet
chos nyid	*dharmatā*	actual reality
chos nyid yongs su grub pa'i mtshan nyid	*dharmapariniṣpannalakṣaṇa*	consummate nature relating to actual reality
chos gnas pa nyid	*dharmasthititā*	abiding nature of reality
chos rnams kyi gnas lugs		abiding nature of all phenomena
chos mi dge ba rnams kyi de bzhin nyid	*akuśaladharmatathatā*	reality of non-virtuous phenomena
mchod gtor	*bali*	torma-offering
'chab pa	*mrakṣa*	hypocrisy
'chi 'pho skye ba shes pa	*cyutyutpattijñāna*	knowledge of the nature of passing away and rebirth
'chi 'pho dang skye ba mngon par shes pa	*cyutopapādābhijñā*	supernormal cognitive power concering death and subsequent lives
'chi sa	*mṛtyubhūmi*	level of death
'jig rten [gyi] lam		mundane spiritual path

['jig rten] chos brgyad	*aṣṭa[laukika]dharma*	eight [worldly] concerns
'jig rten pa	*laukika*	mundane [gods and humans]
'jig lta	*satkāyadṛṣṭi*	mundane view
'jig pa'i sred pa	*vibhavatṛṣṇā*	craving associated with decay/ perishable phenomena
'jig tshogs la/ su lta ba	*satkāyadṛṣṭi*	view concerning mundane aggregates
'jig tshogs la lta ba nyi shu	*viṃśatisatkāyadṛṣṭi*	twenty viewpoints concerning mundane aggregates
'jigs skyob	*bhayatrāṇa*	protection from fear
'jigs pa med pa yongs su grub pa	*abhayapariniṣpanna*	consummate nature devoid of fear
'jug ldog	*pravṛttinivṛtti*	[sensory] engagement and reversal
'jug pa	*pravṛtti*	engagement, sensory engagement
'jug pa'i rnam shes	*pravṛttivijñāna*	engaged [modes of] consciousness
'jug pa'i sems drug		six modes of engaged consciousness
'jug tshul	*pravṛtti*	process of engagement
'jug shes tshogs [drug]		[six] modes of engaged consciousness
rje'u rigs	*vaiśyavarṇa*	mercantile class
rjes thob	*pṛṣṭhalabdha*	post-meditative experience
rjes dran	*anusmṛti*	recollection [of past lives]
rjes dran drug	*ṣaḍanusmṛti*	six recollections
'jog byed	*vyavasthāpaka*	determinative aspect(s) [of dependent origination]
brjed ngas pa	*muṣitasmṛtitā*	forgetfulness
brjod 'dod	*ācikhyāsā*	supposition
brjod pa'i rnam par rtog pa	*vacanavikalpa*	imaginations of verbal expression
nyan thos	*śrāvaka*	pious attendant
nyan thos kyi theg pa	*śrāvakayāna*	vehicle of pious attendants
nyan rang gi theg pa		vehicles of the pious attendants and hermit buddhas
nyams nas thob pa	*vihīnaprāpti*	acquisition of something that had been lost
nyams len	*anubhava*	experiential cultivation
nying mtshams sbyor ba	*pratisaṃdhi*	moment of conception/ reincarnation
nye bar 'jog pa	*upasthāpanā*	intensified [mental] placement

nye bar nyon mongs	*upakleśa*	subsidiary dissonant mental state
nye [bar] nyon [mongs] nyi shu	*viṃsatyopakleśa*	twenty subsidiary dissonant mental states
nye bar sbyar ba	*upanayana*	propulsion
nye bar spyod pa	*upabhoga*	indulgence, engagement
nye bar spyod pa po	*upabhogin*	experiencer of sensory engagement
nye bar len pa bzhi	*caturupādāna*	four kinds of grasping
nyer bsdogs pa	*samantaka*	preparation [in meditative concentration]
nyer spyod	*upacāra*	sensory environment, environmental role, resources
nyer spyod can gyi rten 'brel	*aupabhogikapratītyasamutpāda*	dependent origination associated with sensory engagement
nyer spyod yongs su bzung bar sred pa		craving that grasps after [material] resources
nyes dmigs	*ādinava*	disadvantage
nyon mong gi sgrib	*kleśāvaraṇa*	obscuration comprising dissonant mental states
nyon mongs can gyi rnam rtog	*kliṣṭavikalpa*	imaginations associated with dissonant mental states
nyon mong pa can gyi ma rig pa	*kliṣṭāvidyā*	ignorance endowed with dissonant mental states
nyon mongs can gyi sa mang drug	*ṣaṭkleśamahābhūmika*	group of six mental states found in all afflicted minds
nyon mongs can ma yin pa'i rnam rtog	*akliṣṭavikalpa*	imagination associated with non-dissonant mental states
nyon mong pa can ma yin pa'i ma rig pa	*akliṣṭāvidyā*	ignorance devoid of dissonant mental states
nyon mongs chung ngu'i sa pa bcu	*parīttakleśabhūmika*	group of ten mental states found in all slightly afflicted minds
nyon mongs pa'i kun nas nyon mongs pa	*kleśasaṃkleśa*	dissonant mental states arising from [other] dissonant mental states
nyon mongs gsum	*trikleśa*	three categories of dissonant mental states
nyon yid [kyi rnam par shes pa]	*kliṣṭamanovijñāna*	dissonant mental consciousness
gnyid [pa]	*middha*	drowsiness, sleep
gnyis min brgyad	*aṣṭanaivasaṃjñīnāsaṃjñīvāda*	eight views on neither percipient nor non-percipient immortality

gnyen po'i yan lag	*pratipakṣāṅga*	antidotal aspect(s)
mnyam nyid	*samatā*	sameness
myam nyid kyi ye shes	*samatājñāna*	pristine cognition of sameness
mnyam bzhag	*samasaṃsthāpa*	meditative equipoise
mnyam gzhag	*samāhita*	meditative equipoise
rnying ma		Nyingma [school]
rnyed thob	*labdhaprāpti*	new acquisition
snying rje [chen po]	*[mahā]karuṇā*	[great] compassion
snyoms 'jug	*samāpatti*	meditative absorption
snyoms 'jug bzhi	*catuḥsamāpatti*	four meditative absorptions
bsnyen gnas kyi sdom pa	*upavāsasaṃvara*	the vow to fast for one day
ting nge 'dzin	*samādhi*	meditative stability
ting nge 'dzin gyi spyod yul gzugs brnyan	*samādhigocararūpa*	images appearing within the perceptual range of meditative stability
ting nge 'dzin gnas kyi yan lag	*samādhisthāṅga*	aspect of abiding in meditative stability
ting nge 'dzin las skyes pa'i dga' bde	*samādhijaprītisukhā*	joy and bliss arising from meditative stability
gtan du ba'i gzugs	*ānatyantikarūpa*	uninterrupted form(s) [indicative of spiritual progress]
gti mug	*moha*	delusion
gti mug med pa	*amoha*	non-delusion
gter [ma]	*nidhi*	treasure, treasure-text, revelation
btags yod	*prajñaptitaḥ*	imputed existent
btang snyoms	*upekṣā*	equanimity
btang snyoms yang dag	*upekṣāpariśuddhi*	purity of equanimity
rtag lta	*śāśvatavāda*	eternalism
rtag smra bzhi	*śāśvatavāda*	four views positing eternalism
rten cing 'brel bar 'byung ba	*pratītyasamutpāda*	dependent origination
rten gyi sdug bsngal	*ādhāraduḥkha*	suffering of the supportive [physical body]
rten 'brel	*pratītyasamutpāda*	dependent origination
rten 'brel gyi de kho na nyid	*pratītyasamutpādatattva*	real nature of dependent origination
rten 'brel [gyi] yan lag bcu gnyis	*dvādaśāṅgapratītyasamutpāda*	twelve links of dependent origination
rten mtshungs	*āśrayasamprayukta*	concomitance of support
rten mtshungs	*sabhāga*	form(s) with a shared support

rtog ge'i lam las 'das pa'i yongs su grub pa		consummate nature transcending the path of sophistry
rtog pa	*vitarka*	ideation, conceptual cognition
lta ngan la mngon par zhen pa'i rnam rtog	*abhiniveśavikalpa*	imaginations/ notions fixated on negative views
lta ba	*dṛṣṭi*	view
lta ba [log pa]	*mithyādṛṣṭi*	wrong view
lta ba mchog 'dzin	*dṛṣṭiparāmarśa*	adherence to the supremacy of wrong views
lta ba'i rnam par rtog pa		imaginations/ notions of philosophical views
lta ba'i len pa	*dṛṣṭyopādāna*	grasping of erroneous views
ltar snang lnga	*pañcābhāsa*	five ostensible contradictions
ltos 'jog gi rten 'brel		mutually interdependent origination
ltos nas btags pa		referentially imputed
stong pa	*śūnya*	empty
stong pa nyid	*śūnyatā*	emptiness
stong [pa] nyid kyi ting nge 'dzin	*śūnyatāsamādhi*	meditative stability of emptiness
stong pa nyid kyi rten 'brel	*śūnyatāpratītyasamutpāda*	dependent origination of emptiness
stong [pa nyid] bcu drug	*ṣoḍdaśaśūnyatā*	sixteen aspects/ types of emptiness
stong pa spros bral	*niḥprapañcaśūnyatā*	emptiness free from conceptual elaboration
ston pa	*śāstṛ*	Teacher [=Buddha]
stobs	*bala*	power
stobs lnga	*pañcabala*	five powers
stobs bcu	*daśabala*	ten powers
brtul zhugs	*vrata*	austerity/ vow
bstan bcos	*śāstra*	treatise
bstan med thogs bcas	*anidarśanasapratigha*	unrevealed and obstructed [forms]
bstan med thogs med	*anidarśanāpratigha*	unrevealed and unobstructed [forms]
bstan yod thogs bcas	*sanidarśanasapratigha*	revealed and obstructed [forms]
tha snyad	*vyavahāra*	conventional term
tha snyad ming tshig yi ge gsum du snang ba'i rnam rig		apperception [of linguistic concepts] that manifest as conventional terms, phrases, and letters

tha dad pa'i ming	*nānānāma*	diversifying name
thabs	*upāya*	skillful means
thams cad mkhyen pa [nyid]	*sarvajñatā/ sarvajñātā*	omniscience
thar pa	*mokṣa*	release [from rebirth in cyclic existence]
thugs	*citta*	buddha mind
thugs rje	*karuṇā*	compassion
thugs dam		meditative commitment
thun mong gi sngon 'gro		common prerequisite/ preliminary practices
thun mong ma yin pa 'khor lo tha ma'i lugs		tradition of the uncommon final promulgation
the tshom	*vicikitsā*	doubt
theg chen pa	*mahāyānin*	follower of the Greater Vehicle
theg pa	*yāna*	vehicle
theg (pa) chen (po)	*mahāyāna*	Greater Vehicle
theg pa gsum	*triyāna*	three vehicles
theg dman	*hīnayāna*	Lesser Vehicle
theg dman pa	*hīnayānin*	follower of the Lesser Vehicle
theg rim dgu	*navayāna*	nine sequences of the vehicle
thogs bcas kyi gzugs	*sapratigharūpa*	obstructive matter
thob pa	*prāpti*	acquisition
thos pa	*śrūti*	study, learning
mtha' ldan [bzhi]	*antānantavāda*	[four] views on finitude
mtha' mi spong [bzhi]	*amāravikṣepavāda*	[four] views of equivocation
mtha' bzhi	*caturanta*	four extremes
mthar lta	*antadṛṣṭi*	extreme view
mthu stobs kyis rab tu dbye ba'i rten 'brel	*prabhāvaprabhedapratītya-samutpāda*	dependent origination well-distinguished by means of [spiritual] power
mtho ris	*svarga*	higher/ exalted realms [of gods and humans]
mtho ris gsum	*trisvarga*	three higher realms of existence
mthong chos myong 'gyur	*dṛṣṭadharmavedayitvā*	presently perceptible phenomena [of this life]
mthong lam	*darśanamārga*	path of insight
dag pa 'jig rten pa'i gzhan dbang		pure mundane dependent nature
dag pa'i snang ba		pure vision
dang ba	*prasāda*	confidence

dang ba	*accha/ svaccha*	clear
dad pa	*śraddhā*	faith
dam pa'i chos	*saddharma*	sacred teaching
dam tshig	*samaya*	meditative commitment
dam tshig sems dpa'	*samayasattva*	being of meditative commitment, visualized deity
dam rdzas	*samayadravya*	sacrament, sacramental substance
du mar 'dzin pa'i rtog pa	*nānātvavikalpa*	imaginations of multiplicity
dug gsum	*triviṣa*	three poisons
dus	*kāla*	time
dus mchod		anniversary offering ceremony
dus thams cad du yongs su grub pa		consummate nature present at all times
dus mtshungs	*kālasamprayukta*	concomitance of time
dus la btags pa'i mtshan nyid	*kālaparikalpitalakṣaṇa*	defining characteristics imputed with regard to time
dus su snang ba'i rnam rig		apperception of temporal divisions that become manifest
de kho na yid	*tattva*	nature of reality
de kho na nyid kyi gnas lugs	*tattvasthiti*	abiding nature of reality
de kho na nyid kyi yongs su grub pa		consummate nature of the real
de ma thag rkyen	*samanantarapratyaya*	immediate condition
de bzhin nyid	*tathatā*	absolute reality, suchness
de bzhin nyid kyi rgyu mtshan	*tathatānimitta*	appearances of absolute reality
de bzhin nyid la snyoms par zhugs dus kyi 'du shes		perception coincidental with meditative equipoise in reality
de bzhin nyid gsum	*trayatathatā*	three aspects of reality
de bzhin du smra ba'i rnam par rtog pa		imaginations focusing on absolute reality
de bzhin gshegs pa	*tathāgata*	Buddha
de la brten pa'i sdug bsngal	*ādheyaduḥkha*	suffering based on [the physical body]
de'i mtshungs kyi gzugs	*tatsabhāgarūpa*	form(s) resembling those with a shared support
don	*artha*	object, meaning, purpose
don so sor yang dag pa rang rig	*arthapratisaṃvid*	genuine analytic knowledge of meaning
don lnga	*pañcārtha*	five sense objects
don dam gyi dngos po	*paramārthavastu*	absolute entity

don dam gyi rten 'brel	*paramārthapratītyasamutpāda*	ultimate aspect of dependent origination
don dam stong pa nyid kyi rten 'brel	*paramārthaśūnyatāpratītya-samutpāda*	dependent origination of emptiness, the ultimate reality
don dam [pa]	*paramārtha*	ultimate reality
don dam [pa'i] bden pa	*paramārthasatya*	ultimate truth
don dam pa'i gnas lugs		abiding nature of ultimate reality
don dam pa'i yid		absolute mentation
don byed nus pa	*arthakriyāsamartha*	causally effective
don bsdu	*aṅgasamāsa*	synthesis [of dependent origination]
don la ming du rtog pa	*yathārthanāmā-bhiniveśavikalpa*	imagination of names in relation to meaning [i.e., naïve substantialism]
drag pa'i las	*rudrakriyā*	rite of wrath
drang srong	*ṛṣi*	hermit sage
dran pa	*smṛti*	mindfulness, recollection
dran pa nye [bar] bzhag [pa]	*smṛtyupasthāna*	foundation of mindfulness
dran pa yang dag	*smṛtipariśuddhi*	purity of recollection
dri [ma]	*gandha*	odor
dri med yongs grub	*vimalapariniṣpanna*	immaculate consummate nature
drug pa'i yid		mentation of the sixth [mode of engaged consciousness]
gdags byed	*prajñāpana*	designator
gdags gzhi	*prajñaptivastu*	basis of designation
gdol rigs	*caṇḍāla*	[social] outcaste
bdag	*ātma*	self
bdag ngal dub kyi mtha'	*ātmaklamathānta*	extreme of self-mortification
bdag tu smra ba'i nye bar len pa	*ātmavādopādāna*	grasping after belief in an [inherently existing] self
bdag tu 'dzin pa	*ātmagraha*	apprehension of self, egotistical grasping
bdag [po'i] rkyen	*adhipatipratyaya*	predominant condition
bdag po'i 'bras bu	*adhipatiphala*	predominant result
bdag med [pa]	*nairātmya*	selflessness
bdag med pa gnyis	*nairātmyadvaya*	two aspects of selflessness
bdag med pa'i de kho na nyid	*nairātmyatattva*	real nature of selflessness
bdud bzhi	*caturmāra*	four demonic forces
bde 'gro	*sugati*	happy beings [of the higher realms]

bde ba	*sukha*	bliss
bde bar gshegs pa	*sugata*	Buddha
bde bar gshegs pa'i snying po	*sugatagarbha*	buddha nature, seed of buddhahood
bden [pa] bzhi	*catur[ārya]satya*	four [sublime] truths
mdo	*sūtra*	sūtra, discourse
mdo sde pa	*sautrāntika*	Sautrāntika
'du byed	*saṃskāra*	formative predisposition(s)
'du byed kyi phung po	*saṃskāraskandha*	aggregate of formative predispositions
'du shes	*saṃjñā*	perception
'du shes kyi phung po	*saṃjñāskandha*	aggregate of perceptions
'du shes dang tshor ba 'gog pa	*saṃjñāvedayitanirodha*	cessation of perception and feeling
'du shes med pa	*āsaṃjñika*	state of non-perception
'du shes med pa'i snyoms 'jug	*asaṃjñīsamāpatti*	meditative absorption devoid of perception
'du shes med min gyi snyoms 'jug	*naivasaṃjñānasaṃjñāyatana*	meditative absorption in the activity field of neither perception nor non-perception
'du shes med smra	*asaṃjñīvāda*	views on the non-percipience of the self after death
'du shes yod smra	*saṃjñīvāda*	views holding the self to be percipient after death
'dun pa	*chanda*	will
'dul ba	*damana/ vinaya*	control, discipline
'dus pa'i ming		integrating name
'dus byas dang 'dus ma byas pa'i thob pa	*saṃskṛtāsaṃskṛtaprāpti*	acquisition of conditioned and unconditioned phenomena
'dus ma byas kyi khams	*asaṃskṛtadhātu*	unconditioned sensory base
'dus ma byas bzhi	*caturasamskṛta*	four unconditioned things
'dus ma byas gsum		three categories of unconditioned phenomena
'dod khams kyi mi dge ba		non-virtuous past action(s) associated with the world-system of desire
'dod khams kyi las dge ba		virtuous past action(s) pertaining to the world-system of desire
'dod chags	*rāga*	desire, attachment
'dod pa	*kāma*	desire, attachment
'dod pa	*icchā*	aspiration, wish

'dod pa dang mi 'dod par 'gro ba rab tu dbye ba'i rten 'brel	*iṣṭāniṣṭagativibhāgapratītya-samutpāda*	dependent origination that distinguishes living beings according to desirable and undesirable [realms of rebirth]
'dod pa bsod nyams kyi mtha'	*kāmasukhallikānta*	extreme of over-indulgence
'dod [pa'i] khams	*kāmadhātu*	world-system of desire
'dod pa'i len pa	*kāmopādāna*	grasping after desires
'dod lha rigs drug	*kāmadevaṣaṭkula*	six species of Kāma divinities
rdul phra rab	*paramāṇu*	indivisible atomic particle
rdo rje lta bu'i ting nge 'dzin	*vajropamasamādhi*	adamantine meditative stability
rdo rje'i lus	*vajrakāya*	body of indestructible reality, indestructible body
ldan thob	*samanvāgama*	uninterrupted possession
ldan min 'du byas	*cittaviprayuktasaṃskāra*	formative predisposition(s) disassociated from mind
ldan tshul		quantification
ldog pa	*vyatireka*	distinguisher, counterpart
ldog tshul	*nivṛtti*	process of reversal [of sensory engagement]
sdug bsngal [ba]	*duḥkha*	suffering
sdug bsngal rnams skye ba'i kun nas nyon mongs pa	*janmasaṃkleśa*	dissonant mental states arising from the birth of sufferings
sdug pa	*priya*	attractive [phenomena]
sdug pa dang mi sdug pa rnam par 'byed pa'i rten 'brel	*priyāpriyavibhāgapratītyasam-utpāda*	dependent origination that distinguishes attractive and unattractive [goals]
sdug pa rnam par 'byed pa'i rten 'brel	*priyavibhāgapratītyasamut-pāda*	dependent origination that distinguishes attractive goals
sde snod	*piṭaka*	scriptural compilation
sdom pa	*vrata/ saṃvara*	vow
sdom brtson	*saṃyama*	ascetic endeavor, renunciate endeavor
bsdus pa las gyur pa'i gzugs	*ābhisaṃkṣepikarūpa*	extremely small and concentrated atomic form
nang gi de kho na nyid		real nature of internal [phenomena]
nang gi gzugs dang ba	*ādhyātmakarūpa*	clear and sensitive matter
nang gi gYeng ba	*adhyātmavikṣepa*	internal distraction
nang gi sa bon		internal seeds
nang bcud		sentient inhabitants, inner contents
nang rab tu dang ba	*adhyātmasamprasāda*	intense inner clarity

nam mkha'	*ākāśa*	space
nam mkha' kha dog gcig pa		monochrome sky
nam mkha' mtha' yas skye mched kyi snyoms 'jug	*ākāśānantyāyatanasamāpatti*	meditative absorption of the sensory activity field of infinite space
nur nur po	*kalala*	clotting of the embryo
nus pa mthu can	*samartha*	potential
nus pa so sor nges pa	*samarthapratyaya*	idiosyncratic potency
nor gyi rnam par rtog pa	*dhanavikalpa*	imaginations/ notions of property
gnas skabs	*avasthā*	circumstance
gnas skabs kyi rten 'brel	*avasthānapratītyasamutpāda*	circumstantial dependent origination
gnas skabs ldan pa ma yin pa'i 'du byed		circumstantial formative predisposition disassociated [with mind and mental states]
gnas skabs pa'i yid	*avasthāmanas*	circumstantial mentation
gnas [pa]	*sthiti*	duration
gnas pas zab pa	*sthitigāmbhīrya*	profundity [of ultimate reality] on account of its duration
gnas ma bu pa	*vatsīputrīya*	Vatsīputrīya
gnas lugs [kyi don]	*sthiti*	abiding nature of reality
gnas sam rten [gyi mtshungs]	*āśraya[samprayukta]*	[concomitance of] location/ support
mnar sems med pa	*anāghāta*	absence of enmity
rna'i rnam par shes pa	*śrotravijñāna*	auditory consciousness
rnam grangs brgyad		eightfold reasoning [in proof of the substratum]
rnam grangs pa'i kun btags	*paryāyaparikalpita*	nominal imaginary
rnam grangs sam btags pa'i 'dus ma byas		symbolic or imputed unconditioned phenomena
rnam rtog gi rgyu mtshan	*vikalpanimitta*	appearances of false imagination
rnam thar brgyad	*aṣṭavimokṣa*	eight approaches to liberation
rnam bden pa	*ākāravādin*	Vijñānavādin holding sensa to be veridical
rnam pa mtshungs	*ākārasamprayukta*	concomitance of sensum
rnam par rtog pa	*vikalpa*	[false] imagination, notion, conceptual thought
rnam par dag pas rab tu dbye ba'i rten 'brel	*viśuddhiprabhedapratītyasam-utpāda*	dependent origination well-distinguished by means of purity

rnam par byang ba'i chos kyi rgyu nyid du yongs su grub pa		consummate nature present as the seed of all purificatory teachings
rnam par mi rtog pa'i ye shes	*nirvikalpajñāna*	non-conceptual pristine cognition
rnam par mi 'tshe ba	*ahiṃsa*	non-violence
rnam par gzhag bya 'jog byed kyi ltos bzhag	*vyavasthāpyavyavasthāpaka*	mutual interdependence of the determined and determinative
rnam par gYeng ba'i rnam rtog	*vikṣepavikalpa*	distracting imagination
rnam par rig pa	*pratívid*	apperception
rnam par rig pa tsam	*vijñaptimātra*	mere apperception, apperception alone, ideation alone
rnam par rig pa'i shes pa		apperceptive consciousness
rnam par rig byed	*vijñapti*	apperception
rnam par rig byed kyi gzugs	*vijñaptirūpa*	apperceived [but intangible] form
rnam par rig byed ma yin pa'i gzugs	*avijñaptirūpa*	imperceptible form, non-apperceived form
rnam par shes pa	*vijñāna*	consciousness
rnam par shes pa'i khams	*vijñānadhātu*	sensory base of consciousness
rnam par shes pa'i phung po	*vijñānaskandha*	aggregate of consciousness
rnam par shes pa 'byung ba'i rten 'brel	*vijñānotpattipratītya-samutpāda*	dependent origination through which consciousness arises
rnam par shes pa'i zas	*vijñānāhāra*	nourishment of consciousness
rnam byang	*vyavadāna*	purification
rnam byang gi rten 'brel	*vyavadānapratītyasamutpāda*	dependent origination associated with purified states
rnam smin	*vipāka*	ripening
rnam smin gyi rgyu	*vipākahetu*	ripening cause
rnam smin gyi cha	*vipākabhāga*	maturational aspect [of the substratum consciousness]
rnam smin gyi rnam shes	*vipākavijñāna*	fruitional/ maturational consciousness
rnam smin gyi 'bras bu	*vipākaphala*	ripening result
rnam rdzun pa	*nirākāravādin*	Vijñānavādin holding sensa to be false
rnam zhi	*vyupaśamana*	quiescence
rnam gzhag	*vyavasthāna*	systematic presentation
rnam gYeng gi rnam rtog bcu	*daśavikalpa*	ten aspects of distracting imagination
rnam rig	*vijñapti*	apperception

rnam shes		see *rnam par shes pa*
rnam shes lnga dang mtshungs ldan gyi sim pa bde ba		sensual happiness in affinity with the five types of sensory consciousness
rnam shes mtha' yas skye mched kyi snyoms 'jug	*vijñānāntyāyatanasamāpatti*	meditative absorption of the sensory activity field of infinite consciousness
rnam shes dang mtshungs ldan gyi gdung bas dug bsngal		physical pain in affinity with [sensory] consciousness
rnam shes drug gi 'gyur ba las byung ba mtshan ma snang bar 'gyur ba'i rnam rtog	*nimittābhāsapariṇāmavikalpa*	changeable imaginations mirroring variations of the six modes of [engaged] consciousness
rnam shes drug mtshan snang gi rnam rtog	*nimittābhāsavikalpa*	imaginations mirroring the six modes of [engaged] consciousness
rnam shes tsam bag chags kyi gzugs snang ba lus kyi dbang por snang ba'i rnam rig		apperception that the physical manifestations of propensities which are "only consciousness" appear to the sense faculty of the body
rnam shes tshogs brgyad	*aṣṭavijñāna*	eight modes of consciousness
rnam shes tshogs drug	*ṣaḍvijñāna*	six modes of consciousness
rnal 'byor gyi rgyud	*yogatantra*	Union Tantra
rnal 'byor pa	*yogin*	yogin
sna tshogs pa	*vicitra[hetuphala]*	diversity [of causes and results]
sna'i rnam par shes pa	*ghrāṇavijñāna*	olfactory consciousness
snang ba gzugs	*ābhāsarūpa*	apparent form(s)
snod kyi 'jig rten	*bhājanaloka*	physical environment
snod kyi [rab tu dbye ba'i] rten 'brel	*saṃvartavivartapratītya-samutpāda*	dependent origination [which is an extensive analysis] of the physical environment
dpyod pa	*vicāra*	scrutiny
dpyod pa yid la byed pa	*mīmāṃsāmanaskāra*	attention imbued with scrutiny
dpyod pa'i lhag mthong	*vicāravipaśyana*	higher insight endowed with scrutiny
spobs pa so sor yang dag pa rang rig pa	*pratibhanapratisaṃvid*	genuine analytic knowledge of intellectual brilliance
spyod pa	*caryā*	conduct
spyod pa'i rgyud	*caryātantra*	Conduct Tantra
sprin med	*anabhraka*	Cloudless [realm]
spros pa med pa	*niḥprapañca*	free from conceptual elaboration
pha rol [gyi] sems	*paracitta*	other minds
pha rol tu phyin pa drug	*ṣaṭpāramitā*	six transcendental perfections

phan yon gyi yan lag	*anuśaṃsāṅga*	beneficial aspects(s)
phal chen	*Mahāsaṅghika*	Mahāsaṅghika [school]
phung po	*skandha*	psycho-physical aggregate
phung po lnga	*pañcaskandha*	five psycho-physical aggregates
phung pos bsdus pa'i khams		sensory base subsumed in the psycho-physical aggregates
phung pos ma bsdus pa'i khams		sensory base not subsumed in the psycho-physical aggregates
phyi tha snyad pa'i yul kun rdzob		relative [seeds], comprising objects of external, conventional appearance
phyi don du smra ba	*bāhyārthavādin*	propounder of the existence of external objects
phyi snod		outer container world, physical environment
phyi [ma'i] mtha'	*aparānta*	limits of future time
phyi rol gyi don lnga	*pañcabahyārtha*	five external objects
phyi rol du gYeng ba	*bahirdhāvikṣepa*	external distraction
phyi'i rten 'brel	*bāhyapratītyasamutpāda*	dependent origination of the external [world]
phyi'i sa bon	*bāhyabīja*	external seed(s)
phyin ci ma log pa'i yongs [su] grub [pa]	*aviparyāsaparinispanna*	incontrovertible consummate nature
phyin ci log tu 'khrul pa'i tshul min		absence of erroneous bewilderment
phyin ci log pa	*viparyāsa*	error, perversion
phyir mi ldog pa'i 'khor lo	*avaivartacakra*	irreversible promulgation [of the Buddha's teachings]
phyir mi ldog pa'i yongs su grub pa	*avaivartaparinispanna*	irreversible consummate nature
phra ba'i lus	*sūkṣmakāya*	subtle body
phra ba'i mi rtag pa	*sūkṣmānitya*	subtle impermanence
phrag dog	*īrṣyā*	jealousy
'phags pa	*ārya*	sublime being
'phags pa bden pa bzhi	*caturāryasatya*	four sublime/ noble truths
'phags lam	*āryamārga*	sublime path
'phangs pa'i yan lag	*ākṣiptāṅga*	projected link [of dependent origination]
'phangs pa'i yan lag lnga	*pañcākṣiptāṅga*	five projected links [of dependent origination]
'phen grub rgyu bdun		seven projective and formative causes [of dependent origination]

'phen grub bzhi ldan		fourfold process of projection and formation [of dependent origination]
'phen pa	*ākṣepa*	projection
'phen pa'i rten 'brel	*ākṣepapratītyasamutpāda*	projective dependent origination
'phen byed kyi yan lag	*ākṣepakāṅga*	projective link [of dependent origination]
'phen byed kyi yan lag gnyis	*dvyākṣepakāṅga*	two projective links [of dependent origination]
'phrul dga'	*nirmāṇarata*	Nirmāṇarata [realm]
ba langs spyod	*aparagodānīya*	Aparagodānīya [continent]
bag chags	*vāsanā*	propensity
bag la nyal [phra zhing phra] ba	*anuśaya*	subtle latent tendency
bag med	*pramāda*	carelessness
bag yod	*apramāda*	vigilance
bems po'i rdzas	*acetanavastu*	inert substance
bya ba'i rgyud	*kriyātantra*	Action Tantra
byang chub	*bodhi*	enlightenment
byang chub [kyi] phyogs/ yan lag	*bodhipakṣa/ bodhyaṅga*	branch/ aspect of enlightenment
byang [chub kyi] phyogs so bdun	*saptatriṃśad-bodhipakṣa[dharma]*	thirty-seven aspects of enlightenment
byang chub [kyi] sems	*bodhicitta*	enlightened mind, enlightened attitude
byang chub sems dpa'	*bodhisattva*	bodhisattva
byang chub sems dpa'i spyod dbang	*bodhisattvacaryābhiṣeka*	empowerment of the bodhisattva's conduct
byang chub gsum	*bodhitraya*	three degrees of enlightenment
byams pa	*maitrī*	loving-kindness
bye brag smra ba	*vaibhāṣika*	Vaibhāṣika
byed pa po med pa	*niḥkārtṛka*	without an agent
byed po	*kartṛ*	creator
byed las	*karmavyavasthāna*	function
bram ze'i rigs	*brāhmaṇavarṇa*	priestly class
bla dvags	*adhivacana*	designation
bla na med pa'i rgyud	*yoganiruttaratantra*	Unsurpassed Yogatantra
bla med yang dag par rdzogs pa'i byang chub	*anuttarasamyaksambodhi*	unsurpassed, genuinely perfect enlightenment
dbang bskur	*abhiṣeka*	empowerment
dbang bcu	*daśavaśitā*	ten dominions

dbang po lnga	*pañcendriya*	five sense organs/ faculties
dbang po brtul po	*mṛdvindriya*	dull faculties
dbang po rnon po	*tīkṣṇendriya*	keen faculties
dbang po 'bring	*madhyendriya*	mediocre/ average faculties
dbang po gzugs can lnga'i khams		sensory base(s) of the five physical sense organs
dbang po'i 'gyur ba yongs su gcod pa	*indriyavikāraparicched a*	preclusion modifying the sense faculties
dbang 'byor ba'i gzugs	*vaibhutvikarūpa*	forms deriving from supernormal powers
dbang shes lnga	*pañcendriyajñāna*	five sensory consciousnesses
dbang shes drug		six [modes of engaged] sensory consciousness
dbu ma	*madhyamaka*	Madhyamaka
dbu ma	*avadhūti*	central channel [of the subtle body]
dbu ma pa	*mādhyamika*	Mādhyamika
dbu ma pa rnal 'byor spyod pa	*yogacāramādhyamika*	Yogacārin Mādhyamika
dbu ma rang rgyud pa	*svātantrikamādhyamika*	Mādhyamika upholding independent reasoning
dben pa las skyes pa'i yid la byed pa	*prāvivekyamanaskāra*	attention arising through isolation
dbye ba	*bheda/ vibhāga*	classification
'byung ba	*bhūta*	element
'byung [ba chen po] bzhi	*caturmahābhūta*	four primary elements
'byung ba'i khams		sensory base of the elements
'byung bas zab pa	*vṛttigāmbhīrya*	profundity [of ultimate reality] on account of its functioning
'byor 'brel ba	*yoga*	connection
'bras bu	*phala*	result
'bras bu che	*bṛhatphala*	Great Fruition [realm]
'bras bu'i nye nyon bdun	*saptaphalasaṃkleśa*	seven fruitional dissonant mental states
'bras bu'i dus kyi rnam shes		fruitional [substratum] consciousness
'bras bu'i gzugs	*phalarūpa*	derivative matter
'bras bu'i reg bya	*phalaspraṣṭavya*	fruitional tangible [object]
'brel ba can gyi rten 'brel	*sāṃbandhikapratītyasamut-pāda*	interconnected dependent origination
'brel ba'i ming		relational name
'brel bar rnam par rtog pa	*saṃbandhavikalpa*	imaginations of interdependence

sbyin pa	*dāna*	generosity
sbyin sreg	*homa*	burnt offering
sbyor ba'i mtha' yid la byed pa	*prayoganiṣṭhamanaskāra*	attention imbued with perfected application
sbyor ba'i mtha'i 'bras bu yid la byed pa	*prayoganiṣṭhaphalamanaskāra*	attention to the fruit of perfected application
ma grags pa'i ming		unknown name
ma rgyud	*mātṛtantra*	Mother Tantra
ma chags pa	*alobha*	non-attachment
ma thob pa las thob pa	*aprāptiprāpti*	acquisition of something that had not been acquired
ma dag 'jig rten pa'i gzhan dbang		impure mundane dependent nature
ma dad pa	*aśraddhya*	faithlessness
ma nor ba'i de bzhin nyid	*avitathatā*	unmistaken absolute reality
ma zin pa'i 'byung ba las gyur ba'i sgra	*anupāttamahābhūtahetuka-śabda*	inorganically produced sound [of the primary elements]
ma rig pa	*avidyā*	fundamental ignorance
ma rig pa dang mtshungs ldan gyi las dge sdig		virtuous and negative actions concomitant with ignorance
ma rig pa dang mtshungs ldan gyi dge ba zag bcas		corrupt virtuous actions concomitant with ignorance
ma rig pa dang mtshungs ldan pa'i las mi dge ba		non-virtuous actions concomitant with ignorance
man ngag	*upadeśa*	pith instruction, esoteric instruction
mi skye bar rnam par rtog pa	*anutpādavikalpa*	imaginations of non-birth
mi dge ba bcu	*daśākuśala*	ten non-virtuous actions
mi dge ba'i sa pa chen po gnyis	*dvyayākuśalamahābhūmika*	group of two mental states found in all non-virtuous [minds]
mi 'jigs bzhi	*caturvaiśāradhya*	four fearlessnesses
mi chos bcu drug		sixteen [commonly accepted] human laws
mi rtag pa	*anitya/ anityatā*	impermanence, impermanent
mi sdug pa	*apriya*	unattractive [phenomena]
mi sdug pa rnam par 'byed pa'i rten 'brel	*apriyavibhāgapratītyasamut-pāda*	dependent origination distinguishing unattractive [goals]
mi gstang ba'i ting nge 'dzin	*aśucisamādhi*	meditative stability on impure phenomena
mi 'tshe ba	*ahiṃsa*	non-violence
mi gYo ba	*āniñjya*	immovable state

mi gYo ba'i las	*āniñjyakarma*	unwavering/ non-dynamic [results of] past action(s)
mi srid pa'i dngos med	*asambhavābhāva*	non-substantial phenomena which do not exist/ non-existing non-entities
mi slob pa'i lam	*aśaikṣamārga*	path of no-more-learning
mi gsal ba gnyis		two kinds of invisible [seed]
mig gi skye mched	*cakṣurāyatana*	sensory activity field of the eye
mig gi yul	*cakṣurviṣaya*	sense objects of the eyes
mig shes dbang por snang ba lus can gyi rnam rig		apperception that corporeal forms become manifest to the faculty of visual consciousness
mig shes sogs nye bar longs spyod pa'i rnam rig		apperception of resources associated with visual consciousness and so forth
ming gi rgyu mtshan	*nāmanimtta*	appearances of names
mig [gi rnam par] shes [pa]	*cakṣurvijñāna*	visual consciousness
ming gi tshogs	*nāmakāya*	nominal cluster
ming bzhi'i phung po	*caturnāmaskandha*	fourfold nominal aggregates, [non-material] aggregates "endowed with four names"
ming gzugs	*nāmarūpa*	name and form
ming la don du rtog pa	*yathānāmārthābhiniveśavi-kalpa*	imagination of meanings that accord with names [i.e., naïve realism]
mu stegs	*tīrtha*	extreme, ford, prop, stepping stone
mu stegs can/ byed	*tīrthika*	eternalistic/ philosophical extremist
mu sbyor ba		parameter
me	*agni/ tejas*	fire
me long lta bu'i ye shes	*ādarśajñāna*	mirror-like pristine cognition
mer mer po	*arbuda*	oval formation of the embryo
med pa'i stong pa nyid	*abhāvaśūnyatā*	emptiness of non-existence
med par rtog pa	*abhāvavikalpa*	imaginations of non-existence
mos pa	*adhimokṣa*	resolve
mos pa las byung ba yid la byed pa	*ādhimokṣikamanaskāra*	attention arising through resolve
mya ngan las 'das	*nirvāṇa*	nirvāṇa (= liberation transcending suffering)
dmangs rigs	*śudravarṇa*	laboring class
dmigs rnam	*ālambanākāra*	objective reference and sense data

dmigs pa	*ālambana*	object of reference
dmigs pa yongs grub	*ālambanapariniṣpanna*	consummate nature of the [scriptural] objectives
dmigs pa'i rkyen	*ālambanapratyaya*	referential condition
dmigs mtshungs	*ālambanasamprayukta*	concomitance of objective referent
dmyal ba	*naraka*	hells
rmugs pa	*styāna*	dullness
rmongs pa gsum	*trimoha*	three aspects of delusion
smon lam	*praṇidhāna*	aspiration
gtso bo sems [nyid]		central mind
rtsa nyon	*mūlakleśa*	primary dissonant mental state
rtsa nyon drug	*ṣaḍmūlakleśa*	six primary dissonant mental states
rtsa ba'i rnam rtog [kun gzhi'i rnam shes]	*mūlavikalpa*	fundamental imaginations petaining to substratum consciousness
rtsa ba'i rnam shes	*mūlavijñāna*	fundamental consciousness
rtsa ba'i ma rig pa	*mūlāvidyā*	fundamental ignorance
rtsa rlung thig le	*nāḍī-vāyu-bindu*	energy channels, winds, and generative essences
rtse gcig	*ekotīkaraṇa*	one-pointedness
brtson 'grus	*vīrya*	perseverance
tsha ba	*kaṭuka*	spicy
tshangs pa chen po	*mahābrahmā*	Great Brahmā [realm]
tshangs pa mdun na 'don	*brahmapurohita*	Priest Brahmā [realm]
tshangs ris	*brahmakāyika*	Stratum of Brahmā [realm]
tshangs pa'i theg pa	*brahmāyāna*	vehicle of Brahmā
tshad med	*aprameya*	immeasurable aspiration
tshad med dge	*apramāṇaśubha*	Immeasurable Virtue [realm]
tshad med pa'i 'du shes	*aprameyasaṃjñā*	infinite perception
tshad med 'od	*apramāṇābha*	Immeasurable Radiance [realm]
tshad med bzhi	*caturaprameya*	four immeasurable aspirations
tshig gi tshogs	*padakāya*	phrasal cluster
tshig bsdus pa	*samāsa*	concise explanation
tshul khrims	*śīla*	ethical discipline
tshul khrims kyi bslab pa	*śīlaśikṣā*	training of ethical discipline
tshul khrims dang brtul zhugs mchog 'dzin	*śīlavrataparāmarśa*	adherence to the supremacy of ethical and ascetic disciplines
tshul bzhin gyi rnam rtog	*yoniśovikalpa*	appropriate imaginations

tshul bzhin ma yin pa'i rnam rtog	*ayoniśovikalpa*	inappropriate imaginations
tshe 'di nyid la grol lta	*dṛṣṭidharmanirvāṇavāda*	view(s) concerning the attainment of liberation in this lifetime
tshogs brgyad	*aṣṭavijñāna*	eight modes [of consciousness]
tshogs drug	*ṣaḍvijñāna*	six modes [of consciousness]
tshogs pa	*sāmagrī*	grouping
tshor ba	*vedanā*	feeling, sensation
tshor ba btang snyoms	*vedanopekṣā*	equanimity of feelings
tshor ba'i de bzhin nyid	*vedanātathatā*	reality of feeling
tshor ba'i phung po	*vedanāskandha*	aggregate of feelings
mtshan bcas dang mtshan ma med pa'i rnam rtog	*sanimittanirnimittavikalpa*	symbolic and non-symbolic imagination
mtshan nyid kyi chos	*lakṣaṇadharma*	[mental] phenomena denoting defining characteristics
mtshan nyid kyi rnam par rtog pa	*lakṣaṇavikalpa*	imagination of defining characteristics
mtshan nyid kyis zab pa	*lakṣaṇagāmbhīrya*	profundity [of ultimate reality] on account of its defining characteristics
mtshan nyid med pa	*animitta*	signlessness
mtshan nyid yongs su chad pa'i kun btags	*paricchedaparikalpita*	imaginary nature of delimited characteristics
mtshan nyid rab tu rig pa yid la byed pa	*lakṣaṇapratisaṃ-vedanāmanaskāra*	attention that is aware of individual characteristics
mtshan nyid gsum	*trilakṣaṇa*	three natures
mtshan ma dang bcas pa'i 'du shes	*sanimittasaṃjñā*	symbolic perception
mtshan ma med pa'i 'du shes	*animittasaṃjñā*	non-symbolic perception
mtshan ma la 'ching ba'i gnas		locus binding [engaged consciousness] to substantialist views
mtshan ma'i gYeng ba	*nimittavikṣepa*	distraction of symbolism
mtshan gzhi	*lakṣya*	demonstration, illustration
mtshan gzhi['i] chos	*lakṣyadharma*	factor denoting illustration/ demonstration
mtshungs ldan	*sabhāga/ samprayuktaka*	affinity, concomitance
mtshungs ldan rnam pa lnga	*pañcasamprayuktaka*	five concomitant characteristics
mtshungs par ldan pa ma yin pa'i 'du byed	*cittaviprayuktasaṃskāra*	formative predispositions disassociated with mind
'tshig pa	*pradāśa*	annoyance

'tshol ba po'i rnam rtog	*paryeṣakavikalpa*	investigative [imagination]
'dzam bu gling	*jambudvīpa*	Jambudvīpa [continent]
'dzin pa log pa'i nga rgyal	*mithyāmāna*	perverse pride
rdzas mtshungs	*dravyasamprayukta*	concomitance of substance
rdzas yod	*dravyataḥ*	substantial existent
rdzas yod kyi dngos po	*dravyataḥ vastu*	substantial existent
rdzu 'phrul gyi mngon par shes pa	*ṛddhiviṣayābhijñā*	supernormal cognitive power of the domain of miraculous abilities
gzhi gnas	*śamatha*	calm abiding
zhi gnas rjes mthun pa'i mos pas spyod pa'i sa	*śamathānulobhādhimukti-caryābhūmi*	level of conduct [realized] through resolve in accord with calm abiding
zhi ba	*śamana*	calmness
zhi ba'i las	*śāntikriyā*	rite of pacification
zhi bar gnas pa	*śāntavihāra*	state of quiescence
zhe sdang	*dveṣa*	aversion, hatred
zhe sdang med pa	*adveṣa*	non-hatred
zhen pa rten gyi tshor ba	*snehāśrayavedanā*	feeling associated with greed
gzhag bya	*vyavasthāya*	determined/ relational aspects [of dependent origination]
gzhan skye	*aparotpāda*	extraneous arising [or production from an external cause]
gzhan gyi rgyud la yod pa	*parasāntānika*	present in the mental continuum of others
gzhan gyis bstan pa'i rnam rtog	*parānvayavikalpa*	imaginations disclosed by other intellectual efforts
gzhan gyi don spyi	*anyārthasāmānya*	extraneous object-universal
gzhan [gyi] dbang	*paratantra*	dependent nature
gzhan gyi lus ngag yid gsum la dmigs nas gzhan du snang ba'i rnam rig		apperception of others that becomes manifest with reference to the body, speech, and mind of others
gzhan 'gyur bzhi		four variable mental states
gzhan stong pa		exponent of extraneous emptiness
gzhan 'phrul dbang byed	*paranirmitavaśavartin*	Paranirmitavaśavartin [realm]
gzhan ma yin pa'i de bzhin nyid	*ananyatathatā*	non-extraneous absolute reality
gzhan sems gyi mngon shes	*paracittābhijñā*	knowledge of the minds of others

gzhi	*vastu/ āśraya*	ground [of spiritual realization], basis, basic category, topic
gzhi'i chos nyer gcig		twenty-one aspects associated with the ground
gzhi chos lnga		five foundational factors
za bo/ za ba po	*bhojaka*	consumer
zag bcas kyi chos	*sāsravadharma*	corrupt phenomena/ things
zag pa zad pa'i mngon par shes pa	*āśravakṣayābhijñā*	supernormal cognitive power of the cessation of corruption
zag med kyi sdom pa	*anāśravavrata*	uncorrupted discipline
zang zing dang bcas pa'i tshor ba	*āmiṣavedanā*	disturbed feeling/ feeling of worldliness
zang zing med pa'i tshor ba	*nirāmiṣavedanā*	undisturbed feeling
zad par	*kṛtsna/ kṣaya*	consummation [of the elements]
zad par sa'i ting nge 'dzin	*tejaskṛtsnasamādhi*	meditative stability of the all-consuming earth element
zab 'gal lnga		five profound contradictions [of dependent origination]
zab cing phra ba'i rten 'brel	*gambhīrasūkṣmapratītya-samutpāda*	profound and subtle dependent origination
zas kyi 'tsho bas rnam par dbye ba'i rten 'brel	*āhāropastambhavibhāga-pratītyasamutpāda*	dependent origination distinguished by means of nourishing sustenance
zas bzhi	*caturāhāra*	four kinds of nourishment
zin pa ma yin pas bsdus pa	*anupāttasaṃkṣipta*	organically unretained [form]
zin pa'i 'byung ba las gyur ba'i sgra	*upāttamahābhūtahetukaśabda*	organically produced sound
zin pas bsdus pa	*upāttasaṃkṣipta*	organically retained [form]
gzugs	*rūpa*	physical form(s), visible form(s)
gzugs kyi skye mched	*rūpāyatana*	sensory activity field of [visible] form
gzugs [kyi] khams	*rūpadhātu*	world-system of form
gzugs kyi de bzhin nyid	*rūpatathatā*	reality of physical form
gzugs kyi rnam pa	*rūpākāra*	sensa of physical form
gzugs kyi phung po	*rūpaskandha*	aggregate of physical form(s)
gzugs kyi yan lag	*rūpāṅga*	link of form
gzugs can	*rūpin/ rūpaka*	physical, possessing physical form
gzugs can skye mched bcu	*daśarūpakāyatana*	ten physical sensory activity fields

gzugs can gyi khams bcu	*daśarūpakadhātu*	ten physical sensory bases
gzugs nye bar len pa'i phung po	*rūpopādānaskandha*	compulsively accrued aggregate of physical forms
gzugs brnyen gyi rgyu mtshan	*bimbanimitta*	projected appearance
gzugs med skye mched	*ārūpyāyatana*	formless sensory activity field
gzugs med [kyi] khams	*ārūpyadhātu*	world-system of formlessness
gzugs med khams kyi snyoms 'jug bzhi	*ārūpyadhātucatuḥsamāpatti*	four meditative absorptions associated with the world-system of formlessness
bzung 'dzin	*grāhyagrāhaka*	subject-object dichotomy
bzung 'dzin gyi bag chags	*grāhyagrāhakavāsanā*	propensity of the subject-object dichotomy
bzod pa	*kṣānti*	patience
'od chung	*parīttābha*	Little Radiance [realm]
'og sa	*adhabhūmi*	level below [one's present level]
'od gsal	*ābhāsvara*	Inner Radiance [realm]
'od gsal	*prabhāsvara*	inner radiance
yang dag pa'i rten 'brel	*samyakpratītyasamutpāda*	genuine dependent origination
yang dag pa'i mtha'	*bhūtakoṭi*	genuine goal
yang dag pa'i don	*bhūtārtha*	genuine truth
yang dag pa'i gnas lugs	*samyaksthiti*	genuine abiding nature of reality
yang dag pa'i ye shes	*samyag[nirvikalpa]jñāna*	genuine [non-conceptual] knowledge
yang dag pa'i shes pa'i rgyu mtshan	*samyagājñānimitta*	appearances of genuine [non-conceptual] knowledge
yang dag par blangs pa las byung ba'i gzugs	*sāmādānikarūpa*	forms deriving from genuine commitment
yang dag spong ba	*samyakprahāṇa*	correct training
yan lag bcu gnyis	*dvādaśāṅga*	twelve links [of dependent origination]
yi ge'i tshogs	*vyañjanakāya*	syllabic cluster
yi dvags	*preta*	anguished spirit
yid	*manas*	mentation, mental faculty
yid kyi skye mched	*mano āyatana*	sensory activity field of the mental faculty
yid kyi khams	*manodhātu*	sensory base of the mental faculty
yid kyi rnam [par] shes [pa]	*manovijñāna*	mental consciousness
yid kyi rnam shes za ba po'i rnam rig		apperception of the consumer mental consciousness
yid kyi dbang po	*mana indriya*	sense faculty of the mind

yid ches pa	*adhimukti*	conviction
yid nye bar rgyu ba bco brgyad	*aṣṭādaśamanopavicāra*	eighteen sensory objects that impact upon the mind
yid byed	*manaskāra*	attention, mental activity, mental focus
yid byed kyi bdag rkyen	*manaskārādhipatipratyaya*	predominant condition of mental activity
yid yul	*manoviṣaya*	object of the mental faculty
yid la byed pa drug	*ṣaḍmanaskāra*	six modes of attention
yid la byed pa'i rnam gYeng	*manasikāravikṣepa*	distraction due to mental attention
yid shes		see *yid kyi rnam [par] shes [pa]*
yid shes dang mtshungs ldan gyi sim pa yid bde		mental happiness in affinity with mental consciousness
yid shes dang mtshungs ldan gyi gdung ba yid mi bde		mental unhappiness in affinity with mental consciousness
yin lugs		abiding nature of reality
yul	*deśa/ viṣaya*	location/ space, sense object
yul gyi snang ba'i rnam rig		apperception of geographical features that become manifest
yul nges lnga	*pañcaviṣayaniyata*	five object-determining mental states
yul du 'dzin pa mtshan ma'i rnam rtog	*nimittavikalpa*	symbolic imaginations that apprehend objects
yul drug tu snang ba nye bar spyad bya'i rnam rig		apperception of resources that manifest as the six objects [of sensory consciousness]
yul spyad pas gzugs su yod pa	*viṣayarūpaṇā*	material existence through sensory localization
yul gzugs can lnga'i khams		sensory base(s) of the five physical sense objects
yul la 'jug pa'i rnam rtog	*ālambanavikalpa*	object-oriented imaginations
yul la btags pa'i mtshan nyid	*dikparikalpitalakṣaṇa*	defining characteristics imputed with regard to space
ye shes	*jñāna*	pristine cognition
ye shes kyi sku	*jñānakāya*	body of pristine cognition
ye shes kyi tshogs	*jñānasambhāra*	provision of pristine cognition
ye shes sems dpa'	*jñānasattva*	being of pristine cognition, the actual deity [in contrast to the visualized deity]
yongs grub	*pariniṣpanna*	consummate nature
yongs grub rnam pa dgu		nine aspects of the consummate nature

yongs su mya ngan las 'das	*parinirvāṇa*	final nirvāṇa, conclusive liberation
yongs su 'dzin pa	*parigraha*	embrace
yod pa'i stong pa nyid	*bhāvaśūnyatā*	emptiness of existence
yod par rtog pa	*bhāvavikalpa*	imaginations/ notions of existence
yon tan	*guṇa*	enlightened attribute, erudition, talent, quality
gYeng ba	*vikṣepa*	distraction
gYo	*śāṭhya*	pretentiousness
gYo ba med pa	*nirīhaka*	unmoving
gYo ba med pa'i rkyen	*nirīhakapratyaya*	unmoving condition
rang rkya thub pa		autonomous
rang gi ngo bo nyid du 'dzin pa'i rtog pa	*svabhāvavikalpa*	imaginations/ notions of inherent existence
rang gi lus ngag yid gsum la dmigs nas bdag tu snang ba'i rnam rig		apperception of self that becomes manifest with reference to one's own body, speech, and mind
rang rgyal	*pratyekabuddha*	hermit buddha
rang rgyal gi theg pa	*pratyekabuddhayāna*	vehicle of hermit buddhas
rang bzhin gyi rgyu mtshan	*svabhāvanimitta*	natural appearance
rang bzhin gyi rnam par rtog pa	*svabhāvavikalpa*	imaginations of nature
rang bzhin lnga		five natural properties [of the seeds]
rang bzhin stong pa nyid	*svabhāvaśūnyatā*	emptiness of inherent existence
rang bzhin med pa'i de kho na nyid	*niḥsvabhāvatattva*	real nature devoid of inherent existence
rang bzhin 'od gsal ba'i ye shes	*prakṛtiprabhāsvarajñāna*	pristine cognition of natural inner radiance
rang bzhin yongs grub	*svabhāvapariniṣpanna*	natural consummate nature
rang bzhin gsum	*trisvabhāva*	three natures
rang sa	*svabhūmi*	one's present level
rab [tu] dbye [ba]	*prabheda*	analysis, classification, distinguished variation
rab gnas	*pratiṣṭhā*	consecration
rig pa	*vidyā*	awareness, intelligence, knowledge
rig min spyi'i mtshan nyid	*avijñaptisāmānyalakṣaṇa*	characteristic of an imperceptible universal
rig shes		intelligence
rigs mthun pa	*nikāyasabhāga*	similarity of class, homogeneity

rigs drug	*ṣaḍgati*	six realms/ classes [of sentient beings]
rigs 'dra las 'byung ba	*sajātīya*	emerging from homogenous classes
rigs pa'i rnam par rtog pa	*yuktivikalpa*	imagination of reasoning
rigs pas grub pa	*yuktisiddha*	proven through reason
ril po'i bdag nyid du 'dzin pa	*piṇḍātmagrāha*	apprehension of a composite/ conglomerate self
reg mthong snang gsum		threefold interaction of sensory contact, vision, and perception
reg pa	*sparśa*	[sensory] contact, touch
reg pa'i rnam par shes pa		see *lus kyi rnam par shes pa*
reg pa'i zas	*sparśāhāra*	nourishment of sensory contact
reg pas gzugs su yod pa	*sparśarūpaṇā*	material existence through physical contact
reg bya	*spraṣṭavya*	tangible [object/ sensation]
ro	*rasa*	taste, savor
ro mnyam	*samarasa*	common savor
rlung	*vāyu*	wind, vital energy
lan tshva	*lavaṇa*	salty
len pa'i rnam shes	*ādānavijñāna*	appropriating consciousness
lam	*mārga*	path, spiritual path
lam lnga	*pañcamārga*	five spiritual paths
lam yongs grub	*mārgapariniṣpanna*	consummate nature of the spiritual path
las	*karma*	action(s), past action(s)
las kyi kun nas nyon mongs pa	*karmasaṃkleśa*	dissonant mental state(s) arising from past actions
las kyi lam	*karmamārga*	path influenced by [the impact of] past actions
las [kyi] rlung	*karmavāyu*	vital energy of past actions
las kyi bag chags	*karmavāsanā*	propensity of past actions
las su rung ba	*karmaṇyatā*	physical and mental malleability
las gsum	*triṣkarma*	three kinds of deeds
lugs ldog	*pratiloma*	reversal process [of dependent origination]
lugs 'byung	*anuloma*	arising process [of dependent origination]
lung gi chos	*āgamadharma*	transmitted teachings [of Buddhism]

lung ma bstan	*avyākṛta*	unspecified/ indeterminate
lung ma bstan gyi lta ba bcu bzhi	*caturdaśāvyākṛtavastudṛṣṭi*	fourteen indeterminate/ unspecified views
lung ma bstan rnams kyi de bzhin nyid	*avyākṛtadharmatathatā*	reality of unspecified phenomena
lus kyi rnam par shes pa	*kāyavijñāna*	tactile consciousness
lus 'phags po	*pūrvavideha*	Pūrvavideha [continent]
lus tshor dbang shes lnga dang mtshungs ldan du byung ba'i sems pa		physical sensations originating in affinity with the five types of sensory consciousness
le lo	*kausīdya*	indolence
legs smon		auspicious aspirational prayer
len pa	*upādāna*	grasping, compulsively acquired [aggregates]
log par lta ba	*mithyādṛṣṭi*	heterodox view(s)
shin [tu] sbyangs [pa]	*praśrabdhi*	[physical and mental] refinement
shis pa brjod pa	*āśīrvāda*	benediction
shes pa bcu	*daśajñāna*	ten aspects of knowledge
shes pa'i rdzas	*ājñādravya*	conscious substance
shes bya	*jñeya*	knowable phenomena, phenomenological structures
shes bya thams cad gzhi lnga	*pañcajñeya*	five basic categories of phenomena
shes bya bsdu ba'i gzhi		ground that subsumes [all] phenomenological structures
shes bya'i sgrib	*jñeyāvaraṇa*	obscuration with respect to knowable phenomena
shes bya'i gnas	*jñeyasthiti*	ground of knowable phenomena [= substratum]
shes bzhin	*samprajanya*	alertness
shes bzhin ma yin pa	*asaṃprajanya*	inattentiveness
shes rab	*prajñā*	discriminative awareness
shes rab kyi bslab pa	*prajñāśikṣā*	training of discriminative awareness
shin tu rgyas pa'i sde snod	*mahāvaipulyapiṭaka*	basket/ compilation of the Buddha's extensive teachings
gshin rje	*yama*	Yama, lord of death
gshin [don gyi cho ga]		funerary rite
bshes gnyen	*kalyāṇamitra*	spiritual advisor
sa	*pṛthivī/ bhūmi*	earth/ level
sa bcu	*daśabhūmi*	ten [bodhisattva] levels

sa bcu gsum		thirteen [buddha and bodhisattva] levels
sa bon	*bīja*	seed [of consciousness]
sa bon gyi cha	*bījabhāga*	seminal aspect [of the substratum consciousness]
sa bon thams cad pa'i rnam shes	*sarvabījakālayavijñāna*	store-consciousness of all seeds
sa bon thog med nas brgyud de 'byung ba		indirect origin [of consciousness] from beginningless seeds
sa bon rnam pa drug		six kinds of seed
sa mtshungs pa		abiding on the same level
sangs rgyas	*buddha*	Buddha/ Awakened One
sangs rgyas kyi sa	*buddhabhūmi*	buddha level
sim gdung gnyis ka med pa btang snyoms		equanimity free from both happiness and sorrow
sum cu rtsa gsum	*trayastriṃśa*	Trayastriṃśa [realm]
sems	*ciitta*	mind
sems kyi rnam grangs kyi mngon par shes pa	*paracittaparyāyābhijñā*	supernormal cognitive power that knows the modalities of [other] minds
sems kyi sa mang po bcu	*daśacittamahābhūmika*	group of ten mental states found in all minds
sems kyi bslab pa	*cittaśikṣā*	training of the mind
sems can med pa	*niḥsattva*	non-sentient
sems 'jog pa	*cittasthāpanā*	mental placement
sems dang mtshungs ldan gyi 'du byed	*cittaprayuktasaṃskāra*	formative predisposition(s) associated with mind
sems gnas	*cittasthiti*	mental focus
sems pa	*cetanā*	volition
sems pa'i zas	*cetanāhāra*	nourishment of volition
sems byung	*caitasika*	mental state(s)
sems byung rnga cu nga gcig	*ekapañcāśaccaitasika*	fifty-one mental states
sems byung sems pa		mental process associated with mental states
sems tsam	*cittamātra*	Cittamātra [school]
sems tsam pa	*cittamātrin*	Cittamātrin
sems rtse gcig pa	*cittaikāgratā*	one-pointed mind
sems tshor yid shes dang mtshungs ldan du byung ba'i tshor ba		mental feelings originating in affinity with mental consciousness
sems zhi bar gnas pa'i thabs dgu	*śamathanavakārayacittasthiti*	nine techniques of mental calm abiding

ser sna	*mātsarya*	miserliness
so so'i skye bo	*pṛthagjanatva*	[status of an] ordinary individual
so sor nges pa	*pratiniyama*	distinctive reguar pattern, distinctive regularity
so sor rtog pa'i rnam rtog	*pratyavekṣakavikalpa*	analytical imagination
so sor brtags 'gog	*pratisaṃkhyānirodha*	cessation [of sensory functions] through analytical means
so sor brtags min gyi 'gog pa	*apratisaṃkhyānirodha*	cessation obtained through non-analytical means
srid pa	*bhava*	rebirth process, phenomenal existence
srid pa nyer lnga		twenty-five aspects of phenomenal existence
srid pa la 'dod pa'i sred pa	*kāmatṛṣṇā*	craving that desires rebirth
srid pa gsum	*tribhava*	three levels of existence
srid [pa'i] rtse	*bhavāgra*	summit of [mundane/phenomenal] existence
srid pa'i yan lag	*bhavāṅga*	link of the rebirth process [in dependent origination]
srid pa'i len pa	*bhavopādāna*	grasping of rebirth
srid pa'i sred pa	*bhavatṛṣṇā*	craving associated with rebirth
srung ba med pa bzhi		four [commitments] that are not to be guarded
sred pa	*tṛṣṇā*	craving
srog	*jīva/prāṇa*	vitality, life-force
srog gi dbang po	*jīvitendriya*	faculty of the life-force
slob pa'i lam	*śaikṣamārga*	path(s) of learning
gsang sngags	*guhyamantra*	secret mantra(s)
gsang gnas		secret center [of the subtle/buddha body]
gsar 'gyur		New Translation Schools
gsung	*vāk*	buddha speech
gsung rab	*pravacana*	sacred scripture(s)
gsung rab yan lag bcu gnyis	*dvādaśakadharmapravacana*	twelve branches of the scriptures
bsam gyis mi khyab pa'i dbyings	*acintyadhātu*	inconceivable expanse
bsam gtan	*dhyāna*	meditative concentration
bsam gtan gyi skyon brgyad	*dhyānāṣṭadoṣa*	eight defects associated with meditative concentration
bsam gtan gnyis pa	*dvitīyadhyāna*	second meditative concentration

bsam gtan gnyis pa'i yan lag bzhi	*dvitīyadhyānacaturaṅga*	four aspects of the second meditative concentration
bsam gtan dang po	*prathamadhyāna*	first meditative concentration
bsam gtan dang po'i yan lag lnga	*prathamadhyānapañcāṅga*	five aspects of the first meditative concentration
bsam gtan bzhi	*caturdhyāna*	four meditative concentrations
bsam gtan bzhi pa	*caturthadhyāna*	fourth meditative concentration
bsam gtan bzhi pa'i yan lag bzhi	*caturthadhyānacaturaṅga*	four aspects of the fourth meditative concentration
bsam gtan gsum pa	*tṛtīyadhyāna*	third meditative concentration
bsam gtan gsum pa'i yan lag lnga	*tṛtīyadhyānapañcāṅga*	five aspects of the third meditative concentration
bsam pa	*cintā/ āśaya*	reflection
bsod nams kyi las	*puṇyakarma*	meritorious [past] action(s)
bsod nams 'phel	*puṇyaprasava*	Increasing Merit [realm]
bsod nams min pa'i las	*apuṇyakarma*	non-meritorious [past] action(s)
bslab pa gsum	*triśikṣā*	three higher trainings
bslan 'jog	*avasthāpanā*	integrated placement [in calm abiding]
lha	*deva*	deity, god
lha dang tshangs pa'i theg pa		vehicles of the gods and of Brahmā
lha ma yin	*asura*	antigod
lha mi'i theg pa	*devamanuṣyayāna*	vehicle of gods and humans
lha tshe ring po	*dīrghāyuṣodeva*	long-living god
lha'i rna ba'i mngon [par] shes [pa]	*divyaśrotrābhijñā*	[supernormal cognitive power of] clairaudience
lha'i mig gi mngon [par] shes [pa]	*divyacakṣurabhijñā*	[supernormal power of] clairvoyance
lhag mthong	*vipaśyana*	higher insight
lhag pa'i chos sku chen po	*mahādharmakāya*	superior great buddha body of reality
lhag ma med par mya ngan las 'das pa	*niravaśeṣanirvāṇa*	non-residual nirvāṇa
lhan cig 'jug pa	*sahabhavapravṛtti*	concurrent engagement
lhan cig 'byung ba	*sahabhū*	co-emergent origin [of seeds]

Notes to Part One

1 Dudjom Rinpoche 1991, 1:861.
2 Note that the root verse reads *dbye ba* for *dbyi ba*, as given in the commentary. See below, p. 135.
3 Note that these similes are inverted in the text.
4 The text here reads *mngon 'gro*, but see *SK*, single volume edition, p. 35, for the correct reading, *sngon 'gro*.
5 Parts One and Two are contained in the present volume. Part Three has been eloquently translated and annotated by Elizabeth Callahan (2007) as *Frameworks of Buddhist Philosophy*, and Part Four by Elio Guarisco and Ingrid McLeod (2005) as *Systems of Buddhist Tantra.*
6 As the author has already explained in Book Five, *Buddhist Ethics* (trans. Kalu Rinpoche Translation Group, 1998).
7 The general fields of knowledge are the subject matter of Book Six, Parts One and Two, while the particular approaches of the sūtra and mantra are expounded in Parts Three and Four, respectively.
8 Knowledge of philosophical and spiritual systems (*siddhānta*, *grub mtha'*) is the subject-matter of Book Six of *The Treasury of Knowledge*, whereas the three higher trainings (*triśikṣā*, *bslab pa gsum*) are expounded elsewhere—the training of ethical discipline (*śīla*, *tshul khrims*) in Book Five, the training of the mind (*citta*, *sems*) in Book Eight, and the training of discriminative awareness (*prajñā*, *shes rab*) in Book Seven. Jamgon Kongtrul's source for this section is Buton Rinchendrub, *History of Buddhism* (*Bu ston chos 'byung*), 4–5.
9 Tib. [*mang du*] *thos pa'i phan yon lnga*. This reference is cited in Buton, *History*, 7. The five advantages of erudition are learning with regard to the psycho-physical aggregates (*phung po la mkhas pa*), learning with regard to the sensory bases (*khams la mkhas pa*), learning with regard to the sensory activity fields (*skye mched la mkhas pa*), learning with regard to dependent origination (*rten cing 'brel bar 'byung ba la mkhas pa*), and dependence on these oral teachings but not on other instructions (*de'i gdams ngag dang rjes su bstan pa gzhan rag ma las pa*).
10 Cf. the diverse sources cited in Buton, *History*, 4–7. Among them there is another enumeration of five advantages of listening to the sacred teachings (*dharmaśravaṇa-pañcānuśaṃsa*, *chos mnyan pa'i phan yon lnga*), elucidated in Vasubandhu's *Rational System of Exposition* (*Vyākhyāyukti*, T 4061) and summarized by Jamgon Kongtrul in Book Five of *The Treasury of Knowledge* (translated in Kalu Rinpoche Translation Group 1998, 76). See also Nordrang Orgyan, *Compendium of Buddhist Numeric Terms* (*Chos rnam kun btus*), 1028. Briefly stated, these five advantages are that the subjects of

classical learning will be studied, the subjects of classical learning will be refined, doubts will be abandoned, [mistaken] views will be rectified, and the words and meanings of the teachings will be understood through discriminative awareness.

11 While Asaṅga's writings are traditionally regarded as the source for this section on the four kinds of genuine analytic knowledge, I have not yet been able to locate specific passages or the embedded quotations in his extant works, using ACIP searchable text files.

12 From the Tibetan perspective, the "scriptural compilation" of the Buddhist canon includes all the sūtras and tantras contained in the Kangyur and the *Collected Tantras of the Nyingmapa* (*rNying ma'i rgyud 'bum*), as well as the Nikāya literature of the Theravāda tradition and other sūtras extant in Chinese translation. For a traditional Tibetan overview of the distinctions between the scriptures of the bodhisattvas (*byang chub sems dpa'*) and the scriptures of the pious attendants (*śrāvaka, nyan thos*) presented within the context of the three turnings of the wheel, and so forth, see, e.g., Dudjom Rinpoche 1991, 1:73–87. For further background reading from both Theravāda and Mahāyāna perspectives, see also Law 1933 and Williams 1989. On Jamgon Kongtrul's particular presentation, see Callahan 2007.

13 The twelve branches of the scriptures (*dvādaśāṅgapravacana, gsung rab yan lag bcu gnyis*) altogether comprise discourses (*sūtra, mdo sde*), aphorisms in prose and verse (*geya, dbyangs bsnyad*), prophetic declarations (*vyākaraṇa, lung bstan*), verses (*gāthā, tshig bcad*), proverbs or meaningful expressions (*udāna, ched brjod*), legends or frame stories (*nidāna, gleng gzhi*), extensive teachings (*mahāvaipulya, shin tu rgyas pa*), tales of past lives (*jātaka, skyes rabs*), marvelous events (*adbhutadharma, rmad du byung*), narratives (*avadāna, rtogs brjod*), fables (*itivṛttaka, de lta bu byung ba*), and established instructions (*upadeśa, gtab phab*). See the analysis offered in Buton, *History*, 17–18.

14 This emphasis on the treatises of logic, grammar, and medicine, in that distinctive order, follows Buton, *History*, 24–26. For a more detailed traditional doxography of the classical treatises, see also Dudjom Rinpoche 1991, 1:88–109. The subject-matter of the treatises on logic, grammar, and medicine is specifically summarized below, in the present volume—see pp. 139–176, 125–138, and 317–341, respectively.

15 Works on logic, grammar, and medicine are found within the Buddhist and non-Buddhist traditions of India. Some of the latter are also contained within the Tengyur, e.g., the *Grammar of Pāṇini* (T 4420) and Vāgbhaṭa's *Eight Divisions of Medical Science* (*Aṣṭāṅgahṛdayasaṃhitā*, T 4310).

16 See below, pp. 313–314.

17 Jamgon Kongtrul's source for this passage has not yet been identified. The text mentioned here is not found in the Kangyur under this title; and the verses do not occur in the *Sūtra of the Ascertainment of Meanings: A Lexicon of Buddhist Numerical Categories* (*Arthaviniścayasūtra*, T 317), nor are they found in Ratnakīrti's *Dharmaviniścaya* commentary (T 4084).

18 There are four kinds of genuine analytic knowledge (*catuḥpratisaṃvid, so so yang dag pa rig pa bzhi*): of meanings (*artha, don*), intellectual brilliance (*pratibhāna, spobs pa*), the [sacred] teaching (*dharma, chos*), and etymological definitions (*nirukta, nges tshig*). For a more detailed exposition, see Jamgon Mipham Gyatso's *Gateway to Knowledge* (*mKhas pa'i tshul la 'jug pa'i sgo*), translated in Kunsang 1997–2002, vol. 4, chs. 27–30.

19 This implies that discriminative awareness acquired through meditation should be preceded by that which is cultivated through study and reflection.

20 This text, as stated below, note 21, is quoted by Vasubandhu, and is probably to be identified with the *Prajñaptiśāstra* (Taisho 1538 and 1644), but I have not managed to identify the passage in the corresponding Tibetan versions—either in Maudgalyāyana's *Treatise on the Designation of Causes* (*Kāraṇaprajñapti*, T 4087), which is the most likely source,

or in the related *Treatise on the Designation of Cosmology* (*Lokaprajñapti*, T 4086) and the *Treatise on the Designation of Past Actions* (*Karmaprajñapti*, T 4088).

21 Pruden 1988–1990, 1151–1155.

22 Tib. *rnam par spyod pa'i chos* refers to those teachings which are to be practically applied.

23 This quotation is also cited by Dudjom Rinpoche 1991, 1:98.

24 The text emphasizes that even the study of the ordinary sciences serves to focus the mind upon the ultimate goal of Buddhist practice, which is the cultivation of the provision of pristine cognition (*jñānasambhāra, ye shes kyi tshogs*). See, e.g., Dudjom Rinpoche 1991, 1:192 and 302–303.

25 The *Four Vedas* comprise the early extant corpus of Brāhmaṇical hymns, including the *Ṛgveda*, the *Atharvaveda*, the *Sāmaveda*, and the *Yajurveda*. See bibliography, p. 898. A detailed survey of this literature can be found in Gonda 1975.

26 This is the introductory verse of Tonmi Sambhoṭa's celebrated treatise. See, e.g., *Sum rtags rtsa ba phyogs sgrig* (1992, 2). Cf. also the commentary in Situ Chokyi Jungne's *Great Commentary on the Thirty Verses and Introduction to Gender, entitled Beautiful Pearl Garland, a Neck Ornament of the Learned* (*Sum rtags 'grel chen mkhas pa'i mgul rgyan mu tig phreng mdzes*), 31–32.

27 On the three higher spiritual trainings, see above, note 8.

28 See Pruden 1988–1990, 103–104 and 251–254. The Vaibhāṣikas (*bye brag tu smra ba*) are exponents of the *Great Treasury of Detailed Exposition* (*Mahāvibhāṣa*, Taisho 1545), an influential commentary on the seven Abhidharma treatises maintained by the Sarvāstivāda order, which flourished in Kashmir during the second century CE. See Willemen, Dessein, and Cox (1998), *Sarvāstivāda Buddhist Scholasticism*.

29 Dharmakīrti, *Exposition of Valid Cognition*, DgK., vol. Ce, f. 106a3 (T4210).

30 Ibid., f. 137a7.

31 See Pruden 1988–1990, 251, where the Sautrāntika position is stated somewhat differently—suggesting that they are part of the aggregate of forms and not formative predispositions disassociated from mind. See also below, p. 546. The Sautrāntikas (*mdo sde pa*) are identified as exponents of the Sarvāstivāda order from Gandhāra and Bactria, epitomized by Kumāralāta, who doctrinally opposed the Vaibhāṣikas. See Willemen, Dessein, and Cox 1998, 37 and 123–125.

32 These sixty-four traditional Indic scripts, headed by Brāhmī and Kharoṣṭhī, which are all enumerated in the *Sūtra of Extensive Play* (*Lalitavistarasūtra*, T 95) and other sources, are discussed below, pp. 246–248. On the calligraphy of the Rañjanā script, see also below, pp. 248–250.

33 The eight renowned grammatical treatises (*sgra mdo*) of India are enumerated in Vopadeva's *Dhātupāṭha* (intro, śl. 2) as those of Indra, Candra, Kāśakṛtsna, Āpiśali, Śākaṭāyana, Pāṇini, Amara, and Jinendra. For an alternative listing found in the works of Longdol Lama, see Smith 2001, 191. Among these, reference is made in the present work to the extant treatises of Candra, Pāṇini, and Amara. See below, pp. 110–112, 750, and 382–385. Resources for the further study of Sanskrit phonology are mentioned below, note 35.

34 The four major classical languages of India (*'phags yul gyi skad rigs chen bzhi*) are traditionally enumerated in Tibetan sources as Sanskrit (*legs sbyar*), Prākrit (*phal pa'i skad*), Apabhraṃśa (*zur chags kyi skad*), and Paiśācī (*sha za'i skad*). See, e.g., Dudjom Rinpoche 1991, 1:107.

35 This enumeration of sixteen vowels includes AṂ and AḤ—otherwise there should be fourteen. The full vocalic and consonantal charts, as shown in fig. 1, may be found in Whitney 1896, 2–3, and MacDonnell 1927, 3–4. On the grammarians' distinction between simple and diphthong vowels, see Whitney 1896, 12 (section 30).

36 The five phonetic sets include the velars, palatals, retroflex cerebrals, dentals, and labials, each of which comprises five syllables. The four spirants are ŚA, ṢA, SA, and HA. The full listing of the basic sixteen vowels and thirty-three consonants accords with the chart shown in fig. 1.

37 On these distinctions of vowel length and accent, see Whitney 1896, 27–34. On the relevant section of the *Grammar of Candragomin* (*Candravyākaraṇa*, T 4269), i.e., the *mTshams sbyor lnga bshad pa*, *Yi ge bsdu ba*, which concerns the composition of vowels and consonantal syllables, see Troru Tsenam, *Moonbeams Commentary* (2003), 76.

38 With regard to nasalization, the distinction is actually made between sounds formed by the mouth and nose together ("passing through the nose," *anunāsika*) and those made simply by the non-closure of the nose (*ānunāsikya*). See Whitney 1896, 14 (36). The use of symbols indicating the acceptance of nasalization is also mentioned in Whitney 1896, 25.

39 Troru Tsenam, *Moonbeams Commentary*, 76.

40 On the function of the *visarga* (*rnam gcad*), see Whitney 1896, 23; on the *anusvāra* (*nga ro*), 24–26; on the *jihvāmūlīya* (*lce rtsa can*) and *upadhmānīya* (*mchu can*), 23 and 58. Among them, the *visarga* takes the form of an *h*-breathing, substituting for a final *s* or *r*, and uttered in the articulating position of the preceding vowel. The *anusvāra* is an open nasal, also uttered in the articulating position of the preceding vowel. The *jihvāmūlīya* and *upadhmānīya* are obsolete spirants representing the substitution of a final *s* or *r*, respectively following a velar and a labial hard consonant.

41 Cf. Troru Tsenam, *Moonbeams Commentary*, 76–77.

42 This verse and the commentary which immediately follows are cited verbatim in Troru Tsenam, *Moonbeams Commentary*, 77.

43 The velar phonetic set comprises KA, KHA, GA, GHA and ṄA, on which see Whitney 1896, 15 (39–41). As for the vowel A, see Whitney 1896, 10 (19–21).

44 On the spirant syllable HA, see Whitney 1896, 22 (65–66).

45 With regard to the formation of these vowels and diphthongs, see Whitney 1896, 19–21 (22–30).

46 The retroflex or cacuminal phonetic set comprises ṬA, ṬHA, ḌA, ḌHA, and ṆA, on which see Whitney 1896, 16–17 (45–46).

47 With regard to the semi-vowel RA, see Whitney 1896, 18 (52).

48 This actually refers to contact between the tip of the tongue and the upper incisors, formed when the tip of the tongue is turned back towards the hard palate. On the spirant syllable ṢA, see Whitney 1896, 21–22 (61–62).

49 The dental phonetic set comprises the syllables TA, THA, DA, DHA, and NA, on which see Whitney 1896, 17–18 (47–48).

50 On the semi-vowel LA, see Whitney 1896, 19 (53–54), and on the spirant syllable SA, p. 21 (60).

51 This means that the nasal syllable ṄA is formed in contact with the velum, ÑA in contact with the palate, ṆA when the tip of the tongue is turned back towards the hard palate, NA in contact with the teeth, and MA in contact with the lips.

52 The palatal phonetic set comprises CA, CHA, JA, JHA, and ÑA, on which see Whitney 1896, 15–16 (42–44).

53 On the semi-vowel YA, see Whitney 1896, 19–20 (55–56), and on the spirant syllable ŚA, p. 22 (63–64).

54 The labial phonetic set comprises the syllables PA, PHA, BA, BHA, and MA, on which see Whitney 1896, 18 (49–50).

55 With regard to the formation and pronunciation of the semi-vowel VA, see Whitney 1896, 20 (57–58).

56 Troru Tsenam, *Moonbeams Commentary*, 77.
57 Troru Tsenam, *Moonbeams Commentary*, 77–78.
58 Whitney 1896, 13 (31–32 and 34b), and 18 (51b); also Troru Tsenam, *Moonbeams Commentary*, 77.
59 On these terms, see Whitney 1896, 13–14 (34b and 37d).
60 The first syllable of each phonetic set is classed as an unvoiced and non-aspirate surd; the second is an unvoiced surd, aspirate and spirant; the third is a voiced sonant and non-aspirate; the fourth is a voiced sonant, aspirate and spirant; while the fifth is classed as a voiced sonant and non-aspirate. The semi-vowels are non-aspirates. Along with the true spirants (sibilants and aspiration HA), they also correlate to the distinctive phonetic sets, as shown in the chart (fig. 1). See also Whitney 1896, 14 (37).
61 This observation is made in the *Grammar of Candragomin* (*Candravyākaraṇa*). See, e.g., Troru Tsenam, *Moonbeams Commentary*, 78, which cites Pāṇini as an example.
62 See, e.g., Narthang Lotsāwa's *Method of Mantra Recitation* (*sNgags kyi bklag thabs*).
63 A useful listing of Tibetan language sources for the study of Tibetan phonology and grammar can be found in Drakpa, *Inventory of Tibetan Treatises* (*Bla brang dkar chag*), 60–65. See also the bibliographies in Beyer 1992, Denwood 1999, and Verhagen 2001, as well as the online bibliography at www.tbrc.org, T186.
64 Fig. 2 includes the tables of primary consonants and vowels in the *dbu can* script. The relevant rules are found in Tonmi Sambhota's *Thirty Verses* (*Sum cu pa*) and its commentaries, e.g., Situ Chokyi Jungne, *Great Commentary on the Thirty Verses*, pp. 33–36 on the basic vowels and consonants, and pp. 36–41 on prefixes, suffixes, radicals, and isolates. For a recent account of the formation of syllables, nouns, affixes, and sentences according to the rules of Tibetan grammar, see Pari Sangye, *Elucidation of the Four Grammatical Formations* (*brDa sprod sbyor ba rnam bzhi rab gsal*).
65 See fig. 3, which illustrates the possible combinations of superscript and subscript forms; also the tables of sub-fixed and super-fixed syllables in Hodge 1990, 1–3.
66 On the rules for reduplication, which is employed in Tibetan to mark the end of a sentence, see Stoddard and Tournadre 1992, 68–69; on the functions of the oblique particle (*la don*), 21–43; and on the variable forms of the genitive and instrumental case particles (*i ldan*), 5–20. See also Situ Chokyi Jungne, *Great Commentary on the Thirty Verses*, pp. 41ff.
67 These six comprise the thematic particle *ni* (*ni sgra*); the conjunctive particle *dang* (*dang sgra*); the demonstrative particle *de* (*de sgra*), including both *'di* and *de*; the general particles (*spyi sgra*), including *ci*, *ji*, *su*, and *gang*, which are interrogative, indefinite, or correlative; the negative particles (*dgag sgra*), including *ma*, *mi*, *min*, and *med*; and the possessive particles (*bdag sgra*), including the suffixed *-pa*, *-po*, *-ba*, *-bo*, *-ma*, and *-mo*, as well as *ldan*, *mkhan*, etc. On all these six types of non-variable particle, see Stoddard and Tournadre 1992, 93–125.
68 With regard to the important syntactical distinction between agentives and objectives (*bdag gzhan*) in Tibetan, see Stoddard and Tournadre 1992, 262–271. The formation of the three tenses of the verbal roots—present, past, and future—along with the imperative forms is discussed in the same work, pp. 182ff., and useful verb charts are appended to Zhang Yisun et al., eds., *The Great Tibetan-Chinese Dictionary* (*Bod rgya tshig mdzod chen mo*). The verbal categories (*bya byed*) comprise both differentiative or transitive forms (*bye byed tha dad pa*) and non-differentiative or intransitive forms (*bya byed tha mi dad pa*), on which see Stoddard and Tournadre 1992, 245–261.
69 This quotation derives from Pang Lodro Tenpa's *Clarification of the Three Clusters* (*Tshogs gsum gsal ba*). There are parallel prose passages in Sthiramati's commentary on Vasubandhu's *Pañcaskandhaprakaraṇa* (T 4066), on which see Engle 2009, 322–324.

70 See Whitney 1896, 88–90 (261–268) on declension in general and the nominative in particular. Also Situ Chokyi Jungne, *Great Commentary on the Thirty Verses*, pp. 233–234.

71 This applies to *dharma* and *deva*, but not to *ātman*, where the singular form is *ātma*, the dual form *ātmanī* and the plural form *ātmāni*. See Whitney 1896, 105–106 (308–310) concerning the dual and plural inflections; also Situ Chokyi Jungne, *Great Commentary on the Thirty Verses*, pp. 234–235.

72 The so-called eighth or vocative case (*'bod sgra*) is not traditionally enumerated here. On the usage of *la don* to indicate the accusative, dative, and locative in Tibetan, see Stoddard and Tournadre 1992, 21–43; and Situ Chokyi Jungne, *Great Commentary on the Thirty Verses*, pp. 235–236 (accusative), pp. 236–238 (dative), and pp. 240–241 (locative). Regarding the particles *nas* and *las*, indicating the ablative, see Stoddard and Tournadre 1992, 44–50, and Situ Chokyi Jungne, op. cit., pp. 238–239. On the variants of the genitive particle *kyi*, see Stoddard and Tournadre 1992, 5–10 and Situ Chokyi Jungne, op. cit., pp. 239–240; and on the variants of the instrumental particle *kyis*, Stoddard and Tournadre 1992, 11–20 and Situ Chokyi Jungne, op. cit., p. 236.

73 The rules governing the choice of these variant particles are given in Stoddard and Tournadre 1992, 21–22 on *la don*; pp. 5–6 and 11–12 on *i ldan*; and p. 44 on the ablative particles *nas* and *las*.

74 On the rules governing reduplication the end of a sentence or paragraph, see Stoddard and Tournadre 1992, 68–70; also Situ Chokyi Jungne, *Great Commentary on the Thirty Verses*, pp. 41–46.

75 These categories of variant particles which cannot stand alone (*phrad gzhan dbang can*) are all discussed in Stoddard and Tournadre 1992. The same list and the mnemonic that follows are found in Situ Chokyi Jungne, *Great Commentary on the Thirty Verses*, pp. 242–243.

76 The first part of these mnemonic verses may be translated as follows:

Even **though** one may excel **in** accuracy **and** clarity,
One should become learned **in** [elementary] discourses
Associated with entry **into** the Buddhist teaching,
And then consider ethical discipline.
A noble action should be well designed.
It should be conceived. It should be accomplished. It should be considered.
It should be executed. It should be demonstrated. May the gods be victorious!
It should be examined. It should be demonstrated!
Practicing **Buddhists**—whether **accomplished** or **neophyte**—
[Should be] **endowed with** virtue, **without** pollution **or** degeneration.
Now **then**, what is the **reason for** this, **O** Children! **O** Friends!
It is because they are **continuing to** traverse [the path]!
I've heard **that** this is **both** happy **and** joyful.
There is **a** report **that** this is bright and **that** it is beautiful.
It's said that a discussion should **some**time be held.
If you ask, "Who is there? **If you ask,** "What is it?"
If you say, "I didn't do it," then **let it be** done!

77 The last part of the mnemonic could be translated as follows:

Though [thoughts] may be settled, **though** they may move, **though** they may recall,
Whether they are running, **or** setting out, **or** standing still,
Whether they are in front, **or** behind, **or** well conceived,
Whether they are actualized, **or** planned, **or** over-elaborated,
Or whether they are vast,

One should know, explain, and fully comprehend
That **all** of them are resources [indicative of] wealth.
As many as they are, they are **all capable of possessing** happiness.

78 Cf. the more complete listing in Situ Chokyi Jungne, *Great Commentary on the Thirty Verses*, pp. 243–244.

79 The allocation of verbal action to both the agentive and objective aspects clearly differentiates Tibetan syntax from that of Indo-European languages, which emphasize the distinction between subject and predicate. For a detailed explanation of these semantic nuances of sentence construction, see Stoddard and Tournadre 1992, 262–271.

80 On the formation of the three tenses and the imperative, see Stoddard and Tournadre 1992, 182ff.

81 See also the examples given in Stoddard and Tournadre 1992, 263–268.

82 See the tables of verb tenses appended to Zhang Yisun et al., *Great Tibetan-Chinese Dictionary*, and the analytical charts listed in Stoddard and Tournadre 1992, 182–194.

83 On these distinctions between transitive and non-transitive verbs, see also the examples listed in Stoddard and Tournadre 1992, 245–261.

84 This is the well-known technique that all Tibetan children follow when learning to spell aloud.

85 See especially Sonam Tsemo's *Elementary Guide to Pronunciation* (*Yi ge'i klag thabs byis pa bde blag tu 'jug pa*).

86 There are convenient pocket-size editions of these works, including *Sum rtags rtsa ba phyogs sgrig*, published by Sichuan Nationalities Publishing House in Chengdu, and the root verses are also included within various commentaries, among which Situ Chokyi Jungne's *Great Commentary on the Thirty Verses* is highly influential.

87 On Tonmi Sambhoṭa's contribution to the formation of the Tibetan writing system, see also below, pp. 251 and 782.

88 These eight form the subject matter of the *'Jug pa'i gnas brgyad*, on which see below, p. 123.

89 Tib. *zin pa'i 'byung ba las 'gyur ba'i sgra*, sounds from a sentient source, are contrasted with *ma zin pa'i 'byung ba las 'gyur ba'i sgra*, sounds from an inanimate source. See below, p. 481.

90 In the *Treasury of Phenomenology* (*Abhidharmakośa*, T 4089–90), Vasubandhu occasionally distinguishes between exponents of Abhidharma who adopt an empirical or phenomenological approach and the Vedic grammarians, such as Bhartṛhari, who offer a linguistic interpretation. See, e.g., Pruden 1988–1990, 413–414; also the discussion on names, syntactically bound words or phrases, and syllables, 250–254. On the grammarians as a distinct sub-group within the non-Buddhist philosophical systems, see below, pp. 412–413.

91 The functionality of universals in the context of Buddhist logic is mentioned below, p. 156. The Tibetan term *'jug ldog byed pa* suggests predication and the meaningful application of terminology in specific instances.

92 In transcribing the grammatical conventions of Pāṇini and later Sanskrit grammarians, capital letters are generally employed as meta-linguistic symbols or technical markers (*anubandha*, *rjes 'brel*), which denote a list of related phonemes, forming the so-called *pratyāhāra* listing. See below, pp. 135–136.

93 On this distinction between object-universals and sound-universals or term-universals, see Dreyfus 1997, 221–222.

94 As stated in the anonymous *Commentary on the Eight Elements of Linguistic Application* (*gNas brgyad chen po'i 'grel pa*) (T 4351), pp. 27–28 of the Bod ljong mi rigs dpe skrun khang edition, these are enumerated as (1) adhesion to a given meaning in [association

with] its representation (*rnam pa nyid la don de nyid du mngon zhen*); (2) adhesion to the representation of a given meaning, embodying the representations of both sounds and letters (*sgra'i rnam pa yi ge'i rnam pa'i bdag la don gyi rnam pa nyid du mngon zhen*); (3) adhesion to representation in [association with] the characteristic nature of sounds or phonemes (*sgra rang gi mtshan nyid la rnam pa nyid du mngon zhen*), and (4) adhesion to names in [association with] the representations of sound-universals and the representations of syllables (*sgra spyi'i rnam pa'ang yi ge'i gzugs kyi rnam par ming la mngon zhen*).

95 The root text (T 4350) is by Che Khyidruk, which some Tibetan sources consider to be an epithet of the great translator Kawa Peltsek. On this text and its anonymous commentary (T 4351), see Verhagen 1991, 6–7; Inaba 1954, 24–29; Simonsson 1957, 243–244; and Miller 1963, 486–487.

96 Śāntideva, *Introduction to the Conduct of a Bodhisattva*, ch. 5, v. 32.

97 Nāgārjuna, *Fundamental Stanzas of Madhyamaka*, ch. 24, v. 10.

98 Cf. the comments of Dudjom Rinpoche 1991, 1:98.

99 This is also quoted by Dudjom Rinpoche 1991, 1:98.

100 Maitreya, *Ornament of the Sūtras of the Greater Vehicle*, ch. 11, v. 60. See Jamspal et al. 2004, 141.

101 A wide-ranging appraisal of Sanskrit grammatical literature can be found in Scharfe 1977. See also Cardona 1988, who analyzes the intricate system of Pāṇini's *Aṣṭādhyāyī* (translated in Joshi and Roodbergen 1992–2007), and Thakur 2006 on the system of Candragomin. For Jamgon Kongtrul's own survey, see Ngawang Zangpo 2010, 379–385. Jamgon Kongtrul's presentation owes much to the writings of Situ Chokyi Jungne of Palpung (1699–1774), who was one of the most influential Tibetan authorities on Sanskrit language and the related *vedāṅga* literature. For a survey of his contributions to grammatical studies, see Verhagen 2001, 2:161–182; and for a summary of his life, albeit in relation to his work as a painter and commissioner of art, see Jackson 2009, 3–19. Among the four major lineages of Sanskrit grammar that are extant within the Tibetan tradition, precedence is given, not to the *Grammar of Pāṇini*, but to the *Kalāpasūtra* (T 4282), the *Candravyākaraṇa* (T 4269), and the *Sārasvatavyākaraṇa* (T 4297). On their distinctive transmissions, see above, p. 11. Verhagen 2001 surveys the extant Tibetan versions of classical Sanskrit grammars in detail in vol. 1, and in vol. 2 he considers the Tibetan indigenous assimilation of Sanskrit grammar. An earlier important appraisal is also found in Smith 2001, 190–201. Detailed listings of the relevant Tibetan commentaries on the four grammatical systems of *Sārasvata*, *Candra*, *Kalāpa* and *Pāṇini* can be found in Drakpa, *Inventory of Tibetan Treatises*, 13–19; also online at www.tbrc.org, T282. Contemporary Sanskrit grammars follow the Western philological approach of Whitney 1896, with the notable exception of Goldman 1999.

102 This threefold division of the elements of Sanskrit grammar has been traced to Pang Lodro Tenpa (1276–1342). See Verhagen 2001, 2:70–79.

103 In Sanskrit grammar, the verbal roots have primacy and are considered as "genuine," whereas the nominal stems are "imputed." With regard to the latter, see below, pp. 131–132. About two thousand verbal roots in Sanskrit are traditionally listed, of which between eight and nine hundred have actually been used. On this and the distinctions between traditional and modern ways of classifying verbal roots, see Whitney 1896, 35–36 (102–105). For further detail, see also Whitney 1963, where the verbal roots are listed according to their Sanskrit alphabetical sequence.

104 According to Jamyang Gyatso, *Explanation of Elision* (*rJes 'brel sogs dbyi tshul bshad pa*), 620–621, this explanation derives from an as yet unidentified tract or passage entitled

Clarification of Sensual Grace in the Wish-fulfilling Commentary (*Kā ma dhe nur sgeg pa gsal ba*). The first category of those listed is by far the most common.

105 These chapters include verbal roots belonging to all the main nine classes, altogether numbering three hundred and thirty-five according to the *Paradigm of Verbal Roots* from the *Kalāpasūtra*. See Jamyang Gyatso, *Explanation of Elision*, 620. The full text of the *Paradigms of Verbal Roots* (*Kalāpa'i byings mdo*, ch. 9), including the root text (*rtsa ba*, T 4282) and its commentary (*'grel pa*, T 4285) is also included in Troru Tsenam, *Anthology of Sanskrit Grammatical Texts* (*sGra gzhung phyogs bsgrigs*), 404–557. The formally listed verbs, which originally would have been conjugated aloud, include three subcategories: (1) reflexive verbs conjugated in the middle voice (*ātmanepada, bdag don gyi tshig can*), (2) transitive verbs conjugated in the active voice (*parasmaipada, gzhan don gyi tshigs can*), and (3) verbs capable of being conjugated in either voice (*ubhayapada, gnyis ka'i tshig can*). See Troru Tsenam, *Commentary on the Grammar of Sārasvata* (*brDa sprod pa dbyangs can gyi mdo'i 'grel pa*), 198–200, and Whitney 1896, 200–201 (527–531).

Among the nine classes of verbs, discussed in the nine chapters, Class One is exemplified by *bhū* ("to become"), which has *bhava* as its present stem (ch. 1). Class Two is exemplified by *ad* ("to eat"), to which the personal terminations are added directly (ch. 2). Class Four is exemplified by *div* ("to play"), which adds *–ya* to the unaccented but unstrengthened root (ch. 3). Class Five is exemplified by *su* ("to press out"), which adds *-nu* or *-no* to the root (ch. 4). Class Six is exemplified by *tud* ("to push"), in which the root is unstrengthened (ch. 5). Class Seven is exemplified by *rudh* ("to obstruct"), in which a nasal precedes the final consonant of the stem (ch. 6). Class Eight is exemplified by *tan* ("to stretch"), which adds *-nu* or *-no* to the root (ch. 7). Class Nine is exemplified by *krī* ("to buy"), in which *-nā* or *-nī* may be added to the root (ch. 8). Class Three is exemplified by *hu* ("to sacrifice"), in which the root is preceded by reduplication. Pieter Verhagen (email communication, 7 May 2009) remarks that Jamgon Kongtrul appears to be following the *Paradigms of Verbal Roots* (*Dhātupāṭha*), which accords with the *Kalāpavyākaraṇa*, where nine classes of verbs are distinguished, in contrast to those of the Pāṇini and Cāndra traditions. The latter are known to distinguish ten classes, adding the derivative Class Ten verbs, exemplified by *cur* ("to steal"), in which *-aya* is generally added to the strengthened root (ch. 9). For a Western philological presentation of all these verbal classes, see Whitney 1896, 599–779.

106 Pieter Verhagen has noted (email communication, 7 May 2009) that *adolayati* may possibly derive from the root *dul* ("to raise"), combined with the verbal preposition *ā*. Cf. Monier-Williams 2005, 488 s.v. *dul* and 498 s.v. *dola*; also Whitney 1963, 75. Another possible source of this derivative is *ā -tul* ("lift up"), which has a Vedic attestation as a Class Ten infinitive. Cf. Monier-Williams 2005, 135. On the termination *–ayati* in Buddhist hybrid Sanskrit, see also Edgerton 1953, 1:185.

107 It is said in Jayadeva's *Commentary on the Grammar of Mañjuśrī* (*Mañjuśrīśabdavyākaraṇa*, T 4280) that some twenty such verbal roots have been obliquely mentioned in the major treatises of Candragomin, Kalāpa, and Pāṇini. See Jamyang Gyatso, *Explanation of Elision*, 621.

108 Some of the special *pratyāhāra* abbreviations devised by Pāṇini are mentioned in the following pages. These are formed by the attachment of technical markers (*anubandha, rjes su 'brel ba*) to an affix, indicating the various meta-rules for substitution, replacement and restricted usage. In transliterated form the technical markers are given in upper case, in order to distinguish them from the actual roots and affixes. On the role of the technical markers in the paradigms of the verbal roots, see also Palshule 1961. Among them, *yaK* indicates that a denominative affix *–ya* is to be suffixed to the short form of the root, commonly found in the perfect tense and benedictive. See Cardona 1988, 35.

109 Twenty-four such nouns are listed in Jamyang Gyatso, *Explanation of Elision*, 621. On *saN*, the desiderative termination, see the following note.

110 These twelve derivative suffixes comprise (1) the desiderative suffix *–saN* (as in the example *pipāsāmi*, "I wish to drink"); (2) the denominative suffix *–kāmyaC* (as in the example *putrakāmyati*, "He longs for a son"); (3) the denominative suffix *KyaC* (as in the example *putrīyati*, "He seeks a son"); (4) the denominative zero suffix *-vIP* (as in the example *aśvati*, "He behaves like a horse"); (5) the denominative suffix *KyaṄ* (as in the example *aśvāyate*, "He behaves like a horse"); (6) the denominative suffix *KyaṢ* (as in the example *lohitāyati*, "It turns red," "It reddens"); (7) the denominative suffix *-yaK* (as in the aforementioned example *kaṇḍūyati*, "It itches," "He scratches"); (8) the intensive suffix *-yaṄ* (as in the example *pāpacyate*, "He repeatedly cooks"); (9) the causative suffix *ṆiC* (as in the example *corayati*, "He causes/induces [someone] to steal"); (10) the periphrastic suffix *-āya* (as in the example "*paṇāyitā*, "He should be praised"); (11) the periphrastic suffix *-īyaṄ* (as in the example *ṛtīyatā*, "He should be censured!"); and (12) the periphrastic suffix *-ṇiṄ* (as in the example *kāmyitā*, "He should be desired!"). Among them, five are attached to the preceding verbal root directly, namely, *-saN*, *-yaṄ*, *-āya*, *-īyaṄ*, and *-ṇiṄ* (the last of these can also be attached directly to a nominal stem). Five of them can be attached directly to gender terminations, namely, *-kāmyaC*, *KyaC*, *-vIP*, *KyaṢ* and *KyaṄ*, whereas *-yaK* can only be attached directly to a nominal stem. *ṆiC* can be attached directly to both gender terminations and verbal roots. These are all discussed in Troru Tsenam, *Moonbeams Commentary*, 153–175. See also Verhagen 2001, 1:273. On the formation of causatives, see Whitney 1896, 1041–1052; on intensives, 1000–1025; on desideratives, 1026–1040; and on denominatives, 1053–1068.

111 The deleted agentive suffix *-v*, indicated by the void or zero-equivalent *pratyāhāra* (*KvIP*), is discussed in Cardona 1988, 435. See also Troru Tsenam, *Moonbeams Commentary*, 298–299.

112 On this distinction between the active voice (*parasmaipada*) and the middle voice (*ātmanepada*) in Sanskrit, see Whitney 1896, 528–531.

113 The *Commentary on the Grammar of Sārasvata* (*Sārasvatavyākaraṇa*) by Puñjarāja, though presently unavailable, was accessible to Situ Chokyi Jungne during the eighteenth century, and is cited extensively in his own re-translation of the root text, entitled *mTsho ldan ma'i brda sprod pa'i rab byed*, and in other works. See Verhagen 2001,1:177, 198; also 2:127.

114 This passage is quoted in Anubhūtisvabhāva's *Grammar of Sārasvata* (T 4297), 362. The text was re-translated from Sanskrit under the title *mTsho ldan ma'i rab byed* by Situ Chokyi Jungne, and is contained in b*Ka' brgyud pa'i gsung rab*, 1: 381–602. On the latter's *Light Rays/ Ocean of Eloquent Speech: A Commentary on the Sārasvata Grammar* (*mTsho ldan ma'i brda sprod gzung gi 'grel pa legs bshad ngag gi 'od zer/ rol mtsho*), see also Verhagen 2001, 2:161–163.

115 Anubandhas ending in *Ṅ* are said to indicate following inflections of the middle voice; those ending in *Ñ* indicate following inflections of either voice (*ubhayapada*); while those ending in other letters indicate following inflections of the active voice. See Jamyang Gyatso, *Explanation of Elision*, 622.

116 The *pratyāhāra aC* indicates vowel *a* with moderate *guṇa* strengthening of the root, while *GHaÑ* indicates the vowel *a* with an extreme *vṛddhi* strengthening of the root. On the distinctions between *guna* and *vṛddhi* strengthening, see, e.g., Whitney 1896, 81–84 (235–243).

117 Eighteen verbal suffixes, indicated by *tiṄ* (*tiṄantapada*), and twenty-one nominal suffixes, indicated by *sUP* (*subantapada*), are recognized. These are all enumerated below, note 126.

118 See p. 122.

119 The source for this sixfold classification is unclear, but see Troru Tsenam, *Commentary on the Grammar of Sārasvata*, 55–56.

120 This verse is attributed to the poet and grammarian Vyāḍi, whose *Commentary on Grammatical Rules* (*Paribhāṣavṛtti*), concerning the meta-rules of Pāṇinian grammar, is still extant. The list of synonyms does not appear to be included in either of the extant versions of the *Wish-fulfilling Commentary of Amarasiṃha* (*Amaraṭīkākāmadhenu*, contained in the Kangyur, T 4300), or in the later translation made by Situ Chokyi Jungne, entitled *Ming dang rtags rjes su ston pa'i bstan bcos 'chi med mdzod kyi rgya cher 'grel pa 'dod 'jo'i ba mo* (Collected Works, vol. Nga). It is, however, found in the supplementary text to the final part of the *Treasury of Amarasiṃha* (*Amarakośa*), entitled *Addendum to the Last Part of the Wish-fulfilling Commentary on the Treasury of Amarasiṃha* (*mDzod 'grel 'dod 'jo'i 'phros glegs bam 'og ma*), which was also translated into Tibetan by Situ Chokyi Jungne, Collected Works, vol. Ca, 314. On these writings, see Smith 2001, 204.

121 Situ Chokyi Jungne, Collected Works, vol. Ca, 314, cites the commentary of Ugra (*Drag po*), which states that "citizen" includes within its range of meanings wine-seller, oil-presser, and potter, while "pattern" refers to numeric sequences, and so forth. With regard to the three attributes—lightness of being, motility, and dullness or inertia—and their natural equilibrium, from the standpoint of Sāṃkhya philosophy, see below, p. 407.

122 This verse is found in Situ Chokyi Jungne, Collected Works, vol. Ca, 314. Cf. Satyadevamiśra 2005, 359: *prakṛti yonī liṅge ca.*

123 The third and final part of the *Treasury of Amarasiṃha* concerns gender-based variations of meaning, which are discussed in Situ Chokyi Jungne's aforementioned supplementary translation of the *Addendum*.

124 On indeclinables, see Whitney 1896, 403–417 (1096–1135).

125 These twelve kinds of termination are listed above, note 110.

126 *TiṄ* is a collective name for the personal terminations used in the conjugation of verbs. See Whitney 1896, 551–552. The enumeration of eighteen includes the first, second, and third person, singular, dual, and plural in respect of primary endings (which denote present indicative, future, and subjunctive) and secondary endings (which denote the imperfect, conditional, aorist, and optative). Perfect tense endings are derived from the former and imperatives from the latter. These distinctions apply to verbal roots of the active voice. Those of the middle voice are different.

127 *L-yig* indicates a group of ten tenses and moods, in which all the ten terms begin with the coded letter *l*. These comprise the present indicative (lAṬ), perfect (lIṬ), periphrastic future (lUṬ), future (lṚṬ), subjunctive (lEṬ), imperative (lOṬ), imperfect (lAṄ), optative (lIṄ), aorist (lUṄ) and conditional (lṚṄ). See Verhagen 1991, 251.

128 Here the expression *pada* (*tshig*), rendered as "phrases," would indicate bound syntactical word forms in contrast to the verbal roots themselves.

129 See also the sections on the *Kalāpa Grammar* in Troru Tsenam, *Commentary on the Grammar of Sārasvata*, 416–556.

130 Troru Tsenam, *Moonbeams Commentary*, 8–11, and the commentary on 279ff.

131 Troru Tsenam, *Commentary on the Grammar of Sārasvata*, 429–431, and the commentary on 513–521.

132 These primary nominal suffixes include *tra* and *tha* (appended to nouns of all genders); *a*, *man*, *ra*, and *van* (forming masculine and neuter substantives); *an*, *tṛ*, *ma*, *yu*, and *va* (forming masculine substantives); *u* and *una* (forming mostly masculine substantives); *mi* (forming masculine and feminine substantives); *i*, *ū*, *ti*, *ni*, and *nu* (forming feminine substantives); *ana*, *as*, *is*, *us*, and *ru* (forming neuter substantives); *at*, *āna*, and *māna*

(present and future participial suffixes); *anīya*, *tavya*, and *ya* (gerundive suffixes); *iyāṃs* and *iṣṭha* (comparative and superlative suffixes); *ta* and *na* (forming past participles and substantives); *tum* (forming the infinitive); and *vāṃs* (forming the perfect tense).

133 These are all mentioned, above, note 110. See also Whitney 1896, 1065; and Verhagen 2001, 1:273.

134 On these feminine terminations, see Whitney 1896, 332, 334, and 1210, and Troru Tsenam, *Moonbeams Commentary*, 459ff.

135 These are discussed specifically, from II.4–IV.4. See Troru Tsenam, *Moonbeams Commentary*, 18–20, and the commentary on 482–684. The secondary nominal suffixes, which represent a further stage of derivation from the verbal root and the primary nominal suffixes, include *a* (forming masculine and neuter adjectives preceded by *vṛddhi*), *ā* (forming feminine adjectives),*ānī* and *ī* (forming feminine nouns), *āyana* and *i* (forming masculine patronymics), *in*, *ma*, *maya*, *ya*, *ra*, *la*, *mat*, *vat*, *van*, and *vin* (forming possessive suffixes), *īna* (forming directional adjectives), *īya* (forming adjectives), *ka* and *ika* (forming diminutives and adjectives), *tana* (forming temporal adjectives), *tama* (forming superlatives and ordinals), *tara* (forming comparatives), *tā* and *tva* (forming feminine and neuter abstract nouns), *tya* (forming masculine and neuter nouns), *tha* (forming ordinal numbers), and *bha* (forming masculine nouns).

136 The standard twenty-one case endings are *s* (nominative singular), *au* (nominative dual), *as* (nominative plural), *am* (accusative singular), *au* (accusative dual), *as* (accusative plural), *ā* (instrumental singular), *bhyām* (instrumental dual), *bhis* (instrumental plural), *e* (dative singular), *bhyām* (dative dual), *bhyas* (dative plural), *as* (ablative singular), *bhyām* (ablative dual), *bhyas* (ablative plural), *as* (genitive singular), *os* (genitive dual), *ām* (genitive plural), *i* (locative singular), *os* (locative dual), and *su* (locative plural). On these, see Whitney 1896, 310, and more comprehensively on the subject of declension, 261–320.

137 This comment is derived from Vararuci's *Summation of Gender* (*Liṅgasaṃgraha*) and auto-commentary, which were translated into Tibetan by Situ Chokyi Jungne. See Verhagen 2001, 2:112. More generally on Vararuci, see Chimpa and Chattopadhyaya 1970, 85–86, 111–115, and 202–203; also Smith 2001, 198; and Verhagen 2001, 1:74–75, 170–171, 182, 184, and 195.

138 On these distinctions, see Verhagen 2001, 2:23–24, and for further detail on the term *bhāva/ dngos po* from both grammatical and logical perspectives, see 2:301–303. Also, Troru Tsenam, *Commentary on the Grammar of Sārasvata*, 224–230.

139 Note that the root verse reads *dbye ba* for *dbyi ba*, as given in the commentary. See below.

140 On these transformations, contingent on a preceding preposition, see Whitney 1896, 104, where distinctions are made according to the different approaches of traditional and modern grammarians and lexicographers. See also Jamyang Gyatso, *Explanation of Elision*, 625.

141 On the role of *anubandha* in general, see above, note 108; also Jamyang Gyatso, *Explanation of Elision*, 623ff. An important Tibetan source for the interpretation of *anubandha* is Situ Chokyi Jungne's *Treatise on Sanskrit Grammar, explained according to the Grammar of Candragomin, entitled Ship Transporting Precious Gems [of Eloquence] Launching onto the Ocean of the Grammatical Textual Tradition* (*Legs bshad rin chen 'dren pa'i gru gzings*), on which see Verhagen 2001, 2:169–180.

142 Altogether ten vowels and twenty-two consonants may function as technical markers. The former comprise the vowels A, Ā, I, Ī, U, Ū, Ṛ, Ḷ, E, and O, of which four (A, Ī, U, and Ṛ) may be attached directly to roots. The twenty-two consonants comprise K, KH, GH, Ṅ, C, J, Ñ, Ṭ, ṬH, Ḍ, Ṇ, T, N, P, M, Ś, Ṣ, and S. See, e.g., Verhagen 2001, 1:38–39, where the verbal roots mentioned in *sGra 'byor 'bam gnyis* are listed.

Examples of verbal roots with a following vocalic technical marker include *vidA* ("knowing") and *śāsU* ("learning"), from which the forms *vidyā* ("knowledge") and *śāstṛ* ("teacher") are respectively derived. The examples of a preceding consonantal technical marker, *Ṭu-* and *Ḍu-*, which are given here, suggest that vowels are combined with the voicing of consonants in specific forms of nominal derivation (*gsal byed kyi srog tu dbyangs sbyar ba'i rjes 'brel*). See Jamyang Gyatso, *Explanation of Elision*, 624; also Kelzang Ngawang Damcho, *Extensive Exegesis of the Sārasvata Grammar* (*dByangs can sgra mdo'i rgyas bshad*), 43 for an example of the marker *Ḍu-*. As for *–IR*, given here to illustrate technical markers combining both vowels and consonants, see Kelzang Ngawang Damcho, op. cit., 39, which offers the example *yujIR* ("joining"), from which the word *yoga* ("union") is derived.

143 See above, note 110 and 116.

144 The technical marker *lAṬ* (mis-transcribed as *PAṬ*), as mentioned above in note 127, suggests the present indicative, while *ṄasI* represents the ablative singular case-ending *–as*. On the latter, see Cardona 1988, 31.

145 On *-T* (*takāra, t-yig*) as a technical marker indicating gender, see Kelzang Ngawang Damcho, *Extensive Exegesis*, 582–584. Pieter Verhagen points out (email communication, 7 May 2009) that the technical marker *-aT* indicates a short letter *-a*, and *-āT* indicates a long vowel *-ā*, whereas *-a* without the technical marker is considered neutral, either long or short.

146 Should this *pratyāhāra* not take the form *nUM*. See Cardona 1988, 40, according to which "the augment *n* (*nUM*) is inserted after the last vowel of a neuter stem that ends in a vowel, a non-nasal stop, or a spirant." See also Troru Tsenam, *Moonbeams Commentary*, 885–888, where the examples given suggest that the augments here are those representing singular, dual, and plural inflections.

147 On indeclinable words (*avyayībhāvānubandha*), see Whitney 1896, 1096–1135, and on their derivatives, 1202 and 1205. On permitted finals, see 122 and 139–152.

148 All the ten permitted final vowels which occur as technical markers (*anubandha*) and have the function of facilitating the pronunciation of a given sound (*brjod par byed pa'i don*) are implied here, exemplified by the syllable A. They are all listed above, note 142. Jamyang Gyatso, *Explanation of Elision*, 623, adds that although these vowels that facilitate pronunciation are generally not elided, they may be elided in special circumstances. Whitney 1896, 125–128, describes the possible vowel combinations that may occur when a final inherent A is followed by an initial vowel.

149 Jamyang Gyatso, *Explanation of Elision*, 625, lists some examples of the technical markers that denote peculiarities of inflection (*khyad par gyi don*), and which are dropped when the inflections are applied. Among them are those denoting inflections indicative of declension (*gnas don*), gender (*rtags don*), number (*grangs don*), and action (*bya ba'i don*). Copious examples may also be found throughout Mamhikawi's *Application of Terminations Indicative of Declension: A Commentary on the Kalāpasūtra* (*Kalāpasūtravṛtti syādvibhaktiprakriyā*, T 4288), vol. She, ff. 54b–97a; and in Sarvadhara's *Analysis of the Terminations Indicating Verbal Morphology from the Kalāpa Grammar* (*Tyādyantaprakriyāvicārita*, T 4289), vol. She, ff. 103b, 105a, and so forth. The rules governing elision in all such cases are also explained in the *Joyous Music: Mind Treasury of Proverbs* (*dPer brjod blo gter dgyes pa'i rol mo* (attributed to Paṇchen Tenpei Wangchuk), according to the tradition of the *Kalāpasūtra*, and in Situ Chokyi Jungne's *Ship Transporting Precious Gems* [*of Eloquence*], according to the tradition of the *Grammar of Candragomin* (*Candravyākaraṇa*).

150 Some of these technical markers (*anubandha*), which are attached directly to the verbal roots or to substantives, are listed by Jamyang Gyatso, *Explanation of Elision*, 623–624.

151 These are: pra- (*rab-tu*), parā- (*mchog-tu*), apa- (*lhag par*), sam- (*yang dag par*), anu- (*rjes su*), ava- (*phul du*), nir- (*bral bar*), dur- (*ngan par*), vi- (*rnam par*), ā- (*legs par*), ni- (*nges par*), adhi- (*shin tu*), api- (*slar*), ati- (*dag par*), su- (*bde bar*), ut- (*mtho bar*), abhi- (*mngon par*), prati- (*yongs su*), and upa- (*nye bar*). See Whitney 1896, 1123–1130.

152 Here the text reads *thob* ("obtain").

153 Final *K* as a technical marker indicates the absence of *guṇa* vowel strengthening.

154 On the rules that govern vowel strengthening, see Whitney 1896, 27 and 235–243.

155 This passage derives from Kelzang Ngawang Damcho, *Extensive Exegesis*, 520–521, *yuvor anākau, yu vu dag gi ana aka dag go*. Cf. Pāṇini, 7.1.1. On *yu*, see Whitney 1896, 1165; on *ana*, 1150; and on *aka*, 1181.

156 In certain secondary suffixes, final *ch* is substituted by *īya*, Cf. Pāṇini, 4th and 5th *adhyāya* at several places (e.g., Abhyankar 1961, 157, s.v. *cha*). On *īya*, see also Whitney 1896, 1215c.

157 See above, note 126.

158 See Kelzang Ngawang Damcho, *Extensive Exegesis*, 585.

159 This occurs after a stem ending in *a*, as when *vṛkṣae* becomes *vṛkṣāya*. See Cardona 1988, 21.

160 Whitney 1896, 98–259 offers a comprehensive exposition of *sandhi* and its rules.

161 See specifically Whitney 1896, 234–254.

162 See, e.g., Troru Tsenam, *Commentary on the Grammar of Sārasvata*, 164–197.

163 These comprise six categories of descriptive compound, two of dual compounds, two of indeclinable compounds, eight of dependent compounds, seven of exocentric compounds, and four types of coordinative compound. See Verhagen 1991, 190.

164 The lineages of Buddhist logic derive from the classical Indian works of Dignāga, Dharmakīrti, and their commentators, which are contained in the *Tshad ma* section of the Tengyur. Jamgon Kongtrul recounts the origins of this literary genre in Ngawang Zangpo 2010: 385–392. The indigenous Tibetan commentarial tradition is more extensive—see Drakpa, *Inventory of Tibetan Treatises*, 617–624 and www.tbrc.org, T370, which currently lists 135 texts. Among them are Kadampa works such as Chapa Chokyi Senge's *Dispelling Mental Darkness: Root Text and Commentary Integrating [Dharmakīrti's] Seven Treatises on Valid Cognition* (*Tshad ma sde bdun bsdus pa yid gi mun sel*) and Chomden Rigpei Raldri's *Ornamental Flower of [Dharmakīrti's] Seven Treatises on Valid Cognition* (*Tshad ma sde bdun rgyan gyi me tog*), as well as Bodong Paṇchen's *Exegesis on the Systematic Presentation of Valid Cognition according to Buddhism, as stated in Dharmakīrti's Drops of Reasoning* (*Rigs thigs las gsungs pa'i nang pa'i tshad ma'i rnam gzhag bshad pa*). Important Sakya writings on logic include Sakya Paṇḍita's *Treasure of Valid Logical Reasoning* (*Tshad ma rigs gter*), and the commentaries elucidating his writings and those of Dharmakīrti which were composed, in particular, by Zilungpa Śākya Chokden and Gorampa Sonam Senge. Within the Kagyu school, Karmapa VII Chodrak Gyatso's *Ocean of the Textual Tradition of Logical Reasoning* (*Rigs pa'i gzhung lugs kyi rgya mtsho*) has been most influential. Gelukpa authors have placed great emphasis on the study of logic—their most influential exemplars including Khedrubje Gelek Pelzangpo's *Ornament of the Seven Treatises Clearing Mental Obscurity* (*Tshad ma sde bdun gyi rgyan yid kyi mun sel*), Paṇchen Sonam Drakpa's *Commentary on Difficult Points in the Exposition of Valid Cognition, entitled Complete Revelation of Enlightened Intention* (*rGyas pa'i bstan bcos tshad ma rnam 'grel gyi dka' 'grel dgongs pa rab gsal*), and Phurbuchok Tsultrim Jampa Gyatso's *Magic Key of the Path of Reason:* A *Presentation of the Collected Topics, Analyzing the Meaning of Valid Cognition* (*Tshad ma'i gzhung don 'byed pa'i bsdus grva rnam gzhag rigs lam 'phrul gyi lde mig*). Finally, Nyingma contributions are exemplified by the more recent writings of Jamgon Mipham Gyatso.

165 Tib. *phyi rabs la*, lit., "among later generations." The term *bsdus pa* could refer to the original Tibetan commentarial summaries of the writings of Dharmakīrti, but in this context it most likely refers to the later refinements of these summaries in the *Collected Topics* (*bsDus grva*), on which see below, note 242; also Dreyfus 1997, 22, and Rogers 2009, 21–25 and 281ff.

166 The first chapter of Sakya Paṇchen's *Treasure of Valid Logical Reasoning*, entitled "Examination of the Object" (*yul brtag rab tu byed pa*), is a useful primary source for this section. See root verses, pp. 4–5, and auto-commentary, pp. 39–58.

167 On the definition of substance in terms of its causal effectiveness, see Dreyfus 1997, 77ff., and on the distinction between compounded and uncompounded phenomena, Pruden 1988, 1:59ff.

168 See below, pp. 147–151, on cognitive phenomena.

169 With regard to the use of the term "predominant condition" or "empowering condition" in Buddhist phenomenology, see below, Part Two, pp. 524–527; also Pruden 1988, 1:303–304.

170 Sources that discuss the distinction between positive and negative concomitance include Kajiyama 1958. Along with the property of the thesis (*pakṣadharmatvam*, *phyogs chos*), these form the "three recognized logical criteria" (*trairūpya*, *tshul gsum*). See also Dreyfus 1997, 171 and 510.

171 This distinction is succinctly defined in Dreyfus 1997, 547: "The direct cause produces its effect immediately after its disappearance, in opposition to the indirect causes, which are not immediately effective."

172 The four secondary conditions (*caturpratyaya*) are discussed below, Part Two, p. 527.

173 Tib. *mdun gyi rdul chung tha gcig*. Such particles are arguably either non-substantial or substantial. See also Negi, *Tibetan Sanskrit Dictionary* (*Bod skad dang legs sbyar gyi tshig mdzod chen mo*) 16 vols. (Sarnath: Central Institute of Higher Tibetan Studies, 1993–2005), 2664, which quotes the *Sūtra of Extensive Play* (*Lalitavistarasūtra*), stating that there are seven indivisible atomic particles (*paramāṇu*, *rdul phra rab*) forming a single atom (*truṭi*, *rdul chung ngu*).

174 See above, p. 107; also on the momentariness of the continuum of time, see Dreyfus 1997, 60–65. Pruden 1988–1990, 474–475, discusses measures of time.

175 Dreyfus 1997, 250–260, compares the concept of "object-universals" (*don spyi*) from contrasting Gelukpa and Sakyapa standpoints.

176 Chapa Chokyi Senge's exposition of this typology is presented, along with Sakya critiques, in Dreyfus 1997, 379–399, and the non-deceptiveness of applied objects is also discussed, 300–310. Apparent objects specifically are said to include real things, object-universals, and non-existents (382).

177 On these three categories of appraisable objects, see Tillemans 1999, 28–30.

178 See Dreyfus 1997, 48–50 and 67–72, on further distinctions between *rang mtshan* and *spyi mtshan*.

179 The philosophical implications of Dharmakīrti's views on direct perception and inference are discussed in Dreyfus 1997, 296–298 and 312–315.

180 Just as impurities are said to be ascertained by the process of burning, cutting, and polishing, so the scriptures are similarly to be investigated through these three types of scrutiny (*dpyad pa gsum*). In this regard, Śāntarakṣita in his *Summation of the Real* (*Tattvasaṃgraha*), vv. 3340–3344, compares the study of the Buddhist scriptures to the purification of gold by burning, cutting, and polishing. See also Dudjom Rinpoche 1991, 1:122, and Tillemans 1999, 30 and 47–51, on scripturally based inference, which equates *dpyad pa gsum* with the "three criteria" (*tshul gsum*)—inference through the power of fact, inference based on conviction, and inference based on universal acceptance.

181 On this verse from Nāgārjuna's *Precious Garland* (*Ratnāvalī*), see Tillemans 1999, 48.
182 The fifth chapter of Sakya Paṇchen's *Treasure of Valid Logical Reasoning*, entitled "Examination of the Signified and the Signifier" (*brjod bya rjod byed brtag rab tu byed pa*), refers to this distinction. See root verses, pp. 11–13, and auto-commentary, pp.114–128. Also, Dreyfus 1997, 272–275.
183 On this distinction, made by Sakyapa logicians, see Dreyfus 1997, 163.
184 The second chapter of Sakya Paṇchen's *Treasure of Valid Logical Reasoning*, entitled "Examination of the Cognizing Intellect" (*shes byed kyi blo brtag rab tu byed pa*), also discusses this subject. See root verses, pp. 5–7, and auto-commentary, pp. 58–71.
185 Dreyfus 1997, 272–275.
186 Dreyfus 1997, 432.
187 Tib. *'jug ldog gi gzhi*. Thubten Jinpa Langri notes (email communication, 29 March 2010) that this expression relates to the demonstrations or illustrations (*mtshon gzhi*) of descriptive attributes in the context of their actual usage, as in the construction of meaningful sentences. On the related expression *'jug ldog byed pa*, see above, note 91.
188 Further information on universals and type-universals can be found in Dreyfus 1997, chs. 7–9.
189 These comprise earth, water, fire, air, visible objects, odors or smells, tastes, and tangible objects. As such they are composites of the material elements, for which reason they are regarded in Geluk epistemological thinking as metaphorical rather than real universals. See Dreyfus 1997, 107–109.
190 On divergent Sakya and Geluk interpretations of Dharmakīrti's view concerning predicate and subject oriented expressions, see Dreyfus 1997, 185–187.
191 Dreyfus 1997, 245 refers also to the "preclusion of the contradictory" (*dngos 'gal gcod pa*).
192 Cf. the discussion on conceived and actual signifiers in Dreyfus 1997, 273–274, which is based on Sakya sources, principally the writings of Gorampa.
193 For Jamgon Kongtrul's presentation of the five psycho-physical aggregates—forms, feelings, perceptions, formative predispositions, and consciousness—see below, Part Two, pp. 477–531. The fourfold aggregate excludes form, in the case of sentient individuals who are said to inhabit the world-system of formlessness (*ārūpyadhātu*).
194 Jamgon Kongtrul's presentation of valid and invalid cognition follows below, p. 151ff.
195 On the relationship between conceptual cognition and universals, see Dreyfus 1997, 144–146.
196 Regarding this distinction between generally and specifically characterized phenomena, see above, note 178.
197 For an evaluation of this development of Indian and Tibetan thought, see Williams 1998.
198 Jamgon Kongtrul's presentation of the six or eight modes of consciousness is given below, Part Two, pp. 511–530.
199 These are discussed individually in Part Two, pp. 492–506, on the basis of their analysis in Asaṅga's *Compendium of Phenomenology* (*Abhidharmasamuccaya*).
200 An important source for the examination of direct perception (*mngon sum brtag rab tu byed pa*) is the ninth chapter of Sakya Paṇchen's *Treasure of Valid Logical Reasoning*. See root verses, pp. 23–26, and auto-commentary, pp. 226–264.
201 For Jamgon Kongtrul's summary of sense organs and sense objects in Buddhist phenomenology, see below, Part Two, pp. 479–489.
202 On the functionality of mental consciousness in Buddhist phenomenology, see below, pp. 527–530.
203 See Williams 1998 on the role of reflexive awareness.

204 On these distinctions between pious attendants, hermit buddhas, and bodhisattvas, including their different experiences of the path of insight, see, for example, the Nyingma presentation in Dudjom Rinpoche 1991, 1:223–237; and Jamgon Kongtrul's own account in Callahan 2007: 85–174.

205 On the threefold criteria, see below, pp. 159–160; also Tillemans 1999, 38–39. The last two chapters of Sakya Paṇchen's *Treasure of Valid Logical Reasoning*, entitled "Examination of Inference for One's Own Sake" (*rang don rjes dpag brtag rab tu byed pa*) and "Examination of Inference for the Sake of Others" (*gzhan don rjes dpag brtag pa'i rab tu byed pa*), are important sources. See root verses, pp. 26–36, and auto-commentary, pp. 264–369.

206 See above, note 180. On the three types of inference outlined here, see also Rogers 2009, 305–306 and 444–447.

207 On this distinction and their common validity, see Dreyfus 1997, 392, which states: "A perception able to induce immediate ascertainment is an internally valid cognition. A perception unable to do so is an externally valid cognition."

208 Contradiction or exclusion is discussed in Dreyfus 1997, 144–147 and 158–160; also Rogers 2009, 253–259. The seventh chapter of Sakya Paṇchen's *Treasure of Valid Logical Reasoning*, entitled "Examination of Contradiction" (*gal ba brtag rab tu byed pa*), is also an important source. See root verses, pp. 17–19, and auto-commentary, pp. 167–178.

209 On relation, see Dreyfus 1997, 136, 140, and 174–175; also the sixth chapter of Sakya Paṇchen's *Treasure of Valid Logical Reasoning*, entitled "Examination of Relations" (*'brel pa brtag rab tu byed pa*). See root verses, pp. 13–17, and auto-commentary, pp. 128–167.

210 The two types of negation, as differentiated by Śāntarakṣita, are discussed in Dreyfus 1997, 233–249.

211 On proof, see Dreyfus 1997, 234–236 and 247–249; also the fourth chapter of Sakya Paṇchen's *Treasure of Valid Logical Reasoning*, entitled "Examination of Proof and Elimination" (*sgrub pa dang gzhan sel brtag rab tu byed pa*). See root verses, pp. 8–11, and auto-commentary, pp. 82–114.

212 The "examination of universals" (*spyi dang bye brag brtag rab tu byed pa*) is presented in the third chapter of Sakya Paṇchen's *Treasure of Valid Logical Reasoning*: root verses, pp. 7–8, and auto-commentary, pp. 71–82.

213 This definition of particulars or individuations is reiterated in Dreyfus 1997, 171–174. Primary sources include the third chapter of Sakya Paṇchen's treatise.

214 The concepts of identity and difference are discussed in Dreyfus 1997, 173–179.

215 On the distinction between perceptions or non-conceptual subjects as affirmative engagement and conceptual subjects as eliminative engagement, see Dreyfus 1997, 265.

216 Śāntarakṣita differentiates all three types of elimination. See Dreyfus 1997, 241ff. See also the fourth chapter of Sakya Paṇchen's *Treasure of Valid Logical Reasoning*: root verses, pp. 8–11, and auto-commentary, pp. 82–114.

217 The eighth chapter of Sakya Paṇchen's *Treasure of Valid Logical Reasoning* is entitled "Examination of Defining Characteristics" (*mtshan nyid brtag rab tu byed pa*): root verses, pp. 19–23, and auto-commentary, pp. 179–226.

218 The three substantially existent properties of defining characteristics are also enumerated as "the presence of a defining characteristic (*mtshan nyid yin pa*), the establishment of a defining characteristic upon its demonstration (*rang gi mtshan gzhi'i steng du grub pa*), and the lack of engagement in other defining characteristics extraneous to its own demonstrable object (*rang gi mtshon bya las gzhan pa'i mtshan nyid mi byed pa*)." See Zhang Yisun et al., *Great Tibetan-Chinese Dictionary*, 2854.

219 See, e.g., Dreyfus 1997, 272–275, on signification, and 299–301, on engagement or application.

220 The practical application of the relationship between definition, definiendum, and illustration is explored in Rogers 2009, 288–297.

221 The eight ostensible factors (*ltar snang brgyad*) may be identified as the incomplete counterparts of the eight approaches to logical entailment (*khyab pa sgo brgyad*), on which see below, pp. 175–176. They are all identified as unreliable modes of epistemology.

222 On substance-phenomena and distinguishing counterpart phenomena, see Dreyfus 1997, 158–168.

223 For a more detailed discussion on these three criteria, see Rogers 2009, 33–77 on the first, 109–122 on the second, 102–128 on the third, and 360–363 on all combined. The tenth chapter of Sakya Paṇchen's *Treasure of Valid Logical Reasoning*, entitled "Examination of Reasoning for One's Own Sake" (*rang don brtag rab tu byed pa*), is a key primary source. See root verses, pp. 26–32, and auto-commentary, pp. 264–330.

224 The distinction between *sapakṣa* and *vipakṣa* is discussed in Tillemans 1999, 89–116. See also Rogers 2009, 100–107.

225 On these three criteria in relation to universals, see Dreyfus 1997, 199–200.

226 The three axioms are mentioned in Dreyfus 1997, 477, with references to Gorampa Sonam Senge's *Explanation of Difficult Points in [Sa-paṇ's] Treasury of Valid Cognition* (*Tshad ma rig gter gyi dka' gnas rnam par bshad pa*). Among these three, the axiom of the result relates to causal inferences; the axiom of identity governs inferences determined by the internal relations between a subject of phenomena and its phenomena; while the axiom of the absence of the objective referent applies to negative inferences, such as the *modus tollens* of classical Western logic. See also Dudjom Rinpoche 1991, vol. 1, n95. On the nuances of the last of these axioms, see also Tillemans 1999, 153ff.; and on the axiom of identity in particular, see Steinkellner 1991, 311–324.

227 The distinction between genuine reason that is made for one's own sake (*rang don gyi rtags*) and for the sake of others (*gzhan don gyi rtags*) is analyzed, for example, in chs. 10 and 11 of Sakya Paṇḍita's *Tshad ma rigs pa'i gter.* For a brief discussion on the distinctions between proof of meaning (*don sgrub*) and conventional terms (*tha snyad sgrub*), see also Rogers 2009, 284–286; and for an extensive discussion on genuine reason or correct signs in general, ibid., 149–326.

228 These three types of ostensible evidence are all presented below, with examples, pp. 173–175. See also Rogers 2009, 327–357; and specifically on uncertain evidence, Tillemans 1999, 97–100.

229 The use of correct analogous examples and non-analogous examples in Sakya Paṇchen's *Treasure of Valid Logical Reasoning* is discussed in Tillemans 1999, 98. See also Rogers 2009, 103–107.

230 The technical jargon utilized in the context of formal debate is examined by Tillemans 1999, 117–149. Cf. Rogers 2009, 25–29.

231 With regard to the distinctions between the antagonist and the respondent, whether actual or intentionally imagined, see Rogers 2009, 312–317. The last chapter of Sakya Paṇchen's *Treasure of Valid Logical Reasoning* is entitled "Examination of Reasoning for the Sake of Others" (*gzhan don rjes dpag rab tu byed pa*). See root verses, pp. 32–36, and auto-commentary, pp. 330–366.

232 On correct and ostensible statements of proof, see Perdue 1976; also Rogers 2009, 132–138 and 363ff.

233 On correct and ostensible refutation, see Perdue 1976.

234 Jamgon Kongtrul's presentation of consequential reasoning is summarized below, pp. 169–172, and in greater detail in Callahan 2007, 223–247. For a general survey of the applications of consequential reasoning in Madhyamaka, see Ruegg 1981; for interpretations of Candrakīrti's exposition, Huntington and Wangchen 1989, Padmakara Transla-

tion Group 2002, and Dewar 2008; and for recent research, Dreyfus and McClintock 2003.

235 On the formal language and procedures of debate, see Tillemans 1999, 117ff.

236 Such as in the works of Phurbuchok, on which see below, note 242.

237 This fundamental distinction is made at the start of Sakya Paṇchen's auto-commentary to *Treasure of Valid Logical Reasoning*, ch. 1, p. 39. Subsequently these two lines were adopted by Gorampa Sonam Senge to encapsulate the entire content of his extensive commentary, entitled *Faultless Commentary on the Intention of the Seven Treatises and Their Sūtra Revealing the Meaning* [*of Sa-paṇ's*] *Treasury of Logical Reasoning* (*sDe bdun mdo dang bcas pa'i dgongs pa phyin ci ma log par 'grel pa tshad ma rigs pa'i gter gyi don gsal bar byed pa*). Dreyfus 1997 refers to this influential treatise; specifically on *spyi ldog*, see 501n39.

238 The formal title of this extensive text, which seeks to identify Dhamakīrti with the Tibetan philosophical view of Great Madhyamaka, is *Oceanic Textbook on Logical Reasoning Where the Rivers of All Eloquence of Valid Cognition Converge* (*Tshad ma legs par bshad pa thams cad kyi chu bo yongs su 'du ba'i rigs pa'i gzhung lugs kyi rgya mtsho*), contained in *bKa' brgyud pa'i gsung rab*, vols. 6–7. A few references may be found in Dreyfus 1997, 484n36, 485n11, and 486n25. Also, on the influence of this work and its author upon Zilungpa Shākya Chokden, see Dreyfus 1997, 28–29 and 431.

239 On Ngok Loden Sherab, see Kuijp 1983, 372–387. On Chapa Choseng, see also Kuijp 1978, 359–369, and Dreyfus 1997, 22 and passim. Chapa Choseng's composition, entitled *Dispelling Mental Darkness: Root-text and Commentary Integrating* [*Dharmakīrti's*] *Seven Treatises on Valid Cognition* (*Tshad ma bsdus pa yid kyi mun sel*), is regarded as the precursor of the *Collected Topics* (*bsdus grva*) genre. On this, see Longdol Lama's *Enumeration of Terms Based on* [*the Treatises of*] *Logic, Including the Exposition of Valid Cognition* (*Tshad ma rnam 'grel sogs gtan tshigs rig pa las byung ba'i ming gi rnam grangs*), in his Collected Works, 1:608–610. Chapa's early realistic interpretation of Dharmakīrti is also discussed in Dreyfus 1997, 276.

240 This passage is found in Longdol Lama, *Enumeration of Terms*, pp. 608–609. It is addressed to the monks of Kyemotshal in Dreyul, Rinpung County. The monastery was founded in 1449 by Jamchen Rabjampa Sangyepel (1411–1485), a student of Rongton Mawei Senge. It was renowned for its dialectical college, established by Rinpung Norbu Zangpo. See Ferrari 1958, 163.

241 I have tentatively suggested that the topic *snga btsan bar btsan phyi btsan* should be interpreted as "cogency (*btsan thabs*) of the antagonist (*snga rgol*), the mediator (*bar mi*), and the respondent (*phyi rgol*)." Thubten Jinpa Langri concurs (email communication, 29 March 2010) that this refers to the scope of the language employed by different parties in the context of a debate, adding that the equivalent topic listed by later Geluk writers is termed "formal procedures for accepting [an argument] (*khas blangs song tshul*)." Another, less probable, alternative is that this expression could be interpreted to mean "cogency of the premise, middle term, and conclusion."

242 Longdol Lama, *Enumeration of Terms*, 608–609, explains how this enumeration of eighteen collected topics is based on the tradition of Chapa Choseng, contrasting it with later Geluk presentations such as Tsenpo Ngawang Trinle's arrangement, which includes concise, intermediate, and extensive listings, respectively in eleven, fifteen, and twenty-one topics. The refinement and culimation of this three-stage exposition of the *Collected Topics* (*bsDus grva che 'bring chung gsum*) is found in the *Yongs 'dzin bsdus grva*, otherwise known as the *Magic Key of the Path of Reasoning* (*Rigs lam 'phrul gyi lde mig*) which was composed by Phurbuchok Tsultrim Jampa Gyatso Pelzangpo (1825–1901), a contemporary of Jamgon Kongtrul. On this work, see also Rogers 1980 and the transla-

tions in Rogers 2009; also Perdue 1976; and Lati Rinpoche, Hopkins, and Napper 1986. Other important precursors of Phurbuchok's *Collected Topics* include Tsongkhapa's *Gateway to the Seven Sections on Logic Clearing the Obscuration of Aspirants* (*sDe bdun la 'jug pa'i sgo don gnyer yid kyi mun sel*), Khedrub Gelek Pelzangpo's *Ornament of the Seven Treatises Clearing Mental Obscurity* (*Tshad ma sde bdun gyi rgyan yid kyi mun sel*) and Konchok Tenpei Dronme's *Magic Key Opening a Hundred Doors of Logical Reasoning* (*Rigs lam sgo brgya 'byed pa'i 'phrul gyi lde mig*).

243 For Jamgon Kongtrul's presentation of the five sensory activity fields, see below, Part Two, pp. 537–540; and on superimposition (*sgro 'dogs*), Dreyfus 1997, 68 and 77.

244 See below, Part Two, pp. 526–530.

245 For an analysis of the distinction between extraneous or non-apperceptive awareness (*anyasaṃvedana, gzhan rig*) and intrinsic or reflexive awareness (*svasaṃvedana, rang rig*), see Williams 1998.

246 On the sensory activity field of phenomena and the fifty-one mental states, see below, Part Two, pp. 483–484 and 496–506, respectively.

247 The sixteen aspects of the four truths (*caturāryasatya, bden bzhi*) are enumerated in, e.g., Dudjom Rinpoche 1991, 2:173–174. Cf. Jamgon Kongtrul's explanation in Callahan 2007, 115–119.

248 Jamgon Kongtrul summarizes the distinctions between the perception of a sublime pious attendant or bodhisattva and that of a buddha in Book Six, Part Three of the present work. See Callahan 2007.

249 This is a reference to a passage in Dharmakīrti's *Proof of Other Minds* (*Santānāntarasiddhi-nāma-prakaraṇa*, T 4219), Tshad ma, vol. Che, f. 359a, which states: "The comprehension of all objects by the Transcendent Lord [Buddha] is inconceivable because it goes beyond the [mundane] cognition of all sensa and expressible objects (*bcom ldan 'das kyis don thams cad su chud pa ni bsam gyis mi khyab ste / rnam pa thams cad du shes pa dang brjod pa'i yul las 'das pa'i phyir ro*)." In other words, the direct perception of the buddhas, being inconceivable, is excluded from the categories that are listed here. On the rationale for the inclusion of yoga as a means of direct perception, see Tillemans 1999, 245n32.

250 See above, note 247; also Callahan 2007, 115–119.

251 Regarding Jamgon Kongtrul's summary of the two kinds of selflessness, see Callahan 2007, 162–164, 204–205, and 234.

252 Dreyfus 1997, 140, 143.

253 Jamgon Kongtrul's analysis of dissonant and purified mental states (*sems kyi steng gi kun byang*), along with their seeds, can be found below, in Part Two, pp. 498–506.

254 On the importance of renunciation and antidotes (*spang gnyen*), see, e.g., Padmakara Translation Group 1994, 263ff.

255 See Tillemans 1999, 27–51, on the validity of scriptural authority.

256 See above, note 226.

257 On the three kinds of scrutiny, see above, note 180; and on concealed intention, see the discussion in Dudjom Rinpoche 1991, 1:217–222.

258 According to Khenpo Tsultrim Gyatso, the source of the verses cited in this section is the *Collected Topics of Logical Reasoning* (*Rigs bsdus*) of Zhamar VI Garwang Chokyi Wangchuk—a text which is generally thought to be no longer extant, but which may still possibly resurface when the Collected Works of Zhamar VI are published. Thanks to Karl Brunnhölzl for this observation.

259 Tib. *snga btsan phyi btsan*. See above, note 241.

260 Tib. *skor 'bebs.* Thubten Jinpa Langri points out that these iterations would include the use of double negatives, and so forth.

261 For Jamgon Kongtrul's presentation of Great Madhyamaka, see Callahan 2007, 249–268; also Dudjom Rinpoche 1991, 1:206–216.

262 The determination of selflessness and freedom from conceptual elaboration are the fruitional achievements of Madhyamaka. See, e.g., Dewar 2008, 314–428.

263 Garwang Chokyi Wangchuk (1584–1630) was a student of the Ninth Karmapa Wangchuk Dorje and teacher of the Tenth Karmapa, Choying Dorje. See Douglas and White 1976, 82–83.

264 See above, note 228.

265 Cf. the discussion on unestablished reasoning in Rogers 2009, 350–357 and 465–468.

266 Also, on contradictory reasoning, see Rogers 2009, 329–333 and 453–456.

267 Unascertained reasoning is also examined in Rogers 2009, 338–350 and 457–464.

268 Here the text reads "if *x* is not the evidence" (*rtags de nyid min pas*), but see Nyima and Dorje 2001, 648.

269 *SK*, 246, reads *mthun khyab* for *thur khyab*.

270 According to Taktsang Lotsāwa Sherab Rinchen's *Ocean of Wealth* (*dPal 'byor rgya mtsho, dPal ldan sa skya pa'i gsung rab*, vol. 3), part 1, p. 162, this passage appears to be extracted specifically from the *Analysis of Monastic Discipline* (*Vinayavibhaṅga*).

271 Skt. *aupadhikapuṇya*, Tib. *rdzas las byung ba'i bsod nams*.

272 For an influential practical guide to the cultivation of the four immeasurable aspirations, comprising loving-kindness, compassion, empathetic joy, and equanimity, see Patrul Rinpoche's explanation in Padmakara Translation Group 1994, 195–217.

273 The origins of the Nirgranthas, from which the Jains are said to have evolved, are discussed in Basham 1959, 290, and in Dundas 2002, 121. Some artistic endeavors were included by the Jains in a list of proscribed "joyful" activities (*paramādācaraṇa*). See Dasgupta 1922, 1:200. Equally, Basham 1959, 294, and Sharma 1965, 124 and 130, refer to the importance in Jainism of abstinence from the negative influence of property and material possessions (*parigrahapāpa*). Yet there are other Jain sources deeming arts and crafts to be respectable pursuits, not for the *nirgrantha* ascetics but for the laity. See Jaini 1979, 172, and the significant contribution of Jain sculpture of the Mathurā school cannot be denied. Jamgon Kongtrul's brief presentation of Jainism can be found below, pp. 414–415.

274 Cf. Dudjom Rinpoche 1991, 1:98. The indigenous Indian literature concerning the fine arts (*śilpaśāstra, bzo rig*) includes commentaries on specific chapters or elements of the Buddhist tantras, some of which are contained in the Tengyur and mentioned by Jamgon Kongtrul in the following pages. Among them are the works of Kuladatta, Jagaddarpaṇa, Śākyamitra, and Ātreya. For Kongtrul's account of the origins of sacred art and writing, see Ngawang Zangpo 2010, 395–405. The genre also includes a wide range of non-Buddhist texts, on which see T. Hopkins 1971 and Boner 1966. A fairly short listing of indigenous Tibetan commentaries on the fine arts can be found in Drakpa, *Inventory of Tibetan Treatises*, 22–23; also online at www.tbrc.org, T361. Among them, Sakya Paṇḍita's *Treatise on Artistic Form* (*bZo rig sku gzugs kyi bstan bcos*), Khedrub Gelek Pelzangpo's *Iconometry of Kālacakra* (*Dus 'khor gyi thig rtsa*), and Jamgon Mipham Gyatso's *Cornucopia of Practical Techniques Pertaining to the Arts* (*bZo gnas nyer mkho'i za ma tog*) are well known in different traditions.

275 Taktsang Lotsāwa Sherab Rinchen, *Ocean of Wealth*, 165.

276 This verse is also quoted in Taktsang Lotsāwa Sherab Rinchen, *Ocean of Wealth*, 165–166.

277 Taktsang Lotsāwa Sherab Rinchen, *Ocean of Wealth*, 166.

278 The one-day observances (*upavāsa, bsnyen gnas*) form one category of the *prātimokṣa* vows of monastic discipline (*vinaya*). There are eight specific observances, including the four primary vows not to kill, steal, lie, or commit sexual misconduct, and the

supporting vows to renounce intoxicants, luxurious or high seats, indulgence in song, dance, and ornaments, and eating during the afternoon. On the categories of the outer mantra vehicles of Action Tantra, Conduct Tantra, and Yoga Tantra, in which the deities are not depicted in sexual embrace (*chags bral*), see, e.g., Dudjom Rinpoche 1991, 1:268–273. Jamgon Kongtrul's particular presentation of the one-day observances is contained in Kalu Rinpoche Translation Group 1998, 92–93; and his explanation of the commitments observed according to the outer tantras can be found in the same work, pp. 230–242.

279 For an account of the significance of empowerment ceremonies (*abhiṣeka*), through which the meditator is introduced to the practices of the inner vehicles of the way of secret mantra, see Dorje 1987, 783–811 and 865–881; and on the various classifications of the associated commitments (*saṃvara*) and sacraments (*dam rdzas*), see Dorje 1991, 71–95. Useful works on the making of offering tormas (*mchod gtor*) include Rigdzin Jigme Lingpa's *Illustrations of Torma Offerings According to the Innermost Spirituality of Longchenpa* (*Klong chen snying thig gi gtor ma'i dpe'u ris*), text and illustrations; also Nebesky-Wojkowitz 1956, 347–454; and Beyer 1973, 217–222 and 340–346. Jamgon Kongtrul's presentation of the commitments of inner tantra can be found in Kalu Rinpoche Translation Group 1998, 256ff.; while his analysis of the inner mantra vehicles, comprising Mahāyoga, Anuyoga, and Atiyoga as well as Father Tantra, Mother Tantra, and Non-dual Tantra, is contained in Guarisco and McLeod 2005, 141ff.

280 Vairocana is the peaceful meditational deity indicative of buddha body, while Vighnāntaka is an aspect of Mahābala and gatekeeper of the assembled peaceful deities, who eliminates obstacles. For descriptions of Vairocana, see Jigme Chokyi Dorje, *Great Anthology of Buddhist Icons* (*Bod brgyud nang bstan lha tshogs chen mo*), 217; Willson and Brauen 2000, 104d; Vessantara 1993, 117–126; Dorje 1987, 649; and Dorje 2005, 97. A description of Vighnāntaka can be found in Jigme Chokyi Dorje, op. cit., 803–804, and Willson and Brauen 2000, 214 and 448.

281 Each tantra text has its distinctive maṇḍala ritual, as, for example, in Dorje 1987, 746–845. Anthologies of maṇḍala rituals according to the later tantras are found in compilations such as Abhayākaragupta's *Indestructible Garland* (*Vajrāvalī*, T 3140), Chim Namka Drak's *Hundred Sādhanas of Narthang* (*sNar thang rgya rtsa*), Tāranātha's *Hundred Sādhanas of Precious Origin* (*Rin 'byung rgya rtsa*), and Jamyang Loter Wangpo's *Compendium of All the Tantras* (*rGyud sde kun btus*). On the first three of these, see Willson and Brauen 2000, and on the last, see Chandra, Tachikawa, and Watanabe 2006.

282 The empowerment of the rosary is said to confer the advantages of the branches of enlightenment, along with an ability to retain mantra and meditative stability. See Dorje 1987, 795. For descriptions of the meditational deity Amitābha, who represents buddha speech, see Jigme Chokyi Dorje, *Great Anthology*, 216; Willson and Brauen 2000, 246; Vessantara 1993, 93–103; Dorje 1987, 649; and Dorje 2005, 97.

283 Taktsang Lotsāwa Sherab Rinchen, *Ocean of Wealth*, p. 165.

284 Taktsang Lotsāwa Sherab Rinchen, *Ocean of Wealth*, p. 165.

285 This verse could also be interpreted to mean "they should joyfully meditate in accordance with the [two] stages (*rim gyis dga' spro sgom pa'o*)." For a brief summary on the distinctions between the two stages of generation and perfection in meditation, see, e.g., Dudjom Rinpoche 1991, 1:279–281; also Guarisco and McLeod 2008, 59–135.

286 When deities are visualized in meditation, the form of the deity that is visually generated by the meditator is known as the "being of commitment" (*samayasattva, dam tshig sems dpa'*). This is differentiated from the "being of pristine cognition" (*jñānasattva, ye shes sems dpa'*) or the actual meditational deity, who is invited to enter the visualized form. See, e.g., Dorje 1987, 797–801.

287 This shows that nineteenth-century Tibet was not immune to the controversies that even now sometimes surround the buying and selling of sacred objects.
288 Cf. Snellgrove 1959, 1:114–115 and 2:86–87.
289 These assistants are interpreted to be the female consort of the artist, functioning as a medium. See Snellgrove 1959.
290 An account of the elaborate rituals entailed in preparing the canvas (*paṭa*) in accordance with this text can be found in Kapstein 2001, 257–280. See also Macdonald 1962, which includes a useful bibliography documenting earlier studies of this tantra text. The advantages and disadvantages of sacred painting and sculpture are also discussed in Gyurme Rabgye, *Wondrous Garland of Tales Concerning Tibetan Painting Traditions* (*Bod kyi srol rgyun ri mo'i skor brjod pa'i ngo mtshar gtam phreng*), 140–145.
291 Several references to canonical sūtras, tantras, and śāstras are made in the passages that follow. Recent Tibetan-language studies on iconometry include Konchok Tendzin, *The Fine Arts: A Drop of Water on a Hair-tip* (*bZo gnas skra rtse'i chu thigs*), 231–261; Yeshe Sherab's *Iconometric Drawings and Illustrations Based on the Fine Arts, entitled A Drop of Minium* (*Rig pa bzo yi 'byung ba thig ris dpe dang bcas pa li khri'i thigs pa*), 28–115; Gyurme Rabgye's *Wondrous Garland of Tales*; and Yonten Tsering's *The Supreme Arts: Seeing All Perspectives* (*bZo mchog lha mo kun mthong*). Secondary-language sources consulted here include Jackson and Jackson 1984; Peterson 1980; Jackson 1996; Brauen 1997; Skorupski 2002; Jackson 2009; and Beer 2003.
292 These verses are found in the Sanskrit edition, ch. 5, vv. 171–173. See B. Banerjee 1985, 242–243.
293 The iconometric proportions of the standing buddha image are illustrated in fig. 4. Detailed listings of the symbolic "word-numerals" utilized in the *Kālacakra Tantra* can be found in B. Banerjee 1985, appendix 1, and in Kilty 2004, 605–609. Here, "sun" (Skt. *sūrya* and *arka*, Tib. *nyi ma*) suggests the number 12 because there are twelve *āditya*—charioteers of the sun in Purāṇic mythology.
294 In fig. 4 the measurement of 25 relative finger-widths from the crown protuberance to the throat is presented slightly differently, in the divisions 4, 4.5, 12.5, and 4, but overall the result is the same.
295 The text reads *ma-nu*, i.e., 14 (which is so named because there are fourteen subdivisions of the four classes of traditional Indian society). However, this number refers not to the height but to the length of the soles of the feet. See Yeshe Sherab, *Iconometric Drawings*, 31 and 42, where this point is clarified. The height of the feet is not specifically mentioned in the tantra but is included in the drawings based upon it.
296 Similarly, the knees and their measurement are omitted in the text, but see fig. 4 and Yeshe Sherab, *Iconometric Drawings*, 30–31, as well as references to the relevant iconometric diagrams in the following notes.
297 This makes the total number of vertical relative finger-widths 125. Sanskrit *tattva* (*de nyid*), meaning "reality" suggests the number 25 because according to the Sāṃkhya philosophy, reality comprises twenty-five categories (*tattva*). Veda (*rigs byed*) suggests the number 4 because there are four Vedas.
298 The measurements of the elbows and wrists are not specified in the tantra text, but they are included in all the diagrams based upon it. The horizontal measurement of each side of the body is therefore 62.5, making a total of 125 relative finger-widths. Among the coded word-numerals given here, *ākāśa* (*mkha'*), or "sky," implies zero, and *akṣa* (*mig*), or "eye," suggests the number two—hence twenty, which is abbreviated as *khākṣi*. *Rāja* (*rgyal po*), meaning "king," suggests the number 16 because there were sixteen petty kings of ancient India including Magadha, in the lifetime of the Buddha. For the relevant charts and diagrams, see also Yeshe Sherab, *Iconometric Drawings*, 31; Peterson 1980, 245–246; also Jackson and Jackson 1984, 51.

299 Whether measured horizontally or vertically, and including the knees, elbows, and wrists which are implied but not explicitly indicated in the text.

300 Tib. *phyed dang bcas pa'i bzhi*. *SK*, 251, reads *phyed dang bcas pa'i gzhi*. See Yeshe Sherab, *Iconometric Drawings*, 30, for the correct reading.

301 The Sanskrit *jalanidhi* (*chu gter*), meaning "ocean," suggests the number 4 because four oceans were traditionally enumerated.

302 See fig. 5. This combined measurement of twenty-five relative "finger-widths" accords with the list given in Jackson and Jackson 1984, 51.

303 On the maṇḍala rites of the *Wheel of Time*, see Dalai Lama and Hopkins 1985, and Bryant 1992, 133ff.

304 Peterson 1980, 242, points out that Pema Karpo interprets this category of icons (*lha'i gzugs*) to refer specifically to the buddha image.

305 On the drawing of axial lines, see below, note 340.

306 This verse from ch. 30 of the *Exegetical Tantra of the Emergence of Cakrasaṃvara* (*Śrīmahāsaṃvarodayatantrarāja*) is quoted more extensively by Tāranātha at the start of his *Origin of Happiness: A Description of Iconometric Proportions* ([*rGyal ba'i*] *sku gzugs kyi cha tshad bde skyid 'byung gnas*), ff. 1b2–2b1. Fig. 6, representing this system, is based on Sangye Gyatso's *Removal of the Tarnish* [*of Deluded Appearances*] (*Vaiḍūrya dkar po las dris lan 'khrul snang gYa' sel*), as found in Yeshe Sherab, *Iconometric Drawings*, 56–57. See also the illustrations in Yonten Tsering, *The Supreme Arts*, 12–13 and 16–17. The main distinction here is that the sub-measurements of twelve and a half found in the Kālacakra system are replaced by measurements of twelve finger-widths. Peterson 1980, 246, shows how, in the Cakrasaṃvara system, the vertical measurements of the seated buddha figure comprise three units of four relative finger-widths (protuberance, hairline, nose, and chin), along with three units of twelve relative finger-widths, representing the heart, navel, and genitalia, and another two units of four, representing the hips and the edge of the plinth. The horizontal measurements are similar to those of the Kālacakra system except that the distance from the center of the chest to the armpit is twelve rather than twelve and a half finger-widths. Various large measures can then be established on the basis of that grid of 120 finger-widths. According to Jackson and Jackson 1984, 52, these large palm-length measures are each based on the standard of twelve finger-widths. Among them, the measurements of ten and nine large units are reserved respectively for peaceful bodhisattvas and peaceful female deities—their Class II and Class III figures—the former measuring 120 finger-widths and the latter 108 finger-widths. The division of twelve large measurements is reserved for semi-wrathful meditational deities, such as Hevajra, Cakrasaṃvara, and Kālacakra. See Peterson 1980, 240. On Kuladatta's interpretation of the twelve and ten palm-length measures, see also Skorupski 2002, 137–139.

307 The face-length and palm-length measures are identical. See below, p. 194; also Jackson and Jackson 1984, 50, on the general classifications of these anthropometric measurements.

308 The suggestion here is that this text refers only to the primary grid and not to the derivatives that were actually in use at that time in North India and Nepal. Tāranātha offers further technical details regarding these disparities in his *Origin of Happiness*, ff. 5b4–6b2.

309 See Jackson and Jackson 1984, 52, Class IV, where this measurement, amounting to 96 finger-widths, is reserved for the larger wrathful deities.

310 However, according to Peterson 1980, 242ff., this text is closer to the *Emergence of Cakrasaṃvara* in positing an iconometric measurement of 120 finger-widths, albeit with some differences outlined in the chart on p. 246 of that work.

311 Three maṇḍalas from this work, which is attributed to Jagaddarpaṇa ('Gro ba'i me long), are included by Abhayākaragupta in his *Indestructible Garland*. See Willson and Brauen 2000, 397.

312 Tāranātha, *Origin of Happiness*, f. 8a1.

313 Tib. *mtho* is precisely defined as the "span of the thumb to the extended middle finger."

314 Regarding this use of anthropometric terminology and the smaller measurements, see Yeshe Sherab, *Iconometric Drawings*, 29, Jackson and Jackson 1984, 50; and Skorupski 2002, 66–67.

315 See figs. 4–11, which illustrate the distinctions between these measurements.

316 Respectively these three categories have 125, 120, and 108 finger-widths—the last of which is also equivalent to 9 face-measures. Jackson and Jackson 1984, 51–52, altogether outlines six categories, following the tradition of the Sakya artist Legdrub Gyatso, of which the first (125 finger-widths) is reserved for buddhas; the second (120 finger-widths), for bodhisattvas; the third (9 face measures, or 108 finger-widths), for female deities; the fourth (8 face-measures, or 96 finger-widths), for tall wrathful deities; the fifth (5 or 6 face-measures, or 72 finger-spans), for short protector deities; and the sixth (with a vertical measurement of 98 or 84 finger-widths, and a horizontal measurement of 96 finger-widths), for human figures, including pious attendants and hermit buddhas. Peterson 1980, 240, outlines the eightfold classification employed by Menla Dondrub, on which see below, pp. 207–212.

317 Yamāntaka is a wrathful bull-headed meditational deity (*yi dam*) of the Unsurpassed Tantra class and also of Mahāyoga, who also functions as a gatekeeper in the assembly of peaceful deities; Vajrapāṇi, symbolizing spiritual power, is one of the three principal bodhisattvas, alongside Mañjughoṣa and Avalokiteśvara. Both have many diverse forms and aspects. For descriptions of Yamāntaka, see Jigme Chokyi Dorje, *Great Anthology*, 342, 344–353, and 795; Willson and Brauen 2000, 74–75, 272, and 460; Vessantara 1993, 268–271; Dorje 1987, 653; and Dorje 2005, 101. For descriptions of diverse aspects of Vajrapāṇi, see Jigme Chokyi Dorje, op. cit., 545–577 and 803–804; Willson and Brauen 2000, 153–162; Vessantara 1993, 159–169; Dorje 1987, 651; and Dorje 2005, 99.

318 This no doubt reflects the importance of the *mgon khang* in Tibetan temples, on which see Dorje 2002, 161–177.

319 Cf. Skorupski 2002, 138–139. Jackson and Jackson 1984, 53, and Peterson 1980, 240, both suggest that the smaller of these scales comprises 5 palm-length measures, or 60 relative finger-widths. The former states that the distinction here is between those larger forms of the protector deities that include the lower abdomen and hair and those that exclude such features. Peterson, following the Menla Dondrub tradition, points out that the distinction is made between major or supramundane protectors and minor or mundane protectors.

Mahākāla is a revered protector of the supramundane class according to all Tibetan traditions. Again there are many diverse forms, for descriptions of which see Jigme Chokyi Dorje, *Great Anthology*, 955–1015; Willson and Brauen 2000, 340–393; Vessantara 1993, 298–300; and Linrothe and Watt 2004, 44–98.

320 On the position of Ratnarakṣita, see Tāranātha, *Origin of Happiness*, f. 12b1, and Jackson and Jackson 1984, 147. The elephant-headed Gaṇapati (Tshogs bdag) is revered in the Tibetan tradition as an eliminator of obstacles. For descriptions, see Jigme Chokyi Dorje, *Great Anthology*, 1069–1070; Willson and Brauen 2000, 334–336; and Vessantara 1993, 298.

321 This text (full title: *rGyal ba'i sku gzugs kyi cha tshad bstan pa bde skyid 'byung gnas*) is contained in the Collected Works of Tāranātha, vol. Tsha, no. 19 (26 folios). See Hor rgyal, ed., *Jo nang dkar chag shel dkar phreng mdzes*, 63.

322 Tāranātha, *Origin of Happiness*, ff. 22b7–23a7.

323 This scale accords with the fourth category in 96 finger-widths, as outlined above. The distinction between the peaceful buddhas and the corresponding wrathful herukas is elaborately revealed in texts such as Dorje 1987, chs. 6–16, and Dorje 2005.

324 For descriptions of the female buddha Buddhalocanā (Sangs rgyas spyan ma), the natural purity of the earth or water element, and consort of the Buddha Akṣobhya, see Willson and Brauen 2000, 199; and Dorje 2005, 98 and 389. Tārā (sGrol ma), the compassionate savioress who protects living beings from fear and offers long life, has many diverse forms, for descriptions of which see Jigme Chokyi Dorje, *Great Anthology*, 578–628; Willson and Brauen 2000, 133–152 and 275–299; Vessantara 1993, 171–193; and Mullin and Watt 2003, 54–99. The sow-headed Vajravārāhī stands alone, or functions as the consort of either Cakrasaṃvara or Hayagrīva. Once again there are many aspects, on which see Jigme Chokyi Dorje, op. cit., 286–322; Willson and Brauen 2000, 56–63 and 257–263; Vessantara 1993, 284–285; and Mullin and Watt 2003.

325 I.e., they partake mostly of the second category in 120 finger-widths.

326 Śakra is an epithet of the Brāhmaṇical deity Indra, who functions as a mundane protector in Tibetan Buddhism.

327 Tib. *mtho dgu* is equivalent to 108 finger-widths—the third category enumerated here. Jackson and Jackson 1984, 53, makes a similar observation regarding this category.

328 Hence the sixth category, as outlined in Jackson and Jackson 1984, 53.

329 This tradition whereby hermit buddhas (*pratyekabuddha*) are drawn against a scale of 108 finger-widths (the third category) is also mentioned in Jackson and Jackson 1984, 53n21. For a summary of the distinctions between pious attendants and hermit buddhas, see, e.g., Dudjom Rinpoche 1991, 1:223–231, and for Jamgon Kongtrul's more detailed analysis, Callahan 2007, 85–158.

330 Tāranātha, *Origin of Happiness*, f. 23b3–4.

331 Cakrasaṃvara, Hevajra, and Kālacakra are the foremost wrathful meditational deities of the Unsurpassed Tantras, according to the New Translation Schools. Among them, for illustrations and descriptions of the many aspects of Cakrasaṃvara, see Jigme Chokyi Dorje, *Great Anthology*, 236–285 and 955–1015; Willson and Brauen 2000, 68–69 and 227–228; Linrothe and Watt 2004, 196–201; and Vessantara 1993, 263–268. For Hevajra, see Jigme Chokyi Dorje, op. cit., 354–368; Willson and Brauen 2000, 461–465 and 470–473; Linrothe and Watt 2004, 202–205; and Vessantara 1993, 271–273. For Kālacakra, see Jigme Chokyi Dorje, op. cit., 369–379; Willson and Brauen 2000, 72–73 and 497; and Vessantara 1993, 275–277.

332 I.e., iconometric images of the third category in 108 finger-widths.

333 I.e., iconometric images of the fourth category in 96 finger-widths. For descriptions and illustrations of the bull-headed meditational deities Black Yamāri, Red Yamāri, and Vajrabhairava, see Jigme Chokyi Dorje, *Great Anthology*, 354–368; Willson and Brauen 2000, 74–75, 272, and 508–510; Linrothe and Watt 2004, 206–209; and Vessantara 1993, 268–271. The horse-headed meditational deity Hayagrīva functions as both a meditational deity and a gatekeeper of the assembly of peaceful deities. For diverse aspects, see Jigme Chokyi Dorje, op. cit.,, 676–694; Willson and Brauen 2000, 163–172; Vessantara 1993, 306; Dorje 1987, 653; and Dorje 2005, 101 and 393.

334 The eight closest sons (*nye sras brgyad*) are the foremost male bodhisattvas: Kṣitigarbha, Maitreya, Samantabhadra, Ākāśagarbha, Avalokiteśvara, Mañjughoṣa, Nivāraṇaviśkambhin, and Vajrapāṇi. Among them, reference has already been made to Vajrapāṇi. These figures are collectively described in Jigme Chokyi Dorje, *Great Anthology*, 111–115; and in Dorje 2005, 98–99. Some of them have many diverse aspects, particularly Avalokiteśvara and Mañjughoṣa—the former is described in Jigme Chokyi Dorje,

op. cit., 444–493; Willson and Brauen 2000, 100–132; Vessantara 1993, 137–147; and Dorje 1987, 654; and the latter in Jigme Chokyi Dorje, op. cit., 508–544; Willson and Brauen 2000, 185–189 and 426–428; Vessantara 1993, 149–158; and Dorje 1987, 654. For a description of the bodhisattva Samantabhadra, whose sacred abode is Emei Shan near Chengdu, see Willson and Brauen 2000, 248; and Dorje 1987, 651.

335 Rematī, a wrathful aspect of the protectress Śrīdevī, on which see Jigme Chokyi Dorje, *Great Anthology*, 1040–1048; also Willson and Brauen 2000, 395–396 and 398–402; Vessantara 1993, 300–303; and Linrothe and Watt 2004, 168–171.

336 For descriptions of Yama, lord of death, see Jigme Chokyi Dorje, *Great Anthology*, 1016–1026; also Willson and Brauen 2000, 404–406; Vessantara 1993, 272; Linrothe and Watt 2004, 172–184; and Dorje 2005, 317–341.

337 This comment derives from Tāranātha's *Origin of Happiness*, f. 16a1–3.

338 Obsolete styles would include the Jiugangpa style of the fourteenth and fifteenth centuries and the Khyenri style, developed at Gongkar Chode by Jamyang Khyentse Wangchuk (fl. late fifteenth century). Gyurme Rabgye, *Wondrous Garland of Tales*, 44–47, suggests that Jiugangpa of Yarto was the first prominent artist to integrate the motifs of Newar and Pāla Buddhist painting with the indigenous Tibetan and Zhangzhung tradition; and that the later Tibetan styles of Khyenri, Menri, and Gardri all diverged from him. The same work identifies nine distinctive features of the Jiugangpa style, including the prominence of the central deity and stacking of peripheral figures in a series of cartouches, with background figures fading out so that they display only the torso or head, and a penchant for minium-based pigments, peaceful deities that are golden brown, and wrathful deities that are stocky and short. The other main obsolete style—the Khyenri—is described in the same work (pp. 51–53) in terms of four particular features, which include dynamic and flexible posture of the peaceful and female deities, a preference for red lac pigments, and a distinctive portrayal of wrathful physiognomy which is slightly red, with prominent features. Among the two contemporary traditions that are outlined here by Jamgon Kongtrul, the Encampment style, which integrated elements of Chinese landscape technique, was widely propagated in Kham by Namka Tashi (fl. 1560–1590) during the lifetime of the Ninth Karmapa Wangchuk Dorje (1556–1603), and as stated here, bases its iconometric classification on the Collected Works of Buton Rinchendrub (1290–1364), which contain diverse and elaborate maṇḍala rituals (e.g., vol. 14). The other is the classical Menri style, attributed to Menthangpa Menla Dondrub of Lhodrak (fl. 1450–1480), who was active at Tashilhunpo in Tsang. His teachers appear to have worked on the Gyantse Kumbum. On the origins and development of this tradition, see Jackson 1996, 103ff. Gyurme Rabgye, *Wondrous Garland of Tales*, 53–56, identifies five distinctive features of the Encampment style, and on pp. 47–51 he also lists five distinctive features of the Menri style, including decorative elements and the use of pigments that are bright, somewhat light in tone, and lustrous, with the central figure larger than the surrounding peripheral figures. For further background on artistic styles in Tibet, see Smith 2001, 251–258; Jackson 1996; and Jackson 1997, 254–261. Examples of the Menri style are ubiquitous. See, for example, Huang Ti, *Tibetan Painted Scrolls* (*Bod kyi thang kha*). Recent studies of the Encampment style include an album illustrating the highly regarded work of Tanglha Tsewang (Konchok Tendzin, *The Collection of Thanglha Tsewang* [*Thang lha tshe dbang phyogs bris gces bsgrigs bzo rig mig rgyan*]) and an in-depth analysis of the contribution of Situ Chokyi Jungne to the development of this style in Jackson 2009. It is interesting to observe that Kongtrul makes no mention of the distinctive and contemporary Repkong style.

339 The iconometric system of Buton Rinchendrub is summarized by Rongta Lobzang Damcho Gyatso (1863–1917) in his *Clear Explanation of Many Practical Iconometric*

Techniques, entitled Beautiful Face Ornament of the Fine Arts (*Thig gi lag len du ma gsal bar bshad pa bzo rig mdzes pa'i kha rgyan*), 134. Buton's interest in the subject may also be extrapolated from his monumental commentary on maṇḍala construction, entitled *Sunlight Rays Clarifying the Maṇḍala* (*dKyil 'khor gsal byed nyi ma'i 'od zer*), contained in *bKa' brgyud pa'i gsung rab*, 3:61–730. Cf. Gyurme Rabgye, *Wondrous Garland of Tales*, 56, who comments that Buton and Taktsang Lotsāwa both wrote copiously on iconometric measurement for icons and stūpas. With regard to the eight great iconometric scales of the Menri school, see below, note 356.

340 See the illustrations of the techniques used for drawing these axial lines in Jackson and Jackson 1984, 47.

341 See figs. 4–5. On the distinctions between these two aspects of the buddha body of form—the buddha body of emanation (*nirmāṇakāya*) and the buddha body of perfect resource (*saṃbhogakāya*), see, e.g., Dudjom Rinpoche 1991, 1:123–138, and for illustrations of the peaceful buddhas of the five enlightened families (*pañcakula, rigs lnga*), albeit in the Repkong style, see Dorje 2005, 269ff. Jackson and Jackson 1984, 50, outlines some details concerning the iconometric distinctions between the depictions of these two aspects, including both in Class I.

342 See figs. 8–9. It is important to note that the iconometry of the standing bodhisattva Mahākāruṇika, depicted in fig. 8, varies from the scale of 120 finger-widths on account of its complexity, as has been noted in Jackson and Jackson 1984, 52.

343 See figs. 10–11; also Peterson 1980, 240. Jackson and Jackson 1984, 51 includes them in Class I. Note that the iconometry of Cakrasaṃvara depicted in fig. 10 represents the horizontal scale of twelve palm-lengths [i.e., 125 finger-widths], while the vertical scale is different.

344 This is equivalent to Jackson and Jackson 1984, Class III. However, the iconometry of Green Tārā, illustrated in fig. 12, is based on a scale smaller than 108 finger-widths.

345 See figs. 13–14. This is equivalent to Jackson and Jackson 1984, Class IV. Note, however, that the complex iconometry of Vajrabhairava, depicted in fig. 13, varies from the scale of 96 finger-widths.

346 See fig. 15. This is equivalent to Jackson and Jackson 1984, Class V.

347 See fig. 16. Not depicted in Jackson and Jackson 1984, but attributed to Ratnarakṣita, on whom see above, p. 195.

348 See fig. 17. This class is not depicted in Jackson and Jackson 1984, but mentioned in Rongta Lobzang Damcho Gyatso's work, on which see Jackson and Jackson 1984, 147. The "black-cloaked" Bernakchen is an aspect of Mahākāla, particularly prominent in the Karma Kagyu school. See above, note 319.

349 See fig. 18. These are equivalent to Jackson and Jackson's Class VI. Traditional Buddhist cosmology holds that our world, known as the southern or "rose-apple" continent (Jambudvīpa) is particularly conducive to the practice of Buddhism. For Jamgon Kongtrul's description of it, see Kalu Rinpoche Translation Group 1995, 131–145.

350 Cf. the proportions stipulated in, for example, fig. 12. The creator divinity of Hinduism, Brahmā, is revered in Tibetan Buddhism as a mundane protector deity. See also below, p. 412, and pp. 426–436.

351 See fig. 18. Jackson and Jackson 1984, 53, offers this description within their Class VI, based on the proportions given by Jamgon Mipham Gyatso.

352 See Jackson and Jackson 1984, 51n13, which refers to Jamgon Mipham Gyatso's restatement of Drigungpa's view.

353 The full title is *Extracts from the Mirror of Great Sunlight, concerning the Geometry of the Maṇḍala* (*Nyi ma chen po'i me long las skyil 'khor gyi thig rtsa nyer mkho khol du phyung ba*).

354 This appears to conflict with the view expressed by Sangye Gyatso, *Removal of the Tar-*

nish 1:485, according to which sculpted images of the buddha should utilize a scale of 125 relative finger-widths and painted images a scale of 120. On this, see Peterson 1980, 243 and 247; also Yonten Tsering, *The Supreme Arts*, whose drawings are all based on the 120 scale. Jackson and Jackson 1984, 144–145, point out that this distinction made by Sangye Gyatso regarding the media in which buddha images are prepared is not generally accepted, even in the Menri tradition. Rather, in Menri, the 125 scale is reserved for buddha images and the 120 scale is utilized for bodhisattvas.

355 Menthangpa Menla Dondrub's influential treatise entitled *bDe bar gshegs pa'i sku gzugs kyi [cha tshad] rab tu byed pa yid bzhin nor bu* was republished in Gangtok in 1983.

356 These eight iconometric scales are summarized in Sangye Gyatso's *Removal of the Tarnish* 1:460–485, and in Peterson 1980, 240, following the same source, as well as in Jamgon Mipham Gyatso's *Radiant Sunlight of Iconometry* (*sKu gzugs kyi thig rtsa rab gsal nyi ma*). Briefly stated, the eight scales comprise (1) buddhas, including the buddha body of emanation (*nirmāṇakāya*) and the buddha body of perfect resource (*saṃbhogakāya*), scaled at 125 finger-widths, or 12 large units; (2) semi-wrathful meditational deities (*zhi ma khro*), such as Kālacakra, Hevajra, and Cakrasaṃvara, scaled at 125 finger-widths, or 12 large units; (3) peaceful male bodhisattvas, scaled at 120 finger-widths, or 10 large units; (4) female deities, scaled at 108 finger-widths, or 9 large units; (5) wrathful meditational deities and Yama acolytes, scaled at 96 finger-widths, or 8 large units; (6) human figures, scaled at 84 finger-widths, or 7 large units; (7) Mahākāla and other supramundane protectors, scaled at 72 finger-widths, or 6 large units; and (8) mundane protectors, scaled at 60 finger-widths, or 5 large units.

357 Kilty 2004, 154 and 207, indicates that the anthropometric measurements of the phenomenal world will vary according to the diverse past actions (*karma*) of sentient beings. The same source, 193–194, also refers to the different finger-width measurements within the subtle body that the vital energy of past actions and the vital energy of pristine cognition will travel. On the movement of vital energy within the central channel of the subtle body, see Kilty 2004, 177–207 and 391ff.; also *TMP*, 39–40 and 195–196.

358 These attributes of the buddha body are enumerated in Maitreya's *Ornament of Emergent Realization* (*Abhisamayālaṃkāra*, T 3786), vv. 13–17 and 21–32, translated in Dorje 1987, 405–409.

359 One of the sources for the nine dramatic airs is the *Tantra of Hevajra*, Part 2, ch. 5, v. 26.

360 In Tāranātha's *Origin of Happiness*, ff. 14a1–2.

361 Cf. the depiction of Vajrakīla in Yeshe Sherab, *Iconometric Drawings*, 89.

362 Fig. 19, derived from Yeshe Sherab, *Iconometric Drawings*, 37, illustrates the distinctive grids used for male and female facial representation. Konchok Tendzin, *The Fine Arts*, 268ff., also mentions iconic physiognomy but in no greater detail. Jackson and Jackson 1984, 139–140, discusses facial features, including the eyes.

363 This passage is as yet unidentified, although interpreted by Tāranātha, *Origin of Happiness*, 14b.2–15a1.

364 See fig. 19, derived from Jackson and Jackson 1984, 138.

365 This passage is reproduced in Konchok Tendzin, *The Fine Arts*, 272–273, and interpreted in Tāranātha, *Origin of Happiness*, ff. 16a3–17a1. For an analysis of the diverse postures, see Willson and Brauen 2000, 485–488.

366 See fig. 20. Some of these postures are illustrated in Kunzang Dorje's *Illustrations of the Essential Physical Exercises for the Control of Energy Channels and Winds according to the Vital Attainment of the Awareness-holder* (*Zab chos rig 'dzin srog sgrub las rtsa rlung 'khrul 'khor lus gnad dpe'u ris*), including the contorted turtle posture on pp. 42–43. See also Thubten Phuntsok, *Physical Exercises of the Energy Channels and Winds* (*rTsa rlung 'phrul 'khor*), 1–67, which is based on the *bDe mchog snyan brgyud kyi 'phrul 'khor rtsa ba drug la yan lag so dgu'i dpe ris*. According to Tāranātha, *Origin of Happiness*, f.

16b2–4, the "turtle" posture is a variant of the aforementioned squatting posture, in which "the buttocks do not touch the ground and the lower part of the body and the legs assume the form of a turtle" (*de nyid la 'phongs sa la ma reg tsam du smad pa ni rus sbal gyi rkang stabs so*); while the "fly" posture is another variant of the same posture in which "one knee is raised and the other supported from below, while the body tilts slightly forwards" (*rkang pa phyogs gcig pus mo 'bur ba dang / phyogs gcig rgyab tu btegs nas lus cung zad mdun du bdud ba ni / bung ba'i rkang stabs so*).

367 See fig. 21. This passage is also found in Konchok Tendzin, *The Fine Arts*, 283. The ornaments are explained in Tāranātha, *Origin of Happiness*, f. 17b.

368 These verses derive from Tāranātha, *Origin of Happiness*, f. 17b5–6, where only the first line reads slightly differently: *de la sngon gyi ri mo ba rnams na re*.

369 For a detailed account of the transmission of the oral teachings (*bka' ma*) of the Nyingma school, see Dudjom Rinpoche 1991, 1:597–739.

370 See fig. 22; also Thinley Norbu 1999, 80.

371 The Mother Tantras are generally exemplified by those tantra texts that are devoted to the meditational deity Cakrasaṃvara. For Jamgon Kongtrul's detailed exposition of all categories of Mother Tantra, see Guarisco and McLeod 2008, 153–189.

372 Cf. Konchok Tendzin, *The Fine Arts*, 283–284. The sacred thread of Brahmā, which is a revered symbol of the priestly class in Indian society, is worn only by men.

373 See fig. 23; also Konchok Tendzin, *The Fine Arts*, 284–285.

374 As indicated in Thinley Norbu 1999, 84, these respectively symbolize the subjugation of desire, delusion, and hatred.

375 Thinley Norbu 1999, 84–85. These colored snakes represent the four classes of traditional Indian society, along with the untouchable outcastes, on which see Basham 1959, 138–148.

376 Thinley Norbu 1999, 84.

377 Thinley Norbu 1999, 85.

378 See fig. 25. This verse is also quoted in Thinley Norbu 1999, 85.

379 Tib. *rdo rje glag* could be interpreted to mean "indestructible occiput" or "indestructible back," but see Thinley Norbu 1999, 85.

380 Cf. Thinley Norbu 1999, where the iron discus (*rgya bye'u lcags*) is identified as a crossed vajra (*viśvavajra*).

381 The exact source of these verses is as yet unidentified, but they are interpreted closely by Tāranātha, *Origin of Happiness*, ff. 17b6–18b7.

382 See fig. 25 (1). Open-pronged vajras of this type are associated with wrathful deities, and closed-prong vajras with peaceful deities. Cf. the description of the vajra emblem, and the accompanying illustrations, in Beer 2003, 87–92.

383 See fig. 25 (2); also Beer 2003, 102–107.

384 See fig. 25 (3–4). The club is illustrated and described in Beer 2003, 137–139, and the assortment of bows and arrows similarly depicted on pp. 115–123.

385 See fig. 25 (5–6). On the former, see Beer 2003, 128–129; and on the latter, 135.

386 See fig. 25 (7); and the illustration in Beer 2003, 90. It is an emblem associated with the peaceful deities.

387 See fig. 25 (8–9). Also, for an illustration of the former, see Beer 2003, 89, and on the latter, 137.

388 See fig. 25 (10); also Beer 2003, 107–110.

389 See fig. 25 (11–16). For a description and illustration of the sword, see Beer 2003, 123–124; for the water-knife, which is also called the wave-bladed knife (*churika*), 127–128; for the spear-flag or military standard, which should perhaps read *paṭaka* or *kuntapaṭaka*, 135; for the curved knife, 112–114; for the battle-axe, 144–145; and for the wooden pestle, 152.

390 See fig. 25 (17–19). The long spear (*kunta*, *mdung*) and the pike, or dart (*mdung thung*), are described in Beer 2003, 135. For the shield, see 124–125.

391 *SK*, 261, reads *bho ke*. See the reading (*bho kang*) and identification (*zangs dung*) given in Tāranātha, *Origin of Happiness*, f. 18b7.

392 These various sorts of drums are described in Tāranātha, *Origin of Happiness*, f. 18b1–6. Among them, the kettledrum (*rdza rnga*) is illustrated in fig. 25 (20); the "round drum" (*rnga zlum*) is illustrated in fig. 25 (21) and described as having a slight vent in its lower side for insertion of the drum-stick; the *paṭaha* drum is said to resemble a *ḍamaru*, with a slender middle, though the covers are half as wide as their height. The *ḍāka* is described as a covered drum, resembling the lid of an upturned container. On the playing of drums, see also below, pp. 294–295.

393 See fig. 25 (22). On the ritual bell, see below, pp. 292–293; also Beer 2003, 92–95; also Helffer 1985, 37–41.

394 See fig. 26 and the elegant color illustration in Zhang Yisun et al., *Great Tibetan-Chinese Dictionary* (appendix). The *Bla ma'i yon tan yongs gzung gi rgyud* is not contained in the Kangyur, but extracted quotations from it are found in Karmapa Mikyo Dorje's *Mirror of Great Sunlight* (*Nyi ma chen po'i me long*), 269–270.

395 See Konchok Tendzin, *The Fine Arts*, 295–297. As for the inner meaning of the symbolism, the various parts of the throne symbolize the attributes cultivated by bodhisattvas. These comprise (1) the ten powers (*daśabala*, *stobs bcu*; *MVT*, nos. 760–769), i.e., power over reflection, superior aspiration, application, discriminative awareness, aspirational prayer, vehicles, modes of conduct, transformations, enlightenment, and teachings; (2) the ten dominions (*daśavaśitā*, *dbang bcu*; *MVT*, 771–780) over life, deeds, necessities, devotion, aspirational prayer, miraculous abilities, birth, teaching, mind, and pristine cognition; (3) the four higher transcendental perfections (*MVT*, 920–923), namely, aspirational prayer, skillful means, power, and pristine cognition; (4) the seven branches of enlightenment (*saptabodhyaṅga*, *byang chub kyi phyogs*; *MVT*, 988–995), namely, recollection, doctrinal analysis, perseverance, delight, refinement, meditative stability, and equanimity; (5) the ultimate reality (*paramārtha*, *don dam*) or emptiness; (6) relative appearances (*saṃvṛti*, *kun rdzob*), and (7) enlightened attributes (*gu ṇa*, *yon tan*) untainted by the three obscurations concerning knowable phenomena, dissonant mental states, and propensities.

396 This mythical creature is alternatively represented as a spotted antelope (*kṛṣṇasāra*). See Nyima and Dorje 2001, 356.

397 On the cultivation of these six transcendental perfections (*satpāramitā*, *pha rol tu phyin pa drug*; *MVT*, 914–919), which are the cornerstone of the bodhisattva path, see, e.g., Padmakara Translation Group 1994, 234–261, and Padmakara Translation Group 1997 and 2007.

398 See fig. 26. The relevant passage is found in Taktsang Lotsāwa Sherab Rinchen, *Ocean of Wealth*, pp. 204ff. There are also illustrations of the ornate oval backrests in Jackson and Jackson 1984, 165.

399 For background information, see Chogay Trichen 1979. Tsami Sangye Drakpa is best known as an exponent of the *Tantra of the Wheel of Time* (*Kālcaktratantra*, T 362) and the tantras of Mahākāla. See Roerich 1976, 530, 699, and passim. One of the three questionable tantras which had been retranslated by Tsami was the *Tantra of the Wrathful Lord Mahākāla: The Origin of Secret Accomplishment* (*Śrīvajramahākālakrodhanāthara hasyasiddhibhavatantra*, T 416). Thanks to Gene Smith for this identification. On this basis the comments attributed here to Situ Chokyi Jungne may possibly be found in Tsami's writings on Mahākāla, e.g., the *Compendium of Spiritual Accomplishment based on Glorious Mahākāla, the King of Tantras* (*dPal nag po chen po'i rgyud kyi rgyal po dngos grub kun las btus pa*), which is contained in his Collected Works, vol. Ja, no. 2.

Zenkar Rinpoche notes that some of Karmapa Rangjung Dorje's observations, made in his own catalogue to the Kangyur, are believed to have been retained in colophons to the Tshalpa Kangyur.

400 Concerning the entry of the being of pristine cognition into a visualized image, see above, p. 185, and note 286.

401 In some traditional systems green was substituted with black. See Bodong Paṇchen, *Exegesis on Making Artistic Representations of Buddha Body, Speech, and Mind: A Discourse on the Gateway to Knowledge* (*mKhas pa 'jug pa'i mdo bzo rig sku gsung thugs kyi rten bzhengs tshul bshad pa*), in Collected Works, 2:255–256. Cf. Jackson and Jackson 1984, 91. The application of color and shading are discussed specifically in Jackson and Jackson 1984, 91–93 and 111–127.

402 This precise citation is unidentified. Jackson and Jackson 1984, 93n8, remarks that the same listing occurs in a school textbook published in India, but this in all probability derives from Jamgon Kongtrul himself.

403 This could perhaps also read *ja kha*, "tea brown." See Jackson and Jackson 1984, 92.

404 See Jackson and Jackson 1984, 91–93. Nordrang Orgyan, *Compendium of Buddhist Numeric Terms*, 3412–3413, simply attributes this listing to our present work.

405 See fig. 27. On shading techniques, see specifically Jackson and Jackson 1984, 111ff., and on outlining, 129ff.

406 See fig. 28. These are enumerated in Konchok Tendzin, *The Fine Arts*, 299, as follows: "The four designs of the four elements (*'byung bzhi*), namely, earth which is a repository of precious gems, wind-borne clouds, flames which are the essence of heat, and water [missing!], as well as the design of the borders (*mu khyud patra*), the designs that are interwoven (*slas pa'i patra*), such as the heart orb (*śrīvatsa*, *dpal be'u*) and the ball of thread (*gru gu*), designs that are ornate (*sprad pa'i patra*), such as the frog and the chain-mail armor, and designs of stacked letters (*yi ge gzugs gyur gyi patra*). Many of these decorative motifs and patterns are illustrated in Jackson and Jackson 1984, 166–170, while the elemental symbols are described in Dorje 2001, ch. 2, and in Beer 2003, 82.

407 See fig. 29. These distinctive flames are also depicted in Jackson and Jackson 1984, 159.

408 Source not located. This statement on the distinctions between various national styles of painting is clearly of interest to contemporary historians of Tibetan art.

409 An eighty-two-deity maṇḍala of the Yoganirutttara class, associated with Cakrasaṃvara. See illustration no. 80 in Chandra, Tachikawa, and Watanabe 2006, 83.

410 The thirty-seven aspects of enlightenment (*saptatriṃśabodhipakṣadharma*, *byang phyogs so bdun*) which are cultivated by pious attendants and bodhisattvas comprise (1–4) the four foundations of mindfulness (*catuḥsmṛtyupasthāna*, *dran pa nyer gzhag*; *MVT*, 953–956) of body, feeling, mind, and phenomena; (5–8) the four correct trainings (*catuḥsamyakprahāṇa*, *yang dag spong bzhi*; *MVT*, 958–961) which ensure that future non-virtuous actions are not developed, that past non-virtuous actions are renounced, that future virtuous actions are developed, and that past virtuous actions continue; (9–12) the four supports for miraculous ability (*catvāra ṛddhipādāḥ*, *rdzu 'phrul rkang bzhi*; *MVT*, 967–970) that combine renunciation with the meditative stabilities of aspiration, mind, perseverance, and scrutiny; (13–17) the five faculties (*pañcendriya*, *dbang po lnga*; *MVT*, 977–981) of faith, perseverance, recollection, meditative stability, and discriminative awareness; (18–22) the five powers (*pañcabala*, *stobs lnga*; *MVT*, 983–987) of faith, perseverance, recollection, meditative stability, and discriminative awareness; (23–29) the seven branches of enlightenment (*saptabodhyaṅga*, *byang chub kyi phyogs bdun*; *MVT*, 988–995), namely, recollection, doctrinal analysis, perseverance, delight, refinement, meditative stability, and equanimity; and (30–37) the eightfold

path (*aṣṭaṅgāryamārga, 'phags lam yan lag brgyad*; *MVT*, 996–1004) comprising correct view, correct thought, correct speech, correct activities, correct livelihood, correct effort, correct recollection, and correct meditative stability.

411 A forty-nine-deity maṇḍala of the Yoganiruttara class, associated with Hevajra. See illustration no. 110 in Chandra, Tachikawa, and Watanabe 2006, 112. There is also a related fifty-three-deity maṇḍala, as described in Jigme Chokyi Dorje, *Great Anthology*, 365–367.

412 According to Abhidharma sources, one cubit is equivalent to 24 finger-widths. Descriptions of the five peaceful buddhas and the five enlightened families (*pañcakula, rigs lnga*) are found in Jigme Chokyi Dorje, *Great Anthology*, 215–217; Willson and Brauen 2000, 483–488; Vessantara 1993, 55–126; Dorje 2005, 97–98 and 288–402; and Beer 2003, 234–236.

413 Illustrations of the thirty-two-deity maṇḍala of the *Tantra of the Secret Assembly* (*Guhyasamājatantra*, T 442–443) are found in Chandra, Tachikawa, and Watanabe 2006, 45–46 (nos. 42–43). See also Jigme Chokyi Dorje, *Great Anthology*, 227–229. On the significance of the base line (*rtsa thig*), see below, note 420.

414 An authoritative Indic work on maṇḍalas compiled by Abhayākaragupta, on which see Willson and Brauen 2000, 188–207 and 397–420.

415 In the context of Indo-Tibetan Buddhism, the concept of the benign universal monarch or emperor (*cakravartin*) who rules in accordance with the law of the sacred teachings of Buddhism is one that has permeated Buddhist literature since the time of Aśoka. Their appearance in the world is considered a unique and rare event. *Yojana* (*dpag tshad*) refers to an ancient Indian unit of length, generally held to be four thousand arm-spans, i.e., about eight thousand yards. See Vasubandhu's *Treasury of Phenomenology* (*Abhidharmakośa*), ch. 3, vv. 87–88.

416 The status of an arhat ("worthy one" or "foe destroyer") is the fruitional achievement of those who have attained freedom from cyclic existence by eliminating the formative predispositions and dissonant mental states that give rise to compulsive existence in a cycle of death and rebirth.

417 I am grateful to Karma Gongde, a colleague of Gene Smith at TBRC, for locating this quotation, which is found in vol. Di, f. 77b, of Dīpaṃkarabhadra's *Four Hundred and Fifty Verse Maṇḍala Rite of the Secret Assembly* (*Śrīguhyasamājamaṇḍalavidhi*, T 1865). There is an extant commentary by Tsongkhapa on this work, entitled *Memorandum concerning the Cycle of the Four Hundred and Fifty Verse Commentary* (*bZhi brgya lnga bcu pa'i skor gyi zin bris*).

418 This quotation is as yet unidentified, but an interesting presentation of the generic maṇḍala drawing outlined here can be found in Gungru Sherab Zangpo's *Dissertation and Pith Instructions on the Geometry of the Maṇḍala* (*dKyil 'khor gyi thig gi rab tu byed pa man ngag dang bcas pa*), dPal ldan sa skya pa'i gsung rab, 3:120–132.

419 *SK*, 266, reads *zhi ba* for *bzhi ba*.

420 When the celestial palace containing a maṇḍala is drawn two-dimensionally and of course without perspective, the base line (*rtsa thig*) represents the bottom of the walls and the parapet line (*mda' yab ring thig*) represents the top of the walls. The latter is drawn outside the former and is therefore the longer of the two. The base line is ideally scaled at twice the length of the inner maṇḍala (i.e., 16 large units), and the parapet line is twice the diameter of the circle surrounding the maṇḍala (i.e., 24 large units). See figs. 30–32; also Bryant 1992, 184. For a cross-section of the parts of the maṇḍala, see Rigdzin Jigme Lingpa, *Illustrations of Torma Offerings*, 293–294.

421 Cf. Śraddhākaravarman, *Concise Commentary on Forming the Gridlines of the Maṇḍala* (*Saṃkṣiptamaṇḍalasūtra*, T 2505) and its auto-commentary (T 2506). See also figs.

30–31. The positions of the base line and the parapet line are more easily understood when the palace is constructed three-dimensionally, as, for example, in Bryant 1992, 184 and 189.

422 This is stated in Buton Rinchendrub, *Sunlight Rays Clarifying the Maṇḍala: Part One: The Maṇḍala Array of the Root Tantra of the Summation of the Real* (*dKyil 'khor gsal byed nyi ma'i 'od zer zhes bya ba'i skabs dang po las rtsa rgyud de nyid bsdus pa'i dkyil 'khor gyi bkod pa*), in bKa' brgyud pa'i gsung rab, 3:64. See also figs. 30–31 and the drawing of the *Guhyagarbha* maṇḍala in Dorje 1987, 1368 (insert), where the aperture of the gate measures one eighth of the base line.

423 These maṇḍalas with variant gate-width measurements are illustrated in Chandra, Tachikawa, and Watanabe 2006: the thirteen-deity *Saṃvarodaya* maṇḍala, 75 (no. 72); the 1037-deity *Trailokyavijaya* maṇḍala, 27 (no. 23); and the 1271-deity maṇḍala array of the *Vajraśekharatantra* (T 480), 28 (no. 24). Textual descriptions of various maṇḍalas can be found in Buton, *Sunlight Rays*, 63ff. Cf. Skorupski 2002, 67, which mentions gate-width measures equivalent to one-eighth, one-ninth, and one-tenth of the palace's walls.

424 The four parts of the gate are the door (*sgo*), its exterior passageway (*sgo khyud*), the portal wings (*sgo 'gram*), and the portal side-walls (*sgo logs*). See Karmapa VIII Mikyo Dorje, *Mirror of Great Sunlight* (*Nyi ma chen po'i me long*), 98–99.

425 Different measurements of the four gateway parts are found in different maṇḍalas. In the case of the first model, where the four elements of the gate form two equal pairs (*gnyis gnyis mnyam pa*), it is said that the door and its exterior passageway are equal in their proportions, while the portal wings and side-walls are similarly equal in their proportions. See Karmapa VIII, *Mirror of Great Sunlight*, 120; also fig. 31, a drawing by Robert Beer, illustrating the Cakrasaṃvara mandala, where the gate and passageway each measure one large unit and the portal wings and portal side-walls each measure two small units, in accordance with the instructions of Karmapa Dusum Khyenpa.

426 Tib. *gnyis mnyam gnyis mi mnyam*. I have yet to find an example illustrating portal wings and side-walls of unequal measure.

427 Tib. *bzhi mnyam nyid*. The model in which all four parts of the gate are of equal measure is most commonly found, as in Guhyasamāja and Kālacakra. For detail, see Karmapa VIII, *Mirror of Great Sunlight*, 98–99.

428 The tiered pediments (*toraṇa*, *rta babs*) above the gates of the palace have several clearly defined layers or beams—generally four, eight, or eleven in number—which are stacked upon an arch, comprising a supporting pedimental beam (*rta rkang*), and a bow-shaped keystone (*mun pa pa ti*) with a bow-shaped "ox-back" extrados (*glang rgyab mig sum*). See fig. 31; also the illustrations and chart in Rigdzin Jigme Lingpa, *Illustrations of Torma Offerings*, pp. 293–294.

429 According to Konchok Tendzin, *The Fine Arts*, 206, this should read "Painted scrolls of Indian and Newar origin have diverse sorts of [measurement for the tiered pediment]" (*rgya bal bris thang ci rigs 'byung*).

430 This position seems to accord with that of Śraddhākaravarman. See Buton, *Sunlight Rays*, 67. Ratnākaraśānti's *Commentary on the Four Hundred and Fifty Verse Maṇḍala Rite of the Secret Assembly* (*Śrīguhyasamājamaṇḍalavidhiṭīkā*, T 1871) is also known as the *'Jig rten snang byed* in the sNar-thang and gSer-bris editions of the Tengyur. Thanks to E. Gene Smith for this identification.

431 On this tradition, see Gungru Sherab Zangpo, *Dissertation and Pith Instructions*, 130–131. These four pedimental beams (*snam bu bzhi* or *bang rim bzhi*), which are illustrated in fig. 31(2) and the elevation plans found in Rigdzin Jigme Lingpa, *Illustrations of Torma Offerings*, p. 281, form a simple structure when compared with the more ornate eight-banded or eleven-banded pedimental arch. This type of pediment is generally

associated with the outer tantras of Acala, Avalokiteśvara, Tārā, etc. The four bands are known respectively as the foundation layer (*rmang*), the high pavilion (*bre*), the large capping stone (*bad che*), and the small capping stone (*bad chung*). See Karmapa VIII, *Mirror of Great Sunlight*, 38. It is also said that when, as here, the tiered pediment is one gate-measure in height, it will be three gate-measures in width. See Karmapa VIII, *Mirror of Great Sunlight*, 123.

432 As indicated in Buton, *Sunlight Rays*, p. 65, the eleven decorative tiered beams of the pediment respectively depict (1) bejeweled waterspouts (*rin chen shar bu*); (2) jewels (*rin po che*), (3) horse hooves (*rta rmig*), (4) gold (*gser*), (5) water monsters (*chu srin*), (6) gold (*gser*), (7) hooves (*rmig pa*), (8) jewels (*rin po che*), (9) hooves (*rmig pa*), (10) gold (*gser*), and (11) eaves (*mda' yab kyi snam bu*). This arrangement, as illustrated in fig. 31(1), is found in the Cakrasaṃvara maṇḍala, on which see above, note 425. By contrast, the maṇḍala of Vajrasattva generally has an eight-banded pediment, as illustrated in figs. 30 and 31(3).

433 The distinctions between these different methods of measuring the eleven pedimental beams are discussed in Gungru Sherab Zangpo, *Dissertation and Pith Instructions*, 128–130, corresponding respectively to the accounts given in the *Indestructible Garland* (*Vajrāvalī*) and the *Compendium of Rituals* (*Kriyāsamuccaya*, T 3305), and in Karmapa VIII, *Mirror of Great Sunlight*, 123–124. These sources suggest that the two designs for pediments with eleven beams mentioned here, i.e., two plus nine (*gnyis mnyam dgu mnyam*), or five, plus three plus three (*lnga mnyam gsum gsum mnyam*) are general models, subject to complicated adaptations in practice. For example, Karmapa VIII, op. cit., suggests that in the former case the first or lowest beam is sixteen small units; the second, third, and fourth are eighteen; the fifth and sixth are eight; while the seventh, eighth, ninth, and tenth are seven small units; and the eleventh is only five small units. In the latter case, the same source suggests that the outer third of the third and seventh beams should be marked out, along with the inner third of the fifth beam.

434 This arrangement with three beams of equal width and one unequal is mentioned in Gungru Sherab Zangpo, *Dissertation and Pith Instructions*, 132. However, more commonly, pediments with four beams are depicted with the upper beams progressively shorter than the lower beams, as shown in fig. 31(2).

435 See their depiction surrounding the pediments in figs. 30 and 31, and the analysis offered by Buton, *Sunlight Rays*, 72.

436 The six features of the gates (*sgo drug*) may include the decorative features, two of which flank each side of the doorways, known as dark recesses (*mun pa*), columns (*ka ba*), and column decorations (*ka rgyan*). Alternatively they may include the above-mentioned four parts of the gate, with the addition of the columns and their decoration. See Rigdzin Jigme Lingpa, *Illustrations of Torma Offerings*, 281–282. On the measurement of the gates and columns, see also Skorupski 2002, 67. The seats of the deities (*devālaya*) at the heart of the maṇḍala are drawn last.

437 Rājagṛha (rGyal khab ri bo), modern Rajgir in Bihar, near which many of the Mahāyāna sūtras were reputedly delivered on the slopes of the sacred Vulture Peak (Gṛdhrakūṭa). See the spire of the Guhyagarbha maṇḍala palace, depicted in fig. 33.

438 Tib. *man ngag thig* could also refer to the temporary constructional lines of the maṇḍala. The drawing of several specific maṇḍalas is presented in Gungru Sherab Zangpo, *Dissertation and Pith Instructions*, 132–160; also Buton, *Sunlight Rays*, 63ff.

439 See fig. 32 and Bryant 1992, 177ff., on the preparation of the Kālacakra sand maṇḍala. Cf. also Skorupski 2002, 106, on the procedure for the application of colors.

440 Tib. *sgo yi nyi shu cha*. The bands of color represent the twenty aspects of the gates themselves, including the side-pillars, decorations, dark recesses, pedimental beams, and vajra prongs. See fig. 32.

441 For an illustration of the 634-deity Kālacakra maṇḍala, see Chandra, Tachikawa, and Watanabe 2006, 88 (no. 97).

442 This maṇḍala is described in Gungru Sherab Zangpo, *Dissertation and Pith Instructions*, 132–135; for an illustration of the 32-deity Guhyasamāja maṇḍala, see Chandra, Tachikawa, and Watanabe 2006, 46 (no. 45). For textual description, see Jigme Chokyi Dorje, *Great Anthology*, 227–229.

443 The 23-deity Sampuṭa maṇḍala is described in Gungru Sherab Zangpo, *Dissertation and Pith Instructions*, 141–142; also in Jigme Chokyi Dorje, *Great Anthology*, 367–368.

444 The reading of this verse in the Derge xylograph edition differs slightly. See T 806, f. 127b3.

445 These philosophical extremists (*mu stegs can*) include followers of the Brāhmaṇical traditions and Jainism, on which see below, pp. 398–415.

446 There are illustrations of seven Vajrapāṇi maṇḍalas in Chandra, Tachikawa, and Watanabe 2006, nos. 19, 29, 33–34, 36, 46, and 49. For textual description on the diverse forms and aspects of Vajrapāṇi, see above, note 317.

447 This quotation is attributed to T 369, but not yet found therein.

448 The distinction between the Ancient Translations (*rnying ma*) and the New Translations (*gsar ma*) is made owing to the hiatus following the disintegration of the Tibetan empire in the ninth century and before the subsequent restoration of Buddhism in the Tibetan heartlands by Dromton, Drokmi, and Marpa, and other progenitors of the "new" traditions. Adherents of the earlier translations, who are largely within the Nyingma tradition, have conserved both orally transmitted teachings (*bka' ma*) and revealed teachings (*gter ma*). On the distinction between Nyingma and Sarma, see Dudjom Rinpoche 1991, 1:887–895, and for the biographies of the diverse oral and revealed lineages, ibid., 597–881.

449 See fig. 33. A detailed description of this celestial palace according to the *Tantra of the Secret Nucleus* (*Guhyagarbhatantra*, T 832) is found in Dorje 1987, ch. 1, pp. 372–383, and the illustration of its round spire specifically on p. 373 (insert). On various distinctive aspects of this tantra text and its maṇḍala, see also Dudjom Rinpoche 1991, 1:914–917.

450 Lochen Dharmaśrī's *Ornament of the Enlightened Intention of the Lord of Secrets* (*gSang bdag dgongs rgyan*), *NK* 76:78–79, explains that the causal pediments symbolize the eight approaches to liberation (*rnam thar brgyad*) and the fruitional pediments symbolize the eight vehicles below Atiyoga. Figs. 30 and 31(3) illustrate the eight pedimental bands. Cf. Dorje 1987, 382–383, and the drawing on p. 1368 (insert).

451 *Sūtra of Extensive Play*, ch. 10.

452 The listing of these sixty-four ancient scripts has long been recognized as problematic in the Tibetan commentarial tradition. In the seventeenth century, Sangye Gyatso in his *Removal of the Tarnish of Deluded Appearances*, 2:5–12, tabulated four distinctly varying traditions, pointing out that Taktsang Lotsāwa had actually counted sixty-seven. Therefore he sought to compare the listings offered in the manuscript of the Gyantse Serdri Kangyur Thempangma (*rgyal rtse gser bris bka' 'gyur them spangs ma*), which had been modelled on the calligraphic style of Khyungpo Yutri, along with the Tshalpa Kangyur manuscript, and the Tibetan commentaries of Taktsang Lotsāwa and Mondro Paṇḍita. The last of the four, which Sangye Gyatso personally favors, is the tradition of his mentor Mondro Paṇḍita, outlined in the *Answers to Questions concerning Astrology and Divination* (*sKar nag rtsis kyi dri len*). This is also the listing favored by Jamgon Kongtrul, and repeated with some minor variations in the recent work of Konchok Tendzin, *The Fine Arts*. The problem is that this list omits some of the later scripts included within the Sanskrit sources and canonical Tibetan manuscripts. Therefore, comparing Jamgon Kongtul's list of the sixty-four ancient scripts with those found in the Sanskrit edition

of the *Sūtra of Extensive Play* (*Lalitavistarasūtra*), p. 88, in Negi, *Tibetan Sanskrit Dictionary*, 5759–60, and even in Konchok Tendzin, op. cit., 153–154, there are still several discrepancies. The list as presented here seeks to integrate these different readings, for which reason the following points of divergence have been particularly noted:

No. 10 is missing in the *Lalitavistara* but given as *Ya va na'i yi ge* (Bactrian Greek) in Negi *Tibetan Sanskrit Dictionary*, 5759, though unnumbered. No. 11 is given as *a-hu* in *SK* and *āhu* in Konchok Tendzin, and as *bag le ba'i yi ge* in Negi. No. 20, given as *bru sha'i yi ge* in Negi, would be equivalent to Burushaski or Dardic. Lūna is missing before no. 23 in *SK* and Konchok Tendzin, and may be a corrupt interpolation. Both *SK* and Konchok Tendzin reverse nos. 34 and 35. The Skt. edition reverses nos. 38 and 39, and inserts Vikṣepa between nos. 42 and 43, but it should be no. 47. *SK* and Konchok Tendzin both separate no. 46 as two entries into Lekha and Pratilekha while Negi gives the Tibetan as *sprin yig dang lan gyi yi ge*. No. 48 should read *rnam 'thor* (Negi) not *rnam gzhag* as in *SK* and Konchok Tendzin. No. 49, *chung min*, should read *rings med*, as in Negi. The Skt. edition and Negi add Nikṣepāvarta between nos. 52 and 53. Negi combines nos. 53 and 54, Dviruttarapadasaṃdhi and Yāvaddaśottarapadasaṃdhi, in a single entry. The Skt. edition has no. 57 as two separate entries—Vidyānulomā and Vimiśritā. Konchok Tendzin has no. 58 as two separate entries, Ṛṣi and Tapastaptā. Negi has *lha'i nges pa* instead of *gsal ba* for no. 59. No. 61, Gaganaprekṣiṇī, is omitted in *SK* and Konchok Tendzin. No. 64 is missing in *SK* and Konchok Tendzin.

Among these sixty-four scripts, many are associated with non-humans and other worlds. Those that are attested historically within the sub-Himalayan regions, around the time when the *Lalitavistara* was recorded in writing (circa third century CE), include Brāhmī, an abugida script possibly derived from Aramaic but written from left to right, that evolved from the sixth century BCE and is best known from surviving Aśokan inscriptions. Kharoṣṭhī, also known as Gandhārī, is another Aramaic-based abugida script, written from right to left, which had currency in the Kuṣānic Empire of Central Asia and along the Silk Route, from approximately the third century BCE until the third century CE. There are extant Aśokan edicts written in Kharoṣṭhī, along with Gandhāra manuscripts, on which see Majumdar 2008; Saloman, Allchin, and Barnard 1999; and Saloman and Glass 2000. Several others in the list appear to be regional derivatives, including Puṣkarasārin (in Gandhāra), Aṅga (in Campā on the Bihar-Nepal border), Vaṅga (proto-Bengali), Maṅgalya (possibly associated with Maṅgalapura in Oḍḍiyāna), Magadhā or Magadhī (in Central Bihar); Śakāri (dialect of the Indoscythian Śākas); Drāviḍa (in South India), Kirāta (among hill tribes of the northeast), Dākṣiṇya (in the Deccan), Ugra (in Malabar), Darada (or Dardic Burushaski in Gilgit), and Khāṣya (in Assam). Others are quite distinct, including Hūṇa (the language of the Huns) and Chinese. Mukherjee 2007 speculates that the shell-script may be identified with either Avamūrdha or Śāstravartā. Regarding the *Lalitavistara*, which is the primary source, see also Khosla 1991.

453 Rañjanā is the form of Guptan Brāhmī which evolved among the Newars during the eleventh century and is still utilized for the inscription of Newari and Sanskrit texts, particularly in Nepal and Tibet. On Rañjanā calligraphy, see below, pp. 248–250. An example of the hollow-bodied script (*khog seng*) can be seen in Changlung Paṇḍita Ngawang Lobzang Tenpei Gyaltsen, *Multiple Illustrations of Scripts from India, China, Russia, Kashmir, Nepal, Tibet, and Mongolia* (*rGya dkar rgya nag rgya ser ka smir bal bod hor gyi yi ge dang dpe ris rnam grangs mang ba*), f. 14a3.

454 Sangye Gyatso in his *Removal of the Tarnish of Deluded Appearances*, 2:12, enumerates these fifteen variant scripts from Rañjanā through to Vartula as the first fifteen of sixty-six distinct scripts that were to be found in Tibet at one time or another. Among them, Dharika may perhaps be identified with Śāradā, a western derivative of Guptan

Brāhmī, which evolved in Kashmir from the eighth century. An example of Tibetan-transcribed Dharika script can be found in Changlung Paṇḍita, *Multiple Illustrations of Scripts*, f. 7a3. Its recognized subcategories include the "tailless" Laṇḍā scripts which evolved from circa the eighth century, such as Old Kashmiri, Gurmukhī (the script for Punjabi), and Khojk (the script devised for Urdu), and the Takri scripts, such as Dogri, Kishtwari, Sirmauri, and Chamiyali, used by the hill tribes of present-day Jammu and Kashmir and Himachal Pradesh. Nāgarī, which is an eastern derivative of Guptan Brāhmī, evolved from around the eighth century and also has many subcategories, among which Devanāgarī, the script of modern Hindi, Marathi, and Gujarati, is best known. Other subcategories include Nandināgarī and proto-Bengali (the basis for the Bengali, Assamese, Kaithi, and Oriya scripts). See Rastogi 1980, 88–98. Examples of Tibetan-transcribed Nāgarī script are also found in Changlung Paṇḍita, *Multiple Illustrations of Scripts*, ff. 7b3–8a2. According to Professor Harry Falk (oral communication, 16 March 2010), some of the scripts depicted in this work resemble standard manuscript Nāgarī and others do not, and there is a suggestion that some of the variants may have been contrived or invented for specific purposes.

455 Vartula is said to have a mythical origin among the subterranean water spirits, in contrast to the celestial origins of Nāgarī, on which see the previous note. The heads of the letters in Vartula, which may have some affinity with the Siddham scripts, prominently curl downwards. For examples with Tibetan transcription, see Tseten Zhabdrung, *Examples of Vartula Calligraphy* (*Vartu'i ma phyi*), and Pari Sangye, *The Writing of Tibetan: Wishing All to See* (*Bod yig 'bri tshul mthong ba kun smon*), 153–157.

456 Probably subcategories of Śāradā, on which see note 454 above. Changlung Paṇḍita, *Multiple Illustrations of Scripts*, f. 7b1, includes an example of a Tibetan-transcribed Kashmiri script, placing it immediately after Dharika in the series of variants.

457 This is probably to be identified as the script of Kaliṅga, prior to the diffusion of Oriya. Cf. the example of Tibetan-transcribed Gauḍa script in Changlung Paṇḍita, *Multiple Illustrations of Scripts*, f. 9a3–4. On the poetic tradition of Gauḍa, see also below, pp. 362–363.

458 The origin of the Ghahura script is presently unidentified. An example of Tibetan-transcribed Ghahura script can be found in Changlung Paṇḍita, *Multiple Illustrations of Scripts*, f. 9b1–2.

459 Probably a subcategory of Laṇḍā, that was prevalent in Sindh. Cf. Changlung Paṇḍita, *Multiple Illustrations of Scripts*, f. 10a1.

460 The Ghaula scripts are as yet unidentified. It has been speculated that this might refer to Cola, one of the Southern Brāhmī scripts, which is related to Tamil, but this is not apparent from the Tibetan-transcribed example in Changlung Paṇḍita, *Multiple Illustrations of Scripts*, f. 8b1–2.

461 A script associated with Pāli, which is a form of middle Indo-Āryan Prākrit. See the Tibetan-transcribed example in Changlung Paṇḍita, *Multiple Illustrations of Scripts*, f. 8a3–4.

462 Probably to be identified with Kāmākhya, in the Duars between Bhutan and Assam. See the Tibetan-transcribed example of Kamata script in Changlung Paṇḍita, *Multiple Illustrations of Scripts*, f. 10a3–4. On Kāmākhya, see also Aris 1979, 174, and Dudjom Rinpoche 1991, 1:803.

463 See Chimpa and Chattopadhyaya 1970, 330, where Pukhaṅ and Marko are both said to be coastal regions, most probably equivalent to Chittagong and the neighboring Burmese coastline. Tibetan-transcribed examples of these scripts are found in Changlung Paṇḍita, *Multiple Illustrations of Scripts*—the former on f. 10b3–4 and the latter on f. 8b3–4.

464 Tib. *zangs gling*. This refers to Tamluk on the Bengal coast; the script is probably identifiable with Changlung Paṇḍita's "ocean end script" (*rgya mtsho'i yig*), illustrated on f. 12a1–2 of the same work.

465 The "script of the *rākṣasas*" may possibly refer to Sinhalese. On the association of the *rākṣasa* Rāvaṇa with Sri Laṅkā, see, e.g., Dudjom Rinpoche 1991, 1:454–456.

466 See also below, p. 272 and note 541. Sangye Gyatso, *Removal of the Tarnish of Deluded Appearances*, 12, counts these fifteen scripts from Kashmiri through to the script of the *rākṣasas* as numbers 16–30 among the stylized scripts that were once found in Tibet.

467 Figs. 34–35 show the letters of the Rañjanā script, juxtaposed with Tibetan, with calligraphic gridlines in place. Cf. Sangye Gyatso, *Removal of the Tarnish of Deluded Appearances*, 13, and the discussion and grids in Tseten Zhabdrung, *Commentary on Rañjanā Calligraphy* (*Lañja'i thig 'grel*), 1–2, which points out that, including the allocation for the tails of the letters, there are altogether seven vertical grid squares (*dpangs su cha chen bdun*).

468 This reading accords with Sangye Gyatso, *Removal of the Tarnish of Deluded Appearances*, 13, and Konchok Tendzin, *The Fine Arts*, 155: *a shad ces ring cha can dang / pha yi rgyab lag sogs min pa. SK*, 271, however, reads *ring cha dang po'i rgyab lag sogs min pa*. Tseten Zhabdrung, *Commentary on Rañjanā Calligraphy*, 2b, points out that there are several letters that have the extended backhand stroke (*mtshams gron can*) and therefore require 3.5 horizontal grid squares. Those that do not (*mtshams gron med*) include U, Ū, Ḷ, Ḹ, TSA, ṬHA, ḌA, ḌHA, TA, THA, DA, DHA, BA, BHA, RA, LA, VA, ŚA, and HA.

469 See fig. 36. Generally this is the case, but as Tseten Zhabdrung, *Commentary on Rañjanā Calligraphy*, f. 2b, points out, Ḷ and Ḹ are allocated 3.5 horizontal grid squares, while TA and NA are allocated two, and BHA and RA 2.5. For the calligraphic proportions of those other letters, such as PHA, that do have the extended backhand stroke, see op. cit., f. 4a–b.

470 Recent works on the calligraphy of Rañjanā and Vartula include Tseten Zhabdrung, *Commentary on Rañjanā Calligraphy*; Gu Wenyi and Shi Xueli, *Compilation of the Various Types of Calligraphy of Scholars in the Land of Snow, entitled Precious Garland* (*Gangs can mkhas pa'i phyag bris sna tshogs phyogs bsdus rin chen phreng ba*), 140ff.; Pari Sangye, *The Writing of Tibetan*, 147–157; Paldu, *Exegesis on Tibetan Writing and Calligraphy, entitled Lion's Roar* (*Bod kyi yi ge'i rnam bshad seng ge'i nga ro*), 105–111; and Konchok Tendzin, *The Fine Arts*, 154–156.

471 Sangye Gyatso, *Removal of the Tarnish of Deluded Appearances*, 2:17–33, in fact lists all the variant Tibetan scripts and others that are extant in Tibet in his aforementioned list of sixty-six, starting with no. 31 (the headed block-letter script, *gzab chen*) and concluding with no. 66 (numeric script, *angi'i yi ge*). Pari Sangye, *The Writing of Tibetan*, 6, includes a useful chart which indicates the relationships between these scripts. Thus, he points out that (1) the block letter scripts (*gzab ma*) include both the headed block-letter script (*gzab chen/ dbu can/ yig dkar*) and the headless block-letter script (*gzab chung/ dbu med*). (2) The italic scripts (*'bru ma*) include both the headless thick-stroked italic script (*'bru chen*) and its thin-stroked variation (*'bru chung*). The former gave rise to the formal handwriting script (*bshur ma*) which includes the rounded script (*zlum bris*), the book script (*dpe bris*), and common writing (*dkyus ma*), while the latter gave rise to the short handwriting script (*bshur thung*) and the punctuated italic script (*'bru tsha*). (3) The cursive script (*gshar ma*) gave rise to the intermediate script (*bar bris*) and the common script (*dkyus yig*), which in turn includes the speed writing script (*rgyugs bris*) and the shorthand script (*'khyugs bris*)—both being classed as letter-writing scripts (*'phrin yig*). All of these scripts except the headed block-letter script may also be known as "dark scripts" (*yig nag*). On Tibetan writing systems in general, see the recent work by

Pari Sangye, *Elucidation of the Four Grammatical Formations* (*brDa sprod sbyor ba rnam bzhi rab gsal*) (Beijing: Mi rigs dpe skrun khang, 2008).

472 Dungkar Lobzang Trinle, "Initial Thoughts Concerning the Development of the Tibetan Writing Systems (Bod kyi skad yig 'phel rgyas gtong phyogs skor gyi thog ma'i bsam tshul)," in Khagang Tashi Tsering, ed., *Studies on Ancient Tibetan Writing and Orthography* (*Bod kyi yig rnying zhib 'jug*) (Beijing: Mi rigs dpe skrun khang, 2003), 621, points out that this refers to an inscription carved in rock by Tonmi Sambhoṭa during the reign of King Songtsen Gampo at the Jen Khonang (*'jan khog snang*) Lhakhang to the east of Lhasa in present-day Meldro Gungkar County. The text is said to have been in the form of a poetic eulogy to the king. This style of writing was known as *sbal nang na la bgrad 'dra*. The insertions given in square brackets throughout this section are derived from this same work, and they can also be found in the other recent sources listed here.

473 *Cha ngar*, not *phyi dar*, as given in the text. See Dungkar Lobzang Trinle, "Initial Thoughts," 621.

474 Dungkar Lobzang Trinle, "Initial Thoughts," 621, and Pari Sangye, *The Writing of Tibetan*, 6, refer to this as "resembling greenish-blue barley grains spread out on a [mat of] white felt" (*nas sngon po phying dkar gyi steng du bkram pa 'dra ba*).

475 Dungkar Lobzang Trinle, "Initial Thoughts," 621, refers to him as Dre Shotram ('Bre sho khram). On the inscription of the Samye obelisk, see Sonam Kyi, *An Inventory of Tibetan Obelisk Inscriptions and Bells* (*Bod kyi rdo ring yi ge dang dril bu'i kha byang*) (Beijing: Mi rigs dpe skrun khang, 1984), 121–123, and Konchok Tseten, "The Obelisk Inscription of the Samye Edict, and Its Annotations (bSam yas bka' gtsigs rdo ring gi yi ge dang de'i mchan 'grel)," in Khagang Tashi Tsering, ed., *Studies*, 51–58; and on the edicts summarized in the inscription, which commemorated the establishment of Buddhism as the national religion of Tibet, see Richardson 1998, 89–99. The obelisk is illustrated on plate 11 of that work. For an example of this script "resembling a string of pearls," see Khagang Tashi Tsering, ed., *Studies*, 806.

476 Dungkar Lobzang Trinle, "Initial Thoughts," 621, refers to him as Drewa Yonten ('Bre ba yon tan) rather than Te Yonten (The yon tan).

477 Dungkar Lobzang Trinle, "Initial Thoughts," 621, refers to them as Dra (Gra) and Sho (Shod) rather than Go (rGod).

478 *SK* reads *sna ma*, but see Konchok Tendzin, *The Fine Arts*, 158.

479 Dungkar Lobzang Trinle, "Initial Thoughts," 621, refers to them as Dro Nyatri (sGro gnya' khri) and Shākya Dorje, adding that their style was known as "new effort" (*bad gsar*) and based on the old obelisk inscriptions.

480 Contemporary scholarship holds that both the headed and headless block-letter scripts may have been preceded in Tibet by the headless italic scripts (*'bru tsha*), on which see below, p. 258. These are said to have evolved not from Guptan Brāhmī or Siddham, but from the Marchung script and its Zhangzhung antecedent, in far western Tibet, which in turn probably evolved from Tajik (*stag gzigs spungs yig*), a subcategory of Kharoṣṭhī. See the examples of these scripts in Khagang Tashi Tsering, ed., *Studies*, 804–805; Pari Sangye, *The Writing of Tibetan*, 89–93; and Paldu, *Exegesis on Tibetan Writing*, 93 and 123–124. With regard to the language and history of Zhangzhung, see Hummel 2000; Pasar Tsultrim Tenzin 2008; and Namkhai Norbu, *Light of Kailash: Legends of Zhangzhung and Tibet* (*Zhang bod lo rgyus ti se'i 'od*) (Beijing: Krung go'i bod kyi shes rig dpe skrun khang, 1996), 97–107.

481 Dungkar Lobzang Trinle, "Initial Thoughts," 621, suggests that his style was modeled on the writing of the revered translator Kawa Peltsek. Khyungpo Yutri Bar lived during the hiatus between the early and later promulgations of the Buddhist teachings, and his model calligraphy for u-chen (*dbu can*)—the headed block-letter script—was consid-

ered as the standard to emulate from that time onwards. His calligraphy is exemplified in the Serdri Kangyur Tempangma (*gSer bris bka' 'gyur them spangs ma*) from Gyantse, and was later copied by Dalai Lama V as the model for the Drepung gilded Kangyur manuscript (*gSer bris 'dzam gling gYas bzhag*). See Dungkar Lobzang Trinle, *Great Dictionary of Dungkar* (*Dung dkar tshig mdzod chen mo*) (Beijing: Krun go'i bod rig pa dpe skrun khang, 2002), 336. Pari Sangye, *The Writing of Tibetan*, 49, adds that Khyungpo Yutri Bar's original treatise was entitled *Miraculous Lamp* (*'Phrul gyi sgron me*).

482 Paldu, *Exegesis on Tibetan Writing*, 63, comments that these two traditions arose directly among the students of the calligraphers Chakdor (Phyag rdor) and Kajung (Ka byung). The "frog tradition" (*sbal lugs*), also known as Kham calligraphy (*khams bris*), became widespread in the upper reaches of Kham and around Bachen, while the "popular tradition" (*mang lugs*) developed around Phenyul and Sakya, for which reason it was also known as the Ngor tradition (*ngor lugs*). However, he associates these traditions with the development of *dbu med* rather than *dbu can*. For illustrations of the headless block-letter script (*gzab chung* or *dbu med*), see Gu Wenyi and Shi Xueli, *Compilation of the Various Types of Calligraphy*, 92–97.

483 According to Sangye Gyatso, *Removal of the Tarnish of Deluded Appearances*, 2:17, the three verse quotations which follow here derive from the *Supplement* (*Lhan thabs*) composed by Rongpo, a successor of Khyungpo Yutri. Pari Sangye, *The Writing of Tibetan*, 53, refers to the *Precious Chest Clarifying Calligraphic Proportions* (*Yi ge'i thig ris gsal ba'i rin chen sgrom bu*) of the "great master Rongpo." Paldu, *Exegesis on Tibetan Writing*, 98, observes that these quotations are still cherished as a supplementary instruction (*man ngag zur du phyung ba*) on the importance of drawing particular strokes in calligraphy. However, Jamgon Kongtrul may well have taken this section from Sangye Gyatso, *Removal of the Tarnish of Deluded Appearances*, 17–18. Note too that Pari Sangye omits the last two lines, but in the second line reads *gcig pur gces* for *gcig pur skyes*, suggesting perhaps that this line contains two separates items. Then, on p. 50, he includes a commentarial verse, indicating that "paying attention to the leg stroke is as if paying attention to the buddhas, paying attention to the shoulder stroke is as if paying attention to the bodhisattvas," and so forth.

484 The calligraphic gridlines and stoke sequences for each of the Tibetan consonants, including CHA, are illustrated in fig. 37. See also Yeshe Sherab, *Iconometric Drawings*, 122. Note that *SK* here reads *sgros chags* for *gong chags*.

485 See below, p. 258. Sangye Gyatso, *Removal of the Tarnish of Deluded Appearances*, 17, reads *chig 'khor skyes*.

486 These are found in the letters NGA, TA, and DA. See fig. 37; also Gu Wenyi and Shi Xueli, *Compilation of the Various Types of Calligraphy*, 38 and 40; and Yeshe Sherab, *Iconometric Drawings*, 119–133.

487 These are found in the subjoined letters U, YA, RA, LA, and VA. See fig. 37; also the illustrations in Gu Wenyi and Shi Xueli, *Compilation of the Various Types of Calligraphy*, 54–55 and 58–61.

488 These are found in the letters NYA and A. See fig. 37; also Gu Wenyi and Shi Xueli, *Compilation of the Various Types of Calligraphy*, 39 and 43; and Yeshe Sherab, *Iconometric Drawings*, 119–133.

489 The text reads *pho ba*.

490 These are found in the letters NYA, TA, and HA. See fig. 37; also Gu Wenyi and Shi Xueli, *Compilation of the Various Types of Calligraphy*, 39–40 and 45.

491 The text reads *khong 'dren*.

492 These are found in the letters KA, GA, NYA, TA, DA, NA, and SHA. See fig. 37; also Gu Wenyi and Shi Xueli, *Compilation of the Various Types of Calligraphy*, 38–45.

493 Tib. *rtar zhon phyi 'brang.*

494 The former are found in the letters PA, PHA, BA, MA, LA, SHA, SA, and A, and the latter in the letter ZA. See fig. 37; also Gu Wenyi and Shi Xueli, *Compilation of the Various Types of Calligraphy*, 41 and 43. The thick-ended stroke is also called *gnyen*.

495 See fig. 37. These are the letters CHA, NA, MA, TSHA, and SHA. See also Gu Wenyi and Shi Xueli, *Compilation of the Various Types of Calligraphy*, 39.

496 Paldu, *Exegesis on Tibetan Writing*, 97–98 adds that these verses are essentially a technique for perfecting calligraphic skill, by counting the points on one's finger-tips. His listing, following Sangye Gyatso, *Removal of the Tarnish of Deluded Appearances*, p. 17, is also different: (1) a noble head stroke, (2) an elegant abdominal stroke, (3) a delicate edge stroke (*'jam dkar sna*), (4) a smartly drawn tapering lip stroke, (5) a stylish upright stroke, (6) a rounded "shield-like" curve (*zlum phubs can*), (7) a brightly drawn eye stroke, (8) a graceful downward stroke, (9) a skillful body stroke, (10) a precise ink edge stroke, (11) a flexible "waist" stroke, (12) a swift secondary stroke, (13) a robust "shoulder" stroke (*mkhrang dpung*), and (14) a closing "neck" stroke (*'dzum ske can*).

497 *SK*, 272, reads *bang mgo la 'don* for *bzang mgo la 'don*. See Paldu, *Exegesis on Tibetan Writing*, 97.

498 Paldu, *Exegesis on Tibetan Writing*, 97 reads *drang mar 'then la 'don*.

499 Comments in square brackets have been added in accordance with the explanations of Konchok Tendzin, *The Fine Arts*, 165, and Paldu, *Exegesis on Tibetan Writing*, 95–97, which derive from Sangye Gyatso, *Removal of the Tarnish of Deluded Appearances*, 17.

500 Sic! *tshag mgo*.

501 See fig. 37; also Paldu, *Exegesis on Tibetan Writing*, 97, which derives from Sangye Gyatso, *Removal of the Tarnish of Deluded Appearances*, pp. 17–18.

502 Tib. *gdan thabs brkyang pa. SK*, 273, reads *ldan thabs brkyang pa*.

503 See also Sangye Gyatso, *Removal of the Tarnish of Deluded Appearances*, 18, and Paldu, *Exegesis on Tibetan Writing*, 98.

504 I.e., radicals, prefixes, and suffixes.

505 See Fig 37. The detailed calligraphic measurements for each letter are given individually in Sangye Gyatso, *Removal of the Tarnish of Deluded Appearances*, 18–32; in Pari Sangye, *The Writing of Tibetan*, 54–63; in Yeshe Sherab, *Iconometric Drawings*, 119–133, along with illustrations; in Gu Wenyi and Shi Xueli, *Compilation of the Various Types of Calligraphy*, 38–45; and in Konchok Tendzin, *The Fine Arts*, 166–172. These works accurately describe the measurements of the strokes forming each individual letter in terms of the horizontal and vertical grid lines—the squares that are delineated are known as "black units" (*nag cha*) and those that are left blank are known as "white units" (*dkar cha*).

The strokes applicable for each of the thirty basic letters are sequentially described as follows. (1) KA: long "head" stroke (*mgo ring*); "fang" stroke (*mche ba*); "mid-arm" stroke (*dbus lag*); and "leg" stroke (*rkang pa*). (2) KHA: long "head" stroke (*mgo ring*); "arm" stroke (*lag pa*); "shoulder" stroke (*dpung pa*); "abdominal" stroke (*sbo*) [with concave *mnyen* above]; and downward "clavicle" stroke (*sog pa*) with "tapering lip" (*zag mchu*). (3) GA: long "head" stroke (*mgo ring*); basic "shoulder" stroke (*dpung rtsa*); "abdominal" stroke (*sbo*); "mid-arm" stroke (*dbus lag*); and "leg" stroke (*rkang pa*). (4) NGA: mid-length "head" stroke (*mgo 'bring*); "short shoulder" stroke (*dpung thung*); and "abdominal" stroke (*sbo*) with "tapering lip" (*zag mchu*). (5) CA: mid-length "head" stroke (*mgo 'bring*); "neck" stroke (*ske*); "suspended" lip stroke (*mchu 'phyang*); and "waist" stroke (*rked pa*). (6) CHA: mid-length "head" stroke (*mgo 'bring*); "neck" stroke (*ske*); convex "lip" stroke (*gong chags*); and closing lower curve (*'og 'dzum*). (7) JA: long "head" stroke (*mgo ring*); "shoulder" stroke (*dpung pa*); "transverse" stroke (*le gu*), or "central arm" stroke (*dkyil lag*); and "abdominal" stroke (*sbo*) with "tapering lip" (*zag mchu*). (8) NYA: mid-length "head" stroke (*mgo 'bring*); "upper shield-like" curving stroke (*stod phub*); "neck" stroke (*nya ske*); lower curving "shield-like" stroke (*smad phub*); and "mid-arm" stroke (*dbus lag*) [also called mid-length "leg" stroke (*rkang 'bring*)]. (9) TA: mid-length "head" stroke (*mgo 'bring*); short "shoulder" stroke (*dpung thung*) [also divided into *dpung chung* and *gzhung shing*]; lower curving "shield-like" stroke (*smad phub*) or "body" stroke (*khog 'dren*); and mid-length "leg" stroke (*rkang 'bring*). (10) THA: mid-length "head" stroke (*mgo 'bring*); "upper bend" stroke (*stod 'khyug*) or "shield-arm" stroke (*phub lag*); "lower bend" stroke (*smad 'khyug*) or "threshold" stroke (*rked them*); "abdominal" stroke (*sbo*) with "tapering lip"(*zag mchu*); and "upright" stroke (*yar 'phul*). (11) DA: mid-length "head" stroke (*mgo 'bring*); "neck" stroke (*ske mtshem*) or "short shoulder" stroke (*dpung thung*); "abdominal" stroke (*sbo*); and "mid-leg" stroke (*rkang 'bring*) with "tapering lip" (*zag mchu*). (12) NA: mid-length "head" stroke (*mgo 'bring*); "neck" stroke (*ske*); "waist" stroke (*rked pa*); "mid-leg" stroke (*rkang 'bring*) with "tapering lip" (*zag mchu*); and closing lower "eye" curve (*'og 'dzum*). (13) PA: short "head" stroke (*mgo thung*); "shoulder" stroke (*dpung pa*); "abdominal" stroke (*sbo*) with "tapering lip" (*zag mchu*); and "upright" stroke (*yas 'phul*) [also called *yar 'phul*]. (14) PHA: short "head" stroke (*mgo thung*); "shoulder" stroke (*dpung pa*); "abdominal" stroke (*sbo*) with "tapering lip" (*zag mchu*); "upright" stroke (*yas 'phul*) [also called *yar 'phul*]; and "acute abdominal" stroke (*sbo drang/ 'phred chod*). (15) BA: mid-length "head" stroke (*mgo 'bring*); "shoulder head" stroke (*dpung mgo*); "abdominal" stroke (*sbo*) with "tapering lip" (*zag mchu*); and "upright" stroke (*yas 'phul*) [also called *yar 'phul*]. (16) MA: short "head" stroke (*mgo thung*); "neck" stroke (*ske*); "waist" stroke (*rked pa*) with "tapering lip" (*zags mchu*); closing lower "eye" curve (*'og 'dzum/ mig zlum*); and "upright" stroke (*yas 'phul*) [also called *yar 'phul*]. (17) TSA: same as CA with addition of the superscript arm (*phod btags pa*). (18) TSHA: same as CHA with addition of the superscript arm (*phod btags pa*). (19) DZA: same as JA with addition of the superscript arm (*phod btags pa*). (20) VA: short "head" stroke (*mgo 'thung*); curving "shield-like" stroke (*phub*); "neck" stroke (*ske*); "*ba*-head" stroke (*ba mgo*); "shoulder" stroke (*dpung ba*); "abdominal" stroke (*sbo*) with "tapering lip" (*zag mchu*); "upright" stroke (*yas 'phul*) [also called *yar 'phul*]; and superscript "hand" stroke (*lag pa/ phod*). (21) ZHA: mid-length "head" stroke (*mgo 'bring*); curving "shield-arm" stroke (*phub lag*); "neck" stroke (*nyag ske*); "waist" stroke (*rked pa*) or "mid-leg" stroke (*rkang 'bring*) with "tapering lip" (*zag mchu*); and closing lower "eye" curve (*'og 'dzum*). (22) ZA: mid-length "head" stroke (*mgo 'bring*); "waist" stroke (*rked pa*) or "thick-ended" stroke (*mthar rgyas*) [also known as "linking" stroke (*mnyen*)]; "abdominal" stroke (*sbo*) with "tapering lip" (*zag mchu*) [also known as *'phred 'dren*]; and "transverse" stroke (*le gu*). (23) 'A: "head" stroke with italic point (*mgo zur gseg*); curving "upper shield-like" stroke (*stod phub*); "stomach" stroke (*pho ba*); and transverse stroke (*le gu*) with "tapering lip" (*zag mchu*). (24) YA: short "head" stroke (*mgo 'thung*); curving "egg" stroke (*sgo nga*) or "shield-like" stroke (*phub*); upright "mid-arm" stroke (*dpung lag*); "transverse" stroke (*le gu*) with "tapering lip" (*zag mchu*) or "waterfall" (*chu 'bab*); and "upright" stroke (*yas 'phul*) [also called *yar 'phul*]. (25) RA: mid-length "head" stroke (*mgo 'bring*); "neck" stroke (*ske*); "abdominal" stroke (*sbo*); and "waist" stroke (*rked pa*) with "tapering lip" (*zag mchu*). (26) LA: short "head" stroke (*mgo 'thung*); curving "shield-like" stroke (*phub*); "back" stroke (*rgyab*); "abdominal" stroke (*sbo*) or "transverse" stroke (*le gu*) with "tapering lip" stroke (*zag mchu*); and "upright" stroke (*yas 'phul*) [also called *yar 'phul*]. (27) SHA: short "head" stroke (*mgo 'thung*); thin "neck" stroke (*ske*); "transverse" stroke (*le gu*); "white eye" stroke (*mig dkar/ mig sha*); and "leg" stroke (*rkang pa*). (28) SA: short "head" stroke (*mgo 'thung*); "shoulder" stroke (*dpung pa*); "transverse" stroke (*le gu*); "mid-arm" stroke (*dbus lag*) or "main diagonal" stroke (*gzhung 'phred*) with "tapering lip" (*zag mchu*); and "upright" stroke (*yas 'phul*) [also called *yar 'phul*]. (29) HA: mid-length "head" stroke (*mgo 'bring*); "shoulder" stroke (*dpung pa*) or "arm" stroke (*lag pa*); "transverse" stroke (*le gu*); and lower curving "shield-like" stroke (*smad phub*) combined with mid-length "leg" stroke (*rkang 'bring*), also known as "lip shield" stroke (*mchu phub*). (30) A: short "head" stroke (*mgo 'thung*); "shoulder" stroke (*dpung pa*); "powerful" bend stroke (*mthu ba*); "main diagonal" stroke (*gzhung 'phred*), with "tapering lip" (*zag mchu*); and "upright" stroke (*yas 'phul*) [also called *yar 'phul*].

506 This is also mentioned in Pari Sangye, *The Writing of Tibetan*, 7. Paldu, *Exegesis on Tibetan Writing*, 62, states that the Li tradition originated with Tonmi Sambhoṭa and it implied "refined writing" (*legs bris*). It is said to have been prevalent in Khyungpo and in Ngari but no longer survives. The extant Den tradition dates from the era of King Trisong Detsen, Denma Tsemang being one of the twenty-five recognized disciples of Padmasambhava, on whom see Dudjom Rinpoche 1991, 1:535 and 756.

507 These italic scripts (*'bru tsha*) are considered by contemporary scholars to have predated the block-letter scripts. On their origin, see above, note 480. Pari Sangye, *The Writing of Tibetan*, discusses them in greater detail (pp. 6–7, and 89–96, with illustrations). See also Gu Wenyi and Shi Xueli, *Compilation of the Various Types of Calligraphy*, 67–73.

508 Some of these variant scripts are illustrated in Pari Sangye, *The Writing of Tibetan*, 69–88 (on *sug ring* and *sug thung*) and 97–108 (on the common letter-writing scripts). Also see Gu Wenyi and Shi Xueli, *Compilation of the Various Types of Calligraphy*, 74ff. (on *sug ring*), 91 (on *sug thung*), 97ff. (on *gshar ma*), and 99ff. (on *rgyug bris*). Examples of the Baho script are commonly found in surviving government edicts, inscribed on long scrolls of yellow silk.

509 The source of this long passage of verse is unclear, but Pari Sangye, *The Writing of Tibetan*, 11–17, repeats it verbatim and appears to indicate that Jamgon Kongtrul himself may have been the author, even if this is unlikely.

510 *Stellera chamaejasme* (*shog ldum dung lo ma*) is more commonly known in Tibetan as *re lcag pa*, on which see below, note 512. This particular variety with conch-shaped leaves appears not to be specifically identified in Tibetan materia medica.

511 Tib. *a ga ru*, or more precisely *shog shing ar nag* (*Daphne anrantica* Diels or *Wikstroemia canescens* Meissn.), which is used in paper making and also in Tibetan medicine. See Gawei Dorje, *Immaculate Crystal Mirror of [Materia Medica] Illustrations* (*'Khrungs dpe dri med shel gyi me long*) (Beijing: Mi rigs dpe skrun khang, 1995), 165–166, and color photograph no. 324 in that work, which was prepared at the Chamdo Mentsikhang. It is said to resemble *Stellera chamaejasme*, and is differentiated from two other types of *a ga ru*, namely, Chinese eaglewood (*Aquilaria sinensis*) and black eaglewood (*Aquilaria agallocha* Roxb.), both of which also have medicinal use. See ibid., pp. 164–165, and color illustrations nos. 322–323. Karma Chopel, *Illustrations of Nectar-like Materia Medica* (*bDud rtsi sman gyi 'khrungs dpe legs bshad nor bu'i phreng ba*) (Lhasa: Bod ljongs mi dmangs dpe skrung khang, 1993), 94, identifies this as "pale eaglewood" (*ar skya*), among the four subspecies of this plant, all of which he classifies as types of *Stellera chamaejasme* (*re lcag pa*).

512 Tib. *re'u lcag pa*. Also written as *re lcag pa*, the inner bark (*bar shun*) of the roots of common *Stellera chamaejasme* is widely used in traditional paper-making. On this and its medicinal usage also, see Gawei Dorje, *Immaculate Crystal Mirror*, 292, and the color photograph on 640. Synonyms listed here include *shog ldum pa* and *shog shing pa*. See also Karma Chopel, *Illustrations*, 214–215, and Menpa Dawa, *Drawings of Tibetan Materia Medica, entitled Clear Mirror* (*Bod kyi gso rig sman ris gsal ba'i me long*) (Dharamsala: Tibetan Medical and Astro Institute, 1993), 184–185, which also includes a clear illustration of the plant and its root on 356.

513 Tib. *dam rtsi lhod pa.*
514 Tib. *mchong. SK* reads *mchang.*
515 The entire paper-making process, elaborately described in these verses, can still be observed in practice in the Derge Parkhang and elsewhere. See also Paldu, *Exegesis on Tibetan Writing*, 169–175, and Konchok Tendzin, *The Fine Arts*, 172–176, where this description is repeated almost verbatim but in prose rather than verse.
516 See fig. 38. Paldu, *Exegesis on Tibetan Writing*, 150–159, describes this procedure for drawing the calligraphic and margin lines, with illustrations on 151 and 156.
517 The reading here follows Konchok Tendzin, *The Fine Arts*, 176: *phyi rtse 'jam la 'od dang ldan pa / rgyu sra bas sos mnan na 'dred par 'gyur ba de*, rather that *SK*, which reads *rtsi 'jam sos mnan 'dren pa.*
518 This is also stated in Paldu, *Exegesis on Tibetan Writing*, 51, and in Konchok Tendzin, *The Fine Arts*, 176.
519 Tib. *sub ces dkyus yig.* According to Paldu, *Exegesis on Tibetan Writing*, 51, and Konchok Tendzin, *The Fine Arts*, 176, *sub* (miswritten as *sib* in *SK*, 217) refers to ordinary shorthand letter writing. The Naxi (*'jang*), inhabiting the Lijiang area of present-day Yunnan Province, have settlements as far north as Markham County in Tibet and an historical affinity with the Kagyu school. See Debreczeny 2009, and Dorje 2009, 523–527; and on the distinctive pictogram writing system of the Naxi, see Zhao Jin Xiu 1995. Recent works on the religious traditions of the Naxi include Ge A Gan 2000 and Lhagpa Tsering, *Comparative Analysis of the Bon Tradition and the Religious Tradition of Exorcism among the Naxi* (*Bon lugs dang 'jang rigs gto pa'i chos lugs kyi khyad chos dpyad bsdur*) (Beijing: Mi rigs dpe skrun khang, 2003).
520 See also Konchok Tendzin, *The Fine Arts*, 176, and Paldu, *Exegesis on Tibetan Writing*, 51–52, who altogether mention twelve different kinds of pen. Metal-nib pens also include the fountain pen (*lcags smyug chu babs*), but that would be anachronistic in this context. Paldu also suggests, p. 51, that the "southern" pen and the "ravine" pen are suitable on account of the quality of their bamboo, for which reason the former may possibly derive from the southern border area of Lhomon (Bhutan) and Lhodrak, and the latter from the gorges of Tsawarong or Gyelrong in Eastern Tibet, where bamboo is abundant.
521 This procedure is also explained in detail in Paldu, *Exegesis on Tibetan Writing*, 53–58, and in Konchok Tendzin, *The Fine Arts*, 176–177.
522 Tib. *rtse dang so rno grang bag zhol.*
523 See Paldu, *Exegesis on Tibetan Writing*, 58.
524 Tib. *khal*, for which Paldu, *Exegesis on Tibetan Writing*, 59, reads *lan*. The same source, pp. 59–60, describes the whetstone and the sharpening process in greater detail. The best whetstones, we are informed, are from Zhol Yudruk in the Tro Ziltrom region of Derge.
525 Tib. *cung zad btsugs bdar.*
526 See fig. 39. Tib. *mtheb mdzub tshad sbyar 'grims bder gzhog.*
527 See Konchok Tendzin, *The Fine Arts*, 176 (*gris khams gnyis gzhog*), and Paldu, *Exegesis on Tibetan Writing*, 53 (*gris khams gnyis gzhog*).
528 Tib. *rdzing 'dra yur ba 'dra.* See fig. 39 illustrating the different parts of the bamboo pen; also Paldu, *Exegesis on Tibetan Writing*, 55.
529 Tib. *bcad kha gyen gseg rim gcod bya.* Paldu, *Exegesis on Tibetan Writing*, 54, adds that the nib-point should be sharply angled to the right for writing Rañjanā and Vartula, it should be slightly angled to the right for writing the headless Tibetan scripts, it should be slightly angled to the left for writing the block-letter Tibetan script, and it should be cut straight for writing Hor yig. See fig. 39, where different nib cuts are illustrated.

530 Tib. *sum ldan lnga 'dzom zhes pa'i don.* This verse is repeated in Konchok Tendzin, *The Fine Arts*, 176, and Paldu, *Exegesis on Tibetan Writing*, 554, but the reference is unclear. The three parts of the nib are probably the two tines (*kham gnyis*) of the actual nib (*smyug rdzing*), which are separated by the cleft, along with the vent hole (*smyug yur*), while the five attributes may possibly refer to the tines, the tip, the vent hole, the cleft, and the shoulders of the nib. Alternatively, the five attributes could refer more generally to the possession of good paper, knives, pens, black ink, and vermilion.

531 Tib. *tshig 'theng shes dang drang myur ldan. SK*, 277, reads *'then* for *'theng.*

532 Tib. *sgros dag skyen gsum 'dzom pa.*

533 Tib. *nya sbrid pa* is unidentified, but may have once been a corruption for "fish gall" (*nya 'khris*) which was an important ingredient in the making of some traditional Chinese inks. More likely, it is to be taken as an alternative spelling for *nya 'khrid pa*, meaning either the cherry tree (Zhang Yisun et al., *Great Tibetan-Chinese Dictionary*, 928) or *Sibiraea angustata* (Karma Chopel, *Illustrations*, 122). Jamgon Mipham Gyatso's *Cornucopia of Practical Techniques Pertaining to the Arts*, Collected Works, 1:76–78, describes nine different ingredients for making ink, but makes no mention of this. See Cuppers 1989.

534 Tib. *sbyin chu'i dvangs ma.* Gum arabic is generally used, or else an adhesive prepared from boiled leather.

535 The procedures for making ink are described in greater detail in Konchok Tendzin, *The Fine Arts*, 177–181.

536 Konchok Tendzin, *The Fine Arts*, 178, suggests that in this case, it will not spoil in summer (*dbyar mi rul*). See also Jackson and Jackson 1984, 84.

537 I.e., *Melandrium glandulosum* (Tib. *sug pa* or *lug sug*). This identification follows Gawei Dorje, *Immaculate Crystal Mirror*, 303–304, which also described the related plant *Silene tenuis* Willd. (*ra sug*). These are both illustrated in the same work, nos. 671–672. Karma Chopel, *Illustrations*, 280–282, identifies the two varieties of *sug pa* respectively as *Melandrium apelatum* and *Cypsophila acutifolia.* The alternative identification of *Silene* is also found in *TMP*, 229.

538 I.e., *Saussurea hieracioides* Hook (*spyi bzhur*), on which see Karma Chopel, *Illustrations*, 296–297.

539 Cf. Konchok Tendzin, *The Fine Arts*, 438–439; also Jackson and Jackson 1984, 80–82.

540 This point is elaborated in Konchok Tendzin, *The Fine Arts*, 180.

541 Konchok Tendzin, *The Fine Arts*, 181–182, digresses on this subject, mentioning among the most renowned of these indigenous Tibetan scripts, the "new script of Dorjeden" (*rdo rje gdan gyi yig gsar*), the "new script of Ganden" (*dga' ldan yig gsar*), and the "new script of Chak Lotsāwa (*chag lo'i yig gsar*). Others mentioned here include two kinds of "ḍākinī script" (*mkha' 'gro brda' yig*), namely, *zeg chen* and *zeg chung*, along with the aforementioned Tāmaralipi script (*o rgyan zangs gling gi yi ge*), and the script of the *rākṣasas* (*srin po'i yig ge*), and variants of the Nepali and Mongol scripts. His account is based on Sangye Gyatso, *Removal of the Tarnish of Deluded Appearances*, 2:33, who tallies these remaining scripts to complete his aforementioned enumeration of sixty-six. See above, note 454; also Changlung Paṇḍita, *Multiple Illustrations of Scripts*, ff. 12b3–14a, which illustrates some of these "new scripts."

542 For examples of the symbolic script of the ḍākinīs (*brda' yig*), and the scripts used in transcribing revealed teachings (*gter yig*), see Thondup 1986, 125–136.

543 From the time when the first eight stūpas were constructed to contain the relics of Śākyamuni Buddha, this type of funerary reliquary has been revered as a symbol of the indestructible buddha mind (*citta, thugs*) and the buddha body of actual reality (*dharmakāya, chos sku*) underlying the buddha body of form (*rupakāya, gzugs kyi sku*). On these distinctions, see, e.g., Dudjom Rinpoche 1991, 1:115–148. For interest-

ing accounts of the symbolism and modalities of the stūpa, drawn mainly from Indian sources, see Snodgrass 1992 and Roth 2009.

544 The description of these five types of stūpa, which follows, is also found verbatim in earlier works, notably in Taktsang Lotsāwa, *Ocean of Wealth*, pp. 175ff., and in Sangye Gyatso, *Removal of the Tarnish of Deluded Appearances*, 34ff., and it is restated in recent works such as Konchok Tendzin, *The Fine Arts*, 183–184.

545 This is a subtitle of the *Sūtra Which Gathers All Intentions* (*mDo dgongs pa 'dus pa*, T 829, Dg. *NGB* vol. 7), on which see Dudjom Rinpoche 1991, 1:911–913.

546 For Jamgon Kongtrul's account of distinctions between the three world-systems, see Kalu Rinpoche Translation Group 1995; also Dudjom Rinpoche 1991, 1:57–62, and the chart on pp. 14–15 of that work; and in the context of mundane spiritual paths, see also below, pp. 427–439.

547 See fig. 40, showing the distinct elements of a stūpa. The distinction between the outer world and living beings within it is drawn in the first two chapters of the *Tantra of the Wheel of Time*, on which see Kilty 2004, 73–207.

548 The immeasurable and limitless abode is a synonym for Akaniṣṭha, highest of the world-systems of form (*rūpadhātu*), on which see Kalu Rinpoche Translation Group 1995, also Dorje 1987, 357–372. On the cultivation of these four immeasurable aspirations, see above, note 272.

549 This source is unidentified in either the Derge Kangyur or the Nyingma Gyudbum under this title. The same quotation can be found in Gyurme Rabgye, *Wondrous Garland of Tales*, 83.

550 This quotation has not been located in Ratnarakṣita's *Commentary on the Tantra of the Emergence of Cakrasaṃvara* (*Saṃvarodayamahātantrarāja-padminī-nāma-pañjikā*, T 1420). Gyurme Rabgye, *Wondrous Garland of Tales*, 83–84, attributes it generally to the *Tantra of the Emergence of Cakrasaṃvara.*

551 For Jamgon Kongtrul's description of the four continents, see Kalu Rinpoche Translation Group 1995.

552 This is an alternative title for the *Eight Volumes of Nectar* (*bDud rtsi bam brgyad*, T 841).

553 For a more elaborate account of the taming of Rudra, embodiment of rampant ego-hood, see Dorje 1987, 1075–1095, and Dorje 2005, 138–142. For a description of the Eight Mātaraḥ (*ma mo brgyad*), see Dorje 2005, 105–106.

554 Tib. *ge'u-do-sha*. Konchok Tendzin, *The Fine Arts*, 184, reads *ge'u don na*.

555 Here the text reads only *bde skyid*, but see Konchok Tendzin, *The Fine Arts*, 184.

556 Among these eight stūpas only the Bodhnath Stūpa in Nepal appears to survive intact. For contemporary descriptions, see Dorje 2004, 711–712, and Dowman 1995, 30–35. The Śaṅkarakūṭa Stūpa was located near Bodh Gaya.

557 On the distinctions between these three vehicles, see above, note 204.

558 Cf. Gyurme Rabgye, *Wondrous Garland of Tales*, 85. On Nāgārjuna's description, see below, pp. 278–282.

559 On these four classes of tantra, see above, note 278; and for a brief description of the exemplary stūpas representing the outer and inner tantras at Gomar Gonpa in Amdo, see Dorje 2009, 729.

560 This implies that pious attendants may have an umbrella spire with rings numbering up to four, corresponding to their four fruitional results, while buddhas have thirteen, representing the ten bodhisattva and three buddha levels combined. For Jamgon Kongtrul's perspective on these fruitional realizations, see also Callahan 2007, 141–150, 156–158, and 172. These contrasting types of stūpa are conveniently illustrated in Longchen Choying Tobden Dorje's *Precious Treasury of the Sūtras and Tantras* (*mDo rgyud rin po che'i mdzod*), 5:340.

561 This quotation is not found in the most plausible source, the *Sūtra That Analyzes Past*

Actions (*Karmavibhaṅgasūtra*, T 338–339), which comments extensively on the advantages of constructing stūpas to hold buddha relics. Jamgon Kongtrul seems to have taken the citation directly from Taktsang Lotsāwa, *Ocean of Wealth*, p. 177.

562 Comments have been added in parenthesis in the following description of the eight stūpa designs, based on Taktsang Lotsāwa, *Ocean of Wealth*, 177–179; Sangye Gyatso, *Removal of the Tarnish of Deluded Appearances*, 36–37; Konchok Tendzin, *The Fine Arts*, 185–186; and Yeshe Sherab, *Iconometric Drawings*, 137–140.

563 See fig. 41 (1); also Yeshe Sherab, *Iconometric Drawings*, 142, and Yonten Tsering, *The Supreme Arts*, 208, where it is termed *pad spungs mchod rten*. On Kapilavastu, part of the ancient Kosala kingdom, which is generally identified by UNESCO with Tilaurakot, 25 km east of Lumbinī, see, e.g., Jain n.d., 52–53; Joshi 1967, 28, which is based on the descriptions of the Chinese monks Fa Xian and Xuan Zang; and Woodhatch 1997, 305. An alternative site at Piprahwa, south of Lumbinī (110 km north of Gorakhpur), has also been suggested by Indian archaeologists. On Lumbinī specifically, see Jain n.d., 29–30; Woodhatch 1997, 302–305; and Joshi 1967, 28–29. For a traditional Mahāyāna account of the birth of Śākyamuni Buddha here, see, e.g., Dudjom Rinpoche 1991, 1:416–417.

564 The text reads Rājagṛha (*rgyal po'i khab*), but see Konchok Tendzin, *The Fine Arts*, 185.

565 See fig. 41 (2); also Yeshe Sherab, *Iconometric Drawings*, 141, and Yonten Tsering, *The Supreme Arts*, 209. On Vajrāsana, modern Bodh Gaya in Bihar, see, e.g., Jain n.d., 30–36; Joshi 1967, 32–33; and Dare and Stott 2008, 750–752. For a traditional Mahāyāna account of the manifest enlightenment of Śākyamuni Buddha here, see, e.g., Dudjom Rinpoche 1991, 1:419–423.

566 See fig. 41 (3); also Yeshe Sherab, *Iconometric Drawings*, 145, and Yonten Tsering, *The Supreme Arts*, 211. On Sārnāth near Vārāṇasī, in Uttar Pradesh, see, e.g., Jain n.d., 36–42; Joshi 1967, 29–30; and Dare and Stott 2008, 182–184. For a traditional Mahāyāna account of the first promulgation of the teachings by Śākyamuni Buddha here, see, e.g., Dudjom Rinpoche 1991, 1:423.

567 See fig. 41 (4); also Yeshe Sherab, *Iconometric Drawings*, 143, and Yonten Tsering, *The Supreme Arts*, 210, where it is termed [*bkra shis*] *sgo mang mchod rten*. On Śrāvastī, 150 km from Lucknow in Uttar Pradesh, see, e.g., Jain n.d., 50–52, and Joshi 1967, 28.

568 See fig. 41 (5); also Yeshe Sherab, *Iconometric Drawings*, 144, and Yonten Tsering, *The Supreme Arts*, 212. On Vaiśālī, in Bihar, see, e.g., Joshi 1967, 30–31, and Dare and Stott 2008, 743.

569 See fig. 41 (6); also Yeshe Sherab, *Iconometric Drawings*, 146, and Yonten Tsering, *The Supreme Arts*, 213. For a traditional Mahāyāna account of the activities of Śāriputra and Maudgalyāyana, see, e.g., Dudjom Rinpoche 1991, 1:425–426.

570 See fig. 41 (7); also Yeshe Sherab, *Iconometric Drawings*, 148, and Yonten Tsering, *The Supreme Arts*, 214.

571 See fig. 41 (8); also Yeshe Sherab, *Iconometric Drawings*, 147, and Yonten Tsering, *The Supreme Arts*, 215. On Kuśinagara, in Uttar Pradesh, see, e.g., Jain, n.d., 42–44, Joshi 1967, 29, and Dare and Stott 2008, 145. For a traditional Mahāyāna account of the final nirvāṇa, see, e.g., Dudjom Rinpoche 1991, 1:425–426.

572 About six miles.

573 On the symbolism of the life-supporting pole or axis inside the stūpa, see Snodgrass 1992, 320–324.

574 Konchok Tendzin, *The Fine Arts*, 188, adds that the contributions of the later writers were not substantially different from that of Buton Rinchendrub, who personally had drawn a depiction of the Dhānyakaṭaka Stūpa on a painted scroll. He also includes Lochen Dharmaśrī in the list. Of those mentioned here, Buton Rinchendrub com-

posed the *Proportional Measurements of the Enlightenment Stūpa* (*Byang chub chen po'i mchod rten gyi cha tshad*). Taktsang Lotsāwa's *Ocean of Wealth* (*dPal 'byor rgya mtsho*) has already been mentioned. Trengkheb Palden Zangpo (*'Phreng kheb dpal ldan bzang po*), fl. sixteenth century, was the author of the *Treatise on the Fine Arts, entitled Clear Mirror of the Sūtras and Tantras* (*bZo rig pa'i bstan bcos mdo rgyud gsal ba'i me long*). See Jackson and Jackson 1984, 145.

575 Sangye Gyatso (1655–1705) was renowned for constructing the great reliquary stūpa of the Fifth Dalai Lama, which is known as the "Unique Ornament of the World" (*'dzam gling rgyan gcig*). This magnificent golden reliquary is fully documented in his *mChod rten 'dzam gling rgyan gcig gi dkar chag*. The same author also examines stūpas in his *Removal of the Tarnish of Deluded Appearances*, 2:34–47, specifying the preferred measurements of each section in great detail, and pointing out slight flaws in the designs of those earlier contributors.

576 See fig. 40, above, which identifies the distinct elements of the stūpa. The "lion throne" podium (*seng khri*), also known as the "large face" slab (*nemī*, *gdong chen*), is the fourth element from the ground, on which animal figurines can be painted. The "small capping" slab is either the first or second above that, and the "virtuous foundation" slab is two above the latter. See also Konchok Tendzin, *The Fine Arts*, fig. 69, and Yeshe Sherab, *Iconometric Drawings*, 148. The grid, depicted above in fig. 42, illustrates the proportions of the Stūpa of Supreme Enlightenment. See also Yeshe Sherab, *Iconometric Drawings*, 141.

577 *Tantra of the Wheel of Time*, ch. 5. On these measurements, see also above, p. 280–281.

578 On this text, see above, p. 207 and note 353.

579 The elements described in the following verses are illustrated in figs. 40–42.

580 Also known as *ba ga*, Skt. *jagatī*.

581 Also known as the *bum gdan*, Skt. *kaṇṭhikā*.

582 Tib. *pho 'khor mo 'khor bcu gsum*, Skt. *cakrāvalī*.

583 The following passages on symbolism are also cited in Taktsang Lotsāwa, *Ocean of Wealth*, 185–186.

584 Tib. *rgyu'i chos rnams*. The causal attributes symbolized in the lower parts of the stūpa, as illustrated in fig. 42, mirror the qualities expounded in the causal vehicles of dialectics (*rgyu mtshan nyid theg pa*), which are accumulated by bodhisattvas on the spiritual path to enlightenment. They therefore include the six recollections (*ṣaḍanusmṛti*, *rjes dran drug*), namely, recollection of the spiritual teacher, the buddha, the sacred teachings, the monastic community, ethical discipline and generosity; and the four immeasurable aspirations (*caturaprameya*, *tshad med bzhi*), namely, loving-kindness, compassion, empathetic joy, and equanimity; as well as the thirty-seven aspects of enlightenment (*saptatriṃśabodhipakṣyadharma*, *byang phyogs chos so bdun*), which comprise the four foundations of mindfulness (*dran pa nyer gzhag bzhi*), the four correct trainings (*yang dag spong bzhi*), the four supports for miraculous ability (*rdzu 'phrul rkang bzhi*), the five faculties (*dbang po lnga*), the five powers (*stobs lnga*), the seven branches of enlightenment (*byang chub yan lag bdun*), and the eightfold sublime path (*yan lag brgyad kyi 'phags lam*). These thirty-seven aspects are all enumerated above. See note 410; also Snodgrass 1992, 367–368, and Skorupski 2002, 165–168.

585 The essential attributes acquired by buddhas are symbolized in the upper parts of the stūpa. Specifically the axial pole of the stūpa symbolizes the ten aspects of knowledge (*shes pa bcu*) possessed by the buddhas, namely, (1) knowledge of the sacred teachings (which is omitted in the text); (2) the recollection of past lives (3) the knowledge of other minds; (4–7) the knowledge of the four truths, namely, suffering, its causes, its cessation, and the path leading to its cessation; (8) knowledge that the corrupt formative

predispositions of past actions have ceased to exist; and (9) knowledge that they will not resurface or (10) be regenerated in a subsequent life.

586 The remaining attributes acquired by the buddhas and symbolized in the uppermost parts of the stūpa include skillful means (*upāya, thabs*), discriminative awareness (*prajñā, shes rab*), the ten powers (*daśabala, stobs bcu*), the three essential recollections (*trayasmṛtyupasthāna, dran pa nye bar bzhag pa gsum*), compassion (*karuṇā, thugs rje*), and the buddha body of reality (*dharmakāya, chos sku*). Among them, the ten powers of the buddhas comprise the power of knowing positive and negative contingencies; the power of knowing the maturation of past actions; the power of knowing diverse volitions; the power of knowing diverse sensory bases; the power of knowing those of supreme acumen and those who are not; the power of knowing the paths that lead everywhere; the power of knowing meditative concentrations, liberation, meditative stabilities, absorptions, dissonant mental states, purification, and acquisition; the power of recollecting past abodes; the power of knowing the transference of consciousness at death and rebirth; and the power of knowing the cessation of corrupt formative predispositions. The three essential recollections of the buddhas comprise recollection that is free from attachment even towards a devotee who is listening to the sacred teachings; recollection that is free from animosity even when one lacking devotion does not heed the sacred teachings; and recollection that is without attachment or animosity, whether the teachings are being listened to or not. On the buddha body of reality, see above, note 543.

587 Tib. *'bras bu'i chos rnams.* Among these fruitional attributes symbolized in the peripheral decorative features of the stūpa, the four fearlessnesses (*caturvaiśāradya, mi 'jigs bzhi ldan*; *MVT*, 130–134) comprise fearlessness in the knowledge of all things, fearlessness in the knowledge of the cessation of corrupt formative predispositions, fearlessness to declare that phenomena obstructing the spiritual path will not transform and resurface, and fearlessness that the spiritual path of renunciation has been realized. The four commitments not to be guarded (*srung ba med pa bzhi*) refer to the understanding that there are no limits to guard because (1) the essence of the commitments is free from transgression and violation, (2) there is an attitude of apathy and evenness because the subject-object dichotomy has been transcended, (3) all diverse commitments are gathered together in the nature of mind, and (4) there is commitment to actual reality itself (*dharmatā, chos nyid*). On this, see Dorje 1991, 86. The four demonic forces (*bdud bzhi*) comprise dissonant mental states, the psycho-physical aggregates, the force of the lord of death, and the force of the egotistical "son of the gods." The blazing major and minor marks (*mtshan dpe 'bar*) of the buddha body of form have already been mentioned (see above, note 358). On the four truths (*bden bzhi*), see also above, note 585. The sixty attributes of buddha speech, endowed with the "voice of Brahmā" (*tshangs dbyangs drug cu'i gsung*) are enumerated in the *Ornament of the Sūtras of the Greater Vehicle* (*Mahāyānasūtrālaṃkāra*), on which see Jamspal 2004, 156–158. The four facets of pristine cognition (*ye shes bzhi dang ldan*), mentioned here, refer to the four peripheral aspects of pristine cognition, namely the mirror-like pristine cognition, the pristine cognition of sameness, the pristine cognition of discernment, and the pristine cognition of accomplishment. On these see also Jamspal 2004, 98–101; Dudjom Rinpoche 1991, 1:140–142; and Dorje 2005, 250.

588 As for the symbolism of this particular stūpa design, the eight approaches to liberation (*rnam thar brgyad*) comprise (1) the liberation of regarding external forms as a magical display of appearance and emptiness because inner form is unimpeded; (2) the liberation of regarding external forms without reference to inner form; (3) the liberation of regarding all things as emptiness and a pleasant release from subjective apprehension;

(4) the liberation of the activity field of infinite space; (5) the liberation of the activity field of infinite consciousness; (6) the liberation of the activity field of neither cognition nor non-cognition; (7) the liberation of the activity field of nothing-at-all; and (8) the liberation that is cessation with respect to cyclic existence and nirvāṇa. For a more detailed interpretation, see Dorje 1987, 381–382. The twelve links of dependent origination (*pratītyasamutpāda, rten 'brel*) are an important subject discussed in Part Two of the present volume, on which see below, pp. 579–585. The sixteen types of emptiness (*stong pa bcu drug*) are enumerated as internal emptiness, external emptiness, both internal and external emptiness, the emptiness of emptiness, great emptiness, emptiness of the ultimate reality, emptiness of conditioned phenomena, emptiness of unconditioned phenomena, emptiness of that which is beyond extremes, emptiness of that which has neither beginning nor end, emptiness of that which is not be to abandoned, emptiness of nature, emptiness of all things, emptiness of all individual defining characteristics, emptiness of the non-referential, and emptiness of the essential nature that is without inherent existence. For a detailed analysis, see Dewar 2008, 429–490.

589 From the standpoint of Abhidharma, the rebirth process (*bhava, srid pa*) is considered to be one of the twelve links of dependent origination (*pratītyasamutpāda, rten 'brel*), on which see below, pp. 594–604. For a detailed presentation from the Nyingma perspective, see also Dorje 2005, 273–303. Conceptual elaboration (*prapañca, spros pa*), the absence of which is characteristic of emptiness (*stong pa nyid*), is the focus of Madhyamaka philosophy. For Jamgon Kongtrul's presentation, see Callahan 2007.

590 Concerning the three poisons—attachment, aversion, and delusion—from the standpoint of Abhidharma, see below, pp. 499–504. On the eight approaches to liberation (*rnam thar brgyad*), see above, note 588.

591 See above, pp. 188–190; also Konchok Tendzin, *The Fine Arts*, 198–199.

592 Cf. the illustration of the buddha image superimposed upon a stūpa in Gyurme Rabgye, *Wondrous Garland of Tales*, 88.

593 Taktsang Lotsāwa, *Ocean of Wealth*, p. 186.

594 Belo Tsewang Kunkhyab (*'Be lo tshe dbang kun khyab*) was a student of Situ Chokyi Jungne, on whom see Smith 2001, 94; also the biography in Dro Jinpa, ed., *Catalogue of the Collected Works of Hundreds of Learned and Accomplished Masters from Upper Dokham* (*Yul mdo khams stod kyi mkhas grub brgya rtsa'i gsung 'bum dkar chag phyogs gcig tu bsgrigs pa dvangs gsal shel gyi me long*) (Ziling: Qinghai mi rigs dpe skrun khang, 2008), 382–385. His extant writings include a short *Exegesis of Cakrasaṃvara* and the *Biographical Account of the Karma Kamtsang Lineage of Spiritual Attainment, entitled Infinite Jewel Garland of Crystal.*

595 Cf. the description of Khedrub Norzang Gyatso in Kilty 2004, 79–90.

596 On this distinction see Kilty 2004, 76. The first two chapters of the *Tantra of the Wheel of Time* accordingly correspond to the external and inner levels, and the remaining three chapters to the other subtle levels of the generation and perfection stages of meditation.

597 This entire background narrative derives verbatim from Situ Chokyi Jungne's *Inventory to the Likeness of the Intangible Stūpa of Paramādya, entitled Wish-fulfilling Rain of Good Auspices* (*dPal mchog reg pa med pa'i mchod rten gyi snang brnyan dge legs 'dod dgu'i char 'bebs kyi dkar chags utpala'i phreng ba*), contained in his Collected Works, 13 (Pa):727–728. Situ traces this description to the *Pillar Testament* (*bKa' chems ka khol ma*) of Tibet's unifying emperor, Songtsen Gampo. He also notes that the Indian master Śāntagupta and his student Buddhaguptanātha had seen it, and Tāranātha of Jonang had actually drawn it based on the latter's description, before constructing a replica at Takten Phuntsoling. Cf. Chimpa and Chattopadhyaya 1970, 325, where, in the life story of Laṅkājayabhadra, it states, "In this region [close to present day Mangalore] was the

famous Mahābimba caitya, which was unapproachable but the miraculous reflection of which could be seen in the sky." This legend is reproduced without addition in Konchok Tendzin, *The Fine Arts*, 187–198.

598 The source for this quotation is Sakya Paṇḍita's *Analysis of the Three Vows* (*sDom gsum rab dbye*), in dPal ldan sa skya'i gsung rabs, 12a:81. The verse is also cited in Situ Chokyi Jungne, *Inventory*, 727.

599 These comprise the celestial, terrestrial, and subterranean abodes. The description follows Situ Chokyi Junge verbatim. Many aspects of Vajravārāhī and Vajrayoginī are described in English 2002.

600 Rigdzin Tsewang Norbu (1697–1755), a native of Puborgang and prolific scholar of Katok, traveled widely in Tibet, Nepal, Sikkim, and Bhutan. This passage derives not from his Collected Works but from Situ Chokyi Junge, *Inventory*, 728–729, although the line breaks in certain verses are significantly different. The title page of this work illustrates the stūpa and another related stūpa associated with the *Tantra of the Wheel of Time*, ascribing their authentic description to Katok Tsewang Norbu.

601 The three levels of going for refuge (*triśaraṇagamaṇa, skyabs 'gro rim gsum*) could be enumerated as the Buddha, his sacred teachings, and the monastic community, or as these three precious jewels (*triratna, dkon mchog gsum*) combined with the three buddha bodies (*trikāya, sku gsum*) and the three roots of tantric practice (*trimūla, rtsa ba gsum*). The three buddha bodies comprise those of actual reality, perfect resource, and emanation; while the three roots comprise the spiritual teacher (*guru, bla ma*), the meditational deity (*iṣṭadevatā, yi dam*), and the female intermediary (*ḍākinī, mkha' 'gro ma*). On all such aspects of refuge, see Padmakara Translation Group 1994, 171–192. The four philosophical systems (*siddhānta, grub mtha'*) are those of the Vaibhāṣika, Sautrāntika, Cittamātra, and Madhyamaka, for Jamgon Kongtrul's interpretation of which see Callahan 2007.

602 Tib. *dpal mchog thugs gsung sku'i dkyil 'khor*. On the construction of these three maṇḍalas, see Bryant 1992, 185–227.

603 The four delights (*dga' ba bzhi*) are experienced in the context of the perfection stage (*sampannakrama*) of meditation, when the practices of yoga (*sbyor ba*) are applied in order to bring about a coalescence of bliss and emptiness. The generative essences (*thig le*) of the body descend through the central channel of the subtle body and the four delights are sequentially experienced. As they descend from the energy center of the crown fontanelle to the throat center, the pristine cognition of delight (*dga' ba*) is experienced. When they descend from the throat center to the heart center, the pristine cognition of supreme delight (*mchog dga'*) is experienced. When they descend from the heart center to the navel center, the pristine cognition of the absence of delight (*dga' bral*) is experienced. And when they descend from the navel center to the secret center of the genitalia, the co-emergent delight (*lhan skyes dga' ba*) is experienced. Thereafter, the generative essences are retained within the body and drawn upwards through the central channel, permeating each of the energy centers of the body in turn with unceasing bliss and non-conceptual pristine cognition. See Dorje 1987, 899–914; and, in the context of Kālacakra, Kilty 2004, 375ff.

604 The buddha body of supreme bliss (*mahāsukhakāya, bde chen gyi sku*), refers to the fruitional attainment in which the expanse of reality and pristine cognition are not differentiated, and bliss is coalesced with emptiness in accordance with the perfection stage of meditation. On the deeds associated with the three buddha bodies in general, see Dudjom Rinpoche 1991, 1:115–148.

605 Tib. *rgyu skar dal*, on which see below, p. 346.

606 Tib. *chos dbyings gsung dbang gi dkyil 'khor*. Here the maṇḍala of the power of buddha

speech is identified with the expanse of actual reality (*dharmadhātu*, *chos kyi dbyings*), which is a synonym for emptiness.

607 This legend would refer to the "naturally created" Svayambhū Stūpa on Padmacula Hill to the northwest of Kathmandu, rather than the Jamachu Stūpa on Nāgārjuna Ban (*glang ru'i ri*), which lies to the north of the city. The full name of the stūpa, commemorating Mañjuśrī's emanation, is Svayambhū Vāgīśvara Dharmadhātu Stūpa. For a description of Svayambhū, see Dorje 2004, 708–710, and of Nāgārjuna Ban, ibid., 716; also Dowman 1995, 24–29. Konchok Tendzin, *The Fine Arts*, 198, repeats this legend verbatim. Jamgon Kongtrul's immediate source for the legend is Situ Chokyi Jungne's *Legend of the Great Stūpa of Svayambhū in Nepal* (*Bal yul rang byung mchod rten chen po'i lo rgyus*), contained in vol. 7 (Ja) of the latter's Collected Works.

608 See above, p. 276.

609 This explanation accords with the teachings of Anuyoga, where empowerments are conferred in accordance with all nine vehicles. For a discussion, see Dudjom Rinpoche 1991, 1:911–913; also Konchok Tendzin, *The Fine Arts*, 199.

610 At present I have not managed to identify Tsamorong Sonam Ozer's *Source of Enlightened Attributes: The Methods of Constructing the Three Representational Supports* (*rTen gsum bzhengs thabs yon tan 'byung gnas*), which is also listed as an important early source in Gyurme Rabgye, *Wondrous Garland of Tales*, 56. Guru Chowang's *Method of Constructing Stūpas* (*mChod rten bzhengs thabs*), derived from the cycle of his revelation *Eight Transmitted Precepts: Consummation of Secrets* (*bKa' brgyad gsang ba yongs rdzogs*) may be identified with his *Illustrations of Temple Construction, from the Consummation of the Three Buddha Bodies* (*sKu gsum yongs rdzogs kyi lha khang gzhengs thabs kyi dpe ris*), which is listed in *rNying ma'i dkar chags* (Potala, 1992), vol. 1, no. 40 and vol. 4, no. 51.

611 The hand-held emblems have already been explained above, pp. 222–225, from the standpoint of iconometry, but in this context they are explained to be representations of buddha mind, arising in association with the diverse hand-gestures (*mudrā*, *phyag rgya*), and employed in ritual contexts. See Dorje 1987, 711–745.

612 This passage derives from Taktsang Lotsāwa, *Ocean of Wealth*, 206, who then offers an elaborate explanation of the vajra and bell according to diverse levels of interpretation (206–212).

613 These prominent Sakya and Geluk authors—Gangkar Dorjedenpa (1432–1492) and Khedrubje Gelek Pelzangpo (1385–1438)—were contemporaries of Taktsang Lotsāwa Sherab Rinchen (b. 1405), the former being one of his foremost students. Unfortunately, their writings on the distinctions between the outer and inner aspects of the ritual bell are not easily identified, and it may be that such references were made by them in the context of their commentarial writings on Hevajra and Cakrasaṃvara respectively.

614 See Taktsang Lotsāwa, *Ocean of Wealth*, 207. Further information can be found in Beer 2003, 87–95, and Helffer 1985. For illustrations of the different types of vajra and bell, see above, fig. 26.

615 This reading follows Taktsang Lotsāwa: *zur dang ldan pa yin pa*, whereas *SK*, 289, offers *zur dang ldan pa min pa*, suggesting that the prongs are not fluted or angled. *Badira* is probably a corrupt reading for *khadira*—acacia.

616 Taktsang Lotsāwa treats those approaches separately—the particular explanation of the *Wheel of Time* on 207–208 and the general explanation of the *Tantra of the Emergence of Cakrasaṃvara* (*Śrīmahāsaṃvarodayatantrarāja*) and the *Tantra of Embrace* (*Sampuṭatantra*) on 208–211. There are also distinctive Nyingma descriptions of the vajra and bell and the techniques employed when playing them, on which see Tashi Gyatso's *Exegesis of the Resources, Implements, and Musical Instruments Pertaining to the Ocean of Awareness-holders of the Indestructible Vehicle according to the Ancient Transla-*

tion School, entitled Ornamental Flower of Mantrins (*sNga 'gyur rdo rje theg pa rig 'dzin rgya mtsho'i long spyod chas rgyan dang rol mo rnam bshad sngags 'chang rgyan gyi me tog*), in *Treatises on the Accoutrements and Music of the Ancient Way of Secret* [*Mantra*] (*gSang rnying rgyan chas dang rol mo'i bstan bcos*), 46–53; Jatson Nyingpo's *Exegesis on Maintenance of the Supreme Sacraments Revered in the Great Vehicle of the Way of Secret Mantra* (*gSang sngags theg pa chen po'i bsten par bya ba'i dam rdzas mchog ji ltar bcang ba'i rnam bshad rnal 'byor pa'i dga' ston*), in the same volume, 212–216; and Sangye Lingpa's *Explanation of the Vajra and Bell, in accordance with the Tantras, Transmissions, and Empowerments* (*rDo rje dril bu'i bshad pa rgyud lung dbang bzhag*), also in the same volume, 257–280.

617 Taktsang Lotsāwa, *Ocean of Wealth*, 212, suggests that further details can be found in the *Compendium of Rituals* (*Kriyāsamuccaya*). See fig. 26; also Beer 2003, 107–110; and for Nyingma descriptions, Tashi Gyatso, *Exegesis of the Resources*, 131–133; and Jatson Nyingpo, *Exegesis on Maintenance of the Supreme Sacraments*, 216–220.

618 These six comprise the vajra, bell, hand-drum, *khaṭvāṅga*, curved knife (*kartṛkā*), and skull. See Nyima and Dorje 2001, 720–721. Among them, the curved knife is illustrated above, fig. 26 (14); see also Beer 2003, 112–114. The skull-cup is described in Beer 2003, 110–112. See also fig. 43 (1).

619 Among these hand emblems, the pair of *homa* ladles, comprising the *sruc* (*dgang gzar*) and the *sruva* (*blugs gzar*), are utilized in burnt offering ceremonies, on which see Dorje 1987, 783–786. The ritual spike (*phur ba*) surmounted by the five-pronged vajra is depicted in fig. 43 (2). See also Beer 2003, 98–101; also Tashi Gyatso, *Exegesis of the Resources*, 69–72; and Jatson Nyingpo, *Exegesis on Maintenance of the Supreme Sacraments*, 229–231. The tantric staff emblazoned with the motif of the crossed vajra (*sna tshogs rdo rjes mtshan pa'i khaṭvāṅga*) is illustrated above, fig. 26 (2). See also Beer 2003, 102–107; also Jatson Nyingpo, op. cit., 221–229.

620 The various hand emblems classified under weaponry are also described and illustrated in Beer 2003, 115–160.

621 There is a brief anonymous text entitled *Method of Attaching Drum-skin Covers* (*rNga spags gYogs thabs*), contained in *gSang rnying rgyan chas dang rol mo'i bstan bcos* (Gangs chen rigs mdzod, vol. 30), p. 363.

622 Candraśrī[ratna], also known as Dawa Palrin or Candragomin, is a learned master associated with Zhalu Monastery (b. circa 1375), and not the renowned Indian master of the same name. The text cited here is his versified composition entitled *Systematic Presentation of Drums and Cymbals* (*rNga sbug gi rnam bzhag*), contained in *gSang rnying rgyan chas dang rol mo'i bstan bcos* (Gangs chen rigs mdzod, vol. 30), pp. 357–359. According to Canzio 1980, 67–72, this work is quoted by later Tibetan commentators on musical treatises, such as Jamyang Sonam Wangpo (1559–1621) and his student Kunga Sonam, who both elucidated Sakya Paṇḍita's *Rol pa'i bstan bcos*.

623 These verses are found in Candraśrī, *Systematic Presentation of Drums and Cymbals*, 357. There, however, the last line reads: *ri dvags rgyal po'i gdong mi bskum*, instead of ... *mi bskul*. See Canzio 1980, 68, where it is explained and illustrated that the great ocean refers to the overall surface of the drum, Mt. Sumeru and the four continents refer to the upper surface of the drum, the rocky boundary is the edge of the drum where the drum-skin is attached to the wooden rim, the plains are the areas of the drum surface adjacent to the rim, and the mountains are the wooden rim itself. The expression "face of the lion, king of wild beasts" (*ri dvags rgyal po'i gdong*), according to Canzio (email communication, 12 November 2009) refers to the "clockwise spiralling gem" motif at the center of the drum, also known as the *nor bu dga' dkyil* or *dga' dbang gYas 'khyil*.

624 The following verses are not found in Candraśrī, *Systematic Presentation of Drums and*

Cymbals, but were probably derived from his text and presented in this form by Jamyang Sonam Wangpo.

625 Here the root verses (Candraśrī, *Systematic Presentation of Drums and Cymbals*, 357) read: *steng nas gnam lcags 'bab pa ltar / mkhas pas rnga sgra mi bskul lo / mya ngan can gyi brang ltar du / mkhas pas rnga sgra mi bskul lo / phongs pa sgo yon slong ba ltar / mkhas pas rnga sgra mi bskul lo / bya bran gshog pa sdeb pa ltar / mkhas pas rnga sgra mi bskul lo.*

626 The ideal place to strike the drum is the lower surface, close to the rim. See the illustration in Canzio 1980, 68.

627 I.e., the beating should be staccato-like, with only one sound per beat. The root verses (Candraśrī, *Systematic Presentation of Drums and Cymbals*, 357) state that the first beat of the drum should be made [with the right hand] slowly striking the lower part of the drum surface close to the left shoulder, and downwards, in the direction of the left hip. Thereafter the beats should be increasingly stronger. The place where the drum should be struck is one knuckle-width above the drum handle. By flexing the finger-joints (*sor tshigs*) slightly, and using the drumstick's own weight, one should deliver three firm beats, followed by three relaxed beats.

628 These last verses are found in Candraśrī, *Systematic Presentation of Drums and Cymbals*, 358. However the root verses read "pearls" (*mu tig*) for gemstones. See also Canzio 1980, 67.

629 These verses are found in Candraśrī, *Systematic Presentation of Drums and Cymbals*, 357–358, interpolated with references to the moods which these styles of drumming should evoke. Thus, it states that during the rites of pacification the drumming should evoke a peaceful mood; during the rites of enrichment it should evoke an elegant and heroic mood; during the rites of subjugation it should evoke an attractive and beautiful mood; and during the rites of wrath it should evoke a harsh and wrathful mood.

630 According to the root verses, this should read *rnga thabs drag la brjid par brdung*.

631 For an alternative translation of this passage, see Canzio 1980, 69. On the four rites (*las bzhi*) specifically, see Dorje 1987, 783–786.

632 Among Nyingma descriptions of drums and drumming technique, see Tashi Gyatso, *Exegesis of the Resources*, 134–137; and Jatson Nyingpo, *Exegesis on Maintenance of the Supreme Sacraments*, 206–208.

633 These verses derive from Candraśrī's *Methodology of Musical Sound* (*Rol mo'i sgra thabs bzhugs*), a manuscript of which is preserved in Dharamsala at the Amnye Machen Institute. According to Ricardo Canzio (email communication, 12 November 2009), Kunga Sonam frequently appears to quote this source. Also, in his unpublished translation of the *Treatise on Music*, ch. 1, Canzio correlates these high, low, and neutral registers to both vocal and instrumental sound.

634 Jamyang Sonam Wangpo, fl. 1559–1621. On this text, see Canzio 1980, 72n3; and his translation of these verses on 69.

635 This verse is found in Candraśrī, *Systematic Presentation of Drums and Cymbals*, 359.

636 Candraśrī, *Systematic Presentation of Drums and Cymbals*, 359, where there are minor variants; also Canzio 1980, 70.

637 Candraśrī, *Systematic Presentation of Drums and Cymbals*, 359.

638 Candraśrī, *Systematic Presentation of Drums and Cymbals*, 359, reads *bzhi 'phar* for *'jab 'phar*, perhaps indicating a "fourfold great rebound" or crescendo (*'phar chen*).

639 Among Nyingma descriptions of the cymbals and their playing techniques, see also Tashi Gyatso, *Exegesis of the Resources*, 133, on the small-bossed cymbals (*sil snyan*), and 137–138 on the large-bossed cymbals (*sbub chal*); also Jatson Nyingpo, *Exegesis on Maintenance of the Supreme Sacraments*, 210–212.

640 This paragraph derives from Sangye Gyatso's *Removal of the Tarnish of Deluded Appear-*

ances, 2:45. Among the Nyingma cycles mentioned here, the cycles of the *Wrathful Deities of the Magical Net* (*sGyu 'phrul khro bo*, *NK*, vols. 13–17, 63–80, and 83–89) are based on the *Tantra of the Secret Nucleus* (*Guhyagarbhatantra*), and the cycles of the *Gathering of the Great Assembly* (*Tshogs chen 'dus pa*, *NK*, vols. 19–28 and 90–99), derive from the *Sūtra Which Gathers All Intentions* (*mDo dgongs pa 'dus pa*). The cycles of the *Eight Transmitted Teachings: Means for Attainment* (*sGrub pa bka' brgyad*), including the revelations of Nyangrel, Guru Chowang, and Rigdzin Godemchen, derive from the primary tantras contained in Dg. *NGB*, vols. 31–32, nos. 375–88; while the cycles of *Vajrakīla* (*rDo rje phur ba*, *NK*, vols. 9–12), the lineages of which are described in Dudjom Rinpoche 1991, 1:710–716, derive from the tantra texts contained in T 439 and Dg. *NGB*, vols. 19 and 27–29.

641 Cf. the masked dance described in Nebesky-Wojkowitz 1956, 402–405.

642 These verses are not found in Candraśrī and may possibly be cited in the aforementioned work by Jamyang Sonam Wangpo. They are also cited in Lochen Dharmaśrī's *Choreographic Memoranda of the Sacred Dances of the Wrathful Herukas and of Glorious Samantabhadra entitled Display of the Deities* (*Khrag 'thung khro bo'i 'chams kyi brjed byang dpal kun tu bzang po'i 'chams kyi brjed byang lha'i rol ga*), *NK*, 14:371–372.

643 A short account of the benefits that accrue from the correct performance of the sacred masked dances can be found in Gyurme Rabgye, *Wondrous Garland of Tales*, 145–147, with particular reference to the Mindroling tradition. See also Tashi Gyatso, *Exegesis of the Resources*, 147–170.

644 These quotations are also found in Lochen Dharmaśrī, *Choreographic Memoranda*, 397–398. The term "seal" (*phyag rgya*, Skt. *mudrā*), according to the sūtras, denotes a secure realization of emptiness. In the tantras it generally refers to the various hand-gestures which accompany mantra recitation, and by extension to the meditational deity's symbolic hand emblem (*phyag mtshan*)—the vajra, bell, and so forth. In this context, therefore, the seals are the resonance of buddha body.

645 The realization of the superior great buddha body of reality (*lhag pa'i chos sku chen po*), in which pure appearances and emptiness are indivisibly coalesced in union with the meditational deity, pertains to the basis or continuum of the ground (*gzhi'i rgyu*) in Mahāyoga. See Dudjom Rinpoche 1991, 1:264 and 275–276.

646 On the root tantras and exegetical tantras of the *Magical Net* (*sGyu 'phrul drva ba rtsa bshad kyi rgyud*) which are contained in Dg. *NGB*, vols. 9–11, see also Dorje 1987, 37–49. The *Supramundane Sūtra entitled Heruka Galpo* (*'Jigs rten las 'das pa'i mdo he ru ka galpo*) is contained in Dg. *NGB*, vols. 18–19. Since they respectively focus on Vajrasattva and Śrīheruka they are regarded as tantras embodying the Vajra family. On the association of the hundred peaceful and wrathful deities of the Magical Net with the five enlightened families, viz. Vajra, Buddha, Ratna, Padma, and Karma, see, e.g., Dorje 2005, 388–402.

647 The lineage of these Mahāyoga tantras, within the Nyingma tradition, originating from Indian masters such as King Indrabhūti, was initially maintained in Tibet by the followers of Padmasambhava, including Ma Rinchenchok and Nyak Jñānakumāra, along with the latter's eight students who were known as the "eight glorious sons" (*dpal gyi bu brgyad*). On the Indian period, see Dudjom Rinpoche 1991, 1:456–484, and on these early Tibetan figures, 510–522 and 601–606. In the ninth century, during the interregnum which followed the expansionist activities of the great Buddhist kings, characterized by the decline of Buddhism during the reign of Langdarma, these teachings were maintained by Nubchen Sangye Yeshe (Dudjom Rinpoche 1991, 1:607–616). This was when the "three wise men," Mar Śākyamuni, Yo Gejung, and Tsang Rabsel, fled to Amdo

in northeast Tibet in order to preserve the Vinaya lineage (Dudjom Rinpoche 1991, 1:525–526). Subsequently, when this lineage was restored in Central Tibet and the later dissemination of Buddhism began, the ancient Nyingma teachings were maintained by the Zur family and their followers from the late tenth century through to the seventeenth century (Dudjom Rinpoche 1991, 1:617–683). Darcharuwa is associated with the revelation of hidden teachings on Vajrakīla during the thirteenth century (Dudjom Rinpoche 1991, 1:714–716). Subsequently, during the lifetime of the Fifth Dalai Lama (1617–1682), the Nyingma teachings were consolidated in Central Tibet at Mindroling Monastery by Terdak Lingpa and Lochen Dharmaśrī, on whom see Dudjom Rinpoche 1991, 1:825–834 and 728–732, respectively.

648 Lochen Dharmaśrī's *Choreographic Memoranda* (see above, note 642) presents the sacred dances of the Mindroling tradition. Cf. the related treatise attributed to the Fifth Dalai Lama, translated and analyzed in Nebesky-Wojkowitz 1997, 110–245; and Nebesky-Wojkowitz 1956, 402. A distinction is made between the basic dance (*rtsa 'chams*) which evokes spiritual realization and in some contexts is known as the "higher rite" (*stod las*) and the exorcist dance (*brub 'chams*), which forcibly removes negative obstacles and is sometimes known as the "lower rite" (*smad las*). On this distinction, see Dudjom Rinpoche 1991, 1:710–716. The wrathful rites of sorcery (*drag po'i las sbyor*) and the dances that accompany them are specifically mentioned in Dorje 1987, 1224–1226 and 1257–1273.

649 Often the structure of the sacred dances is divided into three sections—the preliminaries (*sngon 'gro*), the main part (*dngos gzhi*), and the finale (*rjes*). Tashi Gyatso, *Exegesis of the Resources*, 147–170, for example, divides his exposition into these three parts.

650 Lochen Dharmaśrī, *Choreographic Memoranda*, 369–370, refers to this initial section as the "donning of the costumes" (*chas su 'jug pa*). Cf. the corresponding description in Nebesky-Wojkowitz 1997, 114–119.

651 Lochen Dharmaśrī, *Choreographic Memoranda*, 370–371, refers to this second section as the "oblation" (*gser skyems*). Cf. Nebesky-Wojkowitz 1997, 118–119. On the functionality of the protector deities, see Dorje 2002 and Linrothe and Watt 2004.

652 Lochen Dharmaśrī, *Choreographic Memoranda*, 371–373, refers to this third section as the "entry into the arena" (*'chams rar 'gro ba*). The ten aspects of physical movement that are commonly esteemed (*lus 'gyur thun mong du gces pa'i yan lag bcu*) are those demeanors of the head, upper body, and so forth, which have already been mentioned (see above, pp. 297–298). The three masteries of the seals (*phyag rgya la mkhas pa gsum*) refer to the skill in looking to the left when the seals are executed on the right side of the body, to the right when executed on the left side, and straight ahead when executed in the middle; and thereby to the techniques for executing, transforming, and dissolving the seals (*bca' bsgyur bshig gsum*). The enlightened attributes that conform with the three similes of the bodily ornaments (*lus rgyan dpe gsum*) are the upright motion of the dance costume (*phod kha'i thad sha*), the twirling motion of the hair ringlets (*ral pa'i 'khril bshig*), and the radiant appearance of the body (*lus kyi 'dzum bstan pa*), which respectively resemble a soaring garuḍa, a lion shaking its mane, and a tiger prowling through the forest. See also Pearlman 2002.

653 Lochen Dharmaśrī, *Choreographic Memoranda*, 373–374, refers to this fourth section as the "the dancers standing in their respective sectors" (*rang gnas su 'dug pa*).

654 Lochen Dharmaśrī, *Choreographic Memoranda*, 374–376, refers to this fifth section as the "emanation of the maṇḍala" (*dkyil 'khor spro ba*).

655 These are the four peripheral enlightened families of Vajra, Ratna, Padma, and Karma, on which see above, note 646. Lochen Dharmaśrī, *Choreographic Memoranda*, 376,

refers to this sixth section as the "consecratory blessing of the female consorts" (*yum byin gyis rlobs*).

656 Lochen Dharmaśrī, *Choreographic Memoranda*, 376–378, refers to this seventh section as the "entreaty of the students" (*slob mas gsol bag dab pa*).

657 Lochen Dharmaśrī, *Choreographic Memoranda*, 378, refers to this eighth section as the "entreaty of the master of ceremonies" (*slob dpon gyis gsol bag dab pa*).

658 On this "dance step of indestructible reality" (*rdo rje'i gar*) which crushes the power of negative forces, see Nebesky-Wojkowitz 1956, 404. Lochen Dharmaśrī, *Choreographic Memoranda*, 378–382, refers to this ninth section as the "expulsion of obstructive forces by injunction" (*bka' bsgo bas bgegs bskrad pa*).

659 Lochen Dharmaśrī, *Choreographic Memoranda*, 382–427, refers to this long tenth section as the "dance steps of the deities of the maṇḍala" (*dkyil 'khor lha'i stangs stabs*). It comprises general deportment (*gnad sdoms pas spyi'i khog 'grol ba*, pp. 382–391) and an explanation of the actual dance movements (*'chams tshul dngos bshad*, pp. 391–427). The latter includes both the "general consecration through the preliminary dance steps" (*sngon 'gro'i stangs stabs kyis spyir rlob pa*, pp. 391–398) and the "particular consecration through the dance steps of the main practice" (*dngos gzhi'i stangs stabs kyis bye brag tu rlob pa*, pp. 398–427). The verses cited here derive specifically from p. 391.

660 Tib. *'chams skor gsum*. These constitute the first three preliminary steps of the sacred dance (Lochen Dharmaśrī, *Choreographic Memoranda*, 391–392). Cf. their description in Nebesky-Wojkowitz 1997, 120–125. Note that *SK*, 294, reads *gsur* for *gsum*.

661 Tib. *chos dbyings bskyed pa*. This triple movement (*bskor ba lan gsum*), which inscribes two intersecting triangles, forming the *dharmodaya* (*chos dbyings*) motif, constitutes the second preliminary dance step (Lochen Dharmaśrī, *Choreographic Memoranda*, 392–393). For a description of this symbol, see Beer 2003, 209–211. Cf. the description of this dance movement in Nebesky-Wojkowitz 1997, 124–127.

662 Tib. *snang srid rnams dbang du bsdu ba*. This triple movement (*gYob mo lan gsum*) constitutes the third preliminary dance step (Lochen Dharmaśrī, *Choreographic Memoranda*, 393). Cf. the description in Nebesky-Wojkowitz 1997, 127–129.

663 Tib. *mkha' 'gro rnams dpa' bskyed pa*. This triple movement (*sig sig lan gsum*) constitutes the fourth preliminary dance step (op. cit., pp. 393–394). Cf. the description in Nebesky-Wojkowitz 1997, 128–129.

664 Tib. *dam nyams kyi bla 'gugs pa*. This triple movement (*mgo gug lan gsum*) constitutes the fifth preliminary dance step (Lochen Dharmaśrī, *Choreographic Memoranda*, 394). Cf. the description in Nebesky-Wojkowitz 1997, 129–131.

665 Tib. *dam can rnams 'bod pa*. This triple movement (*sbyugs pa lan gsum*) constitutes the sixth preliminary dance step (Lochen Dharmaśrī, *Choreographic Memoranda*, 394–395). Cf. the description in Nebesky-Wojkowitz 1997, 130–131.

666 Tib. *steng byin gyis rlob pa* refers to the drawing of the eight-spoke wheel of the celestial abode (*gnam 'khor lo rtsibs brgyad du bri ba*), which constitutes the seventh preliminary dance step (Lochen Dharmaśrī, *Choreographic Memoranda*, 395). Tib. *bar byin gyis rlob pa* refers to the drawing of the eight auspicious symbols of the intermediate abode (*bkra shis rtags brgyad*), which constitutes the eighth preliminary dance step (p. 395). Then, Tib. *'og byin gyis rlob pa* refers to the drawing of the eight lotus petals of the terrestrial abode (*padma 'dab brgyad*), which constitutes the ninth preliminary dance step (p. 395). Cf. the description of these three movements in Nebesky-Wojkowitz 1997, 131–133.

667 The "half-vajra dance movement" (*rdo rje phyed 'gros*) is the means of requesting the site for the dance arena (*sa btsal ba*), which constitutes the tenth preliminary dance step (Lochen Dharmaśrī, *Choreographic Memoranda*, 395–396). The "single vajra dance movement" (*rdo rje rkyangs 'gros*) is the means of taming or subduing the dance arena

(*sa 'dul ba*), which constitutes the eleventh preliminary dance step (pp. 396–397). Lastly, the "dance movement of the double vajra" (*rdo rje sbags 'gros*) is the means of consecrating the dance arena, which constitutes the twelfth preliminary dance step (pp. 397–398). Cf. the description of these three movements in Nebesky-Wojkowitz 1997, 132–137. Note that *SK*, 294, reads *sngags* for *sbag*.

668 These verses derive from Lochen Dharmaśrī, *Choreographic Memoranda*, 398, following which, the seven visualization supports are described (pp. 398–403). On the celestial palace and the protective rings that encircle it, see above, pp. 234–245. The dance steps accompanying this supportive visualization are also described in Nebesky-Wojkowitz 1997, 136–147.

669 These verses derive from Lochen Dharmaśrī, *Choreographic Memoranda*, 403–404. The dance movements of the nine classes of deities are described on pp. 403–427; see also Nebesky-Wojkowitz 1997, 146–191.

670 For detailed iconographic descriptions of these nine classes of wrathful deities, according to the *Magical Net*, see Dorje 1987, 1096–1143; also Dorje 2005, 103–112.

671 Lochen Dharmaśrī, *Choreographic Memoranda*, 427–430, refers to this eleventh section as "protection by transfixing with the ritual spike" (*phur bu gdab pas bsrung ba*). For a description of the ritual spike (*kīla*), see above, note 619; and for biographical accounts of how it has been used, see Dudjom Rinpoche 1991, 1:710–716.

672 Lochen Dharmaśrī, *Choreographic Memoranda*, 430–431, refers to this twelfth section as the "elimination of the extremes of eternalism and nihilism" (*rtag chad kyi mtha' bsal ba*). For Jamgon Kongtrul's analysis of the eternalist and nihilist views that were prevalent in ancient India, see below, pp. 396–417.

673 Lochen Dharmaśrī, *Choreographic Memoranda*, 431, refers to this last and thirteenth section as the "dedication and benediction" (*bsngo shis bya ba*).

674 The two provisions (*dvayasambhāra*, *tshogs gnyis*) are the accumulations of merit (*puṇyasambhāra*, *bsod nams kyi tshogs*) and pristine cognition (*jñānasambhāra*, *ye shes kyi tshogs*), which are gathered by bodhisattvas on the path to buddhahood. Among them, merit refers to the wholesome tendencies imprinted in the mind as a result of positive and skillful thoughts, words, and actions that ripen in the experience of happiness and well-being. It is important to dedicate the merit of one's wholesome actions to the benefit of all sentient beings, ensuring that others also experience the results of the positive actions generated. Pristine cognition refers to the modality of buddha mind. Although all sentient beings possess the potential for actualizing pristine cognition within their mental continuum, the psychological confusions and deluded tendencies which defile the mind obstruct the natural expression of these inherent potentials, making them appear instead as aspects of mundane consciousness (*vijñāna*). The fulfillment of these "two provisions" constitutes the fruition of the entire path, according to the Greater Vehicle, resulting in the maturation of the buddha body of form (*rūpakāya*) and the buddha body of reality (*dharmakāya*) respectively.

675 On the four rites of pacification, enrichment, subjugation, and wrath, see above note 629. The "supreme spiritual accomplishment" (*paramasiddhi*, *mchog gi dngos grub*) refers to the attainment of buddhahood.

676 These dances of exorcism (*brub 'chams*) are described in Lochen Dharmaśrī, *Choreographic Memoranda*, 438ff.; also Nebesky-Wojkowitz 1997, 105–108 and 190–241.

677 On the Sakya tradition of Vajrakīla (*phur pa'i rtsa 'chams*), see Dudjom Rinpoche 1991, 1:712; also Nebesky-Wojkowitz 1997, 32–34.

678 For a brief account of the life of Drungpa Ma-se (b. 1386), see Trungpa 1966, 32–34; and for a contemporary description of Zurmang itself, Dorje 2009, 618–622. The life of Tilopā, human progenitor of the Kagyu lineages, is contained in Rinchen Namgyal

and Guru Dhottsha, *The Life and Songs of Lord Tilopā, with a Brief Biography of Naropā* (*rJe btsun ti lo pa'i rnam mgur dang dpal na ro pa'i rnam thar bsdus pa*) (Ziling: Qinghai mi rigs dpe skrun khang, 1992), 1–54. On sacred dances within the Kagyu tradition in general, see also Nebesky-Wojkowitz 1997, 34–42.

679 The sacred dances of the tenth day commemorating key events in the career of Padmasambhava are performed at Nyingma monasteries throughout, Tibet, Sikkim and Bhutan. These principally derive from Guru Chowang's revelation entitled *Spiritual Teacher: Gathering of Secrets* (*Bla ma gsang 'dus*). For the life of Guru Chowang, see Dudjom Rinpoche 1991, 1:760–770; for a brief account of the tenth-day dances in Bhutan, see Dorji 2001; and for those at Katok in East Tibet, see Dorje 2009, 576–579. The benefits of witnessing such spectacles have already been mentioned—see above, note 643. On sacred dance within the Nyingma school in general, see also Nebesky-Wojkowitz 1997, 11–32.

680 This passage is also found, with minor variants, in Sangye Gyatso, *Removal of the Tarnish of Deluded Appearances*, 2:45.

681 Cf. Sangye Gyatso, *Removal of the Tarnish of Deluded Appearances*, 2:45.

682 Cf. Smith 2001, 188–189.

683 These two paragraphs derive from Sangye Gyatso, *Removal of the Tarnish of Deluded Appearances*, 2:45, who adds that the machines listed here are all mentioned in the *Tantra of the Wheel of Time*.

684 On the fashioning of armor, swords, helmets, and weaponry, see Chapel Tseten Phuntsok and Tsering Peljor, eds., *Compilation of Useful Instructions on the Arts* (*bZo rig nyer mkho bdams bsgrigs*), in *Gangs can rig mdzod*, vol. 13 (Lhasa: Bod ljongs bod yig dpe rnying dpe skrun khang, 1990).

685 Note that these similes are inverted in the text.

686 On this text, see Tsering 2003, 41n14.

687 The two kinds of spiritual accomplishment (*dngos grub rnam gnyis*) comprise the supreme accomplishment of buddhahood, on which see above, note 675, and the common accomplishments (*thun mong gi dngos grub*) which are a series of mystical powers gained through meditative practices and based on mantra recitation in the context of specific rituals.

688 This specific citation is presently unidentified, but the incident may have been recounted in this form in the *nidāna* (*gleng gzhi*) literature of the monastic discipline (*vinaya*).

689 On the melodic prosody of Vedic hymns, see below, pp. 368–372; and on the Brāhmaṇa Vedas, see also pp. 412–414 and p. 898.

690 Cf. Sangye Gyatso, *Removal of the Tarnish of Deluded Appearances*, 2:46, who mentions these Kadampa and Nyingma methods, adding that the Nyingma chants comprise six different melodic contours: changing (*'gyur*), descending (*khugs*), ascending (*'degs*), constant or pausing (*'jog*), low (*sbom*), and high (*phra*).

691 These later systems include the well-known overtone harmonic chants of the Gelukpa tradition as well as the chanting traditions of the other new translation schools. On the diverse traditions and their systems of musical notation, see Helffer 1998; also Crossley-Holland 1976; Ellingson 1979; and Kaufmann 1975.

692 Ricardo Canzio, in his unpublished translation of the *Treatise on Music*, ch. 1, p. 4, emphasizes that the term "melodic contour" (*svara, nga ro*) here denotes the pitch, timbre, and duration of a given note. The identification of the four primary aspects of melodic contour with the four sounds (*caturvarṇa*) of Indian music is made in the same article, p. 5.

693 Sakya Paṇḍita's *Treatise on Music* (*Rol mo'i bstan bcos*), 351–352. The twelve subsidiary aspects are also listed in this paragraph.

694 In his as yet unpublished translation of the *Treatise on Music* (Canzio n.d., 5–6), Ricardo

Canzio renders these aspects of the sustaining note respectively as straight (*drang po*), upstanding (*bsgreng pa*), curved (*bkug pa*), upper (*bstod pa*), and lower (*smad pa*), closely following the shapes of the Tibetan vowels to which they correspond. According to Ellingson 1979, the sustaining note (*'dren pa*) may rise (*stod pa*), fall (*smad pa*), pause (*bkug pa*), or go flat (*rgyang pa*).

695 Sakya Paṇḍita, *Treatise on Music*, 352 adds that this may take the form of a single stop or a series of stops, comprising two, three or four beats and so forth. Ellingson 1979 comments that *bkug pa* is a stop, usually with a vowel and pitch change, suggesting that the stops may occur ascendingly. Mao Jizheng 1998 suggests that one beat comprises an ascending and descending contour, and that multiple beats comprise several such humps.

696 Sakya Paṇḍita, *Treatise on Music*, 352 adds that these variations may be long or short in duration. See Canzio n.d., 4. Ellingson 1979 comments that *bsgyur ba* refers to changes in the tune, slight fluctuations, with changes in the vowel, such as from (i) to (u) or (i) to (o).

697 Canzio n.d., 6–7, suggests, following Sakya Paṇḍita's description (*de la khyad par thog mtha' rags*), that the ascending note is soft at the beginning and end and louder in the middle. Ellingson 1979 suggests that it refers to the vocal pitch rising by an octave.

698 In his *Treatise on Music*, p. 354. Cf. the alternative translation of this verse in Canzio n.d., 13.

699 Tib. *rtogs brjod*, Skt. *avadāna*.

700 Tib. *rjes su brjod pa*, Skt. *anuvāda, anubhāṣita*.

701 Sakya Paṇḍita, *Treatise on Music*, 359.

702 The three essentials and six defects are explained in Sakya Paṇḍita, *Treatise on Music*, 360.

703 Sakya Paṇḍita, *Treatise on Music*, 360–361.

704 These verses are quoted by Kunga Sonam. Ricardo Canzio (email communication, 12 November 2009) notes a different reading for this verse, indicating that *yi ge dbyangs* (melodic chanting of syllables) might replace *yo ga dbyangs* (melodic chanting of Yoga Tantra).

705 Candraśrī, *Treatise on Melody entitled Neck Ornament of Clear Intelligence* (*dByangs kyi bstan bcos blo gsal mgul rgyan*). R. Canzio (email communication, 12 November 2009) points out how the listing of the six ceremonial contexts is made by way of annotation in the Candraśrī text (*mchan du ces su*).

706 Sakya Paṇḍita's *Treatise on Music*, 359–360.

707 This reading accords with Sakya Paṇḍita, *Treatise on Music*, 359. *SK* here reads *'jol sgeg* for *'jo sgeg.*

708 "Leader" (*kun 'dren pa*) here could be construed as an epithet of the Buddha.

709 Sakya Paṇḍita, *Treatise on Music*, 359, reads "virtuous flower" (*dge ba'i me tog*), whereas the text reads "joyous flower" (*dga' ba'i me tog*).

710 In Sakya Paṇḍita, *Treatise on Music*, 360, the text reads *'dren pa'i khyad par* for *spel ba'i khyad par*. With regard to the intermingling of melodic contours, see also Canzio, n.d., 7–9.

711 On melodic notation in general, see the sources listed above in note 691.

712 The source of these verses is presently unidentified, though in language they are somewhat reminiscent of Candraśrī. Ricardo Canzio rightly points out (email communication, 14 November 2009) the difficulty of translating these terms more technically without reference to specific *dbyang yig* commentaries of the Sakya-Zhalu tradition or technical explanations from a knowledgeable chant master (*dbu mdzad*). It is also clear

that Tibetan chanting encompasses not only voice pitch but also modifiers of timbre and duration, exhibiting "features of performance or neum modifiers."

713 These verses are also cited by Kunga Sonam. The translation of this passage owes much to the input of Ricardo Canzio.

714 Tib. *rus pa ma shor.*

715 This paragraph derives from Sangye Gyatso, *Removal of the Tarnish of Deluded Appearances*, 2:46

716 Sakya Paṇḍita, *Treatise on Music*, 361.

717 Sakya Paṇḍita, *Treatise on Music*, 361 reads *ji snyed sil snyan sbyor bshad pa*, while *SK*, 299, reads *sbyon bshad pa.*

718 For a detailed analysis of the classifications of the canonical transmitted teachings of the Buddha and the treatises (*śāstra*) composed by later commentators, see Dudjom Rinpoche 1991, 1:73–96.

719 Cf. Sangye Gyatso, *Removal of the Tarnish of Deluded Appearances*, 2:46–47. The three modes of discriminative awareness (*shes rab*) are therefore cultivated by means of study, reflection, and meditation. For a clear summary, see Padmakara Translation Group 1994, 251–252.

720 This enumeration is found in the *Detailed Inspection [of Terminology]* (*Mahāvyutpatti* lexicon, *Bye brag tu rtogs par byed pa*, T 4346), *MVT* nos. 4953–4971. The reference has not been identified in Vasubandhu's *Auto-commentary on the Treasury of Phenomenology* (*Abhidharmakośabhāṣya*, T 4090), as might be suggested by Jamgon Kongrul here, nor in any of the other primary Indian commentaries on the *Treasury of Phenomenology*. In the Collected Works of Longdol Lama, 1:692, where the same enumeration is given, the source is attributed simply to the "*Treasury*" (*mdzod*), but it does not appear to figure in the *Treasury of Amarasiṃha* (*Amarakośa*, T 4299), or its commentary (T 4300). The same listing of the eighteen great topics of knowledge (*aṣṭadaśavidyāsthāna*, *rig pa'i gnas bco brgyad*) can be found in later works, such as Jamgon Mipham Gyatso's *Bilingual Concordance entitled Radiant Jewel Mirror* (*sKad gnyis shan sbyar rab gsal nor bu'i me long*), and in Negi, *Tibetan Sanskrit Dictionary*, 6379. An earlier listing is given by Dharmakīrti, in his *Extensive Exegesis on the Garland of the Tales of Past Lives* (*Jātakamālāṭīkā*, T 4151), Ha, f. 139b, in which "behavior" (*nīti*, *chos lugs*) and "history" (*itihāsaka*, *sngon byung ba*) appear to be missing. This latter commentary concludes by referring the reader to other works, viz. the *Bye brag pa*, the *Don gyi phreng ba*, and the *Rig pa'i bstan bcos*, for which reason I have surmised that the original source could possibly be found in the extant Chinese translation of the *Great Treasury of Detailed Exposition* (*Mahāvibhāṣa*, *Bye brag bshad mdzod*, Taisho 1545). This will require further investigation. See also Dungkar Lobzang Trinle, *Great Dictionary of Dungkar*, pp. 1900–1901.

721 On these sciences, see above, pp. 125–176.

722 This figure and his geomantic revelations are mentioned in Dorje 2001, ch. 1. The text reads *Du ha ra* for *Da hu ra*. Sangye Gyatso, *Removal of the Tarnish of Deluded Appearances*, 2:47, notes that he has discussed this topic elsewhere, in ch. 32 of his *White Beryl: [An Eloquent Treatise on the Astrology of the Phukpa School]. [Phug lugs rtsis kyi legs bshad] vaiḍūrya dkar po*. See also Dorje 2001, ch. 3.

723 E. Gene Smith (email communication, 19 September 2009) notes that of the many treatises on lapidary arts in the Indian tradition, very few were translated into Tibetan. Mahoṣadhi is probably an epithet of Buddhabhaṭṭa, author of the most celebrated classical Sanskrit work on the inspection of gems, entitled *Scrutiny of Gems and Precious Metals* (*Ratnaparīkṣā*), which is translated in Finot 1896. The *White Lotus Bouquet of Investigation* (*dPyad don pad dkar chun po*), also known under the title *Legs par bshad*

pa'i padma dkar po chun po, and attributed to the mantrin Hūṃkarajaya, was published in Gangtok in 1981.

724 I have not yet been able to identify any of these works. Among other relevant sources on the ritual properties of skulls, there are the *Inspection of Skulls: Extracting the Wealth of the Yakṣas* (*Thod brtag gnod sbyin nor 'don*), an extract from the *Tantra of Heruka Galpo* (Dg. *NGB* vols. 18–19), which is contained in Tashi Gyatso et al., *Treatises on the Accoutrements and Music of the Ancient Way of Secret* [*Mantras*] (*gSang rnying rgyan dang rol mo'i bstan bcos*) Gangs chen rigs mdzod series, 30 (Lhasa: 1996), 293–297; Sangye Lingpa's *Spiritual Attainment Associated with the Skull: A Storehouse of Wish-fulfilling Gems* (*Thod sgrub yid bzhin bang mdzod*), ibid., 311–316; Tokden Rabjam Lobzang Dargye's *Inspection of Skulls entitled Jewel Garland* (*Thod brtag nor bu'i phreng ba*), ibid., 301–310; and the *Examination of the Begging Bowl* [*of the Skull*], *According to the Inner Way of Secret Mantra* (*gSang sngags nang gi lhun bzed brtag pa*), ibid., 317–334—a text which is attributed to Drakpa Gyaltsen of Sakya. See also the illustrations at the end of this volume, which indicate the defining characteristics and positive and negative attributes of skulls.

725 Two of these three texts comprising the *Mirror Trilogy* (*Me long skor gsum*), entitled *Treatise on Horses entitled Silver-White Mirror* (*rTa gzhung dngul dkar me long*) and *Inspection of Horses entitled All-radiant Mirror* (*rTa dpyad mthong ba kun gsal me long*), are contained in the *Anthology of Texts and Advice Concerning the Veterinary Treatment of Horses* (*Bod kyi rta'i gso dpyad gzhung lugs mdams bsgrigs*), 3–85 and 273–359, respectively. The works are attributed to Drugu Sengdo Ochen (Gru gu seng mdo 'od chen). The introduction to this publication, p. 1, suggests that he, along with Tayilha the daughter of Chokro, Gamzang the daughter of Dro, Yuzher Lekdri, Drokhong, and others, all composed their tracts on horses at the behest of the Tibetan emperor Trisong Detsen himself. On animal husbandry pertaining to horses, based on Dunhuang manuscripts, see also Blondeau 1972. For accounts of the life of the emperor Trisong Detsen (742–circa 797), who established Buddhism as the state religion, see Shakabpa 1967, 34–46, and Kapstein 2006, 66–77.

726 This is mentioned in Sangye Gyatso's *Removal of the Tarnish of Deluded Appearances*, 2:47, although I have not yet identified the text in question. The Tengyur contains a few tracts on this subject, including two works that have been attributed to Durlabharāja, namely, the *Physical Characteristics* [*of Human Beings*], *Demonstrated by Sāmudrika* (*Sāmudrikavyañjanavarṇana*, T 4336), and the *Inspection of the Physical Characteristics of Human Beings entitled Sāmudrika* (*Sāmudrika-nāma-tanūlakṣaṇaparīkṣā*, T 4338), as well as the anonymous *Synopsis of the Inspection of Human Beings* (*Tanūvicāraṇaśāstrasaṃkṣepa*, T 4337) and the *Tales of Spiritual Accomplishment Achieved through a Female Medium* (*Nārīsiddhilābhākhyāna*, T 4343), on all of which see Smith 2001, 185–186.

727 The term *gtsug lag* is analyzed in Sangye Gyatso, *Removal of the Tarnish*, 1:268–269, where it is pointed out that Sonam Gyaltsen makes a basic distinction between the sciences that relate to meaning (*don gyi gtsug lag*), namely, the trainings in ethical discipline, discriminative awareness, and meditative stability, and the sciences that relate to verbal expression (*brjod kyi gtsug lag*), namely, the transmitted teachings and treatises of Buddhism.

728 The four preceding treatises are all attributed to Nāgārjuna.

729 All but the last-mentioned are treatises of Indian origin. The *Eloquence of Sakya* (*Sa skya'i legs bshad*), full title *Legs par bshad pa rin po che'i gter*, was composed in verse by Sakya Paṇḍita, along with a prose commentary.

730 On Gyalwa Ten-ne (rGyal ba ten ne, 1127–1217), who held both Kadampa and Kagyupa

lineages, see Kozhul Drakpa Jungne and Gyalwa Lobzang Khedrub, eds., *Lexicon of the Learned and Accomplished Masters Who Successively Appeared in the Land of Snows* (*Gangs can mkhas grub rim byon ming mdzod*) (Lanzhou: Gansu mi rigs dpe skrun khang, 1992), 391–393. "Dromtonpa" could refer either to Gyalwa Jungne (1004–1064), the illustrious student of Atiśa and founder of Reting Monastery (ibid., pp. 1252–1254), or to Dromton Zhonu Lodro (b. 1271), who redacted the *Father Teachings of Kadam* (*bKa' gdams pha chos*) in its final form.

731 *MVT*, nos. 4972–5006.

732 Sangye Gyatso, *Removal of the Tarnish*, 1:412–415, points out that there are different enumerations of the sixty-four crafts presented in the *Sūtra of Extensive Play* (*Lalitavistarasūtra*), the *Extensive* [*Commentary*] *on the Minor Transmissions* (*Vinayakṣudrāgama*, T 4115) by Śīlapālita, and the *Detailed Inspection of Terminology* (*Mahāvyutpatti*). He also mentions the sixty-four arts of love presented in the classical Indian treatises on love-making (*'dod pa'i bstan bcos*), such as Vatsyāyana's *Discourse on the Arts of Love* (*Kāmasūtra*) and Rūpabhadra's *Treatise on the Arts of Love* (*Kāmaśāstra*, T 2500), as well as in later indigenous Tibetan compositions by Jamgon Mipham Gyatso (*Treatise on the Arts of Love: A Treasure That Delights the Whole World*, *'Dod pa'i bstan bcos 'jig rten kun tu dga' ba'i gter*), and Gendun Chopel—the latter being translated in J. Hopkins 1992.

733 *MVT*, nos. 5027–5034. On the traditional Indian octave or musical scale, see Basham 1959, 383–387. Here the sequence of the seven notes has been reordered, according to their actual position in the scale. Note that our text reverses the positions of the sixth tone and the middle tone.

734 See above, pp. 212–213 and pp. 297–298.

735 Sangye Gyatso, *Removal of the Tarnish*, 1:413–414, enumerates this alternative list.

736 For Jamgon Kongtrul's account of the higher and lower realms of existence, see Kalu Rinpoche Translation Group 1995. The higher realms are those not frequented by animals, anguished spirits, or hell-bound beings.

737 The three exalted, or higher, realms are those of humans, gods, and antigods, on which see Kalu Rinpoche Translation Group 1995. For a discussion of the meditative and ethical practices associated with rebirth in the exalted realms and with the attainment of definitive excellence, see below, pp. 420–439. The three degrees of enlightenment (*byang chub gsum*) are the fruitional attainments of the pious attendants, hermit buddhas, and bodhisattvas, respectively—on which see Jamgon Kongtrul's presentation in Callahan 2007.

738 The three vehicles (*theg pa gsum*) which reverse suffering and its causes are the three Buddhist vehicles pursued by pious attendants, hermit buddhas, and bodhisattvas. See previous note.

739 These verses derive from Longchen Rabjampa's *Precious Treasury of Wish-fulfilling Gems: A Treatise on the Pith Instructions of the Greater Vehicle* (*Theg pa chen po'i man ngag gi bstan bcos yid bzhin rin po che'i mdzod*), ch. 5, *gNas pa'i bskal pa'i skabs*, Dodrubchen edition, p. 30, lines 2–4. On the life of Longchen Rabjampa (1308–1363), see Dudjom Rinpoche 1991: 575–596.

740 The interpretation of these verses is found in Longchen Rabjampa's *White Lotus Autocommentary on the Precious Treasury of Wish-fulfilling Gems: A Treatise on the Pith Instructions of the Greater Vehicle* (*Theg pa chen po'i man ngag gi bstan bcos yid bzhin rin po che'i mdzod kyi 'grel pa padma dkar po*), ch. 5, Dodrubchen edition, pp. 142–155. Accordingly, the "six classes of sentient beings" (*'gro ba drug*) comprise gods, antigods, humans, animals, anguished spirits, and denizens of the hells.

The "four modes of birth" (*skye ba rnam bzhi*) comprise oviparous, viviparous, photosynthetic (through heat and moisture), and miraculous birth.

The "six grounds" (*gzhi drug*; *SK*, 363, reads *bzhi drug*) comprise the enduring ground of the sustaining elements (*gnas pa'i gzhi*); the dependable ground that offers shelter from harm (*brten pa'i gzhi*); the nutritional ground (*zas kyi gzhi*); the comforting ground (*bde ba'i gzhi*) of clothing, bedding, seats, and so forth; the illuminating ground (*snang ba'i gzhi*) of sunlight, moonlight, lamps, and so forth, which enable physical forms to appear; and the bodily sustaining ground (*lus gnas pa'i gzhi*), which comprises the four nutrients (*zas bzhi*)—food, sensory contact, mental activity, and consciousness.

The "ten measures of time" (*dus bcu*) comprise the aeon; year; month; fortnight; day; night; indivisible time moment (*skad cig*); "minute" (*thang gcig*), consisting of sixty indivisible time moments; the "hour" (*yud tsam pa*), consisting of thirty "minutes"; and the season (*dus tshigs*).

The "seventeen material objectives" (*dngos po bcu bdun*) are said to concern self, parents, offspring, wife, servants, employees, livelihood, friends, advisors, relatives, cousins, fields, houses, merchandise, crops, productivity, and wealth creation.

The "fourteen useful devices" (*yo byad bcu bzhi*) comprise food, beverage, clothing, transportation, ornaments, song and dance, laughter, music, incense, flower garlands, ointments, bowls, [favorable] appearances (*snang ba*), and love-making.

The "eight pursuits of daily life" (*rgyun gyi rjes su spyod pa brgyad*) comprise the examination of others' actions, the wearing of fine clothes, eating and drinking, having respect for the physical body, sleeping, love-making, the effort that love-making entails, and the talk that love-making entails.

The "ten mundane pastimes" (*'jig rten spyod bcu*) comprise talk, conversation, merriment, giving away a bride, taking a bride, sending out invitations, borrowing, over-eating, banqueting, and taking sides in a dispute.

The "three kinds of discourse" (*gtam rnam pa gsum*) comprise discourses concerning the genuine teachings, discourses devoid of the sacred teachings, and ethically neutral discourses excluded from those categories.

The "twenty-two kinds of misconduct" (*nyes rtsom nyer gnyis*) comprise deception with regard to wet measures, deception with regard to weights, deception with regard to dry measures, addiction to misconduct, fighting, finding faults, disputing, contesting, scolding, being enraged, breaking a promise, threatening, menacing, killing, imprisoning, encircling, mutilating, banishing, misleading, deluding, ruthlessly suppressing, and lying.

The "sixty-three categories of sentient being" (*sems can rigs*) comprise denizens of the hells, anguished spirits, animals, gods, humans, antigods, beings of the celestial realms (*bar gyi srid pa*), the ruling classes, the mercantile classes, the working classes, the priestly classes, men, women, hermaphrodites, the wicked, the mediocre, the good, householders, renunciants, hardline ascetics, moderate ascetics, the ordained, the unordained, the desireless, the desireful, those who decisively pursue wrong paths, those who decisively pursue genuine paths, those who decisively pursue neither genuine nor wrong paths, fully ordained monks, fully ordained nuns, trainee nuns, novitiate monks, novitiate nuns, laymen, laywomen, those who recite daily prayers, monastic attendants, established practitioners, middle-ranking practitioners, neophytes, monastic preceptors, masters, naturally qualified persons, disciples, newcomers, monastic officials, those who desire wealth, those who desire celebrity, those of diminished resources, the erudite, those who are learned and meritorious, those who embark upon the teachings in pursuit of the genuine teachings, those who maintain the monastic discipline (*vinaya*), those who maintain the sūtras, those who uphold the path of the *mātaraḥ* spirits, ordinary individuals, those who have seen the truth [of the path], those who are on the paths of learning, those who are on the path of no-more-learning, pious attendants, hermit buddhas, bodhisattvas, and universal monarchs.

The "eight phases of the life-cycle" (*dus brgyad*) comprise fetal and embryonic development, birth, childhood, youth, adolescence, adult maturity, old age, and decrepitude.

The "four ways of entering [the womb]" ([*mngal du*] *'jug pa bzhi*) comprise the womb entry of a universal monarch who is cognizant and enters with alertness, the womb entry of the pious attendant and hermit buddha who is not cognizant and enters without alertness, the entry of the bodhisattva who enters and abides within the womb in a state of alertness, and the entry of other beings who enter and abide within the womb, lacking alertness.

The "six modes of livelihood" (*'tsho ba drug*) comprise farming; trade; animal husbandry; livelihood through one's skills or ability; livelihood through writing, mathematics, and astrological computations; and livelihood through other arts and crafts excluding these.

The "six things to be well guarded" (*kun nas bsrung ba drug*) comprise cohorts of elephants, brigades of cavalry, convoys of chariots, phalanxes of infantry, hordes of wealth, and associations of allies.

The "seven kinds of pride" (*nga rgyal bdun*) comprise [conceited] pride (*ahaṃkāramāna, khengs pa nga rgyal*), exalted pride (*adhimāna, che ba'i nga rgyal*), exaggerated pride (*mānātimāna, nga rgyal las kyang nga rgyal*), egotistical pride (*asmimāna, nga'i snyams pa'i nga rgyal*), manifest pride (*abhimāna, mngon pa'i nga rgyal*), slight pride (*ūnamāna, cung zad snaym pa'i nga rgyal*), and perverse pride (*mithyāmāna, 'dzin pa log pa'i nga rgyal*), on which see also below, p. 500.

The "seven kinds of self-satisfaction" (*rgyags pa rnam pa bdun*) comprise self-satisfaction with one's freedom from disease, self-satisfaction with one's adolescence, self-satisfaction with one's own state of life, self-satisfaction with one's own class, self-satisfaction with one's own physical form, self-satisfaction with one's own power, and self-satisfaction with one's own erudition.

The "four kinds of conventional expression" (*tha snyed bzhi*) comprise conventional expressions that have been acquired through hearing (*thos pa'i tha snyad*), conventional expressions that have been acquired through analysis (*bye brag phyed pa'i tha snyed*), conventional expressions that have been acquired through direct perception (*mthong ba'i tha snyed*), and conventional expressions that have been acquired through consciousness (*rnam par shes pa'i tha snyad*), i.e., through the processes of individual intrinsic awareness.

The "manifold bases of conventional expressions" (*tha snyad mang po'i gzhi*) are the objects or meanings that give rise to these conventional terms, including etymological bases, elaborate bases, and concise bases.

The "six kinds of knowledge" (*mkhas pa drug*) comprise knowledge of the psycho-physical aggregates (*phung po*), sensory bases (*khams*), sensory activity fields (*skye mched*), dependent origination (*rten 'brel*), the abodes [of cyclic existence to be abandoned] and the abodes of [nirvāṇa] that are not [to be abandoned] (*gnas dang gnas ma yin pa*), and the sense faculties (*dbang po*).

The "nine themes of the Buddha's transmitted teachings" ([*sangs rgyas kyi*] *bka'i dngos po dgu*) comprise the theme of sentient beings (*sems can kyi dngos po*), i.e., the psycho-physical aggregates (*phung po*); the theme of resources (*longs spyod kyi dngos po*), i.e., the sensory activity fields (*skye mched*); the theme of birth (*skye ba'i dngos po*), i.e., dependent origination; the theme of duration (*gnas pa'i dngos po*), i.e., the four nutrients; the [two] themes of dissonant mental states and purification (*kun nas nyon mongs pa dang rnam par byang ba'i dngos gzhi*), concerning the four truths; the theme of diversity (*sna tshogs kyi dngos po*), concerning the immeasurable world systems; the theme of the teacher (*ston pa po'i dngos po*), concerning buddhas, bodhisattvas, and pious attendants; and the theme of the teachings (*bstan bya'i dngos po*), concerning the thirty-seven aspects of enlightenment (*chos sum cu rtsa bdun*), on which see above, note 410.

Finally, the "eight themes of cyclic existence" (*'khor gyi dngos po brgyad*) comprise the ruling class, the priestly class, householders, renunciants, the class of the four Great Kings (*rgyal chen bzhi*), the class of the Thirty-three Gods (*sum cu rtsa gsum pa*), [the abode of] Māra, and [the world systems] of Brahmā.

741 The ancient Indian medical science of Āyurveda bridges the Brāhmaṇical and Buddhist traditions. At its roots are the compilations of two celebrated physicians—Caraka and Suśruta, on whom see respectively Kaviratna and Sharma 1996 (for their five-volume translation of the *Carakasaṃhitā*) and Dwivedi and Dwivedi 2007 (on the *Suśrutasaṃhitā*). The Indian literature has also been recently surveyed in Wujastyk 2003 and Kutumbian 2005. Specifically, within the Buddhist tradition, there are treatises by Candranandana, Nāgārjuna, and Vāgbhaṭa extant in the Tengyur. Among them, Vāgbhaṭa's *Eight Divisions of Medical Science* (*Aṣṭāṅgahṛdayasaṃhitā*) has been particularly influential (see Vogel 1965).

Within the Tibetan medical tradition, primacy is given to the *Great Tantra of Secret Instructions on the Eight Branches of the Essence of the Glorious Elixir of Immortality* (*dPal ldan bdud rtsi snying po yan lag brgyad pa gsang ba man ngag gi rgyud chen po*). This text is said to have been transmitted in Tibet by the great translator Vairocana during the eighth century, based on teachings he received from Candranandana and Padmasambhava, in the lifetime of the great physician Yutok Yonten Gonpo the Elder, and to have been concealed as a "treasure-doctrine" (*gter chos*) at Samye, from where it was subsequently revealed by Drapa Ngonshe of Dratang on 19 July 1038. Subsequently the text was redacted and came to be known as the *Four Tantras of Dratang* (*Grva thang rgyud bzhi*). Some contemporary scholars consider the work to have been adapted by Yutok Yonten Gonpo from an earlier Bon medical treatise by Chebu Trishe (*dPyad bu khri shes*), entitled *Four Collections of Medical Science* (*gSo rig 'bum bzhi*). Whatever its origin, the *Four Tantras of Dratang* has become the primary sourcebook for the practice of Buddhist medicine in Tibet, surpassing in its importance even the aforementioned Sanskrit treatises.

By the fifteenth century, two main schools of interpretation had evolved: the Jangpa school, stemming from Rigdzin Namgyal Trakzangpel and including Namgyal Dorje; and the Zurkhar lineage, stemming from Wangchuk Drak and including Zurkhar Nyamnyi Dorje (1439–1475). These and other medical lineages were integrated during the seventeenth century by Sangye Gyatso (1653–1705), the author of the authoritative *Blue Beryl* [*Treatise on Medicine, Clarifying the Four Tantras Which Are the Enlightened Intention of Bhaiṣajyaguru*] (*gSo ba rig pa'i bstan bcos sman bla'i dgongs rgyan rgyud bzhi'i gsal byed baiḍūrya sngon po'i mallika*). Sangye Gyatso additionally authored further treatises on medicine—the *Survey of Medicine* (*sMan gyi khog 'bubs*) and his concise appraisal in ch. 34 of the aforementioned *Removal of the Tarnish of Deluded Appearances*. For an account of Drapa Ngonshe's revelations, see Dudjom Rinpoche 1991, 1:753–754, and *TMP*, 3–15. Jamgon Kongtrul's own account of the origins of medical treatises in the Indo-Tibetan world can be found in Ngawang Zangpo 2010, 405–411. Useful listings of indigenous Tibetan treatises on medicine can be found in Drakpa, *Inventory of Tibetan Treatises*, 1–12, and online at www.tbrc.org, T85.

742 As expounded in Vāgbhaṭa's *Eight Divisions of Medical Science* (*Aṣṭāṅgahṛdayasaṃhitā*), the eight aspects of medicine comprise pathology, patients, regimen, medication, diagnosis, prophylaxis, treatment, and physicians.

743 The *Four Tantras of Dratang* (*Grva thang rgyud bzhi*) comprise the *Root Tantra* (*rTsa rgyud*), the *Exegetical Tantra* (*bShad rgyud*), the *Instructional Tantra* (*Man ngag*

rgyud), and the *Subsequent Tantra* (*Phyi ma'i rgyud*). The distinctions between these are summarized in *TMP*, 14–15. Illustrations and commentary are presented in the same work—the *Root Tantra* on pp. 17–24 (plates 1–4); the *Exegetical Tantra* on 23–90 (plates 5–37); the *Instructional Tantra* on 91–122 (plates 38–53); and the *Subsequent Tantra* on 123–170 (plates 54–77).

744 Buddhist tradition holds the *Root Tantra* (*rTsa ba thugs kyi rgyud*) to have been expounded by Vidyājñāna, the emanation of the buddha mind of Bhaiṣajyaguru, who is identified with the buddha Akṣobhyavajra. Bhaiṣajyaguru, the buddha of medicine, has the potential to emanate as four sibling hermit sages known as Vidyājñāna in order to transform impurities into pristine cognition by teaching the four tantras in succession. For an account of his exposition of the *Root Tantra*, see *TMP*, 19–20. The Tibetan text of the *Root Tantra* is contained in Drapa Ngonshe, *Four Tantras of Dratang*, 1–17, and with interlinear commentary in Sangye Gyatso, *Blue Beryl*, 1:1–49.

745 For a detailed and authoritative Tibetan commentary to the *Root Tantra*, see Sangye Gyatso, *Blue Beryl*, 1:1–49.

746 See fig. 44; also the illustration of the first root with its two stems of physiology and pathology, along with their twelve branches and eighty-eight leaves, in *TMP*, 19–20, and the translation of the corresponding captions (pp. 175–176).

747 These fifteen aspects of the three humors are enumerated in *TMP*, 175. Among them, the five types of wind (*pañcavāta, rlung lnga*) comprise life-sustaining breath (*prāṇa, srog 'dzin*), ascending wind associated with the vocal cords (*udāna, gyen rgyu*), pervasive wind associated with metabolism and muscular movement (*vyāna, khyab byed*), fire-accompanying wind associated with digestion (*samāna, me mnyam*), and descending purgative wind (*apāna, thur sel*). The five types of bile (*pañcpitta, mkhris pa lnga*) comprise digestive bile (*pācaka, 'ju byed*), color-transforming bile associated with chyle (*rañjaka, mdangs sgyur*), energizing bile (*sādhaka, sgrub byed*), vision-producing bile (*ālocaka, mthong byed*), and complexion-clearing bile (*bhrājaka, mdog gsal*). The five types of phlegm (*pañckapha, bad kan lnga*) comprise supporting phlegm (*avalambaka, rten byed*), decomposing phlegm (*kledaka, myag byed*), gustatory phlegm (*bodhaka, myong byed*), sensory stimulating phlegm (*tarpaka, tshim byed*), and adhesive phlegm (*śleṣaka, 'byor byed*).

748 The three poisons (*dug gsum*) are delusion (*moha, gti mug*), attachment (*rāga, 'dod chags*), and aversion (*dveṣa, zhe sdang*), for Jamgon Kongtrul's interpretation of which, from the standpoint of Buddhist phenomenology, see below, pp. 499–504.

749 For anatomical illustrations of the muscles, skin tissue, nerves, blood vessels, and organs, see *TMP*, 29–46, and 185–202.

750 The seven bodily constituents (*lus zungs bdun*) and three impurities (*dri ma*) are listed above. Concerning the five sense organs (*dbang po lnga*), from the perspective of Buddhist phenomenology, see below, pp. 479–480. The five solid viscera (*don lnga*) comprise the heart, lungs, liver, spleen, and kidneys, while the six hollow viscera (*snod drug*) comprise the stomach, gall bladder, large intestine, small intestine, urinary bladder, and the "reservoir for reproductive fluid" (*sam se'u*). See the illustrations in *TMP*, 43–44, and 199–200.

751 *TMP*, 175–176.

752 These nine results which bring fatality are enumerated as (1) exhaustion of the life span, merits, and past actions; (2) disharmony of humoral combination; (3) compound medications which exacerbate the disease; (4) afflictions of the vulnerable points; (5) wind disorders beyond recovery; (6) fevers beyond recovery; (7) cold diseases beyond recovery; (8) unsustainable bodily constituents; and (9) extreme injury caused by elemental demons. See *TMP*, 175–176.

753 The permutations of these twelve contrary humoral imbalances are fully enumerated in *TMP*, 175.
754 See fig. 45; also the illustration of the second root of diagnosis with its three stems of observation (*lta*), pulse palpation (*reg*) and inquiry (*dri ba*), along with their eight branches and thirty-eight leaves, in *TMP*, 21–22, and the translation of the corresponding captions on pp. 177–178.
755 Comments in parenthesis derive from *TMP*, 177–178.
756 See fig. 46; also the illustration of the third root of treatment with its four stems of diet (*zas*), regimen (*spyod*), medication (*sman*), and external therapy (*dpyad*), along with their twenty-seven branches and ninety-eight leaves, in *TMP*, 23–24, and the translation of the corresponding captions on pp. 179–180.
757 These types of food and beverage are all enumerated and illustrated in *TMP*, 179–180. Among them horse flesh, molasses, garlic, and warm milk are suitable for wind disorders; curd, butter, game, dandelion, and water are suitable for bile disorders; while mutton, yak meat, fish, honey, buttermilk, and wine are deemed suitable for phlegm disorders.
758 The appropriate regimen for the treatment of wind disorders includes warm locations and the company of pleasant friends; for bile disorders, cool locations and relaxation; and for phlegm disorders, energetic activity and warm locations. See *TMP*, 179–180.
759 *TMP*, 179–180.
760 The ingredients compounded in broths, medicinal butters, decoctions, powders, pills and *tre-sam* powders are all enumerated and illustrated in *TMP*, 179–180.
761 These are enumerated and illustrated in *TMP*, 179–180.
762 That is to say, medications with a sweet, sour, or salty taste are appropriate for the treatment of wind disorders; those with a sweet, bitter, or astringent taste are suitable for the treatment of bile disorders; and those with a pungent, sour, or astringent taste are suitable for phlegm disorders. As far as potency is concerned, medications with an oily, heavy, or mild potency are appropriate for the treatment of wind disorders; those with a cool, thin, or dull potency are for bile disorders; and those with a sharp, harsh, or light potency are appropriate for phlegm disorders. See *TMP*, 179.
763 Broths are prepared from bones; the four essences of meat, molasses, butter, and garlic; and sheep's head. Medicinal butters are prepared from nutmeg, garlic, myrobalan, five roots (solomon's seal, asparagus, hog fennel, mirabilis, and caltrops), and aconite. Decoctions are prepared from elecampane, moonseed, gentian, and myrobalan. Powders are prepared from camphor, white sandalwood, saffron, and bamboo pith. Pills are prepared from poisons and halite, while the class of *tre-sam* powders is prepared from pomegranate, rhododendron, pongamia, burnt salts, and calcite ash. See *TMP*, 179.
764 The three cathartic procedures for wind disorders are the administering of mild enemata, cleansing combined with pressure on the soles of the feet, and cleansing combined with shaking of the body. The three cathartic procedures for bile disorders include bathing and special purgatives, strong purgatives combined with massage, and mild purgatives including compresses. The two cathartic procedures for phlegm disorders include strong and mild emetics. See *TMP*, 179.
765 These are all enumerated in *TMP*, 179.
766 The Aśoka tree (*Jonesia asoka* Roxb., *mya ngan med pa'i ljon shing*) is famed in the Indian subcontinent for its magnificent red flowers.
767 This quotation is found in the *Root Tantra* (*rTsa ba'i rgyud*). See Drapa Ngonshe, *Four Tantras of Dratang*, 9.
768 For a more detailed analysis, see below, pp. 329–341. Buddhist tradition holds the *Exegetical Tantra* (*bShad rgyud sku yi rgyud*) to have been expounded by Vidyājñāna, the

emanation of the buddha body of Bhaiṣajyaguru, who is identified with the Buddha Vairocana. For an account of his exposition of the *Exegetical Tantra*, see *TMP*, 25–26. The Tibetan text of the *Exegetical Tantra* is contained in Drapa Ngonshe, *Four Tantras of Dratang*, 19–114, and with interlinear commentary in Sangye Gyatso, *Blue Beryl*, 1:51–414.

769 Buddhist tradition holds the *Instructional Tantra* (*Man ngag yon tan gyi rgyud*) to have been expounded by Vidyājñāna, the emanation of the buddha-attributes of Bhaiṣajyaguru, who is identified with the Buddha Ratnasambhava. For an account of his exposition of the *Instructional Tantra*, see *TMP*, 91–92. The Tibetan text of the *Instructional Tantra* is contained in Drapa Ngonshe, *Four Tantras of Dratang*, 115–582, and with interlinear commentary in Sangye Gyatso, *Blue Beryl*, 1:415–end, and 2:536–1153.

770 *SK* reads *bdun* for *bdun cu*.

771 These eight branches of medicine are all illustrated with commentary in *TMP*, vol. 1—general health on pp. 91–106 (plates 31–45); pediatrics on 105–106 (plate 45); gynecological diseases on 107–108 (plate 46); demonic possession on 107–108 (plate 46); wounds and injuries on 109–116 (plates 47–50); poisons on 117–118 (plate 51); the treatment of old age on 119–121 (plates 52–53); and the restoration of virility and treatment of infertility on 121–122 (plate 53).

772 The "eight categories of patients" (*gso yul gyi yan lag brgyad*) therefore comprise general adult patients, children, women, and those who are afflicted by demons, by traumatic injuries, and poison, as well as the elderly and the infertile.

773 Buddhist tradition holds the *Subsequent Tantra* (*Phyi ma phrin las kyi rgyud*) to have been expounded by Vidyājñāna, the emanation of the buddha-activities of Bhaiṣajyaguru, who is identified with the Buddha Amoghasiddhi. For an account of his exposition of the *Subsequent Tantra*, see *TMP*, 123–124. The Tibetan text of the *Subsequent Tantra* is contained in Drapa Ngonshe, *Four Tantras of Dratang*, 583–705, and with interlinear commentary in Sangye Gyatso, *Blue Beryl*, 2:1154–1468. The text is also illustrated with commentary in *TMP*, 123–170 and 279–326.

774 On these four distinctions, see *TMP*, 165–168 (plates 75–76). Specifically, the treatment of imaginary and ostensible diseases is discussed on 165–166, and the treatment of absolute and dependent diseases on 167–168.

775 Among these four general categories of disease, it is said that there are one hundred and one "absolute diseases" harmful to the life span, which can be cured by diet, regimen, medication, and external therapy. There are also one hundred and one "dependent diseases" associated with past actions, where the patient may die even when treated by a skilled physician. In addition, there are one hundred and one "ostensible diseases" which may pass without treatment or with inadequate treatment, but which may pass even sooner when treated. Lastly, there are one hundred and one "imaginary diseases" caused by demons which are cured by proper diagnosis of the pulse and urine and the performance of appropriate rituals. All of these may be further subsumed into two categories—diseases associated with heat and those associated with cold. See *TMP*, 165–169.

776 The same explanation is given and illustrated in *TMP*, 165–166 (plate 75).

777 For a detailed presentation of pulse palpation in Tibetan medicine, see *TMP*, 123–140 (plates 54–62) and 279–296.

778 There is a detailed discussion on urinalysis and examination of the tongue in Tibetan medicine in *TMP*, 139–150 (plates 62–67) and 295–306.

779 These are explained below in detail, p. 339, and illustrated in *TMP*, 165–166 and 321–322.

780 After considering diagnostics, the appropriate curative treatments may then be applied. Among them, there are eight classes of tranquilizing agents, of which it is said that

decoctions "should be administered at the inception of a disease since they are sharp and swift-acting." Medicinal powders "should be prescribed if these are ineffective." Pills "should be given if the disease remains unsubdued." Pastes "help draw out chronic and tenacious diseases." Medicinal butters "increase physical stamina and clear the senses." Medicinal ash "mostly alleviates diseases of a cold nature." Medicinal concentrates "mostly alleviate diseases of a hot nature." Medicinal wine "largely relieves wind disorders." Gemstone and precious metal compounds "are expensive but counter all complications and relapses." Lastly, herbal compounds "are inexpensive and effective against sudden diseases." See *TMP*, 149–150 (plate 67) and 305–306.

781 Among the seven cathartic procedures, preliminary oil therapy involves an external massage application of vegetable oils, butter, bone marrow, and animal extracts or an internal injection of oils through the mouth or rectum. The former is recommended in the treatment of skin or head rashes and the latter for the treatment of internal disorders, especially for the elderly, the debilitated, malnourished, or infertile patient, and those with wind disorders or defective vision. Then, among the five main cathartics (*sbyong byed dngos gzhi las lnga*), purgatives or laxatives (*bshal*) "expel bile and blood disorders"; emetics (*skyugs*) "upwardly extract phlegm or gastric disorders"; nasal medications or snuff (*sna sman*) "relieve disorders of the area above the collar bone"; mild enemas (*'jam rtsi*) "relieve wind and intestinal disorders"; while strong enemas (*ni ru ha*) "relieve constipation and urine retention." There is also the supplementary procedure of channel cleansing (*rtsa sbyong*) by means of powerful drugs. See *TMP*, 149–154 (plates 67–69), also 305–310.

782 Among these six techniques of external therapy, bloodletting (*gtar ga*) "extracts the impure blood produced by diseases of heat"; moxibustion (*bsreg pa*) "debilitates cold diseases when dry leaves, particularly of gerbera, are ignited at specific points on the body"; medicinal compresses (*dugs*) "are applied in the treatment of a humoral imbalance in which phlegm predominates"; fomentation (*lums*) "is an antidote for humoral imbalances with a predominance of bile"; massage with ointment (*byug pa*) "remedies humoral imbalances with a predominance of wind; while minor surgery (*thur ma*) removes "purulence, tumors, fluid, etc." See *TMP*, 153–164 (plates 69–74), also 309–320.

783 The enumeration of twenty-three includes the eight main and two supplementary tranquilizing agents, the seven cathartic procedures, and the six techniques of external therapy; whereas the enumeration of eighteen subsumes medicinal ash, medicinal concentrates, medicinal wine, gemstone and precious metal compounds, and herbal compounds within the five primary tranquilizing agents, viz., decoctions, medicinal powders, pills, pastes, and medicinal butters.

784 These topics provide the framework for the *Exegetical Tantra* (*bShad rgyud*), on which see above, pp. 326–327.

785 Human embryology is discussed in ch. 2 of the *Exegetical Tantra*. See the summary and illustrations in *TMP*, 25–26 (plate 5) and 181–182.

786 This metaphorical representation of human anatomy is discussed in ch. 3 of the *Exegetical Tantra*. See the summaries and illustrations in *TMP*, 27–28 (plate 6) and 183–184. The anatomical disposition of the bones, internal organs, and so forth is presented in *TMP*, 29–32 (plates 7–8).

787 The proportionate measurements of the bodily constituents are discussed in ch. 4 of the *Exegetical Tantra*. See the summaries and illustrations in *TMP*, 27–28 (plate 6) and 183–184. Among the bodily constituents, "the chyle produced by the digestive metabolism is transformed into blood in the liver, enabling the other bodily constituents to form in succession. The impure residue of metabolized chyle forms decomposing phlegm.

The residue of the metabolism of blood into muscle tissue becomes the bile of the gall bladder. The residue of the metabolism of muscle tissue into adipose tissue becomes the secretions of the bodily orifices. The residue of the metabolism of adipose tissue into bone becomes perspiration and sebaceous excrements of the skin. The residue of the metabolism of bone tissue into marrow becomes the teeth, nails, and hair. The residue of the metabolism of bone marrow into reproductive fluid becomes the skin and grease. Finally the residue of the metabolism of reproductive fluid into vital fluids becomes semen or menstrual blood. The whole process beginning with the intake of food and ending with the forming of semen lasts for six days." On this metabolic process, see *TMP*, 47–48.

788 Among these four types of channels, the channel of embryonic formation (*chags pa'i rtsa*), during the course of embryonic development, is said to extend upwards from the navel to generate the brain and the nervous system, outwards to generate the blood vessels, and downwards to generate the genitals. Among the three energy channels of the subtle body, as outlined in tantra texts, the right-side channel (*ro ma*) generates the channels of existence (*srid pa'i rtsa*), or blood vessels, and the channels of connection (*'brel pa'i rtsa*), including the capillaries. The course of the life span principle (*tshe gnas pa'i rtsa*) refers to the dispersal of seminal life-essences which are said to circulate through the body according to the lunar cycle, giving rise to white generative fluids that produce bone tissue in the embryo and red generative fluids that produce blood, flesh, and skin. These, along with the nervous system, are all summarized and illustrated in *TMP*, 33–42 (plates 9–13); also 189–198.

789 The summary of the anterior and posterior vulnerable points of the body, including the solid and hollow viscera, is presented and illustrated in *TMP*, 43–46 (plates 14–15) and 199–202.

790 On this metabolic process, see above, note 787; also *TMP*, 43–46, especially 45 (plates 14–15), and 199–202.

791 This analysis of the bodily constituents, impurities, and humors, deriving from ch. 5 of the *Exegetical Tantra*, is summarized in *TMP*, 47–48 (plate 16), and 203–204. See also above, notes 747–748, and 750.

792 On the distinctions between neutral and positive or negative actions, see below, pp. 421–426.

793 Ch. 6 of the *Exegetical Tantra* explains the distinctions of sex, age, and natural constitution which are determined by humoral combinations, emphasizing the character traits and dietary preferences of those with a preponderance of wind, bile, or phlegm. See *TMP*, 47–48 (plate 16) and 203–204.

794 The diverse signs of physical decay which can be observed by a discerning physician are discussed in ch. 7 of the *Exegetical Tantra*. See *TMP*, 47—52 (plates 16–18) and 203–208; also Dorje 2005, 155–181.

795 These are all discussed in chs. 8–12 of the *Exegetical Tantra*, and illustrated in *TMP*, 53–54 (plate 19) and 209–210.

796 This analysis of the primary causes of disease derives from ch. 8 of the *Exegetical Tantra*. For a discussion of the three poisons and fundamental ignorance from the perspective of Buddhist phenomenology, see below, pp. 588–589 and pp. 579–580, respectively.

797 The secondary causes of disease are discussed in ch. 9 of the *Exegetical Tantra*. See also Sangye Gyatso, *Blue Beryl*, 1:164ff.

798 This process whereby the secondary causes of disease gather and arise, at first covertly and later manifestly, is analyzed by Sangye Gyatso, *Blue Beryl*, 1:165.

799 *SK*, 309, reads *spong ba'i rkyen* for *slong ba'i rkyen*.

800 The specific indications of wind diseases include, for example, "bitter, light, and

rough food, sexual exhaustion, fasting, insomnia, vigorous activity on an empty stomach, excessive loss of blood, diarrhoea, vomiting, exposure to cold winds, periods of mourning or crying, mental anguish, unrestrained chatter, protracted consumption of non-nutritious food, and the retention or straining of natural functions." The specific indications of bile disorders include "sharp, hot, or oily food; or meat, butter, molasses, and wine; surging anger, sleeping in direct sunlight, engaging in hard physical activity, athletic pursuits, being injured while falling from horseback, or being wounded." The specific indications of phlegm disorders include "bitter, sweet, heavy, cooling, and oily foods; herbal concoctions of dandelion, milk, goat meat, fat, bone marrow, stale oils or greens, sour radishes, raw garlic, cold water, tea, unboiled milk, immature curd, unripe grains or pulses; as well as resting after a heavy meal, sleeping in the daytime or in a damp place, and being lightly dressed in winter." See *TMP*, 53–53.

801 The inception of disease through the localization of the humors in specific pathways is discussed in ch. 10 of the *Exegetical Tantra*; see also *TMP*, 53–54. This means that at their inception, wind disorders are located in the bones, bile disorders in the blood and perspiration, and those of phlegm elsewhere. Pathological transformations then settle in the skin and muscle tissue, the channels, ligaments, bones, and internal viscera.

802 The excess, deficiency, or mutual aggravation of the three humors with respect to the bodily constituents and the three impurities are discussed in ch. 11 of the *Exegetical Tantra*; see also *TMP*, 53–54.

803 *SK*, 309, reads *gsum* for *bzhi*, but see Sangye Gyatso, *Blue Beryl*, 1:182; also *TMP*, 53–54.

804 Sangye Gyatso, *Blue Beryl*, 1:191–192, adds that there are no sources which precisely enumerate these twenty-five vulnerable disorders, and that the point is to illustrate how their multilayered permutations are limitless. For example, the third to the twenty-fifth may also occur in various combinations, so that they come to number seven thousand eight hundred altogether. Each of these in turn may partake of nine circumstances (three degrees of excess, three degrees of deficiency, and three degrees of mutual aggravation), raising their number of permutations to seventy thousand and two hundred. Further complexities are successively added, until the number of permutations is seen to be limitless.

805 Chs. 13–22 of the *Exegetical Tantra* consider these four topics. Among them, regimen (*spyod lam*) is the subject of chs. 13–15, on which see *TMP*, 55–56 (plate 20) and 211–212. Dietetics (*'tsho ba zas*) is the subject of chs. 16–18, on which see *TMP*, 57–60 (plates 21 and 22) and 213–216. Compounded medications (*sbyor ba'i sman*) are the subject of chs. 19–21, on which see *TMP*, 61–82 (plates 23–33) and 217–238. Lastly, external therapy (*dpyad pa*) and surgical instruments (*cha byad*) are the subjects of ch. 22, on which see *TMP*, 83–84 (plate 34) and 239–240.

806 As summarized and illustrated in *TMP*, 55–56 (plate 20), continuous daily regimen may enhance the life span by the ingestion of myrobalan and compounds made of gemstones and precious metals, or by wearing protective cords, abandoning dangerous pursuits, regulating sleep and sexual intercourse, and undertaking regular ablutions and massage therapy. It may also enhance the performance of mundane actions which are of benefit to society and actions associated with the authentic practice of Buddhism. Note that *SK*, 310, reads *rgyun tu spyod pa* for *rgyun du spyod pa* and *tshe rkyang* for *tshe rgyang*.

807 As illustrated in *TMP*, 53–54 (plate 20), seasonal regimen (*dus spyod*) refers to the modes of conduct suitable for the six distinct seasons of the year, i.e., early winter, late winter, spring, dry summer, wet summer, and autumn. For example, in early winter and especially in late winter, one should adopt a nutritious diet of sweet, sour, and salty foods, meat broth, milk, oily foods, molasses, and wine. At the same time one should massage the body with sesame oil, wear warm clothing, and stay in the warmest part of the house.

During springtime, one should adopt a diet of bitter, pungent, and astringent foods, barley, roasted meat, honey, hot water, and ginger decoctions. Physical exercise, pea-flour massage, and lingering under trees is also recommended. In the dry summer season, the diet should consist of sweet, oily, light, and cooling foods, such as honey, rice, and beef. One should avoid direct sunlight, bathe in cool water, drink only diluted wine, and wear fine silk or cotton, while promenading in cool shady breezes. During the wet summer season the diet should comprise sweet, sour, and salty foods, such as buttermilk, mutton, and strong wine, and one should keep warm by sunbathing. Then, in the autumn, the diet should comprise sweet, bitter, and astringent foods, and one should wear clothes scented with camphor and white sandalwood and frequent fragrant meadows.

808 Occasional regimen (*gnas skabs kyi spyod pa*), as summarized and illustrated in *TMP*, 53–54 (plate 20) means that natural functions should not be suppressed. These include eating when hungry, drinking when thirsty, yawning when tired, coughing when there is mucus or salivation, and defecating, urinating, and ejaculating sperm, as nature requires.

809 As summarized and illustrated in *TMP*, 57–60 (plates 21–22), foods comprise grains, meats, oils and fats, aromatic herbs or vegetables, and assorted cooked dishes; while beverages include milk, water, and wine. All of these are considered in terms of their medicinal properties.

810 Dietary restrictions are recommended in respect of incompatible foods and beverages—avoiding poisoned foods, or yak meat combined with pork, fish with poultry, fresh curd and new wine, milk and fruits, eggs and fish, chicken with curd, and so forth.

811 Moderation in diet should be universally observed, ensuring a balance between lightness and heaviness, warmth and coolness. In particular, cool and heavy foods should be taken sparingly, so that food occupies two parts of the stomach and drink one part, leaving the remainder for the relevant humors. Over-consumption and under-nourishment are to be avoided.

812 As explained in ch. 19 of the *Exegetical Tantra* (*TMP*, 61–62, plate 23), medications are analyzed according to their six possible tastes: sweet, salty, sour, hot, bitter, and astringent. They may also partake of eight distinct potencies—heaviness, oiliness, coldness, dullness, lightness, roughness, heat, and sharpness—that give rise to seventeen subsidiary attributes, on which see Sangye Gyatso, *Blue Beryl*, 1:250–251. The three post-digestive tastes are sweet, bitter, or sour.

813 While some medications will correspond to the six basic tastes—sweet, salty, sour, hot, bitter, and astringent—most partake of the fifty-seven compounded tastes, which are enumerated in Sangye Gyatso, *Blue Beryl*, 1:253–254. The compounds may comprise two, three, four, five, or all the tastes. Tibetan materia medica are generally classified according to their potency. As enumerated in ch. 20 of the *Exegetical Tantra*, and illustrated in *TMP*, 61–78 (plates 23–31), these include (1) gemstones and precious metals (*rin po che'i sman*), such as gold, silver, copper, iron, pearl, conch, coral, and lapis; (2) minerals (*rdo'i sman*), such as iron hydroxide, whitespar, pyrolusite, haematite, magnetite, halysite, ophicalcite, marcasite, tourmaline, pyrite, cinnabar, minium, glauconite, tin, realgar, orpiment, zinc, chalcedony, limestone, slaked lime, and alabaster; (3) earth-based medications (*sa'i sman*), such as sand, ochre, saltpeter, natron, sulphur, vitriol, lichen, and bitumen; (4) wood or tree-derived medications (*shing sman*), such as camphor, sandalwood, and eaglewood; (5) nectarous medications (*rtsi sman*), such as bezoar, bamboo pith, saffron, safflower, marigold, cardamom, nutmeg, clove, cubeb, musk, and bear bile; (5) plateau medications (*thang sman*), such as kapok, cumin, fennel, dill seed, bishop's weed, saxifrage, hemp, musk mallow, senna, balsam apple, grapes, coriander, sea buckthorn, quince, pomegranate, pepper, ginger, capsicum, cinnamon, bonducella, asafoetida, marsh nut, frankincense, pine resin, sal ammoniac, alum, rock

salt, halite, glauber's salt, borax, myrobalan, hog plum, kidney beans, mango, rose apple, persimmon, elecampane, fleabane root, costus, pongam oil, turmeric, sweetflag, orchid, delphinium, liquorice, moonseed, blackberry, birthwort, ash, pine, acacia, sesban, calabash, and wood apple; (6) herbal medications (*sngo sman*), such as lagotis, primula, sage, swertia, saxifrage, dragonhead, gentian, cerastium, sedum, spleenwort, larkspur, soroseris, dittander, fritillary, ragwort, pleusospermum, hog fennel, chrysanthemum, blue poppy, dodder, wild rose, clover, arenaria, angelica, barberry, henbane, mulberry, iris, ginseng, marrubium, cobra lily, fenugreek, bellflower, figwort, starwort, tansy, lakeweed, burrweed, medlar, marsh mallow, bergenia, wolfberry, bush clover, ephedra, pennycress, sorrel, incarvillea, ergot, anemone, buttercup, rhododendron, clematis, plantain, lettuce, chickweed, asparagus, solomon's seal and caltrops; and (7) animal products derived from horn, bone, flesh, bile, fat, brain, hide, hair, urine, feces, and whole organisms, such as crustaceans. Modern documentations of Tibetan materia medica, including excellent photographs, Latin identifications, and detailed explanations, may be found in Karma Chopel, *Illustrations*, Gawei Dorje, *Immaculate Crystal Mirror*, and Menpa Dawa, *Drawings*.

814 On this distinction between tranquilizing medications (*zhi byed pa'i sman*) and cathartic medications (*sbyongs byed pa'i sman*), which is summarized in *TMP*, 81–82 (plate 33), see above, p. 329.

815 This topic is illustrated and summarized in *TMP*, 83–84 (plate 34) and 239–240.

816 Mild therapy (*'jam pa'i dpyad*) includes cold and warm compresses (*dug*), which can alleviate fevers, angina, colic, nasal bleeding, indigestion, tumors, and certain kidney disorders. It also includes fomentation (*lums*), which can alleviate lameness, muscular spasm, wounds, swellings, serum disorders, spinal deformities, and gynecological diseases. Lastly, it includes massage with ointments (*byugs pa*), which can alleviate roughness of the skin, blood deficiencies, debility, defective vision, insomnia, indigestion, poisoning, and loss of appetite. These are described in detail in the *Subsequent Tantra*, chs. 22–24, on which see *TMP*, 163–164 (plate 74). Note that *SK*, 310, reads *'jam po* for *'jam pa*.

817 Rough therapy (*rtsub pa'i dpyad*) includes bloodletting (*gtar*), which can alleviate fevers, swellings, wounds, podagra, ulcers, serum disorders, leprosy, and erysipelas; moxibustion with gerbera leaves (*sreg*), which can alleviate indigestion, dropsy, morbid pallor, tumors, bile and serum disorders, epilepsy, and phlegm disorders; and minor surgery (*dbug pa*) with stylets, which can alleviate tumors, phlegm disorders, indigestion, blood and serum diseases, abscesses, and dropsy. These are described in detail in the *Subsequent Tantra*, chs. 20–21 and 25, on which see *TMP*, 153–165 (plates 69–74).

818 These surgical instruments—probes, forceps, lancets, stylets, cannulas, cupping horns and bowls, and so forth, are described in ch. 22 of the *Exegetical Tantra*. See the summary and illustrations in *TMP*, 83–84. Comments in parenthesis derive from that source. Rigorous therapy (*drag po'i dpyad*) includes the four techniques of incision (*'dral ba*), excision (*gcod pa*), scraping (*'drud pa*), and extraction (*'byin pa*), which are associated with minor surgery.

819 See above, pp. 333–334.

820 The benefits of such elixirs are discussed, along with their suitability in specific geographical locations, the body types for which they are recommended, and their various compounding methods, in ch. 23 of the *Exegetical Tantra* and ch. 90 of the *Subsequent Tantra*. For summaries and illustrations, see *TMP*, 35–36 (plate 35), and 119–122 (plates 52–53). These include elixirs compounded of white garlic with clarified butter to prevent wind disorders, refined bitumen, gold, silver, copper, and iron ash to prevent diseases of bile, and capsicum with butter and honey to alleviate phlegm disorders.

821 Diagnosis is the subject of chs. 23–26 of the *Exegetical Tantra*, which are summarized and illustrated in *TMP*, 85–86 (plate 35) and 241–242. The actual process of diagnosis is based on visual inspection, pulse palpation, and verbal inquiry, which is analyzed in ch. 23.

822 The physician is obliged to understand the causes and symptoms of humoral imbalance, as well as the suitability of certain remedies. On this, see Sangye Gyatso, *Blue Beryl*, 1:365–367.

823 Diagnosis through subterfuge, which is discussed in ch. 24 of the *Exegetical Tantra*, includes the questioning of others before the physician has even seen the patient and the making of an impressive instantaneous diagnosis when the patient describes his or her symptoms. Failing that, the physician should employ delaying tactics and inference until a correct diagnosis is made. In the worst-case scenarios, the physician is advised to prevaricate until the patient divulges further information. See also Sangye Gyatso, *Blue Beryl*, 1:366–370.

824 This is the subject-matter of ch. 26 of the *Exegetical Tantra*. For further detail, see Sangye Gyatso, *Blue Beryl*, 1:370–373. Each of these alternatives is considered in terms of the physician, the medication, the nurse, and the patient. Nominal treatment is applied to incurable patients whose life span has not yet completely terminated and who can be helped somewhat by an appropriate diet and regimen.

825 These three sorts of therapeutic principles are discussed in chs. 27–28 of the *Exegetical Tantra*; and illustrated with summaries in *TMP*, 85–86 (plate 35) and 241–242.

826 For further detail, see Sangye Gyatso, *Blue Beryl*, 1:374.

827 Sangye Gyatso, *Blue Beryl*, 1:376.

828 Comments in brackets in the following description of the nine special therapeutic principles derive from the text and illustrations in *TMP*, 85–86 (plate 35). Cf. also Sangye Gyatso, *Blue Beryl*, 1:378–379.

829 These common anabolic and catabolic methods of treatment are examined in ch. 29 of the *Exegetical Tantra*, on which see the summaries and illustrations in *TMP*, 87–88 (plate 36) and 243–244. Among them, anabolic procedures entail a rich and nutritious diet, mild enema, purging, massage, and a regimen of sound sleep and relaxation to increase vitality. Catabolic procedures employ tranquilizing agents and cathartic procedures as well as fasting or light diets and strenuous exercise to reduce excess energy. For detail, see Sangye Gyatso, *Blue Beryl*, 1:384–388.

830 These special treatments for fevers and colds, integrating regimen, diet, medication, and external therapy, are discussed in ch. 30 of the *Exegetical Tantra*. See Sangye Gyatso, *Blue Beryl*, 1:388–391; also *TMP*, 87–88 (plate 36) and 243–244. Note that *SK*, 312, reads *snum gro* for *snum dro*.

831 The six primary attributes of a physician are finally discussed in ch. 30 of the *Exegetical Tantra*. See Sangye Gyatso, *Blue Beryl*, 1:392–394, along with the summary and illustrations in *TMP*, 89–90 (plate 37) and 245–246. Comments in parenthesis here derive from *TMP*, 89.

832 On the spiritual cultivation of loving-kindness (*byams pa*) and compassion (*snying rje*), see above, note 272.

833 As indicated in Sangye Gyatso, *Blue Beryl*, 1:393–394 (*TMP*, plate 37), the six commitments of a physician are to establish an attitude of respect for medical teachers, books, and colleagues, as well as for their patients, and to establish an absence of revulsion for pus and blood. The two commitments to be retained are to regard all archetypal lineage holders as protector deities and the apparatus as their hand emblems. The three that bring about understanding enable one to regard all medicines as precious gemstones, nectar, and sacred substances.

834 The twelve defects of an inferior doctor, as explained in Sangye Gyatso, *Blue Beryl*, 1:397–398, and summarized with illustrations in *TMP*, 89–90 (plate 37), are (1) the absence of an authentic lineage, like a fox seizing a king's throne; (2) ignorance of medical treatises, like one born blind who is shown material objects; (3) lack of observational skills or experience, as if setting out on an unknown path; (4) ignorance of diagnostic methods, like someone wandering abroad without friends; (5) inability to carry out pulse palpation or urinalysis, like a bird-hunter who cannot release a hunting bird; (6) inability to make predictions concerning diseases, like a chieftain who cannot deliver a speech; (7) ignorance of therapeutic principles, like someone shooting at a target in the dark; (8) ignorance of diet and regimen, like someone ceding authority to an enemy; (9) inability to prepare tranquilizing agents, like a farmer who does not know agriculture; (10) inability to prepare cathartic compounds, like someone pouring water down a mound of sand; (11) lack of medical instruments, like a warrior without armor or weapons; and (12) ignorance of bloodletting and moxibustion, like a thief in an unattended house.

835 Within the Brāhmaṇical tradition in general, there are considered to be six subsidiary sciences necessary for the comprehension of Vedic texts (*ṣadvedāṅga*), namely, ritual sacrifice (*kalpa*), elocution (*śikṣā*), prosody (*chandas*), etymology (*nirukta*), grammar (*vyākaraṇa*), and astronomy/ astrology (*jyotiṣa*). Among these, according to the mainstream tradition of Indo-Tibetan Buddhism, Sanskrit grammar, which has already been discussed, is classed among the major sciences, while prosody and astrology are included among the minor or subsidiary sciences, and etymology is in some respects related to the minor science of synonymics or lexicography. Ritual sacrifice and elocution are replaced in the Buddhist classification by poetics and dramaturgy. On the six branches of Vedic science, see, e.g., Basham 1959, 164.

836 This citation has not been located in any of the three versions of the *Tantra of the Renunciation* (*Abhyudayatantra*), namely the *Tantra of the Renunciation of Śrīheruka* (*Śrīherukābhyudayatantra*, T 374) and two versions of the *Tantra of the Renunciation of Vajravārāhī* (T 378–379). Nor is it found in the *Sūtra of Renunciation* (*Abhiniṣkramanasūtra*, T 301).

837 Traditional Indian astral and mathematical literature is surveyed in Pingree 1981. The non-Buddhist traditions of astrology are exemplified, in particular, by the works of Varāhamihira, whose *Fivefold Textbook Calculation* (*Pañcasiddhāntaka*) includes tracts of Indian, Bactrian, and Alexandrian Greek origin. See Basham 1959, 491–494. Regarding the influence in Tibet of this anthology and the *Great Compilation* (*Bṛhatsaṃhitā*), attributed to the same author, see also Henning 2007, 99, 175, 220, 302, and 356. Buddhist sources on astrology include important canonical works such as the *Sūtra of the Nucleus of the Sun* (*Sūryagarbhasūtra*, T 41), the *Tantra of the Wheel of Time* (*Kālacakratantra*, T 362), Puṇḍarīka's *Taintless Light* (*Vimalaprabhā*, T 845), and Vasubandhu's *Treasury of Phenomenology* (*Abhidharmakośa*). For Jamgon Kongtrul's account of the origins of this genre, see Ngawang Zangpo 2010, 412–416. The indigenous Tibetan commentarial literature is also extensive. See Drakpa, *Inventory of Tibetan Treatises*, 24–42; and the online listing at www.tbrc.org, T203. These Tibetan works include the commentarial traditions of Sakya (represented by Chogyal Phakpa and Yungton Dorjepel), Zhalu (represented by Buton Rinchendrub), Tsurphu (represented by Karmapa Rangjung Dorje and Pawo Tsuklak Trengwa), the practical "error correction" system (of Go Lotsāwa), the Phugpa system (of Phugpa Lhundrub Gyatso and Norzang Gyatso), the New Phugpa system (represented by Sangye Gyatso and Lochen Dharmaśrī), and the Jonang system (of Drakpa Pelzang and Banda Gelek Gyatso). Henning 2007 reviews much of this material in his excellent work. Many of the calculations he presents derive

from Lochen Dharmaśrī's influential treatise entitled *Sunlight Instructions on Astrology* (*rTsis kyi man ngag nyin mor byed pa'i snang ba*), and Sangye Gyatso's *White Beryl*. The last of these sources extensively analyzes Indo-Tibetan astrology (*dkar rtsis*) in chs. 3–19; its companion treatise, the *Removal of the Tarnish of Deluded Appearances*, covers similar subjects in chs. 1–38. A number of contemporary articles on Indo-Tibetan astrology have also been recently published in Jampa Trinle's *Great Compendium of Tibetan Astrological Science* (*Bod kyi rtsis rig kun 'dus chen mo*) (Chengdu: Sichuan mi rigs dpe skrun khang, 1998), vols. 1–2.

838 For a brief description of this reification process from the Nyingma perspective, see Dudjom Rinpoche 1991, 1:54–56. Jamgon Kongtrul's explanation of the unfolding cycle of dependent origination is presented below, pp. 576–611.

839 The outer and inner worlds respectively form the subject matter of the first two chapters of the *Tantra of the Wheel of Time*, comprising the *Lokadhātupaṭala* and the *Ādhyātmapaṭala*, which are discussed in detail in the commentaries—see Kilty 2004, 75–157 on the former and 161–207 on the latter; also Henning 2007 on the former; and Wallace 2001 on the latter. The threefold distinction of the energy channels, currents, and generative essences (*rtsa rlung thig le*) within the subtle body are discussed in detail in ch. 2 of the *Tantra of the Wheel of Time*. In addition to the aforementioned sources, for Jamgon Kongtrul's presentation of the functionality of the subtle body from the standpoint of the tantras in general, see Guarisco and McLeod 2005, 169–185; and for the presentation and illustration of these same subtle physiological processes from the perspective of the medical tradition, see *TMP*, 39–40 and 195–196. The Sun, Moon and Rāhu (the eclipser) are symbolic names referring respectively to the left-side energy channel (*lalanā, rkyang ma*), the right-side energy channel (*rasanā, ro ma*), and the central energy channel (*avadhūti, dbu ma*) within the subtle body.

840 In other words, the movement of vital energy within the energy channels of an ordinary person's subtle body is said to correlate precisely with the apparent geocentric and heliocentric movement of planetary bodies. See below, pp. 346–348.

841 The term "vital energy" (*vāyu, rlung*) has been frequently mentioned above, in the context of the medical tradition. Here, within the context of the "subtle body" of an individual person, rather than the coarse physical body, it is said that there are ten kinds of vital energy or subtle winds which flow through the 72,000 energy channels (*nāḍī, rtsa 'dab*) of the body. These sustain life and include the energies which support various conceptual states within the individual's mind. At the subtlest level, subtle mind and vital energy are thought of as a single entity. The ten kinds of vital energy comprise five inner vital energies (*nang gi rlung lnga*) which influence the body's inner motility, and five outer vital energies (*phyi'i rlung lnga*) which have specific effects on the outward motility of the body. The former are the vital energies associated with the five elements (earth, water, fire, wind, and space) and their respective color-tones (yellow, white, red, green, and blue). The latter, as indicated above, comprise life-breath (*prāṇa, srog 'dzin*), muscular movement (*vyāna*), digestion (*samāna*), semiotic / vocal movement (*udāna*), and reproduction / waste disposal (*apāna*).

The movement of vital energy through the energy channels of the subtle body is refined in the context of the perfection stage of meditation. Ordinarily, in the case of individuals who have not cultivated such practices, both vital energy and subtle mind are diffused via the right and left energy channels and thereby come to permeate the entire network of the body's minor channels. This dissipated vital energy is known as the "vital energy of past actions" (*las kyi rlung*) because it is activated by dissonant mental states and the influence of past actions predominates, obscuring the inner radiance of the subtle mind. However, when the practices of the perfection stage of meditation are applied, the knots which block their combined movement through the energy centers (*cakra*) located on the central energy channel are untied and both vital energy and subtle mind enter, abide, and dissolve within the central energy channel of the body and then the non-conceptual inner radiance arises, for which reason it becomes known as the "vital energy of pristine cognition" (*ye shes kyi rlung*). From the fruitional perspective of the tantras, as given here, the vital energy of pristine cognition within the central channel is the natural state, from which the vital energies of past actions arise and circulate. Cf. Jamgon Kongtrul's presentation in Guarisco and McLeod 2005, 176–180; also Kilty 2004, 182–183; and Wallace 2001, 56–58.

842 This arising of the material elements through "lightness" and through "motility" accords with the Sāṃkhya (*grangs can pa*) system of Indian philosophy, for Jamgon Kongtrul's analysis of which, see below, p. 407. The *Tantra of the Wheel of Time* emphasizes the interrelatedness of the microcosmic and macrocosmic aspects, specifically associating the respective motion of the so-called "five peaceful planetary bodies" (*zhi gza' lnga*)—Rāhu, Moon, Mercury, Venus, and Ketu—with the generation in nature (*prakṛti, rang bzhin*) of the corresponding elemental sequence—space, wind, fire, water, and earth—and the respective motion of the so-called "five wrathful planetary bodies"—Saturn, Jupiter, Mars, Sun, and Kālāgni—with the generation in primal self (*pradhāna, gtso bo*) of the corresponding elemental sequence—earth, water, fire, wind, and space. For these correspondences between the planetary bodies and the elements, see the chart in Henning 2007, 162. On the distinction between peaceful and wrathful planetary bodies, see also Kilty 2004, 109, and especially Henning 2007, 55–56. The main point is that the former category—Venus, Mercury, and so forth—are within the orbit of the earth and are therefore calculated differently from the outer planets, such as Mars, Jupiter, and Saturn, where the calculations also have to take into account the apparent swing of the Sun on either side of the earth.

843 The apparent orbital motion of the planetary bodies is analyzed according to four quadrants (*rkang pa bzhi*). These four phases of planetary motion (*'gros bzhi*) comprise the "fast" northward motion of the perihelion (*śīghra, myur 'gros*), the "slow" southward motion of the aphelion (*manda, dal 'gros*), the "retrograde" westward motion commencing at the southern limit (*vakra, 'khyogs 'gros*), and the "advancing" eastward motion commencing at the northern limit (*nirgama, 'byung 'gros*). Henning 2007, 56, points out that in the case of the outer or wrathful planetary bodies, the slow motion corresponds to true heliocentric longitude and the fast motion to true geocentric longitude. As for the calculations applicable in terms of these four quadrants, see, e.g., the example of Mars in Henning 2007, 70–71; also 287–288, where these four aspects of planetary motion are summarized.

844 On the external dimensions of the fire and wind elemental maṇḍalas, see Wallace 2001, 68; also Kilty 2004, 79–81.

845 According to the prevailing view of Indian cosmology, an aeon of cosmic or cyclical time (*kalpa*) comprises fourteen secondary cycles (*manvantara*), each of which lasts 306,720,000 years. Each secondary cycle is said to contain seventy-one "great ages" (*mahāyuga*), and each of these is further subdivided into four ages (*caturyuga*) which are of decreasing duration and known respectively as the Perfect Age (*kṛtayuga*), the Third Age (*tretāyuga*), the Second Age (*dvāparayuga*), and the Black or Degenerate Age (*kaliyuga*). Among them, the perfect age is replete with wealth, righteousness, sensual pleasure, and well-being, while the third age lacks one of these attributes, the second lacks two, and the degenerate age lacks all but sensual pleasure. Since these four ages represent a gradual decline in meritorious activities, special meditative practices and spiritual antidotes are associated with each in turn. Specifically, the Perfect Age is most

suited to the practice of the *Kriyā Tantra*; the Third Age, to that of the *Caryā Tantra*; the Second Age, to that of the *Yoga Tantra*; and the present Black or Degenerate Age, to that of the *Unsurpassed Yoga Tantra*. According to the *Wheel of Time*, the four ages are calculated differently, each being said to endure for 5,400 years. See Kilty 2004, 45.

846 See Wallace 2001, 59–60, and Kilty 2004, 79–80, on the mere emptiness or vacuity of the external world. Cf. also the description in Pruden 1998–1990, 474–478. Jamgon Kongtrul's account of the four ages, the subsequent vacuity of planetary bodies, and their correlation with the subtle body is found in Kalu Rinpoche Translation Group 1995, 164–170.

847 For a Tibetan description of inner radiance (*prabhāsvara, 'od gsal*) experienced at the moment of death, see Dorje 2005, 225–234.

848 The odd-numbered solar mansions therefore comprise Aries, Gemini, Leo, Libra, Sagittarius, and Aquarius, while the even-numbered solar mansions comprise Taurus, Cancer, Virgo, Scorpio, and Capricorn. See Wallace 2001, 96–98.

849 On the ascendant conjunctions (*dus sbyor*) pertaining to the twelve solar mansions, see also Henning 2007, 201, and Kilty 2004, 110–121; and on the correlation of the breathing cycle with the twelve ascendant signs, Kilty 2004, 679.

850 See Henning 2007, 12; also Kilty 2004, 188 and the chart on 602.

851 The functionality and artfulness of covert intention, designed to induce non-Buddhists towards the Buddhist teachings, is examined in, e.g., Dudjom Rinpoche 1991, 1:218–222. The reference to the "self" here would suggest that the perspective of the Sāṃkhya school is being artfully co-opted. For Jamgon Kongtrul's interpretation of this philosophical perspective, see below, pp. 405–408.

852 See above, note 845.

853 Henning 2007, 321–342, conveniently summarizes the distinctions between the Tsurphu and Phugpa schools of calendrical astrology in Tibet. The former, founded by Karmapa III Rangjung Dorje (1284–1339) and developed by Pawo Tsuklak Trengwa (1504–1566), follows the practical system of astrology (*byed rtsis*) which adherents of the *Tantra of the Wheel of Time* are said to have artfully absorbed from non-Buddhist sources, while the Phugpa school, based on the writings of Phugpa Lhundrub Gyatso (fl. fifteenth c.) and Norzang Gyatso (1423–1513) adopts a modified textbook system of calculation (*grub rtsis*), taking into account discrepancies between the solar longitudinal calculations of the *Tantra of the Wheel of Time* applicable in India, and those that would apply in Tibet. Both the Tsurphu and Phugpa systems continue to produce annual almanacs, inside and outside Tibet. However, Henning 2007 points out computational errors in both systems because the Brāhmaṇical textbook systems "drifted by neglect into using a sidereal zodiac," and although the *Tantra of the Wheel of Time* adopted an innovative tropical zodiac, its Tibetan interpreters have been mistakenly calculating intercalary months since 849 CE, basing their calendrical tables on the premise that "65 years equals 804 lunar months."

854 For a convenient tabular listing of the sixty years of the Jovian cycle, see Henning 2007, 351–352, and Dorje 2001, 67, where Western dates are also correlated from 1027 through to 2046. For the twelve lunar months of the year, see also Henning 2007, 358–359.

855 Here the subtle body of the practitioner is identified with the fruitional buddha body of indestructible reality (*vajrakāya, rdo rje'i lus*), on which see Dudjom Rinpoche 1991, 1:139–140.

856 These are enumerated above, note 848. See also Kalu Rinpoche Translation Group 1995, 156–157.

857 The twenty-eight constellations (*rgyu skar nyer brgyad*) as represented in the Indian system comprise [0] Aśvinī (Tha skar; Beta Arietis); [1] Bharaṇī (Bra nye; 35 Arietis); [2]

Kṛttikā (sMin drug; Pleiades); [3] Rohiṇī (sNar ma; Aldebaran); [4] Mṛgaśiras (mGo; Lambda Orionis); [5] Ārdrā (Lag; Alpha Orionis); [6] Punarvasū (Nabs so; Pollux); [7] Puṣyā (rGyal; Delta Cancri); [8] Aśleṣā (sKag; Alpha Hydrae); [9] Maghā (mChu; Regulus); [10] Pūrvaphalguṇī (Gre; Zosma); [11] Uttaraphalguṇī (dBo; Denebola); [12] Hastā (Me bzhi; Algorab); [13] Citrā (Nag; Spica); [14] Svāti (Sa ri; Arcturus); [15] Viśākhā (Sa ga; Alpha Librae); [16] Anurādhā (Lha mtshams; Delta Scorpii or Iridis); [17] Jyeṣṭhā (sNron; Alpha Scorpii or Antares); [18] Mūlā (sNrubs; Lambda Scorpii or Shaula); [19] Pūrvāṣāḍhā (Chu stod; Delta Sagittarii); [20] Uttarāṣāḍhā (Chu smad; Pelagus); [21] Śravaṇā (Gro zhin; Vega); [21] Abhijit (Byi zhin; Altair); [22] Dhaniṣṭhā (Mon dre; Beta Delphini); [23] Śatabhiṣā (Mon gru; Lambda Aquarii); [24] Pūrvabhādrapada (Khrums stod; Alpha Pegasi); [25] Uttarabhādrapada (Khrums smad; Gamma Pegasi and Alpha Andromedae); and [26] Revatī (Nam gru; Sigma Piscium). Note that the numbers given are the index numbers used in tabular calculations. In the Indian system, Abhijit and Śravaṇā both have the index number 21, and one or the other would usually be omitted, whereas in the Chinese system all twenty-eight are included. For Jamgon Kongtrul's description of the constellations, see Kalu Rinpoche Translation Group 1995, 157–158.

858 These are enumerated above, note 842. For Jamgon Kongtrul's description of the planetary bodies, see Kalu Rinpoche Translation Group 1995, 158.

859 The twelve terrestrial aspects indicative of past actions (*las kyi sa dum bu bcu gnyis*) are equivalent to the "twelve earthly branches" (*sa'i yan lag bcu gnyis, di zhi*), i.e., the twelve animal signs, which in elemental divination (*'byung rtsis*) give their names to the cycle of years, months, days, and hours, thereby demarcating the four seasons of the year. See Henning 2007, 145; also Dorje 2001, 66–103. However, this could perhaps be interpreted to refer to the twelve links of dependent origination (*rten 'brel bcu gnyis*), with which the zodiacal signs are also associated. See Wallace 2001, 97–100.

860 On the Buddhist and Hindu legends associated with Rāhu, see Cornu 1997, 144–145. As indicated in Henning 2007, 95, Rāhu is actually equivalent to the two nodes of the moon's orbit, where it crosses the ecliptic during its orbit of the earth. The ascending node or "head" (*vaktra, gdong*) is located where the moon crosses the ecliptic traveling northwards, while the descending node, also known as the "tail" (*puccha, mjug ma*) is regarded as a distinct planetary body named Kālāgni. For the basic calculations pertaining to Rāhu, see Henning 2007, 95–98. On the microcosmic level, Rāhu is identified with the central energy channel of the subtle body and may be controlled or understood through the "vajra-like" or adamantine meditative stability (*vajropamasamādhi*).

861 The predictive calculations of lunar and solar eclipses on the basis of Rāhu are discussed in detail in Henning 2007, 98–140, who notes that "since Rāhu moves so slowly around the ecliptic, once every eighteen and a half years, eclipses can occur approximately every six months" (p. 100).

862 On the microcosmic level, within the subtle body, the cycle of the three attributes (lightness, motility, and darkness) corresponds sequentially to a series of three successive "seasons," each lasting two months, while the cycle of the six elements also corresponds sequentially to six successive months of the year. See Wallace 2001, 103. This is related to the occurrence of solar and lunar eclipses once every six months.

863 The calculation of solar eclipses, according to their conditions, magnitude, duration, timing, direction, and color, is discussed in Henning 2007, 125–140. Particular problems arise owing to lack of observational data concerning the curvature of the earth and the tilt of its axis. The calculation of two months equaling a single "season" (*ṛtu*) has just been mentioned. On the calculating of months in terms of the links of dependent origination, see below.

864 The calculation of lunar eclipses, according to their conditions, magnitude, duration, timing, direction, and color, is also examined in Henning 2007, 100–125.

865 See also the tabular correlations between the solar mansions, lunar months, and the twelve links of dependent origination in Wallace 2001, 98–99; and for Jamgon Kongtrul's analysis of the twelve links from the standpoint of Buddhist phenomenology, see below, pp. 579–585.

866 Solar eclipses are reckoned to coincide with the thirtieth day of the lunar month, and lunar eclipses with the fifteenth day. Generally speaking the "link of contact" (*reg pa'i yan lag*) on which this calculation is based will coincide with the thirtieth day, but in calendrical reckoning where the waning phase of the month has precedence it will coincide with the fifteenth day. On this distinction, see also below, p. 354.

867 This is explained by Jamgon Kongtrul in Kalu Rinpoche Translation Group 1995, 158–161. The zodiacal or sidereal day (*khyim zhag*) is a measure of time equivalent to one thirtieth of a single sign of the zodiac, there being therefore 360 of them in a zodiacal year. The calendar or lunar day (*tithi, tshes zhag*) is dependent on the phases of the moon—thirty of them corresponding in duration to the lunar month. The solar day (*dina, nyin zhag*) comprises twelve two-hour periods, commencing from daybreak (*pratyūṣa, nam langs*) at approximately 5 AM, and ending with pre-dawn (*prabhāta, tho rangs*). The solar days are therefore of equal length and correspond to the days of the week, from Monday through to Sunday. For a lucid explanation of the distinctions between them that have bearing on calendrical and astrological calculations, see Henning 2007, 7–21.

868 Wallace 2001, 100.

869 Wallace 2001, 100.

870 The gnomon or "sundial shadow stick" (*daṇḍa/ nāḍī, dbyu gu*) is therefore equivalent to twenty-four minutes. See also Henning 2007, 12.

871 See Henning 2007, 12; also Kilty 2004, 602. Note that *SK* here reads "three hundred and sixty" (*sum brgya drug cu*).

872 For the predictive aspects of planetary calculations, see Dorje 2001, 108–109; also Cornu 1997, 127–244.

873 This passage therefore suggests, on the basis of scriptural authority, that the New Year should commence from the waning phase of the month of Kārttika (*smin drug zla ba*), also known as the "late autumn" month (*stong zla tha chung*) or "early winter month" (*dgun zla ra ba*), coinciding with November-December. See the chart of the twelve months in Henning 2007, 359, Dorje 2001, 88, and Cornu 1997, 172.

874 Caitra coincides with April-May. See the chart of the twelve months in Henning 2007, 359.

875 According to the texts of monastic discipline (*vinaya*), the New Year would commence around November, following the completion of the summer rain retreat (*varṣā, dbyar gnas*), whereas the phenomenological (*abhidharma*) tradition follows the common worldly perspective, which sets the "new year" in springtime (April), when the cycle of life is renewed. Among these other traditions, Āśvina (Tha skar) is identified either with the mid-autumn month (*ston zla 'bring po*) or the late-autumn month (*ston zla chung ngu*), equivalent to October-November. In addition, the months of the Mongolian system, which was introduced to Tibet by Drogon Chogyal Phakpa (thirteenth century), commence from the early spring month (*dpyid ra ba*) of Māgha, coinciding with February-March, although this is somewhat confusingly identified with the tiger month (*stag zla*) in the Tsurphu calendrical tradition, and the dragon month in the Phugpa school. The various traditions associated with "new year," including discrepancies between the Tibetan and Chinese systems, are discussed in Henning 2007, 145–148; see also Dorje 2001, 88.

876 For this reason, the mid-summer month (*dbyar 'bring*) of Āṣāḍha, corresponding to

July-August, or the sixth Mongolian month, is considered to start the year, according to this tradition.

877 The same rationale is presented by Norzang Gyatso. See Kilty 2004, 105; also Henning 2007, 146.

878 See Kilty 2004, 106; Henning 2007, 146.

879 Caitra is said to have been the actual month when the *Tantra of the Wheel of Time* was first taught. See Kilty 2004, 106; also Henning 2007, 16–17, who correctly points out that contemporary Tibetan almanacs still follow this system, counting Caitra (the third Mongolian month) as the first of the year, in contrast to the standard civil Tibetan calendar which places the new year two months earlier.

880 See Kilty 2004, 106, and Henning 2007, 146–147. The former corresponds to Western calendrical reckoning, where the waxing fortnight from new moon to full moon has precedence. However, from the perspective of the *Tantra of the Wheel of Time*, the months are said to be waxing-led or waning-led depending on whether the mean sun enters Aries during the bright or dark half of Caitra. In the latter case, Vaiśākha is posited as the first month of the year, commencing on the full moon day. See also Kilty 2004, 620 and 679.

881 Tib. *sdom brtson dang por ngal ba ltar snang.*

882 On the temporal calculations pertaining to the Buddha's renunciation and attainment of buddhahood, which are important for *bstan rtsis* reckoning, see, e.g., Dudjom Rinpoche 1991, 1:946. Śākyamuni Buddha's enlightenment at Vajrāsana is said to have occurred a moment before the ending of a lunar eclipse in the month of Vaiśākha. On this basis precedence is given to the waning fortnight.

883 This would be based on the practical observations of the Sun entering Aries during the waxing half of the month. See Henning 2007, 146.

884 A distinction is generally drawn between the *Root Tantra of the Wheel of Time*, which, though no longer extant, is said to have followed the traditional Buddhist approach, giving precedence to the waning fortnight, and the extant *Concise Tantra of the Wheel of Time*, which is said to artfully adopt a non-Buddhist position by giving precedence to the waxing fortnight.

885 Also known as *lnga bsdus*, these five components of astrological calculation are discussed in detail in Henning 2007, 40–54.

886 The weekdays, commencing at 05.00, have the following computational values: 0 Saturday (*spen pa*), 1 Sunday (*nyi ma*), 2 Monday (*zla ba*), 3 Tuesday (*mig dmar*), 4 Wednesday (*lhag pa*), 5 Thursday (*phur bu*), and 6 Friday (*pa sangs*). See Henning 2007, 40–43, 357.

887 The calculation of lunar longitude can therefore be made in two ways. The simple calculation, adopted by those who prefer to take shortcuts, takes into account only the exact constellation through which the moon is currently passing at the end of a given calendar date (*tshes 'khyud zla skar*). Alternatively, a secondary calculation can then be made on that basis, in relation to the constellation that the moon will pass through at the start of the following solar day or week day (*res 'grogs zla skar*). Thanks to Edward Henning for this clarification (email communication, 4 November 2009). On this distinction, see also Tang Chi An and Yangchen Lhamo, eds., *Dictionary of Tibetan and Chinese Astrological Terms* (*Bod rgya skar rtsis rig pa'i tshig mdzod*) (Chengdu: Sichuan mi rigs dpe skrun khang, 1985), nos. 277–279. The lunar days of the calendar month are numbered from one to thirty, each demarcating 12 degrees of exact separation between the sun and moon. These thirty lunar days are described in rotation as "joyous" (*dga' ba*), "good" (*bzang po*), "victorious" (*rgyal ba*), "empty" (*stong pa*), and "perfected" (*rdzogs pa*). See also Dorje 2001, 89–90; also Henning 2007, 40–42.

888 The twenty-seven solar constellations, starting with Beta and Gamma Arietis (Aśvinī,

Tha skar) are all enumerated above, with their computational values. See note 857; also Henning 2007, 42–43, 356–357.

889 See Henning 2007, 43–44. Specifically, the longitude of the sun at the end of the lunar day is added to the longitude of the moon at daybreak, creating twenty-seven possible readings, which are all listed in Henning 2007, 359–360. Among them, the first is the "eliminator" (*viṣkambha, sel ba*), which has a computational value of 0, and the last is the "malignant" (*vaidhṛti, khon 'dzin*), which has a computational value of 26.

890 Since these "impacts" correspond to halves of the lunar day, they each represent six degrees of separation between the sun and the moon. See Henning 2007, 44–45. The full listing along with their permutations is given in the same work, pp. 360–362.

891 As indicted above, the three wrathful planets are Mars, Jupiter, and Saturn, while the two peaceful planets are Mercury and Venus. With regard to the calculation of their celestial longitude, see Henning 2007, 55–94. The calculations require the preparation of a step index (*rkang 'dzin*) for each planetary body. In this context, the epicycles of the planets are recognized as having two distinct kinds of step—a progressive northward step from perigee to apogee and a regressive southward step from apogee to perigee. The distinctive motions of the planetary bodies are then allocated to specific quadrants, comprising (1) the early progressive step (*rim pa snga rkang*), in which the planets exhibit a fast motion on entering the first or eastern quadrant at the perigee (*smyur 'gros shar*); (2) the later progressive step (*rim pa phyi rkang*), in which the planets exhibit a slow motion on entering the second or southern quadrant (*dal 'gros lho*); (3) the early regressive step (*rim min snga' rkang*), in which the planets exhibit a retrograde or eccentric motion in the third or western quadrant (*'khyogs 'gros nub*); and (4) the later regressive step (*rim min phyi rkang*), in which they exhibit an advancing motion in the fourth or northern quadrant (*'byung 'gros byang*). See also above, note 843.

892 The calculations pertaining to the head and tail of Rāhu are discussed in Henning 2007, 95–140. See also above, pp. 349–351.

893 All twelve of these ascendant conjunctions (*dus sbyor bcu gnyis*) manifest sequentially in the course of a solar day. See above, note 849.

894 Within the Svarodaya system of divination, which reached Tibet from Jumla in northwest Nepal and is of Shaivite origin, there are twelve groups of primary charts and forty-two secondary charts. According to the scroll depicting the charts of the *Svarodaya Tantra*, which is described in Dorje 1999, 162–165, the charts comprise twelve major groups:

> The first comprises the arising of the Sanskrit vowels and consonants in relation to the planets and constellations (*dbyangs dang gsal byed 'char ba*), the various results engendered by corresponding planetary alignments at diverse periods in the course of human life (*tshe'i gnas skabs 'bras bu*), and the omens associated with the charts of zodiacal conjunction (*dus kyi 'khor lo'i ltas*).
>
> The second group comprises the charts superimposed on inanimate objects, schematic animals and human figures (*bem po srog chags rang rigs gsum*). The third refers to the six onerous charts, said to resemble the exposed tusks of an elephant (*glang chen mche gtsigs 'khor lo drug*). The fourth comprises the sixteen charts associated with eclipses, represented largely by the fluctuations of Rāhu (*rā hu la sogs bcu drug*). The fifth comprises the diverse charts of the zodiacal conjunctions which are calculated having ascertained the position of the nativity or ascendant constellation (*tad kal dus sbyor*). The sixth refers to the six-sectored chart, which provides the calculations for the various fractions of a single zodiacal conjunction (*ma ga ta'i dum bu drug*). The seventh comprises the forty-two subsidiary charts (*bye brag so so'i 'khor lo ni / bcu tshan bzhi dang gnyis lhag pa*), which may be

consulted when setting out on a journey, examining the scarcity of merchandise, investigating thieves, probing the duration of the life span or the circumstances of birth, rebirth, names, individual courses of action, disputations, hostilities, injuries, warfare, fame, compatibility, and antidotes.

The eighth includes the charts depicting the nativity or ascendant constellations, the initial letters of the subject's name, and the constellations corresponding to these initial letters (*skyes skar ming yig ming skar gsum*). The ninth category includes five charts which represent minor activities (*phrin las phran tshegs tsakra lnga*), and the tenth refers to the accurate zodiacal and planetary charts comprising the so-called five left-side paths or sectors and the five right-side ones (*lam lnga'i 'khor lo mi slu ba*). The eleventh concerns the arising of the five deities associated with zodiacal conjunction (*dus kyi lha lnga 'char*), and finally the twelfth is the single chart which determines the authenticity of the entire divinatory system outlined in the *Svarodaya Tantra* (*rgyud 'dir tshad ma'i 'khor lo cig*).

Among these twelve categories of charts, the first is said to resemble a king in that its injunctions must be obeyed. The second resembles a minister, formulating the direction of the king's policy. The third is reminiscent of a soldier, since the quantities suggested by its prognoses are consulted in times of strife. The fourth resembles weapons of war which bring about irrevocable results when they are applied. The fifth resembles queens who are pursued and attended upon by all comers. The sixth resembles the limbs since they indicate the objectives to be followed according to changing circumstances. The seventh, the group of subsidiary charts, resembles messengers or the tools of a blacksmith since they are to be utilized whenever they are needed. The eighth resembles the model of a castle through which vulnerable points of intrusion are examined. The ninth resembles enlightened activities through which the implications of advantageous and disadvantageous decrees are examined. The tenth resembles an aged person in that it is encountered whenever it has to be. The eleventh resembles the workers through whom all things are implemented or rejected. Lastly, the twelfth resembles a reliable person since the authenticity of the charts is examined with reference to it.

895 In addition to the source mentioned in the previous note, see also Phugpa Lhundrub Gyatso's *Extensive Commentary on the Glorious Svarodaya, King of Tantras, Esteeming Martial Conquest, entitled Melody That Utterly Delights the Ford of Eloquence* (*dPal gYul las rnam par rgyal ba gces pa'i rgyud kyi rgayl po dbyangs 'char ba'i rgya cher 'grel ba legs bshad 'jug ngogs mchogs tu dga' ba'i sgra dbyangs*), which is contained in Jampa Trinle, *Great Compendium*, 3:5–485.

896 A detailed presentation and analysis of the system of elemental divination (*'byung rtsis*), based on Sangye Gyatso's *White Beryl*, chs. 20–32, and Lochen Dharmaśrī's *Moonbeams: An Instruction on Elemental Divination* (*'Byung rtsis man ngag zla ba'i 'od zer*), is given in Dorje 2001. The extant Tibetan literature is listed in Drakpa, *Inventory of Tibetan Treatises*, 42–47. See also www.tbrc.org, T1835.

897 Regarding the distinction that is made here, see Dorje 2001, 63: "Elemental divination may conform to the natural order of the elements, according to which wood, fire, earth, iron, and water are all recognized to be non-compounded and of the nature of space; or else it may be undertaken in the context of the bewildered misconception of sentient beings, according to which distinctions are made between the discrete elements, the apparent sense objects formed by them, the intellect which analyzes the elemental relationships, and the mind which apprehends positive and negative consequences. These are known as the four primary 'hidden points of divination' (*gab rtse*)."

898 In *White Beryl*, both the forms *gab rtse* and *gab tshe* are given. *Gab* is defined as "compris-

ing past actions, merits, vitality, and bodies" (*las dang bsod nams srog lus gab*); and *rtse* as the "sharpness of their point of realization" (*de dag rtogs pa'i rtse yi nongs*). Alternatively, *gab* is defined as "an example of the esoteric instructions" (*man ngag dpe la gab pa*), or "an example of sharp vision" (*rno mthong dpe la gab pa*), and *tshe* as "the life span measured on the basis of the natal horoscope" (*tshe rabs las kyi rtsis byas nas / tshe yi ring thung brtsi bas tshe*). The four aspects outlined here form the basis upon which all the charts of elemental divination are prepared and their techniques actually implemented. See Dorje 2001, 64:

> When divinations are undertaken in the context of these four hidden points, the diviner should refer to the elaborate turtle divination chart which comprises nine basic techniques for calculating the relationships formed by the elements. Accordingly, calculations may be based on the five constitutional types (*rus khams lnga*); the twelve or sixty year cycle (*lo bcu gnyis/ lo drug bcu*); the nine numeric squares (*sme ba dgu*); the eight trigrams (*spar kha brgyad*); the twelve months (*zla ba bcu gnyis*); the thirty lunar days of the month (*zhag sum bcu*); the twelve two-hour periods of the day (*dus tshod bcu gnyis*); the eight planets representing the weekdays (*bza' brgyad*); or the twenty-eight constellations (*rgyu skar nyer brgyad*).

899 The range of classical Indian literature on the subject of poetics is surveyed in Gerow, 1977; while Smith 2001, 205–208, reviews the Sanskrit literature on poetics which gained currency in Tibet and the indigenous commentarial tradition to which it gave rise. Jamgon Kongtrul's own account is contained in Ngawang Zangpo 2010, 416–417. Extensive listings of Tibetan works on poetics can also be found in Drakpa, *Inventory of Tibetan Treatises*, 48–53, and at www.tbrc.org, T204.

900 Not located.

901 The three activities of the learned (*mkhas pa'i bya ba gsum*) comprise teaching (*'chad pa*), debate (*rtsod pa*), and composition (*rtsom pa*). See Nyima and Dorje 2001, 392.

902 In the *Mirror of Poetics*, ch. 1, v. 10. Daṇḍin's *Mirror of Poetics* (*Kāvyādarśa*, T 4301) is the foremost treatise on the art of poetics within the Indo-Tibetan classical tradition, in contrast to the works of Bhamāha and Udbhaṭa, which, as Smith 2001, 205, observes, were never translated into Tibetan. Later Tibetan writers also refer to the Sanskrit commentaries on Daṇḍin's work by Ratnaśrī and Vāgindrakīrti. Here, in addition to the versions of the *Mirror of Poetics* that are extant in the Tengyur, I have consulted principally the Sanskrit edition of Ray 2004, which includes the commentary of Śrī Premacandra Tarkavāgīśa, and D.K. Gupta 1970.

There are many indigenous Tibetan commentaries on the *Mirror of Poetics* by luminaries such as the Fifth Dalai Lama, Rinpung Ngawang Jikdrak and Bo Khepa Mipham Gelek Namgyal. Among them the last mentioned authored the influential *Commentary and Proverbs Based on the Mirror of Poetics* (*sNyan ngag me long gi 'grel pa dang dper brjod*). Other readily available works of this genre include Khepa Tobden Rabjampa's *Memorandum on the Mirror of Poetics entitled Clarifying Recollection* (*sNyan ngag me long gi zin tho dran pa'i gsal 'debs*), and Karma Tsewang Pelbar's *Exegetical Commentary on the Mirror of Poetics entitled Novel Sugar Cane Plant* (*bsTan bcos snyan ngag me long gi 'grel bshad sngon med bu ram shing gi ljon pa*), as well as Tseten Zhabdrung's *Summary of the Mirror of Poetics entitled Dawning of Awareness Imbued with Meaning* (*sNyan ngag me long gi spyi don sdeb legs rig pa'i 'char sgo*). Jamyang Drakpa's *Recorded and Roughly Transcribed Guidance based on the Supreme Scholar Tseten Zhabdrung's Summary of the Mirror of Poetics, entitled Oral Transmissions of Our Ancestor* (*mKhas dbang tshe brtan zhabs drung mchog gi snyan ngag spyi don dpe khrid ba sgrar phab pa che long tsam yi ger bkod pa mes po'i zhal lung*), and Konchok Tseten et al., eds., *Anthology of Poetical Proverbs* (*sNyan ngag dper brjod phyogs sgrigs*).

903 Ray 2004, 7–8.
904 On the body of poetry, see D.K. Gupta 1970, 121–122.
905 Particularly clusters of five stanzas.
906 Zhang Yisun et al. 1985, 2340.
907 The last of these has also been described as a "short poem with a story." See D.K. Gupta 1970, 123.
908 *Mahākāvya* takes the form of an extended narrative, with nine specific aspects: it should have a prelude, historical or imaginary subject-matter, expressions of the fruits of the four objects of life, a noble heroic figure, descriptive passages, poetic ornaments, sizable length, poetic sentiments, and metrical cantos. See D.K. Gupta 1970, 123–124.
909 See Ray 2004, 18–21, also D.K. Gupta 1970, 124–126. On Asaṅga's *Compendium of Phenomenology* (*Abhidharmasamuccaya*, T 4049), see below, pp. 476–540.
910 However, he adds that in general the former should be narrated by the hero, while the latter may also be related by another character. See D.K. Gupta 1970, 124–125, and Ray 2004, 18–20.
911 *Rig byed rgya mtsho* could correspond to Vidyāsāgara or possibly to Vidyākara (*rig byed*), although the source of this quotation is clearly not the latter's *Subhāṣitaratnakoṣa*. The name Vedārṇa is also attested in Monier-Williams 2005. It has also been speculated, without corroborating evidence, that the poet in question could be a fourteenth-century philosopher named [Anandapurṇa] Vidyāsāgara (*EIPRB*, 805). Somewhat less likely is the possibility that it refers to Vedadvaipāyana, "Island-born sage of the Vedas," which is among the epithets of the legendary sage Vyāsa (*rgyas pa*), redactor of the Vedas and compiler of the epic poem *Mahābharata*. Towards the end of the *Pūrvasaṃgraha* section of the great epic, there is a remark, "As the formation of the three worlds proceeds from the five elements, so do the inspirations of all poets proceed from this excellent composition. O Brahman, as the four kinds of creatures are dependent on space for their existence, so the purāṇic legends depend upon this ancient history" (after the translation of Ganguli 1883–1896).
912 *Mirror of Poetics*, ch.1, v. 15a. Ray 2004, 12 and 15: *itihāsakathodbhūtamitaradvā sadāśrayam*.
913 D.K. Gupta 1970, 126–128, and Ray 2004, 22ff.
914 Daṇḍin describes Sanskrit as the language of Pāṇini and other sages, Prākrit as the generic term for common language, including the variants of Mahārāṣṭrī, Śaurasenī, Gaudī, Lāṭī, and Paiśācī. Apabhraṃśa is stated to be the language of cowherds of mixed social class (*ābhīra*), and Miśrabhāṣā refers to the employment of diverse forms of language in dramatic contexts. See D.K. Gupta 1970, 127–128, and Ray 2004, 22–24.
915 *Mirror of Poetics*, ch. 2, v. 1. Ray 2004, 72: *kāvyaśobhākarān dharmān alaṃkārān pracakṣate*.
916 *Mirror of Poetics*, ch. 1. On the distinctions between these East and South Indian styles or traditions, see the extensive discussion in D.K. Gupta 1970, 132–181, corresponding to Ray 2004, 28–72. With regard to the ten uncommon attributes in particular, see D.K. Gupta 1970, 143–169.
917 D.K. Gupta 1970, in this passage, points out that double entendre refers to the conveying of multiple shades of meaning in compact expressions.
918 Clarity is here defined as the use of words that are easy to comprehend and without affectation.
919 Phonetic balance refers to the balance between syllables which are soft, hard, and middling.
920 Sweetness here refers to the use of alliteration within a common place of articulation, and an absence of vulgarity.

921 Tenderness implies the general absence of harsh syllables, and at the same time avoiding the looseness of diction that results from all the syllables being soft.

922 Elucidation refers to explicitness of sense rather than implicitness.

923 The Tibetan should read *rgya cher nyid*. See Chandra 1990, 495. Nobleness here implies elevation through the expression of merits or virtues, and the employment of excellent epithets.

924 Chandra 1990, 435, here reads *ājo* for *ojas*. In this context, vigor is defined as the impact of the profusion of compounds which is the essence of prose.

925 Beauty is defined as the absence of exaggerated or grotesque and unnatural expressions, maintaining agreeable and pleasant language at all times.

926 In this context, mental focus refers to metaphorical expressions, in which the attributes of one thing are transferred to another, in accordance with mundane usage.

927 As indicated in D.K. Gupta 1970, 160–165, the traditions of Gauḍa favor laxity of structure, words that are difficult to comprehend, uneven diction, the use of harsh sounds, and expressions that transgress the mundane norms. However, as Gupta also indicates, some of the ten attributes (sweetness, elucidation, vigor, and mental focus) appear to be accepted by both traditions, albeit with varying nuances.

928 Enumerated in the *Mirror of Poetics*, ch. 2. For a detailed discussion of the ornaments of sense, see D.K. Gupta 1970, 200–236. See also the individual entries in Zhang Yisun et al. 1985, which refer to their various subdivisions.

929 These are all listed in Daṇḍin, ch. 2, vv. 4–7. See also Ray 2004, 75.

930 On repetition, which is discussed in ch. 3 of the *Mirror of Poetics*, see D.K. Gupta 1970, 236–238.

931 These include acrostic verse revolving in all directions (*sarvotarabhadra*), acrostic verse revolving in two directions (*ardhabrahma*), and alliteration (*niyama*) whether based on the use of a single vowel or consonant, and so forth. See *Mirror of Poetics*, ch. 3, and D.K. Gupta 1970, 238–239.

932 These sixteen ornaments of enigmatic innuendo (*ṣoḍaśaprahelikā, gab tshig bcu drug*) are enumerated in Daṇḍin, ch. 3; in D.K. Gupta 1970, 239; also in Dudjom Rinpoche 1991, 2:174. They comprise (1) meaning concealed by a concentration of words, (2) real meaning that is lost in the apparent, (3) the use of semantically connected words at great distance from each other, (4) contrived meaning, (5) harmonious or derivative meaning, (6) coarse meaning, (7) the use of synonyms, (8) assumed meaning, (9) abbreviation, (10) hidden meaning, (11) confusing use of synonyms, (12) foolish or vexing use of words, (13) stealth, (14) obfuscation with respect to words, (15) obfuscation with regard to word and meaning, and (16) any combination of the above.

933 *Mirror of Poetics*, ch. 3, vv. 125-126. A detailed discussion of these defects can be found in D.K. Gupta 1970, 170–181.

934 In the *Mirror of Poetics*, ch. 1, v. 103. See Ray 2004, 68–69: *naisargikī ca pratibhāśrutañca bahu nirmmalatam / amandaścābhiyogo/syāḥ kāranaṃ kāvyasampadaḥ.*

935 Śūra, the renowned author of the *Garland of Birth Stories* (*Jātakamālā*, T 4150), is conflated in the Tibetan tradition with Aśvaghoṣa, who composed the *Epic of the Deeds of the Buddha* (*Buddhacaritamahākāvya*, T 4156), the *Eulogy entitled One Hundred and Fifty Verses* (*śatapañcāśatka-nāma-stotra*, T 1147), and the *Verses in Eulogy to the Monastery Gong* (*Gaṇḍīstotragāthā*, T 1149). Historians consider the latter to have been a contemporary of King Kaniṣka (first century CE). See, e.g., Lessing and Wayman 1968, 78n.

936 Śūra is reckoned to have lived in the fourth century CE and Kṣemendra much later, in the tenth or eleventh century. See, e.g., Joshi 1967, 352–354.

937 For a useful introduction to Sanskrit prosody in relation to the great literary compositions of diverse ages, see Mukherji 1976; also Smith 2001, 202. Listings of the extant

Tibetan commentarial literature can be found in Drakpa, *Inventory of Tibetan Treatises*, 20–21, and at www.tbrc.org, T206. Among them, Sakya Paṇḍita's *Variegated Flower Bouquet of Prosody* (*sDeb sbyor sna tshogs me tog chun po*) is particularly influential. The sources to which I have referred in the notes on prosody include the restored Sanskrit edition of *Chandoratnākara* with the auto-commentary of Ratnākaraśānti, edited in Shastri 1990, as well as the Tibetan edition of the same text, with computational tables and charts, in Nyagong Konchok Tseten et al., eds., *Commentary on the Precious Source of Prosody* (*sDeb sbyor rin chen 'byung gnas kyi 'grel ba*), (Beijing: Mi rigs dpe skrun khang, 2003); and Rachel Hall's unpublished article on the mathematics of poetry. Jamgon Kongtrul's summary of the origins of this literary genre can be found in Ngawang Zangpo 2010, 417–418.

938 Ch. 1, v. 11cd. Ray 2004, 9–10.

939 Ch. 1, v. 12cd. See Ray 2004, 10.

940 This is in fact the first of the three subcategories of *vṛtta*. See below.

941 According to other traditional Sanskrit sources such as Piṅgala's *Discourse on Prosody* (*Chandaḥsūtra*), meter classes may begin with verses amounting to only a single syllable per line and range up to verses with lines of twenty-seven syllables or more. Tables listing all the precise meter classes, commencing from those with a single syllable up to those with twenty-seven syllables, may be found in Nyagong Konchok Tseten et al., *Commentary*, 164–165. The same twenty-seven meter classes are also presented with examples in an appendix to Apte 1965, 1035–1041. Seven of the most commonly used meter classes are named after the mythic seven horses that pull the chariot of Aditya across the heavens in the course of a solar day, viz., Gāyatrī (six syllables), Uṣṇih (seven syllables), Anuṣṭubh (eight syllables), Bṛhatī (nine syllables), Paṅktī (ten syllables), Triṣṭubh (eleven syllables), and Jagatī (twelve syllables). For Tibetan controversies regarding the permissible number of syllables in a line of verse, see Shastri 1990, 99.

942 See Nyagong Konchok Tseten et al., *Commentary*, 77–79, and Apte 1965, 1041, who states that these may extend from twenty-seven-syllable lines, as far as 999-syllable lines!

943 For the number of permutations relevant to each of the main twenty-seven meter classes, see the tables in Nyagong Konchok Tseten et al., *Commentary*, 164–165; also fig. 48 below. This number of possible permutations of heavy and light syllables in respect of a given meter class is obtained by doubling the number of possible permutations given for the preceding meter class, i.e., only two permutations are possible for a single-syllable line of verse, but four are possible for a two-syllable line, eight for a three-syllable line, sixteen for a four-syllable line, thirty-two for a five syllable line, sixty-four for a six syllable line, one hundred and twenty eight for a seven syllable line, two hundred and fifty six for an eight syllable line, five hundred and twelve for a nine syllable line, and thus one thousand and twenty-four for a ten-syllable line (Paṅktī).

944 For the example of the Tanumadhyā meter, see Nyagong Konchok Tseten et al., *Commentary*, 23. This is described as the thirteenth of the sixty-four possible permutations of the Gāyatrī meter class.

945 The example of the Kumāralalitā meter is given in Nyagong Konchok Tseten et al., *Commentary*, 24. It is described as the thirtieth of the 128 possible permutations of the Pramoda meter class.

946 For the example of the Samānikā meter, see Nyagong Konchok Tseten et al., *Commentary*, 25. This is described as the one hundred and seventy-first of the 256 possible permutations of the Anuṣṭubh meter class.

947 The example of the Vidyunmāla meter is mentioned in Nyagong Konchok Tseten et al., *Commentary*, 26. It is the first and foremost of the 256 possible permutations of the Anuṣṭubh meter class.

948 For the example of the Śuddhavirāja meter, see Nyagong Konchok Tseten et al.,

Commentary, 28–29. It is the first of the 1024 possible permutations of the Mālinī meter class.

949 Nyagong Konchok Tseten et al., *Commentary*, 21–96.

950 In the Upaṣṭhitapracupitā or Vaktradvāra (*kha sgo*) meter class, each of the four metrical lines of a stanza may have varying combinations of heavy and light syllables. See Nyagong Konchok Tseten et al., *Commentary*, 97.

951 In the Padacaturārdhva meter class (*rkang bzhi 'phel*) each of the four metrical lines of a stanza incrementally increase from eight, to twelve, sixteen, and twenty syllables, i.e., lengthening by four syllables each verse. There are also other variations. See Nyagong Konchok Tseten et al., *Commentary*, 97–103.

952 According to Nyagong Konchok Tseten et al., *Commentary*, 103–106, there are three kinds of Ūrdhvagāmin or Udgatā. In the first of them, the lines of the first hemistich each have ten syllables, the third has eleven and the fourth thirteen; in the second the first three lines have ten syllables and the fourth thirteen; and in the third the first two lines have ten, the third twelve, and the fourth thirteen syllables. See also Apte 1965, 1041.

953 According to Nyagong Konchok Tseten et al., *Commentary*, 106–109, there are three kinds of Mardākrāntā. Generally speaking, the first metrical line will have fourteen syllables, the second thirteen, the third nine, and the fourth fifteen syllables. Among the other two variants, one has eighteen syllables in the third line while the others are unchanged.

954 Frequently the first and third lines or the second and fourth will be equal. According to Nyagong Konchok Tseten et al., *Commentary*, 81–90, there are thirteen types of semi-equal syllabic quantity, including the Upacitraka meter. Apte 1965, 1041, lists only six of them.

955 The term "mora" (*mātrā*, *phyi mo*), also rendered as moric or syllabic instant, refers in phonology to a unit of time as it relates to syllable stress. A single moric instant is defined as the time taken to recite a short syllable. Technically, it is the time taken to snap the fingers or to blink the eyes once. A short syllable is said to comprise one moric instant, and a long syllable, two. To identify a given meter, the short and long syllables should be identified and then calculated in terms of morae.

956 See Nyagong Konchok Tseten et al., *Commentary*, 10. The words "and so forth" appear to include final *sandhi*, *visarga*, and final consonants.

957 *SK*, 326, reads Jāti for Āryā.

958 The Āryā meter represents unequal lines; the Vaitālya meter, semi-equal lines; and the Paiṅgala, equal lines. See Nyagong Konchok Tseten et al., *Commentary*, 201. More specifically, on the Āryā meter and its nine variations, see Apte 1965, 1041–42, and Nyagong Konchok Tseten et al., *Commentary*, 114–126; on Vaitālya, 126–133; and on Paiṅgala, 133–142.

959 This text, translated into Tibetan by Situ Chokyi Jungne, is contained in bKa' brgyud pa'i gsung rab, 1:603–624.

960 These combinations are also well-known in classical Greek meter, i.e., dactyl (long, short, short), cretic (long, short, long), antibachius (long, long, short), molossus (long, long, long), tribach (short, short, short), amphibrach (short, long, short), anapaest (short, short, long), and bachius (short, long, long).

961 Not located.

962 See the commentary in Nyagong Konchok Tseten et al., *Commentary*, 12–14.

963 This passage is found in Nyagong Konchok Tseten et al., *Commentary*, 14.

964 On Hayagrīva, as a Buddhist meditational deity and gatekeeper, see above, p. 197. On Hayagrīva from the perspective of Vedic literature, where the name refers to an incarnation of Viṣṇu, see Mani 1964, 311–312.

965 The astonishing applications (*adbhutaprayoga, ngo mtshar rtogs byed kyi sbyor ba*) are the subject matter of the sixth and final part of the *Chandoratnākara*. See Nyagong Konchok Tseten et al., *Commentary*, 142–170, which includes a number of helpful charts and calculations; also Shastri 1990, 140–160; and Hall, n.d. Hall's study relates to the mathematical field of combinatorics, which includes the mathematics of combinations and permutations—responding to the questions of how many ways there are to do or make something.

966 For an example of a model *prastāra* chart, see fig. 47, which is based on Nyagong Konchok Tseten et al., *Commentary*, 147, where the calculations for one, two, three, and four syllable meters are presented. The same work, pp. 144–148, differentiates the traditions of Ratnākaraśānti and Piṅgala in preparing these general tables. A related table on pp. 164–165 (see fig. 48) shows how the number of possible permutations of heavy and light syllables doubles as the number of syllables in a line of verse increases by one. For example, the six-syllable meter has 64 permutations, the seven-syllable meter has 128, and the eight-syllable meter, 256.

967 This step is listed in Nyagong Konchok Tseten et al., *Commentary*, 163–167, and in Shastri 1990 as the fifth step rather than the second. The tabular chart for the ten-syllable meter class includes 1,024 variant meters, so that the corresponding *prastāra* table is 19 units wide, 2,047 units deep, and comprises 38,893 square units in its extent. Hall, n.d., notes that this calculation is originally attributed to Piṅgala.

968 This is listed as the second step in the Nyagong Konchok Tseten et al., *Commentary*, 148–151, and 185; also in Shastri 1990. See fig. 49. The resulting cadence of heavy and light syllables is determined by dividing the number of the specific meter (e.g., the fourteenth permutation of the six-syllable class) by two, repeatedly, until there is no remainder. An even quotient indicates that the first syllable will be "light," and an odd quotient, that it will be "heavy." Since 14 is an even number, the first syllable will be light. Divided again by two, the quotient will be seven, an odd number, indicating that the second syllable will be heavy. Add one to that, making eight, and again divide by two, so that the next quotient will be four, making the third syllable light. That in turn is divided by two, giving a quotient of two, so that the fourth syllable is also light. Two is divided by two, making one, so that the fifth syllable is heavy. Again adding one, two is once again divided by two, so that the final syllable is heavy. The calculation thus continues until, in the case of our example, six syllables of varied heavy and light cadence are fully present in the sequence: light, heavy, light, light, heavy, heavy. This mathematical focus on the combinations of heavy and light syllables, which can be traced back to Piṅgala, ranks as the earliest known description of the binary numeral system in mathematics.

969 This step (illustrated in fig. 50) is listed as the third in Nyagong Konchok Tseten et al., *Commentary*, 151–154, and 183. The calculation is made by aligning the sequence of heavy and light syllables in a given meter sequentially below the incremental *prastāra* numbers (1, 2, 4, 8, 16, 32, 64, etc). One thus obtains the numbers corresponding to the light syllables in the given meter, ignoring those that correspond to the heavy syllables. The numbers corresponding to the light syllables should then be tallied, and the number one added to the total. In the example given here, we know from the *prastāra* table that the ten-syllable meter class has 1,024 permutations. Aligning the syllables of the given meter (heavy, heavy, heavy, light, light, heavy, light, heavy, light, heavy) sequentially below the first ten numbers of the *prastāra* sequence (1, 2, 4, 8, 16, 32, 64, 128, 256, 512) we find that the light syllables correspond to the numbers 8, 16, 64, and 256. Adding these we obtain the figure 344, to which 1 should be added, making 345. Therefore the *uddiṣṭa* calculation shows that this given meter is the 345th of the 1,024 possible permutations of the ten-syllable meter class. Cf. Hall, n.d., who refers to this calculation as the "grouping of patterns."

970 This step is given as the fourth in Nyagong Konchok Tseten et al., *Commentary* (see fig. 51, p. 189), which contrasts the technique of Piṅgala (pp. 154–157) with that of Ratnākaraśānti (pp. 157–161). The expression "and so forth" here indicates as many intervening syllables as there may be before the final number which represents the number of permutations that have all their syllables light. The chart, known as *meruprastāra*, resembles Pascal's triangle, by which name it is generally known, and as Hall, n.d., points out, it predates Pascal's discovery by as many as eighteen centuries. It assumes the shape of a numeric pyramid in which any number is the sum of the two numbers directly above it on either side. Discounting the apex (number one), the horizontal rows of numbers can extend from two (representing the two-syllable meter class) as far as 26 (representing the 26-syllable meter class). In the example of the four-syllable meter class which is often given, the triangle appears as follows:

1
1 1
1 2 1
1 3 3 1
1 4 6 4 1
. . . .

The numbers displayed in the final line provide the required information—the scale of heavy-light syllables ranging from left to right. Therefore, in this case, there is only one meter (shown on the extreme left) in which all four syllables are "heavy," four meters have three heavy and one light syllable, six meters have two heavy and two short syllables, four meters have one heavy and three light syllables, and only one meter (shown on the extreme right) has all four syllables light. Altogether there are sixteen varying permutations for the four-syllable meter class. This can mathematically be rendered as:

$$(a + b)^4 = 1 \cdot a^4 + 4 \cdot a^3 b + 6 \cdot a^2 b^2 + 4 \cdot ab^3 + 1 \cdot b^4$$

Another example is given in Hall, n.d., which also shows how the later Jain writer Hemacandra (ca. 1150), on this basis, calculated the number of permutations that could be formed from combinations of short and long syllables, and thereby arrived at the so-called Fibonacci sequence (0, 1, 1, 3, 5, 8, 13, 21, 34, 55, 89, 144...) some seventy years before the Italian mathematician after whom it is named.

971 This step is discussed in Nyagong Konchok Tseten et al., *Commentary*, 167–169 and 193. See fig. 52. A grid is prepared, comprising horizontal and vertical units measured in relative finger-widths. In the case of the four-syllable meter class, the horizontal axis has seven units (4 × 2 = 8 – 1 = 7), which include four indicating the presence of heavy or light syllables and three that are blank. The vertical axis will have sixteen units, representing the possible permutations of the four-syllable meter class. This number is then multiplied by two to represent the differentiation between heavy and light syllables (32), and then 1 is subtracted, the answer (31) being the calculation of the *adhvā*, which is positioned in the blank unit at the top of the last of the seven columns. See also Nyagong Konchok Tseten et al., *Commentary*, 193–194.

972 This is the subject of Nyagong Konchok Tseten et al., *Commentary*, 170–175, and 194–195. These may be exemplified by a stanza which has 57 moric instants, 23 light syllables and 40 syllables. On this basis the number of heavy syllables may be calculated in three different ways: 40 (syllables) – 23 (light syllables) = 17 heavy syllables; 57 moric instants – 23 light syllables divided by 2 = 17 heavy syllables; or 57 moric instants – 40 syllables = 17 heavy syllables. Similarly, the number of light syllables may also be calculated in three ways, as in the same example: 57 – (17 × 2) = 23; or (40 × 2) – 57 = 23; or 40 – 17

= 23. Then the overall number of syllables may be calculated in three ways: 17 + 23 = 40; or 57 − 17 = 40; or (57 + 23) ÷ 2 = 40. Finally, the number of moric instants may be calculated, as in the same example: (17 × 2) + 23 = 57; or (40 × 2) − 23 = 57; or 40 + 17 = 57.

973 This verse is also quoted in Karma Lhagsam's *Summary of the Precious Source of Prosody entitled Light That Benefits All* (*sDeb sbyor rin chen 'byung gnas kyi bsdus 'grel kun phan snang ba*), bKa' brgyud pa'i gsung rab, 1:637.

974 Karma Lhagsam, *Summary*, 1:637: *tshigs bcad gsal ba*.

975 The observations of Piṅgala in his *Chandasūtra* are discussed in detail in Mukherji 1976. Ratnākaraśānti is revered within the Indo-Tibetan Buddhist tradition as one of the celebrated eighty-four mahāsiddhas of tantric Buddhism.

976 The classical science of synonymics (*abhidāna, mngon brjod*) is a form of lexicography, based on the format of a traditional thesaurus containing lists of homonyms and synonyms appropriate for the composition of Sanskrit poetry (*kāvya, snyan ngag*). A survey of the traditional Indian sources can be found in Vogel 1979. Foremost among the texts of this genre is the *Treasury of Amarasiṃha* (*Amarakośa*, T 4299), also known as the *Treatise on Nouns and Gender* (*Nāmaliṅgānuśāsana*). The author, Amarasiṃha, is revered as one of the "nine gems" (*navaratna*) in the imperial court of Candragupta II (fl. 400 CE), although other sources assign him to the period of Vikramāditya (fl. seventh century). The popularity of this thesaurus among exponents of classical Indian poetry is attested by its forty-one Sanskrit commentaries, which are formally listed in Rādhākāntadeva's *Śabdakalpadruma* lexicon, and some twenty further commentaries which exist in manuscript form, some in other Indic languages. For a summary of these Indian commentaries, see also the introduction to Miśra 2005.

Amarasiṃha is considered to have been a Buddhist, based on the prominence given in the text to synonyms of the word *Buddha*, although others suggest that he may have followed the Jain tradition. Among the commentaries, only one, the *Wish-fulfilling Commentary* (*Amaraṭīkākāmadhenu*, T 4300), composed by the Buddhist scholar Subhūticandra, was translated into Tibetan. For a survey of its Tibetan translations and the indigenous Tibetan commentarial literature, see Smith 2001, 203–206. Extant Tibetan works on this subject are also listed in Drakpa, *Inventory of Tibetan Treatises*, 57–58, and online at www.tbrc.org, T372. Jamgon Kongtrul briefly summarizes the Tibetan literary endeavors in Ngawang Zangpo 2010, 418–419.

The *Treasury of Amarasiṃha* contains three chapters (*khāṇḍa*). The first, entitled "Celestial Realms and So Forth" (*svargavargādikhāṇḍa*), is divided into twelve sections concerning celestial realms, time, abstract terms, speech, sound, dramaturgy, subterranean abodes, serpents, hells, and water. The second chapter, entitled "Terrestrial Realms and So Forth" (*bhūvargādikhāṇḍa*), is divided into ten sections concerning earth, towns, minerals, vegetables, animals, humans, the priestly class, the royal class, the mercantile class, and the laboring class. The third chapter, entitled "General Topics and So Forth" (*samānyādikhāṇḍa*), or "Adjectives and So Forth" (*viśeṣyanighnavarga*), concerns adjectives, compounds, homonyms, indeclinables, and gender. In the following notes I have referred specifically to the convenient Amdowa edition of the root text, *mNgon brjod 'chi ba med pa'i mdzod* (Qinghai mi rigs dpe skrun khang, 1985) and to the commentary found in Satyadevamiśra 2005.

977 Tib. *btags pa'i sgra bshad gsum po. SK* reads *btags pa'i sgra bshad lnga po.*

978 Homonyms (*nānārtha, don sna tshogs*) are contained in the third section of chapter three, on which see above note 120. See Amarasiṃha, *Treasury*, 1985 edition, 122; also Satyadevamiśra 2005, 343.

979 Amarasiṃha, 1985 edition, 123, and Satyadevamiśra 2005, 344.

980 Amarasiṃha, 1985 edition, 132, and Satyadevamiśra 2005, 363.
981 Amarasiṃha, 1985 edition, 144, and Satyadevamiśra 2005, 388.
982 *SK*, 329, reverses the last two.
983 Amarasiṃha, 1985 edition, 151, and Satyadevamiśra 2005, 401–402.
984 Not located. Cf. Dudjom Rinpoche 1991, 1:106.
985 The *Treasury of Amarasiṃha* (*Amarakośa*) adds "arrow," making ten homonyms. See Satyadevamiśra 2005, 348.
986 This has been identified by Smith 2001, 203, as an alternative title for Śrīdharasena's *Viśvalocana* (T 4453), rather than Śrījñāna's *Abhidhānamaṇimālā* (T 4454).
987 This text (full title: *dPal sgra'i snye ma du ma'i don shes rtogs pa*) is a short glossary of Sanskrit terms (fifteen folios), composed by Tāranātha.
988 Smith 2001, 205n659, lists several indigenous Tibetan works on synonymics. A few have recently been republished, e.g., Rinpung Ngawang Jigdrak's *Treatise on Synonymics: Ornament of the Ears of the Learned* (*mNgon brjod kyi bstan bcos mkhas pa'i rna rgyan*), Buchung's *Dictionary of Synonyms* (*mNgon brjod kyi tshig mdzod*), and the Zhigatse Teacher Training College's *Compilation of Commentaries on Synonymics, entitled Sound of the Conch That Recalls Eloquence* (*mNgon brjod kyi 'grel pa btus bsgrigs legs bshad 'dren pa'i dung sgra*), which is based on the *Treatise on Synonymics entitled Drop of Water in the Ocean* (*mNgon brjod kyi bstan bcos rgya mtsho'i chu thigs*) of Ngulchu Dharmabhadra.
989 Amarasiṃha, 1985 edition, 1; and Satyadevamiśra 2005, *Svargavarga*, pp. 4–5.
990 Amarasiṃha, 1985 edition, 2–3, and Satyadevamiśra 2005, *Svargavarga*, pp. 6–7.
991 *SK*, 330, here reads "*buddhi*" rather than "*budh*."
992 Not located.
993 *SK*, 330, reads *bcu drug*.
994 The essential Sanskrit treatise on dramaturgy, Bharata's *Nāṭyaśāstra*, was not translated into Tibetan. The few indigenous Tibetan compositions on the subject, which is distinct from the Tibetan operatic tradition, are listed in Drakpa, *Inventory of Tibetan Treatises*, 59. At www.tbrc.org, T256, the Sanskrit and Tibetan works are listed together. Tenpei Nyingje was the personal name of Situ VIII Chokyi Jungne (1700–1774). Although there seems to be no distinct work on dramaturgy among his collected writings, since Daṇḍin himself alludes to this subject in his *Mirror of Poetics*, there are some references in Situ Chokyi Jungne's commentary, entitled *Concordance of Terminology based on the Mirror of Poetics* (*sNyan ngag me long gi skad gnyis shan sbyar*), Collected Works, vol. 6 (Cha), no. 4. There is also an important text on stagecraft authored by Konchok Tenpei Dronme (1762–1823), the *Treatise on Dramaturgy entitled Play That Leads Along the Pure Pathway* (*Zlos gar gyi bstan bcos yang dag lam du bkri pa'i rol rtsed*). Among the few classical Sanskrit dramas translated into Tibetan, Harṣadeva's *Utter Delight of the Nāgas* (*Nāgānandanāmanāṭaka*) is contained within the Tengyur (T 4154).
995 A useful summary of all these dramaturgical aspects from the standpoint of the poetic ornaments is given by Daṇḍin in the *Mirror of Poetics* 2:367, on which see D.K. Gupta 1970, 234–235.
996 According to M. Gupta 2010, 115, Abhinavabharati suggests in his commentary on the *Nāṭyaśāstra* that these junctures define the segments that give continuity to the plot (*arthāvayavāḥ*). For Abhinavabharati's interpretation and contextualization of the five junctures, see ibid., 113–127. A detailed examination of the five dramatic junctures can also be found in Bhattacharya 2005, 102–127.
997 For example, actors playing upper-class characters will speak Sanskrit while those depicting lower-class figures will speak vernacular languages.
998 This definition accords with Bharata's *Nāṭyaśāstra*, ch. 19, pp. 37–67 of the Sanskrit edi-

tion by Sharma and Upadhyaya. See also Keith 1924, 298–300, and Bhattacharya 2005, 102–115.

999 The Ratnaśrī commentary on the *Mirror of Poetics* (*Kāvyādarśā*), edited by Thakur and Jha, is published in the Darbhaṅga Sanskrit Series, 1957. The content and distribution of these sixty-four aspects is the subject of Bharata's *Nāṭyaśāstra*, ch. 21, vv. 71ff. Bharata emphasizes that "a play deficient in the limbs will be unfit for successful production." As M. Gupta 2010, 127–128, indicates, the purpose of these junctures and their aspects is sixfold, namely, to express a certain purpose, to expand the plot, to attain a pleasing quality of production, to conceal objects that are to be concealed, to evoke surprise, and to disclose things that should be disclosed. Keith 1924, 299–300, points out that not all of these sixty-four [or sixty-five] aspects of the five dramatic junctures need be employed. Some commentators such as Rudraṭa suggest that they can only be included within their own particular juncture of the play, while other authorities appear to disagree. Also, he stresses that they are subservient to the sentiments that they aim to produce. See also Bhattacharya 2005, 115–127; and for the interpretation of Abhinavabharati, M. Gupta 2010, 127–136.

1000 The Tibetan is missing in *SK*.

1001 The Tibetan is missing here. Bharata, ch. 21, v. 78, suggests *samīhā* while Abhinavabharati suggests *vilāsa*. See the discussion in M. Gupta 2010, 133.

1002 *SK* reads *ma dag pa* for *me tog*.

1003 The Tibetan is missing in *SK*.

1004 Explained in Bharata, ch. 21, v. 84, as *caturvarṇyopagamanaṃ varṇasaṃhāra*.

1005 Keith 1924, 299, suggests that this juncture has only twelve aspects, but Bharata lists thirteen. Note that our text runs the second to the fifth aspects grammatically together.

1006 This is out of order in our text, but see Bharata, ch. 21, v. 86, for its proper position in the sequence. Some sources give *rūpa* instead of *vitarka*. Cf. M. Gupta 2010, 133.

1007 This is achieved by disclosing the reality of some hidden emotion. See M. Gupta 2010, 133.

1008 The Tibetan is missing in *SK*.

1009 Bhattacharya 2005, 125, suggests that this should read *vibodha* (re-awakening to the germ of the plot) rather than *virodha*.

1010 Missing in the Tibetan text.

1011 These are the subject of Bharata, ch. 22, and M. Gupta 2010, 287–314. See also Keith 1924, 326–330, and Bhattacharya 2005, 203–246. Bharata in particular holds that all the ten identifiable categories of Sanskrit play proceed from these four dramatic elements which heroes may display; and that they originate respectively from the *Four Vedas*. Keith 1924, 328, following the commentators Dhanañjaya and Dhanika, points out that the first is based on sound and the other three on sense.

1012 Here *SK* reads *rab tu sred pa*.

1013 See Bharata, ch. 22, vv. 26–35; Bhattacharya 2005, 217–226; and M. Gupta 2010, 300–312 and 71–80. These four contexts are appropriate for male actors, speaking Sanskrit. Among them:

(1) The function of the prologue, read out aloud by the director or lead actor (*sūtradhara*), is to stimulate the interest of the audience and promote good auspices.

(2) The function of the prelude is to allow an actress, jester, or supporting actor to interact with the lead actor on a significant topic. It has five branches or elements (*āṅga*): abrupt dialogue (*udghātya*), general opening of the story (*kathodghatā*), particular presentation (*prayogātiśaya*), personal matters (*pravṛttaka*), and continuity (*avalagita*).

(3) The function of the single-act drama is to be acted by only one or two persons. It has thirteen sub-types: enigmatic dialogue (*udghātya*), fortuitous coincidence of events

(*avalagita*), dialogue expressing unintended meaning (*avaspandita*), comical enigmatic statement (*nālikā*), incoherent chatter (*asatpralāpa*), word play or repartee (*vākkeli*), mutual and untrue words of flattery (*prapañca*), damning with mild praise (*mṛdava*), out vying dialogue (*adhibala*), deceit through the semblance of friendship (*chala*), punning and double entendre (*trigata*), vivid and comic speech (*vyāhāra*), and digression (*gaṇḍa*).

(4) The function of farce is to introduce, usually in the context of a one-act play, either pure comedy or partly salacious and obscene comedy.

1014 See Bharata, ch. 22, vv. 38–45; Bhattacharya 2005, 226–231; and M. Gupta 2010, 292–294. These four contexts are deemed appropriate for the expression of truth (*sattva*), lightness of the heart, and majesty, evoking heroic, marvelous, and furious sentiments.

1015 See Bharata, ch. 22, vv. 46–54; Bhattacharya 2005, 231–238; and M. Gupta 2010, 294–297. These four contexts are suitable for the expression of delicate sentiments, including the erotic sentiments of love and love-making. The parts are frequently played by actresses dressed in fine costumes in conjunction with graceful song, dance, and laughter.

1016 See Bharata, ch. 22, vv. 56–63; Bhattacharya 2005, 238–246; and M. Gupta 2010, 297–300. These four contexts are deemed appropriate for the expression of violent sentiments, evoking energy, courage, and subterfuge.

1017 See Bharata, ch. 17; also Keith 1924, 328–329, who points out that these "include the combination of merits of style with poetic figures."

1018 The Tibetan is missing here.

1019 On the importance of song, dance, and music in dramatic performances, see Keith 1924, 338–339. On the additional dramatic junctures (*saṃdhyantara, mtshams sbyor gzhan pa*), conciliation (*sāma*) and so forth, which number twenty-one, see Bharata, ch. 19, vv. 107–109; also Bhattacharya 2005, 127–128; and M. Gupta 2010, 136–137.

1020 For a detailed discussion of the role and modality of poetic sentiments (*rasa*) in Sanskrit drama, see Keith 1924, 314–326, M. Gupta 2010, 243–286, and Bhattacharya 2005, 290–340. According to Bharata, ch. 6, vv. 15–16, there are eight main sentiments, namely, the erotic (*śṛṅgāra*), comic (*hāsya*), pathetic (*karuṇa*), furious (*raudra*), heroic (*vīra*), terrible (*bhayānaka*), odious (*bībhatsa*), and marvelous (*adbhuta*).

1021 This quotation remains unidentified, although the first line is reminiscent of *Bodhisattvacaryāvatāra*, ch. 6, v. 119.

1022 Śāntideva, *Bodhisattvacaryāvatāra*, ch. 9, v. 5.

1023 The exalted vehicle (*abhyudayayāna, mngon mtho'i theg pa*) is discussed below, pp. 420–439; eternalist and nihilist views are also examined below, pp. 397–416.

1024 Vitapāda (Slob dpon sMan pa'i zhabs) was a student of Buddhajñānapāda and author of eight treatises in the Tengyur pertaining to the cycle of the *Guhyasamājatantra* (T 1866, 1870, 1872, 1874–1878). This specific reference is found in the *Commentary on the Oral Teachings of Mañjuśrī: The Beautiful Flower* (*Sukusuma-nāma-dvikramatattvabhavanāmamukhāgama-vṛtti*, T 1866, Tengyur, Di, pp. 220–222). Jamgon Kongtrul's remarks derive here from Chomden Rigpei Raldri's *Ornamental Flower of Spiritual and Philosophical Systems* (*Grub mtha' rgyan gyi me tog*), f. 3b.

1025 This is a renowned treatise by Bhāvaviveka (ca. 500–570), who pioneered the doxographical classification of Indian spiritual and philosophical systems (*siddhānta*). The one hundred and ten primary views are also enumerated in Gonpo Wangyal, *Numeric Lexicon of Buddhist Terms* (*Chos kyi rnam grangs*, Chengdu: Sichuan mi rigs dpe skrun khang, 1988), 550–552.

1026 The ninety-six astonishing views (*ya mtshan gyi lta ba go drug*), as enumerated in Chopel Kelzang Trinle, *Pearl Necklace of Clear Intelligence: A Numeric Lexicon of Buddhist Technical Terms Compiled from the Sūtras, Tantras and Treatises* (*mDo rgyud bstan bcos kun las btus pa'i chos kyi rnam grangs mu thi la'i phreng ba lo gsal mgul rgyan*, Lanzhou: Gansu mi rigs dpe skrun khang, 2005), 295, comprise fifteen subsidiary views propounded by each of the six extremist teachers who were contemporaries of the Buddha, with the addition of their six main views. See also below, note 1050.

1027 On this text, see Bodhi 1978. The sixty-two views enumerated here include eighteen speculations concerning the past, based on theories of eternalism, partial eternalism, extensionism, endless equivocation, and fortuitous origination; as well as forty-four speculations concerning the future, based on percipient immortality, non-percipient immortality, neither percipient nor non-percipient immortality, annihilationism, and the immediate attainment of nirvāṇa in the present life. See also below, pp. 502–503.

1028 These twenty-eight inauthentic views (*dam pa ma yin pa'i lta ba nyer brgyad*) are listed in Rigdzin 1993, 111; also Chopel Kelzang Trinle, *Pearl Necklace*, 247–248, and Nordrang Orgyan, *Compendium of Buddhist Numeric Terms*, 3280–3281. The last mentioned cites the source as Ratnākaraśānti's *Commentary on the Ornament of Madhyamaka entitled Attainment of the Middle Way* (*Madhyamakālaṃkāravṛttimadhyamaka-pratipadāsiddhi*, Dg. T. Sems tsam, vol. Hi, f. 114a; T 4072). The source attributed in our text (*Dad pa cher 'byung gi mdo*) is also mentioned in Chomden Rigpei Raldri, *Ornamental Flower of Spiritual and Philosophical Systems*, f. 4a, but otherwise remains unidentified (neither T 144 nor T 201).

1029 These twenty-six negative views (*lta ngan nyi shu rtsa drug*) are all enumerated and explained in the first fascicule of the *Sūtra of the Excellent Meditation on Faith in the Greater Vehicle* (*Mahāyānaprasādaprabhāvanasūtra*, T 144, *mdo sde*, Pa, pp. 34–39), although the heading therein names them as the "twenty-eight inauthentic views" (*yang dag ma yin pa'i lta ba nyi shu rtsa brgyad*). The twenty-six are listed as follows: (1) the view of clinging to substantialism (*mtshan mar lta ba*); (2) the view that disregards the view (*lta ba la lta ba ma yin pa'i lta ba*); (3) the view that deprecates conventional reality (*tha snyad la skur 'debs pa'i lta ba*); (4) the view that deprecates totally dissonant mental states (*kun nas nyon mongs ba la skur 'debs pa'i lta ba*); (5) the view that deprecates reality (*de kho na nyid la skur 'debs pa'i lta ba*); (6) the view that eradicates good practice (*sbyor ba sel ba'i lta ba*); (7) the view that grasps after everything (*yongs su 'dzin pa'i lta ba*); (8) the view that is fickle (*sgyur ba'i lta ba*); (9) the view that is not renunciant (*nges par 'byung ba ma yin pa'i lta ba*); (10) the view that there are no inadmissible offences (*kha na ma tho ba med par lta ba*); (11) the view that succumbs to downfall (*dpung bar lta ba*); (12) the view concerning obscuration and so forth (*sgrib pa sogs pa lta ba*); (13) the view that is abusive (*brnyas pa'i lta ba*); (14) the view that is thoroughly disturbed (*rab tu 'khrugs pa'i lta ba*); (15) the view that distorts (*yog bar lta ba*); (16) the view that there are no onerous fruits such as the hells (*myal ba 'bral bu med pa'i lta ba*); (17) the view of progress (*'phel bar lta ba*); (18) the view that is deceptive (*bslu ba'i lta ba*); (19) unsustainable views (*khas mi lan pa'i lta ba*); (20) the view that is deceitful (*gYo ba'i lta ba*); (21) skeptical views (*chad pas bcad pa'i lta ba*); (22) sycophantic views (*bkur sti byed pa'i lta ba*); (23) views based on delusion (*rmongs ba brten pa'i lta ba*); (24) unspeakable views (*mi smra ba'i lta ba*); (25) the great view of egotism (*lta ba chen po*); and (26) the view of manifest pride (*mngon pa'i nga rgyal gyi lta ba*). A different enumeration of twenty-six views that adhere to extremes (*mthar 'dzin nyer drug*) is also found in Chopel Kelzang Trinle, *Pearl Necklace*, 242–243.

1030 These twenty views concerning mundane aggregates (*viṃśatisatkāyadṛṣṭi*, *'jig tshogs la lta ba nyi shu*) are enumerated below, p. 502; see also Chopel Kelzang Trinle, *Pearl Necklace*, 222–223.

1031 These sixteen alien interpretations (*ṣodaśānuvāda*, *pha rol smra ba bcu drug*) are listed in Nordrang Orgyan, *Compendium of Buddhist Numeric Terms*, 2943, who attributes the citation to Maitreya's *Ornament of the Sūtras of the Greater Vehicle* (*Mahāyānasūtrālaṃkāra*, T 4020). However, I have not yet located the list in that work. Jamgon Kongtrul's immediate source is Chomden Rigpei Raldri, *Ornamental Flower of Spiritual and Philosophical Systems*, f. 4a. The sixteen comprise (1) the view that the result is present in the cause (*rgyu la 'bras bu yod par smra ba*); (2) the view that [all things] are conspicuous (*mngon par gsal bar smra ba*); (3) the view that the past and the future exist substantially (*'das pa dang ma 'ongs pa rdzas su yod pa*); (4) the view that upholds an independent self (*bdag tu lta bar smra ba*); (5) the view that upholds permanence (*rtag par lta ba smra ba*); (6) the view that things created in the past are causes (*sngon byas pa rgyur smra ba*); (7) the view that Īśvara and so forth are creators (*dbang phyug la sogs pa byed pa por smra ba*); (8) the view that considers violence as a doctrine (*rnam par 'tshe ba'i chos su smra ba*); (9) the view that propounds extremes and the absence of extremes (*mtha' dang mtha med par smra ba*); (10) the view that does not abandon extremes (*mtha' mi spong bat smra ba*); (11) the view that there are no causes (*rgyu med par smra ba*); (12) nihilism (*chad par smra ba*); (13) the view that espouses non-existence (*med par smra ba*); (14) the view that upholds supremacy (*mchog tu smra ba*); (15) the view that upholds purity (*dag par smra ba*); and (16) the view that espouses virtuous signs and intimations of good luck (*dge mtshan dang bkra shis su smra ba*).

1032 These fourteen unspecified views (*caturdaśāvyākṛta, lung ma bstan gyi lta ba bcu bzhi*) are listed in Rigdzin 1993, 268; also in Chopel Kelzang Trinle, *Pearl Necklace*, 192.

1033 The eight extremist views comprise creation, cessation, nihilism, eternalism, coming, going, diversity, and identity (Dudjom Rinpoche 1991, 2:158); while the fourfold enumeration includes being, non-being, both being and non-being, and neither being nor non-being (ibid., 2:129). The two extremes are identified as either being and non-being, or subject and object (ibid., 2:105).

1034 These comprise animals, anguished spirits, and hell-bound beings.

1035 I have as yet been unable to recall the exact source of this memorable quotation, but the source is most probably Dromton Zhonu Lodro's *Biography of Jowoje Atiśa entitled the Father Teachings of Kadam* (*Jo bo rje dpal ldan atisha'i rnam thar bka' gdams pha chos*). The citation is not mentioned in Pawo Tsuklak Trengwa's *Scholars' Feast of Doctrinal History* (*Chos 'byung mkhas pa'i dga' ston*).

1036 Buddhist phenomenology (*abhidharma*), as the common substratum of both the lesser and greater vehicles is the subject of Part Two, below, pp. 441–611. For Jamgon Kongtrul's detailed analysis of the Buddhist philosophical and spiritual systems, see Callahan 2007.

1037 The full title of this text is *bZang spyod kyi 'grel ba bzhi'i don bsdus nas brjed byang du byas pa*.

1038 *Sūtra of the Descent to Laṅkā*, f. 127b3.

1039 For Jamgon Kongtrul's appraisal of those who advocate mundane materialism (*lokāyatika, 'jig rten rgyang 'phen pa*), see below, pp. 403–405. His source for this entire section is again Chomden Rigpei Raldri, *Ornamental Flower of Spiritual and Philosophical Systems*, ff. 4a–5b.

1040 For a critique of the Vātsīputrīya (*gNas ma bu pa*) who uniquely within the Buddhist tradition postulated the existence of an individual entity (*pudgala*), see Vasubandhu's *Auto-commentary on the Treasury of Phenomenology* (*Abhidharmakośabhāṣya*), translated in Pruden 1988–1990, ch. 9, pp. 1313–1342.

1041 While some sources suggest that those holding such heretical views are cut off from the seed of buddhahood (*rigs chad pa'i log rtog can*), elsewhere it is maintained that the expression "cut off" (*kulotsāda, rigs chad*) is merely used as a rhetorical device to induce non-Buddhists towards genuine spiritual pursuits, and that by definition, the seed of buddhahood (*tathāgatagarbha*) cannot be cut off. See e.g., Dudjom Rinpoche 1991, 1:193–194.

1042 These verses derive from a longer quotation found in Chomden Rigpei Raldri, *Ornamental Flower of Spiritual and Philosophical Systems*, ff. 4b–5a, although the primary source is as yet unidentified. The title may suggest an affinity with Harivarman's *Satyasiddhiśāstra* (Taisho 1646) but this requires further investigation.

1043 In other words, they are said to be capable of realizing five of the six supernormal cognitive powers. On this association with the meditative absorptions of formlessness, see below, p. 438. Whereas both Buddhist and non-Buddhist practitioners may realize these five, only buddhas will achieve supernormal power over the cessation of corrupt states, which terminates cyclic existence.

1044 Tib. *Ye shes rgyas pa*. This discussion is found in T 3852, f. 38a2 onwards. Cf. also Chomden Rigpei Raldri, *Ornamental Flower of Spiritual and Philosophical Systems*, f. 6b.

1045 Exemplified in Taktsang Lotsāwa's *Treatise on the Attainment Free from Extremes, Having Known All Philosophical Systems, entitled Ocean of Eloquent Exegesis* (*Grub mtha' kun shes nas mtha' bral grub pa zhes bya ba'i bstan bcos rnam par bshad pa legs bshad kyi rgya mtsho*).

1046 The influence of Madhyamaka philosophy on the *Vedānta* of Gauḍapāda has been noted in, e.g., Murti 1955, 110–121.

1047 See pp. 403–413.

1048 From the Buddhist perspective, there are four primary causes (*caturupādāna*, *nye bar len pa bzhi*) of involuntary rebirth in cyclic existence, namely, desire, erroneous views, exclusive attachment to vows or rituals, and blind belief in an inherently existing self. See Nyima and Dorje 2001, 1298.

1049 Tibetan lexicons list six original teachers of the nihilist view (*chad smra'i phyi rol pa'i ston pa drug*) who appear to form a distinct lineal succession, namely, (1) Bṛhaspati (Phur bu ba), (2) the hermit sage [Vālmīki] (Drang srong pa), (3) Lokākṣin ('Jig rten mig), (4) Avatārabalin ('Jug stobs can), (5) Galagaṇḍin (Va ba can), and (6) Aśvatara (rTa mchog). See Dungkar Lobzang Trinle, *Great Dictionary of Dungkar*, 809, and Nordrang Orgyan, *Compendium of Buddhist Numeric Terms*, 1364. Among them, the legendary association of Bṛhaspati and Vālmīki, author of the *Rāmāyana*, with this strand of nihilistic philosophy is well documented in Tibetan sources. See, e.g., Dudjom Rinpoche 1991, 1:66. The name Lokākṣin is attested in Monier-Williams 2005, 907, and may be synonymous with Cārvāka—the hedonistic acolyte of Bṛhaspati. Avatārabalin may tentatively be identified with Balarāma, who is sometimes cast as an emanation of Viṣṇu. He is regarded as a commentator on the *Lokāyatikasūtra*. Aśvatara may be identified with Kambalāśvatara, who is mentioned in the *Summation of the Real* (*Tattvasaṃgraha*, T 4266). See Jha 1937, 2:890.

1050 These eighteen exponents of extremist views (*mu stegs kyi ston drug gsum bco brgyad*) are all enumerated in Dungkar Lobzang Trinle, *Great Dictionary of Dungkar*, 1614, and in Nordrang Orgyan, *Compendium of Buddhist Numeric Terms*, 3021. Among them, the last group of six, comprising the sophistic teachers of dialectics (*rtog ge ba drug*), are well attested throughout the Buddhist traditions. They include (1) Purānakāśyapa (Kun tu rgyu 'od srung rdzogs byed), (2) Maskarī Gośālaputra (gNag lhas kyi bu), (3) Sañjayavairaḍīputra (Yang dag rgyal ba can), (4) Ajitakeśakambalin (Mi pham skra'i la ba can), (5) Kakudakatyāyana (sMra 'dod kyi bu), and (6) Nirgranthajñātiputra (gCer bu gnyan gyi bu). See also Rigdzin 1993, 207.

The other twelve appear to be unknown as such in Pāli sources (Bhikkhu Bodhi, email communication, 6 November 2009), and seem to be mentioned as a numeric category only in extant Tibetan works. Among them, the six nihilistic teachers who were masters of meditative absorption (*snyom par 'jug pa drug*) included (1) Udraka Rāmaputra (bDe byed kyi bu lhag spyod); (2) Ārāḍakālāma (sGyu rtsal shel gyi bu ring 'phur); (3) Parivrājika Subhadra (Kun tu rgyu rab bzang); (4) Māṇavaka Sañjaya (Bram ze khye'u kun rgyal); (5) Jaṭilakāśyapa (sTeng rgyas 'od srung ral pa can); and (6) the hermit sage Araṇa (Drang srong nyon mongs med). The six who emulated them (*rjes sgrogs pa drug*) included (1) Brahmāṇa Hetujaya (Bram ze rgyus rgyal); (2) Brahmāṇa Bhadrin (Bram ze bzang ldan); (3) Brahmāṇa Tulyotkṣepa (Bram ze gzhal 'degs); (4) Brahmāṇa Āyuḥ (Bram ze tshangs pa'i tshe); (5) Brahmāṇa Padmagarbha (Bram ze padma'i snying po); and (6) Brahmāṇa Lohita (Bram ze dmar po). Only the foremost of each group is mentioned by name in Chomden Rigpei Raldri, *Ornamental Flower of Spiritual and Philosophical Systems*, f. 8a, and in Jangkya Rolpei Dorje's *Exegesis of Philosophical Systems entitled Beautiful Ornament of the Mound of the Buddhist Teachings* (*Grub mtha' bshad pa thub bstan lhun po'i mdzes rgyan*), f. 12b.

1051 Since the original *Bṛhaspatisūtra* (dated circa 600 BCE) is no longer extant, information relies for the most part on the polemical works of other schools. Translated selections may be found in Radhakrishnan and Moore 1957, 228–249. Jamgon Kongtrul's main sources for this passage are Chomden Rigpei Raldri, *Ornamental Flower of Spiritual and Philosophical Systems*, ff. 7b–10b; and Upa Losal's *Exegetical Treasury of Philosophical Systems* (*Grub mtha' rnam par bshad pa'i mdzod*), ch. 3, pp. 20–30. The latter summarizes the nihilistic perspective, citing quotations found in classical Indian treatises, such as Avalokitavrata's *Commentary on the Lamp of Discriminative Awareness* (*Prajñāpradīpaṭīkā*, T 3859, 111bff.), Bodhibhadra's *Interlinear Commentary on the Compendium of the Nucleus of Pristine Cognition* (*Jñānasārasamuccayanāma-nibandhana*, T 3852, 39bff.), and Kamalaśīla's commentary on the *Tattvasaṃgraha*, ch. 22, on which see Jha 1937, 2:887–935. Cf. also Barron 2007, 64–65.

1052 Chomden Rigpei Raldri, *Ornamental Flower of Spiritual and Philosophical Systems*, f. 8b reads: *bum pa dang ldan pa'i rtsig pa*, rather than merely *rtsig pa*.

1053 Other sources read "when the life span was 20,000 years." See, e.g., Dudjom Rinpoche 1991, 1:64; also Barron 2007, 56.

1054 This text is translated in Sinha 1915. Selections are also found in Radhakrishnan and Moore 1957, 426–445.

1055 The *Sāṃkhyakārikā* of Īśvarakṛṣṇa (third c. CE) is also translated in Sinha 1915, and in a later version by Suryanarayana Sastri (Madras: University of Madras, 1935). Selections are contained in Radhakrishnan and Moore 1957, 426–445. There appears to be an anachronism here in that Patañjali is reckoned to have preceded Īśvarakṛṣṇa by some five hundred years. Within the Brāhmaṇical tradition, he is revered as the author of the *Yogasūtra*, which is translated in Prasada 1924. For selections from this work, see also Radhakrishnan and Moore 1957, 454–485.

1056 *Introduction to Madhyamaka,* ch. 6, v. 121.

1057 Jamgon Kongtrul's presentation of Sāṃkhya summarizes the detailed explanation found in Chomden Rigpei Raldri, *Ornamental Flower of Spiritual and Philosophical Systems*, ff. 10b–22b; and Upa Losal, *Exegetical Treasury*, ch. 4, pp. 30–51. Useful secondary language references to the Sāṃkhya philosophical schools include Larson and Bhattacharya 1987; Dasgupta 1922, 1:208–273; Chakravarti 1975; Jha 1937, 1:25–67 and 192–203; and Barron 2007, 56–60.

1058 Dasgupta 1922, 1:268n, quotes the *Tātparyāṭīkā* concerning the seven kinds of relation in inference for one's own sake, from the Sāṃkhya perspective.

1059 These phases are known successively as (1) the ego-principle imbued with lightness (*sāttvikāhaṃkāra* or *vaikārikāhaṃkāra*), (2) the ego-principle imbued with motility (*rājasikāhaṃkāra*), and (3) the ego-principle imbued with dullness (*tāmasikāhaṃkāra*). See Dasgupta 1922, 1:248–251.

1060 According to Dasgupta 1922, 1:247–248, the modified ego-principle is a synonym for the spiritual ego-principle and not the energetic ego-principle. On p. 251 he also refers to the controversy between the Sāṃkhya and Yoga schools as to whether the five aspects of subtle matter evolve from the "great intelligence" or from the "ego-principle."

1061 Kaṇāda (gZegs can) is generally assigned to the third century BCE and is traditionally regarded as a non-theistic philosopher. For a survey of Indian literature pertaining to the Vaiśeṣika school, see Matilal 1977; and on the philosophy of the Vaiśeṣika (and the related Naiyāyika school), see also Dasgupta 1922, 1:274–366; Potter 1977; and Jha 1937, 1:139–163. Selections from Kaṇāda's *Vaiśeṣikasūtra* can be found in Radhakrishnan and Moore 1957, 387–397. Jamgon Kongtrul's presentation is based on Chomden Rigpei Raldri, *Ornamental Flower of Spiritual and Philosophical Systems*, ff. 25b–31a.

1062 Dasgupta 1922, 1:313–314.

1063 Dasgupta 1922, 1:316, suggests that the two missing attributes are elasticity (*sthitisthāpaka*) and meditation (*bhāvanā*).

1064 Dasgupta 1922, 1:317.

1065 Dasgupta 1922, 1:317–318.

1066 Dasgupta 1922, 1:318–319.

1067 Dasgupta 1922, 1:319.

1068 Dasgupta 1922, 1:355.

1069 Jamgon Kongtrul's presentation of Naiyāyika derives from Chomden Rigpei Raldri, *Ornamental Flower of Spiritual and Philosophical Systems*, ff. 31a–36a. The distinctions between these diverse categories are discussed in Dasgupta 1922, 1:295; for a review of the relevant literature, see Matilal 1977; also Potter 1977.

1070 Mani 1964, 654. Jamgon Kongtrul's presentation of the Aiśvarya derives from Chomden Rigpei Raldri, *Ornamental Flower of Spiritual and Philosophical Systems*, ff. 22b–25b. Cf. Upa Losal, *Exegetical Treasury*, ch. 5, pp. 51–72, which includes within its scope an analysis of the Vaiśeṣika and Naiyāyika perspectives.

1071 Jamgon Kongtrul's summary of the Vaiṣṇava is based on Chomden Rigpei Raldri, *Ornamental Flower of Spiritual and Philosophical Systems*, ff. 36a–40b, and Upa Losal, *Exegetical Treasury*, ch. 6, pp. 72–96. On Mahāvīra, see below, pp. 414–415. Kumārila (*gZhon nu ma len*) philosophically contextualized Śabara's commentary on Jaiminī's *Mimāṃsa Sūtra* in his three main works—the *Exposition of the Verses* (*Ślokavārttika*), which elaborates on Book 1, ch. 1; the *Exposition of the Sacred Sciences* (*Tantrārttika*), which elaborates on Book 1, chs. 2–4 and Books 2–3; and the *Full Exposition* (*Tuptika*), on Books 4–9. Selections from the *Ślokavārttika* are contained in Radhakrishnan and Moore 1957, 498–505.

1072 This is the era recounted in the epic poem *Mahābhārata*.

1073 A useful summary of these ten incarnations can be found in Basham 1959, 304–310.

1074 Padmakara Translation Group 2005, 368–370.

1075 As enumerated in the Maitrāyaṇa Upanisad, these six branches are breath-control (*prāṇāyāma*), sense withdrawal (*pratyāhāra*), meditative concentration (*dhyāna*), retention (*dhāraṇā*), logic (*tarka*), and meditative stability (*samādhi*). See Dasgupta 1922, 1:236.

1076 See immediately below, pp. 412–414; also Upa Losal, *Exegetical Treasury*, ch. 6, pp. 72–96. Among them, the Vaidika (*rig byed pa*) are followers of the Vedas, and equivalent to the Brāhmaṇa.

1077 The Brāhmaṇa are typified by the sage Vyāsa, the diffuser of the Vedas and legendary author of the *Mahābhārata*. Jamgon Kongtrul's brief summary of the Brāhmaṇa derives from Chomden Rigpei Raldri, *Ornamental Flower of Spiritual and Philosophical Systems*, ff. 40b–45b.

1078 This is mentioned in the *Bṛhadāraṇyaka Upaniṣad*. See Radhakrishnan 1953, 201. Jamgon

Kongtrul's summary of the Vedānta-Aupaniṣadika systems is based on Chomden Rigpei Raldri, *Ornamental Flower of Spiritual and Philosophical Systems*, ff. 45b–48b.

1079 Bhartṛhari was an illustrious grammarian, who reputedly died in 650 BCE. See Müller 1919, 90. His aphorisms are contained in Kennedy 1913. For recent studies on the life and works of Bhartṛhari, see Chaturvedi 2009; and for the philosophy of the grammarians, Coward and Raja, 1990. Jamgon Kongtrul's summary of the Vaiyākaraṇa derives from Chomden Rigpei Raldri, *Ornamental Flower of Spiritual and Philosophical Systems*, ff. 54a–56b.

1080 This listing derives from the twelve chapters of Jaiminī's *Mimāṃsā Sūtra*, as detailed by Madhva in the *Nyāyamālāvistara*. See Müller 1919, 200–202. Jamgon Kongtrul's summary of the Mīmāṃsaka derives from Chomden Rigpei Raldri, *Ornamental Flower of Spiritual and Philosophical Systems*, ff. 48b–52b. Selections from the *Mimāṃsā Sūtra* are contained in Radhakrishnan and Moore 1957, 487–498.

1081 Müller 1919, 202–203.

1082 Jamgon Kongtrul's summary of the Cāraka system derives from Chomden Rigpei Raldri, *Ornamental Flower of Spiritual and Philosophical Systems*, ff. 52b–54a.

1083 Jamgon Kongtrul's summary of Jainism is based on the detailed description found in Chomden Rigpei Raldri, *Ornamental Flower of Spiritual and Philosophical Systems*, f. 56bff. Cf. Upa Losal, *Exegetical Treasury*, ch. 7, pp. 96–105. The nine categories (*navapadārtha, tshig don dgu*) of Jainism are enumerated below, p. 415. On Jain philosophy in general, see also Malvania and Soni 2008.

1084 Mahāvīra (599–527 BCE) is himself considered to have been the twenty-fourth in the line. Ṛṣabha and his immediate successors are all reputedly mentioned in the *Yajur Veda*. The full listing is presented, along with their locations, parentage, physical description, and assemblies, in Varṇī 1973 2:376–391. Cf. Dundas 2002, 12–41; also Jaini 1979, 1–38.

1085 On the protection of the three staffs, see Dundas 2002, 164.

1086 Cf. the quotation in Dudjom Rinpoche 1991, 1:66. The source may be Devasūrī's *Ornamental Mirror of Categories: A Guide to Valid Cognition* (*Pramāṇanayatattvālokālaṃkāra*).

1087 Humans here exemplify all vertebrate animals. See Dasgupta 1922, 1:189.

1088 I.e., earth, water, wood or plant-life, fire, and wind are all said to possess only one sense faculty, that of touch. Worms possess two, namely touch and taste, while ants have three—touch, taste, and smell. Bees additionally have vision, and vertebrates have all five sense organs. See Dasgupta 1922, 1:189–190.

1089 Regarding the conduct of Jain ascetics in general, see Sharma 1965, 121–146. On controlled actions, see Dundas 2002, 164–165; on the five vows of ascetic restraint, which include non-violence, truthfulness, non-stealing, absence of sexual misconduct, and detachment, see Jaini 1979, 170–178; and on the five aspects of the cultivation of knowledge, which are said to correspond to five distinct modes of consciousness, see ibid., 121–122. The modes of conduct (*pratimā*) which may be enumerated as eleven or thirteen, concern right views, vows of ascetic discipline, equanimity, fasting, purity of nourishment, continence, celibacy, renunciation of household activity, property, family residence, and clothing. See Jaini 1979, 182–186.

1090 This parasol-shaped abode at the summit of existence is designated in Jain sources as the "Slightly Curving Place" (*īṣaprāgbhāra*) and also as the *siddhaloka*. See Dundas 2002, 90–92, and Jaini 1979, 130.

1091 *Exposition of Valid Cognition*, final verse of ch. 1. This translation is based on the explanation given in Lamrim Ngawang Phuntsok's *Commentary on the Exposition of Valid Cognition* (*Tshad ma rnam 'grel gyi ṭikkā*), 1:298–299.

1092 The commentary, p. 298, adds the words "Saying he is a Brahmin, even though uneducated."

1093 This would probably include the religions of the Abrahamic tradition.

1094 Tib. *sog po'am kla klo stag gzig pa*.

1095 Tib. *nam mkha'i lhas bstan pa*. This should probably read *gnag lhas bstan pa*. On the Ājīvaka, see Basham 1951, and Basham 1959, 297–298; also Jaini 1979, 21–25, 136–138.

1096 This is the fatalistic view that all events are predestined—so virtuous and non-virtuous actions would not have any bearing on the outcome.

1097 The five Pāṇḍava brothers, who are heroic figures in the *Mahābhārata* epic, include Yudhiṣṭhira, Bhīma, Arjuna, Nakula, and Sahadeva. See also Basham 1959, 175 and 410–411. All these comments concerning the aboriginals, the Ājīvakas, and the repetition of the names of the five Pāṇḍava brothers derive from Chomden Rigpei Raldri, *Ornamental Flower of Spiritual and Philosophical Systems*, f. 73a–b.

1098 The distinction between "original" or "revealed" Bon (*brdol bon*) and the modern "transformative" Bon (*bsgyur bon*) is made in traditional Buddhist histories of Tibet. See Stein 1972, 229–247. On modern studies, which refer principally to "transformative" Bon rather than "original" Bon, see, e.g., Snellgrove 1967, Karmay 1972, Kvaerne 1995, Baumer 2002, and Wangyal 2000. Chomden Rigpei Raldri, *Ornamental Flower of Spiritual and Philosophical Systems*, ff. 73b–76b, is the main source for Jamgon Kongtrul's presentation here.

1099 The Tibetan assimilation of these Chinese traditions is discussed in Dorje 2001. Kapstein 2009 also presents a series of recent scholarly articles on the cultural and Buddhistic interaction between Tibet and China.

1100 This expression is defined in Nyima and Dorje 2001, 881, as "continuous happiness, the state of liberation and omniscience."

1101 T 4158, f. 107a3–4.

1102 On this distinction, see below, pp. 423–439.

1103 *SK*, 348, here reads *mngon 'gro*, but see the single volume edition, p. 35, for the correct reading, *sngon 'gro*.

1104 T 4158, f. 107a4.

1105 T 4158, f. 107a4–6, with slight differences noted.

1106 The three kinds of faith (*dad pa rnam pa gsum*) are enumerated as confidence (*dang ba*), aspiration (*'dod pa*), and conviction (*yid ches pa*). See, e.g., Dudjom Rinpoche 1991, 2:113.

1107 For an alternative account of the vehicle of gods and humans (*devamanuṣyayāna*, *lha mi'i theg pa*), based on Nyingma sources, see Dudjom Rinpoche 1991, 1:57–61.

1108 *Tantra of Hevajra*, pt. 2, v. 18cd.

1109 The hierarchy of human and god realms associated with the world system of desire (*kāmadhātu*) is visually presented as a chart in Dudjom Rinpoche 1991, 1:14–15. For Jamgon Kongtrul's perspective on the diverse realms of the world system of desire, see also Kalu Rinpoche Translation Group 1995, 115–119.

1110 See the chart in Dudjom Rinpoche 1991, 1:14–15, also 57–61. The four continents inhabited by human beings (*gling bzhi'i mi*) are Pūrvavideha in the east, Jambudvīpa in the south, Aparagodānīya in the west, and Uttarakuru in the north. The six species of Kāma divinities (*kāmadevaṣaṭkula*, *'dod lha rigs drug*) comprise, in ascending order, Caturmahārājakāyika, Trāyatriṃśa, Yāma, Tuṣita, Nirmāṇarata, and Paranirmitavaśavartin.

1111 *Letter to a Friend*, vv. 45–46.

1112 No such verse is found in *Mūlamadhyamakakārikā* (T 3824), as the text suggests, although it is reminiscent of a hemistich from Nāgārjuna's *Precious Garland* (*Ratnāvalī*), which reads: "happiness comes through ethical discipline" (*khrims kyis bde*). The reading in Āryadeva's *Four Hundred Verses* (*Catuḥśataka*, T 3846), f. 13b, however, is also slightly different: "Through ethical discipline one will proceed to the exalted realms" (*tshul khrims kyis ni mtho ris 'gro*). This is reiterated in Candrakīrti's commentary on that very text (*Catuḥśatakaṭīkā*, T 3865, Ya, f. 138b) and by Śāntarakṣita in his *Auto-commentary on the Ornament of Madhyamaka* (*Madhyamakālaṃkāravṛtti*, T 3885), f. 62b. Another similar reading is found in Dharmikasubhūtighoṣa's *Verses on the Foundation of Recollection of the Sacred Teachings* (*Saddharmasmṛtyupasthānakārikā*, T 4179), f. 39a: "Through ethical discipline the exalted realms will be attained" (*tshul khrims kyis ni mtho ris thob*).

1113 *Introduction to Madhyamaka*, ch. 2, v. 7.

1114 This verse is also found in Dudjom Rinpoche 1991, 1:59.

1115 Cf. Dudjom Rinpoche 1991, 1:59–60.

1116 Tib. *las 'dres ma dang 'phen rdzogs mu mi mthun pa*. Among the twelve links of dependent origination, the first three—fundamental ignorance, formative predispositions, and consciousness—are the actions that project into subsequent lives, while the other links, from name and form through to aging and death, are those that fulfil their actions in the present life. See Patrul Rinpoche's explanations of the workings of *karma* in Padmakara Translation Group 1994, 101–131. For Jamgon Kongtrul's exposition of the links of the cycle of dependent origination, see below, pp. 579–585.

1117 A distinction is made here between the fully ripened effects of past actions (*rnam smin gyi las*), such as rebirth in an inferior realm generated through desire, hatred, or delusion, and the effects that are similar to their causes (*rgyu mthun pa'i las*), as when one is instinctively inclined towards particular modes of action or experience as a residual inheritance of one's past karma. See Padmakara Translation Group 1994, 112–113.

1118 The vehicle of Brahmā (*brahmāyāna, tshangs pa'i theg pa*) is presented from the Nyingma perspective in Dudjom Rinpoche 1991, 1:61–63. The hierarchy of the twelve ordinary realms of form (*so so'i skyes gnas bcu gnyis*) associated with the four meditative concentrations, the five pure abodes (*gtsang gnas lnga*) above them, and the four formless realms (*gzugs med khams pa'i gnas bzhi*) at the summit of cyclic existence is also visually presented as a chart, ibid., 1:14–15. For Jamgon Kongtrul's perspective on the diverse realms of the world systems of form and formlessness, see also Kalu Rinpoche Translation Group 1995, 119–127; and for an analysis of the world-systems of desire, form, and formlessness from the standpoint of Buddhist phenomenology, see below, pp. 417–439; also p. 603. Vimuktisena (rNam grol sde), whose life is recounted in Chimpa and Chattopadhyaya 1970, 188–190, was an influential disciple of Vasubandhu. His treatises include the *Abhisamayālaṃkārakārikā-vārttika*, T 3788.

1119 Vasubandhu analyzes the four meditative concentrations from the standpoint of Abhidharma in his *Auto-commentary on the Treasury of Phenomenology* (*Abhidharmakośabhāsyaṃ*), translated in Pruden 1998–1990, ch. 8, pp. 1215–1219. Cf. also Shiramati's *Commentary on the Five Psycho-physical Aggregates* (*Pañcaskandhaprakaraṇavaibhāṣya*, T 4066), as translated in Engle 2009, 169–178; and from the Theravāda tradition, Ñāṇamoli 1979, 144–198.

1120 On the practice of calm abiding in the Kagyu tradition, see Dakpo Rabjampa Tashi Namgyal's *Elucidation on the Sequence of Meditation according to the Great Seal of Definitive Meaning entitled Moonbeams of Eloquence* (*Nges don phyag rgya chen po'i sgom rim gsal bar byed pa'i legs bshad zla ba'i 'od zer*), 367–380, and the translation in Lhalungpa 2006; also Thrangu Rinpoche 1993, 15–62. Cf. Tarthang Tulku 1973, 80–84; Bodhi 2000, 329–344; and Ñāṇamoli 1979, 84ff.

1121 Thrangu Rinpoche 1993, 54, includes a chart outlining the relationship between these nine techniques of calm abiding and their associated mental powers and levels of engagement, which is based on Asaṅga's *Level of the Pious Attendants* (*Śrāvakabhūmi*, T 4036).

1122 Pruden 1988–1990, ch. 8, pp. 1227–1238; also Thrangu Rinpoche 1993, 58–62.

1123 On impure or disturbed meditative concentration, see Pruden 1988–1990, ch. 8, pp. 1238–1240.

1124 On the practice of higher insight in the Kagyu tradition, see Dakpo Rabjampa Tashi Namgyal, *Elucidation*, 381–399; and the translation in Lhalungpa 2006. For a contemporary commentary on the practice of higher insight, see Thrangu Rinpoche 1993, 63–107. Cf. Bodhi 2000, 330 and 344–356.

1125 The Tibetan equivalent is listed as *mtshan nyid so sor rig pa* (*yid la byed pa*), in Negi *Tibetan Sanskrit Dictionary*, 5820, and in Rigdzin 1993, 249.

1126 The three overt kinds of dissonant mental state (*'dod nyon mngon gyur ba chen po gsum*) are desire, hatred, and delusion. See, e.g., Dudjom Rinpoche 1991, 2:118.

1127 It is through the sixth and final mode of attention that the subtlest traces of the world-system of desire will be abandoned, paving the way for the attainment of the world-system of form.

1128 Higher insight (*vipaśyanā, lhag mthong*), is not therefore solely the preserve of those who would cultivate the god-realms of form and formlessness, but it is also an important technique for the spiritual cultivation of pious attendants (*śrāvaka, nyan thos*) and hermit buddhas (*pratyekabuddha, rang rgyal*). See, e.g., Dudjom Rinpoche 1991, 1:223–231; Callahan 2007, 85–158; and Ñāṇamoli 1979, 257–320.

1129 On the first meditative concentration, see, e.g., Engle 2009, 174–175, and Ñāṇamoli 1979, 151–161.

1130 On the second meditative concentration, see, e.g., Engle 2009, 175–176, and Ñāṇamoli 1979, 161–165.

1131 On the third meditative concentration, see, e.g., Engle 2009, 176–177, and Ñāṇamoli 1979, 165–171.

1132 On the fourth meditative concentration, see, e.g., Engle 2009, 177–178, also Ñāṇamoli 1979, 171–175.

1133 This means that rebirth in the Stratum of Brahmā (*brahmakāyika, tshangs ris*) will be obtained by meditating on the lesser foundation of the first meditative concentration; the realm of Priest Brahmā (*brahmapurohita, tshangs pa mdun na 'don*), by meditating on the mediocre foundation; and Great Brahmā (*mahābrahmā, tshangs pa chen po*), by meditating on the greater foundation. Thereafter, rebirth in the realm of Little Radiance (*parīttābha, 'od chung*) will be obtained by meditating on the lesser foundation of the second meditative concentration; the realm of Immeasurable Radiance (*apramāṇābha, tshad med 'od*), by meditating on the mediocre foundation; and the realm of Inner Radiance (*ābhāsvara, 'od gsal*), by meditating on the greater foundation.

Thereafter again, rebirth in the realm of Little Virtue (*parīttaśubha, dge chung*) will be attained by meditating on the lesser foundation of the third meditative concentration; the realm of Immeasurable Virtue (*apramāṇaśubha, tshad med dge*), by meditating on the mediocre foundation; and the realm of Most Extensive Virtue (*śubhakṛtsna, dge rgyas*), by meditating on the greater foundation. Finally, rebirth in the realm of the Cloudless (*anabhraka, sprin med*) will be attained by meditating on the lesser foundation of the fourth meditative concentration; the realm of Increasing Merit (*puṇyaprasava, bsod nams 'phel*), by meditating on the mediocre foundation; and the realm of Great Fruition (*bṛhatphala, 'bras bu che*), by meditating on the greater foundation. See the full chart in Dudjom Rinpoche 1991, 1:14–15.

1134 On these four formless absorptions, see also Pruden 1998–1990, ch. 8, pp. 1220–1227 and 1271–1273; Engle 2009, 178; and Ñāṇamoli 1979, 354–371.

1135 See also the chart, delineating the hierarchy of these four formless absorptions, in Dudjom Rinpoche 1991, 1:14–15.

1136 The Mahāsaṅghika order is discussed in, e.g., Dutt 1978, 57–97.

1137 On the four immeasurable aspirations, including loving-kindness, compassion, empathetic joy, and equanimity, see above, note 272; also Ñāṇamoli 1979, 321–353.

1138 Generally, this is identified as the supernormal cognitive power of miraculous abilities (*ṛddhyabhijnā, rdzu 'phrul gyi bya ba shes pa'i mngon shes*). On the supernormal cognitive powers, see also Ñāṇamoli 1979, 409–478.

1139 The meditative absorption of cessation (*nirodhasamāpatti, 'gog pa'i snyoms 'jug*) refers to the cessation of the modes of consciousness. See below, p. 508 and p. 515

Notes to Part Two

1 *SK* here reads *rang bzhin yi* for *rang bzhin yis,* but see the single-volume publication, root verses, p. 36.
2 Cf. Pruden 1998–1990, 404.
3 Similar passages distinguishing the Buddhist teachings in these terms are found, for example, in Dudjom Rinpoche 1991, 1:70–71, where this same quotation is cited. The three trainings (*bslab pa gsum*) are those of higher ethics (*tshul khrims*), discriminative awareness (*shes rab*), and mental development (*sems*), cultivated through meditation, which themselves form the basis for Jamgon Kongtrul's doxography in *The Treasury of Knowledge.*
4 All strands of Buddhism can identify with these four seals. See, e.g., Dudjom Rinpoche 1991, 1:70–71.
5 Vasubandhu also differentiates the views of the Vatsīputrīyas, who are within the fold of Buddhism, and those of the non-Buddhist grammarians and Vaiśeṣikas, while being equally critical of all notions of individual continuum (*pudgala, gang zag*) or independently existing self (*ātman, bdag nyid*). See Pruden 1998–1990, 1313–1342 on the former; and 1342–1355 on the latter; and for philosophical background, Kapstein 2001, 29–177. Also, for an appraisal of the doctrine of non-self, and the notion of continuity of personality within the Theravāda tradition, see Collins 1982.
6 On the hierarchy of the form and formless realms at the summit of cyclic existence, see above, pp. 417-419.
7 These verses derive from Chapter Nine of the *Eulogy to the Transcendent Lord Buddha: Praising Him Who Is Worthy of Being Praised, but Otherwise Eulogizing the [Ineffable] Which Cannot Be Eulogized* (*Varṇārhavarṇe-bhagavato buddhasya-stotre-śākyastava*, T 1138), the authorship of which is attributed to Matīcitra in the colophon. The Tibetan tradition identifies him with Śūra. See also note 935 above. The first part of this quotation is also cited in Dudjom Rinpoche 1991, 1:69, and the second part, ibid., 71.
8 See above, pp. 403–405, on the former; and pp. 414–415 on the latter.
9 *Letter to a Friend*, v. 105.
10 The *Viśeṣastava* was composed by Mudgaragomin, also known as Udbhaṭasiddhisvāmin (mTho btsun grub rje). On this figure, see Chimpa and Chattopadhyaya 1970. There are slight discrepancies between this reading and the version found in Derge, T 1109, f. 3a1–2.
11 See Jaini 1979, 130, referring to the "crescent-shaped region (*tanuvāta*), lying beyond the celestial realms," which is regarded by Jains as the permanent abode of liberated souls; also ibid., 270, which mentions the dome-like appearance of the liberated soul (*īṣat-prāghbhārabhūmi*). Cf. Dundas 2002, 104–105.
12 On this distinction between buddha-word and commentary, see the analysis in, e.g., Dudjom Rinpoche 1991, 1:73–109.

13 For Jamgon Kongtrul's detailed presentation of these four systems and their permutations, see Callahan 2007.
14 *Sūtra of the Descent to Laṅkā,* ch. 2, v. 201 and ch. 10, v. 457. This quotation is cited also in Dudjom Rinpoche 1991, 1:82.
15 On this distinction, see above, p. 420.
16 Edward Conze's pioneering translation of the *Abhisamayālaṃkāra* (1954), and his companion edition of *The Large Sutra of Perfect Wisdom* (1975) offer important insights into the structural presentation of the graduated path (*lam rim*). The essential Sanskrit commentaries of Vimuktisena and Haribhadra are presented by Gareth Sparham in his four-volume translation of *Abhisamayālaṃkārāloka* (2006).
17 This quotation is also cited in Dudjom Rinpoche 1991, 1:82.
18 *Sūtra of the Lotus*, ch. 2, v. 54. Cf. Dudjom Rinpoche 1991, 1:83.
19 This quotation appears to be paraphrased from Āryadeva's *Lamp Which Subsumes Conduct* (*Caryāmelāpakapradīpa,* T 1803), f. 94b5–7. The passage cited here and Tripiṭakamāla's following verses allude to the frequently cited distinction between the renunciant conduct of the pious attendants who avoid attachment, the engaged conduct of the bodhisattvas who know the antidote for attachment, and the fearless conduct of the mantrins who are capable of transforming attachment.
20 Maitreya, *Ornament of the Sūtras of the Greater Vehicle*, ch. 11, v. 1a.
21 Cf. Collins 1982, 85ff.
22 For this reason, Dudjom Rinpoche 1991, 1:83 remarks, following Nāgārjuna, that "the paths that are to be traversed until perfect enlightenment are positioned like the rungs of a ladder."
23 Vasubandhu, *Treasury of Phenomenology*, ch. 1, v. 3. Cf. Pruden 1998–1990, 57.
24 Not located.
25 *Sthānāsthānajñānabala, gnas dang gnas ma yin pa mkhyen pa'i stobs.* This is the first of the ten powers of a tathāgata. See *MVT*, no. 119; also Dudjom Rinpoche 1991, 1:167.
26 It is a matter of some debate as to whether the Buddha expounded the Abhidharma directly or implicitly. The Sautrāntikas hold the former view, in contrast to the Vaibhāṣikas who attribute the composition of the Abhidharma to elders such as Maudgalyāyana. See, e.g., Dudjom Rinpoche 1991, 1:440.
27 This is discussed by Vasubandhu in the *Treasury of Phenomenology*, v. 20c–d. See Pruden 1998–1990, 80–81.
28 As explained in the *Treasury of Phenomenology*, the psycho-physical aggregates were therefore expounded to address those who are deluded with respect to mental states, who are of keen faculties, and whose volition is inclined towards concise explanations. The sensory activity fields, by contrast, were expounded to those who are deluded with respect to material forms, who are of mediocre faculties and inclined towards moderate explanations. The sensory bases were then expounded to those deluded with respect to both mental states and material forms, who are of dull faculties and inclined towards extensive explanations. See Pruden 1998–1990, 80–81.
29 Pruden 1998–1990, 399ff.
30 Tib. *thun mong ma yin pa 'khor lo tha ma'i lugs srid pa nyer lnga la sogs pa'i rnam gzhag.* See below, pp. 549–574.
31 This distinction corresponds to that between the two main treatises of Abhidharma in Indo-Tibetan Buddhism—the *Compendium of Phenomenology* (*Abhidharmasamuccaya,* T 4049) composed by Asaṅga and the *Treasury of Phenomenology* (*Abhidharmakośa,* T 4089) composed by Vasubandhu. Among the seven canonical Abhidharma texts of the Theravāda tradition, the corresponding treatise focussing on the relationships and distinctions between the aggregates, sensory bases, and activity fields is the *Dhātukathā,*

on which see the English translation by U Nārada, *Discourse on Elements* (1962). A useful reference to the canonical and indigenous Tibetan commentarial literature on the *Treasury of Phenomenology* can be found in Drakpa, *Inventory of Tibetan Treatises*, 584–588, while www.tbrc.org, T59, offers a more comprehensive listing of Abhidharma literature. See also Potter et al. 1996 and 2009.

32 The text reads *dāśi.*

33 This term is often translated as "formations" by Sanskrit and Pali scholars, or else as "motivational tendencies" or "factors" by Tibetanists. Edgerton 1953 suggests "predispositions" or "conditionings."

34 Not located. The aggregates are designated here as "compulsively accrued" because desire and craving perpetuate the continuation and non-abandonment of future and present aggregates, owing to desire for the future and attachment to the present. See Boin-Webb 2001, 3.

35 Boin-Webb 2001, 3.

36 The former refers to concrete changes occurring in physical forms that are actually present, i.e., physical objects that are capable of being damaged, while the latter refers to imagined forms that can be pointed out—"the imagination of form, through determined or undetermined mental conception." See Boin-Webb 2001, 3.

37 Boin-Webb 2001, 4, and Pruden 1998–1990, 68–70. Also see the discussion on the primary elements in Guenther 1976, 146–151; Engle 2009, 248–252; and Bodhi 2000, 237–238.

38 On the substratum consciousness (*ālaya, kun gzhi*), see below, pp. 513–523.

39 Boin-Webb 2001, 4–5. Here the subtle material faculties of the eyes and so forth are contrasted with their corresponding gross material forms. See also Engle 2009, 252–258; and Bodhi 2000, 238–239.

40 Boin-Webb 2001, 5; and for the Sanskrit terminology, see Negi, *Tibetan Sanskrit Dictionary*, 5474. For an analysis of derivative matter according to the diverse schools of Abhidharma, see Guenther 1976, 151–158.

41 According to Jinaputra's *Exposition of the Compendium of Phenomenology* (*Abhidharmasamuccayavyākhyā*, T 4054), vol. Li, f. 122a, these six sub-categories of the twenty-five attributes comprise defining characteristics (*mtshan nyid*), form (*dbyibs*), degree of benefit and harm (*phan gnod*), functional support (*byed pa'i rten*), functional characteristic (*byed pa'i mtshan nyid*), and embellishment (*rgyan*). For an alternative sixfold enumeration of form, see Nordrang Orgyan, *Compendium of Buddhist Numeric Terms*, 1571.

42 *SK*, 367, reads *'di* for *'dir*. This refers to the context of the Higher Abhidharma of Asaṅga specifically, in contrast to the tradition represented by Vasubandhu.

43 The Higher Abhidharma tradition of Asaṅga does not accept the Sarvāstivāda view posited by Vasubandhu, for example, that apperceived but intangible forms arising from past impulses exist substantially throughout the three times. On this distinction between imputed and substantial existents, see below, pp. 495–496. Among more recent sources elucidating the points raised in Jamgon Kongtrul's presentation of the aggregates, mention should be made of the works of his contemporary, the Jonangpa scholar Banda Gelek Gyatso. The latter's *Ascertaining the General Meaning of the Collected Topics, entitled Precious Lamp Clarifying All Phenomena* (*bsDus grva'i spyi don rnam par nges pa chos thams cad kyi mtshan nyid rab tu gsal bar byed pa rin po che'i sgron me*) and his *Necklace of Youthful Clear Intelligence Analyzing the Psycho-physical Aggregates, entitled Jewel Garland of Eloquence* (*Phung po lnga'i rnam par dbye ba blo gsal gzhon nu'i mgul rgyan legs bshad nor bu'i phreng ba*) are particularly useful for their examination of Abhidharma terminology.

44 Boin-Webb 2001, 5, mentions only three: pleasant, unpleasant, or indifferent forms.

45 The *Yogācāra Level* (*Yogācārabhūmi*, T 4035, Dg. T. Sems tsam, vol. Tshi, f. 34a) enumerates the four categories of sound as (1) virtuous (*dge ba*), (2) non-virtuous (*mi dge ba*), (3) obscured and ethically neutral or unspecified (*bsgribs la lung du ma bstan pa*), and (4) unobscured and ethically unspecified (*ma bsgribs la lung du ma bstan pa*). See Nordrang Orgyan, *Compendium of Buddhist Numeric Terms*, 563.

46 Boin-Webb 2001, 5. For alternative discussions on this and variant Abhidharma notions of sound, see Engle 2009, 258–259, and Guenther 1976, 158–159.

47 *SK*, 368, reads *nga ba* for *ngar ba*.

48 Boin-Webb 2001, 5–6; also Engle 2009, 259, and Guenther 1976, 159–160, who interprets the latter to include natural, accidental, and changing odors.

49 Boin-Webb 2001, 6; also Engle 2009, 259, and Guenther 1976, 160.

50 Boin-Webb 2001, 6, adds heat or warmth, which would increase the overall number to twenty-three, but warmth should be included, as it is in the following paragraph.

51 Boin-Webb 2001, 6.

52 A different sixfold classification of tangible sensations is mentioned in the *Yogācāra Level* (*Yogācārabhūmi*, T 4035, Dg. T. Sems tsam, vol. Tshi, f. 35a), comprising (1) tangible sensations of happiness (*bde ba*), (2) tangible sensations of sorrow (*sdug bsngal*), (3) tangible sensations inducing neither sorrow nor happiness (*sdug bsngal ba yang ma yin bde ba yang ma yin pa*), (4) tangible sensations that are co-emergent or instinctive (*lhan cig skyes pa*), (5) tangible sensations that are disharmonious (*mi mthun pa'i phyogs su bsdus pa*), and (6) tangible sensations of softness (*mnyen par bsdus pa*). See Nordrang Orgyan, *Compendium of Buddhist Numeric Terms*, 1591.

53 On tangible objects, see also Engle 2009, 259–262, and Guenther 1976, 160–163.

54 Cf. Engle 2009, 263–264.

55 Meditation on the human form as a skeleton, in order to generate renunciation and progress towards the first meditative concentration, is discussed in, e.g., Ñāṇamoli 1979, 198–199; also Bodhi 2000, 333.

56 Boin-Webb 2001, 6; also Engle 2009, 264. Specifically on the meditative stabilities associated with the ten consummations of the colors and elements (*kṛtsnāyatana*, Pali *kasina*), see Ñāṇamoli 1979, 122–184; also Guenther 1976, 116–119.

57 Engle 2009, 263–264, and 359–360, prefers the terms "indicated" and "resisted." Sthiramati points out that the first category capable of being revealed and obstructed is exemplified by visual objects, the second is exemplified by auditory, olfactory, gustatory, and tangible sense objects as well as all five sense faculties, and the third is exemplified by mental forms, associated with the sensory activity field of phenomena.

58 Cf. Engle 2009, 367–368. The former include presently existing forms but not those of the past or future, as well as the five sense faculties and a portion of the four sense objects (excluding sound, bodily excretions, fluids, and the roots of hair, teeth, etc.). The latter are said to include mental forms, sounds, bodily excretions, fluids, etc.

59 See Engle 2009, 368–369. The former include, for example, the eye which shares its visual object with visual consciousness, the ear which shares its auditory object with auditory consciousness, and so forth. The latter include the same categories on occasions when the sense faculties are divorced from their respective consciousnesses. Absence of a shared support implies that there is no cross-over between the categories themselves.

60 I.e., this also implicitly includes feelings that are compounded by hearing, smelling, tasting, and touching. See Boin-Webb 2001, 6.

61 Boin-Webb 2001, 7. For a more general discussion on feeling (*tshor ba*), cf. Engle 2009, 267–271, and Guenther 1976, 37–39.

62 *SK*, 371, here reads *rna ba'i bsdus te* ("aurally compounded"). See Boin-Webb 2001, 7.

63 *SK*, 371, here includes a passage of scribal repetition, commencing with *mtshan ma' dang bcas pa'i 'du shes* on line 16 and ending with *sas bsdus pa'i 'du shes* on line 19.

64 Boin-Webb 2001, 7–8. For a general interpretation of perception (*'du shes*), see Engle 2009, 271–272, and Guenther 1976, 39–41.

65 Cf. the detailed exposition of formative predispositions given by Sthiramati in Engle 2009, 273–326.

66 On the eight modes of consciousness, see below, pp. 511–530.

67 The fifty-one mental states are all enumerated below, pp. 496–506.

68 Friedmann 1984, 40–41.

69 The first of these texts is translated in Engle 2009, 229–244, and the latter on 245–369. The appendix also provides the Tibetan translation of Vasubandhu's text along with a reconstruction of the Sanskrit. See also Anacker 1984, 49–82, and particularly p. 72, which refers to the apparent amalgam of the aggregates on the basis of "time, series, aspects, developments, and sense objects."

70 Engle 2009, 274.

71 Cf. Pruden 1998–1990, 205–206; also Engle 2009, 473n177.

72 For a detailed discussion on the five aspects of concomitance and their contradictions from the perspective of Mind Only, see Zilung Paṇchen Śākya Chokden's *Exegesis of the Compendium of Phenomenology entitled Ocean Waves Upholding Yogācāra* (*mNgon pa kun btus pa'i rnam bshad rnal 'byor spyod gzung rgya mtsho'i rlabs phreng*), pp. 53ff. Cf. also Sthiramati's *Commentary on the Treasury of Phenomenology entitled Meaningful Reality* (*Abhidharmakośabhāṣyatīkātattvārtha,* T 4421, vol. Tho), ff. 277a–280a; and the discussion on the concomitance of time, where contrasting Vaibhāṣika and Cittamātra positions are given, in Chim Lobzang Drak's *Ocean of Eloquence Elucidating Phenomenology* (*Chos mngon pa gsal byed legs pas bshad pa'i rgya mtsho*), pp. 116–117.

73 These contrasting positions are summarized in Chapter 11 of Upa Losal's *Exegetical Treasury of Philosophical Systems* (*Grub mtha' rnam par bshad pa'i mdzod*) (Thimphu: Kunzang Topgyel and Mani Dorji, 1979), pp. 174–175:

> There are two interpretations concerning the relationship between mind and mental states, one holding that they are different [in substance] and the other holding that they are identical. The former is the view of Asaṅga and so forth, who hold that if mental states were not substantially existent, feelings and perceptions would also lack substantial existence, and therefore the structure of the five psycho-physical aggregates would be unascertained. Also, an efficient cause that lacks particulars could not distinguish its result as being either substantially existent or substantially non-existent. Also, if mental states possessed attributes that are dissimilar to mind, they would be substantially existent, but if they did not they could not even be provisionally different. Furthermore, the scriptures say that mind is afflicted by desire and purified by faith. Therefore, to be brief, it is because the five aggregates would be deranged, an efficient cause would have no particulars, circumstantial differences would be inadmissible, and the scriptures would be contradicted that the opposite view [of identical substance] is untenable. The latter view, which holds that mind and mental states are identical in substance, is maintained by Śāntarakṣita, who claimed scriptural authority, and by Dharmakīrti, who said that other minds can be appreciated because they are identical in nature and not different. In this latter view, the nature of mind comprises feelings from the experiential perspective, perceptions from the reductionist perspective, and attention, etc., from the object-oriented perspective.

Also, on Śāntarakṣita's position with regard to mind and mental states, see Blumenthal 2004, 81ff; and Padmakara Translation Group 2005, 216–217. In his *Auto-commentary on the Ornament of Madhyamaka* (*Madhyamakālaṃkāravṛtti,* T 3885), f. 64b, Śāntarakṣita refers only obliquely to this identity in the expression "mind together with its cluster of mental states" (*sems byung tshogs dang bcas pa'i sems*). Dharmakīrti's position, suggested in the first part of his *Exposition of Valid Cognition* (*Pramāṇavārttika,* T 4210), is summarized by Dungkar Lobzang Trinle, *Great Dictionary of Dungkar*, 2060, as follows:

> Mind and mental states are substance because they are entities, and substantially existent with respect to an individual mind. Mental states are formed from the substance of mind. The mental states and mind are exclusively established as one, in a symbiotic relationship, on the basis of their single substance. There are no objectifiable mental states apart from the mind; nor is there an objectifiable mind apart from the mental states. Therefore, while an individual mind is established to have many distinctive and dissimilar aspects, the mind and its mental states are not separately established as different in substance.

On the other hand, Candrakīrti's comments negating this identity are made towards the end of ch. 6 of his *Auto-commentary on the Introduction to Madhyamaka* (*Madhyamakāvatārabhāṣya,* T 3862), ff. 301a and 348b, and in the root verses (vv. 48ff.). See also Padmakara Translation Group 2002, 74ff. Dungkar Lobzang Trinle, *Great Dictionary*, 2057, summarizes the position of Candrakīrti and Asaṅga as follows:

> If mind and mental states were not different in substance, the definitive sequence of the five aggregates would not hold because feeling and perception would not be different from mind [=consciousness]; and if these two were of a single substance, they could not have a concomitant causal basis. Also if non-virtuous and virtuous mental states were identical, the mind would turn to both virtue and non-virtue in accord with its essential nature. Therefore one should know that these are different. As for the distinction between them, mind perceives the essential nature of its objects through its own power, whereas mental states perceive its attributes through their own power.

On these contrasting positions regarding mind and its mental states in general, cf. Barron 2007, 92–95; also Waldron 2003, 57–59.

74 These comments by Asaṅga are found in the *Summation of Ascertainment from the Yogācāra Level* (*Yogācārabhūmiviniścayasaṃgrahaṇī,* T 4038), vol. 1, ff. 76b–77a, where he remarks that the bundling of the aggregates (1) establishes the identity of many diverse aspects (*bdag nyid sna tshogs mang po'i don*), and in addition it (2) facilitates engagement with interactive objects (*phan tshun 'dres pa'i dngos pos 'jug pa'i don*), (3) manifestly gathers these objects together (*gcig tu mngon par bsdus pa'i don*), (4) facilitates the increase and decrease of mental luminosity (*'phel ba dang 'bri pa'i don*), (5) facilitates the arising of sense objects in the case of the aggregate of physical forms (*yul de dang der skye ba'i don*), and (6) facilitates conceptualization with regard to referential objects in the case of the other four aggregates (*dmigs pa la rnam par rtogs pa'i don*). He asserts that while the mental aggregates might be held from the Mind Only (Cittamātra) perspective to be identical in substance, this cannot be the case for mental states because six faults (*skyon drug*) would arise with regard to the hierarchical arrangement of the psycho-physical aggregates and their five functions. If mental states and mind were not substantially different, not only would this structure be deranged because feeling and perception could not be differentiated from mind, but the five particular circumstances (*gnas skabs kyi bye brag lnga*) through which they function would be ineffective. Similarly, the six modes of engaged consciousness have their different functional circumstances and objects of reference.

75 Asaṅga also points out in *Summation of Ascertainment from the Yogācāra Level*, vol. 1, f. 77a ff., that differentiation between the circumstances of the aggregates is applicable in cases where they relate to material things owing to the transformations that may occur, as in the production of milk, curd, and butter from a common source, but not

so in the case of immaterial things, where, in the absence of an efficient cause (*byed pa'i rgyu*), transformations of mental states and circumstances are not possible. He goes on to say that the view that would identify "mind only" (*cittamātra*) as a substance runs contrary to the scriptures because it would contradict attested processes pertaining to the sequential purification of the dissonant mental states of desire, hatred, and delusion.

76 The presentation of fifty-one mental states accords with Asaṅga's interpretation in contrast to the position of Vasubandhu, which is outlined below, pp. 544–545, and that of the *Abhidhammasangaha*, which enumerates fifty-two distinct mental states. See Engle 2009, 274–312; also Guenther 1976, 30–96; Lusthaus 2002, 542–543; and Bodhi 2000, 78–99.

77 These five ever-present mental states are discussed in detail below, pp. 496–497.

78 The primary and subsidiary dissonant mental states are enumerated individually below, pp. 499–506.

79 All these subcategories of mental states are outlined below, pp. 496–506. Cf. the distribution of the mental states that may arise in virtuous, non-virtuous, and neutral engagement, as described in Pruden 1998–1990, 196–198.

80 On the meaning of object-universals, see above, p. 123 and p. 145.

81 See, e.g., the Vaibhāṣika view as represented by Vasubandhu, in Pruden 1998–1990, 198.

82 Engle 2009, 313. Sthiramati's distinction, however, is made between substantial and imputed existents on the basis of their respective association and non-association with mind, and not within the category of mental states associated with mind. In his *Commentary on the Treasury of Phenomenology entitled Meaningful Reality* (*Abhidharmakośabhāṣyatīkātattvārtha,* vol. Do), ff. 147b–148a, he makes a similar distinction between substantial and imputed existence in relation to the aggregates in general.

83 The analysis presented in this and the preceding paragraph may derive from Chim Lobzang Drak, *Ocean of Eloquence Elucidating Phenomenology,* pp. 117–118, where it is claimed to represent the Cittamātra classification of mental states rather than that of the Vaibhāṣika. Upa Losal, *Exegetical Treasury of Philosophical Systems*, p. 129, defines a contrasting Vaibhāṣika position, holding only five mental states (non-delusion, wrong view, inattentiveness, recollection, and distraction) to be imputed or non-substantial, and all the other forty-six to be substantial.

84 These form the subject matter of works such as Banda Gelek Gyatso's *Exegesis Elucidating the Systematic Presentation of the Eighty Natural Dissonant Mental States, entitled Mirror That Discloses Their Meaning* (*Rang bzhin brgyad cu'i rnam bzhag gsal bar bshad pa don rab tu gsal ba'i me long*). The eighty "natural states of conceptual thought" comprise forty dissonant mental states based on desire, thirty-three based on hatred, and seven based on delusion. For complete enumerations, see Nordrang Orgyan, *Compendium of Buddhist Numeric Terms*, 3624–3625.

85 See Negi, *Tibetan Sanskrit Dictionary*, 6142. The mental states are enumerated differently in the different traditions of Abhidharma. See Guenther 1976, 96, and the contrasting charts on 260–266; also the chart in Lusthaus 2002, 542–553; and Bodhi 2000, 79 and 379–380. For a detailed analysis in Tibetan, see also Chim Lobzang Drak, *Ocean of Eloquence Elucidating Phenomenology,* pp. 119–131.

86 Vasubandhu's *Thirty Verses*, v. 3. Cf. Anacker 1984, 186; and Cook 1999, 378.

87 Boin-Webb 2001, 9.

88 See the detailed discussion of the five ever-present mental states in Engle 2009, 274–277; also Cook 1999, 68–72; Guenther 1976, 30–48; and Bodhi 2000, 78–81.

89 *Thirty Verses*, v. 10. Cf. Anacker 1984, 187, and Cook 1999, 379.

90 See above, p. 431.

91 For Jamgon Kongtrul's presentation of the four truths (*caturāryasatya*)—suffering, its

cause, the path leading to the cessation of suffering, and the actual cessation of suffering, which are the foundation of the Buddhist spiritual path, see Callahan 2007, 89–122.

92 On these five object-determining mental states, see also Boin-Webb 2001, 9; also Engle 2009, 277–281; and Cook 1999, 164–172.

93 *Thirty Verses*, v. 11. Anacker 1984, 187; also Cook 1999, 379.

94 Boin-Webb 2001, 9–10; also Engle 2009, 281–291; and Cook 1999, 172–184.

95 *Thirty Verses*, vv. 11–12. Anacker 1984, 187; and Cook 1999, 379.

96 Boin-Webb 2001, 11–12; also Engle 2009, 291–295 and 302–303; Cook 1999, 185–186.

97 Cf. the presentation in Engle 2009, 292–295.

98 Boin-Webb 2001, 12–13; also Engle 2009, 296–302; and Cook 1999, 186ff.

99 Boin-Webb 2001, 14–15.

100 Bodhi 1978, 65–80, and the commentary on 125–185. Among the four views positing eternalism (*śāśvatavāda, rtag smra ba*) of the world and the self, three are based on the yogic recollection of past lives and one on reason. Among the four views of partial eternalism (*ekasyaśāśvatavāda, kha cig rtag smra ba*) three are theistic or polytheistic and consider sentient beings to be eternal, while one is rationalistic, considering only formative predispositions to be eternal. Among the two views of fortuitous origin (*adhityasamutpannavāda, rgyu med smra ba*), one refers to the yogin's experience of spontaneity of consciousness and the other to the reasoning of ordinary persons who cannot discern past lives. Among the four views on finitude (*antānantavāda, mtha' ldan smra ba*) there are those holding the world and the self to be finite, infinite, both, or neither. Lastly, the four views of equivocation (*amārävikṣepavāda, mtha' mi spong smra ba*) include prevaricators who (1) fear making false statements, (2) fear giving way to desire or aversion, (3) fear challenges and refutations, and (4) prevaricate due to dullness and stupidity.

101 See Bodhi 1978, 80–88, and the commentary on 185–204. Among them, the sixteen views holding the self to be percipient after death (*saṃjñīvāda, 'du shes yod smra*) include those holding the immortal self to be percipient and also material, immaterial, both material and immaterial, neither material not immaterial, finite, infinite, both finite and infinite, neither finite nor infinite, of uniform perception, of diversified perception, of limited perception, of boundless perception, of exclusive happiness, of exclusive suffering, of both happiness and suffering, and of neither happiness nor suffering.

As for the eight views on the non-percipience of the self after death (*asaṃjñīvāda, 'du shes med smra*), they hold the immortal self to be non-percipient and also material, immaterial, both material and immaterial, finite, infinite, both finite and infinite, and neither finite nor infinite.

The eight views on neither percipient nor non-percipient immortality (*naivasaṃjñināsaṃjñīvāda, gnyis min brgyad*) include those holding the immortal self to be neither percipient nor non-percipient after death, and in addition material, immaterial, both material and immaterial, neither material nor immaterial, finite, infinite, both finite and infinite, and neither finite nor infinite. The seven views on nihilism (*uccedavāda, chad par smra ba*) include those maintaining that the self is annihilated at the moment of death, in seven possible ways—through its identity with the physical body, and through its identity with the god-realms of the world-systems of desire and form, and the four levels of the world-system of formlessness.

Lastly, the five views concerning the attainment of liberation in this lifetime (*dṛṣṭidharmanirvāṇavāda, tshe 'di nyid la grol lta*) hold that, rather than the final nirvāṇa of Buddhist practice, liberation may be attained without relinquishing the physical body and by means of hedonism and through the four meditative concentrations.

102 *Verse Summation of the Transcendental Perfection of Discriminative Awareness*, ch. 25, v. 4.

103 On these non-Buddhist views, see above, pp. 403–415. The Vātsīputrīya, though classed

among the schools of the Lesser Vehicle, are subjected to severe criticism by Vasubandhu on account of their ambivalent positions. See Pruden 1998–1990, 1314–1341.

104 Cf. the brief comment in Boin-Webb 2001, 14, and the summation of these arguments offered by Sthiramati in Engle 2009, 296–301.

105 *Thirty Verses*, vv. 12–14. Anacker 1984, 187, and Cook 1999, 379.

106 *SK*, 381, reads *rnam tshe* for *rnam gYeng*—a scribal error repeating *rnam tshe*.

107 The eight worldly concerns (*chos brgyad*) comprise profit, loss, pleasure, pain, fame, defamation, praise, and blame. See, e.g., Dudjom Rinpoche 1991, 2:162.

108 On the subsidiary dissonant mental states, see Boin-Webb 2001, 15–18; also Engle 2009, 303–310, and Cook 1999, 196–209.

109 *Thirty Verses*, v. 14. Cf. Boin-Webb 2001, 18; also Engle 2009, 310–312; Cook 1999, 210–218; and on ideation and scrutiny specifically, see Guenther 1976, 49–51.

110 These disassociated formative dispositions are discussed in greater detail in Chim Lobzang Drak, *Ocean of Eloquence Elucidating Phenomenology*, pp. 131–168.

111 Tib. *'du byas kyi gnas skabs*.

112 It is not immediately apparent that Upa Losal did in fact consider the disassociated formative predispositions to be distinct from physical forms, mind, and mental states. See his comments, *Exegetical Treasury of Philosophical Systems*, ch. 9, pp. 135–138, where the disassociated formative predispositions are summarized; also p. 140, where he assigns them to one aspect of the aggregate of formative predispositions; and ch. 11, p. 175, where he designates them as "circumstances pertaining to mind and mental states" (*sems dang sems las byung ba'i gnas skabs*).

113 Zenkar Rinpoche suggests that this citation may possibly derive from the two-volume *Chariot of Enlightened Activity* (*Karma shing rta*), authored by Karma Trinlepa II (*Karma phrin las pa gnyis pa*). Other extant texts by him include a treatise entitled *Ornaments of Speech: Well-known Ornamental Proverbs Based on the Mirror of Poetics* (*Tshig rgyan snyan ngag gi bstan bcos me long rgyan gyi dper brjod bklags pas kun shes*). He is to be differentiated from the earlier Karma Trinlepa (1456–1539), a grammarian, also known as Pelkhang Ngawang Chokyi Gyatso, who composed a commentary on Karmapa III's *Profound Inner Meaning* (*Zab mo nang don*) and summarized the views of Karmapa VII Chodrak Gyatso (1454–1506) in his *Replies to Doctrinal Questions* (*Dris lan*). On the latter, see Brunnhölzl 2009, 117, and the biography in Kozhul Drakpa Jungne and Gyalwa Lobzang Khedrub, eds., *Lexicon of the Learned and Accomplished Masters Who Successively Appeared in the Land of Snows* (*Gangs can mkhas grub rim byon ming mdzod*), 1001–1002; also Stearns 2002, 63, and the bibliographical entries on p. 280 of that work.

114 Thanks to Karl Brunnhölzl (email communication 29 March 2010) for his suggestions concerning this passage.

115 See the translations of Vasubandhu's treatise in Anacker 1984, 70–71, and Engle 2009, 229–244.

116 Boin-Webb 2001, 18–21.

117 On this distinction, see Anacker 1984, 78–79, notes 16–18; Pruden 1998–1990, 206–211; also Guenther 1976, 178–179; and Waldron 2003, 72–73.

118 See above, pp. 434–437 and p. 508; also Engle 2009, 314–316.

119 Engle 2009, 316–318; also Anacker 1984, 70–71.

120 Engle 2009, 318–319.

121 These three kinds of deeds (*las gsum*) comprise deeds whose fruit will be experienced in this life (*mthong chos myong 'gyur gyi las*), deeds whose fruit will be experienced in the next life (*skyes nas myong 'gyur gyi las*), and deeds whose fruits will be experienced in other subsequent lives (*lan grangs gzhan du myong 'gyur gyi las*). Cf. Engle 2009, 319.

122 Engle 2009, 319–320, and Anacker 1984, 71.

123 *SK*, 384, reads *lngar ma byung* for *sngar ma byung*. On this see also Anacker 1984, 71, and Engle 2009, 320.

124 Anacker 1984, 71; also Engle 2009, 322.

125 *SK*, 385, reads *bcu gcig* for *bcu gnyis*.

126 Cf. Engle 2009, 322–323.

127 Anacker 1984, 71; also Engle 2009, 323–324.

128 The remaining formative predispositions disassociated with mind and mental states are described in Boin-Webb 2001, 20–21, and Engle 2009, 324–326.

129 Cf. the relevant discussion on non-associated formative predispositions in Pruden 1998–1990, 206ff.

130 The eight modes of consciousness (*tshogs brgyad*) are all explained below. Among them, the first six, which are collectively known as "engaged consciousness" (*pravṛttivijñāna, 'jug pa'i rnam shes*) represent the range of consciousness known to exponents of the Vaibhāṣika and Sautrāntika systems; whereas the full eight, including additionally the dissonant mental consciousness (*kliṣṭamanovijñāna, nyon yid rnam shes*) and the substratum consciousness (*ālayavijñāna, kun gzhi'i rnam shes*) are known within the philosophical systems of the Greater Vehicle, espoused by the Mādhyamika and Cittamātrin. For Jamgon Kongtrul's interpretation of all these four systems, see Callahan 2007. Among the latter two systems, a distinction is made here between the Mādhyamika who regard consciousness as "ordinary" and the Cittamātrin who regard it as "extraordinary."

131 Cf. the distinctions drawn between these terms in Keenan 2003, 17.

132 *SK*, 387, here reads *rgyun stug* for *rgyan stug*.

133 For a detailed exposition of the substratum consciousness, also sometimes known as the storehouse consciousness or the consciousness of the ground-of-all (*ālayavijñāna, kun gzhi'i rnam par shes pa*), see Schmithausen 1987 and Waldron 2003; also Cook 1999, 47–111. For an explanation of its defining characteristics, see also Keenan 2003, 19–21; and Sthiramati's interpretation as rendered in Engle 2009, 328–335. Among the two identifiable facets of the substratum consciousness, the seminal aspect is also known as the potential or consequential aspect (*niṣyandabhāga, rgyu mthun pa'i cha*).

134 Tib. *thog ma med pa'i dus kyi bag chags la brten nas sa bon yongs su smin par gyur pa'i kun gzhi*. See Boin-Webb 2001, 21; also Engle 2009, 328–330, and Anacker 1984, 71–72.

135 Cf. Cook 1999, 44–56; and Chatterjee 1971, 18–19.

136 For a detailed explanation of such demonstrations, see Keenan 2003, 24–32.

137 Cf. Engle 2009, 329–330.

138 Sthiramati (in Engle 2009, 331–335) reiterates this dependence of formless meditative absorption on the substratum consciousness, and goes on to show how erroneously constructed arguments are incapable of eliminating the seeds of dissonant mental states. See also Waldron 2003, 179.

139 See the account of these dual processes in Engle 2009, 338–342; and especially in Waldron 2003, 101–127. The latter work also includes a translated extract (pp. 178–189) from the *Summation of Ascertainment from the Yogācāra Level*, in which it is explained that engagement with the objective referent (*ālambanapravṛtti*) encompasses both the indiscernible receptacle world and the internal propensities that are actually discerned (Waldron 2003, 179). Engagement by means of association (*samprayogapravṛtti*) with the five ever-present mental states is also discussed (ibid., 180–181).

140 Cook 1999, 68–72; also Waldron 2003, 180–181.

141 *SK*, 388, reads *mdung* for *gdung*.

142 Engagement based on interacting conditions (*anyonyapratyayatāpravṛtti*) is termed "reciprocal conditionality" by Waldron 2003, 181–182.

143 Cf. the explanation of concurrent engagement in Waldron 2003, 182–185.

144 On this function of the substratum consciousness, nurturing the seeds of this life and projecting them into the subsequent life, see Engle 2009, 338–340; also Waldron 2003, 182, and Chatterjee 1971, 18–19. A Tibetan description of the intermediate states (*antarābhava, bar do*) in the cycle of life, death, and rebirth is found in Dorje 2005.

145 This process of reversal with reference to the substratum consciousness is discussed in Engle 2009, 340–342, and Waldron 2003, 185–189. See also Dudjom Rinpoche 1991, 1:340. On the transformation of the substratum consciousness into the mirror-like pristine cognition, among the five aspects of pristine cognition, see Karmapa Rangjung Dorje's *Treatise Distinguishing Consciousness and Pristine Cognition* (*rNam shes ye shes 'byed pa'i bstan bcos*), p. 327; and the commentary by Jamgon Kongtrul entitled *Ornament of the Enlightened Intention of Rangjung [Dorje]* (*Rang byung dgongs pa'i rgyan*), p. 366. The relevant passages are translated in Brunnhölzl 2009, 364 (root text) and 292–294 (commentary). Cf. Cook 1999, 347–349.

146 See, e.g., Pruden 1998–1990, 1021; and on this attainment, Cook 1999, 341–345; also Dudjom Rinpoche 1991, 1:226–227.

147 On the three natures, see below, pp. 563–574.

148 Cf. the more detailed explanation of "appropriating consciousness," presented by Sthiramati in Engle 2009, 341–342.

149 Cf. the synonyms for the substratum consciousness enumerated in Cook 1999, 81–82.

150 Keenan 2003, ch. 1, v. 12, p. 17; also Waldron 2003, 130–131.

151 These eight reasons (*rnam grangs brgyad*) for the existence of the substratum are posited almost at the start of Asaṅga's *Summation of Ascertainment from the Yogācāra Level*, where he asserts that if there were no substratum (1) it would be impossible for consciousness to assume [new] states of birth (*gnas len pa mi srid pa*); (2) it would be impossible for consciousness to enter into its initial engagement (*dang po 'jug pa mi srid pa*); (3) it would be impossible for consciousness to engage with clarity (*gsal bar 'jug pa mi srid pa*); (4) it would be impossible for the seeds themselves to exist (*sa bon nyid mi srid pa*); (5) the impact of past actions would be impossible (*las mi srid pa*); (6) physical sensations would be impossible (*lus kyi tshor ba mi srid pa*); and (8) consciousness would not be able to transmigrate at death (*rnam shes 'chi 'pho mi srid pa*). Cf. also the initial verses found in ch. 1 of Asaṅga's *Summary of the Greater Vehicle* (*Mahāyānasaṃgraha*, T 4048) translated in Keenan 2003, 13–17, on which see Waldron 2003, 130 and 102–107. Here, the eight proofs of the substratum consciousness enumerated in the *Summation of Ascertainment* are discussed. A more elaborate argument for the existence of the substratum consciousness is also presented in Cook 1999, 83–111.

152 The implication here is that only buddhas and bodhisattvas on the irreversible levels have the capacity to reverse the subtle distribution of propensities within the substratum consciousness.

153 See Waldron 2003, 140–146, based on ch.1, vv. 29–57, of Asaṅga's *Summary of the Greater Vehicle*, in Keenan 2003, 24–33.

154 The substratum consciousness is characterized by impermanence and constant dynamic—regeneration and ripening of propensities. On those phenomena such as space which are characterized as permanent and uncompounded, see above, pp. 535–537.

155 Cf. the explanation of perfuming or permeation in Keenan 2003, 19–20.

156 This is a well-known metaphor for the production of results similar in class to their seeds. See Negi, *Tibetan Sanskrit Dictionary*, 7079, on the analogy presented in the *Sūtra of the Shoots of Rice* (*Śālistambasūtra*, T 210) and its commentaries, including those by Nāgārjuna (T 3985–3986). The distinction between external and internal seeds is explained in ch.1 of Asaṅga's *Summary of the Greater Vehicle*. See Keenan 2003, 22–23, v. 25.

157 The enumeration of the six kinds of seed (*sa bon rnam pa drug*) is mentioned in Khewang

Yeshe Gyatso's *Exegetical Memorandum on the Ascertainment of Great Madhyamaka according to the Most Extensive Teachings of the Supreme Vehicle* (*Theg mchog shin tu rgyas pa'i dbu ma chen po rnam par nges pa'i rnam bshad kyi zin bris*), p. 147. This text (on which see below, note 241) is Jamgon Kongtrul's principal source for the later chapters of Book Six, Part Two on phenomenology according to the final promulgation of the Buddha's teachings.

158 *SK*, 391, reads *rang bzhin yi* for *rang bzhin yis*. See the root verses, p. 36.

159 Cook 1999, 259–260, alludes to the views of Dignāga with regard to the complex relationship between the seeds and the modes of consciousness. The same text, pp. 56–57, summarizes these five characteristics of seeds or propensities as follows: they are instantaneous, serial, morally determinate, originating from multiple conditions, and producing results similar in type. In Asaṅga's *Summary of the Greater Vehicle*, six attributes or qualities of the seeds are enumerated, viz., momentariness, simultaneity with results, sequential continuity, determinate status, dependence on causes, and productivity of special results. See Keenan 2003, 22–23, v. 25. Jamgon Kongtrul's actual words may imply that Dignāga's treatises on Buddhist logic (T 4203–4209) refer explicitly to the six seeds and their five natural properties, but I have been unable to find any such comments in these works, even in the most likely source, *Examination of Objects of Reference* (*Ālambanaparīkṣā*, T 4205–4206), or in his *Essential Lamp Commentary on the Treasury of Phenomenology* (*Abhidharmakośavṛttimarmadīpa*, T 4095).

160 See Asaṅga's *Summary of the Greater Vehicle*, as translated in Keenan 2003, 20, v. 19.

161 See *Summary of the Greater Vehicle*, v. 16, as translated in Keenan 2003, 20.

162 For Jamgon Kongtrul's restatement of the Sautrāntika tenets, see Callahan 2007, 132–135.

163 In his *Door Illuminating the Hundred Teachings of the Greater Vehicle* (*Theg pa chen po'i chos brgya gsal pa'i sgo'i bstan bcos*, T 4063), translated from Chinese. See also Cook 1999, 51–52.

164 For a more detailed analysis of the dissonant mental consciousness, see Cook 1999, 113–152; also Waldron 2003, 146–150 and 182–183.

165 On all these unwholesome or negative mental states, see above, pp. 499–506. Cf. Cook 1999, 131–132, and Engle 2009, 341.

166 This implies that for realized arhats, the dissonant mental consciousness is no longer active, whereas it continues to function in the case of those who have not yet reached the path of no-more-learning. See also Engle 2009, 341–342.

167 On this transformation, see Karmapa Rangjung Dorje's *Treatise Distinguishing Consciousness and Pristine Cognition*, 327; and the commentary by Jamgon Kongtrul entitled *Ornament of the Enlightened Intention of Rangjung*, 366. The relevant passages are also translated in Brunnhölzl 2009, 364–365 (root text) and 294–296 (commentary). Cf. Dudjom Rinpoche 1991, 1:231–237; also Cook 1999, 348–349. For Asaṅga's exposition of the bodhisattva levels, cf. Keenan 2003, 79–83; and more generally, Williams 1989, 204–214.

168 See, for example, Khewang Yeshe Gyatso, *Exegetical Memorandum*, ch. 4, pp. 146–147.

169 Tib. *rigs pa'i rnam grangs drug*. These are enumerated in Asaṅga's *Summary of the Greater Vehicle* (*Mahāyānasaṃgraha*), ch. 1, as follows: (1) If there were no dissonant mental consciousness, delusion devoid of other dissonant mental states would be impossible. (2) Dissonant mental states would have no locus or support on the analogy of the five sensory consciousnesses which have their own supports in the sense organs. (3) Thinking would be impossible if there were no dissonant mental consciousness. (4) There would be no difference between non-conceptual meditative stability and the meditative stability that destroys thought because dissonant mental consciousness is present in the

former but not in the latter. (5) Unconscious gods who have attained such meditative stabilities would have no self-pride or belief in self because they would be perfect, if there were no dissonant mental consciousness. (6) Self-attachment would only arise in negative states and not in good or neutral states if there were no dissonant mental consciousness. See the translation in Keenan 2003, 15–16. The same listing is also alluded to in Cook 1999, 144–152.

170 *Treasury of Phenomenology*, v. 17a–b. For an alternative translation and Vasubandhu's interpretation, see Pruden 1998–1990, 75.

171 This point is made in Karmapa Rangjung Dorje's *Profound Inner Meaning*, ch. 1, p. 4; and in the auto-commentary, ch.1, p. 80. The former states that "the immediate condition is the immediate [mentation] that remains once any of the [six modes of engaged consciousness], including the sixth or mental consciousness, have ceased" (*de ma thag pa'i rkyen zhes pa/ gang gang 'gags pa de ma thag/ yin te drug pa'i yid dang bcas*). The latter elucidates that

> The immediate condition in respect of the six modes [of engaged consciousness], including the sixth or mental consciousness, is explained to be the immediate consciousness that remains when any aspect of the six modes of consciousness has ceased, and it is identical with the sensory base of the mental faculty, endowed with the potent propensities of the substratum, capable of subsequent regeneration. This same consciousness is the immediate condition for the corresponding [modes of engaged consciousness] that subsequently arise. It is through this condition that the six modes of engaged consciousness are subsequently regenerated, following their cessation, without the intervention of any other cognition.

172 It is unclear who the author implies would have held this opinion. Thanks to Karl Brunnhölzl (email communication, 29 March 2010) for his observations on this passage.

173 The immediate mentation (*de ma thag pa'i yid*) that remains after any of the six modes of engaged consciousness cease to function has a dual purpose, triggering their subsidence into the substratum and their subsequent re-emergence as dissonant mental consciousness and so forth. See Karmapa Rangjung Dorje, *Treatise Distinguishing Consciousness and Pristine Cognition*, pp. 326–327; and the discussion in Jamgon Kongtrul, *Ornament of the Enlightened Intention of Rangjung*, pp. 356–364; also Brunnhölzl 2009, 109–113, and the translations on pp. 363–364 (root verses), and pp. 282–286 (commentary).

174 Brunnhölzl 2009, 109–110, similarly contrasts the stainless and afflicted aspects of mentation.

175 Cf. the elaborate description of the six modes of engaged consciousness presented in Cook 1999, 153–229. On the functionality of the four conditions, see also Lusthaus 2002, 496–507.

176 See above, pp. 525–556.

177 See above, note 173.

178 This interpretation derives from Asaṅga's *Yogācāra Level* (*Yogācārabhūmi*, T 4035), vol. Tshi, f. 3a–b.

179 While the actual verses cited here have not yet been located, the interpretation of the verses and the preceding sentence derives from Asaṅga's *Yogācāra Level* (*Yogācārabhūmi*), vol. Tshi, ff. 64–67a. A similar interpretation is also found in Jinaputra's *Exegesis of the Compendium of Phenomenology* (*Abhidharmasamuccayabhāṣya*, T 4053), vol. Li, f. 103b.

180 *Thirty Verses*, v. 15. Anacker 1984, 187; Cook 1999, 380.

181 Anacker 1984, 187; also Cook 1999, 221–227.

182 On this distinction, see also Pruden 1998–1990, 109–111.

183 A flavor of this complexity can be found in Pruden 1998–1990, 83. Cf. Engle 2009, 361–363.
184 Cf. the definition in Boin-Webb 2001, 28.
185 Cf. Pruden 1998–1990, 78.
186 Asaṅga's presentation of the eighteen sensory bases can be found specifically in the *Level of the Pious Attendants* (*Yogācārabhūmau śrāvakabhūmi,* T 4036), vol. Dzi, f. 92a, while earlier, on ff. 82a–83b, he explores the relationship between these diverse external and internal aspects of the sensory bases. Cf. also the root treatise, *Yogācāra Level* (*Yogācārabhūmi*), ff. 13a–18a.
187 See above, p. 484.
188 Pruden 1998–1990, 74–75.
189 See Engle 2009, 140–141, and Anacker 1984, 72–73, where the four are enumerated as space, the two kinds of cessation, and reality or suchness. Sthiramati's commentary can be found in Engle 2009, 349–353.
190 Boin-Webb 2001, 25–26.
191 As to the determination of which sensory bases can be considered virtuous, non-virtuous, or unspecified, see, e.g., the description offered in Engle 2009, 363–364.
192 On the realization of these two aspects of selflessness—of the individual person and of all phenomena—which distinguishes the Greater Vehicle in general, see Dudjom Rinpoche 1991, 1:234; and for Jamgon Kongtrul's perspective, see Callahan 2007, 162–163.
193 Boin-Webb 2001, 23–24, for Asaṅga's particular explanation of these synonyms.
194 Cf. Pruden 1998–1990, especially 59 and 91–92; also Engle 2009, 359–360.
195 Boin-Webb 2001, 24; Pruden 1998–1990, 60; and Engle 2009, 349–351.
196 Boin-Webb, 2001, 24, and Engle 2009, 351–352. See also the discussion in Pruden 1998–1990, 59–60.
197 As stated above, pp. 434–435, these four pairs of defects are said to be associated successively with the four meditative concentrations. See also Boin-Webb 2001, 24.
198 Boin-Webb 2001, 24.
199 Boin-Webb 2001, 25.
200 Cf. the definition in Boin-Webb 2001, 28.
201 Pruden 1998–1990, 78.
202 See the definition in Monier-Williams 2005, 148.
203 Cf. Boin-Webb 2001, 28: *vijñānāyadvāra.*
204 On this distinction, see also above, p. 537.
205 See the discussion in Pruden 1998–1900, 85–86.
206 For the Vaibhāṣika perspective, see Pruden 1998–1990, 184–185. Among the influential Kadampa commentaries on the five categories, Jamgon Kongtrul has already made reference to Upa Losal's *Exegetical Treasury of Philosophical Systems*. See above, note 112. This treatise summarizes the five basic categories: see pp. 120–124 on form; pp. 124–126 on mind; pp. 126–129 on mental states; pp. 129–138 on circumstantial formative predispositions; and pp. 138–140 on unconditioned states.
207 Boin-Webb 2001, 30. Zilungpa Shākya Chokden (1426–1507) authored two important commentaries on phenomenology: the *Exegesis of the Compendium of Phenomenology entitled Ocean Waves Upholding Yogācāra* (*mNgon pa kun btus pa'i rnam bshad rnal 'byor spyod gzung rgya mtsho'i rlabs phreng*), and the *Exegesis on Difficulties in the Treasury of Phenomenology entitled Great Ocean of Detailed Exposition* (*Chos mngon pa'i mdzod kyi dka' ba'i gnas rnam bshad kyi bstan bcos bye brag tu bshad pa'i mtsho chen po*). It is clear from the latter, Collected Works, vol. 20, p. 3, and other remarks that Zilungpa regards the enumeration of five categories as the common basis of Abhidharma, and the eight topics of the *Treasury of Phenomenology* as a special derivative.

208 See Kalu Rinpoche Translation Group 1995; also Callahan 2007.
209 The following verses correspond to the meter of the root verses of the *Treasury of Phenomenology*, but they are not found therein. The comments in parenthesis follow the explanation given in the Tibetan edition, entitled *mNgon pa mdzod rtsa 'grel*, p. 103.
210 Cf. Pruden 1998–1990, 64.
211 Pruden 1998–1990, 65–66.
212 Cf. Pruden 1998–1990, 66, where the distinction is made on the basis of whether the odors are excessive or not excessive. *SK*, 404, reads *nga ba* for *ngar ba* (strong).
213 Pruden 1998–1990, 66.
214 Pruden 1998–1900, 66–67.
215 See the discussion on imperceptible forms in Pruden 1998–1990, 67–72; also Engle 2009, 262–267, and Guenther 1976, 162–163.
216 This quotation derives from the *Treasury of Phenomenology* (*Abhidharmakośa*), ch. 2, v. 24. See Pruden 1998–1990, 189–190.
217 *Treasury of Phenomenology*, ch. 2, v. 25 (Pruden 1998–1900, 190–193).
218 *Treasury of Phenomenology*, ch. 2, v. 26a–c (Pruden 1998–1990, 193–195).
219 *Treasury of Phenomenology*, ch. 2, v. 26c–d (Pruden 1998–1990, 195).
220 *Treasury of Phenomenology*, ch. 2, v. 27 (Pruden 1998–1900, 196).
221 Cf. Pruden 1998–1900, 196.
222 This means that the following mental states associated with mind are listed in the *Compendium of Phenomenology* (*Abhidharmasamuccaya*) but excluded from the *Treasury of Phenomenology* (*Abhidharmakośa*): non-delusion (*amoha, gti mug med pa*), fundamental ignorance (*avidyā, ma rig pa*), wrong view (*mithyādṛṣṭi, lta ba*), forgetfulness (*muṣitasmṛtitā, brjed ngas pa*), distraction (*vikṣepa, gYeng ba*), and inattentiveness (*asaṃprajanya, shes bzhin ma yin pa*).
223 *Treasury of Phenomenology*, ch. 2, vv. 35–36a. See Pruden 1998–1990, 206 (root verses) and 206–254 (commentary).
224 The discussion on acquisition and non-acquisition is found in Pruden 1998–1990, 206–219.
225 Pruden 1998–1990, 219–221.
226 Pruden 1998–1990, 221–222.
227 Pruden 1998–1990, 223–233.
228 Pruden 1998–1990, 233–238.
229 On the characteristics of birth, aging, duration, and impermanence, see Pruden 1998–1990, 238–250.
230 On nominal clusters and the related phrasal clusters and syllabic clusters, see Pruden 1998–1990, 250–254.
231 Pruden 1998–1990, 206–207.
232 See above, pp. 535–537; and for the Vaibhāṣika perspective specifically, Pruden 1998–1990, 59–61.
233 *Treasury of Phenomenology*, ch. 1, v. 9a–b. See Pruden 1998–1990, 63.
234 *Treasury of Phenomenology*, ch. 1, v. 14a–b. See Pruden 1998–1990, 72.
235 See above, p. 537.
236 *Treasury of Phenomenology*, ch. 1, v. 18a–b. See Pruden 1998–1990, 76.
237 This and the following paragraph are taken almost verbatim from Khewang Yeshe Gyatso's *Exegetical Memorandum*, ch. 2, pp. 76–77. Cf. the discussion in Pruden 1998–1990, 232.
238 On these distinctions between substantial and imputed existents in relation to mental states in particular, see above, pp. 495–496.
239 Cf. *Treasury of Phenomenology*, ch. 6, v. 4; and Pruden 1998–1990, 910–911:

Whatever on its destruction or intellectual analysis
Ceases to convey an idea, like a vase or water,
Is relatively existent; all else is absolutely real.

240 This refers to the phenomenological presentation of the sūtras representing the third turning of the wheel, which logically follows on from the preceding analyses of the Higher Abhidharma, representing the principal phenomenological standpoint of the Greater Vehicle in general, and the Lower Abhidharma, representing the views of the Lesser Vehicle.

241 Jamgon Kongtrul's analysis of these three topics in the pages that follow is based almost entirely on Tāranātha's versified *Ascertainment of Great Madhyamaka according to the Most Extensive Teachings of the Supreme Vehicle* (*Theg mchog shin tu rgyas pa'i dbu ma chen po rnam par nges pa*) and its commentary, the *Exegetical Memorandum*, which was composed by Tāranātha's student Khewang Yeshe Gyatso. Among the three themes, the basis of the phenomenological categories is specifically examined in Tāranātha, op. cit., ch. 2, pp. 5–9, and Khewang Yeshe Gyatso, op. cit., ch. 2, pp. 76–84. The five foundational factors follow in Tāranātha, ch. 5, pp. 19–20, and Khewang Yeshe Gyatso, ch. 5, pp. 156–161; and the three natures are presented in Tāranātha, ch. 5, pp. 120–123, and Khewang Yeshe Gyatso, ch. 5, pp. 161–178.

242 See above, pp. 547–548.

243 Tib. *yid kyi skye mched*. *SK*, 407, reads *chos kyi skye mched*.

244 This passage and the two following paragraphs are taken verbatim from Khewang Yeshe Gyatso, *Exegetical Memorandum*, ch. 5, pp. 83–84. The twenty-one phenomenological categeories are also listed in Dungkar Lobzang Trinle, *Great Dictionary*, 1793, under *gzhi chos nyer gcig*.

245 On these mundane spiritual paths, see above, pp. 423–439.

246 The paths followed by pious attendants and hermit buddhas are outlined, from the perspective of Jamgon Kongtrul, in Callahan 2007. Cf. Dudjom Rinpoche 1991, 1:156–159 and 223–231.

247 For a general introduction, see Williams 1989. The traditional presentation of the Greater Vehicle, from the Nyingma perspective, is found in Dudjom Rinpoche 1991, 1:160–237, and for Jamgon Kongtrul's view, see Callahan 2007, 159ff.

248 The source for this paragraph is Khewang Yeshe Gyatso, *Exegetical Memorandum,* ch. 5, pp. 84–85.

249 The expanse of reality (*dharmadhātu, chos kyi dbyings*) is elucidated particularly in Tāranātha, *Ascertainment of Great Madhyamaka*, ch. 3, pp. 9–13. Jamgon Kongtrul's source for this paragraph is Khewang Yeshe Gyatso, *Exegetical Memorandum,* ch. 5, pp. 85–86. More generally, concerning the nature of the expanse of actual reality, which is a synonym for emptiness, see Thrangu 2004, 121ff., and Scott 2004. On the means of realizing the expanse of reality from the Nyingma perspective, see Barron 2001a, and Barron 2001b.

250 See Khewang Yeshe Gyatso, *Exegetical Memorandum,* ch. 5, pp. 86–87. It is stated in ch. 6 of the *Mahāparinirvāṇasūtra* that these twenty-five realms are transcended as follows, on the basis of their respective meditative stabilities, which are all based in the experience of actual reality: (1) rebirth in the hells is destroyed by the taintless meditative stability (*dri ma med pa'i ting nge 'dzin*); (2) rebirth in the animal realms is destroyed by the irreversible meditative stability (*phyir mi ldog pa'i ting nge 'dzin*); (3) rebirth in the realm of anguished spirits is destroyed by the meditative stability of joyous mind (*sems bde ba'i ting nge 'dzin*); (4) rebirth among antigods is destroyed by means of the joyful meditative stability (*rab tu dga' ba'i ting nge 'dzin*); (5) rebirth in Pūrvavideha is destroyed by the sunlight meditative stability (*nyi ma'i 'od zer gyis ting nge 'dzin*); (6)

rebirth in Aparagodanīya is destroyed by the moonlight meditative stability (*zla ba'i 'od zer gyi ting nge 'dzin*); (7) rebirth in Uttarakuru is destroyed by means of the meditative stability of warmth (*me dbal gyi ting nge 'dzin*); (8) rebirth in Jambudvīpa is destroyed by the illusion-like meditative stability (*sgyu ma lta bu'i ting nge 'dzin*); (9) rebirth in Caturmahārājakāyika is destroyed by the meditative stability in which all things are unmoving (*chos thams cad mi gYo ba'i ting nge 'dzin*); (10) rebirth in Trayatriṃśa is destroyed by the meditative stability that is hard to cultivate (*shin tu gdul dka' ba'i ting nge 'dzin*); (11) rebirth in Yāma is destroyed by agreeable meditative stability (*yid du 'ong ba'i ting nge 'dzin*); (12) rebirth in Tuṣita is destroyed by the meditative stability of consummate blueness (*thams cad sngon po'i ting nge 'dzin*); (13) rebirth in Nirmāṇarata is destroyed by means of the meditative stability of consummate yellowness (*thams cad ser po'i ting nge 'dzin*); (14) rebirth in Paranirmitavaśavartin is destroyed by means of the meditative stability of consummate redness (*thams cad dmar po'i ting nge 'dzin*); (15) rebirth in the abodes of the first meditative concentration is destroyed by the meditative stability of consummate whiteness (*thams cad dkar po'i ting nge 'dzin*); (16) rebirth in Mahābrahmā is destroyed by the diversified meditative stability (*rnam pa sna tshogs kyi ting nge 'dzin*); (17) rebirth in the abodes of the second meditative concentration is destroyed by the coalescent meditative stability (*zung du 'brel ba'i ting nge 'dzin*); (18) rebirth in the abodes of the third meditative concentration is destroyed by the thunderous meditative stability (*'brug sgra'i ting nge 'dzin*); (19) rebirth in the abodes of the fourth meditative concentration is destroyed by the meditative stability of pouring rain (*char pa bab pa'i ting nge 'dzin*); (20) rebirth in non-perceptual Akaṇiṣṭha is destroyed by the sky-like meditative stability (*nam mkha' lta bu'i ting nge 'dzin*); (21) rebirth as a once-returner in the Pure Abodes is destroyed by the mirror-like meditative stability (*me long lta bu'i ting nge 'dzin*); (22) rebirth in Ākāśānantyāyatana is destroyed by means of the desireless or formless meditative stability (*chags pa med pa'i ting nge 'dzin*); (23) rebirth in Vijñānānantyāyatana is destroyed by means of the eternal meditative stability (*rtag pa'i ting nge 'dzin*); (24) rebirth in Ākiṃcanyāyatana is destroyed by means of the delightful meditative stability (*dga' ba'i ting nge 'dzin*); and (25) rebirth in Naivasaṃjñānāsaṃjñāyatana is destroyed by means of the meditative stability of the self (*bdag gi ting nge 'dzin*).

251 There are parallel passages which occur in Suzuki 1932, 193–198. However, the references to dependent origination are substituted therein by references to the eight modes of consciousness.

252 Having established the phenomenological structures of the ground, path, and goal, the process of epistemology, according to the final promulgation, is then examined in the context of the five foundational factors. Khewang Yeshe Gyatso, *Exegetical Memorandum,* ch. 5, p. 156, points out that these five are mentioned, not only in the *Sūtra of the Descent to Laṅkā*, but also rather extensively in the *Sūtra of the Dense Array*. Other classical sources discussing the nuances of these five foundational factors include Asaṅga's *Summation of Ascertainment from the Yogācāra Level* (*Yogācārabhūmiviniścayasaṃgrahaṇī*), vol. 1, ff. 287b–288a; Parahitabhadra's *Exegesis of the First Two Verse Sections of the Ornament of the Sūtras of the Greater Vehicle* (*Sūtrālaṃkārādiślok advayavyākhyāna,* T 4039), vol. Bi, f. 179b; Sthiramati's *Commentary on the Analysis of the Middle and Extremes* (*Madhyāntavibhāgaṭīkā,* T 4032), vol. Bi, f. 253a–b; and Ratnākaraśānti's *Pith Instructions on the Transcendental Perfection of Discriminative Awareness* (*Prajñāpāramitopadeśa,* T 4079), vol. Hi, f. 144b. Among them, the last mentioned summarizes the five factors as follows:

> Names refer to the verbalization of a mental state (*yid kyi brjod pa'i gnas pa'i sgra ni ming*); appearances refer to objects (*don ni rgyu mtshan no*); false imaginations

refer to the imaginary nature which is inauthentic (*rnam par rtog pa ni yang dag pa ma yin pa'i kun tu rtog pa*); the absolute reality is emptiness (*de bzhin nyid ni stong pa nyid do*); and the genuine knowledge (*yang dag pa'i ye shes*) is the supramundane pristine cognition (*'jig rten las 'das pa'i ye shes so*).

Cf. also Suzuki 1932, 193–198; and Suzuki 1930, 26–31 and 154–157. The five factors are further mentioned in the two extant commentaries on the *Laṅkāvatārasūtra* contained in the Tangyur—Jñānaśrībhadra's *Laṅkāvatārasūtravṛtti* (T 4018) and Jñānavajra's *Laṅkāvatārasūtravṛtti-tathāgatahṛdayālamkāra* (T 4019), vol. Pi, ff. 127b–128a. Jamgon Kongtrul's immediate source for the material in this chapter is again Khewang Yeshe Gyatso, *Exegetical Memorandum*, ch. 5, pp. 156–161. For a modern appraisal, see also Sutton 1991, 210–220.

253 Khewang Yeshe Gyatso, *Exegetical Memorandum*, ch. 5, pp. 156–158. Cf. Suzuki 1932, 195.

254 Khewang Yeshe Gyatso, *Exegetical Memorandum*, ch. 5, p. 158. This listing is also found in Asaṅga's *Summation of Ascertainment from the Yogācāra Level*, vol. 2, f. 4a.

255 Khewang Yeshe Gyatso, *Exegetical Memorandum*, ch. 5, pp. 158–159. I have not yet been able to identify a listing of forty names, although Asaṅga's *Summation of Ascertainment from the Yogācāra Level*, vol. 2, f. 4b, subsumes this "inestimable diversity" (*rnam pa sna tshogs dpag tu med pa*) under the following twelve headings: names of conventional origin (*tha snyad las byung ba'i ming*), names of authentic substantives (*yang dag pa'i dngos po'i ming*), collective names (*rigs dang 'brel ba'i ming*), individuating names (*so so dang 'brel ba'i ming*), erudite names (*yon tan las byung ba'i ming*), nicknames (*nya bar brtags pa'i ming*), well-known names (*grags pa'i ming*), unknown names (*ma grags pa'i ming*), clear names (*gsal ba'i ming*), unclear names (*mi gsal ba'i ming*), abbreviated or integrated names (*bsdus pa'i ming*), and diversifying names (*tha dad pa'i ming*).

256 A useful appraisal of false imagination (*vikalpa*) can be found in Brunnhölzl 2009, 14–17. The same term may also be rendered, perhaps more narrowly, as "misconception," "conceptual thought" or "notion," and it has also been translated as "discrimination" in Suzuki 1932, 195.

257 The source for this discussion is once again Khewang Yeshe Gyatso, *Exegetical Memorandum*, ch. 5, p. 159. These technical terms are also found in Negi, *Tibetan Sanskrit Dictionary*, 4964, based on Jinaputra's *Exegesis of the Compendium of Phenomenology* (*Abhidharmasamuccayabhāṣya*), ff. 13–16. Asaṅga's *Summation of Ascertainment from the Yogācāra Level*, vol. 2, f. 4b, lists seven main categories of false imagination: imaginations of symbolic origin (*mtshan ma las byung ba'i rnam rtog*), imaginations of non-symbolic origin (*mtshan ma med pa las byung ba'i rnam rtog*), imaginations which are object-oriented by nature (*yul la rang ngang gis 'jug pa'i rnam rtog*), investigative imaginations (*tshol ba pa'i rnam rtog*), analytical imaginations (*so sor rtog pa'i rnam rtog*), dissonant imaginations (*nyon mongs pa can gyi rnam rtog*) and non-dissonant imaginations (*nyon mongs can ma yin pa'i rnam rtog*).

258 Khewang Yeshe Gyatso, *Exegetical Memorandum*, ch. 5, p. 159. Cf. Suzuki 1932, 196.

259 Khewang Yeshe Gyatso, *Exegetical Memorandum*, ch. 5, p. 159. Cf. Suzuki 1932, 195–196.

260 Khewang Yeshe Gyatso, *Exegetical Memorandum*, ch. 5, pp. 159–160.

261 Tib. *de [bzhin] nyid dang gzhan du brjod du med pa*.

262 See above, pp. 495–496.

263 Cf. Suzuki 1932, 198, also Dharmachakra Translation Committee 2006, 81–82. Generally on the three natures, see also below, pp. 563–574. However, in Cook 1999, 288–289, further complexities in the relationship between the five foundational factors and the three natures are highlighted. Jñānavajra, in his *Commentary on the Sūtra of the Descent to Laṅkā entitled Heart Ornament of the Tathāgatas* (*Laṅkāvatārasūtravṛtti-tathāgatahṛdayālamkāra*, T 4019), Pi, ff. 127b–128a, appears to suggest that both the

absolute reality and the genuine non-conceptual knowledge partake of the consummate nature (*yang dag pa'i ye shes dang de bzhin nyid ni sngar bstan pa ltar yongs su grub pa gnyis kyis bsdus pa'o*).

264 This is the term employed in Sthiramati's *Commentary on the Analysis of the Middle and Extremes*, f. 253a–b. See also Dharmachakra Translation Committee 2006, 82.

265 As indicated above, note 252.

266 Jamgon Kongtrul's analysis of the three natures is based on the verses of Tāranātha, *Ascertainment of Great Madhyamaka*, ch. 5, pp. 20–22, and Khewang Yeshe Gyatso, *Exegetical Memorandum*, ch. 5, pp. 161–178. For a discussion of the three natures in general, cf. Cook 1999, 281–296; Keenan 2003, 37–59; Tola and Dragonetti 2004, 187–244; and Sutton 1991, 220–223. On the contrasting pivotal and pyramidal modals of the Cittamātra and Yogācāra-Madhyamaka, see Sponberg 1983, 96–118.

267 This paragraph is taken verbatim from Khewang Yeshe Gyatso, *Exegetical Memorandum*, ch. 5, pp. 165–166. Dudjom Rinpoche 1991, 1:160, also contrasts the presentation of the imaginary nature from the standpoint of Cittamātra, and on 1:170–172 from the standpoint of Great Madhyamaka. Cf. Cook 1999, 281–284.

268 Khewang Yeshe Gyatso, *Exegetical Memorandum*, ch. 5, p. 166, contrasts the example of a vase and its attributes of size and so forth. This distinction is also mentioned in Asaṅga's *Summary of the Greater Vehicle,* ch. 2, v. 18. See Keenan 2003, 46.

269 Suzuki 1932, 113, ch. 2, v. 195, renders this as ten, but also notes that all the Chinese translations of the text mention twelve aspects.

270 The twelve are all explained in Suzuki 1932, 110–111.

271 Khewang Yeshe Gyatso, *Exegetical Memorandum*, ch. 5, pp. 166. Dudjom Rinpoche 1991, 1:160, also contrasts the presentation of the dependent nature from the standpoint of Cittamātra, and on 1:170–172, from the standpoint of Great Madhyamaka.

272 Khewang Yeshe Gyatso, *Exegetical Memorandum*, ch. 5, p. 166.

273 Khewang Yeshe Gyatso, *Exegetical Memorandum*, ch. 5, pp. 166–167. Suzuki 1930, 161 refers to the six categories of the dependent nature without specifically enumerating them.

274 See Asaṅga's *Summary of the Greater Vehicle,* ch. 2, v. 26, and Keenan 2003, 50–51. Jamgon Kongtrul is again citing Khewang Yeshe Gyatso, *Exegetical Memorandum*, ch. 5, p. 167.

275 Khewang Yeshe Gyatso, *Exegetical Memorandum,* ch. 5, p. 167. This distinction is made in ch. 3 of the *Analysis of the Middle and Extremes* (*Madhyāntavibhāga*), entitled *De kho na'i le'ur bcad pa*. See *The Five Treatises of Maitreya* (*Byams chos sde lnga*) (Beijing: Mi rigs dpe skrun khang, 1991), 162, which states: *gyur med phyin ci ma log pa/ yongs su grub pa rnam pa gnyis//* Also Dharmachakra Translation Committee 2006, 79–80.

276 Khewang Yeshe Gyatso, *Exegetical Memorandum*, ch. 5, pp. 170–171. This list derives from the *Ornament of the Sūtras of the Greater Vehicle.* (*Mahāyānasūtrālaṃkārakārikā*, ch. 11, v. 77. See Jamspal et al. 2004, 150–151. They are additionally mentioned in Asaṅga's *Summary of the Greater Vehicle,* ch. 2, vv. 21–22, on which see Keenan 2003, 47–48. Cf. Rigdzin 1993, 160, where there are some minor differences; and Boin-Webb 2001, 240.

277 These are explained in Khewang Yeshe Gyatso, *Exegetical Memorandum*, ch. 5, pp. 171–172. Cf. Boin-Webb 2001, 239–240; also *Summary of the Greater Vehicle*, ch. 2, v. 20, on which see Keenan 2003, 46–47.

278 See the corresponding antidotes listed in Boin-Webb 2001, 240, and in Keenan 2003, 47–48.

279 These eleven aspects of apperception are interpreted in Khewang Yeshe Gyatso, *Exegetical Memorandum,* ch. 5, pp. 172–173; also the same list is also given in Dungkar Lobzang Trinle, *Great Dictionary*, 1791, under *gzhan dbang las 'phros pa'i rnam rig bcu gcig*.

280 *SK*, 416, reads *yid kyi rnam shes zab po'i rnam rig*.
281 Khewang Yeshe Gyatso, *Exegetical Memorandum*, ch. 5, p. 173.
282 These are listed in Khewang Yeshe Gyatso, *Exegetical Memorandum*, ch. 7, p. 329; and derive from the *Śatasāhasrikāprajñāpāramitā*, as indicated in Negi, *Tibetan Sanskrit Dictionary*, 5260.
283 These comments derive from the *Great Commentary on the Transcendental Perfection of Discriminative Awareness in One Hundred Thousand, Twenty-five Thousand, and Eighteen Thousand Lines* (*Śatasāhasrikāpañcaviṃśatisāhasrikāṣṭadaśa-sāhasrikāprajñāpāramitā-bṛhaṭṭīkā*, T 3808), f. 96a–b, which the Tibetan tradition as a whole ascribes to Vasubandhu. According to the Gelukpa tradition, the author is Daṃṣṭrasena. Vasubandhu's conflation of these two lists of nine aspects of the consummate nature is repeated in Khewang Yeshe Gyatso, *Exegetical Memorandum*, ch. 7, p. 330.
284 See Part One, note 588. These are also enumerated elsewhere, in several sources, e.g., Negi, *Tibetan Sanskrit Dictionary*, 1871; also Anacker 1984, 219.
285 See above, p. 560.
286 This synthesis paraphrases comments made in Khewang Yeshe Gyatso, *Exegetical Memorandum*, ch. 5, pp. 167–168. On this paradox, see Cook 1999, 285–287; also Keenan 2003, 45.
287 This analysis is based on the appraisal of the pyramidal structure of the three natures in accordance with the view of Great Madhyamaka, on which see Dudjom Rinpoche 1991, 1:170–172. The "threefold naturelessness" (*rang ngo bo nyid med pa gsum po*) is sometimes given as a synonym—see Cook 1999, 294–296.
288 These comments, also found in Khewang Yeshe Gyatso, *Exegetical Memorandum*, ch. 5, p. 176, derive ultimately from the *Ornament of the Sūtras of the Greater Vehicle*, ch. 10, v. 27, and v. 41, and Vasubandhu's commentary. See Jamspal et al. 2004, 125–126 and 132–133.
289 This quotation is cited also in Khewang Yeshe Gyatso, *Exegetical Memorandum*, ch. 5, p. 176.
290 This outline of the demonstrations or illustrations of the three natures presented in these three paragraphs derives verbatim from Khewang Yeshe Gyatso, *Exegetical Memorandum*, ch. 5, p. 175. Cf. Dudjom Rinpoche 1991, 1:170–172.
291 Khewang Yeshe Gyatso, *Exegetical Memorandum*, ch. 5, p. 165, emphasizes the common ground of Maitreya and Nāgārjuna in respect of their presentations of the three natures. Among the five treatises of Maitreya, the three natures are discussed particularly in the context of the *Ornament of the Sūtras of the Greater Vehicle* (*Sūtrālaṃkāra*) and the *Analysis of the Middle and Extremes* (*Madhyāntavibhāga*). According to Nāgārjuna's *Commentary on the Sūtra of the Shoots of Rice* (*Śālistambhakasūtraṭīkā*), too, "the imaginary nature comprises external objects, their actions, and appearances," while "the dependent nature comprises the substratum consciousness and the sensory aspects of consciousness derived from it," and "the consummate nature comprises the ultimate truth because it is not an object of false imagination."
292 The exponents of extraneous emptiness (*gzhan stong pa rnams*) are exemplified by Tāranātha. On Vasubandhu's position, see Khewang Yeshe Gyatso, *Exegetical Memorandum*, ch. 5, p. 165. More generally, on the distinction between the views of intrinsic and extraneous emptiness, see, e.g., Dudjom Rinpoche 1991, 1:162–216. Jamgon Kongtrul's perspective is presented in Callahan 2007, 223–268.
293 Cf. Vasubandhu's *Thirty Verses*, vv. 20–21, for translations of which see Anacker 1984, 188; and Cook 1999, 381.
294 See Dudjom Rinpoche 1991, 1:170–172, for the presentation of the three natures from the standpoint of Great Madhyamaka.
295 This Maitreya Chapter (*Shes phyin gyi mdo'i byams zhus kyi le'u*) is contained only in the

mid-length versions of the *Prajñāpāramitā* in eighteen thousand and twenty-five thousand lines. For background on this text in relation to the Great Madhyamaka approach to the three natures, see also Stearns 2002, 90–98.

296 Candrakīrti refers briefly to the three natures (*trisvabhāva, ngo bo nyid gsum*), in ch. 6, f. 283a, of his *Auto-commentary on the Introduction to Madhyamaka* (*Madhyamakāvatārabhāṣya*): *kun tu mi brtags pa 'i phyir te / dngos po byas pa can ma reg par rang bzhin 'ba' zhig mngon sum du mdzad pas de nyid thugs su chud pa'i phyir sangs rgyas zhes brjod do / de'i phyir de ltar brtags pa dang gzhan gyi dbang dang yongs su grub pa zhes bya ba ngo bo nyid gsum rnam par gzhag*. On the other hand, Śāntarakṣita refers to the three natures (*trisvabhāva, rang bzhin gsum*) in his *Auto-commentary on the Ornament of Madhyamaka* (*Madhyamakālaṃkāravṛtti*), where he quotes the *Laṅkāvatārasūtra* as follows (f. 80a): *chos lnga rang bzhin gsum rnam par shes pa brgyad nyid dang bdag med nyid kyi dngos pas ni theg pa chen po thams cad 'dus.*

297 Jamgon Kongtrul's analysis of dependent origination derives from Khewang Yeshe Gyatso, *Exegetical Memorandum,* ch. 5, pp. 177–224. For a general spectrum of interpretations of dependent origination in Buddhism, see, e.g., Bodhi 2000, 292–328 (especially 294–302); also Ñāṇamoli 1979, 592–678; Pruden 1988–1990, 401–438; Friedmann 1984, 46–58; Boin-Webb 2001, 55–61; Keenan 2003, 20–21; Cook 1999, 268–279; Sprung 1979; Napper 2003; Thrangu 2001; and Lusthaus 2002, 52–82.

298 On this distinction, see below, pp. 605–606; also Thrangu 2001, 44–45, and Napper 2003. This particular comment derives from Khewang Yeshe Gyatso, *Exegetical Memorandum*, ch. 5, p. 177.

299 Khewang Yeshe Gyatso, *Exegetical Memorandum*, ch. 5, pp. 177–178. On these dichotomies from the ultimate perspective, see also below, pp. 605–611.

300 Khewang Yeshe Gyatso, *Exegetical Memorandum*, ch. 5, p. 178.

301 Cf. the ten modes of understanding which are listed in Boin-Webb 2001, 55.

302 Nāgārjuna, *Fundamental Stanzas of Madhyamaka*, ch. 24, vv. 18–19.

303 Monier-Williams 2005, 673, also suggests "confirmation" or "experiment" as possible meanings.

304 The same etymology is given in Khewang Yeshe Gyatso, *Exegetical Memorandum,* ch. 5, p. 179. Cf. the elaborate grammatical discussion in Pruden 1998–1990, 413–415.

305 This implies that it lacks an external dynamic driving force. See Boin-Webb 2001, 58.

306 This is also listed in Boin-Webb 2001, 58, where it is said to identify the real meaning (*artha*) of dependent origination.

307 This analysis of fundamental ignorance derives also from Khewang Yeshe Gyatso, *Exegetical Memorandum,* ch. 5, pp. 189–191.

308 As stated by his student Khewang Yeshe Gyatso, *Exegetical Memorandum,* ch. 5, pp. 189–190, the fundamental ignorance endowed with dissonant mental states does not simply refer to the view that substantial entities are truly existent, but rather it implies "delusion with respect to the [notion of] self that arises within the range of the dissonant mental consciousness."

309 Here, Khewang Yeshe Gyatso, *Exegetical Memorandum,* ch. 5, pp. 190–191, makes the point that the view upholding mundane aggregates, on which see above, p. 502, is identified with fundamental ignorance only in terms of its conspicuousness because it is related to ignorance and it is a conspicuous aspect of the latter. However, if this viewpoint were established as an acceptable illustration of ignorance, it would follow that the full range of the ten or six dissonant mental states would be incompletely represented—the view of mundane aggregates being only part of one of them. Cf. the discussion of fundamental ignorance in Pruden 1998–1990, 419–422; and especially 418–419 on the conflation of ignorance with the sixty-two views of mundane aggregates.

310 Khewang Yeshe Gyatso, *Exegetical Memorandum,* ch. 5, p. 191. See also above, pp. 419–439; and Pruden 1988–1990, 415–418.

311 On this identification of the third link of dependent origination specifically with the substratum consciousness, see above, p. 516; also Khewang Yeshe Gyatso, *Exegetical Memorandum,* ch. 5, p. 191. Vasubandhu (Pruden 1988–1990, 418) presents the mainstream or general view, referring to the third link simply as "consciousness." The distinction between the seminal and maturational aspects of the propensities has already been mentioned. See above, pp. 513–520.

312 *SK,* 423, reads *gzhan gyi rgyu la yod pa.*

313 Khewang Yeshe Gyatso, *Exegetical Memorandum,* ch. 5, pp. 191–192. Cf. Pruden 1998–1990, 422–423.

314 Khewang Yeshe Gyatso, *Exegetical Memorandum,* ch. 5, p. 192. Cf. Pruden 1988–1990, 400. See also above, p. 331, on embryology. A slightly variant enumeration may be found in Nyima and Dorje 2001, 916.

315 Khewang Yeshe Gyatso, *Exegetical Memorandum,* ch. 5, p. 192; also Pruden 1998–1990, 403.

316 It is said that sensory contact originates while in the womb but strongly manifests following birth, in the interaction that is described here. See the discussion in Pruden 1988–1990, 423–426, which differentiates between the metaphorical or fruitional aspects of sensory contact and that which is residual (in the womb). Jamgon Kongtrul's wording again follows Khewang Yeshe Gyatso, *Exegetical Memorandum,* ch. 5, p. 192.

317 Khewang Yeshe Gyatso, *Exegetical Memorandum,* ch. 5, pp. 192–193; See also the discussion in Pruden 1988–1990, 426–430, as to whether sensation follows, precedes, or is simultaneous with sensory contact.

318 Khewang Yeshe Gyatso, *Exegetical Memorandum,* ch. 5, pp. 192–193. Cf. Pruden 1988–1990, 431–437, particularly with regard to the distribution of sensations through the three world-systems.

319 Khewang Yeshe Gyatso, *Exegetical Memorandum,* ch. 5, p. 193, cites Dharmakīrti on the manifestations of craving in the three world-systems, pointing out that sensory engagement due to attachment to material resources is distinctively associated with the world-system of desire. Cf. Pruden 1988–1990, 787–788.

320 But see Nyima and Dorje 2001, 1298, which lists "exclusive attachment to vows and rituals" instead of rebirth.

321 On grasping, see Khewang Yeshe Gyatso, *Exegetical Memorandum,* ch. 5, p. 193. Cf. Pruden 1998–1990, 403.

322 Khewang Yeshe Gyatso, *Exegetical Memorandum,* ch. 5, p. 193; and Pruden 1988–1990, 405–406.

323 This and the following paragraph derive from Khewang Yeshe Gyatso, *Exegetical Memorandum,* ch. 5, p. 193. Cf. Pruden 1988–1990, 404.

324 Khewang Yeshe Gyatso, *Exegetical Memorandum,* ch. 5, pp. 193–194. Cf. Pruden 1988–1990, 415–417.

325 See *The Five Treatises of Maitreya* (*Byams chos sde lnga*), p. 158, and the translation contained in Friedmann 1984, 46–52. Cf. the interpretation of the *Compendium of Phenomenology,* contained in Boin-Webb 2001, 57.

326 *SK,* 426, here reads *nyes spyod* for *nyer spyod.*

327 Khewang Yeshe Gyatso, *Exegetical Memorandum,* ch. 5, p. 180.

328 Khewang Yeshe Gyatso, *Exegetical Memorandum,* ch. 5, p. 180. On this distinction between the realizations of pious attendants and hermit buddhas, see also Dudjom Rinpoche 1991, 1:228–229.

329 Khewang Yeshe Gyatso, *Exegetical Memorandum,* ch. 5, pp. 180–181.

330 This analysis of the process of sensory engagement and its reversal outlined in this and the following paragraphs also derives from Khewang Yeshe Gyatso, *Exegetical Memorandum,* ch. 5, pp. 181–182.
331 For a contemporary Tibetan synopsis of the spiritual path followed by pious attendants, see, e.g., Dudjom Rinpoche 1991, 1:223–227.
332 Khewang Yeshe Gyatso, *Exegetical Memorandum,* ch. 5, pp. 182–184. Cf. Boin-Webb 2001, 59.
333 This reading follows the root verses, whereas the commentary (*SK,* 429) reads *snod kyis rab tu dbye ba.*
334 Khewang Yeshe Gyatso, *Exegetical Memorandum,* ch. 5, p. 184. On the five spiritual paths, see above, p. 525, and on the three higher trainings, Part One, note 8.
335 Khewang Yeshe Gyatso, *Exegetical Memorandum,* ch. 5, p. 184; also Boin-Webb 2001, 59.
336 *Ornament of the Sūtras of the Greater Vehicle,* ch. 8, v. 1. Jamspal et al. 2004, 55–56.
337 Although our text reads *thog mar,* other versions of the Tibetan read *thogs med.*
338 In most traditions, this is substituted by clairvoyance (*divyacakṣurabijñā, lha'i mig gi mngon shes*).
339 Cf. Jamspal et al. 2004, 55–56.
340 Those who attain the first five but not knowledge of the ways in which the cycle of rebirth is transcended are classed among the pious attendants and hermit buddhas.
341 Khewang Yeshe Gyatso, *Exegetical Memorandum,* ch. 5, pp. 184–185.
342 Khewang Yeshe Gyatso, *Exegetical Memorandum,* ch. 5, p. 185. See the discussion on these three topics in Pruden 1998–1990, 404ff. Vasubandhu also admits a fourth category—"static" (*āsthika*) dependent origination.
343 Pruden 1988–1990, 405–408; also Cook 1999, 266–279.
344 Khewang Yeshe Gyatso, *Exegetical Memorandum,* ch. 5, p. 185. Cf. Boin-Webb 2001, 56; also Cook 1999, 266–269.
345 Khewang Yeshe Gyatso, *Exegetical Memorandum,* ch. 5, p. 185.
346 Khewang Yeshe Gyatso, *Exegetical Memorandum,* ch. 5, pp. 186–187.
347 Khewang Yeshe Gyatso, *Exegetical Memorandum,* ch. 5, pp. 187–188.
348 Khewang Yeshe Gyatso, *Exegetical Memorandum,* ch. 5, pp. 188–189. Cf. Pruden 1998–1990, 404; and Kunsang 1997, 1:58.
349 See Friedmann 1984, 58. Sthiramati's commentary still appears to mention twelve links, and not eleven, although he alludes to their eleven functions, p. 53. Cf. Anacker 1984, 215–216. Jamgon Kongtrul's interpretation again follows Khewang Yeshe Gyatso, *Exegetical Memorandum,* ch. 5, p. 194–197, and especially pp. 195–196, where the two aspects of suffering are introduced.
350 *SK,* 433, reads *sred* for *srid.* See Khewang Yeshe Gyatso, *Exegetical Memorandum,* ch. 5, p. 197; also Pruden 1988–1990, 404.
351 Khewang Yeshe Gyatso, *Exegetical Memorandum,* ch. 5, p. 197. Friedmann 1984, 53–58; also Pruden 1998–1990, 406–407.
352 This is also cited in Khewang Yeshe Gyatso, *Exegetical Memorandum,* ch. 5, p. 197.
353 Khewang Yeshe Gyatso, *Exegetical Memorandum,* ch. 5, p. 197; also Friedmann 1984, 53–54.
354 Khewang Yeshe Gyatso, *Exegetical Memorandum,* ch. 5, p. 197; also Friedmann 1984, 54.
355 The causes listed in parenthesis in the following paragraph have been inserted in accordance with Sthiramati's commentary. See Friedmann 1984, 54–56; also Anacker 1984, 216. The Tibetan again follows Khewang Yeshe Gyatso, *Exegetical Memorandum,* ch. 5, pp. 197–199.
356 See Friedmann 1984, 55n169.

357 Khewang Yeshe Gyatso, *Exegetical Memorandum,* ch. 5, pp. 198–199; also Friedmann 1984, 54–57.

358 This section is based on a synopsis near the end of Vasubandhu's *Commentary Analyzing the Sūtra of Dependent Origination* (*Pratītyasamutpādādivibhaṅgabhāṣya,* T 3995), f. 52a–b. The Tibetan text is found, along with a more detailed analysis, in Khewang Yeshe Gyatso, *Exegetical Memorandum,* ch. 5, pp. 199–201.

359 This reading follows *SK,* 436: *nus pa mthu can tsam du byas pa.* However, Khewang Yeshe Gyatso, *Exegetical Memorandum,* ch. 5, p. 199, suggests "this same seed is not yet potent" (*nus pa mthu can du ma byas pa*).

360 This relates to a brief comment found in Tāranātha's *Ascertainment of Great Madhyamaka according to the Most Extensive Teachings of the Supreme Vehicle (Theg mchog shin tu rgyas pa'i dbu ma chen po rnam par nges pa),* which reads*: tshe gcig la yang rdzogs pa yod pa ste/ go rim dkrug na yan lag rdzogs pa 'gal.* "[This process of dependent origination] may also be completed within a single lifetime, but it is wrong to say that the [twelve] links will be completed if their order is confused." (*Jo nang dpe tshogs,* vol. 10, printed edition, 2007, p. 24). Thanks to Michael Sheehy for this identification. The exegetical memorandum also contains a commentary on this verse, on which see Khewang Yeshe Gyatso, *Exegetical Memorandum,* ch. 5, p. 187.

361 The nine experiential levels comprise the world system of desire, along with the four meditative concentrations of the world system of form and the four absorptions of the world system of formlessness. See Vasubandhu's *Commentary Analyzing the Sūtra of Dependent Origination,* ff. 50b, 73b.

362 Thanks to Zenkar Rinpoche for this interpretation. Cf. also Pruden 1998–1990, 429ff.

363 The *Commentary Analyzing the Sūtra of Dependent Origination* contains an extensive analysis of each of the twelve links of dependent origination and examines the role of fundamental ignorance in the context of rebirth within the three world-systems. Other works elaborating on the impact of meditation on subsequent rebirth in the higher world-systems include Guṇamati's *Extensive Sub-commentary on the Commentary Analyzing the Sūtra of Dependent Origination* (*Pratītyasamutpādādivibhaṅganirdeśaṭīkā,* T 3996); and Khewang Yeshe Gyatso, *Exegetical Memorandum,* ch. 5, pp. 201–203.

364 Khewang Yeshe Gyatso, *Exegetical Memorandum,* ch. 5, p. 203.

365 Boin-Webb 2001, 58.

366 Tib. *mtha' bzhi* implies that it does not arise from itself, from anything else, from both, or neither.

367 Boin-Webb 2001, 58.

368 Nāgārjuna's *Letter to a Friend,* v. 112. Jamspal et al. 1978, 108. Note that the last line of the stanza reads differently as *sangs rgyas de nyid rig pa rnam mchog mthong,* instead of, as here, *chos mthong de yis de bzhin gshegs pa mthong.* See the translation on p. 59: "One who rightly sees this, sees the most excellent buddha, the knower of reality."

369 The source for this section on the real nature of selflessness is Khewang Yeshe Gyatso, *Exegetical Memorandum,* ch. 5, pp. 203–204.

370 Khewang Yeshe Gyatso, *Exegetical Memorandum,* ch. 5, pp. 204–208, examines the real nature of internal phenomena in five contexts: (1) the false notion of a creator; (2) the ways in which past actions, dissonant mental states, and suffering arise; (3) the supposed existence of external objects; (4) the supposed necessity for the existence of external objects; and (5) the arising of imputed apperception—the last of which, in its unmistaken modality, is designated as the "real nature of internal phenomena."

371 This final section on the "real nature devoid of inherent existence" is elaborated in Khewang Yeshe Gyatso, *Exegetical Memorandum,* ch. 5, pp. 208–211.

372 Khewang Yeshe Gyatso, *Exegetical Memorandum,* ch. 5, p. 208.

373 Khewang Yeshe Gyatso, *Exegetical Memorandum,* ch. 5, p. 209.
374 Boin-Webb 2001, 58.
375 Khewang Yeshe Gyatso, *Exegetical Memorandum,* ch. 5, p. 210.
376 Khewang Yeshe Gyatso, *Exegetical Memorandum,* ch. 5, p. 210.
377 Khewang Yeshe Gyatso, *Exegetical Memorandum,* ch. 5, p. 210.
378 Khewang Yeshe Gyatso, *Exegetical Memorandum,* ch. 5, p. 210. In this and the following paragraph, Jamgon Kongtrul alludes to the coalescence of emptiness and inner radiance (*gsal stong zung 'jug*), characteristic of the innate seed of buddha nature (*prakṛtiṣṭhagotra, rang bzhin gnas rigs*), on the basis of which all sentient beings are said to have the potential to attain buddhahood. See Dudjom Rinpoche 1991, 1:178–205.
379 Khewang Yeshe Gyatso, *Exegetical Memorandum,* ch. 5, pp. 210–211.
380 Khewang Yeshe Gyatso, *Exegetical Memorandum,* ch. 5, p. 211.
381 Khewang Yeshe Gyatso, *Exegetical Memorandum,* ch. 5, p. 211.

Abbreviations

ACIP	Asian Classics Input Project (www.asianclassics.org)
B Budh	Bibliotheca Buddhica. St Petersburg/ Leningrad, 1897–1936
BST	Buddhist Sanskrit Texts. Darbhanga, Bihar: Mithila Institute of Post-Graduate Studies and Research in Sanskrit Learning
Dg.K	The Derge Kangyur (sDe dge bka' 'gyur) xylograph edition. 103 vols. Edited by Situ Chokyi Jungne. Freely accessible online at www.tbrc.org
Dg.NGB	The Derge xylograph edition of the Collected Tantras of the Nyingmapa (rNying ma'i rgyud 'bum). 26 vols. Edited by Katok Getse Gyurme Tsewang Chokdrub. Catalogue by Thubten Chodar. Beijing: Mi rigs dpe skrun khang, 2000
Dg.T	The Derge Tengyur (sDe dge bstan 'gyur) xylograph edition. 213 vols. Edited by Zhuchen Tsultrim Rinchen. Freely accessible online at www.tbrc.org
disc.	Discoverer of revealed teachings (*gter ma*)
EIPRB	Karl Potter, *Encyclopaedia of Indian Philosophies*, vol. 1, Bibliography (revised edition). Princeton: Princeton University Press, 1983. Updated and maintained online by Christine Keyt at http://faculty.washington.edu/kpotter/
GOS	Gaekwad's Oriental Series. Baroda: Oriental Institute
HJK	Hor rgyal, ed. *Jonang Catalogue entitled Beautiful Crystal Garland* (*Jo nang dkar chag shel dkar phreng mdzes*). Beijing: Mi rigs dpe skrun khang, 2005
LTWA	Library of Tibetan Works and Archives. Dharamsala, HP, India
MTTWL	P. Pfandt. *Mahāyāna Texts Translated into Western Languages*. Cologne: In Kommission bei E.J. Brill, 1983
MVT	*Mahāvyutpatti*. Ed. R. Sakaki. Kyoto: 1916–1925
NA	Not available; possibly no longer extant
NK	The Collected Transmitted Teachings of the Nyingmapa (rNying ma'i bka' ma). Currently 120 vols. in the most extended edition (*shin tu rgyas pa*), compiled by Khenpo Munsel and Khenpo Jamyang of Katok. Chengdu: 1999
P	*The Tibetan Tripiṭaka*. Peking Edition. 168 vols. Tokyo-Kyoto: Suzuki Research Foundation, 1955–1961

PZ	Pekar Zangpo, *mDo sde spyi'i rnam bzhag*. Beijing: Mi rigs dpe skrun khang, 2006. A sixteenth-century Tibetan language summary of all the sūtras preserved in the Kangyur
RTD	*Treasury of Revealed Teachings* (*Rin chen gter mdzod*), compiled by Jamgon Kongtrul. Palpung edition, republished in 72 vols.
SK	Jamgon Kongtrul's *Treasury of Knowledge* (*Shes bya kun khyab mdzod*)—the root verses, along with prose auto-commentary entitled *Infinite Ocean of Knowledge* (*Shes bya mtha' yas pa'i rgya mtsho*). 3 vols. Beijing: Mi rigs dpe skrun khang, 1982.
SKB	*Sa skya bka' 'bum. The Complete Works of the Great Masters of the Sa Skya Pa Sect of Tibetan Buddhism.* 15 vols. Tokyo: Toyo Bunko, 1968.
Skt.	Sanskrit
SP	Śatapiṭaka Series. New Delhi: International Academy of Indian Culture
T	H. Ui et al., *A Complete Catalogue of the Tibetan Buddhist Canon*. Tohoku University catalogue of the Derge edition of the canon. Sendai: 1934.
Taisho	J. Takakusu, K. Watanabe, et al., *Taisho shinshu daizokyo*. Tokyo: Taisho Issaikyo Kanko Kai, 1924–1932
TBRC	Tibetan Buddhist Resource Center. Online catalogue at www.tbrc.org
Tib.	Tibetan
Tingkye NGB	Rnying ma'i rgyud 'bum. Collected Tantras of the Nyingmapa. 36 vols. Photo-offset edition, based on the gTing skyes rdzong ms. Thimphu: Dilgo Khyentse Rinpoche, 1973. Catalogue by E. Kaneko, Tokyo: 1982.
TMP	Parfionovitch, Yuri, Gyurme Dorje and Fernand Meyer, *Tibetan Medical Paintings*. London: Serindia Publications, 1992

Bibliography of Works Cited by the Author

Bibliographical references for this volume are presented in two main sections—the first listing works cited by Jamgön Kongtrul in SK*; and the second, the reference bibliography, listing works to which the reader is referred in the back-matter. The bibliography of works cited by the author comprises three distinct alphabetically arranged sections: (1) Scriptural Texts: Vinaya, Sūtra, and Tantra; (2) Indic Treatises; and (3) Indigenous Tibetan Treatises and Spiritual Revelations (*gter ma*).*

1. Scriptural Texts: Vinaya, Sūtra, and Tantra

Analysis [*of Monastic Discipline*]
Vinayavibhaṅga
['Dul ba] rnam 'byed
Dg.K. 'Dul ba, vols. Ca, ff. 21a–Nya, ff. 269a. T 3. See Lamotte 1988, 81–197.

Eight Transmitted Teachings: [*Means for Attainment*]
[sGrub pa] bka' brgyad
Dg.NGB, vols. 15–24; Tingkye NGB, vols. 20–33, especially vols. 31–32, which contain the general tantras (*spyi rgyud*) and the particular tantras (*sgos rgyud*) associated with the original Indian revelation of the *Tantra of the Gathering of the Sugatas of the Eight Transmitted Teachings* (*sGrub chen bka' brgyad bde 'dus kyi rgyud*). This is the Mahāyoga source from which the subsequent Tibetan revelations (*gter ma*) of the Eight Transmitted Teachings (*bka' brgyad*) derive. The eight concern the meditational deities: Yamāntaka (*'Jam dpal gzhin rje gshad pa'i rgyud skor*, Dg.NGB vols. 15–17, Tingkye NGB vols. 20–22, T 838); Hayagrīva/ Aśvottama (*dPal rta mgrin padma dbang chen rta mchog rol pa'i rgyud sde rnams*, Dg.NGB vols. 17–18, Tingkye NGB vols. 23–24); Śrīheruka (*dPal yang dag thugs kyi rgyud sde rnams*, Dg.NGB vols. 18–19, Tingkye NGB vol. 25); Vajrāmṛta (*'Chi med bdud rtsi yon tan gyi rgyud sde rnams*, Dg.NGB vols. 19–20, Tingkye NGB vol. 26, T 841); Vajrakīla/ Vajrakumāra (*bCom ldan 'das dpal rdo rje phur pa'i rgyud sde rnams*, Dg.NGB vols. 20–22, Tingkye NGB vols. 27–29); Mātaraḥ (*Ma mo srid pa'i dzong lung chen mo yum bzung ma'i dngos grub chen mo'i rgyud rnams dang ma mo rtsa rgyud 'bum tig gi skor*, Dg.NGB vols. 22–23, Tingkye NGB vols. 30–31 and 33, T 842); Lokastotrapūjā (*bsTan srung 'jig rten mchod bstod*, Dg.NGB vol. 24, Tingkye NGB vol. 32, T 844); and Vajramantrabhīru (*rMod pa drag sngags*, Dg.NGB vol. 24, Tingkye NGB vol. 32, T 843). The principal Tibetan revelations of this genre include the *Eight Transmitted Teachings: Gathering of the Sugatas* (*bKa' brgyad bde gshegs 'dus pa*) discovered by Nyangrel Nyima Ozer, the *Eight Transmitted Teachings: Consummation of Secrets* (*bKa' brgyad gsang*

ba yongs rdzogs), discovered by Guru Chowang, and the *Eight Transmitted Teachings: Natural Arising* (*bKa' brgyad rang shar*), discovered by Rigdzin Godemchen, which are all contained in *bKa' brgyad phyogs sgrigs*, 20 vols.

Exegetical/ Great Tantra of the Emergence of Cakrasaṃvara
[bShad rgyud] sdom 'byung [gi rgyud chen po]
See [*Tantra of*] *the Emergence of Cakrasaṃvara*

Exegetical Tantra of the Four Indestructible Seats: Mantra Section
Śrīcatuḥpīthākhyātatantrarājamantrāṃśa
[dPal] gdan bzhi pa'i bshad rgyud [kyi rgyal po] sngags kyi cha
Dg.K. rGyud 'bum, vol. Nga, ff. 231b–260a. T 429

Gathering of the Great Assembly
Tshogs chen 'dus pa
NK, vols. 19–28, 90–99, which derive from the principal Anuyoga text entitled *Sūtra Which Gathers All Intentions* (*mDo dgongs pa 'dus pa*, Dg.K. rNying rgyud, vol. Ka, ff. 86b–290a. T 829. Dg.NGB, vol. Ja (7), ff. 110b–314a

King of Tantras: [*the Wheel of Time*]
See [*Tantra of the*] *Wheel of Time*

Maṇḍala Array [*of the Tantra of the Indestructible Peak*]
Vajraśekharatantramaṇḍalavyūha
[rGyud rdo rje rtse mo'i] dkyil 'khor bkod pa
Dg.K. rGyud 'bum, vol. Nya, ff. 142b–274a. T 480

Minor Transmissions
Vinayakṣudrakavastu (also: Kṣudrāgama)
'Dul ba lung phreng tshegs kyi gzhi
Dg.K. 'Dul ba, vols. Tha–Da. T 6

Mother
Yum
See *Sūtra of the Transcendental Perfection of Discriminative Awareness in One Hundred Thousand Lines*

Root Tantra of Mañjuśrī
Mañjuśrīmūlatantra
['Phags pa] 'jam dpal gyi rtsa ba'i rgyud
Dg.K. rGyud 'bum, vol. Na, ff. 108a–351a. T 543.
BST 18 (1964). Translated in Macdonald 1962

Scriptural Compilation of the Bodhisattvas
Bodhisattvapiṭaka
['Phags pa] byang chub sems dpa'i sde snod
Dg.K. dKon brtsegs, vols. Kha, ff. 255b–Ga, f. 205b. T 56
MTTWL 44. Translated in Pagel 1995

[*Secret*] *Tantra of General* [*Rites*]
Sāmānyavidhīnāṃ guhyatantra
gSang ba spyi rgyud
Dg.K. rGyud 'bum, vol. Va, ff. 141a–167b. T 806

Supramundane Sūtra entitled Heruka Galpo
'Jigs rten las 'das pa'i mdo he ru ka gal po
Dg.NGB, vols. Tsha (18), ff. 278a–300, and Dza (19), ff. 1–258b

Supreme Tantra of Manifest Expression
Abhidānottaratantra
mNgon par brjod pa'i rgyud bla ma
Dg.K. rGyud 'bum, vol. Ka, ff. 247a–370a. T 369
An explanatory tantra-text of the Cakrasaṃvara cycle, partly edited and translated in Kalff 1979

Supreme Transmission of Monastic Discipline
Vinayottaragrantha
Lung mchog bla ma
Dg.K. 'Dul ba, vols. Na, f. 1b–Ba, f. 313a. T 7
See Lamotte 1988, pp. 181–197

Sūtra of Extensive Play
Lalitavistarasūtra
rGya cher rol pa
Dg.K. mDo sde, vol. Kha, ff. 1b–216b. T 95
Summarized in PZ, pp. 145–146. *MTTWL* 102. BST 1 (1958). Translated from Foucaux's French version in Bays 1983

Sūtra of [Great] Final Nirvāṇa
Mahāparinirvāṇasūtra
Myang ngan las 'das pa'i [chen po'i] mdo
Dg.K. mDo sde, vols. Nya, f. 1b–Tha, f. 152b. T 119–121
Summarized in PZ, pp. 170–175. *MTTWL* 118. *EIPRB* 88. Translated in Yamamoto 1999–2000

Sūtra of [Great] Skillful Means, Repaying [the Buddha] with Gratitude
Thabs la mkhas pa [chen po sangs rgyas] drin lan bsab pa'i mdo
Da fang bian fo bao en jing
Dg.K. mDo sde, vol. Aḥ, ff. 86a–198b. T 353
Summarized in PZ, pp. 520–521

Sūtra of Inconceivable Secrets
Tathāgatācintyaguhyanirdeśasūtra
gSang ba bsam gyis mi khyab pa'i mdo
Dg.K. dKon brtsegs, vol. Ka, ff. 100a–203a. T 47
Summarized in PZ, pp. 28–32. *MTTWL* 232

Sūtra of the Ascertainment of the Characteristics of Phenomena
Chos rnams kyi mtshan nyid rnam par nges pa'i mdo
NA

[*Sūtra of the*] *Dense Array*
Ghanavyūhasūtra
rGyan stug po bkod pa
Dg.K. mDo sde, vol. Cha, ff. 1b–55b. T 110
EIPRB 340. Summarized in PZ, pp. 163–165

Sūtra of the Descent to Laṅkā
Laṅkāvatārasūtra
mDo sde laṅkar gshegs pa
Dg.K. mDo sde, vol. Ca, ff. 56a–191b. T 107
Summarized in PZ, pp. 159–163. *MTTWL* 103. BST 3 (1963). *EIPRB* 137. Translated in Suzuki 1932

Sūtra of the Enhancement of Faith
Dad pa cher 'byung gi mdo
NA

Sūtra of the Excellent Meditation on Faith in the Greater Vehicle
Mahāyānaprasādaprabhāvanasūtra
Theg pa chen po la dad pa rab tu sgom pa'i mdo
Dg.K. mDo sde, vol. Pa, ff. 6b–34a. T 144
Summarized in PZ, pp. 200–201

Sūtra of the Great Drum
Mahābherihārakasūtra
rNga bo che chen po'i le'u
Dg.K. mDo sde, vol. Dza, ff. 84b–126b. T 222
Summarized in PZ, pp. 300–303

Sūtra of the Lotus
Saddharmapuṇḍarīkasūtra
Dam chos pad dkar
Dg.K. mDo sde, vol. Ja, ff. 1b–180b. T 113
Summarized in PZ, pp. 167–169. *MTTWL* 191. BST 6 (1960). Translated in Kern 1884; Kato et al. 1975

Sūtra of the Net of Brahmā
Brahmajālasūtra
Tshangs pa'i dra ba'i mdo
Dg.K. mDo sde, vol. Aḥ, ff. 70b–86a. T 352
Summarized in PZ, pp. 521–524. Translated from Pali in Bodhi 1978.

Sūtra of the Nucleus of the Sun
Sūryagarbhasūtra
mDo sde nyi ma'i snying po
Dg.K. mDo sde, vol. Za, ff. 91b–245b. T 257
Summarized in PZ, pp. 420–422. *EIPRB* 180. *MTTWL* 225

Sūtra of the Stacked Mansion House
Kūṭāgārasūtra
Khang bu brtsegs pa'i mdo
Dg.K. mDo sde, vol. Sa, ff. 260a–263b. T 332
Summarized in PZ, pp. 498–499

Sūtra of the Ten-Wheeled Kṣitigarbha
Daśacakrakṣitigarbhasūtra
Sa'i snying po'i 'khor lo bcu pa
Dg.K. mDo sde, vol. Zha, ff. 100a–241b. T 239
Summarized in PZ, pp. 332–336. *MTTWL* 101

Sūtra of the Transcendental Perfection of Discriminative Awareness [in Eighteen Thousand Lines]
Aṣṭādaśāhasrikāprajñāpāramitā
Shes rab kyi pha rol tu phyin pa khri brgyad stong pa
Dg.K. Shes phyin, vols. Ka, f. 1b–Ga, f. 206a (3 vols.). T 10
Summarized in PZ, pp. 402–406. *EIPRB* 54. *MTTWL* 20. Translated and edited in Conze 1975

[Sūtra of] the Transcendental Perfection of Discriminative Awareness in Five Hundred Lines
Pañcaśatikaprajñāpāramitā
Shes rab kyi pha rol tu phyin pa lnga brgya pa
Dg.K. Shes phyin, vol. Ka, ff. 104a–120b. T 15
Summarized in PZ, pp. 414–415. *EIPRB* 549.1. *MTTWL* 152

Sūtra of the Transcendental Perfection of Discriminative Awareness in One Hundred Thousand Lines
Śatasāhasrikāprajñāpāramitā
Shes rab kyi pha rol tu phyin pa stong phrag brgya pa
Dg.K. Shes phyin, vols. Ka, f. 1b–A, f. 395a (12 vols.). T 8
Summarized in PZ, pp. 395–399. *EIPRB* 52. *MTTWL* 208

Sūtra of the Transcendental Perfection of Discriminative Awareness [in Twenty-five Thousand Lines]
Pañcaviṃśatisāhasrikāprajñāpāramitā
Shes rab kyi pha rol tu phyin pa stong phrag nyi shu lnga pa
Dg.K. Shes phyin, vols. Ka, f. 1b–Ga, f. 381a (3 vols.). T 9
Summarized in PZ, pp. 399–402. *EIPRB* 53. *MTTWL* 154. Annotated Sanskrit edition by Nalinaksha Dutt. London: Luzac, 1934

Sūtra That Expresses the Goals of Activity
Las kyi mtha' brjod pa'i mdo
NA

Sūtra That Reveals the Ten Abodes
gNas bcu bstan pa'i mdo
Not located

Tantra entitled Summation of the Real
Tattvasaṃgrahatantra
De kho na nyid bsdus pa
Dg.K. rGyud 'bum, vol. Nya, ff. 1b–142a. T 479
Sanskrit edited in Yamada 1981; also in Chandra and Snellgrove 1981

Tantra of Acala
Acalakalpatantrarāja
Mi gYo ba'i rtog pa'i rgyud kyi rgyal po
Dg.K. rGyud 'bum, vol. Ca, ff. 1b–12a. T 432

Tantra of Black Yamāri
Kṛṣṇayamāritantra
gShin rje'i bshed nag po'i rgyud kyi rgyal po
Dg.K. rGyud 'bum, vol. Ja, ff. 164a–167b; 175b–185b. T 473

Tantra of Consecration
Supratiṣṭhatantrasaṃgraha
Rab gnas kyi rgyud
Dg.K. rGyud 'bum, vol. Ta, ff. 146b–150a. T 486

Tantra of Embrace
Sampuṭatantra
Yang dag par sbyor ba'i rgyud kyi rgyal po
Dg.K. rGyud 'bum, vol. Ga, ff. 73b–184a. T 381–382

Tantra of Heruka Galpo
See *Supramundane Sūtra entitled Heruka Galpo*

Tantra of Hevajra
Hevajratantra
dGyes rdor rgyud kyi brtag pa
Dg.K. rGyud 'bum, vol. Nga, ff. 1b–30a. T 417–418
Edited and translated in Snellgrove 1959

Tantra of Red Yamāri
Raktayamāritantrarāja
gShin rje bshed dmar po'i rgyud kyi rgyal po
Dg.K. rGyud 'bum, vol. Ja, ff. 186a–244b. T 474–475

Tantra of Renunciation
Abhyudayatantra
mNgon par 'byung ba'i rgyud
The title of three explanatory tantras pertaining to Cakrasaṃvara, which comprise the *Tantra of the Renunciation of Śrīheruka* (*Śrīherukābhyudayatantra*, Dg.K. rGyud 'bum, vol. Ga, ff. 1b–33b; T 374), and the two-part *Tantra of the Renunciation of Vajravārāhī* (Dg.K. rGyud 'bum, vol. Ga, ff. 60b–72b; T 378–379)

Tantra of Supreme Nectar
bDud rtsi mchog gi rgyud
See *Tantra of the Eight Volumes of Nectar*

Tantra of the Eight Volumes of Nectar
Sarvapañcāmṛtasārasiddhimahadgata-hṛdayaparivartāṣṭaka
bDud rtsi bam brgyad
Dg.K. rNying rgyud, vol. Ga, ff. 202a–222a. T 841. Dg.NGB, vols. Dza (19), ff. 311a–354 and Va (20), ff. 1–168b. Tingkye NGB, vol. 26

[*Tantra of*] *the Emergence of Cakrasaṃvara*
Śrīmahāsaṃvarodayatantrarāja
[bDe mchog bshad rgyud] sdom 'byung [rgyud kyi rgyal po chen po]
Dg.K. rGyud 'bum, vol. Kha, ff. 265a–311a. T 373.
This is an exegetical tantra pertaining to the cycle of Cakrasaṃvara (T 366–369). Partially edited and translated in Tsuda 1974. The root tantra, entitled *Tantrarājaśrīlaghusaṃvara* (*rGyud kyi rgyal po dpal bde mchog nyung ngu*, T 368), is translated in Gray 2007

[*Tantra of the*] *Empowerment of Vajrapāṇi*
Vajrapāṇyabhiṣekatantra
Lag na rdo rje dbang bskur ba'i rgyud chen po
Dg.K. rGyud 'bum, vol. Da, ff. 1b–156b. T 496

Tantra of the Flash of the Splendor [of Pristine Cognition]
Jñānāścaryadyutitantra
rGyud ye shes rngam glog
Dg.K. rNying rgyud, vol. Ka, ff. 290b–358a. T 830. Dg.NGB, vol. Ja (7), ff. 314b–382

[Tantra of] the Four [Indestructible] Seats
Catuḥvajrapīthamahayoginītantrarāja
rGyud kyi rgyal po dpal gdan bzhi pa
Dg.K. rGyud 'bum, vol. Nga, ff. 181a–231b. T 428

Tantra of the Habitual Practice of the Yoginī
Yoginīsañcāryatantra
rNal 'byor ma kun spyod kyi rgyud
Dg.K. rGyud 'bum, vol. Ga, ff. 34a–44b. T 375
An explanatory tantra pertaining to Cakrasaṃvara. Sanskrit and Tibetan texts edited in Pandey 1998

Tantra of the Indestructible Array
Vyūhavajratantra
rDo rje bkod pa'i rgyud
Dg.K. rNying rgyud, vol. Ka, ff. 86b–290a. T 829. Dg.NGB, vol. Ja (7), ff. 110b–314a
A primary tantra-text of the Anuyoga tradition. See also *Gathering of the Great Assembly*

[Tantra of the] Indestructible Garland
Vajramālābhidhānatantra
rDo rje phreng ba mngon par brjod pa'i rgyud
Dg.K. rGyud 'bum, vol. Ca, ff. 208a–277b. T 445
An explanatory tantra pertaining to the *Tantra of the Secret Assembly* (*Guhyasamājatantra*, T 442)

Tantra of the Indestructible Peak
Vajraśekharatantra
gSang ba rnal 'byor chen po'i rgyud rdo rje rtse mo
Dg.K. rGyud 'bum, vol. Nya, ff. 142b–274a. T 480
An explanatory tantra pertaining to the *Tantra of the Summation of the Real* (*Tattvasaṃgrahatantra*, T 479)

[Tantra of] the Indestructible Sky-farers
Vajraḍākanāmamahātantrarāja
rGyud kyi rgyal po chen po dpal rdo rje mkha' 'gro
Dg.K. rGyud 'bum, vol. Kha, ff. 1b–125a. T 370
An explanatory tantra pertaining to the cycle of Cakrasaṃvara

[Tantra of the Indestructible] Tent
Ḍākinīvajrapañjaramahātantra
[mKha' 'gro ma rdo rje] gur gyi rgyud
Dg.K. rGyud 'bum, vol. Nga, ff. 30a–65b. T 419
An explanatory tantra pertaining to Hevajra

Tantra of the Lasso of Skillful Means
Thabs kyi zhags pa'i rgyud
Dg.K. rNying rgyud, vol. Kha, ff. 299a–311a. T 835. Dg.NGB, vol. Pa (13), ff. 286a–298. Tingkye NGB, vol. 19
New authoritative edition in Cantwell and Mayer, forthcoming

[*Tantra of the*] *Magical Net* [*of Vajrasattva*]
Vajrasattvamāyājālatantra
rDo rje sems dpa' sgyu 'phrul dra ba'i rgyud
Dg.NGB, vols. 9–11
One of the four primary divisions of the cycle of the tantras of the *Magical Net* (*Māyājāla*), which, according to Longchen Rabjampa, includes the following main texts:
(1) The *Tantra of the Secret Nucleus* (*Guhyagarbha Tantra*, Dg.NGB, vol. Ta [9], ff. 1–31b; Tingkye NGB, vol. 14; Dg.K. rNying rgyud, vol. Kha, ff. 110b–132a; T 832), which presents mind and pristine cognition as naturally manifesting
(2) The *Forty-Chapter Tantra, from the Magical Net* (Dg.NGB, vol. Tha [10], ff. 135a–182b; Tingkye NGB, vol. 14), which perfectly presents buddha activities
(3) The *Eight-Chapter Tantra, from the Magical Net* (Dg.NGB, vol. Tha [10], ff. 114a–123a; Tingkye NGB, vol. 14), which perfectly presents the maṇḍalas
(4) The *Tantra of the Spiritual Teacher, from the Magical Net* (Dg.NGB, vol. Da [11], ff. 34b–60a; Tingkye NGB, vol. 14; Dg.K, rNying rgyud, vol. Ga, ff. 34b–60a; T 837), which clearly presents the empowerments
(5) The *Tantra of Supplementary Points, from the Magical Net* (Dg.NGB, vol. Tha [10], ff. 182b–238b; Tingkye NGB, vol. 14), which emphatically presents the commitments
(6) The *Eighty-Chapter Tantra, from the Magical Net* (Dg.NGB, vol. Da [11], ff. 148b–248b; Tingkye NGB, vol. 14; Dg.K. rNying rgyud, vol. Kha, ff. 198b–298b; T 834), which extensively presents buddha-attributes
(7) The *Mirror of Indestructible Reality* (Dg.NGB, vol. Da [11], ff. 82b–148a; Tingkye NGB, vol. 15; Dg.K. rNying rgyud, vol. Kha, ff. 132b–198a; T 833), which clearly presents the symbolic body-colors and hand-held implements of the hundred deities
(8) The *Oceanic Tantra, from the Magical Net* (Dg.NGB, vol. Tha [10], ff. 279b–313; Tingkye NGB, vol. 15), which clearly presents the generation stage of meditation
(9) The *Penetrating Tantra, from the Magical Net* (Dg.NGB, vol. Da [11], ff. 249a–294a; Tingkye NGB, vol. 15), which clearly presents the path of skillful means.
Nowadays, the root and exegetical tantras of the *Magical Net* (*sGyu 'phrul drva ba rtsa bshad kyi rgyud*) altogether comprise nineteen distinct texts, which are all contained in Dg.NGB, vols. 9–11, and Tingkye NGB, vols. 14–16 and 19. For further detail, see Dorje 1987, and the updated introduction to that work at the Wisdom Books online reading room.

[*Tantra of the*] *Ocean of Sky-farers*
Ḍākārṇavamahāyoginītantrarāja
mKha 'gro rgya mtsho [rnal 'byor ma'i rgyud]
Dg.K. rGyud 'bum, vol. Kha, ff. 137a–264b. T 372
An explanatory tantra pertaining to Cakrasaṃvara. Apabhraṃśa version edited in Nagendra Narayan Chaudhuri, *Studies in the Apabhraṃśa Texts of the Ḍākārṇavamahāyoginītantrarāja*. Calcutta: Metropolitan Printing and Publishing House, 1935

Tantra of the Secret Assembly
Guhyasamājatantra
gSang ba 'dus pa'i rgyud
Dg.K. rGyud 'bum, vol. Ca, ff. 90a–157b. T 442–443. Dg.NGB, vol. Na (12), ff. 89a–157a.
BST 9 (1965). Translated in F. Fremantle. 1971. "A Critical Study of the Guhyasamāja Tantra." PhD diss. University of London, School of Oriental and African Studies.

[*Tantra of the*] *Secret Nucleus*
Guhyagarbhatantra
rGyud gsang ba'i nying po
Dg.K. rNying rgyud, vol. Kha, ff. 110b–132a. T 832. Dg.NGB, vol. Ta (9), ff. 1–31b. Tingkye NGB, vol. 14
Tibetan text edited and translated in Dorje 1987. See also the revised introduction to that work at the Wisdom Books online reading room

[*Tantra of the*] *Victory over the Three Worlds*
Trailokyavijayamahākalparāja
'Jig rten gsum las rnam par rgyal ba rtog pa'i po chen po
Dg.K. rGyud 'bum, vol. Ta, ff. 10a–58a. T 482

[*Tantra of the*] *Wheel of Time*
[Paramādibuddhoddhṛtaśrī] kālacakratantrarāja
[mChog gi dang po'i sangs rgyas las phyung ba rgyud kyi rgyal po dpal] dus kyi 'khor lo
Dg.K. rGyud 'bum, vol. Ka, ff. 22b–128b. T 362
Also known as the *Concise Tantra* [*of the Wheel of Time*] (*bsDus rgyud*), when contrasted with the longer *Root Tantra* [*of the Wheel of Time*] (*rTsa rgyud*), which is no longer extant, apart from references to it which are found in Puṇḍarīka's commentary (T 1347). SP, vols. 69–70 (1966). Sanskrit also edited in B. Banerjee 1985. Translations include Newman 1987 (ch. 1) and Wallace 2001 (ch. 2). See also Kilty 2004; Simon 1985; Dalai Lama and Hopkins 1985; and Bryant 1992

Tantra That Completely Apprehends the Attributes of a Spiritual Teacher
Bla ma'i yon tan yongs gzung gi rgyud
NA

[*Tantras/ Cycles of*] *Vajrakīla*
Vajrakīla[tantra]
rDo rje phur ba'i rgyud/ skor
A set of tantras and derivative cycles, the former comprising the *Root Fragment of Vajrakīla* (*Vajrakīlamūlatantrakhaṇḍa, Phur ba rtsa ba dum bu*, Dg.K. rGyud 'bum, vol. Ca, ff. 43b–45b, T 439), as well as the *Karmamāla* (Dg.NGB, vol. Na [12], ff. 273a–343; Tingkye NGB, vol. 17), *Phur pa bcu gnyis pa* (Dg.NGB, vol. Pa [13], ff. 176a–251b; Tingkye NGB, vol. 19), and the various tantras of the means for attainment of Vajrakīla (*bCom ldan 'das dpal rdo rje phur pa'i rgyud sde rnams,* Dg.NGB, vols. 20–22; Tingkye NGB, vols. 27–29). Among them, the *Phur pa bcu gnyis pa* is summarized in Mayer 1996, while two of the "means for attainment" tantras are presented in Cantwell and Mayer 2007. The extensive commentary entitled *Phur 'grel 'bum nag* is translated and analyzed in Boord 2002.

Transmissions of Monastic Discipline
Vinayāgama
'Dul ba'i lung
Dg.K. 'Dul ba, vols. Ka–Pa (13 vols.). T 1–7
The primary texts of the Sanskrit *Vinayapiṭaka*, as preserved in Tibetan translation. See Frauwallner 1956

Verse Summation [*of the Transcendental Perfection of Discriminative Awareness*]
Prajñāpāramitāsañcayagāthā
Shes rab kyi pha rol tu phyin pa sdud pa tshigs su bcad pa
Dg.K. Shes phyin, vol. Ka, ff. 1b–10b. T 13
Summarized in PZ, p. 412. *MTTWL* 183. BST 17 (1961). Translated in Conze 1973

Wrathful Deities of the Magical Net
sGyu 'phrul khro bo['i skor]
This may refer to all those tantras of the *Magical Net* cycle (Dg.NGB, vols. 9–11) which include the assembly of wrathful deities (*khro bo'i lha tshogs*), and to the derivative cycles of the oral tradition contained in NK, vols. 13–17 and vols. 63–80, 83–89. The former also specifically include the *Kingly Tantra concerning the Power of the Wrathful Deities, from the Secret Nucleus Which Ascertains the Real* (*gSang ba'i snying po de kho na nyid nges pa'i khro bo stobs kyi rgyud rgyal*, Dg.NGB, vol. 11 [Da], ff. 296–297) and the *Tantra of the Attainment of the Mighty Lords of Yoga through the Power of the Precious Wrathful Deities, from the Magical Net* (*Khro bo rin po che'i stobs kyis rnal 'byor dbang phyug sgrub pa'i sgyu 'phrul dra ba'i rgyud*, Dg.NGB, vol. 11 [Da], ff. 294–296)

2. Indic Treatises

Abhayākaragupta (fl. late eleventh–early twelfth century)
Cornucopia of Esoteric Instructions: [A Commentary on the Tantra of Embrace]
Śrīsampuṭatantrarājatīkāmnāyamañjarī
[dPal yang dag par sbyor ba'i rgyud kyi rgyal po'i rgya cher 'grel pa] man ngag snye ma
Dg.T. rGyud, vol. Cha, ff. 1b–316a. T 1198

[Indestructible] Garland
Vajrāvali-nāma-maṇḍalasādhana
[dKyil 'khor gyi cho ga] rdo rje phreng ba
Dg.T. rGyud, vol. Phu, ff. 1b–94b. T 3140
See Willson and Brauen 2000

Amarasiṃha (fl. fifth or seventh century)
Treasury of Amarasiṃha
Amarakośa
'Chi med mdzod
Dg.T. sGra mod, vol. Se, ff. 126b–243a. T 4299
See note 976; also Miśra 2005; and Vogel 1979, pp. 309–313. Tibetan text: *mNgon brjod 'chi ba med pa'i mdzod* (Qinghai mi rigs dpe skrun khang, 1985)

Amoghodaya (*don yod 'char*) (dates uncertain)
Answers to the Questions of Vimala[kīrti]
Vimalapraśnottararatnamālā
Dri ma med pa'i dris lan
Dg.T. Thun mong, vol. Ngo, ff. 126a–127b. T 4333

Anubhūtisvabhāva (a.k.a. Anubhūtisvarūpa, fl. thirteenth century)
Analysis of the Grammar of Sārasvata
Sārasvatavyākaraṇasūtra
mTsho ldan ma'i rab byed
Retranslation by Situ Chokyi Jungne in bKa' brgyud pa'i gsung rab, 1:381–602

Commentary on the Grammar of Sārasvata
Sārasvatavyākaraṇavṛttiprakriyācaturā
brDa sprod pa'i bstan bcos chen po dbyangs can byā ka ra ṇa'i 'grel pa rab tu bya ba gsal ldan gyi mdo
Dg.T. sGra mod, vol. Se, ff. 10b–125a. T 4298

Grammar of Sārasvata
Sārasvatavyākaraṇasūtra
brDa sprod pa dbyangs can gyi mdo
Dg.T. sGra mod, vol. Se, ff. 1b–9a. T 4297

Āryadeva I (fl. second–third century)
Compendium of the Nucleus of Pristine Cognition
Jñānasārasamuccaya
Ye shes snying po kun las btus pa
Dg.T. dBu ma, vol. Tsha, ff. 26b–28a. T 3851
MTTWL 88. *EIPRB* 414.2

Four Hundred Verses
Catuḥśataka
bsTan bcos bzhi brgya pa
Dg.T. dBu ma, vol. Tsha, ff. 1b–18a. T 3846
MTTWL 53. *EIPRB* 50.2. Translated in Lang 1986

Āryadeva II (fl. eighth century)
Lamp Which Subsumes Conduct
Caryāmelāpakapradīpa
sPyod pa bsdus pa'i sgron me
Dg.T. rGyud, vol. Ngi, ff. 57a–106b. T 1803
Translated in Wedemeyer 2008

Asaṅga (fl. late fourth–early fifth century)
Actual Foundation of the Yogācāra Level
Yogācārabhūmivastu
[rNal 'byor spyod pa'i] sa'i dngos gzhi
Dg.T. Sems tsam, vols. Tshi–Vi (3 vols.). T 4035–4037
MTTWL 259. *EIPRB* 174.10. This is the first of the five parts of the Yogācāra Level, comprising three texts: the *Yogācāra Level* (*Yogācārabhūmi*, T 4035) and its sub-sections: the *Level of the Pious Attendants* (*Śrāvakabhūmi*, T 4036) and the *Level of the Bodhisattvas* (*Bodhisattvabhūmi*, *Byang chub sems dpa'i sa*, T 4037)

Compendium of Phenomenology
Abhidharmasamuccaya
Chos mngon pa kun las btus pa
Dg.T. Sems tsam, vol. Ri, ff. 44b–120a. T 4049
MTTWL 1. *EIPRB* 174.2. Translated from French in Boin-Webb 2001

Level of the Bodhisattvas
Bodhisattvabhūmi
Byang chub sems dpa'i sa
Dg.T. Sems tsam, vol. Vi, ff. 1b–213a. T 4037
MTTWL 41. *EIPRB* 174.10. Partly translated in Tatz 1986 and Willis 1982

Summary of the Greater Vehicle
Mahāyānasaṃgraha
Theg pa chen po bsdus pa
Dg.T. Sems tsam, vol. Ri, ff. 1b–43a. T 4048
MTTWL 125. *EIPRB* 174.7. Translated in Keenan 2003

Summation of Ascertainment from the Yogācāra Level
Yogācārabhūmiviniścayasaṃgrahaṇī
rNal 'byor spyod pa'i sa rnam par gtan la dbab pa bsdu ba
Dg.T. Sems tsam, vols Zhi–Zi (2 vols.). T 4038
EIPRB 174.10. One of the five parts of the Yogācāra Level, partly translated in Waldron 2003

Asvabhāva (fl. early sixth century)
Combined Commentary on the Summary of the Greater Vehicle
Mahāyānasaṃgrahapanibandhana
Theg pa chen po bsdus pa'i bshad sbyar
Dg.T. Sems tsam, vol. Ri, ff. 190b–296a. T 4051
MTTWL 127. *EIPRB* 274.2

Ātreya (Tibetan attribution, fl. sixth century)
Sūtra Requested by Śāriputra
Śāriputrāṣṭakasūtra, also known as the Pratibimbamānalakṣaṇa
Shāri bu kyis zhus pa'i mdo [sKu gzugs kyi cha tshad kyi mtshan nyid]
Dg.T. bZo rig, vol. Ngo, ff. 11a–15b. T 4316. P 5812
See Peterson 1980

Bhāvaviveka (ca. 500–570)
Flame of Dialectics
[Madhyamakahṛdayavṛtti]tarkajvālā
[dBu ma'i snying po'i 'grel pa] rtog ge 'bar ba
Dg.T. dBu ma, vol. Dza, ff. 40b–329b. T 3856
MTTWL 104–105. *EIPRB* 294.2. Partial translation (ch. 3) in Iida 1980

Bodhibhadra (fl. 1000)
Interlinear Commentary on the Compendium of the Nucleus of Pristine Cognition
Jñānasārasamuccaya-nāma-nibandhana
Ye shes snying po kun las bstus pa zhes bya ba'i bshad sbyar
Dg.T. dBu ma, vol. Tsha, ff. 28a–45b. T 3852
MTTWL 89. *EIPRB* 568.2

Bodhisattva (dates uncertain)
Commentary on the Taintless [*Crown Protuberance*]
Sheng pu men ru guang ming ding jie wu gou tuo luo ni du song er jing chao chu bai bu zhi duo lai zhi wu zhi duo jian li yi gui
['Phags pa kun nas sgor 'jug pa'i 'od zer] gtsug gtor dri med [gzungs bklag cing mchod rten brgya rtsa brgyad dam mchod rten lnga gdab pa'i cho ga mdo sde las btus pa]
Dg.T. rGyud, vol. Pu, ff. 140a–175b. T 3068–3078
Collective name for a series of rituals on dhāraṇī and stūpas, translated into Tibetan from the Chinese

Bṛhaspati (fl. 650–600 BCE)
Sūtra of Bṛhaspati
Bṛhaspatisūtra
NA. See Chattopadhyaya 1994

Buddhabaṭṭa (a.k.a. Mahoṣadhi, sixth century)
Scrutiny of Gems and Precious Metals
Ratnaparīkṣā
Rin po che brtag pa
Edition and French translation from Sanskrit in Finot 1896

Cāṇakya (350–275 BCE)
Treatise on the Behavior of Kings
Cāṇakyanītiśāstra
Tsa ra ka'i rgyal po'i lugs kyi bstan bcos
Dg.T. Thun mong, vol. Ngo, ff. 127b–137b. T 4334
Sanskrit edited with commentary in Bist 2001; also Sternbach 1963–70 and 1966. Cf. Dudjom Rinpoche 1991, note 85

Candragomin (fl. seventh century)
Grammar of Candragomin
Candravyākaraṇasutra
Lung ston pa tsandra pa'i mdo
Dg.T. sGra mdo, vol. Re, ff. 1b–29a. T 4269
Sanskrit edition in Liebach 1902. See also Thakur 2006

Candrakīrti (fl. seventh century)
Auto-commentary on the Introduction to Madhyamaka
Madhyamakāvatārabhāṣya
dBu ma la 'jug pa'i bshad pa
Dg.T. dBu ma, vol. 'A, ff. 220b–348a. T 3862
EIPRB 321.2

Introduction to Madhyamaka
Madhyamakāvatāra
dBu ma la 'jug pa
Dg.T. dBu ma, vol. 'A, ff. 201b–219a. T 3861
MTTWL 109. *EIPRB* 321.2. Translated in Huntington and Wangchen, 1989; also in Padmakara Translation Group 2002

Daṇḍin (fl. sixth century)
Mirror of Poetics
Kāvyādarśa
sNyan ngag me long
Dg.T. sGra mdo, vol. Se, ff. 318a–341a. T 4301
Sanskrit and Tibetan versions edited in A. Banerjee 1939. Sanskrit edited with English commentary in Ray 2004. See also Gupta 1970

Dharmakīrti (fl. early seventh century)
Exposition of Valid Cognition
Pramāṇavārttika[kārikā]
Tshad ma rnam 'grel gyi tshig le'u byas pa
Dg.T. Tshad ma, vol. Ce, ff. 94b–151a. T 4210
MTTWL 168. *EIPRB* 344.4. Sanskrit edition in Baudha Bharati Series 3 (1968). English translation (ch. 2) in Nagatomi 1957

Seven Sections [of Valid Cognition]
[Tshad ma] sde bdun
A collective name for the seven principal logical treatises of Dharmakīrti, comprising the *Ascertainment of Valid Cognition* (Pramāṇaviniścaya, Dg.T. Tshad ma, vol. Ce, ff. 152b–230a, T 4211, *MTTWL* 170, *EIPRB* 344.5); the *Exposition of Valid Cognition* (Pramāṇavārttika, Dg.T. Tshad ma, vol. Ce, ff. 94b–151a, T 4210, *MTTWL* 168, *EIPRB* 344.4); the *Inquiry into Relations* (Sambandhaparīkṣā, Dg.T. Tshad ma, vol. Ce, ff. 255a–256a, T 4214, *MTTWL* 195, *EIPRB* 344.6); the *Point of the Axioms* (Hetubindu, Dg.T. Tshad ma, vol. Ce, ff. 238a–255a, T 4213, *MTTWL* 83, *EIPRB* 344.1); the *Point*

of Reason (Nyāyabindu, Dg.T. Tshad ma, vol. Ce, ff. 231b–238a, T 4212, *MTTWL* 147, *EIPRB* 344.3); the *Proof of Other Minds* (Santānāntarasiddhināmaprakaraṇa, Dg.T. Tshad ma, vol. Che, ff. 355b–359a, T 4219, *MTTWL* 200, *EIPRB* 344.7); and the *Reasoning of Polemics* (Vādanyāya, Dg.T. Tshad ma, vol. Che, ff. 326b–355b, T 4218, *EIPRB* 344.8)

Dīpaṃkarabhadra (fl. early eighth century)
Four Hundred and Fifty Verse [*Maṇḍala Rite of the Secret Assembly*]
Śrīguhyasamājamaṇḍalavidhi
dPal gsang ba 'dus pa'i dkyil 'khor gyi cho ga; also known as bZhi brgya lnga bcu pa
Dg.T. rGyud, vol. Di, ff. 69a–87a, T 1865

Durgasiṃha (bGrod dka' seng ge)
Paradigm of Verbal Roots
Dhātusūtra
Byings mdo
Dg.T. sGra mdo, vol. Le, ff. 63a–75a. T 4285
This accords with the system of the Kalāpa Tantra

Īśvarakṛṣṇa (fl. fourth century)
Thirty-Chapter and Six-Chapter Tantras
Sāṃkhyākārikā
rGyud sum cu pa dang drug pa
EIPRB 163.1. Translated from Sanskrit in Sinha 1915. Edited and translated in Suryanarayana Sastri 1935. Extracts also in Radhakrishnan and Moore 1957

Jagaddarpaṇa ('Gro ba'i me long, fl. twelfth century)
Compendium of Rituals [*of the Indestructible Master*]
[Vajrācārya] kriyāsamuccaya
[rDo rje slob dpon gyi] bya ba kun las btus pa
Dg.T. rGyud, vol. Bu, ff. 48a–249a, T 3305

Jayasena (ca. 998)
[*Commentary*] *on the Tantra of the Ocean of Sky-farers*
Ḍākārṇavatantramaṇḍalacakrasādhanaratnapadmarāganidhi
dPal mkha' 'gro rgya mtsho'i rgyud kyi dkyil 'khor gyi 'khor lo'i sgrub thabs padma raga'i gter
Dg.T. rGyud, vol. Za, ff. 1b–35a. T 1516

Jñānakīrti (dates uncertain)
Abridgement of All the Transmitted Teachings Without Exception: A Dissertation on Exegesis
Tattvāvatārākhyasakalasugatavācasaṃkṣiptavyākhyāprakaraṇa
De kho na nyid la 'jug pa shes bya ba bde bar gshegs pa'i bka' ma lus pa mdor bsdus te bshad pa'i rab tu byed pa
Dg.T. rGyud, vol. Tsu, ff. 39a–76a. T 3709

Kamalaśīla (740–795)
Lamp of Madhyamaka
Madhyamakāloka
dBu ma snang ba
Dg.T. dBu ma, vol. Sa, ff. 133b–244b. T 3887
EIPRB 418.8

Kapila (fl. seventh century BCE)
Treatise on the Categories of Reality
Sāṃkhyātattvasamāsaśāstra, also known as Sāṃkhyātpravacanasūtra
Also later version of unknown authorship, dated 1300 (*EIPRB* 776). Translated in Sinha 1915. Extracts also in Radhakrishnan and Moore 1957. See also Chakravarti 1975

Karmasiddhi Utpala (dates uncertain)
Tantra of Martial Conquest/ Svarodaya
Yuddhajaya-nāma-tantrarāja-svarodaya
gYul las rnam par rgyal ba shes pa'i rgyud kyi rgyal po dbyangs 'char ba
Dg.T. bZo rig, vol. Ngo, ff. 49b–91b. T 4322

Kṛṣṇamiśra (fl. late eleventh century)
Defining Characteristics of Prosody entitled Mastery through Learning
Chandasaṃlakṣaṇaśrutabodha
sDeb sbyor rnams kyi mtshan nyid thos pas chub pa
Translated into Tibetan by Situ Chokyi Jungne, bKa' brgyud pa'i gsung rab, 1:603–624

Kṣemendra (late tenth–early eleventh century)
Wish-granting Tree: Narrative of the Bodhisattva
Bodhisattvāvadānakalpalatā
[Byang chub sems dpa'i rtogs pa brjod pa] dpag bsam 'khri shing
Dg.T. sKyes rabs, vol. Ke, ff. 1b–366a. T 4155
EIPRB 677.1. Abridged version by Pema Chopel (Sichuan mi rigs dpe krun khang, 1991) translated in Black 1997

Kuladatta (dates uncertain)
Collection of Rites
Kriyāsaṃgraha
Bya ba bsdus pa
Dg.T. rGyud, vol. Ku, ff. 227b–362a. T 2531
Partial translations in Skorupski 2002 and Tanemura 2004

Mahāvyutpatti
Detailed Inspection [of Terminology]
Bye brag tu rtogs par byed pa
Dg.T. sNa tshogs, vol. Co, ff. 1b–131a. T 4346. *MVT*. B Budh 13 (1911). Edited Sakaki 1916–25; reprint, 1965. Also edited and translated in Csoma de Koros (3 vols., 1910, 1916, and 1944); republished 1984

Maitreya (dates uncertain)
Analysis of the Middle and Extremes
Madhyāntavibhāga
dBus mtha' rnam par 'byed pa'i tshig le'u byas pa
Dg.T. Sems tsam, vol. Phi, ff. 40b–45a. T 4021
MTTWL 112. *EIPRB* 174.6. Translated in Dharmachakra Translation Committee 2006; also in the commentarial literature, e.g., Friedmann 1984 and Anacker 1984

The Five Treatises of Maitreya
Byams chos sde lnga
Beijing: Mi rigs dpe skrun khang, 1991. A Tibetan edition of the root verses of five seminal Mahāyāna treatises attributed to Maitreya, comprising the *Ornament of Emergent Realization* (*Abhisamayālaṃkāra*, Dg.T. Shes phyin, vol. Ka, ff. 1b–13a; T 3786); the *Ornament of the Sūtras of the Greater Vehicle* (*Mahāyānasūtrālaṃkārakārikā*,

Dg.T. Sems tsam, vol. Phi, ff. 1b–39a; T 4020); the *Analysis of the Middle and Extremes* (*Madhyāntavibhāga*, Dg.T. Sems tsam, vol. Phi, ff. 40b–45a; T 4021); the *Analysis of Phenomena and Actual Reality* (*Dharmadharmatāvibhāga*, Dg.T. Sems tsam, vol. Phi, ff. 46b–49a; T 4021); and the *Supreme Continuum of the Greater Vehicle* (*Mahāyānottaratantraśāstra*, Dg.T. Sems tsam, vol. Phi, ff. 54b–73a; T 4024).

Ornament of Emergent Realization
Abhisamayālaṃkāra-[nāma-prajñāpāramitopadeśaśāstrakārikā]
[Shes rab kyi pha rol tu phyin pa'i man ngag gi bstan bcos] mngon par rtogs pa'i rgyan
Dg.T. Shes phyin, vol. Ka, ff. 1b–13a. T 3786
BST 4 (1960). *MTTWL* 2–5. *EIPRB* 174.3. Translated in Conze 1954 and Thrangu 2004; also in the commentarial literature, on which see Sparham 2006

Ornament of the Sūtras of the Greater Vehicle
[Mahāyāna] sūtrālaṃkārakārikā
[Theg pa chen po] mdo sde'i rgyan zhes bya ba'i tshig le'ur byas pa
Dg.T. Sems tsam, vol. Phi, ff. 1b–39a. T 4020
BST 13 (1970). *MTTWL* 129. *EIPRB* 174.8. Translated in Jamspal et al. 2004

Masurakṣa (dates uncertain)
Treatise on Human Behavior
Nītiśāstra
Lugs kyi bstan bcos
Dg.T. Thun mong, vol. Ngo, ff. 137b–143a. T 4335

Matīcitra (a.k.a. Mātṛceta, also attributed to Śura, fl. early third century)
Eulogy to the Transcendent Lord Buddha: Praising Him Who Is Worthy of Being Praised, but otherwise Eulogizing the [Ineffable] Which Cannot Be Eulogized
Varṇārhavarṇastotra
Sangs rgyas bcom ldan 'das la bstod pa bsngags par 'os pa bsngags pa las bstod par mi nus par bstod pa
Dg.T. bsTod tshogs, vol. Ka, ff. 84a–100b. T 1138
MTTWL 247. *EIPRB* 67A.2

Maudgalyāyana (fl. fifth century BCE)
Discourse on Designations
Prajñaptipāda
gDags pa'i mdo
Taisho 1538 and 1644

Mudgaragomin (fl. second century)
Eulogy on Distinctions
Viśeṣastava
Khyad par du 'phags pa'i bstod pa
Dg.T. bsTod tshogs, vol. Ka, ff. 1b–4b. T 1109

Nāgabodhi (dates uncertain)
Twenty Rituals of the Maṇḍala of the Secret Assembly
Guhyasamājamaṇḍalaviṃśatividhi
dPal gsang ba 'dus pa'i dkyil 'khor gyi cho ga nyi shu pa
Dg.T. rGyud, vol. Ngi, ff. 131a–145b. T 1810
Sanskrit text restored by Kimiaki Tanaka in Shingo Einoo, ed., *Genesis and Development of Tantrism*, pp. 425–434. Tokyo: Institute of Oriental Culture, University of Tokyo, 2010.

Nāgārjuna (fl. second century)
Commentary on Enlightened Mind
Bodhicittavivaraṇa
Byang chub sems kyi 'grel pa
Dg.T. rGyud, vol. Ngi, ff. 38a–45a. T 1800–1801
MTTWL 36. *EIPRB* 405.1. Edited and translated in Lindtner 1997

Commentary on the Sūtra of the Shoots of Rice
Śālistambhakasūtraṭīkā
'Phags pa sā lu ljang pa zhes bya ba theg pa chen po'i mdo'i rgya cher 'grel pa
Dg.T. mDo 'grel, vol. Ni, ff. 20b–55b. T 3986

Eulogy to the Expanse of Actual Reality
Dharmadhātustava
Chos kyi dbyings su bstod pa
Dg.T. sTod tshogs, vol. Ka, ff. 63b–67b. T 1118
MTTWL 55. Translated in Ruegg 1971; also in Brunnhölzl 2007

Eulogy to the Stūpas of the Eight Supreme Sacred Places
Aṣṭamahāsthānacaityastotra
gNas chen po brgyad kyi mchod rten la bstod pa
Dg.T. sTod tshogs, vol. Ka, ff. 81b–82b. T 1133–1134
MTTWL 21

[*Explanation of the*] *Nucleus of Dependent Origination according to Madhyamaka*
Madhyamakapratītyasamutpādahṛdaya[vyākhyāna]
rTen cing 'brel bar 'byung ba'i snying po['i rnam par bshad pa]
Dg.T. dBu ma, vol. Tsa, ff. 146b–149a. T 3836–3837
MTTWL 172–173. *EIPRB* 47.6. Translated in Jamieson 2001

Fundamental Stanzas of Madhyamaka [*entitled Discriminative Awareness*] Prajñā-nāma-mūlamadhyamakakārikā
dBu ma rtsa ba'i tshig le'u byas pa
Dg.T. dBu ma, vol. Tsa, ff. 1b–19a. T 3824
BST 10 (1960). *MTTWL* 135. *EIPRB* 47.4. Translated in Padmakara Translation Group 2008; also Streng 1967, Inada 1970, Kalupahana 1986, Garfield 1995, and Batchelor 2000

Hundred Verses on Discriminative Awareness
Prajñāśatakaprakaraṇa
Shes rab brgya pa zhes bya ba'i rab tu byed pa
Dg.T. Thun mong, vol. Ngo, ff. 99b–103a. T 4328

Letter to a Friend
Suhṛllekha
bShes pa'i sprin yig
Dg.T. sPrin yig, vol. Nge, ff. 40b–46b. T 4182
MTTWL 218. *EIPRB* 47.8. Translated in Jamspal et al. 1978 and in Tharchin and Engle 1979

Point of Human Sustenance
Nītiśāstrajantupoṣaṇabindu
sKye bo gso thig
Dg.T. Thun mong, vol. Ngo, ff. 113a–116b. T 4330
Translated from the Mongolian in Frye 1981

Precious Garland
[Rājaparikathā] ratnāvalī
[rGyal po la gtam bya ba] rin chen phreng ba
Dg.T. sPrin yig, vol. Ge, ff. 107a–126a. T 4158
BST 10 (1960). *MTTWL* 189. *EIPRB* 47.7. Translated in Dunne and McClintock 1997

Stem of Discriminative Awareness
Nītiśāstraprajñādaṇḍa
[Lugs kyi bstan bcos] shes rab sdong bu
Dg.T. Thun mong, vol. Ngo, ff. 103a–113a. T 4329

Patañjali (fl. third century BCE)
Sūtra on Yoga
Yogasūtra
EIPRB 131.1. Translated in Prasada 1924. Extracts also in Radhakrishnan and Moore 1957

Piṅgala (fl. ca. second century BCE)
Discourse on Prosody
Chandasūtra
dMar ser can gyi gzhung
Sanskrit edited in Weber 1863

Praśāntamitra (fl. late ninth century)
Commentary on the Nucleus of Indestructible Reality
Vajrahṛdayālaṃkāratantrapañjikā
dPal rdo rje snying po'i rgyan gyi rgyud chen po'i dka' 'grel
Dg.T. rGyud, vol. I, ff. 313a–362a. T 2515

Puṇḍarīka (a.k.a. Avalokitavrata) (dates uncertain)
Taintless Light: A Great [Commentary] on the Wheel of Time
Vimalaprabhānāmamūlatantrānusāriṇīdvādaśasāhaśrīkālaghukālacakratantrarājaṭīkā
bsDus pa'i rgyud kyi rgyal po dus kyi 'khor lo'i 'grel bshad rtsa ba'i rgyud kyi rjes su 'jug pa stong phrag bcu gnyis pa dri ma med pa'i 'od, also known as Dus 'khor 'grel chen
Dg.K. Dus 'khor 'grel bshad, vol. Śrī, ff. 1b–469a. T 845
Sanskrit edition in Jagannatha Upadhyaya, Bibliotheca Indo-Tibetica, vols. 11–13. Sarnath: Central Institute of Higher Tibetan Studies, 1986. See Kilty 2004; also Newman 1987, and Wallace 2001

Puñjarāja (dates uncertain)
Commentary on the Sārasvata Grammar
Sārasvatavyākaraṇavṛtti
brDa sprod pa dbyangs can gyi mdo'i 'grel pa
NA

Ratnākara[śānti] (fl. early eleventh century)
Commentary on the Four Hundred and Fifty Verse Maṇḍala Rite of the Secret Assembly
Śrīguhyasamājamaṇḍalavidhiṭīkā
dPal gsang ba 'dus pa'i dkyil 'khor cho ga'i 'grel pa; also known by the short title 'Jig rten snang byed
Dg.T. rGyud, vol. Ni, ff. 59a–130a. T 1871

Precious Source [of Prosody]
Chandoratnākara
[sDeb sbyor] rin chen 'byung gnas
Dg.T. sGra mdo, vol. Se, ff. 371b–379a. T 4303–4. Tibetan edition, with restored

Sanskrit text and Hindi translation in L. Shastri 1990. Tibetan commentary in Nyagong Konchok Tseten et al., *Commentary on the Precious Source of Prosody*

Ratnarakṣita (dates uncertain)
Lotus Commentary on Difficulties in the Tantra of the Emergence of Cakrasaṃvara
Śrīsaṃvarodayamahātantrarāja-padminī-nāma-pañjikā
dPal sdom pa 'byung ba'i rgyud kyi rgyal po chen po'i dka' 'grel padma can, also known as Kyog bshad (the "Evasive Exegesis")
Dg.T. rGyud, vol. Va, ff. 1b–101b. T 1420

Ratnaśrī[jñāna] (dates uncertain)
Ratnaśrī Commentary on the Mirror of Poetics
Kāvyādarśāratnaśrīvṛtti
Sanskrit edition in Anantalal Thakur and Upendra Jha, Darbhaṅga Mithila Institute, 1957

Śākyaprabha (fl. eighth century)
Sun Commentary on the Monastic Discipline [*of the Novitiate*]
[Āryamūlasarvāstivādi] śrāmaṇerakārikāvṛttiprabhāvatī
['Phags pa gzhi thams cad yod par smra ba'i] dge tshul gyi tshig le'ur byas pa'i 'grel pa
Dg.T. 'Dul ba, vol. Shu, ff. 74a–162b. T 4125

Śālihotra (dates uncertain)
Compendium on the Inspection of the Life Span of Horses
Śālihotrīyāśvāyurvedasaṃhitā
rTa'i tshe'i rig byed sha li ho tras bsdus pa
Dg.T. Thun mong, vol. Ngo, ff. 156b–277a. T 4345

Śāntarakṣita (725–783)
Auto-commentary on the Ornament of Madhyamaka
Madhyamakālaṃkāravṛtti
dBu ma rgyan gyi 'grel pa
Dg.T. dBu ma, vol. Sa, ff. 56b–84a. T 3885
EIPRB 404.1. Edited and translated in Ichigo 1985

Ornament of the Madhyamaka
Madhyamakālaṃkāra
dBu ma rgyan gyi tshig le'u byas pa
Dg.T. dBu ma, vol. Sa, ff. 53a–56b. T 3884
EIPRB 404.1. Translated with commentary in Padmakara Translation Group 2005; also Blumenthal 2004, and Doctor 2004.

Śāntideva (fl. late seventh–early eighth century)
Introduction to the Conduct of a Bodhisattva
Bodhisattvacaryāvatāra
Byang chub sems dpa'i spyod pa la 'jug pa
Dg.T. dBu ma, vol. La, ff. 1b–40a. T 3871
BST 12 (1960). B Budh 28 (1929). *MTTWL* 109. *EIPRB* 368.1. Translated in Padmakara Translation Group 1997; also Matics 1970, Batchelor 1979, Crosby and Skilton 1996, Wallace and Wallace 1997

Śāntigarbha (dates uncertain)
Differentiation of the Parts of a Stūpa
Zhi duo xing zhuang luo suo chu jing
mChod rten gyi cha dbye ba
Dg.T. rGyud, vol. Pu, ff. 173b–175b. T 3078

Sarvadhara (dates uncertain)
Analysis of the Terminations Indicating Verbal Morphology from the Kalāpa Grammar
Tyādyantaprakriyāvicārita
Ti la sogs pa'i mtha'o bya ba rnam par dpyad pa
Dg.T. sGra mdo, vol. She, ff. 97b–235a. T 4289

Sarvavarman (a.k.a. Īśvaravarman or Rājadeva, dates uncertain)
Kalāpa Grammar
Kalāpasūtra
Ka lā pa'i mdo
Dg.T. sGra mdo, vol. Le, ff. 1b–20a. T 4282
See also Scharfe 1977, pp. 162–163

Śīlapālita (fl. eighth century)
Extensive [Commentary] on the Minor Transmissions
Āgamakṣudrakavyākhyāna
Lung phran tshegs kyi rgya cher 'grel
Dg.T. 'Dul ba, vol. Dzu, ff. 1b–232a. T 4115

Śraddhākaravarman (dates uncertain)
Auto-commentary on the Concise Commentary on Forming the Gridlines of the Maṇḍala
Saṃksiptamaṇḍalasūtravṛtti
dKyil 'khor gyi thig gdab pa mdor bsdus pa'i 'grel pa
Dg.T. rGyud, vol. Ri, ff. 207b–215b. T 2506

Concise Commentary on Forming the Gridlines of the Maṇḍala
Saṃksiptamaṇḍalasūtra
dKyil 'khor gyi thig gdab pa mdor bsdus pa
Dg.T. rGyud, vol. Ri, ff. 205b–207b. T 2505

Sthiramati (ca. 470–550)
Commentary [on the Dissertation on] the Five Psycho-physical Aggregates
Pañcaskandhaprakaraṇavaibhāṣya
Phung po lnga'i rab tu byed pa bye brag tu bshad pa
Dg.T. Sems tsam, vol. Shi, ff. 195b–250a. T 4066
EIPRB 304.9. Translated in Engle 2009

Subhūticandra (dates uncertain)
Addendum to the Last Part [of the Wish-fulfilling Commentary on the Treasury of Amarasiṃha]
mDzod 'grel 'dod 'jo'i 'phros glegs bam 'og ma
Tibetan translation from Sanskrit by Situ Chokyi Jungne (Collected Works, vol. Ca)

Wish-fulfilling Commentary [on the Treasury of Amarasiṃha]
Amarakośaṭīkākāmadhenu
'Chi med mdzod kyi rgya cher 'grel pa 'dod 'jo'i ba mo
Dg.T. sGra mdo, vol. Se, ff. 244b–318a. T 4300
Sanskrit edited in Lokesh Chandra, SP 38 (1965). Re-translated into Tibetan by Situ Chokyi Jungne, under the title *Ming dang rtags rjes su ston pa'i bstan bcos 'chi med mdzod kyi rgya cher 'grel pa 'dod 'jo'i ba mo* (Collected Works, vol. Nga). See also Vogel 1979, pp. 314–315

Śūra (fourth century)
Garland of Birth Stories
Jātakamālā

sKyes pa'i rabs kyi rgyud
Dg.T. sKyes rabs, vol. Hu, ff. 1b–135a. T 4150
BST 21 (1959). Translated in Speyer 1895

Sūryagupta (fl. sixth century)
Treasury of the Collection of Topics
Gāthākośa
Tshigs su bcad pa'i mdzod
Dg.T. Thun mong, vol. Ngo, ff. 116b–122a. T 4331

Tripiṭakamāla (dates uncertain)
Lamp of the Three Ways
Nayatrayapradīpa
Tshul gsum sgron ma
Dg.T. rGyud, vol. Tsu, ff. 6b–26b. T 3707

Vararuci (late fourth–early fifth century)
Hundred Verses on the Collection of Topics
Śatagāthā
Tshigs su bcad pa brgya pa
Dg.T. Thun mong, vol. Ngo, 122a–126a. T 4332

Vasubandhu (ca. late fourth–early fifth century)
[*Auto-*] *Commentary on the Treasury* [*of Phenomenology*]
Abhidharmakośabhāṣya
Chos mngon pa'i mdzod kyi bshad pa
Dg.T. mNgon pa, vol. Ku, ff. 26b–258a. T 4090
Tibetan edition in *mNgon pa mdzod rtsa 'grel* (Sichuan mi rigs dpe skrun khang, 1996).
EIPRB 175.1. Translated from the French in Pruden 1988–1990.

Commentary Analyzing the Sūtra of Dependent Origination
Pratītyasamutpādādivibhaṅgabhāṣya
rTen cing 'brel bar 'byung ba dang po'i rnam par dbye ba bshad pa
Dg.T. mDo 'grel, vol. Chi, ff. 1b–61a. T 3995
EIPRB 175.12

[*Dissertation on*] *the Five Psycho-physical Aggregates*
Pañcaskandhaprakaraṇa
Phung po lnga'i rab tu byed pa
Dg.T. Sems tsam, vol. Shi, ff. 11b–17a. T 4059
EIPRB 175.11. Translated, along with Tibetan and reconstructed Sanskrit editions, in Engle 2009; also Anacker 1984

[*Dissertation on the*] *Thirty Verses*
Triṃśikā[kārikāprakaraṇa]
Sum cu pa'i tshig le'u byas pa
Dg.T. Sems tsam, vol. Shi, ff. 1b–3a. T 4055
MTTWL 236. *EIPRB* 175.18. Translated from the Chinese in Cook 1999; also Anacker 1984, Kochumuttom 1982

Rational System of Exposition
Vyākhyāyukti
rNam par bshad pa'i rigs pa
Dg.T. Sems tsam, vol. Shi, ff. 29a–134b. T 4061
EIPRB 175.23

Treasury of Phenomenology
Abhidharmakośa[kārikā]
Chos mngon pa'i mdzod kyi tshig le'ur byas pa
Dg.T. mNgon pa, vol. Ku, ff. 1b–25a. T 4089
B Budh 20 (1917, 1930) and 21 (1918–31). Tibetan edition in *mNgon pa mdzod rtsa 'grel* (Sichuan mi rigs dpe skrun khang, 1996). *EIPRB* 175.1. Translated from the French in Pruden 1988–1990

Vasumitra (fl. second or fourth century)
Auto-commentary on the Great Treasury [of Detailed Exposition]
Mahāvibhāṣakośa
Bye brag bshad mdzod [chen mo], also known as mDzod kyi rang 'grel
Extant in Chinese. Taisho 1545. *EIPRB* 39.1.

Vidyākara (fl. twelfth century)
Precious Treasury of Eloquence
Subhāṣitaratnakoṣa
Sanskrit edition by D.D. Kosambi and V.V. Gokhale. Cambridge, MA: Harvard University Press, 1957. Translated in Ingalls 1965

Vimalamitra (fl. late eighth–early ninth century)
Short [*Commentary on the Tantra of the Secret Nucleus*]
Śrīguhyagarbhapiṇḍārthaṭīkā
gSang ba snying po'i 'grel chung
P. rGyud, vol. Mu, ff. 1a–26a. P 4755

Vitapāda (fl. late ninth century)
Commentary on the Oral Teachings of Mañjuśrī: The Beautiful Flower
Sukusuma-nāma-dvikramatattvabhavanāmukhāgamavṛtti
mDzes pa'i me tog zhes bya ba rim pa gnyis pa'i de kho na nyid bsgom pa zhal gyi lung gi 'grel pa
Dg.T. rGyud, vol. Di, ff. 87a–139b. T 1866

Vyāsa (diffuser/ redactor, dates uncertain)
Four Vedas
Caturveda
Rig byed bzhi
The primary source texts or divine revelations of the Brāhmaṇical tradition of Hinduism, comprising the Ṛgveda, Atharvaveda, Sāmaveda, and Yajurveda. Among them, the ten chapters of the Ṛgveda are extant in thirty distinct manuscript recensions, written in Sharad and Devanagari scripts, twenty-four of which were consulted by Max Müller for his six-volume *editio princeps*, entitled *The Hymns of the Ṛgveda with Sayana's Commentary* (London, 1849–75). On all four Vedas, see Gonda 1975, chs. 3–7

Yaśomitra (fl. early fifth century)
Commentary on the Treasury of Phenomenology
Abhidharmakośaṭīkā
Chos mngon pa'i mdzod kyi 'grel bshad
Dg.T. mNgon pa, vols. Gu–Ngu. T 4092

3. Indigenous Tibetan Treatses and Spiritual Revelations (*gter ma*)

Anon
Citadel of the Wind Goddess
Lung lha mo gnas mkhar
Not located

Anon (ninth century)
Commentary on the Eight Elements of Semantic Application
gNas brgyad chen po'i 'grel pa, also known as sGra'i bstan bcos
Dg.T. sNa tshogs, vol. Co, ff. 165a–173a. T 4351
See Part One, note 95

Anon
Hundred Thousand Scrutinies of the Ḍākinīs
mKha' 'gro brtag 'bum
Not located

Anon
Private Tantra: Black Skull of the Charnel Ground
sGer rgyud dur khrod thod nag
Not located

Anon
Short Chapter on Discrimination
'Byed pa le'u chung
See note 1115

Anon
Tantra entitled Mountain of Corpses, Fortress of Skulls
rGyud bam ri thod mkhar
Not located

Anon
Treatise on Behavior entitled "Holy Ornament"
Lugs kyi bstan bcos dam pa'i rgyan
See note 1114

Candraśrī [Dawa Palrin] (Zla ba dpal rin, b. ca. 1375)
Definitive Presentation of Drums and Cymbals
rNga sbug gi rnam gzhag
In Tashi Gyatso et al., *Treatises on the Accoutrements and Music of the Ancient Way of Secret* [*Mantras*], pp. 357–359

Methodology of Musical Sound
Rol mo'i sgra thabs bzhugs
Unpublished ms. held at Amnye Machen Institute, Dharamsala

Treatise on Melody entitled Neck Ornament of Clear Intelligence
dByangs kyi bstan bcos blo gsal mgul rgyan
Unpublished ms. held at Amnye Machen Institute, Dharamsala

Che Khyidrug (Ce khyi 'brug, ca. 798–815)
Root Verses on the Eight Elements of Semantic Application
gNas brgyad [chen po'i] rtsa ba
Dg.T. sNa tshogs, vol. Co, 163a–165a. T 4350. See Part One, note 95

Chomden Rigpei Raldri (bCom ldan rig pa'i ral gri, 1227–1305)
Ornamental Flower of Philosophical Systems
Grub mtha' rgyan gyi me tog
dBu med ms. in TBRC Holdings (W1CZ1041. 2: 159–446)

Dahura [Nagpo], disc. (Da hu ra nag po, fl. ca. twelfth century)
Tantra of the White, Black, and Variegated Hundred Thousand Stanzas
'Bum dkar nag khra gsum gyi rgyud
A work on geomancy attributed to the Chinese treasure-finder Dahura Nagpo, which was translated into Tibetan, along with his other revelations, such as the *Root Tantra of the Clarifying Lamp: Indicatve of Buddha Body* (*sKu rgyud snang gsal sgron me*), by his student Khampa Trawo
Not located

Drapa Ngonshe, disc. (Gra pa mngon bshes, 1012–1090)
Glorious Great Tantra entitled Essence of Nectar, also known as the Great Tantra of Secret Instructions on the Eight Branches of the Essence of the Glorious Elixir [of Immortality]
dPal ldan bdud rtsi snying po yan lag brgyad pa gsang ba man ngag gi rgyud chen po; short title: Grva thang rgyud bzhi
Sometimes attributed to the authorship of Yutok Yonten Gonpo. Tibetan edition published by Bod kyi gso bo rig pa'i gna' dpe phyogs bsgrigs dpe tshogs, vol. 20 (Beijing: 2005). This work comprises the *Four Tantras* (*rGyud bzhi*), namely, the *Root Tantra* (*rTsa rgyud*), the *Exegetical Tantra* (*bShad rgyud*), the *Instructional Tantra* (*Man ngag gi rgyud*), and the *Subsequent Tantra* (*Phyi ma'i rgyud*), the first two of which are translated in Clark 1995. See also Parfionovitch, Dorje, and Meyer 1992; Meyer 1981; and Rechung Rinpoche 1976

Drugu Sengdo Ochen (Gru gu seng mdo 'od chen, dates uncertain)
Mirror Trilogy
Me long skor gsum
Two of these texts, reputedly translated from Central Asian sources into Tibetan by Drugu Sengdo Ochen, respectively entitled *rTa gzhung dngul dkar me long* and *rTa dpyad mthong ba kun gsal me long*, are contained in *Bod kyi rta'i gso dpyad gzhung lugs mdams bsgrigs*, Gangs can rig mdzod, vol. 13, 1990, pp. 3–85 and pp. 273–359 respectively

Guru Chowang (Gu ru chos dbang, 1212–1270)
Method of Constructing Stūpas
mChod rten bzhengs thabs
Not extant in Chengdu photo-offset edition of the *Eight Transmitted Teachings: Consummation of Secrets* (*bKa' brgyad gsang ba yongs rdzogs*), which is contained in 4 vols. of the *bKa' brgyad phyogs bsgrigs*. It may possibly be related to *sKu gsum yongs rdzogs kyi lha khang gzhengs thabs kyi dpe ris*, which is contained in the same collection, according to rNying ma'i dkar chags (Potala, 1992), vol. 1, no. 40 and vol. 4, no. 51

Gyalwa Ten-ne (rGyal ba ten ne, 1127–1217) and Dromtonpa ('Brom ston pa, 1004–1064)
Garland of the Essential Points of the Religion of the Gods and the Religion of Humans
Lha chos mi chos gnad kyi phreng ba
Not located. See note 730

Hūṃkārajaya (Hūṃ mdzad rgyal ba, dates uncertain)
White Lotus Bouquet of Investigation
dPyad don pad dkar chun po, also known as Legs par bshad pa'i padma dkar po chun po
Gangtok: Sherab Gyaltsen Lama, 1981

Jamyang Sonam Wangpo ('Jam dbyangs bsod nams dbang po, fl. 1559–1621)
Treatise on Musical Instruments entitled The Single Knowledge That Liberates All
Rol mo'i bstan bcos gcig shes kun sgrol
Not located

Karmapa VII Chodrak Gyatso (Karmapa chos grags rgya mtsho, 1454–1506)
Oceanic Textbook of Uncommon Logical Reasoning
Thun min rig gzhung rgya mtsho
Full title: Tshad ma legs par bshad pa thams cad kyi chu bo yongs su 'du ba'i rigs pa'i gzhung lugs kyi rgya mtsho
Contained in bKa' brgyud pa'i gsung rab, vols. 6–7

Karmapa VIII Mikyo Dorje (Karmapa mi bskyod rdo rje, 1507–1554)
Mirror of Great Sunlight
Nyi ma chen po'i me long
Full title: rDo rje theg pa'i yang dag par rdzogs pa'i phyag rgya chen po'i nye bar longs spyod pa'i gnas dang spyod yul gsal bar byed pa'i nyi ma chen po'i me long
Contained in the Collected Works of Karmapa Mi bskyod rdo rje, vol. 26; published with the support of the Bodhi Foundation and the Tsadra Foundation, 2004

Khyungpo Yutri Bar (Khyung po gYu khri bar, fl. late tenth–early eleventh century)
Miraculous Lamp
'Phrul gyi sgron me
Not located

Lochen Dharmaśrī (Lo chen Dharmaśrī, 1654–1717)
Choreographic Memoranda of the Sacred Dances of the Wrathful Herukas and of Glorious Samantabhadra entitled Display of the Deities
[Khrag 'thung khro bo'i] 'chams [kyi brjed byang dpal] kun tu bzang po'i 'chams kyi brjed byang lha'i rol ga
Short title: *Choreographic Treatise of the Sacred Dances entitled Display of Samantabhadra ('Chams yig kun bzang rol pa)*
NK, vol. 14, pp. 365–456

Longchen Rabjampa (Klong chen rab 'byams pa, 1308–1363)
Precious Treasury of Wish-fulfilling Gems: A Treatise on the Pith Instructions of the Greater Vehicle
Theg pa chen po'i man ngag gi bstan bcos yid bzhin rin po che'i mdzod
In the Seven Treasuries of Longchenpa (Klong chen mdzod bdun) (Beijing: dPal brtsegs bod yig dpe rnying zhib 'jug khang, 2009), vols. 118–119. Also Potala edition, vol. 1 (31ff.); Gangtok: Dodrupchen Rinpoche, n.d. (I-Tib-143); and Chengdu: Adzom Chogar, 1999. Ch. 1 translated in Lipman 1977

Menthangpa Menla Dondrub (sMan thang pa sman la don grub, fl. late fifteenth century)
Wish-fulfilling Jewel of Iconometry
[bDe bar gshegs pa'i sku gzugs kyi] cha tshad yid bzhin nor bu
Gangtok: Lama Dawa and Sherab Gyaltsen, 1983. Library of Congress: 83905557

[Pang] Lodro Tenpa (dPang blo gros brtan pa, 1276–1342)
Clarification of the Three Clusters
Tshogs gsum gsal ba
Ziling: Qinghai Nationalities Publishing House, 1998

Phurbuchok Tsultrim Jampa Gyatso Pelzangpo (Phur bu lcog tshul khrims byams pa rgya mtsho dpal bzang po, 1825–1901)
Magic Key of the Path of Reasoning: [Presentation of the Collected Topics, Analyzing the Meaning of Valid Cognition]
[Tshad ma'i gzhung don 'byed pa'i bsdus grva rnam gzhag] rigs lam 'phrul gyi lde mig; also known as the Yongs 'dzin bsdus grva (Collected Topics of the Tutor)
Containing the Rigs lam chung ngu'i rnam bshad (23 folios), the Rigs lam 'bring po'i rnam bshad (30 folios), and the Rigs lam che ba'i rnam bshad (36 folios), along with its blo rigs (27 folios) and rtags rigs (25 folios) subdivisions. Gansu'i mi rigs dpe skrung khang, 1982, 2002, 2005. Translated in Rogers 2009; see also Rogers 1980

Rongpo (Rong po, dates uncertain)
Supplement: [The Radiant Lamp That Clarifies Calligraphy]
Lhan thab [yi ge'i thig ris gsal ba'i rin chen sgrom bu]
Not located

Sakya Paṇchen Kunga Gyaltsen (Sa skya paṇ chen kun dga' rgyal mtshan, 1182–1251)
Analysis of the Three Vows
sDom gsum rab dbye
In dPal ldan sa skya'i gsung rab, 12a:1–127

Eloquence of Sakya
Sa skya'i legs bshad; full title: Legs par bshad pa rin po che'i gter
Root verses and prose commentary, in Collected Works of Sapeṇ Kunga Gyaltsen, Gangs can rig mdzod, 23:213–348 (Bod ljongs bod yig dpe rnying dpe skrun khang, 1992); also Bod ljongs mi rigs dpe skrun khang, 1982. Translated in Davenport 2000

Treasure of Valid Logical Reasoning
Tshad ma rigs gter
In Collected Works of Sapeṇ Kunga Gyaltsen, Gangs can rig mdzod, 24:1–53, with auto-commentary pp. 55–538 (Bod ljongs bod yig dpe rnying dpe skrun khang, 1992). Other versions include *SKB*, vol. 5, no. 1 (1968), Bod ljongs mi dmangs dpe skrun khang (1989), Beijing mi rigs dpe skrun khang (1989), and Sichuan mi rigs dpe skrun khang (1995)

Treatise on Music
Rol mo'i bstan bcos
In Collected Works of Sapeṇ Kunga Gyaltsen, Gangs can rig mdzod, 23:349–363 (Bod ljongs bod yig dpe rnying dpe skrun khang, 1992)

Sangye Gyatso (sDe srid sangs rgyas rgya mtsho, 1655–1705)
Removal of the Tarnish [of Deluded Appearances: Questions and Answers Arising from the White Beryl]
[Vaiḍūrya dkar po las dris lan 'khrul snang] gYa' sel
2 vols. Beijing: Krung go'i bod rig pa dpe skrun khang, 2002

White Beryl: [An Eloquent Treatise on the Astrology of the Phukpa School]
[Phug lugs rtsis kyi legs bshad] vaiḍūrya dkar po
2 vols. Beijing: Krung go'i bod rig pa dpe skrun khang, 1996–1997
Extracts translated in Dorje 2001

Smṛtijñānakīrti (Dran pa ye shes grags, fl. late tenth–early eleventh century)
Commentary on the Sword at the Gateway to Language
Vacanamukhāyudhopamanāmavṛtti
sMra sgo mtshon cha lta bu shes bya ba'i 'grel pa
Dg.T. sGra mdo, vol. She, ff. 277b–281b. T 4295

Sword at the Gateway to Language
Vacanamukhāyudhopama
sMra sgo [mtshon cha]
Dg.T. sGra mdo, vol. She, ff. 277b–281b. T 4295
Beijing: Mi rigs dpe skrun khang, 1980

Śrīdharasena (dPal 'dzin sde, dates uncertain)
Pearl Necklace of Synonymics
Abhidhānaśāstra-viśvalocana-[ityaparabhidhānamuktāvalī]
mNgon brjod kyi bstan bcos sna tshgs gsal ba'am mngon brjod mu tig phreng ba
Dg.T. sNa tshogs, vol. Po, ff. 70b–163b. T 4453

Taktsang Lotsāwa Sherab Rinchen (sTag tshang lo tsā ba shes rab rin chen, b. 1405)
Ocean of Wealth
[rTen gsum bzhugs gnas dang bcas pa'i sgrub tshul] dpal 'byor rgya mtsho
In dPal ldan sa skya pa'i gsung rab, vol. 3, pp. 161–239

Tāranātha, Jetsun (rJe btsun tā ra nā tha, 1575–1634)
Origin of Happiness: A Description of Iconometric Proportions
[rGyal ba'i] sku gzugs kyi cha tshad bstan pa bde skyid 'byung gnas
In the Collected Works of Tāranātha, vol. 18 (Tsha), no. 19. HJK, p. 63

Tonmi Sambhoṭa (a.k.a. Anu, Thon mi sam bho ṭa, fl. seventh century)
Introduction to Gender
[Lung du ston pa] rtags kyi 'jug pa
Dg.T. sNa tshogs, vol. Co, ff. 161b–162b. T 4349
See also references in next entry

Thirty Verses
[Lung du ston pa'i rtsa ba] sum cu pa
Dg.T. sNa tshogs, vol. Co, ff. 160b–161b. T 4348
Tibetan text also in *Sum rtags rtsa ba phyogs sgrig* (Chengdu: Sichuan mi rigs dpe skrun khang, 1992); and in *dKyil grva dka' chen padma'i brda dag phyogs bsgrigs* (Lhasa: Bod ljongs bod yig dpe rnying dpe skrun khang, 2001), pp. 240–248. Concerning this text and its secondary literature, see Minyag Butruk, *dKa' gnad sdom tshig situ dgongs gsal* (Beijing: Mi rigs dpe skrun khang, 2003); also Miller 1976, and Verhagen 2001

Tsamorong Sonam Ozer (rTsa mo rong bsod nams 'od zer, fl. thirteenth century)
Source of Enlightened Attributes: the Methods of Constructing the Three Representational Supports
rTen gsum bzhengs thabs yon tan 'byung gnas
NA

Upa Losal (dBus pa blo gsal, fl. thirteenth century)
Exegetical Treasury of Philosophical Systems
Grub mtha' rnam par bshad pa'i mdzod
Thimphu: Kunzang Topgyel and Mani Dorji, 1979. Also Beijing: Mi rigs dpe skrun khang, 2004

Yeshede (Ye shes sde, fl. late eighth–early ninth century)
Commentary on the Aspirational Prayer of Good Conduct [*in the Form of a Memorandum Combining Four Distinct Commentaries*]
bZang spyod kyi 'grel pa [bzhi'i don bsdus nas brjed byang du byas pa]
Dg.T. sNa tshogs, vol. Jo, ff. 184a–213b. T 4359

Zhamar VI Garwang Chokyi Wangchuk (Zhva dmar gar dbang chos kyi dbang phyug, 1584–1630)
Collected Topics of Logical Reasoning
Rigs kyi bsdus grva
Not located

Zilung Paṇchen Śākya Chokden (Zi lung paṇ chen śā kya mchog ldan, 1428–1507)
Exegesis of the Compendium of Phenomenology entitled Ocean Waves Upholding Yogācāra
mNgon pa kun btus pa'i rnam bshad rnal 'byor spyod gzung rgya mtsho'i rlabs phreng
In Collected Works, vol. 14 (Pha). Thimphu: Kunzang Topgey, 1975

Exegesis on Difficulties in the Treasury of Phenomenology entitled Great Ocean of Detailed Exposition
Chos mngon pa'i mdzod kyi dka' ba'i gnas rnam bshad kyi bstan bcos bye brag tu bshad pa'i mtsho chen po
In Collected Works, vols. 20–21 (Va–Zha). Thimphu: Kunzang Topgey, 1975

Reference Bibliography

This comprises five distinct alphabetically arranged sections: (1) Canonical and Commentarial Collections; (2) Individual Scriptures: Vinaya, Sūtra, and Tantra; (3) Treatises of Indic Origin; (4) Treatises and Revelations (gter ma) of Tibetan Origin; and (5) Works in Other Languages.

1. Canonical and Commentarial Collections

bKa' brgyad phyogs sgrigs
Anthology of Spiritual Revelations Concerning the Meditational Deities of the Eight Transmitted Teachings
20 vols. comprising the revelations of Nyangrel Nyima Ozer, Guru Chowang, and Rigdzin Godemchen.
Chengdu: Zenkar Rinpoche, ca. 1999

bKa' brgyud pa'i gsung rab
Scriptures of the Kagyupa School
Edited by Khenpo Damcho Dawa. 20 vols. Ziling: Qinghai mi rigs dpe skrun khang, 2001–2004

Collected Tantras of the Nyingmapa
rNying ma'i rgyud 'bum
Among extant versions, reference is principally made in the present work to the Derge xylographic edition, which was prepared between 1794 and 1798, under the editorial guidance of Getse Paṇḍita Gyurme Tshewang Chodrub of Katok and Pema Namdak, in 26 long-folio volumes (414 texts), and catalogued in Thubten Chodar, *rNying ma rgyud 'bum gyi dkar chag gsal ba'i me long* (Beijing: Mi rigs dpe skrun khang, 2000). Occasional references are also made to the Tingkye edition, published in Delhi in 1973 by Dilgo Khyentse Rinpoche, in 36 short volumes, and catalogued in Kaneko 1982.

Collected Works of Tāranātha
rJe btsun tā ra nā tha'i gsung 'bum
TBRC holds three editions—the Ladakh edition in 17 vols. (1982–87); the Dzamtang photo-offset edition in 23 vols. (1990s), to which HJK refers; and the extensive Pedurma edition in 45 vols., dPal brtsegs dpe rnying zhib 'jug khang, Beijing: Krung go bod rig pa dpe skrun khang, 2008.

dPal ldan sa skya'i gsung rab
Scriptures of the Glorious Sakya School
25 vols. Beijing: Mi rigs dpe skrun khang, in collaboration with Qinghai mi rigs dpe skrun khang, 2003–2004

Jo nang dpe tshogs
Jonang Publications Series
21 vols. Beijing: Nationalities Publishing House, 2007–2008

Kangyur
bKa' 'gyur
The Collected Translations of the Transmitted Teachings. The TBRC digital library includes six versions, which are freely accessible online, including the Derge Parphud xylograph edition of 1733 (103 vols.), which is catalogued in H. Ui et al., *A Complete Catalogue of the Tibetan Buddhist Canons* (Sendai: Tohoku University, 1934). Other editions consulted in the present work include the Peking edition in 104 vols., republished with catalogue by Suzuki Research Foundation (Tokyo-Kyoto: 1955–61); and the new collated edition, Kangyur Pedurma, published Chengdu (2009), in 108 vols. Mention is also made in the text of three renowned manuscript versions: the Serdri (gilded) Kangyur Thempangma from Gyantse (*rgyal rtse gser bris bka' 'gyur them spangs ma*), which is modelled on the calligraphic style of Khyungpo Yutri, the Serdri (gilded) manuscript from Drepung (*gser bris 'dzam gling gYas bzhag*), and the Tshalpa manuscript.

Nikāya Collection
The Nikāya literature, preserved in the *Suttapiṭaka* of the Theravāda tradition, comprises
(1) The *Dīgha Nikāya*, containing thirty-four discourses, translated in M. Walshe, *The Long Discourses of the Buddha* (Boston: Wisdom Publications, 1987)
(2) The *Majjhima Nikāya,* containing 152 discourses, translated in Bhikkhu Ñāṇamoli and Bhikkhu Bodhi, *The Middle Length Discourses of the Buddha* (Boston: Wisdom Publications, 1995)
(3) The *Saṃyutta Nikāya*, containing fifty-six subdivisions, translated in Bhikkhu Bodhi, *The Connected Discourses of the Buddha* (Boston: Wisdom Publications, 2000)
(4) The *Anguttara Nikāya*, containing 2,344 discourses, translated in Woodward and Hare, *The Book of Gradual Sayings* (Pali Text Society, 1932–1936), 208 of which are retranslated in Nyanaponika Thera and Bhikkhu Bodhi, *Numerical Discourses of the Buddha* (Walnut Creek, CA: AltaMira Press, 1999)
(5) The *Khuddaka Nikāya,* containing 15–18 well-known supplementary texts, some of which have been published separately in translation

Tengyur
bsTan 'gyur
The Collected Translations of Classical Treatises. The TBRC digital library includes four versions, which are freely accessible online, including the Derge xylograph edition of 1737–1744 (213 vols.), compiled and edited by Zhuchen Tsultrim Rinchen, which is catalogued in H. Ui et al., *A Complete Catalogue of the Tibetan Buddhist Canons* (Sendai: Tohoku University, 1934). Other editions consulted in the present work include the Peking edition in 185 vols, republished with catalogue by Suzuki Research Foundation (Tokyo-Kyoto: 1955–61); and the new collated edition, Tengyur Pedurma, in 120 vols. (Chengdu: 1995–2005). Mention is occasionally made in the text of two other renowned manuscript versions: the eighteenth-century Nartang (sNar thang) and Serdri (gilded) Tengyurs.

2. Individual Scriptures: Vinaya, Sūtra, and Tantra

Continuation Tantra Based on the Tantra of the Renunciation of Vajravārāhī: The Inconceivable Pristine Cognition Inseparable from the Buddha Mind of All the Sky-farers
mKha' 'gro ma thams cad kyi thugs gnyis su med pa bsam gyis mi khyab pa'i ye shes rdo rje phag mo mngon par 'byung ba'i rgyud las rgyud phyi ma
Dg.K. rGyud 'bum, vol. Ga, ff. 71a–72b. T 379

Inspection of Skulls: Extracting the Wealth of the Yakṣas
Thod brtag gnod sbyin nor 'don
An extract from the *Tantra of Heruka Galpo* (Dg.NGB, vols. 18–19). Included in *gSang rnying rgyan dang rol mo'i bstan bcos*, Gangs can rig mdzod, vol. 30, pp. 293–297. Bod ljongs bod yig dpe rnying dpe skrun khang, 1996

Sūtra of Renunciation
Abhiniṣkramanasūtra
mNgon par 'byung ba'i mdo
Dg.K. mDo sde, vol. Sa, ff. 1b–125a. T 301

Sūtra of the Ascertainment of Meanings: A Lexicon of Buddhist Numerical Categories
Arthaviniścaya-nāma-dharmaparyāya
Don rnam par nges pa zhes bya ba'i chos kyi rnam grangs
Dg.K. mDo sde, vol. Sa, ff. 170b–188a. T 317
EIPRB 134. Translated in Samtani 2002

Sūtra of the Shoots of Rice
Śālistambasūtra
Sā lu ljang pa zhes bya ba theg pa chen po'i mdo
Dg.K. mDo sde, vol. Tsha, ff. 116b–123b. T 210
EIPRB 49B.1. Edited and translated in Reat 1993

Sūtra That Analyzes Past Actions
Karmavibhaṅgasūtra
Las rnam par 'byed pa/ Las rnam par 'gyur ba
Dg.K. mDo sde, vol. Sa, ff. 277a–310a. T 338–339
EIPRB 3.1

Sūtra Which Gathers All Intentions
mDo dgongs pa 'dus pa
Dg.K. rNying rgyud, vol. Ka, ff. 86b–290a. T 829. Dg.NGB, vol. Ja (7), ff. 110b–314a

Tantra of the Renunciation of Śrīheruka
Śrīherukābhyudayatantra
dPal khrag 'thung mngon par 'byung ba
Dg.K. rGyud 'bum, vol. Ga, ff. 1b–33b. T 374

Tantra of the Renunciation of Vajravārāhī: The Inconceivable Pristine Cognition Inseparable from the Buddha Mind of All the Sky-farers
Ḍākinīsarvacittādvayācintyajñānavajravārāhyabhibhavatantrarāja
mKha' 'gro ma thams cad kyi thugs gnyis su med pa bsam gyis mi khyab pa'i ye shes rdo rje phag mo mngon par 'byung ba'i rgyud kyi rgyal po
Dg.K. rGyud 'bum, vol. Ga, ff. 60b–71a. T 378

Tantra of the Wrathful Lord Mahākāla: The Origin of Secret Accomplishment
Śrīvajramahākālakrodhanātharahasyasiddhibhavatantra
dPal rdo rje nag po chen po khros pa'i mgon po gsang ba dngos grub 'byung ba
Dg.K. rGyud 'bum, vol. Ga, ff. 263b–292a. T 416
Re-translated by Tsami Sangye Drakpa

3. Treatises of Indic Origin

Anon
Consecratory Rite entitled King of Consecrations
Rab tu gnas pa'i cho ga rab gnas kyi rgyal po
Dg.T. rGyud, vol. Ku, ff. 188a–225b. T 2528

Anon
Synopsis of the Inspection of Human Beings
Tanūvicāraṇaśāstrasaṃkṣepa
Mi dpyad kyi bstan bsdus pa
Dg.T. Thun mong, vol. Ngo, ff. 150b–151a. T 4337

Anon
Tales of Spiritual Accomplishment Achieved through a Female Medium
Nārīsiddhilābhākhyāna
Bud med kyis grub pa thob pa'i gtam rgyud
Dg.T. Thun mong, vol. Ngo, ff. 155b–156a. T 4343

Asaṅga (fl. late fourth–early fifth century)
Level of the Pious Attendants: [from the Yogācāra Level]
Śrāvakabhūmi
[rNal 'byor spyod pa'i sa las] nyan thos kyi sa
Dg.T. Sems tsam, vol. Dzi, ff. 1b–195a. T 4036
MTTWL 259. *EIPRB* 174.10

Aśvaghoṣa (ca. 80–150)
Epic of the Deeds of the Buddha
Buddhacaritamahākāvya
Sangs rgyas kyi spyod pa zhes bya ba'i snyan dngags
Dg.T. sKyes rabs, vol. Ge, ff. 1b–103b. T 4156
MTTWL 48. Edited and translated in Johnson 1972

Eulogy entitled One Hundred and Fifty Verses
Śatapañcāśatka-nāma-stotra
brGya lnga bcu pa zhes bya ba'i bstod pa
Dg.T. bsTod tshogs, vol. Ka, ff. 110a–116a. T 1147
MTTWL 207

Verses in Eulogy to the Monastery Gong
Gaṇḍīstotragāthā
Gaṇḍī'i bstod pa tshigs su bcad pa
Dg.T. bsTod tshogs, vol. Ka, ff. 178a–181a. T 1149

Avalokitavrata (fl. seventh century)
Commentary on the Lamp of Discriminative Awareness
Prajnāpradīpaṭīkā

Shes rab sgon ma rgya cher 'grel pa
Dg.T. dBu ma, vols. Va–Za (3 vols.). T 3859
EIPRB 354.1

Bharata (fl. prior to second century)
Treatise on Dramaturgy
Nāṭyaśāstra
Sanskrit edition, Sharma and Upadhyaya 1929
Translated in Vatsyayan 1996

Candrakīrti (fl. seventh century)
Commentary on the Four Hundred Verses
[Bodhisattvayogācāra] catuḥśatakaṭīkā
[Byang chub sems dpa' rnal 'byor spyod pa] bzhi brgya pa'i rgya cher 'grel pa
Dg.T. dBu ma, vol. Ya, ff. 30b–239a. T 3865
MTTWL 54. *EIPRB* 321.1

Devasūrī (fl. twelfth century)
Ornamental Mirror of Categories: A Guide to Valid Cognition
Pramāṇanayatattvālokālaṃkāra
EIPRB 658.1

Dharmakīrti (fl. late sixth–early seventh century)
Extensive Exegesis on the Garland of Tales of Past Lives
Jātakamālāṭīkā
sKyes rabs kyi rgya cher bshad pa
Dg.T. sKyes rabs, vol. Ha, ff. 135b–340a. T 4151

Proof of Other Minds
Santānāntarasiddhi-nāma-prakaraṇa
rGyud gzhan grub pa
Dg.T. Tshad ma, vol. Che, ff. 355b–359a. T 4219
MTTWL 200. *EIPRB* 344.7

Dharmapāla (ca. 530–561)
Door Illuminating the Hundred Teachings of the Greater Vehicle
Da cheng bai fa ming men lun
Theg pa chen po'i chos brgya gsal pa'i sgo'i bstan bcos
Dg.T. Sems tsam, vol. Shi, ff. 145a–146b. T 4063
EIPRB 302

Dharmikasubhūtighoṣa (*Chos ldan rab 'byor dbyangs*, dates uncertain)
Verses on the Foundation of Recollection of the Sacred Teachings
Saddharmasmṛtyupasthānakārikā
Dam pa'i chos dran pa nye bar gzhag pa'i tshig le'ur byas pa
Dg.T. sPrin yig, vol. Ngo, ff. 35b–39a. T 4179

Dignāga (fl. late fifth–mid sixth century)
Auto-commentary on the Compendium of Valid Cognition
Pramāṇasamuccayavṛtti
Tshad ma kun las btus pa'i 'grel pa
Dg.T. Tshad ma, vol. Ce, ff. 14b–85b. T 4204
MTTWL 167. *EIPRB* 268.7

Auto-commentary on the Examination of Objects of Reference
Ālambanaparīkṣāvṛtti
dMigs pa brtag pa'i 'grel pa
Dg.T. Tshad ma, vol. Ce, ff. 86a–87b. T 4206
EIPRB 268.2

Compendium of Valid Cognition
Pramāṇasamuccaya
Tshad ma kun las btus pa zhes bya ba'i rab tu byed pa
Dg.T. Tshad ma, vol. Ce, ff. 1b–13a. T 4203
MTTWL 166. *EIPRB* 268.7

Essential Lamp Commentary on the Treasury of Phenomenology
Abhidharmakośavṛttimarmadīpa
Chos mngon pa'i mdzod kyi 'grel pa gnad kyi sgron me
Dg.T. mNgon pa, vol. Nyu, ff. 95b–214a. T 4095
EIPRB 268.1

Establishing the Circle of Logical Axioms
Hetucakraḍamaru
gTan tshigs kyi 'khor lo gtan la dbab pa
Dg.T. Tshad ma, vol. Ce, ff. 93a–94a. T 4209
MTTWL 84. *EIPRB* 268.4

Examination of Objects of Reference
Ālambanaparīkṣā
dMigs pa brtag pa
Dg.T. Tshad ma, vol. Ce, f. 86a. T 4205
MTTWL 11. *EIPRB* 268.2

Examination of the Three Times
Trikalpaparīkṣā
Dus gsum brtag pa
Dg.T. Tshad ma, vol. Ce, ff. 87b–88b. T 4207
EIPRB 368.8

Introduction to Logical Reasoning
Liang lun ru zheng li
Tshad ma'i bstan bcos rigs pa la 'jug pa
Dg.T. Tshad ma, vol. Ce, ff. 88b–93a. T 4208
EIPRB 368.5

Durlabharāja (dates uncertain)
Inspection of the Physical Characteristics of Human Beings entitled Sāmudrika
Sāmudrika-nāma-tanūlakṣaṇaparīkṣā
Mi'i mtshan nyid brtag pa rgya mtsho
Dg.T. Thun mong, vol. Ngo, ff. 151a–153a. T 4338

Physical Charateristics [of Human Beings], Demonstrated by Sāmudrika
Sāmudrikavyañjanavarṇana
rGya mtshos bstan pa'i mtshan
Dg.T. Thun mong, vol. Ngo, ff. 148b–150b. T 4336
See Smith 2001, p. 187, for this tentatve attribution

Guṇamati (fl. early sixth century)
Extensive Sub-commentary on the Commentary Analyzing the Sūtra of Dependent Origination
Pratītyasamutpādādivibhaṅganirdeśaṭīkā
rTen cing 'grel par 'byung ba dang po dang rnam par dbye ba bstan pa'i rgya cher bshad pa
Dg.T. mDo 'grel, vol. Chi, ff. 61b–234a. T 3996
EIPRB 378C.2

Harṣadeva (ca. 600–646)
Utter Delight of the Nāgas
Nāgānandanāmanāṭaka
Klu kun du dga' ba zhes bya ba'i zlos gar
Dg.T. sKyes rabs, vol. U, ff. 225a–252a. T 4154
Translated in Boyd 1872

Jaiminī (fl. third century BCE)
Mimāṃsa Sūtra
EIPRB 22.1. Edited in M. Goswami. *Mimāṃsa Sūtra*. Varanasi: 1984–1987

Jayadeva (fl. late seventh–early eighth century)
Commentary on the Grammar of Mañjuśrī
Mañjuśrīśabdavyākaraṇa
'Jam dpal gyi sgra brda sprod pa'i 'grel pa stong phrag brgyad pa
Dg.T. sGra mdo, vol. Re, ff. 142b–231a. T 4280

Jinaputra (a.k.a. Rājaputra or Yogamitra, dates uncertain)
Exegesis of the Compendium of Phenomenology
Abhidharmasamuccayabhāṣya
mNgon pa chos kun las btus pa'i bshad pa
Dg.T. Sems tsam, vol. Li, ff. 1b–117a. T 4053
EIPRB 296.1

Exposition of the Compendium of Phenomenology
Abhidharmasamuccayavyākhyā
mNgon pa chos kun las btus pa'i rnam par bshad pa
Dg.T. Sems tsam, vol. Li, ff. 117a–293a. T 4054

Jñānaśrībhadra (fl. late eleventh century)
Commentary on the Sūtra of the Descent to Laṅkā
Laṅkāvatārasūtravṛtti
'Phags pa laṅ kar gshegs pa'i 'grel pa
Dg.T. mDo 'grel, vol. Ni, ff. 1b–262a. T 4018
EIPRB 617.1

Jñānavajra (dates uncertain)
Commentary on the Sūtra of the Descent to Laṅkā entitled Heart Ornament of the Tathāgatas
Laṅkāvatārasūtravṛtti-tathāgatahṛdayālaṃkāra
'Phags pa lang kar gshegs pa zhes bya ba theg pa chen po'i mdo'i 'grel pa de bzhin gshegs pa'i snying po'i rgyan
Dg.T. mDo 'grel, vol. Pi, ff. 1b–310a. T 4019

Kamalaśīla (740–795)
Commentary on Difficulties in the Summation of the Real
Tattvasaṃgrahapañjikā
De kho na nyid bsdus pa'i dka' 'grel
Dg.T. Tshad ma, vol. Ze, ff. 133b–363a. T 4267
EIPRB 418.8

Kumārila (c. 686–745)
Exposition of the Sacred Sciences
Tantravārttika
On Śabara, Book 1, chs. 2–4 and Books 2–3. *EIPRB* 363.2. Edited with Hindi translation in Mahaprabhulal Goswami. Varanasi: Tara Publishing, 1984–1987

Exposition of the Verses
Ślokavārttika
On Śabara, Book 1, ch. 1. *EIPRB* 363.1. Sanskrit edition by Rāma Śāstrī Tailaṅga (Manavalli), Chowkhamba, Varanasi: 1891. Translated in Jha 1985

Full Exposition
Tuptika
On Śabara, Books 4–9. *EIPRB* 363.3

Madhva (fl. fourteenth century)
Extensive Garland of Logic
Nyāyamālāvistara
EIPRB 809.13. Edited by Apayya Diksita, Delhi: 1989

Mamhikawi (dates uncertain)
Application of Terminations indicative of Nominal Declension: A Commentary on the Kalāpasūtra
Kalāpasūtravṛtti syādivibhaktiprakriyā
Ka lā pa'i mdo dang 'grel pa'i si la sogs pa'i rnam 'bye'i bya ba
Dg.T. sGra mdo, vol. She, ff. 54b–97a. T 4288

Maudgalyāyana (fl. sixth–fifth century BCE)
Treatise on the Designation of Causes
Kāraṇaprajñapti
rGyu'i gdags pa
Dg.T. mNgon pa, vol. I, ff. 98a–172b. T 4087

Treatise on the Designation of Cosmology
Lokaprajñapti
'Jig rten gdags pa
Dg.T. mNgon pa, vol. I, ff. 1b–93a. T 4086

Treatise on the Designation of Past Actions
Karmaprajñapti
Las gdags pa
Dg.T. mNgon pa, vol. I, ff. 172b–229a. T 4088

Nāgārjuna (fl. second century)
Commentary on the Sūtra of the Greater Vehicle entitled Shoots of Rice
Śālistambhaka-nāma-mahāyānasūtraṭīkā
Sā lu ljang pa zhes bya ba theg pa chen po'i mdo'i rgya cher 'grel pa
Dg.T. mDo 'grel, vol. Ngi, ff. 20b–55b. T 3986

Verses concerning the [Sūtra of] the Shoots of Rice
Śālistambhakakārikā
Sā lu ljang pa'i tshig le'ur byas pa
Dg.T. mDo 'grel, vol. Ngi, ff. 18a–20b. T 3985

Pāṇini (fl. fourth century BCE)
Grammar of Pāṇini
Pāṇinivyākaraṇasūtra
brDa sprod pa pā ṇi ni'i mdo
Dg.T. sNa tshogs, vol. To, ff. 1b–452a. T 4420
Aṣṭādhyāyī translated in Joshi and Roodbergen 1992–2007. See also Katre 1987 and Cardona 1988

Parahitabhadra (fl. 1000)
Exegesis of the First Two Verse Sections of the Ornament of the Sūtras of the Greater Vehicle
Sūtrālaṃkārādiślokadvayavyākhyāna
mDo sde rgyan gyi tshigs su bcad pa dang po gnyis kyi bshad pa
Dg.T. Sems tsam, vol. Bi, ff. 174b–183b. T 4030
EIPRB 570.1

Radhakāntadeva (1784–1867)
Śabdakalpadruma
A lexicon entitled "Wish-granting Tree of Words." Calcutta: Baptist Mission Press, 1886

Ratnākaraśānti (fl. early eleventh century)
Commentary on the Ornament of Madhyamaka entitled Attainment of the Middle Way
Madhyamakālaṃkāravṛttimadhyamakapratipadāsiddhi
dBu ma rgyan gyi 'grel pa dbu ma'i lam grub pa
Dg.T. Sems tsam, vol. Hi, ff. 102a–120b. T 4072

Pith Instructions on the Transcendental Perfection of Discriminative Awareness
Prajñāpāramitopadeśa
Shes rab kyi pha rol tu phyin pa'i man ngag
Dg.T. Sems tsam, vol. Hi, ff. 133b–162b. T 4079

Ratnakīrti (fl. eleventh century)
Ascertainment of the Sacred Teachings
Dharmaviniścaya-nāma-prakaraṇa
Chos rnam par nge pa zhes bya ba'i rab tu byed pa
Dg.T. Sems tsam, vol. Hi, ff. 217b–223b. T 4084
EIPRB 595.6

Rūpabhadra (dates uncertain)
Treatise on the Arts of Love
Kāmaśāstra
'Dod pa'i bstan bcos
Dg.T. rGyud, vol. Zi, ff. 274b–277a. T 2500

Śabara-[svāmin] (fl. 400)
Commentary of Savara
Savarabhāṣya
On Jaiminī's *Mimāṃsa Sūtra*. *EIPRB* 198.1. Edited in Mahaprabhulal Goswami. Varanasi: Tara Publishing, 1984–1987

Śākāyana (ca. second century BCE)
Maitrāyaṇa Upaniṣad
One of sixteen esoteric instructions pertaining to the Sāmaveda. Translated in Radhakrishnan 1953, pp. 793–859

Śāntarakṣita (725–783)
Summation of the Real
Tattvasaṃgraha
De kho na nyid bsdus pa'i tshig le'u byas pa
Dg.T. Tshad ma, vol. Ze, ff. 1b–133a. T 4266
MTTWL 233. *EIPRB* 404.4. English translation in Jha 1937

Śrījñāna (dates uncertain)
Jewel Necklace of Synonymics, Concerning Homonyms
[Ekaśabdabahvarthapravartana] abhidhānamaṇimālā
sKad dod gcig gis don du mar 'jug pa'i mngon brjod nor bu'i phreng ba
Dg.T. sNa tshogs, vol. Po, ff. 164a–242a. T 4454

Sthiramati (ca. 470–550)
Commentary on the Analysis of the Middle and Extremes
Madhyāntavibhāgaṭīkā
dBu dang mtha' rnam par byed pa'i 'grel bshad
Dg.T. Sems tsam, vol. Bi, ff. 189b–318a. T 4032
MTTWL 114. *EIPRB* 304.5. First part translated in Friedmann 1984

Commentary on the Treasury of Phenomenology entitled Meaningful Reality
Abhidharmakośabhāṣya-ṭīkātattvārtha
Chos mngon pa mdzod kyi bshad pa'i rgya cher 'grel pa don gyi de kho na nyid
Dg.T. sNa tshogs, vols. Tho and Do (2 vols.). T 4421
EIPRB 304.1

Vāgbhaṭa (fl. seventh century)
Eight Divisions of Medical Science
Aṣṭāṅgahṛdayasaṃhitā
Yan lag brgyad pa'i snying po zhes bya ba'i sman dpyad kyi bshad pa
Dg.T. gSo rig pa, vol. He, ff. 44b–335a. T 4310
Edited and translated in Vogel 1965

Varāhamihira (fl. sixth century)
Fivefold Textbook Calculation
Pañcasiddhāntaka
Translated from the Sanskrit in Kuppanna Sastry 1993

Great Compilation
Bṛhatsaṃhitā
Translated from the Sanskrit in Ramakrishna Bhat 1981

Vararuci (late fourth–early fifth century)
Summation of Gender, and Its Auto-commentary
Liṅgasaṃgraha
rTags bsdu rtsa 'grel gsar 'gyur
Translated into Tibetan by Situ Chokyi Jungne, Collected Works, vol. Ca

Vasubandhu/ Daṃṣṭrasena
Great Commentary on the Transcendental Perfection of Discriminative Awareness in One Hundred Thousand, Twenty-five Thousand, and Eighteen Thousand Lines
Śatasāhasrikāpañcaviṃśatisāhasrikāṣṭādaśasāhasrikāprajñāpāramitā-bṛhaṭṭīkā
'Phags pa shes rab kyi pha rol tu phyin pa 'bum pa dang nyi khri lnga stong pa dang khri brgyad stong pa'i rgya cher bshad pa
Dg.T. Shes phyin, vol. Pha, ff. 1b–292b. T 3808

Vatsyāyana (fl. ca. second–fifth century)
Discourse on the Arts of Love
Kāmasūtra
Translated in Burton and Arbuthnot 1883; also Doniger and Kakar 2002

Vopadeva (fl. twelfth century)
Paradigms of Verbal Roots
Dhātupāṭha
Sanskrit edited in Ashu Bodha Vidyabhusana et al., *Kavikalpadrumaḥ Dhātupāthaḥ.* SAMP, 1904

Vyāḍi (late fourth–early fifth century)
Commentary on Grammatical Rules
Paribhāsavṛtti
Sanskrit edited and translated in Wujastyk 1993

Yajñāvalkya (eighth–fifth century BCE)
Bṛhadāraṇyaka Upaniṣad
One of fifty esoteric instructions pertaining to the Yajurveda. Translated in Radhakrishnan 1953, pp. 147–333

4. Treatises and Revelations (*gter ma*) of Tibetan Origin

Anon
Clarification of Sensual Grace in the Wish-fulfilling Commentary
Kā ma dhe nur sgeg pa gsal ba
Not located

Anon (possibly Kawa Peltsek)
Commentary on the Eight Elements of Linguistic Application
gNas brgyad chen po'i 'grel pa
Dg.T. sNa tshogs, vol. Co, ff. 165a–173a. T 4351
Also Lhasa: Bod ljongs mi dmangs dpe skrun khang, 1988

Anon
Method of Attaching Drumskin Covers
rNga spags gYogs thabs
In Tashi Gyatso et al., *Treatises on the Accoutrements and Music of the Ancient Way of Secret* [*Mantras*], p. 363

Banda Gelek Gyatso ('Ba' mda' dge legs rgya mtsho, 1844–1904)
Ascertaining the General Meaning of the Collected Topics, entitled Precious Lamp Clarifying All Phenomena
bsDus grva'i spyi don rnam par nges pa chos thams cad kyi mtshan nyid rab tu gsal bar byed pa rin po che'i sgron me

Collected Works of Banda Gelek Gyatso, dbu med ms, vol. 1 (Ka), 491 pages (Dzamtang: 1997). Also Gangs ljongs shes rig gi nying bcud series (Beijing: Krung go'i bod kyi shes rig dpe skrun khang, 1993)
HJK, p. 86

Exegesis Elucidating the Systematic Presentation of the Eighty Natural [Dissonant Mental States], entitled Mirror That Discloses Their Meaning
Rang bzhin brgyad cu'i rnam bzhag gsal bar bshad pa don rab tu gsal ba'i me long
In the Collected Works of Banda Gelek Gyatso, dbu med ms, vol. 17 (Tsa), 12 pages (Dzamtang: 1997)
HJK, p. 96

Necklace of Youthful Clear Intelligence Analyzing the Psycho-physical Aggregates, entitled Jewel Garland of Eloquence
Phung po lnga'i rnam par dbye ba blo gsal gzhon nu'i mgul rgyan legs bshad nor bu'i phreng ba
Collected Works of Banda Gelek Gyatso, dbu med ms, vol. 18 (Tsha), 189 pages (Dzamtang: 1997)
HJK, p. 102

Belo Tsewang Kunkhyab (Be lo tshe dbang kun khyab, b. 1718)
Biographical Account of the Karma Kamtsang Lineage of Spiritual Attainment, entitled Infinite Jewel Garland of Crystal
sGrub brgyud karma kam tshang gi brgyud pa rin po che'i rnam par thar pa rab 'byams nor bu zla ba chu shel gyi phreng ba
Kunming: Yunnan mi rigs dpe skrun khang, 1998

Exegesis of Cakrasaṃvara
bDe mchog rnam bshad
Listed in Dro Jinpa, *Catalogue of the Collected Works of Hundreds of Learned and Accomplished Masters from Upper Dokham*, p. 382

Bo Khepa [Mipham Gelek Namgyal] (Bod mkhas pa, 1618–1685)
Commentary and Proverbs Based on the Mirror of Poetics
sNyan ngag me long gi 'grel pa dang dper brjod
In *sNyan ngag rtsa 'grel.* Qinghai mi rigs dpe skrun khang, 1981

Bodong Paṇchen [Chok-le Namgyal] (Bo dong paṇ chen, 1376–1451)
Exegesis on Making Artistic Representations of Buddha Body, Speech, and Mind: A Discourse on the Gateway to Knowledge
mKhas pa 'jug pa'i mdo bzo rig sku gsung thugs kyi rten bzhengs tshul bshad pa
In Collected Works, 2:215–265. Delhi: Tibet House, 1969

Exegesis on the Systematic Presentation of Valid Cognition according to Buddhism, as stated in Dharmakīrti's Drops of Reasoning
Rigs thigs las gsungs pa'i nang pa'i tshad ma'i rnam gzhag bshad pa
In Collected Works, vols. 7 and 8. Delhi: Tibet House, 1973

Buchung (Bu chung, fl. late twentieth century)
Dictionary of Synonyms
mNgon brjod kyi tshig mdzod
Lhasa: Bod ljongs mi dmangs dpe skrun khang, 1997

Buton Rinchendrub (Bu ston rin chen grub, 1290–1364)
History of Buddhism entitled Treasury of the Precious Scriptures
bDe bar gshegs pa'i bstan pa'i gsal byed chos kyi 'byung gnas gsung rab rin po che'i mdzod
Beijing: Krung go'i bod kyi shes rig dpe skrun khang, 1988

Proportional Measurements of the Enlightenment Stūpa
Byang chub chen po'i mchod rten gyi cha tshad
Collected Works of Buton, vol. 14 (Pha), no. 12. Lhasa: Zhol Parkhang reprint, 2000

Sunlight Rays Clarifying the Maṇḍala
dKyil 'khor gsal byed nyi ma'i 'od zer
Collected Works of Buton, vol. 17 (Tsa), nos. 3–15. Lhasa: Zhol Parkhang re-print, 2000. Also in bKa' brgyud pa'i gsung rab, 3:61–730. Qinghai Mi rigs dpe skrun khang, 2003

Candraśrī[ratna] (Zla bad pal rin, b. ca. 1375)
Methodology of Musical Sound
Rol mo'i sgra thabs bzhugs
Unpublished ms held at Amnye Machen Institute, Dharamsala

Systematic Presentation of Drums and Cymbals
rNga sbug gi rnam bzhag
In Tashi Gyatso et al., *Treatises on the Accoutrements and Music of the Ancient Way of Secret [Mantras]*, pp. 357–359

Treatise on Melody entitled Neck Ornament of Clear Intelligence
dByangs kyi bstan bcos blo gsal mgul rgyan
Unpublished ms held at Amnye Machen Institute, Dharamsala

Changlung Paṇḍita Ngawang Lobzang Tenpei Gyaltsen (lCang lung paṇḍita, 1770–1845)
Multiple Illustrations of Scripts from India, China, Russia, Kashmir, Nepal, Tibet and Mongolia
rGya dkar rgya nag rgya ser kasmir bal bod hor gyi yi ge dang dpe ris rnam grangs mang ba
Collected Works, vol. 4 (Nga), 29ff. Delhi: Mongolian Lama Gurudeva, 1975–1985. Also Dharamsala: LTWA, 1991

Chapa Chokyi Senge (Phyva pa chos kyi seng ge, 1109–1169)
Dispelling Mental Darkness: Root Text and Commentary Integrating [Dharmakīrti's] Seven Treatises on Valid Cognition
Tshad ma [sde bdun] bsdus pa yid gi mun sel [rtsa 'grel]
Unpublished ms in 96ff. TBRC holdings, W12171-2077

Chapel Tseten Phuntsok and Tsering Peljor, eds.
Compilation of Useful Instructions on the Arts
bZo rig nyer mkho bdams bsgrigs
In Gangs can rig mdzod, vol. 13. Lhasa: Bod ljongs bod yig dpe rnying dpe skrun khang, 1990

Che Khyidruk (Ce khyi 'brug, ca. 798–815)
Root Verses on the Eight Elements of Linguistic Application
gNas brgyad chen po'i rtsa ba
Dg.T. mDo 'grel, vol. Co, ff. 163a–165a. T 4350
Also Lhasa: Bod ljongs mi dmangs dpe skrun khang, 1988

Chebu Trishe (dPyad bu khri shes, dates uncertain)
Four Collections of Medical Science
gSo rig 'bum bzhi
Beijing: Mi rigs dpe skrun khang, 2005

Chim Lobzang Drak ('Chims blo bzang grags, 1299–1375)
Ocean of Eloquence Elucidating Phenomenology
Chos mngon pa gsal byed legs pas bshad pa'i rgya mtsho
In dPal ldan sa skya pa'i gsung rab, vol. 17. Beijing: Mi rigs dpe skrun khang, in collaboration with Qinghai mi rigs dpe skrun khang, 2004

Chim Namka Drak ('Chims nam mkha' grags, 1210–1267/85)
Hundred Sādhanas of Narthang
sNar thang rgya rtsa; also known as Yi dam rgya mtsho'i sgrub thabs rin chen byung gnas
Delhi: Chophal Legdan, 1974–1975. See also Willson and Brauen 2000

Chomden Rikpei Raldri (lCom ldan rig pa'i ral gri, 1227–1305)
Ornamental Flower of [Dharmakīrti's] Seven Treatises on Valid Cognition
Tshad ma sde bdun rgyan gyi me tog
Gangs ljongs shes rig gi nying bcud series. Beijing: Krung go'i bod kyi shes rig dpe skrun khang, 1991

Ornamental Flower of Spiritual and Philosophical Systems
Grub mtha' rgyan gyi me tog
Reprinted from dbu med ms. In the Collected Works of Chomden Rigpei Raldri. 10 vols. Lhasa: Khamtrul Sonam Dondrub, 2006

Chopel Kelzang Trinle (Chos dpal skal bzang phrin las, fl. late twentieth century)
Pearl Necklace of Clear Intelligence: A Numeric Lexicon of Buddhist Technical Terms Compiled from the Sūtras, Tantras, and Treatises
mDo rgyud bstan bcos kun las btus pa'i chos kyi rnam grangs mu thi la'i phreng ba lo gsal mgul rgyan
Lanzhou: Gansu mi rigs dpe skrun khang, 2005

Dakpo Rabjampa Tashi Namgyal (Dvags po rab 'byams pa bkra shis rnam rgyal, 1512–1587)
Elucidation on the Sequence of Meditation according to the Great Seal of Definitive Meaning entitled Moonbeams of Eloquence
Nges don phyag rgya chen po'i sgom rim gsal bar byed pa'i legs bshad zla ba'i 'od zer
In bKa' brgyud pa'i gsung rab, 20:323–773. English translation in Lhalungpa 2006

Drakpa (Grags pa, fl. late twentieth century)
Inventory of Tibetan Treatises entitled Immaculate Crystal Rosary
Bod kyi bstan bcos khag cig gi mtshan byang dri med shel dkar phreng ba; also known as the Bla brang dkar chag
Ziling: Qinghai mi rigs dpe skrun khang, 1985

Drakpa Gyaltsen of Sakya (Grags pa rgyal mtshan, 1147–1216)
Examination of the Begging Bowl [of the Skull], According to the Inner Way of Secret Mantras
gSang sngags nang gi lhun bzed brtag pa
In Tashi Gyatso et al., *Treatises on the Accoutrements and Music of the Ancient Way of Secret [Mantras]*, pp. 317–334

Dro Jinpa ('Bro sbyin pa, fl. twenty-first century)
Catalogue of the Collected Works of Hundreds of Learned and Accomplished Masters from Upper Dokham
Yul mdo khams stod kyi mkhas grub brgya rtsa'i gsung 'bum dkar chag phyogs gcig tu bsgrigs pa dvangs gsal shel gyi me long
Ziling: Qinghai mi rigs dpe skrun khang, 2008

Dromton Lodro Zhonu ('Brom ston blo gros gzhon nu, b. 1271)
Biography of Jowoje Atiśa entitled the Father Teachings of Kadam
Jo bo rje dpal ldan atisha'i rnam thar bka' gdams pha chos
Ziling: Qinghai mi rigs dpe skrun khang, 1994.
See Martin 1997, no. 69

Drugu Sengdo Ochen (Gru gu seng mdo 'od chen, fl. eighth century)
Mirror Trilogy
Me long skor gsum
Including the *Treatise on Horses entitled Silver-White Mirror* (*rTa gzhung dngul dkar me long*) and the *Inspection of Horses entitled All-radiant Mirror* (*rTa dpyad mthong ba kun gsal me long*). Published in *Anthology of Texts and Advice Concerning the Veterinary Treatment of Horses* (*Bod kyi rta'i gso dpyad gzhung lugs mdams bsgrigs*). Gangs chen rig mdzod series, vol. 13. Lhasa: Bod ljongs bod yig dpe rnying dpe skrun khang, 1990

Dungkar Lobzang Trinle (Dung dkar blo bzang phrin las, 1927–1997)
Great Dictionary of Dungkar
Dung dkar tshig mdzod chen mo
Beijing: Krung go'i bod rig pa dpe skrun khang, 2002

Initial Thoughts concerning the Development of the Tibetan Writing Systems
Bod kyi skad yig 'phel rgyas gtong phyogs skor gyi thog ma'i bsam tshul
In Khagang Tashi Tsering, ed., *Studies on Ancient Tibetan Writing and Orthography*

Gawei Dorje (dGa' ba'i rdo rje, b. 1950)
Immaculate Crystal Mirror of [Materia Medica] Illustrations
'Khrungs dpe dri med shel gyi me long
Beijing: Mi rigs dpe skrun khang, 1995

Gendun Chopel (dGe 'dun chos 'phel, 1903–1951)
Treatise on the Arts of Love
'Dod pa'i bstan bcos
Translated in J. Hopkins 1992

Gonpo Gyaltsen et al. (mGon po rgyal mtshan, fl. late twentieth century)
Storehouse of Knowledge: A Catalogue of the Collected Works Compiled from Ethnic [Tibetan] Libraries
Mi rigs dpe mdzod khang gi dpe tho las gsung 'bum skor gyi dkar chag shes bya'i gter mdzod
3 vols. Chengdu: Sichuan mi rigs dpe skrun khang, 1984–1997

Gonpo Wangyal (mGon po dbang rgyal, fl. twentieth century)
Numeric Lexicon of Buddhist Terms
Chos kyi rnam grangs
Chengdu: Sichuan mi rigs dpe skrun khang, 1988

Gorampa Sonam Senge (Go ram pa bsod nams seng ge, 1429–1489)
Explanation of Difficult Points in [Sa-paṇ's] Treasury of Valid Cognition [entitled Clarification of the Seven Sections of Dharmkīrti]
Tshad ma rig gter gyi dka' gnas rnam par bshad pa [sde bdun rab gsal]
SKB, vol. 12. Tokyo: Toyo Bunko, 1968

Faultless Commentary on the Intention of the Seven Treatises and their Sūtra Revealing the Meaning [of Sa-paṇ's] Treasury of Logical Reasoning
sDe bdun mdo dang bcas pa'i dgongs pa phyin ci ma log par 'grel pa tshad ma rigs pa'i gter gyi don gsal bar byed pa
SKB, vol. 11. Tokyo: Toyo Bunko, 1968–69

Gu Wenyi and Shi Xueli (fl. twentieth century)
Compilation of the Various Types of Calligraphy of Scholars in the Land of Snow, entitled Precious Garland
Gangs can mkhas pa'i phyag bris sna tshogs phyogs bsdus rin chen phreng ba
Lanzhou: Gansu mi rigs dpe skrun khang, 1990

Gungru Sherab Zangpo (Gung ru shes rab bzang po, 1411–1475)
Dissertation and Pith Instructions on the Geometry of the Maṇḍala
dKyil 'khor gyi thig gi rab tu byed pa man ngag dang bcas pa
In dPal ldan sa skya pa'i gsung rab, 3:120–132. Beijing: Mi rigs dpe skrun khang, in collaboration with Qinghai mi rigs dpe skrun khang, 2004

Guru Chowang (Gu ru chos dbang, 1212–1270)
Method of Constructing Stūpas
mChod rten bzhengs thabs
Possibly to be identified with *Illustrations of Temple Construction, for the Consummation of the Three Buddha Bodies* (*sKu gsum yongs rdzogs kyi lha khang gzhengs thabs kyi dpe ris*). Contained in the *Eight Transmitted Teachings: Consummation of Secrets* (*bKa' brgyad gsang ba yongs rdzogs*). rNying ma'i dkar chags, vol. 1, no. 40 and vol. 4, no. 51. Lhasa: Potala Archives, 1992

Spiritual Teacher: Gathering of Secrets
Bla ma gsang 'dus
RTD, vol. 7, pp. 461–614

Gyurme Rabgye ('Gyur med rab rgyas, fl. twentieth–twenty-first century)
Wondrous Garland of Tales Concerning Tibetan Painting Traditions
Bod kyi srol rgyun ri mo'i skor brjod pa'i ngo mtshar gtam phreng
Lanzhou: Gansu mi rigs dpe skrun khang, 2001

Hor rgyal, ed.
Jonang Catalogue entitled Beautiful Crystal Garland
Jo nang dkar chag shel dkar phreng mdzes
Beijing: Mi rigs dpe skrun khang, 2005

Huang Ti, ed. (fl. twentieth century)
Tibetan Painted Scrolls
Bod kyi thang kha
Beijing: Rig dngos dpe skrun khang, 1985

Hūṃkārajaya (dates uncertain)
White Lotus Bouquet of Investigation/ Bouquet of White Lotuses of Eloquence

dPyad don pad dkar chun po/ Legs par bshad pa'i padma dkar po chun po
Gangtok: Sherab Gyaltsen Lama, 1981

Jamgon Kongtrul ('Jam mgon kong sprul, 1813–1899)
Clear Interlinear Commentary on the Treatise Distinguishing Consciousness and Pristine Cognition entitled Ornament of the Enlightened Intention of Rangjung [Dorje]
rNam shes ye shes 'byed pa'i bstan bcos kyi tshig don go gsal du 'grel pa rang byung dgongs pa'i rgyan
In bKa' brgyud pa'i gsung rab, 16:331–385. Qinghai mi rigs dpe skrun khang, 2003

Infinite Ocean of Knowledge
Shes bya mtha' yas pa'i rgya mtsho
Prose auto-commentary on the *Treasury of Knowledge*, contained in the same volumes

Treasury of Knowledge
Shes bya kun khyab mdzod
Root verses contained in three-volume publication. Beijing: Mi rigs dpe skrun khang, 1982; Boudhnath: Padma Karpo Translation Committee edition, 2000 (photographic reproduction of the original four-volume Palpung xylograph, 1844)
Translated, along with the auto-commentary, by the Kalu Rinpoche Translation Group in *The Treasury of Knowledge* series (Ithaca, NY: Snow Lion Publications, 1995 to present); mentioned here are Kalu Rinpoche Translation Group 1995 (Book 1) and 1998 (Book 5); Ngawang Zangpo 2010 (Books 2, 3, and 4); Callahan 2007 (Book 6, Part 3); and Guarisco and McLeod 2005 (Book 6, Part 4) and 2008 (Book 8, Part 3).

Jamgon Mipham Gyatso ('Jam mgon mi pham rgya mtsho, 1846–1912)
Bilingual Concordance entitled Radiant Jewel Mirror
sKad gnyis shan sbyar rab gsal nor bu'i me long
In Collected Works of Mipham Gyatso, vol. 4 (Nga), pp. 69-770. Gangs can rig gzhung dpe rnying myur skyob lhan tshogs. Chengdu, 2007.

Collected Works of Jamgon Mipham
Mi pham gsung 'bum
Lhasa: Potala Library imprint, 20 vols. Also Paro: Lama Ngodrup and Sherab Drimey, 1984–1993 (27 vols.); Chengdu: Gangs can rig gzhung dpe rnying myur skyobs lhan tshogs, 2007 (32 vols.); Gangtok: Sonam Topgyay Kazi, 1972 (15 vols.)

Cornucopia of Practical Tecnhiques Pertaining to the Arts
bZo gnas nyer mkho'i za ma tog
In Collected Works of Jamgon Mipham, vol. 1 (Ka). 34 folios
Also Ziling: Qinghai mi rigs dpe skrun khang, 1993

Gateway to Knowledge
mKhas pa'i tshul la 'jug pa'i sgo
In Collected Works of Jamgon Mipham, vol. 6 (Cha). 116 folios
Also Ziling: Qinghai mi rigs dpe skrun khang, 1988, 1992. Translated in Erik Pema Kunsang 1997–2002

Radiant Sunlight of Iconometry
sKu gzugs kyi thig rtsa rab gsal nyi ma
In Collected Works of Jamgon Mipham, vol. 1 (Ka). 35 folios

Treatise on the Arts of Love: A Treasure That Delights the Whole World
'Dod pa'i bstan bcos 'jig rten kun tu dga' ba'i gter
In Collected Works of Jamgon Mipham, vol. 4 (Nga). 33 folios

Jampa Trinle, senior ed. (Byams pa phrin las, b. 1928)
Great Compendium of Tibetan Astrological Science
Bod kyi rtsis rig kun 'dus chen mo
5 vols. Chengdu: Sichuan mi rigs dpe skrun khang, 1998

Jamyang Drakpa ('Jam dbyangs grags pa, fl. late twentieth–early twenty-first century)
Recorded and Roughly Transcribed Guidance based on the Supreme Scholar Tseten Zhabdrung's Summary of the Mirror of Poetics, entitled Oral Transmissions of Our Ancestors
mKhas dbang tshe brtan zhabs drung mchog gi snyan ngag spyi don dpe khrid ba sgrar phab pa che long tsam yi ger bkod pa mes po'i zhal lung
Ziling: Qinghai mi rigs dpe skrun khang, 2001

Jamyang Gyatso ('Jam dbyangs rgya mtsho, dates uncertain)
Explanation of Elision of Anubandhas
rJes 'brel sogs dbyi tshul bshad pa
In Kelzang Ngawang Damcho, ed., *Extensive Exegesis of the Sārasvata Grammar*, pp. 619–627

Jamyang Loter Wangpo ('Jam dbyangs blo gter dbang po, 1847–1914)
Compendium of All the Tantras
rGyud sde kun btus
Delhi: N. Lungtok and N. Gyaltsen, 1971–1972 (30 vols.); Kathmandu: Sachen International, Guru Lama, 2004 (32 vols.)

Jangkya Rolpei Dorje (lCang skya rol pa'i rdo rje, 1717–1786)
Exegesis of Philosophical Systems entitled Beautiful Ornament of the Mound of the Buddhist Teachings
Grub mtha' bshad pa thub bstan lhun po'i mdzes rgyan
Beijing: Krung go bod kyi shes rig dpe skrun khang, 1989

Jatson Nyingpo ('Ja' tshon snying po, 1585–1656)
Exegesis on Maintenance of the Supreme Sacraments Revered in the Great Vehicle of the Way of Secret Mantra
gSang sngags theg pa chen po'i bsten par bya ba'i dam rdzas mchog ji ltar bcang ba'i rnam bshad rnal 'byor pa'i dga' ston
In Tashi Gyatso et al., *Treatises on the Accoutrements and Music of the Ancient Way of Secret [Mantras]*, pp. 212–216

Jigme Chokyi Dorje ('Jigs med chos kyi rdo rje, fl. late twentieth–early twenty-first century)
Great Anthology of Buddhist Icons according to the Tibetan Lineages
Bod brgyud nang bstan lha tshogs chen mo
Ziling: Qinghai mi rigs dpe skrun khang, 2001

Karma Chopel, ed. (Karma chos 'phel, fl. late twentieth century)
Illustrations of Nectar-like Materia Medica
bDud rtsi sman gyi 'khrungs dpe legs bshad nor bu'i phreng ba
Lhasa: Bod ljongs mi dmangs dpe skrung khang, 1993

Karma Lhagsam (Karma lhag bsam, fl. ninteenth century)
Summary of the Precious Source of Prosody entitled Light That Benefits All
sDeb sbyor rin chen 'byung gnas kyi bsdus 'grel kun phan snang ba
In bKa' brgyud pa'i gsung rab, 1:637

Karmapa III Rangjung Dorje (Karmapa rang byung rdo rje, 1284–1339)
Profound Inner Meaning
Zab mo nang don
Root text and auto-commentary in *bKa' brgyud pa'i gsung rab*, 20:1–322

Treatise Distinguishing Consciousness and Pristine Cognition
rNam shes ye shes 'byed pa'i bstan bcos
In *bKa' brgyud pa'i gsung rab*, 16:323–329
English translation in Brunnhölzl 2009

Karma Trinlepa (Karma phrin las pa, 1456–1539)
Commentary on the Profound Inner Meaning
Zab mo nang don gyi rnam bshad snying po gsal bar byed pa'i nyin byed 'od kyi phreng ba
In Collected Works of Rangjung Dorje, vol. 14 (Tram), pp. 1–533. Tsurphu Khenpo Loyag Tashi. Ziling, 2006.

Replies to Doctrinal Questions: Dispelling Mental Darkness
Dris lan yid kyi mun sel
In *Spiritual Songs and Replies to Doctrinal Questions* (*mGur dang dris lan*). Delhi: Ngawang Topgyay, 1975

Karma Trinlepa II (Karma phrin las pa gnyis pa, a.k.a Ngawang Chokyi Gyatso, fl. fifteenth–sixteenth century)
Chariot of Enlightened Activity
Karma shing rta
The Collected Works of Karma Trinle II, 2 vols., n.d., n.p. Published separately and incomplete

Ornaments of Speech: Well-known Ornamental Proverbs based on the Mirror of Poetics
Tshig rgyan snyan ngag gi bstan bcos me long rgyan gyi dper brjod bklags pas kun shes
Dated 1543; contained in the *Chariot of Enlightened Activity*

Karma Tsewang Pelbar (Karma tshe dbang dpal 'bar, fl. eighteenth century)
Exegetical Commentary on the Mirror of Poetics entitled Novel Sugar Cane Plant
bsTan bcos snyan ngag me long gi 'grel bshad sngon med bu ram shing gi ljon pa
Chengdu: Sichuan mi rigs dpe skrun khang, 1994

Kelzang Ngawang Damcho, ed. (sKal bzang ngag dbang dam chos, late twentieth–early twenty-first century)
Extensive Exegesis of the Sārasvata Grammar
dByangs can sgra mdo'i rgyas bshad
Gangs can rig brgya'i 'byed lde mig series, vol. 29. Beijing: Mi rigs dpe skrun khang, 2001

Khagang Tashi Tsering, ed. (Kha sgang bkra shis tshe ring, b. 1956)
Studies on Ancient Tibetan Writing and Orthography
Bod kyi yig rnying zhib 'jug
Beijing: Mi rigs dpe skrun khang, 2003

Khedrub[je] Gelek Pelzangpo (mKhas grub rje dge legs dpal bzang po, 1385–1438)
Ornament of the Seven Treatises Clearing Mental Obscurity
Tshad ma sde bdun gyi rgyan yid kyi mun sel
In Collected Works of Khedrub Gelek Pelzangpo, vol. 10. Lhasa: Zhol xylograph, 1897; New Delhi: Guru Deva, 1982

Khepa Tobden Rabjampa (mKhas pa stobs ldan rab byams pa, b. 1813)
Memorandum on the Mirror of Poetics entitled Prayer of Recollection
sNyan ngag me long gi zin tho dran pa'i gsal 'debs
Ziling: Qinghai mi rigs dpe skrun khang, 1995

Khewang Yeshe Gyatso (mKhas dbang ye shes rgya mtsho, fl. sixteenth–seventeenth centuries)
Exegetical Memorandum on the Ascertainment of Great Madhyamaka according to the Most Extensive Teachings of the Supreme Vehicle
Theg mchog shin tu rgyas pa'i dbu ma chen po rnam par nges pa'i rnam bshad kyi zin bris
In Jo nang dpe tshogs, 10:55–399. Also listed among the Collected Works of Tāranātha, vol. 22 (Za), no. 1, in HJK, p. 72

Konchok Tendzin (dKon mchog bstan 'dzin, b. 1949)
The Collection of Thanglha Tsewang
Thang lha tshe dbang phyogs bris gces bsgrigs bzo rig mig rgyan
Chengdu: Sichuan mi rigs dpe skrun khang, 2006

The Fine Arts: A Drop of Water on a Hair-tip
bZo gnas skra rtse'i chu thigs
Beijing: Krung go'i bod kyi shes rig dpe skrun khang, 1994

Konchok Tenpei Dronme (dKon mchog bstan pa'i sgron me, 1762–1823)
Magic Key Opening a Hundred Doors of Logical Reasoning
Rigs lam sgo brgya 'byed pa'i 'phrul gyi lde mig
Lanzhou: Gansu mi rigs dpe skrun khang, 1997

Treatise on Dramaturgy entitled Play That Leads Along the Pure Pathway
Zlos gar gyi bstan bcos yang dag lam du bkri pa'i rol rtsed
In the Collected Works of Gungtang Konchok Tenpei Dronme, vol. 7 (Ja). 14 folios.
Lhasa: Zhol Parkhang xylograph, 1897

Konchok Tseten (dKon mchog tshe brtan)
The Obelisk Inscription of the Samye Edict, and Its Annotations
bSam yas bka' gtsigs rdo ring gi yi ge dang de'i mchan 'grel
In Khagang Tashi Tsering, ed., *Studies on Ancient Tibetan Writing and Orthography*, pp. 51–58

Konchok Tseten et al., eds.
Anthology of Poetical Proverbs
sNyan ngag dper brjod phyogs sgrigs
Lanzhou: Gansu mi rigs dpe skrun khang, 1984

Kozhul Drakpa Jungne (Ko zhul grags pa 'byung gnas, b. 1955) and Gyalwa Lobzang Khedrub (rGyal ba blo bzang mkhas grub), eds.
Lexicon of the Learned and Accomplished Masters Who Successively Appeared in the Land of Snows
Gangs can mkhas grub rim byon ming mdzod
Lanzhou: Gansu mi rigs dpe skrun khang, 1992

Kunzang Dorje (Kun bzang rdo rje, fl. late twentieth–early twenty-first century)
Illustrations of the Essential Physical Exercises for the Control of Energy Channels and Winds according to the Vital Attainment of the Awareness-holder
Zab chos rig 'dzin srog sgrub las rtsa rlung 'khrul 'khor lus gnad dpe'u ris
Gangtok: n.d.

Lamrim Ngawang Phuntsok (Lam rim ngag dbang phun tshogs, 1922–1997)
Commentary on the Exposition of Valid Cognition
Tshad ma rnam 'grel gyi ṭik-kā
Lhasa: Bod ljongs mi dmangs dpe skrun khang, 1997

Lhagpa Tsering (Lhag pa tshe ring, b. 1965)
Comparative Analysis of the Bon Tradition and the Religious Tradition of Exorcism among the Naxi
Bon lugs dang 'jang rigs gto pa'i chos lugs kyi khyad chos dpyad bsdur
Beijing: Mi rigs dpe skrun khang, 2003

Lobzang Norbu Shastri (Blo bzang nor bu, fl. late twentieth–early twenty-first century)
The Precious Source of Prosody
Chandoratnākara
Bibliotheca Indo-Tibetica Series 18. Sarnath: Central Institute of Higher Tibetan Studies, 1990
Edition of root-text, with auto-comentary in Tibetan and restored Sanskrit, along with Hindi translation

Lochen Dharmaśrī (Lo chen Dharmaśrī, 1654–1717)
Moonbeams: An Instruction on Elemental Divination
'Byung rtsis man ngag zla ba'i 'od zer
Smanrtsis Shesrig Spendzod series. Leh: Dondup Tashi, 1975
Translated in Dorje 2001

Ornament of the Enlightened Intention of the Lord of Secrets
gSang bdag dgongs rgyan
NK, vol. 76. Also in Dg.NGB, vol. Ta (9), ff. 31b–174b, and in the Collected Works of Lochen Dharmaśrī, Dehra Dun edition, vol. 8, ff. 90–337 (1999)

Sunlight Instructions on Astrology
rTsis kyi man ngag nyin mor byed pa'i snang ba
In Collected Works of Lochen Dharmaśrī, Dehra Dun edition, vol. 3, ff. 1–170 (1999)

Longchen Choying Tobden Dorje (Klong chen chos dbyings rdo rje, 1785–1848)
Precious Treasury of the Sūtras and Tantras
mDo rgyud rin po che'i mdzod
5 vols. Chengdu: Sichuan mi rigs dpe skrun khang, 2000

Longchen Rabjampa (Klong chen rab byams pa, 1308–1363)
White Lotus Auto-commentary, on the Precious Treasury of Wish-fulfilling Gems: A Treatise on the Pith Instructions of the Greater Vehicle
Theg pa chen po'i man ngag gi bstan bcos yid bzhin rin po che'i mdzod kyi 'grel pa padma dkar po
In the Seven Treasuries of Longchenpa (Klong chen mdzod bdun) (Beijing: dPal brtsegs bod yig dpe rnying zhib 'jug khang, 2009), vols. 118–119; also Potala edition, vol. 1 (312 ff.); Gangtok: Dodrupchen Rinpoche, n.d. (I–Tib–143); Chengdu: Adzom Chogar, 1999

Longdol Lama [Ngawang Lobzang] (Klong rdol bla ma, 1719–1794)
Collected Works of Longdol Lama
Klong rdol ngag dbang blo bzang gi gsung 'bum
2 vols. Gangs can rig mdzod series, vols. 20–21. Lhasa: Bod ljongs bod yig dpe rnying dpe skrun khang, 1991

Menpa Dawa (sMan pa zla ba, b. 1958)
Drawings of Tibetan Materia Medica, entitled Clear Mirror
Bod kyi gso rig sman ris gsal ba'i me long
Dharamsala: Tibetan Medical and Astro Institute, 1993

Minyag Butruk (Mi nyag bu phrug, 1930–1998)
Rules Concerning Difficult Points, Clarifying the Intention of Situ [Chokyi Jungne]
dKa' gnad sdom tshig si tu dgongs gsal
Beijing: Mi rigs dpe skrun khang, 2003

Mondro Paṇḍita [Wangyal Dorje] (sMon 'gro paṇḍita, fl. late sixteenth–early seventeenth century)
Answers to Questions concerning Astrology and Divination
sKar nag rtsis kyi dri len
Not located

Namkhai Norbu (Nam mkha'i nor bu, b. 1938)
Light of Kailash: Legends of Zhangzhung and Tibet
Zhang bod lo rgyus ti se'i 'od
Beijing: Krung go'i bod kyi shes rig dpe skrun khang, 1996
English translation of *Vol. One: The Early Period* by Donatella Rossi. Merigar: Shang Shung Publications, 2009

Narthang Lotsāwa [Gendunpel] (sNar thang lo tsā ba, fl. fourteenth century)
Method of Mantra Recitation
sNgags kyi bklag thabs
Lanzhou: Gansu mi rigs dpe skrun khang, 1995

Negi, J.S.
Tibetan Sanskrit Dictionary
Bod skad dang legs sbyar gyi tshig mdzod chen mo
16 vols. Sarnath: Central Institute of Higher Tibetan Studies, 1993–2005

Ngulchu Dharmabhadra (rNgul chu chos kyi bzang po, 1772–1851)
Treatise on Synonymics entitled Drop of Water in the Ocean
mNgon brjod kyi bstan bcos rgya mtsho'i chu thigs
Imprint from dNgul chu rdzong xylograph, preserved at Zhol Parkhang. Lhasa: 2000

Nordrang Orgyan (Nor brang o rgyan, b. 1933)
Compendium of Buddhist Numeric Terms
Chos rnam kun btus
3 vols. Beijing: Krung go'i bod rig pa dpe skrun khang, 2008

Nyagong Konchok Tseten et al., eds. (gNya' gong dkon mchog tshe brtan, b. 1946)
Commentary on the Precious Source of Prosody
sDeb sbyor rin chen 'byung gnas kyi 'grel ba
Edited with Khabum and Tsewang Namgyal. Beijing: Mi rigs dpe skrun khang, 2003

Paṇchen Sonam Drakpa (Paṇ chen bsod nams grags pa, 1478–1554)
Commentary on Difficult Points in the Exposition of Valid Cognition entitled Complete Revelation of Enlightened Intention
rGyas pa'i bstan bcos tshad ma rnam 'grel gyi dka' 'grel dgongs pa rab gsal
Beijing: Krung go'i bod kyi shes rig dpe skrun khang, 1998. Also Mundgod: Loling Printing Press, 1989

Paṇchen VIII Tenpei Wangchuk (Paṇ chen bstan pa'i dbang phyug, 1855–1882)
Joyous Music: Mind Treasury of Proverbs
dPer brjod blo gter [tshangs sras] dgyes pa'i rol mo
New Delhi: Chopel Lekden, 1972

Paldu (dPal bsdus, b. 1966)
Exegesis on Tibetan Writing and Calligraphy, entitled Lion's Roar
Bod kyi yi ge'i rnam bshad seng ge'i nga ro
Chengdu: Sichuan mi rigs dpe skrun khang, 2004

Pari Sangye (dPa' ris sangs rgyas, b. 1931)
Elucidation of the Four Grammatical Formations
brDa sprod sbyor ba rnam bzhi rab gsal
Beijing: Mi rigs dpe skrun khang, 2008

The Writing of Tibetan: Wishing All to See
Bod yig 'bri tshul mthong ba kun smon
Ziling: Qinghai mi rigs dpe skrun khang, 1997

Pawo Tsuklak Trengwa (dPa' bo gtsug lag phreng ba, 1504–1566)
Scholar's Feast of Doctrinal History
Chos 'byung mkhas pa'i dga' ston
Beijing: Mi rigs dpe skrun khang, 1986 (2 vols.), 2006 (1 vol.)
See Martin 1997, no. 168

Phugpa Lhundrub Gyatso (Phug pa lhun grub rgya mtsho, fl. fifteenth century)
Extensive Commentary on the Glorious Svarodaya, King of Tantras, Esteeming Martial Conquest, entitled Melody That Utterly Delights the Ford of Eloquence
dPal gYul las rnam par rgyal ba gces pa'i rgyud kyi rgyal po dbyangs 'char ba'i rgya cher 'grel ba legs bshad 'jug ngogs mchogs tu dga' ba'i sgra dbyangs
In Jampa Trinle, ed., *Great Compendium of Tibetan Astrological Science*, vol. 3, pp. 5–485

Rigdzin Jigme Lingpa (Rig 'dzin 'jigs med gling pa, 1730–1798)
Illustrations of Torma Offerings According to the Innermost Spirituality of Longchenpa
Klong chen snying thig gi gtor ma'i dpe'u ris
Delhi: Sangye Dorji, n.d.

Rigdzin Tsewang Norbu (Rig 'dzin tshe dbang nor bu, 1697–1755)
Collected Works of Rigdzin Tsewang Norbu of Katok
Kaḥ thog rig 'dzin tshe dbang nor bu'i bka' 'bum
3 vols. Beijing: Krung go'i bod rig pa dpe skrun khang, 2006

Rinchen Namgyal (Rin chen rnam rgyal) and Guru Dhottsha (Gu ru dho tstsha)
The Life and Songs of Lord Tilopā, with a Brief Biography of Naropā
rJe btsun ti lo pa'i rnam mgur dang dpal na ro pa'i rnam thar bsdus pa
Ziling: Qinghai mi rigs dpe skrun khang, 1992

Rinpung Ngawang Jigdrak (Rin spungs ngag dbang 'jigs grags, 1482/1542–1595)
Treatise on Synonymics: Ornament of the Ears of the Learned
mNgon brjod kyi bstan bcos mkhas pa'i rna rgyan
Beijing: Mi rigs dpe skrun khang, 1985

Rongpo (Rong po, fl. late eleventh–twelfth century)
Precious Chest Clarifying Calligraphic Proportions
Yi ge'i thig ris gsal ba'i rin chen sgrom bu
Not located

Supplement
Lhan thabs
Not located

Rongta Lobzang Damcho Gyatso (Rong rta blo bzang dam chos rgya mtsho, 1863–1917)
Clear Explanation of Many Practical Iconometric Techniques entitled Beautiful Face Ornament of the Fine Arts
Thig gi lag len du ma gsal bar bshad pa bzo rig mdzes pa'i kha rgyan
In Collected Works from Ranyak Gonpa, vol. 2. 83 folios. Lhasa: Potala Archives, republished in 1980s

Sakya Paṇchen [Kunga Gyaltsen] (Sa skya paṇ chen kun dga' rgyal mtshan, 1182–1251)
Gateway to Knowledge
mKhas 'jug
In *Sa paṇ mkhas 'jug rtsa 'grel*, pp. 1–46. Chengdu: Sichuan mi rigs dpe skrun khang, 1998
Analyzed in Gold 2008

Variegated Flower Bouquet of Prosody
sDeb sbyor sna tshogs me tog chun po
In *Sa paṇ kun dga' rgyal mtshan gyi gsung 'bum*, 1:410–647. Gangs can rig mdzod series, 23. Lhasa: Bod ljongs yig dpe rnying dpe skrung khang, 1992

Sangye Gyatso (sDe srid sangs rgyas rgya mtsho, 1653–1705)
Blue Beryl [Treatise on Medicine, Clarifying the Four Tantras Which Are the Enlightened Intention of Bhaiṣajyaguru]
[gSo ba rig pa'i bstan bcos sman bla'i dgongs rgyan rgyud bzhi'i gsal byed] baiḍūrya sngon po['i mallika]
2 vols. Lhasa: Bod ljongs mi dmangs dpe skrun khang, 1982
Illustrated extracts translated in Parfionovitch, Dorje, and Meyer 1992

Survey of Medicine
sMan gyi khog 'bubs
Bod kyi gso ba rig pa'i gna' dpe phyogs bsgrigs dpe tshogs series, 8. Beijing: Mi rigs dpe skrun khang, 2004
Translated in Kilty 2010

Sangye Lingpa, disc. (Sangs rgyas gling pa, 1340–1396)
Explanation of the Vajra and Bell, in accordance with the Tantras, Transmissions, and Empowerments
rDo rje dril bu'i bshad pa rgyud lung dbang bzhag
In Tashi Gyatso et al., *Treatises on the Accoutrements and Music of the Ancient Way of Secret [Mantras]*, pp. 257–280

Spiritual Attainment associated with the Skull: A Storehouse of Wish-fulfilling Gems
Thod sgrub yid bzhin bang mdzod
In Tashi Gyatso et al., *Treatises on the Accoutrements and Music of the Ancient Way of Secret [Mantras]*, pp. 311–316

Situ Chokyi Jungne (Si tu chos kyi 'byung gnas, 1700–1774)
Collected Works of Situ Chokyi Jungne
Si tu chos kyi 'byung gnas kyi gsung 'bum
14 vols. Sansal, Kangra: Sungrab Nyamso Khang, 1990

Compendium of Spiritual Accomplishment based on Glorious Mahākāla, the King of Tantras
dPal nag po chen po'i rgyud kyi rgyal po dngos grub kun las btus pa
In Collected Works of Situ Chokyi Jungne, vol. 7 (Ja), no. 2. 17 pages

Concordance of Terminology based on the Mirror of Poetics
sNyan ngag me long gi skad gnyis shan sbyar
In Collected Works of Situ Chokyi Jungne, vol. 6 (Cha), no. 4. 52 pages

Great Commentary on the Thirty Verses and Introduction to Gender entitled Beautiful Pearl Garland, a Neck Ornament of the Learned
Sum rtags 'grel chen mkhas pa'i mgul rgyan mu tig phreng mdzes
In Collected Works of Situ Chokyi Jungne, vol. 6 (Cha), no. 3. 86 pages

Inventory to the Likeness of the Intangible Stūpa of Paramādya, entitled Wish-fulfilling Rain of Good Auspices
dPal mchog reg pa med pa'i mchod rten gyi snang brnyan dge legs 'dod gu'i char bebs kyi dkar chags utpala'i phreng ba
In Collected Works of Situ Chokyi Jungne, vol. 13 (Pa), no. 3. 7 pages

Legend of the Great Stūpa of Svayambhū in Nepal
Bal yul rang byung mchod rten chen po'i lo rgyus
In Collected Works of Situ Chokyi Jungne, vol. 7 (Ja), no. 5. 15 pages

Light Rays/ Ocean of Eloquent Speech: A Commentary on the Sārasvata Grammar
mTsho ldan ma'i brda sprod gzung gi 'grel pa legs bshad ngag gi 'od zer/ Legs bzhad ngag gi rol tsho
Delhi: Konchok Lhadepa, 1993
See Verhagen 2001

[*Treatise on Sanskrit Grammar, explained according to the Grammar of Candragomin,*] *entitled Ship Transporting Precious Gems* [*of Eloquence*] *Launching onto the Ocean of the Grammatical Textual Tradition*
[Legs par sbyar pa'i sgra'i bstan bcos tsandra pa'i rnam bshad] brda sprod zhung lugs rgya mtshor 'jug cing legs bshad rin chen 'dren pa'i gru gzings
In Collected Works of Situ Chokyi Jungne, vol. 1 (Ka), no. 5. 215 pages

Sonam Kyi, ed. (bSod nams skyid)
An Inventory of Tibetan Obelisk Inscriptions and Bells
Bod kyi rdo ring yi ge dang dril bu'i kha byang
Beijing: Mi rigs dpe skrun khang, 1984

Sonam Tsemo (bSod nams rtse mo, 1142–1182)
Elementary Guide to Pronunciation
Yi ge'i klag thabs byis pa bde blag tu 'jug pa
In Sa skya'i gsung 'bum, vol. 4, pp. 800–809. Lanzhou: Gansu mi rigs dpe skrun khang, in collaboration with Qinghai mi rigs dpe skrun khang, 1994. Compiled by Dorje Rinchen and Norbu Kunga

Songtsen Gampo (Srong btsan sgam po, r. 618–641) (Tibetan attribution)
Pillar Testament
bKa' chems [ka khol ma]
Lanzhou: Gansu mi rigs dpe skrun khang, 1991
Martin 1997, no. 4

Taktsang Lotsāwa [Sherab Rinchen] (sTag tshang lo tsā ba, b. 1405)
Treatise on the Attainment Free from Extremes, Having Known All Philosophical Systems, entitled Ocean of Eloquent Exegesis
sGrub mtha' kun shes nas mtha' bral grub pa zhes bya ba'i bstan bcos rnam par bshad pa legs bshad kyi rgya mtsho
In dPal ldan sa skya'i gsung rab, 10:27–243

Tang Chi An and Yangchen Lhamo [Yangqing Lamu], eds.
Dictionary of Tibetan and Chinese Astrological Terms
Bod rgya skar rtsis rig pa'i tshigs mdzod
Chengdu: Sichuan mi rigs dpe skrun khang, 1985

Tāranātha, Jestun (rJe btsun tā ra nā tha, 1575–1634)
Ascertainment of Great Madhyamaka according to the Most Extensive Teachings of the Supreme Vehicle
Theg mchog shin tu rgyas pa'i dbu ma chen po rnam par nges pa
In the Collected Works of Tāranātha, vol. 18 (Tsha), no. 3. HJK, p. 62. Also in Jo nang dpe tshogs, 10:3-53

History of Buddhism in India [entitled Source of All That Is Desired]
Dam pa'i chos rin po che 'phags pa'i yul du ji ltar dar ba'i tshul gsal bar ston pa dgos 'dod kun 'byung
In the Collected Works of Tāranātha, vol. 16 (Ma), no. 4. HJK, pp. 59–60
Translated in Chimpa and Chattopadhyaya 1970. See also Martin 1997, no. 200

Hundred Sādhanas of Precious Origin: [Means for Attainment of Oceans of Meditational Deities]
[Yi dam rgya mtsho'i sgrub thabs] rin 'byung rgya rtsa
2 vols. Delhi: Chophel Legdan, 1974–1975; Dzamtang Gon: 1999. Also in the Collected Works of Tāranātha, vol. 15 (Ba), nos. 1–2. HJK, p. 59
Expanded by Paṇchen VI Tenpei Nyima in his *Precious Origin: Means for Attainment of Hundreds of Meditational Deities* (*Yi dam rgya mtsho'i sgrub thab rin chen 'byung gnas*). Potala Tashilhunpo xylograph edition, vols. 3–4. Translated in Willson and Brauen 2000, pp. 231–378

Tashi Chopel (bKra shis chos 'phel, fl. ninteenth century)
Record of Teachings Received by Jamgon Kongtrul Yonten Gyatso Damcho Rinpoche: A Storehouse of Jewels Yielding All Desires, Citing his Studies of the Sūtras, Tantras, and Classical Sciences, and the Derivative Writings
'Jam mgon kong sprul yon tan rgya mtshos dam pa'i chos rin po che mdo sngags rig gnas dang bcas pa ji ltar thos shing de dag gang las brgyud pa'i yi ge dgos 'dod kun 'byung nor bu'i bang mdzod
Beijing: Mi rigs dpe skrun khang, 2009

Tashi Gyatso (bKra shis rgya mtsho, dates uncertain)
Exegesis of the Resources, Implements, and Musical Instruments Pertaining to the Ocean of Awareness-holders of the Indestructible Vehicle according to the Ancient Translation School, entitled Ornamental Flower of Mantrins
sNga 'gyur rdo rje theg pa rig 'dzin rgya mtsho'i long spyod chas gos rgyan dang rol mo rnam bshad sngags 'chang rgyan gyi me tog
In Tashi Gyatso et al., *Treatises on the Accoutrements and Music of the Ancient Way of Secret [Mantras]*, pp. 3–170

Tashi Gyatso et al.
Treatises on the Accoutrements and Music of the Ancient Way of Secret [Mantras]
gSang rnying rgyan chas dang rol mo'i bstan bcos
Gangs chen rigs mdzod series, 30. Lhasa: 1996

Thubten Nyima (Thub bstan nyi ma, b. 1943)
An Outline of the Treasury of Knowledge
Shes bya kun khyab kyi sa bcad
Chengdu: Sichuan mi rigs dpe skrun khang, 1990

Thubten Phuntsok, ed. (Thub bstan phun tshogs, b. 1955)
Physical Exercises of the Energy Channels and Winds
rTsa rlung 'phrul 'khor
Chengdu: Sichuan mi rigs dpe skrun khang, 1995

Tibetan Language Teaching and Research Unit, Zhigatse Teacher Training College
Compilation of Commentaries on Synonymics, entitled Sound of the Conch That Recalls Eloquence
mNgon brjod kyi 'grel pa btus bsgrigs legs bshad 'dren pa'i dung sgra
Beijing: Mi rigs dpe skrun khang, 1991

Tokden Rabjam Lobzang Dargye (rTogs ldan rab byams blo bzang dar rgyas, dates uncertain)
Inspection of Skulls entitled Jewel Garland
Thod brtag nor bu'i phreng ba
In Tashi Gyatso et al., *Treatises on the Accoutrements and Music of the Ancient Way of Secret [Mantras]*, pp. 301–310

Trengkheb Palden Zangpo (Phreng kheb dpal ldan bzang po, fl. sixteenth century)
Treatise on the Fine Arts entitled Clear Mirror of the Sūtras and Tantras
bZo rig pa'i bstan bcos mdo rgyud gsal ba'i me long
Dharamsala: Tibetan Cultural Printing Press, 1978

Troru Tsenam (Khro ru tshe rnam, 1928–2005)
Anthology of Sanskrit Grammatical Texts
sGra gzhung phyogs bsgrigs
Beijing: Mi rigs dpe skrun khang, 1995

Commentary on the Grammar of Sārasvata: A Slight Clarification
brDa sprod pa dbyangs can gyi mdo'i 'grel pa nyung ngu rnam gsal
Beijing: Krung go bod kyi shes rig dpe skrun khang, in collaboration with Qinghai Xinhua Bookstore, 1998

Moonbeams Commentary on the Grammar of Candragomin
brDa sprod pa tsandra pa'i mdo 'grel pa zla ba'i 'od zer
2 vols. Beijing: Krung go bod kyi shes rig dpe skrun khang, in collaboration with Qinghai Xinhua Bookstore, 2003

Tseten Zhabdrung [Jigme Rigpei Lodro] (Tshe brtan zhabs drung, 1910–1985)
Commentary on Rañjanā Calligraphy
Lañja'i thig 'grel
Ziling: Qinghai mi rigs dpe skrun khang, 1984

Examples of Vartula Calligraphy
Vartu'i ma phyi
Ziling: Qinghai mi rigs dpe skrun khang, 1981

Summary of the Mirror of Poetics entitled Dawning of Awareness Imbued with Meaning
sNyan ngag me long gi spyi don sdeb legs rig pa'i 'char sgo
Lanzhou: Gansu mi rigs dpe skrun khang, 1994

Tsongkhapa [Lobzang Drakpa] (Tsong kha pa blo bzang grags pa, 1357–1419)
Gateway to the Seven Sections on Logic Clearing the Obscuration of Aspirants
sDe bdun la 'jug pa'i sgo don gnyer yid kyi mun sel
Varanasi: Pleasure of Elegant Sayings Press, 1972

Memorandum concerning the Cycle of the Four Hundred and Fifty Verse Commentary
bZhi brgya lnga bcu pa'i skor gyi zin bris
In Collected Works of Tsongkhapa, vol. 7 (Ja). 6 folios. Lhasa: Zhol Parkhang edition, 1897

Yeshe Sherab (Ye shes shes rab, b. 1927)
Iconometric Drawings and Illustrations Based on the Fine Arts, entitled A Drop of Minium
Rig pa bzo yi 'byung ba thig ris dpe dang bcas pa li khri'i thigs pa
Lhasa: Bod ljongs mi dmangs dpe skrun khang, 2000

Yonten Tsering (Yon tan tshe ring, fl. late twentieth–early twenty-first century)
The Supreme Arts: Seeing All Perspectives
bZo mchog ltad mo kun mthong
Chengdu: Sichuan mi rigs dpe skrun khang, 2000

Zhang Yisun et al., eds.
The Great Tibetan-Chinese Dictionary
Bod rgya tshig mdzod chen mo
3 vols., subsequently reprinted in 2 vols. and 1 vol. Beijing: Mi rigs dpe skrun khang, 1985
Vol. 1 translated in Nyima and Dorje 2001

Zhechen Gyaltsab [Gyurme Pema Namgyal] (Zhe chen rgyal tshab, 1871–1926)
Brief Comments on the Origins of the Eight Chariots of the Lineage of Spiritual Attainment, Headed by the Ancient Translation School, entitled White Lotus Pool of Eloquence
sNga 'gyur rdo rje theg pa gtso bor gyur pa'i sgrub brgyud shing rta brgyad kyi byung ba brjod pa'i gtan mdor bsdus legs bshad padma dkar po'i rdzing bu
Chengdu: Sichuan mi rigs dpe skrun khang, 1994
See also Martin 1997, no. 425.

5. Works in Other Languages

Abhyankar, Kashinath Vasudev. 1961. *A Dictionary of Sanskrit Grammar*. GOS 134. Baroda: Oriental Institute.

Anacker, Stefan. 1984. *Seven Works of Vasubandhu*. Delhi: Motilal Banarsidass.

Apte, V.S. 1965. *The Practical Sanskrit-English Dictionary*. 3rd edition. Delhi: Molilal Banarsidass.

Aris, Michael. 1979. *Bhutan: The Early History of a Himalayan Kingdom*. Warminster: Aris and Phillips.

Aris, Michael and Aung San Suu Kyi, eds. 1980. *Tibetan Studies in Honour of Hugh Richardson*. Warminster: Aris and Phillips.

Aziz, Barbara Minri and Matthew Kapstein, eds. 1985. *Soundings in Tibetan Civilization*. New Delhi: Manohar.

Banerjee, Anukul Chandra, ed. 1939. *Kāvyādarśa*. Calcutta: University of Calcutta.

Banerjee, Biswanath, ed. 1985. *Śrī Kālacakratantra-rāja*. Calcutta: The Asiatic Society.
Barron, Richard, trans. 2001a. *The Precious Treasury of the Basic Space of Phenomena*. By Longchen Rabjam. Junction City, CA: Padma Publishing.
———, trans. 2001b. *A Treasure Trove of Scriptural Transmission*. By Longchen Rabjam. Junction City, CA: Padma Publishing.
———, trans. 2003. *The Autobiography of Jamgön Kongtrul: A Gem of Many Colors*. Tsadra Foundation Series. Ithaca, NY: Snow Lion Publications.
———, trans. 2007. *The Precious Treasury of Philosophical Systems*. By Longchen Rabjam. Junction City, CA: Padma Publishing.
Basham, A.L. 1951. *History and Doctrine of the Ājīvakas*. London: Luzac.
———. 1959. *The Wonder That Was India*. New York: Grove Press.
Batchelor, Stephen. 1979. *Guide to the Bodhisattva's Way of Life*. Dharamsala: LTWA.
———. 2000. *Verses from the Center: A Buddhist Vision of the Sublime*. New York: Riverhead Books.
Baumer, Christoph. 2002. *Bon: Tibet's Ancient Religion*. Bangkok: Orchid Press. Translated from the German by Michael Kohn.
Bays, Gwendolyn, trans. 1983. *The Voice of the Buddha*. 2 vols. Emeryville, CA: Dharma Publishing.
Beer, Robert. 2003. *The Handbook of Tibetan Buddhist Symbols*. Chicago: Serindia Publications.
Beyer, Stephan V. 1973. *The Cult of Tārā*. Berkeley: University of California Press.
———. 1992. *The Classical Tibetan Language*. Albany: State University of New York Press.
Bhattacharya, Syamapada. 2005. *An Evolution of the Topics of Sanskrit Dramaturgy*. Kolkata: Sanskrit Book Depot.
Bist, B.S. 2001. *Cāṇakyanītidarpaṇaḥ*. Delhi: Chaukhambha Sanskrit Pratisthan.
Black, Deborah, trans. 1997. *Leaves of the Heaven Tree*. Emeryville, CA: Dharma Publishing.
Blondeau, Anne-Marie. 1972. *Matériaux pour l'étude de l'hippologie et de l'hippiatrie tibétaines*. Geneva: Librairie Droz.
Blumenthal, James. 2004. *The Ornament of the Middle Way: A Study of the Madhyamaka Thought of Śāntarakṣita*. Ithaca, NY: Snow Lion Publications.
Bodhi, Bhikkhu, trans. 1978. *The Discourse on the All-Embracing Net of Views*. Kandy: Buddhist Publication Society.
———, trans. 2000. *Abhidhammatthasangaha: A Comprehensive Manual of Abhidhamma*. Onalaska: BPS Pariyatti Editions.
Böhtlingk, Otto von. 1887. *Pāṇini's Grammatik mit Übersetzung*. Leipzig: H. Haessel.
Boin-Webb, Sara, trans. 2001. *Abhidharmasamuccaya: The Compendium of the Higher Teaching (Philosophy) by Asanga* by Walpola Rahula. Fremont, CA: Asian Humanities Press.
Boord, Martin J. 2002. *A Bolt of Lightning from the Blue*. Berlin: edition khordong.
Boyd, Palmer, trans. 1872. *Nāgānanda, or, the Joy of the Snake World: A Buddhist Drama in Five Acts*. London: Trübner. Also available as *Nagananda* by Harsha. Sanskrit Drama Series. Cambridge, Ontario: In parentheses Publications, 1999.
Brauen, Martin. 1997. *The Maṇḍala: Sacred Circle in Tibetan Buddhism*. Boston: Shambhala. Translated from the German by Martin Willson.
Brunnhölzl, Karl, trans. 2007. *In Praise of Dharmadhātu*. Ithaca, NY: Snow Lion Publications.
———, trans. 2009. *Luminous Heart: The Third Karmapa on Consciousness, Wisdom, and Buddha Nature*. Ithaca, NY: Snow Lion Publications.
Bryant, Barry. 1992. *The Wheel of Time Sand Mandala*. San Francisco: HarperSanFrancisco.
Burton, Richard and F.F. Arbuthnot, trans. 1883. *Kāmasūtra*. Privately published.
Callahan, Elizabeth, trans. 2007. *The Treasury of Knowledge: Book Six, Part Three: Frameworks of Buddhist Philosophy*. By Jamgön Kongtrul. Ithaca, NY: Snow Lion Publications.

Cantwell, C and R. Mayer. 2007. *The Kīlaya Nirvāṇa Tantra and the Vajra Wrath Tantra: Two Texts from the Ancient Tantra Collection.* Vienna: Osterreichische Akademie der Wissenschaften.

Canzio, Ricardo. 1980. "On the way of playing the drums and cymbals among the Sakyas." In Aris and Aung San Suu Kyi 1980, 67–72.

———. n.d. Translation of Sakya Paṇḍita's *Treatise on Music.* Unpublished.

Cardona, George. (1976) 1988. *Pāṇini: A Survey of Research.* The Hague: Mouton. Reprint, Delhi: Motilal Banarsidass.

Chakravarti, Pulinbihari. 1975. *Origin and Development of the Samkhya System of Thought.* Delhi: Munshiram Manoharlal.

Chandra, Lokesh. 1990. *Tibetan-Sanskrit Dictionary* (compact edition). Kyoto: Rinsen Book Co.

Chandra, Lokesh and David L. Snellgrove. 1981. *Sarvatathāgata-tattva-saṃgraha: Facsimile Reproduction of a Tenth Century Sanskrit Manuscript from Nepal.* New Delhi: Sharada Rani.

Chandra, Lokesh, with Tachikawa and Watanabe. 2006. *The Ngor Maṇḍala Collection.* Nagoya: Mandala Institute.

Chatterjee, A.K. 1971. *Readings on Yogacara Buddhism.* Varanasi: BHU Centre of Advanced Study in Philosophy.

Chattopadhyaya, Debiprasad, ed. 1994. *Cārvāka/Lokāyata: An Anthology of Source Materials and Some Recent Studies.* New Delhi: Indian Council of Philosophical Research, 1990 (1994)

Chaturvedi, M. 2009. *Bhartṛhari: Language, Thought and Reality.* Delhi: Motilal Banarsidass.

Chimpa, Lama and Alaka Chattopadhyaya, trans. 1970. *Tāranātha's History of Buddhism in India.* Simla/ Delhi: Motilal Banarsidass.

Chogay Trichen, Thubten Legshay Gyatsho. 1979. *Gateway to the Temple: Manual of Tibetan Monastic Customs, Art, Building and Celebrations.* English translation by David Paul Jackson. Kathmandu: Ratna Pustak Bhandar.

Clark, Barry, trans. 1995. *The Quintessence Tantras of Tibetan Medicine.* Ithaca, NY: Snow Lion Publications.

Cleary, Thomas. 1984. *The Flower Ornament Scripture.* Boston and London: Shambhala.

Collins, Steven. 1982. *Selfless Persons: Imagery and Thought in Theravāda Buddhism.* Cambridge and New York: Cambridge University Press.

Conze, Edward, trans. 1954. *Abhisamayālaṅkāra.* Serie Orientale Roma 6. Rome: Istituto Italiano per il Medio ed Estremo Oriente.

———, trans. 1973. *The Perfection of Wisdom in Eight Thousand Lines and Its Verse Summary.* Bolinas, CA: Four Seasons Foundation.

———, trans. 1975. *The Large Sutra on Perfect Wisdom.* Berkeley: University of California Press.

Cook, Francis H., trans. 1999. *Three Texts on Consciousness Only.* Berkeley: Numata Center for Buddhist Translation and Research.

Cornu, Phillipe. 1997. *Tibetan Astrology.* Translated from the French by Hamish Gregor. Boston and London: Shambhala.

Coward, H.G., and K.K. Raja. 1990. *The Philosophy of the Grammarians.* Delhi: Motilal Banarsidass.

Crosby, Kate and Andrew Skilton, trans. 1996. *Śāntideva: The Bodhicaryāvatāra.* Oxford: Oxford University Press.

Crossley-Holland, P. 1976. "The Ritual Music of Tibet." In *The Tibet Journal* 1 (3–4): 47–53. Dharamsala: LTWA.

Csoma de Koros, A., trans. 1984. *Sanskrit-Tibetan-English Vocabulary.* Originally published in 3 vols. (1910, 1916, and 1944); reprint, Budapest: Akademiai Kiado.

Cuppers, C. 1989. "On the Manufacture of Ink." In *Ancient Nepal: Journal of the Department of Archaeology* 113 (August-September 1989): 1–7. Kathmandu: Department of Archaeology.

Dalai Lama and Jeffrey Hopkins. 1985. *The Kalachakra Tantra*. London: Wisdom Publications.

Dare, Annie and Stott, David. 2008. *India Handbook*. 15th edition. Bath: Footprint.

Dasgupta, Surendranath. 1922. *A History of Indian Philosophy*. 5 vols. Cambridge: University Press.

Davenport, John T. 2000. *Sakya Paṇḍita's Treasury of Good Advice*. Boston: Wisdom Publications.

Debreczeny, Karl. 2009. "Bodhisattvas South of the Clouds: Situ Paṇchen's Activities and Artistic Inspiration in Yunnan." In Jackson 2009, 223–251.

Denwood, Philip. 1999. *Tibetan*. Amsterdam/ Philadelphia: John Benjamins Publishing Company.

Dewar, Tyler, trans. 2008. *The Karmapa's Middle Way*. Ithaca, NY: Snow Lion Publications.

Dharmachakra Translation Committee, trans. 2006. *Middle Beyond Extremes: Maitreya's Madhyāntavibhāga with Commentaries by Khenpo Shenga and Ju Mipham*. Ithaca, NY: Snow Lion Publications.

Doctor, Thomas, trans. 2004. *Speech of Delight: Mipham's Commentary on Śāntarakṣita's Ornament of the Middle Way by Mipham Jamyang Namgyal Gyatso*. Ithaca, NY: Snow Lion Publications.

Doniger, Wendy and Sudhir Kakar. 2002. *Kāmasūtra*. Delhi: Oxford University Press.

Dorje, Gyurme, trans. 1987. "The Guhyagarbhatantra and its XIVth Century Tibetan Commentary Phyogs bcu mun sel." 3 vols. PhD diss. University of London, School of Oriental and African Studies. Revised introduction available at Wisdom Books online reading room.

———. 1991. "The rNyingma Interpretation of Commitment and Vow." In T. Skorupski, ed. *The Buddhist Forum* 2. London: SOAS.

———. 1999. "The Charts of the Svarodaya." In Robert A. F. Thurman and David Weldon, *Sacred Symbols: The Ritual Art of Tibet*, 162–165. New York: Sotheby's; London: Rossi and Rossi.

———. 2001. *Tibetan Elemental Divination Paintings*. London: Eskenazi and Fogg.

———. 2002. "A Rare Series of Tibetan Banners." In N. Allan, ed., *Pearls of the Orient*, pp. 160–177. Chicago: The Wellcome Trust/ Serindia Publications.

———. 2004. *Tibet Handbook*. 3rd edition. Bath: Footprint.

———. 2005. trans. *The Tibetan Book of the Dead*. London and New York: Penguin.

———. 2009. *Tibet Handbook*. 4th edition. Bath: Footprint.

Dorji, Dasho Sithel. 2001. *The Origins and Description of Bhutanese Mask Dances*. Thimphu: KMT Press.

Douglas, Nik and Meryl White. 1976. *Karmapa: The Black Hat Lama of Tibet*. London: Luzac.

Dowman, Keith. 1995. *Power Places of Kathmandu*. London: Thames and Hudson.

Dreyfus, Georges. 1997. *Recognizing Reality*. Delhi: Sri Satguru Publications.

Dreyfus, Georges and Sara McClintock, eds. 2003. *The Svātantrika-Prāsaṅgika Distinction*. Boston: Wisdom Publications.

Dudjom Rinpoche. 1991. *The Nyingma School of Tibetan Buddhism: Its Fundamentals and History*. 2 vols. Translated by Gyurme Dorje with Matthew Kapstein. Boston: Wisdom Publications.

Dundas, Paul. 2002. *The Jains*. 2nd edition. London and New York: Routledge.

Dunne, John and Sara McClintock, trans. 1997. *Precious Garland*. Boston: Wisdom Publications.

Dutt, Nalinaksa. 1978. *Buddhist Sects in India*. Delhi: Motilal Banarsidass.

Dwivedi, Girish and Shridhar Dwivedi. 2007. *History of Medicine: Sushruta the Clinician: Teacher par Excellence.* Government of India: National Informatics Centre.

Edgerton, Franklin. 1953. *Buddhist Hybrid Sanskrit Grammar and Dictionary.* 2 vols. New Haven: Yale University Press.

Ellingson, Ter. 1979. "'Don Rta Dbyangs Gsum: Tibetan Chant and Melodic Categories." In *Asian Music: Journal of the Society for Asian Music* 10 (2): 112–156.

Engle, Artemis B., trans. 2009. *The Inner Science of Buddhist Practice.* Ithaca, NY: Snow Lion Publications.

English, Elizabeth. 2002. *Vajrayogini.* Boston: Wisdom Publications.

Ferrari, A. 1958. *Mk'yen brtse's Guide to the Holy Places of Central Tibet.* Serie Orientale Roma 16. Rome: Istituto Italiano per il Medio ed Estremo Oriente.

Finot, Louis. 1896. *Les lapidaires indiens.* Paris: Bibliothèque de l'École des hautes études.

Frauwallner, Erich. 1956. *The Earliest Vinaya and the Beginnings of Buddhist Literature.* Serie Orientale Roma 8. Rome: Istituto Italiano per il Medio ed Estremo Oriente.

Friedmann, D.L., trans. 1937 (1984). *Madhyāntavibhāgatīkā.* Originally published Uttrecht: 1937; photographic reprint, Talent: Canon Publications, 1984.

Frye, Stanley, trans. 1981. *Nāgārjuna's Drop of Nourishment for the People.* Dharamsala: LTWA.

Ganguli, K.M., trans. 1883–1896. *Mahābharata.* Delhi: Munshiram Manoharlal Publishers. Available online at www.sacred-texts.com.

Garfield, Jay L., trans. 1995. *The Fundamental Wisdom of the Middle Way.* New York: Oxford University Press.

Ge A Gan. 2000. *The Genealogy of Dongba Deities.* Kunming: Yunnan Mei shu Publishing House.

Gerow, E. 1977. *Indian Poetics.* History of Indian Literature series, vol. 5, pt. 2, fasc. 3. Wiesbaden: Otto Harrassowitz.

Gold, Jonathan, trans. 2008. *Dharma's Gatekeepers.* Albany: State University of New York Press.

Goldman, Robert P. 1987. *Devavāṇīpraveśikā: An Introduction to the Sanskrit Language.* Berkeley: Center for South and Southeast Asia Studies, University of California.

Gonda, J. 1975. *Vedic Literature.* History of Indian Literature series, vol. 1, fasc. 1. Wiesbaden: Otto Harrassowitz.

Gray, David B., trans. 2007. *The Cakrasaṃvara Tantra.* New York: American Institute of Buddhist Studies at Columbia University.

Guarisco, Elio and Ingrid McLeod, trans. 2005. *The Treasury of Knowledge: Book Six, Part Four: Systems of Buddhist Tantra.* By Jamgön Kongtrul. Ithaca, NY: Snow Lion Publications.

———, trans. 2008. *The Treasury of Knowledge: Book Eight, Part Three: The Elements of Tantric Practice.* By Jamgön Kongtrul. Ithaca, NY: Snow Lion Publications.

Guenther, Herbert V. 1976. *Philosophy and Psychology in the Abhidharma.* Boston: Shambhala.

Gupta, D. K. 1970. *A Critical Study of Daṇḍin and His Works.* Delhi: Meharchand Lachhmandas.

Gupta, Manjul. 2010. *A Study of Abhinavabhāratī on Bharata's Nāṭyaśāstra and Avaloka on Dhañanjaya's Daśarūpaka: Dramaturgical Principles.* Delhi: Gyan Publishing, 1945; reprint, 2010.

Hall, Rachel. n.d. "The Mathematics of Poetry." Unpublished article available at www.sju.edu/~rhall/Multi/rhythm2.pdf.

———. 2005. *Math for Poets and Drummers.* Philadelphia: St. Joseph's University.

Helffer, Mireille. 1985. "A Typology of the Tibetan Bell." In Aziz and Kapstein 1985, 37–42.

———. 1998. "Du son au chant vocalisé: la terminologie tibétaine à travers les âges (VIIIe au XIXe siècle)." In *Cahiers de musiques traditionnelles* 11, 141–162.

Henning, Edward. 2007. *Kālacakra and the Tibetan Calendar.* New York: American Institute of Buddhist Studies at Columbia University.

Hodge, Stephen. 1990. *An Introduction to Classical Tibetan.* Warminster: Aris and Phillips.

Hopkins, Jeffrey, trans. 1998. *Buddhist Advice for Living and Liberation: Nagarjuna's Precious Garland*. Ithaca, NY: Snow Lion Publications.

——— et al. 1992. *Tibetan Arts of Love*. By Gedün Chöpel. Ithaca, NY: Snow Lion Publications.

Hopkins, Thomas J. 1971. *The Hindu Religious Tradition*. Encino, CA: Dickenson Publishing Company.

Hummel, Siegbert. 2000. *On Zhang-zhung*. Edited and translated by Guido Vogliotti. Dharamsala: LTWA.

Huntington, C.W, and Geshe Namgyal Wangchen. 1989. *The Emptiness of Emptiness*. Honolulu: University of Hawaii Press.

Hutchings, Robert M. 1952. "The Great Conversation: The Substance of a Liberal Education." In *Great Books of the Western World*, vol. 1. Chicago: Encyclopedia Britannica, Inc.

Ichigo, M. trans. 1985. *Madhyamakālaṃkāra of Śāntarakṣita with His Own Commentary or Vṛtti, and with the Subcommentary or Pañjikā of Kamalaśīla*. Kyoto: Buneido.

Iida, Shotaro. 1980. *Reason and Emptiness*. Tokyo: Hokuseido Press.

Inaba, Shoju. 1954. *Chibetto-go Koten Bunpogaku*. Kyoto: Hozokan.

Inada, Kenneth K. 1970. *Nagarjuna: A Translation of his Mulamadhyamakakarika with an Introductory Essay*. Tokyo: Hokuseido Press.

Ingalls, Daniel H. 1965. *An Anthology of Sanskrit Court Poetry*. Boston: Harvard Oriental Series, 44.

Jackson, David. 1994. "Biography of rNgog Lo-tsā-ba." In P. Kvaerne, *Tibetan Studies*, vol. 1, pp. 372–387. Oslo: The Institute for Comparative Research in Human Culture.

———. 1996. *A History of Tibetan Painting: The Great Painters and Their Traditions*. Vienna: Verlag der Osterreichischen Akademie der Wissenschaften.

———. 1997. "Chronological Notes on the Founding Masters of Tibetan Painting Traditions." In Jane Casey-Singer and Philip Denwood, eds. *Tibetan Art: Towards a Definition of Style*, 254–261. London: Laurence King.

———. 2009. *Patron and Painter: Situ Panchen and the Revival of the Encampment Style*. New York: Rubin Museum of Art.

Jackson, David and Janice Jackson. 1984. *Tibetan Thangka Painting*. London: Serindia Publications.

Jain, A.C. n.d. *Buddha and Buddhist Shrines in India*. Delhi: Jainco.

Jaini, Padmannabh S. 1979. *The Jaina Path of Purification*. Delhi: Motilal Banarsidass.

Jamieson, R.C. 2001. *Nāgārjuna's Verses on the Great Vehicle and the Heart of Dependent Origination*. Delhi: D.K. Printworld.

Jamspal, Lobzang et al., trans. 1978. *Nāgārjuna's Letter to King Gautamīputra*. Delhi: Motilal Banarsidass.

———. 2004. *The Universal Vehicle Discourse Literature*. New York: American Institute of Buddhist Studies at Columbia University.

Jha, Ganganatha, trans. 1937. *The Tattvasaṃgraha of Śāntarakṣita*. 2 vols. Baroda: GOS 80.

———, trans. (1900) 1985. *Exposition of the Verses. Ślokavārttika*. Calcutta: The Asiatic Society. Reprint Delhi: Sri Satguru Publications.

Johnson, E. H. (1936) 1972. *Aśvaghoṣa's Buddhacarita or Acts of the Buddha*. Part I, Sanskrit text; Part II, translation, cantos I–XIV. Reprint, Delhi: Motilal Banarsidass.

Joshi, Lalmani. 1967. *Studies in the Buddhistic Culture of India*. Delhi: Motilal Banarsidass.

Joshi, S. D. and J. A. F. Roodbergen, trans. 1992–2007. *The Aṣṭādhyāyī of Pāṇini*. 14 vols. Continuing series. Delhi: Sahitya Akademi.

Kajiyama, Y. 1958. "On the Theory of Intrinsic Determination of Universal Concomitance in Buddhist Logic." In *The Journal of International Buddhist Studies* 7 (1): 360–364. Lausanne: Dept. of Oriental Languages and Cultures.

Kalff, Martin M. 1979. "Selected Chapters from the Abhidānottara-Tantra: The Union of Female and Male Deities." PhD diss. Columbia University. 2 vols.

Kalu Rinpoche Translation Group, trans. 1995. *The Treasury of Knowledge: Book One: Myriad Worlds.* By Jamgön Kongtrul. Ithaca, NY: Snow Lion Publications.

———, trans. 1998. *The Treasury of Knowledge: Book Five: Buddhist Ethics.* By Jamgön Kongtrul. Ithaca, NY: Snow Lion Publications.

Kalupahana, David J., trans. 1986. *The Philosophy of the Middle Way*. Albany: State University of New York Press.

Kaneko, Eiichi. 1982. *Ko-Tantora zenchū kaidai mokuroku.* Tokyo: Kokusho Kankōkai.

Kapstein, Matthew T. 2001. *Reason's Traces: Identity and Interpretation in Indian and Tibetan Buddhist Thought*. Boston: Wisdom Publications.

———. 2006. *The Tibetans*. Malden and Oxford: Blackwell Publishing.

———, ed. 2009. *Buddhism Between Tibet and China*. Boston: Wisdom Publications.

Karmay, Samten G., trans. (1972) 2001. *The Treasury of Good Sayings.* London: Oxford University Press, 1972; reprint, Delhi: Motilal Banarsidass.

Kato, Bunno et al., trans. 1975. *The Threefold Lotus Sutra*. Tokyo: Kosei Publishing.

Katre, Sumitra M. 1987. *Aṣṭādhyāyī of Pāṇini*. Austin: University of Texas Press.

Kaufmann, Walter. 1975. *Tibetan Buddhist Chant: Musical Notations and Interpretations of a Song Book by the Bkah Brgyud Pa and Sa Skya Pa Sects*. Bloomington: IUP.

Kaviratna, A.C. and P. Sharma, trans. (1897) 1996. *The Charaka Samhita*. 5 vols. Reprint, Indian Medical Science Series. Delhi: Sri Satguru Publications.

Keenan, John P., trans. 2003. *The Summary of the Great Vehicle by Bodhisattva Asaṅga*. Berkeley: Numata Center for Buddhist Translation and Research.

Keith, Arthur B. 1924. *The Sanskrit Drama.* Oxford: Oxford University Press

Kennedy, J. M., trans. 1913. *The Satakas or Wise Sayings of Bhartṛhari.* London: Werner Laurie.

Kern, H., trans. (1884) 1968. *Saddharma-Puṇḍarīka or the Lotus of the True Law.* Oxford: Oxford University Press; reprint, Delhi: Motilal Banarsidass.

Khosla, Sarla. 1991. *Lalitavistara and the Evolution of Buddha Legend.* Delhi: Galaxy Publications.

Kilty, Gavin, trans. 2004. *Ornament of Stainless Light.* Boston: Wisdom Publications.

———, trans. 2010. *Mirror of Beryl.* Boston: Widom Publications.

Kochumuttom, T., trans. 1982. *A Buddhist Doctrine of Experience*. Delhi: Motilal Banarsidass.

Kuijp, Leonard W. J. van der. 1978. "Phya-pa Chos-kyi Seng-ge's Impact on Tibetan Epistemological Theory." *Journal of Indian Philosophy* 5: 355–369.

———. 1983. *Contributions to the Development of Tibetan Buddhist Epistemology*. Wiesbaden: Franz Steiner.

Kunsang, Erik Pema, trans. 1997–2002. *Gateway to Knowledge*. By Jamgon Mipham Rinpoche. 4 vols. Hong Kong: Rangjung Yeshe Publications.

Kuppanna Sastry, T. S., trans. 1993. *Pañcasiddhāntikā: The Astronomical Treatise of Varāhamihira.* Adyar, Madras: P.P.S.T. Foundation.

Kutumbian, P. 2005. *Ancient Indian Medicine.* Hyderabad: Orient.

Kvaerne, Per. 1995. *The Bon Religion of Tibet*. London: Serindia Publications.

Lamotte, Étienne. 1988. *History of Indian Buddhism*. Translated from the French by Sara Webb-Boin. Louvain-la-Neuve: Université catholique de Louvain, Institut orientaliste.

Lang, Karen, trans. 1986. *Āryadeva's Catuḥśataka: On the Bodhisattva's Cultivation of Merit and Knowledge*. Copenhagen: Akademisk Forlag.

Larson, G. J., and R. S. Bhattacharya, eds. 1987. *Sāṃkhya: A Dualistic Tradition in Indian Philosophy*. Delhi: Motilal Banarsidass.

Lati Rinpoche, J. Hopkins, and E. Napper. 1986. *Mind in Tibetan Buddhism*. Ithaca, NY: Snow Lion Publications.

Law, Bimala Chum. 1933. *A History of Pāli Literature.* London: Kegan Paul, Trench, Trubner & Co.

Lessing, Ferdinand D. and Alex Wayman, trans. 1968: *Mkhas Grub rJe's Fundamentals of the Buddhist Tantras.* The Hague: Mouton.

Lhalungpa, Lobsang, trans. 2006. *Mahamudra: The Moonlight Quintessence of Mind and Meditation.* Boston: Wisdom Publications.

Liebach, Brunno, ed. 1902. *Cāndra-Vyākaraṇa, die Grammatik des Candragomin: Sūtra, Uṇādi, Dhātupāṭha.* Abhandlungen für die kunde des Morgenländes 11(4). Leipzig: Brockhaus.

Lindtner, Christian, trans. 1997. *Master of Wisdom: Writings of the Buddhist Master Nāgārjuna.* Emeryville, CA: Dharma Publishing.

Linrothe, Rob and Jeff Watt. 2004. *Demonic Divine: Himalayan Art and Beyond.* New York: Rubin Museum of Art.

Lipman, Kennard. 1977. "How Samsara Is Fabricated from the Ground of Being." Chapter One of *The Wish-Fulfilling Treasury* by Longchenpa. In *Crystal Mirror* 5, 344–364. Emeryville, CA: Dharma Publishing.

Lusthaus, Dan. 2002. *Buddhist Phenomenology.* New York and Abingdon: Routledge Curzon.

Macdonald, Ariane, trans. 1962. *Le Maṇḍala du Mañjuśrīmūlakalpa.* Paris: Adrien Maisonneuve.

MacDonnell, A. A. 1927. *A Sanskrit Grammar for Students.* Oxford: Oxford University Press

Majumdar, N. G. 2008. *A List of Kharoṣṭhī Inscriptions.* Kolkata: The Asiatic Society.

Malvania, D., and J. Soni. 2008. *Jain Philosophy.* Delhi: Motilal Banarsidass.

Mani, Vettam, ed. 1964. *Purāṇic Encyclopaedia.* Delhi: Molilal Banarsidass.

Mao Jizheng. 1998. "Discussion on the Rol-mo'i bstan bcos." In *Essays on the Structure of the Court Musics of East and Southeast Asia.* Taiwan: International Forum for Ethnomusicology.

Martin, Dan. 1997. *Tibetan Histories.* London: Serindia Publications.

Matics, Marion L., trans. 1970. *Entering the Path of Enlightenment.* London: Allen and Unwin.

Matilal, Bimal Krishna. 1977. *Nyāya-Vaiśeṣika.* History of Indian Literature 6, pt. 3, fasc. 2. Wiesbaden: Otto Harrassowitz.

Mayer, Robert. 1996. *A Scripture of the Ancient Tantra Collection.* Oxford: Kiscadale Publications.

Meyer, Fernand. 1981. *Gso-ba rig-pa: Le système médical tibétain.* Paris: Editions du Centre National de la Recherche Scientifique.

Miller, Roy Andrew. 1963. "Thoṇ-mi Sambhota and His Grammatical Treatises." In *Journal of the American Oriental Society* 83, 485–502.

———. 1976. *Studies in the Grammatical Tradition in Tibet.* Amsterdam Studies in the Theory and History of Linguistic Science, Series 3, vol. 6. Amsterdam: Benjamins.

Miśra, Satyadeva et al., trans. 2005. *Amarakośa of Amarasiṃha.* With Kṛṣṇamitra's Commentary in Sanskrit, Vaikunthi Commentary in Hindi, and Annotation of Words in English. Jaipur: Jagdish Sanskrit Pustakalaya.

Misra, Vidyaniwas. 1966. *The Descriptive Technique of Pāṇini.* The Hague: Mouton.

Monier-Williams, Monier. (1899) 2005. *A Sanskrit-English Dictionary.* Oxford: Oxford University Press. Reprint, Delhi: Motilal Banarsidass.

Mukherjee, B. N. 2007. "The So-called Śaṅkha-lipi." In Patel, Pandey, and Rajgor, eds. *The Indic Scripts,* 116–117. Delhi: D. K. Printworld.

Mukherji, Amulyadhan. 1976. *Sanskrit Prosody: Its Evolution.* Calcutta: Rabindra Bharati University.

Müller, Max. 1919. *The Six Systems of Indian Philosophy.* London: Longman's, Green and Co.

Mullin, Glenn H. and Jeff J. Watt. 2003. *Female Buddhas: Women of Enlightenment in Tibetan Mystical Art.* Santa Fe: Clear Light Publishers.

Murti, T.V. 1955. *The Central Philosophy of Buddhism.* London: Allen and Unwin.

Nagarjuna and Sakya Pandita. 1977. *Elegant Sayings.* Emeryville, CA: Dharma Publishing.

Nagatomi, Masatoshi. 1957. "A Study of Dharmakīrti's Pramāṇavārttika: An English Translation and Annotation of the Pramāṇavārttika Book I." PhD diss. Harvard University.

Ñāṇamoli, Bhikkhu, trans. 1979. *The Path of Purification* by Buddhaghosa. Kandy: Buddhist Publication Society.

Napper, Elizabeth. 2003. *Dependent Arising and Emptiness.* Boston: Wisdom Publications.
Nebesky-Wojkowitz, René de. 1956. *Oracles and Demons of Tibet.* The Hague: Mouton.
———. (1976) 1997. *Tibetan Religious Dances: Tibetan Text and Annotated Translation of the 'Chams yig.* Edited by Christoph von Fürer-Haimendorf. The Hague: Mouton, 1976; reprint, Delhi: Paljor Publications, 1997.
Newman, John. 1987. "The Outer Wheel of Time: Vajrayāna Buddhist Cosmology in the Kālacakra Tantra." PhD diss. University of Wisconsin–Madison.
Ngawang Zangpo, trans. 2010. *The Treasury of Knowledge: Books Two, Three, and Four: Buddhism's Journey to Tibet.* By Jamgön Kongtrul. Ithaca, NY: Snow Lion Publications.
Nyima, Tudeng and Gyurme Dorje, trans. 2001. *An Encyclopaedic Tibetan-English Dictionary.* Vol. 1. Beijing and London: Nationalities Publishing House and SOAS.
Padmakara Translation Group, trans. 1993. *Wisdom: Two Buddhist Commentaries.* Peyzac-le-Moustier: Editions Padmakara.
———, trans. 1994. *The Words of My Perfect Teacher.* By Patrul Rinpoche. San Francisco: Harper Collins.
———, trans. 1997. *The Way of the Bodhisattva: A Translation of the Bodhicharyāvatāra by Shantideva.* Boston: Shambhala.
———, trans. 2002. *Introduction to the Middle Way: Candrakīrti's Madhyamakāvatāra with Commentary by Ju Mipham.* Boston: Shambhala.
———, trans. 2005. *The Adornment of the Middle Way: Shantarakshita's Madhyamakalankara with Commentary by Jamgon Mipham.* Boston: Shambhala.
———, trans. 2008. *The Root Stanzas on the Middle Way: Mūlamadhyamaka-kārikā.* By Nāgārjuna. Peyzac-le-Moustier: Editions Padmakara.
———, trans. 2007. *The Nectar of Manjushri's Speech: A Detailed Commentary on Shantideva's Way of the Bodhisattva by Kunzang Pelden.* Boston: Shambhala.
Pagel, Ulrich. 1995. *Bodhisattvapitaka.* Tring: The Institute of Buddhist Studies.
Palshule, G. B. 1961. *The Sanskrit Dhātupāṭhas.* Poona: University of Poona.
Pandey, Janardan Shastri, ed. 1998. *Yoginīsañcāryatantram with Nibandha of Tathāgatarakṣita and Upadeśānusārinivyākhyā of Alakakalaśa* [in Sanskrit]. Rare Buddhist Texts series 21. Sarnath: Central Institute of Higher Tibetan Studies.
Parfionovitch. Y., G. Dorje, and F. Meyer. 1992. *Tibetan Medical Paintings: Illustrations to the Blue Beryl Treatise of Sangye Gyamtso (1653–1705).* London: Serindia Publications.
Pasar Tsultrim Tenzin et al. 2008. *A Lexicon of Zhangzhung and Bonpo Terms.* Osaka: National Museum of Ethnology.
Pearlman, Ellen. 2002. *Tibetan Sacred Dance: A Journey into the Religious and Folk Tradition.* Rochester, VT: Inner Traditions.
Perdue, D. 1976. *Debate in Tibetan Buddhist Education.* Dharamsala: LTWA.
Peterson, Kathleen. 1980. "Sources of Variation in Tibetan Canons of Iconometry." In Aris and Aung San Suu Kyi 1980, 239–248.
Pingree, David. 1981. *Jyotiḥśāstra: Astral and Mathematical Literature.* History of Indian Literature, vol. 6, fasc. 4. Wiesbaden: Otto Harrassowitz.
Potter, Karl. 1977. *Indian Metaphysics and Epistemology.* Delhi: Motilal Banarsidass.
———. 2009a. *Buddhist Philosophy from 100 to 350 AD.* Delhi: Motilal Banarsidass.
———. 2009b. *Buddhist Philosophy from 350–600 AD.* Delhi: Motilal Banarsidass.
Potter, Karl with Robert Buswell et al. 1996. *Abhidharma Buddhism.* Delhi: Motilal Banarsidass.
Prasada, Rama, trans. (1924) 1988. *Patañjali's Yoga Sūtras.* Allahabad: 1924; reprint, Delhi: Munshiram Manoharlal.
Pruden, Leo M., trans. 1988–1990. *Abhidharmakośabhāṣyaṃ* by Vasubandhu. Translated by Louis de La Vallée Poussin. English translation by Leo M. Pruden. 4 vols. Berkeley: Asian Humanities Press.

Radhakrishnan, S. 1953. *The Principal Upaniṣads.* London: Allen and Unwin.

Radhakrishnan, S., and Charles A. Moore, eds. 1957. *A Source Book in Indian Philosophy.* New Jersey: Princeton University Press.

Rāmacandra Kaulācāra. 1966. *Śilpa Prakāśa: Medieval Orissan Sanskrit Text on Temple Architecture.* Translated and annotated by Alice Boner and Sadāśiva Rath Śarma. Leiden: E. J. Brill.

Ramakrishna Bhat, M., trans. 1981. *Varāhamihira's Bṛhat Saṃhitā.* Delhi: Motilal Banarsidass.

Rastogi, N. P. 1980. *Origin of the Brāhmī Script: The Beginning of Alphabet in India.* Varanasi: Chowkhamba Saraswatibhawan.

Ray, Kumudranjan, trans. 2004. *Kāvyādarśaḥ.* Text, English Translation and Commentary of Śrī Premacandra Tarkavāgīśa. Delhi: Oriental Book Centre.

Reat, N. Ross. 1993. *Śālistamba Sūtra.* Delhi: Motilal Banarsidass.

Rechung Rinpoche. 1976. *Tibetan Medicine.* Berkeley/ Los Angeles: University of California Press.

Richardson, Hugh E. 1998. *High Peaks, Pure Earth: Collected Writings on Tibetan History and Culture.* London: Serindia Publications.

Rigdzin, Tsepak. 1993. *Tibetan-English Dictionary of Buddhist Terminology.* Dharamsala: LTWA.

Ringu Tulku. 2006. *The Ri-me Philosophy of Jamgön Kongtrul the Great: A Study of the Buddhist Lineages of Tibet.* Edited by Ann Helm. Boston; London: Shambhala.

Roerich, George, trans. 1976. *The Blue Annals.* 2nd edition. Delhi: Motilal Banarsidass.

Rogers, Katherine Manchester. 1980. "Tibetan Logic." [Dissertation on the *rtags rigs* section of the *Collected Topics*, with commentary of Lati Rinpoche, Denma Locho Rinpoche and Geshe Gendun Lodro.] PhD diss. University of Virginia.

———. 2009. *Tibetan Logic.* Ithaca, NY: Snow Lion Publications.

Roth, Gustav. 2009. "Symbolism of the Buddhist Stūpa." In G. Roth et al., eds. *Stupa: Cult and Symbolism*, 9–33. Śatapiṭaka Series 624. Delhi: International Academy of Indian Culture and Aditya Prakashan.

Ruegg, David S. 1971. "Le Dharmadhātustava de Nāgārjuna." In *Études tibétaines dédiées à la mémoire de Marcelle Lalou*, 446–471. Paris: Adrien Maisonneuve.

———. 1981. *The Literature of the Madhyamaka School of Philosophy in India.* History of Indian Literature, vol. 7, fasc. 1. Wiesbaden: Otto Harrassowitz.

Sakaki, R., ed. 1916–1925. *Mahāvyutpatti.* Reprint, Kyoto: Shingonshu Kyoto Daigaku, 1965.

Salomon, Richard. 1999. *Ancient Buddhist Scrolls from Gandhāra: The British Library Kharoṣṭhī Fragments.* With contributions by Raymond Allchin and Mark Barnard. Seattle, WA: University of Washington Press.

Salomon, Richard. 2000. *A Gāndhārī Version of the Rhinoceros Sūtra: British Library Kharoṣṭhī Fragment 5B.* With a contribution by Andrew Glass. Seattle, WA: University of Washington Press.

Samtani, N. H., trans. 2002. *Gathering the Meanings: The Compendium of Categories: the Arthaviniścaya Sūtra and Its Commentary, Nibandhana.* Berkeley, CA: Dharma Publishing.

Scharfe, Hartmut. 1977. *Grammatical Literature.* History of Indian Literature, vol. 5, part 2, fasc. 2. Wiesbaden: Otto Harrassowitz.

Schmithausen, Lambert. 1987. *Ālayavijñāna: On the Origin and Early Development of a Central Concept of Yogācāra Philosophy.* Tokyo: International Institute for Buddhist Studies.

Scott, Jim, trans. 2004. *Maitreya's Distinguishing Phenomena and Pure Being.* Ithaca, NY: Snow Lion Publications.

Shakabpa, Wangchuk D. 1967. *Tibet: A Political History.* New Haven/ London: Yale University Press.

Sharma, B. N. and B. Upadhyaya. 1929. *The Nāṭyaśāstra of Bharata.* Kashi Sanskrit Series 60. Varanasi.

Sharma, I. C. 1965. *Ethical Philosophies of India*. London: Allen and Unwin.
Shastri, Losang Norbu, ed. 1990. *Chandoratnākara*. Sanskrit edition with the auto-commentary of Ratnākaraśānti. Varanasi: Central Institute of Higher Tibetan Studies.
Simon, Beth, ed. 1985. *The Wheel of Time. The Kalachakra in Context*. Madison: Deer Park Books.
Simonsson, Nils. 1957. *Indo-tibetische Studien. Die Methoden der tibetischen Übersetzer, untersucht im Hinblick auf die Bedeutung ihrer Übersetzungen für die Sanskritphilologie*. Uppsala: Almqvist & Wiksells.
Sinha, Nandalal, trans. 1915. *The Samkhya Philosophy*. Containing the *Tattvasamāsa* and *Sāṃkhyākārikā* with other texts. Allahabad: Panini Office.
Skorupski, Tadeusz. 2002. *Kriyāsaṃgraha: Compendium of Buddhist Rituals* [by Kuladatta]*: An Abridged Version*. Tring: Institute of Buddhist Studies.
Smith, E. Gene. 2001. *Among Tibetan Texts*. Boston: Wisdom Publications.
Snellgrove, David L., trans. 1959. *The Hevajra Tantra*. Two Parts. London: Oxford University Press.
———. 1967. *The Nine Ways of Bon*. London Oriental Series 18. London: Oxford University Press.
Snodgrass, Adrian. 1992. *The Symbolism of the Stupa*. Delhi: Motilal Banarsidass.
Sparham, Gareth, trans. 2006. *Abhisamayālaṃkāra with vṛtti and ālokā/ vṛtti by Ārya Vimuktisena; ālokā by Haribhadra*. Fremont, CA: Jain Publishing.
Speyer, J. S., trans. 1895. *The Jātakamālā of Āryasūra*. London: The Pali Text Society.
Sponberg, Alan. 1983. "The Trisvabhāva Doctrine in India and China." In *Ryukoku Dougairu Buikyo Bunka Kenkyujo Kiyo* 21, 96–118.
Sprung, Mervyn, trans. 1979. *Lucid Exposition of the Middle Way*. London: Routledge & Kegan Paul.
Stearns, Cyrus. 2002. *The Buddha from Dolpo*. Delhi: Motilal Banarsidass.
Stein, Rolf A. 1972. *Tibetan Civilization*. Stanford, CA: Stanford University Press.
Steinkellner, Ernst, ed. 1991. "The Logic of the *svabhāvahetu* in Dharmakīrti's Vādanyāya." In *Studies in the Buddhist Epistemological Tradition: Proceedings of the Second International Dharmakīrti Conference*, 311–324. Vienna: Österreichische Akademie der Wissenschaften.
Sternbach, Ludwik. 1963–70. *Cāṇakya-Nīti Text Tradition*. 3 vols. Vishveshvaranand Indological Series 27–29. Hoshiarpur: Vishveshvaranand Vedic Research Institute.
———. 1966. *The Subhāsita-saṃgraha-s as Treasuries of Cānakya's Sayings*. Vishveshvaranand Indological Series 36. Hoshiarpur: Vishveshvaranand Vedic Research Institute.
Stoddard, Heather and N. Tournadre, trans. 1992. *Le clair miroir: enseignement de la grammaire tibétain*. By sKal-bZang 'Gyur-med. Translated, adapted, and annotated by Heather Stoddard and Nicolas Tournadre. In French. Arvillard: Editions Prajña.
Streng, Frederick J., trans. 1967. *Emptiness: A Study in Religious Meaning*. Nashville, TN: Abingdon Press.
Suryanarayana Sastri, S.S., ed. and trans. 1935. *The Sāṅkhyakārikā of Īśvara Kṛṣṇa*. Madras: University of Madras.
Sutton, Florin G. 1991. *Existence and Enlightenment in the Laṅkāvatāra Sūtra*. Delhi: Sri Satguru Publications.
Suzuki, Daisetz T. 1930. *Studies in the Laṅkāvatāra Sūtra*. Delhi: Munishiram Manoharlal.
———, trans. 1932. *The Laṅkāvatārasūtra*. London: Routledge & Kegan Paul.
Tanemura, Ryugen. 2004. *Kuladatta's Kriyāsaṃgrahapañjikā*. Groningen Oriental Studies 19. Groningen: Egbert Forsten.
Tarthang Tulku et al., trans. 1973. *Calm and Clear*. Emeryville, CA: Dharma Publishing.
Tatz, Mark, trans. 1986. *Asaṅga's Chapter on Ethics with the Commentary of Tsong-Kha-Pa, The Basic Path to Awakening, the Complete Bodhisattva*. Lewiston, NY: Edwin Mellen Press.

Thakur, Amrendra. 2006. *Chāndra System of Grammar: A Structural Study.* Varanasi: Aditya Book Centre.

Tharchin, Geshe Lobsang and Artemus B. Engle, trans. 1979. *Nāgārjuna's Letter: Nāgārjuna's "Letter to a Friend" with a Commentary by the Venerable Rendawa, Zhön-nu Lodrö.* Dharamsala: LTWA.

Thinley Norbu. 1999. *The Small Golden Key.* Boston: Shambhala.

Thrangu, Khenchen Rinpoche, trans. 1993. *The Practice of Tranquillity and Insight.* Ithaca, NY: Snow Lion Publications.

———. 2001. *The Twelve Links of Dependent Origination.* Auckland: Zhyisil Chokyi Ghatsal Publications.

———, trans. 2004. *Maitreya's Distinguishing Dharma and Dharmata.* Auckland: Zhyisil Chokyi Ghatsal Charitable Trust Publications.

Tillemans, Tom J. F. 1999. *Scripture, Logic, Language: Essays on Dharmakirti and His Tibetan Successors.* Boston: Wisdom Publications.

Tola, Fernando and Carmen Dragonetti, trans. 2004. *Being as Consciousness.* Delhi: Motilal Banarsidass.

Thondup, Tulku. 1986. *Hidden Teachings of Tibet: An Explanation of the Terma Tradition of the Nyingma School of Buddhism.* Edited by Harold Talbott. London: Wisdom Publications.

Trungpa, Chogyam. 1966. *Born in Tibet.* London: Allen and Unwin.

Tsering, Tashi. 2003. "Reflections on Thang stong rgyal po as the Founder of the Ache Lhamo Tradition of Tibetan Performing Arts." In *Lungta* 15. Dharamsala: Amnye Machen Institute.

Tsuda, Shinichi. 1974. *The Saṃvarodaya Tantra: Selected Chapters.* Tokyo: The Hokuseido Press.

U Nārada, trans. 1962. *Discourse on Elements [Dhātukathā].* London: Pali Text Society.

Varnī, Jinendra. 1973. *Jainendra Siddhānta Kośa.* 4 vols. Varanasi: Bhāratīya Jñānapīṭha.

Vatsyayan, Kapila, trans. 1996. *Bharata: The Nāṭyaśāstra.* New Delhi: Sahitya Akademi.

Verhagen, Pieter C. 1991. "Sanskrit Grammatical Literature in Tibet." PhD diss. University of Leiden.

———. 2001. *A History of Sanskrit Grammatical Literature in Tibet.* 2 vols. Leiden: E. J. Brill.

Vessantara. 1993. *Meeting the Buddhas.* Glasgow: Windhorse Publications.

Vogel, Claus. 1965. *Vāgbhaṭa's Aṣṭāṅgahṛdayasaṃhitā.* Abhandlung für die Kunde des Morgenlandes 37, 2. Wiesbaden: Franz Steiner Verlag.

———. 1979. *Indian Lexicography.* History of Indian Literature series, vol. 5, fasc. 4. Wiesbaden: Otto Harrassowitz.

Waldron, William S. 2003. *The Buddhist Unconscious: The Ālaya-vijñāna in the Context of Indian Buddhist Thought.* RoutledgeCurzon Critical Studies in Buddhism. London: RoutledgeCurzon.

Wallace, Vesna A. 2001. *The Inner Kālacakratantra: A Buddhist Tantric View of the Individual.* New York/ Oxford: Oxford University Press.

———, trans. 2010. *The Kālacakratantra: The Chapter on Sādhanā together with the Vimalaprabhā Commentary.* New York: American Institute of Buddhist Studies at Columbia University.

Wallace, Vesna, A., and B. Alan Wallace, trans. 1997. *A Guide to the Bodhisattva Way of Life.* By Śāntideva. Ithaca, NY: Snow Lion Publications.

Wangyal, Tenzin Rinpoche. 2000. *Wonders of the Natural Mind.* Delhi: New Age Books.

Weber, Albrecht. 1863. *Chandasūtra.* Edition of Piṅgala's discourse on prosody. Leipzig: *Indische Studien* 8.

Wedemeyer, Christian, trans. 2008. *Āryadeva's Lamp That Integrates Practice.* New York: American Institute of Buddhist Studies at Columbia University.

Whitney, William D. 1896. *Sanskrit Grammar.* 3rd ed. Leipzig: Breitkopf & Härtel.

———. (1885) 1963. *The Roots, Verb-forms and Primary Derivatives of the Sanskrit Language.* Delhi: Motilal Banarsidass.

Willemen, Charles, Bart Dessein, and Collett Cox. 1998. *Sarvāstivāda Buddhist Scholasticism.* Leiden: E. J. Brill.

Williams, Paul. 1989. *Mahāyāna Buddhism.* London/ New York: Routledge.

———. 1998. *The Reflexive Nature of Awareness.* London: Curzon Press.

Willis, Janice D., trans. 1982. *On Knowing Reality.* Delhi: Motilal Banarsidass.

Willson, Martin, and Martin Brauen. 2000. *Deities of Tibetan Buddhism.* Boston: Wisdom Publications.

Woodhatch, Tom. 1997. *Nepal Handbook.* Bath: Footprint.

Wujastyk, Dominik, trans. 1993. *Metarules of Pāṇinian Grammar: The Vyāḍīyaparibhāṣāvṛtti.* Critically edited with translation and commentary. 2 vols. Groningen: Egbert Forsten.

———. 2003. *The Roots of Ayurveda: Selections from Sanskrit Medical Writings.* New York/ London: Penguin Classics.

Yamada, Isshi. 1981. *Sarva-tathāgata-tattva-saṃgraha nāma mahāyāna-sūtra: A Critical Edition Based on the Sanskrit Manuscript and Chinese and Tibetan Translations.* New Delhi: Sharada Rani.

Yamamoto, Kosho, trans. 1999–2000. *The Mahāyāna Mahāparinirvāṇa Sūtra.* 12 vols. Edited by Tony Page. London: Nirvana Publications.

Zhao Jin Xiu. 1995. *Dongba Xiangxingwen Changyong Zici Yizhu.* Kunming: Yunnan People's Publishing House.

Index

The index includes primary sources mentioned in the text and endnotes, but not secondary references or translations, for which the reader should consult the notes and bibliography.